COMPACT
WORLD
ATLAS

LONDON, NEW YORK, MUNICH,
MELBOURNE, DELHI

A DORLING KINDERSLEY PUBLISHING BOOK
www.dk.com

EDITOR-IN-CHIEF
Andrew Heritage

SENIOR MANAGING ART EDITOR
Philip Lord

SENIOR CARTOGRAPHIC MANAGER
David Roberts

SENIOR CARTOGRAPHIC EDITOR
Simon Mumford

PROJECT CARTOGRAPHER
Iorwerth Watkins

PROJECT DESIGNER
Karen Gregory

PROJECT EDITOR
Debra Clapson

SYSTEMS CO-ORDINATOR
Philip Rowles

PRODUCTION
Wendy Penn

First American edition 2001
Published in the United States by Dorling Kindersley Publishing, Inc.,
375 Hudson Street
New York, New York 10014

Copyright © 2001, 2002, 2003, 2004, 2005 Dorling Kindersley Limited, London
Reprinted with revisions 2002. Second Edition 2003.
Reprinted with revisions 2004. Third Edition 2005.
A Penguin Company

A CIP catalog record for this book is available from the Library of Congress

ISBN 0-7566-0965-8

Printed and bound in China by Toppan Printing Co. (Shenzhen) Ltd.

For the very latest information, visit:
www.dk.com and click on the Maps & Atlases icon

KEY TO MAP SYMBOLS

PHYSICAL FEATURES

Elevation

- 4,000m/13,124ft
- 2,000m/6,562ft
- 1,000m/3,281ft
- 500m/1,640ft
- 250m/820ft
- 100m/328ft
- 0
- Below sea level

△ Mountain

▽ Depression

⌂ Volcano

)(Pass/tunnel

◻ Sandy desert

DRAINAGE FEATURES

Major perennial river

Minor perennial river

Seasonal river

Canal

Waterfall

Perennial lake

Seasonal lake

Wetland

ICE FEATURES

Permanent ice cap/ice shelf

Winter limit of pack ice

Summer limit of pack ice

BORDERS

Full international border

Disputed *de facto* border

Territorial claim border

x—x—x Cease-fire line

Undefined boundary

Internal administrative boundary

COMMUNICATIONS

Major road

Minor road

Rail

✈ International airport

SETTLEMENTS

◉ Over 500,000

◉ 100,000 - 500,000

○ 50,000 - 100,000

○ Less than 50,000

● National capital

● Internal administrative capital

MISCELLANEOUS FEATURES

+ Site of interest

ᴖᴖᴖ Ancient wall

GRATICULE FEATURES

Line of latitude/longitude/ Equator

Tropic/Polar circle

25° Degrees of latitude/ longitude

NAMES

Physical features

Andes

Sahara   Landscape features

Ardennes

Land's End   Headland

Mont Blanc   Elevation/volcano/pass
4,807m

Blue Nile   River/canal/waterfall

Ross Ice Shelf   Ice feature

PACIFIC
OCEAN

Sulu Sea   Sea features

Palk Strait

Chile Rise   Undersea feature

Regions

FRANCE   Country

JERSEY   Dependent territory
(to UK)

KANSAS   Administrative region

Dordogne   Cultural region

Settlements

PARIS   Capital city

SAN JUAN   Dependent territory
capital city

Chicago

Kettering   Other settlements

Burke

INSET MAP SYMBOLS

Urban area

City

Park

▪ Place of interest

◻ Suburb/district

CONTENTS

The Political World 6-7

The Physical World 8-9

Time Zones 10

THE
WORLD ATLAS

NORTH &
CENTRAL AMERICA

North & Central America 12-13
Western Canada & Alaska 14-15
Eastern Canada 16-17
USA: The Northeast 18-19
USA: The Southeast 20-21
  Bermuda
USA: Central States 22-23
USA: The West 24-25
  Los Angeles & Hawaii
USA: The Southwest 26-27
Mexico 28-29
Central America 30-31
The Caribbean 32-33
  Jamaica, St. Lucia, & Barbados

SOUTH AMERICA

South America 34-35
Northern South America 36-37
Western South America 38-39
  Galapagos Islands
Brazil .40-41
Southern South America 42-43

The Atlantic Ocean 44-45

AFRICA

Africa .46-47
Northwest Africa 48-49
Northeast Africa 50-51
West Africa 52-53
Central Africa 54-55
  Sao Tome & Principe
Southern Africa 56-57

EUROPE

Europe .58-59
The North Atlantic 60-61
Scandinavia & Finland 62-63
The Low Countries 64-65
The British Isles 66-67
  London
France, Andorra, & Monaco . . .68-69
  Paris, Andorra, & Monaco
Spain & Portugal 70-71
  Azores & Gibraltar
Germany & the Alpine States . .72-73
  Liechtenstein

EUROPE *continued*

Italy 74-75
   San Marino & Vatican City
Central Europe 76-77
Southeast Europe 78-79
   Bosnia & Herzegovina
The Mediterranean 80-81
   Malta & Cyprus . . . .
Bulgaria & Greece 82-83
The Baltic States
   & Belarus 84-85
Ukraine, Moldova,
   & Romania 86-87
European Russia 88-89

NORTH & WEST ASIA

North & West Asia 90-91
Russia & Kazakhstan 92-93
Turkey & the Caucasus 94-95
The Near East 96-97
   West Bank
The Middle East 98-99
Central Asia 100-101

SOUTH & EAST ASIA

South & East Asia 102-103
Western China & Mongolia . .104-105
Eastern China & Korea 106-107
   Hong Kong (Xianggang)
Japan 108-109
   Tōkyō & Nansei-Shotō
South India & Sri Lanka 110-111

North India, Pakistan,
   & Bangladesh 112-113
Mainland Southeast Asia 114-115
Maritime Southeast Asia 116-117
   Singapore

The Indian Ocean 118-119

AUSTRALASIA & OCEANIA

Australasia & Oceania 120-121
The Southwest Pacific 122-123
Western Australia 124-125
Eastern Australia 126-127
   Sydney
New Zealand 128-129

The Pacific Ocean 130-131

Antarctica 132

The Arctic Ocean 133

INDEX – GAZETTEER

Overseas Territories
   & Dependencies 134-135

Countries Factfile 135-151

Geographical Comparisons . .152-153

Index 154-192

THE POLITICAL WORLD

ABBREVIATIONS

AFGH.
Afghanistan

ALB.
Albania

AUT.
Austria

AZ. OR AZERB.
Azerbaijan

B. & H.
Bosnia &
Herzegovina

BELA.
Belarus

BELG.
Belgium

BOTS.
Botswana

BULG.
Bulgaria

CAMB.
Cambodia

C.A.R.
Central African
Republic

CRO.
Croatia

CZ. REP.
Czech Republic

DOM. REP.
Dominican
Republic

EST.
Estonia

EQ. GUINEA
Equatorial
Guinea

HUNG.
Hungary

KYRG.
Kyrgyzstan

LAT.
Latvia

LIECH.
Liechtenstein

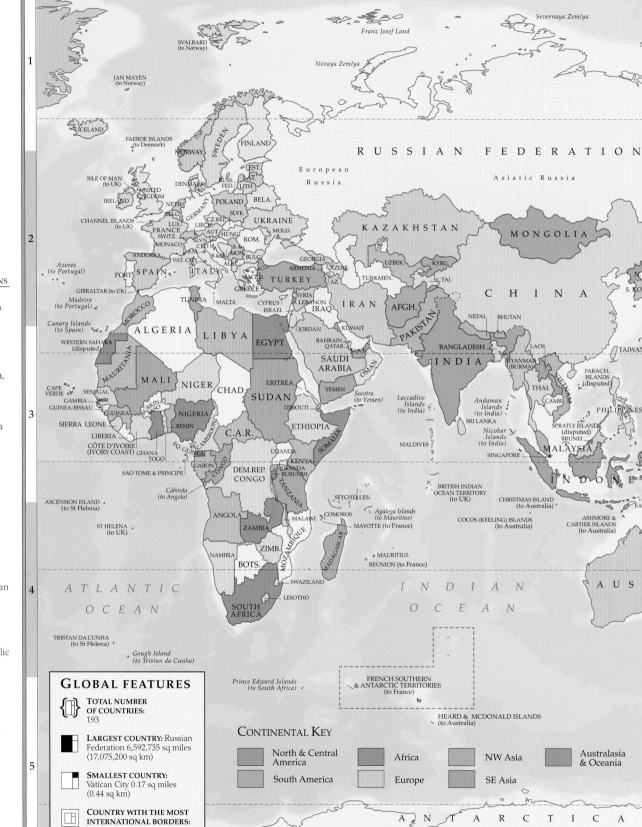

GLOBAL FEATURES

**TOTAL NUMBER
OF COUNTRIES:**
193

LARGEST COUNTRY: Russian
Federation 6,592,735 sq miles
(17,075,200 sq km)

SMALLEST COUNTRY:
Vatican City 0.17 sq miles
(0.44 sq km)

**COUNTRY WITH THE MOST
INTERNATIONAL BORDERS:**
China 14 / Russ. Fed. 14

CONTINENTAL KEY

North & Central America

South America

Africa

Europe

NW Asia

SE Asia

Australasia & Oceania

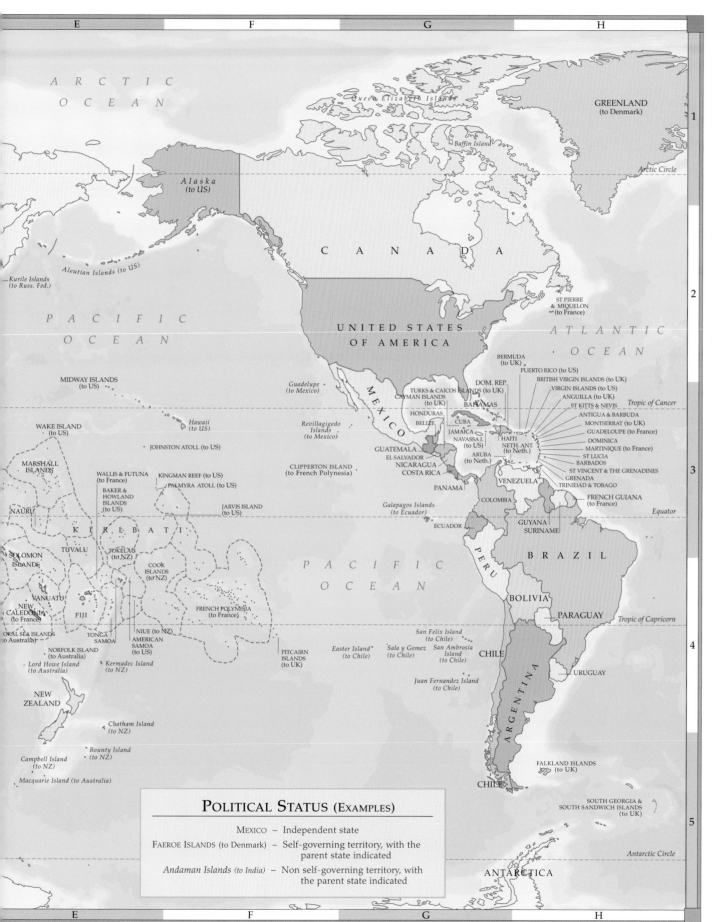

POLITICAL STATUS (EXAMPLES)

MEXICO — Independent state

FAEROE ISLANDS (to Denmark) — Self-governing territory, with the parent state indicated

Andaman Islands (to India) — Non self-governing territory, with the parent state indicated

ABBREVIATIONS

LITH.
Lithuania

LUX.
Luxembourg

MACED.
Macedonia

MOLD.
Moldova

NETH.
Netherlands

NETH. ANT.
Netherland Antilles

PORT.
Portugal

ROM.
Romania

RUSS. FED.
Russian Federation

S. & MON.
Serbia & Montenegro (Yugoslavia)

SLVK.
Slovakia

SLVN.
Slovenia

S. M.
San Marino

SWITZ.
Switzerland

TAJ.
Tajikistan

THAI.
Thailand

TURKMEN.
Turkmenistan

U. A. E.
United Arab Emirates

UZBECK.
Uzbekistan

VAT. CITY
Vatican City

ZIMB.
Zimbabwe

THE PHYSICAL WORLD

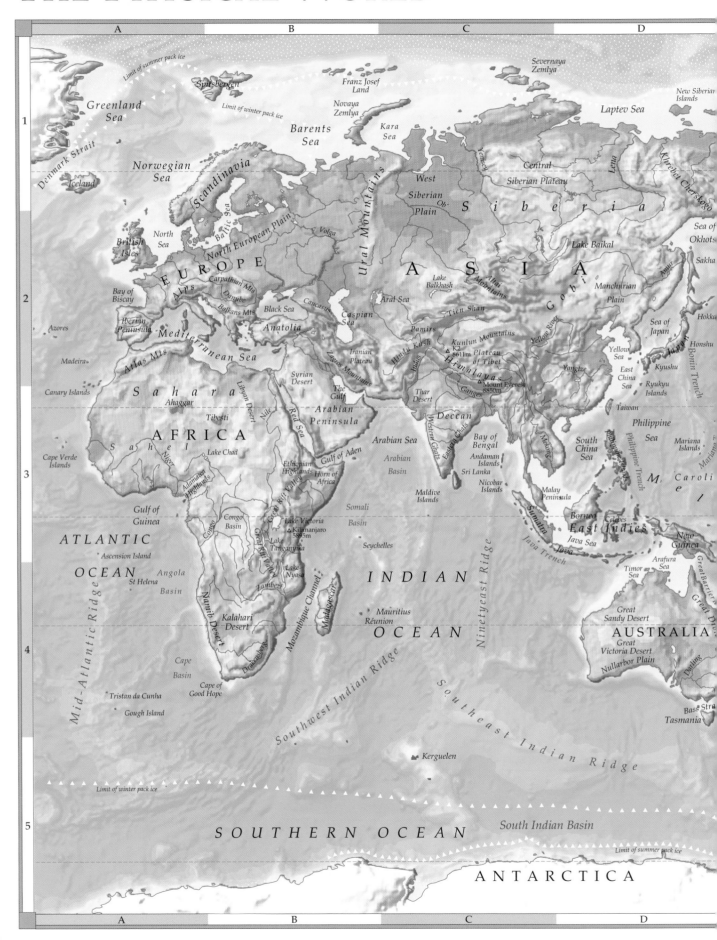

THE PHYSICAL WORLD

Greenland Sea

Denmark Strait

Iceland

Norwegian Sea

Limit of summer pack ice

Spitsbergen

Limit of winter pack ice

Franz Josef Land

Novaya Zemlya

Barents Sea

Kara Sea

Severnaya Zemlya

Laptev Sea

New Siberian Islands

Khrebet Cherskogo

Scandinavia

Baltic Sea

North European Plain

British Isles

North Sea

EUROPE

Bay of Biscay

Alps

Carpathian Mts

Danube

Balkans Mts

Black Sea

Anatolia

Caucasus

Volga

Ural Mountains

West Siberian Plain

Ob

SIBERIA

Yenisey

Central Siberian Plateau

Lena

ASIA

Lake Baikal

Amur

Sea of Okhots

Sakha

Caspian Sea

Aral Sea

Lake Balkhash

Altai Mountains

Tien Shan

Yellow River

Manchurian Plain

Sea of Japan

Hokka

Azores

Iberian Peninsula

Mediterranean Sea

Madeira

Atlas Mts

Canary Islands

Sahara

Ahaggar

Libyan Desert

Tibesti

Nile

Syrian Desert

Iranian Plateau

Zagros Mountains

The Gulf

Red Sea

Arabian Peninsula

Pamirs

Hindu Kush

Indus

K2 8611m

Plateau of Tibet

Himalayas

Kunlun Mountains

Mount Everest 8850m

Ganges

Thar Desert

Deccan

Yangtze

Yellow Sea

East China Sea

Honshu

Kyushu

Ryukyu Islands

Taiwan

Japan

Bonin Trench

AFRICA

Sahel

Niger

Lake Chad

Adamawa Highlands

Cape Verde Islands

Ethiopian Highlands

Gulf of Aden

Horn of Africa

Arabian Sea

Arabian Basin

Western Ghats

Eastern Ghats

Bay of Bengal

Andaman Islands

Sri Lanka

Maldive Islands

Nicobar Islands

Somali Basin

Philippine Sea

Mariana Islands

Philippine Trench

Mariana T

Caroli

South China Sea

Malay Peninsula

Sumatra

Borneo

Celebes

Java Sea

Java

East Indies

New Guinea

ATLANTIC

Gulf of Guinea

Congo

Congo Basin

Great Rift Valley

Lake Victoria

Kilimanjaro 5895m

Lake Tanganyika

Ascension Island

St Helena

Angola Basin

OCEAN

Zambezi

Lake Nyasa

Seychelles

INDIAN

Mauritius

Réunion

OCEAN

Ninetyeast Ridge

Java Trench

Timor Sea

Arafura Sea

Great Barrier Re

Great Di

AUSTRALIA

Great Sandy Desert

Namib Desert

Kalahari Desert

Mozambique Channel

Madagascar

Cape Basin

Drakensberg

Cape of Good Hope

Tristan da Cunha

Gough Island

Mid-Atlantic Ridge

Southwest Indian Ridge

Southeast Indian Ridge

Kerguelen

Great Victoria Desert

Nullarbor Plain

Darling

Bass Stra

Tasmania

SOUTHERN OCEAN

South Indian Basin

Limit of winter pack ice

Limit of summer pack ice

ANTARCTICA

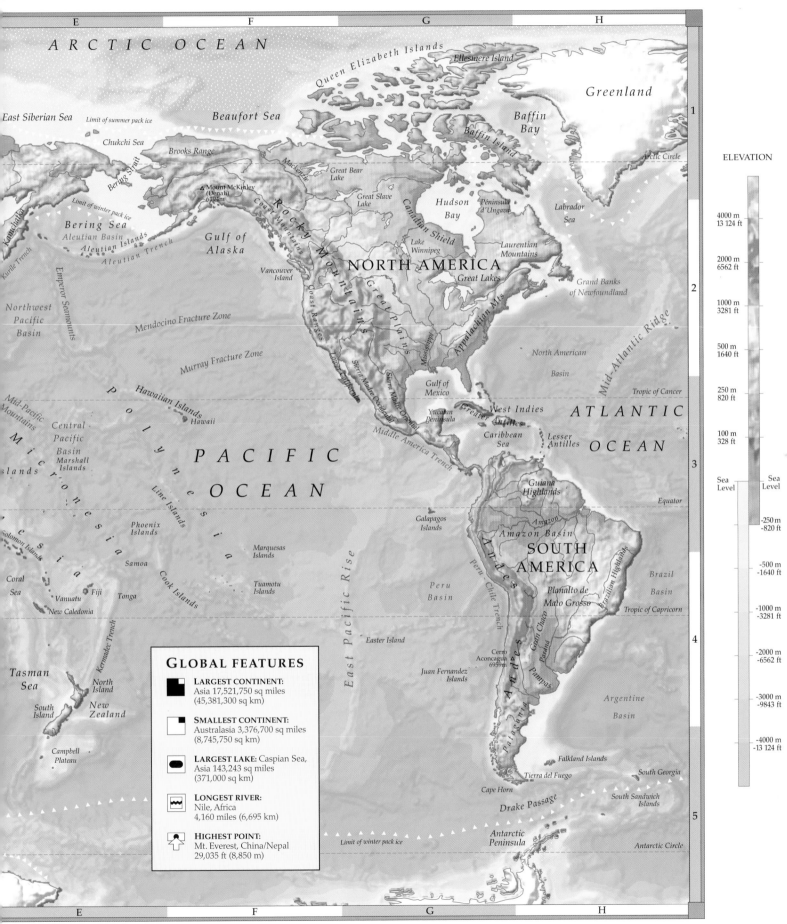

GLOBAL FEATURES

LARGEST CONTINENT:
Asia 17,521,750 sq miles
(45,381,300 sq km)

SMALLEST CONTINENT:
Australasia 3,376,700 sq miles
(8,745,750 sq km)

LARGEST LAKE: Caspian Sea,
Asia 143,243 sq miles
(371,000 sq km)

LONGEST RIVER:
Nile, Africa
4,160 miles (6,695 km)

HIGHEST POINT:
Mt. Everest, China/Nepal
29,035 ft (8,850 m)

ELEVATION

4000 m / 13 124 ft
2000 m / 6562 ft
1000 m / 3281 ft
500 m / 1640 ft
250 m / 820 ft
100 m / 328 ft
Sea Level — Sea Level
-250 m / -820 ft
-500 m / -1640 ft
-1000 m / -3281 ft
-2000 m / -6562 ft
-3000 m / -9843 ft
-4000 m / -13 124 ft

TIME ZONES

The numbers represented thus: +2/-2, indicate the number of hours ahead or behind GMT (Greenwich Mean Time) of each time zone.

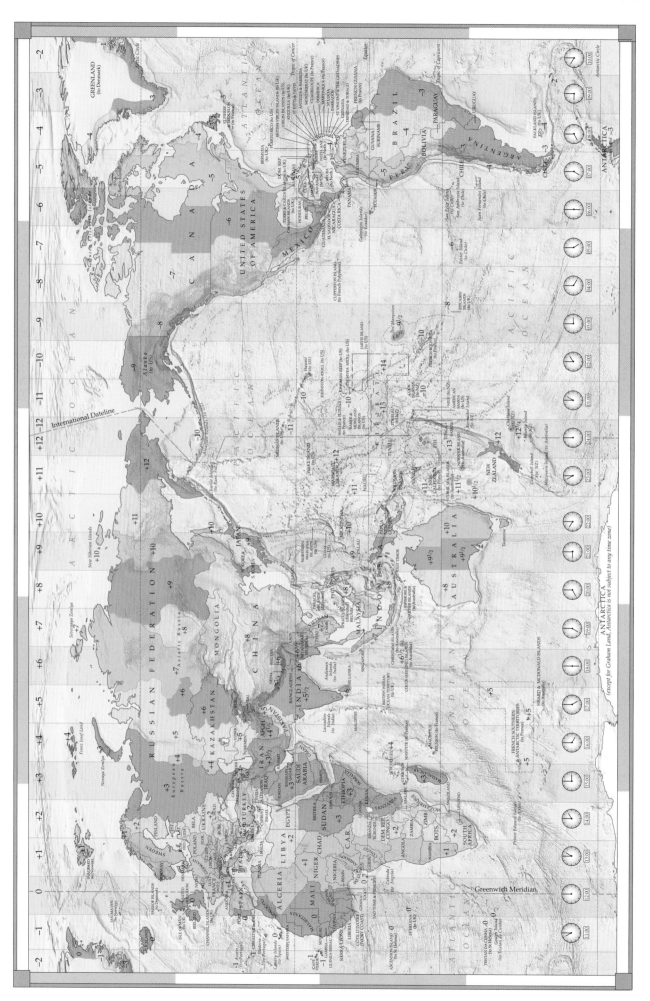

THE
WORLD
ATLAS

NORTH & CENTRAL AMERICA

POPULATION

 Over 500,000

◉ 100,000 - 500,000

○ 50,000 - 100,000

· Less than 50,000

• National capital

(Map content includes labels:)

EUROPE · ASIA

Barents Sea · Svalbard (to Norway) · Mohns Ridge · Greenland Sea · Jan Mayen (to Norway) · Denmark Strait · Iceland · Reykjanes Basin · North Atlantic Mid-Ocean Canyon · Newfoundland · St. John's · Grand Banks of

Nansen Basin · Nansen Cordillera · Wandel Sea · Kap Morris Jesup · Lincoln Sea · Kong Frederik VIII Land · Kong Christian X Land · GREENLAND (to Denmark) · Kong Christian IX Land · Kong Frederik VI Kyst · NUUK · Limit of winter pack ice · Labrador Basin · Labrador Sea · Labrador · Torngat Mountains · Gulf of

Laptev Sea · North Pole · Lomonosov Ridge · Makarov Basin · Mendeleyev Ridge · Alpha Cordillera · ARCTIC OCEAN · Ellesmere Island · Queen Elizabeth Islands · Baffin Bay · Davis Strait · Baffin Island · Peninsule d'Ungava · Ungava Bay · Smallwood Reservoir

East Siberian Sea · Wrangel Island · Chukchi Plateau · Canada Basin · Beaufort Sea · Banks Island · Victoria Island · Prince of Wales Island · Lancaster Sound · Gulf of Boothia · Foxe Basin · Southampton Island · Hudson Bay · Belcher Islands · James Bay · Lake Nipigon · Lake Winnipeg · Winnipeg

Chukchi Sea · Saint Lawrence Island · Nunivak Island · Limit of summer pack ice · Great Bear Lake · Great Slave Lake · Lake Athabasca · Reindeer Lake · CANADA · Saskatoon · Regina · Lake Winnipeg

ASIA · Bering Sea · Norton Sound · Yukon · Alaska (to U.S.) · Brooks Range · Mount McKinley (Denali) 6194m · Arctic Circle · Mackenzie · Mackenzie Mountains · Rocky Mountains · Edmonton · Calgary · Athabasca · Mount Logan 5959m

Bering Strait · Bristol Bay · Alaska Range · Aleutian Range · Anchorage · Gulf of Alaska · Juneau · Alexander Archipelago · Queen Charlotte Islands · Coast Mountains · Vancouver Island · Vancouver · Victoria · Seattle · Mount Rainier 4392m · Cascadia Basin · Cascade Range · Eugene · Boise · Snake

Aleutian Basin · Kodiak Island · Aleutian Trench · Aleutian Islands · PACIFIC OCEAN

THE WORLD ATLAS

A   B   C   D

Poluostrov Kamchatka

160°

170°

△ 93

Arctic Circle

60°

70°

170°

180°

80°

RUSSIAN FEDERATION

Ostrov Vrangelya

ARCTIC

1

Chukchi Sea

Wevok

Point Lay

Barrow

△ 130

Attu Island

Near Islands

Bering Sea

Gambell

Bering Strait

Wales

Kivalina

Deering

Colville River

Prudhoe Bay

Umiat

Kaktovi

2

50°

Rat Islands

Saint Lawrence Island

Norton Sound

Brooks Range

Amchitka Island

170°

Nunivak Island

Alakanuk

Grayling

Yukon River

Kokrines

Fort Yukon

Aklavik

180°

Pribilof Islands

Kwigillingok

Kuskokwim Mts

ALASKA (to US)

Fairbanks

Fort McPherson

Aleutian Islands

Andreanof Islands

Atka

Platinum

Alaska Range

Mount McKinley (Denali) 6194m

McKinley Park

Yukon River

Umnak Island

Dutch Harbor

Bristol Bay

Iliamna Lake

Susitna

3

Unalaska Island

Anchorage

Hope

Gulkana

YUKON

Mackenz

Unimak Island

Alaska Peninsula

Valdez

Chitina

TERRITORY

Belkofski

Shumagin Islands

Kodiak

Cordova

Katalla

Mount Logan 5959m

Whitehorse

ROCK

Kodiak Island

Gulf of Alaska

Yakutat

160°

Haines

Atlin

PACIFIC

Gustavus

Juneau

40°

Alexander Archipelago

Kake

BRITISH

170°

Port Alexander

4

131

Ketchikan

Prince Rupert

OCEAN

Kitimat

Queen Charlotte Islands

Ocean Falls

Queen Charlotte Sound

Mount Waddington 4016m

Port Hardy

Campbell River

160°

N

Vancouver Island

Nanaimo

5

0 km   400

0 miles   400

150°

131

40°

140°

130°

Victoria

A   B   C   D

POPULATION

⊙ Over 500,000

◉ 100,000 – 500,000

○ 50,000 – 100,000

○ Less than 50,000

● Internal administrative capital

NORTH & CENTRAL AMERICA

ELEVATION

4000 m
13 124 ft

2000 m
6562 ft

1000 m
3281 ft

500 m
1640 ft

250 m
820 ft

100 m
328 ft

Sea Level — Sea Level

-250 m
-820 ft

-500 m
-1640 ft

-1000 m
-3281 ft

-2000 m
-6562 ft

-3000 m
-9843 ft

-4000 m
-13 124 ft

OCEAN

Queen Elizabeth Islands

Ellesmere Island

Axel Heiberg Island

Ellef Ringnes Island

Isachsen

Amund Ringnes Island

Prince Patrick Island

Mould Bay

Melville Island

Bathurst Island

Cornwallis Island

Devon Island

Resolute

Banks Island

Viscount Melville Sound

Beaufort Sea

Sachs Harbour

Tuktoyaktuk

Amundsen Gulf

Holman

Victoria Island

McClintock Channel

Somerset Island

Prince of Wales Island

Boothia Peninsula

Gulf of Boothia

Brodeur Peninsula

Lancaster Sound

GREENLAND
(to Denmark)

Knud Rasmussen Land

Nares Strait

Alert

133

Baffin Bay

Davis Strait

Arctic Circle

60

Baffin Island

Cumberland Sound

uvik

Paulatuk

Fort Good Hope

Great Bear Lake

Echo Bay

Mackenzie

Cambridge Bay

King William Island

Pelly Bay

Gjoa Haven

Repulse Bay

Igloolik

Melville Peninsula

Foxe Basin

Nettilling Lake

Amadjuak Lake

Iqaluit

Hudson Strait

Kugluktuk

Burnside

NUNAVUT

Garry Lake

Back

Baker Lake

Southampton Island

Coral Harbour

NORTHWEST TERRITORIES

ungsten

Edzo

Yellowknife

Reliance

Lutselk'e

Great Slave Lake

Fort Simpson

Fort Providence

Fort Liard

Hay River

Fort Smith

Fort Nelson

OLUMBIA

Ware

Dubawnt

Rankin Inlet

Whale Cove

Arviat

Coats Island

Mansel Island

Péninsule d'Ungava

QUÉBEC

Hudson Bay

Churchill

Belcher Islands

James Bay

16

Lake Athabasca

Fort Vermilion

Fort McMurray

Fox Mine

Reindeer Lake

Wollaston Lake

C A N A D A

Southern Indian Lake

Nelson

Thompson

Fort St. John

ALBERTA

Grande Prairie

Athabasca

SASKATCHEWAN

Buffalo Narrows

Flin Flon

Lake Winnipeg

The Pas

MANITOBA

ONTARIO

Prince George

Edmonton

Mount Robson 3954m

Leduc

Red Deer

Kamloops

Calgary

Kelowna

Cranbrook

ancouver

Athabasca

North Saskatchewan

Saskatchewan

Prince Albert

Saskatoon

Kindersley

Yorkton

Regina

Medicine Hat

Lethbridge

Milk River

Qu'Appelle

Brandon

Weyburn

Melita

Estevan

Lake Manitoba

Winnipeg

Lake of the Woods

Lake Superior

Lake Michigan

Lake Huron

23

Eastern Canada

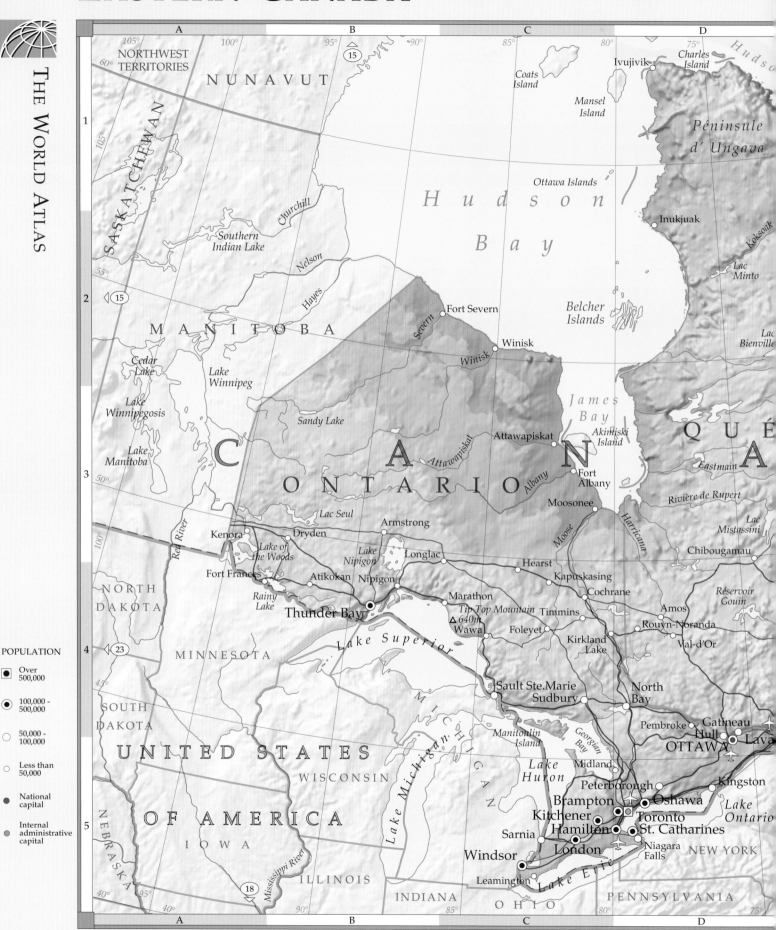

THE WORLD ATLAS

NORTHWEST
TERRITORIES

NUNAVUT

SASKATCHEWAN

MANITOBA

Churchill

Southern
Indian Lake

Nelson

Hayes

Cedar
Lake

Lake
Winnipeg

Lake
Winnipegosis

Lake
Manitoba

Red River

Kenora

Dryden

Lake of
the Woods

Fort Frances

Rainy
Lake

NORTH
DAKOTA

MINNESOTA

SOUTH
DAKOTA

NEBRASKA

UNITED STATES

OF AMERICA

IOWA

WISCONSIN

ILLINOIS

INDIANA

Mississippi River

C A N A D A

ONTARIO

Sandy Lake

Lac Seul

Armstrong

Lake
Nipigon

Longlac

Atikokan

Nipigon

Thunder Bay

Lake Superior

MICHIGAN

Severn

Fort Severn

Winisk

Winisk

Attawapiskat

Attawapiskat

Albany

Moose

Fort
Albany

Moosonee

Hearst

Marathon

Tip Top Mountain
△ 640m
Wawa

Foleyet

Kapuskasing

Cochrane

Timmins

Kirkland
Lake

Sault Ste.Marie

Sudbury

North
Bay

Lake
Michigan

Manitoulin
Island

Georgian
Bay

Lake
Huron

Midland

Peterborough

Brampton

Kitchener

Hamilton

Sarnia

Windsor

London

Leamington

Lake Erie

OHIO

Niagara
Falls

Oshawa

Toronto

St. Catharines

Lake
Ontario

Kingston

NEW YORK

PENNSYLVANIA

Pembroke

Gatineau

Hull

OTTAWA

Laval

Harricana

Amos

Rouyn-Noranda

Val-d'Or

Réservoir
Gouin

Chibougamau

Lac
Mistassini

Rivière de Rupert

Eastmain

Lac
Bienville

Lac
Minto

Koksoak

Péninsule
d' Ungava

Inukjuak

Ivujivik

Charles
Island

Hudson

QUÉ

QUÉ

Hudson

Bay

Coats
Island

Mansel
Island

Ottawa Islands

Belcher
Islands

James
Bay

Akimiski
Island

Coats
Island

15

15

23

18

POPULATION

Over
500,000

100,000 -
500,000

50,000 -
100,000

Less than
50,000

National
capital

Internal
administrative
capital

16

ELEVATION

4000 m
13 124 ft

2000 m
6562 ft

1000 m
3281 ft

500 m
1640 ft

250 m
820 ft

100 m
328 ft

| Sea Level | Sea Level |

-250 m
-820 m

-500 m
-1640 ft

-1000 m
-3281 ft

-2000 m
-6562 ft

-3000 m
-9843 ft

-4000 m
-13 124 ft

Labrador Sea

Baffin Island

Strait

Resolution Island

Button Islands

Akpatok Island

Ungava Bay

Kuujjuaq

Rivière à la Baleine

Caniapiscau

Nain

Hopedale
Makkovik

Cape Harrison

Scheffervillle

NEWFOUNDLAND

Cartwright

Smallwood Reservoir

Lake Melville

Churchill

Réservoir de Caniapiscau

BEC

D

A

& LABRADOR

St.Anthony

Strait of Belle Isle

Laurentian Mountains

Havre-St-Pierre

Réservoir Manicouagan

Sept-Îles

Île d'Anticosti

Corner Brook

Gander

Grand Falls

St.John's

Newfoundland

Baie-Comeau

St.Lawrence

Gaspé

Gulf of St. Lawrence

Cape Race

Lac St-Jean

Matane

Péninsule de Gaspé

Cabot Strait

Channel-Port aux Basques

Chicoutimi

Rimouski

Îles de la Madeleine

ST PIERRE & MIQUELON
(to France)

nquière

Rivière-du-Loup

Bathurst

PRINCE EDWARD ISLAND

Glace Bay
Sydney

La Tuque

Edmundston

NEW BRUNSWICK

Charlottetown

Cape Breton Island

Charlesbourg

Québec

St-Georges

Moncton

Amherst

Oromocto

New Glasgow

Trois-Rivières

Fredericton

Truro

NOVA SCOTIA

Sable Island

Drummondville

Saint John

Montréal

MAINE

Bay of Fundy

Dartmouth
Halifax

Sherbrooke

Liverpool

VERMONT

Yarmouth

ATLANTIC

NEW HAMPSHIRE

MASSACHUSETTS

Cape Cod

OCEAN

N

CONNECTICUT

RHODE ISLAND

USA: The Northeast

POPULATION

- ◙ Over 500,000
- ◉ 100,000 – 500,000
- ○ 50,000 – 100,000
- ○ Less than 50,000
- ● National capital
- ● Internal administrative capital

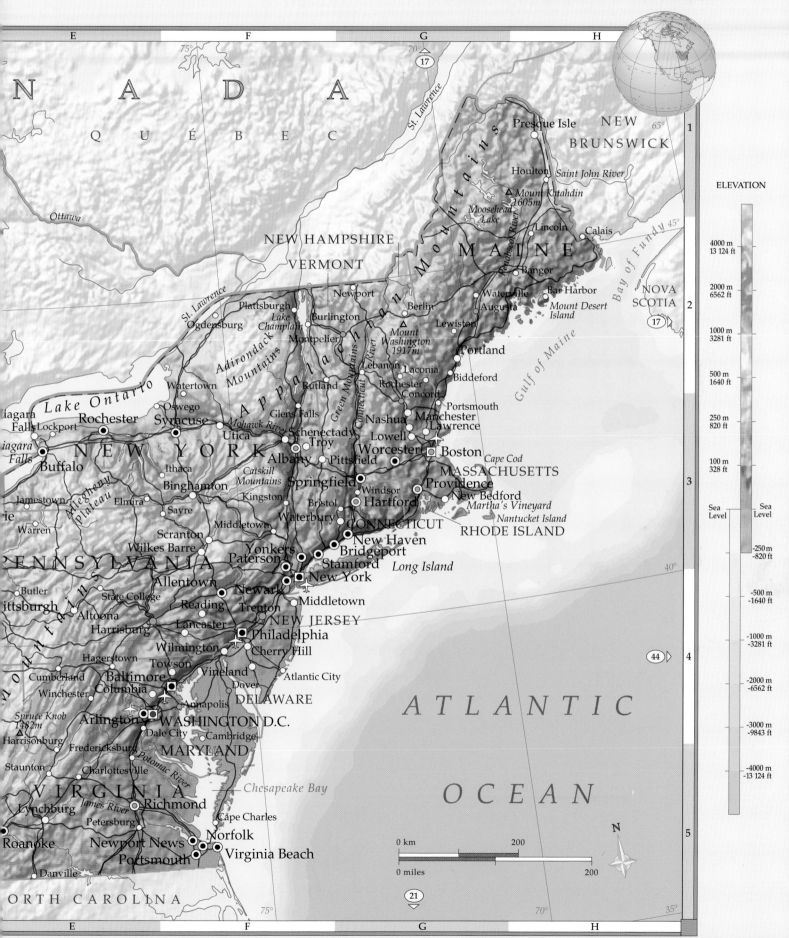

E   F   G   H

ELEVATION

N · A · D · A

QUÉBEC

Ottawa

St. Lawrence

17

NEW
BRUNSWICK

Presque Isle

65°

1

Houlton   *Saint John River*

Mount Katahdin
1605m

*Moosehead
Lake*

Lincoln   Calais

NEW HAMPSHIRE

VERMONT

St. Lawrence

Plattsburgh

Ogdensburg

Lake
Champlain

Burlington

Montpelier

Newport

Berlin

Mount
Washington
1917m

Watervillle

Augusta

Bangor

Bar Harbor

*Mount Desert
Island*

Bay of Fundy   45°

NOVA
SCOTIA

17

2

Adirondack
Mountains

Appalachian Mountains

Green Mountains

Connecticut River

Lewiston

Portland

Gulf of Maine

4000 m
13 124 ft

2000 m
6562 ft

1000 m
3281 ft

Watertown

Lebanon

Rutland

Glens Falls

Laconia

Rochester

Concord

Portsmouth

500 m
1640 ft

Lake Ontario

Oswego

iagara
Falls

Lockport

Rochester

Syracuse

Mohawk River

Utica

Schenectady
Troy

Albany

Nashua

Lowell

Manchester

Lawrence

Portsmouth

250 m
820 ft

iagara
Falls

Buffalo

NEW   YORK

Ithaca

*Catskill
Mountains*

Pittsfield

Worcester

Boston

Cape Cod

100 m
328 ft

3

Jamestown

Allegheny
Plateau

Binghamton

Kingston

Springfield

Windsor

Bristol

Hartford

Providence

New Bedford

MASSACHUSETTS

Martha's Vineyard

Sea
Level

Sea
Level

rie

Elmira

Sayre

Waterbury

Middletown

CONNECTICUT

New Haven

Nantucket Island

RHODE ISLAND

Warren

Scranton

Yonkers

Bridgeport

Stamford

Long Island

-250 m
-820 ft

PENNSYLVANIA

Wilkes Barre

Paterson

New York

40°

-500 m
-1640 ft

Butler

Allentown

State College

Reading

Newark

Middletown

ittsburgh

Altoona

Lancaster

Trenton

NEW JERSEY

-1000 m
-3281 ft

Harrisburg

Philadelphia

Cherry Hill

44

4

Wilmington

Atlantic City

-2000 m
-6562 ft

Hagerstown

Towson

Vineland

Cumberland

Baltimore

Dover

Winchester

Columbia

Annapolis

DELAWARE

-3000 m
-9843 ft

*Spruce Knob
1482m*

Arlington

WASHINGTON D.C.

Harrisonburg

Dale City

Cambridge

-4000 m
-13 124 ft

Staunton

Fredericksburg

MARYLAND

Potomac River

Chesapeake Bay

ATLANTIC

Charlottesville

VIRGINIA

James River

Richmond

OCEAN

Lynchburg

Petersburg

Cape Charles

N

5

Roanoke

Newport News

Norfolk

0 km   200

Danville

Portsmouth

Virginia Beach

0 miles   200

ORTH CAROLINA

21

E   F   G   H

USA: THE SOUTHEAST

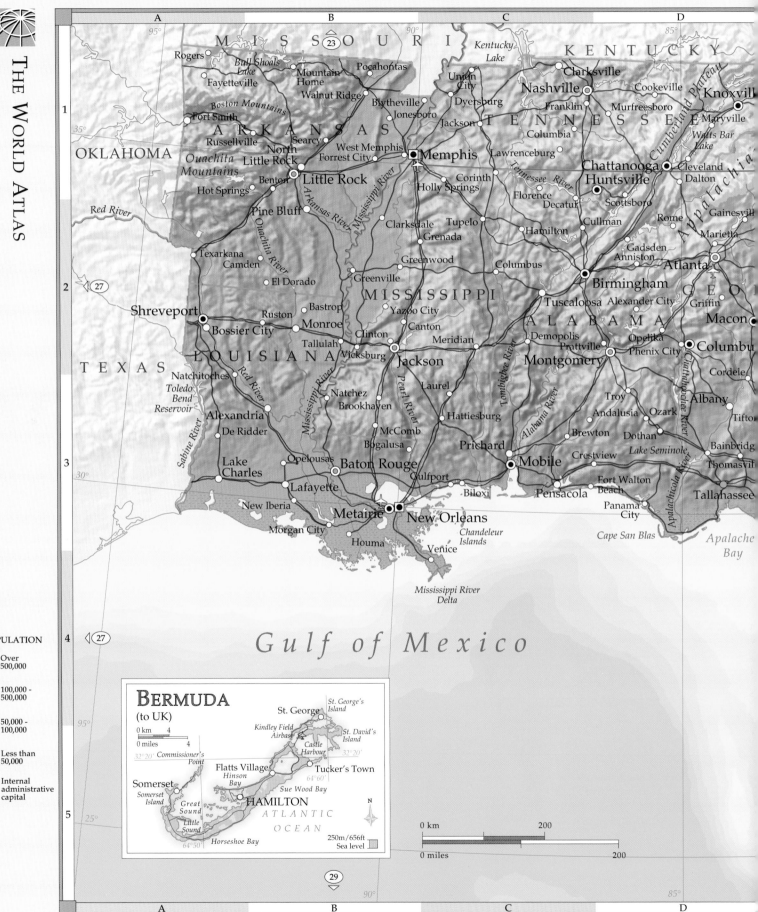

POPULATION

- ◉ Over 500,000
- ◉ 100,000 – 500,000
- ○ 50,000 – 100,000
- ○ Less than 50,000
- ● Internal administrative capital

BERMUDA
(to UK)

0 km 4
0 miles 4

St. George's Island
St. George
Kindley Field Airbase
St. David's Island
Commissioner's Point
Castle Harbour
Flatts Village
Tucker's Town
Hinson Bay
Sue Wood Bay
Somerset
Somerset Island
HAMILTON
Great Sound
Little Sound
ATLANTIC OCEAN
Horseshoe Bay

250m/656ft
Sea level

0 km 200
0 miles 200

Gulf of Mexico

E   F   G   H

VIRGINIA

80°

△ 19

75°

Elizabeth City

Kingsport

Greeneville

Winston
Salem

Greensboro

Durham

Rocky
Mount

High
Point

Raleigh

Greenville

△ Mount Mitchell
2037m

Cary

35°

1

Asheville

NORTH CAROLINA

Goldsboro

New Bern

Cape Hatteras

Gastonia

Charlotte

Fayetteville

Havelock

Pamlico Sound

Spartanburg

Laurinburg

Greenville

Rock Hill

Jacksonville

Onslow
Bay

Union

SOUTH CAROLINA

Florence

Wilmington

Greenwood

Cape Fear

hens

Columbia

Myrtle Beach

Clark
Hill Lake

Aiken

Lake Marion

Long Bay

Augusta

Orangeburg

Georgetown

2

△ 44 ▷

GIA

Milledgeville

North Charleston

Savannah River

Dublin

Statesboro

Charleston

Vidalia

Hilton
Head Island

Altamaha River

Savannah

ELEVATION

Hinesville

4000 m
13 124 ft

Waycross

Brunswick

2000 m
6562 ft

Valdosta

Okefenokee
Swamp

1000 m
3281 ft

A T L A N T I C

500 m
1640 ft

Jacksonville

250 m
820 ft

Lake City

O C E A N

100 m
328 ft

Gainesville

Saint Augustine

30°

3

Lake
George

Sea
Level

Sea
Level

Ocala

Daytona Beach

-250 m
-820 ft

De Land

Deltona

Spring Hill

Orlando

Cape Canaveral

-500 m
-1640 ft

Clear-
water

Lakeland

Melbourne

-1000 m
-3281 ft

argo

Tampa

Lake Kissimmee

△ 44 ▷

4

Tampa
Bay

Saint Petersburg

Fort Pierce

-2000 m
-6562 ft

Sarasota

FLORIDA

Hutchinson
Island

-3000 m
-9843 ft

Port Charlotte

Lake
Okeechobee

West Palm
Beach

Great Abaco

-4000 m
-13 124 ft

Charlotte Harbor

Grand
Bahama Island

Fort Myers

Boca Raton

Naples

Big Cypress
Swamp

Pompano Beach

Fort Lauderdale

N

Miami Beach

BAHAMAS

The Everglades

Miami

Eleuthera Island

Cape Sable

Key Largo

25°

5

New
Providence

Florida
Bay

Florida Keys

Andros Island

Cat Island

Key West

32 ▷

Straits of Florida

San Salvador

80°

75°

E   F   G   H

USA: CENTRAL STATES

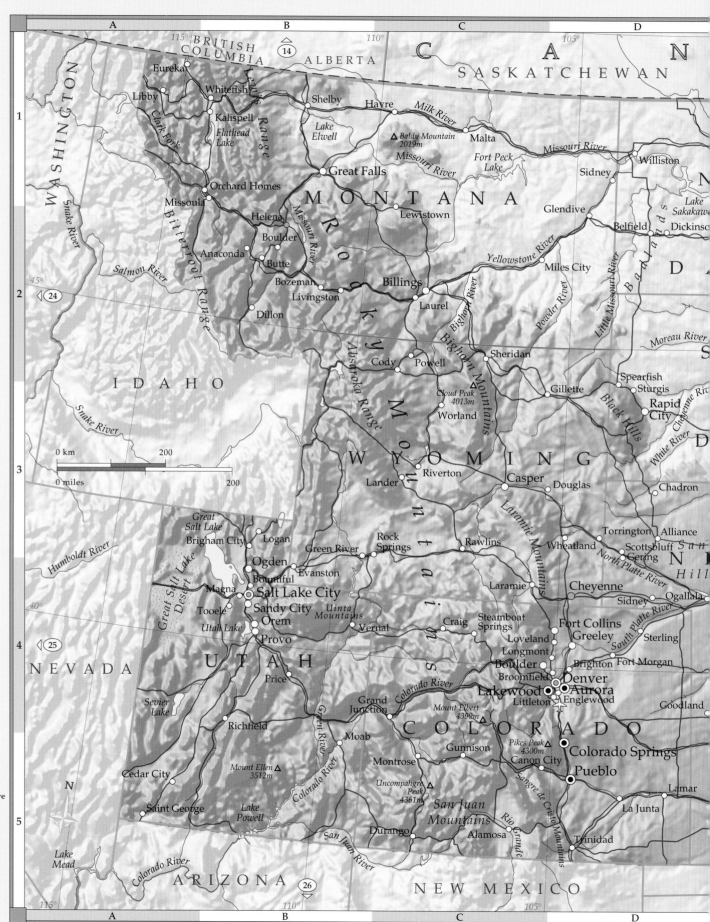

POPULATION

- ⬤ Over 500,000
- ◉ 100,000 - 500,000
- ○ 50,000 - 100,000
- ○ Less than 50,000
- ● Internal administrative capital

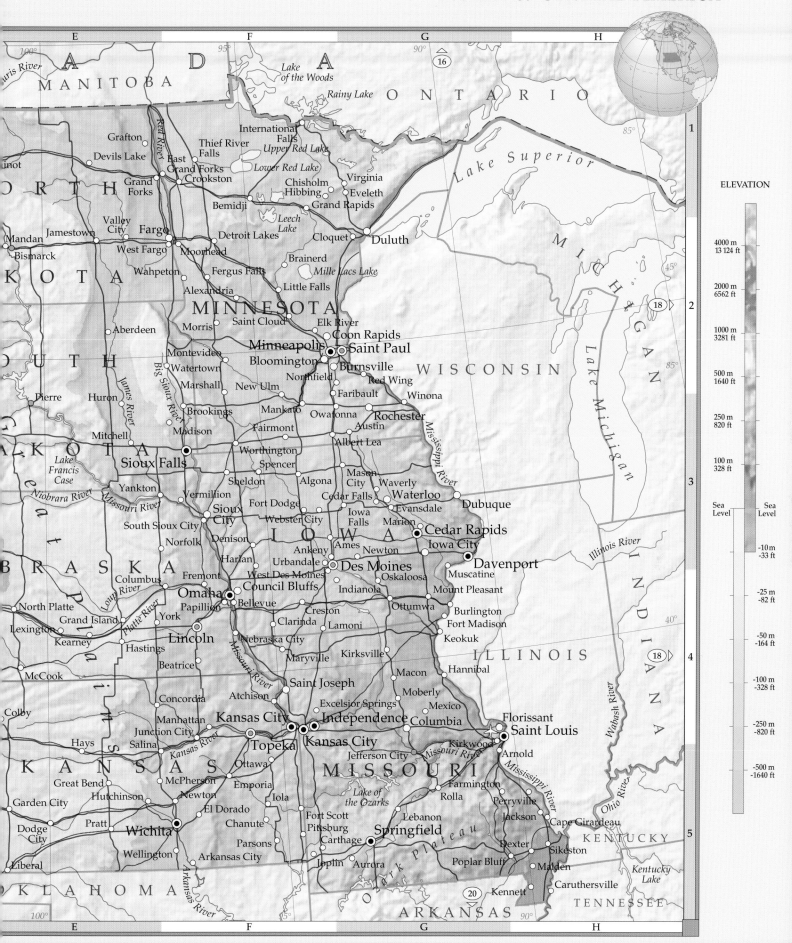

ELEVATION

4000 m 13 124 ft	
2000 m 6562 ft	
1000 m 3281 ft	
500 m 1640 ft	
250 m 820 ft	
100 m 328 ft	
Sea Level	Sea Level
−10 m −33 ft	
−25 m −82 ft	
−50 m −164 ft	
−100 m −328 ft	
−250 m −820 ft	
−500 m −1640 ft	

CANADA

MANITOBA
ONTARIO

Lake of the Woods
Rainy Lake
Upper Red Lake
Lower Red Lake
Lake Superior
MICHIGAN
Lake Michigan

Grafton
Devils Lake
Thief River Falls
International Falls
Virginia
Chisholm
Hibbing
Eveleth
Grand Rapids
Bemidji
Leech Lake

inot
East Grand Forks
Crookston
Grand Forks

NORTH
DAKOTA

Mandan
Bismarck
Jamestown
Valley City
Fargo
West Fargo
Moorhead
Wahpeton
Fergus Falls
Detroit Lakes
Brainerd
Mille Lacs Lake
Little Falls
Duluth
Cloquet

SOUTH
DAKOTA

Aberdeen
Alexandria
MINNESOTA
Morris
Saint Cloud
Elk River
Coon Rapids
Minneapolis
Saint Paul
Bloomington
Burnsville
Northfield
Red Wing

WISCONSIN

Pierre
Huron
Montevideo
Watertown
Marshall
New Ulm
Faribault
Winona

Big Sioux River
James River
Mitchell
Madison
Brookings
Mankato
Owatonna
Rochester
Austin
Fairmont
Albert Lea

Mississippi River

Lake Francis Case
Sioux Falls
Worthington
Spencer
Mason City
Waverly
Algona
Cedar Falls
Waterloo
Evansdale
Dubuque

Niobrara River
Yankton
Vermillion
Sheldon
Fort Dodge
Iowa Falls
Marion
Cedar Rapids

Missouri River

NEBRASKA

South Sioux City
Sioux City
Webster City
Ames
Newton
Iowa City
Davenport

Norfolk
Denison
IOWA
Ankeny
Urbandale
Des Moines
Muscatine

Columbus
Fremont
West Des Moines
Oskaloosa
Harlan
Indianola
Mount Pleasant

North Platte
Grand Island
Loup River
Platte River
York
Omaha
Papillion
Bellevue
Council Bluffs
Creston
Ottumwa
Burlington
Fort Madison

Lexington
Kearney
Lincoln
Clarinda
Lamoni
Keokuk

McCook
Hastings
Beatrice
Maryville
Kirksville
ILLINOIS

Colby
Concordia
Atchison
Saint Joseph
Macon
Hannibal

Manhattan
Kansas City
Excelsior Springs
Independence
Moberly
Mexico
Columbia
Florissant
Saint Louis

Hays
Junction City
Salina
Kansas River
Topeka
Kansas City
Jefferson City
Kirkwood
Arnold

KANSAS
Great Bend
McPherson
Emporia
Ottawa
MISSOURI
Farmington

Garden City
Hutchinson
Newton
Iola
El Dorado
Lake of the Ozarks
Rolla
Perryville
Jackson
Cape Girardeau

Pratt
Wichita
Chanute
Fort Scott
Pittsburg
Lebanon
Springfield
Dexter
Sikeston

Dodge City
Wellington
Parsons
Carthage
Joplin
Aurora
Poplar Bluff
Malden
Caruthersville

Liberal
Arkansas City
Arkansas River
Kennett

OKLAHOMA
ARKANSAS

Missouri River
Mississippi River
Illinois River
Wabash River
Ohio River
Ozark Plateau

INDIANA
KENTUCKY
Kentucky Lake
TENNESSEE

16
18
20

23

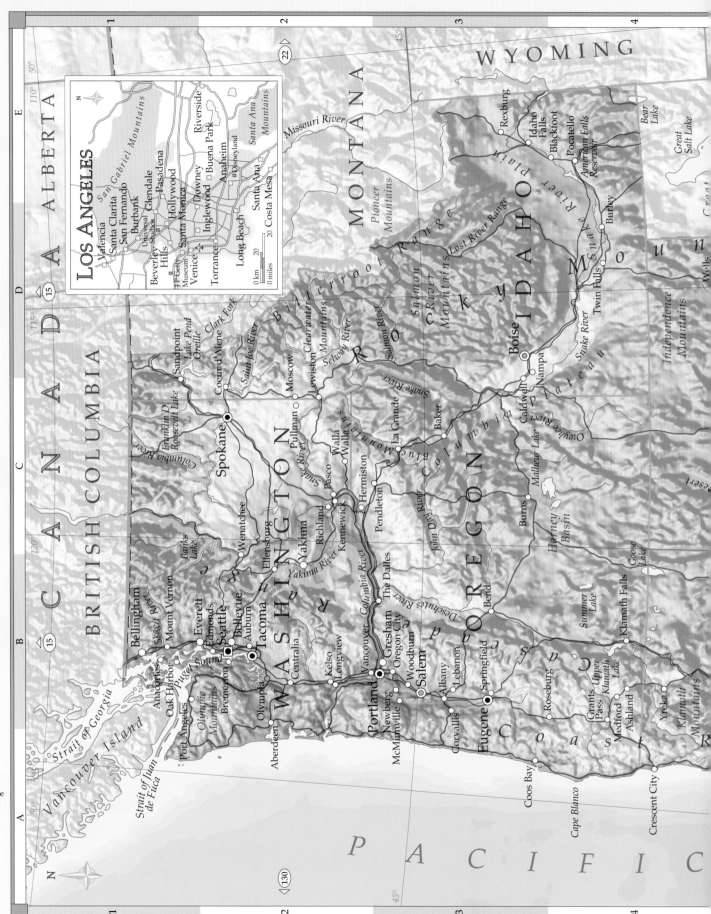

LOS ANGELES

Valencia
Santa Clarita
San Fernando
San Gabriel Mountains
Burbank
Glendale
Pasadena
Universal Studios
Hollywood
Beverley Hills
Getty Museum
Santa Monica
Venice
Inglewood
Downey
Buena Park
Anaheim
Disneyland
Santa Ana
Santa Ana Mountains
Torrance
Long Beach
Costa Mesa

0 km 20
0 miles 20

POPULATION

- ◉ Over 500,000
- ◉ 100,000 – 500,000
- ○ 50,000 – 100,000
- ○ Less than 50,000
- ● Internal administrative capital

Strait of Georgia
Vancouver Island
Strait of Juan de Fuca
PACIFIC

CANADA
BRITISH COLUMBIA
ALBERTA

WASHINGTON
OREGON
IDAHO
MONTANA
WYOMING

ROCKY MOUNTAINS

Rexburg
Idaho Falls
Blackfoot
Pocatello
American Falls Reservoir
Burley
Twin Falls
Bear Lake
Great Salt Lake
Wells

Boise
Nampa
Caldwell
Malheur Lake
Burns
Harney Basin
Independence Mountains

Spokane
Coeur d'Alene
Sandpoint
Lake Pend Oreille
Clark Fork
Franklin D. Roosevelt Lake
Columbia River
Saint Joe River
Moscow
Pullman
Lewiston
Clearwater Mountains
Selway River
Salmon River
Salmon River Mountains
Bitterroot Range
Lost River Range
Pioneer Mountains
Snake River Plain
Snake River
Owyhee River

Wenatchee
Ellensburg
Yakima
Yakima River
Richland
Pasco
Kennewick
Walla Walla
Hermiston
Pendleton
La Grande
Baker
Blue Mountains
Snake River
Banks Lake
Missouri River

Bellingham
Mount Vernon
Anacortes
Oak Harbor
Everett
Edmonds
Seattle
Bellevue
Auburn
Tacoma
Bremerton
Port Angeles
Aberdeen
Olympia
Centralia
Puget Sound
Olympic Mountains
Skagit River

Kelso
Longview
Vancouver
Portland
Gresham
Oregon City
Woodburn
Salem
Newberg
McMinnville
Corvallis
Albany
Lebanon
Springfield
Eugene
Coos Bay
Cape Blanco
Roseburg
Grants Pass
Medford
Ashland
Upper Klamath Lake
Klamath Falls
Klamath Mountains
Yreka
Crescent City
Summer Lake
Goose Lake
Bend
The Dalles
Deschutes River
John Day River
Columbia River
Coast Ranges

WYOMING

ELEVATION

4000 m
13 124 ft

2000 m
6562 ft

1000 m
3281 ft

500 m
1640 ft

250 m
820 ft

100 m
328 ft

Sea
Level

Sea
Level

-250 m
-820 ft

-500 m
-1640 ft

-1000 m
-3281 ft

-2000 m
-6562 ft

-3000 m
-9843 ft

-4000 m
-13 124 ft

UTAH

ARIZONA

MEXICO

NEVADA

CALIFORNIA

Great Basin

Sierra Nevada

Central Valley

San Joaquin Valley

Sacramento Valley

Death Valley

Mojave Desert

Chocolate Mountains

San Rafael Mountains

Santa Lucia Range

PACIFIC OCEAN

Grand Canyon

Lake Powell
Lake Mead
Lake Mohave
Colorado River
Gila River

Henderson
Las Vegas
Alamo
Ely
Tonopah
Hawthorne
Walker Lake
Mono Lake

Reese River
Humboldt River
Schell Creek Range
Ruby Mountains

Carson Sink
Pyramid Lake
Honey Lake
Black Rock
Susanville
Reno
Sparks
Carson City
South Lake Tahoe
Lake Tahoe
Citrus Heights
Chico
Yuba City
Woodland
Sacramento
Fairfield
Napa
Vallejo
Berkeley
Oakland
San Francisco
Palo Alto
Sunnyvale
San Jose
Gilroy
Santa Cruz
Monterey Bay
Monterey
Santa Maria
Lompoc
San Luis Obispo
Atascadero
Salinas
Stockton
Manteca
Modesto
Turlock
Madera
Fresno
Hanford
Selma
Visalia
Tulare Lake Bed
Porterville
Delano
Bakersfield
Ridgecrest
Mount Whitney 4418m
Lancaster
Barstow
Victorville
Santa Barbara
Oxnard
Pasadena
Los Angeles
Long Beach
Huntington Beach
Santa Catalina Island
Santa Rosa Island
San Clemente Island
Channel Islands
San Bernardino
Riverside
Santa Ana
Palm Springs
Salton Sea
Fallbrook
Oceanside
Encinitas
Escondido
El Cajon
Lakeside
San Diego
Chula Vista
Brawley
El Centro
Blythe

Redding
Ukiah
Santa Rosa
Eureka

Colorado River

20
28
28
131

40°
35°
35°
40°

120°
125°

5
6
7
8

HAWAI'I

N

Kaua'i
Ni'ihau
Lihu'e
O'ahu
Wahiawa
Kāne'ohe
Honolulu
Moloka'i
Maui
Wailuku
Mauna Kea 4205m
Hilo
Hawai'i

PACIFIC OCEAN

2000m/6562ft
1000m/3281ft
500m/1640ft
200m/656ft
Sea level

0 km
0 miles

160°
158°
156°
22°
21°
20°

0 km
200
0 miles
200
200
200

USA: THE SOUTHWEST

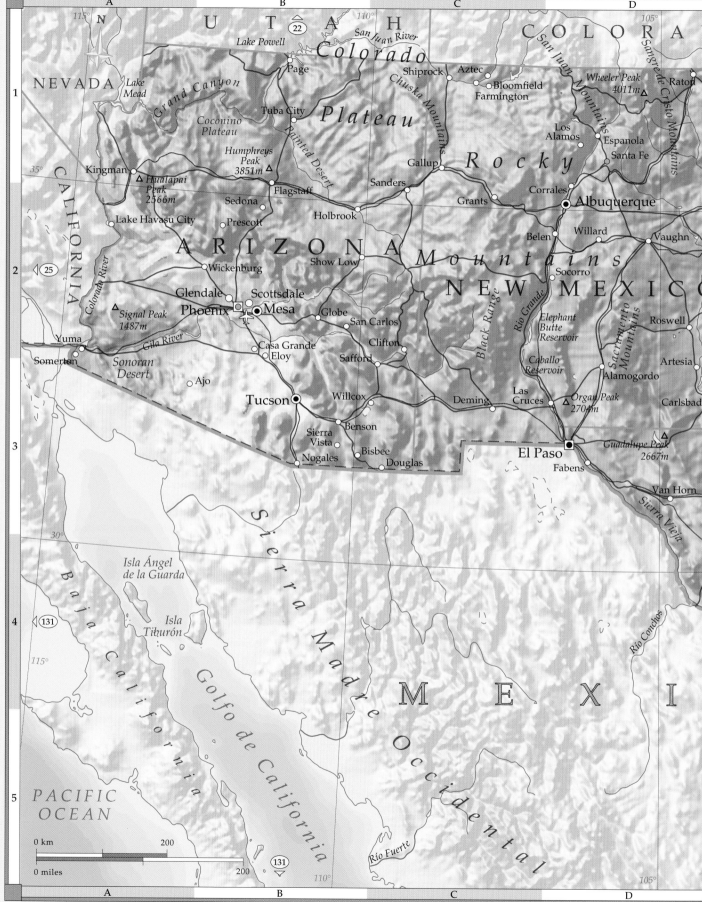

POPULATION

- ◉ Over 500,000
- ◉ 100,000 – 500,000
- ○ 50,000 – 100,000
- ○ Less than 50,000
- ● Internal administrative capital

NEVADA
UTAH
COLORADO
CALIFORNIA
ARIZONA
NEW MEXICO

Lake Powell
San Juan River
Lake Mead
Page
Shiprock
Aztec
Bloomfield
Farmington
Wheeler Peak 4011m
Raton
Grand Canyon
Coconino Plateau
Tuba City
Colorado Plateau
Chuska Mountains
Sangre de Cristo Mountains
San Juan Mountains
Los Alamos
Espanola
Santa Fe
Kingman
Humphreys Peak 3851m
Painted Desert
Gallup
Rocky
Corrales
Albuquerque
Hualapai Peak 2566m
Sedona
Flagstaff
Sanders
Grants
Lake Havasu City
Prescott
Holbrook
Belen
Willard
Vaughn
Wickenburg
Show Low
Mountains
Socorro
Roswell
Glendale
Scottsdale
Colorado River
Signal Peak 1487m
Phoenix
Mesa
Globe
San Carlos
Black Range
Rio Grande
Elephant Butte Reservoir
Yuma
Gila River
Casa Grande
Eloy
Clifton
Safford
Caballo Reservoir
Alamogordo
Artesia
Somerton
Sonoran Desert
Ajo
Willcox
Deming
Las Cruces
Organ Peak 2704m
Carlsbad
Tucson
Benson
Sierra Vista
Bisbee
El Paso
Guadalupe Peak 2667m
Nogales
Douglas
Fabens
Van Horn
Sierra Vieja
Rio Conchos
Isla Ángel de la Guarda
Sierra Madre Occidental
MEXI
Isla Tiburón
Baja California
Golfo de California
PACIFIC OCEAN
Río Fuerte

0 km 200
0 miles 200

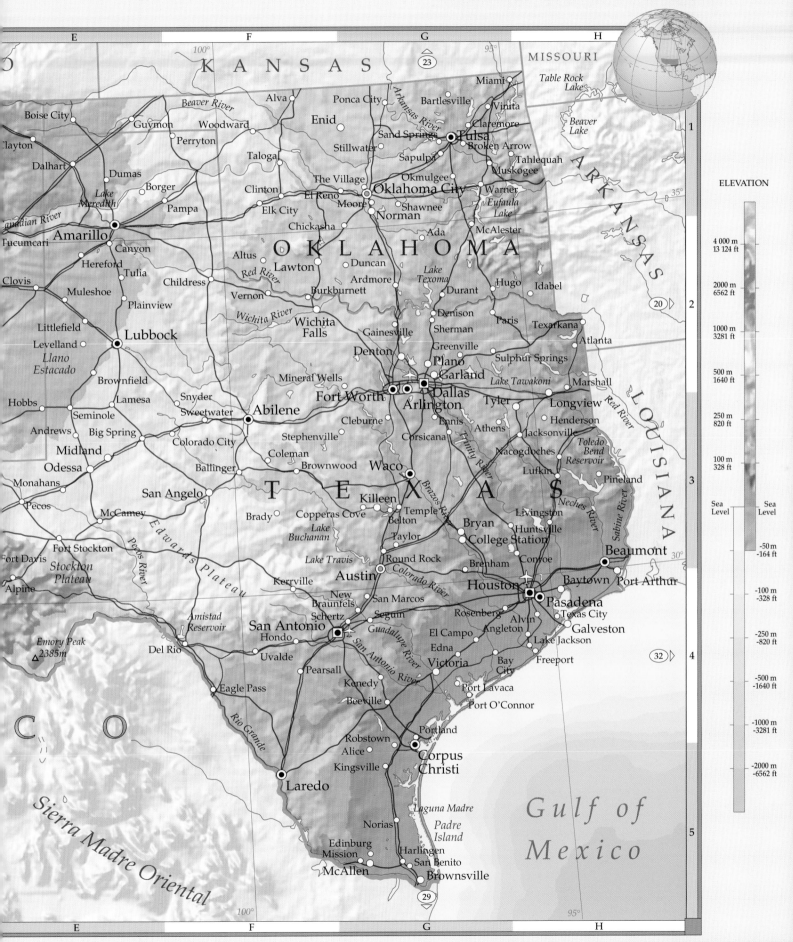

KANSAS

MISSOURI

23

Table Rock Lake

Beaver Lake

Boise City · Guymon · Woodward · Alva · Ponca City · Bartlesville · Miami · Vinita

Clayton · Dalhart · Dumas · Perryton · Enid · Sand Springs · Tulsa · Claremore · Broken Arrow · Tahlequah

Beaver River · *Arkansas River*

Dalhart · Borger · Stillwater · Okmulgee · Sapulpa · Muskogee

Lake Meredith · Pampa · Clinton · The Village · El Reno · Oklahoma City · Warner

Canadian River · Amarillo · Canyon · Elk City · Moore · Shawnee · Norman · *Eufaula Lake*

Tucumcari · Hereford · **OKLAHOMA** · Ada · McAlester

Clovis · Tulia · Altus · Lawton · Duncan · *Lake Texoma* · Hugo · Idabel

Muleshoe · Plainview · *Red River* · Vernon · Burkburnett · Ardmore · Durant

Littlefield · Lubbock · Childress · *Wichita River* · Wichita Falls · Gainesville · Sherman · Paris · Texarkana

Levelland · *Llano Estacado* · Denison · Greenville · Atlanta

Brownfield · Mineral Wells · Denton · Plano · Garland · *Lake Tawakoni* · Marshall

Hobbs · Lamesa · Snyder · Fort Worth · Dallas · Tyler · Longview

Seminole · Sweetwater · Abilene · Arlington · Ennis · Athens · Henderson · *Red River*

Andrews · Big Spring · Colorado City · Cleburne · Corsicana · Jacksonville · *Toledo Bend Reservoir*

Midland · Stephenville · Nacogdoches · Lufkin · Pineland

Odessa · Ballinger · Coleman · Brownwood · Waco · *Trinity River* · *Neches River*

Monahans · **TEXAS** · Killeen · Livingston · *Sabine River*

Pecos · San Angelo · Brady · Copperas Cove · Temple · Bryan · Huntsville

McCamey · *Edwards Plateau* · *Lake Buchanan* · Belton · College Station · Conroe · Beaumont

Fort Stockton · *Pecos River* · Taylor · Brenham · Baytown · Port Arthur

Stockton Plateau · *Lake Travis* · Round Rock · *Colorado River* · Houston · Pasadena

Fort Davis · Alpine · Kerrville · Austin · Rosenberg · Alvin · Texas City

Amistad Reservoir · New Braunfels · San Marcos · El Campo · Angleton · Galveston

San Antonio · Schertz · Seguin · Edna · Lake Jackson

Del Rio · Hondo · Uvalde · *Guadalupe River* · Victoria · Bay City · Freeport

Eagle Pass · Pearsall · *San Antonio River* · Port Lavaca

Kenedy · Port O'Connor

Beeville · Portland

Rio Grande · Robstown · Corpus Christi

Laredo · Alice · Kingsville

Norias · *Laguna Madre* · *Padre Island*

Sierra Madre Oriental · Edinburg · Harlingen

Mission · San Benito

McAllen · Brownsville

Gulf of Mexico

△ Emory Peak 2385m

29

Mexico

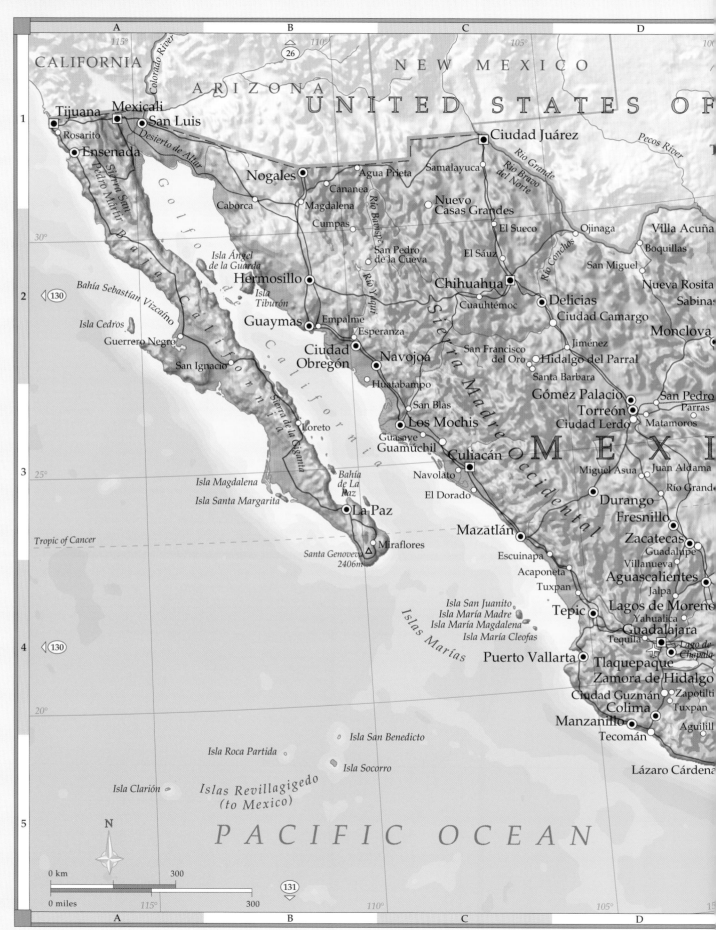

CALIFORNIA

ARIZONA

NEW MEXICO

UNITED STATES OF

Colorado River

Pecos River

Tijuana
Rosarito
Mexicali
San Luis
Ensenada
Desierto de Altar
Nogales
Agua Prieta
Samalayuca
Ciudad Juárez
Rio Grande
Río Bravo del Norte
Cananea
Magdalena
Nuevo Casas Grandes
Caborca
Cumpas
El Sueco
Ojinaga
Villa Acuña
Sierra San Pedro Mártir
Golfo de California
Isla Ángel de la Guarda
San Pedro de la Cueva
El Sáuz
Boquillas
San Miguel
Río Bavispe
Bahía Sebastián Vizcaíno
Hermosillo
Chihuahua
Nueva Rosita
Sabina
Isla Cedros
Isla Tiburón
Cuauhtémoc
Delicias
Monclova
Guerrero Negro
Guaymas
Empalme
Esperanza
Río Yaqui
Ciudad Camargo
San Francisco del Oro
Jiménez
San Ignacio
Ciudad Obregón
Navojoa
Hidalgo del Parral
Santa Barbara
Huatabampo
Gómez Palacio
San Pedro
Sierra Madre Occidental
San Blas
Torreón
Parras
Loreto
Los Mochis
Ciudad Lerdo
Matamoros
Sierra de la Giganta
Guasave
Guamúchil
MEXI
Isla Magdalena
Culiacán
Miguel Asua
Juan Aldama
Bahía de La Paz
Navolato
Río Grand
Isla Santa Margarita
El Dorado
Durango
Tropic of Cancer
La Paz
Fresnillo
Mazatlán
Zacatecas
Santa Genoveva 2406m
Miraflores
Escuinapa
Guadalupe
Acaponeta
Villanueva
Tuxpan
Aguascalientes
Jalpa
Isla San Juanito
Lagos de Moreno
Isla María Madre
Tepic
Yahualica
Isla María Magdalena
Guadalajara
Isla María Cleofas
Tequila
Lago de Chapala
Islas Marías
Puerto Vallarta
Tlaquepaque
Zamora de Hidalgo
Ciudad Guzmán
Zapotilti
Colima
Tuxpan
Manzanillo
Aguilill
Isla San Benedicto
Tecomán
Isla Roca Partida
Lázaro Cárdena
Isla Socorro
Islas Revillagigedo (to Mexico)
Isla Clarión

N

PACIFIC OCEAN

POPULATION

- Over 500,000
- 100,000 - 500,000
- 50,000 - 100,000
- Less than 50,000
- National capital

0 km   300

0 miles   300

E   F   G   H

1

ELEVATION

2

4000 m
13 124 ft

2000 m
6562 ft

1000 m
3281 ft

500 m
1640 ft

250 m
820 ft

100 m
328 ft

Sea
Level

Sea
Level

-250 m
-820 ft

-500 m
-1640 ft

-1000 m
-3281 ft

-2000 m
-6562 ft

-3000 m
-9843 ft

-4000 m
-13 124 ft

3

4

5

ALABAMA
FLORIDA
MISSISSIPPI
LOUISIANA
AMERICA
T E X A S
Brazos River
Red River
Sabine River
Mississippi River
Mississippi River Delta
Colorado River
Piedras Negras
Río Grande
Nuevo Laredo
Sabinas Hidalgo
Ciudad Miguel Alemán
Reynosa
Río Bravo
Matamoros
Padre Island
Monterrey
Saltillo
Montemorelos
Laguna Madre
Linares
Sierra Madre Oriental
Ciudad Victoria
Ciudad Mante
San Luis Potosí
Ciudad Madero
Pánuco
Tampico
Río Verde
Ciudad Valles
Dolores Hidalgo
Tamazunchale
Laguna de Tamiahua
León
Tuxpán
Guanajuato
Poza Rica
Querétaro
Papantla
Irapuato
Tulancingo
Pachuca
Teziutlán
Xalapa
Morelia
MÉXICO
Perote
Tlaxcala
Veracruz
(MEXICO CITY)
Toluca
Alvarado
Córdoba
Cuernavaca
Puebla
Uruapan
Popocatépetl 5452m
Tehuacán
Coatzacoalcos
Zacatepec
San Andrés Tuxtla
Presa del Infiernillo
Cuautla
Tuxtepec
Minatitlán
Taxco
Iguala
Ixtapa
Río Balsas
Huajuapan
Istmo de Tehuantepec
Sierra Madre del Sur
Chilpancingo
Oaxaca
Ocozocuautla
Matías Romero
Ixtepec
Tecpan
Pinotepa Nacional
Tehuantepec
Juchitán
Arriaga
Acapulco
Miahuatlán
Salina Cruz
Pijijiapán
Puerto Escondido
Puerto Angel
Golfo de Tehuantepec
Escuintla
Huixtla
Tapachula
Ciudad Hidalgo

Gulf of Mexico
Tropic of Cancer
Bahía de Campeche
Yucatan Channel
Río Lagartos
Tizimín
Cancún
Progreso
Motul
Isla Cozumel
Mérida
Umán
Valladolid
Ticul
Peto
Oxkutzcab
Tekax
Campeche
Yucatan Peninsula
Champotón
Felipe Carrillo Puerto
Chetumal
Laguna de Términos
Frontera
Comalcalco
Carmen
Fransisco Escárcega
Villahermosa
Macuspana
BELIZE
Teapa
San Cristóbal de Las Casas
Río Usumacinta
Tuxtla
Chiapa de Corzo
Comitán
Presa de la Angostura
Gulf of Honduras
GUATEMALA
HONDURAS
EL SALVADOR

131

20

44

30

95°   90°   85°   30°
25°   85°   20°   15°
100°   95°   90°

E   F   G   H

CENTRAL AMERICA

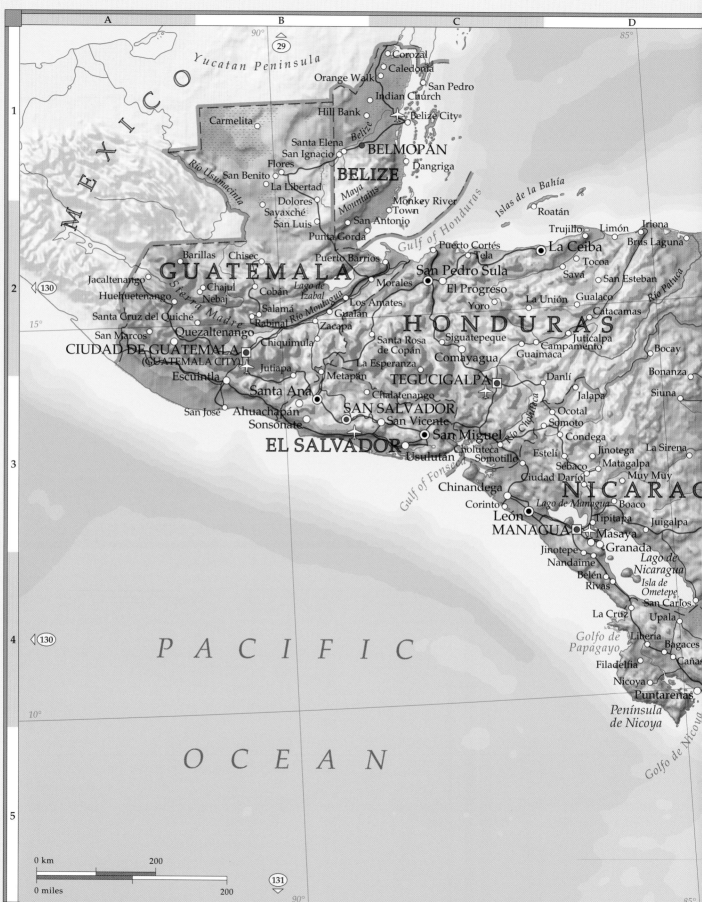

	A	B	C	D

MEXICO

Yucatan Peninsula

Carmelita

Corozal
Caledonia
Orange Walk
San Pedro
Indian Church
Hill Bank
Belize City
Belize

Santa Elena
San Ignacio
Flores
San Benito
La Libertad
BELMOPAN
BELIZE
Dangriga

Dolores
Maya Mountains
Monkey River Town
Sayaxché
San Antonio
San Luis
Punta Gorda

Barillas Chisec
Puerto Barrios
Islas de la Bahía
Roatán
Trujillo Limón Iriona
Brus Laguna

Jacaltenango
Chajul
Nebaj
Cobán
Lago de Izabal
Morales
Puerto Cortés
Tela
San Pedro Sula
La Ceiba
Tocoa
Savá
San Esteban

GUATEMALA
Huehuetenango
Sierra Madre
Salamá
Rabinal *Río Montagua*
Gualán
Zacapa
Los Amates
El Progréso
Yoro
La Unión
Gualaco
Río Patuca
Catacamas

Santa Cruz del Quiché
Chiquimula
HONDURAS

San Marcos
Quezaltenango
Santa Rosa de Copán
Siguatepeque
Comayagua
Campamento
Juticalpa
Bocay
Bonanza

CIUDAD DE GUATEMALA
(GUATEMALA CITY)
Jutiapa
Metapán
La Esperanza
TEGUCIGALPA
Guaimaca
Danlí
Jalapa
Siuna

Escuintla
Santa Ana
Chalatenango
Ocotal
Somoto
Condega

San José
Ahuachapán
Sonsonate
SAN SALVADOR
San Vicente
San Miguel
Río Choluteca
Estelí
Jinotega
La Sirena

EL SALVADOR
Usulután
Choluteca
Somotillo
Sebaco
Matagalpa
Muy Muy

Gulf of Fonseca
Ciudad Daríol
Chinandega
NICARAG

Corinto
Lago de Managua
Boaco
Juigalpa

León
Tipitapa
MANAGUA
Masaya

Jinotepe
Granada
Lago de Nicaragua

Nandaime
Belén
Rivas
Isla de Ometepe

San Carlos
Upala

La Cruz
Golfo de Papágayo
Liberia
Bagaces

Filadelfia
Cañas

Nicoya
Puntarenas

PACIFIC

Península de Nicoya

Golfo de Nicoya

OCEAN

POPULATION

- ◉ Over 500,000
- ◉ 100,000 – 500,000
- ○ 50,000 – 100,000
- ○ Less than 50,000
- ● National capital

0 km   200
0 miles   200

E · F · G · H

80°

N

1

Bajo Nuevo
(to Colombia)

Cayo de Serranilla
(to Colombia)

15°

*Islas Santanilla
(to Honduras)*

guna de Caratasca

Puerto Lempira

Cayo de Serrana
(to Colombia)

2

33

75°

Waspam

Río Coco

Yablis

Tuapi

Cayos Miskitos

Puerto Cabezas

C a r i b b e a n

Mosquito Coast

Prinzapolka

Isla de Providencia
(to Colombia)

S e a

Barra de Río Grande

3

UA

Laguna de Perlas

Isla de San Andrés
(to Colombia)

El Rama

Islas del Maíz

Bluefields

Punta Gorda

San Juan del Norte

10°

o San Juan

erto
Viejo

36

4

COSTA RICA

Istmo de Panamá

Quesada

Siquirres

El Porvenir

Gulf of

uela

Heredia

Portobelo

Darien

SAN JOSÉ

Limón

Colón

Ailigandí

Cartago

Guabito

Cristóbal

Cordillera de San Blas

Cerro Chirripó
Grande
3819m

Cordillera de

Almirante

Laguna
de Chiriquí

Panama Canal

Lago Bayano

Puerto Obaldía

epos

Golfo de los

Lago Gatún

San Miguelito

Buenos Aires

Talamanca

Mosquitos

Balboa

PANAMÁ

Chimán

Serranía del Darién

Cortés

Volcán Barú 3475m

(PANAMA CITY)

Palmar Sur

Boquete

Cordillera Central

Capira

La Palma

Yaviza

Bahía
e Coronado

La Concepción

Penonomé

Archipiélago
de las Perlas

Isla
del Rey

El Real

Península de Osa

David

P A N A M A

Aguadulce

Garachiné

5

Golfo Dulce

Santiago

Golfo

Chitré

de Panamá

Golfo
de Chiriquí

Guarumal

Ocú

Las Tablas

Jaqué

Península de
Azuero

Isla de Coiba

Isla
Cébaco

131

80°

E · F · G · H

COLOMBIA

32

33

36

131

ELEVATION

4000 m 13 124 ft
2000 m 6562 ft
1000 m 3281 ft
500 m 1640 ft
250 m 820 ft
100 m 328 ft
Sea Level / Sea Level
-250 m -820 ft
-500 m -1640 ft
-1000 m -3281 ft
-2000 m -6562 ft
-3000 m -9843 ft
-4000 m -13 124 ft

THE CARIBBEAN

N

UNITED STATES OF AMERICA

Gulf of Mexico

Tropic of Cancer

Grand Bahama Island
Freeport
Marsh Harbour
Great Abaco

The Everglades

Bimini Islands
Berry Islands
Northeast Providence Channel

Nicholls Town
NASSAU
New Providence
Eleuthera Island
Rock Sound

Florida Keys

Straits of Florida

Andros Town
Andros Island
Cat Island
San Salvador

Cay Sal

Exuma Cays
Exuma Sound

BAHAMAS

Anguilla Cays

George Town
Rum Cay
Long Island

Great Exuma Island

Archipiélago de Camagüey

Clarence Town
Crooked Island

Crooked Island Passage

LA HABANA (HAVANA)
Guanabacoa
Cárdenas
Matanzas
Sagua la Grande
Artemisa
Pinar del Río
Consolación del Sur
La Fé
Cienfuegos
Santa Clara
Placetas

Nueva Gerona
Isla de la Juventud
Cayo Largo
Archipiélago de los Canarreos
Sancti Spíritus
Ciego de Ávila
Morón
Nuevitas

Bahía de Cochinos

C U B A

Camagüey
Las Tunas
Holguín
Bayamo
Manzanillo
Palma Soriano
Guantánamo
Santiago de Cuba

Archipiélago de los Jardines de la Reina

Ragged Island Range
Acklins Island
Mayaguana Passage
Mayaguana

Little Inagua
Lake Rosa
Matthew Town
Great Inagua

Caicos Passage

Cap-Haïtien
Gonaïves

HAIT

Guantánamo Bay (to US)

Windward Passage

Cayman Brac
Little Cayman

NAVASSA ISLAND (to US)

Jérémie
PORT-AU-PRINCE

GEORGE TOWN
Grand Cayman

CAYMAN ISLANDS (to UK)

Île de la Gonâve

Cayes
Jacmel

G r e a t e r

Montego Bay
Spanish Town
Portmore
KINGSTON

JAMAICA

Pedro Cays

Jamaica Channel

A

C a r i b b e a n

HONDURAS

NICARAGUA

COSTA RICA

COLOMBIA

Inset map: JAMAICA

JAMAICA

Caribbean Sea

Montego Bay
Lucea
Falmouth
Runaway Bay
St Ann's Bay
Ocho Rios
Annotto Bay
Buff Bay
Port Antonio

Cambridge
The Cockpit Country
Christiana
Ewarton

Savanna-La-Mar
Mandeville
Spanish Town
Blue Mountain Peak △ 2258m

Black River
May Pen
Old Harbour
Spanish Town
KINGSTON
Portmore
Morant Bay

Portland Bight

Caribbean Sea

N

0 km 20
0 miles 20

2000m/6562ft
1000m/3281ft
500m/1640ft
200m/656ft
Sea level

POPULATION

- ◉ Over 500,000
- ◎ 100,000 – 500,000
- ○ 50,000 – 100,000
- ∘ Less than 50,000
- ● National capital

0 km 200
0 miles 200

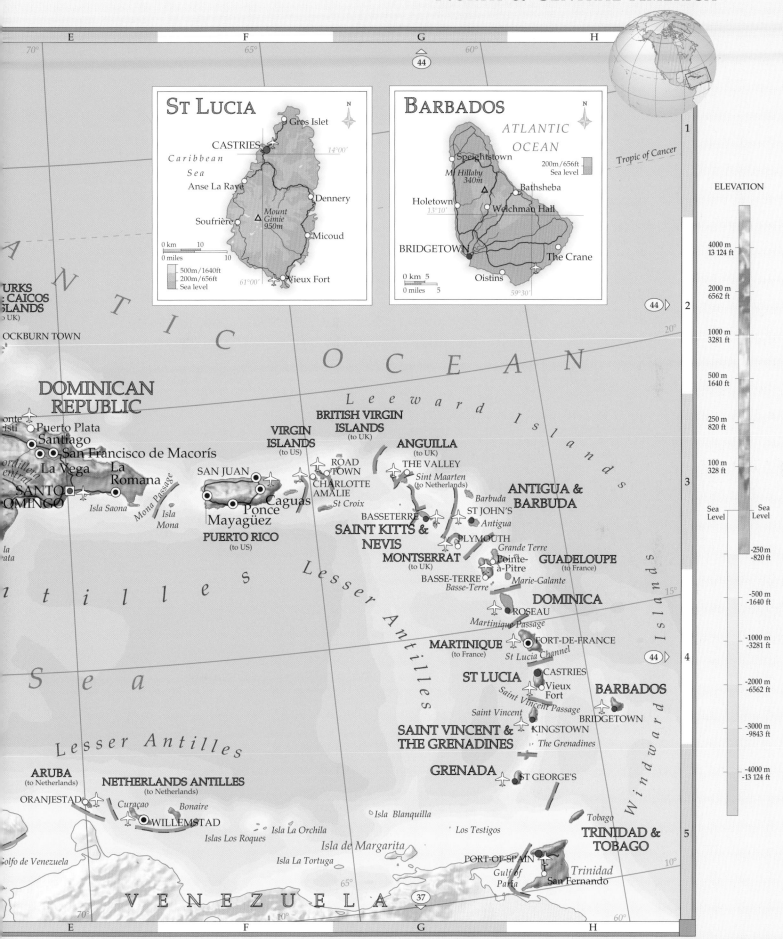

ST LUCIA

N

Gros Islet

CASTRIES ✈

Caribbean Sea

14°00'

Anse La Raye

Dennery

Soufrière

△ Mount Gimie 950m

Micoud

0 km   10
0 miles   10

500m/1640ft
200m/656ft
Sea level

61°00'

✈ Vieux Fort

BARBADOS

N

ATLANTIC OCEAN

Speightstown

Mt Hillaby 340m △

Bathsheba

Holetown

Welchman Hall

13°10'

200m/656ft
Sea level

BRIDGETOWN

The Crane

0 km   5
0 miles   5

Oistins ✈

59°30'

Tropic of Cancer

ELEVATION

4000 m
13 124 ft

2000 m
6562 ft

1000 m
3281 ft

500 m
1640 ft

250 m
820 ft

100 m
328 ft

Sea Level   Sea Level

-250 m
-820 ft

-500 m
-1640 ft

-1000 m
-3281 ft

-2000 m
-6562 ft

-3000 m
-9843 ft

-4000 m
-13 124 ft

A T L A N T I C   O C E A N

Leeward Islands

20°

TURKS & CAICOS ISLANDS (to UK)

COCKBURN TOWN

DOMINICAN REPUBLIC

onte risti
Puerto Plata
Santiago
San Francisco de Macorís
La Vega
La Romana
Cordillera Central
SANTO DOMINGO ✈
Isla Saona
Mona Passage
Isla Mona
la rata

VIRGIN ISLANDS (to US)

BRITISH VIRGIN ISLANDS (to UK)

ANGUILLA (to UK)
THE VALLEY

SAN JUAN ✈
✈ ROAD TOWN
CHARLOTTE AMALIE ✈
Sint Maarten (to Netherlands)
Caguas
St Croix
Ponce
Mayagüez
PUERTO RICO (to US)

Barbuda

ANTIGUA & BARBUDA

ST JOHN'S ● *Antigua*

BASSETERRE ✈

SAINT KITTS & NEVIS

PLYMOUTH ✈ ○
MONTSERRAT (to UK)
Grande Terre
Pointe-à-Pitre ✈
GUADELOUPE (to France)

BASSE-TERRE
Basse-Terre
Marie-Galante

15°

DOMINICA
✈ ● ROSEAU
Martinique Passage

MARTINIQUE (to France)
✈ ● FORT-DE-FRANCE
St Lucia Channel

ST LUCIA
● CASTRIES
✈ ● Vieux Fort

BARBADOS
✈ ● BRIDGETOWN

Saint Vincent Passage
Saint Vincent

SAINT VINCENT & THE GRENADINES
✈ ● KINGSTOWN
The Grenadines

GRENADA
✈ ● ST GEORGE'S

Windward Islands

A N t i l l e s

Lesser Antilles

C a r i b b e a n   S e a

Lesser Antilles

ARUBA (to Netherlands)
ORANJESTAD ✈
Curaçao
Bonaire
NETHERLANDS ANTILLES (to Netherlands)
✈ ● WILLEMSTAD
Isla La Orchila
Islas Los Roques

Isla Blanquilla
Los Testigos

Tobago

TRINIDAD & TOBAGO

Golfo de Venezuela
Isla de Margarita
Isla La Tortuga

PORT-OF-SPAIN ● ✈
Gulf of Paria
Trinidad
San Fernando

V E N E Z U E L A

SOUTH AMERICA

ATLANTIC OCEAN

Mid-Atlantic Ridge

Equator

Demerara Plain

Amazon Fan

Puerto Rico Trench

Lesser Antilles

Puerto Rico

Venezuelan Basin

Greater Antilles

Hispaniola

Jamaica

Caribbean Sea

Colombian Basin

Panama Basin

Isthmus of Panama

Trinidad

Cumaná

CARACAS

Maracay

Valencia

Barquisimeto

Maracaibo

Barinas

San Cristóbal

VENEZUELA

Orinoco

Meta

COLOMBIA

Cúcuta

Bucaramanga

BOGOTÁ

Ibagué

Medellín

Manizales

Pereira

Cali

Pasto

Cauca

Magdalena

Santa Marta

Barranquilla

Cartagena

Montería

GEORGETOWN

PARAMARIBO

CAYENNE

Linden

GUYANA

SURINAME

FRENCH GUIANA
(to France)

(claimed by Venezuela)

(claimed by Suriname)

Essequibo

Caroní

Guiana Highlands

Tumuc-Humac Mountains

ECUADOR

QUITO

Portoviejo

Chimborazo 6310m

Guayaquil

Gulf of Guayaquil

Machala

Cuenca

Riobamba

Esmeraldas

Equator

Piura

Chiclayo

Trujillo

PERU

Callao

LIMA

Cusco

Arequipa

Tacna

Arica

Peru-Chile Trench

Peru Basin

Andes

Marañón

Ucayali

Napo

Putumayo

Caquetá

Guaviare

Guaviare

Içá

Juruá

Purus

Madeira

Amazon

Rio Negro

Branco

Manaus

Santarém

Belém

São Luís

Teresina

Fortaleza

Mossoró

Natal

João Pessoa

Recife

Maceió

Aracaju

Salvador

BRASÍLIA

Goiânia

Cuiabá

Belo Horizonte

BRAZIL

Amazon Basin

Tocantins

Xingu

Tapajós

Serra do Cachimbo

Chapada dos Parecis

Serra do Roncador

Mato Grosso

Planalto de

Serra Formosa

Planalto da Borborema

São Francisco

Represa de Sobradinho

Brazilian Highlands

Serra do Espinhaço

Abrolhos Bank

Ceará Plain

Represa Balbina

Porto Velho

Rio Branco

Madre de Dios

Beni

BOLIVIA

LA PAZ

Oruro

Cochabamba

SUCRE

Santa Cruz

Altiplano

Lake Titicaca

Pantanal

Paraguay

POPULATION

- ▣ Over 500,000
- ◉ 100,000 - 500,000
- ○ 50,000 - 100,000
- ○ Less than 50,000
- ● National capital

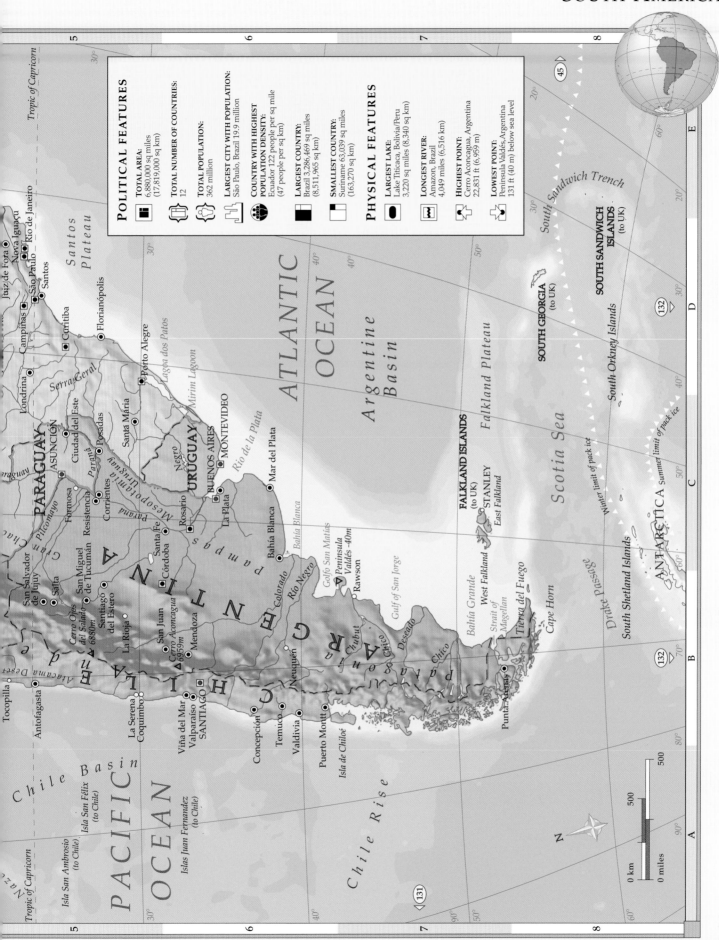

POLITICAL FEATURES

TOTAL AREA:
6,880,000 sq miles
(17,819,000 sq km)

TOTAL NUMBER OF COUNTRIES:
12

TOTAL POPULATION:
362 million

LARGEST CITY WITH POPULATION:
São Paulo, Brazil 19.9 million

COUNTRY WITH HIGHEST POPULATION DENSITY:
Ecuador 122 people per sq mile
(47 people per sq km)

LARGEST COUNTRY:
Brazil 3,286,469 sq miles
(8,511,965 sq km)

SMALLEST COUNTRY:
Suriname 63,039 sq miles
(163,270 sq km)

PHYSICAL FEATURES

LARGEST LAKE:
Lake Titicaca, Bolivia/Peru
3,220 sq miles (8,340 sq km)

LONGEST RIVER:
Amazon, Brazil
4,049 miles (6,516 km)

HIGHEST POINT:
Cerro Aconcagua, Argentina
22,831 ft (6,959 m)

LOWEST POINT:
Peninsula Valdés, Argentina
131 ft (40 m) below sea level

NORTHERN SOUTH AMERICA

ATLANTIC

OCEAN

SAINT VINCENT &
THE GRENADINES

GRENADA

BARBADOS

Isla Blanquilla

Isla de
Margarita

Islas Los Testigos

Tobago

a Tortuga

La Asunción

TRINIDAD &
TOBAGO

Porlamar

Carúpano

Cumaná

Cariaco

Güiria

Gulf of
Paria

Puerto La Cruz

Trinidad

Barcelona

The Serpent's Mouth

San Mateo

Maturín

Anaco

Cantaura

Zaraza

Tucupita

El Tigre

Río Orinoco

Ciudad Guayana

Ciudad
Bolívar

Upata

Z U E L A

Embalse de Guri

Matthews
Ridge

Charity

El Callao

Spring Garden

Aurora

Parika

GEORGETOWN

El Dorado

Cuyuni River

Peters Mine

New
Amsterdam

Totness

PARAMARIBO

Bartica

Nieuw Amsterdam

St-Laurent-
du-Maroni

Rockstone

Salto
Ángel

Linden

Sinnamary

Kamarang

Nieuw
Nickerie

Kourou

Río Caroní

Río Caura

GUYANA

Kaaimanston

Mount Roraima
2810m

Orealla

Apoera

CAYENNE

Río Paragua

Pakaraima Mountains

Kurupukari

W. J. van
Blommesteinmeer

Grand-
Santi

St-Georges

SURINAME

(Venezuela claims all
of Guyana west of
Essequibo River)

Lethem

Juliana Top
1230m

FRENCH
GUIANA
(to France)

Ouanary

Camopi

G u i a n a

H i g h l a

Essequibo River

Courantyne River

Tumuc Hunnac Mountains

Montagnes
de la Trinité

Montagne
Tortue

Río Orinoco

n d s

(claimed by
Suriname)

(claimed by
Suriname)

Acarai Mountains

Río Negro

Equator

B R A Z I L

Amazon

a z o n   B a s i n

Amazon

Amazon

Río Purus

Río Tapajós

ELEVATION

4000 m
13 124 ft

2000 m
6562 ft

1000 m
3281 ft

500 m
1640 ft

250 m
820 ft

100 m
328 ft

Sea
Level

Sea
Level

-250 m
-820 ft

-500 m
-1640 ft

-1000 m
-3281 ft

-2000 m
-6562 ft

-3000 m
-9843 ft

-4000 m
-13 124 ft

WESTERN SOUTH AMERICA

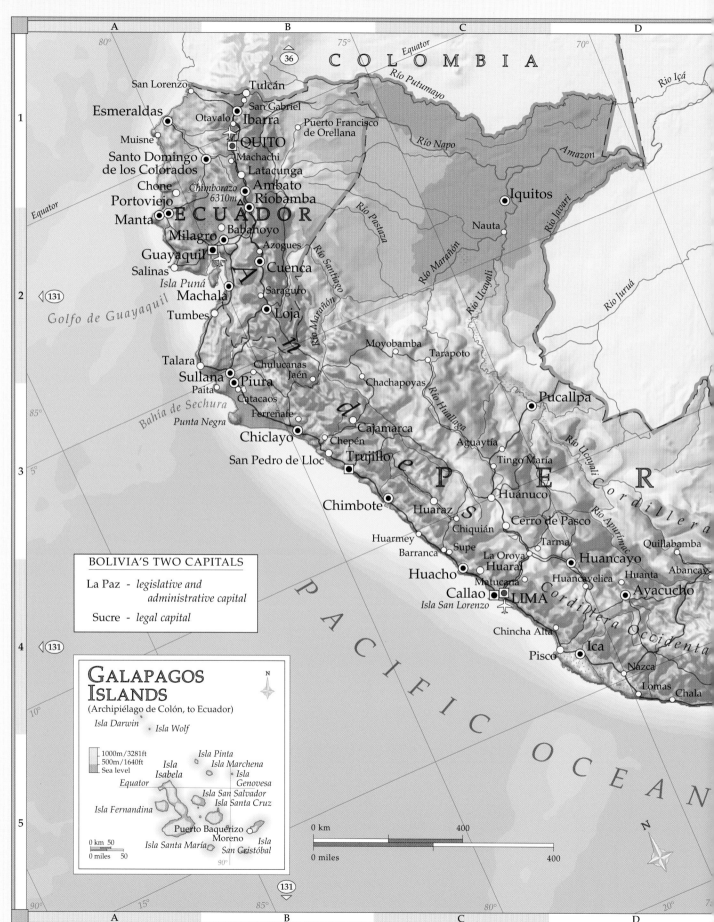

COLOMBIA

San Lorenzo
Tulcán
Esmeraldas
San Gabriel
Otavalo Ibarra
Muisne
Puerto Francisco de Orellana
QUITO
Santo Domingo de los Colorados
Machachi
Chone
Latacunga
Chimborazo 6310m
Ambato
Portoviejo
Riobamba
Manta ECUADOR
Milagro Babahoyo
Guayaquil
Azogues
Salinas
Cuenca
Isla Puná
Saraguro
Machala
Tumbes
Loja

Golfo de Guayaquil

Río Putumayo
Río Napo
Amazon
Iquitos
Nauta
Río Pastaza
Río Santiago
Río Marañón
Río Javari
Río Jurúa
Río Icá

Talara
Sullana
Piura
Chulucanas
Jaén
Paíta
Catacaos
Ferreñafe
Bahía de Sechura
Punta Negra
Chiclayo
Chepén
San Pedro de Lloc
Trujillo
Moyobamba
Tarapoto
Chachapoyas
Cajamarca
Aguaytía
Pucallpa
Río Huallaga
Río Ucayali
Río Apurímac
Cordillera

Chimbote
Huaraz
Chiquián
Huánuco
Tingo María
Cerro de Pasco
Quillabamba
Huarmey
Tarma
Barranca
Supe
La Oroya
Huaral
Huancayo
Huanta
Abancay
Huacho
Matucana
Huancavelica
Callao
LIMA
Isla San Lorenzo
Ayacucho
Chincha Alta
Pisco
Ica
Nazca
Lomas
Chala

Cordillera Occidental

BOLIVIA'S TWO CAPITALS

La Paz - *legislative and administrative capital*

Sucre - *legal capital*

GALAPAGOS ISLANDS

(Archipiélago de Colón, to Ecuador)

Isla Darwin   Isla Wolf

1000m/3281ft	
500m/1640ft	
Sea level	

Isla Pinta
Isla Marchena
Isla Isabela
Isla Genovesa
Equator
Isla San Salvador
Isla Santa Cruz
Isla Fernandina
Puerto Baquerizo Moreno
Isla San Cristóbal
Isla Santa María

0 km 50
0 miles 50

PACIFIC OCEAN

0 km 400
0 miles 400

ELEVATION

4000 m	
13 124 ft	
2000 m	
6562 ft	
1000 m	
3281 ft	
500 m	
1640 ft	
250 m	
820 ft	
100 m	
328 ft	
Sea Level	Sea Level
	−250 m −820 ft
	−500 m −1640 ft
	−1000 m −3281 ft
	−2000 m −6562 ft
	−3000 m −9843 ft
	−4000 m −13 124 ft

Amazon Basin
Amazon
Rio Madeira
Rio Purus
Rio Abunã
Rio Madre de Dios
Rio Beni
Rio Guaporé
Rio Mamoré
Rio San Miguel
Rio Jurruena
Rio São Manuel
Serra do Cachimbo
Chapada dos Parecis
Pantanal
Gran Chaco
Paraguay
Pilcomayo

BRAZIL
BOLIVIA
PARAGUAY
ARGENTINA
CHILE

Fortaleza
Villa Bella
Riberalta
Cobija
Porvenir
Magdalena
Santa Ana
Puerto Maldonado
San Matías
Reyes
San Ignacio
Trinidad
Concepción
Cusco
Sicuani
Nevado Pupuya 5818m
Montero
Warnes
San José
Puerto Suárez
Moho
Puerto Acosta
Portachuelo
Ayaviri
Juliaca
Lake Titicaca
Achacachi
Buena Vista
Santa Cruz
Puno
Copacabana
Cochabamba
Nevado Ampato 6310m
LA PAZ
Ilave
Viacha
Comarapa
Corocoro
Oruro
Aiquile
Volcán Misti 5822m
Huanuni
Arequipa
Uncia
Moquegua
Nevado Sajama 6542m
Challapata
SUCRE
Lagunillas
Monteagudo
amaná
Lago Poopó
Potosí
Mollendo
Ilo
Tacna
Sabaya
La Yarada
Desierto de Atacama
Uyuni
Cotagaita
San Lorenzo
Villa Martín
Tupiza
Tarija
San Pablo
Villazón

Cordillera Oriental
Cordillera Occidental
Altiplano
Cordillera Oriental

Tropic of Capricorn
Tropic of Capricorn

BRAZIL

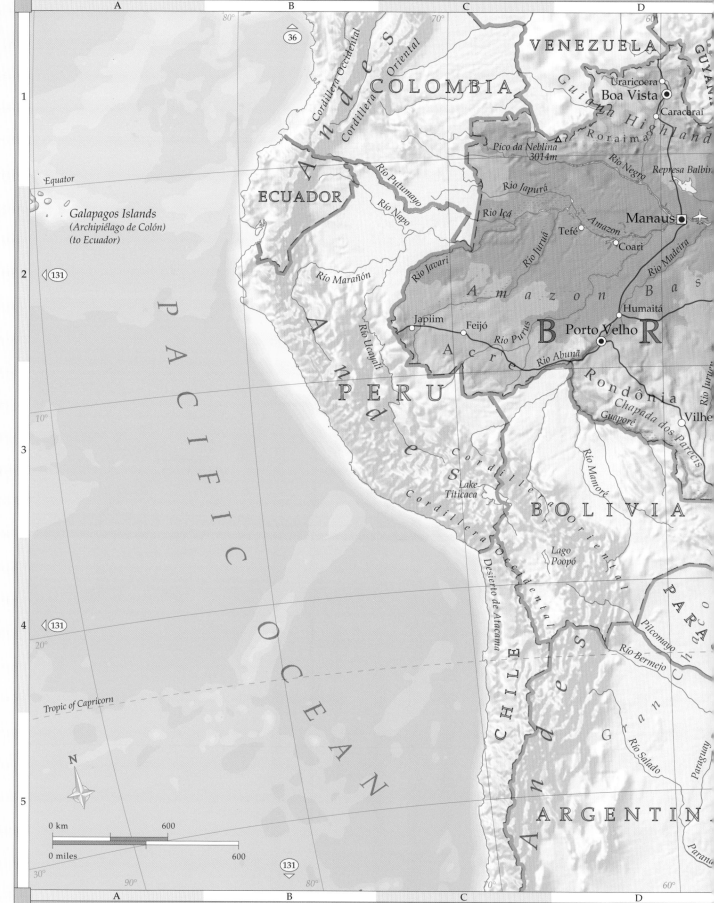

VENEZUELA

GUYANA

COLOMBIA

Cordillera Occidental

Cordillera Oriental

A n d e s

Uraricoera

Boa Vista

Caracaraí

Guiana Highland

Roraima

ECUADOR

Río Putumayo

Río Napo

Equator

Pico da Neblina
3014m

Río Negro

Represa Balbina

Galapagos Islands
(Archipiélago de Colón)
(to Ecuador)

Río Japurá

Río Içá

Manaus

Tefé

Amazon

Coari

Río Iça

Río Javari

A   m   a   z   o   n

Río Madeira

B a s

Río Marañón

Río Iuruá

Río Juruá

Humaitá

Japiim

Feijó

B Porto Velho R

Río Purus

Río Abunã

Acre

Rondônia

Río Juruen

Vilhe

Chapada dos Parecis

Guaporé

P E R U

A
n
d
e
s

Cordillera

Río Mamoré

B O L I V I A

Lake
Titicaca

Cordillera Oriental

Lago
Poopó

PA

Desierto de Atacama

Río Pilcomayo

Río Bermejo

G
r
a
n

C
h
a
c
o

Paraguay

Río Salado

C H I L E

A n d e s

Paraguay

Tropic of Capricorn

ARGENTIN

Paraná

P   A   C   I   F   I   C   O   C   E   A   N

POPULATION

- ⊙ Over 500,000
- ◉ 100,000 – 500,000
- ○ 50,000 – 100,000
- ○ Less than 50,000
- ● National capital

N

0 km   600

0 miles   600

FRENCH GUIANA (to France)
SURINAME

Tumuc Humac Mountains

Mouths of the Amazon

A T L A N T I C   O C E A N

Amapá
Macapá
Ilha Caviana de Fora
Baía de Marajó
Ilha de Marajó
Baía de São Marco
Belém

Alenquer
Amazon
Santarém
São Luís
Parnaíba
Camocim
Fortaleza
Equator

Itaituba
Altamira
Represa de Tucuruí
Bacabal
Piripiri
Teresina
Mossoró
Açu
Atol das Rocas
San Fernando de Noronha (to Brazil)

Rio Tapajós
Rio Xingu
Marabá
Imperatriz
Maranhão
Ceará
Cabo de São Roque
Natal

Pará
Floriano
Picos
Juazeiro do Norte
João Pessoa
Campina Grande
Rio São Manuel
Serra do Cachimbo
A
Z
I
L
Carolina
Balsas
Piauí
Pernambuco
Alagoas
Recife

Serra Formosa
Serra dos Gradaús
Rio Tocantins
Represa de Sobradinho
Juazeiro
Maceió

Rio São Francisco
Tocantins
Chapada Diamantina
Aracaju
Estância
10°

Taguatinga
Bahia
Feira de Santana
Salvador
Baía de Todos os Santos

Cuiabá
Rio Araguaia
Goiás
Planalto
Central
BRASÍLIA
Jananúba
Itabuna
Vitória da Conquista
Canavieiras

Anápolis
Mato Grosso
Jataí
Goiânia
Araguari
Minas
Gerais
Araçuaí
Montes Claros
ondonópolis
Pantanal

Uberlândia
Uberaba
Governador Valadares
Espírito
Santo

Campo Grande
Mato Grosso do Sul
Ribeirão Preto
Belo Horizonte
Vitória

Aquidauana
Divinópolis
Campos

Presidente Epitácio
São Paulo
Juiz de Fora

Marília
Campinas
Nova
Iguaçu
Rio de Janeiro
20°

Londrina
Paraná
São Paulo
Santos
45

Maringá
Represa de Itaipú
Ponta Grossa
Tropic of Capricorn

UAY
Salto do Iguaçu
Rio Iguaçu
Curitiba
Joinville

Paraná
Blumenau
Florianópolis

Santa Catarina
Passo Fundo

anta Maria
Rio Grande
Canoas

Rio Negro
Bagé
Porto Alegre
Lagoa dos Patos

URUGUAY
Rio Grande
Mirim Lagoon

A T L A N T I C   O C E A N

30°

1
2
3
4
5

44
45
45
45

50°
40°
30°
E
F
G
H

ELEVATION

4000 m
13 124 ft

2000 m
6562 ft

1000 m
3281 ft

500 m
1640 ft

250 m
820 ft

100 m
328 ft

Sea Level
Sea Level

-250 m
-820 ft

-500 m
-1640 ft

-1000 m
-3281 ft

-2000 m
-6562 ft

-3000 m
-9843 ft

-4000 m
-13 124 ft

SOUTHERN SOUTH AMERICA

POPULATION

◨ Over 500,000

◉ 100,000 – 500,000

○ 50,000 – 100,000

∘ Less than 50,000

● National capital

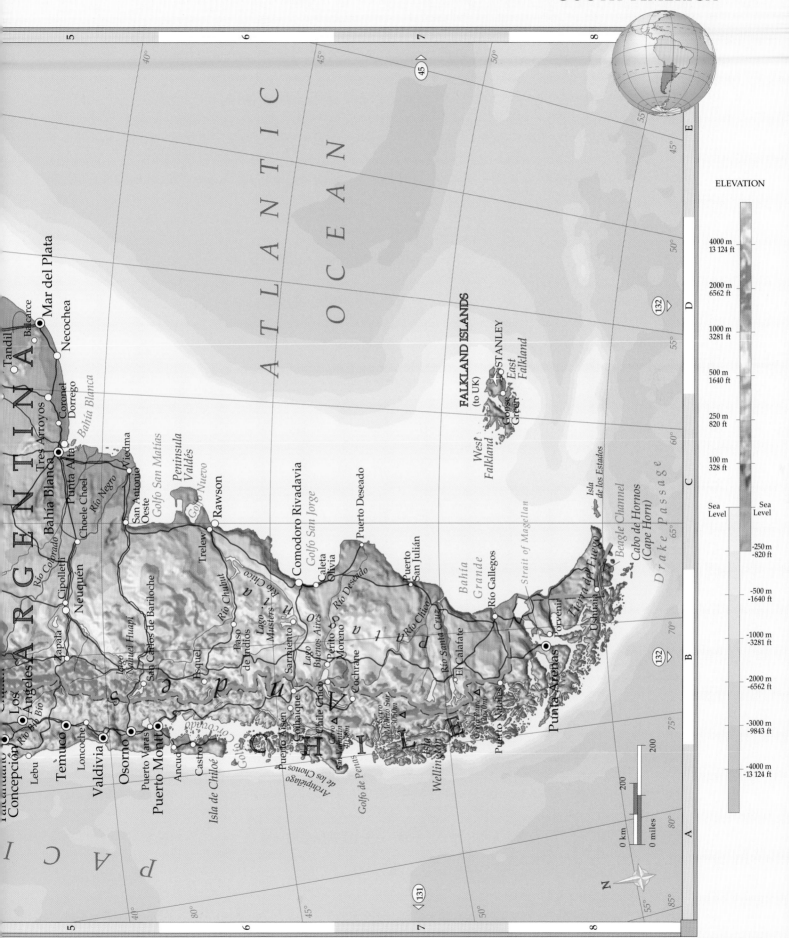

ATLANTIC

OCEAN

PACIFIC

A R G E N T I N A

Tandil
Balcarce
Mar del Plata
Necochea
Coronel
Dorrego
Bahía Blanca
Punta Alta
Tres Arroyos
Bahía Blanca
Viedma
Río Negro
Choele Choel
San Antonio Oeste
Golfo San Matías
Península Valdés
Golfo Nuevo
Rawson
Trelew
Cipolletti
Neuquén
Zapala
San Carlos de Bariloche
Lago Nahuel Huapi
Esquel
Río Colorado
Río Chubut
Paso de Indios
Lago Musters
Sarmiento
Lago Buenos Aires
Río Senguerr
Río Chico
Comodoro Rivadavia
Golfo San Jorge
Caleta Olivia
Río Deseado
Puerto Deseado
Puerto San Julián
Perito Moreno
Cochrane
Chile Chico
Coyhaique
Puerto Aisén
Bahía Grande
Río Gallegos
El Calafate
Río Santa Cruz
Puerto Natales
Cerro San Valentín 4058m
Cerro Murallón 3050m
Río Chico

C H I L E

Concepción
Los Angeles
Río Bío Bío
Lebu
Temuco
Loncoche
Valdivia
Osorno
Puerto Varas
Puerto Montt
Ancud
Castro
Isla de Chiloé
Golfo Corcovado
Golfo de Penas
Archipiélago de los Chonos
Isla Wellington
San Martín
Punta Arenas
Porvenir
Tierra del Fuego
Ushuaia
Beagle Channel
Cabo de Hornos (Cape Horn)
Strait of Magellan
Drake Passage
Isla de los Estados

FALKLAND ISLANDS
(to UK)
West Falkland
Goose Green
East Falkland
STANLEY

45
50
55
132
132
131

ELEVATION

4000 m	13 124 ft
2000 m	6562 ft
1000 m	3281 ft
500 m	1640 ft
250 m	820 ft
100 m	328 ft
Sea Level	Sea Level
-250 m	-820 ft
-500 m	-1640 ft
-1000 m	-3281 ft
-2000 m	-6562 ft
-3000 m	-9843 ft
-4000 m	-13 124 ft

0 km 200
0 miles 200

N

THE ATLANTIC OCEAN

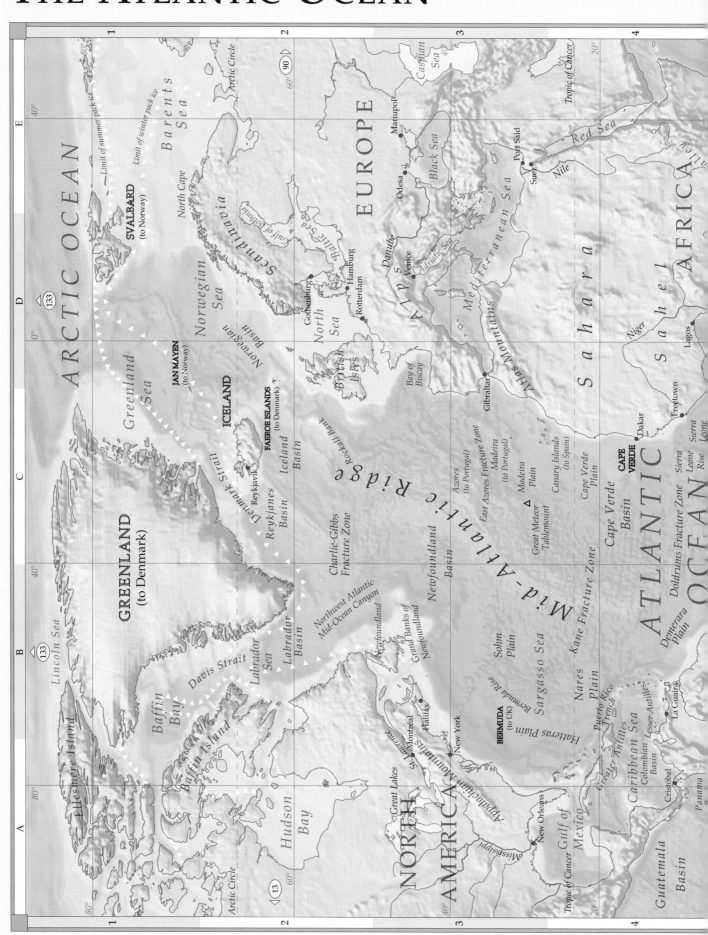

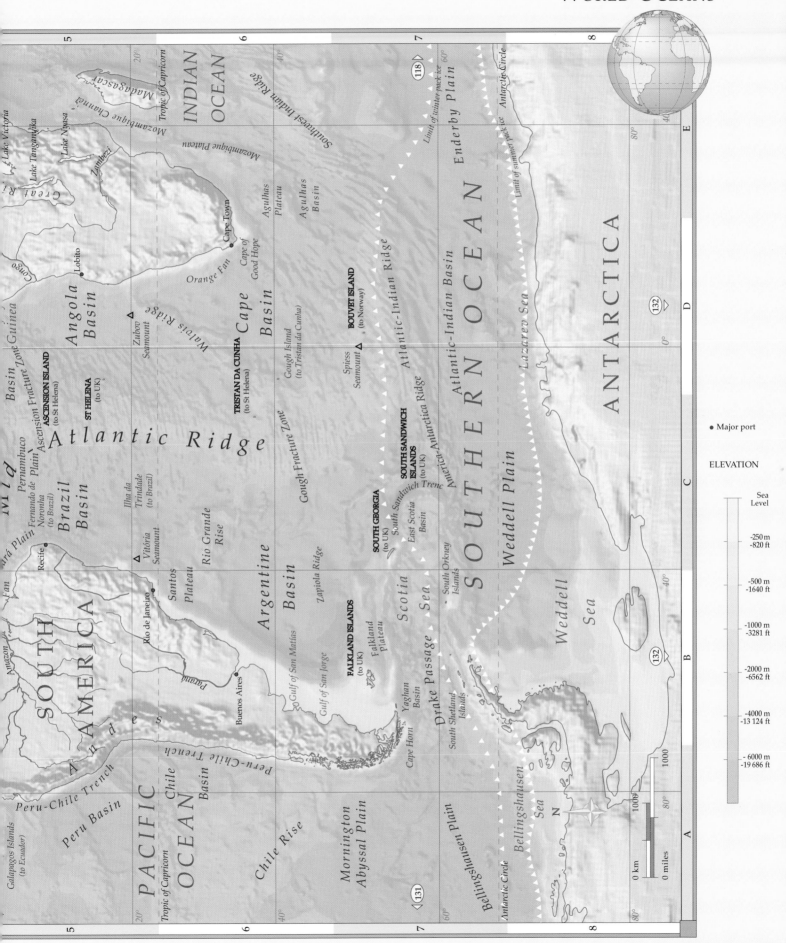

5   6   7   8

E

D

C

B

A

INDIAN OCEAN

Tropic of Capricorn

Madagascar

Mozambique Channel

Lake Victoria

Lake Tanganyika

Lake Nyasa

Zambezi

Great Ri...

Congo

Mozambique Plateau

Southwest Indian Ridge

Cape Town

Agulhas Plateau

Agulhas Basin

Cape of Good Hope

Lobito

Guinea Basin

Angola Basin

Orange Fan

Zubov Seamount

Walvis Ridge

Cape Basin

Gough Island (to Tristan da Cunha)

TRISTAN DA CUNHA (to St Helena)

Spiess Seamount

BOUVET ISLAND (to Norway)

Atlantic-Indian Ridge

Enderby Plain

Limit of summer pack ice

Antarctic Circle

80°

60°

Limit of summer pack ice

Lazarev Sea

ANTARCTICA

SOUTHERN OCEAN

Atlantic-Indian Basin

118

132

0°

ASCENSION ISLAND (to St Helena)

ST HELENA (to UK)

Atlantic Ridge

Mid

Pernambuco

Fernando de Noronha (to Brazil)

Ascension Fracture Zone Plain

Ilha da Trindade (to Brazil)

Brazil Basin

Recife

...ará Plain

...Fan

Vitória Seamount

Rio Grande Rise

Santos Plateau

Rio de Janeiro

Gough Fracture Zone

Zapiola Ridge

Argentine Basin

SOUTH SANDWICH ISLANDS (to UK)

SOUTH GEORGIA (to UK)

South Sandwich Trench

America-Antarctica Ridge

East Scotia Basin

Scotia Sea

South Orkney Islands

Weddell Plain

Weddell Sea

40°

132

● Major port

ELEVATION

Sea Level

-250 m -820 ft

-500 m -1640 ft

-1000 m -3281 ft

-2000 m -6562 ft

-4000 m -13 124 ft

-6000 m -19 686 ft

SOUTH AMERICA

Amazon

Paraná

Buenos Aires

Gulf of San Matías

Gulf of San Jorge

FALKLAND ISLANDS (to UK)

Falkland Plateau

Yaghan Basin

Drake Passage

Cape Horn

South Shetland Islands

South Orkney Islands

Andes

Peru-Chile Trench

Chile Basin

Chile Rise

Galapagos Islands (to Ecuador)

Tropic of Capricorn

PACIFIC OCEAN

Peru-Chile Trench

Peru Basin

Mornington Abyssal Plain

Bellingshausen Plain

Antarctic Circle

Bellingshausen Sea

N

80°

60°

40°

20°

40°

60°

80°

131

0 km   1000

0 miles   1000

AFRICA

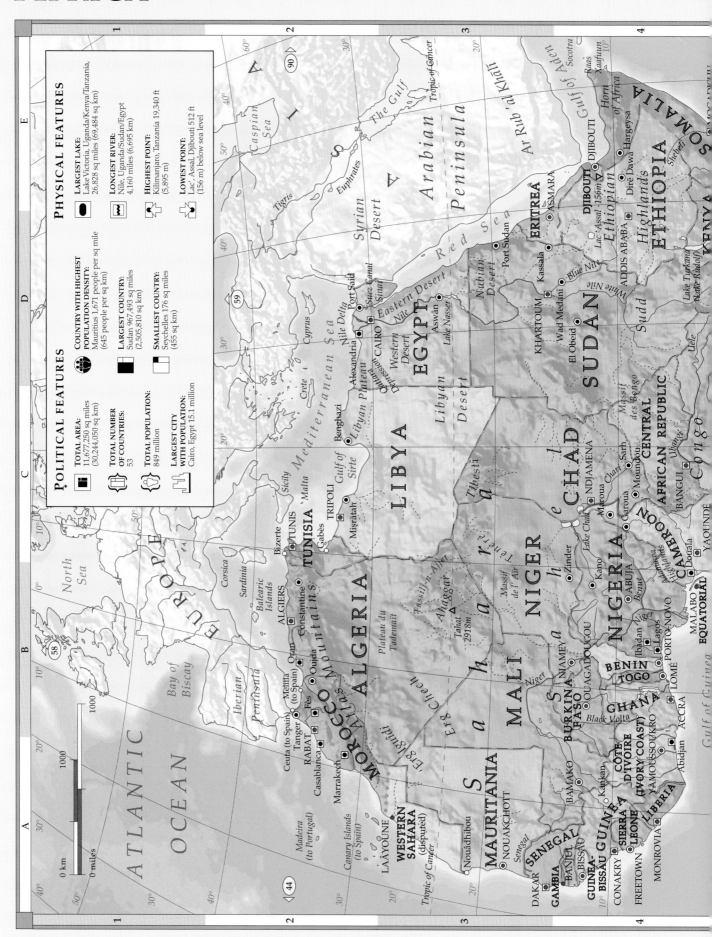

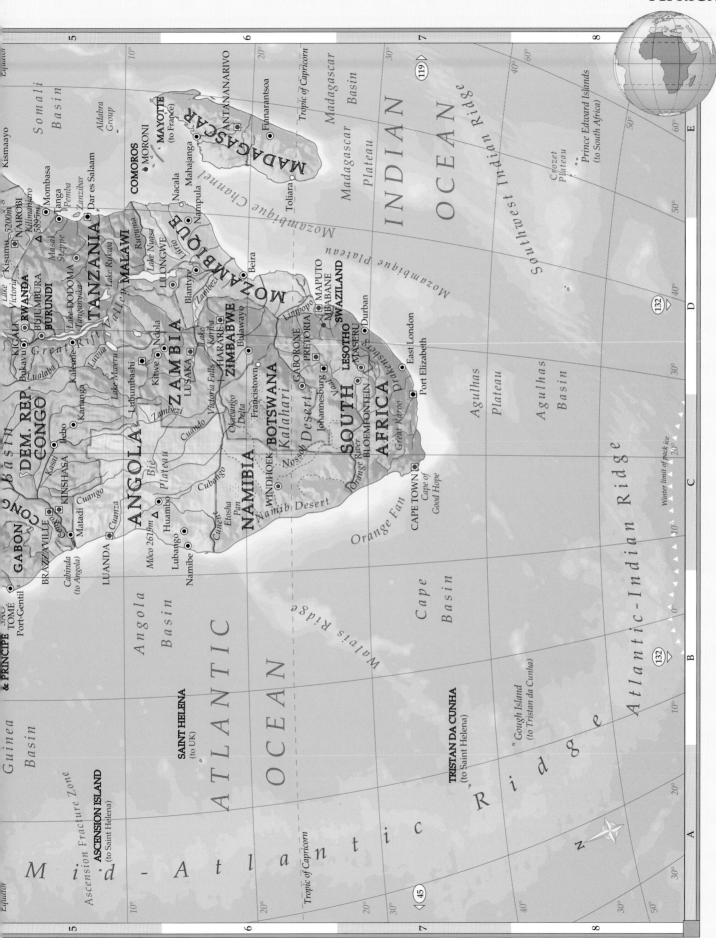

Guinea Basin

Mid-Atlantic

SÃO TOMÉ & PRINCIPE
GABON
Port-Gentil
BRAZZAVILLE
CONGO
Cabinda (to Angola)
Matadi
KINSHASA
DEM. REP. CONGO
Kasai
Kananga
Ilebo
Lualaba
Bukavu
KIGALI
RWANDA
BUJUMBURA
BURUNDI
Lake Tanganyika
Kalemie
Lake Mweru
Lubumbashi
Luapula
Congo Basin

ATLANTIC OCEAN

Ascension Fracture Zone
ASCENSION ISLAND (to Saint Helena)

SAINT HELENA (to UK)

Equator
10°
20°

Tropic of Capricorn

Walvis Ridge

Angola Basin

LUANDA
Cuanza
Cuango
ANGOLA
Bié Plateau
Huambo
Lubango
Môco 2619m
Namibe
Cunene
Cubango
Etosha Pan
Namib Desert
NAMIBIA
WINDHOEK
Nossob
Kalahari
Cuando
Zambezi
ZAMBIA
LUSAKA
Kitwe
Ndola
Victoria Falls
Lake Kariba
BOTSWANA
GABORONE
Francistown
Okavango Delta
Orange River
Orange Fan
Cape Basin

TRISTAN DA CUNHA (to Saint Helena)

Gough Island (to Tristan da Cunha)

Lake Victoria
Kisumu
NAIROBI
Kilimanjaro 5895m
Masai Steppe
DODOMA
TANZANIA
Lake Rukwa
Great Rift Valley
Kasama
Nacala
Nampula
Ruvuma
MALAWI
LILONGWE
Lake Nyasa
Luio
Blantyre
MOZAMBIQUE
Zambezi
HARARE
ZIMBABWE
Bulawayo
Limpopo
PRETORIA
MBABANE
SWAZILAND
MAPUTO
Johannesburg
Vaal
BLOEMFONTEIN
MASERU
LESOTHO
SOUTH AFRICA
Great Karoo
Drakensberg
Durban
East London
Port Elizabeth
CAPE TOWN
Cape of Good Hope

Somali Basin
Kismaayo
Mombasa
Tanga
Pemba
Zanzibar
Dar es Salaam
Aldabra Group
COMOROS
MORONI
MAYOTTE (to France)
Mozambique Channel
Mahajanga
Toliara
ANTANANARIVO
Fianarantsoa
MADAGASCAR
Madagascar Plateau
Madagascar Basin

Beira

INDIAN OCEAN

Southwest Indian Ridge
Mozambique Plateau
Agulhas Plateau
Agulhas Basin

Crozet Plateau
Prince Edward Islands (to South Africa)

Atlantic-Indian Ridge

Winter limit of pack ice

Tropic of Capricorn
10°
20°
30°
40°
50°
60°

10°
20°
30°
40°
50°

Equator

NORTHWEST AFRICA

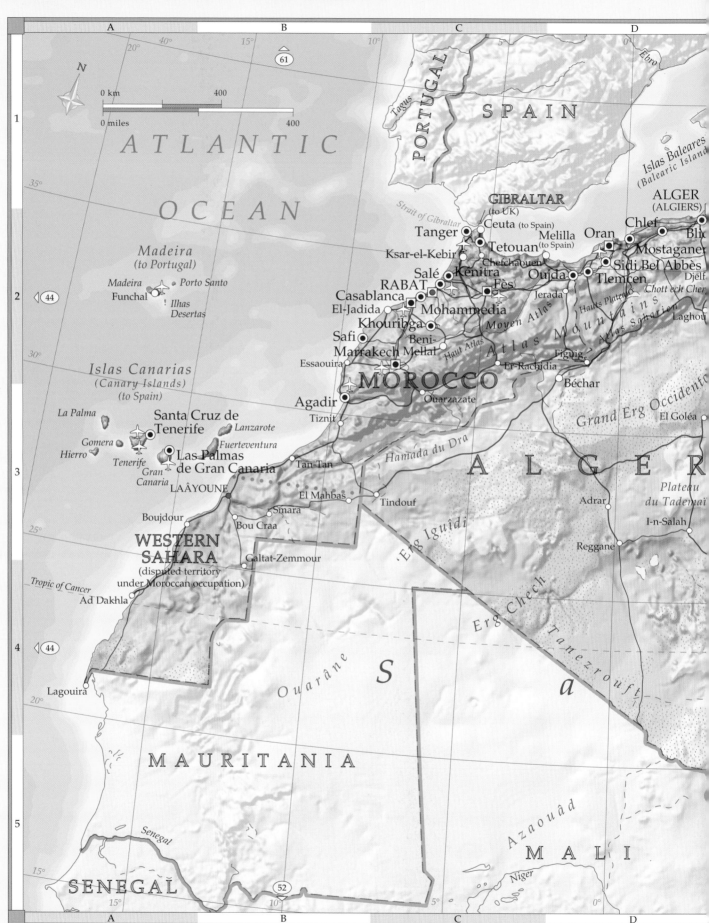

N

0 km 400
0 miles 400

ATLANTIC

OCEAN

PORTUGAL

SPAIN

Tagus

61

Ebro

Islas Baleares
(Balearic Islands)

GIBRALTAR
(to UK)

ALGER
(ALGIERS)

Strait of Gibraltar

Ceuta (to Spain)

Chlef

Tanger

Melilla
(to Spain)

Oran

Blic

Tetouan

Ksar-el-Kebir

Mostaganer

Chefchaouen

Sidi Bel Abbès

Salé
Kénitra

Oujda

Tlemcen

Djelf

RABAT

Fès

Jerada

Chott ech Cher

Casablanca

Mohammedia

Hauts Plateaux

El-Jadida

Moyen Atlas

Atlas Saharien

Khouribga

Laghou

Safi

Beni-

Haut Atlas

Atlas Mountains

Marrakech Mellal

Essaouira

Er-Rachidia

Figuig

MOROCCO

Ouarzazate

Béchar

Agadir

Grand Erg Occidental

Tiznit

El Goléa

Madeira
(to Portugal)

Madeira • *Porto Santo*

Funchal

Ilhas
Desertas

Islas Canarias
(Canary Islands)
(to Spain)

La Palma

Gomera

Santa Cruz de
Tenerife

Lanzarote

Fuerteventura

Hierro

Tenerife

Las Palmas
de Gran Canaria

Gran
Canaria

LAÂYOUNE

Tan-Tan

Hamada du Dra

A L G E R

Adrar

Plateau
du Tademaï

Erg Iguîdi

El Mahbas

Smara

Tindouf

I-n-Salah

Boujdour

Bou Craa

Reggane

WESTERN
SAHARA
(disputed territory
under Moroccan occupation)

Calat-Zemmour

Tropic of Cancer

Ad Dakhla

Ouarâne

S

Erg Chech

Tanezrouft

a

POPULATION

▣ Over
500,000

◉ 100,000 –
500,000

○ 50,000 –
100,000

○ Less than
50,000

● National
capital

Lagouira

M A U R I T A N I A

Azaouâd

M A L I

Senegal

SENEGAL

Niger

52

44

44

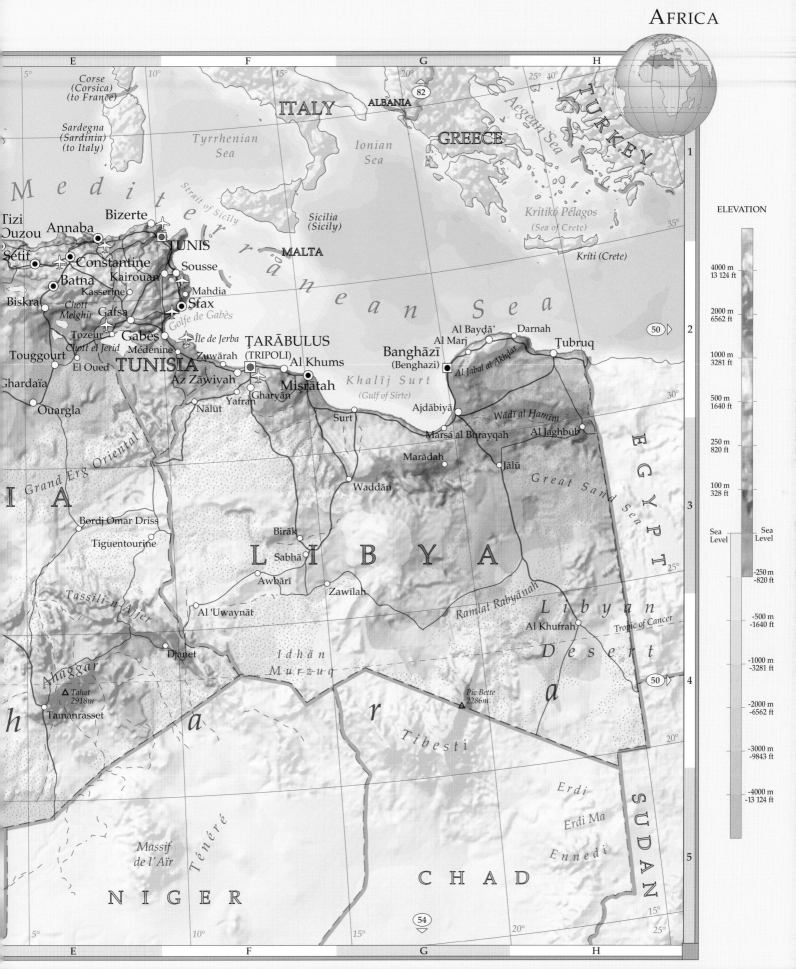

E 5° 10° F 15° G 20° 25° 40° H

ITALY

ALBANIA 82

Corse (Corsica) (to France)

Sardegna (Sardinia) (to Italy)

Tyrrhenian Sea

Ionian Sea

GREECE

Aegean Sea

TURKEY

1

Kritiko Pélagos (Sea of Crete)

35°

Kríti (Crete)

M e d i t e r r a n e a n   S e a

Tizi Ouzou
Annaba
Bizerte
Sétif
Constantine
TUNIS
Batna
Sousse
Kairouan
Kasserine
Mahdia
Biskra
Gafsa
Sfax
Chott Melghir
Tozeur
Gabes
Golfe de Gabès
Île de Jerba
Médenine
Zuwārah
ṬARĀBULUS (TRIPOLI)
Al Khums
Banghāzī (Benghazi)
Al Bayḍā'
Al Marj
Darnah
Ṭubruq

Strait of Sicily

Sicilia (Sicily)

MALTA

ELEVATION

4000 m
13 124 ft

2000 m
6562 ft

50

2

Al Jabal al Akhḍar

1000 m
3281 ft

Ghardaïa
El Oued
TUNISIA
Chott el Jerid
Ouargla
Nālūt
Yafran
Gharyān
Az Zāwiyah
Miṣrātah
Surt
Khalīj Surt (Gulf of Sirte)
Ajdābiyā
Marsá al Burayqah
Marādah
Jālū

30°

Wādī al Ḥamīm

E G Y P T

500 m
1640 ft

Touggourt

Grand Erg Oriental

Waddān

Great Sand Sea

250 m
820 ft

100 m
328 ft

3

I A

Bordj Omar Driss

Tiguentourine

Birāk

L
Sabhā

I B Y A

Awbārī

Zawīlah

25°

Ramlat Rabyānah

Sea Level

Sea Level

-250 m
-820 ft

Tassili-n-Ajjer

Al 'Uwaynāt

Libyan

Al Khufrah

Tropic of Cancer

-500 m
-1640 ft

50

4

Djanet

Idhān Murzuq

Desert

-1000 m
-3281 ft

Ahaggar
△ *Tahat 2918m*
Tamanrasset

△ *Pic Bette 2286m*

20°

Tibesti

-2000 m
-6562 ft

h

a

r

a

-3000 m
-9843 ft

S U D A N

Erdi

Erdi Ma

Ennedi

-4000 m
-13 124 ft

Massif de l'Aïr

Ténéré

5

N I G E R

C H A D

15°

54

E 5° 10° F 15° G 20° H 25°

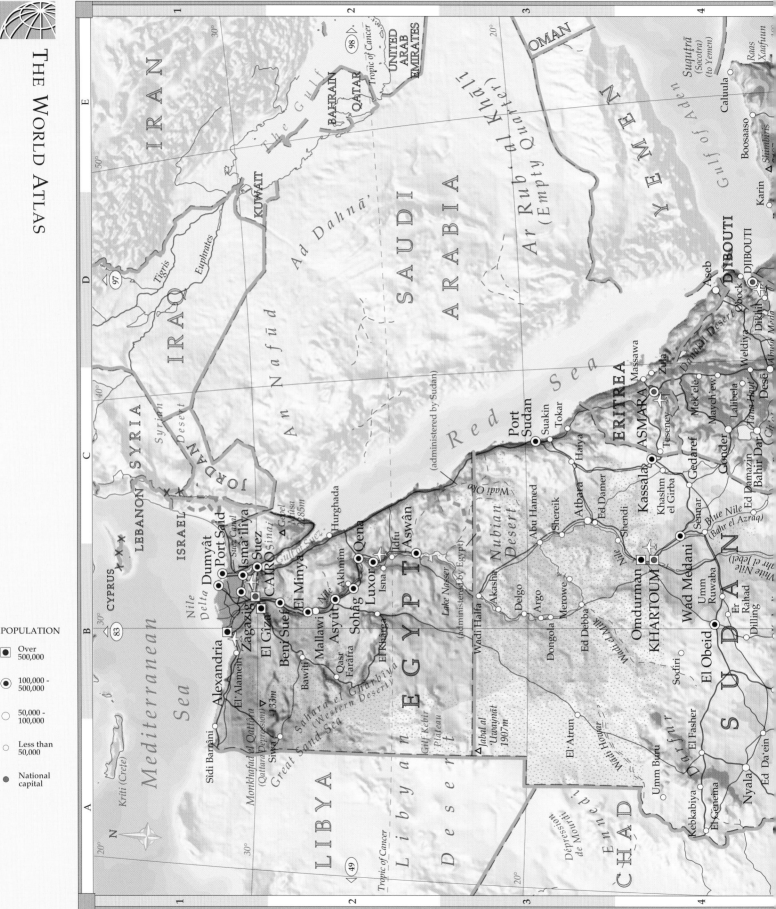

POPULATION

- ◉ Over 500,000
- ◉ 100,000 - 500,000
- ○ 50,000 - 100,000
- ○ Less than 50,000
- ● National capital

Mediterranean Sea

Kriti (Crete)

CYPRUS 83

LEBANON
SYRIA
ISRAEL
JORDAN

Syrian Desert

IRAQ
IRAN
KUWAIT

Tigris
Euphrates

97

BAHRAIN
QATAR
UNITED ARAB EMIRATES
98

Tropic of Cancer

The Gulf

An Nafūd

Ad Dahnā'

SAUDI ARABIA

Ar Rub' al Khālī (Empty Quarter)

OMAN

YEMEN

Suquṭrā (Socotra) (to Yemen)

Raas Xaafuun

Calula

Gulf of Aden

Boosaaso
Slumbiris
Karin

DJIBOUTI
DJIBOUTI
Aseb
Obock
Dikhil
Weldiya
Desē

Danakil Desert

Red Sea

Port Sudan
Suakin
Tokar

(administered by Sudan)

ERITREA
ASMARA
Massawa
Zula

Teseney
Mek'elē
Maych'ew
Lalibela
Gonder
Bahir Dar
Ed Damazin

Kassala
Khashm el Girba
Gedaref

Haya
Ed Damer
Atbara
Shereik
Abu Hamed

Nubian Desert
(administered by Egypt)

Wadi Oko

Akasha
Delgo
Argo
Merowe
Ed Debba
Dongola

Shendi
Sennar
Blue Nile (Bahr el Azraq)

Omdurman
KHARTOUM
Wad Medani
Umm Ruwaba
Er Rahad
Dilling

White Nile (Bahr el Jebel)

El Obeid
Sodiri
Umm Buru

S U D A N

Kebkabiya
El Geneina
El Fasher
Nyala
Ed Da'ein

Darfur

Depression de Mourdi

Ennedi

C H A D

LIBYA

Libyan Desert

Sahara el Gharbiya (Western Desert)

Great Sand Sea

Gilf Kebir Plateau

Jabal al 'Uwaynāt 1907m

El 'Atrun

Wādī el Milk

Wādī Howar

EGYPT

Lake Nasser

Aswân
Idfu
Isna
Luxor
Qena
Sohâg
Akhmîm
Asyût
Mallawi
Qasr Farâfra
Bawîti
El Kharga

Nile

Beni Suef
El Minya
CAIRO
El Gîza
Zagazig
Isma'iliya
Suez
Port Said
Dumyât

Gebel Mûsa 2285m

Hurghada
Gulf of Suez

Suez Canal

Nile Delta

Alexandria
El 'Alamein
Monkhafad el Qattâra (Qattara Depression) -133m
Siwa

Sîdi Barrâni

N

49

Tropic of Cancer

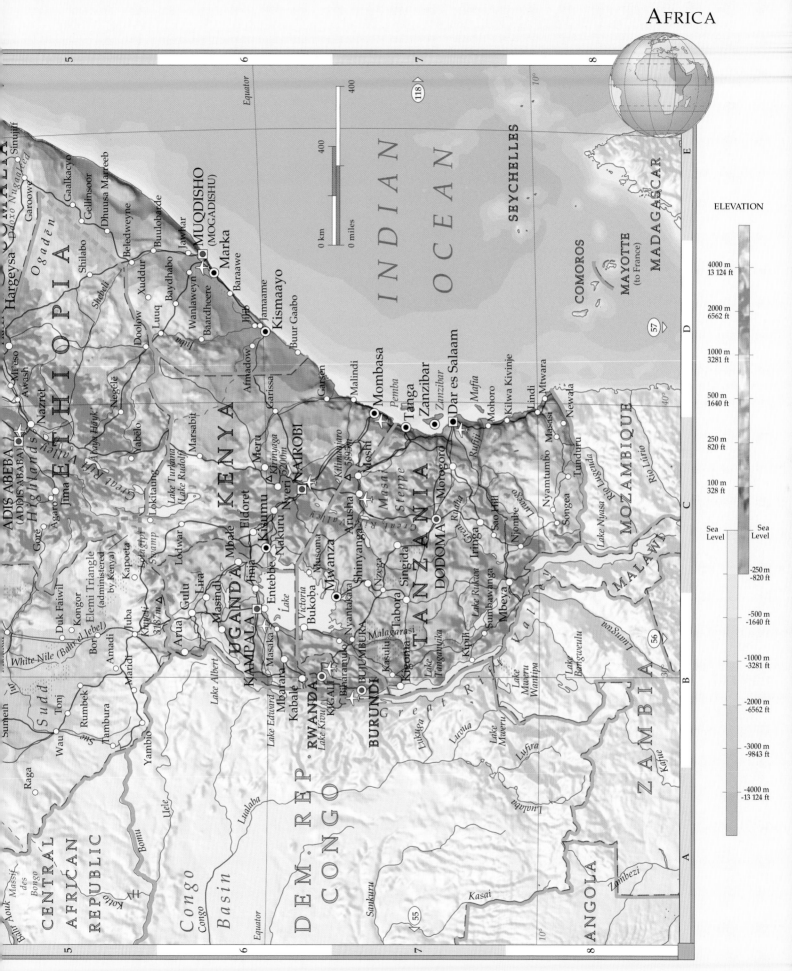

INDIAN OCEAN

ELEVATION

4000 m
13 124 ft

2000 m
6562 ft

1000 m
3281 ft

500 m
1640 ft

250 m
820 ft

100 m
328 ft

Sea Level — Sea Level

-250 m
-820 ft

-500 m
-1640 ft

-1000 m
-3281 ft

-2000 m
-6562 ft

-3000 m
-9843 ft

-4000 m
-13 124 ft

WEST AFRICA

WESTERN SAHARA
(disputed territory under Moroccan occupation)

Aïn Ben Tili

Bîr Mogreïn

Fdérik · Zouérat

Touâjîl

Choûm

Nouâdhibou

Akchâr

Atâr · Chinguetti

Akjoujt · Oujeft

M A U R I T A N I A

El Mreyyé

Idîni · Tidjikja · Tîchît

Boutilimit · Magta Lahjar · Boûmdeïd

Aoukâr

Rkîz · Aleg

Rosso · Kaédi · Ouâlâta

Richard Toll · Dagana · Timbedgha · Néma

Saint Louis · Kiffa · 'Ayoûn el 'Atroûs · Amourj

Louga · Matam · Kobenni · Bassikoun

Mékhe · **SENEGAL** · Sélibabi

DAKAR · Thiès · Mbaké · Nioro · Ténenkou

Mbour · Diourbel · Kayes · Niger

Sokone · **Kaolack** · Kolokani · Ségou

BANJUL · **GAMBIA** · Tambacounda · Toukoto · Bani

Bignona · Kolda · Gambia · Kita · Koulikoro

Ziguinchor · Sédhiou · Bafing · **BAMAKO** · Koutia

Bafata · Koutia

BISSAU · Gaoual · Sikas

GUINEA-BISSAU · Boké · Labé · Dinguiraye · Bagoé · Bougouni

Kindia · Pita · Niger · Siguiri · Sikas

G U I N E A · Mamou · Kankan · Ferkessédou

CONAKRY · Faranah · Tokounou · Odienné · Korho

Makeni · Kissidougou · Boundiali

SIERRA LEONE · Beyla · **CÔTE D'IVOIRE (IVORY COAST)**

FREETOWN · Bo · Kenema · Nzérékoré · Katiola

Gbanga · Danane · Gagnoa

Tubmanburg · **YAMOUSSOUKRO**

Harbel · Zwedru · Divo

MONROVIA · Buchanan · Sassandr

LIBERIA · Harper · San-Pédro

CAPE VERDE

Ilhas de Barlavento

Santo Antão · Mindelo · Pedra Lume

São Vicente · Sal

São Nicolau · Boa Vista

Santiago · Maio

Fogo · **PRAIA**

Ilhas de Sotavento

A T L A N T I C

O C E A N

Tropic of Cancer

POPULATION

- ⊡ Over 500,000
- ◉ 100,000 – 500,000
- ○ 50,000 – 100,000
- ∘ Less than 50,000
- ● National capital

0 km   400

0 miles   400

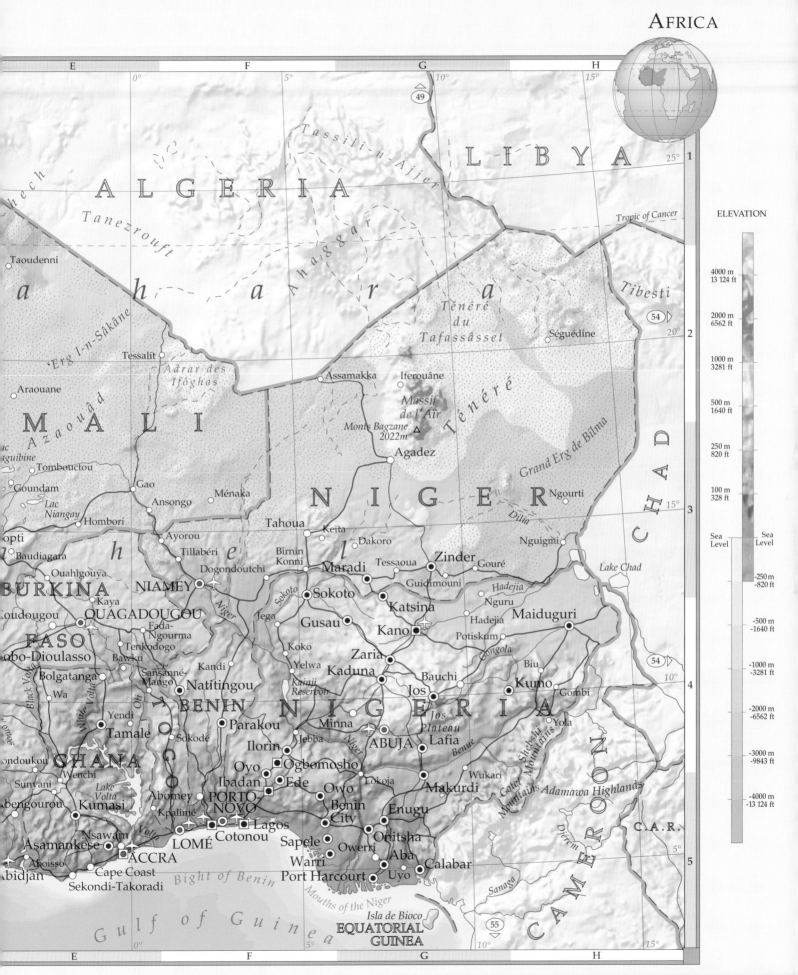

ELEVATION

4000 m
13 124 ft

2000 m
6562 ft

1000 m
3281 ft

500 m
1640 ft

250 m
820 ft

100 m
328 ft

Sea
Level

Sea
Level

-250 m
-820 ft

-500 m
-1640 ft

-1000 m
-3281 ft

-2000 m
-6562 ft

-3000 m
-9843 ft

-4000 m
-13 124 ft

LIBYA

ALGERIA

Tassili-n-Ajjer

Tanezrouft

Ahaggar

Tibesti

Tropic of Cancer

Taoudenni

Sahara

Ténéré
du
Tafassâsset

Séguédine

Erg I-n-Sâkâne

Araouane

Tessalit

Adrar des
Ifôghas

Assamakka

Iferouâne

Massif
de l'Aïr

Ténéré

Grand Erg de Bilma

MALI

Azaouâd

Monts Bagzane
2022m

Lac
Aguibine

Tombouctou

Gao

Agadez

CHAD

Goundam

Lac
Niangay

Ansongo

Ménaka

NIGER

Ngourti

opti

Hombori

Tahoua

Keïta

Dilia

Baudiagara

Ayorou

Dakoro

Nguigmi

Tillabéri

Birnin
Konni

Maradi

Tessaoua

Zinder

Gouré

Lake Chad

Ouahigouya

Dogondoutchi

Niger

Sokoto

Guidimouni

Hadejia

NIAMEY

Jega

Sokoto

Katsina

Nguru

Maiduguri

BURKINA

Kaya

Gusau

Kano

Hadejia

Potiskum

OUAGADOUGOU

Jega

Zaria

Gongola

Biu

FASO

Fada-
Ngourma

Koko

Kaduna

Bauchi

Kumo

obo-Dioulasso

Tenkodogo

Yelwa

Jos

Gombi

Bolgatanga

Bawku

Kandi

Kainji
Reservoir

Jos
Plateau

Yola

Wa

Sansanné-
Mango

Natitingou

NIGERIA

Shebeli Mountains

Black Volta

Yendi

BENIN

Minna

Lafia

Benue

Adamawa Highlands

Tamale

Sokodé

Parakou

Jebba

ABUJA

Wukari

oundoukou

GHANA

Ilorin

Oyo

Ogbomosho

Lokoja

Makurdi

CAMEROON

Sunyani

Wenchi

Ibadan

Ede

Owo

C.A.R.

bengourou

Kumasi

Abomey

PORTO-
NOVO

Benin
City

Enugu

Onitsha

Dierem

Nsawam

Kpalimé

Lagos

Sapele

Owerri

Aba

Calabar

Asamankese

LOMÉ

Cotonou

Warri

Uyo

Aboisso

ACCRA

Port Harcourt

Sanaga

Abidjan

Cape Coast

Bight of Benin

Sekondi-Takoradi

Mouths of the Niger

Gulf of Guinea

Isla de Bioco

EQUATORIAL
GUINEA

Lake
Volta

White Volta

Red Volta

Oti

Volta

Kumasi

Lac
Faguibine

CENTRAL AFRICA

SÃO TOMÉ & PRÍNCIPE

Príncipe
Santo António
Ilha Caroço
Tinhosa Grande
Tinhosa Pequena

SÃO TOMÉ
Santana
São Cruz
Santa Cruz
Porto Alegre
Ilha das Cabras
Neves
Pico de São Tomé 2024m
Ilha das Rôlas
Equator

Gulf of Guinea

0 km   20
0 miles   20

2000m/6562ft
1000m/3281ft
500m/1640ft
200m/656ft

EGYPT

ALGERIA

LIBYA

Libyan Desert

Ramlat Rabyānah

Idhān Murzuq

NIGER

Ténéré

Massif de l'Aïr

Massif d'Abo

Tibesti
Aozou
Bardaï
Zouar

Erg du Djourab

Faya

Koro Toro

Ounianga Kébir

Fada

Erdi Ma

Depression du Mourdi

Ennedi

SUDAN

Darfur

Sudd

White Nile (Bahr el Jebel)

White Nile (Bahr el Jebel)

CHAD

S a h a r a

Erg du Djourab

Massif du Kapka

Biltine
Abéché
Goz Beïda
Mangalmé
Mongo
Abou-Déïa
Am Timan
Birao

Ati
Moussoro
Mao
Bol
Nokou
Lake Chad
Haïe Chad

NDJAMENA
Koussérie
Massenya
Chari Baguirmi
Bongor
Fianga
Kélo
Léré
Lac de Léré
Bongor

Massaguet

CENTRAL AFRICAN REPUBLIC

Ouanda Djallé
Ndélé
Bria
Raga Bandoro
Dékoa
Bakala
Grimari
Sibut
Bambari
Ippy
Kabo
Markounda
Bossangoa
Bouar
Baoro
Bossembélé
Djéma
Obo
Bomu

Massif des Bongo

Kotto

Bamingui

Sarh
Kyabé
Maro
Bahr Aouk
Doba
Gore
Koumra
Moundou
Baïbokoum
Bébédjia

CAMEROON

Maroua
Guider
Garoua
Mbé
Ngaoundéré
Banyo
Foumban
Bamenda
Nkongsamba

NIGERIA

Jos Plateau

Shebshi Mountains

Adamawa Highlands

Benue
Niger
Hadejia

Tropic of Cancer

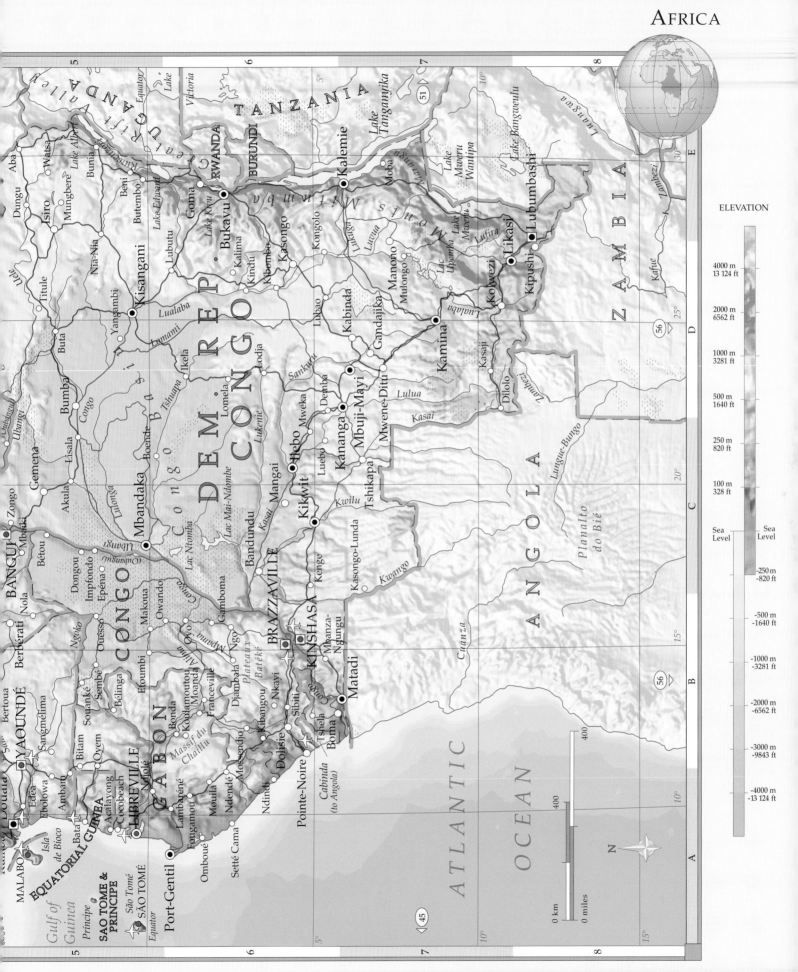

SOUTHERN AFRICA

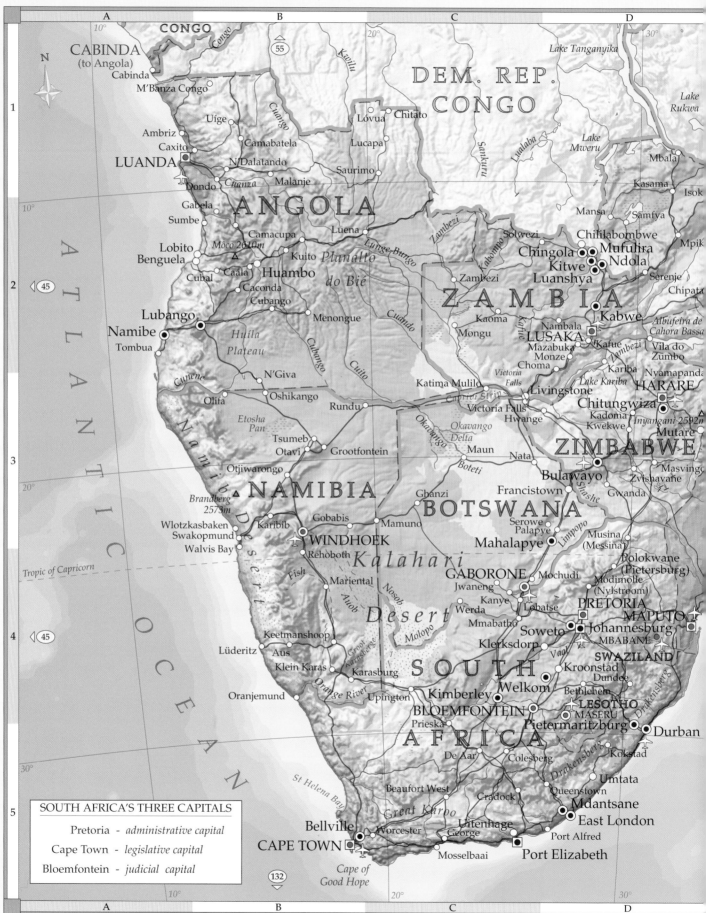

POPULATION

- ◉ Over 500,000
- ◉ 100,000 – 500,000
- ○ 50,000 – 100,000
- ○ Less than 50,000
- ● National capital

SOUTH AFRICA'S THREE CAPITALS

Pretoria - *administrative capital*

Cape Town - *legislative capital*

Bloemfontein - *judicial capital*

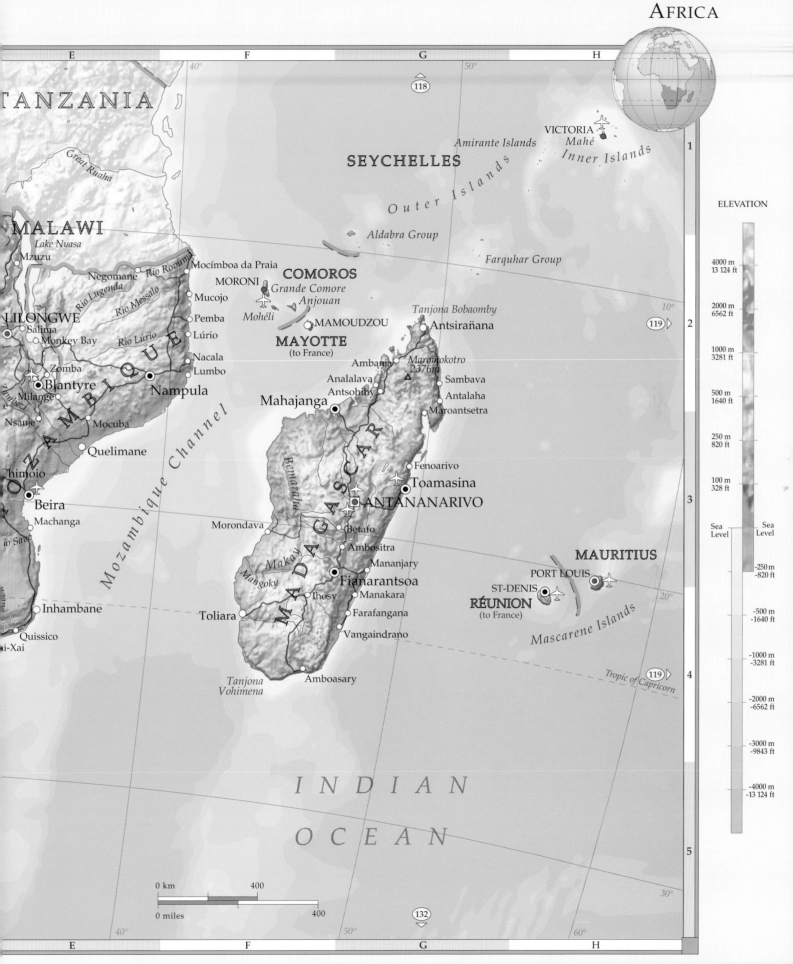

E   F   G   H

40°   50°

⌂ 118

TANZANIA

1

Great Ruaha

VICTORIA   Mahé
Amirante Islands   ✈

SEYCHELLES   Inner Islands

MALAWI

Outer Islands

Lake Nyasa

Mzuzu

Aldabra Group

Negomane   Rio Rovuma   Mocímboa da Praia

ELEVATION

Rio Lugenda   Mucojo   COMOROS   Farquhar Group   10°

MORONI   Grande Comore

Rio Messalo   Anjouan

LILONGWE   Pemba   ✈   Mohéli

Salima   Lúrio   MAMOUDZOU   Tanjona Bobaomby   ⌂ 119   2

Monkey Bay   Rio Lúrio   Nacala   MAYOTTE   Antsiranana

Zomba   Lumbo   (to France)

4000 m
13 124 ft

Blantyre   Ambanja   Maromokotro
2376m

Milange   Nampula   Analalava

Nsanje   Mocuba   Antsohihy   Sambava   2000 m
6562 ft

Mahajanga   Antalaha

Quelimane   Maroantsetra   1000 m
3281 ft

Chimoio   M A D A G A S C A R

Bemaraha   500 m
1640 ft

Fenoarivo

Beira   Toamasina   250 m
820 ft

Machanga   ANTANANARIVO

io Save   Betafo   100 m
328 ft   3

Morondava   Ambositra

Makay   Mananjary   MAURITIUS

m   Mangoky   Fianarantsoa   PORT LOUIS   Sea
Level   Sea
Level

Inhambane   Ihosy   Manakara   ST-DENIS   ✈

Quissico   Toliara   Farafangana   RÉUNION   -250 m
-820 ft

i-Xai   (to France)

Vangaindrano   -500 m
-1640 ft

Mascarene Islands   20°

Amboasary   -1000 m
-3281 ft

Tanjona
Vohimena   Tropic of Capricorn   ⌂ 119   4

Mozambique Channel

-2000 m
-6562 ft

I N D I A N   -3000 m
-9843 ft

-4000 m
-13 124 ft

O C E A N

5

0 km   400

0 miles   400   30°

⌂ 132

40°   50°   60°

E   F   G   H

POLITICAL FEATURES

TOTAL AREA:
4,809,200 sq miles (12,456,000 sq km)

TOTAL NUMBER OF COUNTRIES: 43

TOTAL POPULATION: 707 million

LARGEST CITY WITH POPULATION:
Moscow, European Russia 15.5 million

COUNTRY WITH HIGHEST POPULATION DENSITY:
Monaco 42,840 people per sq mile (16,477 people per sq km)

LARGEST COUNTRY:
European Russia 1,527,341 sq miles (3,955,818 sq km)

SMALLEST COUNTRY:
Vatican City, Italy 0.17 sq miles (0.44 sq km)

PHYSICAL FEATURES

LARGEST LAKE:
Lake Lagoda, European Russia 7,100 sq miles (18,390 sq km)

LONGEST RIVER:
Volga, European Russia 2,290 miles (3,688 km)

HIGHEST POINT:
El'brus, Caucasus, European Russia 18,510ft (5,642 m)

LOWEST POINT:
Volga Delta, Caspian Sea, European Russia 92 ft (28m) below sea level

POPULATION

- Over 500,000
- 100,000 – 500,000
- 50,000 – 100,000
- Less than 50,000
- National capital

Barents Sea

North Cape

Murmansk

Kola Peninsula

Ostrov Kolguyev

Arctic Circle

Ob'

Irtysh

133

White Sea

Archangel

Northern Dvina

Ural Mountains

R U S S I A N

Perm'

90

Lake Onega

Tampere

Turku   HELSINKI

Åland

Uppsala

STOCKHOLM   TALLINN

Saint Petersburg

Lake Ladoga

F E D E R A T I O N

Vologda

Ufa

Yaroslavl'

Kazan'

ESTONIA

Nizhniy Novgorod

Ul'yanovsk

Orenburg

LATVIA

MOSCOW

Samara

Ural

RĪGA

LITHUANIA

KALININGRAD (to Russ.Fed).

Vitsyebsk

Volga Uplands

Volga

Aral Sea

Syr Darya

VILNIUS

Kaunas

iningrad

ańsk

MINSK

Central Russian Upland

Babruysk

Homyel'

Voronezh

Ural

ydgoszcz

BELARUS

Pripet Marshes

Amu Darya

WARSAW

Brest

Dnieper Lowlands

Don

Volgograd

ódź

Bug

KIEV

Kharkiv

OLAND

Kraków

L'viv

Dniester

UKRAINE

Dnieper

Dnipropetrovs'k

Donets'k

Astrakhan'

Volga Delta -28m

OVAKIA

Carpathian Mountains

Chernivtsi

Rostov-na-Donu

Caspian Sea

UDAPEST

MOLDOVA

CHIŞINĂU

Sea of Azov

Stavropol'

UNGARY

Cluj-Napoca

Odesa

ROMANIA

Braşov

Crimea

Caucasus

El'brus 5642m

BELGRADE

BUCHAREST

Simferopol'

SERB. & MON. (YUGO.)

Danube

Constanţa

Black Sea

BULGARIA

Varna

SOFIA

Balkan Mountains

Burgas

SKOPJE

MACED.

TURKEY

TIRANA

LBANIA

Aegean Sea

Anatolia

Zagros Mountains

GREECE

ATHENS

Piraeus

Peloponnese

Irákleio

Cyprus

Tigris

Euphrates

96

Crete

Sea

E   20°   30°   40°   50°   F   70°   60°   G   70°   80°   H   80°   70°   50°   40°   60°   30°   50°

1   2   3   4   5

THE WORLD ATLAS

Arctic Circle

90°

Hudson Bay

Southampton Island

Foxe Basin

N U N A V U T

Gulf of Boothia

Devon Island

Ellesmere Island

Nares Strait

Knud Rasmussen La.

Qaanaaq

Innaanganeq

Savissivik

Qimusseriarsuaq

C A N A D A

80°

Baffin Island

Baffin Bay

Kullorsuaq

Upernavik

Péninsule d'Ungava

QUÉBEC

Hudson Strait

Cumberland Sound

Frobisher Bay

Limit of summer pack ice

Uummannaq

Qeqertarsuaq

Qeqertarsuaq

Qeqertarsuup Tunua

Qasigiannguit

70°

Arnaud

George

Ungava Bay

Davis Strait

Sisimiut

Kong Frederik IX Land

Maniitsoq

NUUK

G R E E N L A N D

(to Denmark)

Kong Christian IX Land

Gunnbjørn Fj.
3700

Mont Forel
3360m

Paamiut

Ivittuut

Ammassalik

Kong Frederik VI Kyst

Labrador Sea

NEWFOUNDLAND & LABRADOR

60°

Qaqortoq

Nanortalik

Nunap Isua
(Kap Farvel)

Denmark

Limit of winter pack ice

Reykjanes Basin

ATLANTIC

OCEAN

50°

40°

30°

POPULATION

- ⊙ Over 500,000
- ◉ 100,000 - 500,000
- ○ 50,000 - 100,000
- ○ Less than 50,000
- ● National capital

0 km   400

0 miles   400

E 60° 50° 40° 30° 20° 10° F 0° 10° 20° 30° 40° G 50° H

ARCTIC
OCEAN

△ 133

*Lincoln
Sea*

Kap Morris Jesup

*Wandel
Sea*

Zemlya
Frantsa-Iosifa

Kvitøya

SVALBARD
(to Norway)

Nordaustlandet

Novaya
Zemlya

Independence Fjord

Nord

Kong Karls Land

Spitsbergen

Barentsøya

*Barents
Sea*

88 ▷

LONGYEARBYEN
Barentsberg

Edgeøya

Storfjorden

Kong Frederik VIII Land

Limit of winter pack ice

*Greenland
Sea*

Bjørnøya
(to Norway)

*Kong Christian X
Land*

Limit of summer pack ice

Nordkapp
(North Cape)

△ Petermann Bjerg
2940m

Daneborg

FINLAND

3

Kong Oscar Fjord

Ittoqqortoormiit

Mohns Ridge

JAN MAYEN
(to Norway)

S
W
E
D
E
N

Kangertittivaq
Kangikajik

*Norwegian
Sea*

Vestfjorden

Arctic Circle

62 ▷

4

Strait

Norwegian Basin

ICELAND

*Gulf
of
Bothnia*

Bolungarvík
Siglufjördhur   Raufarhöfn
Ísafjördhur
Húsavík
Akureyri
Stykkishólmur   Seydhisfjördhur
REYKJAVÍK   Neskaupstadhur
Selfoss   *Vatnajökull*
Thorlákshöfn   Djúpivogur
Hvannadalshnúkur
2119m
Surtsey   Vestmannaeyjar

FAEROE ISLANDS
(to Denmark)

N
O
R
W
A
Y

5

TÓRSHAVN

N

*Shetland
Islands*

63 ▷

E 50° 20° F 10° G 0° H 60° 20°

ELEVATION

4000 m
13 124 ft

2000 m
6562 ft

1000 m
3281 ft

500 m
1640 ft

250 m
820 ft

100 m
328 ft

Sea
Level
Sea
Level

-250 m
-820 ft

-500 m
-1640 ft

-1000 m
-3281 ft

-2000 m
-6562 ft

-3000 m
-9843 ft

-4000 m
-13 124 ft

SCANDINAVIA & FINLAND

POPULATION

- ◉ Over 500,000
- ◉ 100,000 – 500,000
- ○ 50,000 – 100,000
- ○ Less than 50,000
- ● National capital

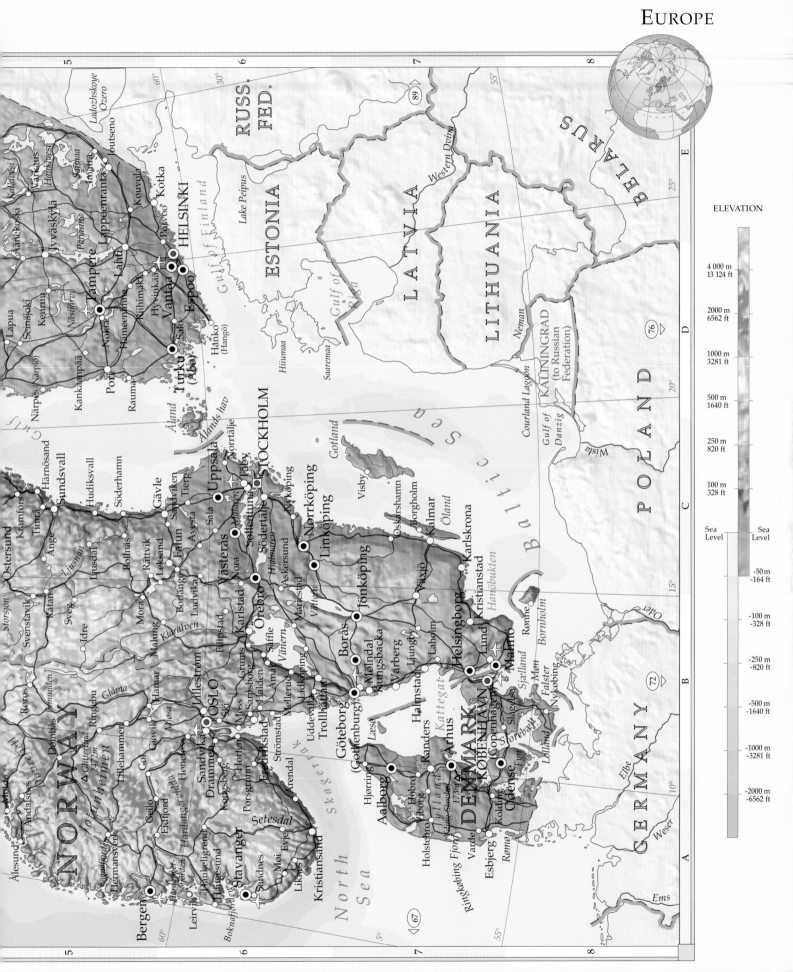

ELEVATION

4 000 m 13 124 ft	
2000 m 6562 ft	
1000 m 3281 ft	
500 m 1640 ft	
250 m 820 ft	
100 m 328 ft	
Sea Level	Sea Level
-50 m -164 ft	
-100 m -328 ft	
-250 m -820 ft	
-500 m -1640 ft	
-1000 m -3281 ft	
-2000 m -6562 ft	

RUSS. FED.

BELARUS

ESTONIA

LATVIA

LITHUANIA

KALININGRAD (to Russian Federation)

POLAND

GERMANY

NORWAY

DENMARK

Gulf of Finland

Gulf of Riga

Baltic Sea

Ladozhskoye Ozero

Lake Peipus

Hiiumaa

Saaremaa

Gotland

Öland

Bornholm

HELSINKI
Tampere
Espoo
Vantaa
Turku (Åbo)
Hanko (Hangö)
Lappeenranta
Kotka
Kouvola
Lahti
Porvoo
Hyvinkää
Riihimäki
Hämeenlinna
Nokia
Salo
Pori
Rauma
Kankaanpää
Seinäjoki
Keuruu
Jyväskylä
Äänekoski
Kalajärsi
Varkaus
Hankasi
Imatra
Savanna
Lapua

STOCKHOLM
Uppsala
Norrtälje
Täby
Norrköping
Linköping
Nyköping
Södertälje
Eskilstuna
Västerås
Örebro
Karlstad
Jönköping
Borås
Göteborg (Gothenburg)
Mölndal
Kungsbacka
Varberg
Halmstad
Laholm
Ljungby
Växjö
Kalmar
Oskarshamn
Borgholm
Karlskrona
Kristianstad
Helsingborg
Lund
Malmö
Landskrona
Visby
Gävle
Sandviken
Falun
Ludvika
Borlänge
Avesta
Sala
Mora
Bollnäs
Söderhamn
Hudiksvall
Sundsvall
Härnösand
Timrå
Ånge
Östersund
Klamfors
Leksand
Rättvik
Nässjö
Vimmerby
Mariestad
Lidköping
Skövde
Trollhättan
Vänersborg
Uddevalla
Strömstad

OSLO
Drammen
Sandvika
Lillestrøm
Moss
Horten
Sarpsborg
Halden
Fredrikstad
Tønsberg
Larvik
Skien
Porsgrunn
Kongsberg
Hønefoss
Gjøvik
Hamar
Lillehammer
Gol
Geilo
Eidfjord
Bergen
Voss
Stavanger
Sandnes
Haugesund
Kristiansand
Arendal
Mandal
Moi
Evje
Sirdal
Ålesund
Åndalsnes
Dombås
Røros
Molde
Kristiansund
Ringebu

KØBENHAVN (Copenhagen)
Ålborg
Århus
Odense
Esbjerg
Randers
Kolding
Vejle
Horsens
Holstebro
Viborg
Hjørring
Herning
Varde
Slagelse
Næstved
Roskilde

Jylland
Sjælland
Fyn
Lolland
Falster
Møn
Læsø
Storebælt
Kattegat
Skagerrak
North Sea
Bodn Fjord
Setesdal
Hardangerfjord

Gulf of Danzig
Courland Lagoon
Neman
Western Dvina
Wisła
Oder
Elbe
Weser
Ems

Åland
Ålands hav

Glomma
Klarälven
Dalälven
Ljusnan
Indalsälven
Vänern
Vättern

Hanöbukten
Ronne

Glittertind 2472m
Jotunheimen

Storsjön

THE LOW COUNTRIES

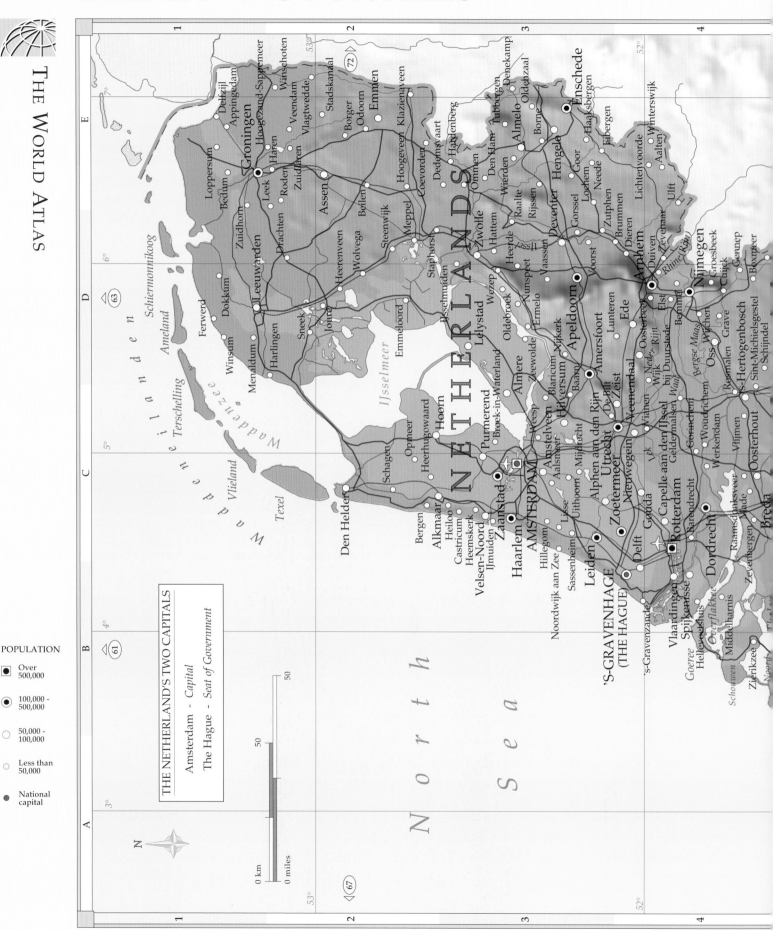

POPULATION

- ■ Over 500,000
- ◉ 100,000 – 500,000
- ○ 50,000 – 100,000
- ○ Less than 50,000
- ● National capital

THE NETHERLAND'S TWO CAPITALS

Amsterdam - *Capital*
The Hague - *Seat of Government*

50
50
50

0 km
0 miles

N

Labels on map

NETHERLANDS

North Sea
Wadden Zee
IJsselmeer
Texel
Vlieland
Terschelling
Ameland
Schiermonnikoog
Waddeneilanden

Den Helder
Groningen
Leeuwarden
Assen
Emmen
Enschede
Nijmegen
Arnhem
Apeldoorn
Amersfoort
AMSTERDAM
Zaanstad
Haarlem
Leiden
'S-GRAVENHAGE (THE HAGUE)
Rotterdam
Dordrecht
Utrecht
Zwolle
Deventer
Breda
'S-Hertogenbosch

Delfzijl
Appingedam
Winschoten
Veendam
Hoogezand-Sappemeer
Vlagtwedde
Stadskanaal
Borger
Odoorn
Klazienaveen
Hoogeveen
Coevorden
Hardenberg
Den Ham
Tubbergen
Denekamp
Oldenzaal
Almelo
Borne
Hengelo
Haaksbergen
Eibergen
Lichtenvoorde
Aalten
Winterswijk
Ulft
Zevenaar
Duiven
Elst
Groesbeek
Cuijk
Boxmeer
Gennep
Grave
Wijchen
Oss
Sint-Michielsgestel
Schijndel
Rosmalen
Oosterhout
Made
Zevenbergen
Middelharnis
Zierikzee

Loppersum
Bedum
Zuidhorn
Leek
Haren
Roden
Zuidlaren
Drachten
Beilen
Steenwijk
Wolvega
Heerenveen
Meppel
Heerde
Raalte
Rijssen
Ommen
Dedemsvaart
Staphorst
IJsselmuiden
Hattem
Wezep
Vaassen
Nunspeet
Ermelo
Harderwijk
Nijkerk
Baarn
Soest
Lunteren
Ede
Wageningen
Renkum
Dieren
Brummen
Zutphen
Lochem
Needle
Goor
Gorssel
Voorst

Dokkum
Ferwerd
Winsum
Menaldum
Harlingen
Sneek
Joure
Balk

Emmeloord
Lelystad
Oldebroek
Zeewolde
Almere

Purmerend
Hoorn
Broek-in-Waterland
Schagen
Opmeer
Heerhugowaard
Alkmaar
Heiloo
Bergen
Castricum
Heemskerk
Velsen-Noord
IJmuiden
Zandvoort
Hillegom
Lisse
Sassenheim
Noordwijk aan Zee
Uithoorn
Aalsmeer
Amstelveen
Weesp
Hilversum
Blaricum
Bussum
Naarden
De Bilt
Zeist
Veenendaal
Rhenen

Zoetermeer
Nieuwegein
Vianen
Wijk bij Duurstede
Culemborg
Geldermalsen
Zaltbommel
Tiel

Delft
Gouda
Alphen aan den Rijn
Capelle aan den IJssel
Woudrichem
Gorinchem
Werkendam
Vlijmen

'S-Gravenzande
Vlaardingen
Spijkenisse
Hellevoetsluis
Barendrecht
Raamsdonksveer
Zevenbergen

Goeree
Overflakkee
Schouwen
Noord

Rhine (Rijn)
Neder Rijn
Lek
Waal
Bergse Maas

Wadden

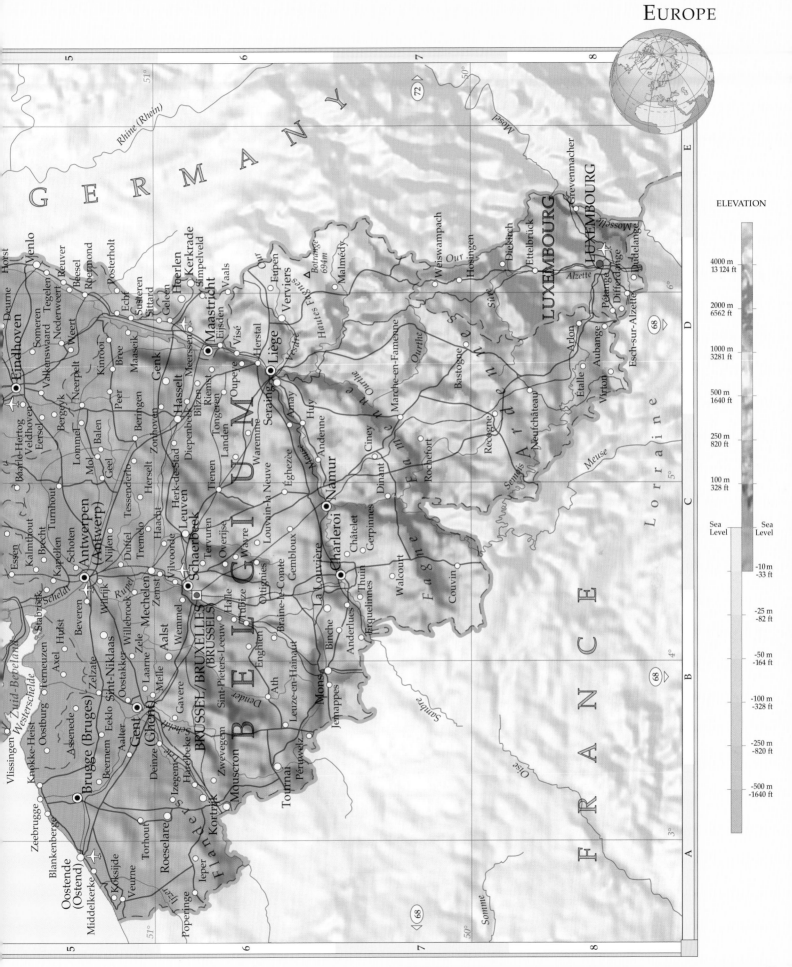

ELEVATION

4000 m	13 124 ft
2000 m	6562 ft
1000 m	3281 ft
500 m	1640 ft
250 m	820 ft
100 m	328 ft
Sea Level	Sea Level
	-10 m / -33 ft
	-25 m / -82 ft
	-50 m / -164 ft
	-100 m / -328 ft
	-250 m / -820 ft
	-500 m / -1640 ft

THE BRITISH ISLES

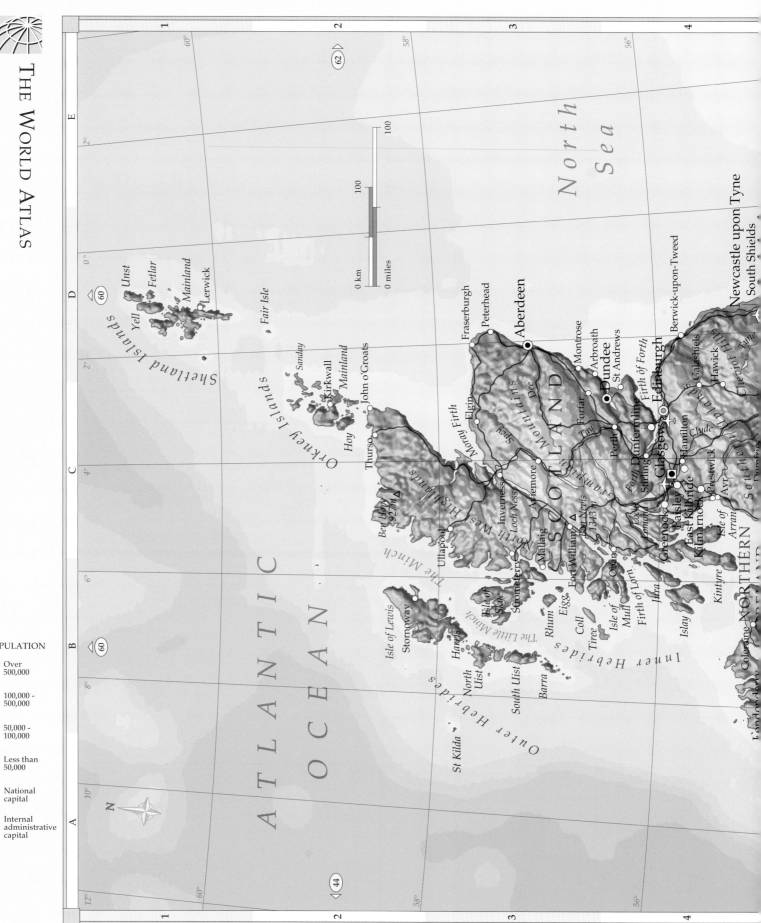

POPULATION

- ⊡ Over 500,000
- ◉ 100,000 - 500,000
- ○ 50,000 - 100,000
- ○ Less than 50,000
- ● National capital
- ● Internal administrative capital

Scale

100 km · 0 km
100 miles · 0 miles

Map labels

North Sea

ATLANTIC OCEAN

Shetland Islands
Unst
Fetlar
Yell
Mainland
Lerwick

Fair Isle

Orkney Islands
Sanday
Kirkwall
Mainland
Hoy
John o'Groats

Thurso

Moray Firth
Elgin
Spey
Grampian Mountains
Dee
Fraserburgh
Peterhead
Aberdeen

Montrose
Arbroath
Forfar
Dundee
St Andrews
Firth of Tay
Tay
Perth

Ben Hope 927m
North West Highlands
Inverness
Loch Ness
Aviemore
Ullapool

Stromeferry
Mallaig
Loch Linnhe
Fort William
Ben Nevis 1343m
Oban

Dunfermline
Firth of Forth
Edinburgh
Stirling
Forth
Glasgow
Hamilton
Clyde
Greenock
Paisley
East Kilbride
Kilmarnock
Prestwick
Ayr
Isle of Arran
Kintyre

Berwick-upon-Tweed
Galashiels
Hawick
Cheviot Hills
Southern Uplands
Dumfries

Newcastle upon Tyne
South Shields
Tyne

The Minch
Isle of Lewis
Stornoway
Harris
North Uist
South Uist
Barra
Outer Hebrides
St Kilda

Isle of Skye
Rhum
Eigg
Coll
Tiree
The Little Minch
Isle of Mull
Firth of Lorn
Jura
Islay
Inner Hebrides

SCOTLAND

NORTHERN
Coleraine
Londonderry

60 (D)
60 (B)
62 (E)
44 (A)

60° 58° 56°
2° 0° 2° 4° 6° 8° 10° 12°

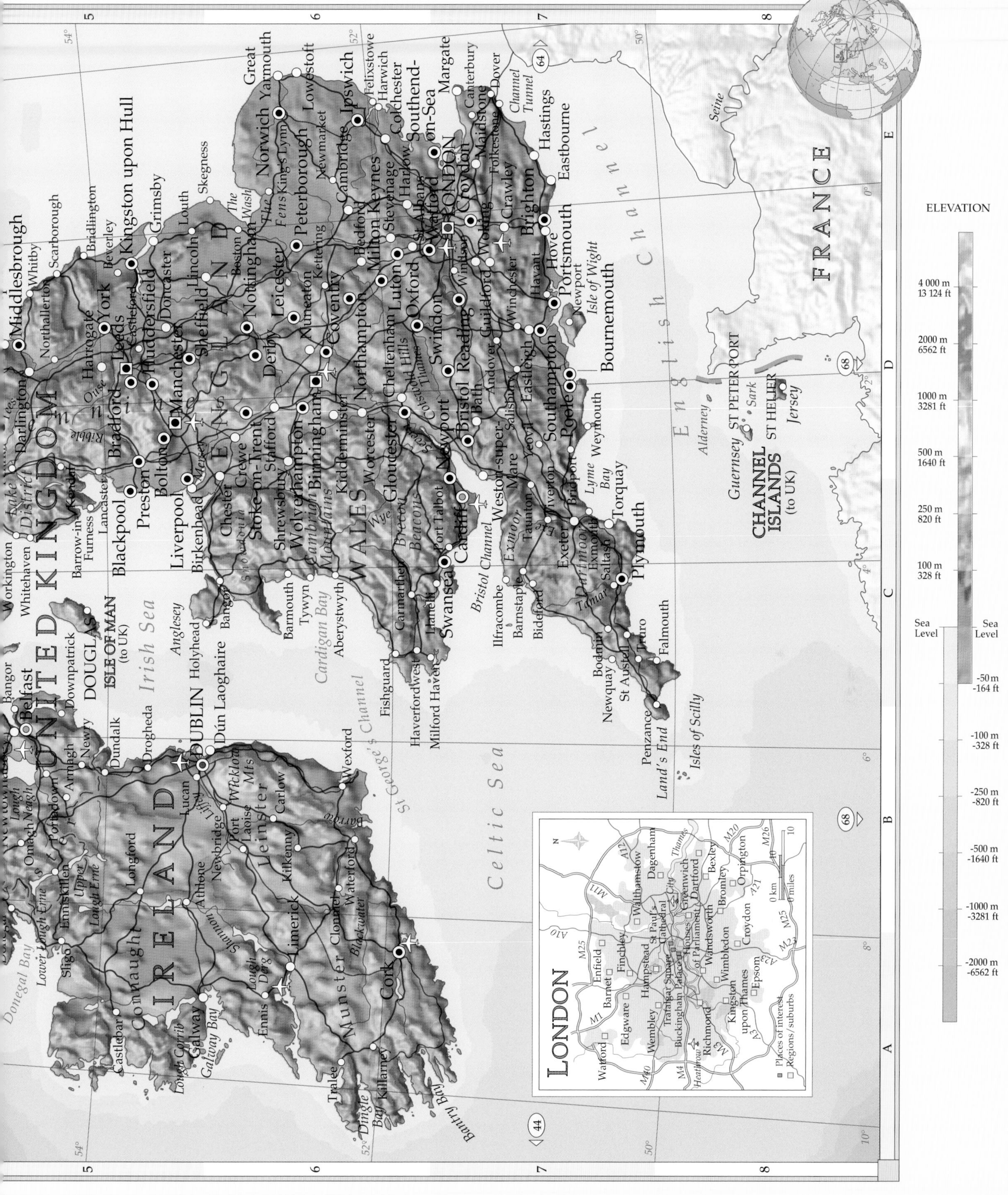

ELEVATION

4 000 m	13 124 ft
2000 m	6562 ft
1000 m	3281 ft
500 m	1640 ft
250 m	820 ft
100 m	328 ft

Sea Level	Sea Level
-50 m	-164 ft
-100 m	-328 ft
-250 m	-820 ft
-500 m	-1640 ft
-1000 m	-3281 ft
-2000 m	-6562 ft

FRANCE

Seine

English Channel

Channel Tunnel

UNITED KINGDOM

ENGLAND

WALES

IRELAND

ISLE OF MAN (to UK)

CHANNEL ISLANDS (to UK)

Irish Sea

Celtic Sea

St George's Channel

Cardigan Bay

Bristol Channel

Lyme Bay

Isle of Wight

Guernsey — ST PETER PORT — Sark — Alderney — ST HELIER — Jersey

Land's End — Isles of Scilly

England and Wales place names:
Middlesbrough, Whitby, Scarborough, Northallerton, Harrogate, York, Bridlington, Beverley, Kingston upon Hull, Grimsby, Leeds, Bradford, Huddersfield, Doncaster, Sheffield, Lincoln, Skegness, Louth, Manchester, Bolton, Preston, Blackpool, Liverpool, Birkenhead, Chester, Crewe, Stoke-on-Trent, Stafford, Shrewsbury, Wolverhampton, Birmingham, Derby, Nottingham, Leicester, Nuneaton, Coventry, Kidderminster, Worcester, Northampton, Kettering, Peterborough, King's Lynn, Norwich, Great Yarmouth, Lowestoft, Ipswich, Felixstowe, Harwich, Colchester, Newmarket, Cambridge, Bedford, Milton Keynes, Luton, Stevenage, Harlow, Southend-on-Sea, LONDON, Croydon, Watford, Oxford, Cheltenham, Gloucester, Swindon, Reading, Guildford, Crawley, Brighton, Hove, Worthing, Chichester, Havant, Portsmouth, Southampton, Eastleigh, Winchester, Andover, Salisbury, Bath, Bristol, Newport, Cardiff, Swansea, Port Talbot, Carmarthen, Llanelli, Haverfordwest, Milford Haven, Fishguard, Aberystwyth, Tywyn, Barmouth, Bangor, Holyhead, Anglesey, Lancaster, Kendal, Workington, Whitehaven, Barrow-in-Furness, Darlington, Canterbury, Margate, Dover, Folkestone, Hastings, Eastbourne, Maidstone, Bournemouth, Poole, Weymouth, Yeovil, Taunton, Exeter, Exmouth, Torquay, Plymouth, Truro, Falmouth, Penzance, Newquay, St Austell, Bodmin, Barnstaple, Bideford, Ilfracombe, Newport, Westbury, Weston-super-Mare, Bridgwater

Ireland place names:
Belfast, Bangor, Downpatrick, Newry, Newtownards, Armagh, Dungannon, Omagh, Enniskillen, Sligo, Castlebar, Galway, Ennis, Limerick, Tralee, Killarney, Cork, Clonmel, Waterford, Wexford, Kilkenny, Carlow, Athlone, Longford, Mullingar, Portlaoise, Naas, Newbridge, DUBLIN, Dún Laoghaire, Dundalk, Drogheda, Lucan

Scotland/North:
DOUGLAS

Wash, The Fens, The Wolds, Pennines, Cambrian Mountains, Brecon Beacons, Exmoor, Dartmoor, Bodmin Moor, Wicklow Mts, Leinster, Munster, Connaught, Cotswold Hills

Rivers/features: Ribble, Ouse, Trent, Severn, Wye, Thames, Tamar, Avon, Shannon, Barrow, Liffey, Lough Neagh, Lough Erne, Upper Lough Erne, Lower Lough Erne, Lough Corrib, Lough Derg, Blackwater, Donegal Bay, Galway Bay, Dingle Bay, Bantry Bay

LONDON inset map:
LONDON — N
Enfield, Barnet, Finchley, Edgware, Wembley, Hampstead, Waltham, Dagenham, Bexley, Bromley, Orpington, Greenwich, Dartford, Croydon, Epsom, Wimbledon, Kingston upon Thames, Richmond, Heathrow, Watford, Wandsworth, Trafalgar Square, St Paul's Cathedral, Houses of Parliament, Buckingham Palace, City
Roads: M1, M11, M25, M26, M20, M23, M3, M4, M40, A1, A10, A12, A13
Thames
□ Places of interest
▢ Regions / suburbs
0 km 10 / 0 miles 10

54° 52° 50° 52° 50°

67

FRANCE, ANDORRA & MONACO

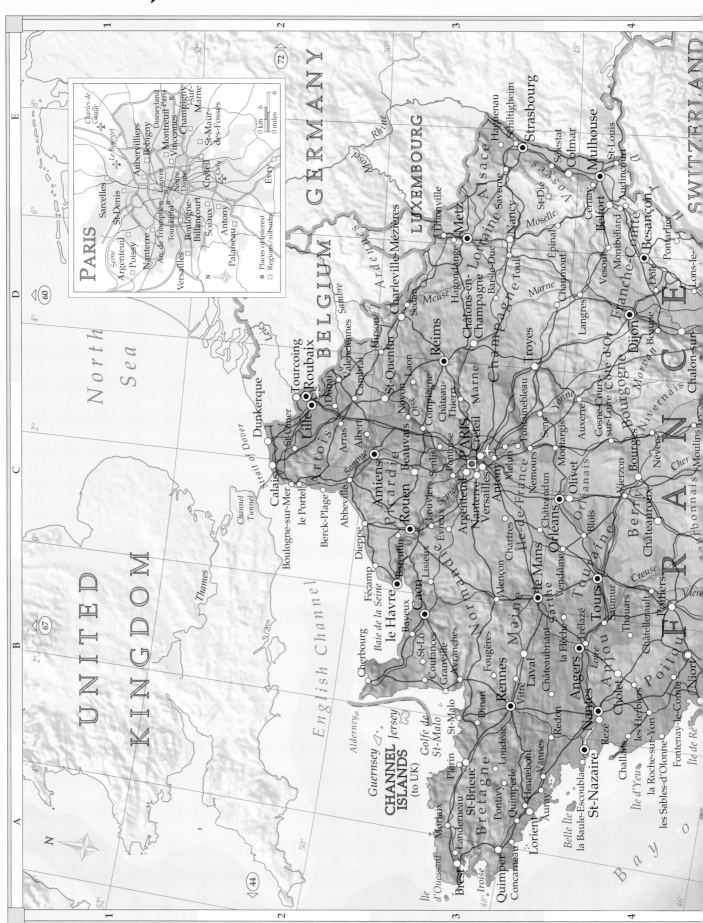

PARIS

POPULATION

- ◉ Over 500,000
- ◉ 100,000 – 500,000
- ○ 50,000 – 100,000
- ○ Less than 50,000
- ● National capital

■ Places of interest
Regions / suburbs

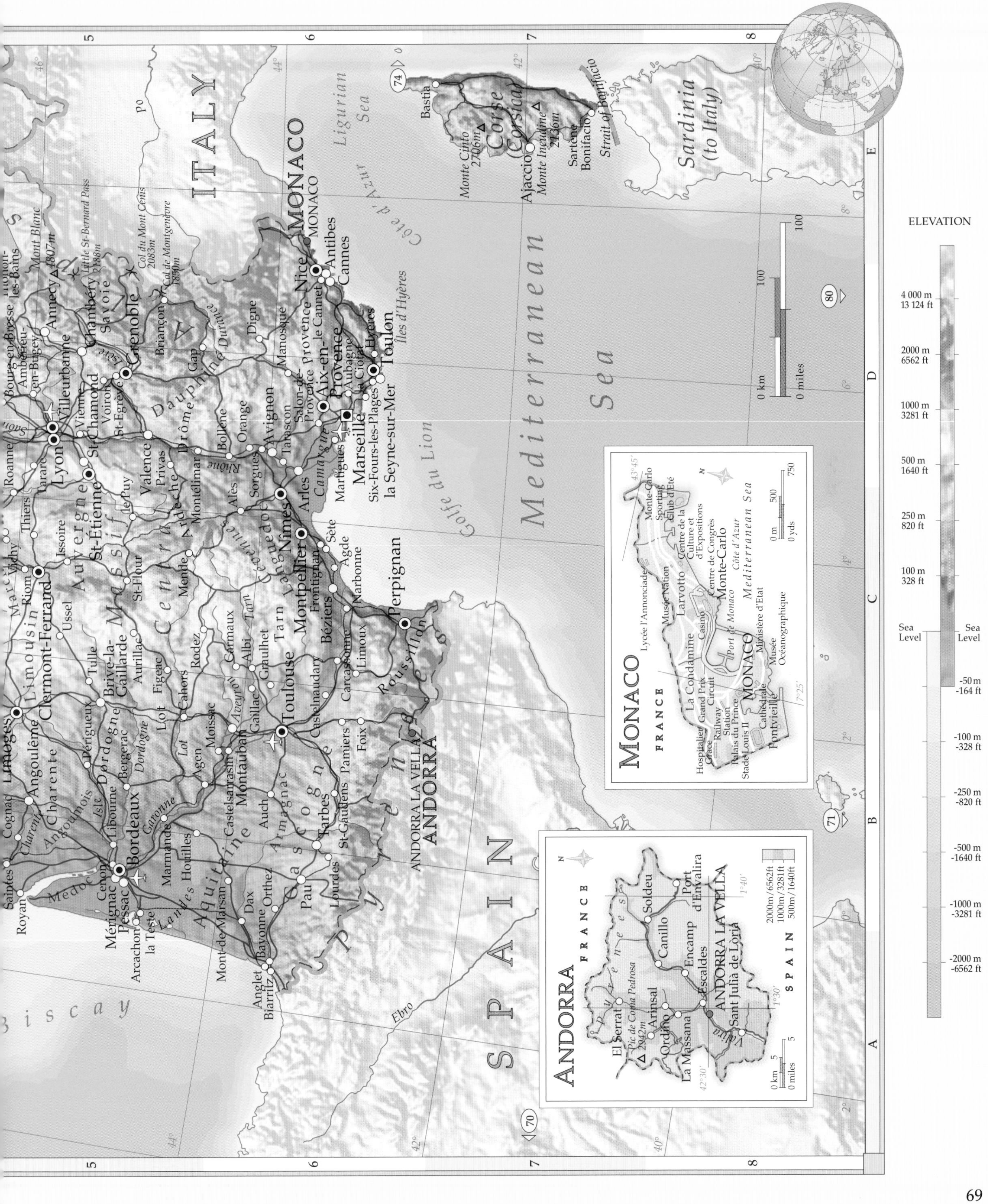

ITALY

Mont Blanc
4807m

Little St-Bernard Pass
Col du Mont Cenis
Col de Montgenèvre 2083m
2188m 1850m

Thonon-les-Bains
Annecy
Bourg-en-Bresse
Amberieu-en-Bugey
Savoie
Chambery
Grenoble
Briançon
Gap
Vienne
St-Chamond
Voiron
St-Egrève
Roanne
Tarare
Lyon
Villeurbanne
Digne
Drôme
Dauphiné
Durance

Thiers
Vichy
Roanne
Mâcon
Privas
Valence
le Puy
Montélimar
Ardèche
Orange
Bollène
Sorgues
Avignon
Tarascon
Salon-de-Provence
Aix-en-Provence
le Cannet
Nice
Antibes
Cannes

MONACO
MONACO

Issoire
St-Flour
Clermont-Ferrand
Rion
Ussel
Aurillac
Mende
Alès
Nîmes
Arles
Martigues
la Ciotat
Toulon
Six-Fours-les-Plages
la Seyne-sur-Mer
Aubagne
Marseille
Sète
Agde
Frontignan
Montpellier
Béziers
Narbonne

Tulle
Brive-la-Gaillarde
Figeac
Rodez
Albi
Carmaux
Graulhet
Gaillac
Castres
Mazamet
Limoux
Carcassonne
Castelnaudary
Perpignan

Limoges
Angoulême
Périgueux
Bergerac
Cahors
Montauban
Toulouse
Pamiers
Foix
St-Girons
St-Gaudens

Saintes
Cognac
Angoulême
Libourne
Bordeaux
Cenon
Pessac
Mérignac
Arcachon
la Teste
Bayonne
Anglet
Biarritz
Agen
Marmande
Mont-de-Marsan
Dax
Orthez
Pau
Tarbes
Lourdes
Auch

ANDORRA LA VELLA
ANDORRA

SPAIN

Biscay

Ebro

Ligurian Sea

Côte d'Azur

Îles d'Hyères

Golfe du Lion

Mediterranean Sea

Corse (Corsica)
Bastia
Monte Cinto 2706m
Ajaccio
Monte Incudine 2136m
Sartène
Bonifacio
Strait of Bonifacio

Sardinia (to Italy)

ELEVATION

4 000 m
13 124 ft

2000 m
6562 ft

1000 m
3281 ft

500 m
1640 ft

250 m
820 ft

100 m
328 ft

Sea Level | Sea Level

-50 m
-164 ft

-100 m
-328 ft

-250 m
-820 ft

-500 m
-1640 ft

-1000 m
-3281 ft

-2000 m
-6562 ft

0 km 100
0 miles 100

MONACO
FRANCE

Lycée l'Annonciade
Musée-Nation
Monte-Carlo
Sporting Club d'Été
Larvotto
Centre de la Culture et d'Expositions
La Condamine
Casino
Centre de Congrès
Grand Prix Circuit
Monte-Carlo
Côte d'Azur
Hospitalier Princesse Grace
Railway Station
Palais du Prince
Stade Louis II
MONACO
Ministère d'État
Musée Océanographique
Cathédrale
Fontvieille

Mediterranean Sea

0 m 500
0 yds 750

ANDORRA
FRANCE

Pyrénées

El Serrat
Soldeu
Pic de Coma Pedrosa 2942m
Canillo
Encamp
Port d'Envalira
Arinsal
Ordino
La Massana
Escaldes
ANDORRA LA VELLA
Sant Julià de Lòria
Valira

SPAIN

2000m/6562ft
1000m/3281ft
500m/1640ft

0 km 5
0 miles 5

69

SPAIN & PORTUGAL

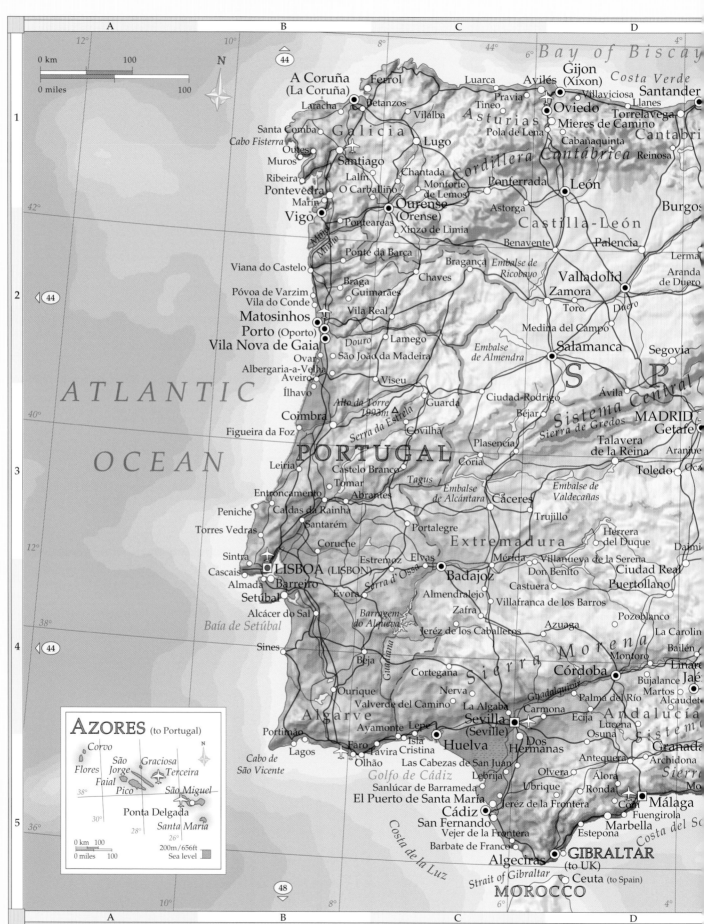

POPULATION

⬛ Over 500,000

◉ 100,000 - 500,000

○ 50,000 - 100,000

○ Less than 50,000

⬤ National capital

AZORES (to Portugal)

Corvo

Flores

São Jorge   Graciosa

Faial   Terceira

Pico

São Miguel

Ponta Delgada

Santa Maria

0 km 100

0 miles 100

200m/656ft
Sea level

FRANCE

redo
Bermeo
Zarautz
Eibar
Irún
Donostia-San Sebastián
Bilbao
Tolosa
País Vasco
Bergara
Vitoria-Gasteiz
Pamplona
(Iruña)
Miranda
de Ebro
Estella
Navarra
Jaca
Monte Perdido
3348m
ANDORRA
Figueres
Logroño
La Rioja
Arnedo
Calahorra
Huesca
La Seo d'Urgel
Ripoll
Girona
(Gerona)
Berga
Manlleu
Banyoles
Palafrugell
Sistema Ibérico
Tudela
Tarazona
Soria
Ejea de
los Caballeros
Barbastro
Monzón
Balaguer
Cataluña
Vic
Palamós
Blanes
El Burgo
de Osma
Zaragoza
Lleida
(Lérida)
Cervera
Tárrega
Sabadell
Terrassa
Arenys de Mar
Mataró
Costa Brava
Calatayud
Fraga
Aragón
Daroca
Vilafranca del Penedès
Valls
Barcelona
L'Hospitalet de Llobregat
Sitges
Medinaceli
Alcañiz
Reus
El Vendrell
Sierra de
Guadarrama
Teruel
Tortosa
Tarragona
Guadalajara
Alcalá de Henares
orrejón de Ardoz
Javalambre
2020m
Amposta
Sant Carles de la Ràpita
Vinaròs
Ciutadella de Menorca
Menorca
(Minorca)
Tagus
Cuenca
Onda
Castelló de la Plana
Pollença
Mahón
Tarancón
Burriana
Vall d'Uxó
Sa Pobla
Castilla-La Mancha
Burjassot
Sagunto
Costa del Azahar
Palma
Manacor
Mota del Cuervo
Torrent
Valencia
Golfo de
Valencia
Llucmajor
Felanitx
Campo de Criptana
Socuéllamos
Catarroja
Sueca
Tomelloso
Manzanares
La Solana
ldepeñas
La Roda
Júcar
Algemesí
Cullera
Gandía
Oliva
Dénia
Eivissa
(Ibiza)
Cabrera
Mallorca
(Majorca)
Albacete
Xàtiva
Almansa
Alcoy
Villanueva de los Infantes
Villena
Benidorm
Eivissa
Islas Baleares
(Balearic Islands)
Hellín
Jumilla
Elda
Villajoyosa
Formentera
Beas de Segura
Segura
Monovar
San Juan de Alicante
Moratalla
Cieza
Elche
(Elx)
Alicante (Alacant)
Villacarrillo
Mula
Callosa de Segura
beda
Cazorla
Murcia
Orihuela
Murcia
Béticos
Huéscar
Totana
La Unión
Baza
Lorca
Cartagena
Guadix
Aguilas
Mulhacén
3481m
Mojácar
Nevada
Berja
Almería
Adra

Golfe du Lion

Mediterranean Sea

ALGERIA

68

74

75

49

ELEVATION

4000 m 13 124 ft	
2000 m 6562 ft	
1000 m 3281 ft	
500 m 1640 ft	
250 m 820 ft	
100 m 328 ft	
Sea Level	Sea Level
-250 m -820 ft	
-500 m -1640 ft	
-1000 m -3281 ft	
-2000 m -6562 ft	
-3000 m -9843 ft	
-4000 m -13 124 ft	

GIBRALTAR (to UK)

N
5° 21'
SPAIN
Gibraltar
Airport
North Mole
Gibraltar
Harbour
The Rock
Catalan
Bay
Catalan Bay
36° 8'
Summit
426m
Sandy
Bay
Bay of Gibraltar
Rosía
Buena Vista
Rosía
Bay
Little
Bay
Europa Point
Strait of Gibraltar
200m/656ft
Sea level
0 km   1
0 mile   1

Germany & The Alpine States

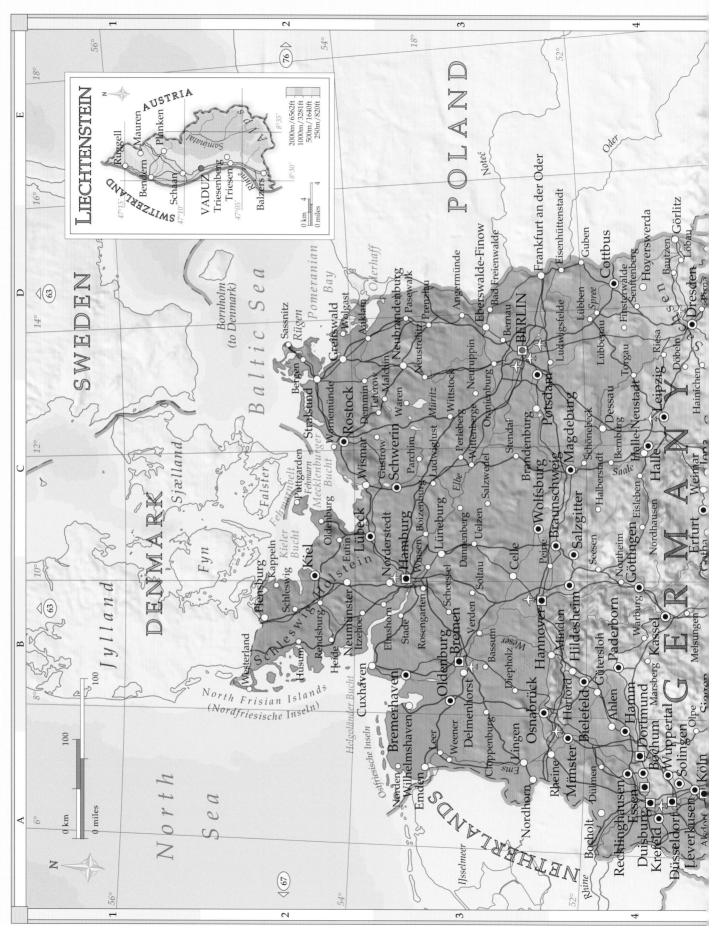

LIECHTENSTEIN

AUSTRIA

SWITZERLAND

Ruggell
Mauren
Planken
Bendern
Schaan
Triesenberg
VADUZ
Triesenberg
Triesen
Balzers

2000m/6562ft
1000m/3281ft
500m/1640ft
250m/820ft

0 km   4
0 miles   4

POPULATION

■ Over 500,000

◉ 100,000 - 500,000

○ 50,000 - 100,000

○ Less than 50,000

● National capital

0 km   100
0 miles   100

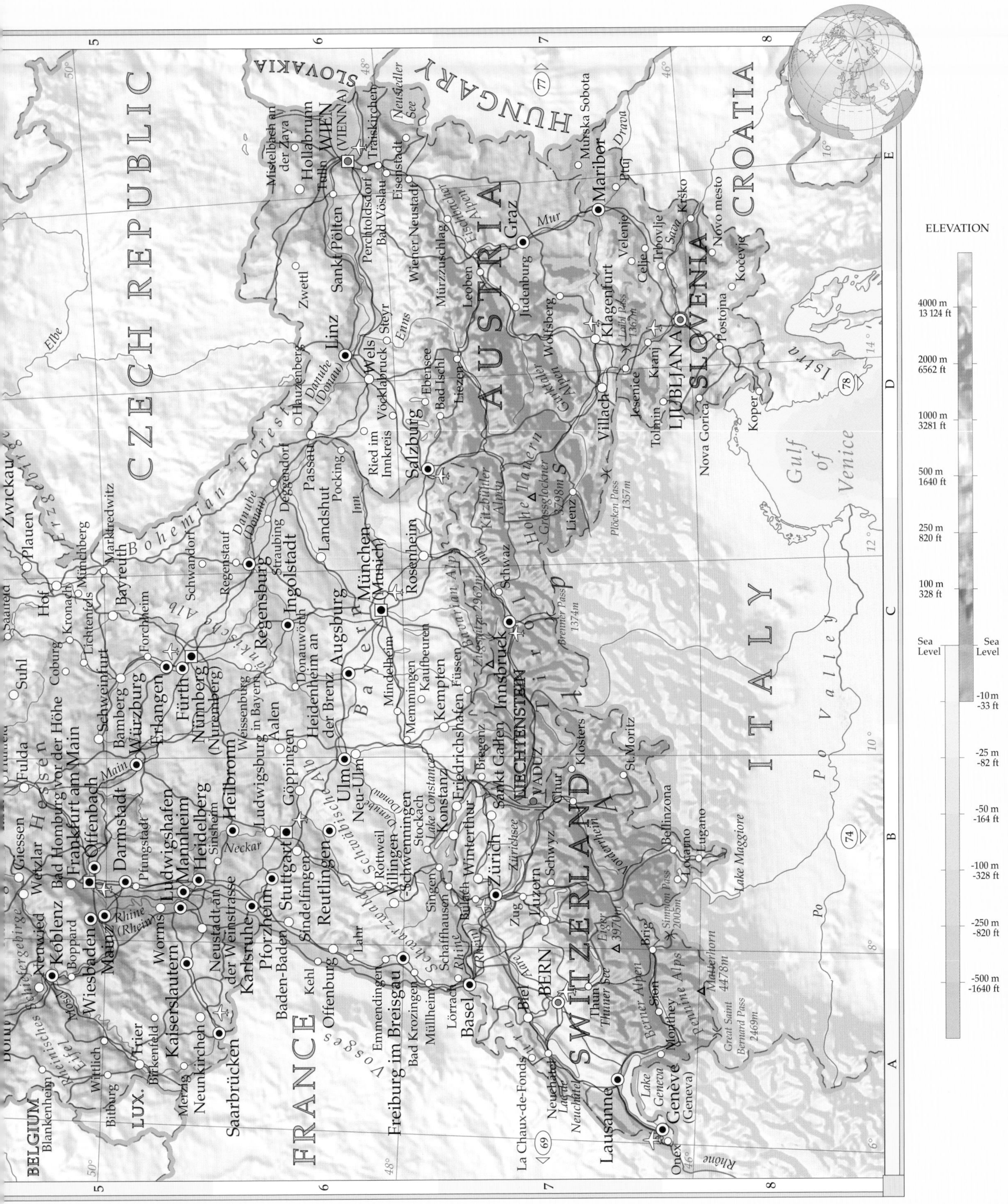

ELEVATION

4000 m	13 124 ft
2000 m	6562 ft
1000 m	3281 ft
500 m	1640 ft
250 m	820 ft
100 m	328 ft
Sea Level	Sea Level
-10 m	-33 ft
-25 m	-82 ft
-50 m	-164 ft
-100 m	-328 ft
-250 m	-820 ft
-500 m	-1640 ft

CZECH REPUBLIC

SLOVAKIA

HUNGARY

AUSTRIA

SLOVENIA

CROATIA

ITALY

SWITZERLAND

FRANCE

BELGIUM

LUX.

LIECHTENSTEIN

Mistelbach an der Zaya · Hollabrunn · WIEN (VIENNA) · Neusiedler See · Mürska Sobota
Poysdorf · Tulln · Traiskirchen · Neusiedl · Ptuj · Drava
Perchtoldsdorf · Eisenstadt · Maribor · Krško
Bad Vöslau · Wiener Neustadt · Velenje · Celje · Trbovlje · Sava
Sankt Pölten · Mürzzuschlag · Graz · Mur · Jesenice · Kranj · LJUBLJANA · Novo mesto
Zwettl · Leoben · Jugenburg · Klagenfurt · Laibl Pass 1367m · Kočevje · Istria
Linz · Wels · Enns · Steyr · Liezen · Wolfsberg · Villach · Tolmin · Postojna · Kranj
Danube (Donau) · Ebensee · Bad Ischl · Spittal · Nova Gorica · Koper
Hauzenberg · Vöcklabruck · Salzburg · Gulf of Venice
Ried im Innkreis · Pocking · Hohe Tauern · Grossglockner 3798m · Plöcken Pass 1357m · Lienz
Passau · Deggendorf · Kitzbühler Alpen
Schwandorf · Regenstauf · Landshut · München (Munich) · Rosenheim · Schwaz · Brenner Pass 1374m
Regensburg · Ingolstadt · Innsbruck · Tirol
Straubing · Donauwörth · Augsburg · Mindelheim · Kaufbeuren · Kempten · Zugspitze 2962m
Nürnberg (Nuremberg) · Fürth · Erlangen · Bamberg · Würzburg · Schweinfurt
Weissenburg in Bayern · Aalen · Friedrichshafen · Füssen
Heidenheim an der Brenz · Memmingen · Bregenz · Lake Constance · Konstanz
Bayreuth · Kronach · Coburg · Lichtenfels · Forchheim
Bohemian Forest · Elbe · Erzgebirge · Zwickau · Plauen · Hof · Marktredwitz · Münchberg
Suhl · Coburg · Schweinfurt
Heilbronn · Ludwigsburg · Sinsheim · Stuttgart · Sindelfingen · Göppingen · Ulm · Neu-Ulm
Villingen-Schwenningen · Rottweil · Reutlingen · Schwäbische Alb
Heidelberg · Mannheim · Ludwigshafen · Worms · Darmstadt · Pfungstadt
Offenbach · Frankfurt am Main · Wiesbaden · Mainz · Bad Homburg vor der Höhe
Giessen · Wetzlar · Fulda · Hessen
Koblenz · Neuwied · Boppard · Mosel · Rhine (Rhein) · Bingen · Neustadt an der Weinstrasse
Trier · Wittlich · Bitburg · Birkenfeld · Kaiserslautern · Neunkirchen · Saarbrücken · Karlsruhe · Baden-Baden · Pforzheim
Kehl · Offenburg · Lahr · Freiburg im Breisgau · Emmendingen · Bad Krozingen · Müllheim · Lörrach · Basel
Neuchâtel · Lac de Neuchâtel · La Chaux-de-Fonds · Biel · Aare · BERN · Thun · Thuner See
Lausanne · Lake Geneva · Genève (Geneva) · Onex · Rhône · Montreux · Berner Alpen · Pennine Alps · Great Saint Bernard Pass 2469m · Matterhorn 4478m
Schaffhausen · Bülach · Winterthur · Zürich · Zug · Luzern · Schwyz · Zürichsee · Rhein
Sankt Gallen · VADUZ · Chur · Klosters · St. Moritz · Nordrhein · Splügen · Simplon Pass 2005m · Eiger 3970m · Brig
Bellinzona · Locarno · Lugano · Lake Maggiore · Po Valley · Po

Saalfeld · Schmalkalden-gebirge · Rhön · Eifel · Rheinisches · Blankenheim · Hunsrück · Vosges

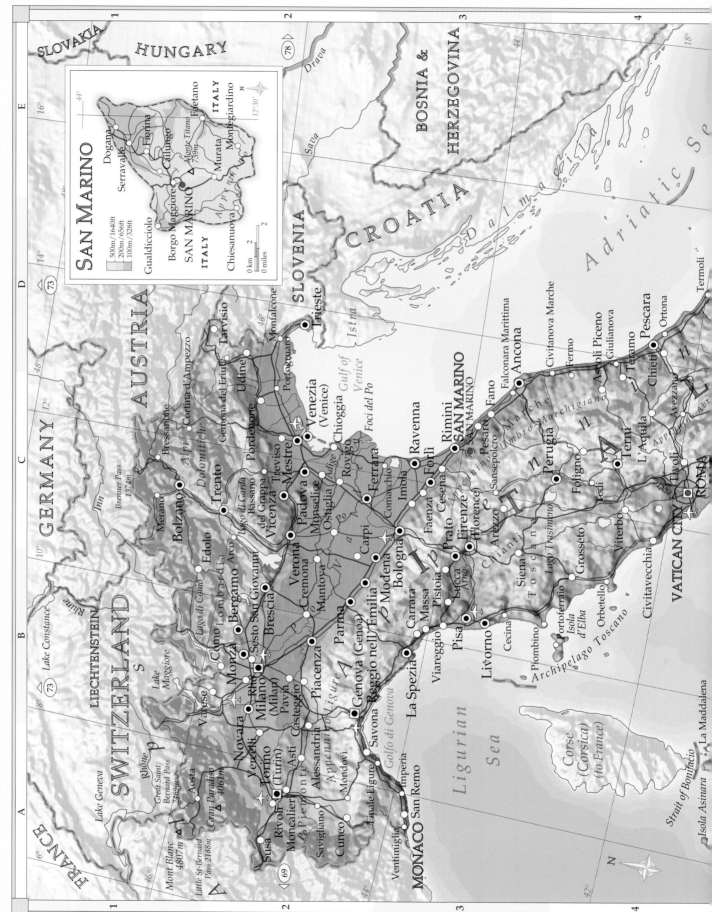

POPULATION

- ■ Over 500,000
- ◉ 100,000 – 500,000
- ○ 50,000 – 100,000
- ○ Less than 50,000
- ● National capital

SAN MARINO

Dogana
Serravalle
Fiorina
Cailungo
Faetano
Monte Titano 739m
Murata
Montegiardino
Gualdicciolo
Borgo Maggiore
SAN MARINO
ITALY
Chiesanuova

500m/1640ft
200m/656ft
100m/328ft

0 km   2
0 miles   2

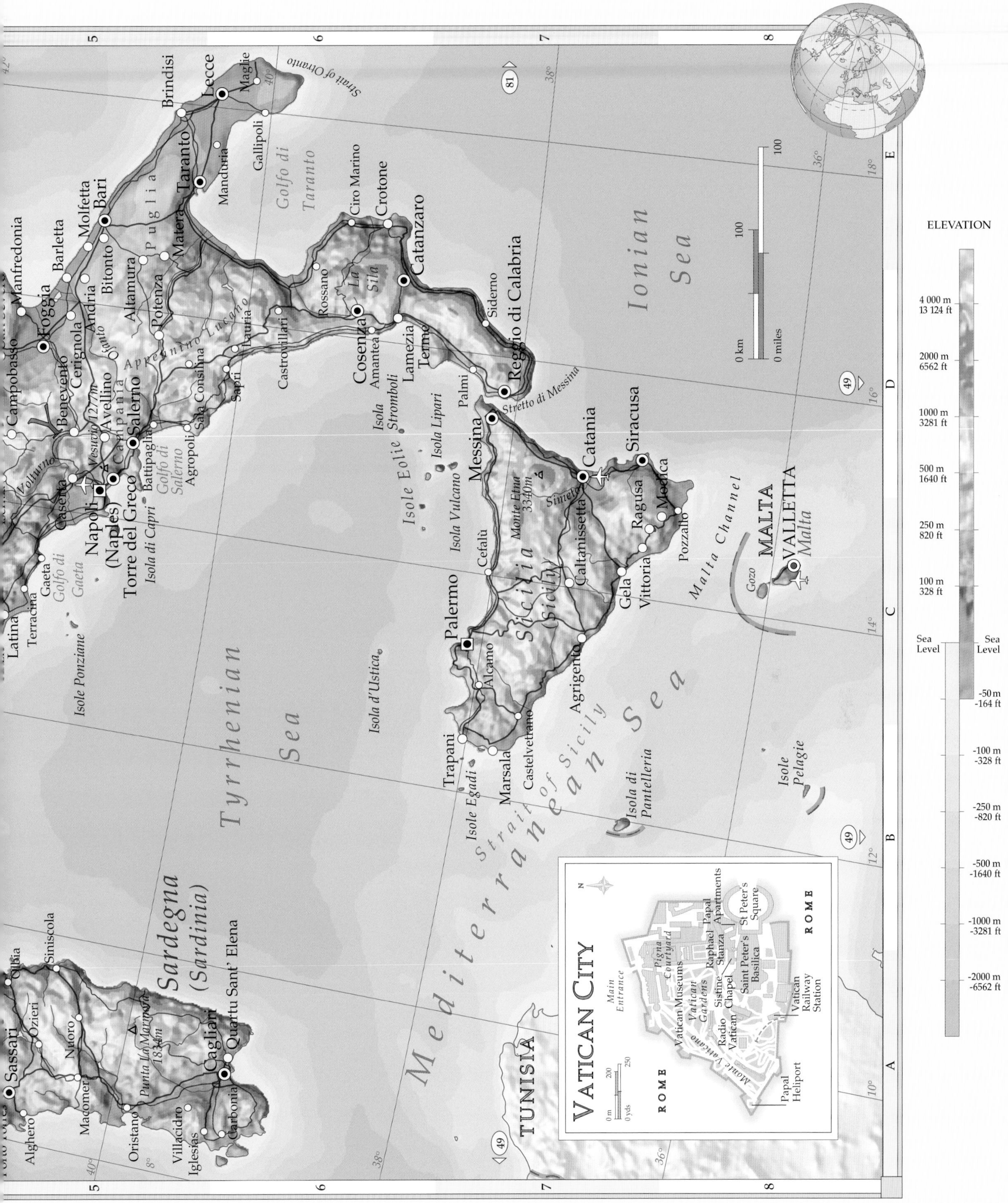

5   6   7   8

42°

40°

38°

36°

18°   16°   14°   12°   10°   8°

E   D   C   B   A

81

49

49

49

Strait of Otranto

Maglie
Lecce
Brindisi
Gallipoli
Taranto
Manduria
Bari
Molfetta
Matera
Bitonto
Altamura
Andria
Barletta
Manfredonia
Foggia
Cerignola
Benevento
Campobasso
Puglia
Golfo di Taranto
Ciro Marino
Crotone
Catanzaro
Rossano
La Sila
Cosenza
Amantea
Stromboli
Lamezia
Terme
Siderno
Reggio di Calabria
Palmi
Potenza
Castrovillari
Sala Consilina
Sapri
Agropoli
Battipaglia
Golfo di Salerno
Salerno
Avellino
Vesuvio 1277m
Caserta
Napoli (Naples)
Torre del Greco
Isola di Capri
Gaeta
Golfo di Gaeta
Terracina
Latina
Isole Ponziane
Appennino Lucano
Lucano
Campania
Ionian Sea
Stretto di Messina
Messina
Catania
Siracusa
Monte Etna 3340m
Simeto
Caltanissetta
Ragusa
Modica
Pozzallo
Gela
Vittoria
Isola Lipari
Isola Vulcano
Isole Eolie
Isola Stromboli
Isola d'Ustica
Cefalù
Palermo
Alcamo
Sicilia (Sicily)
Agrigento
Castelvetrano
Marsala
Trapani
Isole Egadi
Strait of Sicily
Malta Channel
Gozo
MALTA
VALLETTA
Malta
Isole Pelagie
Isola di Pantelleria
TUNISIA
Tyrrhenian Sea
Mediterranean Sea
Sardegna (Sardinia)
Sassari
Olbia
Siniscola
Ozieri
Nuoro
Macomer
Oristano
Punta La Marmora 1834m
Villacidro
Iglesias
Carbonia
Cagliari
Quartu Sant' Elena
Alghero

ELEVATION

4 000 m	13 124 ft
2000 m	6562 ft
1000 m	3281 ft
500 m	1640 ft
250 m	820 ft
100 m	328 ft
Sea Level	Sea Level
-50 m	-164 ft
-100 m	-328 ft
-250 m	-820 ft
-500 m	-1640 ft
-1000 m	-3281 ft
-2000 m	-6562 ft

100
100
0 km   0 miles

VATICAN CITY

N

ROME

Main Entrance
Pigna Courtyard
Vatican Gardens
Vatican Museums
Radio Vatican
Raphael Stanza
Sistine Chapel
Monte Vaticano
Papal Apartments
St Peter's Square
Saint Peter's Basilica
Vatican Railway Station
Papal Heliport
ROME
ROME
0 m   200
0 yds   250

5   6   7   8

CENTRAL EUROPE

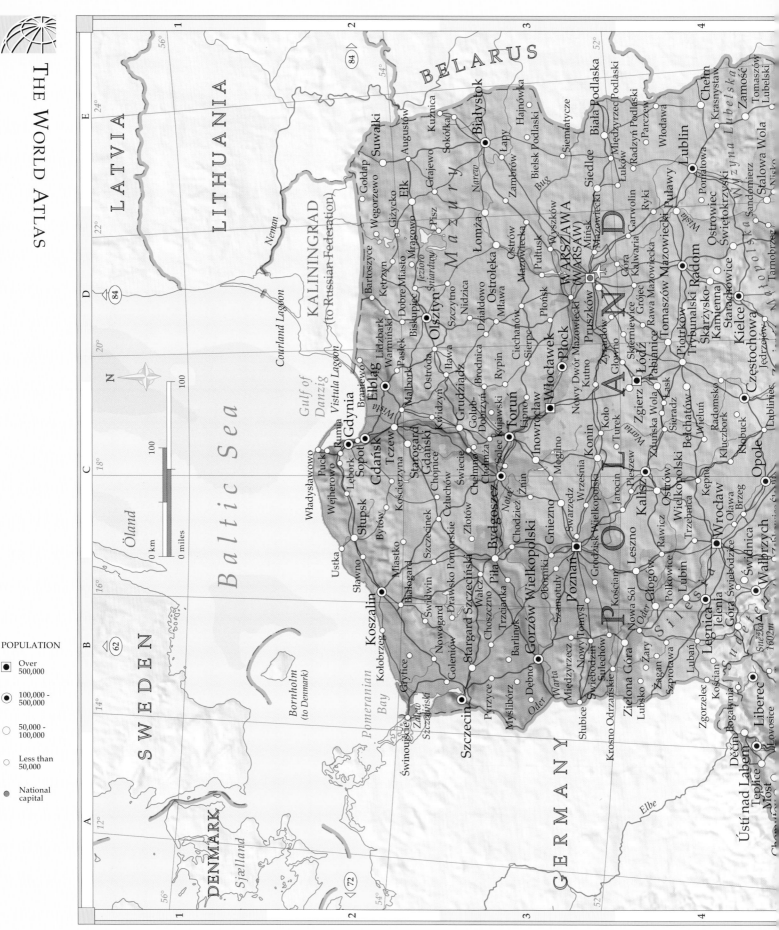

POPULATION

- ● Over 500,000
- ◉ 100,000 – 500,000
- ○ 50,000 – 100,000
- ○ Less than 50,000
- ● National capital

LATVIA

LITHUANIA

SWEDEN

DENMARK

Sjælland

GERMANY

BELARUS

KALININGRAD
(to Russian Federation)

Baltic Sea

Gulf of Danzig

Pomeranian Bay

Bornholm
(to Denmark)

Öland

Courland Lagoon

Vistula Lagoon

Neman

POLAND

Białystok
Suwałki
Augustów
Kuźnica
Sokółka
Goldap
Wegorzewo
Gizycko
Ełk
Grajewo
Hajnówka
Bielsk Podlaski
Siemiatycze
Międzyrzec Podlaski
Biała Podlaska
Radzyń Podlaski
Parczew
Chełm
Krasnystaw
Tomaszów Lubelski
Zamość
Lubelski
Lublin
Puławy
Łuków
Garwolin
Ryki
Ponfiatowa
Stalowa Wola
Nisko
Tarnobrzeg
Sandomierz
Świętokrzyskie
Ostrowiec
Starachowice
Kielce
Skarżysko-Kamienna
Radom
Piotrków Trybunalski
Tomaszów Mazowiecki
Rawa Mazowiecka
Skierniewice
Kalwaria
Góra Kalwaria
Grójec
Pruszków
WARSZAWA (WARSAW)
Mińsk Mazowiecki
Wyszków
Pułtusk
Siedlce
Zambrów
Łomża
Ostrów Mazowiecka
Ostrołęka
Maków Mazowiecki
Ciechanów
Płońsk
Mława
Działdowo
Nidzica
Szczytno
Olsztyn
Bartoszyce
Kętrzyn
Mrągowo
Pisz
Dobre Miasto
Biskupiec
Lidzbark Warmiński
Braniewo
Pasłek
Elbląg
Malbork
Ostróda
Iława
Brodnica
Rypin
Sierpc
Włocławek
Nowy Dwór Mazowiecki
Kutno
Gostynin
Płock
Grudziądz
Golub-Dobrzyń
Kwidzyn
Chełmno
Toruń
Inowrocław
Solec Kujawski
Chełmża
Świecie
Chojnice
Tuchola
Starogard Gdański
Tczew
Gdańsk
Sopot
Gdynia
Rumia
Puck
Wejherowo
Lębork
Władysławowo
Słupsk
Bytów
Kościerzyna
Kartuzy
Ustka
Sławno
Koszalin
Białogard
Świdwin
Mastko
Szczecinek
Złotów
Piła
Wałcz
Drawsko Pomorskie
Choszczno
Trzcianka
Chodzież
Wągrowiec
Gniezno
Września
Konin
Koło
Turek
Łódź
Zgierz
Pabianice
Łask
Sieradz
Zduńska Wola
Bełchatów
Wieluń
Radomsko
Kłobuck
Lubliniec
Częstochowa
Opole
Brzeg
Oława
Wrocław
Strzelin
Świdnica
Wałbrzych
Kamienna Góra
Nowa Ruda
Kłodzko
Jelenia Góra
Legnica
Lubin
Głogów
Polkowice
Nowa Sól
Zielona Góra
Żagań
Żary
Lubsko
Szprotawa
Zgorzelec
Lubań
Bolesławiec
Leszno
Kościan
Rawicz
Góra
Wolsztyn
Nowy Tomyśl
Grodzisk Wielkopolski
Szamotuły
Oborniki
Poznań
Swarzędz
Środa Wielkopolska
Jarocin
Pleszew
Kalisz
Ostrów Wielkopolski
Kępno
Krotoszyn
Grodzisk
Krosno Odrzańskie
Słubice
Sulechów
Świebodzin
Międzyrzecz
Gorzów Wielkopolski
Barlinek
Dębno
Myślibórz
Pyrzyce
Stargard Szczeciński
Goleniów
Nowogard
Gryfice
Kołobrzeg
Gryfino
Świnoujście
Szczecin
Police
Zalew Szczeciński

Silesia
Sudety
Śnieżka 1602m

Wisła
Narew
Bug
Noteć
Warta
Oder
Odra
Elbe

Mazury
Jezioro Śniardwy
Wyżyna Lubelska
Małopolska

Liberec
Decín bgałynia
Lovosice
Ústí nad Labem
Teplice
Most
Chomutov

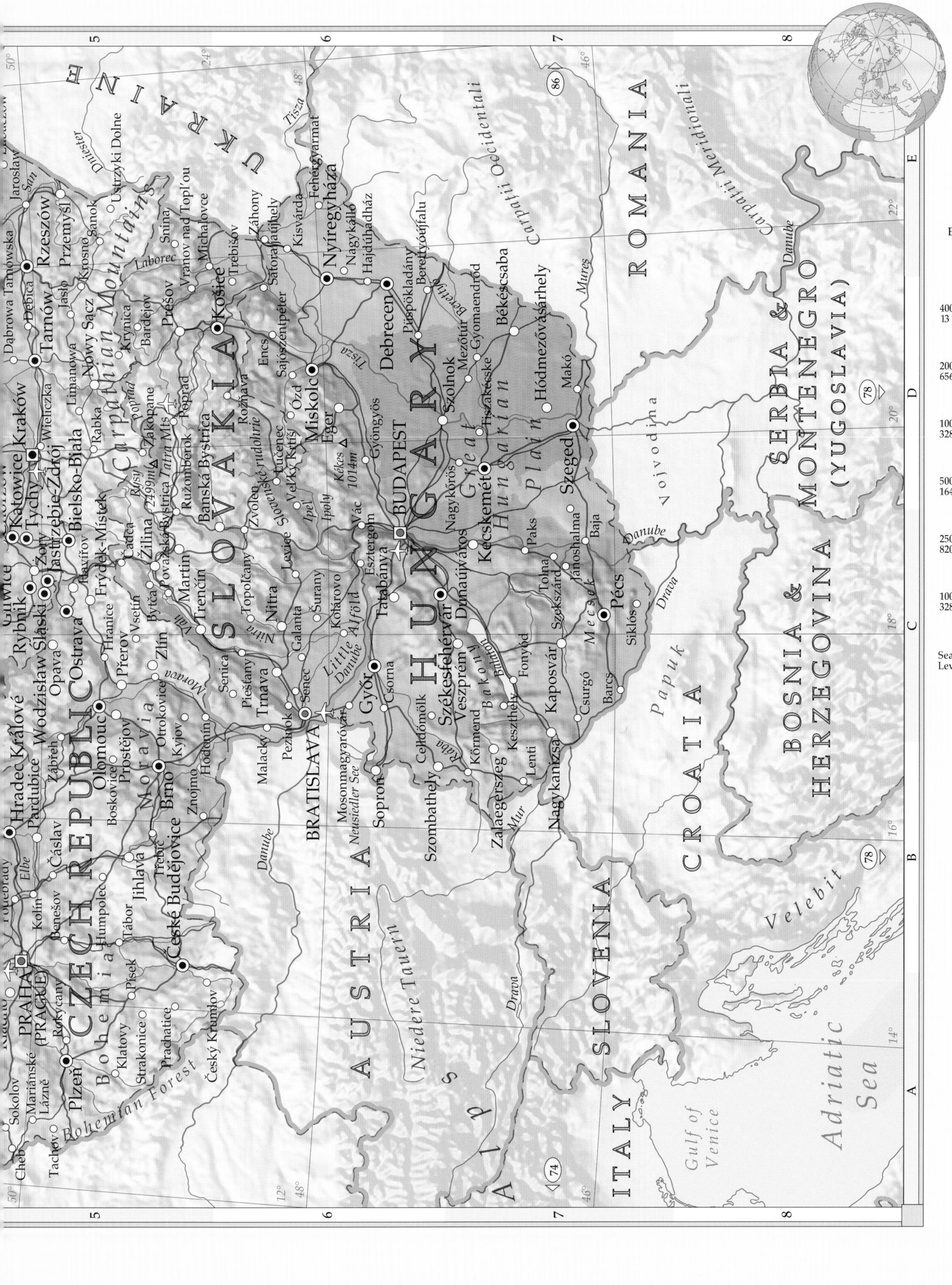

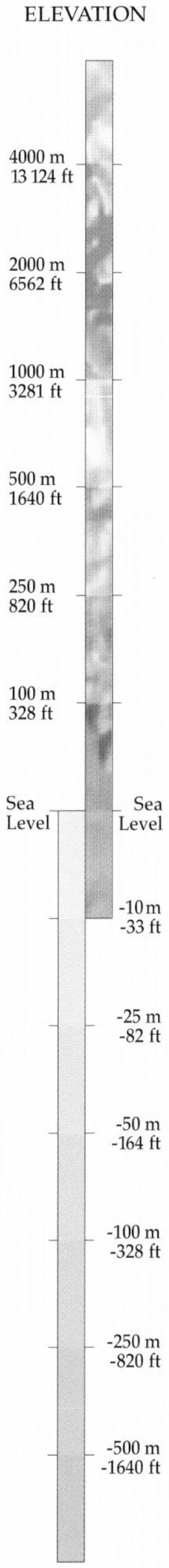

ELEVATION

4000 m
13 124 ft

2000 m
6562 ft

1000 m
3281 ft

500 m
1640 ft

250 m
820 ft

100 m
328 ft

Sea Level

Sea Level

-10 m
-33 ft

-25 m
-82 ft

-50 m
-164 ft

-100 m
-328 ft

-250 m
-820 ft

-500 m
-1640 ft

UKRAINE

ROMANIA

SERBIA & MONTENEGRO (YUGOSLAVIA)

BOSNIA & HERZEGOVINA

CROATIA

SLOVENIA

ITALY

AUSTRIA

HUNGARY

SLOVAKIA

CZECH REPUBLIC

Carpathian Mountains

Carpaţii Occidentali

Carpaţii Meridionali

Great Hungarian Plain

Little Alföld

Vojvodina

Bohemia

Moravia

Niedere Tauern

Alps

Bohemian Forest

Adriatic Sea

Gulf of Venice

Velebit

Bakony

Mecsek

Papuk

BUDAPEST

BRATISLAVA

PRAHA (PRAGUE)

Debrecen

Miskolc

Szeged

Nyíregyháza

Košice

Kraków

Katowice

Brno

Ostrava

Kecskemét

Pécs

Győr

Székesfehérvár

Szolnok

Békéscsaba

Hódmezővásárhely

Kaposvár

Nagykanizsa

Zalaegerszeg

Szombathely

Sopron

Veszprém

Tatabánya

Esztergom

Vác

Dunaújváros

Paks

Szekszárd

Baja

Tolna

Makó

Gyula

Gyomaendrőd

Mezőtúr

Tiszakécske

Nagykőrös

Cegléd

Gyöngyös

Eger

Ózd

Salgótarján

Sátoraljaújhely

Kisvárda

Záhony

Nagykálló

Hajdúnánás

Hajdúszoboszló

Berettyóújfalu

Püspökladány

Fehérgyarmat

Mátészalka

Rzeszów

Tarnów

Dębica

Przemyśl

Jarosław

Nowy Sącz

Bielsko-Biała

Rybnik

Tychy

Jastrzębie-Zdrój

Wodzisław Śląski

Żory

Gliwice

Opava

Olomouc

Přerov

Zlín

Frýdek-Místek

Třinec

Hranice

Vsetín

Prostějov

Kroměříž

Uherské Hradiště

Hodonín

Kyjov

Znojmo

Břeclav

Jihlava

Havlíčkův Brod

Žďár

Třebíč

Tábor

Pelhřimov

Humpolec

České Budějovice

Strakonice

Písek

Klatovy

Plzeň

Rokycany

Beroun

Kladno

Kolín

Kutná Hora

Čáslav

Benešov

Příbram

Mělník

Mladá Boleslav

Nymburk

Hradec Králové

Pardubice

Žamberk

Svitavy

Boskovice

Blansko

Žilina

Martin

Trenčín

Nitra

Trnava

Senec

Galanta

Komárno

Nové Zámky

Levice

Zvolen

Banská Bystrica

Ružomberok

Poprad

Prešov

Michalovce

Trebišov

Humenné

Snina

Bardejov

Krynica

Krosno

Sanok

Jasło

Limanowa

Rabka

Zakopane

Rožňava

Lučenec

Rimavská Sobota

Topoľčany

Piešťany

Senica

Malacky

Pezinok

Dunajská Streda

Sereď

Šaľa

Kolárovo

Šurany

Štúrovo

Šahy

Spišská Nová Ves

Kežmarok

Stará Ľubovňa

Mosonmagyaróvár

Neusiedler See

Kőszeg

Körmend

Lenti

Celldömölk

Keszthely

Fonyód

Siófok

Balaton

Barcs

Csurgó

Siklós

Mohács

Sárvár

Pápa

Ajka

Komló

Csorna

Dombóvár

Mátészalka

High Tatra Mts

Rysy

Gerlachovský štít 2655 m

Tatra

2499 m

Kékes 1014 m

Danube

Tisza

Tisza

Mureş

Drava

Drava

Mura

Sava

Danube

Ipoly

Ipeľ

Hron

Nitra

Váh

Morava

Elbe

Dunajec

San

Dniester

Vah

77

SOUTHEAST EUROPE

THE WORLD ATLAS

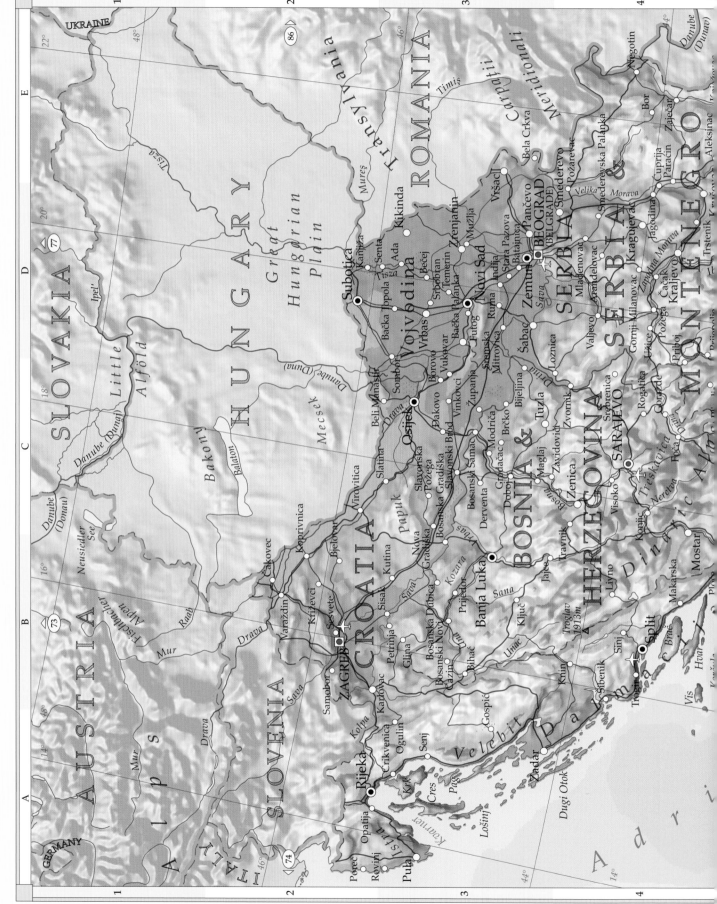

POPULATION

- Over 500,000
- 100,000 – 500,000
- 50,000 – 100,000
- Less than 50,000
- National capital

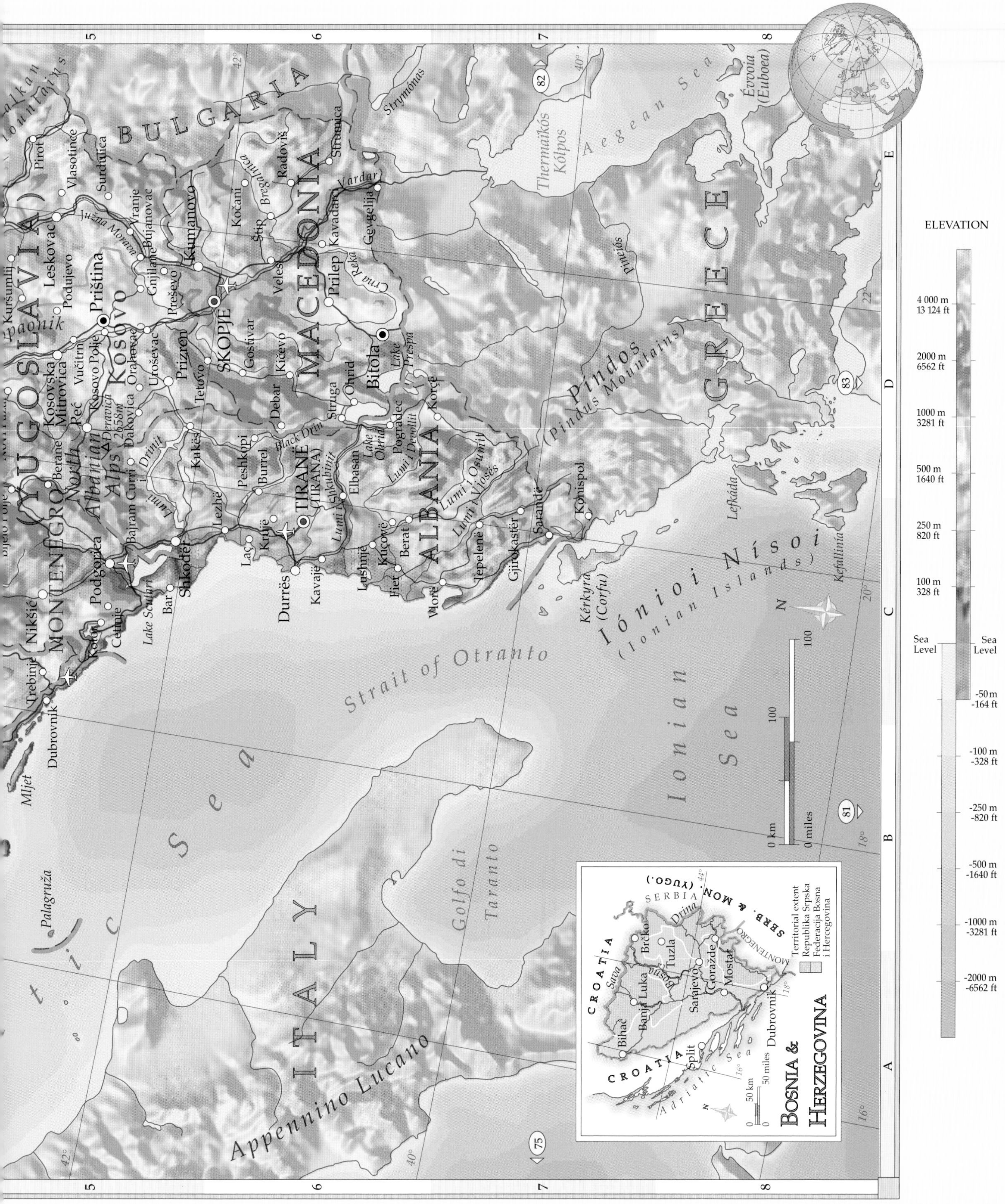

BULGARIA

(YUGOSLAVIA)

MACEDONIA

GREECE

ALBANIA

MONTENEGRO

Kosovo

Pindos (Pindus Mountains)

Aegean Sea

Thermaïkós Kólpos

Strymónas

Évvoia (Euboea)

Pineiós

Lefkáda

Kefallinía

Kérkyra (Corfu)

Iónioi Nísoi (Ionian Islands)

Ionian Sea

Strait of Otranto

Golfo di Taranto

Appennino Lucano

ITALY

Adriatic Sea

Mljet

Palagruža

Pirot
Vlasotince
Surdulica
Leskovac
Podujevo
Vranje
Bujanovac
Južna Morava
Kumanovo
Radoviš
Strumica
Kočani
Štip
Bregalnica
Kavadarci
Gevgelija
Vardar
Prilep
Crna Reka
Veles
Bitola
Lake Prespa
Gostivar
Kičevo
Ohrid
Lake Ohrid
Debar
Struga
Pogradec
Lumi i Drinit
Korçë
Lumi i Osumit
Lumi i Vjosës
Tepelenë
Gjirokastër
Sarandë
Konispol
Kursumlij
Kopaonik
Priština
Kosovska Mitrovica
Vučitrn
Kosovo Polje
Peć
Orahovac
Uroševac
Gnjilane
Preševo
Prizren
Tetovo
SKOPJE
Skopje
Berane
North Albanian Alps
Đakovica
Drenica
2658m
Kukës
Peshkopi
Burrel
Elbasan
Lumi i Shkumbin
Kavajë
Lushnjë
Fier
Berat
Kuçovë
Vlorë
Durrës
Lac
Krujë
TIRANË (TIRANA)
Lezhë
Bajram Curri
Drinit
Shkodër
Lake Scutari
Bar
Kotor
Cetinje
Podgorica
Nikšić
Trebinje
Dubrovnik
Niksic

ELEVATION

4 000 m 13 124 ft
2000 m 6562 ft
1000 m 3281 ft
500 m 1640 ft
250 m 820 ft
100 m 328 ft
Sea Level
-50 m -164 ft
-100 m -328 ft
-250 m -820 ft
-500 m -1640 ft
-1000 m -3281 ft
-2000 m -6562 ft

BOSNIA & HERZEGOVINA

CROATIA
SERBIA
SRB. & MON. (YUGO.)
MONTENEGRO
Sava
Brčko
Drina
Tuzla
Banja Luka
Bihać
Sarajevo
Goražde
Mostar
Split
Dubrovnik
Adriatic Sea

Territorial extent
Republika Srpska
Federacija Bosna i Hercegovina

THE MEDITERRANEAN

POPULATION

- ■ Over 500,000
- ◉ 100,000 – 500,000
- ○ 50,000 – 100,000
- ○ Less than 50,000
- ● National capital

MALTA

Mediterranean Sea

Gozo

Victoria · Nadur

Comino (Kemmuna)

Mġarr

Mellieħa

St Julian's

Sliema

Mosta

VALLETTA

Hamrun

Paola

Rabat

Birżebbuġa

Malta

250m/820ft
100m/328ft
Sea Level

0 km   10
0 miles   10

CYPRUS

Mediterranean Sea

Agialoúsa (Yenierenköy)

TURKISH REPUBLIC OF NORTHERN CYPRUS (recognized only by Turkey)

Lápithos (Lapta)

Kerýneia (Girno)

Mórfou (Güzelyurt)

Kythréa (Değirmenlik)

Kólpos Ammóchostos (Gazimağusa Körfezi)

Pólis

NICOSIA

Ammóchostos (Gazimağusa) (Famagusta)

Troódos

Dekéleia

Lárnaka

Páfos

Sovereign Base Area (to UK)

Sovereign Base Area (to UK)

Akrotírion

Lemesós (Limassol)

1000m/3281ft
500m/1640ft
250m/820ft
Sea Level

0 km   25
0 miles   25

80

ELEVATION

4000 m
13 124 ft

2000 m
6562 ft

1000 m
3281 ft

500 m
1640 ft

250 m
820 ft

100 m
328 ft

Sea
Level

Sea
Level

-250 m
-820 ft

-500 m
-1640 ft

-1000 m
-3281 ft

-2000 m
-6562 ft

-3000 m
-9843 ft

-4000 m
-13 124 ft

SLOVAKIA
WIEN (VIENNA)
USTRIA
LJUBLJANA
LVN.
ZAGREB
CROATIA
Rijeka
BOSNIA & HERZ.
SARAJEVO
cara
Dalmatia
Adriatic Sea
Bari
Napoli (Naples)
Vesuvio 1277m
Lecce
Strait of Otranto
Golfo di Taranto
Cosenza
Catanzaro
Ionian Sea
Monte Etna 3340m
Catania
Siracusa
VALLETTA
MALTA

Danube
BUDAPEST
HUNGARY
Great Hungarian Plain
Tisza
Satu Mare
Târgu Mures
Novi Sad
BEOGRAD (BELGRADE)
SERBIA & MONTENEGRO (YUGOSLAVIA)
Sava
Pristina
Carpathian Mountains
ROMANIA
Carpatii Meridonali
BUCURESTI (BUCHAREST)
Danube
BULGARIA
SOFIYA (SOFIA)
Balkan Mountains
Rhodope Mountains
SKOPJE
MACED.
TIRANË (TIRANA)
ALBANIA
Pindos (Pindus) Mts
Kérkyra (Corfu)
Kefallinía
Zákynthos
GREECE
Thessaloníki (Salonica)
Límnos
Lárisa
Aegean Sea
Chíos
ATHÍNA (ATHENS)
Kýthira
Mirtóo Pelagos
Kykládes (Cyclades)
Sámos
Dodekánisos (Dodecanese)
Kritikó Pélagos (Sea of Crete)
Irákleio
Kríti (Crete)

Bâlti
MOLD.
CHISINĂU
Dnister
Odesă
Galati
Constanta
Varna
Burgas
Edirne
İstanbul Bogazi (Bosporus)
İstanbul
Marmara Denizi
Bursa
Balikesir
Izmir
Antalya
Ródos (Rhodes)
Kárpathos
Antalya Körfezi

86
UKRAINE
Kakhovs'ka Vodoskhovyshche
Dnieper
Berdyans'k
Sea of Azov
Kryms'kyy Pivostrov
Kerch
RUSS. FED.
Sevastopol'
Novorossiysk
Black Sea
95
Küre Daglari
Zonguldak
Samsun
Ordu
Kizil Irmak
ANKARA
TURKEY
Tuz Gölü
Kayseri
Toros Daglari
Adana
Gaziantep
İskenderun Körfezi
Halab (Aleppo)
NICOSIA
CYPRUS
Lárnaka
Lemesós (Limassol)
SYRIA
LEBANON
BEYROUTH (BEIRUT)
DIMASHQ (DAMASCUS)
97
Hefa
ISRAEL
Tel Aviv-Yafo
Gaza
JERUSALEM
'AMMĀN
Dead Sea
Euphrates

Mediterranean Sea
Darnah
Banghāzī (Benghazi)
Misrātah
Khalīj Surt (Gulf of Sirte)
Surt
Ajdābiyā
Tubruq
Libyan Plateau
Alexandria
Nile Delta
Port Said
Suez Canal
CAIRO
El Giza
Suez
JORDAN
Elat
Al 'Aqabah
Sinai
Gulf of Suez
SAUDI ARABIA
Waddān
Great Sand Sea
Munkhafad al Qattāra (Qattara Depression)
LIBYA
Libyan Desert
EGYPT
Nile
Sahara el Sharqiya (Eastern Desert)
Red Sea

0 km   400
0 miles   400

50

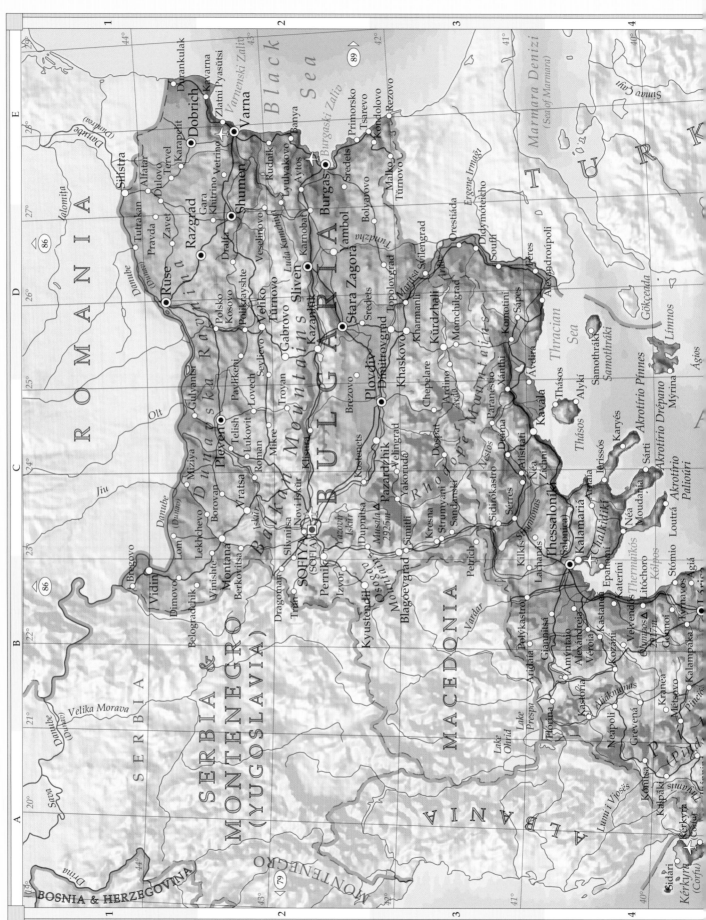

POPULATION

- ● Over 500,000
- ◉ 100,000 - 500,000
- ○ 50,000 - 100,000
- ○ Less than 50,000
- ● National capital

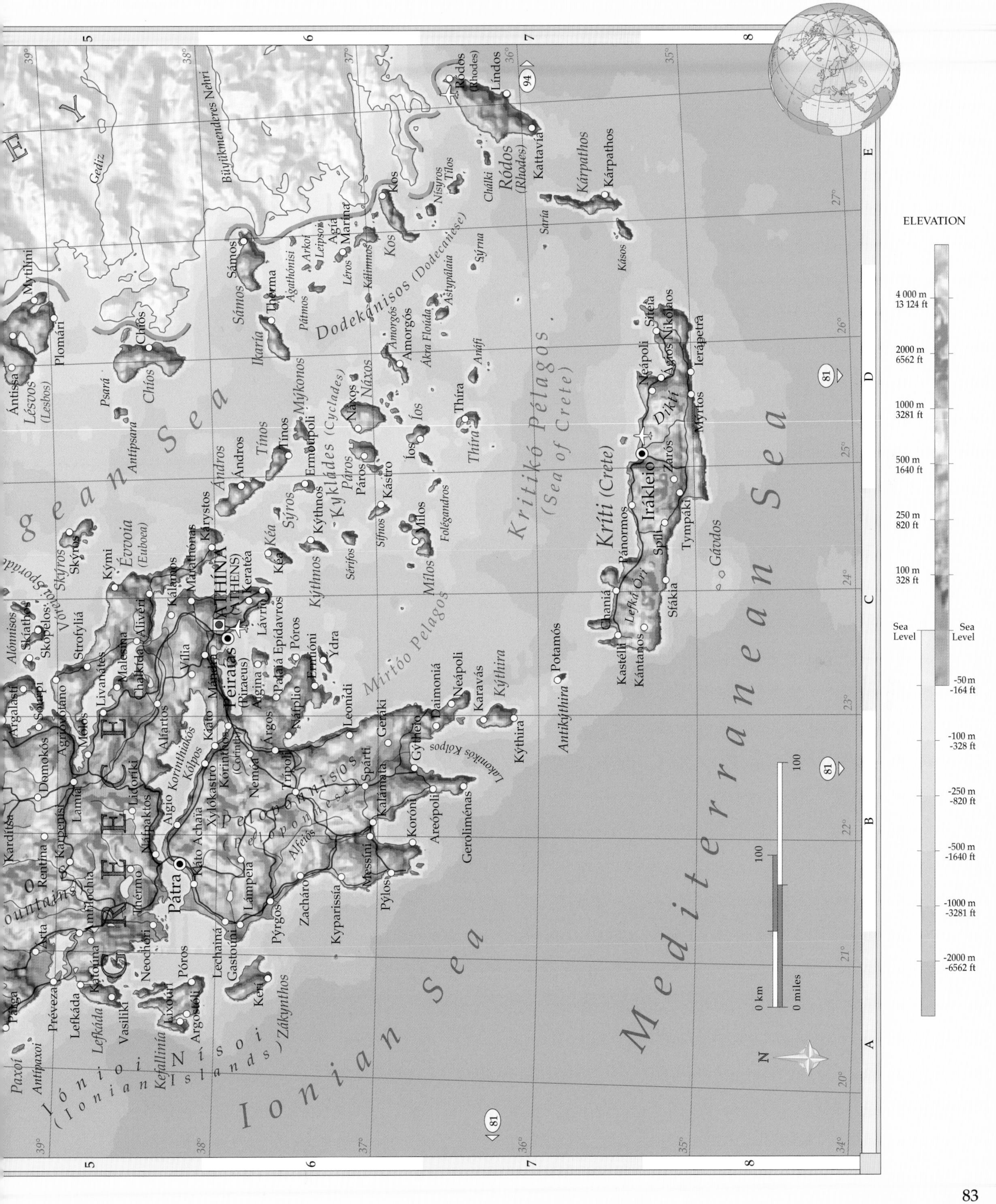

GREECE

TURKEY

Ionian Sea

Aegean Sea

Mediterranean Sea

Kritikó Pélagos (Sea of Crete)

Mirtóo Pélagos

Lakonikós Kólpos

Korinthiakós Kólpos

Dodekánisos (Dodecanese)

Kykládes (Cyclades)

Iónioi Nísoi (Ionian Islands)

Peloponnisos

Place names:

Antissa, Lésvos (Lesbos), Mytilíni, Plomári, Antípsara, Psará, Chíos, Chíos, Sámos, Sámos, Ikaría, Thérma, Agathónisi, Pátmos, Léros, Arkoí, Leipsoí, Agía Marína, Kálimnos, Kos, Kos, Nísyros, Tílos, Chálki, Ródos (Rhodes), Ródos (Rhodes), Líndos, Kattaviá, Kárpathos, Kárpathos, Kásos, Sýria, Astypálaia, Anáfi, Amorgós, Amorgós, Akra Floúda, Náxos, Náxos, Íos, Íos, Thíra, Thíra, Thíra, Síros, Sýros, Ermoúpoli, Mýkonos, Tínos, Tínos, Ándros, Ándros, Skýros, Skýros, Alónnisos, Skíathos, Skópelos, Strofyliá, Kými, Évvoia (Euboea), Chalkída, Alivéri, Kárystos, Kéa, Kéa, Kýthnos, Kýthnos, Sérifos, Sífnos, Síkinos, Folégandros, Mílos, Mílos, Kástro, Páros, Páros, Kératéa, Lávrio, Pórto Ráfti, Marathónas, Kálamos, Vília, Megára, Máni, Pórto, AthÍNA (ATHENS), Peiraiás (Piraeus), Salamína, Aígina, Palaiá Epídavros, Póros, Méthana, Ermióni, Ýdra, Náfplio, Epídavros, Árgos, Korinthos (Corinth), Kórinthos, Korinthos, Xylókastro, Néméa, Trípoli, Spárti, Leonídi, Geráki, Gýtheio, Daimoniá, Neápoli, Karavás, Kýthira, Kýthira, Antikýthira, Potamós, Gerolimenás, Areópoli, Koróni, Messíni, Kalamáta, Pýlos, Kyparissía, Zacháro, Pyrgos, Lámpeia, Gastoúni, Lecháiná, Keri, Zákynthos, Argostóli, Lixoúri, Póros, Neochóri, Vasilikí, Lefkáda, Préveza, Karoúna, Amfilochía, Arta, Rentína, Karpenísi, Lamía, Domokós, Karditsa, Karpenísi, Thérmo, Mesolóngi, Agrínio, Naúpaktos, Agio, Aígio, Páine, Káto Acháïa, Pátra, Litochóri, Neochóri, Amfíkleia, Livanátes, Aliártos, Stefáni, Vóïo, Antipaxoí, Paxoí, Mountains, Olympus Mountains

Crete section:

Kastélli, Kántanos, Chaniá, Lefká Ori, Sfakiá, Panormós, Irákleio, Zarós, Spíli, Tympáki, Myrtos, Díkti, Iterápetra, Agios Nikólaos, Neápoli, Sitía, Myrtos, Gávdos

Krfti (Crete)

Rivers / features: Gediz, Büyükmenderes Nehri, Alfeiós

ELEVATION

4 000 m	13 124 ft
2000 m	6562 ft
1000 m	3281 ft
500 m	1640 ft
250 m	820 ft
100 m	328 ft
Sea Level	Sea Level
-50 m	-164 ft
-100 m	-328 ft
-250 m	-820 ft
-500 m	-1640 ft
-1000 m	-3281 ft
-2000 m	-6562 ft

0 km   100

0 miles   100

N

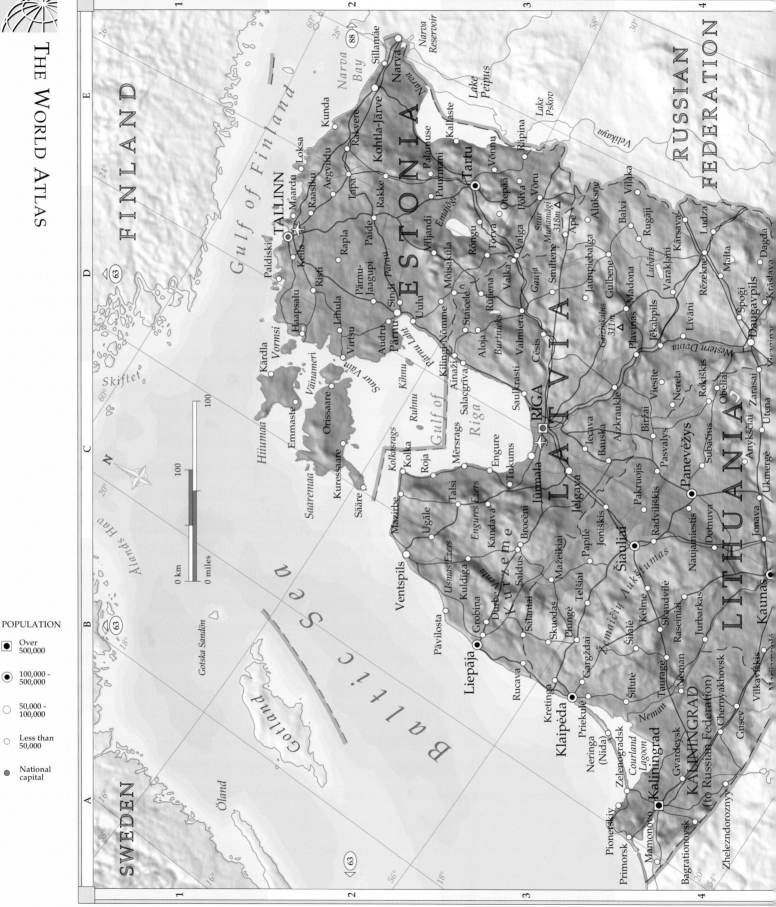

POPULATION

- Over 500,000
- 100,000 – 500,000
- 50,000 – 100,000
- Less than 50,000
- National capital

SWEDEN

FINLAND

Gulf of Finland

Skiftet

Ålands Hav

Gotska Sandön

Gotland

Öland

Baltic Sea

TALLINN

Paldiski
Keila
Maardu
Loksa
Raasiku
Aegviidu
Tapa
Rakke
Rakvere
Kohtla-Järve
Sillamäe
Narva

Narva Bay
Narva Reservoir

Lake Peipus
Lake Pskov

Velikaya

Kunda

ESTONIA

Haapsalu
Risti
Rapla
Paide
Lihula
Virtsu
Audru
Sindi
Pärnu
Pärnu-Jaagupi

Kärdla
Hiiumaa
Vormsi
Emmaste
Orissaare
Kuressaare
Saaremaa
Sääre

Väinameri
Suur Väin

Kihnu
Ruhnu

Viljandi
Mõisaküla
Õru
Rõngu
Tõrva
Valga
Valka

Emajõgi
Tartu
Elva
Puurmani
Põltsamaa
Põlva
Võru
Võnnu
Räpina
Kallaste

Suur Munamägi
318m

Ape
Altiüksne
Balvi
Viļaka
Rugāji
Kārsava
Ludza
Malta
Rēzekne
Dagda
Krāslava
Daugavpils
Spoģi

RUSSIAN FEDERATION

Kilingi-Nõmme
Ainaži
Staicele
Aloja
Rūjiena
Burtnieks
Valmiera
Cēsis
Saulkrasti

LATVIA

Salacgrīva
Engure
Mērsrags
Kolkasrags
Kolka
Roja

Gulf of Riga

RIGA
Jūrmala
Tukums

Ventspils
Pāvilosta

Kurzeme

Mazirbe
Ugāle
Talsi
Usmas Ezers
Kuldīga
Durbe
Saldus
Broceni
Engures Ezers
Kandava
Venta

Jelgava
Iecava
Bauska
Aizkraukle
Gaizinkalns 311m
Plaviņas
Jēkabpils
Līvāni
Varakļāni
Madona
Lubāns
Gulbene
Jaunpiebalga
Gauja

Western Dvina

Nereta
Viesīte
Birži
Pasvalys
Rokiškis
Obeliai
Zarasai
Utena
Ukmergė

LITHUANIA

Liepāja
Grobiņa
Rucava

Salantai
Skuodas
Plungė
Telšiai
Mažeikiai
Papilė
Joniškis
Pakruojis
Radviliškis
Panevėžys
Naujamiestis
Dotnuva
Jonava
Kaunas

Žemaičiu Aukštumas

Kretinga
Gargždai
Klaipėda
Priekulė
Neringa (Nida)
Courland Lagoon
Zelenogradsk
Pionerskiy
Primorsk

KALININGRAD
(to Russian Federation)

Gvardeysk
Chernyakhovsk
Gusev
Neman

Šilutė
Šilalė
Kelmė
Raseiniai
Skaudvilė
Jurbarkas
Tauragė
Neman

Vilkaviškis

Bagrationovsk
Mamonovo
Zelenodorozny
Gvardeysk

N

0 km 100
0 miles 100

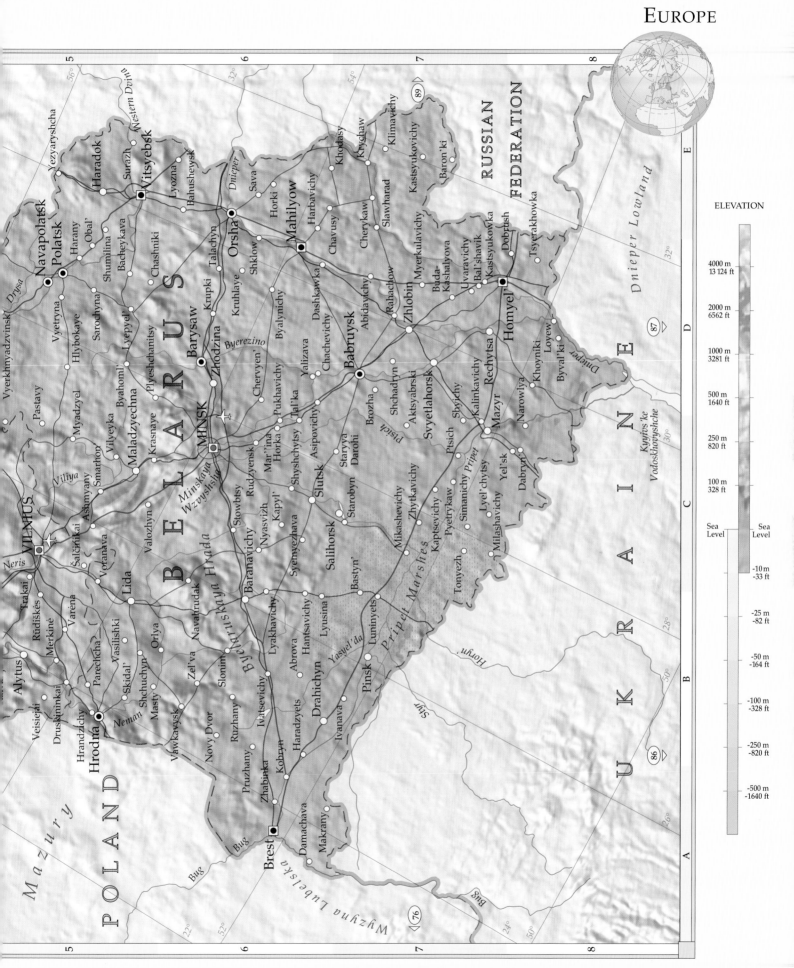

ELEVATION

| 4000 m 13 124 ft |
| 2000 m 6562 ft |
| 1000 m 3281 ft |
| 500 m 1640 ft |
| 250 m 820 ft |
| 100 m 328 ft |
| Sea Level | Sea Level |
| -10 m -33 ft |
| -25 m -82 ft |
| -50 m -164 ft |
| -100 m -328 ft |
| -250 m -820 ft |
| -500 m -1640 ft |

RUSSIAN FEDERATION

BELARUS

POLAND

UKRAINE

Mazury

Dnieper Lowland

Pripet Marshes

VILNIUS

Navapolatsk
Polatsk
Haradok
Vitsyebsk
Yezyaryshcha
Surazh
Lyozna
Balushewsk
Western Dvina

Minsk
Barysaw
Zhodzina
Orsha
Mahilyow
Horki
Shklow
Talachyn
Kruhlaye
Krupki

Babruysk
Zhlobin
Homyel
Rechytsa
Mazyr
Kalinkavichy

Hrodna
Brest
Pinsk
Baranavichy
Slonim
Lida

Ukraine, Moldova & Romania

POPULATION

- ⬛ Over 500,000
- ◉ 100,000 - 500,000
- ○ 50,000 - 100,000
- ○ Less than 50,000
- ● National capital

Dnieper
(Dnyapro)

E 32° F 34° G 36° H 38° 40°

1

Horodnya
Shchors
Shostka
Chernihiv
Krolevets'
Hlukhiv
Konotop
Bakhmach
Nizhyn
Romny
Sumy
Nosivka
Oster
Kyyivs'ke
Vodoskhovyshche
Brovary
Pryluky
Yahotyn
Pyryatyn
Okhtyrka
Lebedyn
KYYIV
KIEV
Boyarka
Vasyl'kiv
Fastiv
Kaniv's'ke
Vodoskhovyshche
Hrebinka
Lubny
Myrhorod
Lyubotyn
Merefa
Zolochiv
Derhachi
Kharkiv
Bila Tserkva
Bohuslav
Kaniv
Zolotonosha
Poltava
Donets
Izyum
Starobil's'k
Horodyshche
Cherkasy
Hlobyne
Kremenchuts'ke
Vodoskhovyshche
Kreminna
Rubizhne
Zvenyhorodka
Smila
Chyhyryn
Slov''yans'k
Syeverodonets'k
Shpola
Kramators'k
Lysychans'k
Tal'ne
Oleksandrivka
Svitlovods'k
Kremenchuk
Dniprodzerzhyns'ke
Vodoskhovyshche
Zolote
Luhans'k
Uman'
Mala Vyska
Znam''yanka
Oleksandriya
Novomoskovs'k
Kostyantynivka
Holovanivs'k
Dniprodzerzhyns'k
Pavlohrad
Horlivka
Stakhanov
Kirovohrad
Dnipropetrovs'k
Ulyanivka
Zhovti Vody
P''yatykhatky
Synel'nykove
Yenakiyeve
Krasnodon
Vil'shanka
Dolyns'ka
Pokrovs'ke
Makiyivka
Krasnyy Luch
Pervomays'k
Bobrynets'
Kryvyy Rih
Torez
Kryve Ozero
Arbyzynka
Inhulets'
Zaporizhzhya
Donets'k
Amvrosiyivka
Novyy Buh
Ordzhonikidze
Nikopol
Orikhiv
Volnovakha
Dokuchayevs'k
Voznesens'k
Marhanets
Dniprorudne
Polohy
Kam''yanka-Dniprovs'ka
Tokmak
Mariupol'
Novoazovs'k
Kakhovs'ka
Vodoskhovyshche
Molochans'k
Southrennyy Buh
Black
Sea
Mykolayiv
Dnieper
(Dnipro)
Kakhovka
Melitopol'
Gulf of Taganrog
Zhovtneve
Akinovka
Prymors'k
Berdyans'k
Yeya
Ochakiv
Kherson
Odesa
Hola Prystan'
Tsyurupyns'k
Novotroyits'ke
Illichivs'k
Chaplynka
Heniches'k
Kalanchak
Armyans'k
Sea of Azov
Krasnoperekops'k
RUSSIAN
FEDERATION
Chornomors'ke
Rozdol'ne
Dzhankoy
Kerch Strait
Krasnohvardiys'ke
Zatoka
Syvash
Kerch
Kuban'
Yevpatoriya
Nyzhn'ohirs'kyy
Lenine
Saky
Kryms'kyy
Pivostriv
Simferopol'
Feodosiya
Bakhchysaray
Sevastopol'
Alushta
Krymski Hory
Yalta
Alupka

RUSSIAN
FEDERATION

Srednerusskaya
Vozvyshennost'

Don

Psel

Oskil

Kup''yans'k

Black Sea

ELEVATION

4 000 m	13 124 ft
2000 m	6562 ft
1000 m	3281 ft
500 m	1640 ft
250 m	820 ft
100 m	328 ft
Sea Level	Sea Level
-50 m	-164 ft
-100 m	-328 ft
-250 m	-820 ft
-500 m	-1640 ft
-1000 m	-3281 ft
-2000 m	-6562 ft

0 km 100
0 miles 100

88
94

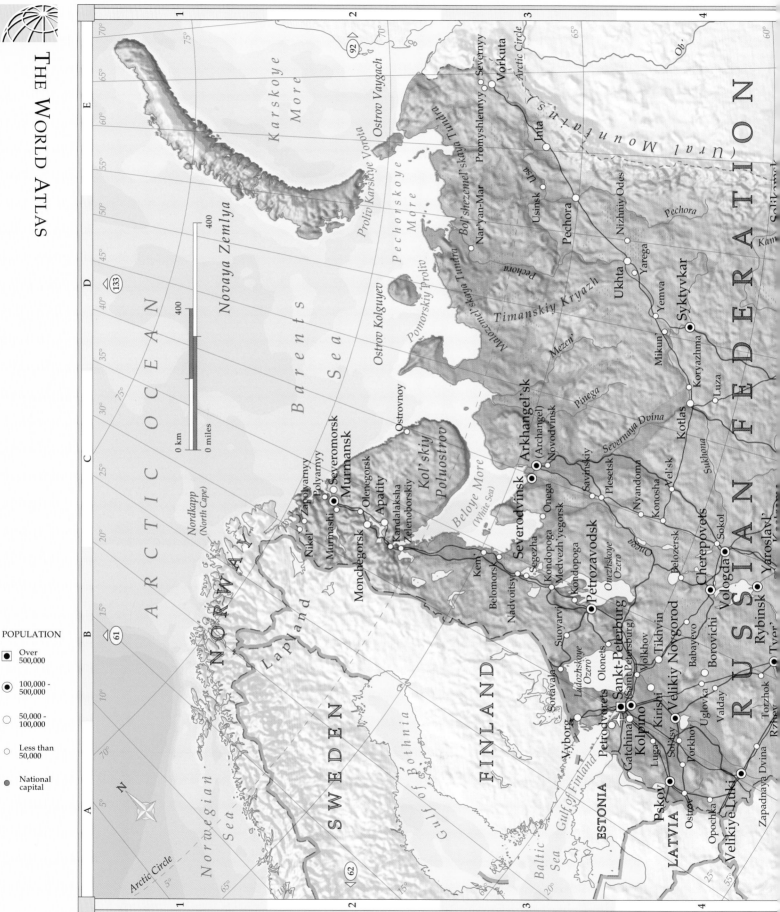

POPULATION

- Over 500,000
- 100,000 – 500,000
- 50,000 – 100,000
- Less than 50,000
- National capital

ARCTIC OCEAN

Karskoye More

Novaya Zemlya

Barents Sea

Pechorskoye More

Beloye More (White Sea)

NORWAY

SWEDEN

FINLAND

ESTONIA

LATVIA

RUSSIAN FEDERATION

Vorkuta
Severnyy
Promyshlennyy
Inta
Usinsk
Usa
Pechora
Naryan-Mar
Nizhniy Odes
Pechora
Kam
Yarega
Ukhta
Yemva
Mikun'
Syktyvkar
Koryazhma
Luza
Kotlas
Vel'sk
Sukhona
Nyandoma
Konosha
Cherepovets
Vologda
Sokol
Yaroslavl'
Rybinsk
Tver'
Rzhev
Torzhok
Valday
Uglovka
Borovichi
Babayevo
Velikiy Novgorod
Tikhvin
Volkhov
Kirishi
Sankt-Peterburg (Saint Petersburg)
Kolpino
Gatchina
Petrodvorets
Vyborg
Luga
Sol'tsy
Porkhov
Pskov
Ostrov
Opochka
Velikiye Luki
Zapadnaya Dvina

Arkhangel'sk (Archangel)
Novodvinsk
Severodvinsk
Onega
Savinskiy
Plesetsk
Belozersk

Murmansk
Severomorsk
Polyarnyy
Zapolyarnyy
Nikel'
Murmashi
Olenegorsk
Apatity
Monchegorsk
Kandalaksha
Zelenoborskiy
Ostrovnoy

Kol'skiy Poluostrov

Petrozavodsk
Kondopoga
Medvezh'yegorsk
Segezha
Nadvoitsy
Belomorsk
Kem'
Suoyarvi
Sortavala
Olonets
Ladozhskoye Ozero
Onezhskoye Ozero

Ural Mountains

Timanskiy Kryazh

Malozemel'skaya Tundra
Bol'shezemel'skaya Tundra

Severnaya Dvina
Mezen'
Pinega

Lapland

Nordkapp (North Cape)

Ostrov Kolguyev
Ostrov Vaygach

Proliv Karskiye Vorota
Pomorskiy Proliv

Norwegian Sea
Gulf of Bothnia
Baltic Sea
Gulf of Finland

Arctic Circle

400 km
400 miles
0 km
0 miles

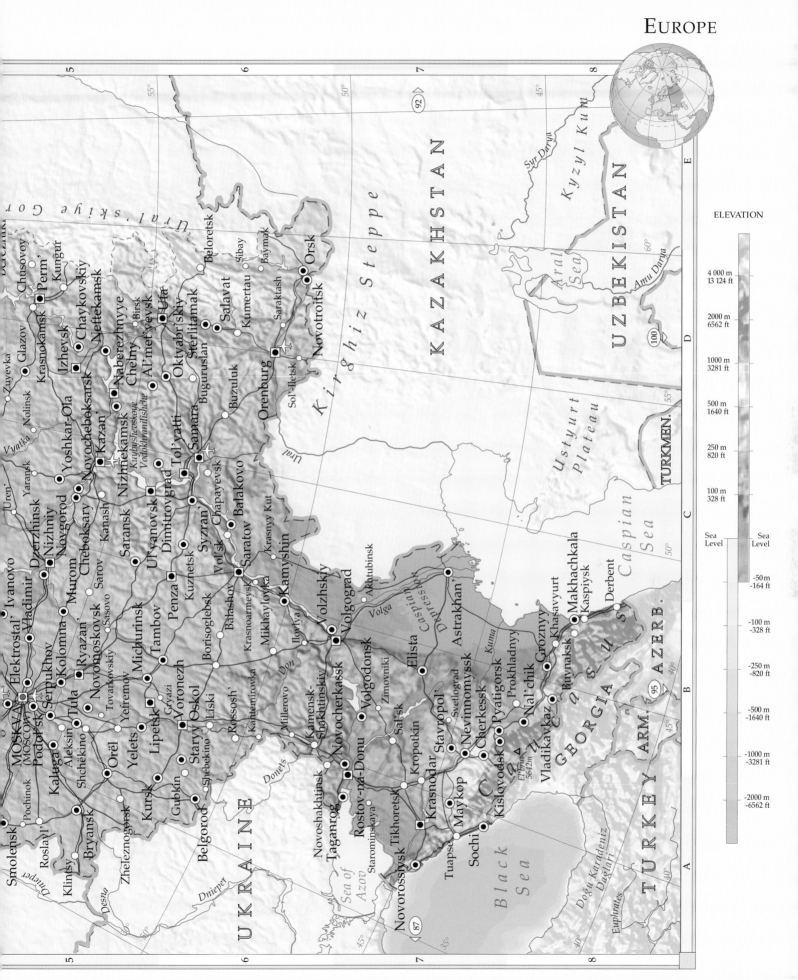

ELEVATION

4 000 m
13 124 ft

2000 m
6562 ft

1000 m
3281 ft

500 m
1640 ft

250 m
820 ft

100 m
328 ft

Sea Level	Sea Level

-50 m
-164 ft

-100 m
-328 ft

-250 m
-820 ft

-500 m
-1640 ft

-1000 m
-3281 ft

-2000 m
-6562 ft

KAZAKHSTAN

UZBEKISTAN

Kyzyl Kum

Syr Darya

Aral Sea

Amu Darya

Kirghiz Steppe

Ustyurt Plateau

TURKMEN.

Caspian Sea

Orsk
Novotroitsk
Orenburg
Sol'-Iletsk
Saraktash
Kumertau
Silbay
Baymak
Salavat
Sterlitamak
Oktyabr'skiy
Beloretsk
Ufa
Birsk
Al'met'yevsk
Chelny
Naberezhnyye Chelny
Buzuluk
Buguruslan
Samara
Tol'yatti
Chapayevsk
Balakovo
Balashov
Krasnyy Kut
Saratov
Vol'sk
Syzran'
Dimitrovgrad
Ul'yanovsk
Kuybyshevskoye Vodokhranilishche
Kazan'
Novocheboksarsk
Cheboksary
Yoshkar-Ola
Nizhnekamsk

Perm'
Chaykovskiy
Chusovoy
Kungur
Krasnokamsk
Izhevsk
Glazov
Zuyevka
Nolinsk
Yaransk
Kanash
Sarov
Saransk
Kuznetsk
Penza
Borisoglebsk
Michurinsk
Kamyshin
Volzhskiy
Volgograd
Akhtubinsk
Ilovlya
Kotel'nikovo
Astrakhan'
Elista
Kuma
Makhachkala
Kaspiysk
Derbent
Buynaksk
Grozny
Khasavyurt
Nal'chik
Prokhladnyy
Pyatigorsk
Cherkessk
Nevinnomyssk
Stavropol'
Kropotkin
Sal'sk
Zimovniki
Svetlograd
Maykop
Sochi
Tuapse
Novorossiysk
Krasnodar
Tikhoretsk
Rostov-na-Donu
Taganrog
Novoshakhtinsk
Shakhty
Kamensk-Shakhtinskiy
Millerovo
Kantemirovka
Rossosh'
Liski
Staryy Oskol
Gubkin
Shebekino
Belgorod
Kursk
Zheleznogorsk
Bryansk
Klintsy
Roslavl'
Smolensk
Pochinok
Kaluga
Aleksin
Shchëkino
Tula
Orël
Yefremov
Yelets
Lipetsk
Gryazi
Voronezh
Tambov
Sasovo
Shatsk
Ryazan
Novomoskovsk
Tovarkovskiy
Kolomna
Serpukhov
Podol'sk
Elektrostal'
MOSKVA
MOSCOW
Ivanovo
Vladimir
Dzerzhinsk
Nizhniy Novgorod
Murom
Uren'
Vyatka
Vyazniki

UKRAINE

Dnieper
Desna
Dnieper
Donets
Don

Sea of Azov
Starominskaya

Black Sea

Doğu Karadeniz Dağları
TURKEY
Euphrates
ARM.
AZERB.
GEORGIA
Caucasus
El'brus 5642m
Vladikavkaz
Kislovodsk

Ural
Volga
Don
Caspian Depression

NORTH & WEST ASIA

A   B   C   D

20j   40j   60j   80j   100j

△133 *Franz Josef Land*   A R C T I C

Severnaya Zemly

Ostrov Komsomolets

1

Summer limit of pack ice   *Ostrov Oktyabr skoy Revolyutsii*
Ostrov Bol shevik

Winter limit of pack ice

Novaya Zemlya   *Kara Sea*   *Poluostrov Taymyr*   *Ozero Taymy*

Norwegian Sea   *North Cape*   *Barents Sea*   *East Novaya Zemlya Trench*   *North Siberia*   *Kheta*

Ostrov Kolguyev   *Kotuy*

70j   • Murmansk   *Kola Peninsula*   • Noril sk   *Central Siberian Plateau*   *Kureyka*

2

Arctic Circle   *White Sea*   R U S S I A N   *Lower Tunguska*   F E

△59   • Archangel   *West Siberian Plain*   *Stony Tunguska*   *Si*

Gulf of Bothnia   *Northern Dvina*   *Ural Mountains*   *Ob'*   *Irtysh*   *Ob*   *Angara*

Baltic Sea   *Lake Onega*   • Vologda   Perm'   • Yekaterinburg   *Irtush*   • Tomsk   *Chulym*

60j   • Saint Petersburg   *Lake Ladoga*   Nizhniy Novgorod   • Chelyabinsk   • Novosibirsk   • Krasnoyarsk

• Yaroslavl   *Volga*   Kazan'   Ufa   • Omsk   • Novokuznetsk

MOSCOW ◉   *Central Russian Upland*   Samara   *Ishim*   • ASTANA   *Sayanskiy Khrebet*

Kaliningrad   Ul yanovsk   • ● Saratov   Orenburg   • Karaganda   • Semipalatinsk   *Altai Mountains*   Irkut

3   KALININGRAD   • Voronezh   *Volga*   Ural sk   *Kirghiz Steppe*   • ● ASTANA   A   • S

50j   (to Russ. Fed.)   • Volgograd   *Ural*   *Kazakh Uplands*   *Ozero Zaysan*

E U R O P E   Rostov-na-Donu   *Don*   K A Z A K H S T A N   *Lake Balkhash*

Danube   • Astrakhan'   *Aral sk*   *Syr Darya*   *Ili*   • Almaty   *Tien Shan*

Stavropol'   *Aral Sea*   *Kyzyl Kum*   *Kyzylorda*   • Taraz   △ Pik Pobedy 7443m

Black Sea   *El brus 5642m* △   *Caucasus*   *Caspian Sea*   Aktau   *Ustyurt Plateau*   UZBEKISTAN   • BISHKEK   KYRGYZSTAN   G

Istanbul •   GEORGIA   T'BILISI   *Daşoguz*   *Amu Darya*   TASHKENT   DUSHANBE

40j   *Kre Daglari*   ARMENIA   AZERB.   BAKU   TURKMENISTAN   • TAJIKISTAN

ANKARA ◉   YEREVAN   *Garagum*   *Hindu Kush*   *Kunlun Mountains*

Anatolia   *Lake Van*   Tabriz   AŞGABAT   KABUL • Jalalabad

T U R K E Y   Gaziantep   TEHRAN ◉   Herat •   AFGHANISTAN   *Khyber Pass*   *Himalayas*

Adana   Aleppo   Mosul   Qom •   I R A N

4   CYPRUS   SYRIA   IRAQ   *Zagros Mountains*   *Tigris*   Isfahan •   *Iranian Plateau*   *Thar Desert*

Mediterranean Sea   △81   BEIRUT   DAMASCUS   BAGHDAD ◉   *Syrian Desert*   *Euphrates*   Basra •   Shiraz •   Zahedan •   *Ganges*

LEBANON   ISRAEL   AMMAN ◉   Bandar-e 'Abbas •   *Indus Fan*

JERUSALEM ◉   ▽ JORDAN   KUWAIT ◉   *The Gulf*   Dubai •   MUSCAT •   *Murray Ridge*   *Ganges Fan*

30j   *Dead Sea -392m*   KUWAIT   MANAMA ◉   DOHA ◉   U.A.E.   *Gulf of Oman*   Sur •

An Nafud   BAHRAIN ◉   U.A.E.   MUSCAT •

A F R I C A   RIYADH ◉   QATAR   ABU DHABI   *Indus*

Tropic of Cancer   *Nile*   *Red Sea*   SAUDI ARABIA   *Arabian Peninsula*

20j   JEDDA •   O M A N

At Ta'if •   *Ar Rub' al Khali*

N   SANA •   *Bay of Bengal*

YEMEN   *Socotra (to Yemen)*   *Arabian Sea*

Ta'izz •   • Aden   *Mekon*

0 km   800   *Gulf of Aden*

10j   0 miles   800   △47

20j   40j   60j   80j   100j

A   B   C   D

POPULATION

◉ Over 500,000

◉ 100,000 - 500,000

○ 50,000 - 100,000

○ Less than 50,000

● National capital

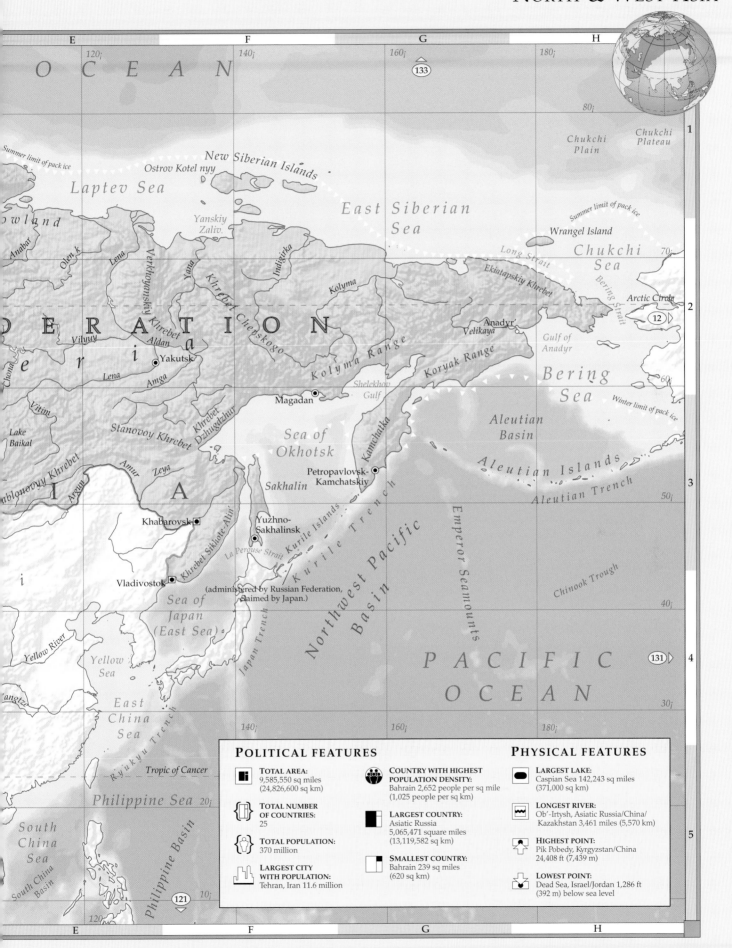

RUSSIA & KAZAKHSTAN

POPULATION

- ■ Over 500,000
- ◉ 100,000 – 500,000
- ○ 50,000 – 100,000
- ○ Less than 50,000
- ● National capital

NETH.
NORWAY
DENMARK
SWEDEN
GERMANY
FINLAND
SVALBARD (to Norway)
Zemlya Frantsa-Iosifa
ARCTI
Barents Sea
Nordkapp (North Cape)
Murmansk
Kandalaksha
KALININGRAD (to Russ. Fed.)
Gulf of Bothnia
Gulf of Finland
Baltic Sea
Kaliningrad
POLAND
LITH.
LAT.
EST.
Sankt-Peterburg
Ladozhskoye Ozero
Kol'skiy Poluostrov
Beloye More
Novaya Zemlya
Karskoye More
Ostrov Belyy
Ostrov Kolguyev
Dikson
BELARUS
Pskov
Velikiy Novgorod
Petrozavodsk
Onezhskoye Ozero
Severodvinsk
Arkhangel'sk
Nar'yan-Mar
Pechora
Poluostrov Yamal
Obskaya Guba
Talnak
Smolensk
Cherepovets
Vel'sk
Severnaya Dvina
Ukhta
Vorkuta
Salekhard
Ob'
Noril'sk
MOLDOVA
MOSKVA (MOSCOW)
Tver'
Vologda
Yaroslavl'
Kotlas
Syktyvkar
Ural'skiye Gory
Igarka
Bryansk
Tula
Kineshma
Vladimir
Nizhniy Novgorod
Kirov
Glazov
Solikamsk
Nadym
Nyagan'
Zapadno-Sibirskaya
UKRAINE
Belgorod
Ryazan'
Penza
Kazan'
Perm'
Serov
Khanty-Mansiysk
Voronezh
Tambov
Ul'yanovsk
Izhevsk
Lesnoy
Yekaterinburg
Surgut
Ravnina
Nizhnevartovsk
Mikhaylovka
Tol'yatti
Naberezhnyye Chelny
Chelyabinsk
Tobol'sk
RUSSIAN
Sea of Azov
Rostov-na-Donu
Saratov
Samara
Ufa
Tyumen'
Ishim
Chulym
Krasnodar
Balakovo
Volgograd
Sterlitamak
Ishim
Irtysh
Ob'
Black Sea
Sochi
Stavropol'
Ural'sk
Ural
Orenburg
Magnitogorsk
Orsk
Petropavlovsk
Omsk
Seversk
Tomsk
Strelka
Caucasus
El'brus 5692m
Nal'chik
Astrakhan'
Aktobe
Alga
Rudnyy
Kostanay
Kokshetau
Novosibirsk
Krasnoyarsk
GEORGIA
Vladikavkaz
Groznyy
Makhachkala
Atyrau
Emba
Atbasar
Shchuchinsk
Tuntugur
Kemerovo
ARM.
AZERBAIJAN
Fort-Shevchenko
Shalkar
KAZAKHSTAN
ASTANA
Pavlodar
Barnaul
Novokuznetsk
Abakan
Caspian Sea
Aktau
Zhanaozen
Ustyurt Plateau
Aral Sea
Aral'sk
Temirtau
Saran'
Karaganda
Semipalatinsk
Leninogorsk
Kyzy
IRAN
TURKMENISTAN
UZBEKISTAN
Syr Darya
Ayteke Bi
Dzhusaly
Zhezkazgan
Kyzylorda
Kazakhskiy Melkosopochnik
Shar
Zyryanovsk
Zapadny
Ust'-Kamenogorsk
Balkhash
Ayagoz
Ozero Zaysan
Goro Belukha 4506m
Kyzyl Kum
Turkestan
Kentau
Ozero Balkhash
Altai Mountains
Amu Darya
Arys'
Karatau
Shu
Taldykorgan
Tekeli
Shymkent
Taraz
Almaty (Alma-Ata)
TAJIKISTAN
AFGHANISTAN
Kyrghiz Range
KYRGYZSTAN
Tien Shan
CHINA

61
86
98
100
Arctic Circle
Winter limit of pack-ice
Summer limit of pack-ice

ALASKA
(to US)

ELEVATION

4000 m
13 124 ft

2000 m
6562 ft

1000 m
3281 ft

500 m
1640 ft

250 m
820 ft

100 m
328 ft

Sea
Level

Sea
Level

-250 m
-820 ft

-500 m
-1640 ft

-1000 m
-3281 ft

-2000 m
-6562 ft

-3000 m
-9843 ft

-4000 m
-13 124 ft

*Chukchi
Sea*

Bering Strait

Arctic Circle

OCEAN

*Ostrov
Komsomolets*

Ostrov Oktyabr'skoy Revolyutsii

*Severnaya
Zemlya*

*Ostrov
Bol'shevik*

*Ostrov
Vrangelya*

Proliv Longa

Pevek

Ekiatapskiy Khrebet

Anadyr'

Anadyr'

*Anadyrskiy
Zaliv*

*Bering
Sea*

*Vostochno-Sibirskoye
More*

*Novosibirskiye
Ostrova*

*Ostrov
Novaya Sibir'*

Ambarchik
Cherskiy

Alazeya

Koryakskoye Nagor'ye

Ostrov Karaginskiy

luostrov Taymyr

Ostrov Kotel'nyy

*Ostrov Bol'shoy
Lyakhovskiy*

Indigirka

Kolyma

Ossora

*Zaliv
Shelikhova*

Ust'-Kamchatsk

Vulkan Klyucheyskaya

*More
Laptevykh*

Ust'-Olenëk

Tiksi

Kazach'ye

Yana

Khrebet Cherskogo

Susuman

Atka

*Sopka
4750m*

Atlasovo

*Ozero
Taymyr*

Magadan

Mil'kovo

*Poluostrov
Kamchatka*

vero-Sibirskaya Nizmennost'

Kheta

Anabar

Kotuy

Olenëk

Verkhoyanskiy Khrebet

Lena

Petropavlovsk-
Kamchatskiy

Olenëk

*Plato
itorana*

Aldan

Okhotsk

*Okhotskoye
More*

Pervyy Kuril'skiy Proliv

Srednesibirskoye
Ploskogor'ye

zhnyaya Tunguska

Yakutsk

Vilyuy

Nyurba

Lena

Amga

Aldan

Khrebet Dzhugdzhur

*Ostrov
Paramushir*

I B I R
(SIBERIA)

Mirnyy

Chunya

Suntar

Olëkminsk

Olëkma

*Shantarskiye
Ostrova*

Ostrov Sakhalin

Ostrov Urup

FEDERATION

Angara

Ust'-Ilimsk

Bodaybo

Neryungri

Vitim

Amur

Ostrov Iturup

Kuril'sk

Kansk

Ust'-Kut

Tynda

Skovorodino

Komsomol'sk-
na-Amure

Khrebet Sikhote-Alin

Yuzhno-Sakhalinsk

Bratsk

*Ozero
Baykal*

Amur

Svobodnyy

Khabarovsk

La Pérouse Strait

Tulun

Lena

Yablonovyy Khrebet

Blagoveshchensk

Birobidzhan

Khor

Usol'ye-Sibirskoye

Shilka

Chita

Bikin

an

Angarsk

Olovyannaya

(administered by
Russian Federation,
claimed by Japan)

Eastern Sayan

Irkutsk

Ulan-Ude

Krasnokamensk

*Kuril'skiye Ostrova
(Kurile Islands)*

Kyakhta

Zabaykal'sk

CHINA

Ussuriysk

MONGOLIA

G o b i

Vladivostok

Nakhodka

JAPAN

*Sea of
Japan
(East Sea)*

**NORTH
KOREA**

TURKEY & THE CAUCASUS

ROMANIA

Lacul Razim
Lacul Sinoie

UKRAINE

Kryms'kyy
Pivostriv

Black Sea

BULGARIA

Varnenski
Zaliv

Burgaski
Zaliv

Maritsa

Kırklareli
Edirne

Çorlu

Tekirdag

İstanbul Boğazı
(Bosporus)

Ergene Nehri

İstanbul
İzmit
Adapazarı

Cide
İnebolu
Sinop
Gerze

Zonguldak
Bartın
Küre Dağları
Kastamonu
Bafra
Samsun

Devrek
Karabük
Kargı
Ünye

Çerkeş
Merzifon
Ordu

Yalova
İznik Gölü
Bolu
Gerede
Çankırı
Kızıl Irmak
Çorum
Canik Dağları

Bandırma
Bursa
Bilecik
Kalecik
Alaca
Tokat

Çanakkale

Marmara Denizi
Sea of Marmara

Balıkesir

Bozüyük
Eskişehir
ANKARA
Sorgun
Yıldızeli

Çanakkale
Boğazı
(Dardanelles)

Edremit
Ayvalık

Kütahya
Kırıkkale
Sivas

Lésvos
Simav
Polatlı
Şarkışla
Boğazlıyan

Hırfanlı
Barajı
Bünyan
Hekimh

Menemen
Manisa
Akhisar
Gediz
Kulu
İncesu
Gürün

Chíos
İzmir
Uşak
Afyon
Tuz Gölü
Nevşehir
Kayseri

Ödemiş
Aksaray

Sámos
Aydın
Nazilli
Alaşehir
Akşehir
Niğde
Göksun

Söke
Büyükmenderes Nehri
Dinar
Beyşehir
Gölü
Konya
Ereğli
Kahramanmaraş

Milas
Denizli
Burdur
Isparta
Suğla Gölü
Karaman
Ceyhan
Tarsus
Gaziante

Bodrum
Tavas
Burdur
Gölü
Mut
Mersin
Adana
Osmaniye

Marmaris
Muğla
Antalya
Manavgat
İskenderun
Kilis

Dalaman
Alanya
Silifke
Antakya
Kırıkhan

Dodekánisos
(Dodecanese)
Fethiye
Kaş
Finike
Antalya
Körfezi
Anamur

Ródos
(Rhodes)

Kárpathos

TURKISH REPUBLIC OF
NORTHERN CYPRUS
(recognised only by Turkey)

CYPRUS

Orantes

Mediterranean
Sea

LEBANON

GREECE

TURKEY

Anatolia

Toros Dağları

POPULATION

- Over 500,000
- 100,000 - 500,000
- 50,000 - 100,000
- Less than 50,000
- National capital

0 km   200
0 miles   200

RUSSIAN

FEDERATION

Caspian

Sea

Caucasus

Gagra
Gudaut'a
Sokhumi
Och'amch'ire
Abkhazia Enguri Mestia
Kazbek
5047m
P'ot'i
K'ut'aisi South
Ossetia
GEORGIA
Samtredia
Gori
Tsalka
T'BILISI
Rust'avi
Zaqatala
Xaçmaz
Quba
Siyäzän
K'obulet'i
Bat'umi *Ajaria* Akhalts'ikhe
Hopa
Lesser Cau
Şäki
Greater Caucasus
Märäzä
Sumqayıt
Artvin
Trabzon Rize
Of
Pazar
Doğu Karadeniz Dağlari
Gyumri
Kars
Artik
Sevan
Vanadzor
Gäncä
Mingäçevir
Yevlax
BAKI
(BAKU)
Giresun
Çoruh Nehri
ARMENIA
YEREVAN *Sevana Lich*
AZERBAIJAN
Nagorno-
Karabakh
Imişli
Qazimämmäd
Äli Bayramı
ümüşhane
Sarıkamış
İspir
Horasan
Aras
Artashat
Xankändi
Biläsuvar
Pasinler
Askale *Büyükağrı Dağı
(Mount Ararat)*
5137m
AZERBAIJAN
Goris
Aras
ahiye
Erzincan Ağrı
Erzurum
Doğubayazıt
Naxçıvan
Länkäran
Kemah
Tercan
Patnos
Erciş
Muradiye
*Euphrates
Firat Nehri)*
Keban
Baraji
Bingöl
Muş
Tatvan
*Van
Gölü*
Van
*Daryācheh-ye
Orūmīyeh*
*Reshteh-ye Kühhā-ye Alborz
(Elburz Mountains)*
Elazığ
Silvan
Bitlis
Gevaş
Malatya
Toroslar Dağları
Siirt
Adıyaman Diyarbakır
Batman
Silverek
Şırnak
Mardin
Kurdistan
IRAN
*Atatürk
Baraji*
Viranşehir
Nusaybin
Şanlıurfa
Ceylanpınar
Tigris
*Kühhā-ye Zagros
(Zagros Mountains)*
*Buhayrat
al Asad*
Al Jazīrah
Euphrates
Jabal Bishrī
IRAQ
RIA
*Buhayrat
ath
Tharthār*

89
100
98
98

E F G H

40° 45° 45° 50°
40°
50°
35°

1
2
3
4
5

ELEVATION

4 000 m
13 124 ft

2000 m
6562 ft

1000 m
3281 ft

500 m
1640 ft

250 m
820 ft

100 m
328 ft

Sea
Level

Sea
Level

-50 m
-164 ft

-100 m
-328 ft

-250 m
-820 ft

-500 m
-1640 ft

-1000 m
-3281 ft

-2000 m
-6562 ft

THE NEAR EAST

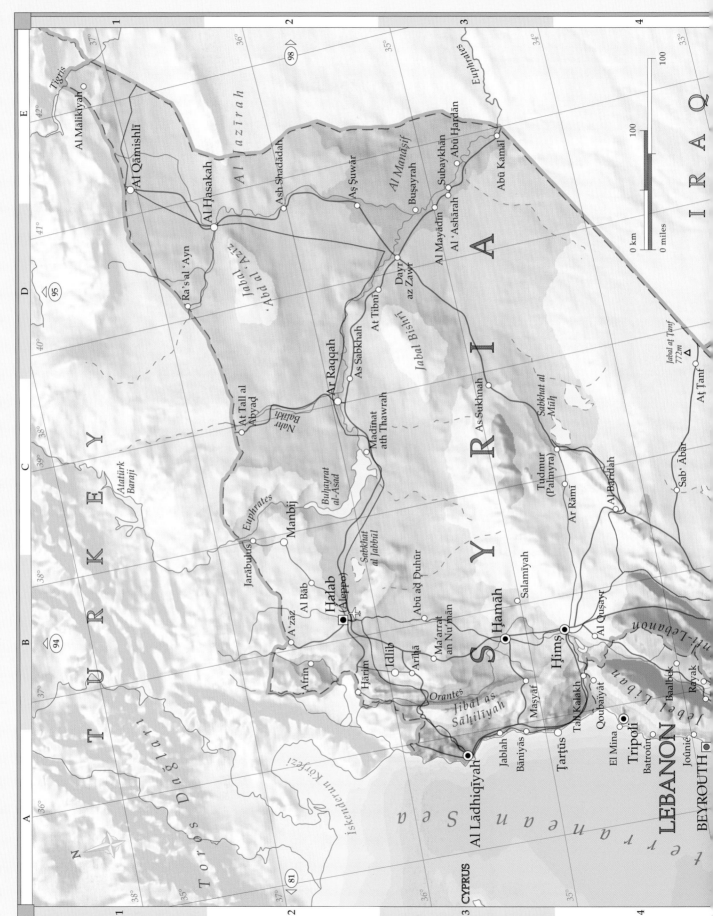

POPULATION

- ⊡ Over 500,000
- ◉ 100,000 – 500,000
- ○ 50,000 – 100,000
- ○ Less than 50,000
- ● National capital

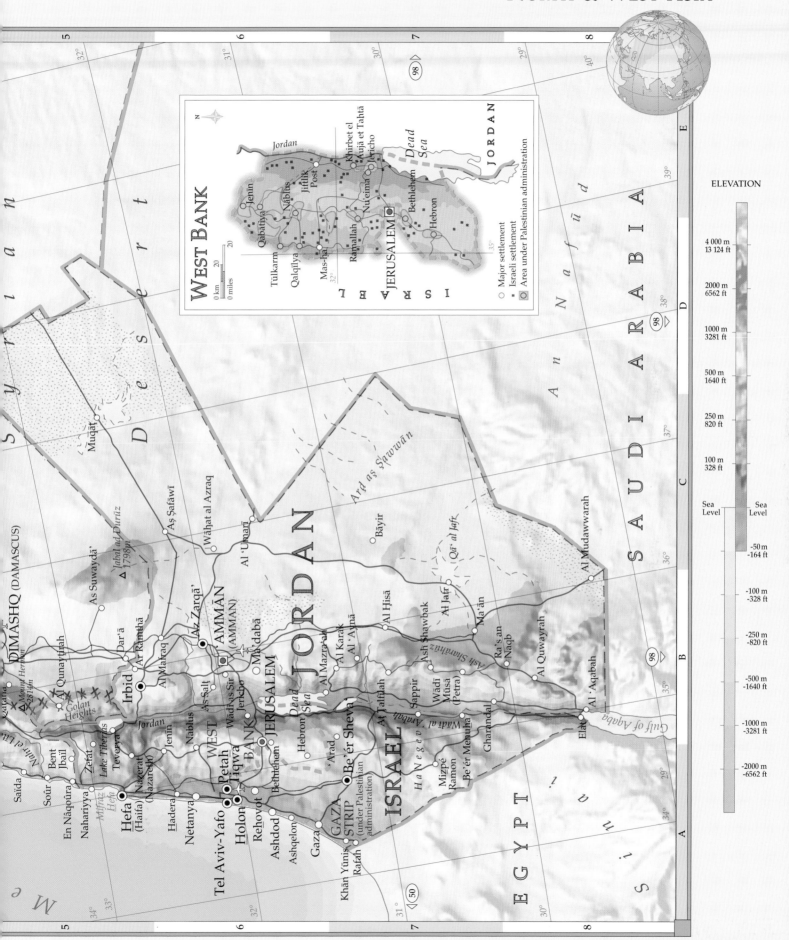

WEST BANK

N

Jordan

Khirbet el   'Auja et Tahtā
Jenin   Jiftik Post   Jericho
Qabātiya   Nāblus   Nu'eima
                                          Bethlehem
Tūlkarm   Ramallah   Hebron
Qalqīlya   Mas-ha   JERUSALEM
Mas-ha

DEAD SEA

JORDAN

ISRAEL

0 km   20
0 miles   20

○ Major settlement
■ Israeli settlement
◉ Area under Palestinian administration

ELEVATION

4 000 m	13 124 ft
2000 m	6562 ft
1000 m	3281 ft
500 m	1640 ft
250 m	820 ft
100 m	328 ft
Sea Level	Sea Level
-50 m	-164 ft
-100 m	-328 ft
-250 m	-820 ft
-500 m	-1640 ft
-1000 m	-3281 ft
-2000 m	-6562 ft

Syrian

Desert

An Nafūd

SAUDI ARABIA

DIMASHQ (DAMASCUS)

Mount Hermon
2814m

Golan
Heights

Muqāt

Al Qunayṭirah
As Suwaydā'

Jabal ad Durūz
1798m

Aṣ Ṣafāwi

Wāḥat al Azraq

Al 'Umarī

Ard aṣ Ṣawwān

Bāyir

Qā' al Jafr

JORDAN

Dar'ā
Ar Ramthā
Al Mafraq
Az Zarqā'
AMMAN
(AMMAN)
Mādabā
Al Mazra'ah
Al Karak
Al 'Aynā
Al Hisā

Ash Shawbak
Al Jafr
Ma'ān

Al Mudawwarah

Ash Sharāh

Ra's an Naqb

Al Quwayrah

Bent Jbaïl
Zefat
Irbid
Al Mafraq
As-Salt
Wādi as Sir
Jericho

JERUSALEM

Dead Sea

Hebron

Be'ér Menuha

Sour
Nahariyya
Naẕerat (Nazareth)
Teverya
Lake Tiberias
Jordan
Nāblus
Jenin
WEST BANK
Petah Tiqwa
Bethlehem
Hebron
Arad
Be'ér Sheva'

At Ṭafīlah
Sappir
Wādī Mūsā (Petra)
Gharandal

Saida
En Nāqoūra
Mizrās Heh

Hefa (Haifa)
Holon
Hadera
Netanya
Tel Aviv-Yafo
Reḥovot
Ashdod
Ashqelon
Gaza

ISRAEL

Ha Negev

Mizpé Ramon

Elat

Gulf of Aqaba

GAZA STRIP
(under Palestinian administration)

Khān Yūnis
Rafah

EGYPT

Mediterranean

Wādi al 'Arabah

Al 'Aqabah

THE MIDDLE EAST

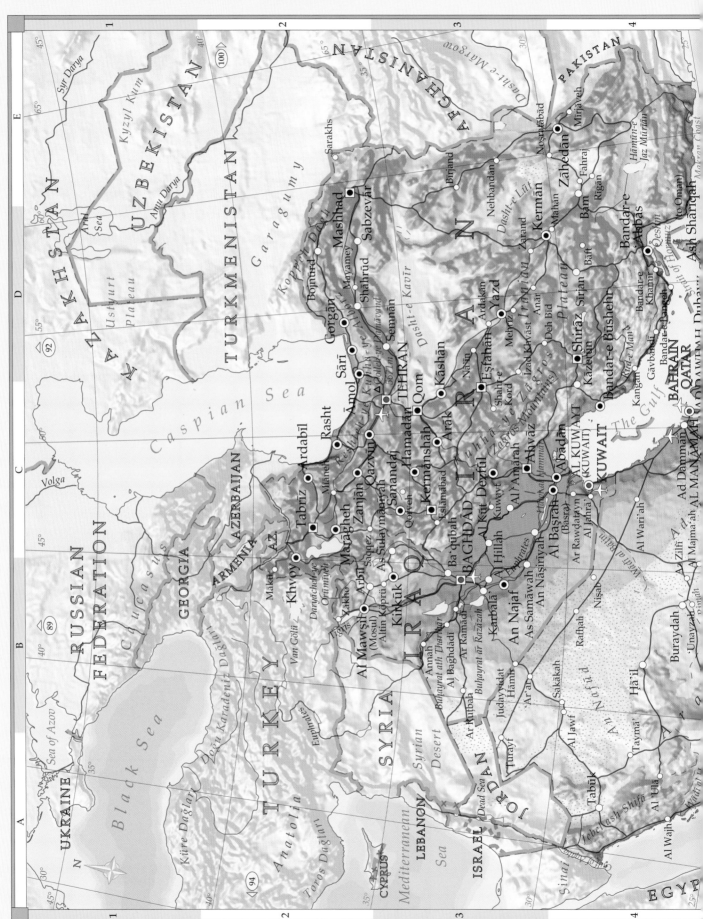

POPULATION

- ◉ Over 500,000
- ◉ 100,000 – 500,000
- ○ 50,000 – 100,000
- ○ Less than 50,000
- ● National capital

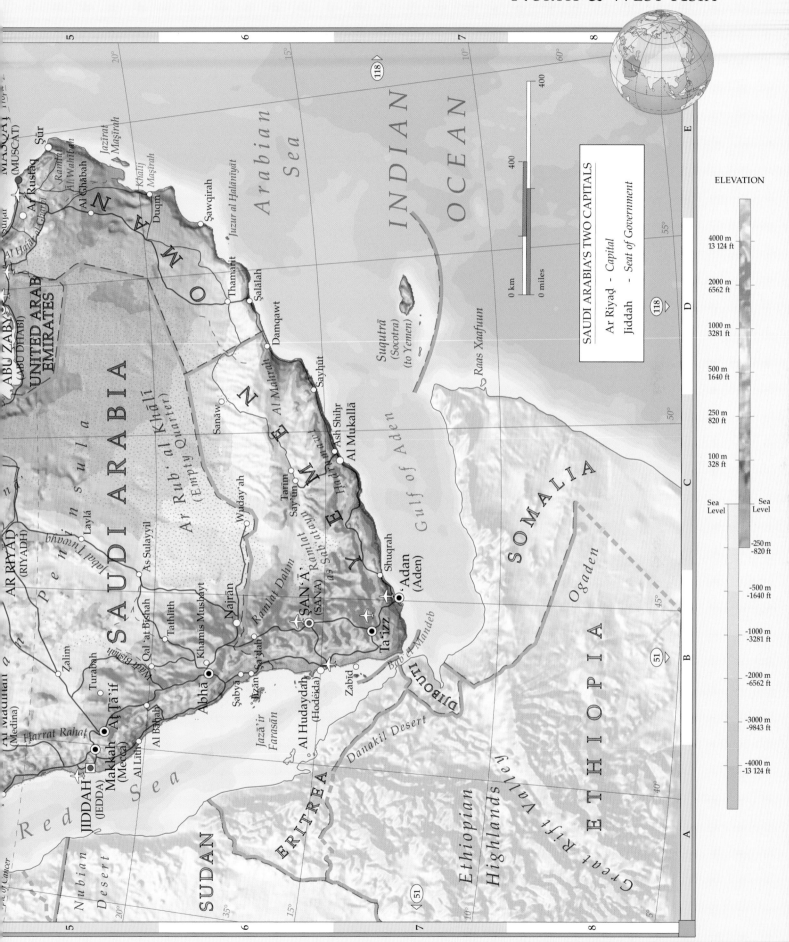

MASQAŢ (MUSCAT)
Şūr
Ar Rustāq
Suḩār
Jazīrat Maşīrah
Ramlat
Al Wahībah
Khalīj Maşīrah
Al Ghābah
Al Ḩajar al Gharbī
Duqm

UNITED ARAB EMIRATES
ABU ZABY (ABU DHABI)

O M A N

Şawqirah

Thamarīt

Ar Rub' al Khālī
(Empty Quarter)

Juzur al Ḩalānīyāt

Arabian Sea

INDIAN OCEAN

118

55°

50°

45°

Suquţrā
(Socotra)
(to Yemen)

Raas Xaafuun

SAUDI ARABIA

Peninsula

Layla
Laylá
Jabal Ţuwayq

Salālah
Damqawt
Al Mahrah
Sayḩūt
Ash Shiḩr
Al Mukallā

Sanāw
Wudayah
Tarīm
Say'ūn
Ḩaḑramawt
Ramlat as Sab'atayn

Ramlat Dalim

Wādī Bīshah
Najrān
As Sulayyil
Khamis Mushayt
Qal 'at Bishah
Tathlīth
Sa'dah
Jīzān
Şabya
Jazā'ir Farasān

Ạbhā
Al Bāḩah
Zabīd

SAN'Ā (SANA)
Y E M E N
Şan'ā
Ta'izz
Shuqrah
Adan (Aden)
Bāb el Mandeb

Gulf of Aden

SOMALIA

Ogaden

AR RIYĀḐ (RIYADH)

Al Madinah (Medina)
Ḩarrat Rahaţ
Aţ Ṭā'if
Makkah (Mecca)
JIDDAH (JEDDA)
Al Līth
Ẕalim
Turabah

Red Sea

Al Hudaydah (Hodeida)

DJIBOUTI

SUDAN

ERITREA

ETHIOPIA

Ethiopian Highlands

Great Rift Valley

Danakil Desert

Nubian Desert

Tr. of Cancer

20°

15°

118

51

51

35°
40°
45°
50°
55°
60°

SAUDI ARABIA'S TWO CAPITALS	
Ar Riyāḑ -	*Capital*
Jiddah -	*Seat of Government*

400
400
0 km
0 miles

ELEVATION

4000 m 13 124 ft	
2000 m 6562 ft	
1000 m 3281 ft	
500 m 1640 ft	
250 m 820 ft	
100 m 328 ft	
Sea Level	Sea Level
-250 m -820 ft	
-500 m -1640 ft	
-1000 m -3281 ft	
-2000 m -6562 ft	
-3000 m -9843 ft	
-4000 m -13 124 ft	

Central Asia

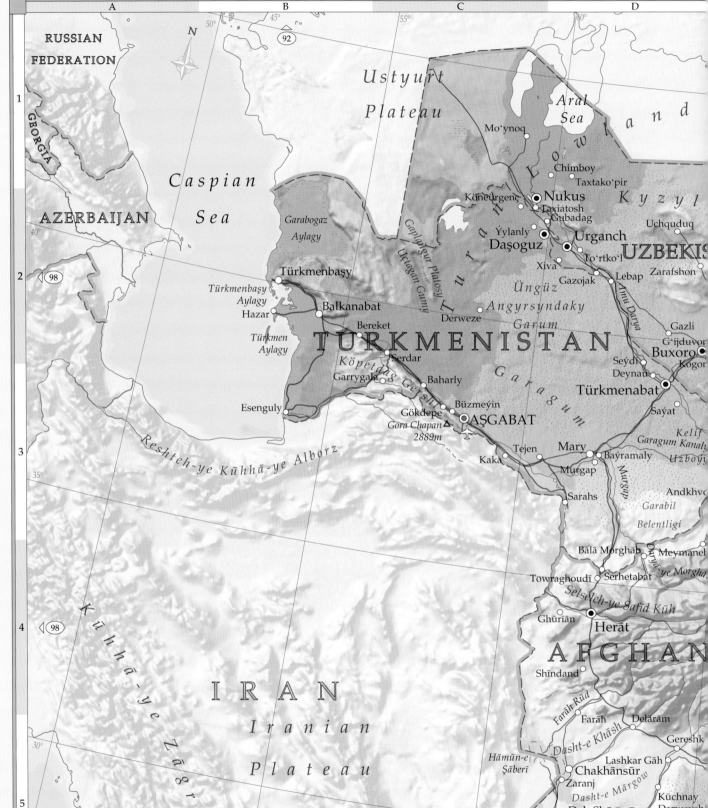

RUSSIAN FEDERATION

GEORGIA

AZERBAIJAN

Caspian Sea

Ustyurt Plateau

Aral Sea

Turan Lowland

Kyzyl

Mo'ynoq

Chimboy

Taxtako'pir

Köneürgenç

Nukus

Taxiatosh

Gubadag

Garabogaz Aylagy

Üçtagan Gumy

Gaplaňgyr platosy

Ýylanly

Daşoguz

Uchquduq

Urganch

UZBEKIS

Xiva

To'rtko'l

Gazojak

Lebap

Zarafshon

Türkmenbaşy

Türkmenbaşy Aylagy

Hazar

Balkanabat

Bereket

Derweze

Üngüz Angyrsyndaky Garum

Anu Darya

Gazli

G'ijduvon

Buxoro

Kogor

Türkmen Aylagy

Köpetdag Gerşi

Serdar

TURKMENISTAN

Garagum

Seýdi

Deynau

Garrygala

Baharly

Türkmenabat

Esenguly

Gökdepe

Büzmeýin

Gora Chapan 2889m

AŞGABAT

Tejen

Mary

Saýat

Kelif

Garagum Kanaly

Uzboýy

Reshteh-ye Kūhhā-ye Alborz

Kaka

Murgap

Bāýramaly

Murgap

Sarahs

Andkhv

Garabil Belentligi

Bālā Morghāb

Meymaneh

Kūhhā-ye Zāgros

Towraghoudī

Serhetabat

Daryā-ye Morghā

Selseleh-ye Safid Kūh

Ghūrīān

HERĀT

AFGHAN

IRAN

Shīndand

Iranian Plateau

Farāh Rūd

Farāh

Delārām

Gereshk

Dasht-e Khāsh

Hāmūn-e Şāberī

Lashkar Gāh

Chakhānsūr

Zaranj

Dasht-e Mārgow

Kūchnay Darweysha

Deh Shū

Daryā-ye Helmand

Rīgestā

Chāgai Hills

POPULATION

- ▣ Over 500,000
- ◉ 100,000 – 500,000
- ○ 50,000 – 100,000
- ○ Less than 50,000
- ● National capital

0 km   200

0 miles   200

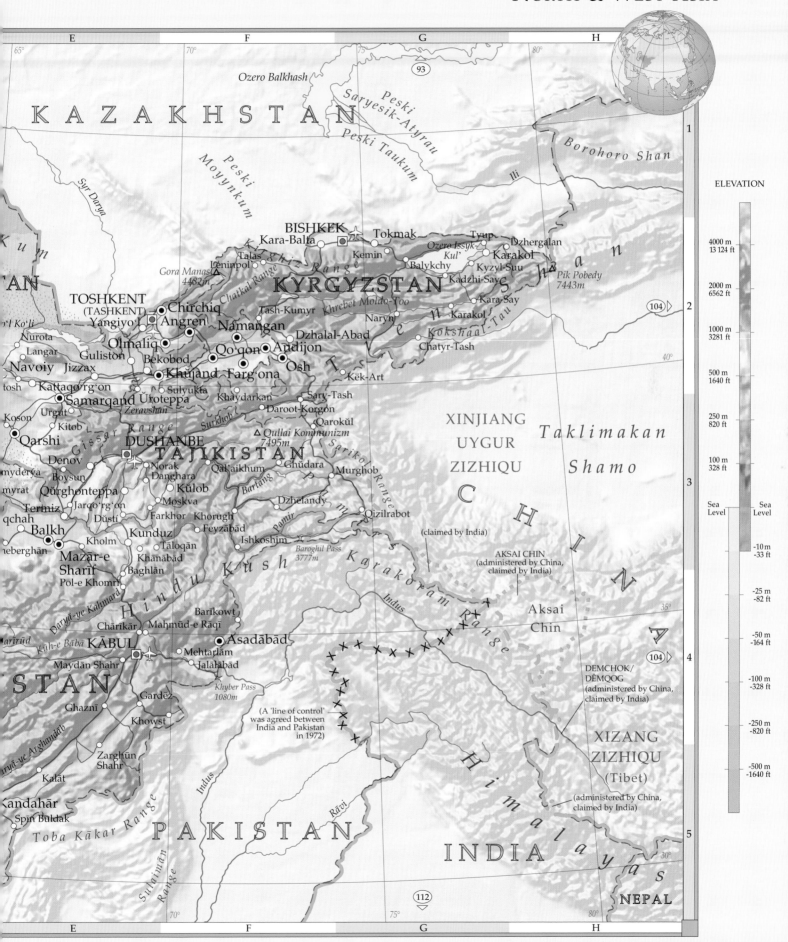

KAZAKHSTAN

Ozero Balkhash

Peski Saryesik-Atyrau

Peski Taukum

Peski Moyynkum

Syr Darya

Borohoro Shan

Ili

1

ELEVATION

BISHKEK
Kara-Balta
Tokmak
Tyup
Dzhergalan
Ozero Issyk-Kul'
Karakol
Talas
Kemin
Balykchy
Kyzyl-Suu
Leninpol
Kadzhi-Say
Gora Manas
4482m
Chatkal Range
Kirghiz Range
Kara-Say
Pik Pobedy
7443m

TOSHKENT
(TASHKENT)
KYRGYZSTAN
Khrebet Moldo-Too
Karakol
Yangiyo'l
Chirchiq
Tash-Kumyr
Naryn
Angren
Namangan
Kokshaal-Tau
O'l Ko'li
Olmaliq
Qo'qon
Dzhalal-Abad
Chatyr-Tash
Nurota
Guliston
Andijon
Langar
Bekobod
Osh
Navoiy
Jizzax
Khŭjand
Farg'ona
Kŭk-Art
tosh
Kattaqo'rg'on
Sulyukta
Khaydarkan
Sary-Tash
Samarqand
Ŭroteppa
Zeravshan
Daroot-Korgon
Urgut
Range
Koson
Kitob
Surkhob
Qarokŭl
Qarshi
Gissar
Range
△ *Qullai Kommunizm*
7495m
myderya
DUSHANBE
Denov
Norak
Qal'aikhum
Ghŭdara
Boysun
Danghara
Murghob
myrat
Qŭrghonteppa
TAJIKISTAN
Bartang
Dzhelandy
qchah
Jarqo'rg'on
Kŭlob
Moskva
Sarikol Range
Pamir
Qizilrabot
Termiz
Dŭstí
Farkhor
Khorugh
Balkh
Kunduz
Feyzābād
Ishkoshim
neberghān
Kholm
Baroghil Pass
3777m
Mazār-e
Sharīf
Khānabād
Tāloqān
Baghlān
Pol-e Khomrī

XINJIANG
UYGUR
ZIZHIQU

Taklimakan Shamo

C H I N A

(claimed by India)

AKSAI CHIN
(administered by China,
claimed by India)

Aksai
Chin

2

3

4

4000 m
13 124 ft

2000 m
6562 ft

1000 m
3281 ft

500 m
1640 ft

250 m
820 ft

100 m
328 ft

Sea
Level

Sea
Level

−10 m
−33 ft

−25 m
−82 ft

−50 m
−164 ft

−100 m
−328 ft

−250 m
−820 ft

−500 m
−1640 ft

Darya-ye Kahmard
Hindu Kush
Barīkowt
Karakoram Range
Indus
Chārīkār
Mahmūd-e Rāqī
STAN
KĀBUL
Asadābād
DEMCHOK/
DÊMQOG
(administered by China,
claimed by India)
Maydān Shahr
Mehtarlām
harirūd
Kūh-e Bābā
Jalālābād
Ghaznī
Khyber Pass
1080m
Gardēz
XIZANG
ZIZHIQU
(Tibet)
Khowst
(administered by China,
claimed by India)
Zarghūn
Shahr
(A 'line of control'
was agreed between
India and Pakistan
in 1972)
Indus
Kalāt
Darya-ye Arghandāb
andahār
Indus
Rāvi
Spin Buldak
Toba Kākar Range
Sulaiman Range
P A K I S T A N
Himalayas
INDIA
NEPAL

5

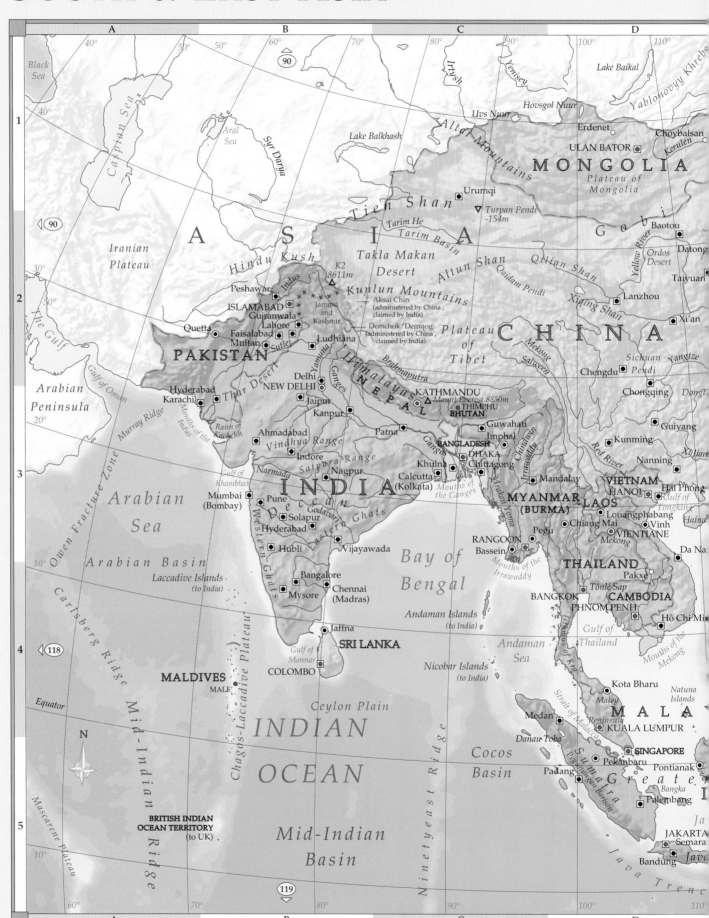

A B C D

1

POPULATION

- Over 500,000
- 100,000 - 500,000
- 50,000 - 100,000
- Less than 50,000
- National capital

Black Sea
Caspian Sea
Aral Sea
Syr Darya
Lake Balkhash
Irtysh
Yenisey
Lake Baikal
Hovsgol Nuur
Yablohovyy Khrebet
Uvs Nuur
Erdenet
Choybalsan
ULAN BATOR
Kerulen
MONGOLIA
Plateau of Mongolia

Urumqi
Turpan Pendi -154m
Gobi
Baotou
Ordos Desert
Datong

Iranian Plateau
Hindu Kush
Tien Shan
Tarim He
Tarim Basin
Takla Makan Desert
K2 8611m
Kunlun Mountains
Altun Shan
Aksai Chin (administered by China, claimed by India)
Qilian Shan
Qaidam Pendi
Xiqing Shan
Lanzhou
Taiyuan
Xi'an

PAKISTAN
Peshawar
ISLAMABAD
Gujranwala
Lahore
Quetta
Faisalabad
Multan
Sutlej
Jammu and Kashmir
Ludhiana
Demchok/Demqog (administered by China, claimed by India)
Plateau of Tibet
CHINA
Mekong
Salween
Sichuan Pendi
Chengdu
Chongqing
Yangtze
Dong

The Gulf
Arabian Peninsula
Arabian Sea
Gulf of Oman
Murray Ridge
Mouths of the Indus
Thar Desert
Delhi
NEW DELHI
Jaipur
Ganges
Yamuna
Kanpur
Himalayas
NEPAL
KATHMANDU
Mount Everest 8850m
THIMPHU
BHUTAN
Brahmaputra
Guwahati
Imphal
Chindwin
Guiyang
Kunming
Nanning
Xi Jian

Karachi
Hyderabad
Rann of Kachchh
Ahmadabad
Vindhya Range
Indore
Narmada
Satpura Range
Nagpur
INDIA
Patna
Ganges
BANGLADESH
DHAKA
Khulna
Chittagong
Calcutta (Kolkata)
Mouths of the Ganges
Mandalay
Arakan Yoma
Irrawaddy
MYANMAR (BURMA)
Red River
VIETNAM
HANOI
Hai Phong
Gulf of Tongking
Haino

Owen Fracture Zone
Arabian Sea
Arabian Basin
Gulf of Khambhat
Mumbai (Bombay)
Pune
Godavari
Solapur
Deccan
Hyderabad
Eastern Ghats
Western Ghats
Vijayawada
Hubli
Bangalore
Mysore
Chennai (Madras)
Bay of Bengal
Mouths of the Irrawaddy
RANGOON
Bassein
Pegu
LAOS
Louangphabang
Chiang Mai
VIENTIANE
Vinh
Mekong
Da Na

Laccadive Islands (to India)
Carlsberg Ridge
Mid-Indian Ridge
Jaffna
SRI LANKA
Gulf of Mannar
COLOMBO
Andaman Islands (to India)
Nicobar Islands (to India)
THAILAND
Pakxe
Tônlé Sap
BANGKOK
CAMBODIA
PHNOM PENH
Hô Chi Mir
Gulf of Thailand
Andaman Sea
Gulf of
Da Na

MALDIVES
MALE
Equator
N
Ceylon Plain
INDIAN OCEAN
Ninetyeast Ridge
Islands of Kra
Malay Peninsula
Kota Bharu
Natuna Islands
MALA
Medan
Strait of Malacca
KUALA LUMPUR
Danau Toba
SINGAPORE
Pekanbaru
Pontianak
Sumatra
Padang
Greater
Bangka
Palembang

Mascarene Plateau
BRITISH INDIAN OCEAN TERRITORY (to UK)
Chagos-Laccadive Plateau
Cocos Basin
Mid-Indian Basin
JAKARTA
Semara
Bandung
Java Tren
Ja

102

E · 130° · 50° · F · 140° · 150° · 160° · G · 170° · 40° · 180° · H

130

Amur

Sakhalin

Kurile Islands

Kurile Trench

Great Khingan Range

Qiqihar

Manchuria Plain

Harbin

Lake Khanka

Sapporo

Hokkaido

Northwest Pacific Basin

Changchun

Liao He

Shenyang

Sea of Japan (East Sea)

JAPAN

Honshu

Sendai

Japan Trench

Shatskiy Rise

Dandong

Yalu

NORTH KOREA

PYONGYANG

BEIJING

Tianjin

Dalian

SOUTH KOREA

SEOUL

Nagoya

TOKYO

Yokohama

Kyoto

Fuji-san 3776m

hijiazhuang

Jinan

Bo Hai

Osaka

Hiroshima

Shikoku

Qingdao

Yellow Sea

Korea Strait

Kitakyushu

Kyushu

ngzhou

130

Nanjing

East China Sea

Shanghai

Shikoku Basin

Wuhan

Hangzhou

Nanchang

Ryukyu Islands

Ryukyu Trench

hangsha

Wuyi Shan

Fuzhou

TAIPEI

PACIFIC

OCEAN

20°

hantou

TAIWAN

Philippine Basin

Kyushu-Palau Ridge

West Mariana Basin

130

Guangzhou

Kaohsiung

Philippine Sea

Hong Kong (Xianggang)

Macao Aomen

Luzon Strait

ARACEL ISLANDS (disputed)

Luzon

Baguio

Mariana Trench

South China Sea

Mindoro

MANILA

10°

China Basin

PHILIPPINES

Panay

Samar

Yap Trench

M i c r o n e s i a

SPRATLY ISLANDS (disputed)

Bacolod

Cebu

Eauripik Rise

Equator

130

Negros

Palawan

Sulu Sea

Zamboanga

Mindanao

Davao

M e l a n e s i a

Ontong Java Rise

RUNEI

BANDAR SERI BEGAWAN

Celebes Sea

Halmahera

Bismarck Archipelago

Solomon Islands

A

Borneo

Manado

Moluccas

Jayapura

Solomon Sea

Balikpapan

Seram

Ambon

Pegunungan Maoke

unda Islands

Banjarmasin

Celebes

Buru

Banda Sea

New Guinea

DONESIA

a

Ujungpandang

Flores Sea

Lesser Sunda Islands

Flores

DILI

Arafura Sea

Surabaya

Bali

EAST TIMOR

Coral Sea

Malang

Sumba

Timor

Timor Trough

Timor Sea

120

A U S T R A L I A

120° · 130° · F · 140° · G · 150° · H · 160°

E · F · G · H

POLITICAL FEATURES

TOTAL AREA:
7,936,200 sq miles
(20,554,700 sq km)

TOTAL NUMBER OF COUNTRIES:
24

TOTAL POPULATION:
3,483 million

LARGEST CITY WITH POPULATION:
Tokyo, Japan 33.9 million

COUNTRY WITH HIGHEST POPULATION DENSITY:
Singapore 18,200 people per sq mile
(7,049 people per sq km)

LARGEST COUNTRY:
China 3,705,386 sq miles
(9,596,960 sq km)

SMALLEST COUNTRY:
Maldives 116 sq miles
(300 sq km)

PHYSICAL FEATURES

LARGEST LAKE:
Tônlé Sap, Cambodia
1,000 sq miles (2,850 sq km)

LONGEST RIVER:
Chang Jiang (Yangtze), China
3,965 miles (6,380 km)

HIGHEST POINT:
Mount Everest, China/Nepal
29,035 ft (8,850 m)

LOWEST POINT:
Turpan Pendi (Turfan Basin), China
505 ft (154 m) below sea level

0 km   1000

0 miles   1000

1

2

3

4

5

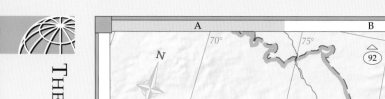

THE WORLD ATLAS

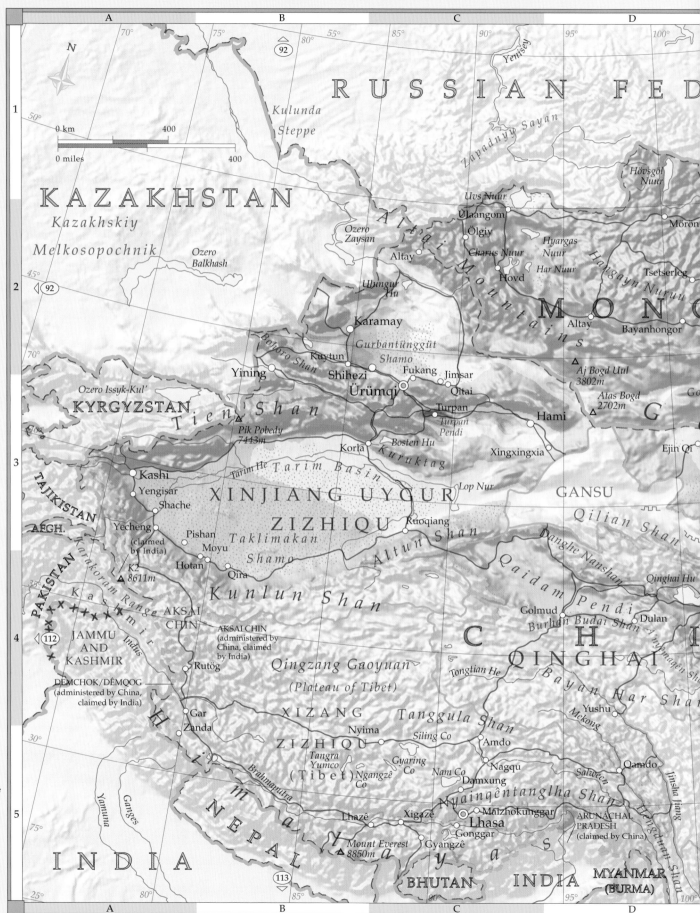

RUSS. FED.

ERATION

OLIA

OLIA

NEI MONGOL ZIZHIQU (Inner Mongolia)

N A

Ozero Baykal

Sühbaatar
Darhan
Erdenet
Bulgan
Dzuunmod
ULAANBAATAR
(ULAN BATOR)
Öndörhaan
Baruun-Urt
Saynshand
Dalandzadgad
Altayn Nuruu
Selenga
Onon
Onon Gol
Choybalsan
Kerulen
Erenhot
Hailar
Manzhouli
Hulun Nur
Menengiyn Tal
Xilinhot
Ergun Zuoqi
Jagdaqi
Argun (Ergun He)
Shilka
Amur (Heilong Jiang)
Hulingol
Tongliao
Chifeng
Da Hinggan Ling
93

HEILONGJIANG
JILIN
Lake Khanka
Liao He
LIAONING
Lihodong Wan
NORTH KOREA
Korea Bay
Bo Hai
SOUTH KOREA
Sea of Japan
(East Sea)
Yellow Sea
JAPAN
106
108

Xining
Wuhai
Labrai Shan
Tengger Shamo
NINGXIA HUIZU ZIZHIQU
GANSU
Jining
Hohhot
Baotou
Huang He
Mu Us Shamo
Great Wall of China
SHANXI
SHAANXI
Han Shui
HENAN
BEIJING
TIANJIN
HEBEI
SHANDONG
Huang He (Yellow River)
JIANGSU
Lang Shan

SICHUAN
CHONGQING
HUBEI
Chang Jiang (Yangtze)
HUNAN
YUNNAN
GUIZHOU
ANHUI
ZHEJIANG
JIANGXI
FUJIAN
SHANGHAI
East China Sea
Nansei-shotō (to Japan)
Tropic of Cancer
TAIWAN

ELEVATION

4 000 m	13 124 ft
2000 m	6562 ft
1000 m	3281 ft
500 m	1640 ft
250 m	820 ft
100 m	328 ft
Sea Level	Sea Level
-50 m	-164 ft
-100 m	-328 ft
-250 m	-820 ft
-500 m	-1640 ft
-1000 m	-3281 ft
-2000 m	-6562 ft

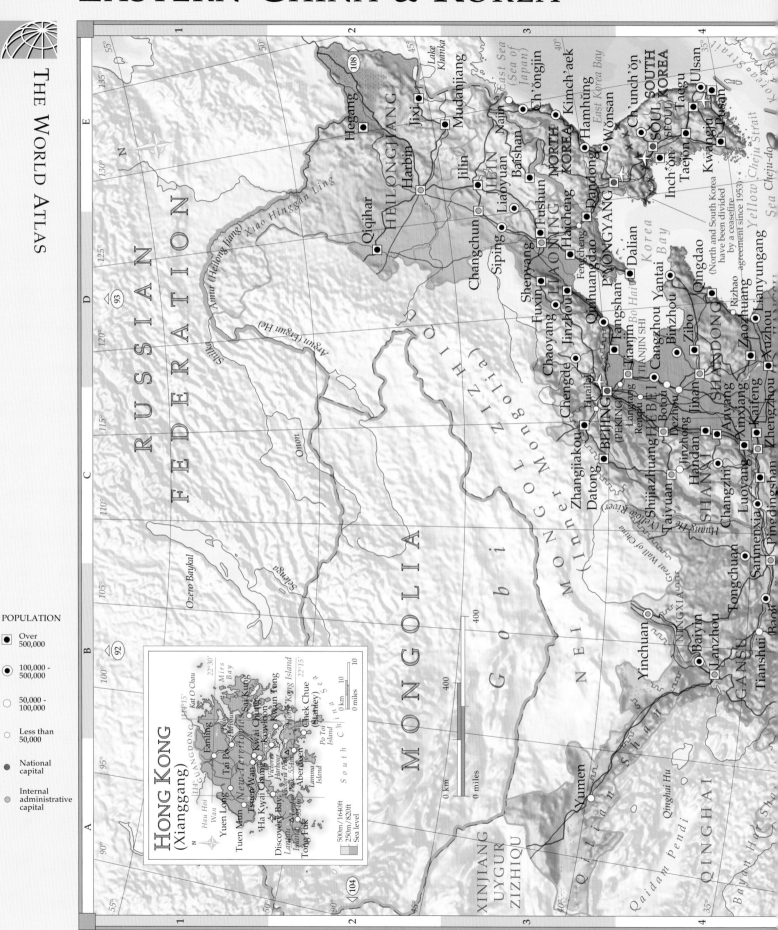

POPULATION

- ◉ Over 500,000
- ◉ 100,000 – 500,000
- ○ 50,000 – 100,000
- ○ Less than 50,000
- ● National capital
- ● Internal administrative capital

HONG KONG (Xianggang)

Hau Hoi Wan
Mirs Bay
Kat O Chau
Fanling
Sai Kung
Yuen Long
Tuen Mun
New Territories
Kwai Chung
Kowloon
Tai Po
Tsuen Wan
Ma Wan
Victoria
Harbour
Kwun Tong
Hong Kong Island
'Ha Kwai Chung
Discovery Bay
Lantau Island
Aberdeen
Chek Chue (Stanley)
Lamma Island
Po Toi Island
Tong Fuk
South China Sea

500m/1640ft
250m/820ft
Sea level

RUSSIAN FEDERATION

Ozero Baykal
Shilka
Amur (Heilong Jiang)
Argun (Ergun He)
Onon
Selenga
Selenga

Xiao Hinggan Ling

MONGOLIA

Nei Mongol Zizhiqu (Inner Mongolia)

Gobi
Gobi

HEILONGJIANG
Hegang
Jixi
Mudanjiang
Harbin
Qiqihar

Lake Khanka

East Sea (Sea of Japan)

JILIN
Jilin
Changchun
Siping
Baishan
Liaoyuan

Najin
Ch'ŏngjin
Kimch'aek
East Korea Bay

NORTH KOREA
Hamhŭng
Wŏnsan
PYONGYANG
Namp'o
Fengcheng
Dandong

Ch'unch'ŏn
SŎUL (SEOUL)
Inch'ŏn
Ch'ŏnan
SOUTH KOREA
Taejŏn
Taegu
Ulsan
Kwangju
Pusan
Yellow Sea / Cheju-do
Cheju Strait

(North and South Korea have been divided by a ceasefire agreement since 1953)

LIAONING
Fushun
Haicheng
Shenyang
Fuxin
Chaoyang
Chengde
Jinzhou
Qinhuangdao
Dalian
Haid Bo Hai
Korea Bay
Korea

HEBEI
Zhangjiakou
Datong
Tangshan
TIANJIN SHI
Tianjin
Langfang
Renqiu
Botou
Dezhou
BEIJING (PEKING)
Shijiazhuang
Jinzhou
Handan
Baiyin
Lanzhou

SHANXI
Taiyuan
Changzhi
Yongchuan

SHANDONG
Jinan
Zibo
Yantai
Binzhou
Qingdao
Rizhao
Laozhuang
Linyi
Lianyungang
Anyang
Xinxiang
Luoyang
Sanmenxia
Pingdingshan
Zhengzhou

GANSU
Yumen
Tianshui
Bayan Har Shan

NINGXIA
Yinchuan

QINGHAI
Qinghai Hu
Qaidam pendi

XINJIANG UYGUR ZIZHIQU

Qilian Shan

Great Wall of China
Huang He (Yellow River)
Huang He

0 km 400
0 miles 400

0 km 10
0 miles 10

JAPAN

East China Sea

Okinawa

Nansei-shoto (part of Japan)

(China and Taiwan claim all of each other's territory)

Tropic of Cancer

PACIFIC OCEAN

PHILIPPINES

TAIWAN
Chilung
TAIPEI
Taichung
Chiai
T'ainan
Kaohsiung

Luzon Strait

Taiwan Strait

ELEVATION

4 000 m	13 124 ft
2000 m	6562 ft
1000 m	3281 ft
500 m	1640 ft
250 m	820 ft
100 m	328 ft
Sea Level	Sea Level
-50 m	-164 ft
-100 m	-328 ft
-250 m	-820 ft
-500 m	-1640 ft
-1000 m	-3281 ft
-2000 m	-6562 ft

South China Sea

SPRATLY ISLANDS
(disputed by China, Malaysia, Philippines, Taiwan and Vietnam)
Flat Island
Nanshan Island
Thitu Island
Loaita Island
Namyit Island
Len Dao
Spratly Island

PARACEL ISLANDS
(disputed by China, Taiwan and Vietnam)
Amphitrite Group
Crescent Group
Triton Island

Yangzhou
Suzhou
Shanghai
Wuxi
Jiaxing
Ningbo
Hangzhou
Wenzhou
Shangrao
ZHEJIANG
Jinhua
Huzhou
Jingdezhen
Fuzhou
FUJIAN
Yong'an
Nanping
Quanzhou
Xiamen
Shantou
Hong Kong (Xianggang)
Macao (Aomen)
Guangzhou
Dongguan
Jiangmen
GUANGDONG
Zhaoqing
Yulin
Maoming
Zhanjiang
Haikou
Xuwen
Danzhou
Dongfang
Hainan Dao
HAINAN
Gulf of Tongking

Huaihan
Nanjing
Hefei
ANHUI
Wuhu
Anqing
Wuhan
HUBEI
Yichang
Huangshi
Jiujiang
JIANGXI
Nanchang
Xiangtan
Changsha
HUNAN
Loudi
Hengyang
Shaoguan
Ganzhou
Longyan
Zhangzhou
Chenzhou
Lengshuitan
Quanzhou
GUANGXI ZHUANGZU ZIZHIQU
Liuzhou
Guilin
Nanning
Beihai
Qinzhou
Suixi

Huayin
Xinyang
SHAANXI
Nanyang
Guangyuan
SICHUAN
Miaoyang
Wanxian
Chongqing
CHONGQING
Neijiang
Zigong
Zunyi
GUIZHOU
Guiyang
Anshun
Gejiu
Kunming
YUNNAN
Baoshan
Dali
Xichang
Leshan
Ya'an
Chengdu
Litang
Sichuan Pendi
Yalong Jiang
Jinsha Jiang

XIZANG ZIZHIQU (Tibet)

INDIA

MYANMAR (BURMA)

Tropic of Cancer

Hengduan Shan
Wuliang Shan
Mekong
Jinghong
Salween

LAOS

THAILAND

CAMBODIA

VIETNAM

Red River

Gulf of Thailand

Jinsha Jiang
Dadu
Dongting Hu
CHANGJIANG

130
117
114
114

JAPAN

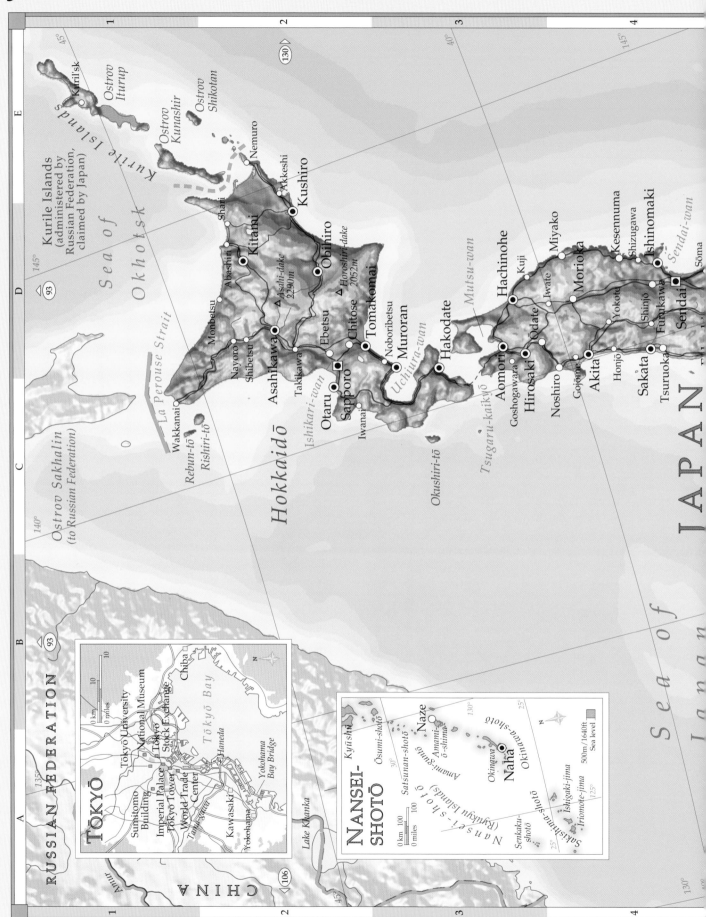

POPULATION

- ● Over 500,000
- ◉ 100,000 - 500,000
- ○ 50,000 - 100,000
- ○ Less than 50,000
- ● National capital

RUSSIAN FEDERATION

CHINA

Amur

Lake Khanka

TŌKYŌ

Tōkyō Bay

Chiba

Tokyo University
National Museum
Tokyo Stock Exchange
Sumitomo Building
Imperial Palace
Tōkyō Tower
World Trade Center
Haneda
Yokohama Bay Bridge
Kawasaki
Yokohama
Tama-gawa

NANSEI-SHOTŌ

Kyūshū
Ōsumi-shotō
Satsunan-shotō
Amami-guntō
Naze
Amami-ō-shima
Okinawa
Naha
Okinawa-shotō
Sakishima-shotō
Ishigaki-jima
Iriomote-jima
Senkaku-shotō
Nansei-shotō (Ryūkyū Islands)

500m/1640ft
Sea level

Sea of Okhotsk

Kuril'sk
Ostrov Iturup
Ostrov Shikotan
Ostrov Kunashir
Ostrov Shikotan
Kurile Islands (administered by Russian Federation, claimed by Japan)

Kurile Islands

Nemuro
Akkeshi
Kushiro
Shari
Kitami
Abashiri
Monbetsu
Obihiro
△ Asahi-dake 2290m
△ Horoshiri-dake 2052m
Asahikawa
Nayoro
Shibetsu
Takikawa
Chitose
Ebetsu
Tomakomai
Noboribetsu
Muroran
Uchiura-wan
Hakodate
Otaru
Sapporo
Iwanai
Ishikari-wan
Wakkanai
Rebun-tō
Rishiri-tō
La Perouse Strait

Ostrov Sakhalin (to Russian Federation)

Hokkaidō

Okushiri-tō

Tsugaru-kaikyō

Mutsu-wan

Hachinohe
Kuji
Aomori
Iwate
Miyako
Goshogawara
Hirosaki
Odate
Morioka
Noshiro
Yokote
Shizugawa
Gojōme
Akita
Shinjō
Furukawa
Honjō
Sakata
Tsuruoka
Kesennuma
Ishinomaki
Sendai
Sōma
Sendai-wan

JAPAN

Sea of Japan

Sea of Japan

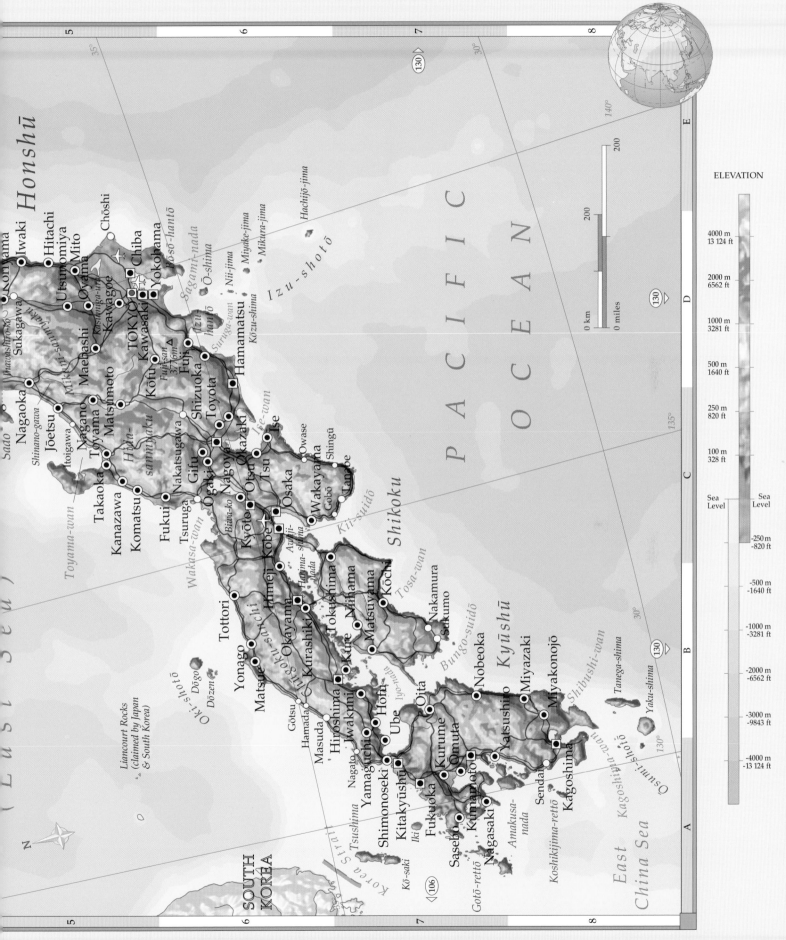

Honshū

Iwaki

(*East Sea*)

Kōriyama

Iwaki
Hitachi
Utsunomiya
Mito
Chōshi
Sukagawa
Oyama
Chiba
Yokohama
Kawagoe
Kawasaki
TOKYO
Maebashi
Nagano
Matsumoto
Fuji
Shizuoka
Kōfu
Fuji-san 3776m △
Hamamatsu
Nagaoka
Nagaoka
Jōetsu
Toyama
Shinano-gawa
Takaoka
Kanazawa
Komatsu
Fukui
Gifu
Nakatsugawa
Ōgaki Nagoya
Ōtsu
Okazaki
Toyota
Ise
Tsu
Owase
Shingū
Wakayama
Gobō
Tanabe
Kyōto
Kōbe
Ōsaka

Sado
Toyama-wan
Oki-shotō
Dōgo
Dōzen

Hida-sanmyaku
Kiso-sammyaku

Wakasa-wan
Tsuruga
Biwa-ko

Tottori
Matsue
Yonago
Gōtsu
Hamada
Masuda
Nagato

Chūgoku-sanchi

Himeji
Okayama
Kurashiki
Tokushima
Kure
Iwakuni
Mihama
Matsuyama
Kōchi
Nakamura
Sukumo

Awaji-shima
Hama-nada

Shikoku

Tosa-wan

Hiroshima
Hōfu
Ube
Ōita
Nobeoka
Miyazaki
Miyakonojō

Kyūshū

Bungo-suidō
Iyo-nada

Yamaguchi
Shimonoseki
Kitakyūshū
Fukuoka
Saseho
Nagasaki
Kumamoto
Ōmuta
Kurume
Yatsushiro
Sendai
Kagoshima

Tsushima
Iki
Kō-saki
Gotō-rettō
Amakusa-nada
Koshikijima-rettō

Korea Strait

SOUTH KOREA

N

Liancourt Rocks
(claimed by Japan
& South Korea)

Izu-shotō

Hachijō-jima
Miyake-jima
Mikura-jima
Nii-jima
Ō-shima
Kōzu-shima
Izu-hantō
Suruga-wan
Sagami-nada
Bōsō-hantō

PACIFIC OCEAN

Tanega-shima
Yaku-shima
Shibushi-wan
Kagoshima-wan
Ōsumi-shotō
Ōsumi-suidō

East China Sea

⟨130⟩
⟨130⟩
⟨130⟩
⟨106⟩

ELEVATION

4000 m	13 124 ft
2000 m	6562 ft
1000 m	3281 ft
500 m	1640 ft
250 m	820 ft
100 m	328 ft
Sea Level	Sea Level
-250 m	-820 ft
-500 m	-1640 ft
-1000 m	-3281 ft
-2000 m	-6562 ft
-3000 m	-9843 ft
-4000 m	-13 124 ft

200
200
0 km
0 miles

SOUTH INDIA & SRI LANKA

Arabian

Sea

Amīndīvi Islands

Lakshadweep (Laccadive Islands) (to India)

Kavaratti Island

Kalpeni Island

Nine Degree Channel

Minicoy Island

Eight Degree Channel

Ihavandippolhu Atoll

MALDIVES

Faadhippolhu Atoll

Horsburgh Atoll

Male' Atoll

Ari Atoll

● **MALE'**

Felidhu Atoll

Mulaku Atoll

Kolhumadulu Atoll

Hadhdhunmathi Atoll

North Huvadhu Atoll

South Huvadhu Atoll

Equator

Gan ⬡ 118

Addu Atoll

Kalyān
Mumbai (Bombay)
Pune
Ahmadnagar
Bārāmati
Nizāmābād
Solāpur
Sāngli
Kolhāpur
Belgaum
Pānji
Hubli
Gadag
Dāvangere
Shimoga
Bhadrāvati
Udupi
Mangalore
Kāsargod
Cannanore
Calicut
Coimbatore
Trichūr
Ernākulam
Cochin
Alleppey
Quilon
Trivandrum
Nāgercoil

Nānded
Jagdalpur
Karimnagar
Vizianagaram
Secunderābād
Visākhapatnam
Gulbarga
Hyderābād
Rājahmundri
Kākināda
Rāichūr
Vijayawada
Kurnool
Machilīpatnam
Nandyāl
Chirāla
Tādpatri
Kāvali
Anantapur
Ongole
Cuddapah
Nellore
Tumkūr
Bangalore
Vellore
Chennai (Madras)
Mandya
Kanchīpuram
Krishnagiri
Tiruppattūr
Mysore
Salem
Pondicherry
Erode
Neyveli
Tiruchchirāppalli
Dindigul
Madurai
Rājapālaiyam
Jaffna
Quilon
Tuticorin
Mannar
SRI LANKA
Vavuniya
Trincomalee
Puttalam
Anurādhapura
Batticaloa
Matale
Negombo
Kandy
COLOMBO
Sri Jayawardanapura
Kalutara
Ratnapura
Galle
Matara

Godāvari
Andhra Pradesh
Krishna
Deccan
Karnātaka
Tungabhadra Reservoir
Tamil Nādu
Coromandel Coast
Malabār Coast
Palk Strait
Gulf of Mannar

INDIAN

POPULATION

- ▪ Over 500,000
- ⊙ 100,000 – 500,000
- ○ 50,000 – 100,000
- ○ Less than 50,000
- ● National capital

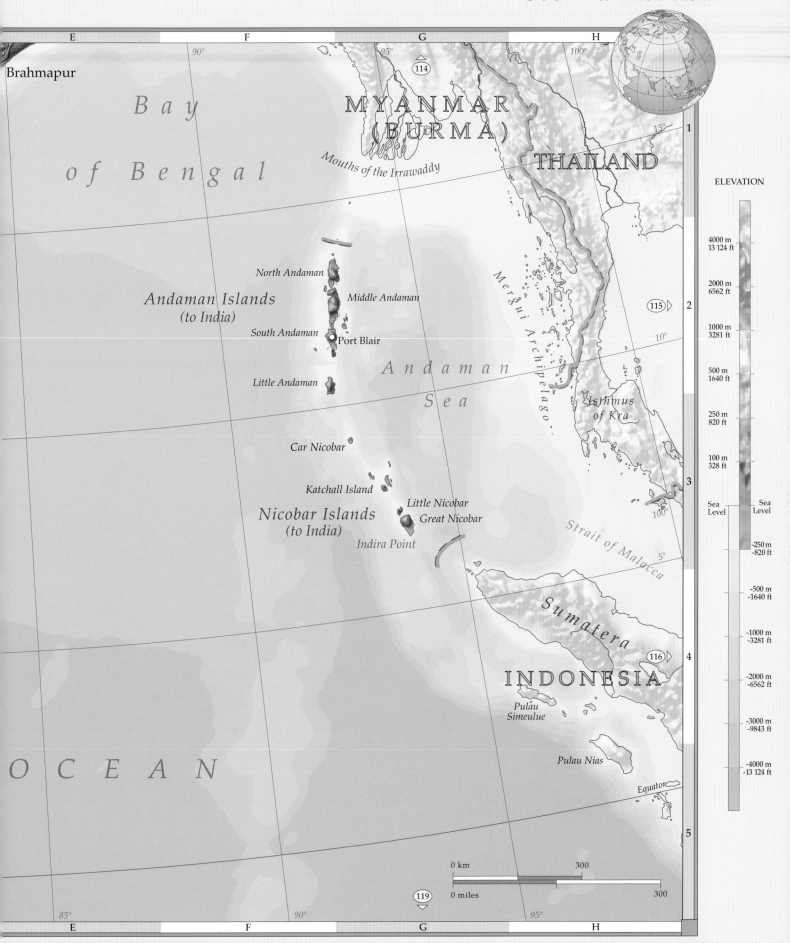

Brahmapur

Bay

of Bengal

MYANMAR
(BURMA)

Mouths of the Irrawaddy

THAILAND

North Andaman

Andaman Islands
(to India)

Middle Andaman

South Andaman

Port Blair

Little Andaman

Andaman

Sea

Mergui Archipelago

*Isthmus
of Kra*

Car Nicobar

Katchall Island

Nicobar Islands
(to India)

Little Nicobar

Great Nicobar

Indira Point

Strait of Malacca

Sumatera

INDONESIA

*Pulau
Simeulue*

Pulau Nias

Equator

OCEAN

ELEVATION

4000 m
13 124 ft

2000 m
6562 ft

1000 m
3281 ft

500 m
1640 ft

250 m
820 ft

100 m
328 ft

Sea
Level

Sea
Level

-250 m
-820 ft

-500 m
-1640 ft

-1000 m
-3281 ft

-2000 m
-6562 ft

-3000 m
-9843 ft

-4000 m
-13 124 ft

0 km   300

0 miles   300

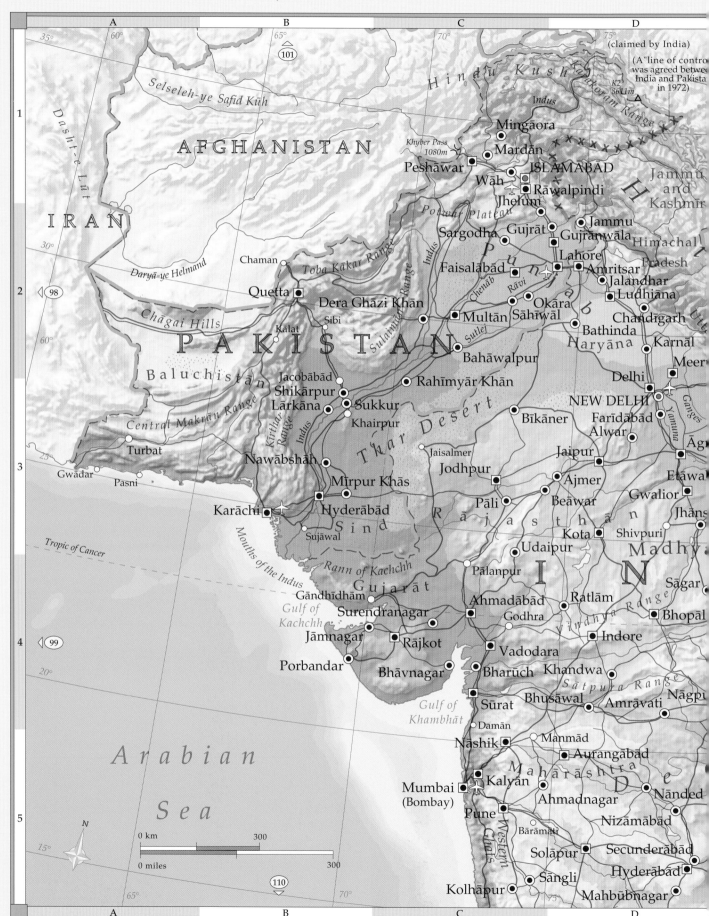

(claimed by India)

(A "line of control"
was agreed between
India and Pakistan
in 1972)

K2
8611m

AFGHANISTAN

Selseleh-ye Safīd Kūh

Dasht-e Lūt

Hindu Kush

Karakoram Range

Indus

Mingaora

Khyber Pass
1080m

Mardān

Peshāwar

Wāh

ISLĀMĀBĀD

Jhelum

Rāwalpindi

Jammu
and
Kashmir

Potwar Plateau

IRAN

Sargodha

Gujrāt

Jammu

Chaman

Toba Kākar Range

Indus

Quetta

Sulaimān Range

Faisalābād

Sargodha

Chenab

Rāvi

Okāra

Sāhīwal

Lahore

Gujrānwāla

Amritsar

Jalandhar

Ludhiāna

Chandīgarh

Himachal
Pradesh

Daryā-ye Helmand

Kālat

Sibi

Dera Ghāzi Khan

Multān

Sutlej

Bahāwalpur

Bathinda

Karnāl

Haryāna

Delhi

Meer

PAKISTAN

Chāgai Hills

Baluchistan

Jacobābād

Shikārpur

Lārkāna

Sukkur

Rahīmyār Khān

Thar Desert

NEW DELHI

Faridābād

Alwar

Āg

Central Makrān Range

Kīrthar Range

Khairpur

Bīkāner

Indus

Jaisalmer

Nawābshāh

Jaipur

Ajmer

Turbat

Mīrpur Khās

Jodhpur

Pāli

Beāwar

Etāwa

Gwalior

Gwādar

Pasni

Karāchi

Hyderābād

Sind

Kota

Shivpuri

Jhāns

Udaipur

Madhya

Tropic of Cancer

Sujāwal

Rājasthan

Pālanpur

Sāgar

Mouths of the Indus

Rann of Kachchh

Gujarāt

Gāndhīdhām

Ahmadābād

Godhra

Ratlām

Bhopāl

Vindhya Range

Surendranagar

Indore

Gulf of
Kachchh

Jāmnagar

Rājkot

Vadodara

Khandwa

Sātpura Range

Porbandar

Bhāvnagar

Bharūch

Nāgp

Gulf of
Khambhāt

Sūrat

Bhusāwal

Amrāvati

Dāman

Manmād

Arabian

Nāshik

Aurangābād

Maharāshtra

Nānded

Sea

Mumbai
(Bombay)

Kalyān

Ahmadnagar

Nizāmābād

Pune

Bārāmati

D

Secunderābād

Solāpur

Hyderābād

Sangli

Kolhāpur

Mahbūbnagar

N

0 km   300

0 miles   300

POPULATION

⊙ Over
500,000

⊙ 100,000 -
500,000

○ 50,000 -
100,000

○ Less than
50,000

● National
capital

E   F   G   H

XINJIANG
Uygur Zizhiqu

Kunlun Shan

QINGHAI

SICHUAN

1

C H I N A

AKSAI CHIN
(administered by China,
claimed by India)

Qingzang Gaoyuan
(Plateau of Tibet)

Tanggula Shan

Jinsha Jiang

Mekong
(Lancang Jiang)

DEMCHOK/
DÊMQOG
(administered by China,
claimed by India)

XIZANG ZIZHIQU
(Tibet)

Nyainqêntanglha Shan

ARUNĀCHAL
PRADESH
(claimed by China)

2

104

104

Brahmaputra

H   i   m   a   l   a   y   a   s

Dibrugarh

NEPAL

Annapurna
8091m

Pokhara

Mount Everest
8850m

Kula Kangri
7554m

THIMPHU

Brahmaputra

Jorhāt

Bareilly

Salyan

Bhaktapur

Gangtok

BHUTAN

Assam

Bahraich

KATHMANDU

Lalitpur Darjiling

Shiliguri

Bongaigaon

Kohīma

daun

Uttar Pradesh

Faizābād

Gorakhpur

Biratnagar

Koch Bihar

Dispur

Shillong

Meghālaya

Imphāl

3

ucknow

Kānpur

Jaunpur

Mau

Chhapra

Saidpur

Dinajpur

Rangpur

Guwāhāti

Allahābād

Varanasi

Patna

Bhāgalpur

Bihār

Jamalpur

Sylhet

Silchar

Bihar Sharīf

Ganges

BANGLADESH

Murwāra

Jabalpur

Gaya

Chota
Nāgpur

Rājshāhi

Pabna

Brahmanbaria

DHAKA

Comilla

Tropic of Cancer

I   N   D   I   A

Jhārkhand

Dhanbād

Asānsol

Bānkura

Jessore

Khulna

MYANMAR
(BURMA)

Bokāro

Chhattisgarh

Rānchi

West Bengal

Ganges

Bilāspur

Korba

Jamshedpur

Hāora

Chittagong

Gondia

Rāulakela

Kharagpur

Calcutta
(Kolkata)

Barisal

114

4

Raipur

Sambalpur

Bāleshwar

Mouths of the Ganges

Nāndgaon

Durg

Mahānadi

Orissa

Irrawaddy

handrapur

Jagdalpur

Cuttack

Bhubaneshwar

Puri

Bay of
Bengal

arimnagar

ndhra Pradesh

Brahmapur

Srīkākulam

Vizianagaram

Visākhapatnam

5

arangal

Rājahmundry

Kākināda

Eastern Ghats

Godāvari

111

Mouths of the
Irrawaddy

E   F   G   H

ELEVATION

4 000 m
13 124 ft

2000 m
6562 ft

1000 m
3281 ft

500 m
1640 ft

250 m
820 ft

100 m
328 ft

Sea
Level

Sea
Level

-50 m
-164 ft

-100 m
-328 ft

-250 m
-820 ft

-500 m
-1640 ft

-1000 m
-3281 ft

-2000 m
-6562 ft

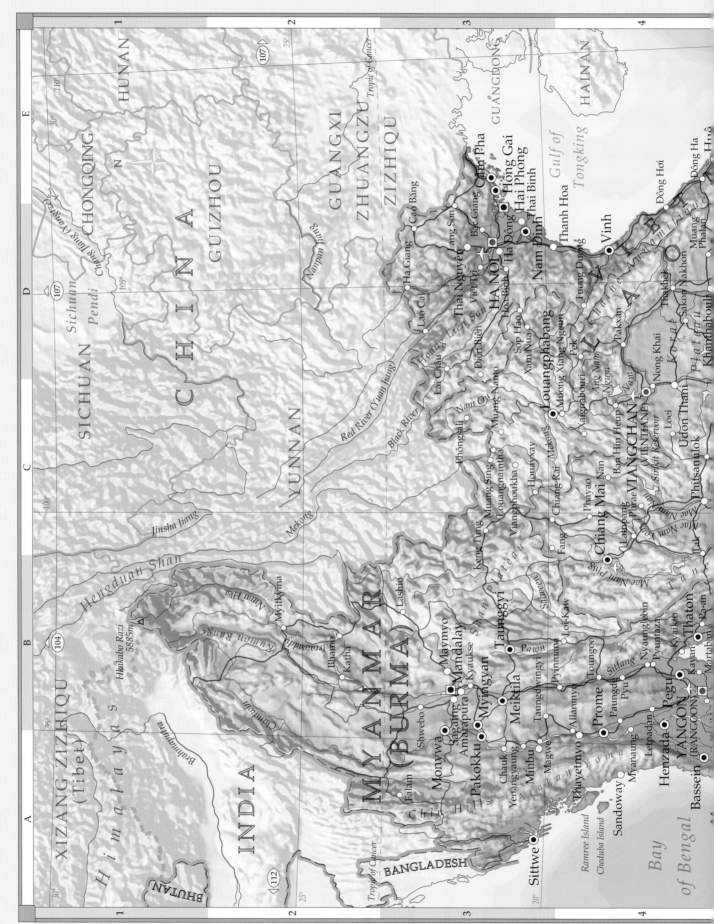

South China Sea

Kepulauan Natuna
(to Indonesia)

Mouths of the Mekong
Côn Dao

Mouths of the Irrawaddy

THAILAND

Nakhon Sawan
Nakhon
Ratchasima
Lop Buri
Sara Buri
Buriram
Surin
Ubon Ratchathani
Muang
Khôngxédôn
Pakxé
Champasak
Chon Buri
Samut Prakan
KRUNG
THEP
(BANGKOK)
Srinagarind
Reservoir
Ayutthaya
Ratchaburi
Phetchaburi
Nakhon Pathom
Ao Krung
Thep
Ban Hua Hin

Pattaya

CAMBODIA

Phumi
Sâmraông
Krâlănh
Bătdâmbâng
Rêăng Kesei
Bâvĕng
Chanthaburi
Pôŭthĭsăt
Moŭng Roĕsei
Krăvănh Ôdŏngk
Krâchéh
Stœ̆ng Trêng
Phumi Muang Không
Stœ̆ng Sên
Tônlé Srêpôk
Tônlé San
Vôŭng
Vôchôey
Samakkhixai
Phumi Prêk
Kâmpóng Thum
Kâmpóng Chhnăng
Suông
Kâmpóng Cham
Prey Vêng
Svay Riêng
Mekong
Kâmpôt
Kâmpóng Spœ̆
Kâmpóng Saôm
PHNUM PENH
Tuôl Sap
Chuor Phnum

Tônlé Sap
Ko Chang
Gulf of Thailand

VIETNAM

Tam Ky
Quảng Ngai
Quy Nhon
Tuy Hoa
Plây Cu
Vrôchey
Đi Linh
Nha Trang
Da Lat
Cam Ranh
Kâmpóng-Trâp Cham
Phan Rang-
Phan Thiết
Hô Chí Minh
Biên Hoa
Vung Tau
My Tho
Long
Xuyên
Ca Mau
Tra Vinh
Cân Tho
Sóc Trăng
Bac Liêu
Rach Gia
Châu Đôc
Vinh
Rach Gia

MALAYSIA

Narathiwat
Pattani
Yala
Songkhla
Hat Yai
Thale Luang
Phatthalung
Pak Phanang
Nakhon Si Thammarat
Thung Song
Surat Thani
Sichon
Ko Phangan
Ko Samui
Lang Suan
Chumphon
Ko Ta Ru Tao
Trang
Ko Lanta
Phuket
Ko Phuket
Phang-Nga
Ranong
Pulau Pinang
Pulau Langkawi

Malay Peninsula
Malay
Strait of Malacca

INDONESIA

Sumatera
(Sumatra)
Pulau Simeulue

Tavoy

Ye
Tenasserim
Mergui
Mali Kyun
Kadan Kyun
Daung Kyun
Letsôk-aw Kyun
Lanbi Kyun
Zadetkyi Kyun
Mergui Archipelago
Bilauktaung Range

Andaman Sea

Andaman Islands (to India)

North Andaman
Middle Andaman
South Andaman
Little Andaman
Car Nicobar

Nicobar Islands (to India)

Katchall Island
Little Nicobar
Great Nicobar

INDIAN OCEAN

ELEVATION

4 000 m	13 124 ft
2000 m	6562 ft
1000 m	3281 ft
500 m	1640 ft
250 m	820 ft
100 m	328 ft
Sea Level	Sea Level
-50 m	-164 ft
-100 m	-328 ft
-250 m	-820 ft
-500 m	-1640 ft
-1000 m	-3281 ft
-2000 m	-6562 ft

200

200

0 km

0 miles

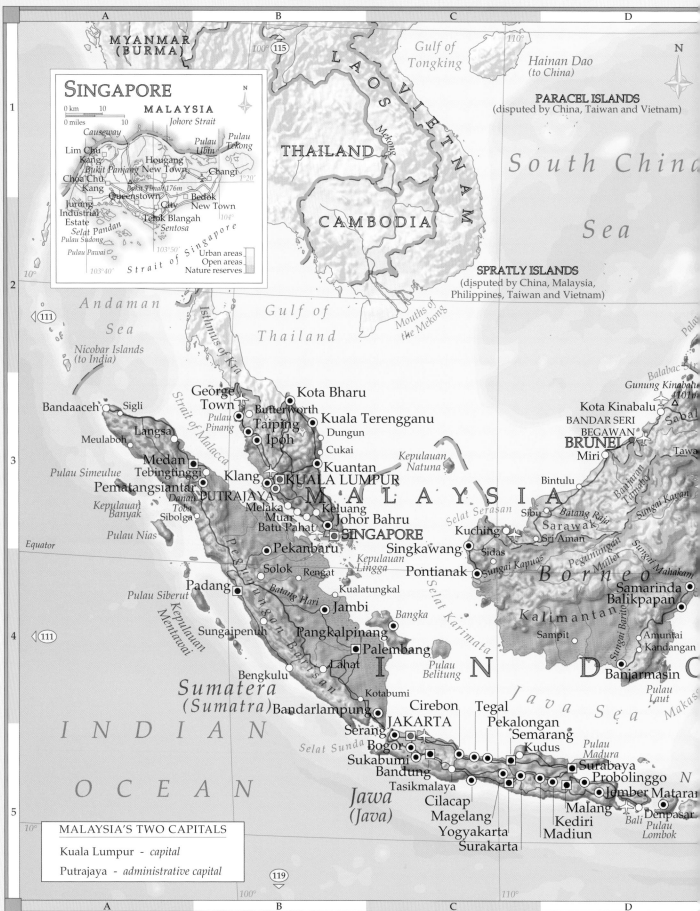

THE INDIAN OCEAN

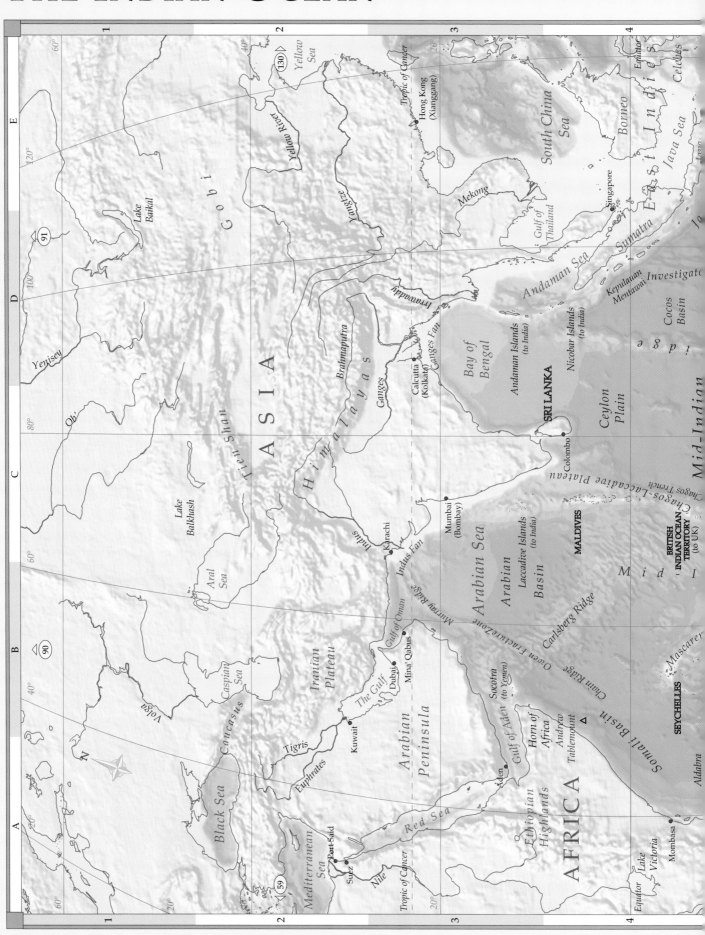

Yellow Sea

Gobi

Yellow River

Lake Baikal

Yenisey

Ob'

Tien Shan

A S I A

Hong Kong (Xianggang)

Tropic of Cancer

South China Sea

Borneo

East Indies

Celebes

Java Sea

Sumatra

Singapore

Mekong

Yangtze

Andaman Sea

Kepulauan Mentawai

Investigato

Cocos Basin

Irrawaddy

Brahmaputra

Himalayas

Ganges

Ganges Fan

Calcutta (Kolkata)

Bay of Bengal

Andaman Islands (to India)

Nicobar Islands (to India)

SRI LANKA

Ceylon Plain

Colombo

Mid-Indian

Chagos-Laccadive Plateau

Chagos Trench

Lake Balkhash

Aral Sea

Indus

Karachi

Indus Fan

Mumbai (Bombay)

Arabian Sea

Laccadive Islands (to India)

Arabian Basin

MALDIVES

BRITISH INDIAN OCEAN TERRITORY (to UK)

M i d - I

Caspian Sea

Volga

Iranian Plateau

The Gulf

Dubai

Mina' Qabus

Gulf of Oman

Murray Ridge

Carlsberg Ridge

Owen Fracture Zone

Chain Ridge

Somali Basin

Mascaren

SEYCHELLES

Caucasus

Black Sea

Tigris

Kuwait

Euphrates

Arabian Peninsula

Socotra (to Yemen)

Gulf of Aden

Horn of Africa

Andrew Tablemount

Ethiopian Highlands

AFRICA

Aden

Mediterranean Sea

Port Said

Suez

Nile

Red Sea

Tropic of Cancer

Equator

Lake Victoria

Mombasa

Aldabra

60°

40°

120°

100°

80°

60°

40°

20°

60°

20°

Equator

130

91

90

59

N

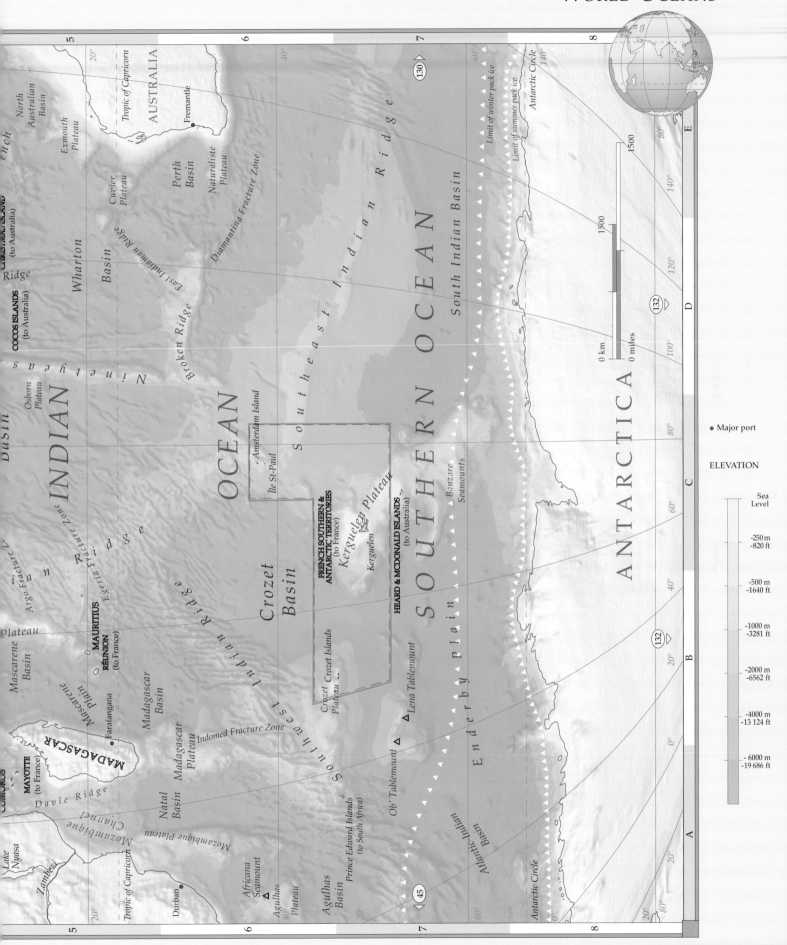

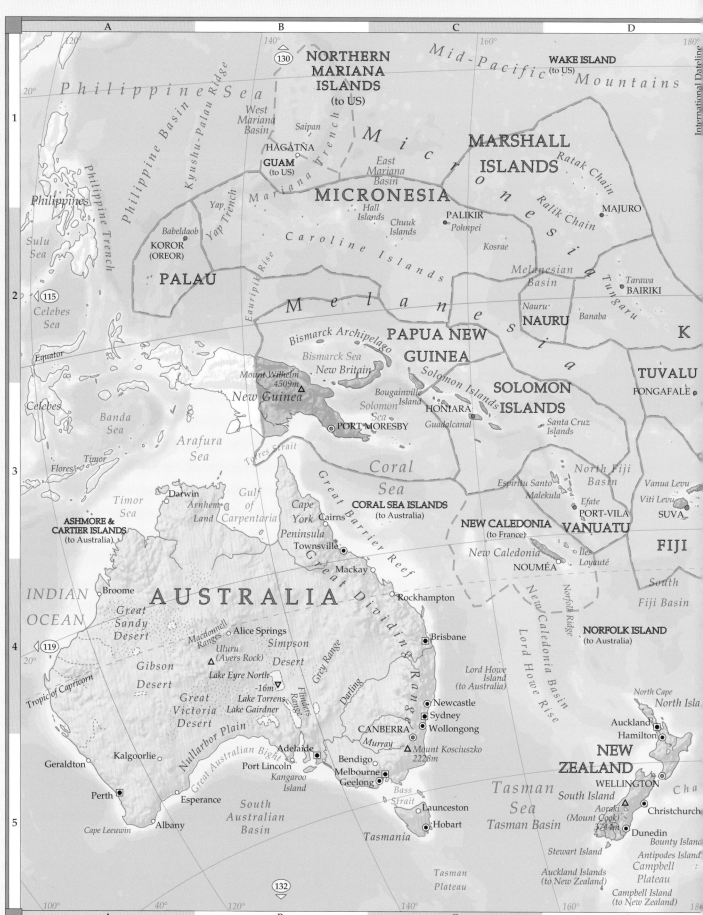

POPULATION

- ◉ Over 500,000
- ◉ 100,000 - 500,000
- ○ 50,000 - 100,000
- ○ Less than 50,000
- ● National capital

Map labels (A–D columns, 1–5 rows):

Philippine Sea · Philippine Basin · Kyushu-Palau Ridge · Mariana Trench · NORTHERN MARIANA ISLANDS (to US) · West Mariana Basin · Saipan · Micronesia · MARSHALL ISLANDS · WAKE ISLAND (to US) · Mid-Pacific Mountains · Ratak Chain · Philippine Trench · HAGÁTÑA · GUAM (to US) · East Mariana Basin · MICRONESIA · Ralik Chain · MAJURO · Yap · Yap Trench · Hall Islands · Chuuk Islands · PALIKIR · Pohnpei · Philippines · Babeldaob · KOROR (OREOR) · Caroline Islands · Kosrae · Sulu Sea · Eauripik Rise · PALAU · Melanesian Basin · Tarawa · BAIRIKI · Celebes Sea · Melanesia · Nauru · Banaba · Tungaru · NAURU · K · Equator · Bismarck Archipelago · PAPUA NEW GUINEA · Bismarck Sea · New Britain · Solomon Islands · SOLOMON ISLANDS · TUVALU · FONGAFALE · Celebes · Mount Wilhelm 4509m · New Guinea · Bougainville Island · Solomon Sea · HONIARA · Guadalcanal · Santa Cruz Islands · Banda Sea · PORT MORESBY · Timor · Flores · Arafura Sea · Torres Strait · Coral Sea · Espíritu Santo · North Fiji Basin · Vanua Levu · Viti Levu · Timor Sea · Darwin · Arnhem Land · Gulf of Carpentaria · Cape York · CORAL SEA ISLANDS (to Australia) · Malekula · Efate · SUVA · PORT-VILA · ASHMORE & CARTIER ISLANDS (to Australia) · Peninsula · Cairns · Great Barrier Reef · NEW CALEDONIA (to France) · VANUATU · FIJI · Townsville · New Caledonia · Îles Loyauté · NOUMÉA · South Fiji Basin · INDIAN OCEAN · Broome · Great Sandy Desert · Mackay · Great Dividing Range · Rockhampton · AUSTRALIA · New Caledonia Ridge · Norfolk Ridge · Lord Howe Basin · Macdonnell Ranges · Alice Springs · Simpson Desert · Brisbane · Lord Howe Island (to Australia) · NORFOLK ISLAND (to Australia) · Tropic of Capricorn · Gibson Desert · Uluru (Ayers Rock) · Grey Range · Lord Howe Rise · North Cape · Lake Eyre North -16m · Darling · Newcastle · North Island · Great Victoria Desert · Lake Torrens · Flinders Range · Sydney · Auckland · Lake Gairdner · Wollongong · Hamilton · Kalgoorlie · Nullarbor Plain · CANBERRA · Murray · Mount Kosciuszko 2228m · NEW ZEALAND · Geraldton · Adelaide · Bendigo · Melbourne · Geelong · Perth · Port Lincoln · Kangaroo Island · Bass Strait · WELLINGTON · Esperance · Great Australian Bight · Tasman Sea · South Island · Aoraki (Mount Cook) 3724m · Christchurch · Albany · South Australian Basin · Launceston · Tasman Basin · Dunedin · Cape Leeuwin · Hobart · Bounty Islands · Tasmania · Stewart Island · Antipodes Islands · Tasman Plateau · Auckland Islands (to New Zealand) · Campbell Plateau · Campbell Island (to New Zealand)

E   F   G   H

160°   140°   20°   120°

Hawaiian Islands (to US)

JOHNSTON ATOLL (to US)

Clarion Fracture Zone

1

PACIFIC

Central Pacific Basin

Christmas Ridge

KINGMAN REEF (to US)

OCEAN

PALMYRA ATOLL (to US)

Clipperton Fracture Zone

Teraina Tabuaeran

BAKER & HOWLAND ISLANDS (to US)

JARVIS ISLAND (to US)

Kiritimati

Line Islands

Equator

131

2

K I R I B A T I

Phoenix Islands

Malden Island
Starbuck Island

Galapagos Fracture Zone

TOKELAU (to NZ)

Northern Cook Islands   *Penrhyn*

Manihiki

Millennium Island
Flint Island

Marquesas Islands

...bie Ridge

WALLIS FUTUNA (to France)

SAMOA
Savai'i

Manihiki Plateau

Samoa Basin

Penrhyn Basin

Marquesas Fracture Zone

3

TĀ'UTU   *Upolu*
ĀPIA   ○**PAGO PAGO**

TONGA
Tutuila

AMERICAN SAMOA (to US)

COOK ISLANDS (to NZ)

Tuamotu Islands

Tiki Basin

Tuamotu Fracture Zone

Kava'u Group

NIUE (to NZ)

Society Islands

PAPEETE
Tahiti

KU'ALOFA

Southern Cook Islands

AVARUA
Rarotonga

FRENCH POLYNESIA
(to France)

Tonga Trench

Îles Australes

Austral Fracture Zone

131

Îles Gambier

PITCAIRN ISLANDS (to UK)
Pitcairn Island

20°

4

...rmadec Islands New Zealand)

Marotiri

Tropic of Capricorn

Kermadec Trench

Louisville Ridge

Southwest Pacific Basin

N

140°   120°

132

...a Rise
Chatham Islands (to New Zealand)

40°

P

0 km	1000

0 miles	1000

5

POLITICAL FEATURES

TOTAL AREA:
3,376,700 sq miles
(8,745,750 sq km)

TOTAL NUMBER OF COUNTRIES:
14

TOTAL POPULATION:
31.4 million

LARGEST CITY WITH POPULATION:
Sydney, Australia
4.25 million

COUNTRY WITH HIGHEST POPULATION DENSITY:
Nauru 1,522 people per sq mile
(599 people per sq km)

LARGEST COUNTRY:
Australia 2,967,892 sq miles
(7,686,850 sq km)

SMALLEST COUNTRY:
Nauru 8 sq miles
(21 sq km)

PHYSICAL FEATURES

LARGEST LAKE:
Lake Eyre, Australia
3,700 sq miles (9,583 sq km)

LONGEST RIVER:
Murray-Darling, Australia 2,330 miles
(3,750 km)

HIGHEST POINT:
Mt. Wilhelm Papua New Guinea
14,794 ft (4,509 m)

LOWEST POINT:
Lake Eyre, Australia
52 ft (16 m) below sea level

E   F   G   H

160°

THE SOUTHWEST PACIFIC

A   B   C   D

140°   150°   160°   170°

130

Saipan
Tinian
Rota
NORTHERN MARIANA ISLANDS (to US)

GUAM (to US)
HAGÁTÑA

MARSHALL ISLANDS

Enewetak Atoll
Bikini Atoll
Rongelap Atoll
Ailuk Atoll
Wotje Atoll
Maloelap
Ujelang Atoll
Kwajalein Atoll
Namu Atoll
Majuro Atoll
Ailinglaplap Atoll
Jaluit Atoll
Mili Atoll
Ebon Atoll

10°

Yap

MICRONESIA

Babeldaob
KOROR (OREOR)

PALAU

117

Caroline Islands

Chuuk Islands

PALIKIR
Pohnpei

Kosrae

Makin

Tarawa
BAIRIKI

Equator

Abemam
Nonout

NAURU

Banaba

Admiralty Islands
St. Matthias Group
Bismarck Archipelago
Bismarck Sea
New Ireland

New Guinea

Madang
Mount Wilhelm 4509m
Lae
PAPUA NEW GUINEA
New Britain

Bougainville Island

Choiseul
Santa Isabel
Malaita
SOLOMON ISLANDS

INDONESIA

Central Range

Owen Stanley Range
Gulf of Papua

PORT MORESBY

Solomon Sea

New Georgia Islands
HONIARA
Guadalcanal

Santa Cruz Islands

10°

Arafura Sea

D'Entrecasteaux Islands

Torres Strait

San Cristobal
Rennell

Louisiade Archipelago

Arnhem Land
Groote Eylandt
Gulf of Carpentaria

Cape York Peninsula

Coral Sea

Banks Islands

Espíritu Santo
Maéwo
Pentecost
Ambrym
Epi

124

Barkly Tableland

Great Barrier Reef

CORAL SEA ISLANDS (to Australia)

NEW CALEDONIA (to France)

Malekula
Efate
PORT-VILA
VANUATU
Erromango
Tanna
Aneityum

20°

NORTHERN

Tropic of Capricorn

TERRITORY

QUEENSLAND

Great Dividing Range

New Caledonia

Ouvéa
Îles Loyauté
Lifou
Maré

NOUMÉA

Macdonnell Ranges

AUSTRALIA

127

A   B   C   D

140°   150°   160°   170°

POPULATION

- ▣ Over 500,000
- ◉ 100,000 - 500,000
- ○ 50,000 - 100,000
- ∘ Less than 50,000
- ● National capital

180°   170°   160°   150°

N

International Dateline

131

0 km   750
0 miles   750

1

10°

PACIFIC OCEAN

ELEVATION

KINGMAN REEF
(to US)

PALMYRA ATOLL
(to US)

Teraina

Tabuaeran

131

4000 m
13 124 ft

BAKER & HOWLAND
ISLANDS
(to US)

JARVIS ISLAND
(to US)

Kiritimati
(Christmas Island)

2000 m
6562 ft

1000 m
3281 ft

2

Equator

Beru
Nikunau
mana
Arorae

K   I   R   I   B   A   T   I

Line Islands

500 m
1640 ft

Kanton
Birnie Island

Enderbury Island

McKean Island

Malden Island

250 m
820 ft

Nikumaroro

Orona   Manra

Starbuck Island

100 m
328 ft

anumea Atoll
Niutao
Nanumaga
Nui Atoll
Nukufetau
Funafuti
Atoll
Nukulaelae

Phoenix Islands

P
o
l
y
n
e
s
i
a

3

FONGAFALE

Atafu Atoll

Nukunonu
Atoll

TOKELAU
(to New Zealand)

Fakaofo Atoll

Rakahanga

Penrhyn

Vostok Island

Millennium
Island

Sea
Level

Sea
Level

10°

Niulakita

Manihiki

-250 m
-820 ft

TUVALU

WALLIS &
FUTUNA
(to France)

AMERICAN
SAMOA
(to US)

Northern Cook
Islands

Flint Island

otuma

Île Uvea
MATA'UTU

SAMOA

Savai'i   ĀPIA
PAGO PAGO

-500 m
-1640 ft

Île Futuna

Upolu
Tutuila

Ta'ū

COOK
ISLANDS
(to New Zealand)

-1000 m
-3281 ft

131

4

Cikobia

Niuatoputapu

Vanua Levu

TONGA

Raiatea

PAPEETE

Îles Tuamotu

Nadi
Viti
Levu

SUVA

Lau Group

Vava'u
Group

Palmerston

Manuae

Archipel de la Société

Tahiti

-2000 m
-6562 ft

-4000 m
-13124 ft

Kadavu

ALOFI

Southern Cook
Islands

Takutea

20°

Tofua

Ha'apai
Group

-6000 m
-19 686 ft

FIJI

NUKU'ALOFA

Tongatapu
'Eua

NIUE
(to New Zealand)

AVARUA

Rarotonga

Mangaia

FRENCH POLYNESIA
(to France)

Tongatapu
Group

Îles Australes

Tropic of Capricorn

International Dateline

5

131

Marotiri

180°   170°   160°   150°

WESTERN AUSTRALIA

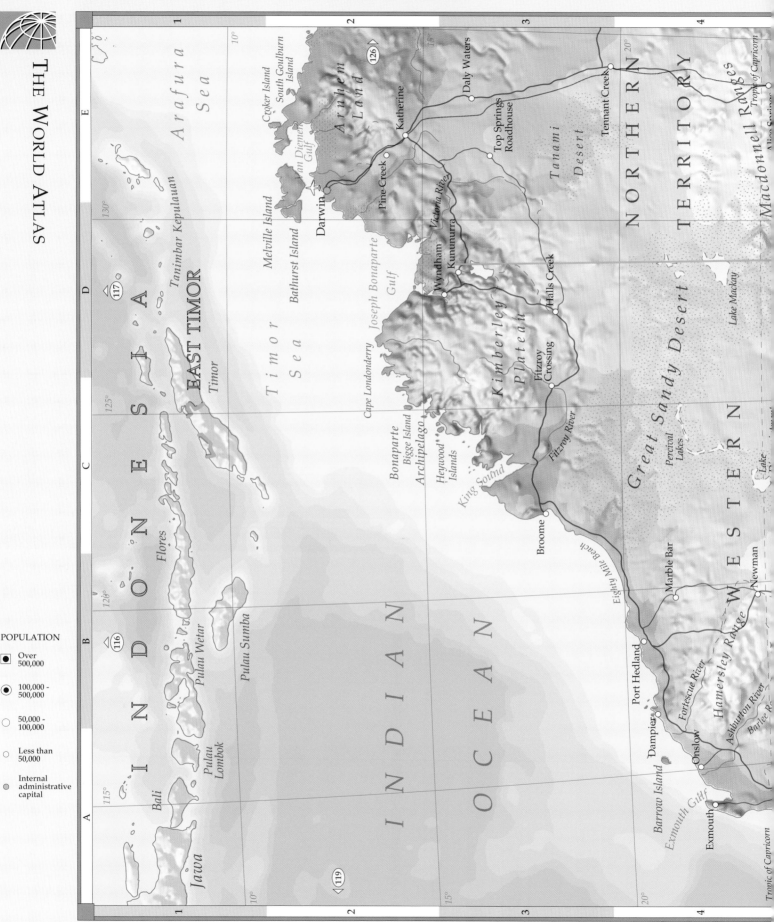

POPULATION

- ■ Over 500,000
- ◉ 100,000 - 500,000
- ○ 50,000 - 100,000
- ○ Less than 50,000
- ● Internal administrative capital

Arafura Sea

Tanimbar Kepulauan

EAST TIMOR

Timor

INDONESIA

Bali

Flores

Pulau Wetar

Pulau Sumba

Pulau Lombok

Jawa

Timor Sea

Melville Island

Croker Island

South Goulburn Island

Bathurst Island

Van Diemen Gulf

Arnhem Land

Darwin

Pine Creek

Katherine

Daly Waters

Top Springs Roadhouse

Tanami Desert

Tennant Creek

NORTHERN TERRITORY

Macdonnell Ranges

Tropic of Capricorn

Alice Springs

Joseph Bonaparte Gulf

Cape Londonderry

Victoria River

Kununurra

Wyndham

Halls Creek

Kimberley Plateau

Fitzroy Crossing

Fitzroy River

Great Sandy Desert

Lake Mackay

Percival Lakes

Lake

Bonaparte Archipelago

Bigge Island

Heywood Islands

King Sound

Broome

Eighty Mile Beach

INDIAN OCEAN

Port Hedland

Marble Bar

Newman

Hamersley Range

WESTERN

Dampier

Onslow

Fortescue River

Ashburton River

Barlee R.

Barrow Island

Exmouth Gulf

Exmouth

Tropic of Capricorn

115° 120° 125° 130°

10° 15° 20°

ELEVATION

4000 m
13 124 ft

2000 m
6562 ft

1000 m
3281 ft

500 m
1640 ft

250 m
820 ft

100 m
328 ft

Sea Level — Sea Level

-250 m
-820 ft

-500 m
-1640 ft

-1000 m
-3281 ft

-2000 m
-6562 ft

-3000 m
-9843 ft

-4000 m
-13 124 ft

AUSTRALIA

SOUTH AUSTRALIA

Musgrave Ranges

Uluru (Ayers Rock)
△ 867m

Great Victoria Desert

Coober Pedy

Tarcoola

Lake Everard

Penong

Lake Gairdner

Ceduna

Elliston

Port Lincoln

Eucla

Great Australian Bight

Nullarbor Plain

Reid

INDIAN OCEAN

Zanthus

Balladonia

Lake Rebecca

Lake Carey

Kalgoorlie

Coolgardie

Lake Cowan

Norseman

Esperance

Lake Wells

Lake Carnegie

Robinson Range

Meekatharra

Mount Magnet

Lake Barlee

Lake Moore

Southern Cross

Merredin

Northam

Brookton

Narrogin

Wagin

Katanning

Collie

Manjimup

Albany

Gascoyne River

Murchison River

Carnarvon

Bernier Island

Dorre Island

Shark Bay

Dirk Hartog Island

Denham

Kalbarri

Geraldton

Moora

Gingin

Perth

Fremantle

Rockingham

Mandurah

Bunbury

Busselton

Augusta

0 km

0 miles

400

400

N

Eastern Australia

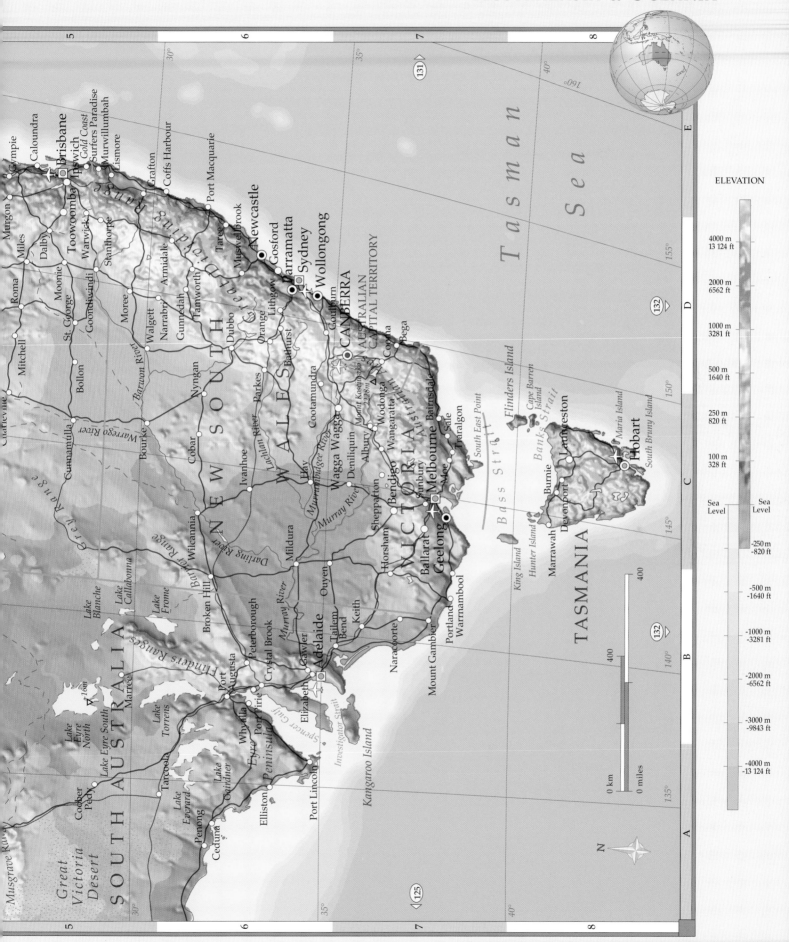

ELEVATION

4000 m	13 124 ft
2000 m	6562 ft
1000 m	3281 ft
500 m	1640 ft
250 m	820 ft
100 m	328 ft
Sea Level	Sea Level
-250 m	-820 ft
-500 m	-1640 ft
-1000 m	-3281 ft
-2000 m	-6562 ft
-3000 m	-9843 ft
-4000 m	-13 124 ft

NEW ZEALAND

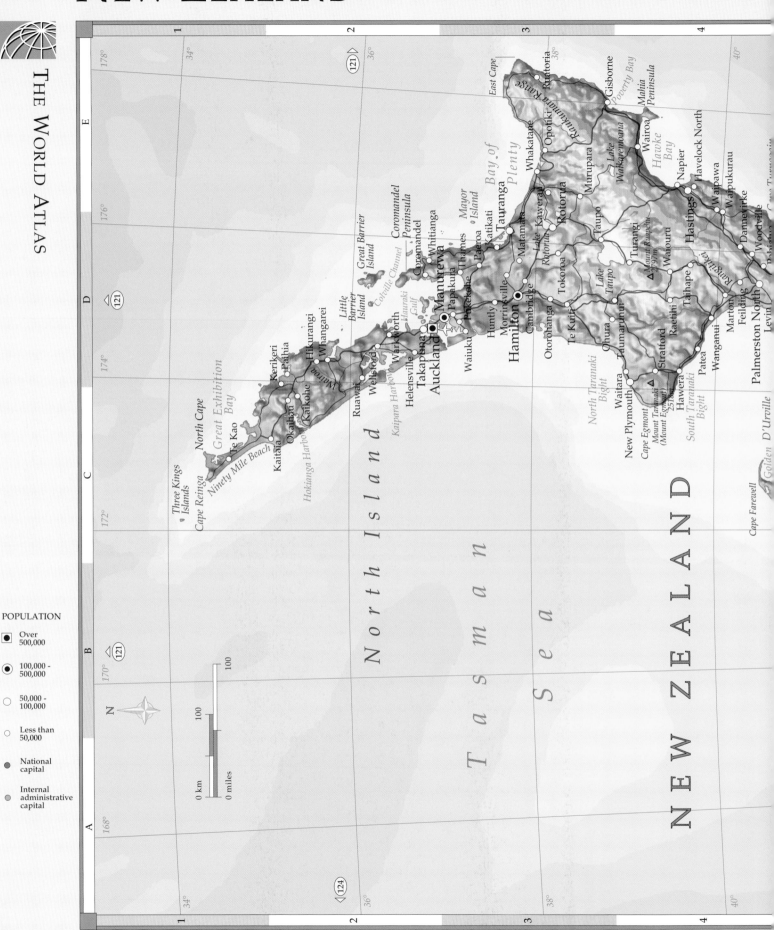

POPULATION

- Over 500,000
- 100,000 – 500,000
- 50,000 – 100,000
- Less than 50,000
- National capital
- Internal administrative capital

N

100

100

0 km

0 miles

Three Kings Islands

Cape Reinga

North Cape

Te Kao

Great Exhibition Bay

Ninety Mile Beach

Kaitaia

Okaihau

Kaikohe

Kerikeri

Pahia

Hokianga Harbour

Hikurangi

Whangarei

Wairoa

Ruawai

Dargaville

Kaipara Harbour

Warkworth

Helensville

Takapuna

Auckland

Manukau

Waiuku

Pukekohe

Papakura

Huntly

Morrinsville

Hamilton

Cambridge

Te Kuiti

Otorohanga

Waitara

New Plymouth

Cape Egmont

Mount Taranaki (Mount Egmont) 2518m

Hawera

Stratford

Ohura

Taumarunui

Mount Ruapehu 2797m

Turangi

Raetihi

Waiouru

Taihape

Patea

Wanganui

Marton

Feilding

Palmerston North

Levin

North Taranaki Bight

South Taranaki Bight

North Island

Little Barrier Island

Great Barrier Island

Coromandel Peninsula

Coromandel

Whitianga

Thames

Paeroa

Katikati

Tauranga

Matamata

Kawerau

Lake Rotorua

Rotorua

Lake Rotoiti

Tokoroa

Lake Taupo

Taupo

Whakatane

Opotiki

Murupara

Lake Waikaremoana

Wairoa

Mahia Peninsula

Napier

Hastings

Havelock North

Waipawa

Waipukurau

Dannevirke

Woodville

Mayor Island

Bay of Plenty

East Cape

Gisborne

Poverty Bay

Raukumara Range

Ruatoria

Hauraki Gulf

Coville Channel

Kaiwaka

Hawke Bay

Rangitikei

Cape Farewell

Golden D'Urville

Tasman Sea

NEW ZEALAND

ELEVATION

4000 m	13 124 ft
2000 m	6562 ft
1000 m	3281 ft
500 m	1640 ft
250 m	820 ft
100 m	328 ft
Sea Level	Sea Level
-250 m	-820 ft
-500 m	-1640 ft
-1000 m	-3281 ft
-2000 m	-6562 ft
-3000 m	-9843 ft
-4000 m	-13 124 ft

South Island

PACIFIC OCEAN

Lower Hutt
WELLINGTON
Porirua
Cape Palliser
Cape Campbell
Seddon
Clarence
Blenheim
Kaikoura
Kaikoura Peninsula
Nelson
Picton
Moutere
Richmond
Mount Owen 1875m
Richmond Range
Murchison
Cheviot
Hanmer Springs
Springs Junction
Waipara
Rangiora
Kaiapoi
Christchurch
Lyttelton
Banks Peninsula
Pegasus Bay
Otira
Arthur's Pass 920m
Oxford
Darfield
Ashburton
Lake Brunner
Reefton
Hinds
Canterbury Plains
Canterbury Bight
Seddonville
Westport
Cape Foulwind
Karamea Bight
Runanga
Greymouth
Hokitika
Ross
Rakaia
Mayfield
Geraldine
Temuka
Timaru
Studholme
Oamaru
Hampden
Abut Head
Whataroa
Fox Glacier
Aoraki (Mount Cook) 3744m
Mount Cook
Fairlie
Waimate
Waitaki
Jackson Head
Haast
Lake Pukaki
Lake Hawea
Wanaka
Lake Wanaka
Lake Wakatipu
Queenstown
Cromwell
Alexandra
Lumsden
Lake Te Anau
Lake Manapouri
Milford Sound
Milford
George Sound
Caswell Sound
Lake Monowai
Lake Hauroka
Resolution Island
West Cape
Mataura
Eyre Mts
Livingstone Mts
Clutha
Lake Wakatipu
Winton
Riverton
Waiau
Gore
Mataura
Invercargill
Tokanui
Toetoes Bay
Foveaux Strait
Codfish Island
Halfmoon Bay
Ruapuke Island
Stewart Island
South West Cape
Muttonbird Islands
Te Waewae Bay
Mosgiel
Milton
Clutha
Balclutha
Dunedin
Otago Peninsula
Lake Ellesmere

THE PACIFIC OCEAN

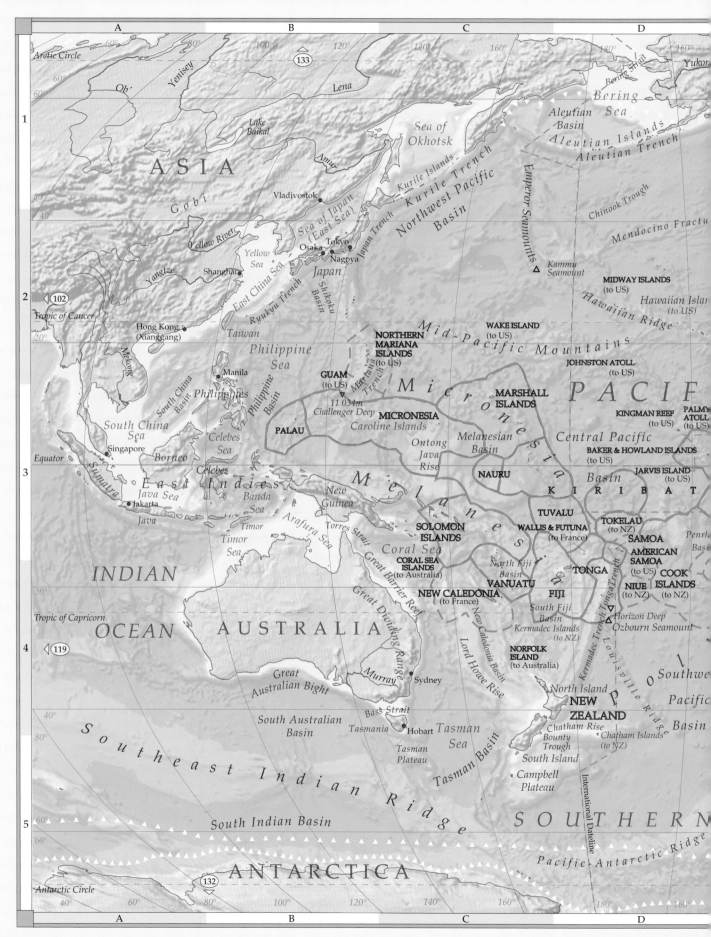

ASIA

Arctic Circle

Ob'
Yenisey
Lena

Lake Baikal

Sea of Okhotsk

Bering Strait

Yukon

Bering Sea

Aleutian Basin

Aleutian Islands

Aleutian Trench

Gobi

Vladivostok

Kurile Islands

Kurile Trench

Northwest Pacific Basin

Emperor Seamounts

Chinook Trough

Mendocino Fracture

Sea of Japan (East Sea)

Yellow River

Tokyo

Osaka

Nagoya

Japan

Japan Trench

Kammu Seamount

MIDWAY ISLANDS (to US)

Hawaiian Islands (to US)

Yellow Sea

Shikoku Basin

Shanghai

Yangtze

Ryukyu Trench

East China Sea

Mid-Pacific Mountains

Hawaiian Ridge

Tropic of Cancer

Hong Kong (Xianggang)

Taiwan

Philippine Sea

WAKE ISLAND (to US)

NORTHERN MARIANA ISLANDS (to US)

JOHNSTON ATOLL (to US)

PACIFIC

Mekong

Manila

Philippines

Philippine Basin

GUAM (to US)

11 034m Challenger Deep

Mariana Trench

Micronesia

MARSHALL ISLANDS

KINGMAN REEF (to US)

PALMYRA ATOLL (to US)

South China Basin

South China Sea

PALAU

MICRONESIA

Caroline Islands

Melanesian Basin

Central Pacific

Singapore

Celebes Sea

Borneo

Ontong Java Rise

NAURU

KIRIBATI

Basin

BAKER & HOWLAND ISLANDS (to US)

JARVIS ISLAND (to US)

Equator

Sumatra

Java Sea

Celebes

East Indies

Melanesia

New Guinea

TUVALU

WALLIS & FUTUNA (to France)

TOKELAU (to NZ)

Jakarta

Banda Sea

SOLOMON ISLANDS

SAMOA

Penrhyn Basin

Java

Timor

Arafura Sea

Torres Strait

Great Barrier Reef

Coral Sea

North Fiji Basin

AMERICAN SAMOA (to US)

Timor Sea

CORAL SEA ISLANDS (to Australia)

VANUATU

TONGA

COOK ISLANDS (to NZ)

INDIAN

NEW CALEDONIA (to France)

FIJI

NIUE (to NZ)

Tropic of Capricorn

AUSTRALIA

Great Dividing Range

New Caledonia Basin

South Fiji Basin

Kermadec Islands (to NZ)

Horizon Deep

Ozbourn Seamount

OCEAN

NORFOLK ISLAND (to Australia)

Great Australian Bight

Murray

Sydney

Lord Howe Rise

North Island

Southwest Pacific Basin

South Australian Basin

Bass Strait

Tasmania

Hobart

Tasman Sea

NEW ZEALAND

Chatham Rise

Bounty Trough

Chatham Islands (to NZ)

Tasman Plateau

Tasman Basin

South Island

Campbell Plateau

South Indian Basin

SOUTHERN

Southeast Indian Ridge

International Dateline

Pacific-Antarctic Ridge

Antarctic Circle

ANTARCTICA

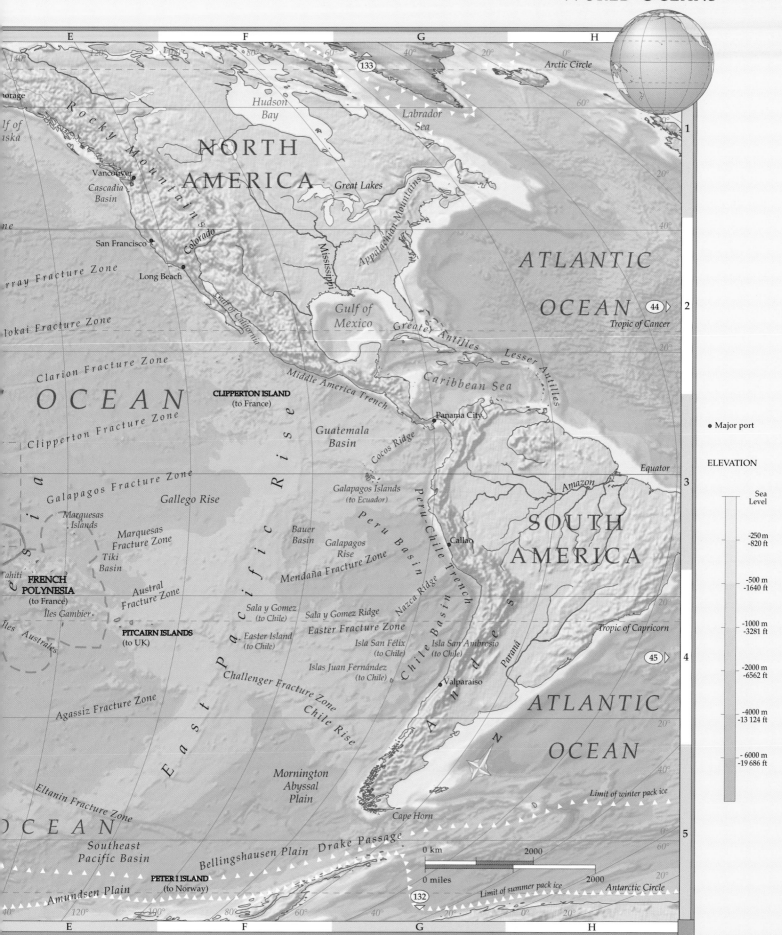

NORTH AMERICA

SOUTH AMERICA

ATLANTIC OCEAN

OCEAN

Hudson Bay

Labrador Sea

Arctic Circle

Rocky Mountains

Great Lakes

Vancouver

Cascadia Basin

San Francisco

Long Beach

Colorado

Mississippi

Appalachian Mountains

Gulf of California

Gulf of Mexico

Greater Antilles

Caribbean Sea

Lesser Antilles

Panama City

Tropic of Cancer

Murray Fracture Zone

Molokai Fracture Zone

Clarion Fracture Zone

CLIPPERTON ISLAND (to France)

Middle America Trench

Clipperton Fracture Zone

Guatemala Basin

Cocos Ridge

Galapagos Fracture Zone

Gallego Rise

Galapagos Islands (to Ecuador)

Peru Basin

Equator

Amazon

Marquesas Islands

Marquesas Fracture Zone

Tiki Basin

Bauer Basin

Galapagos Rise

Callao

East Pacific Rise

Peru-Chile Trench

Tahiti

FRENCH POLYNESIA (to France)

Îles Gambier

Austral Fracture Zone

Mendaña Fracture Zone

Sala y Gomez (to Chile)

Sala y Gomez Ridge

Easter Fracture Zone

Nazca Ridge

Tropic of Capricorn

Îles Australes

PITCAIRN ISLANDS (to UK)

Easter Island (to Chile)

Isla San Félix (to Chile)

Isla San Ambrosio (to Chile)

Chile Basin

Andes

Paraná

Islas Juan Fernández (to Chile)

Valparaiso

Challenger Fracture Zone

Chile Rise

ATLANTIC OCEAN

Agassiz Fracture Zone

Eltanin Fracture Zone

Mornington Abyssal Plain

Cape Horn

OCEAN

Southeast Pacific Basin

Bellingshausen Plain

Drake Passage

PETER I ISLAND (to Norway)

Amundsen Plain

Limit of winter pack ice

Limit of summer pack ice

Antarctic Circle

• Major port

ELEVATION

Sea Level

-250 m / -820 ft

-500 m / -1640 ft

-1000 m / -3281 ft

-2000 m / -6562 ft

-4000 m / -13 124 ft

-6000 m / -19 686 ft

0 km   2000

0 miles   2000

N

ANTARCTICA

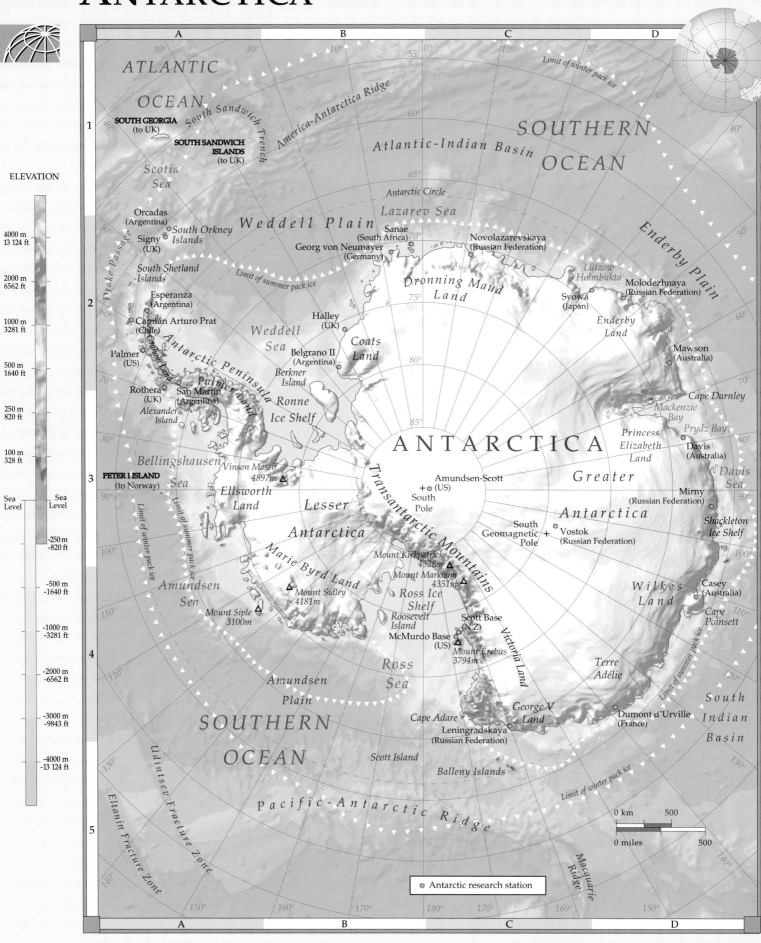

ELEVATION

4000 m	13 124 ft
2000 m	6562 ft
1000 m	3281 ft
500 m	1640 ft
250 m	820 ft
100 m	328 ft
Sea Level	Sea Level
-250 m	-820 ft
-500 m	-1640 ft
-1000 m	-3281 ft
-2000 m	-6562 ft
-3000 m	-9843 ft
-4000 m	-13 124 ft

ATLANTIC OCEAN

SOUTHERN OCEAN

SOUTH GEORGIA (to UK)

SOUTH SANDWICH ISLANDS (to UK)

South Sandwich Trench

America-Antarctica Ridge

Atlantic-Indian Basin

Scotia Sea

Antarctic Circle

Lazarev Sea

Weddell Plain

Enderby Plain

Orcadas (Argentina)

South Orkney Islands

Signy (UK)

Sanae (South Africa)

Georg von Neumayer (Germany)

Novolazarevskaya (Russian Federation)

Drake Passage

South Shetland Islands

Limit of summer pack ice

Dronning Maud Land

Lützow Holmbukta

Molodezhnaya (Russian Federation)

Syowa (Japan)

Enderby Land

Esperanza (Argentina)

Halley (UK)

Capitán Arturo Prat (Chile)

Weddell Sea

Coats Land

Mawson (Australia)

Palmer (US)

Antarctic Peninsula

Belgrano II (Argentina)

Berkner Island

Cape Darnley

Rothera (UK)

Graham Land

Palmer Land

Ronne Ice Shelf

Mackenzie Bay

Prydz Bay

San Martín (Argentina)

Alexander Island

Princess Elizabeth Land

Davis (Australia)

Bellingshausen Sea

Vinson Massif 4897m △

Davis Sea

PETER I ISLAND (to Norway)

Ellsworth Land

ANTARCTICA

Greater Antarctica

Mirny (Russian Federation)

Amundsen-Scott (US)

South Pole

Lesser Antarctica

Transantarctic Mountains

South Geomagnetic Pole +

Vostok (Russian Federation)

Shackleton Ice Shelf

Limit of winter pack ice

Limit of summer pack ice

Marie Byrd Land

Mount Kirkpatrick 4528m △

Mount Sidley 4181m △

Mount Markham 4351m △

Wilkes Land

Casey (Australia)

Amundsen Sea

Ross Ice Shelf

Cape Poinsett

Mount Siple 3100m △

Roosevelt Island

Scott Base (N.Z.)

McMurdo Base (US)

Mount Erebus 3794m

Victoria Land

Terre Adélie

Amundsen Plain

Ross Sea

SOUTHERN OCEAN

Cape Adare

George V Land

Dumont d'Urville (France)

South Indian Basin

Leningradskaya (Russian Federation)

Scott Island

Balleny Islands

Udintsev Fracture Zone

Eltanin Fracture Zone

Pacific-Antarctic Ridge

Limit of winter pack ice

Macquarie Ridge

| 0 km | 500 |
| 0 miles | 500 |

● Antarctic research station

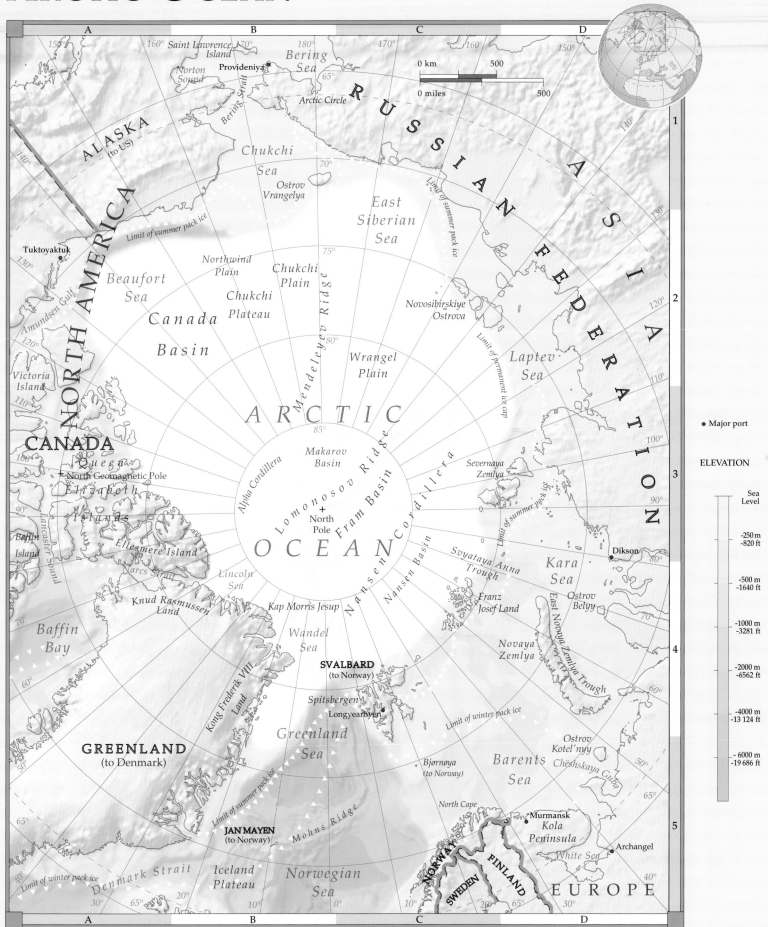

ALASKA (to US)

NORTH AMERICA

Saint Lawrence Island

Norton Sound

Providenya

Bering Sea

R U S S I A N

Arctic Circle

Chukchi Sea

Ostrov Vrangelya

East Siberian Sea

Limit of summer pack ice

Tuktoyaktuk

Beaufort Sea

Northwind Plain

Chukchi Plain

Canada Basin

Chukchi Plateau

Novosibirskiye Ostrova

F E D E R A T I O N

Limit of permanent ice cap

Laptev Sea

Victoria Island

Wrangel Plain

Mendeleyev Ridge

CANADA

A R C T I C

Makarov Basin

Severnaya Zemlya

Queen

North Geomagnetic Pole

Elizabeth

Alpha Cordillera

Lomonosov Ridge

North Pole

Fram Basin

Nansen Cordillera

Limit of summer pack ice

Islands

Kara Sea

Dikson

Baffin Island

OCEAN

Ostrov Belyy

Lancaster Sound

Ellesmere Island

Nares Strait

Lincoln Sea

Knud Rasmussen Land

Kap Morris Jesup

Nansen Basin

Svyataya Anna Trough

Franz Josef Land

East Novaya Zemlya Trough

Baffin Bay

Kong Frederik VIII Land

Wandel Sea

SVALBARD (to Norway)

Novaya Zemlya

Ostrov Kotel'nyy

GREENLAND (to Denmark)

Spitsbergen

Longyearbyen

Greenland Sea

Limit of winter pack ice

Bjørnøya (to Norway)

Barents Sea

Chëshskaya Guba

North Cape

Limit of summer pack ice

JAN MAYEN (to Norway)

Mohns Ridge

Murmansk

Kola Peninsula

White Sea

Archangel

Limit of winter pack ice

Denmark Strait

Iceland Plateau

Norwegian Sea

NORWAY

SWEDEN

FINLAND

EUROPE

0 km 500
0 miles 500

● Major port

ELEVATION

Sea Level

-250 m -820 ft

-500 m -1640 ft

-1000 m -3281 ft

-2000 m -6562 ft

-4000 m -13 124 ft

- 6000 m -19 686 ft

OVERSEAS TERRITORIES AND DEPENDENCIES (sidebar)

OVERSEAS TERRITORIES AND DEPENDENCIES

DESPITE THE RAPID PROCESS of decolonization since the end of the Second World War, around 10 million people in more than 50 territories around the world continue to live under the protection of France, Australia, the Netherlands, Denmark, Norway, New Zealand, the United Kingdom or the USA. These remnants of former colonial empires may have persisted for economic, strategic or political reasons, and are administered in a variety of ways.

AUSTRALIA

ASHMORE & CARTIER ISLANDS
Indian Ocean
Status External territory
Claimed 1978
Capital *not applicable*
Population None
Area 2 sq miles (5.2 sq km)

 CHRISTMAS ISLAND
Indian Ocean
Status External territory
Claimed 1958
Capital Flying Fish Cove
Population 1,275
Area 52 sq miles (134.6 sq km)

COCOS ISLANDS
Indian Ocean
Status External territory
Claimed 1955
Capital No official capital
Population 670
Area 5.5 sq miles (14.24 sq km)

CORAL SEA ISLANDS
South Pacific
Status External territory
Claimed 1969
Capital None
Population 8 (meteorologists)
Area Less than 1.16 sq miles (3 sq km)

HEARD & MCDONALD ISLANDS
Indian Ocean
Status External territory
Claimed 1947
Capital *not applicable*
Population None
Area 161 sq miles (417 sq km)z

 NORFOLK ISLAND
South Pacific
Status External territory
Claimed 1774
Capital Kingston
Population 2,181
Area 13.3 sq miles (34.4 sq km)

DENMARK

 FAEROE ISLANDS
North Atlantic
Status External territory
Claimed 1380
Capital Tórshavn
Population 43,382
Area 540 sq miles (1,399 sq km)

 GREENLAND
North Atlantic
Status External territory
Claimed 1380
Capital Nuuk
Population 56,076
Area 840,000 sq miles (2,175,516 sq km)

FRANCE

CLIPPERTON ISLAND
East Pacific
Status Dependency of French Polynesia
Claimed 1930
Capital *not applicable*
Population None
Area 2.7 sq miles (7 sq km)

FRENCH GUIANA South America
Status Overseas department
Claimed 1817
Capital Cayenne
Population 152,300
Area 35,135 sq miles (90,996 sq km)

 FRENCH POLYNESIA
South Pacific
Status Overseas territory
Claimed 1843
Capital Papeete
Population 219,521
Area 1,608 sq miles (4,165 sq km)

GUADELOUPE West Indies
Status Overseas department
Claimed 1635
Capital Basse-Terre
Population 419,500
Area 687 sq miles (1,780 sq km)

MARTINIQUE West Indies
Status Overseas department
Claimed 1635
Capital Fort-de-France
Population 381,200
Area 425 sq miles (1,100 sq km)

MAYOTTE Indian Ocean
Status Territorial collectivity
Claimed 1843
Capital Mamoudzou
Population 131,320
Area 144 sq miles (374 sq km)

NEW CALEDONIA South Pacific
Status Overseas territory
Claimed 1853
Capital Nouméa
Population 196,836
Area 7,374 sq miles (19,103 sq km)

RÉUNION Indian Ocean
Status Overseas department
Claimed 1638
Capital Saint-Denis
Population 697,000
Area 970 sq miles (2,512 sq km)

ST. PIERRE & MIQUELON
North America
Status Territorial collectivity
Claimed 1604
Capital Saint-Pierre
Population 6,600
Area 93.4 sq miles (242 sq km)

WALLIS & FUTUNA
South Pacific
Status Overseas territory
Claimed 1842
Capital Matā'Utu
Population 15,000
Area 106 sq miles (274 sq km)

NETHERLANDS

 ARUBA
West Indies
Status Autonomous part of the Netherlands
Claimed 1643
Capital Oranjestad
Population 88,000
Area 75 sq miles (194 sq km)

 NETHERLANDS ANTILLES
West Indies
Status Autonomous part of the Netherlands
Claimed 1816
Capital Willemstad
Population 207,175
Area 308 sq miles (800 sq km)

NEW ZEALAND

 COOK ISLANDS
South Pacific
Status Associated territory
Claimed 1901
Capital Avarua
Population 20,200
Area 113 sq miles (293 sq km)

 NIUE
South Pacific
Status Associated territory
Claimed 1901
Capital Alofi
Population 2,080
Area 102 sq miles (264 sq km)

TOKELAU
South Pacific
Status Dependent territory
Claimed 1926
Capital *not applicable*
Population 1,577
Area 4 sq miles (10.4 sq km)

NORWAY

BOUVET ISLAND
South Atlantic
Status Dependency
Claimed 1928
Capital *not applicable*
Population None
Area 22 sq miles (58 sq km)**JAN MAYEN**
North Atlantic
Status Dependency
Claimed 1929
Capital *not applicable*
Population None
Area 147 sq miles (381 sq km)

PETER I ISLAND
Southern Ocean
Status Dependency
Claimed 1931
Capital *not applicable*
Population None
Area 69 sq miles (180 sq km)

SVALBARD Arctic Ocean
Status Dependency
Claimed 1920
Capital Longyearbyen
Population 3,231
Area 24,289 sq miles (62,906 sq km)

UNITED KINGDOM

 ANGUILLA
West Indies
Status Dependent territory
Claimed 1650
Capital The Valley
Population 10,300
Area 37 sq miles (96 sq km)

ASCENSION ISLAND
South Atlantic
Status Dependency of St. Helena
Claimed 1673
Capital Georgetown
Population 1,099
Area 34 sq miles (88 sq km)

 BERMUDA
North Atlantic
Status Crown colony
Claimed 1612
Capital Hamilton
Population 60,144
Area 20.5 sq miles (53 sq km)

BRITISH INDIAN OCEAN TERRITORY Indian Ocean
Status Dependent territory
Claimed 1814
Capital Diego Garcia
Population 930
Area 23 sq miles (60 sq km)

 BRITISH VIRGIN ISLANDS West Indies
Status Dependent territory
Claimed 1672
Capital Road Town
Population 17,896
Area 59 sq miles (153 sq km)

 CAYMAN ISLANDS West Indies
Status Dependent territory
Claimed 1670
Capital George Town
Population 35,000
Area 100 sq miles (259 sq km)

 FALKLAND ISLANDS South Atlantic
Status Dependent territory
Claimed 1832
Capital Stanley
Population 2,564
Area 4,699 sq miles (12,173 sq km)

 GIBRALTAR Southwest Europe
Status Crown colony
Claimed 1713
Capital Gibraltar
Population 27,086
Area 2.5 sq miles (6.5 sq km)

 GUERNSEY Channel Islands
Status Crown dependency
Claimed 1066
Capital St Peter Port
Population 56,681
Area 25 sq miles (65 sq km)

 ISLE OF MAN British Isles
Status Crown dependency
Claimed 1765
Capital Douglas
Population 71,714
Area 221 sq miles (572 sq km)

 JERSEY Channel Islands
Status Crown dependency
Claimed 1066
Capital St. Helier
Population 85,150
Area 45 sq miles (116 sq km)

 MONTSERRAT West Indies
Status Dependent territory
Claimed 1632
Capital Plymouth (uninhabited)
Population 2,850
Area 40 sq miles (102 sq km)

 PITCAIRN ISLANDS South Pacific
Status Dependent territory
Claimed 1887
Capital Adamstown
Population 55
Area 1.35 sq miles (3.5 sq km)

 ST. HELENA South Atlantic
Status Dependent territory
Claimed 1673
Capital Jamestown
Population 6,472
Area 47 sq miles (122 sq km)

SOUTH GEORGIA & THE SOUTH SANDWICH ISLANDS South Atlantic
Status Dependent territory
Capital *not applicable*
Claimed 1775
Population No permanent residents
Area 1,387 sq miles (3,592 sq km)

TRISTAN DA CUNHA South Atlantic
Status Dependency of St. Helena
Claimed 1612
Capital Edinburgh
Population 297
Area 38 sq miles (98 sq km)

 **TURKS & CAICOS ISLANDS** West Indies
Status Dependent territory
Claimed 1766
Capital Cockburn Town
Population 13,800
Area 166 sq miles (430 sq km)

NORWAY

 AMERICAN SAMOA South Pacific
Status Unincorporated territory
Claimed 1900
Capital Pago Pago
Population 60,000
Area 75 sq miles (195 sq km)

BAKER & HOWLAND ISLANDS South Pacific
Status Unincorporated territory
Claimed 1856
Capital *not applicable*
Population None
Area 0.54 sq miles (1.4 sq km)

 GUAM West Pacific
Status Unincorporated territory
Claimed 1898
Capital Hagåtña
Population 149,249
Area 212 sq miles (549 sq km)

JARVIS ISLAND South Pacific
Status Unincorporated territory
Claimed 1856
Capital *not applicabl*
Population None
Area 1.7 sq miles (4.5 sq km)

 NORTHERN MARIANA ISLANDS West Pacific
Status Commonwealth territory
Claimed 1947
Capital Saipan
Population 58,846
Area 177 sq miles (457 sq km)

 PALMYRA ATOLL Central Pacific
Status Unincorporated territory
Claimed 1898
Capital *not applicable*
Population None
Area 5 sq miles (12 sq km)

 PUERTO RICO West Indies
Status Commonwealth territory
Claimed 1898
Capital San Juan
Population 3.8 million
Area 3,458 sq miles (8,959 sq km)

VIRGIN ISLANDS West Indies
Status Unincorporated territory
Claimed 1917
Capital Charlotte Amalie
Population 101,809
Area 137 sq miles (355 sq km)

WAKE ISLAND Central Pacific
Status Unincorporated territory
Claimed 1898
Capital *not applicable*
Population 302
Area 2.5 sq miles (6.5 sq km)

COUNTRY PROFILES

THIS FACTFILE IS INTENDED as a guide to a world that is continually changing as political fashions and personalities come and go. Nevertheless, all the material in these factfiles has been researched from the most up-to-date and authoritative sources to give an incisive portrait of the geographical, political, and social characteristics that make each country so unique.

There are currently 193 independent countries in the world - more than at any previous time - and 59 dependencies. Antarctica is the only land area on Earth that is not officially part of, and does not belong to, any single country.

AFGHANISTAN

Page 100 D4

In 2001, following a US-led offensive, the hard-line Muslim taliban *militia was replaced by a new interim government under Hamid Karazi*

Official name Islamic State of Afghanistan
Formation 1919
Capital Kabul
Population 23.9 million / 95 people per sq mile (37 people per sq km)
Total area 250,000 sq. miles (647,500 sq. km)
Languages Pashtu, Tajik, Dari, Farsi, Uzbek, Turkmen
Religions Sunni Muslim 84%, Shi'a Muslim 15%, other 1%
Ethnic mix Pashtun 38%, Tajik 25%, Hazara 19%, other 18%
Government Transitional regime
Currency New afghani = 100 puls
Literacy rate 36%
Calorie consumption 1539 calories

ALBANIA

Page 79 C6

Lying at the southeastern end of the Adriatic Sea, Albania held its first multiparty elections in 1991, after nearly five decades of communism.

Official name Republic of Albania
Formation 1912
Capital Tirana
Population 3.2 million / 302 people per sq mile (117 people per sq km)
Total area 11,100 sq. miles (28,748 sq. km)
Languages Albanian, Greek
Religions Sunni Muslim 70%, Orthodox Christian 20%, Roman Catholic 10%
Ethnic mix Albanian 86%, Greek 12%, other 2%
Government Parliamentary system
Currency Lek = 100 qindarka (qintars)
Literacy rate 99%
Calorie consumption 2900 calories

ALGERIA

Page 48 C3

Algeria achieved independence from France in 1962. Today, its military-dominated government faces a severe challenge from Islamic extremists.

Official name People's Democratic Republic of Algeria
Formation 1962
Capital Algiers
Population 31.8 million / 35 people per sq mile (13 people per sq km)
Total area 919,590 sq. miles (2,381,740 sq. km)
Languages Arabic, Tamazight (Kabyle, Shawia, Tamashek), French
Religions Sunni Muslim 99%, Christian and Jewish 1%
Ethnic mix Arab 75%, Berber 24%, European and Jewish 1%
Government Presidential system
Currency Algerian dinar = 100 centimes
Literacy rate 69%
Calorie consumption 2987 calories

ANDORRA

Page 69 B6

A tiny landlocked principality, Andorra lies high in the eastern Pyrenees between France and Spain. It held its first full elections in 1993.

Official name Principality of Andorra
Formation 1278
Capital Andorra la Vella
Population 69,150 / 384 people per sq mile (149 people per sq km)
Total area 181 sq. miles (468 sq. km)
Languages Spanish, Catalan, French, Portuguese
Religions Roman Catholic 94%, other 6%
Ethnic mix Spanish 46%, Andorran 28%, French 8%, other 18%
Government Parliamentary system
Currency Euro = 100 cents
Literacy rate 99%
Calorie consumption Not available

ANGOLA

Page 56 B2

Located in southwest Africa, Angola has been in a state of civil war following its independence from Portugal, except for a brief period from 1994–98.

Official name Republic of Angola
Formation 1975
Capital Luanda
Population 13.6 million / 28 people per sq mile (11 people per sq km)
Total area 481,351 sq. miles (1,246,700 sq. km)
Languages Portuguese, Umbundu, Kimbundu, Kikongo
Religions Roman Catholic 50%, Protestant 20%, other 30%
Ethnic mix Ovimbundu 37%, other 25%, Kimbundu 25%, Bakongo 13%
Government Presidential system
Currency Readjusted kwanza = 100 lwei
Literacy rate 40%
Calorie consumption 1953 calories

ANTIGUA & BARBUDA

Page 33 H3

Lying on the Atlantic edge of the Leeward Islands, Antigua and Barbuda's area includes the uninhabited islet of Redonda.

Official name Antigua and Barbuda
Formation 1981
Capital St. John's
Population 67,897 / 399 people per sq mile (154 people per sq km)
Total area 170 sq. miles (442 sq. km)
Languages English, English patois
Religions Anglican 45%, Other Protestant 42%, Roman Catholic 10%, Rastafarian 1%, other 2%
Ethnic mix Black African 95%, other 5%
Government Parliamentary system
Currency Eastern Caribbean dollar = 100 cents
Literacy rate 87%
Calorie consumption 2381 calories

ARGENTINA

Page 43 B5

Most of the southern half of South America is occupied by Argentina. The country returned to civilian rule in 1983 after a series of military coups.

Official name Republic of Argentina
Formation 1816
Capital Buenos Aires
Population 38.4 million / 36 people per sq mile (14 people per sq km)
Total area 1,068,296 sq. miles (2,766,890 sq. km)
Languages Spanish, Italian, Amerindian languages
Religions Roman Catholic 90%, Protestant 2%, Jewish 2%, other 6%
Ethnic mix Indo-European 83%, Mestizo 14%, Jewish 2%, Amerindian 1%
Government Presidential system
Currency Argentine peso = 100 centavos
Literacy rate 97%
Calorie consumption 3171 calories

ARMENIA

Page 95 F3

Smallest of the former USSR's republics, Armenia lies in the Lesser Caucasus mountains. Territorial war with Azerbaijan ended in a 1994 ceasefire.

Official name Republic of Armenia
Formation 1991
Capital Yerevan
Population 3.1 million / 269 people per sq mile (104 people per sq km)
Total area 11,506 sq. miles (29,800 sq. km)
Languages Armenian, Azeri, Russian
Religions Armenian Apostolic Church (Orthodox) 94%, other 6%
Ethnic mix Armenian 93%, Azeri 3%, Russian 2%, other 2%
Government Presidential system
Currency Dram = 100 luma
Literacy rate 99%
Calorie consumption 1991 calories

AUSTRALIA

Page 120 A4

An island continent located between the Indian and Pacific oceans, Australia was settled by Europeans 200 years ago, but now has many Asian immigrants.

Official name Commonwealth of Australia
Formation 1901
Capital Canberra
Population 19.7 million / 7 people per sq mile (3 people per sq km)
Total area 2,967,893 sq. miles (7,686,850 sq. km)
Languages English, Italian, Cantonese, Greek, Arabic, Vietnamese, Aboriginal languages
Religions Christian 64%, Other 36%
Ethnic mix European 92%, Asian 5%, Aboriginal and other 3%
Government Parliamentary system
Currency Australian dollar = 100 cents
Literacy rate 99%
Calorie consumption 3126 calories

AUSTRIA

Page 73 D7

Bordering eight countries in the heart of Europe, Austria was created in 1920 after the collapse of the Austro-Hungarian Empire the previous year.

Official name Republic of Austria
Formation 1918
Capital Vienna
Population 8.1 million / 254 people per sq mile (98 people per sq km)
Total area 32,378 sq. miles (83,858 sq. km)
Languages German, Croatian, Slovenian, Hungarian (Magyar)
Religions Roman Catholic 78%, Nonreligious 9%, Other (including Jewish and Muslim) 8%, Protestant 5%
Ethnic mix Austrian 93%, Croat, Slovene, and Hungarian 6%, other 1%
Government Parliamentary system
Currency Euro = 100 cents
Literacy rate 99%
Calorie consumption 3799 calories

AZERBAIJAN

Page 95 G2

Situated on the western coast of the Caspian Sea, Azerbaijan was the first Soviet republic to declare independence from Moscow in 1991.

Official name Republic of Azerbaijan
Formation 1991
Capital Baku
Population 8.4 million / 251 people per sq mile (97 people per sq km)
Total area 33,436 sq. miles (86,600 sq. km)
Languages Azeri, Russian
Religions Shi'a Muslim 68%, Sunni Muslim 26%, Russian Orthodox 3%, Armenian Apostolic Church (Orthodox) 2%, other 1%
Ethnic mix Azeri 90%, Dagestani 3%, Russian 3%, Armenian 2%, other 2%
Government Presidential system
Currency Manat = 100 gopik
Literacy rate 97%
Calorie consumption 2474 calories

BAHAMAS

Page 32 C1

Located in the western Atlantic, off the Florida coast, the Bahamas comprise some 700 islands and 2,400 cays, only 30 of which are inhabited.

Official name Commonwealth of the Bahamas
Formation 1973
Capital Nassau
Population 314,000 / 81 people per sq mile (31 people per sq km)
Total area 5382 sq. miles (13,940 sq. km)
Languages English, English Creole, French Creole
Religions Baptist 32%, Anglican 20%, Roman Catholic 19%, other 17%, Methodist 6%, Church of God 6%
Ethnic mix Black African 85%, other 15%
Government Parliamentary system
Currency Bahamian dollar = 100 cents
Literacy rate 96%
Calorie consumption 2777 calories

BAHRAIN

Page 98 C4

Bahrain is an archipelago of 33 islands between the Qatar peninsula and the Saudi Arabian mainland. Only three of these islands are inhabited.

Official name Kingdom of Bahrain
Formation 1971
Capital Manama
Population 724,000 / 2652 people per sq mile (1025 people per sq km)
Total area 239 sq. miles (620 sq. km)
Languages Arabic
Religions Muslim (mainly Shi'a) 99%, other 1%
Ethnic mix Bahraini 70%, Iranian, Indian, and Pakistani 24%, Other Arab 4%, European 2%
Government Monarchy
Currency Bahraini dinar = 1000 fils
Literacy rate 89%
Calorie consumption Not available

BANGLADESH

Page 113 G3

Bangladesh lies at the north of the Bay of Bengal. It seceded from Pakistan in 1971 and, after much political instability, returned to democracy in 1991.

Official name People's Republic of Bangladesh
Formation 1971
Capital Dhaka
Population 147 million / 2837 people per sq mile (1096 people per sq km)
Total area 55,598 sq. miles (144,000 sq. km)
Languages Bengali, Urdu, Chakma, Marma (Magh), Garo, Khasi, Santhali, Tripuri, Mro
Religions Muslim (mainly Sunni) 87%, Hindu 12%, other 1%
Ethnic mix Bengali 98%, other 2%
Government Parliamentary system
Currency Taka = 100 poisha
Literacy rate 41%
Calorie consumption 2187 calories

BELGIUM

Page 65 B6

Located in northwestern Europe, Belgium's history has been marked by the division between its Flemish- and French-speaking communities.

Official name Kingdom of Belgium
Formation 1830
Capital Brussels
Population 10.3 million / 813 people per sq mile (314 people per sq km)
Total area 11,780 sq. miles (30,510 sq. km)
Languages Dutch, French, German
Religions Roman Catholic 88%, Muslim 2%, other 10%
Ethnic mix Fleming 58%, Walloon 33%, other 6%, Italian 2%, Moroccan 1%
Government Parliamentary system
Currency Euro = 100 cents
Literacy rate 99%
Calorie consumption 3682 calories

BHUTAN

Page 113 G3

The landlocked Buddhist kingdom of Bhutan is perched in the eastern Himalayas between India and China. Gradual reforms protect its cultural identity.

Official name Kingdom of Bhutan
Formation 1656
Capital Thimphu
Population 2.3 million / 127 people per sq mile (49 people per sq km)
Total area 18,147 sq. miles (47,000sq. km)
Languages Dzongkha, Nepali, Assamese
Religions Mahayana Buddhist 70%, Hindu 24%, other 6%
Ethnic mix Bhute 50%, Nepalese 25%, other 25%
Government Monarchy
Currency Ngultrum = 100 chetrum
Literacy rate 47%
Calorie consumption Not available

BOTSWANA

Page 56 C3

Once the British protectorate of Bechuanaland, Botswana lies landlocked in southern Africa. Diamonds provide it with a prosperous economy.

Official name Republic of Botswana
Formation 1966
Capital Gaborone
Population 1.8 million / 8 people per sq mile (3 people per sq km)
Total area 231,803 sq. miles (600,370 sq. km)
Languages Setswana, English, Shona, San, Khoikhoi, isiNdebele
Religions Traditional beliefs 50%, Christian (mainly Protestant) 30%, Other (including Muslim) 20%
Ethnic mix Tswana 98%, other 2%
Government Presidential system
Currency Pula = 100 thebe
Literacy rate 79%
Calorie consumption 2292 calories

BARBADOS

Page 33 H4

Barbados is the most easterly of the Caribbean Windward Islands. Under British rule for 339 years, it became fully independent in 1966.

Official name Barbados
Formation 1966
Capital Bridgetown
Population 270,000 / 1627 people per sq mile (628 people per sq km)
Total area 166 sq. miles (430 sq. km)
Languages Bajan (Barbadian English), English
Religions Anglican 40%, Nonreligious 17%, Pentecostal 8%, Methodist 7%, Roman Catholic 4%, other 24%
Ethnic mix Black African 90%, other 10%
Government Parliamentary system
Currency Barbados dollar = 100 cents
Literacy rate 99%
Calorie consumption 2992 calories

BELIZE

Page 30 B1

The last Central American country to gain independence, this former British colony lies on the eastern shore of the Yucatan Peninsula.

Official name Belize
Formation 1981
Capital Belmopan
Population 256,000 / 29 people per sq mile (11 people per sq km)
Total area 8867 sq. miles (22,966 sq.km)
Languages English Creole, Spanish, English, Mayan, Garifuna (Carib)
Religions Roman Catholic 62%, Anglican 12%, Methodist 6%, Mennonite 4%, other 17%
Ethnic mix Mestizo 44%, Creole 30%, Maya 11%, Garifuna 7%, Asian Indian 4%, other 4%
Government Parliamentary system
Currency Belizean dollar = 100 cents
Literacy rate 77%
Calorie consumption 2886 calories

BOLIVIA

Page 39 F3

Bolivia lies landlocked high in central South America. Mineral riches once made it the region's wealthiest state. Today, it is the poorest.

Official name Republic of Bolivia
Formation 1825
Capital La Paz (administrative); Sucre (judicial)
Population 8.8 million / 21 people per sq mile (8 people per sq km)
Total area 424,162 sq. miles (1,098,580 sq. km)
Languages Aymara, Quechua, Spanish
Religions Roman Catholic 93%, other 7%
Ethnic mix Quechua 37%, Aymara 32%, Mixed race 13%, European 10%, other 8%
Government Presidential system
Currency Boliviano = 100 centavos
Literacy rate 87%
Calorie consumption 2267 calories

BRAZIL

Page 40 C2

Brazil covers more than half of South America and is the site of the world's largest rain forest. The country has immense natural resources.

Official name Federative Republic of Brazil
Formation 1822
Capital Brasília
Population 179 million / 55 people per sq mile (21 people per sq km)
Total area 3,286,470 sq. miles (8,511,965 sq. km)
Languages Portuguese, German, Italian, Spanish, Polish, Japanese.
Religions Roman Catholic 74%, Protestant 15%, Atheist 7%, other 4%,
Ethnic mix Black 53%, Mixed race 40%, White 6%, other 1%
Government Presidential system
Currency Real = 100 centavos
Literacy rate 86%
Calorie consumption 3002 calories

BELARUS

Page 85 B6

Formerly known as White Russia, Belarus lies landlocked in eastern Europe. The country reluctantly became independent of the USSR in 1991.

Official name Republic of Belarus
Formation 1991
Capital Minsk
Population 9.9 million / 124 people per sq mile (48 people per sq km)
Total area 80,154 sq. miles (207,600 sq. km)
Languages Belarussian, Russian
Religions Orthodox Christian 60%, Roman Catholic 8%, other 32%
Ethnic mix Belarussian 78%, Russian 13%, Polish 4%, Ukrainian 3%, other 2%
Government Presidential system
Currency Belarussian rouble = 100 kopeks
Literacy rate 99%
Calorie consumption 2925 calories

BENIN

Page 53 F4

Stretching north from the West African coast, Benin became one of the pioneers of African democratization in 1990, ending years of military rule.

Official name Republic of Benin
Formation 1960
Capital Porto-Novo
Population 6.7 million / 157 people per sq mile (61 people per sq km)
Total area 43,483 sq. miles (112,620 sq. km)
Languages Fon, Bariba, Yoruba, Adja, Houeda, Somba, French
Religions Voodoo 50%, Muslim 30%, Christian 20%
Ethnic mix Fon 47%, Adja 12%, Bariba 10%, other 31%
Government Presidential system
Currency CFA franc = 100 centimes
Literacy rate 40%
Calorie consumption 2455 calories

BOSNIA & HERZEGOVINA

Page 78 B3

At the heart of the western Balkans, Bosnia and Herzegovina was the focus of the bitter conflict surrounding the breakup of former Yugoslavia.

Official name Bosnia and Herzegovina
Formation 1992
Capital Sarajevo
Population 4.2 million / 213 people per sq mile (82 people per sq km)
Total area 19,741 sq. miles (51,129 sq. km)
Languages Serbo-Croat
Religions Muslim (mainly Sunni) 40%, Orthodox Christian 31%, Roman Catholic 15%, Protestant 4%, other 10%
Ethnic mix Bosniak 48%, Serb 38%, Croat 14%
Government Parliamentary system
Currency Marka = 100 pfeninga
Literacy rate 95%
Calorie consumption 2845 calories

BRUNEI

Page 116 D3

Lying on the northwestern coast of the island of Borneo, Brunei is surrounded and divided in two by the Malaysian state of Sarawak.

Official name Sultanate of Brunei
Formation 1984
Capital Bandar Seri Begawan
Population 358,000 / 176 people per sq mile (68 people per sq km)
Total area 2228 sq. miles (5770 sq. km)
Languages Malay, English, Chinese
Religions Muslim (mainly Sunni) 66%, Buddhist 14%, Christian 10%, other 10%
Ethnic mix Malay 67%, Chinese 16%, Indigenous 6%, other 11%
Government Monarchy
Currency Brunei dollar = 100 cents
Literacy rate 94%
Calorie consumption 2814 calories

BULGARIA

Page 82 C2

Located in southeastern Europe, Bulgaria has made slow progress toward democracy since the fall of its communist regime in 1990.

Official name Republic of Bulgaria
Formation 1908
Capital Sofia
Population 7.9 million / 185 people per sq mile (71 people per sq km)
Total area 42,822 sq. miles (110,910 sq. km)
Languages Bulgarian, Turkish, Romani
Religions Orthodox Christian 83%, Muslim 12%, other 4%, Roman Catholic 1%
Ethnic mix Bulgarian 84%, Turkish 9%, Roma 5%, other 2%
Government Parliamentary system
Currency Lev = 100 stotinki
Literacy rate 99%
Calorie consumption 2626 calories

BURKINA FASO

Page 53 E4

Known as Upper Volta until 1984, the West African state of Burkina Faso has been under military rule for most of its post-independence history.

Official name Burkina Faso
Formation 1960
Capital Ouagadougou
Population 13 million / 123 people per sq mile (47 people per sq km)
Total area 105,869 sq. miles (274,200 sq. km)
Languages Mossi, Fulani, French, Tuareg, Dyula, Songhai
Religions Muslim 55%, Traditional beliefs 35%, Roman Catholic 9%, other Christian 1%
Ethnic mix Mossi 50%, other 50%
Government Presidential system
Currency CFA franc = 100 centimes
Literacy rate 25%
Calorie consumption 2485 calories

BURUNDI

Page 51 B7

Small, landlocked Burundi lies just south of the Equator, on the Nile-Congo watershed in Central Africa. Since 1993 it has been marked by violent ethnic conflict.

Official name Republic of Burundi
Formation 1962
Capital Bujumbura
Population 6.8 million / 687 people per sq mile (265 people per sq km)
Total area 10,745 sq. miles (27,830 sq. km)
Languages Kirundi, French, Kiswahili
Religions Christian (mainly Roman Catholic) 60%, Traditional beliefs 39%, Muslim 1%
Ethnic mix Hutu 85%, Tutsi 14%, Twa 1%
Government Transitional regime
Currency Burundi franc = 100 centimes
Literacy rate 50%
Calorie consumption 1612 calories

CAMBODIA

Page 115 D5

Located in mainland Southeast Asia, Cambodia has emerged from two decades of civil war and invasion from Vietnam.

Official name Kingdom of Cambodia
Formation 1953
Capital Phnom Penh
Population 14.1 million / 207 people per sq mile (80 people per sq km)
Total area 69,900 sq. miles (181,040 sq. km)
Languages Khmer, French, Chinese, Vietnamese, Cham
Religions Buddhist 93%, Muslim 6%, Christian 1%
Ethnic mix Khmer 90%, Vietnamese 4%, Chinese 1%, other 5%
Government Parliamentary system
Currency Riel = 100 sen
Literacy rate 69%
Calorie consumption 1967 calories

CAMEROON

Page 54 A4

Situated on the central West African coast, Cameroon was effectively a one-party state for 30 years. Multiparty elections were held in 1992.

Official name Republic of Cameroon
Formation 1960
Capital Yaoundé
Population 16 million /89 people per sq mile (34 people per sq km)
Total area 183,567 sq. miles (475,400 sq. km)
Languages Bamileke, Fang, Fulani, French, English
Religions Traditional beliefs 25%, Christian 53%, Muslim 22%.
Ethnic mix Cameroon highlanders 31%, Equatorial Bantu 19%, Kirdi 11%, other 21%
Government Presidential system
Currency CFA franc = 100 centimes
Literacy rate 68%
Calorie consumption 2242 calories

CANADA

Page 15 E4

Canada extends from its US border norh to the Arctic Ocean. In recent years, French-speaking Quebec has sought independence from the rest of the country.

Official name Canada
Formation 1867
Capital Ottawa
Population 31.5 million / 9 people per sq mile (3 people per sq km)
Total area 3,717,792 sq. miles (9,984,670 sq. km)
Languages English, French, Chinese, Italian, German, Ukrainian, Inuktitut,
Religions Roman Catholic 44%, Protestant 29%, nonreligious 27%
Ethnic mix British origin 44%, French origin 25%, other European 20%, other 11%
Government Parliamentary system
Currency Canadian dollar = 100 cents
Literacy rate 99%
Calorie consumption 3176 calories

CAPE VERDE

Page 52 A2

Off the west coast of Africa, in the Atlantic Ocean, lies the group of islands that make up Cape Verde, a Portuguese colony until 1975.

Official name Republic of Cape Verde
Formation 1975
Capital Praia
Population 463,000 / 298 people per sq mile (115 people per sq km)
Total area 1557 sq. miles (4033 sq. km)
Languages Portuguese Creole, Portuguese
Religions Roman Catholic 97%, other 3%
Ethnic mix Mestiço 60%, African 30%, other 10%
Government Mixed presidential–parliamentary system
Currency Cape Verde escudo = 100 centavos
Literacy rate 76%
Calorie consumption 3308 calories

CENTRAL AFRICAN REPUBLIC

Page 54 C4

This landlocked country lies between the basins of the Chad and Congo rivers. Its arid north sustains less than 2% of the population.

Official name Central African Republic
Formation 1960
Capital Bangui
Population 3.9 million / 16 people per sq mile (6 people per sq km)
Total area 240,534 sq. miles (622,984 sq. km)
Languages Sango, Banda, Gbaya, French
Religions Traditional beliefs 60%, Christian 35%, Muslim 5%
Ethnic mix Baya 34%, Banda 27%, Mandjia 21%, Sara 10%, other 8%
Government Transitional regime
Currency CFA franc = 100 centimes
Literacy rate 49%
Calorie consumption 1949 calories

CHAD

Page 54 C3

Landlocked in north central Africa, Chad has been torn by intermittent periods of civil war since it gained independence from France in 1960.

Official name Republic of Chad
Formation 1960
Capital N'Djamena
Population 8.6 million / 18 people per sq mile (7 people per sq km)
Total area 495,752 sq. miles (1,284,000 sq. km)
Languages French, Sara, Arabic, Maba
Religions Muslim 55%, Traditional beliefs 35%, Christian 10%
Ethnic mix Nomads (Tuareg and Toubou) 38%, Sara 30%, other 17%, Arab 15%
Government Presidential system
Currency CFA franc = 100 centimes
Literacy rate 46%
Calorie consumption 2245 calories

CHILE

Page 42 B3

Chile extends in a ribbon down the west coast of South America. It returned to democracy in 1989 after a referendum rejected its military dictator.

Official name Republic of Chile
Formation 1818
Capital Santiago
Population 15.8 million / 55 people per sq mile (21 people per sq km)
Total area 292,258 sq. miles (756,950 sq. km)
Languages Spanish, Amerindian languages
Religions Roman Catholic 80%, other and nonreligious 20%
Ethnic mix Mixed race and European 90%, Amerindian 10%
Government Presidential system
Currency Chilean peso = 100 centavos
Literacy rate 96%
Calorie consumption 2868 calories

CHINA

Page 104 C4

This vast East Asian country was dominated by Mao Zedong, who founded the Communist republic, and Deng Xiaoping, his successor (1976–1997).

Official name People's Republic of China
Formation 960
Capital Beijing
Population 1.3 billion / 362 people per sq mile (140 people per sq km)
Total area 3,705,386 sq. miles (9,596,960 sq. km)
Languages Mandarin, Wu, Cantonese, Hsiang, Min, Hakka, Kan
Religions Nonreligious 59%, Traditional beliefs 20%, other 13%, Buddhist 6%, Muslim 2%
Ethnic mix Han 92%, other 8%,
Government One-party state
Currency Renminbi (Yuan) = 10 jiao
Literacy rate 91%
Calorie consumption 2963 calories

COLOMBIA

Page 36 B3

Lying in northwest South America, Colombia is one of the world's most violent countries, with powerful drugs cartels and guerrilla activity.

Official name Republic of Colombia
Formation 1819
Capital Bogotá
Population 44.2 million / 110 people per sq mile (43 people per sq km)
Total area 439,733 sq. miles (1,138,910 sq. km)
Languages Spanish, Wayuu, Páez, and other Amerindian languages
Religions Roman Catholic 95%, other 5%
Ethnic mix Mestizo 58%, White 20%, other 22%
Government Presidential system
Currency Colombian peso = 100 centavos
Literacy rate 92%
Calorie consumption 2580 calories

COMOROS

Page 57 F2

In the Indian Ocean, between Mozambique and Madagascar, lie the Comoros, comprising three main islands, and a number of smaller islets.

Official name Union of the Comoros
Formation 1975
Capital Moroni
Population 768,000 / 892 people per sq mile (344 people per sq km)
Total area 838 sq. miles (2170 sq. km)
Languages Arabic, Comoran, French
Religions Muslim (mainly Sunni) 98%, Roman Catholic 1%, other 1%
Ethnic mix Comoran 97%, other 3%
Government Presidential system
Currency Comoros franc = 100 centimes
Literacy rate 56%
Calorie consumption 1735 calories

CONGO

Page 55 B5

Astride the Equator in west central Africa, this former French colony emerged from 26 years of Marxist-Leninist rule in 1990.

Official name Republic of the Congo
Formation 1960
Capital Brazzaville
Population 3.7 million / 28 people per sq mile (11 people per sq km)
Total area 132,046 sq. miles (342,000 sq. km)
Languages Kongo, Teke, Lingala, French
Religions Traditional beliefs 50%, Roman Catholic 25%, Protestant 23%, Muslim 2%
Ethnic mix Bakongo 48%, Sangha 20%, Teke 17%, Mbochi 12%, other 3%
Government Presidential system
Currency CFA franc = 100 centimes
Literacy rate 83%
Calorie consumption 2221 calories

CONGO, DEM. REP.

Page 55 C6

Straddling the Equator in east central Africa, Dem. Rep. Congo is one of Africa's largest countries. It achieved independence from Belgium in 1960.

Official name Democratic Republic of the Congo
Formation 1960
Capital Kinshasa
Population 52.8 million / 60 people per sq mile (23 people per sq km)
Total area 905,563 sq. miles (2,345,410 sq. km)
Languages Kiswahili, Tshiluba, Kikongo, Lingala, French
Religions Roman Catholic 37%, Protestant 13%, Traditional beliefs 50%, other 55%
Ethnic mix Bantu and Hamitic 45%, other 55%
Government Transitional regime
Currency Congolese franc = 100 centimes
Literacy rate 63%
Calorie consumption 1535 calories

COSTA RICA

Page 31 E4

Costa Rica is the most stable country in Central America. Its neutrality in foreign affairs is long-standing, but it has very strong ties with the US.

Official name Republic of Costa Rica
Formation 1838
Capital San José
Population 4.2 million / 213 people per sq mile (82 people per sq km)
Total area 19,730 sq. miles (51,100 sq. km)
Languages Spanish, English Creole, Bribri, Cabecar
Religions Roman Catholic 76%, other (including Protestant) 24%
Ethnic mix Mestizo and European 96%, Black 2%, Chinese 1%, Amerindian 1%
Government Presidential system
Currency Costa Rican colón = 100 centimos
Literacy rate 96%
Calorie consumption 2761 calories

CÔTE D'IVOIRE

Page 52 D4

One of the larger nations along the coast of West Africa, Côte d'Ivoire remains under the influence of its former colonial ruler, France.

Official name Republic of Côte d'Ivoire
Formation 1960
Capital Yamoussoukro
Population 16.6 million / 135 people per sq mile (52 people per sq km)
Total area 124,502 sq. miles (322,460 sq. km)
Languages Akan, French, Kru, Voltaic
Religions Muslim 38%, Traditional beliefs 25%, Roman Catholic 25%, Protestant 6%, other 6%
Ethnic mix Baoulé 23%, Bété 18%, Senufo 15%, Agni-Ashanti 14%, Mandinka 11%, other 19%
Government Presidential system
Currency CFA franc = 100 centimes
Literacy rate 50%
Calorie consumption 2594 calories

CROATIA

Page 78 B2

Post-independence fighting in this former Yugoslav republic, thwarted its plans to capitalize on its prime location along the east Adriatic coast.

Official name Republic of Croatia
Formation 1991
Capital Zagreb
Population 4.4 million / 202 people per sq mile (78 people per sq km)
Total area 21,831 sq. miles (56,542 sq. km)
Languages Croatian
Religions Roman Catholic 88%, Orthodox Christian 4%, Muslim 1%, other 7%
Ethnic mix Croat 90%, Serb 4%, Bosniak 1%, other 5%
Government Parliamentary system
Currency Kuna = 100 lipas
Literacy rate 98%
Calorie consumption 2678 calories

CUBA

Page 32 C

Cuba is the largest island in the Caribbean and the only Communist country in the Americas. It has been led by Fidel Castro since 1959.

Official name Republic of Cuba
Formation 1902
Capital Havana
Population 11.3 million / 264 people per sq mile (102 people per sq km)
Total area 42,803 sq. miles (110,860 sq. km)
Languages Spanish
Religions Nonreligious 49%, Roman Catholic 40%, Atheist 6%, Protestant 1%, other 4%
Ethnic mix White 66%, European–African 22%, Black 12%
Government One-party state
Currency Cuban peso = 100 centavos
Literacy rate 97%
Calorie consumption 2643 calories

CYPRUS

Page 80 C5

Cyprus lies in the eastern Mediterranean. Since 1974, it has been partitioned between the Turkish-occupied north and the Greek south.

Official name Republic of Cyprus
Formation 1960
Capital Nicosia
Population 802,000 / 225 people per sq mile (87 people per sq km)
Total area 3571 sq. miles (9250 sq. km)
Languages Greek, Turkish
Religions Orthodox Christian 78%, Muslim 18%, other 4%
Ethnic mix Greek 85%, Turkish 12%, other 3%
Government Presidential system
Currency Cyprus pound (Turkish lira in TRNC) = 100 cents (Cyprus pound); 100 kurus (Turkish lira)
Literacy rate 97%
Calorie consumption 3302 calories

CZECH REPUBLIC

Page 77 A5

Once part of Czechoslovakia in eastern Europe, it became independent in 1993, after peacefully dissolving its federal union with Slovakia.

Official name Czech Republic
Formation 1993
Capital Prague
Population 10.2 million / 335 people per sq mile (129 people per sq km)
Total area 30,450 sq. miles (78,866 sq. km)
Languages Czech, Slovak, Hungarian (Magyar)
Religions Roman Catholic 39%, Atheist 38%, Protestant 3%, Hussite 2%, other 18%
Ethnic mix Czech 81%, Moravian 13%, Slovak 6%
Government Parliamentary system
Currency Czech koruna = 100 haleru
Literacy rate 99%
Calorie consumption 3097 calories

DENMARK

Page 63 A7

The country occupies the Jutland peninsula and over 400 islands in Scandinavia. Greenland and the Faeroe Islands are self-governing associated territories.

Official name Kingdom of Denmark
Formation 950
Capital Copenhagen
Population 5.4 million / 330 people per sq mile (127 people per sq km)
Total area 16,639 sq. miles (43,094 sq. km)
Languages Danish
Religions Evangelical Lutheran 89%, Roman Catholic 1%, other 10%
Ethnic mix Danish 96%, other (including Scandinavian and Turkish) 3%, Faeroese and Inuit 1%
Government Parliamentary system
Currency Danish krone = 100 øre
Literacy rate 99%
Calorie consumption 3454 calories

DJIBOUTI

Page 50 D4

A city state with a desert hinterland, Djibouti lies in northeast Africa. Once known as French Somaliland, its economy relies on its port.

Official name Republic of Djibouti
Formation 1977
Capital Djibouti
Population 703,000 / 79 people per sq mile (30 people per sq km)
Total area 8494 sq. miles (22,000 sq. km)
Languages Somali, Afar, French, Arabic
Religions Muslim (mainly Sunni) 94%, Christian 6%
Ethnic mix Issa 60%, Afar 35%, other 5%
Government Presidential system
Currency Djibouti franc = 100 centimes
Literacy rate 66%
Calorie consumption 2218 calories

DOMINICA

Page 33 H4

The Caribbean island Dominica resisted European colonization until the 18th century, when it first came under the French, and then, the British

Official name Commonwealth of Dominica
Formation 1978
Capital Roseau
Population 69,655 / 240 people per sq mile (93 people per sq km)
Total area 291 sq. miles (754 sq. km)
Languages French Creole, English
Religions Roman Catholic 77%, Protestant 15%, other 8%
Ethnic mix Black 91%, Mixed race 6%, Carib 2%, other 1%
Government Parliamentary system
Currency Eastern Caribbean dollar = 100 cents
Literacy rate 76%
Calorie consumption 2995 calories

DOMINICAN REPUBLIC

Page 33 E2

The republic occupies the eastern two-thirds of the island of Hispaniola in the Caribbean. Frequent coups and a strong US influence mark its recent past.

Official name Dominican Republic
Formation 1865
Capital Santo Domingo
Population 8.7 million / 466 people per sq mile (180 people per sq km)
Total area 18,679 sq. miles (48,380 sq. km)
Languages Spanish, French Creole
Religions Roman Catholic 92%, other and nonreligious 8%
Ethnic mix Mixed race 75%, White 15%, Black 10%
Government Presidential system
Currency Dominican Republic peso = 100 centavos
Literacy rate 84%
Calorie consumption 2333 calories

EAST TIMOR

Page 116 F5

This new nation occupies the eastern half of the island of Timor. Invaded by Indonesia in 1975, it declared independence in 1999.

Official name Democratic Republic of Timor-Leste
Formation 2002
Capital Dili
Population 778,000 / 138 people per sq mile (53 people per sq km)
Total area 5756 sq. miles (14,874 sq. km)
Languages Tetum (Portuguese/Austronesian), Bahasa Indonesia, and Portuguese
Religions Roman Catholic 95%, other 5%
Ethnic mix Papuan groups approx 85%, Indonesian approx 13%, Chinese 2%
Government Parliamentary system
Currency US dollar = 100 cents
Literacy rate 59%
Calorie consumption Not available

ECUADOR

Page 38 A2

Ecuador sits high on South America's western coast. Once part of the Inca heartland, its territory includes the Galapagos Islands, to the west.

Official name Republic of Ecuador
Formation 1830
Capital Quito
Population 13 million / 122 people per sq mile (47 people per sq km)
Total area 109,483 sq. miles (283,560 sq. km)
Languages Spanish, Quechua, other Amerindian languages
Religions Roman Catholic 93%, Protestant, Jewish, and other 7%
Ethnic mix Mestizo 55%, Amerindian 25%, White 10%, Black 10%
Government Presidential system
Currency US dollar = 100 cents
Literacy rate 91%
Calorie consumption 2792 calories

EGYPT

Page 50 B2

Egypt occupies the northeast corner of Africa. Its essentially pro-Western, military-backed regime is being challenged by Islamic fundamentalists.

Official name Arab Republic of Egypt
Formation 1936
Capital Cairo
Population 71.9 million / 187 people per sq mile (72 people per sq km)
Total area 386,660 sq. miles (1,001,450 sq. km)
Languages Arabic, French, English, Berber
Religions Muslim (mainly Sunni) 94%, Coptic Christian and other 6%
Ethnic mix Eastern Hamitic 90%, Nubian, Armenian, and Greek 10%
Government Presidential system
Currency Egyptian pound = 100 piastres
Literacy rate 56%
Calorie consumption 3385 calories

EL SALVADOR

Page 30 B3

El Salvador is Central America's smallest state. A 12-year war between US-backed government troops and left-wing guerrillas ended in 1992.

Official name Republic of El Salvador
Formation 1841
Capital San Salvador
Population 6.5 million / 812 people per sq mile (314 people per sq km)
Total area 8124 sq. miles (21,040 sq. km)
Languages Spanish
Religions Roman Catholic 80%, Evangelical 18%, other 2%
Ethnic mix Mestizo 94%, Amerindian 5%, White 1%
Government Presidential system
Currency Salvadorean colón & US dollar = 100 centavos (colón); 100 cents (US dollar)
Literacy rate 80%
Calorie consumption 2512 calories

EQUATORIAL GUINEA

Page 55 A5

The country comprises the Rio Muni mainland and five islands on the west coast of central Africa. Free elections were first held in 1988.

Official name Republic of Equatorial Guinea
Formation 1968
Capital Malabo
Population 494,000 / 46 people per sq mile (18 people per sq km)
Total area 10,830 sq. miles (28,051 sq. km)
Languages Spanish, Fang, Bubi
Religions Roman Catholic 90%, other 10%
Ethnic mix Fang 85%, Bubi 4%, other 11%
Government Presidential system
Currency CFA franc = 100 centimes
Literacy rate 84%
Calorie consumption Not available

ERITREA

Page 50 C3

Lying on the shores of the Red Sea, Eritrea effectively seceded from Ethiopia in 1993, following a 30-year war for independence.

Official name State of Eritrea
Formation 1993
Capital Asmara
Population 4.1 million / 90 people per sq mile (35 people per sq km)
Total area 46,842 sq. miles (121,320 sq. km)
Languages Tigrinya, English, Tigre, Afar, Arabic, Bilen, Kunama, Nara, Saho, Hadareb
Religions Christian 45%, Muslim 45%, other 10%
Ethnic mix Tigray and Kunama 40%, Tigray 50%, Afar 4%, Saho 3%, other 3%
Government Transitional regime
Currency Nakfa = 100 cents
Literacy rate 57%
Calorie consumption 1690 calories

ESTONIA

Page 84 D2

Estonia is the smallest and most developed of the three Baltic states. It has the highest standard of living of any of the former Soviet republics.

Official name Republic of Estonia
Formation 1991
Capital Tallinn
Population 1.3 million / 75 people per sq mile (29 people per sq km)
Total area 17,462 sq. miles (45,226 sq. km)
Languages Estonian, Russian
Religions Evangelical Lutheran 56%, Orthodox Christian 25%, other 19%
Ethnic mix Estonian 62%, Russian 30%, other 8%
Government Parliamentary system
Currency Kroon = 100 senti
Literacy rate 99%
Calorie consumption 3048 calories

ETHIOPIA

Page 51 C5

Located in northeast Africa, Ethiopia was a Marxist regime from 1974–91. It has suffered a series of economic, civil, and natural crises.

Official name Federal Democratic Republic of Ethiopia
Formation 1896
Capital Addis Ababa
Population 70.7 million / 165 people per sq mile (64 people per sq km)
Total area 435,184 sq. miles (1,127,127 sq. km)
Languages Amharic, Tigrinya, Galla, Sidamo, Somali, English, Arabic
Religions Orthodox Christian 40%, Muslim 40%, other 20%.
Ethnic mix Oromo 40%, Amhara 25%, Sidamo 9%, Berta 6%, other 20%
Government Parliamentary system
Currency Ethiopian birr = 100 cents
Literacy rate 42%
Calorie consumption 2037 calories

FIJI

Page 123 E5

A volcanic archipelago, Fiji comprises 882 islands in the southern Pacific Ocean. Ethnic Fijians and Indo-Fijians have been in conflict since 1987.

Official name Republic of the Fiji Islands
Formation 1970
Capital Suva
Population 839,000 / 119 people per sq mile (46 people per sq km)
Total area 7054 sq. miles (18,270 sq. km)
Languages Fijian, English, Hindi, Urdu, Tamil, Telugu
Religions Hindu 38%, Methodist 37%, Roman Catholic 9%, other 16%.
Ethnic mix Melanesian 48%, Indian 46%, other 6%
Government Parliamentary system
Currency Fiji dollar = 100 cents
Literacy rate 93%
Calorie consumption 2789 calories

FINLAND

Page 62 D4

Finland's distinctive language and national identity have been influenced by both its Scandinavian and its Russian neighbors.

Official name Republic of Finland
Formation 1917
Capital Helsinki
Population 5.2 million / 44 people per sq mile (17 people per sq km)
Total area 130,127 sq. miles (337,030 sq. km)
Languages Finnish, Swedish, Sámi
Religions Evangelical Lutheran 89%, Orthodox Christian 1%, Roman Catholic 1%, other 9%
Ethnic mix Finnish 93%, other (including Sámi) 7%
Government Parliamentary system
Currency Euro = 100 cents
Literacy rate 99%
Calorie consumption 3202 calories

FRANCE

Page 68 B4

Straddling Western Europe from the English Channel to the Mediterranean Sea, France, is one of the world's leading industrial powers.

Official name French Republic
Formation 987
Capital Paris
Population 60.1 million / 283 people per sq mile (109 people per sq km)
Total area 211,208 sq. miles (547,030 sq. km)
Languages French, Provençal, German, Breton, Catalan, Basque
Religions Roman Catholic 88%, Muslim 8%, Protestant 2%, other 2%
Ethnic mix French 90%, North African 6%, German 2%, other 2%
Government Mixed presidential–parliamentary system
Currency Euro = 100 cents
Literacy rate 99%
Calorie consumption 3629 calories

GABON

Page 55 A5

A former French colony straddling the Equator on Africa's west coast, it returned to multiparty politics in 1990, after 22 years of one-party rule.

Official name Gabonese Republic
Formation 1960
Capital Libreville
Population 1.3 million / 13 people per sq mile (5 people per sq km)
Total area 103,346 sq. miles (267,667 sq. km)
Languages Fang, French, Punu, Sira, Nzebi, Mpongwe
Religions Christian 55%, Traditional beliefs 40%, other 4%, Muslim 1%
Ethnic mix Fang 35%, other Bantu 29%, Eshira 25%, European and other African 9%, French 2%
Government Presidential system
Currency CFA franc = 100 centimes
Literacy rate 71%
Calorie consumption 2602 calories

GERMANY

Page 72 B4

Europe's strongest economic power, Germany's democratic west and Communist east were re-unified in 1990, after the fall of the east's regime.

Official name Federal Republic of Germany
Formation 1871
Capital Berlin
Population 82.5 million / 611 people per sq mile (236 people per sq km)
Total area 137,846 sq. miles (357,021 sq. km)
Languages German, Turkish
Religions Protestant 34%, Roman Catholic 33%, other 30%, Muslim 3%
Ethnic mix German 92%, other 3%, other European 3%, Turkish 2%
Government Parliamentary system
Currency Euro = 100 cents
Literacy rate 99%
Calorie consumption 3567 calories

GRENADA

Page 33 G5

The Windward island of Grenada became a focus of attention in 1983, when the US mounted an invasion to sever its growing links with Cuba.

Official name Grenada
Formation 1974
Capital St. George's
Population 89,258 / 681 people per sq mile (263 people per sq km)
Total area 131 sq. miles (340 sq. km)
Languages English, English Creole
Religions Roman Catholic 68%, Anglican 17%, other 15%
Ethnic mix Black African 82%, Mulatto (mixed race) 13%, East Indian 3%, other 2%
Government Parliamentary system
Currency Eastern Caribbean dollar = 100 cents
Literacy rate 94%
Calorie consumption 2749 calories

GUINEA-BISSAU

Page 52 B4

Known as Portuguese Guinea during its days as a colony, Guinea-Bissau is situated on Africa's west coast, bordered by Senegal and Guinea.

Official name Republic of Guinea-Bissau
Formation 1974
Capital Bissau
Population 1.5 million / 138 people per sq mile (53 people per sq km)
Total area 13,946 sq. miles (36,120 sq. km)
Languages Portuguese Creole, Balante, Fulani, Malinke, Portuguese
Religions Traditional beliefs 52%, Muslim 40%, Christian 8%
Ethnic mix Balante 25%, Mandinka 12%, Fula 20% Mandyako 11%, other 13%
Government Transitional regime
Currency CFA franc = 100 centimes
Literacy rate 40%
Calorie consumption 2481 calories

GAMBIA

Page 52 B3

A narrow state on the west coast of Africa, The Gambia was renowned for its stability until its government was overthrown in a coup in 1994.

Official name Republic of the Gambia
Formation 1965
Capital Banjul
Population 1.4 million / 363 people per sq mile (140 people per sq km)
Total area 4363 sq. miles (11,300 sq. km)
Languages Mandinka, Fulani, Wolof, Jola, Soninke, English
Religions Sunni Muslim 90%, Christian 9%, Traditional beliefs 1%
Ethnic mix Mandinka 42%, Fulani 18%, Wolof 16%, Jola 10%, Serahuli 9%, other 5%
Government Presidential system
Currency Dalasi = 100 butut
Literacy rate 38%
Calorie consumption 2300 calories

GHANA

Page 53 E5

Once known as the Gold Coast, Ghana in West Africa has experienced intermittent periods of military rule since independence in 1957.

Official name Republic of Ghana
Formation 1957
Capital Accra
Population 20.9 million / 235 people per sq mile (91 people per sq km)
Total area 92,100 sq. miles (238,540 sq. km)
Languages Twi, Fanti, Ewe, Ga, Adangbe, Gurma, Dagomba (Dagbani)
Religions Christian 69%, Muslim 16%, Traditional beliefs 9%, other 6%
Ethnic mix Ashanti and Fanti 52%, Moshi-Dagomba 16%, Ewe 12%, other 11%, Ga and Ga-adanbe 8%, Yoruba 1%
Government Presidential system
Currency Cedi = 100 psewas
Literacy rate 74%
Calorie consumption 2670 calories

GUATEMALA

Page 30 A2

The largest state on the Central American isthmus, Guatemala returned to civilian rule in 1986, after 32 years of repressive military rule.

Official name Republic of Guatemala
Formation 1838
Capital Guatemala City
Population 12.3 million / 294 people per sq mile (113 people per sq km)
Total area 42,042 sq. miles (108,890 sq. km)
Languages Quiché, Mam, Cakchiquel, Kekchí, Spanish
Religions Roman Catholic 65%, Protestant 33%, other and nonreligious 2%
Ethnic mix Amerindian 60%, Mestizo 30%, other 10%
Government Presidential system
Currency Quetzal = 100 centavos
Literacy rate 70%
Calorie consumption 2203 calories

GUYANA

Page 37 F3

The only English-speaking country in South America, Guyana gained independence from Britain in 1966, and became a republic in 1970.

Official name Cooperative Republic of Guyana
Formation 1966
Capital Georgetown
Population 765,000 / 10 people per sq mile (4 people per sq km)
Total area 83,000 sq. miles (214,970 sq. km)
Languages English Creole, Hindi, Tamil, Amerindian languages, English
Religions Christian 57%, Hindu 33%, Muslim 9%, other 1%
Ethnic mix East Indian 52%, Black African 38%, other 10%
Government Presidential system
Currency Guyana dollar = 100 cents
Literacy rate 97%
Calorie consumption 2515 calories

GEORGIA

Page 95 F2

Located on the eastern shore of the Black Sea, Georgia's northern provinces have been torn by civil war since independence from the USSR in 1991.

Official name Georgia
Formation 1991
Capital Tbilisi
Population 5.1 million / 190 people per sq mile (73 people per sq km)
Total area 26,911 sq. miles (69,700 sq. km)
Languages Georgian, Russian, Azeri, Armenian, Mingrelian, Ossetian,
Religions Georgian Orthodox 65%, Muslim 11%, Russian Orthodox 10%, Armenian Orthodox 8%, other 6%
Ethnic mix Georgian 70%, Armenian 8%, Russian 6%, Azeri 6%, other 10%
Government Presidential system
Currency Lari = 100 tetri
Literacy rate 99%
Calorie consumption 2247 calories

GREECE

Page 83 A5

Greece is the southernmost Balkan nation. Surrounded by the Mediterranean, Aegean, and Ionian Seas, it has a strong seafaring tradition.

Official name Hellenic Republic
Formation 1829
Capital Athens
Population 11 million / 218 people per sq mile (84 people per sq km)
Total area 50,942 sq. miles (131,940 sq. km)
Languages Greek, Turkish, Macedonian, Albanian
Religions Orthodox Christian 98%, Muslim 1%, other 1%
Ethnic mix Greek 98%, other 2%
Government Parliamentary system
Currency Euro = 100 cents
Literacy rate 97%
Calorie consumption 3754 calories

GUINEA

Page 52 C4

Facing the Atlantic Ocean, on the west coast of Africa, Guinea became the first French colony in Africa to gain independence, in 1958.

Official name Republic of Guinea
Formation 1958
Capital Conakry
Population 8.5 million / 90 people per sq mile (35 people per sq km)
Total area 94,925 sq. miles (245,857 sq. km)
Languages Fulani, Malinke, Soussou, French
Religions Muslim 65%, Traditional beliefs 33%, Christian 2%
Ethnic mix Fulani 30%, Malinke 30%, Soussou 15%, Kissi 10%, other tribes 10%, other 5%
Government Presidential system
Currency Guinea franc = 100 centimes
Literacy rate 41%
Calorie consumption 2362 calories

HAITI

Page 32 D3

Haiti shares the Caribbean island of Hispaniola with the Dominican Republic. At independence, in 1804, it became the world's first Black republic.

Official name Republic of Haiti
Formation 1804
Capital Port-au-Prince
Population 8.3 million / 780 people per sq mile (301 people per sq km)
Total area 10,714 sq. miles (27,750 sq. km)
Languages French Creole, French
Religions Roman Catholic 80%, Protestant 16%, other (including Voodoo) 3%, Nonreligious 1%
Ethnic mix Black African 95%, Mulatto (mixed race) and European 5%
Government Transitional regime
Currency Gourde = 100 centimes
Literacy rate 52%
Calorie consumption 2045 calories

HONDURAS

Page 30 C2

Honduras straddles the Central American isthmus. The country returned to full democratic civilian rule in 1984, after a succession of military regimes.

Official name Republic of Honduras
Formation 1838
Capital Tegucigalpa
Population 6.9 million / 160 people per sq mile (62 people per sq km)
Total area 43,278 sq. miles (112,090 sq. km)
Languages Spanish, Garífuna (Carib), English Creole
Religions Roman Catholic 97%, Protestant 3%
Ethnic mix Mestizo 90%, Black African 5%, Amerindian 4%, White 1%
Government Presidential system
Currency Lempira = 100 centavos
Literacy rate 80%
Calorie consumption 2406 calories

HUNGARY

Page 77 C6

Hungary is bordered by seven states in Central Europe. It has changed its economic and political policies to develop closer ties with the EU.

Official name Republic of Hungary
Formation 1918
Capital Budapest
Population 9.9 million / 278 people per sq mile (107 people per sq km)
Total area 35,919 sq. miles (93,030 sq. km)
Languages Hungarian (Magyar)
Religions Roman Catholic 52%, Calvinist 16%, other 15%, Nonreligious 14%, Lutheran 3%
Ethnic mix Magyar 90%, other 7%, Roma 2%, German 1%
Government Parliamentary system
Currency Forint = 100 fillér
Literacy rate 99%
Calorie consumption 3520 calories

ICELAND

Page 61 E4

Europe's westernmost country, Iceland lies in the North Atlantic, straddling the mid-Atlantic ridge. Its spectacular, volcanic landscape is largely uninhabited.

Official name Republic of Iceland
Formation 1944
Capital Reykjavík
Population 290,000 / 7 people per sq mile (3 people per sq km)
Total area 39,768 sq. miles (103,000 sq. km)
Languages Icelandic
Religions Evangelical Lutheran 93%, Nonreligious 6%, other (mostly Christian) 1%
Ethnic mix Icelandic 94%, Danish 1%, other 5%
Government Parliamentary system
Currency Icelandic króna = 100 aurar
Literacy rate 99%
Calorie consumption 3231 calories

INDIA

Page 112 D4

Separated from the rest of Asia by the Himalayan mountain ranges, India forms a subcontinent. It is the world's second most populous country.

Official name Republic of India
Formation 1947
Capital New Delhi
Population 1.07 billion / 928 people per sq mile (358 people per sq km)
Total area 1,269,338 sq. miles (3,287,590 sq. km)
Languages Hindi, English, Urdu, Bengali, Marathi, Telugu, Tamil, Bihari, Gujarati, Kanarese
Religions Hindu 83%, Muslim 11%, Christian 2%, Sikh 2%, other 1%
Ethnic mix Indo-Aryan 72%, Dravidian 25%, Mongoloid and other 3%
Government Parliamentary system
Currency Indian rupee = 100 paise
Literacy rate 61%
Calorie consumption 2487 calories

INDONESIA

Page 116 C4

Formerly the Dutch East Indies, Indonesia, the world's largest archipelago, stretches over 5,000 km (3,100 miles), from the Indian Ocean to the Pacific Ocean.

Official name Republic of Indonesia
Formation 1949
Capital Jakarta
Population 220 million / 317 people per sq mile (122 people per sq km)
Total area 741,096 sq. miles (1,919,440 sq. km)
Languages Javanese, Sundanese, Madurese, Bahasa Indonesia, Dutch
Religions Muslim 87%, Protestant 6%, Roman Catholic 3%, other 4%
Ethnic mix Javanese 45%, other 25%, Sundanese 14%, Coastal Malays 8%, Madurese 8%
Government Presidential system
Currency Rupiah = 100 sen
Literacy rate 88%
Calorie consumption 2904 calories

IRAN

Page 98 B3

Since the 1979 revolution led by Ayatollah Khomeini, which sent Iran's Shah into exile, this Middle Eastern country has become the world's largest theocracy.

Official name Islamic Republic of Iran
Formation 1502
Capital Tehran
Population 68.9 million / 109 people per sq mile (42 people per sq km)
Total area 636,293 sq. miles (1,648,000 sq. km)
Languages Farsi, Azeri, Luri, Gilaki, Mazanderani, Kurdish, Turkmen, Arabic,
Religions Shi'a Muslim 93%, Sunni Muslim 6%, other 1%
Ethnic mix Persian 50%, Azari 24%, Kurdish 8%, Lur and Bakhtiari 8%, other 10%
Government Islamic theocracy
Currency Iranian rial = 100 dinars
Literacy rate 77%
Calorie consumption 2931 calories

IRAQ

Page 98 B3

Oil-rich Iraq is situated in the central Middle East. Since the removal of the monarchy in 1958, it has experienced considerable political turmoil.

Official name Republic of Iraq
Formation 1932
Capital Baghdad
Population 25.2 million / 149 people per sq mile (58 people per sq km)
Total area 168,753 sq. miles (437,072 sq. km)
Languages Arabic, Kurdish, Turkic languages, Armenian, Assyrian
Religions Shi'a Muslim 62%, Sunni Muslim 33%, other (including Christian) 5%
Ethnic mix Arab 79%, Kurdish 16%, Persian 3%, Turkmen 2%
Government Transitional regime
Currency New Iraqi dinar = 1000 fils
Literacy rate 40%
Calorie consumption 2197 calories

IRELAND

Page 67 A6

The Republic of Ireland occupies about 85% of the island of Ireland, with the remainder (Northern Ireland) being part of the United Kingdom.

Official name Ireland
Formation 1922
Capital Dublin
Population 4 million / 150 people per sq mile (58 people per sq km)
Total area 27,135 sq. miles (70,280 sq. km)
Languages English, Irish Gaelic
Religions Roman Catholic 88%, Anglican 3%, other and nonreligious 9%
Ethnic mix Irish 93%, other 4%, British 3%
Government Parliamentary system
Currency Euro = 100 cents
Literacy rate 99%
Calorie consumption 3666 calories

ISRAEL

Page 97 A7

Israel was created as a new state in 1948 on the east coast of the Mediterranean. Following wars with its Arab neighbors, it has extended its boundaries.

Official name State of Israel
Formation 1948
Capital Jerusalem
Population 6.4 million / 815 people per sq mile (315 people per sq km)
Total area 8019 sq. miles (20,770 sq. km)
Languages Hebrew, Arabic, Yiddish, German, Russian, Polish, Romanian, Persian
Religions Jewish 80%, Muslim (mainly Sunni) 16%, Druze and other 2%, Christian 2%
Ethnic mix Jewish 80%, other 20%
Government Parliamentary system
Currency Shekel = 100 agorot
Literacy rate 95%
Calorie consumption 3512 calories

ITALY

Page 74 B3

Projecting into the Mediterranean Sea in Southern Europe, Italy is an ancient land, but also one of the continent's newest unified states.

Official name Italian Republic
Formation 1861
Capital Rome
Population 57.4 million / 506 people per sq mile (195 people per sq km)
Total area 116,305 sq. miles (301,230 sq. km)
Languages Italian, German, French, Rhaeto-Romanic, Sardinian
Religions Roman Catholic 85%, other and nonreligious 13%, Muslim 2%
Ethnic mix Italian 94%, Sardinian 2%, other 4%
Government Parliamentary system
Currency Euro = 100 cents
Literacy rate 99%
Calorie consumption 3680 calories

JAMAICA

Page 32 C3

First colonized by the Spanish and then, from 1655, by the English, Jamaica was the first of the Caribbean island nations to achieve independence, in 1962.

Official name Jamaica
Formation 1962
Capital Kingston
Population 2.7 million / 646 people per sq mile (249 people per sq km)
Total area 4243 sq. miles (10,990 sq. km)
Languages English Creole, English
Religions Church of God 18%, Baptist 10%, Anglican 7%, other and nonreligious 45%, other Protestant 20%
Ethnic mix Black African 75%, Mulatto (mixed race) 13%, European and Chinese 11%, East Indian 1%
Government Parliamentary system
Currency Jamaican dollar = 100 cents
Literacy rate 88%
Calorie consumption 2705 calories

JAPAN

Page 108 C4

Japan comprises four principal islands and over 3,000 smaller ones. With the emperor as constitutional head, it is now the world's most powerful economy.

Official name Japan
Formation 1590
Capital Tokyo
Population 128 million / 878 people per sq mile (339 people per sq km)
Total area 145,882 sq. miles (377,835 sq. km)
Languages Japanese, Korean, Chinese
Religions Shinto and Buddhist 76%, Buddhist 16%, other (including Christian) 8%
Ethnic mix Japanese 99%, other (mainly Korean) 1%
Government Parliamentary system
Currency Yen = 100 sen
Literacy rate 99%
Calorie consumption 2746 calories

JORDAN

Page 97 B6

The kingdom of Jordan lies east of Israel. In 1993, King Hussein responded to calls for greater democracy by agreeing to multiparty elections.

Official name Hashemite Kingdom of Jordan
Formation 1946
Capital Amman
Population 5.5 million / 160 people per sq mile (62 people per sq km)
Total area 35,637 sq. miles (92,300 sq. km)
Languages Arabic
Religions Muslim (mainly Sunni) 92%, other (mostly Christian) 8%
Ethnic mix Arab 98%, Circassian 1%, Armenian 1%
Government Monarchy
Currency Jordanian dinar = 1000 fils
Literacy rate 91%
Calorie consumption 2769 calories

KIRIBATI

Page 123 F3

Part of the British colony of the Gilbert and Ellice Islands until independence in 1979, Kiribati comprises 33 islands in the mid-Pacific Ocean.

Official name Republic of Kiribati
Formation 1979
Capital Bairiki (Tarawa Atoll)
Population 98,549 / 360 people per sq mile (139 people per sq km)
Total area 277 sq. miles (717 sq. km)
Languages English, Kiribati
Religions Roman Catholic 53%, Kiribati Protestant Church 39%, other 8%
Ethnic mix Micronesian 96%, other 4%
Government Nonparty system
Currency Australian dollar = 100 cents
Literacy rate 99%
Calorie consumption 2922 calories

LAOS

Page 114 D4

A former French colony, independent in 1953, Laos lies landlocked in Southeast Asia. It has been under communist rule since 1975.

Official name Lao People's Democratic Republic
Formation 1953
Capital Vientiane
Population 5.7 million / 64 people per sq mile (25 people per sq km)
Total area 91,428 sq. miles (236,800 sq. km)
Languages Lao, Mon-Khmer, Yao, Vietnamese, Chinese, French
Religions Buddhist 85%, other (including animist) 15%
Ethnic mix Lao Loum 66%, Lao Theung 30%, Lao Soung 2%, other 2%
Government One-party state
Currency New kip = 100 at
Literacy rate 66%
Calorie consumption 2309 calories

LESOTHO

Page 56 D4

The landlocked kingdom of Lesotho is entirely surrounded by South Africa, which provides all its land transportation links with the outside world.

Official name Kingdom of Lesotho
Formation 1966
Capital Maseru
Population 1.8 million / 154 people per sq mile (59 people per sq km)
Total area 11,720 sq. miles (30,355 sq. km)
Languages English, Sesotho, isiZulu
Religions Christian 90%, Traditional beliefs 10%
Ethnic mix Sotho 97%, European and Asian 3%
Government Parliamentary system
Currency Loti = 100 lisente
Literacy rate 81%
Calorie consumption 2320 calories

KAZAKHSTAN

Page 92 B4

Second largest of the former Soviet republics, mineral-rich Kazakhstan has the potential to become the major Central Asian economic power.

Official name Republic of Kazakhstan
Formation 1991
Capital Astana
Population 15.4 million / 15 people per sq mile (6 people per sq km)
Total area 1,049,150 sq. miles (2,717,300 sq. km)
Languages Kazakh, Russian, Ukrainian, Tatar, German, Uzbek, Uighur
Religions Muslim (mainly Sunni) 47%, Orthodox Christian 44%, other 9%
Ethnic mix Kazakh 53%, Russian 30%, Ukrainian 4%, Tatar 2%, German 2%, other 9%
Government Presidential system
Currency Tenge = 100 tiyn
Literacy rate 99%
Calorie consumption 2477 calories

KUWAIT

Page 98 C4

Kuwait lies on the northwest extreme of the Persian Gulf. The state was a British protectorate from 1914 until 1961, when full independence was granted.

Official name State of Kuwait
Formation 1961
Capital Kuwait City
Population 2.5 million / 363 people per sq mile (140 people per sq km)
Total area 6880 sq. miles (17,820 sq. km)
Languages Arabic, English
Religions Sunni Muslim 45%, Shi'a Muslim 40%, Christian, Hindu, and other 15%
Ethnic mix Kuwaiti 45%, other Arab 35%, South Asian 9%, other 7%, Iranian 4%
Government Monarchy
Currency Kuwaiti dinar = 1000 fils
Literacy rate 83%
Calorie consumption 3170 calories

LATVIA

Page 84 C3

Situated on the east coast of the Baltic Sea, Lativa, like its Baltic neighbors, became independent in 1991. It retains a large Russian population.

Official name Republic of Latvia
Formation 1991
Capital Riga
Population 2.3 million / 92 people per sq mile (36 people per sq km)
Total area 24,938 sq. miles (64,589 sq. km)
Languages Latvian, Russian
Religions Lutheran 55%, Roman Catholic 24%, Orthodox Christian 9%, other 12%
Ethnic mix Latvian 57%, Russian 32%, Belarussian 4%, Ukrainian 3%, Polish 2%, other 2%
Government Parliamentary system
Currency Lats = 100 santims
Literacy rate 99%
Calorie consumption 2809 calories

LIBERIA

Page 52 C5

Liberia faces the Atlantic Ocean in equatorial West Africa. Africa's oldest republic, it was established in 1847. Today, it is torn by civil war.

Official name Republic of Liberia
Formation 1847
Capital Monrovia
Population 3.4 million / 91 people per sq mile (35 people per sq km)
Total area 43,000 sq. miles (111,370 sq. km)
Languages Kpelle, Vai, Bassa, Kru, Grebo, Kissi, Gola, Loma, English
Religions Christian 68%, Traditional beliefs 18%, Muslim 14%
Ethnic mix Indigenous tribes (16 main groups) 95%, Americo-Liberians 5%
Government Transitional regime
Currency Liberian dollar = 100 cents
Literacy rate 56%
Calorie consumption 1946 calories

KENYA

Page 51 C6

Kenya straddles the Equator on Africa's east coast. It became a multiparty democracy in 1992 and has been led by President Moi since 1978.

Official name Republic of Kenya
Formation 1963
Capital Nairobi
Population 32 million / 146 people per sq mile (56 people per sq km)
Total area 224,961 sq. miles (582,650 sq. km)
Languages Kiswahili, English, Kikuyu, Luo, Kalenjin, Kamba
Religions Christian 60%, Traditional beliefs 25%, Muslim 6%, other 9%
Ethnic mix Kikuyu 21%, Luhya 14%, Luo 13%, Kalenjin 11%, Kamba 11%, other 30%
Government Presidential system
Currency Kenya shilling = 100 cents
Literacy rate 84%
Calorie consumption 2058 calories

KYRGYZSTAN

Page 101 F2

A mountainous, landlocked state in Central Asia. The most rural of the ex-Soviet republics, it only gradually developed its own cultural nationalism.

Official name Kyrgyz Republic
Formation 1991
Capital Bishkek
Population 5.1 million / 67 people per sq mile (26 people per sq km)
Total area 76,641 sq. miles (198,500 sq. km)
Languages Kyrgyz, Russian, Uzbek, Tatar, Ukrainian
Religions Muslim (mainly Sunni) 70%, Orthodox Christian 30%
Ethnic mix Kyrgyz 57%, Russian 19%, Uzbek 13%, Tatar 2%, Ukrainian 2%, other 7%
Government Presidential system
Currency Som = 100 tyyn
Literacy rate 97%
Calorie consumption 2882 calories

LEBANON

Page 96 A4

Lebanon is dwarfed by its two powerful neighbors, Syria and Israel. The state started rebuilding in 1989, after 14 years of intense civil war.

Official name Republic of Lebanon
Formation 1941
Capital Beirut
Population 3.7 million / 937 people per sq mile (362 people per sq km)
Total area 4015 sq. miles (10,400 sq. km)
Languages Arabic, French, Armenian, Assyrian
Religions Muslim 70%, Christian 30%
Ethnic mix Arab 94%, Armenian 4%, other 2%
Government Parliamentary system
Currency Lebanese pound = 100 piastres
Literacy rate 87%
Calorie consumption 3184 calories

LIBYA

Page 49 F3

Situated on the Mediterranean coast of North Africa, Libya is a Muslim dictatorship, politically marginalized by the West for its terrorist links.

Official name Great Socialist People's Libyan Arab Jamahariyah
Formation 1951
Capital Tripoli
Population 5.6 million / 8 people per sq mile (3 people per sq km)
Total area 679,358 sq. miles (1,759,540 sq. km)
Languages Arabic, Tuareg
Religions Muslim (mainly Sunni) 97%, other 3%
Ethnic mix Arab and Berber 95%, other 5%
Government One-party state
Currency Libyan dinar = 1000 dirhams
Literacy rate 82%
Calorie consumption 3333 calories

LIECHTENSTEIN

Page 73 B7

Tucked in the Alps between Switzerland and Austria, Liechtenstein became an independent principality of the Holy Roman Empire in 1719.

Official name Principality of Liechtenstein
Formation 1719
Capital Vaduz
Population 33,145 / 535 people per sq mile (207 people per sq km)
Total area 62 sq. miles (160 sq. km)
Languages German, Alemannish dialect, Italian
Religions Roman Catholic 81%, other 12%, Protestant 7%
Ethnic mix Liechtensteiner 62%, Foreign residents 38%
Government Parliamentary system
Currency Swiss franc = 100 rappen/centimes
Literacy rate 99%
Calorie consumption Not available

LITHUANIA

Page 84 B4

The largest, most powerful and stable of the Baltic states, Lithuania was the first Baltic country to declare independence from Moscow, in 1991.

Official name Republic of Lithuania
Formation 1991
Capital Vilnius
Population 3.4 million / 135 people per sq mile (52 people per sq km)
Total area 25,174 sq. miles (65,200 sq. km)
Languages Lithuanian, Russian
Religions Roman Catholic 83%, other 12%, Protestant 5%
Ethnic mix Lithuanian 80%, Russian 9%, Polish 7%, Belarussian 2%, other 2%
Government Parliamentary system
Currency Litas (euro is also legal tender) = 100 centu
Literacy rate 99%
Calorie consumption 3384 calories

LUXEMBOURG

Page 65 D8

Making up part of the plateau of the Ardennes in Western Europe, Luxembourg is Europe's last independent duchy and one of its richest states.

Official name Grand Duchy of Luxembourg
Formation 1867
Capital Luxembourg-Ville
Population 453,000 / 454 people per sq mile (175 people per sq km)
Total area 998 sq. miles (2586 sq. km)
Languages Luxembourgish, German, French
Religions Roman Catholic 97%, Protestant, Orthodox Christian, and Jewish 3%
Ethnic mix Luxembourger 73%, Foreign residents 27%
Government Parliamentary system
Currency Euro = 100 cents
Literacy rate 99%
Calorie consumption 3701 calories

MACEDONIA

Page 79 D6

Landlocked in the southern Balkans, Macedonia has been affected by sanctions imposed on its northern trading partners and by Greek antagonism.

Official name Republic of Macedonia
Formation 1991
Capital Skopje
Population 2.02 million / 204 people per sq mile (79 people per sq km)
Total area 9781 sq. miles (25,333 sq. km)
Languages Macedonian, Albanian, Serbo-Croat
Religions Orthodox Christian 59%, Muslim 26%, Roman Catholic 4%, Protestant 1%, other 10%
Ethnic mix Macedonian 64%, Albanian 25%, Turkish 4%, Roma 3%, other 4%
Government Mixed presidential–parliamentary system
Currency Macedonian denar = 100 deni
Literacy rate 94%
Calorie consumption 2552 calories

MADAGASCAR

Page 57 F4

Lying in the Indian Ocean, Madagascar is the world's fourth largest island. Free elections in 1993 ended 18 years of radical socialist government.

Official name Republic of Madagascar
Formation 1960
Capital Antananarivo
Population 17.4 million / 77 people per sq mile (30 people per sq km)
Total area 226,656 sq. miles (587,040 sq. km)
Languages Malagasy, French
Religions Traditional beliefs 52%, Christian (mainly Roman Catholic) 41%, Muslim 7%
Ethnic mix other Malay 46%, Merina 26%, Betsimisaraka 15%, Betsileo 12%, other 1%
Government Presidential system
Currency Ariary = 5 iraimbilanja
Literacy rate 67%
Calorie consumption 2072 calories

MALAWI

Page 57 E1

A former British colony, Malawi lies landlocked in southeast Africa. Its name means "the land where the sun is reflected in the water like fire."

Official name Republic of Malawi
Formation 1964
Capital Lilongwe
Population 12.1 million / 333 people per sq mile (129 people per sq km)
Total area 45,745 sq. miles (118,480 sq. km)
Languages Chewa, Lomwe, Yao, Ngoni, English
Religions Protestant 55%, Roman Catholic 20%, Muslim 20%, Traditional beliefs 5%
Ethnic mix Bantu 99%, other 1%
Government Presidential system
Currency Malawi kwacha = 100 tambala
Literacy rate 62%
Calorie consumption 2168 calories

MALAYSIA

Page 116 B3

Malaysia's three separate territories include Malaya, Sarawak, and Sabah. A financial crisis in 1997 ended a decade of spectacular financial growth.

Official name Federation of Malaysia
Formation 1963
Capital Kuala Lumpur; Putrajaya (administrative)
Population 24.4 million / 192 people per sq mile (74 people per sq km)
Total area 127,316 sq. miles (329,750 sq. km)
Languages Bahasa Malaysia, Malay, Chinese, Tamil, English
Religions Muslim 53%, Buddhist 19%, Chinese faiths 12%, other 16%
Ethnic mix Malay 48%, Chinese 29%, Indigenous tribes 12%, other 11%
Government Parliamentary system
Currency Ringgit = 100 sen
Literacy rate 89%
Calorie consumption 2927 calories

MALDIVES

Page 110 A4

Only 200 of the more than 1,000 Maldivian small coral islands in the Indian Ocean, are inhabited. Government rests in the hands of a few influential families.

Official name Republic of Maldives
Formation 1965
Capital Male'
Population 318,000 / 2741 people per sq mile (1060 people per sq km)
Total area 116 sq. miles (300 sq. km)
Languages Dhivehi (Maldivian), Sinhala, Tamil, Arabic
Religions Sunni Muslim 100%
Ethnic mix Arab–Sinhalese–Malay 100%
Government Nonparty system
Currency Rufiyaa = 100 lari
Literacy rate 97%
Calorie consumption 2587 calories

MALI

Page 53 E2

Landlocked in the heart of West Africa, Mali held its first free elections in 1992, more than 30 years after it gained independence from France.

Official name Republic of Mali
Formation 1960
Capital Bamako
Population 13 million / 28 people per sq mile (11 people per sq km)
Total area 478,764 sq. miles (1,240,000 sq. km)
Languages Bambara, Fulani, Senufo, Soninke, French
Religions Muslim (mainly Sunni) 80%, Traditional beliefs 18%, other 2%
Ethnic mix Bambara 32%, other 26%, Fulani 14%, Senufo 12%, Soninka 9%, Tuareg 7%
Government Presidential system
Currency CFA franc = 100 centimes
Literacy rate 26%
Calorie consumption 2376 calories

MALTA

Page 80 A5

The Maltese archipelago lies off southern Sicily, midway between Europe and North Africa. The only inhabited islands are Malta, Gozo, and Kemmuna.

Official name Republic of Malta
Formation 1964
Capital Valletta
Population 394,000 / 3177 people per sq mile (1231 people per sq km)
Total area 122 sq. miles (316 sq. km)
Languages Maltese, English
Religions Roman Catholic 98%, other and nonreligious 2%
Ethnic mix Maltese 96%, other 4%
Government Parliamentary system
Currency Maltese lira = 100 cents
Literacy rate 93%
Calorie consumption 3496 calories

MARSHALL ISLANDS

Page 122 D1

A group of 34 atolls, the Marshall Islands were under US rule as part of the UN Trust Territory of the Pacific Islands until 1986. The economy depends on US aid.

Official name Republic of the Marshall Islands
Formation 1986
Capital Majuro
Population 56,429 / 806 people per sq mile (312 people per sq km)
Total area 70 sq. miles (181 sq. km)
Languages Marshallese, English, Japanese, German
Religions Protestant 90%, Roman Catholic 8%, other 2%
Ethnic mix Micronesian 97%, other 3%
Government Presidential system
Currency US dollar = 100 cents
Literacy rate 91%
Calorie consumption Not available

MAURITANIA

Page 52 C2

Situated in northwest Africa, two-thirds of Mauritania's territory is desert. A former French colony, it achieved independence in 1960.

Official name Islamic Republic of Mauritania
Formation 1960
Capital Nouakchott
Population 2.9 million / 7 people per sq mile (3 people per sq km)
Total area 397,953 sq. miles (1,030,700 sq. km)
Languages Hassaniyah Arabic, Wolof, French
Religions Sunni Muslim 100%
Ethnic mix Maure 81%, Wolof 7%, Tukolor 5%, Soninka 3%, other 4%
Government Presidential system
Currency Ouguiya = 5 khoums
Literacy rate 41%
Calorie consumption 2764 calories

MAURITIUS

Page 57 H3

Located to the east of Madagascar in the Indian Ocean, Mauritius became a republic 25 years after it gained independence. Tourism is a mainstay of its economy.

Official name Republic of Mauritius
Formation 1968
Capital Port Louis
Population 1.2 million / 1671 people per sq mile (645 people per sq km)
Total area 718 sq. miles (1860 sq. km)
Languages French Creole, Hindi, Urdu, Tamil, Chinese, English, French
Religions Hindu 52%, Roman Catholic 26%, Muslim 17%, Protestant 2%, other 3%,
Ethnic mix Indo-Mauritian 68%, Creole 27%, Sino-Mauritian 3%, Franco-Mauritian 2%
Government Parliamentary system
Currency Mauritian rupee = 100 cents
Literacy rate 84%
Calorie consumption 2995 calories

MOLDOVA

Page 86 D3

The smallest and most densely populated of the ex-Soviet republics, Moldova has strong linguistic and cultural links with Romania to the west.

Official name Republic of Moldova
Formation 1991
Capital Chisinau
Population 4.3 million / 330 people per sq mile (128 people per sq km)
Total area 13,067 sq. miles (33,843 sq. km)
Languages Moldovan, Ukrainian, Russian
Religions Orthodox Christian 98%, Jewish 2%
Ethnic mix Moldovan 65%, Ukrainian 14%, Russian 13%, Gagauz 4%, other 4%
Government Parliamentary system
Currency Moldovan leu = 100 bani
Literacy rate 99%
Calorie consumption 2712 calories

MOROCCO

Page 48 C2

A former French colony in northwest Africa, independent in 1956, Morocco has occupied the disputed territory of Western Sahara since 1975.

Official name Kingdom of Morocco
Formation 1956
Capital Rabat
Population 30.6 million / 178 people per sq mile (69 people per sq km)
Total area 172,316 sq. miles (446,300 sq. km)
Languages Arabic, Tamazight (Berber), French, Spanish
Religions Muslim (mainly Sunni) 99%, other (mostly Christian) 1%
Ethnic mix Arab 70%, Berber 29%, European 1%
Government Monarchy
Currency Moroccan dirham = 100 centimes
Literacy rate 51%
Calorie consumption 3046 calories

NAMIBIA

Page 56 B3

Located in southwestern Africa, Namibia became free of South African control in 1990, after years of uncertainty and guerrilla activity.

Official name Republic of Namibia
Formation 1990
Capital Windhoek
Population 2 million / 6 people per sq mile (2 people per sq km)
Total area 318,694 sq. miles (825,418 sq. km)
Languages Ovambo, Kavango, English, Bergdama, German, Afrikaans
Religions Christian 90%, Traditional beliefs 10%
Ethnic mix Ovambo 50%, other tribes 16%, Kavango 9%, other 9%, Damara 8%, Herero 8%
Government Presidential system
Currency Namibian dollar = 100 cents
Literacy rate 83%
Calorie consumption 2745 calories

MEXICO

Page 28 D3

Located between the United States of America and the Central American states, Mexico was a Spanish colony for 300 years until 1836.

Official name United Mexican States
Formation 1836
Capital Mexico City
Population 104 million / 140 people per sq mile (54 people per sq km)
Total area 761,602 sq. miles (1,972,550 sq. km)
Languages Spanish, Nahuatl, Mayan, Zapotec, Mixtec, Otomi, Totonac, Tzotzil, Tzeltal
Religions Roman Catholic 88%, Protestant 5%, other 7%
Ethnic mix Mestizo 60%, Amerindian 30%, European 9%, other 1%
Government Presidential system
Currency Mexican peso = 100 centavos
Literacy rate 91%
Calorie consumption 3160 calories

MONACO

Page 69 E6

A jet-set image and a thriving service sector define the modern identity of this tiny enclave on the Côte d'Azur in southeastern France.

Official name Principality of Monaco
Formation 1861
Capital Monaco-Ville
Population 32,130 / 42840 people per sq mile (16477 people per sq km)
Total area 0.75 sq. miles (1.95 sq. km)
Languages French, Italian, Monégasque, English
Religions Roman Catholic 89%, Protestant 6%, other 5%
Ethnic mix French 47%, Monégasque 17%, Italian 16%, other 20%
Government Monarchy
Currency Euro = 100 cents
Literacy rate 99%
Calorie consumption Not available

MOZAMBIQUE

Page 57 E3

Mozambique lies on the southeast African coast. It was torn by a civil war between the Marxist government and a rebel group from 1977–1992.

Official name Republic of Mozambique
Formation 1975
Capital Maputo
Population 18.9 million / 62 people per sq mile (24 people per sq km)
Total area 309,494 sq. miles (801,590 sq. km)
Languages Makua, Xitsonga, Sena, Lomwe, Portuguese
Religions Traditional beliefs 56%, Christian 30%, Muslim 14%
Ethnic mix Makua Lomwe 47%, Tsonga 23%, Malawi 12%, Shona 11%, Yao 4%, other 3%
Government Presidential system
Currency Metical = 100 centavos
Literacy rate 47%
Calorie consumption 1980 calories

NAURU

Page 122 D3

Nauru lies in the Pacific, 4,000 km (2,480 miles) northeast of Australia. Phosphate deposits have made its citizens among the richest in the world.

Official name Republic of Nauru
Formation 1968
Capital None
Population 12,570 / 1552 people per sq mile (599 people per sq km)
Total area 8.1 sq. miles (21 sq. km)
Languages Nauruan, Kiribati, Chinese, Tuvaluan, English
Religions Nauruan Congregational Church 60%, Roman Catholic 35%, other 5%
Ethnic mix Nauruan 62%, other Pacific islanders 25%, Chinese and Vietnamese 8%, European 5%
Government Parliamentary system
Currency Australian dollar = 100 cents
Literacy rate 95%
Calorie consumption Not available

MICRONESIA

Page 122 B1

The Federated States of Micronesia, situated in the western Pacific, comprise 607 islands and atolls grouped into four main island states.

Official name Federated States of Micronesia
Formation 1986
Capital Palikir (Pohnpei Island)
Population 108,143 / 399 people per sq mile (154 people per sq km)
Total area 271 sq. miles (702 sq. km)
Languages Trukese, Pohnpeian, Mortlockese, Kosraean, English
Religions Roman Catholic 50%, Protestant 48%, other 2%
Ethnic mix Micronesian 100%
Government Nonparty system
Currency US dollar = 100 cents
Literacy rate 81%
Calorie consumption Not available

MONGOLIA

Page 104 D2

Lying between Russia and China, Mongolia is a vast and isolated country with a small population. Over two-thirds of the country is desert.

Official name Mongolia
Formation 1924
Capital Ulan Bator
Population 2.6 million / 4 people per sq mile (2 people per sq km)
Total area 604,247 sq. miles (1,565,000 sq. km)
Languages Khalkha Mongolian, Kazakh, Chinese, Russian
Religions Tibetan Buddhist 96%, Muslim 4%
Ethnic mix Mongol 90%, Kazakh 4%, Chinese 2%, Russian 2%, other 2%
Government Mixed presidential–parliamentary system
Currency Tugrik (tögrög) = 100 möngö
Literacy rate 98%
Calorie consumption 1974 calories

MYANMAR (BURMA)

Page 114 A3

Myanmar forms the eastern shores of the Bay of Bengal and the Andaman Sea in Southeast Asia. Since 1988 it has been ruled by a repressive military regime.

Official name Union of Myanmar
Formation 1948
Capital Rangoon (Yangon)
Population 49.5 million / 195 people per sq mile (75 people per sq km)
Total area 261,969 sq. miles (678,500 sq. km)
Languages Burmese, Shan, Karen, Rakhine, Chin, Yangbye, Kachin, Mon
Religions Buddhist 87%, Christian 6%, Muslim 4%, Hindu 1%, other 2%
Ethnic mix Burman (Bamah) 68%, Shan 9%, Karen 6%, Rakhine 4%, other 13%
Government Military-based regime
Currency Kyat = 100 pyas
Literacy rate 85%
Calorie consumption 2822 calories

NEPAL

Page 113 E3

Nepal lies between India and China, on the shoulder of the southern Himalayas. The elections of 1991 ended a period of absolute monarchy.

Official name Kingdom of Nepal
Formation 1769
Capital Kathmandu
Population 25.2 million / 477 people per sq mile (184 people per sq km)
Total area 54,363 sq. miles (140,800 sq. km)
Languages Nepali, Maithili, Bhojpuri
Religions Hindu 90%, Buddhist 5%, Muslim 3%, other (including Christian) 2%
Ethnic mix Nepalese 52%, Maithili 11%, Tibeto-Burmese 10%, Bhojpuri 8%, other 19%
Government Monarchy
Currency Nepalese rupee = 100 paise
Literacy rate 44%
Calorie consumption 2459 calories

NETHERLANDS

Page 64 C3

Astride the delta of five major rivers in northwest Europe, the Netherlands has a long trading tradition. Rotterdam is the world's largest port.

Official name Kingdom of the Netherlands
Formation 1648
Capital Amsterdam; The Hague (administrative)
Population 16.1 million / 1229 people per sq mile (475 people per sq km)
Total area 16,033 sq. miles (41,526 sq. km)
Languages Dutch, Frisian
Religions Roman Catholic 36%, Protestant 27%, Muslim 3%, other 34%
Ethnic mix Dutch 82%, Surinamese 2%, Turkish 2%, Moroccan 2%, other 12%
Government Parliamentary system
Currency Euro = 100 cents
Literacy rate 97%
Calorie consumption 3282 calories

NEW ZEALAND

Page 128 A4

One of the Pacific Rim countries, New Zealand lies southeast of Australia, and comprises the North and South Islands, separated by the Cook Strait.

Official name New Zealand
Formation 1947
Capital Wellington
Population 3.9 million / 38 people per sq mile (15 people per sq km)
Total area 103,737 sq. miles (268,680 sq. km)
Languages English, Maori
Religions Anglican 24%, Presbyterian 18%, Nonreligious 16%, Roman Catholic 15%, Methodist 5%, other 22%
Ethnic mix European 77%, Maori 12%, other 6%, Pacific islanders 5%
Government Parliamentary system
Currency New Zealand dollar = 100 cents
Literacy rate 99%
Calorie consumption 3235 calories

NICARAGUA

Page 30 D3

Nicaragua lies at the heart of Central America. An 11-year war between left-wing Sandinistas and right-wing US-backed Contras ended in 1989.

Official name Republic of Nicaragua
Formation 1838
Capital Managua
Population 5.5 million / 120 people per sq mile (46 people per sq km)
Total area 49,998 sq. miles (129,494 sq. km)
Languages Spanish, English Creole, Miskito
Religions Roman Catholic 80%, Protestant Evangelical 17%, other 3%
Ethnic mix Mestizo 69%, White 14%, Black 8%, Amerindian 5%, Zambo 4%
Government Presidential system
Currency Córdoba oro = 100 centavos
Literacy rate 77%
Calorie consumption 2256 calories

NIGER

Page 53 F3

Niger lies landlocked in West Africa, but it is linked to the sea by the River Niger. Since 1973 it has suffered civil unrest and two major droughts.

Official name Republic of Niger
Formation 1960
Capital Niamey
Population 12 million / 25 people per sq mile (9 people per sq km)
Total area 489,188 sq. miles (1,267,000 sq. km)
Languages Hausa, Djerma, Fulani, Tuareg, Teda, French
Religions Muslim 85%, Traditional beliefs 14%, other 1%
Ethnic mix Hausa 54%, Djerma and Songhai 21%, Fulani 10%, Tuareg 9%, other 6%
Government Presidential system
Currency CFA franc = 100 centimes
Literacy rate 17%
Calorie consumption 2118 calories

NIGERIA

Page 53 F4

Africa's most populous state Nigeria, in West Africa, is a federation of 30 states. It adopted civilian rule in 1999 after 33 years of military government.

Official name Federal Republic of Nigeria
Formation 1960
Capital Abuja
Population 124 million / 353 people per sq mile (136 people per sq km)
Total area 356,667 sq. miles (923,768 sq. km)
Languages Hausa, English, Yoruba, Ibo
Religions Muslim 50%, Christian 40%, Traditional beliefs 10%
Ethnic mix Hausa 21%, Yoruba 21%, Ibo 18%, Fulani 11%, other 29%
Government Presidential system
Currency Naira = 100 kobo
Literacy rate 67%
Calorie consumption 2747 calories

NORTH KOREA

Page 106 E3

North Korea comprises the northern half of the Korean peninsula. A communist state since 1948, it is largely isolated from the outside world.

Official name Democratic People's Republic of Korea
Formation 1948
Capital Pyongyang
Population 22.7 million / 488 people per sq mile (189 people per sq km)
Total area 46,540 sq. miles (120,540 sq. km)
Languages Korean, Chinese
Religions Atheist 100%
Ethnic mix Korean 100%
Government One-party state
Currency North Korean won = 100 chon
Literacy rate 99%
Calorie consumption 2201 calories

NORWAY

Page 63 A5

The Kingdom of Norway traces the rugged western coast of Scandinavia. Settlements are largely restricted to southern and coastal areas.

Official name Kingdom of Norway
Formation 1905
Capital Oslo
Population 4.5 million / 38 people per sq mile (15 people per sq km)
Total area 125,181 sq. miles (324,220 sq. km)
Languages Norwegian (*Bokmål* "book language" and *Nynorsk* "new Norsk"), Sámi
Religions Evangelical Lutheran 89%, Roman Catholic 1%, other 10%
Ethnic mix Norwegian 93%, other 6%, Sámi 1%
Government Parliamentary system
Currency Norwegian krone = 100 øre
Literacy rate 99%
Calorie consumption 3382 calories

NIGERIA

OMAN

Page 99 D6

Situated on the eastern coast of the Arabian Peninsula, Oman is the least developed of the Gulf states, despite modest oil exports.

Official name Sultanate of Oman
Formation 1951
Capital Muscat
Population 2.9 million / 35 people per sq mile (14 people per sq km)
Total area 82,031 sq. miles (212,460 sq. km)
Languages Arabic, Baluchi, Farsi, Hindi, Punjabi
Religions Ibadi Muslim 75%, other Muslim and Hindu 25%
Ethnic mix Arab 88%, Baluchi 4%, Persian 3%, Indian and Pakistani 3%, African 2%
Government Monarchy
Currency Omani rial = 1000 baizas
Literacy rate 74%
Calorie consumption Not available

PAKISTAN

Page 112 B2

Once a part of British India, Pakistan was created in 1947 as an independent Muslim state. Today, the country is divided into four provinces.

Official name Islamic Republic of Pakistan
Formation 1947
Capital Islamabad
Population 154 million / 516 people per sq mile (199 people per sq km)
Total area 310,401 sq. miles (803,940 sq. km)
Languages Punjabi, Sindhi, Pashtu, Urdu, Baluchi, Brahui
Religions Sunni Muslim 77%, Shi'a Muslim 20%, Hindu 2%, Christian 1%
Ethnic mix Punjabi 56%, Pathan 15%, Sindhi 14%, Mohajir 7%, other 8%
Government Presidential system
Currency Pakistani rupee = 100 paisa
Literacy rate 44%
Calorie consumption 2457 calories

PALAU

Page 122 A2

The Palau archipelago, a group of over 200 islands, lies in the western Pacific Ocean. In 1994, it became the world's newest independent state.

Official name Republic of Palau
Formation 1994
Capital Koror
Population 19,717 / 101 people per sq mile (39 people per sq km)
Total area 177 sq. miles (458 sq. km)
Languages Palauan, English, Japanese, Angaur, Tobi, Sonsorolese
Religions Christian 66%, Modekngei 34%
Ethnic mix Micronesian 87%, Filipino 8%, Chinese and other Asian 5%
Government Nonparty system
Currency US dollar = 100 cents
Literacy rate 98%
Calorie consumption Not available

PANAMA

Page 31 F5

Southernmost of the Central American countries. The Panama Canal (returned to Panama from US control in 2000) links the Pacific and Atlantic oceans.

Official name Republic of Panama
Formation 1903
Capital Panama City
Population 3.1 million / 106 people per sq mile (41 people per sq km)
Total area 30,193 sq. miles (78,200 sq. km)
Languages English Creole, Spanish, Amerindian languages, Chibchan languages
Religions Roman Catholic 86%, Protestant 6%, other 8%
Ethnic mix Mestizo 60%, White 14%, Black 12%, Amerindian 8%, other 6%
Government Presidential system
Currency Balboa = 100 centesimos
Literacy rate 92%
Calorie consumption 2386 calories

PAPUA NEW GUINEA

Page 122 B3

Achieving independence from Australia in 1975, PNG occupies the eastern section of the island of New Guinea and several other island groups.

Official name Independent State of Papua New Guinea
Formation 1975
Capital Port Moresby
Population 5.7 million / 33 people per sq mile (13 people per sq km)
Total area 178,703 sq. miles (462,840 sq. km)
Languages Pidgin English, Papuan, English, Motu, 750 native languages
Religions Protestant 60%, Roman Catholic 37%, other 3%
Ethnic mix Melanesian and mixed race 100%
Government Parliamentary system
Currency Kina = 100 toeas
Literacy rate 65%
Calorie consumption 2193 calories

PARAGUAY

Page 42 D2

Landlocked in central South America. Its post-independence history has included periods of military rule. Free elections were held in 1993.

Official name Republic of Paraguay
Formation 1811
Capital Asunción
Population 5.9 million /
38 people per sq mile (15 people per sq km)
Total area 157,046 sq. miles
(406,750 sq. km)
Languages Guaraní, Spanish, German
Religions Roman Catholic 96%, Protestant (including Mennonite) 4%
Ethnic mix Mestizo 90%, other 8%, Amerindian 2%
Government Presidential system
Currency Guaraní = 100 centimos
Literacy rate 92%
Calorie consumption 2576 calories

PERU

Page 38 C3

Once the heart of the Inca empire, before the Spanish conquest in the 16th century, Peru lies on the Pacific coast of South America.

Official name Republic of Peru
Formation 1824
Capital Lima
Population 27.2 million /
55 people per sq mile (21 people per sq km)
Total area 496,223 sq. miles
(1,285,200 sq. km)
Languages Spanish, Quechua, Aymara
Religions Roman Catholic 95%, other 5%
Ethnic mix Amerindian 50%, Mestizo 40%, White 7%, other 3%
Government Presidential system
Currency New sol = 100 centimos
Literacy rate 85%
Calorie consumption 2610 calories

PHILIPPINES

Page 117 E1

An archipelago of 7,107 islands between the South China Sea and the Pacific. After 21 years of dictatorship, democracy was restored in 1986.

Official name Republic of the Philippines
Formation 1946
Capital Manila
Population 80 million / 695 people per sq mile (268 people per sq km)
Total area 115,830 sq. miles
(300,000 sq. km)
Languages Filipino, Tagalog, Cebuano, Hiligaynon, Samaran, Ilocano, Bicolano, English
Religions Roman Catholic 83%, Protestant 9%, Muslim 5%, other 3%
Ethnic mix Malay 95%, other 5%
Government Presidential system
Currency Peso = 100 centavos
Literacy rate 93%
Calorie consumption 2372 calories

POLAND

Page 76 B3

With its seven international borders and strategic location in the heart of Europe, Poland has always played an important role in European affairs.

Official name Republic of Poland
Formation 1918
Capital Warsaw
Population 38.6 million / 328 people per sq mile (127 people per sq km)
Total area 120,728 sq. miles (312,685 sq. km)
Languages Polish
Religions Roman Catholic 93%, other and nonreligious 5%, Orthodox Christian 2%
Ethnic mix Polish 97%, Silesian 1%, other 2%
Government Parliamentary system
Currency Zloty = 100 groszy
Literacy rate 99%
Calorie consumption 3397 calories

PORTUGAL

Page 70 B3

Facing the Atlantic on the western side of the Iberian Peninsula, Portugal is the most westerly country on the European mainland.

Official name Republic of Portugal
Formation 1139
Capital Lisbon
Population 10.1 million /
284 people per sq mile (110 people per sq km)
Total area 35,672 sq. miles
(92,391 sq. km)
Languages Portuguese
Religions Roman Catholic 97%, Protestant 1%, other 2%
Ethnic mix Portuguese 98%, African and other 2%
Government Parliamentary system
Currency Euro = 100 cents
Literacy rate 93%
Calorie consumption 3751 calories

QATAR

Page 98 C4

Projecting north from the Arabian Peninsula into the Persian Gulf, Qatar's reserves of oil and gas make it one of the region's wealthiest states.

Official name State of Qatar
Formation 1971
Capital Doha
Population 610,000 /
144 people per sq mile (55 people per sq km)
Total area 4416 sq. miles
(11,437 sq. km)
Languages Arabic
Religions Muslim (mainly Sunni) 95%, other 5%
Ethnic mix Arab 40%, Indian 18%, Pakistani 18%, Iranian 10%, other 14%
Government Monarchy
Currency Qatar riyal = 100 dirhams
Literacy rate 82%
Calorie consumption Not available

ROMANIA

Page 86 B4

Romania lies on the Black Sea coast. Since the overthrow of its communist regime in 1989, it has been slowly converting to a free-market economy.

Official name Romania
Formation 1878
Capital Bucharest
Population 22.3 million / 251 people per sq mile (97 people per sq km)
Total area 91,699 sq. miles
(237,500 sq. km)
Languages Romanian, Hungarian (Magyar), Romani, German
Religions Romanian Orthodox 87%, Roman Catholic 5%, Protestant 4%, other 4%
Ethnic mix Romanian 89%, Magyar 7%, Roma 3%, other 1%
Government Presidential system
Currency Romanian leu = 100 bani
Literacy rate 97%
Calorie consumption 3407 calories

RUSSIAN FEDERATION

Page 92 D4

Still the world's largest state, despite the breakup of the USSR in 1991, the Russian Federation is struggling to capitalize on its diversity.

Official name Russian Federation
Formation 1480
Capital Moscow
Population 143 million / 22 people per sq mile (8 people per sq km)
Total area 6,592,735 sq. miles
(17,075,200 sq. km)
Languages Russian, Tatar, Ukrainian, Chavash, various other national languages
Religions Orthodox Christian 75%, Muslim 10%, other 15%
Ethnic mix Russian 82%, Tatar 4%, Ukrainian 3%, Chavash 1%, other 10%
Government Presidential system
Currency Russian rouble = 100 kopeks
Literacy rate 99%
Calorie consumption 3014 calories

RWANDA

Page 51 B6

Rwanda lies just south of the Equator in east central Africa. Since independence from France in 1962, ethnic tensions have dominated politics.

Official name Republic of Rwanda
Formation 1962
Capital Kigali
Population 8.4 million / 872 people per sq mile (337 people per sq km)
Total area 10,169 sq. miles
(26,338 sq. km)
Languages Kinyarwanda, French, Kiswahili, English
Religions Roman Catholic 56%, Traditional beliefs 25%, Muslim 10%, Protestant 9%
Ethnic mix Hutu 90%, Tutsi 9%, other (including Twa) 1%
Government Presidential system
Currency Rwanda franc = 100 centimes
Literacy rate 69%
Calorie consumption 2086 calories

SAINT KITTS & NEVIS

Page 33 G3

Separated by a channel, the two islands of Saint Kitts and Nevis are part of the Leeward Islands chain in the Caribbean. Nevis is the less developed of the two.

Official name Federation of Saint Christopher and Nevis
Formation 1983
Capital Basseterre
Population 38,763 / 279 people per sq mile (108 people per sq km)
Total area 101 sq. miles (261 sq. km)
Languages English, English Creole
Religions Anglican 33%, Methodist 29%, Moravian 9%, Roman Catholic 7%, other 22%
Ethnic mix Black 94%, Mixed race 3%, other and Amerindian 2%, White 1%
Government Parliamentary system
Currency Eastern Caribbean dollar = 100 cents
Literacy rate 98%
Calorie consumption 2997 calories

SAINT LUCIA

Page 33 G4

Among the most beautiful of the Caribbean Windward Islands, Saint Lucia retains both French and British influences from its colonial history.

Official name Saint Lucia
Formation 1979
Capital Castries
Population 162,157 /
687 people per sq mile (266 people per sq km)
Total area 239 sq. miles
(620 sq. km)
Languages English, French Creole
Religions Roman Catholic 90%, other 10%
Ethnic mix Black 90%, Mulatto (mixed race) 6%, Asian 3%, White 1%
Government Parliamentary system
Currency Eastern Caribbean dollar = 100 cents
Literacy rate 95%
Calorie consumption 2849 calories

SAINT VINCENT & THE GRENADINES

Page 33 G4

Formerly ruled by Britain, these volcanic islands form part of the Caribbean Windward Islands.

Official name Saint Vincent and the Grenadines
Formation 1979
Capital Kingstown
Population 116,812 / 892 people per sq mile (344 people per sq km)
Total area 150 sq. miles (389 sq. km)
Languages English, English Creole
Religions Anglican 47%, Methodist 28%, Roman Catholic 13%, other 12%
Ethnic mix Black 66%, Mulatto (mixed race) 19%, Asian 6%, White 4%, other 5%
Government Parliamentary system
Currency Eastern Caribbean dollar = 100 cents
Literacy rate 83%
Calorie consumption 2609 calories

SAMOA

Page 123 F4

The southern Pacific islands of Samoa gained independence from New Zealand in 1962. Four of the nine islands are inhabited.

Official name Independent State of Samoa
Formation 1962
Capital Apia
Population 178,000 / 163 people per sq mile (63 people per sq km)
Total area 1104 sq. miles (2860 sq. km)
Languages Samoan, English
Religions Christian 99%, other 1%
Ethnic mix Polynesian 90%, Euronesian 9%, other 1%
Government Parliamentary system
Currency Tala = 100 sene
Literacy rate 99%
Calorie consumption Not available

SAN MARINO

Page 74 C3

Perched on the slopes of Monte Titano in the Italian Appennino, San Marino has maintained its independence since the 4th century AD.

Official name Republic of San Marino
Formation 1631
Capital San Marino
Population 28,119 / 1172 people per sq mile (461 people per sq km)
Total area 23.6 sq. miles (61 sq. km)
Languages Italian
Religions Roman Catholic 93%, other and nonreligious 7%
Ethnic mix Sammarinese 80%, Italian 19%, other 1%
Government Parliamentary system
Currency Euro = 100 cents
Literacy rate 99%
Calorie consumption Not available

SAO TOME & PRINCIPE

Page 55 A5

A former Portuguese colony off Africa's west coast, comprising two main islands and smaller islets. The 1991 elections ended 15 years of Marxism.

Official name Democratic Republic of São Tomé and Príncipe
Formation 1975
Capital São Tomé
Population 175,883 / 474 people per sq mile (183 people per sq km)
Total area 386 sq. miles (1001 sq. km)
Languages Portuguese Creole, Portuguese
Religions Roman Catholic 84%, other 16%
Ethnic mix Black 90%, Portuguese and Creole 10%
Government Presidential system
Currency Dobra = 100 centimos
Literacy rate 83%
Calorie consumption 2567 calories

SAUDI ARABIA

Page 99 B5

Occupying most of the Arabian Peninsula, the desert kingdom of Saudi Arabia, rich in oil and gas, covers an area the size of Western Europe.

Official name Kingdom of Saudi Arabia
Formation 1932
Capital Riyadh; Jiddah (administrative)
Population 24.2 million / 30 people per sq mile (11 people per sq km)
Total area 756,981 sq. miles (1,960,582 sq. km)
Languages Arabic
Religions Sunni Muslim 85%, Shi'a Muslim 15%
Ethnic mix Arab 90%, Afro-Asian 10%
Government Monarchy
Currency Saudi riyal = 100 halalat
Literacy rate 78%
Calorie consumption 2841 calories

SENEGAL

Page 52 B3

A former French colony, Senegal achieved independence in 1960. Its capital, Dakar, stands on the westernmost cape of Africa.

Official name Republic of Senegal
Formation 1960
Capital Dakar
Population 10.1 million / 136 people per sq mile (52 people per sq km)
Total area 75,749 sq. miles (196,190 sq. km)
Languages Wolof, Pulaar, Serer, Diola, Mandinka, Malinke, Soninke, French
Religions Sunni Muslim 90%, Traditional beliefs 5%, Christian 5%
Ethnic mix Wolof 43%, Toucouleur 24%, Serer 15%, Diola 4%, Malinke 3%, other 11%
Government Presidential system
Currency CFA franc = 100 centimes
Literacy rate 39%
Calorie consumption 2277 calories

SERBIA & MONTENEGRO (YUGOSLAVIA)

Page 78 D4

Serbia and Montenegro is the successor state to the former Yugoslavia.

Official name Serbia and Montenegro
Formation 1992
Capital Belgrade
Population 10.5 million / 266 people per sq mile (103 people per sq km)
Total area 39,517 sq. miles (102,350 sq. km)
Languages Serbo-Croat, Albanian, Hungarian (Magyar)
Religions Orthodox Christian 65%, other 12%, Muslim 19%, Roman Catholic 4%
Ethnic mix Serb 62%, Albanian 17%, Montenegrin 5%, other 16%
Government Parliamentary system
Currency Dinar (Serbia); euro (Montenegro)
Literacy rate 98%
Calorie consumption 2778 calories

SEYCHELLES

Page 57 G1

A former British colony comprising 115 islands in the Indian Ocean. Under one-party rule for 16 years, it became a multiparty democracy in 1993.

Official name Republic of Seychelles
Formation 1976
Capital Victoria
Population 80,469 / 774 people per sq mile (298 people per sq km)
Total area 176 sq. miles (455 sq. km)
Languages French Creole, English, French
Religions Roman Catholic 90%, Anglican 8%, other (including Muslim) 2%
Ethnic mix Creole 89%, Indian 5%, Chinese 2%, other 4%
Government Presidential system
Currency Seychelles rupee = 100 cents
Literacy rate 92%
Calorie consumption 2461 calories

SIERRA LEONE

Page 52 C4

The West African state of Sierra Leone achieved independence from the British in 1961. Today, it is one of the world's poorest nations.

Official name Republic of Sierra Leone
Formation 1961
Capital Freetown
Population 5 million / 181 people per sq mile (70 people per sq km)
Total area 27,698 sq. miles (71,740 sq. km)
Languages Mende, Temne, Krio, English
Religions Muslim 30%, Traditional beliefs 30%, Christian 10%, other 30%
Ethnic mix Mende 35%, Temne 32%, Limba 8%, Kuranko 4%, other 21%
Government Presidential system
Currency Leone = 100 cents
Literacy rate 36%
Calorie consumption 1913 calories

SINGAPORE

Page 116 A1

A city state linked to the southernmost tip of the Malay Peninsula by a causeway, Singapore is one of Asia's most important commercial centers.

Official name Republic of Singapore
Formation 1965
Capital Singapore
Population 4.3 million / 18220 people per sq mile (7049 people per sq km)
Total area 250 sq. miles (648 sq. km)
Languages Mandarin, Malay, Tamil, English
Religions Buddhist 55%, Taoist 22%, Muslim 16%, Hindu, Christian, and Sikh 7%
Ethnic mix Chinese 77%, Malay 14%, Indian 8%, other 1%
Government Parliamentary system
Currency Singapore dollar = 100 cents
Literacy rate 93%
Calorie consumption Not available

SLOVAKIA

Page 77 C6

Landlocked in Central Europe, Slovakia has been independent since 1993. It is the less developed half of the former Czechoslovakia.

Official name Slovak Republic
Formation 1993
Capital Bratislava
Population 5.4 million / 285 people per sq mile (110 people per sq km)
Total area 18,859 sq. miles (48,845 sq. km)
Languages Slovak, Hungarian (Magyar), Czech
Religions Roman Catholic 60%, Atheist 10%, Protestant 8%, Orthodox Christian 4%, other 18%
Ethnic mix Slovak 85%, Magyar 11%, Roma 1%, Czech 1%, other 2%
Government Parliamentary system
Currency Slovak koruna = 100 halierov
Literacy rate 99%
Calorie consumption 2894 calories

SLOVENIA

Page 73 D8

Northernmost of the former Yugoslav republics, Slovenia has the closest links with Western Europe. In 1991, it gained independence with little violence.

Official name Republic of Slovenia
Formation 1991
Capital Ljubljana
Population 2 million / 256 people per sq mile (99 people er sq km)
Total area 7820 sq. miles 20,253 sq. km)
Languages Slovene, Serbo-Croat
Religions Roman Catholic 96%, Muslim 1%, other 3%
Ethnic mix Slovene 83%, Serb 2%, Croat 2%, Bosniak 1%, other 12%
Government Parliamentary system
Currency Tolar = 100 stotinov
Literacy rate 99%
Calorie consumption 2935 calories

SOLOMON ISLANDS

Page 122 C3

The Solomon archipelago comprises several hundred islands scattered in the southwestern Pacific. Independence from Britain came in 1978.

Official name Solomon Islands
Formation 1978
Capital Honiara
Population 477,000 / 44 people per sq mile (17 people per sq km)
Total area 10,985 sq. miles (28,450 sq. km)
Languages English, Pidgin English, Melanesian Pidgin
Religions Anglican 34%, Roman Catholic 19%, South Seas Evangelical Church 17%, Methodist 11%, other 19%
Ethnic mix Melanesian 94%, other 6%
Government Parliamentary system
Currency Solomon Islands dollar = 100 cents
Literacy rate 77%
Calorie consumption 2272 calories

SOMALIA

Page 51 E5

Italian and British Somaliland were united in 1960 to create this semiarid state occupying the horn of Africa. It has suffered years of civil war.

Official name Somalia
Formation 1960
Capital Mogadishu
Population 9.9 million / 41 people per sq mile (16 people per sq km)
Total area 246,199 sq. miles (637,657 sq. km)
Languages Somali, Arabic, English, Italian
Religions Sunni Muslim 98%, Christian 2%
Ethnic mix Somali 85%, other 15%
Government Transitional regime
Currency Somali shilling = 100 centesimi
Literacy rate 24%
Calorie consumption 1628 calories

SPAIN

Page 70 D2

Lodged between mainland Europe and Africa, the Atlantic and the Mediterranean, Spain has occupied a pivotal position since it was united in 1492.

Official name Kingdom of Spain
Formation 1492
Capital Madrid
Population 41.1 million / 213 people per sq mile (82 people per sq km)
Total area 194,896 sq. miles (504,782 sq. km)
Languages Spanish, Catalan, Galician, Basque
Religions Roman Catholic 96%, other 4%
Ethnic mix Castilian Spanish 72%, Catalan 17%, Galician 6%, Basque 2%, other 2%, Roma 1%
Government Parliamentary system
Currency Euro = 100 cents
Literacy rate 98%
Calorie consumption 3422 calories

SURINAME

Page 37 G3

Suriname is a former Dutch colony on the north coast of South America. Democracy was restored in 1991, after almost 11 years of military rule.

Official name Republic of Suriname
Formation 1975
Capital Paramaribo
Population 436,000 / 7 people per sq mile (3 people per sq km)
Total area 63,039 sq. miles (163,270 sq. km)
Languages Sranan, Dutch, Javanese, Sarnami Hindi, Saramaccan, Chinese
Religions Hindu 27%, Protestant 25%, Roman Catholic 23%, Muslim 20%, Traditional beliefs 5%
Ethnic mix Creole 34%, South Asian 34%, Javanese 18%, Black 9%, other 5%
Government Parliamentary system
Currency Suriname dollar = 100 cents
Literacy rate 94%
Calorie consumption 2643 calories

SWITZERLAND

Page 73 A7

One of the world's most prosperous countries, with a long tradition of neutrality in foreign affairs, it lies at the center of Western Europe.

Official name Swiss Confederation
Formation 1291
Capital Bern
Population 7.2 million / 469 people per sq mile (181 people per sq km)
Total area 15,942 sq. miles (41,290 sq. km)
Languages German, Swiss-German, French, Italian, Romansch
Religions Roman Catholic 46%, Protestant 40%, other, 12%, Muslim 2%
Ethnic mix German 65%, French 18%, Italian 10%, other 6%, Romansch 1%
Government Parliamentary system
Currency Swiss franc = 100 rappen/centimes
Literacy rate 99%
Calorie consumption 3440 calories

SOUTH AFRICA

Page 56 C4

South Africa is the most southerly nation on the African continent. The multiracial elections of 1994 overturned 80 years of white minority rule.

Official name Republic of South Africa
Formation 1934
Capital Pretoria; Cape Town; Bloemfontein
Population 45 million / 95 people per sq mile (37 people per sq km)
Total area 471,008 sq. miles (1,219,912 sq. km)
Languages English, Afrikaans, 9 other African languages
Religions Christian 68%, Traditional beliefs and animist 29%, other 3%
Ethnic mix Black 79%, White 10%, Colored 9%, Asian 2%
Government Presidential system
Currency Rand = 100 cents
Literacy rate 86%
Calorie consumption 2921 calories

SRI LANKA

Page 110 D3

The island republic of Sri Lanka is separated from India by the narrow Palk Strait. Since 1983, the Sinhalese and Tamil population have been in conflict.

Official name Democratic Socialist Republic of Sri Lanka
Formation 1948
Capital Colombo
Population 19.1 million / 764 people per sq mile (295 people per sq km)
Total area 25,332 sq. miles (65,610 sq. km)
Languages Sinhala, Tamil, English
Religions Buddhist 69%, Hindu 15%, Muslim 8%, Christian 8%
Ethnic mix Sinhalese 74%, Tamil 18%, Moor 7%, other 1%
Government Mixed presidential–parliamentary system
Currency Sri Lanka rupee = 100 cents
Literacy rate 92%
Calorie consumption 2274 calories

SWAZILAND

Page 56 D4

The tiny southern African kingdom of Swaziland gained independence from Britain in 1968. It is economically dependent on South Africa.

Official name Kingdom of Swaziland
Formation 1968
Capital Mbabane
Population 1.1 million / 166 people per sq mile (64 people per sq km)
Total area 6704 sq. miles (17,363 sq. km)
Languages English, siSwati, isiZulu, Xitsonga
Religions Christian 60%, Traditional beliefs 40%
Ethnic mix Swazi 97%, other 3%
Government Monarchy
Currency Lilangeni = 100 cents
Literacy rate 81%
Calorie consumption 2593 calories

SYRIA

Page 96 B3

Stretching from the eastern Mediterranean to the River Tigris, Syria's borders were created on its independence from France in 1946.

Official name Syrian Arab Republic
Formation 1941
Capital Damascus
Population 17.8 million / 250 people per sq mile (97 people per sq km)
Total area 71,498 sq. miles (184,180 sq. km)
Languages Arabic, French, Kurdish, Armenian, Circassian
Religions Sunni Muslim 74%, other Muslim 16%, Christian 10%
Ethnic mix Arab 89%, Kurdish 6%, other 3%, Armenian, Turkmen, and Circassian 2%
Government One-party state
Currency Syrian pound = 100 piasters
Literacy rate 83%
Calorie consumption 3038 calories

SOUTH KOREA

Page 106 E4

South Korea occupies the southern half of the Korean peninsula. It was separated from the communist North in 1948.

Official name Republic of Korea
Formation 1948
Capital Seoul
Population 47.7 million / 1251 people per sq mile (483 people per sq km)
Total area 38,023 sq. miles (98,480 sq. km)
Languages Korean, Chinese
Religions Mahayana Buddhist 47%, Protestant 38%, Roman Catholic 11%, Confucianist 3%, other 1%
Ethnic mix Korean 100%
Government Presidential system
Currency South Korean won = 100 chon
Literacy rate 98%
Calorie consumption 3055 calories

SUDAN

Page 50 B4

The largest country in Africa, part of Sudan borders the Red Sea. In 1989, an army coup installed a military Islamic fundamentalist regime.

Official name Republic of the Sudan
Formation 1956
Capital Khartoum
Population 33.6 million / 35 people per sq mile (13 people per sq km)
Total area 967,493 sq. miles (2,505,810 sq. km)
Languages Arabic, Dinka, Nuer, Nubian, Beja, Zande, Bari, Fur, Shilluk
Religions Muslim (mainly Sunni) 70%, Traditional beliefs 20%, other 10%,
Ethnic mix Arab 40%, Dinka and Beja 7%, other Black 52%, other 1%
Government Presidential system
Currency Sudanese pound or dinar = 100 piastres
Literacy rate 60%
Calorie consumption 2288 calories

SWEDEN

Page 62 B4

The largest Scandinavian country in both population and area, Sweden's strong industrial base helps to fund its extensive welfare system.

Official name Kingdom of Sweden
Formation 1523
Capital Stockholm
Population 8.9 million / 56 people per sq mile (22 people per sq km)
Total area 173,731 sq. miles (449,964 sq. km)
Languages Swedish, Finnish, Sámi
Religions Evangelical Lutheran 82%, Roman Catholic 2%, Muslim 2%, Orthodox Christian 1%, other 13%
Ethnic mix Swedish 88%, Foreign-born or first-generation immigrant 10%, Finnish and Sámi 2%
Government Parliamentary system
Currency Swedish krona = 100 öre
Literacy rate 99%
Calorie consumption 3164 calories

TAIWAN

Page 107 D6

The island republic of Taiwan lies 130 km (80 miles) off the southeast coast of mainland China. China considers it to be one of its provinces.

Official name Republic of China (ROC)
Formation 1949
Capital Taipei
Population 22.6 million / 1815 people per sq mile (701 people per sq km)
Total area 13,892 sq. miles (35,980 sq. km)
Languages Amoy Chinese, Mandarin Chinese, Hakka Chinese
Religions Buddhist, Confucianist, and Taoist 93%, Christian 5%, other 2%
Ethnic mix Indigenous Chinese 84%, Mainland Chinese 14%, Aboriginal 2%
Government Presidential system
Currency Taiwan dollar = 100 cents
Literacy rate 96%
Calorie consumption Not available

TAJIKISTAN

Page 101 F3

Tajikistan lies landlocked on the western slopes of the Pamirs in Central Asia. The Tajiks' language and traditions are similar to those of Iran.

Official name Republic of Tajikistan
Formation 1991
Capital Dushanbe
Population 6.2 million / 112 people per sq mile (43 people per sq km)
Total area 55,251 sq. miles (143,100 sq. km)
Languages Tajik, Uzbek, Russian
Religions Sunni Muslim 80%, other 15%, Shi'a Muslim 5%
Ethnic mix Tajik 62%, Uzbek 24%, Russian 8%, Tatar 1%, Kyrgyz 1%, other 4%
Government Presidential system
Currency Somoni = 100 diram
Literacy rate 99%
Calorie consumption 1662 calories

TOGO

Page 53 F4

Togo lies sandwiched between Ghana and Benin in West Africa. The 1993–94 presidential elections were the first since its independence in 1960.

Official name Republic of Togo
Formation 1960
Capital Lomé
Population 4.9 million / 233 people per sq mile (90 people per sq km)
Total area 21,924 sq. miles (56,785 sq. km)
Languages Ewe, Kabye, Gurma, French
Religions Traditional beliefs 50%, Christian 35%, Muslim 15%
Ethnic mix Ewe 46%, Kabye 27%, other African 26%, European 1%
Government Presidential system
Currency CFA franc = 100 centimes
Literacy rate 60%
Calorie consumption 2287 calories

TUNISIA

Page 49 E2

Tunisia, in North Africa, has traditionally been one of the more liberal Arab states, but is now facing a challenge from Islamic fundamentalists.

Official name Republic of Tunisia
Formation 1956
Capital Tunis
Population 9.8 million / 163 people per sq mile (63 people per sq km)
Total area 63,169 sq. miles (163,610 sq. km)
Languages Arabic, French
Religions Muslim (mainly Sunni) 98%, Christian 1%, Jewish 1%
Ethnic mix Arab and Berber 98%, Jewish 1%, European 1%
Government Presidential system
Currency Tunisian dinar = 1000 millimes
Literacy rate 73%
Calorie consumption 3293 calories

TUVALU

Page 123 E3

The former Ellice Islands, linked to the Gilbert Islands as a British colony until 1978, Tuvalu is an isolated chain of nine atolls in the Central Pacific.

Official name Tuvalu
Formation 1978
Capital Fongafale, on Funafuti Atoll
Population 11,305 / 1130 people per sq mile (435 people per sq km)
Total area 10 sq. miles (26 sq. km)
Languages Tuvaluan, Kiribati, English
Religions Church of Tuvalu 97%, other 1%, Baha'i 1%, Seventh-day Adventist 1%
Ethnic mix Polynesian 96%, other 4%
Government Nonparty system
Currency Australian dollar and Tuvaluan dollar = 100 cents
Literacy rate 98%
Calorie consumption Not available

TANZANIA

Page 51 B7

The East African state of Tanzania was formed in 1964 by the union of Tanganyika and Zanzibar. A third of its area is game reserve or national park.

Official name United Republic of Tanzania
Formation 1964
Capital Dodoma
Population 37 million / 108 people per sq mile (42 people per sq km)
Total area 364,898 sq. miles (945,087 sq. km)
Languages Kiswahili, Sukuma, English
Religions Muslim 33%, Christian 33%, Traditional beliefs 30%, other 4%
Ethnic mix Native African (over 120 tribes) 99%, European and Asian 1%
Government Presidential system
Currency Tanzanian shilling = 100 cents
Literacy rate 77%
Calorie consumption 1997 calories

TONGA

Page 123 E4

Northeast of New Zealand, in the South Pacific, Tonga is an archipelago of 170 islands, 45 of which are inhabited. Politics is effectively controlled by the king.

Official name Kingdom of Tonga
Formation 1970
Capital Nuku'alofa
Population 108,141 / 389 people per sq mile (150 people per sq km)
Total area 289 sq. miles (748 sq. km)
Languages English, Tongan
Religions Free Wesleyan 41%, Roman Catholic 16%, Church of Jesus Christ of Latter-day Saints 14%, Free Church of Tonga 12%, other 17%
Ethnic mix Polynesian 99%, other 1%
Government Monarchy
Currency Pa'anga (Tongan dollar) = 100 seniti
Literacy rate 99%
Calorie consumption Not available

TURKEY

Page 94 B3

Lying partly in Europe, but mostly in Asia, Turkey's position gives it significant influence in the Mediterranean, Black Sea, and Middle East.

Official name Republic of Turkey
Formation 1923
Capital Ankara
Population 71.3 million / 240 people per sq mile (93 people per sq km)
Total area 301,382 sq. miles (780,580 sq. km)
Languages Turkish, Kurdish, Arabic, Circassian, Armenian, Greek, Georgian, Ladino
Religions Muslim (mainly Sunni) 99%, other 1%
Ethnic mix Turkish 70%, Kurdish 20%, Arab 2%, other 8%
Government Parliamentary system
Currency Turkish lira = 100 kurus
Literacy rate 87%
Calorie consumption 3343 calories

UGANDA

Page 51 B6

Uganda lies landlocked in East Africa. It was ruled by one of Africa's more eccentric leaders, the dictator Idi Amin Dada, from 1971–1980.

Official name Republic of Uganda
Formation 1962
Capital Kampala
Population 25.8 million / 335 people per sq mile (129 people per sq km)
Total area 91,135 sq. miles (236,040 sq. km)
Languages Luganda, Nkole, English
Religions Roman Catholic 38%, Protestant 33%, Traditional beliefs 13%, Muslim (mainly Sunni) 8%, other 8%
Ethnic mix Bantu tribes 50%, Sudanese 5%, other 45%
Government Nonparty system
Currency New Uganda shilling = 100 cents
Literacy rate 69%
Calorie consumption 2398 calories

THAILAND

Page 115 C5

Thailand lies at the heart of mainland Southeast Asia. Continuing rapid industrialization has resulted in massive congestion in the capital.

Official name Kingdom of Thailand
Formation 1238
Capital Bangkok
Population 62.8 million / 318 people per sq mile (123 people per sq km)
Total area 198,455 sq. miles (514,000 sq. km)
Languages Thai, Chinese, Malay, Khmer, Mon, Karen, Miao
Religions Buddhist 95%, Muslim 4%, other (including Christian) 1%
Ethnic mix Thai 83%, Chinese 12%, Malay 3%, Khmer and other 2%
Government Parliamentary system
Currency Baht = 100 stang
Literacy rate 93%
Calorie consumption 2486 calories

TRINIDAD & TOBAGO

Page 33 H5

The former British colony of Trinidad and Tobago is the most southerly of the West Indies, lying just 15 km (9 miles) off the coast of Venezuela.

Official name Republic of Trinidad and Tobago
Formation 1962
Capital Port-of-Spain
Population 1.3 million / 656 people per sq mile (253 people per sq km)
Total area 1980 sq. miles (5128 sq. km)
Languages English Creole, English, Hindi, French, Spanish
Religions Christian 60%, Hindu 24%, other 16%
Ethnic mix East Indian 40%, Black 40%, Mixed race 19%, other 1%
Government Parliamentary system
Currency Trinidad and Tobago dollar = 100 cents
Literacy rate 99%
Calorie consumption 2756 calories

TURKMENISTAN

Page 100 B2

Stretching from the Caspian Sea into the deserts of Central Asia, the ex-Soviet state of Turkmenistan has adjusted better than most to independence.

Official name Turkmenistan
Formation 1991
Capital Ashgabat
Population 4.9 million / 26 people per sq mile (10 people per sq km)
Total area 188,455 sq. miles (488,100 sq. km)
Languages Turkmen, Uzbek, Russian, Kazakh, Tatar
Religions Sunni Muslim 87%, Orthodox Christian 11%, other 2%
Ethnic mix Turkmen 77%, Uzbek 9%, Russian 7%, other 4%, Kazakh 2%, Tatar 1%
Government One-party state
Currency Manat = 100 tenga
Literacy rate 98%
Calorie consumption 2738 calories

UKRAINE

Page 86 C2

Bordered by seven states, the former "breadbasket of the Soviet Union" balances assertive nationalism with concerns over its relations with Russia.

Official name Ukraine
Formation 1991
Capital Kiev
Population 47.7 million / 205 people per sq mile (79 people per sq km)
Total area 223,089 sq. miles (603,700 sq. km)
Languages Ukrainian, Russian, Tatar
Religions Christian (mainly Orthodox) 95%, Jewish 1%, other 4%
Ethnic mix Ukrainian 73%, Russian 22%, Jewish 1%, other 4%
Government Presidential system
Currency Hryvna = 100 kopiykas
Literacy rate 99%
Calorie consumption 3008 calories

UNITED ARAB EMIRATES

Page 99 D5

Bordering the Persian Gulf on the northern coast of the Arabian Peninsula, is the United Arab Emirates, a working federation of seven states.

Official name United Arab Emirates
Formation 1971
Capital Abu Dhabi
Population 3 million / 93 people per sq mile (36 people per sq km)
Total area 32,000 sq. miles (82,880 sq. km)
Languages Arabic, Farsi, Indian and Pakistani languages, English
Religions Muslim (mainly Sunni) 96%, Christian, Hindu, and other 4%
Ethnic mix Asian 60%, Emirian 25%, other Arab 12%, European 3%
Government Monarchy
Currency UAE dirham = 100 fils
Literacy rate 77%
Calorie consumption 3340 calories

UNITED KINGDOM

Page 67 B5

Separated from continental Europe by the North Sea and the English Channel, the UK comprises England, Wales, Scotland, and Northern Ireland.

Official name United Kingdom of Great Britain and Northern Ireland
Formation 1707
Capital London
Population 59.3 million / 636 people per sq mile (245 people per sq km)
Total area 94,525 sq. miles (244,820 sq. km)
Languages English, Welsh, Scottish Gaelic, Irish Gaelic
Religions Anglican 45%, Roman Catholic 9%, Presbyterian 4%, other 42%
Ethnic mix English 80%, Scottish 9%, Northern Irish 3%, Welsh 3%, other 5%,
Government Parliamentary system
Currency Pound sterling = 100 pence
Literacy rate 99%
Calorie consumption 3368 calories

UNITED STATES OF AMERICA

Page 13 B5

Stretching across the most temperate part of North America, and with many natural resources, the USA is the sole truly global superpower.

Official name United States of America
Formation 1776
Capital Washington D.C.
Population 294 million / 83 people per sq mile (32 people per sq km)
Total area 3,717,792 sq. miles (9,626,091 sq. km)
Languages English, Spanish, Chinese, French, German, Italian, Russian, Polish
Religions Protestant 52%, Roman Catholic 25%, Jewish 2%, other 21%
Ethnic mix White 69%, Hispanic 13%, Black American/African 13%, Asian 4%, Native American 1%
Government Presidential system
Currency US dollar = 100 cents
Literacy rate 99%
Calorie consumption 3766 calories

URUGUAY

Page 42 D4

Uruguay is situated in southeastern South America. It returned to civilian government in 1985, after 12 years of military dictatorship.

Official name Eastern Republic of Uruguay
Formation 1828
Capital Montevideo
Population 3.4 million / 50 people per sq mile (19 people per sq km)
Total area 68,039 sq. miles (176,220 sq. km)
Languages Spanish
Religions Roman Catholic 66%, Jewish 2%, Protestant 2%, other and nonreligious 30%
Ethnic mix White 90%, other 10%
Government Presidential system
Currency Uruguayan peso = 100 centésimos
Literacy rate 98%
Calorie consumption 2848 calories

UZBEKISTAN

Page 100 D2

Sharing the Aral Sea coastline with its northern neighbor, Kazakhstan, Uzbekistan lies on the ancient Silk Road between Asia and Europe.

Official name Republic of Uzbekistan
Formation 1991
Capital Tashkent
Population 26.1 million / 151 people per sq mile (58 people per sq km)
Total area 172,741 sq. miles (447,400 sq. km)
Languages Uzbek, Russian, Tajik, Kazakh
Religions Sunni Muslim 88%, Orthodox Christian 9%, other 3%
Ethnic mix Uzbek 71%, Russian 8%, Tajik 5%, Kazakh 4%, other 12%,
Government Presidential system
Currency Som = 100 tiyin
Literacy rate 99%
Calorie consumption 2197 calories

VANUATU

Page 122 D4

An archipelago of 82 islands and islets in the Pacific Ocean, it was ruled jointly by Britain and France from 1906 until independence in 1980.

Official name Republic of Vanuatu
Formation 1980
Capital Port Vila
Population 212,000 / 45 people per sq mile (17 people per sq km)
Total area 4710 sq. miles (12,200 sq. km)
Languages Bislama, English, French,
Religions Presbyterian 37%, Anglican 15%, Roman Catholic 15%, Traditional beliefs 8%, Seventh-day Adventist 6%, , other 19%
Ethnic mix Melanesian 94%, other 3%, Polynesian 3%
Government Parliamentary system
Currency Vatu = 100 centimes
Literacy rate 34%
Calorie consumption 2565 calories

VATICAN CITY

Page 75 A8

The Vatican City, seat of the Roman Catholic Church, is a walled enclave in the city of Rome. It is the world's smallest fully independent state.

Official name State of the Vatican City
Formation 1929
Capital Vatican City
Population 911 / 5359 people per sq mile (2070 people per sq km)
Total area 0.17 sq. miles (0.44 sq. km)
Languages Italian, Latin
Religions Roman Catholic 100%
Ethnic mix The current pope is Polish, ending nearly 500 years of Italian popes. Cardinals are from many nationalities, but Italians form the largest group. Most of the resident lay persons are Italian.
Government Papal state
Currency Euro = 100 cents
Literacy rate 99%
Calorie consumption Not available

VENEZUELA

Page 36 D2

Located on the north coast of South America, Venezuela has the continent's most urbanized society. Most people live in the northern cities.

Official name Bolivarian Republic of Venezuela
Formation 1830
Capital Caracas
Population 25.7 million / 75 people per sq mile (29 people per sq km)
Total area 352,143 sq. miles (912,050 sq. km)
Languages Spanish, Amerindian languages
Religions Roman Catholic 89%, Protestant and other 11%
Ethnic mix Mestizo 69%, White 20%, Black 9%, Amerindian 2%
Government Presidential system
Currency Bolívar = 100 centimos
Literacy rate 93%
Calorie consumption 2376 calories

VIETNAM

Page 114 D4

Situated in the far east of mainland Southeast Asia, the country is still rebuilding after the devastating 1962–1975 Vietnam War.

Official name Socialist Republic of Vietnam
Formation 1976
Capital Hanoi
Population 81.4 million / 648 people per sq mile (250 people per sq km)
Total area 127,243 sq. miles (329,560 sq. km)
Languages Vietnamese, Chinese, Thai, Khmer, Muong, Nung, Miao, Yao, Jarai
Religions Buddhist 55%, other and nonreligious 38%, Christian 7%
Ethnic mix Vietnamese 88%, Chinese 4%, Thai 2%, other 6%
Government One-party state
Currency Dông = 10 hao = 100 xu
Literacy rate 93%
Calorie consumption 2533 calories

YEMEN

Page 99 C7

Located in southern Arabia, Yemen was formerly two countries – a socialist regime in the south, and a republic in the north. Both united in 1990.

Official name Republic of Yemen
Formation 1990
Capital Sana
Population 20 million / 92 people per sq mile (36 people per sq km)
Total area 203,849 sq. miles (527,970 sq. km)
Languages Arabic
Religions Sunni Muslim 55%, Shi'a Muslim 42%, Christian, Hindu, and Jewish 3%
Ethnic mix Arab 95%, Afro-Arab 3%, Indian, Somali, and European 2%
Government Presidential system
Currency Yemeni rial = 100 sene
Literacy rate 49%
Calorie consumption 2050 calories

ZAMBIA

Page 56 C2

Zambia lies landlocked at the heart of southern Africa. In 1991, it made a peaceful transition from single-party rule to multiparty democracy.

Official name Republic of Zambia
Formation 1964
Capital Lusaka
Population 10.8 million / 38 people per sq mile (15 people per sq km)
Total area 290,584 sq. miles (752,614 sq. km)
Languages Bemba, Tonga, Nyanja, Lozi, Lala-Bisa, Nsenga, English
Religions Christian 63%, Traditional beliefs 36%, Muslim and Hindu 1%
Ethnic mix Bemba 34%, other African 65%, European 1%
Government Presidential system
Currency Zambian kwacha = 100 ngwee
Literacy rate 80%
Calorie consumption 1885 calories

ZIMBABWE

Page 56 D3

The former British colony of Southern Rhodesia became fully independent as Zimbabwe in 1980, after 15 years of troubled white minority rule.

Official name Republic of Zimbabwe
Formation 1980
Capital Harare
Population 12.9 million / 86 people per sq mile (33 people per sq km)
Total area 150,803 sq. miles (390,580 sq. km)
Languages Shona, isiNdebele, English
Religions Syncretic (Christian/traditional beliefs) 50%, Christian 25%, Traditional beliefs 24%, other (including Muslim) 1%
Ethnic mix Shona 71%, Ndebele 16%, other African 11%, White 1%, Asian 1%
Government Presidential system
Currency Zimbabwe dollar = 100 cents
Literacy rate 90%
Calorie consumption 2133 calories

LARGEST COUNTRIES

Russ. Fed.	.6,592,735 sq miles	(17,075,200 sq km)
Canada	.3,855,171 sq miles	(9,984,670 sq km)
USA	.3,717,792 sq miles	(9,629,091 sq km)
China	.3,705,386 sq miles	(9,596,960 sq km)
Brazil	.3,286,470 sq miles	(8,511,965 sq km)
Australia	.2,967,893 sq miles	(7,686,893 sq km)
India	.1,269,339 sq miles	(3,287,590 sq km)
Argentina	.1,068,296 sq miles	(2,766,890 sq km)
Kazakhstan	.1,049,150 sq miles	(2,717,300 sq km)
Sudan	.967,493 sq miles	(2,505,810 sq km)

SMALLEST COUNTRIES

Vatican City	.0.17 sq miles	(0.44 sq km)
Monaco	.0.75 sq miles	(1.95 sq km)
Nauru	.8 sq miles	(21 sq km)
Tuvalu	.10 sq miles	(26 sq km)
San Marino	.24 sq miles	(61 sq km)
Liechtenstein	.62 sq miles	(160 sq km)
Marshall Islands	.70 sq miles	(181 sq km)
St. Kitts & Nevis	.101 sq miles	(261 sq km)
Maldives	.116 sq miles	(300 sq km)
Malta	.122 sq miles	(316 sq km)

LARGEST ISLANDS

(TO THE NEAREST 1,000 - OR 100,000 FOR THE LARGEST)

Greenland	.849,400 sq miles	(2,200,000 sq km)
New Guinea	.312,000 sq miles	(808,000 sq km)
Borneo	.292,222 sq miles	(757,050 sq km)
Madagascar	.229,300 sq miles	(594,000 sq km)
Sumatra	.202,300 sq miles	(524,000 sq km)
Baffin Island	.183,800 sq miles	(476,000 sq km)
Honshu	.88,800 sq miles	(230,000 sq km)
Britain	.88,700 sq miles	(229,800 sq km)

RICHEST COUNTRIES

(GNP PER CAPITA, IN US$)

Liechtenstein	.50,000
Luxembourg	.39,470
Norway	.38,730
Switzerland	.36,170
USA	.35,400
Japan	.34,010
Denmark	.30,260
Iceland	.27,960
Monaco	.27,500
Sweden	.25,970

POOREST COUNTRIES

(GNP PER CAPITA, IN US$)

Congo, Dem. Rep.	.100
Burundi	.100
Ethiopia	.100
Somalia	.120
Guinea-Bissau	.130
Sierra Leone	.140
Liberia	.140
Malawi	.160
Tajikistan	.180
Niger	.180

MOST POPULOUS COUNTRIES

China	.1,304,200,000
India	.1,065,500,000
USA	.294,000,000
Indonesia	.219,900,000
Brazil	.178,500,000
Pakistan	.153,600,000
Bangladesh	.146,700,000

MOST POPULOUS COUNTRIES *continued*

Russian Federation	.143,200,000
Japan	.127,700,000
Nigeria	.124,000,000

LEAST POPULOUS COUNTRIES

Vatican City	.921
Tuvalu	.11,305
Nauru	.12,570
Palau	.19,717
San Marino	.28,119
Monaco	.32,130
Liechtenstein	.33,145
St. Kitts & Nevis	.38,763
Marshall Islands	.56,429
Antigua & Barbuda	.67,897

MOST DENSELY POPULATED COUNTRIES

Monaco	.42,840 people per sq mile	(16,477 per sq km)
Singapore	18,220 people per sq mile	(7,049 per sq km)
Vatican City	.5,359 people per sq mile	(2,070 per sq km)
Malta	.3,177 people per sq mile	(1,231 per sq km)
Bangladesh	.2,837 people per sq mile	(1,096 per sq km)
Maldives	.2,741 people per sq mile	(1,060 per sq km)
Bahrain	.2,652 people per sq mile	(1,025 per sq km)
Taiwan	.1,815 people per sq mile	(701 per sq km)
Mauritius	.1,671 people per sq mile	(645 per sq km)
Barbados	.1,627 people per sq mile	(628 per sq km)

MOST SPARSELY POPULATED COUNTRIES

Mongolia	.4 people per sq mile	(2 per sq km)
Namibia	.6 people per sq mile	(2 per sq km)
Suriname	.7 people per sq mile	(3 per sq km)
Mauritania	.7 people per sq mile	(3 per sq km)
Iceland	.7 people per sq mile	(3 per sq km)
Australia	.7 people per sq mile	(3 per sq km)
Libya	.8 people per sq mile	(3 per sq km)
Botswana	.8 people per sq mile	(3 per sq km)
Canada	.9 people per sq mile	(3 per sq km)
Guyana	.10 people per sq mile	(4 per sq km)

MOST WIDELY SPOKEN LANGUAGES

1. Chinese (Mandarin)	6. Arabic
2. English	7. Bengali
3. Hindi	8. Portuguese
4. Spanish	9. Malay-Indonesian
5. Russian	10. French

COUNTRIES WITH THE MOST LAND BORDERS

14: China *(Afghanistan, Bhutan, Myanmar, India, Kazakhstan, Kyrgyzstan, Laos, Mongolia, Nepal, North Korea, Pakistan, Russian Federation, Tajikistan, Vietnam)*

14: Russ. Fed. *(Azerbaijan, Belarus, China, Estonia, Finland, Georgia, Kazakhstan, Latvia, Lithuania, Mongolia, North Korea, Norway, Poland, Ukraine)*

10: Brazil *(Argentina, Bolivia, Colombia, French Guiana, Guyana, Paraguay, Peru, Suriname, Uruguay, Venezuela)*

9: Congo, Dem. Rep. *(Angola, Burundi, Central African Republic, Congo, Rwanda, Sudan, Tanzania, Uganda, Zambia)*

9: Germany *(Austria, Belgium, Czech Republic, Denmark, France, Luxembourg, Netherlands, Poland, Switzerland)*

9: Sudan *(Central African Republic, Chad, Congo, Dem. Rep., Egypt, Eritrea, Ethiopia, Kenya, Libya, Uganda)*

8: Austria *(Czech Republic, Germany, Hungary, Italy, Liechtenstein, Slovakia, Slovenia, Switzerland)*

8: France *(Andorra, Belgium, Germany, Italy, Luxembourg, Monaco, Spain, Switzerland)*

8: Tanzania *(Burundi, Congo, Dem. Rep., Kenya, Malawi, Mozambique, Rwanda, Uganda, Zambia)*

8: Turkey *(Armenia, Azerbaijan, Bulgaria, Georgia, Greece, Iran, Iraq, Syria)*

LONGEST RIVERS

Nile (NE Africa)	.4,160 miles	(6,695 km)
Amazon (South America)	.4,049 miles	(6,516 km)
Yangtze (China)	.3,915 miles	(6,299 km)
Mississippi/Missouri (US)	.3,710 miles	(5,969 km)
Ob'-Irtysh (Russ. Fed.)	.3,461 miles	(5,570 km)
Yellow River (China)	.3,395 miles	(5,464 km)
Congo (Central Africa)	.2,900 miles	(4,667 km)
Mekong (Southeast Asia)	.2,749 miles	(4,425 km)
Lena (Russian Federation)	.2,734 miles	(4,400 km)
Mackenzie (Canada)	.2,640 miles	(4,250 km)

HIGHEST MOUNTAINS
(HEIGHT ABOVE SEA LEVEL)

Everest	.29,035 ft	(8,850 m)
K2	.28,253 ft	(8,611 m)
Kanchenjunga I	.28,210 ft	(8,598 m)
Makalu I	.27,767 ft	(8,463 m)
Cho Oyu	.26,907 ft	(8,201 m)
Dhaulagiri I	.26,796 ft	(8,167 m)
Manaslu I	.26,783 ft	(8,163 m)
Nanga Parbat I	.26,661 ft	(8,126 m)
Annapurna I	.26,547 ft	(8,091 m)
Gasherbrum I	.26,471 ft	(8,068 m)

LARGEST BODIES OF INLAND WATER
(WITH AREA AND DEPTH)

Caspian Sea	143,243 sq miles (371,000 sq km)	3,215 ft (980 m)
Lake Superior	32,151 sq miles (83,270 sq km)	1,289 ft (393 m)
Lake Victoria	26,560 sq miles (68,880 sq km)	328 ft (100 m)
Lake Huron	23,436 sq miles (60,700 sq km)	751 ft (229 m)
Lake Michigan	22,402 sq miles (58,020 sq km)	922 ft (281 m)
Lake Tanganyika	12,703 sq miles (32,900 sq km)	4,700 ft (1,435 m)
Great Bear Lake	12,274 sq miles (31,790 sq km)	1,047 ft (319 m)
Lake Baikal	11,776 sq miles (30,500 sq km)	5,712 ft (1,741 m)
Great Slave Lake	10,981 sq miles (28,440 sq km)	459 ft (140 m)
Lake Erie	9,915 sq miles (25,680 sq km)	197 ft (60 m)

DEEPEST OCEAN FEATURES

Challenger Deep, Marianas Trench (Pacific)	.36,201 ft	(11,034 m)
Vityaz III Depth, Tonga Trench (Pacific)	.35,704 ft	(10,882 m)
Vityaz Depth, Kurile-Kamchatka Trench (Pacific)	.34,588 ft	(10,542 m)
Cape Johnson Deep, Philippine Trench (Pacific)	.34,441 ft	(10,497 m)
Kermadec Trench (Pacific)	.32,964 ft	(10,047 m)
Ramapo Deep, Japan Trench (Pacific)	.32,758 ft	(9,984 m)
Milwaukee Deep, Puerto Rico Trench (Atlantic)	.30,185 ft	(9,200 m)
Argo Deep, Torres Trench (Pacific)	.30,070 ft	(9,165 m)
Meteor Depth, South Sandwich Trench (Atlantic)	.30,000 ft	(9,144 m)
Planet Deep, New Britain Trench (Pacific)	.29,988 ft	(9,140 m)

GREATEST WATERFALLS
(MEAN FLOW OF WATER)

Boyoma (Congo, Dem. Rep.)	600,400 cu. ft/sec	(17,000 cu.m/sec)
Khône (Laos/Cambodia)	.410,000 cu. ft/sec	(11,600 cu.m/sec)
Niagara (USA/Canada)	.195,000 cu. ft/sec	(5,500 cu.m/sec)
Grande (Uruguay)	.160,000 cu. ft/sec	(4,500 cu.m/sec)
Paulo Afonso (Brazil)	.100,000 cu. ft/sec	(2,800 cu.m/sec)
Urubupunga (Brazil)	.97,000 cu. ft/sec	(2,750 cu.m/sec)
Iguaçu (Argentina/Brazil)	.62,000 cu. ft/sec	(1,700 cu.m/sec)
Maribondo (Brazil)	.53,000 cu. ft/sec	(1,500 cu.m/sec)
Victoria (Zimbabwe)	.39,000 cu. ft/sec	(1,100 cu.m/sec)
Kabalega (Uganda)	.42,000 cu. ft/sec	(1,200 cu.m/sec)

HIGHEST WATERFALLS

Angel (Venezuela)	.3,212 ft	(979 m)
Tugela (South Africa)	.3,110 ft	(948 m)
Utigard (Norway)	.2,625 ft	(800 m)
Mongefossen (Norway)	.2,539 ft	(774 m)
Mtarazi (Zimbabwe)	.2,500 ft	(762 m)
Yosemite (USA)	.2,425 ft	(739 m)
Ostre Mardola Foss (Norway)	.2,156 ft	(657 m)
Tyssestrengane (Norway)	.2,119 ft	(646 m)
*Cuquenan (Venezuela)	.2,001 ft	(610 m)
Sutherland (New Zealand)	.1,903 ft	(580 m)

* indicates that the total height is a single leap

LARGEST DESERTS

Sahara	.3,450,000 sq miles	(9,065,000 sq km)
Gobi	.500,000 sq miles	(1,295,000 sq km)
Ar Rub al Khali	.289,600 sq miles	(750,000 sq km)
Great Victorian	.249,800 sq miles	(647,000 sq km)
Sonoran	.120,000 sq miles	(311,000 sq km)
Kalahari	.120,000 sq miles	(310,800 sq km)
Kara Kum	.115,800 sq miles	(300,000 sq km)
Takla Makan	.100,400 sq miles	(260,000 sq km)
Namib	.52,100 sq miles	(135,000 sq km)
Thar	.33,670 sq miles	(130,000 sq km)

NB – Most of Antarctica is a polar desert, with only 50 mm of precipitation annually

HOTTEST INHABITED PLACES

Djibouti (Djibouti)	.86° F	(30 °C)
Timbouctou (Mali)	.84.7° F	(29.3 °C)
Tirunelveli (India)	.84.7° F	(29.3 °C)
Tuticorin (India)	.84.7° F	(29.3 °C)
Nellore (India)	.84.5° F	(29.2 °C)
Santa Marta (Colombia)	.84.5° F	(29.2 °C)
Aden (Yemen)	.84° F	(28.9 °C)
Madurai (India)	.84° F	(28.9 °C)
Niamey (Niger)	.84° F	(28.9 °C)
Hodeida (Yemen)	.83.8° F	(28.8 °C)

DRIEST INHABITED PLACES

Aswân (Egypt)	.0.02 in	(0.5 mm)
Luxor (Egypt)	.0.03 in	(0.7 mm)
Arica (Chile)	.0.04 in	(1.1 mm)
Ica (Peru)	.0.1 in	(2.3 mm)
Antofagasta (Chile)	.0.2 in	(4.9 mm)
El Minya (Egypt)	.0.2 in	(5.1 mm)
Asyût (Egypt)	.0.2 in	(5.2 mm)
Callao (Peru)	.0.5 in	(12.0 mm)
Trujillo (Peru)	.0.55 in	(14.0 mm)
El Faiyûm (Egypt)	.0.8 in	(19.0 mm)

WETTEST INHABITED PLACES

Buenaventura (Colombia)	.265 in	(6,743 mm)
Monrovia (Liberia)	.202 in	(5,131 mm)
Pago Pago (American Samoa)	.196 in	(4,990 mm)
Moulmein (Myanmar)	.191 in	(4,852 mm)
Lae (Papua New Guinea)	.183 in	(4,645 mm)
Baguio (Luzon Island, Philippines)	180 in	(4,573 mm)
Sylhet (Bangladesh)	.176 in	(4,457 mm)
Padang (Sumatra, Indonesia)	.166 in	(4,225 mm)
Bogor (Java, Indonesia)	.166 in	(4,225 mm)
Conakry (Guinea)	.171 in	(4,341 mm)

INDEX

GLOSSARY OF ABBREVIATIONS
This Glossary provides a comprehensive guide to the abbreviations used in this Atlas, and in the Index.

A
abbrev. abbreviated
Afr. Afrikaans
Alb. Albanian
Amh. Amharic
anc. ancient
Ar. Arabic
Arm. Armenian
Az. Azerbaijani

B
Basq. Basque
Bel. Belorussian
Ben. Bengali
Bibl. Biblical
Bret. Breton
Bul. Bulgarian
Bur. Burmese

C
Cam. Cambodian
Cant. Cantonese
Cast. Castilian
Cat. Catalan
Chin. Chinese
Cro. Croat
Cz. Czech

D
Dan. Danish
Dut. Dutch

E
Eng. English
Est. Estonian
est. estimated

F
Faer. Faeroese
Fij. Fijian
Fin. Finnish
Flem. Flemish
Fr. French
Fris. Frisian

G
Geor. Georgian
Ger. German
Gk. Greek
Guj. Gujarati

H
Haw. Hawaiian
Heb. Hebrew
Hind. Hindi
hist. historical
Hung. Hungarian

I
Icel. Icelandic
Ind. Indonesian
Ir. Irish
It. Italian

J
Jap. Japanese

K
Kaz. Kazakh
Kir. Kirghiz
Kor. Korean
Kurd. Kurdish

L
Lao. Laotian
Lapp. Lappish
Lat. Latin
Latv. Latvian
Lith. Lithanian
Lus. Lusatian

M
Mac. Macedonian
Mal. Malay
Malg. Malagasy
Malt. Maltese
Mong. Mongolian

N
Nepali. Nepali
Nor. Norwegian

O
off. officially

P
Pash. Pashtu
Per. Persian
Pol. Polish
Port. Portuguese
prev. previously

R
Rmsch. Romansch
Roman. Romanian
Rus. Russian

S
SCr. Serbo-Croatian
Serb. Serbian
Slvk. Slovak
Slvn. Slovene
Som. Somali
Sp. Spanish
Swa. Swahili
Swe. Swedish

T
Taj. Tajik
Th. Thai
Tib. Tibetan
Turk. Turkish
Turkm. Turkmenistan

U
Uigh. Uighur
Ukr. Ukrainian
Uzb. Uzbek

V
var. variant
Vtn. Vietnamese

W
Wel. Welsh

X
Xh. Xhosa

Y
Yugo. Yugoslavia

INDEX

A

Aachen 72 A4 *Dut.* Aken, *Fr.* Aix-la-Chapelle; *anc.* Aquae Grani, Aquisgranum. Nordrhein-Westfalen, W Germany
Aaiún *see* Laâyoune
Aalborg 58 D3 *var.* Ålborg, Ålborg-Nørresundby; *anc.* Alburgum. Nordjylland, N Denmark
Aalen 73 B6 Baden-Württemberg, S Germany
Aalsmeer 64 C3 Noord-Holland, C Netherlands
Aalst 65 B6 *Fr.* Alost. Oost-Vlaanderen, C Belgium
Aalten 64 E4 Gelderland, E Netherlands
Aalter 65 B5 Oost-Vlaanderen, NW Belgium
Äänekoski 63 D5 Länsi-Suomi, W Finland
Aar *see* Aare
Aare 73 A7 *var.* Aar. *River* W Switzerland
Aarhus *see* Århus
Aat *see* Ath
Aba 53 G5 Abia, S Nigeria
Aba 55 E5 Orientale, NE Dem. Rep. Congo
Abā as Su'ūd *see* Najrān
Abaco Island *see* Great Abaco
Ābādān 98 C4 Khūzestān, SW Iran
Abai *see* Blue Nile
Abakan 92 D4 Respublika Khakasiya, S Russian Federation
Abancay 38 D4 Apurímac, SE Peru
Abariringa *see* Kanton
Abashiri 108 D2 *var.* Abasiri. Hokkaidō, NE Japan
Abasiri *see* Abashiri
Ābaya Hāyk' 51 C5 *Eng.* Lake Margherita, *It.* Abbaia. *Lake* SW Ethiopia
Ābay Wenz *see* Blue Nile
Abbeville 68 C2 *anc.* Abbatis Villa. Somme, N France
'Abd al 'Azīz, Jabal 96 D2 *mountain range* NE Syria
Abéché 54 C3 *var.* Abécher, Abeshr. Ouaddaï, SE Chad
Abécher *see* Abéché
Abela *see* Ávila
Abemama 122 D2 *var.* Apamama; *prev.* Roger Simpson Island. *Atoll* Tungaru, W Kiribati
Abengourou 53 E5 E Côte d'Ivoire
Aberdeen 66 D3 *anc.* Devana. NE Scotland, UK
Aberdeen 23 E2 South Dakota, N USA
Aberdeen 24 B2 Washington, NW USA
Abergwaun *see* Fishguard
Abertawe *see* Swansea
Aberystwyth 67 C6 W Wales, UK
Abeshr *see* Abéché
Abhā 99 B6 'Asīr, SW Saudi Arabia
Abidavichy 85 D7 *Rus.* Obidovichi. Mahilyowskaya Voblasts', E Belarus
Abidjan 53 E5 S Côte d'Ivoire
Abilene 27 F3 Texas, SW USA
Abingdon *see* Pinta, Isla
Abkhazia 95 E1 *autonomous republic* NW Georgia
Åbo 85 D6 Länsi-Suomi, W Finland
Aboisso 53 E5 SE Côte d'Ivoire
Abo, Massif d' 54 B1 *mountain range* NW Chad
Abomey 53 F5 S Benin
Abou-Déïa 54 C3 Salamat, SE Chad
Abrantes 70 B3 *var.* Abrántes. Santarém, C Portugal
Abrolhos Bank 34 E4 *undersea feature* W Atlantic Ocean
Abrova 85 B6 *Rus.* Obrovo. Brestskaya Voblasts', SW Belarus
Abrud 86 B4 *Ger.* Gross-Schlatten, *Hung.* Abrudbánya. Alba, SW Romania
Abruzzese, Appennino 74 C4 *mountain range* C Italy
Absaroka Range 22 B2 *mountain range* Montana/Wyoming, NW USA
Abū aḍ Ḍuhūr 96 B3 *Fr.* Aboudouhour. Idlib, NW Syria
Abu Dhabi *see* Abū Ẓaby
Abu Hamed 50 C3 River Nile, N Sudan
Abū Ḥardān 96 E3 *var.* Hajîne. Dayr az Zawr, E Syria
Abuja 53 G4 *country capital* (Nigeria) Federal Capital District, C Nigeria
Abū Kamāl 96 E3 *Fr.* Abou Kémal. Dayr az Zawr, E Syria
Abula *see* Ávila
Abunã, Rio 40 C2 *var.* Río Abuná. *River* Bolivia/Brazil
Abut Head 129 B6 *headland* South Island, NZ
Ābuyē Mēda 50 D4 *mountain* C Ethiopia
Abū Ẓabī *see* Abū Ẓaby
Abū Ẓaby 99 C5 *var.* Abū Ẓabī, *Eng.* Abu Dhabi. *Country capital* (UAE) Abū Ẓaby, C UAE
Abyla *see* Ávila
Acalayong 55 A5 SW Equatorial Guinea
Acaponeta 28 D4 Nayarit, C Mexico
Acapulco 29 E5 *var.* Acapulco de Juárez. Guerrero, S Mexico
Acapulco de Juárez *see* Acapulco
Acarai Mountains 37 F4 *Sp.* Serra Acaraí. *Mountain range* Brazil/Guyana
Acarigua 36 D2 Portuguesa, N Venezuela
Accra 53 E5 *country capital* (Ghana) SE Ghana
Achacachi 39 E4 La Paz, W Bolivia
Acklins Island 32 C2 *island* SE Bahamas
Aconcagua, Cerro 42 B4 *mountain* W Argentina
Açores *see* Azores
A Coruña 70 B1 *Cast.* La Coruña, *Eng.* Corunna; *anc.* Caronium. Galicia, NW Spain
Acre 40 C2 *off.* Estado do Acre. *State* W Brazil
Açu 41 G2 *var.* Assu. Rio Grande do Norte, E Brazil
Ada 27 G2 Oklahoma, C USA
Ada 78 D3 Serbia, N Serbia and Montenegro (Yugo.)
Adalia, Gulf of *see* Antalya Körfezi
Adama *see* Nazrēt
Adamawa Highlands 54 B4 *plateau* NW Cameroon
'Adan 99 B7 *Eng.* Aden. SW Yemen
Adana 94 D4 *var.* Seyhan. Adana, S Turkey
Adapazarı 94 B2 *prev.* Ada Bazar. Sakarya, NW Turkey
Adare, Cape 132 B4 *headland* Antarctica
Ad Dahnā' 98 C4 *desert* E Saudi Arabia
Ad Dakhla 48 A4 *var.* Dakhla. SW Western Sahara
Ad Dalanj *see* Dilling
Ad Damar *see* Ed Damer
Ad Damazīn *see* Ed Damazin
Ad Dāmir *see* Ed Damer
Ad Dammān 98 C4 *var.* Dammām. Ash Sharqīyah, NE Saudi Arabia
Ad Dāmūr *see* Damoûr
Ad Dawḥah 98 C4 *Eng.* Doha. *Country capital* (Qatar) C Qatar
Aḍ Ḍiffah *see* Libyan Plateau
Addis Ababa *see* Ādīs Ābeba
Addu Atoll 110 A5 *atoll* S Maldives
Adelaide 127 B6 *state capital* South Australia
Aden *see* 'Adan
Aden, Gulf of 99 C7 *gulf* SW Arabian Sea
Adige 74 C2 *Ger.* Etsch. *River* N Italy
Adirondack Mountains 19 F2 *mountain range* New York, NE USA
Ādīs Ābeba 51 C5 *Eng.* Addis Ababa. *Country capital* (Ethiopia) C Ethiopia
Adıyaman 95 E4 Adıyaman, SE Turkey
Adjud 86 C4 Vrancea, E Romania
Admiralty Islands 122 B3 *island group* N PNG
Adra 71 E5 Andalucía, S Spain
Adrar 48 D3 C Algeria
Adrar des Iforas *see* Ifôghas, Adrar des
Adrian 18 C3 Michigan, N USA
Adriatic Sea 81 E2 *Alb.* Deti Adriatik, *It.* Mare Adriatico, *SCr.* Jadransko More, *Slvn.* Jadransko Morje. *Sea* N Mediterranean Sea
Adycha 93 F2 *river* NE Russian Federation
Aegean Sea 83 C5 *Gk.* Aigaíon Pélagos, Aigaío Pélagos, *Turk.* Ege Denizi. *Sea* NE Mediterranean Sea
Aegviidu 84 D2 *Ger.* Charlottenhof. Harjumaa, NW Estonia
Aelana *see* Al 'Aqabah
Aelok *see* Ailuk Atoll
Aelōnlaplap *see* Ailinglaplap Atoll
Aeolian Islands *see* Eolie, Isole
Afar Depression *see* Danakil Desert
Afghanistan 100 C4 *Per.* Dowlat-e Eslāmī-ye Afghānestān; *prev.* Republic of Afghanistan. *Country* C Asia
Afmadow 51 D6 Jubbada Hoose, S Somalia
Africa 46 *continent*
Africa, Horn of 46 E4 *physical region* Ethiopia/Somalia
Africana Seamount 119 A6 *undersea feature* SW Indian Ocean
'Afrīn 96 B2 Ḥalab, N Syria
Afyon 94 B3 *prev.* Afyonkarahisar. Afyon, W Turkey
Agadez 53 G3 *prev.* Agadès. Agadez, C Niger
Agadir 48 B3 SW Morocco
Agana/Agaña *see* Hagåtña
Āgaro 51 C5 C Ethiopia
Agassiz Fracture Zone 121 G5 *tectonic feature* S Pacific Ocean
Agathónisi 83 D6 *island* Dodekánisos, Greece, Aegean Sea
Agde 69 C6 *anc.* Agatha. Hérault, S France
Agedabia *see* Ajdābiyā
Agen 69 B5 *anc.* Aginnum. Lot-et-Garonne, SW France
Aghri Dagh *see* Büyükağrı Dağı
Agiá 82 B4 *var.* Ayiá. Thessalía, C Greece
Agialoúsa 80 D4 *var.* Yenierenköy. NE Cyprus
Agía Marína 83 E6 Léros, Dodekánisos, Greece, Aegean Sea
Ágios Nikólaos 83 D8 *var.* Áyios Nikólaos. Kríti, Greece, E Mediterranean Sea
Āgra 112 D3 Uttar Pradesh, N India
Agram *see* Zagreb
Ağrı 95 F3 *var.* Karaköse; *prev.* Karakılısse. Ağrı, NE Turkey
Agri Dagi *see* Büyükağrı Dağı
Agrigento 75 C7 *Gk.* Akragas; *prev.* Girgenti. Sicilia, Italy, C Mediterranean Sea
Agriovótano 83 C5 Évvoia, C Greece
Agropoli 75 D5 Campania, S Italy
Aguachica 36 B2 Cesar, N Colombia
Aguadulce 31 F5 Coclé, S Panama
Agua Prieta 28 B1 Sonora, NW Mexico
Aguascalientes 28 D4 Aguascalientes, C Mexico
Aguaytía 38 C3 Ucayali, C Peru
Aguilas 71 E4 Murcia, SE Spain
Aguililla 28 D4 Michoacán de Ocampo, SW Mexico
Agulhas Basin 47 D8 *undersea feature* SW Indian Ocean
Agulhas Plateau 45 D6 *undersea feature* SW Indian Ocean
Ahaggar 53 F2 *high plateau region* SE Algeria
Ahlen 72 B4 Nordrhein-Westfalen, W Germany
Ahmadābād 112 C4 *var.* Ahmedabad. Gujarāt, W India
Ahmadnagar 112 C5 *var.* Ahmednagar. Mahārāshtra, W India
Ahmedabad *see* Ahmadābād
Ahmednagar *see* Ahmadnagar
Ahuachapán 30 B3 Ahuachapán, W El Salvador
Ahvāz 98 C3 *var.* Ahwāz; *prev.* Nāsiri. Khūzestān, SW Iran
Ahvenanmaa *see* Åland
Ahwāz *see* Ahvāz
Aïdin *see* Aydın
Aígina 83 C6 *var.* Aíyina, Egina. Aígina, C Greece
Aígio 83 B5 *var.* Egio; *prev.* Aíyion. Dytikí Ellás, S Greece
Aiken 21 E2 South Carolina, SE USA
Ailigandí 31 G4 San Blas, NE Panama
Ailinglaplap Atoll 122 D2 *var.* Aelōnlaplap. *Atoll* Ralik Chain, S Marshall Islands
Ailuk Atoll 122 D1 *var.* Aelok. *Atoll* Ratak Chain, NE Marshall Islands
Ainaži 84 D3 *Est.* Heinaste, *Ger.* Hainasch. Limbaži, N Latvia
'Aïn Ben Tili 52 D1 Tiris Zemmour, N Mauritania
Aintab *see* Gaziantep
Aïoun el Atrous *see* 'Ayoûn el 'Atroûs
Aïoun el Atroûss *see* 'Ayoûn el 'Atroûs
Aiquile 39 F4 Cochabamba, C Bolivia
Aïr *see* Aïr, Massif de l'
Air du Azbine *see* Aïr, Massif de l'
Aïr, Massif de l' 53 G2 *var.* Aïr, Air du Azbine, Asben. *Mountain range* NC Niger
Aiud 86 B4 *Ger.* Strassburg, *Hung.* Nagyenyed; *prev.* Engeten. Alba, SW Romania
Aix *see* Aix-en-Provence
Aix-en-Provence 69 D6 *var.* Aix; *anc.* Aquae Sextiae. Bouches-du-Rhône, SE France
Aíyina *see* Aígina
Aíyion *see* Aígio
Aizkraukle 84 C4 Aizkraukle, S Latvia
Ajaccio 69 E7 Corse, France, C Mediterranean Sea
Ajaria 95 F2 *autonomous republic* SW Georgia
Aj Bogd Uul 104 D2 *mountain* SW Mongolia
Ajdābiyā 49 G2 *var.* Agedabia, Ajdābiyah. NE Libya
Ajdābiyah *see* Ajdābiyā
Ajjinena *see* El Geneina
Ajmer 112 D3 *var.* Ajmere. Rājasthān, N India
Ajmere *see* Ajmer
Ajo 26 A3 Arizona, SW USA
Akaba *see* Al 'Aqabah
Akamagaseki *see* Shimonoseki
Akasha 50 B3 Northern, N Sudan
Akchâr 52 C2 *desert* W Mauritania
Akhalts'ikhe 95 F2 SW Georgia
Akhisar 94 A3 Manisa, W Turkey
Akhmîm 50 B2 *anc.* Panopolis. C Egypt
Akhtubinsk 89 C7 Astrakhanskaya Oblast', SW Russian Federation
Akimiski Island 16 C3 *island* Northwest Territories, C Canada
Akinovka 87 F4 Zaporiz'ka Oblast', S Ukraine
Akita 108 D4 Akita, Honshū, C Japan
Akjoujt 52 C2 *prev.* Fort-Repoux. Inchiri, W Mauritania
Akkeshi 108 E2 Hokkaidō, NE Japan
Aklavik 14 D3 Northwest Territories, NW Canada
Akmola *see* Astana
Akpatok Island 17 E1 *island* Northwest Territories, E Canada
Akra Dhrepanon *see* Drépano, Akrotírio
Akra Kanestron *see* Palioúri, Akrotírio
Akron 18 D4 Ohio, N USA
Akrotiri *see* Akrotírion
Akrotírion 80 C5 *var.* Akrotiri. *UK air base* S Cyprus
Aksai Chin 102 B2 *Chin.* Aksayqin. *Disputed region* China/India
Aksaray 94 C4 Aksaray, C Turkey
Akşehir 94 B4 Konya, W Turkey
Aktau 92 A4 *Kaz.* Aqtaū; *prev.* Shevchenko. Mangistau, W Kazakhstan
Aktobe 92 B4 *Kaz.* Aqtöbe. *prev.* Aktyubinsk. Aktyubinsk, NW Kazakhstan
Aktsyabrski 85 C7 *Rus.* Oktyabr'skiy; *prev.* Karpilovka. Homyel'skaya Voblasts', SE Belarus
Aktyubinsk *see* Aktobe
Akula 55 C5 Equateur, NW Dem. Rep. Congo
Akureyri 61 E4 Nordhurland Eystra, N Iceland
Akyab *see* Sittwe
Alabama 29 G1 *off.* State of Alabama; also known as Camellia State, Heart of Dixie, The Cotton State, Yellowhammer State. *State* S USA
Alabama River 20 C3 *river* Alabama, S USA
Alaca 94 C3 Çorum, N Turkey
Alacant *see* Alicante
Alagoas 41 G2 *off.* Estado de Alagoas. *State* E Brazil
Alajuela 31 E4 Alajuela, C Costa Rica
Alakanuk 14 C2 Alaska, USA
Al 'Alamayn *see* El 'Alamein
Al 'Amārah 98 C3 *var.* Amara. E Iraq
Alamo 25 D6 Nevada, W USA
Alamogordo 26 D3 New Mexico, SW USA
Alamosa 22 C5 Colorado, C USA
Åland 63 C6 *var.* Aland Islands, *Fin.* Ahvenanmaa. *Island group* SW Finland
Aland Islands *see* Åland
Aland Sea *see* Ålands Hav
Ålands Hav 63 C6 *var.* Aland Sea. *Strait* Baltic Sea/Gulf of Bothnia
Alanya 94 C4 Antalya, S Turkey
Alappuzha *see* Alleppey
Al 'Aqabah 97 B8 *var.* Akaba, Aqaba, 'Aqaba; *anc.* Aelana, Elath. Ma'ān, SW Jordan
Alasca, Golfo de *see* Alaska, Gulf of
Alaşehir 94 A4 Manisa, W Turkey
Al 'Ashārah 96 E3 *var.* Ashara. Dayr az Zawr, E Syria
Alaska 14 C3 *off.* State of Alaska; also known as Land of the Midnight Sun, The Last Frontier, Seward's Folly; *prev.* Russian America. *State* NW USA
Alaska, Gulf of 14 C4 *var.* Golfo de Alasca. *Gulf* Canada/USA
Alaska Peninsula 14 C3 *peninsula* Alaska, USA
Alaska Range 12 B2 *mountain range* Alaska, USA
Al-Asnam *see* Chlef
Al Awaynāt *see* Al 'Uwaynāt
Al 'Aynā 97 B7 Al Karak, W Jordan
Alazeya 93 G2 *river* NE Russian Federation
Al Bāb 96 B2 Ḥalab, N Syria
Albacete 71 E3 Castilla-La Mancha, C Spain
Al Baghdādī 98 B3 *var.* Khān al Baghdādī. SW Iraq
Al Bāha *see* Al Bāḥah
Al Bāḥah 99 B5 *var.* Al Bāha. Al Bāḥah, SW Saudi Arabia
Al Baḥr al Mayyit *see* Dead Sea
Alba Iulia 86 B4 *Ger.* Weissenburg, *Hung.* Gyulafehérvár; *prev.* Bălgrad, Karlsburg, Károly-Fehérvár. Alba, W Romania
Albania 79 C7 *Alb.* Republika e Shqipërisë, Shqipëria; *prev.* People's Socialist Republic of Albania. *Country* SE Europe
Albany 16 C3 *river* Ontario, S Canada
Albany 19 F3 *state capital* New York, NE USA
Albany 20 D3 Georgia, SE USA
Albany 24 B3 Oregon, NW USA
Albany 125 B7 Western Australia
Al Bāridah 96 C4 *var.* Bāridah. Ḥimṣ, C Syria
Al Baṣrah 98 C3 *Eng.* Basra; *hist.* Busra, Bussora. SE Iraq
Al Batrūn *see* Batroûn
Al Bayḍā' 49 G2 *var.* Beida. NE Libya
Albemarle Island *see* Isabela, Isla
Albemarle Sound 21 G1 *inlet* W Atlantic Ocean
Albergaria-a-Velha 70 B2 Aveiro, N Portugal
Albert 68 C3 Somme, N France
Alberta 15 E4 *province* SW Canada
Albert Edward Nyanza *see* Edward, Lake
Albert, Lake 51 B6 *var.* Albert Nyanza, Lac Mobutu Sese Seko. *Lake* Uganda/Dem. Rep. Congo
Albert Lea 23 F3 Minnesota, N USA
Albert Nyanza *see* Albert, Lake
Albi 69 C6 *anc.* Albiga. Tarn, S France
Ålborg *see* Aalborg
Ålborg-Nørresundby *see* Aalborg
Alborz, Reshteh-ye Kūhhā-ye 98 C2 *Eng.* Elburz Mountains. *Mountain range* N Iran
Albuquerque 26 D2 New Mexico, SW USA
Al Burayqah *see* Marsá al Burayqah
Alburgum *see* Aalborg
Albury 127 C7 New South Wales, SE Australia
Alcácer do Sal 70 B4 Setúbal, W Portugal
Alcalá de Henares 71 E3 *Ar.* Alkal'a; *anc.* Complutum. Madrid, C Spain
Alcamo 75 C7 Sicilia, Italy, C Mediterranean Sea
Alcañiz 71 F2 Aragón, NE Spain
Alcántara, Embalse de 70 C3 *reservoir* W Spain
Alcaudete 92 D4 Andalucía, S Spain
Alcázar *see* Ksar-el-Kebir
Alcoi *see* Alcoy
Alcoy 71 F4 *var.* Alcoi. País Valenciano, E Spain
Aldabra Group 57 G2 *island group* SW Seychelles
Aldan 93 F3 *river* NE Russian Federation
al Dar al Baida *see* Rabat
Alderney 68 A2 *island* Channel Islands
Aleg 52 C3 Brakna, SW Mauritania
Aleksandropol' *see* Gyumri
Aleksin 89 B5 Tul'skaya Oblast', W Russian Federation
Aleksinac 78 E4 Serbia, SE Serbia and Montenegro (Yugo.)
Alençon 68 B3 Orne, N France
Alenquer 41 E2 Pará, NE Brazil
Aleppo *see* Ḥalab
Alert 15 F1 Ellesmere Island, Nunavut, N Canada
Alès 69 C6 *prev.* Alais. Gard, S France
Aleşd 86 B3 *Hung.* Élesd. Bihor, SW Romania
Alessandria 74 B2 *Fr.* Alexandrie. Piemonte, N Italy
Ålesund 63 A5 Møre og Romsdal, S Norway
Aleutian Basin 91 G3 *undersea feature* Bering Sea
Aleutian Islands 14 A3 *island group* Alaska, USA
Aleutian Range 12 A2 *mountain range* Alaska, USA
Aleutian Trench 91 H3 *undersea feature* S Bering Sea
Alexander Archipelago 14 D4 *island group* Alaska, USA
Alexander City 20 D2 Alabama, S USA
Alexander Island 132 A3 *island* Antarctica
Alexandra 129 B7 Otago, South Island, NZ
Aléxandreia 82 B4 *var.* Alexándria. Kentrikí Makedonía, N Greece
Alexandria 50 B1 *Ar.* Al Iskandarīyah. N Egypt
Alexándria *see* Aléxandreia
Alexandria 20 B3 Louisiana, S USA
Alexandria 23 F2 Minnesota, N USA
Alexandria 86 C5 Teleorman, S Romania

Alexandroúpoli 82 D3 var. Alexandroúpolis, Turk. Dedeagaç, Dedeagach. Anatolikí Makedonía kai Thráki, NE Greece
Alexandroúpolis see Alexandroúpoli
Al Fāshir see El Fasher
Alfatar 82 E1 Silistra, NE Bulgaria
Alfeiós 83 B6 prev. Alfiós, anc. Alpheius, Alpheus. River S Greece
Alföld see Great Hungarian Plain
Alga 92 B4 Kaz. Algha. Aktyubinsk, NW Kazakhstan
Algarve 70 B4 cultural region S Portugal
Algeciras 70 C5 Andalucía, SW Spain
Algemesí 71 F3 País Valenciano, E Spain
Al-Genain see El Geneina
Alger 49 E1 var. Algiers, El Djazaïr, Al Jazair. Country capital (Algeria) N Algeria
Algeria 48 C3 Country N Africa
Algerian Basin 58 C5 var. Balearic Plain undersea feature W Mediterranean Sea
Al Ghābah 99 E5 var. Ghaba. C Oman
Alghero 75 A5 Sardegna, Italy, C Mediterranean Sea
Al Ghurdaqah see Hurghada
Algiers see Alger
Al Golea see El Goléa
Algona 23 F3 Iowa, C USA
Al Ḥajār al Gharbī 99 D5 mountain range N Oman
Al Ḥasakah 96 D2 var. Al Hasijah, El Haseke, Fr. Hassetché. Al Ḥasakah, NE Syria
Al Hasijah see Al Ḥasakah
Al Ḥillah 98 B3 var. Hilla. C Iraq
Al Ḥisā 97 B7 Aṭ Ṭafīlah, W Jordan
Al Ḥudaydah 99 B6 Eng. Hodeida. W Yemen
Al Hufūf 98 C4 var. Hofuf. Ash Sharqīyah, NE Saudi Arabia
Aliákmonas 82 B4 prev. Aliákmon, anc. Haliacmon. River N Greece
Alíartos 83 C5 Stereá Ellás, C Greece
Alicante 71 F4 Cat. Alacant;. País Valenciano, SE Spain
Alice 27 G5 Texas, SW USA
Alice Springs 126 A4 Northern Territory, C Australia
Aliki see Alykí
Alima 55 B6 river C Congo
Alindao 54 C4 Basse-Kotto, S Central African Republic
Aliquippa 18 D4 Pennsylvania, NE USA
Alistráti 82 C3 Kentrikí Makedonía, NE Greece
Alivéri 83 C5 var. Alivérion. Évvoia, C Greece
Alivérion see Alivéri
Al Jabal al Akhḑar 49 G2 mountain range NE Libya
Al Jabal ash Sharqī see Anti-Lebanon
Al Jafr 97 B7 Ma'ān, S Jordan
Al Jaghbūb 49 H3 NE Libya
Al Jahrā' 98 C4 var. Al Jahrah, Jahra. C Kuwait
Al Jahrah see Al Jahrā'
Al Jawf 98 B4 var. Jauf. Al Jawf, NW Saudi Arabia
Al Jazair see Alger
Al Jazīrah 96 E2 physical region Iraq/Syria
Al Jīzah see El Gîza
Al Junaynah see El Geneina
Al Karak 97 B7 var. El Kerak, Karak, Kerak; anc. Kir Moab, Kir of Moab. Al Karak, W Jordan
Al-Kasr al-Kebir see Ksar-el-Kebir
Al Khalīl see Hebron
Al Khārijah see El Khârga
Al Khufrah 49 H4 SE Libya
Al Khums 49 F2 var. Homs, Khoms, Khums. NW Libya
Alkmaar 64 C2 Noord-Holland, NW Netherlands
Al Kūt 98 C3 var. Kūt al 'Amārah, Kut al Imara. E Iraq
Al-Kuwait see Al Kuwayt
Al Kuwayt 98 C4 var. Al-Kuwait, Eng. Kuwait, Kuwait City; prev. Qurein. Country capital (Kuwait) E Kuwait
Al Lādhiqīyah 96 A3 Eng. Latakia, Fr. Lattaquié; anc. Laodicea, Laodicea ad Mare. Al Lādhiqīyah, W Syria
Allahābād 113 E3 Uttar Pradesh, N India
Allanmyo 114 B4 Magwe, C Myanmar
Allegheny Plateau 19 E3 mountain range New York/Pennsylvania, NE USA
Allentown 19 F4 Pennsylvania, NE USA
Alleppey 110 C3 var. Alappuzha; prev. Alleppi. Kerala, SW India
Alleppi see Alleppey
Alliance 22 D3 Nebraska, C USA
Al Līth 99 B5 Makkah, SW Saudi Arabia
Alma-Ata see Almaty
Almada 70 B4 Setúbal, W Portugal
Al Madīnah 99 A5 Eng. Medina. Al Madīnah, W Saudi Arabia
Al Mafraq 97 B6 var. Mafraq. Al Mafraq, N Jordan
Al Mahdīyah see Mahdia
Al Mahrah 99 C6 mountain range E Yemen
Al Majma'ah 98 B4 Ar Riyāḑ, C Saudi Arabia
Al Mālikīyah 96 E1 Al Ḥasakah, NE Syria
Al Manāmah 98 C4 Eng. Manama. Country capital (Bahrain) N Bahrain
Al Manāşif 96 E3 mountain range E Syria
Almansa 71 F4 Castilla-La Mancha, C Spain
Al Marj 49 G2 var. Barka, It. Barce. NE Libya
Almaty 92 C5 var. Alma-Ata. Almaty, SE Kazakhstan
Al Mawşil 98 B2 Eng. Mosul. N Iraq
Al Mayādīn 96 D3 var. Mayadin, Fr. Meyadine. Dayr az Zawr, E Syria
Al Mazra' see Al Mazra'ah
Al Mazra'ah 97 B6 var. Al Mazra', Mazra'a. Al Karak, W Jordan
Almelo 64 E3 Overijssel, E Netherlands
Almendra, Embalse de 70 C2 reservoir Castilla-León, NW Spain
Almendralejo 70 C4 Extremadura, W Spain
Almere 64 C3 var. Almere-stad. Flevoland, C Netherlands
Almere-stad see Almere
Almería 71 E5 Ar. Al-Mariyya; anc. Unci, Lat. Portus Magnus. Andalucía, S Spain
Al'met'yevsk 89 D5 Respublika Tatarstan, W Russian Federation
Al Mīnā' see El Mina
Al Minyā see El Minya
Almirante 31 E4 Bocas del Toro, NW Panama
Al Mudawwarah 97 B8 Ma'ān, SW Jordan
Al Mukallā 99 C6 var. Mukalla. SE Yemen
Al Obayyid see El Obeid
Alofi 123 F4 dependent territory capital (Niue) W Niue
Aloja 84 D3 Limbaži, N Latvia
Alónnisos 83 C5 island Vóreioi Sporádes, Greece, Aegean Sea
Álora 70 D5 Andalucía, S Spain
Alor, Kepulauan 117 E5 island group E Indonesia
Al Oued see El Oued
Alpen see Alps
Alpena 18 D2 Michigan, N USA
Alpes see Alps
Alpha Cordillera 133 B3 var. Alpha Ridge. Undersea feature Arctic Ocean
Alpha Ridge see Alpha Cordillera
Alphen see Alphen aan den Rijn
Alphen aan den Rijn 64 C3 var. Alphen. Zuid-Holland, C Netherlands
Alpi see Alps
Alpine 27 E4 Texas, SW USA
Alpi Transilvaniei see Carpaţii Meridionali
Alps 80 C1 Fr. Alpes, Ger. Alpen, It. Alpi. Mountain range C Europe
Al Qaḑārif see Gedaref
Al Qāmishlī 96 E1 var. Kamishli, Qamishly. Al Ḥasakah, NE Syria
Al Qaşrayn see Kasserine
Al Qayrawān see Kairouan
Al-Qsar see Ksar-el-Kebir
Al Qubayyāt see Qoubaïyât
Alqueva, Barragem do 70 C4 reservoir S Portugal
Al Qunayţirah 97 B5 var. El Kuneitra, El Quneitra, Kuneitra, Qunaytra. Al Qunayţirah, SW Syria
Al Quşayr 96 B4 var. El Quseir, Quşayr, Fr. Kousseir. Ḥimş, W Syria
Al Quwayrah 97 B8 var. El Quweira. Ma'ān, SW Jordan
Alsace 68 E3 cultural region NE France
Alsdorf 72 A4 Nordrhein-Westfalen, W Germany
Alt see Olt
Alta 62 D2 Fin. Alattio. Finnmark, N Norway
Altai see Altai Mountains
Altai Mountains 104 C2 var. Altai, Chin. Altay Shan, Rus. Altay. Mountain range Asia/Europe
Altamaha River 21 E3 river Georgia, SE USA
Altamira 41 E2 Pará, NE Brazil
Altamura 75 E5 anc. Lupatia. Puglia, SE Italy
Altar, Desierto de 28 A1 var. Sonoran Desert. Desert Mexico/USA see also Sonoran Desert
Altay 104 C2 Chin. A-le-t'ai, Mong. Sharasume; prev. Ch'eng-hua, Chenghwa. Xinjiang Uygur Zizhiqu, NW China
Altay see Altai Mountains
Altay 104 D2 Govĭ-Altay, W Mongolia
Altay Shan see Altai Mountains
Altin Köprü 98 B3 var. Altun Kupri. N Iraq
Altiplano 39 F4 physical region W South America
Alton 18 B5 Illinois, N USA
Alton 18 B4 Missouri, C USA
Altoona 19 E4 Pennsylvania, NE USA
Alto Paraná see Paraná
Altun Kupri see Altin Köprü
Altun Shan 104 C3 var. Altyn Tagh. Mountain range NW China
Altus 27 F2 Oklahoma, C USA
Altyn Tagh see Altun Shan
Al Ubayyiḑ see El Obeid
Alūksne 84 D3 Ger. Marienburg. Alūksne, NE Latvia
Al 'Ulā 98 A4 Al Madīnah, NW Saudi Arabia
Al 'Umarī 97 C6 'Ammān, E Jordan
Alupka 87 F5 Respublika Krym, S Ukraine
Alushta 87 F5 Respublika Krym, S Ukraine
Al 'Uwaynāt 49 F4 var. Al Awaynāt. SW Libya
Alva 27 F1 Oklahoma, C USA
Alvarado 29 F4 Veracruz-Llave, E Mexico
Alvin 27 H4 Texas, SW USA
Al Wajh 98 A4 Tabūk, NW Saudi Arabia
Alwar 112 D3 Rājasthān, N India
Al Wari'ah 98 C4 Ash Sharqīyah, N Saudi Arabia
Alykí 82 C4 var. Aliki. Thásos, N Greece
Alytus 85 B5 Pol. Olita. Alytus, S Lithuania
Alzette 65 D8 river S Luxembourg
Amadeus, Lake 125 D5 seasonal lake Northern Territory, C Australia
Amadi 51 B5 Western Equatoria, SW Sudan
Amadjuak Lake 15 G3 lake Baffin Island, Nunavut, N Canada
Amakusa-nada 109 A7 gulf Kyūshū, SW Japan
Åmål 63 B6 Västra Götaland, S Sweden
Amami-guntō 108 A3 island group SW Japan
Amami-ō-shima 108 A3 island S Japan
Amantea 75 D6 Calabria, SW Italy
Amapá 41 E1 Amapá, NE Brazil
Amara see Al 'Amārah
Amarapura 114 B3 Mandalay, C Myanmar
Amarillo 27 E2 Texas, SW USA
Amay 65 C6 Liège, E Belgium
Amazon 41 E1 Sp. Amazonas. River Brazil/Peru
Amazon Basin 40 D2 basin N South America
Amazon, Mouths of the 41 F1 delta NE Brazil
Ambam 55 B5 Sud, S Cameroon
Ambanja 57 G2 Antsirañana, N Madagascar
Ambarchik 93 G2 Respublika Sakha (Yakutiya), NE Russian Federation
Ambato 38 B1 Tungurahua, C Ecuador
Ambérieu-en-Bugey 69 D5 Ain, E France
Amboasary 57 F4 Toliara, S Madagascar
Ambon 117 F4 prev. Amboina, Amboyna. Pulau Ambon, E Indonesia
Ambositra 57 G3 Fianarantsoa, SE Madagascar
Ambrim see Ambrym
Ambriz 56 A1 Bengo, NW Angola
Ambrym 122 D4 var. Ambrim. Island C Vanuatu
Amchitka Island 14 A2 island Aleutian Islands, Alaska, USA
Amdo 104 C5 Xizang Zizhiqu, W China
Ameland 64 D1 Fris. It Amelân. Island Waddeneilanden, N Netherlands
America-Antarctica Ridge 45 C7 undersea feature S Atlantic Ocean
American Falls Reservoir 24 E4 reservoir Idaho, NW USA
American Samoa 123 E4 US unincorporated territory W Polynesia
Amersfoort 64 D3 Utrecht, C Netherlands
Ames 23 F3 Iowa, C USA
Amfilochía 83 A5 var. Amfilokhía. Dytikí Ellás, C Greece
Amfilokhía see Amfilochía
Amga 93 F3 river NE Russian Federation
Amherst 17 F4 Nova Scotia, SE Canada
Amida see Diyarbakır
Amiens 68 C3 anc. Ambianum, Samarobriva. Somme, N France
Amíndaion see Amýntaio
Amindeo see Amýntaio
Amīndīvi Islands 110 A2 island group Lakshadweep, India, N Indian Ocean
Amirante Islands 57 G1 var. Amirantes Group. Island group C Seychelles
Amirantes Group see Amirante Islands
Amistad Reservoir 27 F4 var. Presa de la Amistad. Reservoir Mexico/USA
'Ammān 97 B6 var. Amman; anc. Philadelphia, Bibl. Rabbah Ammon, Rabbath Ammon. Country capital (Jordan) 'Ammān, NW Jordan
Amman see 'Ammān
Ammassalik 60 D4 var. Angmagssalik. S Greenland
Ammóchostos 80 D5 var. Famagusta, Gazimağusa. E Cyprus
Āmol 98 D2 var. Amul. Māzandarān, N Iran
Amorgós 83 D6 island Kykládes, Greece, Aegean Sea
Amorgós 83 D6 Amorgós, Kykládes, Greece, Aegean Sea
Amos 16 D4 Québec, SE Canada
Amourj 52 D3 Hodh ech Chargui, SE Mauritania
Amoy see Xiamen
Ampato, Nevado 39 E4 mountain S Peru
Amposta 71 F2 Cataluña, NE Spain
Amrāvati 112 D4 prev. Amraoti. Mahārāshtra, C India
Amritsar 112 D2 Punjab, N India
Amstelveen 64 C3 Noord-Holland, C Netherlands
Amsterdam 64 C3 country capital (Netherlands) Noord-Holland, C Netherlands
Amsterdam Island 119 C6 island NE French Southern and Antarctic Territories
Am Timan 54 C3 Salamat, SE Chad
Amu Darya 100 D2 Rus. Amudar'ya, Taj. Dar"yoi Amu, Turkm. Amyderya, Uzb. Amudaryo; anc. Oxus. River C Asia
Amu-Dar'ya see Amyderya
Amul see Āmol
Amund Ringnes Island 15 F2 island Nunavut, N Canada
Amundsen Basin see Fram Basin
Amundsen Gulf 15 E2 gulf Northwest Territories, N Canada
Amundsen Plain 132 A4 undersea feature S Pacific Ocean
Amundsen-Scott 132 B3 US research station Antarctica
Amundsen Sea 132 A4 sea S Pacific Ocean
Amuntai 116 D4 prev. Amoentai. Borneo, C Indonesia
Amur 93 G4 Chin. Heilong Jiang. River China/Russian Federation
Amvrosiyivka 87 H3 Rus. Amvrosiyevka. Donets'ka Oblast', SE Ukraine
Amyderya 101 E3 Rus. Amu-Dar'ya. Lebapskiy Velayat, NE Turkmenistan
Amýntaio 82 B4 var. Amindeo; prev. Amíndaion. Dytikí Makedonía, N Greece
Anabar 93 E2 river NE Russian Federation
An Abhainn Mhór see Blackwater
Anaco 37 E2 Anzoátegui, NE Venezuela
Anaconda 22 B2 Montana, NW USA
Anacortes 24 B1 Washington, NW USA
Anadolu Dağları see Doğu Karadeniz Dağları
Anadyr' 93 G1 river NE Russian Federation
Anadyr' 93 H1 Chukotskiy Avtonomnyy Okrug, NE Russian Federation
Anadyr, Gulf of see Anadyrskiy Zaliv
Anadyrskiy Zaliv 93 H1 Eng. Gulf of Anadyr. Gulf NE Russian Federation
Anáfi 83 D7 anc. Anaphe. Island Kykládes, Greece, Aegean Sea
'Ānah see 'Annah
Anaheim 24 E2 California, W USA
Anaiza see 'Unayzah
Analalava 57 G2 Mahajanga, NW Madagascar
Anamur 94 C5 İçel, S Turkey
Anantapur 110 C2 Andhra Pradesh, S India
Anápolis 41 F3 Goiás, C Brazil
Anār 98 D3 Kermān, C Iran
Anatolia 94 C4 plateau C Turkey
Anatom see Aneityum
Añatuya 42 C3 Santiago del Estero, N Argentina
An Bhearú see Barrow
Anchorage 14 C3 Alaska, USA
Ancona 74 C3 Marche, C Italy
Ancud 43 B6 prev. San Carlos de Ancud. Los Lagos, S Chile
Åndalsnes 63 A5 Møre og Romsdal, S Norway
Andalucía 70 D4 cultural region S Spain
Andalusia 20 C3 Alabama, S USA
Andaman Islands 102 B4 island group India, NE Indian Ocean
Andaman Sea 102 C4 sea NE Indian Ocean
Andenne 65 C6 Namur, SE Belgium
Anderlues 65 B7 Hainaut, S Belgium
Anderson 18 C4 Indiana, N USA
Andes 42 B3 mountain range W South America
Andhra Pradesh 113 E5 state E India
Andijon 101 F2 Rus. Andizhan. Andijon Wiloyati, E Uzbekistan
Andikíthira see Antikýthira
Andipaxi see Antípaxoi
Andípsara see Antípsara
Ándissa see Ántissa
Andkhvoy 100 D3 Fāryāb, N Afghanistan
Andorra 69 A7 Cat. Valls d'Andorra, Fr. Vallée d'Andorre. Country SW Europe
Andorra see Andorra la Vella
Andorra la Vella 69 A8 var. Andorra, Fr. Andorre la Vielle, Sp. Andorra la Vieja. Country capital (Andorra) C Andorra
Andorra la Vieja see Andorra la Vella
Andorre la Vielle see Andorra la Vella
Andover 67 D7 S England, UK
Andøya 62 C2 island C Norway
Andreanof Islands 14 A3 island group Aleutian Islands, Alaska, USA
Andrews 27 E3 Texas, SW USA
Andrew Tablemount 118 A4 var. Gora Andryu. Undersea feature W Indian Ocean
Andria 75 D5 Puglia, SE Italy
An Droichead Nua see Newbridge
Ándros 83 C6 island Kykládes, Greece, Aegean Sea
Ándros 83 D6 Ándros, Kykládes, Greece, Aegean Sea
Andros Island 32 B2 island NW Bahamas
Andros Town 32 C1 Andros Island, NW Bahamas
Aneityum 122 D5 var. Anatom; prev. Kéamu. Island S Vanuatu
Ānewetak see Enewetak Atoll
Angara 93 E4 river C Russian Federation
Angarsk 93 E4 Irkutskaya Oblast', S Russian Federation
Ånge 63 C5 Västernorrland, C Sweden
Ángel de la Guarda, Isla 28 B2 island NW Mexico
Angeles 117 E1 off. Angeles City. Luzon, N Philippines
Angel Falls see Ángel, Salto
Ángel, Salto 37 E3 Eng. Angel Falls. Waterfall E Venezuela
Ångermanälven 62 C4 river N Sweden
Angermünde 72 D3 Brandenburg, NE Germany
Angers 68 B4 anc. Juliomagus. Maine-et-Loire, NW France
Anglesey 67 C5 island NW Wales, UK
Anglet 69 A6 Pyrénées-Atlantiques, SW France
Angleton 27 H4 Texas, SW USA
Angmagssalik see Ammassalik
Ang Nam Ngum 114 C4 lake C Laos
Angola 56 B2 prev. People's Republic of Angola, Portuguese West Africa. Country SW Africa
Angola Basin 47 B5 undersea feature E Atlantic Ocean
Angostura, Presa de la 29 G5 reservoir SE Mexico
Angoulême 69 B5 anc. Iculisma. Charente, W France
Angoumois 69 B5 cultural region W France
Angren 101 F2 Toshkent Wiloyati, E Uzbekistan
Anguilla 33 G3 UK dependent territory E West Indies
Anguilla Cays 32 B2 islets SW Bahamas
Anhui 106 C5 var. Anhui Sheng, Anhwei, Wan. Admin. region province E China
Anhui Sheng see Anhui
Anhwei see Anhui
Anina 86 A4 Ger. Steierdorf, Hung. Stájerlakanina; prev. Ştaierdorf-Anina, Steierdorf-Anina, Steyerlak-Anina. Caraş-Severin, SW Romania
Anjou 68 B4 cultural region NW France
Anjouan 57 F2 var. Nzwani, Johanna Island. Island SE Comoros
Ankara 94 C3 prev. Angora, anc. Ancyra. Country capital (Turkey) Ankara, C Turkey
Ankeny 23 F3 Iowa, C USA
Anklam 72 D2 Mecklenburg-Vorpommern, NE Germany
Anykščiai 84 C4 Anykščiai, E Lithuania
An Longfort see Longford
An Mhuir Cheilteach see Celtic Sea
Annaba 49 E1 prev. Bône. NE Algeria
An Nafūd 98 B4 desert NW Saudi Arabia
'Annah 98 B3 var. 'Ānah. NW Iraq
An Najaf 98 B3 var. Najaf. S Iraq
Annamitique, Chaîne 114 D4 mountain range C Laos
Annapolis 19 F4 state capital Maryland, NE USA
Annapurna 113 E3 mountain C Nepal
An Nāqūrah see En Nâqoûra
Ann Arbor 18 C3 Michigan, N USA
An Nāşirīyah 98 C3 var. Nasiriya. SE Iraq
Annecy 69 D5 anc. Anneciacum. Haute-Savoie, E France
An Nīl al Azraq see Blue Nile
Anniston 20 D2 Alabama, S USA
Annotto Bay 32 B4 C Jamaica
An Ómaigh see Omagh
Anqing 106 D5 Anhui, E China
Anse La Raye 33 F1 NW Saint Lucia
Anshun 106 B6 Guizhou, S China
Ansongo 53 E3 Gao, E Mali
An Srath Bán see Strabane
Antakya 94 D4 anc. Antioch, Antiochia. Hatay, S Turkey
Antalaha 57 G2 Antsirañana, NE Madagascar
Antalya 94 B4 prev. Adalia, anc. Attaleia, Bibl. Attalia. Antalya, SW Turkey
Antalya, Gulf of see Antalya Körfezi
Antalya Körfezi 94 B4 var. Gulf of Adalia, Eng. Gulf of Antalya. Gulf SW Turkey
Antananarivo 57 G3 prev. Tananarive. Country capital (Madagascar) Antananarivo, C Madagascar
Antarctica 132 B3 continent
Antarctic Peninsula 132 A2 peninsula Antarctica
Antep see Gaziantep
Antequera 70 D5 anc. Anticaria, Antiquaria. Andalucía, S Spain
Antequera see Oaxaca
Antibes 69 D6 anc. Antipolis. Alpes-Maritimes, SE France
Anticosti, Île d' 17 F3 Eng. Anticosti Island. Island Québec, E Canada
Antigua 33 G3 island S Antigua and Barbuda, Leeward Islands
Antigua and Barbuda 33 G3 country E West Indies
Antikýthira 83 B7 var. Andikíthira. Island S Greece
Anti-Lebanon 96 B4 var. Jebel esh Sharqi, Ar. Al Jabal ash Sharqī, Fr. Anti-Liban. Mountain range Lebanon/Syria
Anti-Liban see Anti-Lebanon
Antípaxoi 83 A5 var. Andipaxi. Island Iónioi Nísoi, Greece, C Mediterranean Sea
Antipodes Islands 120 D5 island group, S NZ
Antípsara 83 D5 var. Andípsara. Island E Greece
Ántissa 83 D5 var. Ándissa. Lésvos, E Greece
An tIúr see Newry
Antofagasta 42 B2 Antofagasta, N Chile
Antony 68 E2 Hauts-de-Seine, N France
Antserana see Antsirañana
An tSionainn see Shannon
Antsirañana 57 G2 var. Antserana; prev. Antsirane, Diégo-Suarez. Antsirañana, N Madagascar
Antsirane see Antsirañana
Antsohihy 57 G2 Mahajanga, NW Madagascar
An-tung see Dandong
Antwerp see Antwerpen
Antwerpen 87 C5 Eng. Antwerp, Fr. Anvers. Antwerpen, N Belgium
Anuradhapura 110 D3 North Central Province, C Sri Lanka
Anyang 106 C4 Henan, C China
A'nyêmaqên Shan 104 D4 mountain range C China
Anzio 75 C5 Lazio, C Italy
Aomen see Macao
Aomori 108 D3 Aomori, Honshū, C Japan
Aóos see Vjosës, Lumi i
Aoraki 129 B6 prev. Aorangi, Mount Cook. Mountain South Island, NZ
Aorangi see Aoraki
Aosta 74 A1 anc. Augusta Praetoria. Valle d'Aosta, NW Italy
Ao Thai see Thailand, Gulf of
Aoukâr 52 D3 var. Aouker. Plateau C Mauritania
Aouk, Bahr 54 C4 river Central African Republic/Chad
Aouker see Aoukâr
Aozou 54 C1 Borkou-Ennedi-Tibesti, N Chad
Apalachee Bay 20 D3 bay Florida, SE USA
Apalachicola River 20 D3 river Florida, SE USA
Apamama see Abemama
Apaporis, Río 36 C4 river Brazil/Colombia
Apatity 88 C2 Murmanskaya Oblast', NW Russian Federation
Ape 84 D3 Alūksne, NE Latvia
Apeldoorn 64 D3 Gelderland, E Netherlands
Apennines see Appennino
Āpia 123 F4 country capital (Samoa) Upolu, SE Samoa
Apoera 37 G3 Sipaliwini, NW Suriname
Apostle Islands 18 B1 island group Wisconsin, N USA
Appalachian Mountains 13 D5 mountain range E USA
Appennino 74 E2 Eng. Apennines. Mountain range Italy/San Marino
Appingedam 64 E1 Groningen, NE Netherlands
Appleton 18 B2 Wisconsin, N USA
Apure, Río 36 C2 river W Venezuela
Apurímac, Río 38 D3 river S Peru
Apuseni, Munţii 86 A4 mountain range W Romania
'Aqaba see Al 'Aqabah
Aqaba, Gulf of 98 A4 var. Gulf of Elat, Ar. Khalīj al 'Aqabah; anc. Sinus Aelaniticus. Gulf NE Red Sea
Āqchah 101 E3 var. Āqcheh. Jowzjān, N Afghanistan
Āqcheh see Āqchah
Aquae Augustae see Dax
Aquae Sextiae see Aix-en-Provence
Aquae Tarbelicae see Dax
Aquidauana 41 E4 Mato Grosso do Sul, S Brazil
Aquila see L'Aquila
Aquila degli Abruzzo see L'Aquila
Aquitaine 69 B6 cultural region SW France
'Arabah, Wādī al 135 B7 Heb. Ha'Arava. Dry watercourse Israel/Jordan
Arabian Basin 102 A4 undersea feature N Arabian Sea

Arabian Desert see Eastern Desert
Arabian Peninsula 99 B5 peninsula SW Asia
Arabian Sea 102 A3 sea NW Indian Ocean
Aracaju 41 G3 state capital Sergipe, E Brazil
Araçuai 41 F3 Minas Gerais, SE Brazil
Arad 86 A4 Arad, W Romania
'Arad 97 B7 Southern, S Israel
Arafura Sea 120 A3 Ind. Laut Arafuru. Sea W Pacific Ocean
Aragón 93 E2 cultural region E Spain
Araguaia, Río 41 E3 var. Araguaya. River C Brazil
Araguari 41 F3 Minas Gerais, SE Brazil
Araguaya see Araguaia, Río
Arāk 98 C3 prev. Sultānābād. Markazī, W Iran
Arakan Yoma 114 A3 mountain range W Myanmar
Aral Sea 100 C1 Kaz. Aral Tengizi, Rus. Aral'skoye More, Uzb. Orol Dengizi. Inland sea Kazakhstan/Uzbekistan
Aral'sk 92 B4 Kaz. Aral. Kyzylorda, SW Kazakhstan
Aranda de Duero 70 D2 Castilla-León, N Spain
Arandelovac 78 D4 prev. Arandjelovac. Serbia, C Serbia and Montenegro (Yugo.)
Aranjuez 70 D3 anc. Ara Jovis. Madrid, C Spain
Araouane 53 E2 Tombouctou, N Mali
'Ar'ar 98 B3 Al Ḥudūd ash Shamālīyah, NW Saudi Arabia
Aras 95 G3 Arm. Arak's, Az. Araz Nehri, Per. Rūd-e Aras, Rus. Araks; prev. Araxes. River SW Asia
Arauca 36 C2 Arauca, NE Colombia
Arauca, Río 36 C2 river Colombia/Venezuela
Arbela see Arbīl
Arbīl 98 B2 var. Erbil, Irbīl, Kurd. Hawlēr; anc. Arbela. N Iraq
Arbroath 66 D3 anc. Aberbrothock. E Scotland, UK
Arbyzynka 87 E3 Rus. Arbuzinka. Mykolayivs'ka Oblast', S Ukraine
Arcachon 69 B5 Gironde, SW France
Arcata 24 A4 California, W USA
Archangel see Arkhangel'sk
Archangel Bay see Chëshskaya Guba
Archidona 70 D5 Andalucía, S Spain
Archipel des Australes see Australes, Îles
Archipel des Tuamotu see Tuamotu, Îles
Archipel de Tahiti see Société, Archipel de la
Arco 74 C2 Trentino-Alto Adige, N Italy
Arctic-Mid Oceanic Ridge see Nansen Cordillera
Arctic Ocean 172 B3 ocean
Arda 82 C3 var. Ardhas, Gk. Ardas. River Bulgaria/Greece see also Ardas
Arda see Ardas
Ardabīl 98 C2 var. Ardebil. Ardabīl, NW Iran
Ardakān 98 D3 Yazd, C Iran
Ardas 82 D3 var. Ardhas, Bul. Arda. River Bulgaria/Greece see also Arda
Ardas see Arda
Arḑ aş Şawwān 97 C7 var. Ardh es Suwwān. Plain S Jordan
Ardebil see Ardabīl
Ardèche 69 C5 cultural region E France
Ardennes 65 C8 plateau W Europe
Ardhas see Ardas
Ardh es Suwwan see Arḑ aş Şawwān
Ardino 82 D3 Kŭrdzhali, S Bulgaria
Ard Mhacha see Armagh
Ardmore 27 G2 Oklahoma, C USA
Arelas see Arles
Arelate see Arles
Arendal 63 A6 Aust-Agder, S Norway
Arenys de Mar 71 G2 Cataluña, NE Spain
Areópoli 83 B7 prev. Areópolis. Pelopónnisos, S Greece
Arequipa 39 E4 Arequipa, SE Peru
Arezzo 74 C3 anc. Arretium. Toscana, C Italy
Argalastí 83 C5 Thessalía, C Greece
Argenteuil 68 D1 Val-d'Oise, N France
Argentina 43 B5 Country S South America
Argentina Basin see Argentine Basin
Argentine Basin 35 C7 var. Argentina Basin. Undersea feature SW Atlantic Ocean
Argentine Rise see Falkland Plateau
Arghandāb, Daryā-ye 101 E5 river SE Afghanistan
Argirocastro see Gjirokastër
Argo 50 B3 Northern, N Sudan
Argo Fracture Zone 119 C5 tectonic feature C Indian Ocean
Árgos 83 B6 Pelopónnisos, S Greece
Argostóli 83 A5 var. Argostólion. Kefallinía, Iónioi Nísoi, Greece, C Mediterranean Sea
Argostólion see Argostóli
Argun 103 E1 Chin. Ergun He, Rus. Argun'. River China/Russian Federation
Argyrokastron see Gjirokastër
Århus 63 B7 var. Aarhus. Århus, C Denmark
Aria see Herāt
Ari Atoll 110 A4 atoll C Maldives
Arica 42 B1 hist. San Marcos de Arica. Tarapacá, N Chile
Aridaía 82 B3 var. Aridea, Aridhaía. Dytikí Makedonía, N Greece
Aridea see Aridaía
Aridhaía see Aridaía
Arīḩā 96 B3 var. Arīhā. Idlib, W Syria
Arīḩā see Jericho
Arinsal 69 A7 NW Andorra
Arizona 26 A2 off. State of Arizona; also known as Copper State, Grand Canyon State. Admin. region state SW USA
Arkansas 20 A1 off. State of Arkansas; also known as The Land of Opportunity. State S USA
Arkansas City 23 F5 Kansas, C USA
Arkansas River 27 G1 river C USA
Arkhangel'sk 92 B2 Eng. Archangel. Arkhangel'skaya Oblast', NW Russian Federation
Arkoí 83 E6 island Dodekánisos, Greece, Aegean Sea
Arles 69 D6 var. Arles-sur-Rhône; anc. Arelas, Arelate. Bouches-du-Rhône, SE France
Arles-sur-Rhône see Arles
Arlington 27 G2 Texas, SW USA
Arlington 19 E4 Virginia, NE USA
Arlon 65 D8 Dut. Aarlen, Ger. Arel; Lat. Orolaunum. Luxembourg, SE Belgium
Armagh 67 B5 Ir. Ard Mhacha. S Northern Ireland, UK
Armagnac 69 B6 cultural region S France
Armenia 95 F3 var. Ajastan, Arm. Hayastani Hanrapetut'yun; prev. Armenian Soviet Socialist Republic. Country SW Asia
Armenia 36 B3 Quindío, W Colombia
Armidale 127 D6 New South Wales, SE Australia
Armstrong 16 B3 Ontario, S Canada
Armyans'k 87 F4 Rus. Armyansk. Respublika Krym, S Ukraine
Arnaía 82 C4 var. Arnea. Kentrikí Makedonía, N Greece
Arnaud 60 A3 river Quebec, E Canada
Arnea see Arnaía
Arnedo 71 E2 La Rioja, N Spain
Arnhem 64 D4 Gelderland, SE Netherlands
Arnhem Land 126 A2 physical region Northern Territory, N Australia
Arno 74 B3 river C Italy
Arnold 23 G4 Missouri, C USA
Arorae 123 E3 atoll Tungaru, W Kiribati
Arquipélago da Madeira see Madeira
Arquipélago dos Açores see Azores
Ar Rahad see Er Rahad
Ar Ramādī 98 B3 var. Ramadi, Rumadiya. SW Iraq
Ar Rāmī 96 C4 Ḩimş, C Syria
Ar Ramthā 97 B5 var. Ramtha. Irbid, N Jordan
Arran, Isle of 66 C4 island SW Scotland, UK
Ar Raqqah 96 C2 var. Rakka; anc. Nicephorium. Ar Raqqah, N Syria
Arras 68 C2 anc. Nemetocenna. Pas-de-Calais, N France
Ar Rawḑatayn 98 C4 var. Raudhatain. N Kuwait
Arriaga 29 G5 Chiapas, SE Mexico
Ar Riyāḑ 99 C5 Eng. Riyadh. Country capital (Saudi Arabia) Ar Riyāḑ, C Saudi Arabia
Ar Rub 'al Khālī 99 C6 Eng. Empty Quarter, Great Sandy Desert. Desert SW Asia
Ar Rustāq 99 E5 var. Rostak, Rustaq. N Oman
Ar Ruţbah 98 B3 var. Rutba. SW Iraq
Árta 83 A5 anc. Ambracia. Ípeiros, W Greece
Artashat 95 F3 S Armenia
Artemisa 32 B2 La Habana, W Cuba
Artesia 48 D3 New Mexico, SW USA
Arthur's Pass 129 C6 pass South Island, NZ
Artigas 42 D3 prev. San Eugenio, San Eugenio del Cuareim. Artigas, N Uruguay
Art'ik 95 F2 W Armenia
Artois 68 C2 cultural region N France
Artsyz 86 D4 Rus. Artsiz. Odes'ka Oblast', SW Ukraine
Artvin 95 F2 Artvin, NE Turkey
Arua 51 B6 NW Uganda
Aruângua see Luangwa
Aruba 36 C1 var. Oruba. Dutch autonomous region S West Indies
Aru, Kepulauan 117 G4 Eng. Aru Islands; prev. Aroe Islands. Island group E Indonesia
Arunāchal Pradesh 113 G3 cultural region NE India
Arusha 51 C7 Arusha, N Tanzania
Arviat 15 G4 prev. Eskimo Point. Nunavut, C Canada
Arvidsjaur 62 C4 Norrbotten, N Sweden
Arys' 92 B5 Kaz. Arys. Yuzhnyy Kazakhstan, S Kazakhstan
Asadābād 101 F4 var. Asaḑābād; prev. Chaghasarāy. Kunar, E Afghanistan
Asad, Buḩayrat al- 134 C2 Eng. Lake Assad. Lake N Syria
Asahi-dake 108 D2 mountain Hokkaidō, N Japan
Asahikawa 108 D2 Hokkaidō, N Japan
Asamankese 53 E5 SE Ghana
Āsānsol 113 F4 West Bengal, NE India
Asben see Aïr, Massif de l'
Ascension Fracture Zone 47 A5 tectonic feature C Atlantic Ocean
Ascension Island 63 A5 dependency of St. Helena C Atlantic Ocean
Ascoli Piceno 74 C4 anc. Asculum Picenum. Marche, C Italy
Aseb 50 D4 var. Assab, Amh. Āseb. SE Eritrea
Aşgabat 100 C3 Rus. Ashgabat; prev. Ashkhabad, Poltoratsk. Country capital (Turkmenistan) Akhalskiy Velayat, C Turkmenistan
Ashara see Al 'Ashārah
Ashburton 129 C6 Canterbury, South Island, NZ
Ashburton River 124 A4 river Western Australia
Ashdod 97 A6 anc. Azotos, Lat. Azotus. Central, W Israel
Asheville 21 E1 North Carolina, SE USA
Ashgabat see Aşgabat
Ashkelon see Ashqelon
Ashland 24 B4 Oregon, NW USA
Ashland 18 B1 Wisconsin, N USA
Ashmore and Cartier Islands 120 A3 Australian external territory E Indian Ocean
Ashmyany 85 C5 Rus. Oshmyany. Hrodzyenskaya Voblasts', W Belarus
Ashqelon 97 A6 var. Ashkelon. Southern, C Israel
Ash Shadādah 96 D2 var. Ash Shaddādah, Jisr ash Shadadi, Shaddādī, Shedadi, Tell Shedadi. Al Ḩasakah, NE Syria
Ash Shaddādah see Ash Shadādah
Ash Shām see Dimashq
Ash Sharāh 97 B7 var. Esh Sharā. Mountain range W Jordan
Ash Shāriqah 98 D4 Eng. Sharjah. Ash Shāriqah, NE UAE
Ash Shawbak 97 B7 Ma'ān, W Jordan
Ash Shiḩr 99 C6 SE Yemen
Asia 25 C2 continent
Asinara, Isola 74 A4 island W Italy
Asipovichy 85 D6 Rus. Osipovichi. Mahilyowskaya Voblasts', C Belarus
Aşkale 95 E3 Erzurum, NE Turkey
Askersund 63 C6 Örebro, C Sweden
Asmara 50 C4 Amh. Āsmera. Country capital (Eritrea) C Eritrea
Assab see Aseb
As Sabkhah 96 D2 var. Sabkha. Ar Raqqah, NE Syria
Assad, Lake see Asad, Buḩayrat al-
Aş Şafāwī 97 C6 Al Mafraq, N Jordan
Aş Şaḩrā' al Gharbīyah see Sahara el Gharbîya
Aş Şaḩrā' al Lībīyah see Libyan Desert
Aş Şaḩrā' ash Sharqīyah see Eastern Desert
As Salamīyah see Salamīyah
'Assal, Lac 46 E4 lake W Djibouti
As Salţ 97 B6 var. Salt. Al Balqā', NW Jordan
Assamaka see Assamakka
Assamakka 53 F2 var. Assamaka. Agadez, NW Niger
As Samāwah 98 B3 var. Samawa. S Iraq
Assen 64 E2 Drenthe, NE Netherlands
Assenede 65 B5 Oost-Vlaanderen, NW Belgium
Assiout see Asyût
Assiut see Asyût
Assouan see Aswân
Assu see Açu
Assuan see Aswân
As Sukhnah 96 C3 var. Sukhne, Fr. Soukhné. Ḩimş, C Syria
As Sulaymānīyah 98 C3 var. Sulaimaniya, Kurd. Slēmānī. NE Iraq
As Sulayyil 99 B5 Ar Riyāḑ, S Saudi Arabia
Aş Şuwār 96 D2 var. Şuwār. Dayr az Zawr, E Syria
As Suwaydā' 97 B5 var. El Suweida, Es Suweida, Suweida, Fr. Soueida. As Suwaydā', SW Syria
Astacus see İzmit
Astana 92 C4 prev. Akmola, Akmolinsk, Tselinograd, Kaz. Aqmola. country capital (Kazakhstan) Akmola, N Kazakhstan
Astarabad see Gorgān
Asterābād see Gorgān
Asti 74 A2 anc. Asta Colonia, Asta Pompeia, Hasta Colonia, Hasta Pompeia. Piemonte, NW Italy
Astipálaia see Astypálaia
Astorga 70 C1 anc. Asturica Augusta. Castilla-León, N Spain
Astrabad see Gorgān
Astrakhan' 89 C7 Astrakhanskaya Oblast', SW Russian Federation
Asturias 70 C1 cultural region NW Spain
Astypálaia 83 D7 var. Astipálaia, It. Stampalia. Island Kykládes, Greece, Aegean Sea
Asunción 42 D2 country capital (Paraguay) Central, S Paraguay
Aswân 50 B2 var. Assouan, Assuan; anc. Syene. SE Egypt
Asyût 50 B2 var. Assiout, Assiut, Siut; anc. Lycopolis. C Egypt
Atacama Desert see Atacama, Desierto de
Atacama, Desierto de 42 B2 Eng. Atacama Desert. Desert N Chile
Atafu Atoll 123 E3 island NW Tokelau
Atamyrat 100 D3 prev. Kerki. Lebapskiy Velayat, E Turkmenistan
Aţâr 52 C2 Adrar, W Mauritania
Atas Bogd 104 D3 mountain SW Mongolia
Atascadero 25 B7 California, W USA
Atatürk Barajı 95 E4 reservoir S Turkey
Atbara 50 C3 var. 'Aţbārah. River Nile, NE Sudan
'Aţbārah see Atbara
Atbasar 92 C4 Akmola, N Kazakhstan
Atchison 23 F4 Kansas, C USA
Ath 65 B6 var. Aat. Hainaut, SW Belgium
Athabasca 15 E5 var. Athabaska. River Alberta, SW Canada
Athabasca 15 E5 Alberta, SW Canada
Athabasca, Lake 15 F4 lake Alberta/Saskatchewan, SW Canada
Athabaska see Athabasca
Athens see Athína
Athens 21 E2 Georgia, SE USA
Athens 18 D4 Ohio, N USA
Athens 27 G3 Texas, SW USA
Atherton 126 D3 Queensland, NE Australia
Athína 83 C6 Eng. Athens; prev. Athínai, anc. Athenae. Country capital (Greece) Attikí, C Greece
Athlone 67 B5 Ir. Baile Átha Luain. C Ireland
Ath Thawrah see Madīnat ath Thawrah
Ati 54 C3 Batha, C Chad
Atikokan 16 B4 Ontario, S Canada
Atka 14 A3 Atka Island, Alaska, USA
Atka 93 G3 Magadanskaya Oblast', E Russian Federation
Atlanta 20 D2 state capital Georgia, SE USA
Atlanta 27 H2 Texas, SW USA
Atlantic City 19 F4 New Jersey, NE USA
Atlantic-Indian Basin 45 D7 undersea feature SW Indian Ocean
Atlantic-Indian Ridge 47 B8 undersea feature SW Indian Ocean
Atlantic Ocean 44 B4 ocean
Atlas Mountains 48 C2 mountain range NW Africa
Atlasovo 93 H3 Kamchatskaya Oblast', E Russian Federation
Atlas Saharien 48 D2 var. Saharan Atlas. Mountain range Algeria/Morocco
Atlas Tellien 80 C3 Eng. Tell Atlas. Mountain range N Algeria
Atlin 14 D4 British Columbia, W Canada
Aţ Ţafīlah 97 B7 var. Et Tafila, Tafila. Aţ Ţafīlah, W Jordan
Aţ Ţā'if 99 B5 Makkah, W Saudi Arabia
At Tall al Abyaḑ 96 C2 var. Tall al Abyaḑ, Tell Abyad, Fr. Tell Abiad. Ar Raqqah, N Syria
Aţ Ţanf 96 D4 Ḩimş, S Syria
Attapu see Samakhixai
Attawapiskat 16 C3 river Ontario, S Canada
Attawapiskat 16 C3 Ontario, C Canada
At Tibnī 96 D2 var. Tibnī. Dayr az Zawr, NE Syria
Attopeu see Samakhixai
Attu Island 14 A2 island Aleutian Islands, Alaska, USA
Atyrau 92 B4 prev. Gur'yev. Atyrau, W Kazakhstan
Aubagne 69 D6 anc. Albania. Bouches-du-Rhône, SE France
Aubange 65 D8 Luxembourg, SE Belgium
Aubervilliers 68 E1 Seine-St-Denis, N France
Auburn 46 B2 Washington, NW USA
Auch 69 B6 Lat. Augusta Auscorum, Elimberrum. Gers, S France
Auckland 128 D2 Auckland, North Island, NZ
Auckland Islands 120 C5 island group S NZ
Audincourt 68 E4 Doubs, E France
Audru 84 D2 Ger. Audern. Pärnumaa, SW Estonia
Augathella 127 D5 Queensland, E Australia
Augsburg 73 C6 Fr. Augsbourg; anc. Augusta Vindelicorum. Bayern, S Germany
Augusta 19 G2 state capital Maine, NE USA
Augusta 21 E2 Georgia, SE USA
Augusta 125 A7 Western Australia
Augustów 76 E2 Rus. Avgustov. Podlaskie, NE Poland
'Aujā et Tahtā see. Khirbet el 'Aujā et Tahtā
Aulie Ata/Auliye-Ata see Taraz
Auob 56 B4 var. Oup. River Namibia/South Africa
Aurangābād 112 D5 Mahārāshtra, C India
Auray 68 A3 Morbihan, NW France
Aurès, Massif de l' 80 C4 mountain range NE Algeria
Aurillac 69 C5 Cantal, C France
Aurora 22 D4 Colorado, C USA
Aurora 18 B3 Illinois, N USA
Aurora 23 G5 Missouri, C USA
Aurora 37 F2 NW Guyana
Aus 56 B4 Karas, SW Namibia
Ausa see Vic
Austin 27 G3 state capital Texas, S USA
Austin 23 G3 Minnesota, N USA
Australes, Îles 121 F4 var. Archipel des Australes, Îles Tubuai, Tubuai Islands, Eng. Austral Islands. Island group SW French Polynesia
Austral Fracture Zone 121 H4 tectonic feature S Pacific Ocean
Australia 120 A4 Country
Australian Alps 127 C7 mountain range SE Australia
Australian Capital Territory 127 D7 prev. Federal Capital Territory. Territory SE Australia
Austral Islands see Australes, Îles
Austria 73 D7 Ger. Österreich. Country C Europe
Auvergne 69 C5 cultural region C France
Auxerre 68 C4 anc. Autesiodorum, Autissiodorum. Yonne, C France
Avarua 123 G5 dependent territory capital (Cook Islands) Rarotonga, S Cook Islands
Ávdira 82 C3 Anatolikí Makedonía kai Thráki, NE Greece
Aveiro 70 B2 anc. Talabriga. Aveiro, W Portugal
Avela see Ávila
Avellino 75 D5 anc. Abellinum. Campania, S Italy
Avesta 63 C6 Kopparberg, C Sweden
Aveyron 69 C6 river S France
Avezzano 74 C4 Abruzzo, C Italy
Aviemore 66 C3 N Scotland, UK
Avignon 69 D6 anc. Avenio. Vaucluse, SE France
Avila see Ávila
Ávila 70 D3 var. Avila; anc. Abela, Abula, Abyla, Avela. Castilla-León, C Spain
Avilés 70 C1 Asturias, NW Spain
Avranches 68 B3 Manche, N France
Awaji-shima 109 C6 island SW Japan
Āwash 51 D5 var. Hawash. River C Ethiopia
Awbārī 49 F3 SW Libya
Ax see Dax
Axel 65 B5 Zeeland, SW Netherlands
Axel Heiberg Island 15 E1 var. Axel Heiburg. Island Nunavut, N Canada
Axel Heiburg see Axel Heiberg Island
Ayacucho 38 D4 Ayacucho, S Peru
Ayagoz 130 C5 var. Ayaguz, Kaz. Ayaköz; prev. Sergiopol. Vostochnyy Kazakhstan, E Kazakhstan
Ayaguz see Ayagoz
Ayaköz see Ayagoz
Ayamonte 70 C4 Andalucía, S Spain
Ayaviri 39 E4 Puno, S Peru
Aydarko'l Ko'li 101 E2 var. Aydarkŭl, Rus. Ozero Aydarkul'. Lake C Uzbekistan
Aydarkŭl see Aydarko'l Ko'li
Aydın 94 A4 var. Aïdin; anc. Tralles. Aydın, SW Turkey
Ayers Rock see Uluru
Ayeyarwady see Irrawaddy
Ayiá see Agiá
Ayios Evstratios see Efstrátios, Ágios
Áyios Nikólaos see Ágios Nikólaos
Ayorou 53 E3 Tillabéri, W Niger
'Ayoûn el 'Atroûs 52 D3 var. Aïoun el Atrous, Aïoun el Atroûss. Hodh el Gharbi, SE Mauritania
Ayr 66 C4 W Scotland, UK
Ayteke Bi 130 B4 . Kaz. Zhangaqazaly, prev. Novokazalinsk Kyzylorda, SW Kazakhstan
Aytos 82 E2 Burgas, E Bulgaria
Ayutthaya 115 C5 var. Phra Nakhon Si Ayutthaya. Phra Nakhon Si Ayutthaya, C Thailand
Ayvalık 94 A3 Balıkesir, W Turkey
Azahar, Costa del 71 F3 coastal region E Spain
Azaouâd 53 E3 desert C Mali
A'zāz 96 B2 Ḩalab, NW Syria
Azerbaijan 95 G2 Az. Azărbaycan, Azărbaycan Respublikasi; prev. Azerbaijan SSR. Country SE Asia
Azimabad see Patna
Azogues 38 B2 Cañar, S Ecuador
Azores 70 A4 var. Açores, Ilhas dos Açores, Port. Arquipélago dos Açores. Island group Portugal, NE Atlantic Ocean
Azores-Biscay Rise 58 A3 undersea feature E Atlantic Ocean
Azoum, Bahr 54 C3 seasonal river SE Chad
Azov, Sea of 81 H1 Rus. Azovskoye More, Ukr. Azovs'ke More. Sea NE Black Sea
Azraq, Wāḩat al 135 C6 oasis N Jordan
Aztec 26 C1 New Mexico, SW USA
Azuaga 70 C4 Extremadura, W Spain
Azuero, Península de 31 F5 peninsula S Panama
Azul 43 D5 Buenos Aires, E Argentina
Azur, Côte d' 85 E6 Coastal region SE France
Az Zaqāzīq see Zagazig
Az Zarqā' 97 B6 var. Zarqa. Az Zarqā', NW Jordan
Az Zāwiyah 49 F2 var. Zawia. NW Libya
Az Zilfī 98 B4 Ar Riyāḑ, N Saudi Arabia
Æsernia see Isernia

B

Ba 78 D3 prev. Mba. Viti Levu, W Fiji
Baalbek 96 B4 var. Ba'labakk; anc. Heliopolis. E Lebanon
Bá an Daingin see Dingle Bay
Baardheere 51 D6 var. Bardere, It. Bardera. Gedo, SW Somalia
Baarle-Hertog 65 C5 Antwerpen, N Belgium
Baarn 64 C3 Utrecht, C Netherlands
Babadag 86 D5 Tulcea, SE Romania
Babahoyo 38 B2 prev. Bodegas. Los Ríos, C Ecuador
Bābā, Kūh-e 101 E4 mountain range C Afghanistan
Babayevo 88 B4 Vologodskaya Oblast', NW Russian Federation
Babeldaob 122 A1 var. Babeldaop, Babelthuap. Island N Palau
Babeldaop see Babeldaob
Bab el Mandeb 99 B7 strait Gulf of Aden/Red Sea
Babelthuap see Babeldaob
Bá Bheanntraí see Bantry Bay
Babruysk 85 D7 Rus. Bobruysk. Mahilyowskaya Voblasts', E Belarus
Babuyan Channel 117 E1 channel N Philippines
Babuyan Island 117 E1 island N Philippines
Bacabal 41 F2 Maranhão, E Brazil
Bacău 86 C4 Hung. Bákó. Bacău, NE Romania
Bắc Giang 114 D3 Ha Bắc, N Vietnam
Bacheykava 85 D5 Rus. Bocheykovo. Vitsyebskaya Voblasts', N Belarus
Back 37 F3 river Nunavut, N Canada
Bačka Palanka 78 D3 prev. Palanka. Serbia, NW Serbia and Montenegro (Yugo.)
Bačka Topola 78 D3 Hung. Topolya; prev. Hung. Bácstopolya. Serbia, N Serbia and Montenegro (Yugo.)
Bac Liêu 115 D6 var. Vinh Loi. Minh Hai, S Vietnam
Bacolod 103 E4 off. Bacolod City. Negros, C Philippines
Bacolod City see Bacolod
Bácsszenttamás see Srbobran
Badajoz 70 C4 anc. Pax Augusta. Extremadura, W Spain
Baden-Baden 73 B6 anc. Aurelia Aquensis. Baden-Württemberg, SW Germany
Bad Freienwalde 72 D3 Brandenburg, NE Germany
Bad Hersfeld 72 B4 Hessen, C Germany
Bad Homburg see Bad Homburg vor der Höhe
Bad Homburg vor der Höhe 73 B5 var. Bad Homburg. Hessen, W Germany
Bá Dhún na nGall see Donegal Bay
Bad Ischl 73 D7 Oberösterreich, N Austria
Bad Krozingen 73 A6 Baden-Württemberg, SW Germany
Badlands 22 D2 physical region North Dakota, N USA
Badu Island 126 C1 island Queensland, NE Australia
Bad Vöslau 73 E6 Niederösterreich, NE Austria
Baetic Cordillera see Béticos, Sistemas
Baetic Mountains see Béticos, Sistemas
Bafatá 52 C4 C Guinea-Bissau
Baffin Bay 15 G2 bay Canada/Greenland
Baffin Island 15 G2 island Nunavut, NE Canada
Bafing 52 C3 river W Africa
Bafoussam 54 A4 Ouest, W Cameroon
Bafra 94 D2 Samsun, N Turkey
Bāft 98 D4 Kermān, S Iran
Bagaces 30 D4 Guanacaste, NW Costa Rica
Bagdad see Baghdād
Bagé 41 E5 Rio Grande do Sul, S Brazil
Baghdād 98 B3 var. Bagdad, Eng. Baghdad. Country capital (Iraq) C Iraq
Baghlān 101 E3 Baghlān, NE Afghanistan
Bago see Pegu
Bagoé 52 D4 river Côte d'Ivoire/Mali
Bagrationovsk 84 A4 Ger. Preussisch Eylau. Kaliningradskaya Oblast', W Russian Federation
Bagrax Hu see Bosten Hu
Baguio 117 E1 off. Baguio City. Luzon, N Philippines

Bagzane, Monts 53 *F3 mountain* N Niger
Bahama Islands *see* Bahamas
Bahamas 32 *C2 Country* N West Indies
Bahamas 13 *D6 var.* Bahama Islands. *Island group* N West Indies
Baharly 100 *C3 var.* Bäherden, *Rus.* Bakharden; *prev.* Bakherden. Akhalskiy Velayat, C Turkmenistan
Bahāwalpur 112 *C2* Punjab, E Pakistan
Bäherden *see* Baharly
Bahia 41 *F3 off.* Estado da Bahia. *State* E Brazil
Bahía Blanca 43 *C5* Buenos Aires, E Argentina
Bahía, Islas de la 30 *C1 Eng.* Bay Islands. *Island group* N Honduras
Bahir Dar 50 *C4 var.* Bahr Dar, Bahrdar Giyorgis. NW Ethiopia
Bahraich 113 *E3* Uttar Pradesh, N India
Bahrain 98 *C4 Ar.* Al Baḩrayn; *prev.* Bahrein, *anc.* Tylos or Tyros. *Country* SW Asia
Baḩr al Milḩ *see* Razāzah, Buḩayrat ar
Baḩrat Lūṭ *see* Dead Sea
Bahrat Tabariya *see* Tiberias, Lake
Bahr Dar *see* Bahir Dar
Bahrdar Giyorgis *see* Bahir Dar
Bahr el Azraq *see* Blue Nile
Bahr el Jebel *see* White Nile
Bahret Lut *see* Dead Sea
Bahr Tabariya, Sea of *see* Tiberias, Lake
Bahushewsk 85 *E6 Rus.* Bogushëvsk. Vitsyebskaya Voblasts', NE Belarus
Baia Mare 86 *B3 Ger.* Frauenbach, *Hung.* Nagybánya; *prev.* Neustadt. Maramureş, NW Romania
Baia Sprie 86 *B3 Ger.* Mittelstadt, *Hung.* Felsőbánya. Maramureş, NW Romania
Baïbokoum 54 *B4* Logone-Oriental, SW Chad
Baidoa *see* Baydhabo
Baie-Comeau 17 *E3* Québec, SE Canada
Baikal, Lake *see* Baykal, Ozero
Baile Átha Luain *see* Athlone
Bailén 70 *D4* Andalucía, S Spain
Baile na Mainistreach *see* Newtownabbey
Băileşti 86 *B5* Dolj, SW Romania
Ba Illi 54 *B3* Chari-Baguirmi, SW Chad
Bainbridge 20 *D3* Georgia, SE USA
Bā'ir *see* Bāyir
Bairiki 122 *D2 country capital* (Kiribati) Tarawa, NW Kiribati
Bairnsdale 127 *C7* Victoria, SE Australia
Baishan 107 *E3 prev.* Hunjiang. Jilin, NE China
Baiyin 106 *B4* Gansu, C China
Baja 77 *C7* Bács-Kiskun, S Hungary
Baja California 26 *A4 Eng.* Lower California. *Peninsula* NW Mexico
Baja California 28 *B2 state* NW Mexico
Bajo Boquete *see* Boquete
Bajram Curri 79 *D5* Kukës, N Albania
Bakala 54 *C4* Ouaka, C Central African Republic
Bakan *see* Shimonoseki
Baker 24 *C3* Oregon, NW USA
Baker and Howland Islands 123 *E2 US unincorporated territory* W Polynesia
Baker Lake 15 *F3* Nunavut, N Canada
Bakersfield 25 *C7* California, W USA
Bakharden *see* Baharly
Bakhchysaray 87 *F5 Rus.* Bakhchisaray. Respublika Krym, S Ukraine
Bakhmach 87 *F1* Chernihivs'ka Oblast', N Ukraine
Bākhtarān *see* Kermānshāh
Bakı 95 *H2 Eng.* Baku. *Country capital* (Azerbaijan) E Azerbaijan
Bakony 77 *C7 Eng.* Bakony Mountains, *Ger.* Bakonywald. *Mountain range* W Hungary
Baku *see* Bakı
Balabac Island 107 *C8 island* W Philippines
Balabac Strait 116 *D2 var.* Selat Balabac. *Strait* Malaysia/Philippines
Ba'labakk *see* Baalbek
Balaguer 93 *F2* Cataluña, NE Spain
Balakovo 89 *C6* Saratovskaya Oblast', W Russian Federation
Bālā Morghāb 100 *D4* Laghmān, NW Afghanistan
Balashov 89 *B6* Saratovskaya Oblast', W Russian Federation
Balaton *C7 var.* Lake Balaton, *Ger.* Plattensee. *Lake* W Hungary
Balaton, Lake *see* Balaton
Balbina, Represa 40 *D1 reservoir* NW Brazil
Balboa 31 *G4* Panamá, C Panama
Balcarce 43 *D5* Buenos Aires, E Argentina
Balclutha 129 *B7* Otago, South Island, NZ
Baldy Mountain 22 *C1 mountain* Montana, NW USA
Bâle *see* Basel
Baleares, Islas 71 *G3 Eng.* Balearic Islands. *Island group* Spain, W Mediterranean Sea
Balearic Islands *see* Baleares, Islas
Balearic Plain *see* Algerian Basin
Baleine, Rivière à la 17 *E2 river* Québec, E Canada
Balen 65 *C5* Antwerpen, N Belgium
Bāleshwar 113 *F4 prev.* Balasore. Orissa, E India
Bali 116 *D5 island* C Indonesia
Balıkesir 94 *A3* Balıkesir, W Turkey
Balīkh, Nahr 96 *C2 river* N Syria
Balikpapan 116 *D4* Borneo, C Indonesia
Balkanabat 100 *B2 var.* Nebitdag. Balkanskiy Velayat, W Turkmenistan
Balkan Mountains 82 *C2 Bul./SCr.* Stara Planina. *Mountain range* Bulgaria/Serbia and Montenegro (Yugo.)
Balkh 101 *E3 anc.* Bactra. Balkh, N Afghanistan
Balkhash 92 *C5 Kaz.* Balqash. Karaganda, SE Kazakhstan
Balkhash, Lake *see* Balkhash, Ozero
Balkhash, Ozero 92 *C5 Eng.* Lake Balkhash, *Kaz.* Balqash. *Lake* SE Kazakhstan
Balladonia 125 *C6* Western Australia
Ballarat 127 *C7* Victoria, SE Australia
Balleny Islands 132 *B5 island group* Antarctica
Ballinger 27 *F3* Texas, SW USA
Balochistān *see* Baluchistān
Balş 86 *B5* Olt, S Romania
Balsas 41 *F2* Maranhão, E Brazil
Balsas, Río 29 *E5 var.* Río Mexcala. *River* S Mexico
Bal'shavik 85 *D7 Rus.* Bol'shevik. Homyel'skaya Voblasts', SE Belarus
Balta 86 *D3* Odes'ka Oblast', SW Ukraine
Bălţi 86 *D3 Rus.* Bel'tsy. N Moldova
Baltic Sea 63 *C7 Ger.* Ostee, *Rus.* Baltiskoye More. *Sea* N Europe
Baltimore 19 *F4* Maryland, NE USA
Baltkrievija *see* Belarus
Baluchistān 112 *B3 var.* Balochistān, Beluchistan. *Admin. region province* SW Pakistan
Balvi 84 *D4* Balvi, NE Latvia
Balykchy 101 *G2 Kir.* Ysyk-Köl; *prev.* Issyk-Kul', Rybach'ye. Issyk-Kul'skaya Oblast', NE Kyrgyzstan
Balzers 72 *E2* S Liechtenstein
Bam 98 *E4* Kermān, SE Iran
Bamako 52 *D4 country capital* (Mali) Capital District, SW Mali
Bambari 54 *C4* Ouaka, C Central African Republic
Bamberg 73 *C5* Bayern, SE Germany
Bamenda 54 *A4* Nord-Ouest, W Cameroon
Banaba 122 *D2 var.* Ocean Island. *Island* Tungaru, W Kiribati
Bandaaceh 138 *A3 var.* Banda Atjeh; *prev.* Koetaradja, Kutaradja, Kutaraja. Sumatera, W Indonesia
Banda Atjeh *see* Bandaaceh
Bandama 52 *D5 var.* Bandama Fleuve. *River* S Côte d'Ivoire
Bandama Fleuve *see* Bandama
Bandar 'Abbās *see* Bandar-e 'Abbās
Bandarbeyla 51 *E5 var.* Bender Beila, Bender Beyla. Bari, NE Somalia
Bandar-e 'Abbās 98 *D4 var.* Bandar 'Abbās; *prev.* Gombroon. Hormozgān, S Iran
Bandar-e Būshehr 98 *C4 var.* Būshehr, *Eng.* Bushire. Būshehr, S Iran
Bandar-e Khamīr 98 *D4* Hormozgān, S Iran
Bandar-e Langeh 98 *D4 var.* Bandar-e Lengeh, Lingeh. Hormozgān, S Iran
Bandar-e Lengeh *see* Bandar-e Langeh
Bandar Kassim *see* Boosaaso
Bandarlampung 116 *C4 prev.* Tanjungkarang, Teloekbetoeng, Telukbetung. Sumatera, W Indonesia
Bandar Maharani *see* Muar
Bandar Masulipatnam *see* Machilīpatnam
Bandar Seri Begawan 116 *D3 prev.* Brunei Town. *Country capital* (Brunei) N Brunei
Bandar Sri Aman *see* Sri Aman
Banda Sea 117 *F5 var.* Laut Banda. *Sea* E Indonesia
Bandiagara 53 *E3* Mopti, C Mali
Bandırma 94 *A3 var.* Penderma. Balıkesir, NW Turkey
Bandundu 55 *C6 prev.* Banningville. Bandundu, W Dem. Rep. Congo
Bandung 116 *C5 prev.* Bandoeng. Jawa, C Indonesia
Bangalore 110 *C2* Karnātaka, S India
Bangassou 54 *D4* Mbomou, SE Central African Republic
Banggai, Kepulauan 117 *E4 island group* C Indonesia
Banghāzī 49 *G2 Eng.* Bengazi, Benghazi, *It.* Bengasi. NE Libya
Bangka, Pulau 116 *C4 island* W Indonesia
Bangkok *see* Krung Thep
Bangkok, Bight of *see* Krung Thep, Ao
Bangladesh 113 *G3 prev.* East Pakistan. *Country* S Asia
Bangor 67 *B5 Ir.* Beannchar. E Northern Ireland, UK
Bangor 19 *G2* Maine, NE USA
Bangor 67 *C6* NW Wales, UK
Bangui 55 *B5 country capital* (Central African Republic) Ombella-Mpoko, SW Central African Republic
Bangweulu, Lake 51 *B8 var.* Lake Bengweulu. *Lake* N Zambia
Ban Hat Yai *see* Hat Yai
Ban Hin Heup 114 *C4* Viangchan, C Laos
Ban Houayxay *see* Houayxay
Ban Houei Sai *see* Houayxay
Ban Hua Hin 115 *C6 var.* Hua Hin. Prachuap Khiri Khan, SW Thailand
Bani 52 *D3 river* S Mali
Banias *see* Bāniyās
Banī Suwayf *see* Beni Suef
Bāniyās 96 *B3 var.* Banias, Baniyas, Paneas. Ṭarṭūs, W Syria
Baniyas *see* Bāniyās
Banja Luka 78 *B3* Republika Srpska, NW Bosnia and Herzegovina
Banjarmasin 116 *D4 prev.* Bandjarmasin. Borneo, C Indonesia
Banjul 52 *B3 prev.* Bathurst. *Country capital* (Gambia) W Gambia
Banks Island 15 *E2 island* Banks Island, Northwest Territories, NW Canada
Banks Islands 122 *D4 Fr.* Îles Banks. *Island group* N Vanuatu
Banks Lake 24 *B1 reservoir* Washington, NW USA
Banks Peninsula 129 *C6 peninsula* South Island, NZ
Banks Strait 127 *C8 strait* SW Tasman Sea
Bānkura 113 *F4* West Bengal, NE India
Ban Mak Khaeng *see* Udon Thani
Banmo *see* Bhamo
Bañolas *see* Banyoles
Ban Pak Phanang *see* Pak Phanang
Ban Sichon *see* Sichon
Banská Bystrica 77 *C6 Ger.* Neusohl, *Hung.* Besztercebánya. Banskobystrický Kraj, C Slovakia
Bantry Bay 67 *A7 Ir.* Bá Bheanntraí. *Bay* SW Ireland
Banya 82 *E2* Burgas, E Bulgaria
Banyak, Kepulauan 116 *A3 prev.* Kepulauan Banjak. *Island group* NW Indonesia
Banyo 54 *B4* Adamaoua, NW Cameroon
Banyoles 71 *G2 var.* Bañolas. Cataluña, NE Spain
Banzare Seamounts 119 *C7 undersea feature* S Indian Ocean
Baoji 106 *B4 var.* Pao-chi, Paoki. Shaanxi, C China
Baoro 54 *B4* Nana-Mambéré, W Central African Republic
Baoshan 106 *A6 var.* Pao-shan. Yunnan, SW China
Baotou 105 *F3 var.* Pao-t'ou, Paotow. Nei Mongol Zizhiqu, N China
Ba'qūbah 98 *B3 var.* Qubba. C Iraq
Baquerizo Moreno *see* Puerto Baquerizo Moreno
Bar 79 *C5 It.* Antivari. Montenegro, SW Serbia and Montenegro (Yugo.)
Baraawe 51 *D6 It.* Brava. Shabeellaha Hoose, S Somalia
Baraji, Hirfanli 94 *C3 lake* C Turkey
Bārāmati 112 *C5* Mahārāshtra, W India
Baranavichy 85 *B6 Pol.* Baranowicze, *Rus.* Baranovichi. Brestskaya Voblasts', SW Belarus
Barbados 33 *G1 country* SE West Indies
Barbastro 71 *F2* Aragón, NE Spain
Barbate de Franco 70 *C5* Andalucía, S Spain
Barbuda 33 *G3 island* N Antigua and Barbuda
Barcaldine 126 *C4* Queensland, E Australia
Barce *see* Al Marj
Barcelona 71 *G2 anc.* Barcino, Barcinona. Cataluña, E Spain
Barcelona 37 *E2* Anzoátegui, NE Venezuela
Barcoo *see* Cooper Creek
Barcs 77 *C7* Somogy, SW Hungary
Bardaï 54 *C1* Borkou-Ennedi-Tibesti, N Chad
Bardejov 77 *D5 Ger.* Bartfeld, *Hung.* Bártfa. Prešovský Kraj, E Slovakia
Bardera *see* Baardheere
Bardere *see* Baardheere
Bareilly 113 *E3 var.* Bareli. Uttar Pradesh, N India
Bareli *see* Bareilly
Barendrecht 64 *C4* Zuid-Holland, SW Netherlands
Barentin 68 *C3* Seine-Maritime, N France
Barentsberg 61 *G2* Spitsbergen, W Svalbard
Barentsøya 61 *G2 island* E Svalbard
Barents Sea 88 *C2 Nor.* Barents Havet, *Rus.* Barentsevo More. *Sea* Arctic Ocean
Barents Trough 59 *E1 undersea feature* SW Barents Sea
Bar Harbor 19 *H2* Mount Desert Island, Maine, NE USA
Bari 75 *E5 var.* Bari delle Puglie; *anc.* Barium. Puglia, SE Italy
Bārīdah *see* Al Bārīdah
Bari delle Puglie *see* Bari
Barikot *see* Barīkowṭ
Barīkowṭ 101 *F4 var.* Barikot. Kunar, NE Afghanistan
Barillas 30 *A2 var.* Santa Cruz Barillas. Huehuetenango, NW Guatemala
Barinas 36 *C2* Barinas, W Venezuela
Barisal 113 *G4* Khulna, S Bangladesh
Barisan, Pegunungan 116 *B4 mountain range* Sumatera, W Indonesia
Barito, Sungai 116 *D4 river* Borneo, C Indonesia
Barium *see* Bari
Barka *see* Al Marj
Barkly Tableland 126 *B3 plateau* Northern Territory/Queensland, N Australia
Bârlad 86 *D4 prev.* Bîrlad. Vaslui, E Romania
Barlavento, Ilhas de 52 *A2 var.* Windward Islands. *Island group* N Cape Verde
Bar-le-Duc 68 *D3 var.* Bar-sur-Ornain. Meuse, NE France
Barlee, Lake 125 *B6 lake* Western Australia
Barlee Range 124 *A4 mountain range* Western Australia
Barletta 75 *D5 anc.* Barduli. Puglia, SE Italy
Barlinek 76 *B3 Ger.* Berlinchen. Zachodniopomorskie, NW Poland
Barmouth 67 *C6* NW Wales, UK
Barnaul 92 *D4* Altayskiy Kray, C Russian Federation
Barnet 67 *A7* SE England, UK
Barnstaple 67 *C7* SW England, UK
Baroghil Pass 101 *F3 var.* Kowtal-e Barowghīl. *Pass* Afghanistan/Pakistan
Baron'ki 85 *E7 Rus.* Boron'ki. Mahilyowskaya Voblasts', E Belarus
Barquisimeto 36 *C2* Lara, NW Venezuela
Barra 66 *B3 island* NW Scotland, UK
Barra de Río Grande 31 *E3* Región Autónoma Atlántico Sur, E Nicaragua
Barragem de Sobradinho *see* Sobradinho, Represa de
Barranca 38 *C3* Lima, W Peru
Barrancabermeja 36 *B2* Santander, N Colombia
Barranquilla 36 *B1* Atlántico, N Colombia
Barreiro 70 *B4* Setúbal, W Portugal
Barrier Range 127 *C6 hill range* New South Wales, SE Australia
Barrow 67 *B6 Ir.* An Bhearú. *River* SE Ireland
Barrow 14 *D2* Alaska, USA
Barrow-in-Furness 67 *C5* NW England, UK
Barrow Island 124 *A4 island* Western Australia
Barstow 25 *C7* California, W USA
Bar-sur-Ornain *see* Bar-le-Duc
Bartang 101 *F3 river* SE Tajikistan
Bartica 37 *F3* N Guyana
Bartın 94 *C2* Bartın NW Turkey
Bartlesville 27 *G1* Oklahoma, C USA
Bartoszyce 76 *D2 Ger.* Bartenstein. Warmińsko-Mazurskie, NE Poland
Baruun-Urt 105 *F2* Sühbaatar, E Mongolia
Barú, Volcán 31 *E5 var.* Volcán de Chiriquí. *Volcano* W Panama
Barwon River 127 *D5 river* New South Wales, SE Australia
Barysaw 85 *D6 Rus.* Borisov. Minskaya Voblasts', NE Belarus
Basarabeasca 86 *D4 Rus.* Bessarabka. SE Moldova
Basel 73 *A7 Eng.* Basle, *Fr.* Bâle. Basel-Stadt, NW Switzerland
Basilan 117 *E3 island* SW Philippines
Basle *see* Basel
Basra *see* Al Başrah
Bassano del Grappa 74 *C2* Veneto, NE Italy
Bassein 114 *A4 var.* Pathein. Irrawaddy, SW Myanmar
Basse-Terre 33 *G4 dependent territory capital* (Guadeloupe) Basse Terre, SW Guadeloupe
Basse Terre 33 *G4 island* W Guadeloupe
Basseterre 33 *G3 country capital* (Saint Kitts and Nevis) Saint Kitts, Saint Kitts and Nevis
Bassikounou 52 *D3* Hodh ech Chargui, SE Mauritania
Bass Strait 127 *C7 strait* SE Australia
Bassum 72 *B3* Niedersachsen, NW Germany
Bastia 69 *E7* Corse, France, C Mediterranean Sea
Bastogne 65 *D7* Luxembourg, SE Belgium
Bastrop 20 *B2* Louisiana, S USA
Bastyn' 85 *B7 Rus.* Bostyn'. Brestskaya Voblasts', SW Belarus
Basuo *see* Dongfang
Bata 55 *A5* NW Equatorial Guinea
Batabanó, Golfo de 32 *A2 gulf* W Cuba
Batajnica 78 *D3* Serbia, N Serbia and Montenegro (Yugo.)
Batangas 117 *E2 off.* Batangas City. Luzon, N Philippines
Bătdâmbâng 115 *C5 prev.* Battambang. Bătdâmbâng, NW Cambodia
Batéké, Plateaux 55 *B6 plateau* S Congo
Bath 67 *D7 hist.* Akermanceaster, *anc.* Aquae Calidae, Aquae Solis. SW England, UK
Bathinda 112 *D2* Punjab, NW India
Bathsheba 33 *G1* E Barbados
Bathurst 17 *F4* New Brunswick, SE Canada
Bathurst 127 *D6* New South Wales, SE Australia
Bathurst Island 124 *D2 island* Northern Territory, N Australia
Bathurst Island 15 *F2 island* Parry Islands, Nunavut, N Canada
Bāṭin, Wādī al 136 *C4 dry watercourse* SW Asia
Batman 95 *E4 var.* İluh. Batman, SE Turkey
Batna 49 *E2* NE Algeria
Baton Rouge 20 *B3 state capital* Louisiana, S USA
Batroûn 96 *A4 var.* Al Batrūn. N Lebanon
Batticaloa 110 *D3* Eastern Province, E Sri Lanka
Battipaglia 75 *D5* Campania, S Italy
Bat'umi 95 *F2* W Georgia
Batu Pahat 116 *B3 prev.* Bandar Penggaram. Johor, Peninsular Malaysia
Bauchi 53 *G4* Bauchi, NE Nigeria
Bauer Basin 131 *F3 undersea feature* E Pacific Ocean
Bauska 84 *C3 Ger.* Bauske. Bauska, S Latvia
Bautzen 72 *D4 Lus.* Budyšin. Sachsen, E Germany
Bavarian Alps 73 *C7 Ger.* Bayrische Alpen. *Mountain range* Austria/Germany
Bavispe, Río 28 *C2 river* NW Mexico
Bawîṭi 50 *B2* N Egypt
Bawku 53 *E4* N Ghana
Bayamo 32 *C3* Granma, E Cuba
Bayan Har Shan 104 *D4 var.* Bayan Khar. *Mountain range* C China
Bayanhongor 104 *D2* Bayanhongor, C Mongolia
Bayan Khar *see* Bayan Har Shan
Bayano, Lago 31 *G4 lake* E Panama
Bay City 18 *C3* Michigan, N USA
Bay City 27 *G4* Texas, SW USA
Baydhabo 51 *D6 var.* Baydhowa, Isha Baydhabo, *It.* Baidoa. Bay, SW Somalia
Baydhowa *see* Baydhabo
Bayern 73 *C6 cultural region* SE Germany
Bayeux 68 *B3 anc.* Augustodurum. Calvados, N France
Bāyir 97 *C7 var.* Bā'ir. Ma'ān, S Jordan
Baykal, Ozero 93 *E4 Eng.* Lake Baikal. *Lake* S Russian Federation
Baymak 89 *D6* Respublika Bashkortostan, W Russian Federation
Bayonne 69 *A6 anc.* Lapurdum. Pyrénées-Atlantiques, SW France
Baýramaly 100 *D3 var.* Bayramaly; *prev.* Bayram-Ali. Maryyskiy Velayat, S Turkmenistan
Bayreuth 73 *C5 var.* Baireuth. Bayern, SE Germany
Bayrūt *see* Beyrouth
Baytown 27 *H4* Texas, SW USA
Baza 71 *E4* Andalucía, S Spain
Beagle Channel 43 *C8 channel* Argentina/Chile
Béal Feirste *see* Belfast
Beannchar *see* Bangor
Bear Lake 24 *E4 lake* Idaho/Utah, NW USA
Beas de Segura 71 *E4* Andalucía, S Spain
Beata, Isla 33 *E3 island* SW Dominican Republic
Beatrice 23 *F4* Nebraska, C USA
Beaufort Sea 14 *D2 sea* Arctic Ocean
Beaufort West 56 *C5 Afr.* Beaufort-Wes. Western Cape, SW South Africa
Beaumont 27 *H3* Texas, SW USA
Beaune 68 *D4* Côte d'Or, C France
Beauvais 68 *C3 anc.* Bellovacum, Caesaromagus. Oise, N France
Beaver Island 18 *C2 island* Michigan, N USA
Beaver Lake 27 *H1 reservoir* Arkansas, C USA
Beaver River 27 *F1 river* Oklahoma, C USA
Beāwar 112 *C3* Rājasthān, N India
Bečej 78 *D3 Ger.* Altbetsche, *Hung.* Óbecse, Rácz-Becse; *prev.* Magyar-Becse, Stari Bečej. Serbia, N Serbia and Montenegro (Yugo.)
Béchar 48 *D2 prev.* Colomb-Béchar. W Algeria
Beckley 18 *D5* West Virginia, NE USA
Bedford 67 *D6* E England, UK
Bedum 64 *E1* Groningen, NE Netherlands
Be'er Menuḥa 97 *B7 var* Be'er Menukha. Southern, S Israel
Be'er Menukha *see* Be'ér Menuḥa
Beernem 65 *A5* West-Vlaanderen, NW Belgium
Beersheba *see* Be'ér Sheva'
Be'ér Sheva' 97 *A7 var.* Beersheba, *Ar.* Bir es Saba. Southern, S Israel
Beesel 65 *D5* Limburg, SE Netherlands
Beeville 27 *G4* Texas, SW USA
Bega 127 *D7* New South Wales, SE Australia
Beida *see* Al Bayḍā'
Beihai 106 *B6* Guangxi Zhuangzu Zizhiqu, S China
Beijing 106 *C3 var.* Pei-ching, *Eng.* Peking; *prev.* Pei-p'ing. *Country/municipality capital* (China) Beijing Shi, E China
Beilen 64 *E2* Drenthe, NE Netherlands
Beira 57 *E3* Sofala, C Mozambique
Beirut *see* Beyrouth
Beit Leḥm *see* Bethlehem
Beiuş 86 *B3 Hung.* Belényes. Bihor, NW Romania
Beja 70 *B4 anc.* Pax Julia. Beja, SE Portugal
Béjar 70 *C3* Castilla-León, N Spain
Bejraburi *see* Phetchaburi
Békéscsaba 77 *D7 Rom.* Bichiş-Ciaba. Békés, SE Hungary
Bekobod 101 *E2 Rus.* Bekabad; *prev.* Begovat. Toshkent Wiloyati, E Uzbekistan
Bela Crkva 78 *E3 Ger.* Weisskirchen, *Hung.* Fehértemplom. Serbia, W Serbia and Montenegro (Yugo.)
Belarus 85 *B6 var.* Belorussia, *Latv.* Baltkrievija; *prev.* Belorussian SSR, *Rus.* Belorusskaya SSR. *Country* E Europe
Belau *see* Palau
Belchatow *see* Bełchatów
Bełchatów 76 *C4 var.* Belchatow. Łódzkie, C Poland
Belcher Islands 16 *C2 Fr.* Îles Belcher. *Island group* Northwest Territories, SE Canada
Beledweyne 51 *D5 var.* Belet Huen, *It.* Belet Uen. Hiiraan, C Somalia
Belém 41 *F1 var.* Pará. *State capital* Pará, N Brazil
Belen 26 *D2* New Mexico, SW USA
Belén 30 *D4* Rivas, SW Nicaragua
Belet Huen *see* Beledweyne
Belet Uen *see* Beledweyne
Belfast 67 *B5 Ir.* Béal Feirste. *Admin capital* E Northern Ireland, UK
Belfield 22 *D2* North Dakota, N USA
Belfort 68 *E4* Territoire-de-Belfort, E France
Belgaum 110 *B1* Karnātaka, W India
Belgium 65 *B6 Dut.* België, *Fr.* Belgique. *Country* NW Europe
Belgorod 89 *A6* Belgorodskaya Oblast', W Russian Federation
Belgrade *see* Beograd
Belgrano II 132 *A2 Argentinian research station* Antarctica
Belice *see* Belize City
Beligrad *see* Berat
Beli Manastir 78 *C3 Hung.* Pélmonostor; *prev.* Monostor. Osijek-Baranja, NE Croatia
Bélinga 55 *B5* Ogooué-Ivindo, NE Gabon
Belitung, Pulau 116 *C4 island* W Indonesia
Belize 30 *B1 Sp.* Belice; *prev.* British Honduras, Colony of Belize. *Country* Central America
Belize 30 *B1 river* Belize/Guatemala
Belize *see* Belize City
Belize City 30 *C1 var.* Belize, *Sp.* Belice. Belize, NE Belize
Belkofski 14 *B3* Alaska, USA
Belle Île 68 *A4 island* NW France
Belle Isle, Strait of 17 *G3 strait* Newfoundland and Labrador, E Canada
Belleville 18 *B4* Illinois, N USA
Bellevue 23 *F4* Iowa, C USA
Bellevue 24 *B2* Washington, NW USA
Bellingham 24 *B1* Washington, NW USA
Belling Hausen Mulde *see* Southeast Pacific Basin
Bellingshausen Abyssal Plain *see* Bellingshausen Plain
Bellingshausen Plain 131 *F5 var.* Bellingshausen Abyssal Plain. *Undersea feature* SE Pacific Ocean
Bellingshausen Sea 132 *A3 sea* Antarctica
Bellinzona 73 *B8 Ger.* Bellenz. Ticino, S Switzerland
Bello 36 *B2* Antioquia, W Colombia
Bellville 56 *B5* Western Cape, SW South Africa
Belmopan 30 *C1 country capital* (Belize) Cayo, C Belize
Belogradchik 82 *B1* Vidin, NW Bulgaria
Belo Horizonte 41 *F4 prev.* Bello Horizonte. *State capital* Minas Gerais, SE Brazil
Belomorsk 88 *B3* Respublika Kareliya, NW Russian Federation
Beloretsk 89 *D6* Respublika Bashkortostan, W Russian Federation
Belorussia/Belorussian SSR *see* Belarus
Belorusskaya SSR *see* Belarus
Beloye More 88 *C3 Eng.* White Sea. *Sea* NW Russian Federation

INDEX

Belozersk 88 B4 Vologodskaya Oblast', NW Russian Federation
Belton 27 G3 Texas, SW USA
Beluchistan see Baluchistān
Belukha, Gora 92 D5 mountain Kazakhstan/Russian Federation
Belyy, Ostrov 92 D2 island N Russian Federation
Bemaraha 57 F3 var. Plateau du Bemaraha. Mountain range W Madagascar
Bemidji 23 F1 Minnesota, N USA
Bemmel 64 D4 Gelderland, SE Netherlands
Benaco see Garda, Lago di
Benavente 70 D2 Castilla-León, N Spain
Bend 24 B3 Oregon, NW USA
Bender Beila see Bandarbeyla
Bender Beyla see Bandarbeyla
Bender Cassim see Boosaaso
Bendern 72 E1 NW Liechtenstein
Bender Qaasim see Boosaaso
Bendery see Tighina
Bendigo 127 C7 Victoria, SE Australia
Benešov 77 B5 Ger. Beneschau. Středočesky Kraj, W Czech Republic
Benevento 75 D5 anc. Beneventum, Malventum. Campania, S Italy
Bengal, Bay of 102 C4 bay N Indian Ocean
Bengbu 106 D5 var. Peng-pu. Anhui, E China
Benghazi see Banghāzī
Bengkulu 116 B4 prev. Bengkoeloe, Benkoelen, Benkulen. Sumatera, W Indonesia
Benguela 56 A2 var. Benguella. Benguela, W Angola
Benguella see Benguela
Bengweulu, Lake see Bangweulu, Lake
Ben Hope 66 B2 mountain N Scotland, UK
Beni 34 B4 var. El Beni. Admin. region department N Bolivia
Beni 55 E5 Nord Kivu, NE Dem. Rep. Congo
Benidorm 71 F4 País Valenciano, SE Spain
Beni-Mellal 48 C2 C Morocco
Benin 53 F4 prev. Dahomey. Country W Africa
Benin, Bight of 53 F5 gulf W Africa
Benin City 53 F5 Edo, SW Nigeria
Beni, Río 39 E3 river N Bolivia
Beni Suef 50 B2 var. Banī Suwayf. N Egypt
Ben Nevis 66 C3 mountain N Scotland, UK
Benson 26 B3 Arizona, SW USA
Bent Jbaïl 97 A5 var. Bint Jubayl. S Lebanon
Benton 20 B1 Arkansas, C USA
Benue 54 B4 Fr. Bénoué. River Cameroon/Nigeria
Benue 53 G4 state SE Nigeria
Beograd 78 D3 Eng. Belgrade, Ger. Belgrad; anc. Singidunum. Country capital. Serbia, N Serbia and Montenegro (Yugo.)
Berane 79 D5 prev. Ivangrad. Montenegro, SW Serbia and Montenegro (Yugo.)
Berat 79 C6 var. Berati, SCr. Beligrad. Berat, C Albania
Berati see Berat
Berau, Teluk 117 G4 var. MacCluer Gulf. Bay Papua, E Indonesia
Berbera 50 D4 Woqooyi Galbeed, NW Somalia
Berbérati 55 B5 Mambéré-Kadéï, SW Central African Republic
Berck-Plage 68 C2 Pas-de-Calais, N France
Berdyans'k 87 G4 Rus. Berdyansk; prev. Osipenko. Zaporiz'ka Oblast', SE Ukraine
Berdychiv 108 D2 Rus. Berdichev. Zhytomyrs'ka Oblast', N Ukraine
Bereket 100 B2 prev. Gazandzhyk, Kazandzhik, Turkm. Gazanjyk. Balkanskiy Velayat, W Turkmenistan
Berehove 86 B3 Cz. Berehovo, Hung. Beregszász, Rus. Beregovo. Zakarpats'ka Oblast', W Ukraine
Berettyó 77 D7 Rom. Barcău; prev. Berătău, Beretău. River Hungary/Romania
Berettyóújfalu 77 D6 Hajdú-Bihar, E Hungary
Berezhany 86 C2 Pol. Brzeżany. Ternopil's'ka Oblast', W Ukraine
Berezniki 89 D5 Permskaya Oblast', NW Russian Federation
Berga 71 G2 Cataluña, NE Spain
Bergamo 74 B2 anc. Bergomum. Lombardia, N Italy
Bergara 71 E1 País Vasco, N Spain
Bergen 63 A5 Hordaland, S Norway
Bergen 72 D2 Mecklenburg-Vorpommern, NE Germany
Bergen 64 C2 Noord-Holland, NW Netherlands
Bergerac 69 B5 Dordogne, SW France
Bergeyk 65 C5 Noord-Brabant, S Netherlands
Bergse Maas 64 D4 river S Netherlands
Beringen 65 C5 Limburg, NE Belgium
Bering Sea 14 A2 sea N Pacific Ocean
Bering Strait 14 C2 Rus. Beringov Proliv. Strait Bering Sea/Chukchi Sea
Berja 71 E5 Andalucía, S Spain
Berkeley 25 B6 California, W USA
Berkner Island 132 A2 island Antarctica
Berkovitsa 82 C2 Montana, NW Bulgaria
Berlin 72 D3 country capital (Germany) Berlin, NE Germany
Berlin 19 G2 New Hampshire, NE USA
Bermejo, Río 42 C2 river N Argentina
Bermeo 71 E1 País Vasco, N Spain
Bermuda 13 D6 var. Bermuda Islands, Bermudas; prev. Somers Islands. UK crown colony NW Atlantic Ocean
Bermuda Islands see Bermuda
Bermuda Rise 13 E6 undersea feature C Sargasso Sea
Bermudas see Bermuda
Bern 73 A7 Fr. Berne. Country capital (Switzerland) Bern, W Switzerland
Bernau 72 D3 Brandenburg, NE Germany
Bernburg 72 C4 Sachsen-Anhalt, C Germany
Berne see Bern
Berner Alpen 73 A7 var. Berner Oberland, Eng. Bernese Oberland. Mountain range SW Switzerland
Berner Oberland see Berner Alpen
Bernese Oberland see Berner Alpen
Bernier Island 125 A5 island Western Australia
Berry 90 C4 cultural region C France
Berry Islands 32 C1 island group N Bahamas
Bertoua 55 B5 Est, E Cameroon
Beru 123 E2 var. Peru. Atoll Tungaru, W Kiribati
Berwick-upon-Tweed 66 D4 N England, UK
Berytus see Beyrouth
Besançon 68 D4 anc. Besontium, Vesontio. Doubs, E France
Beskra see Biskra
Betafo 57 G3 Antananarivo, C Madagascar
Betanzos 70 B1 Galicia, NW Spain
Bethlehem 97 B6 Ar. Beit Laḥm, Heb. Bet Lehem. C West Bank
Bethlehem 56 D4 Free State, C South Africa
Béticos, Sistemas 70 D4 var. Sistema Penibético, Eng. Baetic Cordillera, Baetic Mountains. Mountain range S Spain
Bet Lehem see Bethlehem
Bétou 55 C5 La Likouala, N Congo
Bette, Picco see Bette, Pic
Bette, Pic 49 G4 var. Bīkkū Bīttī, It. Picco Bette. Mountain S Libya
Bette, Picco see Bette, Pic
Beulah 18 C2 Michigan, N USA
Beuthen see Bytom
Beveren 65 B5 Oost-Vlaanderen, N Belgium
Beverley 67 D5 E England, UK
Bexley 67 B8 SE England, UK
Beyla 52 D4 Guinée-Forestière, SE Guinea
Beyrouth 96 A4 var. Bayrūt, Eng. Beirut; anc. Berytus. Country capital (Lebanon) W Lebanon
Beyşehir 94 B4 Konya, SW Turkey
Beyşehir Gölü 94 B4 lake C Turkey
Béziers 69 C6 anc. Baeterrae, Baeterrae Septimanorum, Julia Beterrae. Hérault, S France
Bhadrāvati 110 C2 Karnātaka, SW India
Bhāgalpur 113 F3 Bihār, NE India
Bhaktapur 113 F3 Central, C Nepal
Bhamo 114 B2 var. Banmo. Kachin State, N Myanmar
Bharūch 112 C4 Gujarāt, W India
Bhāvnagar 112 C4 prev. Bhaunagar. Gujarāt, W India
Bhopāl 112 D4 Madhya Pradesh, C India
Bhubaneshwar 113 F5 prev. Bhubaneswar, Bhuvaneshwar. Orissa, E India
Bhuket see Phuket
Bhusāwal 112 D4 prev. Bhusaval. Mahārāshtra, C India
Bhutan 113 G3 var. Druk-yul. Country S Asia
Biak, Pulau 139 G4 island E Indonesia
Biała Podlaska 76 E3 Lubelskie, E Poland
Białogard 76 B2 Ger. Belgard. Zachodniopomorskie, NW Poland
Białystok 76 E3 Rus. Belostok, Bielostok. Podlaskie, NE Poland
Biarritz 69 A6 Pyrénées-Atlantiques, SW France
Bicaz 86 C3 Hung. Békás. Neamț, NE Romania
Biddeford 19 G2 Maine, NE USA
Bideford 67 C7 SW England, UK
Biel 73 A7 Fr. Bienne. Bern, W Switzerland
Bielefeld 72 B4 Nordrhein-Westfalen, NW Germany
Bielsko-Biała 77 C5 Ger. Bielitz, Bielitz-Biala. Śląskie, S Poland
Bielsk Podlaski 76 E3 Podlaskie, NE Poland
Bien Bien see Điện Biên
Biên Hoa 115 E6 Đông Nai, S Vietnam
Bienville, Lac 16 D2 lake Québec, C Canada
Bié, Planalto do 56 B2 var. Bié Plateau. Plateau C Angola
Bié Plateau see Bié, Planalto do
Big Cypress Swamp 21 E5 wetland Florida, SE USA
Bigge Island 124 C2 island Western Australia
Bighorn Mountains 22 C2 mountain range Wyoming, C USA
Bighorn River 22 C2 river Montana/Wyoming, NW USA
Bignona 52 B3 SW Senegal
Big Sioux River 23 E2 river Iowa/South Dakota, N USA
Big Spring 27 E3 Texas, SW USA
Bihać 78 B3 Federacija Bosna I Hercegovina, NW Bosnia and Herzegovina
Bihār 113 F3prev. Behar. Admin. region state N India
Biharamulo 51 B7 Kagera, NW Tanzania
Bihosava 85 D5 Rus. Bigosovo. Vitsyebskaya Voblasts', NW Belarus
Bijeljina 78 C3 Republika Srpska, NE Bosnia and Herzegovina
Bijelo Polje 79 D5 Montenegro, SW Serbia and Montenegro (Yugo.)
Bīkāner 112 C3 Rājasthān, NW India
Bikin 93 G4 Khabarovskiy Kray, SE Russian Federation
Bikini Atoll 122 C1 var. Pikinni. Atoll Ralik Chain, NW Marshall Islands
Bīkkū Bīttī see Bette, Pic
Bilāspur 113 E4 Madhya Pradesh, C India
Biläsuvar 95 H3 Rus. Bilyasuvar; prev. Pushkino. SE Azerbaijan
Bila Tserkva 87 E2 Rus. Belaya Tserkov'. Kyyivs'ka Oblast', N Ukraine
Bilauktaung Range 115 C6 var. Thanintari Taungdan. Mountain range Myanmar/Thailand
Bilbao 71 E1 Basq. Bilbo. País Vasco, N Spain
Bilecik 94 B3 Bilecik, NW Turkey
Billings 22 C2 Montana, NW USA
Bilma, Grand Erg de 53 H3 desert NE Niger
Biloela 126 D4 Queensland, E Australia
Biloxi 20 C3 Mississippi, S USA
Biltine 54 C3 Biltine, E Chad
Bilwi see Puerto Cabezas
Bilzen 87 D6 Limburg, NE Belgium
Bimini Islands 32 C1 island group W Bahamas
Binche 65 B7 Hainaut, S Belgium
Bindloe Island see Marchena, Isla
Binghamton 19 F3 New York, NE USA
Bingöl 95 E3 Bingöl, E Turkey
Bint Jubayl see Bent Jbaïl
Bintulu 116 D3 Sarawak, East Malaysia
Binzhou 106 D4 Shandong, E China
Bío Bío, Río 43 B5 river C Chile
Bioco, Isla de 55 A5 var. Bioko, Eng. Fernando Po, Sp. Fernando Póo; prev. Macías Nguema Biyogo. Island NW Equatorial Guinea
Bioko see Bioco, Isla de
Birāk 49 F3 var. Brak. C Libya
Birao 54 D3 Vakaga, NE Central African Republic
Biratnagar 113 F3 Eastern, SE Nepal
Bir es Saba see Be'ér Sheva'
Birhār Sharīf 113 F3 Bihar, N India
Bīrjand 98 E3 Khorāsān, E Iran
Birkenfeld 73 A5 Rheinland-Pfalz, SW Germany
Birkenhead 67 C5 NW England, UK
Birmingham 20 C2 Alabama, S USA
Birmingham 67 C6 C England, UK
Bir Moghrein see Bîr Mogreïn
Bîr Mogreïn 52 C1 var. Bir Moghrein; prev. Fort-Trinquet. Tiris Zemmour, N Mauritania
Birnie Island 123 E3 atoll Phoenix Islands, C Kiribati
Birni-Nkonni see Birnin Konni
Birnin Konni 53 F3 var. Birni-Nkonni. Tahoua, SW Niger
Birobidzhan 93 G4 Yevreyskaya Avtonomnaya Oblast', SE Russian Federation
Birsk 89 D5 Respublika Bashkortostan, W Russian Federation
Biržai 84 C4 Ger. Birsen. Biržai, NE Lithuania
Birżebbuġa 80 B5 SE Malta
Bisbee 26 B3 Arizona, SW USA
Biscay, Bay of 58 B4 Sp. Golfo de Vizcaya, Port. Baía de Biscaia. Bay France/Spain
Biscay Plain 58 B3 undersea feature SE Bay of Biscay
Bīshah, Wādī 99 B5 dry watercourse C Saudi Arabia
Bishkek 101 G2 var. Pishpek; prev. Frunze. Country capital (Kyrgyzstan) Chuyskaya Oblast', N Kyrgyzstan
Bishop's Lynn see King's Lynn
Bishrī, Jabal 96 D3 mountain range E Syria
Biskara see Biskra
Biskra 49 E2 var. Beskra, Biskara. NE Algeria
Biskupiec 76 D2 Ger. Bischofsburg. Warmińsko-Mazurskie, NE Poland
Bislig 117 F2 Mindanao, S Philippines
Bismarck 23 E2 state capital North Dakota, N USA
Bismarck Archipelago 122 B3 island group NE PNG
Bismarck Sea 122 B3 sea W Pacific Ocean
Bisnulok see Phitsanulok
Bissau 52 B4 country capital (Guinea-Bissau) W Guinea-Bissau
Bistrița 86 B3 Ger. Bistritz, Hung. Beszterce; prev. Nösen. Bistrița-Năsăud, N Romania
Bitam 55 B5 Woleu-Ntem, N Gabon
Bitburg 73 A5 Rheinland-Pfalz, SW Germany
Bitlis 95 F3 Bitlis, SE Turkey
Bitola 79 D6 Turk. Monastir; prev. Bitolj. S FYR Macedonia
Bitonto 75 D5 anc. Butuntum. Puglia, SE Italy
Bitterroot Range 24 D2 mountain range Idaho/Montana, NW USA
Bitung 117 F3 prev. Bitoeng. Sulawesi, C Indonesia
Biu 53 H4 Borno, E Nigeria
Biwa-ko 109 C6 lake Honshū, SW Japan
Bizerte 49 E1 Ar. Banzart, Eng. Bizerta. N Tunisia
Bjelovar 78 B2 Hung. Belovár. Bjelovar-Bilogora, N Croatia
Bjørnøya 61 F3 Eng. Bear Island. Island N Norway
Blackall 126 C4 Queensland, E Australia
Black Drin 79 D6 Alb. Lumi i Drinit të Zi, SCr. Crni Drim. River Albania/FYR Macedonia
Blackfoot 24 E4 Idaho, NW USA
Black Forest see Schwarzwald
Black Hills 22 D3 mountain range South Dakota/Wyoming, N USA
Blackpool 67 C5 NW England, UK
Black Range 26 C2 mountain range New Mexico, SW USA
Black River 114 C3 Chin. Babian Jiang, Lixian Jiang, Fr. Rivière Noire, Vtn. Sông Đa. River China/Vietnam
Black River 32 A5 W Jamaica
Black Rock Desert 25 C5 desert Nevada, W USA
Black Sand Desert see Garagum
Black Sea 94 B1 var. Euxine Sea, Bul. Cherno More, Rom. Marea Neagră, Rus. Chernoye More, Turk. Karadeniz, Ukr. Chorne More. Sea Asia/Europe
Black Sea Lowland 87 E4 Ukr. Prychornomors'ka Nyzovyna. Depression SE Europe
Black Volta 53 E4 var. Borongo, Mouhoun, Moun Hou, Fr. Volta Noire. River W Africa
Blackwater 67 A6 Ir. An Abhainn Mhór. River S Ireland
Blagoevgrad 82 C3 prev. Gorna Dzhumaya. Blagoevgrad, SW Bulgaria
Blagoveshchensk 93 G4 Amurskaya Oblast', SE Russian Federation
Blake Plateau 13 D6 var. Blake Terrace. Undersea feature W Atlantic Ocean
Blake Terrace see Blake Plateau
Blanca, Bahía 43 C5 bay E Argentina
Blanca, Costa 71 F4 physical region SE Spain
Blanche, Lake 127 B5 lake South Australia
Blanc, Mont 69 D5 It. Monte Bianco. Mountain France/Italy
Blanco, Cape 24 A4 headland Oregon, NW USA
Blanes 71 G2 Cataluña, NE Spain
Blankenberge 65 A5 West-Vlaanderen, NW Belgium
Blankenheim 73 A5 Nordrhein-Westfalen, W Germany
Blanquilla, Isla 37 E1 var. La Blanquilla. Island N Venezuela
Blantyre 57 E2 var. Blantyre-Limbe. Southern, S Malawi
Blantyre-Limbe see Blantyre
Blaricum 64 C3 Noord-Holland, C Netherlands
Blenheim 129 C5 Marlborough, South Island, NZ
Blida 48 D2 var. El Boulaida, El Boulaïda. N Algeria
Bloemfontein 56 C4 var. Mangaung. Country capital (South Africa-judicial capital) Free State, C South Africa
Blois 68 C4 anc. Blesae. Loir-et-Cher, C France
Bloomfield 26 C1 New Mexico, SW USA
Bloomington 18 B4 Illinois, N USA
Bloomington 18 C4 Indiana, N USA
Bloomington 23 F2 Minnesota, N USA
Bloomsbury 126 D3 Queensland, NE Australia
Bluefield 18 D5 West Virginia, NE USA
Bluefields 31 E3 Región Autónoma Atlántico Sur, SE Nicaragua
Blue Mountain Peak 32 B5 mountain E Jamaica
Blue Mountains 24 C3 mountain range Oregon/Washington, NW USA
Blue Nile 46 D4 var. Abai, Bahr el Azraq, Amh. Ābay Wenz, Ar. An Nīl al Azraq. River Ethiopia/Sudan
Blue Nile 50 C4 state E Sudan
Blumenau 41 E5 Santa Catarina, S Brazil
Blythe 25 D8 California, W USA
Blytheville 20 C1 Arkansas, C USA
Bo 52 C4 S Sierra Leone
Boaco 30 D3 Boaco, S Nicaragua
Boa Vista 52 A3 island Ilhas de Barlavento, E Cape Verde
Boa Vista 40 D1 state capital Roraima, NW Brazil
Bobaomby, Tanjona 57 G2 Fr. Cap d'Ambre. Headland N Madagascar
Bobigny 68 E1 Seine-St-Denis, N France
Bobo-Dioulasso 52 D4 SW Burkina faso
Bobrynets' 87 E3 Rus. Bobrinets. Kirovohrads'ka Oblast', C Ukraine
Boca Raton 21 F5 Florida, SE USA
Bocay 30 D2 Jinotega, N Nicaragua
Bocche del Po see Po, Foci del
Bocholt 72 A4 Nordrhein-Westfalen, W Germany
Bochum 72 A4 Nordrhein-Westfalen, W Germany
Bocşa 86 A4 Ger. Bokschen, Hung. Boksánbánya. Caraş-Severin, SW Romania
Bodaybo 93 F4 Irkutskaya Oblast', E Russian Federation
Boden 62 D4 Norrbotten, N Sweden
Bodmin 67 C7 SW England, UK
Bodø 62 C3 Nordland, C Norway
Bodrum 94 A4 Muğla, SW Turkey
Boende 55 C5 Equateur, C Dem. Rep. Congo
Boetoeng see Buton, Pulau
Bogale 114 B4 Irrawaddy, SW Myanmar
Bogalusa 20 B3 Louisiana, S USA
Bogatynia 76 B4 Ger. Reichenau. Dolnośląskie, SW Poland
Boğazlıyan 94 D3 Yozgat, C Turkey
Bogor 116 C5 Dut. Buitenzorg. Jawa, C Indonesia
Bogotá 36 B3 prev. Santa Fe, Santa Fe de Bogotá. Country capital (Colombia) Cundinamarca, C Colombia
Bo Hai 106 D4 var. Gulf of Chihli. Gulf NE China
Bohemia 77 A5 Cz. Čechy, Ger. Böhmen. Cultural and historical region W Czech Republic
Bohemian Forest 73 C5 Cz. Český Les, Šumava, Ger. Böhmerwald. Mountain range C Europe
Böhmisch-Krumau see Český Krumlov
Bohol Sea 117 E2 var. Mindanao Sea. Sea S Philippines
Bohoro Shan 104 B2 mountain range NW China
Bohuslav 87 E2 Rus. Boguslav. Kyyivs'ka Oblast', N Ukraine
Boise 24 D3 var. Boise City. State capital Idaho, NW USA
Boise City see Boise
Boise City 27 E1 Oklahoma, C USA
Boizenburg 72 C3 Mecklenburg-Vorpommern, N Germany
Bojador see Boujdour
Bojnūrd 98 D2 var. Bujnurd. Khorāsān, N Iran
Bokāro 113 F4 Bihār, N India
Boké 52 C4 Guinée-Maritime, W Guinea
Bokhara see Buxoro
Boknafjorden 85 A6 fjord S Norway
Bol 54 B3 Lac, W Chad
Bolgatanga 53 E4 N Ghana
Bolhrad 86 D4 Rus. Bolgrad. Odes'ka Oblast', SW Ukraine
Bolívar, Pico 36 C2 mountain W Venezuela
Bolivia 39 F3 Country W South America
Bollène 69 D6 Vaucluse, SE France
Bollnäs 85 C5 Gävleborg, C Sweden
Bollon 127 D5 Queensland, C Australia
Bologna 74 C3 Emilia-Romagna, N Italy
Bol'shevik, Ostrov 93 E2 island Severnaya Zemlya, N Russian Federation
Bol'shezemel'skaya Tundra 88 E3 physical region NW Russian Federation
Bol'shoy Lyakhovskiy, Ostrov 93 F2 island NE Russian Federation
Bolton 67 D5 prev. Bolton-le-Moors. NW England, UK
Bolu 94 B3 Bolu, NW Turkey
Bolungarvík 61 E4 Vestfirdhir, NW Iceland
Bolyarovo 82 D3 prev. Pashkeni. Yambol, E Bulgaria
Bolzano 74 C1 Ger. Bozen; anc. Bauzanum. Trentino-Alto Adige, N Italy
Boma 55 B6 Bas-Zaïre, W Dem. Rep. Congo
Bombay see Mumbai
Bomu 54 D4 var. Mbomou, Mbomu, M'Bomu. River Central African Republic/Dem. Rep. Congo
Bonaire 33 F5 island E Netherlands Antilles
Bonanza 30 D2 Región Autónoma Atlántico Norte, NE Nicaragua
Bonaparte Archipelago 124 C2 island group Western Australia
Bon, Cap 80 D3 headland N Tunisia
Bonda 55 B6 Ogooué-Lolo, C Gabon
Bondoukou 53 E4 E Côte d'Ivoire
Bone see Watampone
Bone, Teluk 117 E4 bay Sulawesi, C Indonesia
Bongaigaon 113 G3 Assam, NE India
Bongo, Massif des 54 D4 var. Chaîne des Mongos. Mountain range NE Central African Republic
Bongor 54 B3 Mayo-Kébbi, SW Chad
Bonifacio 69 E7 Corse, France, C Mediterranean Sea
Bonifacio, Strait of 74 A4 Fr. Bouches de Bonifacio, It. Bocche de Bonifacio. Strait C Mediterranean Sea
Bonn 73 A5 Nordrhein-Westfalen, W Germany
Bononia see Boulogne-sur-Mer
Boosaaso 50 E4 var. Bandar Kassim, Bender Qaasim, Bosaso, It. Bender Cassim. Bari, N Somalia
Boothia, Gulf of 15 F2 gulf Nunavut, NE Canada
Boothia Peninsula 15 F2 prev. Boothia Felix. Peninsula Nunavut, NE Canada
Boppard 73 A5 Rheinland-Pfalz, W Germany
Boquete 31 E5 var. Bajo Boquete. Chiriquí, W Panama
Boquillas 28 D2 var. Boquillas del Carmen. Coahuila de Zaragoza, NE Mexico
Boquillas del Carmen see Boquillas
Bor 51 B5 Jonglei, S Sudan
Bor 78 E4 Serbia, E Serbia and Montenegro (Yugo.)
Borås 63 B7 Västra Götaland, S Sweden
Borborema, Planalto da 34 E3 plateau NE Brazil
Bordeaux 69 B5 anc. Burdigala. Gironde, SW France
Bordj Omar Driss 49 E3 E Algeria
Børgefjell 62 C4 mountain range C Norway
Borger 64 E2 Drenthe, NE Netherlands
Borger 27 E1 Texas, SW USA
Borgholm 63 C7 Kalmar, S Sweden
Borgo Maggiore 74 E1 NW San Marino
Borisoglebsk 89 B6 Voronezhskaya Oblast', W Russian Federation
Borlänge 63 C6 Kopparberg, C Sweden
Borne 64 E3 Overijssel, E Netherlands
Borneo 116 C4 island Brunei/Indonesia/Malaysia
Bornholm 63 B8 island E Denmark
Borohoro Shan 101 H1 mountain range NW China
Borongo see Black Volta
Borovan 82 C2 Vratsa, NW Bulgaria
Borovichi 88 B4 Novgorodskaya Oblast', W Russian Federation
Borovo 78 C3 Vukovar-Srijem, NE Croatia
Borşa 86 C3 Hung. Borsa. Maramureş, N Romania
Boryslav 86 B2 Pol. Borysław, Rus. Borislav. L'vivs'ka Oblast', NW Ukraine
Bosanska Dubica 78 B3 var. Kozarska Dubica. Republika Srpska, NW Bosnia and Herzegovina
Bosanska Gradiška 78 B3 var. Gradiška. Republika Srpska, N Bosnia and Herzegovina
Bosanski Novi 78 B3 var. Novi Grad. Republika Srpska, NW Bosnia and Herzegovina
Bosanski Šamac 78 C3 var. Šamac, Republika Srpska, N Bosnia and Herzegovina
Bosaso see Boosaaso
Boskovice 77 B5 Ger. Boskowitz. Brněnský Kraj, SE Czech Republic
Bosna 78 C4 river N Bosnia and Herzegovina
Bosna I Hercegovina, Federacija Admin. region republic Bosnia and Herzegovina
Bosnia and Herzegovina 78 B3 Country SE Europe
Bōsō-hantō 109 D6 peninsula Honshū, S Japan
Bosphorus see İstanbul Boğazı
Bosporus see İstanbul Boğazı
Bosporus Cimmerius see Kerch Strait
Bosporus Thracius see İstanbul Boğazı
Bossangoa 54 C4 Ouham, C Central African Republic
Bossembélé 54 C4 Ombella-Mpoko, C Central African Republic
Bossier City 20 A2 Louisiana, S USA
Bosten Hu 104 C3 var. Bagrax Hu. Lake NW China
Boston 67 E6 prev. St.Botolph's Town. E England, UK
Boston 19 G3 state capital Massachusetts, NE USA
Boston Mountains 20 B1 mountain range Arkansas, C USA

Botany 126 E2 New South Wales, SE Australia
Botany Bay 126 E2 inlet New South Wales, SE Australia
Boteti 56 C3 var. Botletle. River N Botswana
Bothnia, Gulf of 63 D5 Fin. Pohjanlahti, Swe. Bottniska Viken. Gulf N Baltic Sea
Botletle see Boteti
Botoşani 86 C3 Hung. Botosány. Botoşani, NE Romania
Botou 106 C4 prev. Bozhen. Hebei, E China
Botrange 65 D6 mountain E Belgium
Botswana 56 C3 Country S Africa
Bouar 54 B4 Nana-Mambéré, W Central African Republic
Bou Craa 48 B3 var. Bu Craa. NW Western Sahara
Bougainville Island 120 B3 island NE PNG
Bougaroun, Cap 80 C3 headland NE Algeria
Bougouni 52 D4 Sikasso, SW Mali
Boujdour 48 A3 var. Bojador. W Western Sahara
Boulder 22 C4 Colorado, C USA
Boulder 22 B2 Montana, NW USA
Boulogne see Boulogne-sur-Mer
Boulogne-Billancourt 68 D1 prev. Boulogne-sur-Seine. Hauts-de-Seine, N France
Boulogne-sur-Mer 68 C2 var. Boulogne; anc. Bononia, Gesoriacum, Gessoriacum. Pas-de-Calais, N France
Boûmdeïd 52 C3 var. Boumdeït. Assaba, S Mauritania
Boumdeït see Boûmdeïd
Boundiali 52 D4 N Côte d'Ivoire
Bountiful 22 B4 Utah, W USA
Bounty Basin see Bounty Trough
Bounty Islands 120 D5 island group S NZ
Bounty Trough 130 C5 var. Bounty Basin. Undersea feature S Pacific Ocean
Bourbonnais 68 C4 Illinois, N USA
Bourg see Bourg-en-Bresse
Bourgas see Burgas
Bourge-en-Bresse see Bourg-en-Bresse
Bourg-en-Bresse 69 D5 var. Bourg, Bourge-en-Bresse. Ain, E France
Bourges 68 C4 anc. Avaricum. Cher, C France
Bourgogne 68 C4 Eng. Burgundy. Cultural region E France
Bourke 127 C5 New South Wales, SE Australia
Bournemouth 67 D7 S England, UK
Boutilimit 52 C3 Trarza, SW Mauritania
Bouvet Island 45 D7 Norwegian dependency S Atlantic Ocean
Bowen 126 D3 Queensland, NE Australia
Bowling Green 18 B5 Kentucky, S USA
Bowling Green 18 C3 Ohio, N USA
Boxmeer 64 D4 Noord-Brabant, SE Netherlands
Boyarka 87 E2 Kyyiv's'ka Oblast', N Ukraine
Boysun 101 E3 Rus. Baysun. Surkhondaryo Wiloyati, S Uzbekistan
Bozeman 22 B2 Montana, NW USA
Bozüyük 94 B3 Bilecik, NW Turkey
Brač 78 B4 var. Brach, It. Brazza; anc. Brattia. Island S Croatia
Brach see Brač
Bradford 67 D5 N England, UK
Brady 27 F3 Texas, SW USA
Braga 70 B2 anc. Bracara Augusta. Braga, NW Portugal
Bragança 70 C2 Eng. Braganza; anc. Julio Briga. Bragança, NE Portugal
Brahmanbaria 113 G4 Chittagong, E Bangladesh
Brahmapur 113 F5 Orissa, E India
Brahmaputra 113 H3 var. Padma, Tsangpo, Ben. Jamuna, Chin. Yarlung Zangbo Jiang, Ind. Bramaputra, Dihang, Siang. River S Asia
Brăila 86 D4 Brăila, E Romania
Braine-le-Comte 65 B6 Hainaut, SW Belgium
Brainerd 23 F2 Minnesota, N USA
Brak see Birāk
Bramaputra see Brahmaputra
Brampton 16 D5 Ontario, S Canada
Branco, Rio 34 C3 river N Brazil
Brandberg 56 A3 mountain NW Namibia
Brandenburg 72 C3 var. Brandenburg an der Havel. Brandenburg, NE Germany
Brandenburg an der Havel see Brandenburg
Brandon 15 F5 Manitoba, S Canada
Braniewo 76 D2 Ger. Braunsberg. Warmińsko-Mazurskie, NE Poland
Brasília 41 F3 country capital (Brazil) Distrito Federal, C Brazil
Braşov 86 C4 Ger. Kronstadt, Hung. Brassó; prev. Oraşul Stalin. Braşov, C Romania
Bratislava 77 C6 Ger. Pressburg, Hung. Pozsony. Country capital (Slovakia) Bratislavský Kraj, SW Slovakia
Bratsk 93 E4 Irkutskaya Oblast', C Russian Federation
Brattia see Brač
Braunschweig 72 C4 Eng./Fr. Brunswick. Niedersachsen, N Germany
Brava, Costa 71 H2 coastal region NE Spain
Bravo del Norte, Río see Grande, Rio
Bravo del Norte, Río see Bravo, Río
Bravo del Norte, Río see Grande, Rio
Bravo, Río 28 C1 var. Río Bravo del Norte, Rio Grande. River Mexico/USA
Bravo, Río see Grande, Rio
Brazil 40 C2 Port. República Federativa do Brasil, Sp. Brasil; prev. United States of Brazil. Country South America
Brazil Basin 45 C5 var. Brazilian Basin, Brazil'skaya Kotlovina. Undersea feature W Atlantic Ocean
Brazilian Basin see Brazil Basin
Brazilian Highlands see Central, Planalto
Brazil'skaya Kotlovina see Brazil Basin
Brazos River 27 G3 river Texas, SW USA

Brazza see Brač
Brazzaville 55 B6 country capital (Congo) Capital District, S Congo
Brecht 65 C5 Antwerpen, N Belgium
Brecon Beacons 67 C6 mountain range S Wales, UK
Breda 64 C4 Noord-Brabant, S Netherlands
Bree 65 D5 Limburg, NE Belgium
Bregalnica 79 E6 river E FYR Macedonia
Bregenz 35 B7 anc. Brigantium. Vorarlberg, W Austria
Bregovo 82 B1 Vidin, NW Bulgaria
Brčko 78 C3 Republika Srpska, NE Bosnia and Herzegovina
Bremen 72 B3 Fr. Brême. Bremen, NW Germany
Bremerhaven 72 B3 Bremen, NW Germany
Bremerton 24 B2 Washington, NW USA
Brenham 27 G3 Texas, SW USA
Brenner Pass 74 C1 var. BrennerSattel, Fr. Col du Brenner, Ger. Brennerpass, It. Passo del Brennero. Pass Austria/Italy
Brennerpass see Brenner Pass
Brenner Sattel see Brenner Pass
Brescia 74 B2 anc. Brixia. Lombardia, N Italy
Bressanone 74 C1 Ger. Brixen. Trentino-Alto Adige, N Italy
Brest 85 A6 Pol. Brześć nad Bugiem, Rus. Brest-Litovsk; prev. Brześć Litewski. Brestskaya Voblasts', SW Belarus
Brest 68 A3 Finistère, NW France
Bretagne 68 A3 Eng. Brittany; Lat. Britannia Minor. Cultural region NW France
Brewton 20 C3 Alabama, S USA
Brezovo 82 D2 prev. Abrashlare. Plovdiv, C Bulgaria
Bria 54 D4 Haute-Kotto, C Central African Republic
Briançon 69 D5 anc. Brigantio. Hautes-Alpes, SE France
Bridgeport 19 F3 Connecticut, NE USA
Bridgetown 33 G2 country capital (Barbados) SW Barbados
Bridlington 67 D5 E England, UK
Bridport 67 D7 S England, UK
Brig 73 A7 Fr. Brigue, It. Briga. Valais, SW Switzerland
Brigham City 22 B3 Utah, W USA
Brighton 22 D4 Colorado, C USA
Brighton 67 E7 SE England, UK
Brindisi 75 E5 anc. Brundisium, Brundusium. Puglia, SE Italy
Brisbane 127 E5 state capital Queensland, E Australia
Bristol 67 D7 anc. Bricgstow. SW England, UK
Bristol 19 F3 Connecticut, NE USA
Bristol 18 D5 Virginia, NE USA
Bristol Bay 14 B3 bay Alaska, USA
Bristol Channel 67 C7 inlet England/Wales, UK
Britain 58 C3 var. Great Britain. Island UK
British Columbia 14 D4 Fr. Colombie-Britannique. Province SW Canada
British Indian Ocean Territory 119 B5 UK dependent territory C Indian Ocean
British Isles 67 island group NW Europe
British Virgin Islands 33 F3 var. Virgin Islands. UK dependent territory E West Indies
Brive-la-Gaillarde 69 C5 prev. Brive, anc. Briva Curretia. Corrèze, C France
Brno 77 B5 Ger. Brünn. Brněnský Kraj, SE Czech Republic
Broceni 84 B3 Saldus, SW Latvia
Brodeur Peninsula 15 F2 peninsula Baffin Island, Nunavut, NE Canada
Brodnica 76 C3 Ger. Buddenbrock. Kujawski-pomorskie, C Poland
Broek-in-Waterland 64 C3 Noord-Holland, C Netherlands
Broken Arrow 27 G1 Oklahoma, C USA
Broken Bay 126 E1 bay New South Wales, SE Australia
Broken Hill 127 B6 New South Wales, SE Australia
Broken Ridge 119 D6 undersea feature S Indian Ocean
Bromley 67 B8 SE England, UK
Brookhaven 20 B3 Mississippi, S USA
Brookings 23 F3 South Dakota, N USA
Brooks Range 14 D2 mountain range Alaska, USA
Brookton 125 B6 Western Australia
Broome 124 B3 Western Australia
Broomfield 22 C4 Colorado, C USA
Broucsella see Brussel
Brovary 87 E2 Kyyivs'ka Oblast', N Ukraine
Brownfield 27 E2 Texas, SW USA
Brownville 27 G5 Texas, SW USA
Brownwood 27 F3 Texas, SW USA
Brozha 85 D7 Mahilyowskaya Voblasts', E Belarus
Brugge 65 A5 Fr. Bruges. West-Vlaanderen, NW Belgium
Brummen 64 D3 Gelderland, E Netherlands
Brunei 116 D3 Mal. Negara Brunei Darussalam. Country SE Asia
Brunner, Lake 129 C5 lake South Island, NZ
Brunswick 21 E3 Georgia, SE USA
Brusa see Bursa
Brus Laguna 30 D2 Gracias a Dios, E Honduras
Brussa see Bursa
Brussel var. Brussels, Fr. Bruxelles, Ger. Brüssel; anc. Broucsella. Country capital (Belgium) Brussels, C Belgium see also Bruxelles
Brüssel see Brussel
Brussels see Brussel
Bruxelles see Brussel
Bryan 27 G3 Texas, SW USA
Bryansk 89 A5 Bryanskaya Oblast', W Russian Federation
Brzeg 76 C4 Ger. Brieg; anc. Civitas Altae Ripae. Opolskie, S Poland
Bucaramanga 36 B2 Santander, N Colombia

Buchanan 52 C5 prev. Grand Bassa. SW Liberia
Buchanan, Lake 27 F3 reservoir Texas, SW USA
Bucharest see Bucureşti
Bu Craa see Bou Craa
Bucureşti 86 C5 Eng. Bucharest, Ger. Bukarest; prev. Altenburg, anc. Cetatea Dambovitei. Country capital (Romania) Bucureşti, S Romania
Buda-Kashalyova 85 D7 Rus. Buda-Koshelëvo. Homyel'skaya Voblasts', SE Belarus
Budapest 77 C6 off. Budapest Főváros, SCr. Budimpešta. Country capital (Hungary) Pest, N Hungary
Budaun 112 D3 Uttar Pradesh, N India
Buena Park 46 E2 California, W USA
Buenaventura 36 A3 Valle del Cauca, W Colombia
Buena Vista 71 H5 S Gibraltar
Buena Vista 39 G4 Santa Cruz, C Bolivia
Buenos Aires 42 D4 hist. Santa Maria del Buen Aire. Country capital (Argentina) Buenos Aires, E Argentina
Buenos Aires 31 E5 Puntarenas, SE Costa Rica
Buenos Aires, Lago 43 B6 var. Lago General Carrera. Lake Argentina/Chile
Buffalo 19 E3 New York, NE USA
Buffalo Narrows 15 F4 Saskatchewan, C Canada
Buff Bay 32 B5 E Jamaica
Buftea 86 C5 Bucureşti, S Romania
Bug 59 E3 Bel. Zakhodni Buh, Eng. Western Bug, Rus. Zapadnyy Bug, Ukr. Zakhidnyy Buh. River E Europe
Buga 36 B3 Valle del Cauca, W Colombia
Bughotu see Santa Isabel
Buguruslan 89 D6 Orenburgskaya Oblast', W Russian Federation
Buhayrat Nāşir see Nasser, Lake
Buheiret Nâsir see Nasser, Lake
Bujalance 70 D4 Andalucía, S Spain
Bujanovac 79 E5 Serbia, SE Serbia and Montenegro (Yugo.)
Bujnurd see Bojnūrd
Bujumbura 51 B7 prev. Usumbura. Country capital (Burundi) W Burundi
Bukavu 55 E6 prev. Costermansville. Sud Kivu, E Dem. Rep. Congo
Bukhara see Buxoro
Bukhoro see Buxoro
Bukoba 51 B6 Kagera, NW Tanzania
Bülach 73 B7 Zürich, NW Switzerland
Bulawayo 56 D3 var. Buluwayo. Matabeleland North, SW Zimbabwe
Buldur see Burdur
Bulgan 105 E2 Bulgan, N Mongolia
Bulgaria 82 C2 Bul. Bŭlgariya; prev. People's Republic of Bulgaria. Country SE Europe
Bull Shoals Lake 20 B1 reservoir Arkansas/Missouri, C USA
Bulukumba 117 E5 prev. Boeloekoemba. Sulawesi, C Indonesia
Buluwayo see Bulawayo
Bumba 55 D5 Equateur, N Dem. Rep. Congo
Bunbury 125 A7 Western Australia
Bundaberg 126 E4 Queensland, E Australia
Bungo-suidō 109 B7 strait SW Japan
Bunia 55 E5 Orientale, NE Dem. Rep. Congo
Bünyan 94 D3 Kayseri, C Turkey
Buraida see Buraydah
Buraydah 98 B4 var. Buraida. Al Qaşīm, N Saudi Arabia
Burdur 94 B4 var. Buldur. Burdur, SW Turkey
Burdur Gölü 94 B4 salt lake SW Turkey
Burē 50 C4 W Ethiopia
Burgas 82 E2 var. Bourgas. Burgas, E Bulgaria
Burgaski Zaliv 82 E2 gulf E Bulgaria
Burgos 70 D2 Castilla-León, N Spain
Burhan Budai Shan 104 D4 mountain range C China
Buri Ram see Buriram
Buriram 115 D5 var. Buri Ram, Puriramya. Buri Ram, E Thailand
Burjassot 71 F3 País Valenciano, E Spain
Burkburnett 27 F2 Texas, SW USA
Burketown 126 B3 Queensland, NE Australia
Burkina see Burkina Faso
Burkina Faso 53 E4 var. Burkina; prev. Upper Volta. Country W Africa
Burley 24 D4 Idaho, NW USA
Burlington 23 G4 Iowa, C USA
Burlington 19 F2 Vermont, NE USA
Burma see Myanmar
Burnie 127 C8 Tasmania, SE Australia
Burns 24 C3 Oregon, NW USA
Burnside 15 F3 river Nunavut, NW Canada
Burnsville 23 F2 Minnesota, N USA
Burrel 79 D6 var. Burreli. Dibër, C Albania
Burreli see Burrel
Burriana 71 F3 País Valenciano, E Spain
Bursa 94 B3 var. Brussa, anc. Prusa. Bursa, NW Turkey
Burtnieks 84 C3 var. Burtnieku Ezers. Lake N Latvia
Burtnieku Ezers see Burtnieks
Burundi 51 B7 prev. Kingdom of Burundi, Urundi. Country C Africa
Buru, Pulau 117 F4 prev. Boeroe. Island E Indonesia
Buşayrah 96 D3 Dayr az Zawr, E Syria
Büshehr see Bandar-e Büshehr
Bushire see Bandar-e Büshehr
Busselton 125 A7 Western Australia
Buta 55 D5 Orientale, N Dem. Rep. Congo
Butembo 55 E5 Nord Kivu, NE Dem. Rep. Congo
Butler 19 E4 Pennsylvania, NE USA
Buton, Pulau 117 E4 var. Pulau Butung; prev. Boetoeng. Island C Indonesia
Butte 22 B2 Montana, NW USA
Butterworth 116 B3 Pinang, Peninsular Malaysia

Button Islands 17 E1 island group Northwest Territories, NE Canada
Butuan 117 F2 off. Butuan City. Mindanao, S Philippines
Buulobarde 51 D5 var. Buulo Berde. Hiiraan, C Somalia Africa
Buulo Berde see Buulobarde
Buur Gaabo 51 D6 Jubbada Hoose, S Somalia
Buxoro 100 D2 var. Bokhara, Bukhoro, Rus. Bukhara. Bukhoro Wiloyati, C Uzbekistan
Buynaksk 89 B8 Respublika Dagestan, SW Russian Federation
Büyükağrı Dağı 95 F3 var. Aghri Dagh, Agri Dagi, Koh I Noh, Masis, Eng. Great Ararat, Mount Ararat. Mountain E Turkey
Büyükmenderes Nehri 94 A4 river SW Turkey
Buzău 86 C4 Buzău, SE Romania
Büzmeyin 100 C3 Rus. Byuzmeyin; prev. Bezmein. Akhalskiy Velayat, C Turkmenistan
Buzuluk 89 D6 Akmola, C Kazakhstan
Byahoml' 85 D5 Rus. Begoml'. Vitsyebskaya Voblasts', N Belarus
Byalynichy 85 D6 Rus. Belynichi. Mahilyowskaya Voblasts', E Belarus
Bydgoszcz 76 C3 Ger. Bromberg. Kujawskie-pomorskie, C Poland
Byelaruskaya Hrada 85 B6 Rus. Belorusskaya Gryada. Ridge N Belarus
Byerezino 85 D6 Rus. Berezina. River C Belarus
Byron Island see Nikunau
Bytom 77 C5 Ger. Beuthen. Śląskie, S Poland
Bytča 77 C5 Žilinský Kraj, N Slovakia
Bytów 76 C2 Ger. Bütow. Pomorskie, N Poland
Byuzmeyin see Büzmeyin
Byval'ki 85 D8 Homyel'skaya Voblasts', SE Belarus
Byzantium see İstanbul

C

Caála 56 B2 var. Kaala, Robert Williams, Port. Vila Robert Williams. Huambo, C Angola
Caazapá 42 D3 Caazapá, S Paraguay
Caballo Reservoir 26 C3 reservoir New Mexico, SW USA
Cabañaquinta 70 D1 Asturias, N Spain
Cabanatuan 117 E1 off. Cabanatuan City. Luzon, N Philippines
Cabimas 36 C1 Zulia, NW Venezuela
Cabinda 56 A1 var. Kabinda. Cabinda, NW Angola
Cabinda 56 A1 var. Kabinda. Admin. region province NW Angola
Cabora Bassa, Lake see Cahora Bassa, Albufeira de
Caborca 28 B1 Sonora, NW Mexico
Cabot Strait 17 G4 strait E Canada
Cabras, Ilha das 54 E2 island S Sao Tome and Principe
Cabrera 71 G3 anc. Capraria. Island Islas Baleares, Spain, W Mediterranean Sea
Cáceres 70 C3 Ar. Qazris. Extremadura, W Spain
Cachimbo, Serra do 41 E2 mountain range C Brazil
Caconda 56 B2 Huíla, C Angola
Cadca 77 C5 Hung. Csaca. Žilinský Kraj, N Slovakia
Cadillac 18 C2 Michigan, N USA
Cadiz 117 E2 off. Cadiz City. Negros, C Philippines
Cádiz 70 C5 anc. Gades, Gadier, Gadir, Gadire. Andalucía, SW Spain
Cádiz, Golfo de 70 B5 Eng. Gulf of Cadiz. Gulf Portugal/Spain
Cadiz, Gulf of see Cádiz, Golfo de
Caen 68 B3 Calvados, N France
Caene see Qena
Caenepolis see Qena
Caerdydd see Cardiff
Caer Gybi see Holyhead
Caesarea Mazaca see Kayseri
Cafayate 42 C2 Salta, N Argentina
Cagayan de Oro 117 E2 off. Cagayan de Oro City. Mindanao, S Philippines
Cagliari 75 A6 anc. Caralis. Sardegna, Italy, C Mediterranean Sea
Caguas 33 F3 E Puerto Rico
Cahora Bassa, Albufeira de 56 D2 var. Lake Cabora Bassa. Reservoir NW Mozambique
Cahors 69 C5 anc. Cadurcum. Lot, S France
Cahul 86 D4 Rus. Kagul. S Moldova
Caicos Passage 32 D2 strait Bahamas/Turks and Caicos Islands
Caiffa see Hefa
Cailungo 74 E1 N San Marino
Caiphas see Hefa
Cairns 126 D3 Queensland, NE Australia
Cairo 50 B2 Ar. Al Qāhirah, var. El Qâhira. Country capital (Egypt) N Egypt
Caisleán an Bharraigh see Castlebar
Cajamarca 38 B3 prev. Caxamarca. Cajamarca, NW Peru
Čakovec 78 B2 Ger. Csakathurn, Hung. Csáktornya; prev. Ger. Tschakathurn. Medimurje, N Croatia
Calabar 53 G5 Cross River, S Nigeria
Calabozo 36 D2 Guárico, C Venezuela
Calafat 86 B5 Dolj, SW Romania
Calafate see El Calafate
Calahorra 71 E2 La Rioja, N Spain
Calais 19 H2 Maine, NE USA
Calais 68 C2 Pas-de-Calais, N France
Calama 42 B2 Antofagasta, N Chile
Calamianes see Calamian Group
Calamian Group 107 C7 var. Calamianes. Island group N Philippines
Calamocha 71 E3 Aragón, NE Spain
Călan 86 B4 Ger. Kalan, Hung. Kalán. Hunedoara, SW Romania
Calarasi see Călărași
Călărași 86 D3 var. Călăras, Rus. Kalarash. C Moldova
Călărași 86 C5 Călărași, SE Romania

Calatayud 71 E2 Aragón, NE Spain
Calbayog 117 E2 off. Calbayog City. Samar, C Philippines
Calcutta 113 G4 var. Kolkata. West Bengal, NE India
Caldas da Rainha 70 B3 Leiria, W Portugal
Caldera 42 B3 Atacama, N Chile
Caldwell 24 C3 Idaho, NW USA
Caledonia 30 C1 Corozal, N Belize
Caleta see Catalan Bay
Caleta Olivia 43 B6 Santa Cruz, SE Argentina
Calgary 15 E5 Alberta, SW Canada
Cali 36 B3 Valle del Cauca, W Colombia
Calicut 110 C2 var. Kozhikode. Kerala, SW India
California 25 B7 off. State of California; also known as El Dorado, The Golden State. State W USA
California, Golfo de 28 B2 Eng. Gulf of California; prev. Sea of Cortez. Gulf W Mexico
California, Gulf of see California, Golfo de
Călimănești 86 B4 Vâlcea, SW Romania
Callabonna, Lake 127 B5 lake South Australia
Callao 38 C4 Callao, W Peru
Callosa de Segura 71 F4 País Valenciano, E Spain
Calmar see Kalmar
Caloundra 127 E5 Queensland, E Australia
Caltanissetta 75 C7 Sicilia, Italy, C Mediterranean Sea
Caluula 50 E4 Bari, NE Somalia
Camabatela 56 B1 Cuanza Norte, NW Angola
Camacupa 56 B2 var. General Machado, Port. Vila General Machado. Bié, C Angola
Camagüey 32 C2 prev. Puerto Príncipe. Camagüey, C Cuba
Camagüey, Archipiélago de 32 C2 island group C Cuba
Camaná 39 E4 Arequipa, SW Peru
Camargue 69 D6 physical region SE France
Ca Mau 115 D6 prev. Quan Long. Minh Hai, S Vietnam
Cambodia 115 D5 var. Democratic Kampuchea, Roat Kampuchea, Cam. Kampuchea; prev. People's Democratic Republic of Kampuchea. Country SE Asia
Cambrai 68 C2 Flem. Kambryk; prev. Cambray, anc. Cameracum. Nord, N France
Cambrian Mountains 67 C6 mountain range C Wales, UK
Cambridge 67 E6 Lat. Cantabrigia. E England, UK
Cambridge 19 F4 Maryland, NE USA
Cambridge 18 D4 Ohio, NE USA
Cambridge 32 A4 W Jamaica
Cambridge 128 D3 Waikato, North Island, NZ
Cambridge Bay 15 F3 district capital Victoria Island, Nunavut, NW Canada
Camden 20 B2 Arkansas, C USA
Cameroon 54 A4 Fr. Cameroun. Country W Africa
Camocim 41 F2 Ceará, E Brazil
Camopi 37 H3 E French Guiana
Campamento 30 C2 Olancho, C Honduras
Campania 75 D5 cultural region SE Italy
Campbell, Cape 129 D5 headland South Island, NZ
Campbell Island 120 D5 island S NZ
Campbell Plateau 120 D5 undersea feature SW Pacific Ocean
Campbell River 14 D5 Vancouver Island, British Columbia, SW Canada
Campeche 29 G4 Campeche, SE Mexico
Campeche, Bahía de 29 F4 Eng. Bay of Campeche. Bay E Mexico
Câm Pha 114 E3 Quang Ninh, N Vietnam
Câmpina 86 C4 prev. Cîmpina. Prahova, SE Romania
Campina Grande 41 G2 Paraíba, E Brazil
Campinas 41 F4 São Paulo, S Brazil
Campobasso 75 D5 Molise, C Italy
Campo de Criptana see Campo de Criptana
Campo de Criptana 71 E3 var. Campo Criptana. Castilla-La Mancha, C Spain
Campos dos Goitacazes see Campos
Campo Grande 41 E4 state capital Mato Grosso do Sul, SW Brazil
Campos 41 F4 var. Campo dos Goitacazes. Rio de Janeiro, SE Brazil
Câmpulung 86 B4 prev. Câmpulung-Muşcel, Cîmpulung. Argeş, S Romania
Campus Stellae see Santiago
Cam Ranh 115 E6 Khanh Hoa, S Vietnam
Canada 12 B4 country N North America
Canada Basin 12 C2 undersea feature Arctic Ocean
Canadian River 27 E2 river SW USA
Çanakkale 94 A3 var. Dardanelli; prev. Chanak, Kale Sultanie. Çanakkale, W Turkey
Çanakkale Boğazı 94 A2 Eng. Dardanelles. Strait NW Turkey
Cananea 28 B1 Sonora, NW Mexico
Canarias, Islas 48 A2 Eng. Canary Islands. Island group Spain, NE Atlantic Ocean
Canary Islands see Canarias, Islas
Canarreos, Archipiélago de los 32 B2 island group W Cuba
Canary Islands see Canarias, Islas
Cañas 30 D4 Guanacaste, NW Costa Rica
Canaveral, Cape 21 E4 headland Florida, SE USA
Canavieiras 41 G3 Bahia, E Brazil
Canberra 120 C4 country capital (Australia) Australian Capital Territory, SE Australia
Cancún 29 H3 Quintana Roo, SE Mexico
Candia see Irákleio
Canea see Chaniá
Cangzhou 106 D4 Hebei, E China
Caniapiscau 17 E2 river Québec, E Canada
Caniapiscau, Réservoir de 16 D3 reservoir Québec, C Canada

Canik Dağları 94 D2 mountain range N Turkey
Canillo 69 A7 C Andorra
Çankırı 94 C3 var. Chankiri; anc. Gangra, Germanicopolis. Çankın, N Turkey
Cannanore 110 B2 var. Kananur, Kannur. Kerala, SW India
Cannes 69 D6 Alpes-Maritimes, SE France
Canoas 41 E5 Rio Grande do Sul, S Brazil
Canon City 22 C5 Colorado, C USA
Cantabria 70 D1 cultural region N Spain
Cantábrica, Cordillera 70 C1 mountain range N Spain
Cantaura 37 E2 Anzoátegui, NE Venezuela
Canterbury 67 E7 hist. Cantwaraburh, anc. Durovernum, Lat. Cantuaria. SE England, UK
Canterbury Bight 129 C6 bight South Island, NZ
Canterbury Plains 129 C6 plain South Island, NZ
Cân Thơ 115 E6 Cân Thơ, S Vietnam
Canton see Guangzhou
Canton 20 B2 Mississippi, S USA
Canton 18 D4 Ohio, N USA
Canton Island see Kanton
Canyon 27 E2 Texas, SW USA
Cao Bằng 114 D3 var. Caobang. Cao Bằng, N Vietnam
Caobang see Cao Bằng
Cape Barren Island 127 C8 island Furneaux Group, Tasmania, SE Australia
Cape Basin 47 B7 undersea feature S Atlantic Ocean
Cape Breton Island 17 G4 Fr. Île du Cap-Breton. Island Nova Scotia, SE Canada
Cape Charles 19 F5 Virginia, NE USA
Cape Coast 53 E5 prev. Cape Coast Castle. S Ghana
Cape Farewell see Uummannarsuaq
Cape Girardeau 23 H5 Missouri, C USA
Cape Horn see Hornos, Cabo de
Capelle aan den IJssel 64 C4 Zuid-Holland, SW Netherlands
Cape Palmas see Harper
Cape Town 56 B5 var. Ekapa, Afr. Kaapstad, Kapstad. Country capital (South Africa-legislative capital) Western Cape, SW South Africa
Cape Verde 52 A2 Port. Cabo Verde, Ilhas do Cabo Verde. Country E Atlantic Ocean
Cape Verde Basin 44 C4 undersea feature E Atlantic Ocean
Cape Verde Plain 44 C4 undersea feature E Atlantic Ocean
Cape York Peninsula 126 C2 peninsula Queensland, N Australia
Cap-Haïtien 32 D3 var. Le Cap. N Haiti
Capira 31 G5 Panamá, C Panama
Capitán Arturo Prat 132 A2 Chilean research station South Shetland Islands, Antarctica
Capitán Pablo Lagerenza 42 D1 var. Mayor Pablo Lagerenza. Chaco, N Paraguay
Capri, Isola di 75 C5 island S Italy
Caprivi Strip 56 C3 Ger. Caprivizipfel; prev. Caprivi Concession. Cultural region NE Namibia
Caquetá 34 B3 off. Departamanto del Caquetá. Province S Colombia
Caquetá, Río 36 C5 var. Rio Japurá, Yapurá. River Brazil/Colombia see also Japurá, Rio
CAR see Central African Republic
Caracal 86 B5 Olt, S Romania
Caracaraí 40 D1 Rondônia, W Brazil
Caracas 36 D1 country capital (Venezuela) Distrito Federal, N Venezuela
Caratasca, Laguna de 31 E2 lagoon NE Honduras
Carballiño see O Carballiño
Carbondale 18 B5 Illinois, N USA
Carbonia 75 A6 var. Carbonia Centro. Sardegna, Italy, C Mediterranean Sea
Carbonia Centro see Carbonia
Carcassonne 69 C6 anc. Carcaso. Aude, S France
Cárdenas 32 B2 Matanzas, W Cuba
Cardiff 67 C7 Wel. Caerdydd. Admin capital S Wales, UK
Cardigan Bay 67 C6 bay W Wales, UK
Carei 86 B3 Ger. Gross-Karol, Karol, Hung. Nagykároly; prev. Careii-Mari. Satu Mare, NW Romania
Carey, Lake 125 B6 lake Western Australia
Cariaco 37 E1 Sucre, NE Venezuela
Caribbean Sea 32 C4 sea W Atlantic Ocean
Carlisle 66 C4 anc. Caer Luel, Luguvallium, Luguvallum. NW England, UK
Carlow 67 B6 Ir. Ceatharlach. SE Ireland
Carlsbad 26 D3 New Mexico, SW USA
Carlsberg Ridge 118 B4 undersea feature S Arabian Sea
Carlsruhe see Karlsruhe
Carmana see Kermān
Carmarthen 67 C6 SW Wales, UK
Carmaux 69 C6 Tarn, S France
Carmel 18 C4 Indiana, N USA
Carmelita 30 B1 Petén, N Guatemala
Carmen 29 G4 var. Ciudad del Carmen. Campeche, SE Mexico
Carmona 70 C4 Andalucía, S Spain
Carnaro see Kvarner
Carnarvon 125 A5 Western Australia
Carnegie, Lake 125 B5 salt lake Western Australia
Car Nicobar 111 F3 island Nicobar Islands, India, NE Indian Ocean
Caroço, Ilha 54 E1 island N Sao Tome and Principe
Carolina 41 F2 Maranhão, E Brazil
Caroline Island see Millennium Island
Caroline Islands 84 C2 island group C Micronesia
Caroní, Río 37 E3 river E Venezuela
Caronium see A Coruña
Carora 36 C1 Lara, N Venezuela
Carpathian Mountains 59 E4 var. Carpathians, Cz./Pol. Karpaty, Ger. Karpaten. Mountain range E Europe
Carpathians see Carpathian Mountains
Carpații Meridionali 86 B4 var. Alpi Transilvaniei, Carpații Sudici, Eng. South Carpathians, Transylvanian Alps, Ger. Südkarpaten, Transsylvanische Alpen, Hung. Déli-Kárpátok, Erdélyi-Havasok. Mountain range C Romania
Carpații Occidentali 77 E7 Eng. Western Carpathians. Mountain range W Romania
Carpații Sudici see Carpații Meridionali
Carpentaria, Gulf of 126 B2 gulf N Australia
Carpi 74 C2 Emilia-Romagna, N Italy
Carrara 74 B3 Toscana, C Italy
Carson City 25 C5 state capital Nevada, W USA
Carson Sink 25 C5 salt flat Nevada, W USA
Cartagena 71 F4 anc. Carthago Nova. Murcia, SE Spain
Cartagena 36 B1 var. Cartagena de los Indes. Bolívar, NW Colombia
Cartagena de los Indes see Cartagena
Cartago 31 E4 Cartago, C Costa Rica
Carthage 23 F5 Missouri, C USA
Cartwright 17 F2 Newfoundland and Labrador, E Canada
Carúpano 37 E1 Sucre, NE Venezuela
Caruthersville 23 H5 Missouri, C USA
Cary 21 F1 North Carolina, SE USA
Casablanca 48 C2 Ar. Dar-el-Beida. NW Morocco
Casa Grande 26 B2 Arizona, SW USA
Cascade Range 24 B3 mountain range Oregon/Washington, NW USA
Cascadia Basin 12 A4 undersea feature NE Pacific Ocean
Cascais 70 B4 Lisboa, C Portugal
Caserta 75 D5 Campania, S Italy
Casey 132 D4 Australian research station Antarctica
Casino 69 C8 New South Wales, SE Australia
Čáslav 77 B5 Ger. Tschaslau. Středočesky Kraj, C Czech Republic
Casper 22 C3 Wyoming, C USA
Caspian Depression 89 B7 Kaz. Kaspīy Mangy Oypaty, Rus. Prikaspiyskaya Nizmennost'. Depression Kazakhstan/Russian Federation
Caspian Sea 92 A4 Az. Xäzär Dänizi, Kaz. Kaspiy Tengizi, Per. Baḥr-e Khazar, Daryā-ye Khazar, Rus. Kaspiyskoye More. Inland sea Asia/Europe
Cassai see Kasai
Castamoni see Kastamonu
Casteggio 96 B2 Lombardia, N Italy
Castelló de la Plana 71 F3 var. Castellón. País Valenciano, E Spain
Castellón see Castelló de la Plana
Castelnaudary 69 C6 Aude, S France
Castelo Branco 70 C3 Castelo Branco, C Portugal
Castelsarrasin 69 B6 Tarn-et-Garonne, S France
Castelvetrano 75 C7 Sicilia, Italy, C Mediterranean Sea
Castilla-La Mancha 71 E3 cultural region NE Spain
Castilla-León 70 C2 cultural region NW Spain
Castlebar 67 A5 Ir. Caisleán an Bharraigh. W Ireland
Castleford 67 D5 N England, UK
Castle Harbour 20 B5 inlet Bermuda, NW Atlantic Ocean
Castricum 64 C3 Noord-Holland, W Netherlands
Castries 33 F1 country capital (Saint Lucia) N Saint Lucia
Castro 43 B6 Los Lagos, W Chile
Castrovillari 75 D6 Calabria, SW Italy
Castuera 70 D4 Extremadura, W Spain
Caswell Sound 129 A7 sound South Island, NZ
Catacamas 30 D2 Olancho, C Honduras
Catacaos 38 B3 Piura, NW Peru
Catalan Bay 71 H4 var. Caleta. Bay E Gibraltar
Cataluña 71 G2 cultural region N Spain
Catamarca see San Fernando del Valle de Catamarca
Catania 75 D7 Sicilia, Italy, C Mediterranean Sea
Catanzaro 75 D6 Calabria, SW Italy
Catarroja 71 F3 País Valenciano, E Spain
Cat Island 32 C1 island C Bahamas
Catskill Mountains 19 F3 mountain range New York, NE USA
Cauca, Río 36 B2 river N Colombia
Caucasia 36 B2 Antioquia, NW Colombia
Caucasus 59 G4 Rus. Kavkaz. Mountain range Georgia/Russian Federation
Caura, Río 37 E3 river C Venezuela
Cavalla 52 D5 var. Cavally, Cavally Fleuve. River Côte d'Ivoire/Liberia
Cavally see Cavalla
Cavally Fleuve see Cavalla
Caviana de Fora, Ilha 41 E1 var. Ilha Caviana. Island N Brazil
Caxito 56 B1 Bengo, NW Angola
Cayenne 37 H3 de6pendent territory capital (French Guiana) NE French Guiana
Cayes 32 D3 var. Les Cayes. SW Haiti
Cayman Brac 32 B3 island E Cayman Islands
Cayman Islands 32 B3 UK dependent territory W West Indies
Cay Sal 32 B2 islet SW Bahamas
Cazin 78 B3 Federacija Bosna I Hercegovina, NW Bosnia and Herzegovina
Cazorla 71 E4 Andalucía, S Spain
Ceadâr-Lunga see Ciadîr-Lunga
Ceará 41 F2 off. Estado do Ceará. State C Brazil
Ceara Abyssal Plain see Ceará Plain
Ceará Plain 34 E3 var. Ceara Abyssal Plain. Undersea feature W Atlantic Ocean
Ceatharlach see Carlow
Cébaco, Isla 31 F5 island SW Panama
Cebu 117 E2 off. Cebu City. Cebu, C Philippines
Cecina 74 B3 Toscana, C Italy
Cedar City 22 A5 Utah, W USA
Cedar Falls 23 G3 Iowa, C USA
Cedar Lake 16 A2 lake Manitoba, C Canada
Cedar Rapids 23 G3 Iowa, C USA
Cedros, Isla 28 A2 island W Mexico
Ceduna 127 A6 South Australia
Cefalu 75 C7 anc. Cephaloedium. Sicilia, Italy, C Mediterranean Sea
Celebes see Sulawesi
Celebes Sea 117 E3 Ind. Laut Sulawesi. Sea Indonesia/Philippines
Celje 73 E7 Ger. Cilli. C Slovenia
Celldömölk 99 C6 Vas, W Hungary
Celle 72 B3 var. Zelle. Niedersachsen, N Germany
Celtic Sea 67 B7 Ir. An Mhuir Cheilteach. Sea SW British Isles
Celtic Shelf 58 B3 undersea feature E Atlantic Ocean
Cenderawasih, Teluk 117 G4 var. Teluk Irian, Teluk Sarera. Bay W Pacific Ocean
Cenon 69 B5 Gironde, SW France
Central African Republic 54 C4 var. République Centrafricaine, abbrev. CAR; prev. Ubangi-Shari, Oub angui-Chari, Territoire de l'Oubangui-Chari. Country C Africa
Central, Cordillera 33 E3 mountain range C Dominican Republic
Central, Cordillera 31 F5 mountain range C Panama
Central, Cordillera 117 E1 mountain range Luzon, N Philippines
Central, Cordillera 36 B3 mountain range W Colombia
Central Group see Inner Islands
Centralia 24 B2 Washington, NW USA
Central Indian Ridge see Mid-Indian Ridge
Central Makrān Range 112 A3 mountain range W Pakistan
Central Pacific Basin 120 D1 undersea feature C Pacific Ocean
Central, Planalto 41 F3 var. Brazilian Highlands. Mountain range E Brazil
Central Range 122 B3 mountain range NW PNG
Central Russian Upland see Srednerusskaya Vozvyshennost'
Central Siberian Plateau see Srednesibirskoye Ploskogor'ye
Central Siberian Uplands see Srednesibirskoye Ploskogor'ye
Central, Sistema 70 D3 mountain range C Spain
Central Valley 25 B6 valley California, W USA
Cephaloedium see Cefalu
Ceram see Seram, Pulau
Ceram Sea 117 F4 Ind. Laut Seram. Sea E Indonesia
Cerasus see Giresun
Cereté 36 B2 Córdoba, NW Colombia
Cerignola 75 D5 Puglia, SE Italy
Cerigo see Kýthira
Çerkeş 94 C2 Çankın, N Turkey
Cernay 90 E4 Haut-Rhin, NE France
Cerro Chirripó see Chirripó Grande, Cerro
Cerro de Mulhacén see Mulhacén
Cerro de Pasco 38 C3 Pasco, C Peru
Cervera 71 F2 Cataluña, NE Spain
Cesena 74 C3 anc. Caesena. Emilia-Romagna, N Italy
Cēsis 84 D3 Ger. Wenden. Cēsis, C Latvia
České Budějovice 77 B5 Ger. Budweis. Budějovický Kraj, S Czech Republic
Český Krumlov 77 A5 var. Böhmisch-Krumau, Ger. Krummau. Budějovický Kraj, S Czech Republic
Cetinje 79 C5 It. Cettigne. Montenegro, SW Serbia and Montenegro (Yugo.)
Ceuta 48 C2 enclave Spain, N Africa
Cévennes 69 C6 mountain range S France
Ceyhan 94 D4 Adana, S Turkey
Ceylanpınar 95 E4 Şanlıurfa, SE Turkey
Ceylon Plain 102 B4 undersea feature N Indian Ocean
Ceyre to the Caribs see Marie-Galante
Chachapoyas 38 B2 Amazonas, NW Peru
Chachevichy 85 D6 Rus. Chechevichi. Mahilyowskaya Voblasts', E Belarus
Chaco see Gran Chaco
Chad 54 C3 Fr. Tchad. Country C Africa
Chad, Lake 54 B3 Fr. Lac Tchad. Lake C Africa
Chadron 22 D3 Nebraska, C USA
Chadyr-Lunga see Ciadîr-Lunga
Chāgai Hills 112 A2 var. Chāh Gay. Mountain range Afghanistan/Pakistan
Chaghasarāy see Asadābād
Chagos-Laccadive Plateau 102 B4 undersea feature N Indian Ocean
Chagos Trench 119 C5 undersea feature N Indian Ocean
Chāh Gay see Chāgai Hills
Chaillu, Massif du 55 B6 mountain range C Gabon
Chaîne des Dangrek see Dângrêk, Chuŏr Phnum
Chaîne des Mitumba see Mitumba, Monts
Chaîne des Mongos see Bongo, Massif des
Chain Ridge 118 B4 undersea feature W Indian Ocean
Chajul 30 B2 Quiché, W Guatemala
Chakhānsūr 100 D5 Nīmrūz, SW Afghanistan
Chala 38 D4 Arequipa, SW Peru
Chalatenango 30 C3 Chalatenango, N El Salvador
Chalcidice see Chalkidikí
Chalcis see Chalkída
Chálki 83 E7 island Dodekánisos, Greece, Aegean Sea
Chalkída 83 C5 var. Halkida; prev. Khalkís, anc. Chalcis. Evvoia, E Greece
Chalkidikí 82 C4 var. Khalkidhikí; anc. Chalcidice. Peninsula NE Greece
Challans 90 B4 Vendée, NW France
Challapata 39 F4 Oruro, SW Bolivia
Challenger Deep 130 B3 undersea feature W Pacific Ocean
Challenger Fracture Zone 131 F4 tectonic feature SE Pacific Ocean
Châlons-en-Champagne 68 D3 prev. Châlons-sur-Marne, hist. Arcae Remorum, anc. Carolopois. Marne, NE France
Chalon-sur-Saône 68 D4 anc. Cabillonum. Saône-et-Loire, C France
Cha Mai see Thung Song
Chaman 112 B2 Baluchistān, SW Pakistan
Chambéry 69 D5 anc. Camberia. Savoie, E France
Champagne 68 D3 Yukon Territory, W Canada
Champaign 18 B4 Illinois, N USA
Champasak 115 D5 Champasak, S Laos
Champlain, Lake 19 F2 lake Canada/USA
Champotón 29 G4 Campeche, SE Mexico
Chanak see Çanakkale
Chañaral 42 B3 Atacama, N Chile
Chanchiang see Zhanjiang
Chandeleur Islands 20 C3 island group Louisiana, S USA
Chandīgarh 112 D2 Punjab, N India
Chandrapur 113 E5 Mahārāshtra, C India
Changan see Xi'an
Changane 57 E3 river S Mozambique
Changchun 106 D3 var. Ch'angch'un, Ch'ang-ch'un; prev. Hsinking. Jilin, NE China
Ch'angch'un see Changchun
Chang Jiang 106 B5 var. Yangtze Kiang, Eng. Yangtze. River C China
Changkiakow see Zhangjiakou
Chang, Ko 115 C6 island S Thailand
Changsha 106 C5 var. Ch'angsha, Ch'ang-sha. Hunan, S China
Ch'angsha see Changsha
Changzhi 106 C4 Shanxi, C China
Chaniá 83 C7 var. Hania, Khaniá, Eng. Canea; anc. Cydonia. Kríti, Greece, E Mediterranean Sea
Chañi, Nevado de 42 B2 mountain NW Argentina
Chankiri see Çankırı
Channel Islands 67 C8 Fr. Îles Normandes. Island group S English Channel
Channel Islands 25 B8 island group California, W USA
Channel-Port aux Basques 17 G4 Newfoundland, Newfoundland and Labrador, SE Canada
Channel, The see English Channel
Channel Tunnel 68 C2 tunnel France/UK
Chantabun see Chanthaburi
Chantaburi see Chanthaburi
Chantada 70 C1 Galicia, NW Spain
Chanthaburi 115 C6 var. Chantabun, Chantaburi. Chantaburi, S Thailand
Chanute 23 F5 Kansas, C USA
Chaouèn see Chefchaouen
Chaoyang 106 D3 Liaoning, NE China
Chapala, Lago de 28 D4 lake C Mexico
Chapan, Gora 100 B3 mountain C Turkmenistan
Chapayevsk 89 C6 Samarskaya Oblast', W Russian Federation
Chaplynka 87 F4 Khersons'ka Oblast', S Ukraine
Charcot Seamounts 58 B3 undersea feature E Atlantic Ocean
Charente 69 B5 cultural region W France
Charente 69 B5 river W France
Chari 54 B3 var. Shari. River Central African Republic/Chad
Chārīkār 101 E4 Parwān, NE Afghanistan
Charity 37 F2 NW Guyana
Charkhlik see Ruoqiang
Charkhliq see Ruoqiang
Charleroi 87 C7 Hainaut, S Belgium
Charlesbourg 17 E4 Québec, SE Canada
Charles de Gaulle 68 E1 international airport (Paris) Seine-et-Marne, N France
Charles Island 16 D1 island Northwest Territories, NE Canada
Charles Island see Santa María, Isla
Charleston 18 D5 state capital West Virginia, NE USA
Charleston 21 F2 South Carolina, SE USA
Charleville 127 D5 Queensland, E Australia
Charleville-Mézières 68 D3 Ardennes, N France
Charlie-Gibbs Fracture Zone 44 C2 tectonic feature N Atlantic Ocean
Charlotte 21 E1 North Carolina, SE USA
Charlotte Amalie 33 F3 prev. Saint Thomas. Dependent territory capital (Virgin Islands (US)) Saint Thomas, N Virgin Islands (US)
Charlotte Harbor 21 E5 inlet Florida, SE USA
Charlottesville 19 E5 Virginia, NE USA
Charlottetown 17 F4 Prince Edward Island, Prince Edward Island, SE Canada
Charsk see Shar
Charters Towers 126 D3 Queensland, NE Australia
Chartres 68 C3 anc. Autricum, Civitas Carnutum. Eure-et-Loir, C France
Charus Nuur 104 C2 lake NW Mongolia
Chashniki 85 D5 Rus. Chashniki. Vitsyebskaya Voblasts', N Belarus
Châteaubriant 68 B4 Loire-Atlantique, NW France
Châteaudun 68 C3 Eure-et-Loir, C France
Châteauroux 68 C4 prev. Indreville. Indre, C France
Château-Thierry 68 C3 Aisne, N France
Châtelet 65 C7 Hainaut, S Belgium
Châtelherault see Châtellerault
Châtellerault 68 B4 var. Châtelherault. Vienne, W France
Chatham Island see San Cristóbal, Isla
Chatham Island Rise see Chatham Rise
Chatham Islands 121 E5 island group NZ, SW Pacific Ocean
Chatham Rise 120 D5 var. Chatham Island Rise. Undersea feature S Pacific Ocean
Chatkal Range 101 F2 Rus. Chatkal'skiy Khrebet. Mountain range Kyrgyzstan/Uzbekistan
Chattahoochee River 20 D3 river SE USA
Chattanooga 20 D1 Tennessee, S USA
Chatyr-Tash 101 G2 Narynskaya Oblast', C Kyrgyzstan
Châu Đốc 115 D6 var. Chauphu, Chau Phu. An Giang, S Vietnam
Chauk 114 A3 Magwe, W Myanmar
Chaumont 68 D4 prev. Chaumont-en-Bassigny. Haute-Marne, N France
Chau Phu see Châu Đốc
Chaves 70 C2 anc. Aquae Flaviae. Vila Real, N Portugal
Chávez, Isla see Santa Cruz, Isla
Chavusy 85 E6 Rus. Chausy. Mahilyowskaya Voblasts', E Belarus
Chaykovskiy 89 D5 Permskaya Oblast', NW Russian Federation
Cheb 77 A5 Ger. Eger. Karlovarský Kraj, W Czech Republic
Cheboksary 89 C5 Chuvashskaya Respublika, W Russian Federation
Cheboygan 18 C2 Michigan, N USA
Chechaouèn see Chefchaouen
Chech, Erg 52 D1 desert Algeria/Mali
Che-chiang see Zhejiang
Cheduba Island 114 A4 island W Myanmar
Chefchaouen 48 C2 var. Chaouèn, Chechaouèn, Sp. Xauen. N Morocco
Chefoo see Yantai
Cheju-do 107 E4 Jap. Saishū; prev. Quelpart. Island S South Korea
Cheju Strait 107 E4 strait S South Korea
Chekiang see Zhejiang
Hazar 100 B2 prev. Cheleken. Balkanskiy Velayat, W Turkmenistan
Chelkar see Shalkar
Chełm 76 E4 Rus. Kholm. Lubelskie, E Poland
Chełmno 76 C3 Ger. Culm, Kulm. Kujawski-pomorskie, C Poland
Chełmża 76 C3 Ger. Culmsee, Kulmsee. Kujawski-pomorskie, C Poland
Cheltenham 67 D6 C England, UK
Chelyabinsk 92 C3 Chelyabinskaya Oblast', C Russian Federation
Chemnitz 72 D4 prev. Karl-Marx-Stadt. Sachsen, E Germany
Chenāb 112 C2 river India/Pakistan
Chengchiatun see Liaoyuan
Ch'eng-chou see Zhengzhou
Chengchow see Zhengzhou
Chengde 106 D3 var. Jehol. Hebei, E China
Chengdu 106 B5 var. Chengtu, Ch'eng-tu. Sichuan, C China
Chenghsien see Zhengzhou
Ch'eng-tu see Chengdu
Chennai 110 D2 prev Madras. Tamil Nādu, S India
Chenxian see Chenzhou
Chen Xian see Chenzhou
Chen Xiang see Chenzhou
Chenzhou 106 C6 var. Chenxian, Chen Xian, Chen Xiang. Hunan, S China
Chepelare 82 C3 Smolyan, S Bulgaria
Chepén 38 B3 La Libertad, C Peru
Cher 68 C4 river C France
Cherbourg 68 B3 anc. Carusbur. Manche, N France
Cherepovets 88 B4 Vologodskaya Oblast', NW Russian Federation
Chergui, Chott ech 48 D2 salt lake NW Algeria
Cherkasy 87 E2 Rus. Cherkassy. Cherkas'ka Oblast', C Ukraine
Cherkessk 89 B7 Karachayevo-Cherkesskaya Respublika, SW Russian Federation
Chernihiv 87 E1 Rus. Chernigov. Chernihivs'ka Oblast', NE Ukraine
Chernivtsi 86 C3 Ger. Czernowitz, Rom. Cernăuţi, Rus. Chernovtsy. Chernivets'ka Oblast', W Ukraine
Cherno More see Black Sea
Chernoye More see Black Sea
Chernyakhovsk 84 A4 Ger. Insterburg. Kaliningradskaya Oblast', W Russian Federation
Cherry Hill 19 F4 New Jersey, NE USA
Cherski Range see Cherskogo, Khrebet
Cherskiy 93 G2 Respublika Sakha (Yakutiya), NE Russian Federation
Cherskogo, Khrebet 93 F2 var. Cherski Range. Mountain range NE Russian Federation
Chervonohrad 86 C2 Rus. Chervonograd. L'vivs'ka Oblast', NW Ukraine
Chervyen' 85 D6 Rus. Cherven'. Minskaya Voblasts', C Belarus
Cherykaw 85 E7 Rus. Cherikov. Mahilyowskaya Voblasts', E Belarus
Chesapeake Bay 19 F5 inlet NE USA
Chesha Bay see Chëshskaya Guba
Chëshskaya Guba 172 D5 var. Archangel Bay, Chesha Bay, Dvina Bay. Bay NW Russian Federation
Chester 67 C6 Wel. Caerleon; hist. Legaceaster, Lat. Deva, Devana Castra. C England, UK
Chetumal 29 H4 var. Payo Obispo. Quintana Roo, SE Mexico
Cheviot Hills 66 D4 hill range England/Scotland, UK
Cheyenne 22 D4 state capital Wyoming, C USA
Cheyenne River 22 D3 river South Dakota/Wyoming, N USA
Chhapra 113 F3 prev. Chapra. Bihār, N India
Chhattīsgarh 113 E4 Admin. region state N India

INDEX

Chiai 106 D6 var. Chia-i, Chiayi, Kiayi, Jiayi, Jap. Kagi. C Taiwan
Chia-i see Chiai
Chiang-hsi see Jiangxi
Chiang Mai 114 B4 var. Chiangmai, Chiengmai, Kiangmai. Chiang Mai, NW Thailand
Chiangmai see Chiang Mai
Chiang Rai 114 C3 var. Chianpai, Chienrai, Muang Chiang Rai. Chiang Rai, NW Thailand
Chiang-su see Jiangsu
Chian-ning see Nanjing
Chianpai see Chiang Rai
Chianti 96 C3 cultural region C Italy
Chiapa see Chiapa de Corzo
Chiapa de Corzo 29 G5 var. Chiapa. Chiapas, SE Mexico
Chiayi see Chiai
Chiba 108 B1 var. Tiba. Chiba, Honshū, S Japan
Chibougamau 16 D3 Québec, SE Canada
Chicago 18 B3 Illinois, N USA
Ch'i-ch'i-ha-erh see Qiqihar
Chickasha 27 G2 Oklahoma, C USA
Chiclayo 38 B3 Lambayeque, NW Peru
Chico 25 B5 California, W USA
Chico, Río 43 B6 river S Argentina
Chico, Río 43 B7 river SE Argentina
Chicoutimi 17 E4 Québec, SE Canada
Chiengmai see Chiang Mai
Chienrai see Chiang Rai
Chiesanuova 96 D2 SW San Marino
Chieti 74 D4 var. Teate. Abruzzo, C Italy
Chifeng 105 G2 var. Ulanhad. Nei Mongol Zizhiqu, N China
Chih-fu see Yantai
Chihli see Hebei
Chihli, Gulf of see Bo Hai
Chihuahua 28 C2 Chihuahua, NW Mexico
Childress 27 F2 Texas, SW USA
Chile 42 B3 Country SW South America
Chile Basin 35 A5 undersea feature E Pacific Ocean
Chile Chico 43 B6 Aisén, W Chile
Chile Rise 35 A7 undersea feature SE Pacific Ocean
Chililabombwe 56 D2 Copperbelt, C Zambia
Chi-lin see Jilin
Chillán 43 B5 Bío Bío, C Chile
Chillicothe 18 D4 Ohio, N USA
Chiloé, Isla de 43 A6 var. Isla Grande de Chiloé. Island W Chile
Chilpancingo 29 E5 var. Chilpancingo de los Bravos. Guerrero, S Mexico
Chilpancingo de los Bravos see Chilpancingo
Chilung 106 D6 var. Keelung, Jap. Kirun, Kirun'; prev. Sp. Santissima Trinidad. N Taiwan
Chimán 31 G5 Panamá, E Panama
Chimborazo 38 A1 volcano C Ecuador
Chimbote 38 C3 Ancash, W Peru
Chimboy 100 D1 Rus. Chimbay. Qoraqalpoghiston Respublikasi, NW Uzbekistan
Chimoio 57 E3 Manica, C Mozambique
China 102 C2 Chin. Chung-hua Jen-min Kung-ho-kuo, Zhonghua Renmin Gongheguo; prev. Chinese Empire. Country E Asia
Chi-nan see Jinan
Chinandega 30 C3 Chinandega, NW Nicaragua
Chincha Alta 38 D4 Ica, SW Peru
Chin-chiang see Quanzhou
Chin-chou see Jinzhou
Chinchow see Jinzhou
Chindwin 114 B2 river N Myanmar
Ch'ing Hai see Qinghai Hu
Chingola 56 D2 Copperbelt, C Zambia
Ching-Tao see Qingdao
Chinguetti 52 C2 var. Chinguetti. Adrar, C Mauritania
Chin Hills 114 A3 mountain range W Myanmar
Chinhsien see Jinzhou
Chinnereth see Tiberias, Lake
Chinook Trough 91 H4 undersea feature N Pacific Ocean
Chioggia 74 C2 anc. Fossa Claudia. Veneto, NE Italy
Chíos 83 D5 var. Hios, Khíos, It. Scio, Turk. Sakiz-Adasi. Chíos, E Greece
Chíos 83 D5 var. Khíos. Island E Greece
Chipata 56 D2 prev. Fort Jameson. Eastern, E Zambia
Chiquián 38 C3 Ancash, W Peru
Chiquimula 30 B2 Chiquimula, SE Guatemala
Chīrāla 110 D1 Andhra Pradesh, E India
Chirchiq 101 E2 Rus. Chirchik. Toshkent Wiloyati, E Uzbekistan
Chiriquí, Golfo de 31 E5 Eng. Chiriqui Gulf. Gulf SW Panama
Chiriquí, Laguna de 31 E5 lagoon NW Panama
Chirripó Grande, Cerro 30 D4 var. Cerro Chirripó. Mountain SE Costa Rica
Chisec 30 B2 Alta Verapaz, C Guatemala
Chisholm 23 F1 Minnesota, N USA
Chisimaio see Kismaayo
Chisimayu see Kismaayo
Chişinău 86 D4 Rus. Kishinev. Country capital (Moldova) C Moldova
Chita 93 F4 Chitinskaya Oblast', S Russian Federation
Chitato 56 C1 Lunda Norte, NE Angola
Chitina 14 D3 Alaska, USA
Chitose 108 D2 var. Titose. Hokkaidō, NE Japan
Chitré 31 F5 Herrera, S Panama
Chittagong 113 G4 Ben. Chāttagām. Chittagong, SE Bangladesh
Chitungwiza 56 D3 prev. Chitangwiza. Mashonaland East, NE Zimbabwe
Chlef 48 D2 var. Ech Cheliff, Ech Chleff; prev. Al-Asnam, El Asnam, Orléansville. NW Algeria
Chocolate Mountains 25 D8 mountain range California, W USA
Chodzież 76 C3 Wielkopolskie, C Poland
Choele Choel 43 C5 Río Negro, C Argentina
Choiseul 122 C3 var. Lauru. Island NW Solomon Islands
Chojnice 76 C2 Ger. Knoitz. Pomorskie, N Poland
Ch'ok'ē 50 C4 var. Choke Mountains. Mountain range NW Ethiopia
Choke Mountains see Ch'ok'ē
Cholet 68 B4 Maine-et-Loire, NW France
Choluteca 30 C3 Choluteca, S Honduras
Choluteca, Río 30 C3 river SW Honduras
Choma 56 D2 Southern, S Zambia
Chomutov 76 A4 Ger. Komotau. Ústecký Kraj, NW Czech Republic
Chona 91 E2 river C Russian Federation
Chon Buri 115 C5 prev. Bang Pla Soi. Chon Buri, S Thailand
Chone 38 A1 Manabí, W Ecuador
Ch'ŏngjin 107 E3 NE North Korea
Chongqing 106 B5 var. Ch'ung-ching, Ch'ung-ch'ing, Chungking, Pahsien, Tchongking, Yuzhou. Chongqing, C China
Chongqing 106 B5 Admin. region province C China
Chonos, Archipiélago de los 43 A6 island group S Chile
Chorne More see Black Sea
Chornomors'ke 87 E4 Rus. Chernomorskoye. Respublika Krym, S Ukraine
Chortkiv 86 C2 Rus. Chortkov. Ternopil's'ka Oblast', W Ukraine
Chorum see Çorum
Chorzów 77 C5 Ger. Königshütte; prev. Królewska Huta. Śląskie, S Poland
Chōshi 109 D5 var. Tyôsi. Chiba, Honshū, S Japan
Choszczno 76 B3 Ger. Arnswalde. Zachodniopomorskie, NW Poland
Chota Nāgpur 113 E4 plateau N India
Chott el-Hodna see Hodna, Chott El
Chott Melrhir see Melghir, Chott
Choûm 52 C2 Adrar, C Mauritania
Choybalsan 105 F2 Dornod, E Mongolia
Christchurch 129 C6 Canterbury, South Island, NZ
Christiana 32 B5 C Jamaica
Christiansand see Kristiansand
Christianshåb see Qasigiannguit
Christiansund see Kristiansund
Christmas Island 119 D5 Australian external territory E Indian Ocean
Christmas Ridge 121 E1 undersea feature C Pacific Ocean
Chuan see Sichuan
Ch'uan-chou see Quanzhou
Chubut 35 B7 off. Provincia de Chubut. Admin. region province S Argentina
Chubut, Río 43 B6 river SE Argentina
Ch'u-chiang see Shaoguan
Chūgoku-sanchi 109 B6 mountain range Honshū, SW Japan
Chuí see Chuy
Chukai see Cukai
Chukchi Plain 133 B2 undersea feature Arctic Ocean
Chukchi Plateau 12 C2 undersea feature Arctic Ocean
Chukchi Sea 12 B2 Rus. Chukotskoye More. Sea Arctic Ocean
Chula Vista 25 C8 California, W USA
Chulucanas 38 B2 Piura, NW Peru
Chulym 92 D4 river C Russian Federation
Chumphon 115 C6 var. Jumporn. Chumphon, SW Thailand
Ch'unch'ŏn 107 E4 Jap. Shunsen. N South Korea
Ch'ung-ching see Chongqing
Chungking see Chongqing
Chunya 93 E3 river C Russian Federation
Chuquicamata 42 B2 Antofagasta, N Chile
Chur 73 B7 Fr. Coire, It. Coira, Rmsch. Cuera, Quera; anc. Curia Rhaetorum. Graubünden, E Switzerland
Churchill 16 B2 river Manitoba/Saskatchewan, C Canada
Churchill 17 F2 river Newfoundland and Labrador, E Canada
Churchill 15 G4 Manitoba, C Canada
Chuska Mountains 26 C1 mountain range Arizona/New Mexico, SW USA
Chusovoy 89 D5 Permskaya Oblast', NW Russian Federation
Chuuk Islands 122 B2 var. Hogoley Islands; prev. Truk Islands. Island group Caroline Islands, C Micronesia
Chuy 42 E4 var. Chuí. Rocha, E Uruguay
Chyhyryn 87 E2 Rus. Chigirin. Cherkas'ka Oblast', N Ukraine
Ciadîr-Lunga 86 D4 var. Ceadâr-Lunga, Rus. Chadyr-Lunga. S Moldova
Cide 94 C2 Kastamonu, N Turkey
Ciechanów 76 D3 prev. Zichenau. Mazowieckie, C Poland
Ciego de Ávila 32 C2 Ciego de Ávila, C Cuba
Ciénaga 36 B1 Magdalena, N Colombia
Cienfuegos 32 B2 Cienfuegos, C Cuba
Cieza 71 E4 Murcia, SE Spain
Cihanbeyli 94 C3 Konya, C Turkey
Cikobia 123 E4 prev. Thikombia. Island N Fiji
Cilacap 116 C5 prev. Tjilatjap. Jawa, C Indonesia
Cill Airne see Killarney
Cill Chainnigh see Kilkenny
Cill Mhantáin see Wicklow
Cincinnati 18 C4 Ohio, N USA
Ciney 65 C7 Namur, SE Belgium
Cinto, Monte 69 E7 mountain Corse, France, C Mediterranean Sea
Cipolletti 43 B5 Río Negro, C Argentina
Cirebon 116 C4 prev. Tjirebon. Jawa, S Indonesia
Ciro Marino 97 E6 Calabria, S Italy
Cisnădie 86 B4 Ger. Heltau, Hung. Nagydisznód. Sibiu, SW Romania
Citlaltépetl see Orizaba, Volcán Pico de
Citrus Heights 25 B5 California, W USA
Ciudad Bolívar 37 E2 prev. Angostura. Bolívar, E Venezuela
Ciudad Acuña see Villa Acuña
Cuidad Camargo 28 D2 Chihuahua, N Mexico
Ciudad Cortés see Cortés
Ciudad Darío 30 D3 var. Dario. Matagalpa, W Nicaragua
Ciudad de Dolores Hidalgo see Dolores Hidalgo
Ciudad de Guatemala 30 B2 var. Gautemala City Eng. Guatemala City; prev. Santiago de los Caballeros. Country capital (Guatemala) Guatemala, C Guatemala
Ciudad del Carmen see Carmen
Ciudad del Este 42 E2 prev. Cuidad Presidente Stroessner, Presidente Stroessner, Puerto Presidente Stroessner. Alto Paraná, SE Paraguay
Ciudad Delicias see Delicias
Ciudad de México see México
Ciudad de Panamá see Panamá
Ciudad Guayana 37 E2 prev. San Tomé de Guayana, Santo Tomé de Guayana. Bolívar, NE Venezuela
Ciudad Guzmán 28 D4 Jalisco, SW Mexico
Ciudad Hidalgo 29 G5 Chiapas, SE Mexico
Ciudad Juárez 28 C1 Chihuahua, N Mexico
Ciudad Lerdo 28 D3 Durango, C Mexico
Ciudad Madero 29 E3 var. Villa Cecilia. Tamaulipas, C Mexico
Ciudad Mante 29 E3 Tamaulipas, C Mexico
Ciudad Miguel Alemán 29 E2 Tamaulipas, C Mexico
Ciudad Obregón 28 B2 Sonora, NW Mexico
Ciudad Ojeda 36 C1 Zulia, NW Venezuela
Ciudad Porfirio Díaz see Piedras Negras
Ciudad Quesada see Quesada
Ciudad Real 70 D3 Castilla-La Mancha, C Spain
Ciudad-Rodrigo 70 C3 Castilla-León, N Spain
Ciudad Valles 29 E3 San Luis Potosí, C Mexico
Ciudad Victoria 29 E3 Tamaulipas, C Mexico
Ciutadella see Ciutadella de Menorca
Ciutadella de Menorca 71 H3 var. Ciutadella. Menorca, Spain, W Mediterranean Sea
Civitanova Marche 74 D3 Marche, C Italy
Civitavecchia 74 C4 anc. Centum Cellae, Trajani Portus. Lazio, C Italy
Claremore 27 G1 Oklahoma, C USA
Clarence 129 C5 river South Island, NZ
Clarence 129 C5 Canterbury, South Island, NZ
Clarence Town 32 D2 Long Island, C Bahamas
Clarinda 23 F4 Iowa, C USA
Clarion Fracture Zone 131 E2 tectonic feature NE Pacific Ocean
Clarión, Isla 28 A5 island W Mexico
Clark Fork 22 A1 river Idaho/Montana, NW USA
Clark Hill Lake 21 E2 var. J.Storm Thurmond Reservoir. Reservoir Georgia/South Carolina, SE USA
Clarksburg 18 D4 West Virginia, NE USA
Clarksdale 20 B2 Mississippi, S USA
Clarksville 20 C1 Tennessee, S USA
Clayton 27 E1 New Mexico, SW USA
Clearwater 21 E4 Florida, SE USA
Clearwater Mountains 24 D2 mountain range Idaho, NW USA
Cleburne 27 G3 Texas, SW USA
Clermont 126 D4 Queensland, E Australia
Clermont-Ferrand 69 C5 Puy-de-Dôme, C France
Cleveland 18 D3 Ohio, N USA
Cleveland 20 D1 Tennessee, S USA
Clifton 26 C2 Arizona, SW USA
Clinton 20 B2 Mississippi, S USA
Clinton 27 F1 Oklahoma, C USA
Clipperton Fracture Zone 131 E3 tectonic feature E Pacific Ocean
Clipperton Island 13 A7 French dependency of French Polynesia E Pacific Ocean
Cloncurry 126 B3 Queensland, C Australia
Clonmel 67 B6 Ir. Cluain Meala. S Ireland
Cloppenburg 72 B3 Niedersachsen, NW Germany
Cloquet 23 G2 Minnesota, N USA
Cloud Peak 22 C3 mountain Wyoming, C USA
Clovis 27 E2 New Mexico, SW USA
Cluain Meala see Clonmel
Cluj-Napoca 86 B3 Ger. Klausenburg, Hung. Kolozsvár; prev. Cluj. Cluj, NW Romania
Clutha 129 B7 river South Island, NZ
Clyde 66 C4 river W Scotland, UK
Coari 40 D2 Amazonas, N Brazil
Coast Mountains 14 D4 Fr. Chaîne Côtière. Mountain range Canada/USA
Coast Ranges 24 A4 mountain range W USA
Coats Island 15 G3 island Nunavut, NE Canada
Coats Land 132 B2 physical region Antarctica
Coatzacoalcos 29 G4 var. Quetzalcoalco; prev. Puerto México. Veracruz-Llave, E Mexico
Cobán 30 B2 Alta Verapaz, C Guatemala
Cobar 127 C6 New South Wales, SE Australia
Cobija 39 E3 Pando, NW Bolivia
Coburg 73 C5 Bayern, SE Germany
Coca see Puerto Francisco de Orellana
Cochabamba 39 F4 hist. Oropeza. Cochabamba, C Bolivia
Cochin 110 C3 var. Kochi. Kerala, SW India
Cochinos, Bahía de 32 B2 Eng. Bay of Pigs. Bay SE Cuba
Cochrane 43 B7 Aisén, S Chile
Cochrane 16 C4 Ontario, S Canada
Cocibolca see Nicaragua, Lago de
Cockburn Town 33 E2 var. Grand Turk. dependent territory capital (Turks and Caicos Islands) Grand Turk Island, SE Turks and Caicos Islands
Cockpit Country, The 32 A4 physical region W Jamaica
Cocobeach 55 A5 Estuaire, NW Gabon
Coconino Plateau 26 B1 plain Arizona, SW USA
Coco, Río 31 E2 var. Río Wanki, Segoviao Wangkí. River Honduras/Nicaragua
Cocos Basin 102 C5 undersea feature E Indian Ocean
Cocos Island Ridge see Cocos Ridge
Cocos Islands 119 D5 island group E Indian Ocean
Cocos Ridge 13 C8 var. Cocos Island Ridge. Undersea feature E Pacific Ocean
Cod, Cape 19 G3 headland Massachusetts, NE USA
Codfish Island 129 A8 island SW NZ
Codlea 86 C4 Ger. Zeiden, Hung. Feketehalom. Braşov, C Romania
Cody 22 C2 Wyoming, C USA
Coeur d'Alene 24 C2 Idaho, NW USA
Coevorden 64 E2 Drenthe, NE Netherlands
Coffs Harbour 127 E6 New South Wales, SE Australia
Cognac 69 B5 anc. Compniacum. Charente, W France
Coiba, Isla de 31 E5 island SW Panama
Coihaique 43 B6 var. Coyhaique. Aisén, S Chile
Coimbatore 110 C3 Tamil Nādu, S India
Coimbra 70 B3 anc. Conimbria, Conimbriga. Coimbra, W Portugal
Coín 70 D5 Andalucía, S Spain
Coirib, Loch see Corrib, Lough
Colby 23 E4 Kansas, C USA
Colchester 67 E6 hist. Colneceaste, anc. Camulodunum. E England, UK
Col du Brenner see Brenner Pass
Coleman 27 F3 Texas, SW USA
Coleraine 66 B4 Ir. Cúil Raithin. N Northern Ireland, UK
Colesberg 56 C5 Northern Cape, C South Africa
Colima 28 D4 Colima, S Mexico
Coll 66 B3 island W Scotland, UK
College Station 27 G3 Texas, SW USA
Collie 125 A7 Western Australia
Colmar 68 E4 Ger. Kolmar. Haut-Rhin, NE France
Cöln see Köln
Cologne see Köln
Colombia 36 B3 Country N South America
Colombian Basin 34 A1 undersea feature SW Caribbean Sea
Colombo 110 C4 country capital (Sri Lanka) Western Province, W Sri Lanka
Colón 31 G4 prev. Aspinwall. Colón, C Panama
Colonia Agrippina see Köln
Colón Ridge 13 B8 undersea feature E Pacific Ocean
Colorado 22 C4 off. State of Colorado; also known as Centennial State, Silver State. State C USA
Colorado City 27 F3 Texas, SW USA
Colorado Plateau 26 B1 plateau W USA
Colorado, Río 43 C5 river E Argentina
Colorado, Río see Colorado River
Colorado River 13 B5 var. Río Colorado. River Mexico/USA
Colorado River 27 G4 river Texas, SW USA
Colorado Springs 22 D5 Colorado, C USA
Columbia 24 B3 river Canada/USA
Columbia 21 E2 state capital South Carolina, SE USA
Columbia 19 E4 Maryland, NE USA
Columbia 23 G4 Missouri, C USA
Columbia 20 C1 Tennessee, S USA
Columbia Plateau 24 C3 plateau Idaho/Oregon, NW USA
Columbus 18 D4 state capital Ohio, N USA
Columbus 20 D2 Georgia, SE USA
Columbus 18 C4 Indiana, N USA
Columbus 20 C2 Mississippi, S USA
Columbus 23 F4 Nebraska, C USA
Colville Channel 128 D2 channel North Island, NZ
Colville River 14 D2 river Alaska, USA
Comacchio 74 C3 var. Commachio; anc. Comactium. Emilia-Romagna, N Italy
Comactium see Comacchio
Comalcalco 29 G4 Tabasco, SE Mexico
Coma Pedrosa, Pic de 69 A7 mountain NW Andorra
Comarapa 39 F4 Santa Cruz, C Bolivia
Comayagua 30 C2 Comayagua, W Honduras
Comer See see Como, Lago di
Comilla 113 G4 Ben. Kumillā. Chittagong, E Bangladesh
Comino 80 A5 Malt. Kemmuna. Island C Malta
Comitán 29 G5 var. Comitán de Domínguez. Chiapas, SE Mexico
Comitán de Domínguez see Comitán
Commachio see Comacchio
Commissioner's Point 20 A5 headland W Bermuda
Communism Peak see Kommunizm, Qullai
Como 74 B2 anc. Comum. Lombardia, N Italy
Comodoro Rivadavia 43 B6 Chubut, SE Argentina
Como, Lago di B2 var. Lario, Eng. Lake Como, Ger. Comer See. Lake N Italy
Como, Lake see Como, Lago di
Comoros 57 F2 Fr. République Fédérale Islamique des Comores. Country W Indian Ocean
Compiègne 68 C3 Oise, N France
Compostella see Santiago
Comrat 86 D4 Rus. Komrat. S Moldova
Conakry 52 C4 country capital (Guinea) Conakry, SW Guinea
Concarneau 68 A3 Finistère, NW France
Concepción 42 D2 var. Villa Concepción. Concepción, C Paraguay
Concepcion see La Concepción
Concepción 43 B5 Bío Bío, C Chile
Concepción 39 G3 Santa Cruz, E Bolivia
Concepción de la Vega see La Vega
Conchos, Río 28 D2 river C Mexico
Conchos, Río 26 D4 river NW Mexico
Concord 19 G3 state capital New Hampshire, NE USA
Concordia 42 D4 Entre Ríos, E Argentina
Concordia 23 E4 Kansas, C USA
Côn Đao 115 E7 var. Con Son. Island S Vietnam
Condate see Cosne-Cours-sur-Loire
Condega 30 D3 Estelí, NW Nicaragua
Congo 55 D5 Fr. Moyen-Congo; prev. Middle Congo. Country C Africa
Congo, Dem. Rep. 55 C6 prev. Zaire, Belgian Congo, Congo (Kinshasa). Country C Africa
Congo 55 C6 var. Kongo, Fr. Zaire. River C Africa
Congo Basin 55 C6 drainage basin W Dem. Rep. Congo
Connacht see Connaught
Connaught 67 A5 var. Connacht, Ir. Chonnacht, Cúige. Cultural region W Ireland
Connecticut 19 F3 off. State of Connecticut; also known as Blue Law State, Constitution State, Land of Steady Habits, Nutmeg State. State NE USA
Connecticut 19 G3 river Canada/USA
Conroe 27 G3 Texas, SW USA
Consolación del Sur 32 A2 Pinar del Río, W Cuba
Con Son see Côn Đao
Constance see Konstanz
Constance, Lake B7 Ger. Bodensee. Lake C Europe
Constanța 86 D5 var. Küstendje, Eng. Constanza, Ger. Konstanza, Turk. Küstence. Constanța, SE Romania
Constantia see Konstanz
Constantine 49 E2 var. Qacentina, Ar. Qoussantîna. NE Algeria
Constantinople see Istanbul
Constanz see Konstanz
Constanza see Constanța
Coober Pedy 127 A5 South Australia
Cookeville 20 D1 Tennessee, S USA
Cook Islands 123 F4 territory in free association with NZ S Pacific Ocean
Cook, Mount see Aoraki
Cook Strait 129 D5 var. Raukawa. Strait NZ
Cooktown 126 D2 Queensland, NE Australia
Coolgardie 125 B6 Western Australia
Cooma 127 D7 New South Wales, SE Australia
Coon Rapids 23 F2 Minnesota, N USA
Cooper Creek 126 C4 var. Barcoo, Cooper's Creek. Seasonal river Queensland/South Australia
Cooper's Creek see Cooper Creek
Coos Bay 24 A3 Oregon, NW USA
Cootamundra 127 D6 New South Wales, SE Australia
Copacabana 39 E4 La Paz, W Bolivia
Copenhagen see København
Copiapó 42 B3 Atacama, N Chile
Copperas Cove 27 G3 Texas, SW USA
Coppermine see Kugluktuk
Coquimbo 42 B3 Coquimbo, N Chile
Corabia 86 B5 Olt, S Romania
Coral Harbour 15 G3 Southampton Island, Nunavut, NE Canada
Coral Sea 120 B3 sea SW Pacific Ocean
Coral Sea Islands 122 B4 Australian external territory SW Pacific Ocean
Corantijn Rivier see Courantyne River
Corcaigh see Cork
Corcovado, Golfo 43 B6 gulf S Chile
Cordele 20 D3 Georgia, SE USA
Cordillera Ibérica see Ibérico, Sistema
Cordoba see Córdoba
Córdoba 70 D4 var. Cordoba, Eng. Cordova; anc. Corduba. Andalucía, SW Spain
Córdoba 42 C3 Córdoba, C Argentina
Córdoba 29 F4 Veracruz-Llave, E Mexico
Cordova see Córdoba
Cordova 14 C3 Alaska, USA
Corduba see Córdoba
Corentyne River see Courantyne River
Corfu see Kérkyra
Coria 70 C3 Extremadura, W Spain
Corinth see Kórinthos
Corinth 20 C1 Mississippi, S USA
Corinth, Gulf of see Korinthiakós Kólpos
Corinthiacus Sinus see Korinthiakós Kólpos
Corinto 30 C3 Chinandega, NW Nicaragua
Cork 67 A6 Ir. Corcaigh. S Ireland
Çorlu 94 A2 Tekirdağ, NW Turkey
Corner Brook 17 G3 Newfoundland, Newfoundland and Labrador, E Canada
Corn Islands see Maíz, Islas del
Cornwallis Island 15 F2 island Nunavut, N Canada
Coro 36 C1 prev. Santa Ana de Coro. Falcón, NW Venezuela
Corocoro 39 F4 La Paz, W Bolivia
Coromandel 128 D2 Waikato, North Island, NZ
Coromandel Coast 110 D2 coast E India
Coromandel Peninsula 128 D2 peninsula North Island, NZ
Coronado, Bahía de 30 D5 bay S Costa Rica

Coronel Dorrego 43 C5 Buenos Aires, E Argentina
Coronel Oviedo 42 D2 Caaguazú, SE Paraguay
Corozal 30 C1 Corozal, N Belize
Corpus Christi 27 G4 Texas, SW USA
Corrales 26 D2 New Mexico, SW USA
Corrib, Lough 67 A5 Ir. Loch Coirib. Lake W Ireland
Corrientes 42 D3 Corrientes, NE Argentina
Corriza see Korçë
Corse 69 E7 Eng. Corsica. Island France, C Mediterranean Sea
Corsica see Corse
Corsicana 27 G3 Texas, SW USA
Cortegana 92 C4 Andalucía, S Spain
Cortés 31 E5 var. Ciudad Cortés. Puntarenas, SE Costa Rica
Cortina d'Ampezzo 74 C1 Veneto, NE Italy
Coruche 70 B3 Santarém, C Portugal
Çoruh Nehri 95 E3 Geor. Chorokhi, Rus. Chorokh. River Georgia/Turkey
Çorum 94 D3 var. Chorum. Çorum, N Turkey
Corunna see A Coruña
Corvallis 24 B3 Oregon, NW USA
Corvo 70 A5 var. Ilha do Corvo. Island Azores, Portugal, NE Atlantic Ocean
Cosenza 75 D6 anc. Consentia. Calabria, SW Italy
Cosne-Cours-sur-Loire 68 C4 var. Cosne-sur-Loire; anc. Condate. Nièvre, C France
Cosne-sur-Loire see Cosne-Cours-sur-Loire
Costa Mesa 24 D2 California, W USA
Costa Rica 31 E4 Country Central America
Cotagaita 39 F5 Potosí, S Bolivia
Côte d'Ivoire 52 D4 Eng. Ivory Coast, Republic of the Ivory Coast. Country W Africa
Côte d'Or 68 D4 cultural region C France
Cotonou 53 F5 var. Kotonu. S Benin
Cotrone see Crotone
Cotswold Hills 67 D6 var. Cotswolds. Hill range S England, UK
Cotswolds see Cotswold Hills
Cottbus 72 D4 prev. Kottbus. Brandenburg, E Germany
Council Bluffs 23 F4 Iowa, C USA
Courantyne River 37 G4 var. Corantijn Rivier, Corentyne River. River Guyana/Suriname
Courland Lagoon 84 A4 Ger. Kurisches Haff, Rus. Kurskiy Zaliv. Lagoon Lithuania/Russian Federation
Coutances 68 B3 anc. Constantia. Manche, N France
Couvin 65 C7 Namur, S Belgium
Coventry 67 D6 anc. Couentrey. C England, UK
Covilhã 70 C3 Castelo Branco, E Portugal
Cowan, Lake 125 B6 lake Western Australia
Coxen Hole see Roatán
Coxin Hole see Roatán
Coyhaique see Coihaique
Cozumel, Isla 29 H3 island SE Mexico
Cradock 56 C5 Eastern Cape, S South Africa
Craig 22 C4 Colorado, C USA
Craiova 86 B5 Dolj, SW Romania
Cranbrook 15 E5 British Columbia, SW Canada
Crane see The Crane
Crawley 67 E7 SE England, UK
Cremona 74 B2 Lombardia, N Italy
Cres 78 A3 It. Cherso; anc. Crexa. Island W Croatia
Crescent City 24 A4 California, W USA
Crescent Group 106 C7 island group C Paracel Islands
Creston 23 F4 Iowa, C USA
Crestview 20 D3 Florida, SE USA
Crete see Kríti
Créteil 68 E2 Val-de-Marne, N France
Crete, Sea of see Kritikó Pélagos
Creuse 68 B4 river C France
Crewe 67 D6 C England, UK
Crikvenica 78 A3 It. Cirquenizza; prev. Cirkvenica, Crjkvenica. Primorje-Gorski Kotar, NW Croatia
Crimea 59 F4 var. Krym, Eng. Crimea, Crimean Oblast; prev. Rus. Krymskaya ASSR, Krymskaya Oblast'. Admin. region province SE Ukraine
Crimean Oblast see Crimea
Cristóbal 31 G4 Colón, C Panama
Cristóbal Colón, Pico 36 B1 mountain N Colombia
Cristuru Secuiesc 86 C4 prev. Cristur, Cristuru Săcuiesc, Sitaş Cristuru, Ger. Kreutz, Hung. Székelykeresztúr, Szitás-Keresztúr. Harghita, C Romania
Crna Reka 79 D6 river S FYR Macedonia
Croatia 78 B3 Ger. Kroatien, SCr. Hrvatska. Country SE Europe
Crocodile see Limpopo
Croia see Krujë
Croker Island 124 E2 island Northern Territory, N Australia
Cromwell 129 B7 Otago, South Island, NZ
Crooked Island 32 D2 island SE Bahamas
Crooked Island Passage 32 D2 channel SE Bahamas
Crookston 23 F1 Minnesota, N USA
Croton see Crotone
Crotona see Crotone
Crotone 75 E6 var. Cotrone; anc. Croton, Crotona. Calabria, SW Italy
Croydon 67 A8 SE England, UK
Crozet Basin 119 B6 undersea feature S Indian Ocean
Crozet Islands 119 B7 island group French Southern and Antarctic Territories
Crozet Plateau 119 B7 var. Crozet Plateaus. Undersea feature SW Indian Ocean
Crozet Plateaus see Crozet Plateau
Crystal Brook 127 B6 South Australia
Csorna 77 C6 Győr-Moson-Sopron, NW Hungary
Csurgó 99 C7 Somogy, SW Hungary
Cuando 56 C2 var. Kwando. River S Africa
Cuango 56 B1 var. Kwango. River Angola/Dem. Rep. Congo see also Kwango
Cuan na Gaillimhe see Galway Bay
Cuanza 56 B1 var. Kwanza. River C Angola
Cuauhtémoc 28 C2 Chihuahua, N Mexico
Cuautla 29 E4 Morelos, S Mexico
Cuba 32 B2 Country W West Indies
Cubal 56 B2 Benguela, W Angola
Cubango 56 B2 var. Kavango, Kavengo, Kubango, Okavango, Okavanggo. River S Africa see also Okavango
Cubango 56 B2 var. Kuvango, Port. Vila Artur de Paiva, Vila da Ponte. Huíla, SW Angola
Cúcuta 36 C2 var. San José de Cúcuta. Norte de Santander, N Colombia
Cuddapah 110 C2 Andhra Pradesh, S India
Cuenca 71 E3 anc. Conca. Castilla-La Mancha, C Spain
Cuenca 38 B2 Azuay, S Ecuador
Cuernavaca 29 E4 Morelos, S Mexico
Cuiabá 41 E3 prev. Cuyabá. State capital Mato Grosso, SW Brazil
Cúige see Connaught
Cúige Laighean see Leinster
Cúige Mumhan see Munster
Cuijck 64 D4 Noord-Brabant, SE Netherlands
Cúil Raithin see Coleraine
Cuito 56 B2 var. Kwito. River SE Angola
Cukai 116 B3 var. Chukai, Kemaman. Terengganu, Peninsular Malaysia
Culiacán 28 C3 var. Culiacán Rosales, Culiacán-Rosales. Sinaloa, C Mexico
Culiacán-Rosales see Culiacán
Cullera 71 F3 País Valenciano, E Spain
Cullman 20 C2 Alabama, S USA
Culmsee see Chełmża
Culpepper Island see Darwin, Isla
Cumaná 37 E1 Sucre, NE Venezuela
Cumbal, Nevada de 36 A4 mountain SW Colombia
Cumberland 19 E4 Maryland, NE USA
Cumberland Plateau 20 D1 plateau E USA
Cumberland Sound 15 H3 inlet Baffin Island, Nunavut, NE Canada
Cumpas 28 B2 Sonora, NW Mexico
Cunene 47 C6 var. Kunene. River Angola/Namibia see also Kunene
Cunene 56 A3 province S Angola
Cuneo 74 A2 Fr. Coni. Piemonte, NW Italy
Cunnamulla 127 C5 Queensland, E Australia
Ćuprija 78 E4 Serbia, E Serbia and Montenegro (Yugo.)
Curaçao 33 E5 island Netherlands Antilles
Curicó 42 B4 Maule, C Chile
Curitiba 41 E4 prev. Curytiba. State capital Paraná, S Brazil
Curtea de Argeş 86 C4 var. Curtea-de-Arges. Argeş, S Romania
Curtea-de-Arges see Curtea de Argeş
Curtici 86 A4 Ger. Kurtitsch, Hung. Kürtös. Arad, W Romania
Curtis Island 126 E4 island Queensland, SE Australia
Cusco 39 E4 var. Cuzco. Cusco, C Peru
Cusset 69 C5 Allier, C France
Cutch, Gulf of see Kachchh, Gulf of
Cuttack 113 F4 Orissa, E India
Cuvier Plateau 119 E6 undersea feature E Indian Ocean
Cuxhaven 72 B2 Niedersachsen, NW Germany
Cuyuni, Río see Cuyuni River
Cuyuni River 37 F3 var. Río Cuyuni. River Guyana/Venezuela
Cuzco see Cusco
Cyclades see Kykládes
Cydonia see Chaniá
Cymru see Wales
Cyprus 80 C4 Gk. Kypros, Turk. Kıbrıs, Kıbrıs Cumhuriyeti. Country E Mediterranean Sea
Cythera see Kýthira
Cythnos see Kýthnos
Czech Republic 77 A5 Cz. Česká Republika. Country C Europe
Częstochowa 76 C4 Ger. Czenstochau, Tschenstochau, Rus. Chenstokhov. Śląskie, S Poland
Człuchów 76 C3 Ger. Schlochau. Pomorskie, N Poland

D

Dabajuro 36 C1 Falcón, NW Venezuela
Dabeiba 36 B2 Antioquia, NW Colombia
Dąbrowa Tarnowska 77 D5 Małopolskie, S Poland
Dabryn' 85 C8 Rus. Dobryn'. Homyel'skaya Voblasts', SE Belarus
Dagana 52 B3 N Senegal
Dagda 84 D4 Krāslava, SE Latvia
Dagenham 67 B8 SE England, UK
Dağliq Qarabağ see Nagorno-Karabakh
Dagupan 117 E1 off. Dagupan City. Luzon, N Philippines
Da Hinggan Ling 105 G1 Eng. Great Khingan Range. Mountain range NE China
Dahm, Ramlat 99 B6 desert NW Yemen
Daimiel 70 D3 Castilla-La Mancha, C Spain
Daimoniá 83 B7 Pelopónnisos, S Greece
Dairen see Dalian
Dakar 52 B3 country capital (Senegal) W Senegal
Dakhla see Ad Dakhla
Dakoro 53 G3 Maradi, S Niger
Đakovica 79 D5 var. Djakovica, Alb. Gjakovë. Serbia, S Serbia and Montenegro (Yugo.)
Đakovo 78 C3 var. Djakovo, Hung. Diakovár. Osijek-Baranja, E Croatia
Dalai see Hulun Nur
Dalain Hob see Ejin Qi
Dalaman 94 A4 Muğla, SW Turkey
Dalandzadgad 105 E3 Ömnögovĭ, S Mongolia
Đa Lat 115 E6 Lâm Đông, S Vietnam
Dalby 127 D5 Queensland, E Australia
Dale City 19 E4 Virginia, NE USA
Dalhart 27 E1 Texas, SW USA
Dali 106 A6 var. Xiaguan. Yunnan, SW China
Dalian 106 D4 var. Dairen, Dalien, Lüda, Ta-lien, Rus. Dalny. Liaoning, NE China
Dalien see Dalian
Dallas 27 G2 Texas, SW USA
Dalmacija 78 B4 Eng. Dalmatia, Ger. Dalmatien, It. Dalmazia. Cultural region S Croatia
Dalny see Dalian
Dalton 20 D1 Georgia, SE USA
Daly Waters 126 A2 Northern Territory, N Australia
Damachava 85 A6 var. Damachova, Pol. Domaczewo, Rus. Domachëvo. Brestskaya Voblasts', SW Belarus
Damachova see Damachava
Damān 112 C4 Damān and Diu, W India
Damara 54 C4 Ombella-Mpoko, S Central African Republic
Damas see Dimashq
Damasco see Dimashq
Damascus see Dimashq
Damāvand, Qolleh-ye 98 D3 mountain N Iran
Dammām see Ad Dammān
Damoûr 97 A5 var. Ad Dāmūr. W Lebanon
Dampier 124 A4 Western Australia
Dampier, Selat 117 F4 strait Papua, E Indonesia
Damqawt 99 D6 var. Damqut. E Yemen
Damqut see Damqawt
Damxung 104 C5 Xizang Zizhiqu, W China
Danakil Desert 50 D4 var. Afar Depression, Danakil Plain. Desert E Africa
Danakil Plain see Danakil Desert
Danané 52 D5 W Côte d'Ivoire
Đa Năng 115 E5 prev. Tourane. Quang Nam-Đa Năng, C Vietnam
Danborg see Daneborg
Dandong 106 D3 var. Tan-tung; prev. An-tung. Liaoning, NE China
Daneborg 61 E3 var. Danborg. N Greenland
Dänew see Deynau
Dangerous Archipelago see Tuamotu, Îles
Danghara 101 E3 Rus. Dangara. SW Tajikistan
Danghe Nanshan 104 D3 mountain range W China
Dangla see Tanggula Shan
Dângrêk, Chuŏr Phnum 115 D5 var. Phanom Dang Raek, Phanom Dong Rak, Fr. Chaîne des Dangrek. Mountain range Cambodia/Thailand
Dangriga 30 C1 prev. Stann Creek. Stann Creek, E Belize
Danish West Indies see Virgin Islands (US)
Danlí 30 D2 El Paraíso, S Honduras
Danmarksstraedet see Denmark Strait
Dannenberg 72 C3 Niedersachsen, N Germany
Dannevirke 128 D4 Manawatu-Wanganui, North Island, NZ
Danube 59 E4 Bul. Dunav, Cz. Dunaj, Ger. Donau, Hung. Duna, Rom. Dunărea. River C Europe
Danville 19 E5 Virginia, NE USA
Dan Xian see Danzhou
Danxian/Dan Xian see Danzhou
Danzhou 106 C7 prev. Dan Xian, Danxian, Nada. Hainan, S China
Danziger Bucht see Danzig, Gulf of
Danzig, Gulf of 76 C2 var. Gulf of Danzig, Ger. Danziger Bucht, Pol. Zakota Pomorskiea, Rus. Gdan'skaya Bukhta. Gulf N Poland
Daqm see Duqm
Dar'ā 97 B5 var. Der'a, Fr. Déraa. Dar'ā, SW Syria
Darabani 86 C3 Botoşani, NW Romania
Daraut-Kurgan see Daroot-Korgon
Dardanelli see Çanakkale
Dar es Salaam 51 C7 Dar es Salaam, E Tanzania
Darfield 129 C6 Canterbury, South Island, NZ
Darfur 50 A4 var. Darfur Massif. Cultural region W Sudan
Darfur Massif see Darfur
Darhan 105 E2 Selenge, N Mongolia
Darien, Gulf of 36 A2 Sp. Golfo del Darién. Gulf S Caribbean Sea
Darién, Serranía del 31 H5 mountain range Colombia/Panama
Dario see Ciudad Darío
Darjeeling see Darjiling
Darjiling 113 F3 prev. Darjeeling. West Bengal, NE India
Darling River 127 C6 river New South Wales, SE Australia
Darlington 67 D5 N England, UK
Darmstadt 73 B5 Hessen, SW Germany
Darnah 49 G2 var. Dérna. NE Libya
Darnley, Cape 132 D2 headland Antarctica
Daroca 71 E2 Aragón, NE Spain
Daroot-Korgon 101 F3 var. Daraut-Kurgan. Oshskaya Oblast', SW Kyrgyzstan
Dartford 67 B8 SE England, UK
Dartmoor 67 C7 moorland SW England, UK
Dartmouth 17 F4 Nova Scotia, SE Canada
Darvaza see Derweze
Darwaza see Derweze
Darwin 124 D2 prev. Palmerston, Port Darwin. Territory capital Northern Territory, N Australia
Darwin, Isla 38 A4 var. Culpepper Island. Island W Ecuador
Daryācheh-ye Hāmūn see Şāberī, Hāmūn-e
Daryācheh-ye Sīstān see Şāberī, Hāmūn-e
Daryā-ye Morghāb see Murgab
Daryā-ye Pāmīr see Pamir
Daryoi Pomir see Pamir
Dashhowuz see Daşoguz
Dashkawka 85 D6 Rus. Dashkovka. Mahilyowskaya Voblasts', E Belarus
Dashkhovuz see Daşoguz
Daşoguz 100 C2 var. Dashhowuz, Dashkhovuz; prev. Tashauz. Dashkhovuzskiy Velayat, N Turkmenistan
Datong 106 C3 var. Tatung, Ta-t'ung. Shanxi, C China
Daugavpils 84 D4 Ger. Dünaburg; prev. Rus. Dvinsk. Municipality Daugvapils, SE Latvia
Daung Kyun 115 B6 island S Myanmar
Dauphiné 69 D5 cultural region E France
Dāvangere 110 C2 Karnātaka, W India
Davao 117 F3 off. Davao City. Mindanao, S Philippines
Davao Gulf 117 F3 gulf Mindanao, S Philippines
Davenport 23 G3 Iowa, C USA
David 31 E5 Chiriquí, W Panama
Davie Ridge 119 A5 undersea feature W Indian Ocean
Davis 132 D3 Australian research station Antarctica
Davis Sea 132 D3 sea Antarctica
Davis Strait 60 B3 strait Baffin Bay/Labrador Sea
Dawei see Tavoy
Dax 69 B6 var. Ax; anc. Aquae Augustae, Aquae Tarbelicae. Landes, SW France
Dayr az Zawr 96 D3 var. Deir ez Zor. Dayr az Zawr, E Syria
Dayton 18 C4 Ohio, N USA
Daytona Beach 21 E4 Florida, SE USA
De Aar 56 C5 Northern Cape, C South Africa
Dead Sea 97 B6 var. Bahret Lut, Lacus Asphaltites, Ar. Al Baḩr al Mayyit, Baḩrat Lūt, Heb. Yam HaMelaḥ. Salt lake Israel/Jordan
Deán Funes 42 C3 Córdoba, C Argentina
Death Valley 25 C7 valley California, W USA
Deatnu 62 D2 Fin. Tenojoki, Nor. Tana. River Finland/Norway see also Tenojoki
Debar 79 D6 Ger. Dibra, Turk. Debre. W FYR Macedonia
Debica 77 D5 Podkarpackie, SE Poland
De Bildt see De Bilt
De Bilt 64 C3 var. De Bildt. Utrecht, C Netherlands
Dębno 76 B3 Zachodniopomorskie, NW Poland
Debrecen 77 D6 Ger. Debreczin, Rom. Debreţin; prev. Debreczen. Hajdú-Bihar, E Hungary
Decatur 20 C1 Alabama, S USA
Decatur 18 B4 Illinois, N USA
Deccan 112 D5 Hind. Dakshin. Plateau C India
Děčín 76 B4 Ger. Tetschen. Ústecký Kraj, NW Czech Republic
Dedeagaç see Alexandroúpoli
Dedeagach see Alexandroúpoli
Dedemsvaart 64 E3 Overijssel, E Netherlands
Dee 66 C3 river NE Scotland, UK
Deering 14 C2 Alaska, USA
Deggendorf 73 D6 Bayern, SE Germany
Değirmenlik 80 C5 N Cyprus
Deh Bīd 98 D3 Fārs, C Iran
Dehli see Delhi
Deh Shū 100 D5 var. Deshu. Helmand, S Afghanistan
Deinze 65 B5 Oost-Vlaanderen, NW Belgium
Deir ez Zor see Dayr az Zawr
Deirgeirt, Loch see Derg, Lough
Dej 86 B3 Hung. Dés; prev. Deés. Cluj, NW Romania
Dékoa 54 C4 Kémo, 163C Central African Republic
De Land 21 E4 Florida, SE USA
Delano 25 C7 California, W USA
Delārām 100 D5 Farāh, SW Afghanistan
Delaware 19 F4 off. State of Delaware; also known as Blue Hen State, Diamond State, First State. State NE USA
Delaware 18 D4 Ohio, N USA
Delft 64 B4 Zuid-Holland, W Netherlands
Delfzijl 64 E1 Groningen, NE Netherlands
Delgo 50 B3 Northern, N Sudan
Delhi 112 D3 var. Dehli, Hind. Dilli; hist. Shahjahanabad. Delhi, N India
Delicias 28 D2 var. Ciudad Delicias. Chihuahua, N Mexico
Déli-Kárpátok see Carpaţii Meridionali
Delmenhorst 72 B3 Niedersachsen, NW Germany
Del Rio 27 F4 Texas, SW USA
Deltona 21 E4 Florida, SE USA
Demba 55 D6 Kasai Occidental, C Dem. Rep. Congo
Dembia 54 D4 Mbomou, SE Central African Republic
Demchok var. Dêmqog. Disputed region China/India see also Dêmqog
Demchok 104 A4 var. Dêmqog. China/India see also Dêmqog
Demerara Plain 34 C2 undersea feature W Atlantic Ocean
Deming 26 C3 New Mexico, SW USA
Demmin 72 C2 Mecklenburg-Vorpommern, NE Germany
Demopolis 20 C2 Alabama, S USA
Dêmqog var. Demchok. Disputed region China/India see also Demchok
Denali see McKinley, Mount
Denau see Denov
Dender 65 B6 Fr. Dendre. River W Belgium
Denekamp 64 E3 Overijssel, E Netherlands
Den Haag see 's-Gravenhage
Den Ham 64 E3 Overijssel, E Netherlands
Denham 125 A5 Western Australia
Den Helder 64 C2 Noord-Holland, NW Netherlands
Dénia 71 F4 País Valenciano, E Spain
Deniliquin 127 C7 New South Wales, SE Australia
Denison 23 F3 Iowa, C USA
Denison 27 G2 Texas, SW USA
Denizli 94 B4 Denizli, SW Turkey
Denmark 63 A7 Dan. Danmark; anc. Hafnia. Country N Europe
Denmark Strait 60 D4 var. Danmarksstraedet. Strait Greenland/Iceland
Dennery 33 F1 E Saint Lucia
Denov 101 E3 var. Denow, Rus. Denau. Surkhondaryo Wiloyati, S Uzbekistan
Denow see Denov
Denpasar 116 D5 prev. Paloe. Bali, C Indonesia
Denton 27 G2 Texas, SW USA
D'Entrecasteaux Islands 122 B3 island group SE PNG
Denver 22 D4 state capital Colorado, C USA
Der'a see Dar'ā
Déraa see Dar'ā
Dera Ghāzi Khān 112 C2 var. Dera Ghāzikhān. Punjab, C Pakistan
Dera Ghāzikhān see Dera Ghāzi Khān
Đeravica 79 D5 mountain S Serbia and Montenegro (Yugo.)
Derbent 89 B8 Respublika Dagestan, SW Russian Federation
Derby 67 D6 C England, UK
Dereli see Gónnoi
Derg, Lough 67 A6 Ir. Loch Deirgeirt. Lake W Ireland
Derhachi 87 G2 Rus. Dergachi. Kharkivs'ka Oblast', E Ukraine
De Ridder 20 A3 Louisiana, S USA
Dérna see Darnah
Derry see Londonderry
Derventa 78 B3 Republika Srpska, N Bosnia and Herzegovina
Derweze 100 C2 var. Darvaza, Darwaza. Akhalskiy Velayat, C Turkmenistan'
Deschutes River 24 B3 river Oregon, NW USA
Desē 50 C4 var. Desse, It. Dessie. N Ethiopia
Deseado, Río 43 B7 river S Argentina
Desertas, Ilhas 48 A2 island group Madeira, Portugal, NE Atlantic Ocean
Deshu see Deh Shū
Desierto de Altar see Sonoran Desert
Des Moines 23 F3 state capital Iowa, C USA
Desna 87 E2 river Russian Federation/Ukraine
Dessau 72 C4 Sachsen-Anhalt, E Germany
Desse see Desē
Dessie see Desē
Detroit 18 D3 Michigan, N USA
Detroit Lakes 23 F2 Minnesota, N USA
Deurne 65 D5 Noord-Brabant, SE Netherlands
Deva 86 B4 Ger. Diemrich, Hung. Déva. Hunedoara, W Romania
Đevđelija see Gevgelija
Deventer 64 D3 Overijssel, E Netherlands
Devils Lake 23 E1 North Dakota, N USA
Devoll see Devollit, Lumi i
Devollit, Lumi i 79 D6 var. Devoll. River SE Albania
Devon Island 15 F2 prev. North Devon Island. Island Parry Islands, Nunavut, NE Canada
Devonport 127 C8 Tasmania, SE Australia
Devrek 94 C2 Zonguldak, N Turkey
Dexter 23 H5 Missouri, C USA
Deynau 100 D3 var. Dyanev, Turkm. Dänew. Lebapskiy Velayat, NE Turkmenistan
Dezfūl 98 C3 var. Dizful. Khūzestān, SW Iran
Dezhou 106 D4 Shandong, E China
Dhaka 113 G4 prev. Dacca. Country capital (Bangladesh) Dhaka, C Bangladesh
Dhanbād 113 F4 Bihār, NE India
Dhekélia 80 C5 Eng. Dhekelia. Gk. Dekéleia. UK air base SE Cyprus
Dhidhimótikhon see Didymóteicho
Dhíkti Ori see Díkti
Dhodhekánisos see Dodekánisos
Dhomokós see Domokós
Dhráma see Dráma
Dhrepanon, Akrotírio see Drépano Akrotírio
Dhuusa Marreeb 51 E5 var. Dusa Marreb, It. Dusa Mareb. Galguduud, C Somalia
Diakovár see Đakovo
Diamantina, Chapada 41 F3 mountain range E Brazil
Diamantina Fracture Zone 119 E6 tectonic feature E Indian Ocean
Diarbekr see Diyarbakır
Dibrugarh 113 H3 Assam, NE India
Dickinson 22 D2 North Dakota, N USA
Didimotiho see Didymóteicho
Didymóteicho 82 D3 var. Dhidhimótikhon, Didimotiho. Anatolikí Makedonía kai Thráki, NE Greece
Diégo-Suarez see Antsirañana
Diekirch 65 D7 Diekirch, C Luxembourg
Điên Biên 114 D3 var. Bien Bien, Dien Bien Phu. Lai Châu, N Vietnam
Dien Bien Phu see Điên Biên
Diepenbeek 65 D6 Limburg, NE Belgium
Diepholz 72 B3 Niedersachsen, NW Germany
Dieppe 68 C2 Seine-Maritime, N France
Dieren 64 D4 Gelderland, E Netherlands
Differdange 65 D8 Luxembourg, SW Luxembourg
Digne 69 D6 var. Digne-les-Bains. Alpes-de-Haute-Provence, SE France
Digne-les-Bains see Digne
Digoin 68 C4 Saône-et-Loire, C France
Digul, Sungai 117 H5 prev. Digoel. River Papua, E Indonesia
Dihang see Brahmaputra
Dijon 68 D4 anc. Dibio. Côte d'Or, C France
Dikhil 50 D4 SW Djibouti
Dikson 92 D2 Taymyrskiy (Dolgano-Nenetskiy) Avtonomnyy Okrug, N Russian Federation

Díkti *83 D8 var.* Dhíkti Ori. *Mountain range* Kríti, Greece, E Mediterranean Sea
Dili *117 F5 var.* Dilli, Dilly. *Country capital* (East Timor), N East Timor
Dilia *53 G3 var.* Dillia. *River* SE Niger
Di Linh *115 E6* Lâm Đông, S Vietnam
Dilli *see* Delhi
Dilli *see* Dili
Dillia *see* Dilia
Dilling *50 B4 var.* Ad Dalanj. Southern Kordofan, C Sudan
Dillon *22 B2* Montana, NW USA
Dilly *see* Dili
Dilolo *55 D7* Ngounié, S Gabon
Dimashq *97 B5 var.* Ash Shām, Esh Sham, *Eng.* Damascus, *Fr.* Damas, *It.* Damasco. *Country capital* (Syria) Dimashq, SW Syria
Dimitrovgrad *82 D3* Khaskovo, S Bulgaria
Dimitrovgrad *89 C6* Ul'yanovskaya Oblast', W Russian Federation
Dimovo *82 B1* Vidin, NW Bulgaria
Dinajpur *113 F3* Rajshahi, NW Bangladesh
Dinan *68 B3* Côtes d'Armor, NW France
Dinant *65 C7* Namur, S Belgium
Dinar *94 B4* Afyon, SW Turkey
Dinara *see* Dinaric Alps
Dinaric Alps *78 C4 var.* Dinara. *Mountain range* Bosnia and Herzegovina/Croatia
Dindigul *110 C3* Tamil Nādu, SE India
Dingle Bay *67 A6 Ir.* Bá an Daingin. *Bay* SW Ireland
Dinguiraye *52 C4* Haute-Guinée, N Guinea
Diourbel *52 B3* W Senegal
Dirē Dawa *51 D5* E Ethiopia
Dirk Hartog Island *125 A5 island* Western Australia
Disappointment, Lake *124 C4 salt lake* Western Australia
Dispur *113 G3* Assam, NE India
Divinópolis *41 F4* Minas Gerais, SE Brazil
Divo *52 D5* S Côte d'Ivoire
Diyarbakır *95 E4 var.* Diarbekr; *anc.* Amida. Dıyarbakır, SE Turkey
Dizful *see* Dezfūl
Djajapura *see* Jayapura
Djakovica *see* Đakovica
Djakovo *see* Đakovo
Djambala *55 B6* Plateaux, C Congo
Djambi *see* Jambi
Djanet *49 E4 prev.* Fort Charlet. SE Algeria
Djéblé *see* Jablah
Djelfa *48 D2 var.* El Djelfa. N Algeria
Djéma *54 D4* Haut-Mbomou, E Central African Republic
Djérablous *see* Jarābulus
Djerba *see* Jerba, Île de
Djérem *54 B4 river* C Cameroon
Djevdjelija *see* Gevgelija
Djibouti *50 D4 var.* Jibuti; *prev.* French Somaliland, French Territory of the Afars and Issas, *Fr.* Côte Française des Somalis, Territoire Français des Afars et des Issas. *Country* E Africa
Djibouti *50 D4 var.* Jibuti. *Country capital* (Djibouti) E Djibouti
Djourab, Erg du *54 C2 dunes* N Chad
Djúpivogur *61 E5* Austurland, SE Iceland
Dnieper *59 F4 Bel.* Dnyapro, *Rus.* Dnepr, *Ukr.* Dnipro. *River* E Europe
Dnieper Lowland *87 E2 Bel.* Prydnyaprowskaya Nizina, *Ukr.* Prydniprovs'ka Nyzovyna. *Lowlands* Belarus/Ukraine
Dniester *59 E4 Rom.* Nistru, *Rus.* Dnestr, *Ukr.* Dnister; *anc.* Tyras. *River* Moldova/Ukraine
Dnipro *see* Dnieper
Dniprodzerzhyns'k *87 F3 Rus.* Dneprodzerzhinsk; *prev.* Kamenskoye. Dnipropetrovs'ka Oblast', E Ukraine
Dniprodzerzhyns'ke Vodoskhovyshche *87 F3 Rus.* Dneprodzerzhinskoye Vodokhranilishche. *Reservoir* C Ukraine
Dnipropetrovs'k *87 F3 Rus.* Dnepropetrovsk; *prev.* Yekaterinoslav. Dnipropetrovs'ka Oblast', E Ukraine
Dniprorudne *87 F3 Rus.* Dneprorudnoye. Zaporiz'ka Oblast', SE Ukraine
Doba *54 C4* Logone-Oriental, S Chad
Döbeln *72 D4* Sachsen, E Germany
Doberai, Jazirah *117 G4 Dut.* Vogelkop. *Peninsula* Papua, E Indonesia
Doboj *78 C3* Republika Srpska, N Bosnia and Herzegovina
Dobre Miasto *76 D2 Ger.* Guttstadt. Warmińsko-Mazurskie, NE Poland
Dobrich *82 E1 Rom.* Bazargic; *prev.* Tolbukhin. Dobrich, NE Bulgaria
Dobrush *85 D7* Homyel'skaya Voblasts', SE Belarus
Dodecánese *see* Dodekánisos
Dodekánisos *83 D6 var.* Nóties Sporádes, *Eng.* Dodecanese; *prev.* Dhodhekánisos. *Island group* SE Greece
Dodge City *23 E5* Kansas, C USA
Dodoma *47 D5 country capital* (Tanzania) Dodoma, C Tanzania
Dodoma *51 C7 region* C Tanzania
Dogana *74 E1* NE San Marino
Dōgo *109 B6 island* Oki-shotō, SW Japan
Dogondoutchi *53 F3* Dosso, SW Niger
Doğubayazıt *95 F3* Ağrı, E Turkey
Doğu Karadeniz Dağları *95 E3 var.* Anadolu Dağları. *Mountain range* NE Turkey
Doha *see* Ad Dawḩah
Doire *see* Londonderry
Dokkum *64 D1* Friesland, N Netherlands
Dokuchayevs'k *87 G3 var.* Dokuchayevsk. Donets'ka Oblast', SE Ukraine
Dokuchayevsk *see* Dokuchayevs'k
Doldrums Fracture Zone *44 C4 tectonic feature* W Atlantic Ocean
Dôle *68 D4* Jura, E France
Dolisie *55 B6 prev.* Loubomo. Le Niari, S Congo
Dolomites *see* Dolomitiche, Alpi
Dolomiti *see* Dolomitiche, Alpi
Dolomitiche, Alpi *74 C1 var.* Dolomiti, *Eng.* Dolomites. *Mountain range* NE Italy
Dolores *42 D4* Buenos Aires, E Argentina
Dolores *30 B1* Petén, N Guatemala
Dolores *42 D4* Soriano, SW Uruguay
Dolores Hidalgo *29 E4 var.* Ciudad de Dolores Hidalgo. Guanajuato, C Mexico
Dolyna *86 B2 Rus.* Dolina. Ivano-Frankivs'ka Oblast', W Ukraine
Dolyns'ka *87 F3 Rus.* Dolinskaya. Kirovohrads'ka Oblast', S Ukraine
Domachëvo *see* Damachava
Domaczewo *see* Damachava
Dombås *63 B5* Oppland, S Norway
Domel Island *see* Letsôk-aw Kyun
Domeyko *42 B3* Atacama, N Chile
Dominica *33 H4 Country* E West Indies
Dominica Channel *see* Martinique Passage
Dominican Republic *33 E2 country* C West Indies
Domokós *83 B5 var.* Dhomokós. Stereá Ellás, C Greece
Don *89 B6 var.* Duna, Tanais. *River* SW Russian Federation
Donau *see* Danube
Donauwörth *73 C6* Bayern, S Germany
Don Benito *70 C3* Extremadura, W Spain
Doncaster *67 D5 anc.* Danum. N England, UK
Dondo *56 B1* Cuanza Norte, NW Angola
Donegal *67 B5 Ir.* Dún na nGall. NW Ireland
Donegal Bay *67 A5 Ir.* Bá Dhún na nGall. *Bay* NW Ireland
Donets *87 G2 var.* Sivers'kyy Donets', *Rus.* Severskiy Donets. Serra Acaraí. *river* Russian Federation/Ukraine
Donets'k *87 G3 Rus.* Donetsk; *prev.* Stalino. Donets'ka Oblast', E Ukraine
Dongfang *106 B7 var.* Basuo. Hainan, S China
Dongguan *106 C6* Guangdong, S China
Đông Ha *114 E4* Quang Tri, C Vietnam
Đông Hoi *114 D4* Quang Binh, C Vietnam
Dongliao *see* Liaoyuan
Dongola *50 B3 var.* Donqola, Dunqulah. Northern, N Sudan
Dongou *55 C5* La Likouala, NE Congo
Dongting Hu *106 C5 var.* Tung-t'ing Hu. *Lake* S China
Donji Vakuf *var.* Srbobran, Federacija Bosna I Hercegovina, N Serbia and Montenegro (Yugo.)
Donostia-San Sebastián *71 E1* País Vasco, N Spain
Donqola *see* Dongola
Doolow *51 D5* E Ethiopia
Doornik *see* Tournai
Door Peninsula *18 C2 peninsula* Wisconsin, N USA
Dooxo Nugaaleed *51 E5 var.* Nogal Valley. *Valley* E Somalia
Dordogne *69 B5 cultural region* SW France
Dordogne *69 B5 river* W France
Dordrecht *64 C4 var.* Dordt, Dort. Zuid-Holland, SW Netherlands
Dordt *see* Dordrecht
Dorohoi *86 C3* Botoşani, NE Romania
Dorotea *62 C4* Västerbotten, N Sweden
Dorre Island *125 A5 island* Western Australia
Dort *see* Dordrecht
Dortmund *72 A4* Nordrhein-Westfalen, W Germany
Dos Hermanas *70 C4* Andalucía, S Spain
Dospad Dagh *see* Rhodope Mountains
Dospat *82 C3* Smolyan, S Bulgaria
Dothan *20 D3* Alabama, S USA
Dotnuva *84 B4* Kėdainiai, C Lithuania
Douai *68 C2 prev.* Douay, *anc.* Duacum. Nord, N France
Douala *55 A5 var.* Duala. Littoral, W Cameroon
Douglas *67 C5 dependent territory capital* (Isle of Man) E Isle of Man
Douglas *26 C3* Arizona, SW USA
Douglas *22 D3* Wyoming, C USA
Douro *70 B2 Sp.* Duero. *River* Portugal/Spain *see also* Duero
Dover *67 E7 Fr.* Douvres; *Lat.* Dubris Portus. SE England, UK
Dover *19 F4 state capital* Delaware, NE USA
Dover, Strait of *68 C2 var.* Straits of Dover, *Fr.* Pas de Calais. *Strait* England, UK/France
Dover, Straits of *see* Dover, Strait of
Dovrefjell *63 B5 plateau* S Norway
Downpatrick *67 B5 Ir.* Dún Pádraig. SE Northern Ireland, UK
Dōzen *109 B6 island* Oki-shotō, SW Japan
Drač *see* Durrës
Drachten *64 D2* Friesland, N Netherlands
Drăgăşani *86 B5* Vâlcea, SW Romania
Dragoman *82 B2* Sofiya, W Bulgaria
Dra, Hamada du *48 C3 var.* Hammada du Drâa, Haut Plateau du Dra. *Plateau* W Algeria
Drahichyn *85 B6 Pol.* Drohiczyn Poleski, *Rus.* Drogichin. Brestskaya Voblasts', SW Belarus
Drakensberg *56 D5 mountain range* Lesotho/South Africa
Drake Passage *35 B8 passage* Atlantic Ocean/Pacific Ocean
Dralfa *82 D2* Tŭrgovishte, N Bulgaria
Dráma *82 C3 var.* Dhráma. Anatolikí Makedonía kai Thráki, NE Greece
Drammen *63 B6* Buskerud, S Norway
Drau *see* Drava
Drava *78 C3 var.* Drau, *Eng.* Drave, *Hung.* Dráva. *River* C Europe *see also* Drau
Dráva *see* Drava
Drave *see* Drava
Drawsko Pomorskie *76 B3 Ger.* Dramburg. Zachodniopomorskie, NW Poland
Drépano, Akrotírio *82 C4 var.* Akra Dhrepanon. *Headland* N Greece
Dresden *72 D4* Sachsen, E Germany
Drin *see* Drinit, Lumi i
Drina *78 C3 river* Bosnia and Herzegovina/Serbia and Montenegro (Yugo.)
Drinit, Lumi i *79 D5 var.* Drin. *River* NW Albania
Drobeta-Turnu Severin *86 B5 prev.* Turnu Severin. Mehedinţi, SW Romania
Drogheda *67 B5 Ir.* Droichead Átha. NE Ireland
Drohobych *86 B2 Pol.* Drohobycz, *Rus.* Drogobych. L'vivs'ka Oblast', NW Ukraine
Droichead Átha *see* Drogheda
Drôme *69 D5 cultural region* SE France
Dronning Maud Land *132 B2 physical region* Antarctica
Drummondville *17 E4* Québec, SE Canada
Druskininkai *85 B5 Pol.* Druskienniki. Druskininkai, S Lithuania
Dryden *16 B3* Ontario, C Canada
Drysa *85 D5 Rus.* Drissa. *River* N Belarus
Duala *see* Douala
Dubai *see* Dubayy
Dubăsari *86 D3 Rus.* Dubossary. NE Moldova
Dubawnt *15 F4 river* Northwest Territories/Nunavut, NW Canada
Dubayy *98 D4 Eng.* Dubai. Dubayy, NE UAE
Dubbo *127 D6* New South Wales, SE Australia
Dublin *67 B5 Ir.* Baile Átha Cliath; *anc.* Eblana. *Country capital* (Ireland), E Ireland
Dublin *21 E2* Georgia, SE USA
Dubno *86 C2* Rivnens'ka Oblast', NW Ukraine
Dubrovnik *79 B5 It.* Ragusa. Dubrovnik-Neretva, SE Croatia
Dubuque *23 G3* Iowa, C USA
Dudelange *65 D8 var.* Forge du Sud, *Ger.* Dudelingen. Luxembourg, S Luxembourg
Dudelingen *see* Dudelange
Duero *70 D2 Port.* Douro. *River* Portugal/Spain *see also* Douro
Duesseldorf *see* Düsseldorf
Duffel *65 C5* Antwerpen, C Belgium
Dugi Otok *78 A4 var.* Isola Grossa, *It.* Isola Lunga. *Island* W Croatia
Duisburg *72 A4 prev.* Duisburg-Hamborn. Nordrhein-Westfalen, W Germany
Duiven *64 D4* Gelderland, E Netherlands
Duk Faiwil *51 B5* Jonglei, SE Sudan
Dulan *104 D4 var.* Qagan Us. Qinghai, C China
Dulce, Golfo *31 E5 gulf* S Costa Rica
Dülmen *72 A4* Nordrhein-Westfalen, W Germany
Dulovo *82 E1* Silistra, NE Bulgaria
Duluth *23 G2* Minnesota, N USA
Dūmā *97 B5 Fr.* Douma. Dimashq, SW Syria
Dumas *27 E1* Texas, SW USA
Dumfries *66 C4* S Scotland, UK
Dumont d'Urville *132 C4 French research station* Antarctica
Dumyât *50 B1 Eng.* Damietta. N Egypt
Duna *see* Danube
Duna *see* Don
Dunaj *see* Danube
Dunaújváros *77 C7 prev.* Dunapentele, Sztálinváros. Fejér, C Hungary
Dunav *see* Danube
Dunavska Ravnina *82 C2 Eng.* Danubian Plain. *Plain* N Bulgaria
Duncan *27 G2* Oklahoma, C USA
Dundalk *67 B5 Ir.* Dún Dealgan. NE Ireland
Dún Dealgan *see* Dundalk
Dundee *66 C4* E Scotland, UK
Dundee *56 D4* KwaZulu/Natal, E South Africa
Dunedin *129 B7* Otago, South Island, NZ
Dunfermline *66 C4* C Scotland, UK
Dungu *55 E5* Orientale, NE Dem. Rep. Congo
Dungun *116 B3 var.* Kuala Dungun. Terengganu, Peninsular Malaysia
Dunkerque *68 C2 Eng.* Dunkirk, *Flem.* Duinekerke; *prev.* Dunquerque. Nord, N France
Dún Laoghaire *67 B6 Eng.* Dunleary; *prev.* Kingstown. E Ireland
Dún na nGall *see* Donegal
Dún Pádraig *see* Downpatrick
Dunqulah *see* Dongola
Dunărea *see* Danube
Dupnitsa *82 C2 prev.* Marek, Stanke Dimitrov. Kyustendil, W Bulgaria
Duqm *99 E5 var.* Daqm. E Oman
Durance *69 D6 river* SE France
Durango *28 D3 var.* Victoria de Durango. Durango, W Mexico
Durango *22 C5* Colorado, C USA
Durankulak *82 E1 Rom.* Răcari; *prev.* Blatnitsa, Duranulac. Dobrich, NE Bulgaria
Durant *27 G2* Oklahoma, C USA
Durazzo *see* Durrës
Durban *56 D4 var.* Port Natal. KwaZulu/Natal, E South Africa
Durbe *84 B3 Ger.* Durben. Liepāja, W Latvia
Durg *113 E4 prev.* Drug. Madhya Pradesh, C India
Durham *67 D5 hist.* Dunholme. N England, UK
Durham *21 F1* North Carolina, SE USA
Durostorum *see* Silistra
Durrës *79 C6 var.* Durrësi, Dursi, *It.* Durazzo, *SCr.* Drač, *Turk.* Draç. Durrës, W Albania
Durrësi *see* Durrës
Dursi *see* Durrës
Durūz, Jabal ad *97 C5 mountain* SW Syria
D'Urville Island *128 C4 island* C NZ
Dusa Mareb *see* Dhuusa Marreeb
Dusa Marreb *see* Dhuusa Marreeb
Dushanbe *101 E3 var.* Dyushambe; *prev.* Stalinabad, *Taj.* Stalinobod. *Country capital* (Tajikistan) W Tajikistan
Düsseldorf *72 A4 var.* Duesseldorf. Nordrhein-Westfalen, W Germany
Dŭstí *101 E3 Rus.* Dusti. SW Tajikistan
Dutch Harbor *14 B3* Unalaska Island, Alaska, USA
Dutch New Guinea *see* Papua
Duzdab *see* Zāhedān
Dvina *see* Severnaya Dvina
Dvina Bay *see* Chëshskaya Guba
Dyanev *see* Deynau
Dyersburg *20 C1* Tennessee, S USA
Dyushambe *see* Dushanbe
Dza Chu *see* Mekong
Dzerzhinsk *89 C5* Nizhegorodskaya Oblast', W Russian Federation
Dzhalal-Abad *101 F2 Kir.* Jalal-Abad. Dzhalal-Abadskaya Oblast', W Kyrgyzstan
Dzhambul *see* Taraz
Dzhankoy *87 F4* Respublika Krym, S Ukraine
Dzhelandy *101 F3* SE Tajikistan
Dzhergalan *101 G2 Kir.* Jyrgalan. Issyk-Kul'skaya Oblast', NE Kyrgyzstan
Dzhugdzhur, Khrebet *93 G3 mountain range* E Russian Federation
Dzhusaly *92 B4 Kaz.* Zholsaly. Kyzylorda, SW Kazakhstan
Działdowo *76 D3* Warmińsko-Mazurskie, NE Poland
Dzuunmod *105 E2* Töv, C Mongolia

E

Eagle Pass *27 F4* Texas, SW USA
East Açores Fracture Zone *see* East Azores Fracture Zone
East Antarctica *see* Greater Antarctica
East Australian Basin *see* Tasman Basin
East Azores Fracture Zone *44 C3 var.* East Açores Fracture Zone. *Tectonic feature* E Atlantic Ocean
Eastbourne *67 E7* SE England, UK
East Cape *128 E3 headland* North Island, NZ
East China Sea *103 E2 Chin.* Dong Hai. *Sea* W Pacific Ocean
Easter Fracture Zone *131 G4 tectonic feature* E Pacific Ocean
Easter Island *131 F4 var.* Rapa Nui, *island* E Pacific Ocean
Eastern Desert *46 D3 var.* Aş Şaḩrā' ash Sharqīyah, *Eng.* Arabian Desert, Eastern Desert. *Desert* E Egypt
Eastern Ghats *102 B3 mountain range* SE India
Eastern Sayans *93 E4 Mong.* Dzüün Soyonï Nuruu, *Rus.* Vostochnyy Sayan. *Mountain range* Mongolia/Russian Federation
East Falkland *43 D8 var.* Isla Soledad. *Island* E Falkland Islands
East Grand Forks *23 E1* Minnesota, N USA
East Indiaman Ridge *119 D6 undersea feature* E Indian Ocean
East Indies *130 A3 island group* SE Asia
East Kilbride *66 C4* S Scotland, UK
East Korea Bay *107 E3 bay* E North Korea
Eastleigh *67 D7* S England, UK
East London *56 D5 Afr.* Oos-Londen; *prev.* Emonti, Port Rex. Eastern Cape, S South Africa
Eastmain *16 D3 river* Québec, C Canada
East Mariana Basin *120 B1 undersea feature* W Pacific Ocean
East Novaya Zemlya Trench *90 C1 var.* Novaya Zemlya Trench. *Undersea feature* W Kara Sea
East Pacific Rise *131 F4 undersea feature* E Pacific Ocean
East Saint Louis *18 B4* Illinois, N USA
East Scotia Basin *45 C7 undersea feature* SE Scotia Sea
East Sea *108 A4 var.* Sea of Japan *Rus.* Yapanskoye More. *Sea* NW Pacific Ocean *see also* Japan, Sea of
East Siberian Sea *see* Vostochno-Sibirskoye More
East Timor *117 F5 var.* Loro Sae *prev.* Portuguese Timor, Timor Timur. Country, SE Asia
Eau Claire *18 A2* Wisconsin, N USA
Eauripik Rise *120 B2 undersea feature* W Pacific Ocean
Ebensee *73 D6* Oberösterreich, N Austria
Eberswalde-Finow *72 D3* Brandenburg, E Germany
Ebetsu *108 D2 var.* Ebetu. Hokkaidō, NE Japan
Ebetu *see* Ebetsu
Ebolowa *55 A5* Sud, S Cameroon
Ebon Atoll *122 D2 var.* Epoon. *Atoll* Ralik Chain, S Marshall Islands
Ebro *71 E2 river* NE Spain
Ebusus *see* Eivissa
Ech Cheliff *see* Chlef
Ech Chleff *see* Chlef
Echo Bay *15 E3* Northwest Territories, NW Canada
Echt *65 D5* Limburg, SE Netherlands
Ecija *70 D4 anc.* Astigi. Andalucía, SW Spain
Ecuador *38 B1 Country* NW South America
Ed Da'ein *50 A4* Southern Darfur, W Sudan
Ed Damazin *50 C4 var.* Ad Damazīn. Blue Nile, E Sudan
Ed Damer *50 C3 var.* Ad Damar, Ad Dāmir. River Nile, NE Sudan
Ed Debba *50 B3* Northern, N Sudan
Ede *64 D4* Gelderland, C Netherlands
Ede *53 F5* Osun, SW Nigeria
Edéa *55 A5* Littoral, SW Cameroon
Edeyin Murzuq *see* Murzuq, Idhān
Edfu *see* Idfu
Edgeøya *61 G2 island* S Svalbard
Edgware *67 A7* SE England, UK
Edinburg *27 G5* Texas, SW USA
Edinburgh *66 C4 admin capital* S Scotland, UK
Edirne *94 A2 Eng.* Adrianople; *anc.* Adrianopolis, Hadrianopolis. Edirne, NW Turkey
Edmonds *24 B2* Washington, NW USA
Edmonton *15 E5* Alberta, SW Canada
Edmundston *17 E4* New Brunswick, SE Canada
Edna *27 G4* Texas, SW USA
Edolo *74 B1* Lombardia, N Italy
Edremit *94 A3* Balıkesir, NW Turkey
Edward, Lake *55 E5 var.* Albert Edward Nyanza, Edward Nyanza, Lac Idi Amin, Lake Rutanzige. *Lake* Uganda/Zaire
Edward Nyanza *see* Edward, Lake
Edwards Plateau *27 F3 plain* Texas, SW USA
Eeklo *65 B5 var.* Eekloo. Oost-Vlaanderen, NW Belgium
Edzo *53 E4 prev.* Rae-Edzo. Northwest Territories, NW Canada
Eekloo *see* Eeklo
Eersel *65 C5* Noord-Brabant, S Netherlands
Efate *122 D4 var.* Éfaté *Fr.* Vaté; *prev.* Sandwich Island. *Island* C Vanuatu
Effingham *18 B4* Illinois, N USA
Eforie Sud *86 D5* Constanţa, E Romania
Efstrátios, Ágios *82 D4 var.* Ayios Evstratios. *Island* E Greece
Egadi, Isole *75 B7 island group* S Italy
Eger *77 D6 Ger.* Erlau. Heves, NE Hungary
Egeria Fracture Zone *119 C5 tectonic feature* W Indian Ocean
Éghezèe *65 C6* Namur, C Belgium
Egina *see* Aígina
Egio *see* Aígio
Egmont, Mount *see* Taranaki, Mount
Egmont, Cape *128 C4 headland* North Island, NZ
Egoli *see* Johannesburg
Egypt *50 B2 Ar.* Jumhūrīyah Mişr al 'Arabīyah; *prev.* United Arab Republic, *anc.* Aegyptus. *Country* NE Africa
Eibar *71 E1* País Vasco, N Spain
Eibergen *64 E3* Gelderland, E Netherlands
Eidfjord *63 A5* Hordaland, S Norway
Eier-Berg *see* Suur Munamägi
Eifel *73 A5 plateau* W Germany
Eiger *95 B7 mountain* C Switzerland
Eigg *66 B3 island* W Scotland, UK
Eight Degree Channel *110 B3 channel* India/Maldives
Eighty Mile Beach *124 B4 beach* Western Australia
Eijsden *65 D6* Limburg, SE Netherlands
Eilat *see* Elat
Eindhoven *65 D5* Noord-Brabant, S Netherlands
Eipel *see* Ipel'
Eipel *see* Ipoly
Eisenhüttenstadt *72 D4* Brandenburg, E Germany
Eisenstadt *73 E6* Burgenland, E Austria
Eisleben *72 C4* Sachsen-Anhalt, C Germany
Eivissa *71 G3 var.* Iviza, *Cast.* Ibiza; *anc.* Ebusus. *Island* Islas Baleares, Spain, W Mediterranean Sea
Eivissa *71 G3 var.* Iviza, *Cast.* Ibiza; *anc.* Ebusus. Eivissa, Spain, W Mediterranean Sea
Ejea de los Caballeros *71 E2* Aragón, NE Spain
Ejin Qi *104 D3 var.* Dalain Hob. Nei Mongol Zizhiqu, N China
Ekapa *see* Cape Town
Ekiatapskiy Khrebet *93 G1 mountain range* NE Russian Federation
El 'Alamein *50 B1 var.* Al 'Alamayn. N Egypt
El Asnam *see* Chlef
Elat *97 B8 var.* Eilat, Elath. Southern, S Israel
Elat, Gulf of *see* Aqaba, Gulf of
Elath *see* Al 'Aqabah
Elath *see* Elat
El'Atrun *50 B3* Northern Darfur, NW Sudan
Elazığ *95 E3 var.* Elâzîğ, Elâziz. Elâzığ, E Turkey
Elâzîz *see* Elazığ
Elba, Isola d' *74 B4 island* Archipelago Toscano, C Italy
Elbasan *79 D6 var.* Elbasani. Elbasan, C Albania
Elbasani *see* Elbasan
Elbe *58 D3 Cz.* Labe. *River* Czech Republic/Germany
El Beni *see* Beni
Elbert, Mount *22 C4 mountain* Colorado, C USA
Elbing *see* Elbląg
Elbląg *76 C2 var.* Elblag, *Ger.* Elbing. Warmińsko-Mazurskie, NE Poland
El Boulaida *see* Blida
El'brus *89 A8 var.* Gora El'brus. *Mountain* SW Russian Federation
El Burgo de Osma *71 E2* Castilla-León, C Spain
El Cajon *25 C8* California, W USA
El Calafate *43 B7 var.* Calafate. Santa Cruz, S Argentina
El Callao *37 E2* Bolívar, E Venezuela
El Campo *27 G4* Texas, SW USA
El Carmen de Bolívar *36 B2* Bolívar, NW Colombia
El Centro *25 D8* California, W USA
Elche *71 F4 var.* Elx; *anc.* Ilici, *Lat.* Illicis. País Valenciano, E Spain
Elda *93 F4* País Valenciano, E Spain
El Djazaïr *see* Alger
El Djelfa *see* Djelfa
El Dorado *20 B2* Arkansas, C USA
El Dorado *37 F2* Bolívar, E Venezuela
El Dorado *23 F5* Kansas, C USA
El Dorado *28 C3* Sinaloa, C Mexico
Eldorado *42 E3* Misiones, NE Argentina
Eldoret *51 C6* Rift Valley, W Kenya
Elektrostal' *89 B5* Moskovskaya Oblast', W Russian Federation
Elemi Triangle *51 B5 disputed region* Kenya/Sudan
Elephant Butte Reservoir *26 C2 reservoir* New Mexico, SW USA
Eleuthera Island *32 C1 island* N Bahamas

INDEX

El Fasher 50 A4 var. Al Fāshir. Northern Darfur, W Sudan
El Ferrol see Ferrol
El Ferrol del Caudillo see Ferrol
El Gedaref see Gedaref
El Geneina 50 A4 var. Ajjinena, Al-Genain, Al Junaynah. Western Darfur, W Sudan
Elgin 18 B3 Illinois, N USA
Elgin 66 C3 NE Scotland, UK
El Gîza 50 B1 var. Al Jīzah, Gîza, Gizeh. N Egypt
El Goléa 48 D3 var. Al Golea. C Algeria
El Hank 52 D1 cliff N Mauritania
El Haseke see Al Ḩasakah
Elista 111 B7 Respublika Kalmykiya, SW Russian Federation
Elizabeth 127 B6 South Australia
Elizabeth City 21 G1 North Carolina, SE USA
Elizabethtown 18 C5 Kentucky, S USA
El-Jadida 48 C2 prev. Mazagan. W Morocco
Ełk 76 E2 Ger. Lyck. Warmińsko-Mazurskie, NE Poland
Elk City 27 F1 Oklahoma, C USA
El Kerak see Al Karak
El Khalil see Hebron
El Khârga 50 B2 var. Al Khārijah. C Egypt
Elkhart 18 C3 Indiana, N USA
El Khartûm see Khartoum
Elk River 23 F2 Minnesota, N USA
El Kuneitra see Al Qunayṭirah
Ellef Ringnes Island 15 E1 island Nunavut, N Canada
Ellen, Mount 22 B5 mountain Utah, W USA
Ellensburg 24 B2 Washington, NW USA
Ellesmere Island 15 F1 island Queen Elizabeth Islands, Nunavut, N Canada
Ellesmere, Lake 129 C6 lake South Island, NZ
Elliston 127 A6 South Australia
Ellsworth Land 132 A3 physical region Antarctica
El Mahbas 48 B3 var. Mahbés. SW Western Sahara
El Mina 96 B4 var. Al Mīnā'. N Lebanon
El Minya 50 B2 var. Al Minyā, Minya. C Egypt
Elmira 19 E3 New York, NE USA
El Mreyyé 52 D2 desert E Mauritania
Elmshorn 72 B3 Schleswig-Holstein, N Germany
El Muglad 50 B4 Western Kordofan, C Sudan
El Obeid 50 B4 var. Al Obayyid, Al Ubayyiḍ. Northern Kordofan, C Sudan
El Ouâdi see El Oued
El Oued 49 E2 var. Al Oued, El Ouâdi, El Wad. NE Algeria
Eloy 26 B2 Arizona, SW USA
El Paso 26 D3 Texas, SW USA
El Porvenir 31 G4 San Blas, N Panama
El Progreso 30 C2 Yoro, NW Honduras
El Puerto de Santa María 70 C5 Andalucía, S Spain
El Quds see Jerusalem
El Quneitra see Al Qunayṭirah
El Quseir see Al Quṣayr
El Queira see Al Quwayrah
El Rama 31 E3 Región Autónoma Atlántico Sur, SE Nicaragua
El Real 31 H5 var. El Real de Santa María. Darién, SE Panama
El Real de Santa María see El Real
El Reno 27 F1 Oklahoma, C USA
El Salvador 30 B3 Country Central America
El Sáuz 28 C2 Chihuahua, N Mexico
El Serrat 69 A7 N Andorra
Elst 64 D4 Gelderland, E Netherlands
El Sueco 28 C2 Chihuahua, N Mexico
El Suweida see As Suwaydā'
Eltanin Fracture Zone 131 E5 tectonic feature SE Pacific Ocean
El Tigre 37 E2 Anzoátegui, NE Venezuela
Elvas 70 C4 Portalegre, C Portugal
El Vendrell 71 G2 Cataluña, NE Spain
El Vigía 36 C2 Mérida, NW Venezuela
El Wad see El Oued
Elwell, Lake 22 B1 reservoir Montana, NW USA
Elx see Elche
Ely 25 D5 Nevada, W USA
El Yopal see Yopal
Emajõgi 84 D3 Ger. Embach. River SE Estonia
Emba 92 B4 Kaz. Embi. Aktyubinsk, W Kazakhstan
Emden 72 A3 Niedersachsen, NW Germany
Emerald 126 D4 Queensland, E Australia
Emerald Isle see Montserrat
Emesa see Ḩimş
Emmaste 84 C2 Hiiumaa, W Estonia
Emmeloord 64 D2 Flevoland, N Netherlands
Emmen 64 E2 Drenthe, NE Netherlands
Emmendingen 73 A6 Baden-Württemberg, SW Germany
Emory Peak 27 E4 mountain Texas, SW USA
Empalme 28 B2 Sonora, NW Mexico
Emperor Seamounts 91 G3 undersea feature NW Pacific Ocean
Emporia 23 F5 Kansas, C USA
Empty Quarter see Ar Rub 'al Khālī
Ems 72 A3 Dut. Eems. River NW Germany
Encamp 69 A8 C Andorra
Encarnación 42 D3 Itapúa, S Paraguay
Encinitas 25 C8 California, W USA
Encs 77 D6 Borsod-Abaúj-Zemplén, NE Hungary
Endeavour Strait 126 C1 strait Queensland, NE Australia
Enderbury Island 123 F3 atoll Phoenix Islands, C Kiribati
Enderby Land 132 C2 physical region Antarctica
Enderby Plain 132 D2 undersea feature S Indian Ocean
Enewetak Atoll 122 C1 var. Ānewetak, Eniwetok. Atoll Ralik Chain, W Marshall Islands
Enfield 67 A7 SE England, UK
Engannim see Jenīn
Enghien 65 B6 Dut. Edingen. Hainaut, SW Belgium
England 67 D5 Lat. Anglia. National region UK
Englewood 22 D4 Colorado, C USA
English Channel 67 D8 var. The Channel, Fr. la Manche. Channel NW Europe
Engure 84 C3 Tukums, W Latvia
Engures Ezers 84 B3 lake NW Latvia
Enguri 95 F1 Rus. Inguri. River NW Georgia
Enid 27 F1 Oklahoma, C USA
Enikale Strait see Kerch Strait
Eniwetok see Enewetak Atoll
En Nâqoûra 97 A5 var. An Nāqūrah. SW Lebanon
Ennedi 54 D2 plateau E Chad
Ennis 67 A6 Ir. Inis. W Ireland
Ennis 27 G3 Texas, SW USA
Enniskillen 67 B5 var. Inniskilling, Ir. Inis Ceithleann. SW Northern Ireland, UK
Enns 73 D6 river C Austria
Enschede 64 E3 Overijssel, E Netherlands
Ensenada 28 A1 Baja California, NW Mexico
Entebbe 51 B6 S Uganda
Entroncamento 70 B3 Santarém, C Portugal
Enugu 53 G5 Enugu, S Nigeria
Eolie, Isole 75 C6 var. Isole Lipari, Eng. Aeolian Islands, Lipari Islands. Island group S Italy
Epanomí 82 B4 Kentrikí Makedonía, N Greece
Epéna 55 B5 La Likouala, NE Congo
Eperies see Prešov
Eperjes see Prešov
Epi 122 D4 var. Épi. Island C Vanuatu
Épi see Epi
Épinal 68 D4 Vosges, NE France
Epiphania see Ḩamāh
Epitoli see Pretoria
Epoon see Ebon Atoll
Epsom 67 A8 SE England, UK
Equatorial Guinea 55 A5 Country C Africa
Erautini see Johannesburg
Erbil see Arbīl
Erciş 95 F3 Van, E Turkey
Erdélyi-Havasok see Carpaţii Meridionali
Erdenet 105 E2 Bulgan, N Mongolia
Erdi 54 C2 plateau NE Chad
Erdi Ma 54 D2 desert NE Chad
Erebus, Mount 132 B4 mountain Ross Island, Antarctica
Ereğli 94 C4 Konya, S Turkey
Erenhot 105 F2 var. Erlian. Nei Mongol Zizhiqu, NE China
Erevan see Yerevan
Erfurt 72 C4 Thüringen, C Germany
Ergene Irmağı 94 A2 var. Ergene Irmağı. River NW Turkey
Erg Iguid see Iguîdi, 'Erg
Ergun He see Argun
Ergun Zuoqi 105 F1 Nei Mongol Zizhiqu, N China
Erie 18 D3 Pennsylvania, NE USA
Erie, Lake 18 D3 Fr. Lac Érié. Lake Canada/USA
Eritrea 50 C4 Tig. Ērtra. Country E Africa
Erivan see Yerevan
Erlangen 73 C5 Bayern, S Germany
Erlian see Erenhot
Ermelo 64 D3 Gelderland, C Netherlands
Ermióni 83 C6 Pelopónnisos, S Greece
Ermoúpoli 83 D6 var. Hermoupolis; prev. Ermoúpolis. Sýros, Kykládes, Greece, Aegean Sea
Ermoúpolis see Ermoúpoli
Ernākulam 110 C3 Kerala, SW India
Erode 110 C2 Tamil Nādu, SE India
Erquelinnes 65 B7 Hainaut, S Belgium
Er-Rachidia 48 C2 var. Ksar al Soule. E Morocco
Er Rahad 50 B4 var. Ar Rahad. Northern Kordofan, C Sudan
Erromango 122 D4 island S Vanuatu
Ertis see Irtysh
Erzgebirge 73 C5 Cz. Krušné Hory, Eng. Ore Mountains. Mountain range Czech Republic/Germany see also Krušné Hory
Erzincan 95 E3 var. Erzinjan. Erzincan, E Turkey
Erzinjan see Erzincan
Erzurum 95 E3 prev. Erzerum. Erzurum, NE Turkey
Esbjerg 63 A7 Ribe, W Denmark
Escaldes 69 A8 C Andorra
Escanaba 18 C2 Michigan, N USA
Esch-sur-Alzette 65 D8 Luxembourg, S Luxembourg
Escondido 25 C8 California, W USA
Escuinapa 28 D3 var. Escuinapa de Hidalgo. Sinaloa, C Mexico
Escuinapa de Hidalgo see Escuinapa
Escuintla 29 G5 Chiapas, SE Mexico
Escuintla 30 B2 Escuintla, S Guatemala
Esenguly 100 B3 var. Gasan-Kuli. Balkanskiy Velayat, W Turkmenistan
Eşfahān 98 C3 Eng. Isfahan; anc. Aspadana. Eşfahān, C Iran
Esh Sham see Dimashq
Esh Sharā see Ash Sharāh
Eskişehir 94 B3 var. Eskishehr. Eskişehir, W Turkey
Eskishehr see Eskişehir
Eslāmābād 98 C3 var. Eslāmābād-e Gharb; prev. Harunabad, Shāhābād. Kermānshāhān, W Iran
Eslāmābād-e Gharb see Eslāmābād
Esmeraldas 38 A1 Esmeraldas, N Ecuador
Esna see Isna
Espanola 26 D1 New Mexico, SW USA
Esperance 125 B7 Western Australia
Esperanza 132 A2 Argentinian research station Antarctica
Esperanza 28 B2 Sonora, NW Mexico
Espinal 36 B3 Tolima, C Colombia
Espinhaço, Serra do 34 D4 mountain range SE Brazil
Espírito Santo 41 F4 off. Estado do Espírito Santo. State E Brazil
Espiritu Santo 122 C4 var. Santo. Island W Vanuatu
Espoo 63 D6 Swe. Esbo. Etelä-Suomi, S Finland
Esquel 43 B6 Chubut, SW Argentina
Essaouira 48 B2 prev. Mogador. W Morocco
Es Semara see Smara
Essen 72 A4 var. Essen an der Ruhr. Nordrhein-Westfalen, W Germany
Essen 65 C5 Antwerpen, N Belgium
Essen an der Ruhr see Essen
Essequibo River 37 F3 river C Guyana
Es Suweida see As Suwaydā'
Estacado, Llano 27 E2 plain New Mexico/Texas, SW USA
Estados, Isla de los 43 C8 prev. Eng. Staten Island. Island S Argentina
Estância 41 G3 Sergipe, E Brazil
Estelí 30 D3 Estelí, NW Nicaragua
Estella 71 E1 Bas. Lizarra. Navarra, N Spain
Estepona 92 D5 Andalucía, S Spain
Estevan 15 F5 Saskatchewan, S Canada
Estonia 84 D2Est. Eesti Vabariik, Ger. Estland, Latv. Igaunija; prev. Estonian SSR, Rus. Estonskaya SSR. Country NE Europe
Estrela, Serra da 70 C3 mountain range C Portugal
Estremoz 70 C4 Évora, S Portugal
Esztergom 77 C6 Ger. Gran; anc. Strigonium. Komárom-Esztergom, N Hungary
Étalle 65 D8 Luxembourg, SE Belgium
Etāwah 112 D3 Uttar Pradesh, N India
Ethiopia 51 C5 prev. Abyssinia, People's Democratic Republic of Ethiopia. Country E Africa
Ethiopian Highlands 51 C5 var. Ethiopian Plateau. Plateau N Ethiopia
Ethiopian Plateau see Ethiopian Highlands
Etna, Monte 75 C7 Eng. Mount Etna. Volcano Sicilia, Italy, C Mediterranean Sea
Etna, Mount see Etna, Monte
Etosha Pan 56 B3 salt lake N Namibia
Etoumbi 55 B5 Cuvette, NW Congo
Et Tafila see Aţ Ţafīlah
Ettelbrück 65 D8 Diekirch, C Luxembourg
'Eua 123 E5 prev. Middleburg Island. Island Tongatapu Group, SE Tonga
Euboea see Évvoia
Eucla 125 D6 Western Australia
Euclid 18 D3 Ohio, N USA
Eufaula Lake 27 G1 var. Eufaula Reservoir. Reservoir Oklahoma, C USA
Eufaula Reservoir see Eufaula Lake
Eugene 24 B3 Oregon, NW USA
Eupen 65 D6 Liège, E Belgium
Euphrates 90 B4 Ar. Al Furāt, Turk. Firat Nehri. River SW Asia
Eureka 25 A5 California, W USA
Eureka 22 A1 Montana, NW USA
Europa Point 71 H5 headland S Gibraltar
Europe 12 E1 continent
Eutin 72 C2 Schleswig-Holstein, N Germany
Euxine Sea see Black Sea
Evansdale 23 G3 Iowa, C USA
Evanston 18 B3 Illinois, N USA
Evanston 22 B4 Wyoming, C USA
Evansville 18 B5 Indiana, N USA
Eveleth 23 G1 Minnesota, N USA
Everard, Lake 127 A6 salt lake South Australia
Everest, Mount 104 B5 Chin. Qomolangma Feng, Nep. Sagarmatha. Mountain China/Nepal
Everett 24 B2 Washington, NW USA
Everglades, The 21 F5 wetland Florida, SE USA
Evje 63 A6 Aust-Agder, S Norway
Évora 70 B4 anc. Ebora, Lat. Liberalitas Julia.Évora, C Portugal
Évreux 68 C3 anc. Civitas Eburovicum. Eure, N France
Évros see Maritsa
Évry 68 E2 Essonne, N France
Évvoia 79 E8 Lat. Euboea. Island C Greece
Ewarton 32 B5 C Jamaica
Excelsior Springs 23 F4 Missouri, C USA
Exe 67 C7 river SW England, UK
Exeter 67 C7 anc. Isca Damnoniorum. SW England, UK
Exmoor 67 C7 moorland SW England, UK
Exmouth 67 C7 SW England, UK
Exmouth 124 A4 Western Australia
Exmouth Gulf 124 A4 gulf Western Australia
Exmouth Plateau 119 E5 undersea feature E Indian Ocean
Extremadura 70 C3 cultural region W Spain
Exuma Cays 32 C1 islets C Bahamas
Exuma Sound 32 C1 sound C Bahamas
Eyre Mountains 129 A7 mountain range South Island, NZ
Eyre North, Lake 127 A5 salt lake South Australia
Eyre Peninsula 127 A6 peninsula South Australia
Eyre South, Lake 127 A5 salt lake South Australia

F

Faadhippolhu Atoll 110 B4 var. Fadiffolu, Lhaviyani Atoll. Atoll N Maldives
Fabens 26 D3 Texas, SW USA
Fada 54 C2 Borkou-Ennedi-Tibesti, E Chad
Fada-Ngourma 53 E4 E Burkina faso
Fadiffolu see Faadhippolhu Atoll
Faenza 74 C3 anc. Faventia. Emilia-Romagna, N Italy
Faeroe-Iceland Ridge 58 C1 undersea feature NW Norwegian Sea
Faeroe-Shetland Trough 58 C2 undersea feature NE Atlantic Ocean
Faeroes Islands 61 E5 Dan. Færøerne, Faer. Føroyar. Danish external territory N Atlantic Ocean
Faetano 74 E2 E San Marino
Făgăraş 86 C4 Ger. Fogarasch, Hung. Fogaras. Braşov, C Romania
Fagibina, Lake see Faguibine, Lac
Fagne 65 C7 hill range S Belgium
Faguibine, Lac 53 E3 var. Lake Fagibina. Lake NW Mali
Fahlun see Falun
Fahraj 98 E4 Kermān, SE Iran
Faial 70 A5 var. Ilha do Faial. Island Azores, Portugal, NE Atlantic Ocean
Fairbanks 14 D3 Alaska, USA
Fairfield 25 B6 California, W USA
Fair Isle 66 D2 island NE Scotland, UK
Fairlie 129 B6 Canterbury, South Island, NZ
Fairmont 23 F3 Minnesota, N USA
Faisalābād 112 C2 prev. Lyallpur. Punjab, NE Pakistan
Faizābād see Feyzābād
Faizābād 113 E3 Uttar Pradesh, N India
Fakaofo Atoll 123 F3 island SE Tokelau
Falam 114 A3 Chin State, W Myanmar
Falconara Marittima 74 C3 Marche, C Italy
Falkland Islands 43 D7 var. Falklands, Islas Malvinas. UK dependent territory SW Atlantic Ocean
Falkland Plateau 35 D7 var. Argentine Rise. Undersea feature SW Atlantic Ocean
Falklands see Falkland Islands
Fallbrook 25 C8 California, W USA
Falmouth 67 C7 SW England, UK
Falmouth 32 A4 W Jamaica
Falster 63 B8 island SE Denmark
Fălticeni 86 C3 Hung. Falticsén. Suceava, NE Romania
Falun 63 C6 var. Fahlun. Kopparberg, C Sweden
Famagusta see Ammóchostos
Famagusta Bay see Kólpos Ammóchostos
Famenne 65 C7 physical region SE Belgium
Fang 114 C3 Chiang Mai, NW Thailand
Fano 74 C3 anc. Colonia Julia Fanestris, Fanum Fortunae. Marche, C Italy
Farafangana 57 G4 Fianarantsoa, SE Madagascar
Farāh 100 D4 var. Farah, Fararud. Farāh, W Afghanistan
Farāh Rūd 100 D4 river W Afghanistan
Faranah 52 C4 Haute-Guinée, S Guinea
Fararud see Farāh
Farasān, Jazā'ir 99 A6 island group SW Saudi Arabia
Farewell, Cape 128 C4 headland South Island, NZ
Farewell, Cape see Nunap Isua
Farghona see Farg'ona
Fargo 23 F2 North Dakota, N USA
Farg'ona 101 F2 var. Farghona, Rus. Fergana; prev. Novyy Margilan. Farghona Wiloyati, E Uzbekistan
Faribault 23 F2 Minnesota, N USA
Farīdābād 112 D3 Haryāna, N India
Farkhor 101 E3 Rus. Parkhar. SW Tajikistan
Farmington 23 G5 Missouri, C USA
Farmington 26 C1 New Mexico, SW USA
Faro 70 B5 Faro, S Portugal
Farquhar Group 57 G2 island group S Seychelles
Farvel, Kap see Nunap Isua
Fastiv 87 E2 Rus. Fastov. Kyyivs'ka Oblast', NW Ukraine
Fauske 84 C3 Nordland, C Norway
Faxaflói 60 D5 Eng. Faxa Bay. Bay W Iceland
Faya 54 C2 prev. Faya-Largeau, Largeau. Borkou-Ennedi-Tibesti, N Chad
Fayetteville 20 A1 Arkansas, C USA
Fayetteville 21 F1 North Carolina, SE USA
Fdérick see Fdérik
Fdérik 52 C2 var. Fdérick, Fr. Fort Gouraud. Tiris Zemmour, NW Mauritania
Fear, Cape 21 F2 headland Bald Head Island, North Carolina, SE USA
Fécamp 68 B3 Seine-Maritime, N France
Federation of the separate territories of see Malaysia
Fehérgyarmat 77 E6 Szabolcs-Szatmár-Bereg, E Hungary
Fehmarn 72 C2 island N Germany
Fehmarnbelt 72 C2 var Fehmarn Belt, Dan. Fehmern Bælt. Strait Denmark/Germany
Fehmern Bælt see Fehmarnbelt
Feijó 40 C2 Acre, W Brazil
Feilding 128 D4 Manawatu-Wanganui, North Island, NZ
Feira see Feira de Santana
Feira de Santana 41 G3 var. Feira. Bahia, E Brazil
Felanitx 71 G3 anc. Canati, Felaniche. Mallorca, Spain, W Mediterranean Sea
Felidhu Atoll 110 B4 atoll C Maldives
Felipe Carrillo Puerto 29 H4 Quintana Roo, SE Mexico
Felixstowe 67 E6 E England, UK
Femunden 63 B5 lake S Norway
Fengcheng 106 D3 var. Feng-cheng, Fenghwangcheng. Liaoning, NE China
Feng-cheng see Fengcheng
Fenghwangcheng see Fengcheng
Fengtien see Liaoning
Fenoarivo 57 G3 Toamasina, E Madagascar
Fens, The 67 E6 wetland E England, UK
Feodosiya 87 F5 var. Kefe, It. Kaffa; anc. Theodosia. Respublika Krym, S Ukraine
Féres 82 D3 Anatolikí Makedonía kai Thráki, NE Greece
Fergus Falls 23 F2 Minnesota, N USA
Ferkessédougou 52 D4 N Côte d'Ivoire
Ferghana see Farg'ona
Fermo 74 C4 anc. Firmum Picenum. Marche, C Italy
Fernandina, Isla 38 A5 var. Narborough Island. Island Galapagos Islands, Ecuador, E Pacific Ocean
Fernando de Noronha 41 H2 island E Brazil
Fernando Po see Bioco, Isla de
Fernando Póo see Bioco, Isla de
Ferrara 74 C2 anc. Forum Alieni. Emilia-Romagna, N Italy
Ferreñafe 38 B3 Lambayeque, W Peru
Ferro see Hierro
Ferrol 70 B1 var. El Ferrol; prev. El Ferrol del Caudillo. Galicia, NW Spain
Ferwerd 64 D1 Fris. Ferwert. Friesland, N Netherlands
Fès 48 C2 Eng. Fez. N Morocco
Feteşti 86 D5 Ialomiţa, SE Romania
Fethiye 94 B4 Muğla, SW Turkey
Fetlar 66 D1 island NE Scotland, UK
Feyzābād 101 F3 var. Faizabad, Faizābād, Feyzābād, Fyzabad. Badakhshān, NE Afghanistan
Fianarantsoa 57 F3 Fianarantsoa, C Madagascar
Fianga 54 B4 Mayo-Kébbi, SW Chad
Fier 79 C6 var. Fieri. Fier, SW Albania
Fieri see Fier
Figeac 69 C5 Lot, S France
Figig see Figuig
Figueira da Foz 70 B3 Coimbra, W Portugal
Figueres 71 G2 Cataluña, E Spain
Figuig 48 D2 var. Figig. E Morocco
Fiji 123 E5 Fij. Viti. Country SW Pacific Ocean
Filadelfia 30 D4 Guanacaste, W Costa Rica
Filiaşi 86 B5 Dolj, SW Romania
Filipstad 63 B6 Värmland, C Sweden
Finale Ligure 74 A3 Liguria, NW Italy
Finchley 67 A7 SE England, UK
Findlay 18 C4 Ohio, N USA
Finike 94 B4 Antalya, SW Turkey
Finland 62 D4 Fin. Suomen Tasavalta, Suomi. Country N Europe
Finland, Gulf of 63 D6 Est. Soome Laht, Fin. Suomenlahti, Ger. Finnischer Meerbusen, Rus. Finskiy Zaliv, Swe. Finska Viken. Gulf E Baltic Sea
Finnmarksvidda 62 D2 physical region N Norway
Finsterwalde 72 D4 Brandenburg, E Germany
Fiordland 129 A7 physical region South Island, NZ
Fiorina 74 E1 NE San Marino
Firenze 74 C3 Eng. Florence; anc. Florentia. Toscana, C Italy
Fischbacher Alpen 73 E7 mountain range E Austria
Fish 56 B4 var. Vis. River S Namibia
Fishguard 67 C6 Wel. Abergwaun. SW Wales, UK
Fisterra, Cabo 70 B1 headland NW Spain
Fitzroy Crossing 124 C3 Western Australia
Fitzroy River 124 C3 river Western Australia
Flagstaff 26 B2 Arizona, SW USA
Flanders 65 A6 Dut. Vlaanderen, Fr. Flandre. Cultural region Belgium/France
Flathead Lake 22 B1 lake Montana, NW USA
Flat Island 106 C8 island NE Spratly Islands
Flatts Village 20 B5 var. The Flatts Village. C Bermuda
Flensburg 72 B2 Schleswig-Holstein, N Germany
Flinders Island 127 C8 island Furneaux Group, Tasmania, SE Australia
Flinders Ranges 127 B6 mountain range South Australia
Flinders River 126 C3 river Queensland, NE Australia
Flin Flon 15 F5 Manitoba, C Canada
Flint 18 C3 Michigan, N USA
Flint Island 123 G4 island Line Islands, E Kiribati
Floreana, Isla see Santa María, Isla
Florence see Firenze
Florence 20 C1 Alabama, S USA
Florence 21 F2 South Carolina, SE USA
Florencia 36 B4 Caquetá, S Colombia
Florentia see Firenze
Flores 70 A5 island Azores, Portugal, NE Atlantic Ocean
Flores 117 E5 island Nusa Tenggara, C Indonesia
Flores 30 B1 Petén, N Guatemala
Flores Sea 116 D5 Ind. Laut Flores. Sea C Indonesia
Floriano 41 F2 Piauí, E Brazil
Florianópolis 41 F5 prev. Destêrro. State capital Santa Catarina, S Brazil
Florida 21 E4 off. State of Florida; also known as Peninsular State, Sunshine State. State SE USA
Florida 42 D4 Florida, S Uruguay
Florida Bay 21 E5 bay Florida, SE USA
Florida Keys 21 E5 island group Florida, SE USA
Florida, Straits of 32 B1 strait Atlantic Ocean/Gulf of Mexico
Flórina 82 B4 var. Phlórina. Dytikí Makedonía, N Greece
Florissant 23 G4 Missouri, C USA
Floúda, Akrotírio 83 D7 headland Astypálaia, Kykládes, Greece, Aegean Sea
Foča 78 C4 var. Srbinje, Republika Srpska, SE Bosnia and Herzegovina
Focşani 86 C4 Vrancea, E Romania
Foggia 75 D5 Puglia, SE Italy
Fogo 52 A3 island Ilhas de Sotavento, SW Cape Verde
Foix 69 B6 Ariège, S France
Folégandros 83 C7 island Kykládes, Greece, Aegean Sea
Foleyet 16 C4 Ontario, S Canada
Foligno 74 C4 Umbria, C Italy
Folkestone 67 E7 SE England, UK
Fond du Lac 18 B2 Wisconsin, N USA
Fongafale 123 E3 var. Funafuti. Country capital (Tuvalu) Funafuti Atoll, SE Tuvalu
Fonseca, Gulf of 30 C3 Sp. Golfo de Fonseca. Gulf Central America
Fontainebleau 68 C3 Seine-et-Marne, N France
Fontenay-le-Comte 68 B4 Vendée, NW France

Fontvieille 69 B8 SW Monaco
Fonyód 77 C7 Somogy, W Hungary
Foochow *see* Fuzhou
Forchheim 73 C5 Bayern, SE Germany
Forel, Mont 60 D4 *mountain* SE Greenland
Forfar 66 C3 E Scotland, UK
Forge du Sud *see* Dudelange
Forlì 74 C3 *anc.* Forum Livii. Emilia-Romagna, N Italy
Formentera 93 G4 *anc.* Ophiusa, *Lat.* Frumentum. *Island* Islas Baleares, Spain, W Mediterranean Sea
Formosa 42 D2 Formosa, NE Argentina
Formosa, Serra 41 E3 *mountain range* C Brazil
Formosa Strait *see* Taiwan Strait
Forrest City 20 B1 Arkansas, C USA
Fort Albany 16 C3 Ontario, C Canada
Fortaleza 41 G2 *prev.* Ceará. *State capital* Ceará, NE Brazil
Fortaleza 39 F2 Pando, N Bolivia
Fort-Bayard *see* Zhanjiang
Fort-Cappolani *see* Tidjikja
Fort Collins 22 D4 Colorado, C USA
Fort Davis 27 E3 Texas, SW USA
Fort-de-France 33 H4 *prev.* Fort-Royal. *Dependent territory capital* (Martinique) W Martinique
Fort Dodge 23 F3 Iowa, C USA
Fortescue River 124 A4 *river* Western Australia
Fort Frances 16 B4 Ontario, S Canada
Fort Good Hope 15 E3 *var.* Good Hope. Northwest Territories, NW Canada
Fort Gouraud *see* Fdérik
Forth 66 C4 *river* C Scotland, UK
Forth, Firth of 66 C4 *estuary* E Scotland, UK
Fort-Lamy *see* Ndjamena
Fort Lauderdale 21 F5 Florida, SE USA
Fort Liard 15 E4 *var.* Liard. Northwest Territories, W Canada
Fort Madison 23 G4 Iowa, C USA
Fort McMurray 15 E4 Alberta, C Canada
Fort McPherson 14 D3 *var.* McPherson. Northwest Territories, NW Canada
Fort Morgan 22 D4 Colorado, C USA
Fort Myers 21 E5 Florida, SE USA
Fort Nelson 15 E4 British Columbia, W Canada
Fort Peck Lake 22 C1 *reservoir* Montana, NW USA
Fort Pierce 21 F4 Florida, SE USA
Fort Providence 15 E4 *var.* Providence. Northwest Territories, W Canada
Fort St.John 15 E4 British Columbia, W Canada
Fort Scott 23 F5 Kansas, C USA
Fort Severn 16 C2 Ontario, C Canada
Fort-Shevchenko 92 A4 Mangistau, W Kazakhstan
Fort Simpson 15 E4 *var.* Simpson. Northwest Territories, W Canada
Fort Smith 15 E4 *district capital* Northwest Territories, W Canada
Fort Smith 20 B1 Arkansas, C USA
Fort Stockton 27 E3 Texas, SW USA
Fort-Trinquet *see* Bîr Mogreïn
Fort Vermilion 15 E4 Alberta, W Canada
Fort Walton Beach 20 C3 Florida, SE USA
Fort Wayne 18 C4 Indiana, N USA
Fort William 66 C3 N Scotland, UK
Fort Worth 27 G2 Texas, SW USA
Fort Yukon 14 D3 Alaska, USA
Fougamou 55 A6 Ngounié, C Gabon
Fougères 68 B3 Ille-et-Vilaine, NW France
Fou-hsin *see* Fuxin
Foulwind, Cape 129 B5 *headland* South Island, NZ
Foumban 54 A4 Ouest, NW Cameroon
Fou-shan *see* Fushun
Foveaux Strait 129 A8 *strait* S NZ
Foxe Basin 15 G3 *sea* Nunavut, N Canada
Fox Glacier 129 B6 West Coast, South Island, NZ
Fox Mine 15 F4 Manitoba, C Canada
Fraga 71 F2 Aragón, NE Spain
Fram Basin 133 C3 *var.* Amundsen Basin. *Undersea feature* Arctic Ocean
France 68 B4 *It./Sp.* Francia; *prev.* Gaul, Gaule, *Lat.* Gallia. *Country* W Europe
Franceville 55 B6 *var.* Massoukou, Masuku. Haut-Ogooué, E Gabon
Francfort prev *see* Frankfurt am Main
Franche-Comté 68 D4 *cultural region* E France
Francis Case, Lake 23 E3 *reservoir* South Dakota, N USA
Francisco Escárcega 29 G4 Campeche, SE Mexico
Francistown 56 D3 North East, NE Botswana
Franconian Jura *see* Fränkische Alb
Frankenalb *see* Fränkische Alb
Frankenstein *see* Ząbkowice Śląskie
Frankenstein in Schlesien *see* Ząbkowice Śląskie
Frankfort 18 C5 *state capital* Kentucky, S USA
Frankfort on the Main *see* Frankfurt am Main
Frankfurt *see* Frankfurt am Main
Frankfurt am Main 73 B5 *var.* Frankfurt, *Fr.* Francfort; prev. *Eng.* Frankfort on the Main. Hessen, SW Germany
Frankfurt an der Oder 72 D3 Brandenburg, E Germany
Fränkische Alb 73 C6 *var.* Frankenalb, *Eng.* Franconian Jura. *Mountain range* S Germany
Franklin 20 C1 Tennessee, S USA
Franklin D.Roosevelt Lake 24 C1 *reservoir* Washington, NW USA
Frantsa-Iosifa, Zemlya 92 D1 *Eng.* Franz Josef Land. *Island group* N Russian Federation
Franz Josef Land *see* Frantsa-Iosifa, Zemlya
Fraserburgh 66 D3 NE Scotland, UK
Fraser Island 126 E4 *var.* Great Sandy Island. *Island* Queensland, E Australia
Fredericksburg 19 E5 Virginia, NE USA
Fredericton 17 F4 New Brunswick, SE Canada
Frederikshåb *see* Paamiut
Fredrikstad 63 B6 Østfold, S Norway
Freeport 32 C1 Grand Bahama Island, N Bahamas
Freeport 27 H4 Texas, SW USA
Freetown 52 C4 *country capital* (Sierra Leone) W Sierra Leone
Freiburg *see* Freiburg im Breisgau
Freiburg im Breisgau 73 A6 *var.* Freiburg, *Fr.* Fribourg-en-Brisgau. Baden-Württemberg, SW Germany
Fremantle 125 A6 Western Australia
Fremont 23 F4 Nebraska, C USA
French Guiana 37 H3 *var.* Guiana, Guyane. *French overseas department* N South America
French Polynesia 121 F4 *French overseas territory* C Polynesia
French Southern and Antarctic Territories 119 B7 *Fr.* Terres Australes et Antarctiques Françaises. *French overseas territory* S Indian Ocean
Fresnillo 28 D3 *var.* Fresnillo de González Echeverría. Zacatecas, C Mexico
Fresnillo de González Echeverría *see* Fresnillo
Fresno 25 C6 California, W USA
Frías 42 C3 Catamarca, N Argentina
Fribourg-en-Brisgau *see* Freiburg im Breisgau
Friedrichshafen 73 B7 Baden-Württemberg, S Germany
Frobisher Bay 60 B3 *inlet* Baffin Island, Northwest Territories, NE Canada
Frohavet 62 B4 *sound* C Norway
Frome, Lake 127 B6 *salt lake* South Australia
Frontera 29 G4 Tabasco, SE Mexico
Frontignan 91 C6 Hérault, S France
Frostviken *see* Kvarnbergsvattnet
Frøya 62 A4 *island* W Norway
Frunze *see* Bishkek
Frýdek-Místek 77 C5 *Ger.* Friedek-Mistek. Ostravský Kraj, E Czech Republic
Fu-chien *see* Fujian
Fu-chou *see* Fuzhou
Fuengirola 70 D5 Andalucía, S Spain
Fuerte Olimpo 42 D2 *var.* Olimpo. Alto Paraguay, NE Paraguay
Fuerte, Río 26 C5 *river* C Mexico
Fuerteventura 48 B3 *island* Islas Canarias, Spain, NE Atlantic Ocean
Fuhkien *see* Fujian
Fu-hsin *see* Fuxin
Fuji 109 D6 *var.* Huzi. Shizuoka, Honshū, S Japan
Fujian 106 D6 *var.* Fu-chien, Fuhkien, Fujian Sheng, Fukien, Min. Admin. region *province* SE China
Fujian Sheng *see* Fujian
Fuji-san 109 C6 *var.* Fujiyama, *Eng.* Mount Fuji. *Mountain* Honshū, SE Japan
Fujiyama *see* Fuji-san
Fukang 104 C2 Xinjiang Uygur Zizhiqu, W China
Fukien *see* Fujian
Fukui 109 C6 *var.* Hukui. Fukui, Honshū, SW Japan
Fukuoka 109 A7 *var.* Hukuoka; *hist.* Najima. Fukuoka, Kyūshū, SW Japan
Fukushima 108 D4 *var.* Hukusima. Fukushima, Honshū, C Japan
Fulda 73 B5 Hessen, C Germany
Funafuti *see* Fongafale
Funafuti Atoll 123 E3 *atoll* C Tuvalu
Funchal 48 A2 Madeira, Portugal, NE Atlantic Ocean
Fundy, Bay of 17 F5 *bay* Canada/USA
Furnes *see* Veurne
Fürth 73 C5 Bayern, S Germany
Furukawa 108 D4 *var.* Hurukawa. Miyagi, Honshū, C Japan
Fushun 106 D3 *var.* Fou-shan, Fu-shun. Liaoning, NE China
Fu-shun *see* Fushun
Fusin *see* Fuxin
Füssen 73 C7 Bayern, S Germany
Futog 78 D3 Serbia, NW Serbia and Montenegro (Yugo.)
Futuna, Île 123 E4 *island* S Wallis and Futuna
Fuxin 106 D3 *var.* Fou-hsin, Fu-hsin, Fusin. Liaoning, NE China
Fuzhou 106 D6 *var.* Foochow, Fu-chou. Fujian, SE China
Fuzhou 106 D5 *prev.* Linchuan. Jiangxi, S China
Fyn 63 B8 *Ger.* Fünen. *Island* C Denmark
Fyzabad *see* Feyẓābād

G

Gaafu Alifu Atoll *see* North Huvadhu Atoll
Gaafu Dhaalu Atoll *see* South Huvadhu Atoll
Gaalkacyo 51 E5 *var.* Galka'yo, *It.* Galcaio. Mudug, C Somalia
Gabela 56 B2 Cuanza Sul, W Angola
Gabès 49 E2 *var.* Qābis. E Tunisia
Gabès, Golfe de 49 F2 *Ar.* Khalīj Qābis. *Gulf* E Tunisia
Gabon 55 B6 *Country* C Africa
Gaborone 56 C4 *prev.* Gaberones. *Country capital* (Botswana) South East, SE Botswana
Gabrovo 82 D2 Gabrovo, N Bulgaria
Gadag 110 C1 Karnātaka, W India
Gadsden 20 D2 Alabama, S USA
Gaeta 75 C5 Lazio, C Italy
Gaeta, Golfo di 75 C5 *var.* Gulf of Gaeta. *Gulf* C Italy
Gaeta, Gulf of *see* Gaeta, Golfo di
Gäfle *see* Gävle
Gafsa 49 E2 *var.* Qafṣah. W Tunisia
Gagnoa 52 D5 C Côte d'Ivoire
Gagra 95 E1 NW Georgia
Gaillac 69 C6 *var.* Gaillac-sur-Tarn. Tarn, S France
Gaillac-sur-Tarn *see* Gaillac
Gaillimh *see* Galway
Gainesville 21 E3 Florida, SE USA
Gainesville 20 D2 Georgia, SE USA
Gainesville 27 G2 Texas, SW USA
Gairdner, Lake 127 A6 *salt lake* South Australia
Gaiziņkalns 84 C3 *var.* Gaizina Kalns. *Mountain* E Latvia
Gaizina Kalns *see* Gaiziņkalns
Galán, Cerro 42 B3 *mountain* NW Argentina
Galanta 77 C6 *Hung.* Galánta. Trnavský Kraj, W Slovakia
Galapagos Fracture Zone 131 E3 *tectonic feature* E Pacific Ocean
Galapagos Islands 131 F3 *var.* Islas de los Galápagos,*Tortoise Islands. Island group* Ecuador, E Pacific Ocean
Galapagos Rise 131 F3 *undersea feature* E Pacific Ocean
Galashiels 66 C4 SE Scotland, UK
Galaţi 86 D4 *Ger.* Galatz. Galaţi, E Romania
Galcaio *see* Gaalkacyo
Galesburg 18 B3 Illinois, N USA
Galicia 70 B1 *cultural region* NW Spain
Galicia Bank 58 B4 *undersea feature* E Atlantic Ocean
Galilee, Sea of *see* Tiberias, Lake
Galka'yo *see* Gaalkacyo
Galle 110 D4 *prev.* Point de Galle. Southern Province, SW Sri Lanka
Gallego Rise 131 F3 *undersea feature* E Pacific Ocean
Gallegos *see* Río Gallegos
Gallipoli 75 E6 Puglia, SE Italy
Gällivare 62 C3 Norrbotten, N Sweden
Gallup 26 C1 New Mexico, SW USA
Galtat-Zemmour 48 B3 C Western Sahara
Galveston 27 H4 Texas, SW USA
Galway 67 A5 *Ir.* Gaillimh. W Ireland
Galway Bay 67 A6 *Ir.* Cuan na Gaillimhe. *Bay* W Ireland
Gambell 14 C2 Saint Lawrence Island, Alaska, USA
Gambia 52 C3 *Fr.* Gambie. *River* W Africa
Gambia 52 B3 *Country* W Africa
Gambier, Îles 121 G4 *island group* E French Polynesia
Gamboma 55 B6 Plateaux, E Congo
Gan *see* Gansu
Gan *see* Jiangxi
Gan 110 B5 Addu Atoll, C Maldives
Gäncä 95 G2 *Rus.* Gyandzha; *prev.* Kirovabad, Yelisavetpol. W Azerbaijan
Gandajika 55 D7 Kasai Oriental, S Dem. Rep. Congo
Gander 17 G3 Newfoundland, Newfoundland and Labrador, SE Canada
Gāndhīdhām 112 C4 Gujarāt, W India
Gandía 71 F3 País Valenciano, E Spain
Ganges 113 F3 *Ben.* Padma. *River* Bangladesh/India *see also* Padma
Ganges Cone *see* Ganges Fan
Ganges Fan 118 D3 *var.* Ganges Cone. *Undersea feature* N Bay of Bengal
Ganges, Mouths of the 113 G4 *delta* Bangladesh/India
Gangra *see* Çankırı
Gangtok 113 F3 Sikkim, N India
Gansu 106 B4 *var.* Gan, Gansu Sheng, Kansu. Admin. region *province* N China
Gansu Sheng *see* Gansu
Ganzhou 106 D6 Jiangxi, S China
Gao 53 E3 Gao, E Mali
Gaoual 52 C4 Moyenne-Guinée, N Guinea
Gaoxiong *see* Kaohsiung
Gap 69 D5 *anc.* Vapincum. Hautes-Alpes, SE France
Gaplaňgyr Platosy 100 C2 *Rus.* Kaplangky, Plato. *Ridge* Turkmenistan/Uzbekistan
Gar 104 A4 *var.* Gar Xincun. Xizang Zizhiqu, W China
Garabil Belentligi 100 D3 *Rus.* Karabil', Vozvyshennost'. *Mountain range* S Turkmenistan
Garabogaz Aylagy 100 B2 *Rus.* Zaliv Kara-Bogaz-Gol. *Bay* Balkanskiy Velayat, W Turkmenistan
Garachiné 31 G5 Darién, SE Panama
Garagum 100 C3 *var.* Garagumy, Qara Qum, *Eng.* Black Sand Desert, Kara Kum; *prev.* Peski Karakumy. *Desert* C Turkmenistan
Garagum Kanaly 100 D3 *var.* Kara Kum Canal, Karakumskiy Kanal, *Turkm.* Garagumskiy Kanaly. *Canal* C Turkmenistan
Garagumskiy Kanal *see* Garagum Kanaly
Garagumy *see* Garagum
Gara Khitrino 82 D2 Shumen, NE Bulgaria
Garda, Lago di 74 C2 *var.* Benaco, *Eng.* Lake Garda, *Ger.* Gardasee. *Lake* NE Italy
Garda, Lake *see* Garda, Lago di
Gardasee *see* Garda, Lago di
Garden City 23 E5 Kansas, C USA
Gardeyz *see* Gardēz
Gardēz 101 E4 *var.* Gardeyz, Gordiaz. Paktīā, E Afghanistan
Gargždai 84 B3 Gargždai, W Lithuania
Garissa 51 D6 Coast, E Kenya
Garland 27 G2 Texas, SW USA
Garman, Loch *see* Wexford
Garoe *see* Garoowe
Garonne 69 B5 *anc.* Garumna. *River* S France
Garoowe 51 E5 *var.* Garoe. Nugaal, N Somalia
Garoua 54 B4 *var.* Garua. Nord, N Cameroon
Garrygala 100 C3 *Rus.* Kara-Kala. Balkanskiy Velayat, W Turkmenistan
Garry Lake 15 F3 *lake* Nunavut, N Canada
Garsen 51 D6 Coast, S Kenya
Garua *see* Garoua
Garwolin 76 D4 Mazowieckie, C Poland
Gar Xincun *see* Gar
Gary 18 B3 Indiana, N USA
Garzón 36 B4 Huila, S Colombia
Gasan-Kuli *see* Esenguly
Gascogne 69 B6 *Eng.* Gascony. *Cultural region* S France
Gascoyne River 125 A5 *river* Western Australia
Gaspé 17 F3 Québec, SE Canada
Gaspé, Péninsule de 17 E4 *var.* Péninsule de la Gaspésie. *Peninsula* Québec, SE Canada
Gastonia 21 E1 North Carolina, SE USA
Gastoúni 83 B6 Dytikí Ellás, S Greece
Gatchina 88 B4 Leningradskaya Oblast', NW Russian Federation
Gatineau 16 D4 Québec, SE Canada
Gatún, Lago 31 F4 *reservoir* C Panama
Gauja 84 D3 *Ger.* Aa. *River* Estonia/Latvia
Gauteng *see* Johannesburg
Gāvbandī 98 D4 Hormozgān, S Iran
Gávdos 83 C8 *island* SE Greece
Gavere 65 B6 Oost-Vlaanderen, NW Belgium
Gävle 63 C6 *var.* Gäfle; *prev.* Gefle. Gävleborg, C Sweden
Gawler 127 B6 South Australia
Gaya 113 F3 Bihār, N India
Gayndah 127 E5 Queensland, E Australia
Gaza 97 A6 *Ar.* Ghazzah, *Heb.* 'Azza. NE Gaza Strip
Gaz-Achak *see* Gazojak
Gaza Strip 97 A7 *Ar.* Qiṭā' Ghazzah. *Disputed region* SW Asia
Gazi Antep *see* Gaziantep
Gaziantep 94 D4 *var.* Gazi Antep; *prev.* Aintab, Antep. Gaziantep, S Turkey
Gazimağusa *see* Ammóchostos
Gazimağusa Körfezi *see* Kólpos Ammóchostos
Gazli 100 D2 Bukhoro Wiloyati, C Uzbekistan
Gazojak 100 D2 *var.* Gaz-Achak. Lebapskiy Velayat, NE Turkmenistan
Gbanga 52 D5 *var.* Gbarnga. N Liberia
Gbarnga *see* Gbanga
Gdansk 76 C2 *Fr.* Dantzig, *Ger.* Danzig. Pomorskie, N Poland
Gdan'skaya Bukhta *see* Danzig, Gulf of
Pomorskie, Gulf of *see* Danzig, Gulf of
Gdynia 76 C2 *Ger.* Gdingen. Pomorskie, N Poland
Gedaref 50 C4 *var.* Al Qaḍārif, El Gedaref. Gedaref, E Sudan
Gediz 94 B3 Kütahya, W Turkey
Gediz Nehri 94 A3 *river* W Turkey
Geel 65 C5 *var.* Gheel. Antwerpen, N Belgium
Geelong 127 C7 Victoria, SE Australia
Ge'e'mu *see* Golmud
Gefle *see* Gävle
Geilo 63 A5 Buskerud, S Norway
Gejiu 106 B6 *var.* Kochiu. Yunnan, S China
Gëkdepe *see* Gökdepe
Gela 75 C7 *prev.* Terranova di Sicilia. Sicilia, Italy, C Mediterranean Sea
Geldermalsen 64 C4 Gelderland, C Netherlands
Geleen 65 D6 Limburg, SE Netherlands
Gelinsoor *see* Gellinsoor
Gellinsoor 51 E5 *var.* Gelinsoor. Mudug, NE Somalia
Gembloux 65 C6 Namur, Belgium
Gemena 55 C5 Equateur, NW Dem. Rep. Congo
Gemona del Friuli 74 D2 Friuli-Venezia Giulia, NE Italy
Genck *see* Genk
General Alvear 42 B4 Mendoza, W Argentina
General Eugenio A.Garay 42 C1 Guairá, S Paraguay
General Machado *see* Camacupa
General Santos 117 F3 *off.* General Santos City. Mindanao, S Philippines
Geneva *see* Genève
Geneva, Lake A7 *Fr.* Lac de Genève, Lac Léman, le Léman, *Ger.* Genfer See. *Lake* France/Switzerland
Genève 73 A7 *Eng.* Geneva, *Ger.* Genf, *It.* Ginevra. Genève, SW Switzerland
Genf *see* Genève
Genk 65 D6 *var.* Genck. Limburg, NE Belgium
Gennep 64 D4 Limburg, SE Netherlands
Genoa *see* Genova
Genova 80 D1 *Eng.* Genoa, *Fr.* Gênes; *anc.* Genua. Liguria, NW Italy
Genova, Golfo di 74 A3 *Eng.* Gulf of Genoa. *Gulf* NW Italy
Genovesa, Isla 38 B5 *var.* Tower Island. *Island* Galapagos Islands, Ecuador, E Pacific Ocean
Gent 65 B5 *Eng.* Ghent, *Fr.* Gand. Oost-Vlaanderen, NW Belgium
Geok-Tepe *see* Gökdepe
George 60 A4 *river* Newfoundland and Labrador/Quebec, E Canada
George 56 C5 Western Cape, S South Africa
George, Lake 21 E3 *lake* Florida, SE USA
Georges Bank 13 D5 *undersea feature* W Atlantic Ocean
George Sound 129 A7 *sound* South Island, NZ
Georges River 126 D2 *river* New South Wales, SE Australia
George Town 32 B3 *var.* Georgetown. *Dependent territory capital* (Cayman Islands) Grand Cayman, SW Cayman Islands
George Town 116 B3 *var.* Penang, Pinang. Pinang, Peninsular Malaysia
George Town 32 C2 Great Exuma Island, C Bahamas
Georgetown 37 F2 *country capital* (Guyana) N Guyana
Georgetown 21 F2 South Carolina, SE USA
George V Land 132 C4 *physical region* Antarctica
Georgia 95 F2 *Geor.* Sak'art'velo, *Rus.* Gruzinskaya SSR, Gruziya; *prev.* Georgian SSR. *Country* SW Asia
Georgia 20 D2 *off.* State of Georgia; also known as Empire State of the South, Peach State. *State* SE USA
Georgian Bay 18 D2 *lake bay* Ontario, S Canada
Georgia, Strait of 24 A1 *strait* British Columbia, W Canada
Georg von Neumayer 132 A2 *German research station* Antarctica
Gera 72 C4 Thüringen, E Germany
Geráki 83 B6 Pelopónnisos, S Greece
Geraldine 129 B6 Canterbury, South Island, NZ
Geraldton 125 A6 Western Australia
Geral, Serra 35 D5 *mountain range* S Brazil
Gerede 94 C2 Bolu, N Turkey
Gereshk 100 D5 Helmand, SW Afghanistan
Gering 22 D3 Nebraska, C USA
Germanicopolis *see* Çankırı
Germany 72 B4 *Ger.* Bundesrepublik Deutschland, Deutschland. *Country* N Europe
Geroliménas 83 B7 Pelopónnisos, S Greece
Gerona *see* Girona
Gerpinnes 65 C7 Hainaut, S Belgium
Gerunda *see* Girona
Gerze 94 D2 Sinop, N Turkey
Gesoriacum *see* Boulogne-sur-Mer
Gessoriacum *see* Boulogne-sur-Mer
Getafe 70 D3 Madrid, C Spain
Gevaş 95 F3 Van, SE Turkey
Gevgeli *see* Gevgelija
Gevgelija 79 E6 *var.* Đevđelija, Djevdjelija, *Turk.* Gevgeli. SE FYR Macedonia
Ghaba *see* Al Ghābah
Ghana 53 E5 *Country* W Africa
Ghanzi 56 C3 *var.* Khanzi. Ghanzi, W Botswana
Gharandal 97 B7 Ma'ān, SW Jordan
Ghardaïa 48 D2 N Algeria
Gharvān *see* Gharyān
Gharyān 49 F2 *var.* Gharvān. NW Libya
Ghaznī 101 E4 *var.* Ghazni. Ghaznī, E Afghanistan
Ghazni *see* Ghaznī
Gheel *see* Geel
Gheorgheni 86 C4 *prev.* Gheorghieni, Sînt-Miclăuş, *Ger.* Niklasmarkt, *Hung.* Gyergyószentmiklós. Harghita, C Romania
Ghijduwon *see* G'ijduvon
Ghŭdara 101 F3 *var.* Gudara, *Rus.* Kudara. SE Tajikistan
Ghurdaqah *see* Hurghada
Ghūrīān 100 D4 Herāt, W Afghanistan
Giannitsá 82 B4 *var.* Yiannitsá. Kentrikí Makedonía, N Greece
Gibraltar 71 G4 *UK dependent territory* SW Europe
Gibraltar, Bay of 71 G5 *bay* Gibraltar/Spain
Gibraltar, Strait of 70 C5 *Fr.* Détroit de Gibraltar, *Sp.* Estrecho de Gibraltar. *Strait* Atlantic Ocean Mediterranean Sea
Gibson Desert 125 B5 *desert* Western Australia
Giedraičiai 85 C5 Molėtai, E Lithuania
Giessen 95 B5 Hessen, W Germany
Gifu 109 C6 *var.* Gihu. Gifu, Honshū, SW Japan
Giganta, Sierra de la 28 B3 *mountain range* W Mexico
Gihu *see* Gifu
G'ijduvon 100 D2 *var.* Ghijduwon, *Rus.* Gizhduvan. Bukhoro Wiloyati, C Uzbekistan
Gijón 70 D1 *var.* Xixón. Asturias, NW Spain
Gilani *see* Gnjilane
Gila River 26 A2 *river* Arizona, SW USA
Gilbert River 126 C3 *river* Queensland, NE Australia
Gilf Kebir Plateau 50 A2 *Ar.* Haḍabat al Jilf al Kabīr. *Plateau* SW Egypt
Gillette 22 D3 Wyoming, C USA
Gilroy 25 B6 California, W USA
Gimie, Mount 33 F1 *mountain* C Saint Lucia
Gimma *see* Jīma
Ginevra *see* Genève
Gingin 125 A6 Western Australia
Giohar *see* Jawhar
Girardot 36 B3 Cundinamarca, C Colombia
Giresun 95 E2 *var.* Kerasunt; *anc.* Cerasus, Pharnacia. Giresun, NE Turkey
Girin *see* Jilin
Girne *see* Kerýneia
Girona 71 G2 *var.* Gerona; *anc.* Gerunda. Cataluña, NE Spain
Gisborne 128 E3 Gisborne, North Island, NZ
Gissar Range 101 E3 *Rus.* Gissarskiy Khrebet. *Mountain range* Tajikistan/Uzbekistan
Githio *see* Gýtheio
Giulianova 74 D4 Abruzzo, C Italy
Giumri *see* Gyumri
Giurgiu 86 C5 Giurgiu, S Romania
Gîza *see* El Gîza
Gizeh *see* El Gîza
Gizhduvan *see* G'ijduvon
Giżyeko 76 D2 Warmiúsko-Mazurskie, NE Poland
Gjakovë *see* Đakovica
Gjilan *see* Gnjilane
Gjinokastër *see* Gjirokastër
Gjirokastër 79 C7 *var.* Gjirokastra; *prev.* Gjinokastër, *Gk.* Argyrokastron, *It.* Argirocastro. Gjirokastër, S Albania
Gjirokastra *see* Gjirokastër
Gjoa Haven 15 F3 King William Island, Nunavut, NW Canada
Gjøvik 63 B5 Oppland, S Norway
Glace Bay 17 G4 Cape Breton Island, Nova Scotia, SE Canada
Gladstone 126 E4 Queensland, E Australia
Glåma 63 B5 *river* SE Norway
Glasgow 66 C4 S Scotland, UK

Glavn'a Morava see Velika Morava
Glazov 89 D5 Udmurtskaya Respublika, NW Russian Federation
Glendale 26 B2 Arizona, SW USA
Glendive 22 D2 Montana, NW USA
Glens Falls 19 F3 New York, NE USA
Glina 78 B3 Sisak-Moslavina, NE Croatia
Glittertind 63 A5 mountain S Norway
Gliwice 77 C5 Ger. Gleiwitz. Śląskie, S Poland
Globe 26 B2 Arizona, SW USA
Głogów 76 B4 Ger. Glogau, Glogow. Dolnośląskie
Gloucester 67 D6 hist. Caer Glou, Lat. Glevum. C England, UK
Głowno 76 D4 Łódź, C Poland
Gniezno 76 C3 Ger. Gnesen. Wielkopolskie, C Poland
Gnjilane 79 D5 var. Gilani, Alb. Gjilan. Serbia, S Serbia and Montenegro (Yugo.)
Goa see Panaji
Gobabis 56 B3 Omaheke, E Namibia
Gobi 104 D3 desert China/Mongolia
Gobō 109 C6 Wakayama, Honshū, SW Japan
Godāvari 102 B3 var. Godavari. River C India
Godhavn see Qeqertarsuaq
Godhra 112 C4 Gujarāt, W India
Godoy Cruz 42 B4 Mendoza, W Argentina
Godthaab see Nuuk
Godthåb see Nuuk
Goeree 64 B4 island SW Netherlands
Goes 65 B5 Zeeland, SW Netherlands
Goettingen see Göttingen
Gogebic Range 18 B1 hill range Michigan/Wisconsin, N USA
Goiânia 41 E3 prev. Goyania. State capital Goiás, C Brazil
Goiás 41 E3 Goiás, C Brazil
Gojōme 108 D4 Akita, Honshū, NW Japan
Gökçeada 82 D4 var. Imroz Adası, Gk. Imbros. Island NW Turkey
Gökdepe 100 C3 var. Gëkdepe, Geok-Tepe. Akhalskiy Velayat, C Turkmenistan
Göksun 94 D4 Kahramanmaraş, C Turkey
Gol 63 A5 Buskerud, S Norway
Golan Heights 97 B5 Ar. Al Jawlān, Heb. HaGolan. Mountain range SW Syria
Gołdap 76 E2 Ger. Goldap. Warmińsko-Mazurskie, NE Poland
Gold Coast 127 E5 cultural region Queensland, E Australia
Golden Bay 128 C4 bay South Island, NZ
Goldsboro 21 F1 North Carolina, SE USA
Goleniów 76 B3 Ger. Gollnow. Zachodniopomorskie, NW Poland
Golmo see Golmud
Golub-Dobrzyń 76 C3 Kujawski-pomorskie, C Poland
Golmud 104 D4 var. Ge'e'mu, Golmo, Chin. Ko-erh-mu. Qinghai, C China
Goma 55 E6 Nord Kivu, NE Dem. Rep. Congo
Gombi 53 H4 Adamawa, E Nigeria
Gombroon see Bandar-e 'Abbās
Gomera 48 A3 island Islas Canarias, Spain, NE Atlantic Ocean
Gómez Palacio 28 D3 Durango, C Mexico
Gonaïves 32 D3 var. Les Gonaïves. N Haiti
Gonâve, Île de la 32 D3 island C Haiti
Gondar see Gonder
Gonder 50 C4 var. Gondar. N Ethiopia
Gondia 113 E4 Mahārāshtra, C India
Gonggar 104 C5 Xizang Zizhiqu, W China
Gongola 53 G4 river E Nigeria
Gonni see Gónnoi
Gónnoi 82 B4 var. Gonni, Gónnos; prev. Dereli. Thessalía, C Greece
Gónnos see Gónnoi
Good Hope see Fort Good Hope
Good Hope, Cape of 56 B5 Afr. Kaap de Goede Hoop, Kaap die Goeie Hoop. Headland SW South Africa
Goodland 22 D4 Kansas, C USA
Goondiwindi 127 D5 Queensland, E Australia
Goor 64 E3 Overijssel, E Netherlands
Goose Green 43 D7 var. Prado del Ganso. East Falkland, Falkland Islands
Goose Lake 24 B4 var. Lago dos Gansos. Lake California/Oregon, W USA
Göppingen 73 B6 Baden-Württemberg, SW Germany
Gora Andryu see Andrew Tablemount
Gora El'brus see El'brus
Góra Kalwaria 114 D4 Mazowieckie, C Poland
Gorakhpur 113 E3 Uttar Pradesh, N India
Goražde 78 C4 Federacija Bosna I Hercegovina, SE Bosnia and Herzegovina
Gordiaz see Gardēz
Gore 129 B7 Southland, South Island, NZ
Gorē 51 C5 C Ethiopia
Goré 54 C4 Logone-Oriental, S Chad
Gorgān 98 D2 var. Astarabad, Astrabad, Gurgan; prev. Asterābād, anc. Hyrcania. Golestān, N Iran
Gori 95 F2 C Georgia
Gorinchem 64 C4 var. Gorkum. Zuid-Holland, C Netherlands
Goris 95 G3 SE Armenia
Gorkum see Gorinchem
Görlitz 72 D4 Sachsen, E Germany
Gornji Milanovac 78 C4 Serbia, C Serbia and Montenegro (Yugo.)
Gorontalo 117 E4 Sulawesi, C Indonesia
Gorontalo, Teluk see Tomini, Gulf of
Gorssel 64 D3 Gelderland, E Netherlands
Gory Putorana see Putorana, Plato
Gorzów Wielkopolski 76 B3 Ger. Landsberg, Landsberg an der Warthe. Lubuskie, W Poland
Gosford 127 D6 New South Wales, SE Australia
Goshogawara 108 D3 var. Gosyogawara. Aomori, Honshū, C Japan
Gospić 78 A3 Lika-Senj, C Croatia
Gostivar 79 D6 W FYR Macedonia
Gosyogawara see Goshogawara
Göteborg 63 B7 Eng. Gothenburg. Västra Götaland, S Sweden
Gotel Mountains 53 G5 mountain range E Nigeria
Gotha 72 C4 Thüringen, C Germany
Gothenburg see Göteborg
Gothenburg 58 D3 Nebraska, C USA
Gotland 63 C7 island SE Sweden
Gotō-rettō 109 A7 island group SW Japan
Gotska Sandön 84 B1 island SE Sweden
Gōtsu 109 B6 var. Gôtu. Shimane, Honshū, SW Japan
Göttingen 72 B4 var. Goettingen. Niedersachsen, C Germany
Gôtu see Gōtsu
Gouda 64 C4 Zuid-Holland, C Netherlands
Gough Fracture Zone 45 C6 tectonic feature S Atlantic Ocean
Gough Island 47 B8 island Tristan da Cunha, S Atlantic Ocean
Gouin, Réservoir 16 D4 reservoir Québec, SE Canada
Goulburn 127 D6 New South Wales, SE Australia
Goundam 53 E3 Tombouctou, NW Mali
Gouré 53 G3 Zinder, SE Niger
Governador Valadares 41 F4 Minas Gerais, SE Brazil
Govĭ Altayn Nuruu 105 E3 mountain range S Mongolia
Goya 42 D3 Corrientes, NE Argentina
Goz Beïda 54 C3 Ouaddaï, SE Chad
Gozo 75 C8 Malt. Ghawdex. Island N Malta
Graciosa 70 A5 var. Ilha Graciosa. Island Azores, Portugal, NE Atlantic Ocean
Gradačac 78 C3 Federacija Bosna I Hercegovina, N Bosnia and Herzegovina
Gradaús, Serra dos 41 E3 mountain range C Brazil
Gradiška see Bosanska Gradiška
Grafton 127 E5 New South Wales, SE Australia
Grafton 23 E1 North Dakota, N USA
Graham Land 132 A2 physical region Antarctica
Grajewo 76 E3 Podlaskie, NE Poland
Grampian Mountains 66 C3 mountain range C Scotland, UK
Granada 70 D5 Andalucía, S Spain
Granada 30 D3 Granada, SW Nicaragua
Gran Canaria 48 A3 var. Grand Canary. Island Islas Canarias, Spain, NE Atlantic Ocean
Gran Chaco 42 D2 var. Chaco. Lowland plain South America
Grand see Cockburn Town
Grand Bahama Island 32 B1 island N Bahamas
Grand Banks of Newfoundland 12 E4 undersea feature NW Atlantic Ocean
Grand Canary see Gran Canaria
Grand Canyon 26 A1 canyon Arizona, SW USA
Grand Cayman 32 B3 island SW Cayman Islands
Grande, Bahía 43 B7 bay S Argentina
Grande Comore 57 F2 var. Njazidja, Great Comoro. Island NW Comoros
Grande de Chiloé, Isla see Chiloé, Isla de
Grande Prairie 15 E4 Alberta, W Canada
Grand Erg Occidental 48 D3 desert W Algeria
Grand Erg Oriental 49 E3 desert Algeria/Tunisia
Grande, Rio 13 B6 var. Río Bravo, Sp. Río Bravo del Norte, Bravo del Norte. River Mexico/USA
Grande, Rio 27 F4 river Texas, SW USA
Grande, Rio see Bravo, Río
Grande, Río 29 E2 river S Mexico
Grande Terre 33 G3 island E West Indies
Grand Falls 17 G3 Newfoundland, Newfoundland and Labrador, SE Canada
Grand Forks 23 E1 North Dakota, N USA
Grand Island 23 E4 Nebraska, C USA
Grand Junction 22 C4 Colorado, C USA
Grand Rapids 18 C3 Michigan, N USA
Grand Rapids 23 F1 Minnesota, N USA
Grand-Santi 37 G3 W French Guiana
Gran Lago see Nicaragua, Lago de
Gran Malvina, Isla see West Falkland
Gran Paradiso 74 A2 Fr. Grand Paradis. Mountain NW Italy
Gran Santiago see Santiago
Grants 26 C2 New Mexico, SW USA
Grants Pass 24 B4 Oregon, NW USA
Granville 68 B3 Manche, N France
Graulhet 69 C6 Tarn, S France
Grave 64 D4 Noord-Brabant, SE Netherlands
Grayling 14 C2 Alaska, USA
Graz 73 E7 prev. Gratz. Steiermark, SE Austria
Great Abaco 32 C1 var. Abaco Island. Island N Bahamas
Great Alfold see Great Hungarian Plain
Great Ararat see Büyükağrı Dağı
Great Australian Bight 125 D7 bight S Australia
Great Barrier Island 128 D2 island N NZ
Great Barrier Reef 126 D2 reef Queensland, NE Australia
Great Basin 25 C5 basin W USA
Great Bear Lake 15 E3 Fr. Grand Lac de l'Ours. Lake Northwest Territories, NW Canada
Great Belt see Storebælt
Great Bend 23 E5 Kansas, C USA
Great Bermuda see Bermuda
Great Britain see Britain
Great Comoro see Grande Comore
Great Dividing Range 126 D4 mountain range NE Australia
Greater Antarctica 132 C3 var. East Antarctica. Physical region Antarctica
Greater Antilles 32 D3 island group West Indies
Greater Caucasus 95 G2 Az. Bas Qafqaz Silsiläsi, Geor. Kavkasioni, Rus. Bol'shoy Kavkaz. Mountain range Asia/Europe
Greater Sunda Islands 102 D5 var. Sunda Islands. Island group Indonesia
Great Exhibition Bay 128 C1 inlet North Island, NZ
Great Exuma Island 32 C2 island C Bahamas
Great Falls 22 B1 Montana, NW USA
Great Hungarian Plain 77 C7 var. Great Alfold, Plain of Hungary, Hung. Alföld. Plain SE Europe
Great Inagua 32 D2 var. Inagua Islands. Island S Bahamas
Great Indian Desert see Thar Desert
Great Karroo see Great Karoo
Great Lakes 13 C5 lakes Ontario, Canada/USA
Great Meteor Seamount see Great Meteor Tablemount
Great Meteor Tablemount 44 B3 var. Great Meteor Seamount. Undersea feature E Atlantic Ocean
Great Nicobar 111 G3 island Nicobar Islands, India, NE Indian Ocean
Great Plain of China 103 E2 plain E China
Great Plains 23 E3 var. High Plains. Plains Canada/USA
Great Rift Valley 51 C5 var. Rift Valley. Depression Asia/Africa
Great Ruaha 51 C7 river S Tanzania
Great Saint Bernard Pass 74 A1 Fr. Col du Grand-Saint-Bernard, It. Passo di Gran San Bernardo. Pass Italy/Switzerland
Great Salt Desert see Kavīr, Dasht-e
Great Salt Lake 22 A3 salt lake Utah, W USA
Great Salt Lake Desert 22 A4 plain Utah, W USA
Great Sand Sea 49 H3 desert Egypt/Libya
Great Sandy Desert 124 C4 desert Western Australia
Great Sandy Island see Fraser Island
Great Slave Lake 15 E4 Fr. Grand Lac des Esclaves. Lake Northwest Territories, NW Canada
Great Sound 20 A5 bay Bermuda, NW Atlantic Ocean
Great Victoria Desert 125 C5 desert South Australia/Western Australia
Great Wall of China 106 C4 ancient monument N China
Great Yarmouth 67 E6 var. Yarmouth. E England, UK
Gredos, Sierra de 70 D3 mountain range W Spain
Greece 83 A5 Gk. Ellás; anc. Hellas. Country SE Europe
Greece 59 E5 New York, NE USA
Greeley 22 D4 Colorado, C USA
Green Bay 18 B2 lake bay Michigan/Wisconsin, N USA
Green Bay 18 B2 Wisconsin, N USA
Greeneville 21 E1 Tennessee, S USA
Greenland 60 D3 Dan. Grønland, Inuit Kalaallit Nunaat. Danish external territory NE North America
Greenland Sea 61 F2 sea Arctic Ocean
Green Mountains 19 G2 mountain range Vermont, NE USA
Greenock 66 C4 W Scotland, UK
Green River 18 C5 river Kentucky, C USA
Green River 22 B4 river Utah, W USA
Green River 22 B3 Wyoming, C USA
Greensboro 21 F1 North Carolina, SE USA
Greenville 20 B2 Mississippi, S USA
Greenville 21 F1 North Carolina, SE USA
Greenville 21 E1 South Carolina, SE USA
Greenville 27 G2 Texas, SW USA
Greenwich 67 B8 SE England, UK
Greenwood 20 B2 Mississippi, S USA
Greenwood 21 E2 South Carolina, SE USA
Gregory Range 126 C3 mountain range Queensland, E Australia
Greifswald 72 D2 Mecklenburg-Vorpommern, NE Germany
Grenada 33 G5 country SE West Indies
Grenada 20 C2 Mississippi, S USA
Grenadines, The 33 H4 island group Grenada/St Vincent and the Grenadines
Grenoble 69 D5 anc. Cularo, Gratianopolis. Isère, E France
Gresham 24 B3 Oregon, NW USA
Grevenà 82 B4 Dytikí Makedonía, N Greece
Grevenmacher 65 E8 Grevenmacher, E Luxembourg
Greymouth 129 B5 West Coast, South Island, NZ
Grey Range 127 C5 mountain range New South Wales/Queensland, E Australia
Greytown see San Juan del Norte
Griffin 20 D2 Georgia, SE USA
Grimari 54 C4 Ouaka, C Central African Republic
Grimsby 67 E5 prev. Great Grimsby. E England, UK
Grobiņa 84 B3 Ger. Grobin. Liepāja, W Latvia
Grodzisk Wielkopolski 76 B3 Wielkolpolskie, C Poland
Groesbeek 64 D4 Gelderland, SE Netherlands
Grójec 76 D4 Mazowieckie, C Poland
Groningen 64 E1 Groningen, NE Netherlands
Groote Eylandt 126 B2 island Northern Territory, N Australia
Grootfontein 56 B3 Otjozondjupa, N Namibia
Groot Karasberge 56 B4 mountain range S Namibia
Groot Karoo see Great Karoo
Gros Islet 33 F1 N Saint Lucia
Grosse Morava see Velika Morava
Grosseto 74 B4 Toscana, C Italy
Grossglockner 73 C7 mountain W Austria
Groznyy 89 B8 Chechenskaya Respublika, SW Russian Federation
Grudziądz 76 C3 Ger. Graudenz. Kujawski-pomorskie, C Poland
Grums 63 B6 Värmland, C Sweden
Gryazi 89 B6 Lipetskaya Oblast', W Russian Federation
Gryfice 76 B2 Ger. Greifenberg, Greifenberg in Pommern. Zachodniopomorskie, NW Poland
Guabito 31 E4 Bocas del Toro, NW Panama
Guadalajara 71 E3 Ar. Wad Al-Hajarah; anc. Arriaca. Castilla-La Mancha, C Spain
Guadalajara 28 D4 Jalisco, C Mexico
Guadalcanal 122 C3 island C Solomon Islands
Guadalquivir 70 D4 river W Spain
Guadalupe 28 D3 Zacatecas, C Mexico
Guadalupe Peak 26 D3 mountain Texas, SW USA
Guadalupe River 27 G4 river SW USA
Guadarrama, Sierra de 71 E2 mountain range C Spain
Guadeloupe 33 H3 French overseas department E West Indies
Guadiana 70 C4 river Portugal/Spain
Guadix 71 E4 Andalucía, S Spain
Guaimaca 30 C2 Francisco Morazán, C Honduras
Guajira, Península de la 36 B1 peninsula N Colombia
Gualaco 30 D2 Olancho, C Honduras
Gualán 30 B2 Zacapa, C Guatemala
Gualdicciolo 74 D1 NW San Marino
Gualeguaychú 42 D4 Entre Ríos, E Argentina
Guam 122 B1 US unincorporated territory W Pacific Ocean
Guamúchil 28 C3 Sinaloa, C Mexico
Guanabacoa 32 B2 La Habana, W Cuba
Guanajuato 29 E4 Guanajuato, C Mexico
Guanare 36 C2 Portuguesa, N Venezuela
Guanare, Río 36 D2 river W Venezuela
Guangdong 106 C6 var. Guangdong Sheng, Kuang-tung, Kwangtung, Yue. Admin. region province S China
Guangdong Sheng see Guangdong
Guangxi see Guangxi Zhuangzu Zizhiqu
Guangxi Zhuangzu Zizhiqu 106 C6 var. Guangxi, Gui, Kuang-hsi, Kwangsi, Eng. Kwangsi Chuang Autonomous Region. Admin. region autonomous region S China
Guangyuan 106 B5 var. Kuang-yuan, Kwangyuan. Sichuan, C China
Guangzhou 106 C6 var. Kuang-chou, Kwangchow, Eng. Canton. Guangdong, S China
Guantánamo 32 D3 Guantánamo, SE Cuba
Guantánamo Bay 32 D3 US military installation, SE Cuba
Guaporé, Río 40 D3 var. Río Iténez. River Bolivia/Brazil see also Iténez, Río
Guarda 70 C3 Guarda, N Portugal
Guarumal 31 F5 Veraguas, S Panama
Guasave 28 C3 Sinaloa, C Mexico
Guatemala 30 A2 Country Central America
Guatemala Basin 13 B7 undersea feature E Pacific Ocean
Guatemala City see Ciudad de Guatemala
Guaviare 34 B2 off. Comisaría Guaviare. Province S Colombia
Guaviare, Río 36 D3 river E Colombia
Guayaquil 38 A2 var. Santiago de Guayaquil. Guayas, SW Ecuador
Guayaquil, Golfo de 38 A2 var. Gulf of Guayaquil. Gulf SW Ecuador
Guayaquil, Gulf of see Guayaquil, Golfo de
Guaymas 28 B2 Sonora, NW Mexico
Gubadag 100 C2 Turkm. Tel'man; prev. Tel'mansk. Dashkhovuzskiy Velayat, N Turkmenistan
Guben 72 D4 var. Wilhelm-Pieck-Stadt. Brandenburg, E Germany
Gudara see Ghŭdara
Gudaut'a 95 E1 NW Georgia
Guéret 68 C4 Creuse, C France
Guernsey 67 D8 UK dependent territory NW Europe
Guerrero Negro 28 A2 Baja California Sur, NW Mexico
Gui see Guangxi Zhuangzu Zizhiqu
Guiana see French Guiana
Guiana Highlands 40 D1 var. Macizo de las Guayanas. Mountain range N South America
Guidder see Guider
Guider 54 B4 var. Guidder. Nord, N Cameroon
Guidimouni 53 G3 Zinder, S Niger
Guildford 67 D7 SE England, UK
Guilin 106 C6 var. Kuei-lin, Kweilin. Guangxi Zhuangzu Zizhiqu, S China
Guimarães 70 B2 var. Guimaráes. Braga, N Portugal
Guinea 52 C4 var. Guinée; prev. French Guinea, People's Revolutionary Republic of Guinea. Country W Africa
Guinea Basin 47 A5 undersea feature E Atlantic Ocean
Guinea-Bissau 52 B4 Fr. Guinée-Bissau, Port. Guiné-Bissau; prev. Portuguese Guinea. Country W Africa
Guinea, Gulf of 46 B4 Fr. Golfe de Guinée. Gulf E Atlantic Ocean
Güiria 37 E1 Sucre, NE Venezuela
Guiyang 106 B6 var. Kuei-Yang, Kuei-yang, Kueyang, Kweiyang; prev. Kweichu. Guizhou, S China
Guizhou 106 B6 var. Guizhou Sheng, Kuei-chou, Kweichow, Qian. Admin. region province S China
Guizhou Sheng see Guizhou
Gujarāt 112 C4 var. Gujerat. Admin. region state W India
Gujerat see Gujarāt
Gujrānwāla 112 D2 Punjab, NE Pakistan
Gujrāt 112 D2 Punjab, E Pakistan
Gulbarga 110 C1 Karnātaka, C India
Gulbene 84 D3 Ger. Alt-Schwanenburg. Gulbene, NE Latvia
Gulfport 20 C3 Mississippi, S USA
Gulf, The 98 C4 var. Persian Gulf, Ar. Khalīj al 'Arabī, Per. Khalīj-e Fars. Gulf SE Asia
Guliston 101 E2 Rus. Gulistan. Sirdaryo Wiloyati, E Uzbekistan
Gulja see Yining
Gulkana 14 D3 Alaska, USA
Gulu 51 B6 N Uganda
Gulyantsi 82 C1 Pleven, N Bulgaria
Guma see Pishan
Gümülcine see Komotiní
Gümüljina see Komotiní
Gümüşane see Gümüşhane
Gümüşhane 95 E3 var. Gümüşane, Gumushkhane. Gümüşhane, NE Turkey
Gumushkhane see Gümüşhane
Güney Doğu Toroslar 95 E4 mountain range SE Turkey
Gunnbjørn Fjeld 60 D4 var. Gunnbjörns Bjerge. Mountain C Greenland
Gunnbjörns Bjerge see Gunnbjørn Fjeld
Gunnedah 127 D6 New South Wales, SE Australia
Gunnison 22 C5 Colorado, C USA
Gurbantünggüt Shamo 104 B2 desert W China
Gurgan see Gorgān
Guri, Embalse de 37 E2 reservoir E Venezuela
Gurktaler Alpen 73 D7 mountain range S Austria
Gürün 94 D3 Sivas, C Turkey
Gusau 53 G4 Zamfara, NW Nigeria
Gusev 84 B4 Ger. Gumbinnen. Kaliningradskaya Oblast', W Russian Federation
Gustavus 14 D4 Alaska, USA
Güstrow 72 C3 Mecklenburg-Vorpommern, NE Germany
Gütersloh 72 B4 Nordrhein-Westfalen, W Germany
Guwāhāti 113 G3 prev. Gauhāti. Assam, NE India
Guyana 37 F3 prev. British Guiana. Country N South America
Guyane see French Guiana
Guymon 27 E1 Oklahoma, C USA
Güzelyurt seeMórfou
Gvardeysk 84 A4 Ger. Tapaiu. Kaliningradskaya Oblast', W Russian Federation
Gwādar 112 A3 var. Gwadur. Baluchistān, SW Pakistan
Gwadur see Gwādar
Gwalior 112 D3 Madhya Pradesh, C India
Gwanda 56 D3 Matabeleland South, SW Zimbabwe
Gwy see Wye
Gyangzê 104 C5 Xizang Zizhiqu, W China
Gyaring Co 104 C5 lake W China
Gympie 127 E5 Queensland, E Australia
Gyomaendrőd 77 D7 Békés, SE Hungary
Gyöngyös 77 D6 Heves, NE Hungary
Győr 77 C6 Ger. Raab; Lat. Arrabona. Győr-Moson-Sopron, NW Hungary
Gýtheio 83 B6 var. Githio; prev. Yíthion. Pelopónnisos, S Greece
Gyumri 95 F2 var. Giumri, Rus. Kumayri; prev. Aleksandropol', Leninakan. W Armenia

H

Haabai see Ha'apai Group
Haacht 65 C6 Vlaams Brabant, C Belgium
Haaksbergen 64 E3 Overijssel, E Netherlands
Ha'apai Group 123 F4 var. Haabai. Island group C Tonga
Haapsalu 84 D2 Ger. Hapsal. Läänemaa, W Estonia
Haarlem 64 C3 prev. Harlem. Noord-Holland, W Netherlands
Haast 129 B6 West Coast, South Island, NZ
Hachijō-jima 109 D6 var. Hatizyô Zima. Island Izu-shotō, SE Japan
Hachinohe 108 D3 Aomori, Honshū, C Japan
Hadama see Nazrēt
Haddummati Atoll see Hadhdhunmathi Atoll
Hadejia 53 G3 river N Nigeria
Hadejia 53 G4 Jigawa, N Nigeria
Hadera 97 A6 var. Khadera. Haifa, C Israel
Hadhdhunmathi Atoll 110 A5 var. Haddummati Atoll, Laamu Atoll. Atoll S Maldives
Ha Đông 114 D3 var. Hadong. Ha Tây, N Vietnam
Hadong see Ha Đông
Ḩaḑramawt 99 C6 Eng. Hadhramaut. Mountain range S Yemen
Haerbin see Harbin
Haerhpin see Harbin
Hafren see Severn
Hagåtña 160 B1 var. Agana/Agaña. Dependent territory capital (Guam), NW Guam
Hagerstown 19 E4 Maryland, NE USA
Ha Giang 114 D3 Ha Giang, N Vietnam
Hagondange 68 D3 Moselle, NE France
Haguenau 68 E3 Bas-Rhin, NE France
Haicheng 106 D3 Liaoning, NE China
Haidarabad see Hyderābād
Haifa see Ḩefa
Haifong see Hai Phong
Haikou 106 C7 var. Hai-k'ou, Hoihow, Fr. Hoï-Hao. Hainan, S China
Hai-k'ou see Haikou
Ḩā'il 98 B4 off. Minţaqah Ḩā'il. Province N Saudi Arabia
Hai-la-erh see Hailar
Hailar 105 F1 var. Hai-la-erh; prev. Hulun. Nei Mongol Zizhiqu, N China
Hailuoto 62 D4 Swe. Karlö. Island W Finland

Hainan 106 B7 *var.* Hainan Sheng, Qiong. Admin. region *province* S China
Hainan Dao 106 C7 *island* S China
Hainan Sheng *see* Hainan
Haines 14 D4 Alaska, USA
Hainichen 72 D4 Sachsen, E Germany
Hai Phong 114 D3 *var.* Haifong, Haiphong. N Vietnam
Haiphong *see* Hai Phong
Haiti 32 D3 C West Indies
Haiya 50 C3 Red Sea, NE Sudan
Hajdúhadház 77 D6 Hajdú-Bihar, E Hungary
Hajîne *see* Abū Ḩardān
Hajnówka 76 E3 *Ger.* Hermhausen. Podlaskie, NE Poland
Hakodate 108 D3 Hokkaidō, NE Japan
Ḩalab 96 B2 *Eng.* Aleppo, *Fr.* Alep; *anc.* Beroea. Ḩalab, NW Syria
Ḩalāniyāt, Juzur al 137 D6 *var.* Jazā'ir Bin Ghalfān, *Eng.* Kuria Muria Islands. *Island group* S Oman
Halberstadt 72 C4 Sachsen-Anhalt, C Germany
Halden 63 B6 *prev.* Fredrikshald. Østfold, S Norway
Halfmoon Bay 129 A8 *var.* Oban. Stewart Island, Southland, NZ
Halifax 17 F4 Nova Scotia, SE Canada
Halkida *see* Chalkída
Halle 65 B6 *Fr.* Hal. Vlaams Brabant, C Belgium
Halle 72 C4 *var.* Halle an der Saale. Sachsen-Anhalt, C Germany
Halle an der Saale *see* Halle
Halle-Neustadt 72 C4 Sachsen-Anhalt, C Germany
Halley 132 B2 *UK research station* Antarctica
Hall Islands 120 B2 *island group* C Micronesia
Halls Creek 124 C3 Western Australia
Halmahera, Pulau 117 F3 *prev.* Djailolo, Gilolo, Jailolo. *Island* E Indonesia
Halmahera Sea 117 F4 *Ind.* Laut Halmahera. *Sea* E Indonesia
Halmstad 63 B7 Halland, S Sweden
Hama *see* Ḩamāh
Hamada 109 B6 Shimane, Honshū, SW Japan
Hamadān 98 C3 *anc.* Ecbatana. Hamadān, W Iran
Ḩamāh 96 B3 *var.* Hama; *anc.* Epiphania, *Bibl.* Hamath. Ḩamāh, W Syria
Hamamatsu 109 D6 *var.* Hamamatu. Shizuoka, Honshū, S Japan
Hamamatu *see* Hamamatsu
Hamar 63 B5 *prev.* Storhammer. Hedmark, S Norway
Hamath *see* Ḩamāh
Hamburg 72 B3 Hamburg, N Germany
Ḩamḑ, Wādī al 136 A4 *dry watercourse* W Saudi Arabia
Hämeenlinna 63 D5 *Swe.* Tavastehus. Etelä-Suomi, S Finland
Hamersley Range 124 A4 *mountain range* Western Australia
Hamhŭng 107 E3 C North Korea
Hami 104 C3 *var.* Ha-mi, *Uigh.* Kumul, Qomul. Xinjiang Uygur Zizhiqu, NW China
Ha-mi *see* Hami
Hamilton 20 C2 Alabama, S USA
Hamilton 16 D5 Ontario, S Canada
Hamilton 66 C4 S Scotland, UK
Hamilton 128 D3 Waikato, North Island, NZ
Ḩamīm, Wādī al 87 G2 *river* NE Libya
Hamīs Musait *see* Khamīs Mushayt
Hamiton 20 A5 *dependent territory capital* (Bermuda) C Bermuda
Hamm 72 B4 *var.* Hamm in Westfalen. Nordrhein-Westfalen, W Germany
Hammada du Drâa *see* Dra, Hamada du
Hammamet, Golfe de 80 D3 *Ar.* Khalīj al Ḩammāmāt. *Gulf* NE Tunisia
Ḩammār, Hawr al 136 C3 *lake* SE Iraq
Hamm in Westfalen *see* Hamm
Hampden 129 B7 Otago, South Island, NZ
Hampstead 67 A7 SE England, UK
Hamrun 80 B5 C Malta
Hânceşti *see* Hînceşti
Handan 106 C4 *var.* Han-tan. Hebei, E China
Haneda 108 A2 *international airport* (Tōkyō) Tōkyō, Honshū, S Japan
HaNegev 97 A7 *Eng.* Negev. *Desert* S Israel
Hanford 25 C6 California, W USA
Hangayn Nuruu 104 D2 *mountain range* C Mongolia
Hang-chou *see* Hangzhou
Hangchow *see* Hangzhou
Hangö *see* Hanko
Hangzhou 106 D5 *var.* Hang-chou, Hangchow. Zhejiang, SE China
Hania *see* Chaniá
Hanka, Lake *see* Khanka, Lake
Hanko 63 D6 *Swe.* Hangö. Etelä-Suomi, SW Finland
Han-k'ou *see* Wuhan
Hankow *see* Wuhan
Hanmer Springs 129 C5 Canterbury, South Island, NZ
Hannibal 23 G4 Missouri, C USA
Hannover 72 B3 *Eng.* Hanover. Niedersachsen, NW Germany
Hanöbukten 63 B7 *bay* S Sweden
Ha Nôi 114 D3 *Eng.* Hanoi, *Fr.* Ha noï. *Country capital* (Vietnam) N Vietnam
Hanoi *see* Ha Nôi
Han Shui 105 E4 *river* C China
Han-tan *see* Handan
Hantsavichy 85 B6 *Pol.* Hancewicze, *Rus.* Gantsevichi. Brestskaya Voblasts', SW Belarus
Hanyang *see* Wuhan
Hanzhong 106 B5 Shaanxi, C China
Hāora 113 F4 *prev.* Howrah. West Bengal, NE India
Haparanda 62 D4 Norrbotten, N Sweden
Haradok 85 E5 *Rus.* Gorodok. Vitsyebskaya Voblasts', N Belarus
Haradzyets 85 B6 *Rus.* Gorodets. Brestskaya Voblasts', SW Belarus
Haramachi 108 D4 Fukushima, Honshū, E Japan
Harany 85 D5 *Rus.* Gorany. Vitsyebskaya Voblasts', N Belarus
Harare 56 D3 *prev.* Salisbury. *Country capital* (Zimbabwe) Mashonaland East, NE Zimbabwe
Harbavichy 85 E6 *Rus.* Gorbovichi. Mahilyowskaya Voblasts', E Belarus
Harbel 52 C5 W Liberia
Harbin 107 E2 *var.* Haerbin, Ha-erh-pin, Kharbin; *prev.* Haerhpin, Pingkiang, Pinkiang. Heilongjiang, NE China
Hardangerfjorden 63 A6 *fjord* S Norway
Hardangervidda 63 A6 *plateau* S Norway
Hardenberg 64 E3 Overijssel, E Netherlands
Harelbeke 65 A6 *var.* Harlebeke. West-Vlaanderen, W Belgium
Harem *see* Ḩārim
Haren 64 E2 Groningen, NE Netherlands
Hārer 51 D5 E Ethiopia
Hargeisa *see* Hargeysa
Hargeysa 51 D5 *var.* Hargeisa. Woqooyi Galbeed, NW Somalia
Hariana *see* Haryāna
Hari, Batang 116 B4 *prev.* Djambi. *River* Sumatera, W Indonesia
Ḩārim 96 B2 *var.* Harem. Idlib, W Syria
Harima-nada 109 B6 *sea* S Japan
Harīrūd *var.* Tedzhen, *Turkm.* Tejen. *River* Afghanistan/Iran *see also* Tedzhen
Harlan 23 F3 Iowa, C USA
Harlebeke *see* Harelbeke
Harlingen 64 D2 *Fris.* Harns. Friesland, N Netherlands
Harlingen 27 G5 Texas, SW USA
Harlow 67 E6 E England, UK
Harney Basin 24 B4 *basin* Oregon, NW USA
Härnösand 63 C5 *var.* Hernösand. Västernorrland, C Sweden
Har Nuur 104 C2 *lake* NW Mongolia
Harper 52 D5 *var.* Cape Palmas. NE Liberia
Harricana 16 D3 *river* Québec, SE Canada
Harris 66 B3 *physical region* NW Scotland, UK
Harrisburg 19 E4 *state capital* Pennsylvania, NE USA
Harrisonburg 19 E4 Virginia, NE USA
Harrison, Cape 17 F2 *headland* Newfoundland and Labrador, E Canada
Harris Ridge *see* Lomonosov Ridge
Harrogate 67 D5 N England, UK
Hârşova 86 D5 *prev.* Hîrşova. Constanţa, SE Romania
Harstad 62 C2 Troms, N Norway
Hartford 19 G3 *state capital* Connecticut, NE USA
Hartlepool 67 D5 N England, UK
Harunabad *see* Eslāmābād
Harwich 67 E6 E England, UK
Haryāna 112 D2 *var.* Hariana. Admin. region *state* N India
Hasselt 65 C6 Limburg, NE Belgium
Hassetché *see* Al Ḩasakah
Hastings 128 E4 Hawke's Bay, North Island, NZ
Hastings 23 E4 Nebraska, C USA
Hastings 67 E7 SE England, UK
Haţeg 86 B4 *Ger.* Wallenthal, *Hung.* Hátszeg; *prev.* Hatzeg, Hötzing. Hunedoara, SW Romania
Hatizyô Zima *see* Hachijō-jima
Hattem 64 D3 Gelderland, E Netherlands
Hatteras, Cape 21 G1 *headland* North Carolina, SE USA
Hatteras Plain 13 D6 *undersea feature* W Atlantic Ocean
Hattiesburg 20 C3 Mississippi, S USA
Hatton Bank *see* Hatton Ridge
Hatton Ridge 58 B2 *var.* Hatton Bank. *Undersea feature* N Atlantic Ocean
Hat Yai 115 C7 *var.* Ban Hat Yai. Songkhla, SW Thailand
Haugesund 63 A6 Rogaland, S Norway
Haukeligrend 63 A6 Telemark, S Norway
Haukivesi 63 E5 *lake* SE Finland
Hauraki Gulf 128 D2 *gulf* North Island, NZ
Hauroko, Lake 129 A7 *lake* South Island, NZ
Haut Atlas 48 C2 *Eng.* High Atlas. *Mountain range* C Morocco
Hautes Fagnes 65 D6 *Ger.* Hohes Venn. *Mountain range* E Belgium
Haut Plateau du Dra *see* Dra, Hamada du
Hauts Plateaux 48 D2 *plateau* Algeria/Morocco
Hauzenberg 73 D6 Bayern, SE Germany
Havana *see* La Habana
Havana 13 D6 Illinois, N USA
Havant 67 D7 S England, UK
Havelock 21 F1 North Carolina, SE USA
Havelock North 128 E4 Hawke's Bay, North Island, NZ
Haverfordwest 67 C6 SW Wales, UK
Havířov 77 C5 Ostravský Kraj, E Czech Republic
Havre 22 C1 Montana, NW USA
Havre-St-Pierre 17 F3 Québec, E Canada
Hawai'i 25 B8 *var.* Hawaii. *Island* Hawaiian Islands, USA, C Pacific Ocean
Hawai'i 25 A8 *off.* State of Hawaii; also known as Aloha State, Paradise of the Pacific, *var.* Hawaii. *State* USA, C Pacific Ocean
Hawaiian Islands 130 D2 *prev.* Sandwich Islands. *Island group* Hawaii, USA, C Pacific Ocean
Hawaiian Ridge 91 H4 *undersea feature* N Pacific Ocean
Hawash *see* Āwash
Hawea, Lake 129 B6 *lake* South Island, NZ
Hawera 128 D4 Taranaki, North Island, NZ
Hawick 66 C4 SE Scotland, UK
Hawke Bay 128 E4 *bay* North Island, NZ
Hawlēr *see* Arbīl
Hawthorne 25 C6 Nevada, W USA
Hay 127 C6 New South Wales, SE Australia
Hayes 16 B2 *river* Manitoba, C Canada
Hay River 15 E4 Northwest Territories, W Canada
Hays 23 E5 Kansas, C USA
Haysyn 86 D3 *Rus.* Gaysin. Vinnyts'ka Oblast', C Ukraine
Hazar 100 B2 *prev.* Cheleken. Balkanskiy Velayat, W Turkmenistan
Heard and McDonald Islands 119 B7 *Australian external territory* S Indian Ocean
Hearst 16 C4 Ontario, S Canada
Heathrow 67 A8 *international airport* (London)SE England, UK
Hebei 106 C4 *var.* Hebei Sheng, Hopeh, Hopei, Ji; *prev.* Chihli. Admin. region *province* E China
Hebei Sheng *see* Hebei
Hebron 97 A6 *var.* Al Khalīl, El Khalil, *Heb.* Ḩevron; *anc.* Kiriath-Arba. S West Bank
Hebrus *see* Maritsa
Heemskerk 64 C3 Noord-Holland, W Netherlands
Heerde 64 D3 Gelderland, E Netherlands
Heerenveen 64 D2 *Fris.* It Hearrenfean. Friesland, N Netherlands
Heerhugowaard 64 C2 Noord-Holland, NW Netherlands
Heerlen 65 D6 Limburg, SE Netherlands
Heerwegen *see* Polkowice
Ḩefa 97 A5 *var.* Haifa; *hist.* Caiffa, Caiphas, *anc.* Sycaminum. Haifa, N Israel
Ḩefa, Mifraz 97 A5 *Eng.* Bay of Haifa. *Bay* N Israel
Hefei 106 D5 *var.* Hofei; *hist.* Luchow. Anhui, E China
Hegang 107 E2 Heilongjiang, NE China
Hei *see* Heilongjiang
Heide 72 B2 Schleswig-Holstein, N Germany
Heidelberg 73 B5 Baden-Württemberg, SW Germany
Heidenheim *see* Heidenheim an der Brenz
Heidenheim an der Brenz 73 B6 *var.* Heidenheim. Baden-Württemberg, S Germany
Heilbronn 73 B6 Baden-Württemberg, SW Germany
Heilongjiang 106 D2 *var.* Hei, Heilongjiang Sheng, Hei-lung-chiang, Heilungkiang. Admin. region *province* NE China
Heilongjiang Sheng *see* Heilongjiang
Heiloo 64 C3 Noord-Holland, NW Netherlands
Hei-lung-chiang *see* Heilongjiang
Heilungkiang *see* Heilongjiang
Heimdal 63 B5 Sør-Trøndelag, S Norway
Hekimhan 94 D3 Malatya, C Turkey
Helena 22 B2 *state capital* Montana, NW USA
Helensville 128 D2 Auckland, North Island, NZ
Helgoland Bay *see* Helgoländer Bucht
Helgoländer Bucht 72 A2 *var.* Helgoland Bay, Heligoland Bight. *Bay* NW Germany
Heligoland Bight *see* Helgoländer Bucht
Heliopolis *see* Baalbek
Hellevoetsluis 64 B4 Zuid-Holland, SW Netherlands
Hellín 71 E4 Castilla-La Mancha, C Spain
Helmand, Daryā-ye *var.* Rūd-e Hīrmand. *River* Afghanistan/Iran *see also* Hīrmand, Rūd-e
Helmond 65 D5 Noord-Brabant, S Netherlands
Helsingborg 63 B7 *prev.* Hälsingborg. Skåne, S Sweden
Helsinki 63 D6 *Swe.* Helsingfors. *Country capital* (Finland) Etelä-Suomi, S Finland
Henan 106 C5 *var.* Henan Sheng, Honan, Yu. Admin. region *province* C China
Henan Sheng *see* Henan
Henderson 18 B5 Kentucky, S USA
Henderson 25 D7 Nevada, W USA
Henderson 27 H3 Texas, SW USA
Hengchow *see* Hengyang
Hengduan Shan 106 A5 *mountain range* SW China
Hengelo 64 E3 Overijssel, E Netherlands
Hengnan *see* Hengyang
Hengyang 106 C6 *var.* Hengnan, Heng-yang; *prev.* Hengchow. Hunan, S China
Heng-yang *see* Hengyang
Heniches'k 87 F4 *Rus.* Genichesk. Khersons'ka Oblast', S Ukraine
Hennebont 68 A3 Morbihan, NW France
Henzada 114 B4 Irrawaddy, SW Myanmar
Herakleion *see* Irákleio
Herāt 100 D4 *var.* Herat; *anc.* Aria. Herāt, W Afghanistan
Herat *see* Herāt
Heredia 31 E4 Heredia, C Costa Rica
Hereford 27 E2 Texas, SW USA
Herford 72 B4 Nordrhein-Westfalen, NW Germany
Herk-de-Stad 65 C6 Limburg, NE Belgium
Hermansverk 63 A5 Sogn Og Fjordane, S Norway
Hermhausen *see* Hajnówka
Hermiston 24 C2 Oregon, NW USA
Hermon, Mount 97 B5 *Ar.* Jabal ash Shaykh. *Mountain* S Syria
Hermosillo 28 B2 Sonora, NW Mexico
Hermoupolis *see* Ermoúpoli
Hernösand *see* Härnösand
Herrera del Duque 70 D3 Extremadura, W Spain
Herselt 65 C5 Antwerpen, C Belgium
Herstal 65 D6 *Fr.* Héristal. Liège, E Belgium
Hessen 73 B5 *cultural region* C Germany
Ḩevron *see* Hebron
Heydebrech *see* Kędzierzyn-Kole
Heywood Islands 124 C3 *island group* Western Australia
Hibbing 23 F1 Minnesota, N USA
Hidalgo del Parral 28 C2 *var.* Parral. Chihuahua, N Mexico
Hida-sanmyaku 109 C5 *mountain range* Honshū, S Japan
Hierro 48 A3 *var.* Ferro. *Island* Islas Canarias, Spain, NE Atlantic Ocean
High Plains *see* Great Plains
High Point 21 E1 North Carolina, SE USA
High Veld *see* Great Karoo
Hiiumaa 84 C2 *Ger.* Dagden, *Swe.* Dagö. *Island* W Estonia
Hikurangi 128 D2 Northland, North Island, NZ
Hildesheim 72 B4 Niedersachsen, N Germany
Hilla *see* Al Ḩillah
Hillaby, Mount 33 G1 *mountain* N Barbados
Hill Bank 30 C1 Orange Walk, N Belize
Hillegom 64 C3 Zuid-Holland, W Netherlands
Hilo 25 B8 Hawai'i, USA, C Pacific Ocean
Hilton Head Island 21 E2 South Carolina, SE USA
Hilversum 64 C3 Noord-Holland, C Netherlands
Himalaya *see* Himalayas
Himalayas 113 E2 *var.* Himalaya, *Chin.* Himalaya Shan. *Mountain range* S Asia
Himalaya Shan *see* Himalayas
Himeji 109 C6 *var.* Himezi. Hyōgo, Honshū, SW Japan
Himezi *see* Himeji
Ḩimş 96 B4 *var.* Homs; *anc.* Emesa. Ḩimş, C Syria
Hînceşti 86 D4 *var.* Hânceşti; *prev.* Kotovsk. C Moldova
Hinchinbrook Island 126 D3 *island* Queensland, NE Australia
Hinds 129 C6 Canterbury, South Island, NZ
Hindu Kush 101 F4 *Per.* Hendū Kosh. *Mountain range* Afghanistan/Pakistan
Hinesville 21 E3 Georgia, SE USA
Hinnøya 62 C3 *island* C Norway
Hinson Bay 20 A5 *bay* W Bermuda
Hios *see* Chíos
Hirosaki 108 D3 Aomori, Honshū, C Japan
Hiroshima 109 B6 *var.* Hirosima. Hiroshima, Honshū, SW Japan
Hirosima *see* Hiroshima
Hirson 68 D3 Aisne, N France
Hispaniola 34 B1 *island* Dominion Republic/Haiti
Hitachi 109 D5 *var.* Hitati. Ibaraki, Honshū, S Japan
Hitati *see* Hitachi
Hitra 62 A4 *prev.* Hitteren. *Island* S Norway
Hjälmaren 63 C6 *Eng.* Lake Hjalmar. *Lake* C Sweden
Hjørring 63 B7 Nordjylland, N Denmark
Hkakabo Razi 114 B1 *mountain* Myanmar/China
Hlobyne 87 F2 *Rus.* Globino. Poltavs'ka Oblast', NE Ukraine
Hlukhiv 87 F1 *Rus.* Glukhov. Sums'ka Oblast', NE Ukraine
Hlybokaye 85 D5 *Rus.* Glubokoye. Vitsyebskaya Voblasts', N Belarus
Hoa Binh 114 D3 Hoa Binh, N Vietnam
Hoang Liên Sơn 114 D3 *mountain range* N Vietnam
Hobart 127 C8 *prev.* Hobarton, Hobart Town. *State capital* Tasmania, SE Australia
Hobbs 27 E3 New Mexico, SW USA
Hobro 63 A7 Nordjylland, N Denmark
Hô Chi Minh 115 E6 *var.* Ho Chi Minh City; *prev.* Saigon. S Vietnam
Ho Chi Minh City *see* Hô Chi Minh
Hódmezővásárhely 77 D7 Csongrád, SE Hungary
Hodna, Chott El 118 C4 *var.* Chott el-Hodna, *Ar.* Shatt al-Hodna. *Salt lake* N Algeria
Hodonín 77 C5 *Ger.* Göding. Brněnský Kraj, SE Czech Republic
Hoë Karoo *see* Great Karoo
Hof 73 C5 Bayern, SE Germany
Hofei *see* Hefei
Hōfu 109 B7 Yamaguchi, Honshū, SW Japan
Hofuf *see* Al Hufūf
Hogoley Islands *see* Chuuk Islands
Hohe Tauern 73 C7 *mountain range* W Austria
Hohhot 105 F3 *var.* Huhehot, Huhuohaote, *Mong.* Kukukhoto; *prev.* Kweisui, Kwesui. Nei Mongol Zizhiqu, N China
Hôi An 115 E5 *prev.* Faifo. Quang Nam-Đa Nǎng, C Vietnam
Hoï-Hao *see* Haikou
Hoihow *see* Haikou
Hokianga Harbour 128 C2 *inlet* SE Tasman Sea
Hokitika 129 B5 West Coast, South Island, NZ
Hokkaidō 108 C2 *prev.* Ezo, Yeso, Yezo. *Island* NE Japan
Hola Prystan' 87 E4 *Rus.* Golaya Pristan. Khersons'ka Oblast', S Ukraine
Holbrook 26 B2 Arizona, SW USA
Holetown 33 G1 *prev.* Jamestown. W Barbados
Holguín 32 C2 Holguín, SE Cuba
Hollabrunn 73 E6 Niederösterreich, NE Austria
Hollandia *see* Jayapura
Holly Springs 20 C1 Mississippi, S USA
Holman 15 E3 Victoria Island, Northwest Territories, N Canada
Holmsund 62 D4 Västerbotten, N Sweden
Ḩolon 97 A6 *var.* Kholon. Tel Aviv, C Israel
Holovanivs'k 87 E3 *Rus.* Golovanevsk. Kirovohrads'ka Oblast', C Ukraine
Holstebro 63 A7 Ringkøbing, W Denmark
Holsteinborg *see* Sisimiut
Holsteinsborg *see* Sisimiut
Holstenborg *see* Sisimiut
Holstensborg *see* Sisimiut
Holyhead 67 C5 *Wel.* Caer Gybi. NW Wales, UK
Hombori 53 E3 Mopti, S Mali
Homs *see* Al Khums
Homs *see* Ḩimş
Homyel' 85 D7 *Rus.* Gomel'. Homyel'skaya Voblasts', SE Belarus
Honan *see* Henan
Honan *see* Luoyang
Hondo *see* Honshū
Hondo 27 F4 Texas, SW USA
Honduras 30 C2 *Country* Central America
Honduras, Gulf of 30 C2 *Sp.* Golfo de Honduras. *Gulf* W Caribbean Sea
Hønefoss 63 B6 Buskerud, S Norway
Honey Lake 25 B5 *lake* California, W USA
Hon Gai *see* Hông Gai
Hongay *see* Hông Gai
Hông Gai 114 E3 *var.* Hon Gai, Hongay. Quang Ninh, N Vietnam
Hong Kong 106 A1 *Chin.* Xianggang. S China
Hong Kong Island 106 B2 *Chin.* Xianggang. *Island* S China
Honiara 122 C3 *country capital* (Solomon Islands) Guadalcanal, C Solomon Islands
Honjō 108 D4 *var.* Honzyô. Akita, Honshū, C Japan
Honolulu 25 A8 *admin capital* O'ahu, Hawai'i, USA, C Pacific Ocean
Honshū 109 E5 *var.* Hondo, Honsyû. *Island* SW Japan
Honsyû *see* Honshū
Honzyô *see* Honjō
Hoogeveen 64 E2 Drenthe, NE Netherlands
Hoogezand-Sappemeer 64 E2 Groningen, NE Netherlands
Hoorn 64 C2 Noord-Holland, NW Netherlands
Hopa 95 E2 Artvin, NE Turkey
Hope 14 C3 British Columbia, SW Canada
Hopedale 17 F2 Newfoundland and Labrador, NE Canada
Hopeh *see* Hebei
Hopei *see* Hebei
Hopkinsville 18 B5 Kentucky, S USA
Horasan 95 F3 Erzurum, NE Turkey
Horizon Deep 130 D4 *undersea feature* W Pacific Ocean
Horki 85 E6 *Rus.* Gorki. Mahilyowskaya Voblasts', E Belarus
Horlivka 87 G3 *Rom.* Adâncata, *Rus.* Gorlovka. Donets'ka Oblast', E Ukraine
Hormuz, Strait of 98 D4 *var.* Strait of Ormuz, *Per.* Tangeh-ye Hormoz. *Strait* Iran/Oman
Hornos, Cabo de 43 C8 *Eng.* Cape Horn. *Headland* S Chile
Hornsby 126 E1 New South Wales, SE Australia
Horodnya 87 E1 *Rus.* Gorodnya. Chernihivs'ka Oblast', NE Ukraine
Horodyshche 87 E2 *Rus.* Gorodishche. Cherkas'ka Oblast', C Ukraine
Horokok 86 B2 *Pol.* Gródek Jagielloński, *Rus.* Gorodok, Gorodok Yagellonski. L'vivs'ka Oblast', NW Ukraine
Horoshiri-dake 108 D2 *var.* Horosiri Dake. *Mountain* Hokkaidō, N Japan
Horosiri Dake *see* Horoshiri-dake
Horsburgh Atoll 110 A4 *atoll* N Maldives
Horseshoe Bay 20 A5 *bay* W Bermuda
Horseshoe Seamounts 58 A4 *undersea feature* E Atlantic Ocean
Horsham 127 B7 Victoria, SE Australia
Horst 65 D5 Limburg, SE Netherlands
Horten 63 B6 Vestfold, S Norway
Horyn' 85 B7 *Rus.* Goryn. *River* NW Ukraine
Hosingen 65 D7 Diekirch, NE Luxembourg
Hospitalet *see* L'Hospitalet de Llobregat
Hotan 104 B4 *var.* Khotan, *Chin.* Ho-t'ien. Xinjiang Uygur Zizhiqu, NW China
Ho-t'ien *see* Hotan
Hoting 62 C4 Jämtland, C Sweden
Hot Springs 20 B1 Arkansas, C USA
Houayxay 114 C3 *var.* Ban Houayxay, Ban Houei Sai. Bokèo, N Laos
Houghton 18 B1 Michigan, N USA
Houilles 69 B5 Yvelines, N France
Houlton 19 H1 Maine, NE USA
Houma 20 B3 Louisiana, S USA
Houston 27 H4 Texas, SW USA
Hovd 104 C2 *var.* Khovd. Hovd, W Mongolia
Hove 67 E7 SE England, UK
Hoverla, Hora 86 C3 *Rus.* Gora Goverla. *Mountain* W Ukraine
Hovsgol, Lake *see* Hövsgöl Nuur
Hövsgöl Nuur 104 D1 *var.* Lake Hovsgol. *Lake* N Mongolia
Howar, Wādi 50 A3 *var.* Ouadi Howa. *River* Chad/Sudan *see also* Howa, Ouadi
Hoy 66 C2 *island* N Scotland, UK
Hoyerswerda 72 D4 Sachsen, E Germany
Hradec Králové 77 B5 *Ger.* Königgrätz. Hradecký Kraj, N Czech Republic
Hrandzichy 85 B5 *Rus.* Grandichi. Hrodzyenskaya Voblasts', W Belarus
Hranice 77 C5 *Ger.* Mährisch-Weisskirchen. Olomoucký Kraj, E Czech Republic
Hrebinka 87 E2 *Rus.* Grebenka. Poltavs'ka Oblast', NE Ukraine
Hrodna 85 B5 *Pol.* Grodno. Hrodzyenskaya Voblasts', W Belarus
Hsia-men *see* Xiamen
Hsiang-t'an *see* Xiangtan
Hsi Chiang *see* Xi Jiang
Hsing-k'ai Hu *see* Khanka, Lake
Hsining *see* Xining
Hsinking *see* Changchun
Hsin-yang *see* Xinyang
Hsu-chou *see* Xuzhou
Huacho 38 C4 Lima, W Peru
Hua Hin *see* Ban Hua Hin
Huaihua 106 C5 Hunan, S China
Huailai 106 C3 *prev.* Shacheng. Hebei, E China

Huainan 106 D5 var. Huai-nan, Hwainan. Anhui, E China
Huai-nan see Huainan
Huajuapan 29 F5 var. Huajuapan de León. Oaxaca, SE Mexico
Huajuapan de León see Huajuapan
Hualapai Peak 26 A2 mountain Arizona, SW USA
Huallaga, Río 38 C3 river N Peru
Huambo 56 B2 Port. Nova Lisboa. Huambo, C Angola
Huancavelica 38 D4 Huancavelica, SW Peru
Huancayo 38 D3 Junín, C Peru
Huang He 106 C4 var. Yellow River. River C China
Huangshi 106 C5 var. Huang-shih, Hwangshih. Hubei, C China
Huang-shih see Huangshi
Huanta 38 D4 Ayacucho, C Peru
Huánuco 38 C3 Huánuco, C Peru
Huanuni 39 F4 Oruro, W Bolivia
Huaral 38 C4 Lima, W Peru
Huarás see Huaraz
Huaraz 38 C3 var. Huarás. Ancash, W Peru
Huarmey 38 C3 Ancash, W Peru
Huatabampo 28 C2 Sonora, NW Mexico
Hubli 102 B3 Karnātaka, SW India
Huddersfield 89 D5 N England, UK
Hudiksvall 63 C5 Gävleborg, C Sweden
Hudson Bay 15 G4 bay NE Canada
Hudson Strait 15 H3 Fr. Détroit d'Hudson. Strait Nunavut/Québec, NE Canada
Hudur see Xuddur
Huê 114 E4 Thua Thiên-Huê, C Vietnam
Huehuetenango 30 A2 Huehuetenango, W Guatemala
Huelva 70 C4 anc. Onuba. Andalucía, SW Spain
Huesca 71 F2 anc. Osca. Aragón, NE Spain
Huéscar 71 E4 Andalucía, S Spain
Hughenden 126 C3 Queensland, NE Australia
Hugo 27 G2 Oklahoma, C USA
Huhehot see Hohhot
Huhuohaote see Hohhot
Huíla Plateau 56 B2 plateau S Angola
Huixtla 29 G5 Chiapas, SE Mexico
Hukui see Fukui
Hukuoka see Fukuoka
Hukusima see Fukushima
Hulingol 105 G2 prev. Huolin Gol. Nei Mongol Zizhiqu, N China
Hull see Kingston upon Hull
Hull 16 D4 Québec, SE Canada
Hulst 65 B5 Zeeland, SW Netherlands
Hulun see Hailar
Hu-lun Ch'ih see Hulun Nur
Hulun Nur 105 F1 var. Hu-lun Ch'ih; prev. Dalai Nor. lake NE China
Humaitá 40 D2 Amazonas, N Brazil
Humboldt River 25 C5 river Nevada, W USA
Humphreys Peak 26 B1 mountain Arizona, SW USA
Humpolec 77 B5 Ger. Gumpolds, Humpoletz. Jihlavský Kraj, C Czech Republic
Hunan 106 C6 var. Hunan Sheng, Xiang. Admin. region province S China
Hunan ShEng see Xiang
Hunedoara 86 B4 Ger. Eisenmarkt, Hung. Vajdahunyad. Hunedoara, SW Romania
Hünfeld 73 B5 Hessen, C Germany
Hungary 77 C6 Ger. Ungarn, Hung. Magyarország, Rom. Ungaria, SCr. Mađarska, Ukr. Uhorshchyna; prev. Hungarian People's Republic. Country C Europe
Hungary, Plain of see Great Hungarian Plain
Hunter Island 127 B8 island Tasmania, SE Australia
Huntington 18 D4 West Virginia, NE USA
Huntington Beach 25 B8 California, W USA
Huntly 128 D3 Waikato, North Island, NZ
Huntsville 20 D1 Alabama, S USA
Huntsville 27 G3 Texas, SW USA
Hurghada 50 C2 var. Al Ghurdaqah, Ghurdaqah. E Egypt
Huron 23 E3 South Dakota, N USA
Huron, Lake 18 D2 lake Canada/USA
Hurukawa see Furukawa
Hurunui 129 C5 river South Island, NZ
Húsavík 61 E4 Nordhurland Eystra, NE Iceland
Husum 72 B2 Schleswig-Holstein, N Germany
Hutchinson 23 E5 Kansas, C USA
Hutchinson Island 21 F4 island Florida, SE USA
Huy 65 C6 Dut. Hoei, Hoey. Liège, E Belgium
Huzi see Fuji
Hvannadalshnúkur 61 E5 mountain S Iceland
Hvar 78 B4 It. Lesina; anc. Pharus. Island S Croatia
Hwainan see Huainan
Hwange 56 D3 prev. Wankie. Matabeleland North, W Zimbabwe
Hwangshih see Huangshi
Hyargas Nuur 104 C2 lake NW Mongolia
Hyderābād 112 D5 var. Haidarabad. Andhra Pradesh, C India
Hyderābād 112 B3 var. Haidarabad. Sind, SE Pakistan
Hyères 69 D6 Var, SE France
Hyères, Îles d' 69 D6 island group S France
Hypanis see Kuban'
Hyrcania see Gorgān
Hyvinkää 63 D5 Swe. Hyvinge. Etelä-Suomi, S Finland

I

Ialomiţa 86 C5 river SE Romania
Iaşi 86 D3 Ger. Jassy. Iaşi, NE Romania
Ibadan 53 F5 Oyo, SW Nigeria
Ibagué 36 B3 Tolima, C Colombia
Ibar 78 D4 Alb. Ibër. River C Serbia and Montenegro (Yugo.)
Ibarra 38 B1 var. San Miguel de Ibarra. Imbabura, N Ecuador
Iberian Mountains see Ibérico, Sistema
Iberian Peninsula 58 B4 physical region Portugal/Spain
Iberian Plain 58 B4 undersea feature E Atlantic Ocean
Ibérico, Sistema 71 E2 var. Cordillera Ibérica, Eng. Iberian Mountains. Mountain range NE Spain
Ibiza see Eivissa
Ibo see Sassandra
Ica 38 D4 Ica, SW Peru
Içá see Putumayo, Río
Icaria see Ikaría
Içá, Rio 40 C2 var. Río Putumayo. River NW South America see also Putumayo, Río
Iceland 61 E4 Dan. Island, Icel. Ísland. Country N Atlantic Ocean
Iceland Basin 58 B1 undersea feature N Atlantic Ocean
Icelandic Plateau see Iceland Plateau
Iceland Plateau 172 B5 var. Icelandic Plateau. Undersea feature S Greenland Sea
Iconium see Konya
Idabel 27 H2 Oklahoma, C USA
Idaho 24 D3 off. State of Idaho; also known as Gem of the Mountains, Gem State. State NW USA
Idaho Falls 24 E3 Idaho, NW USA
Idensalmi see Iisalmi
Idfu 50 B2 var. Edfu. SE Egypt
Ídhra see Ýdra
Idi Amin, Lac see Edward, Lake
Idîni 52 B2 Trarza, W Mauritania
Idlib 96 B3 Idlib, NW Syria
Idre 63 B5 Kopparberg, C Sweden
Iecava 84 C3 Bauska, S Latvia
Ieper 65 A6 Fr. Ypres. West-Vlaanderen, W Belgium
Ierápetra 83 D8 Kríti, Greece, E Mediterranean Sea
Ierisós see Ierissós
Ierissós 82 C4 var. Ierisós. Kentrikí Makedonía, N Greece
Iferouâne 53 G2 Agadez, N Niger
Ifôghas, Adrar des 53 E2 var. Adrar des Iforas. Mountain range NE Mali
Igarka 92 D3 Krasnoyarskiy Kray, N Russian Federation
Iglesias 75 A5 Sardegna, Italy, C Mediterranean Sea
Igloolik 15 G2 Nunavut, N Canada
Igoumenítsa 82 A4 Ípeiros, W Greece
Iguaçu, Rio 41 E4 Sp. Río Iguazú. River Argentina/Brazil see also Iguazú, Río
Iguaçu, Salto do 41 E4 Sp. Cataratas del Iguazú; prev. Victoria Falls. Waterfall Argentina/Brazil see also Iguazú, Cataratas del
Iguala 29 E4 var. Iguala de la Independencia. Guerrero, S Mexico
Iguala de la Independencia see Iguala
Iguîdi, 'Erg 48 C3 var. Erg Iguid. Desert Algeria/Mauritania
Ihavandiffulu Atoll see Ihavandippolhu Atoll
Ihavandippolhu Atoll 110 A3 var. Ihavandiffulu Atoll. Atoll N Maldives
Ihosy 57 F4 Fianarantsoa, S Madagascar
Ijmuiden 64 C3 Noord-Holland, W Netherlands
Iisalmi 62 E4 var. Idensalmi. Itä-Suomi, C Finland
IJssel 64 D3 var. Yssel. River Netherlands/Germany
IJsselmeer 64 C2 prev. Zuider Zee. Lake N Netherlands
IJsselmuiden 64 D3 Overijssel, E Netherlands
Ijzer 65 A6 river W Belgium
Ikaría 83 D6 var. Kariot, Nicaria, Nikaria; anc. Icaria. Island Dodekánisos, Greece, Aegean Sea
Ikela 55 D6 Equateur, C Dem. Rep. Congo
Iki 109 A7 island SW Japan
Ilagan 117 E1 Luzon, N Philippines
Ilave 39 E4 Puno, S Peru
Iława 76 D3 Ger. Deutsch-Eylau. Warmińsko-Mazurskie, NE Poland
Ilebo 55 C6 prev. Port-Francqui. Kasai Occidental, W Dem. Rep. Congo
Île-de-France 68 C3 cultural region N France
Îles de la Société see Société, Archipel de la
Îles Tubuai see Australes, Îles
Ilfracombe 67 C7 SW England, UK
Ilha Caviana see Caviana de Fora, Ilha
Ilha de Madeira see Madeira
Ilha do Corvo see Corvo
Ilha do Faial see Faial
Ilha do Pico see Pico
Ilha do Porto Santo see Porto Santo
Ilha Graciosa see Graciosa
Ilhas dos Açores see Azores
Ilha Terceira see Terceira
Ílhavo 70 B2 Aveiro, N Portugal
Ili 90 C3 Kaz. Ile, Rus. Reka Ili. River China/Kazakhstan
Iliamna Lake 14 C3 lake Alaska, USA
Ilici see Elche
Iligan 117 E2 off. Iligan City. Mindanao, S Philippines
Illapel 42 B4 Coquimbo, C Chile
Illichivs'k 87 E4 Rus. Il'ichevsk. Odes'ka Oblast', SW Ukraine
Illicis see Elche
Illinois 18 A4 off. State of Illinois; also known as Prairie State, Sucker State. State C USA
Illinois River 18 B4 river Illinois, N USA
Ilo 39 E4 Moquegua, SW Peru
Iloilo 117 E2 off. Iloilo City. Panay Island, C Philippines
Ilorin 53 F4 Kwara, W Nigeria
Îlots de Bass see Marotiri
Ilovlya 89 B6 Volgogradskaya Oblast', SW Russian Federation
Iluh see Batman
Il'yaly see Ýylanly
Imatra 85 E5 Etelä-Suomi, S Finland
Imbros see Gökçeada
İmişli 95 H3 Rus. Imishli. C Azerbaijan
Imola 74 C3 Emilia-Romagna, N Italy
Imperatriz 41 F2 Maranhão, NE Brazil
Imperia 74 A3 Liguria, NW Italy
Impfondo 55 C5 La Likouala, NE Congo
Imphāl 113 H3 Manipur, NE India
Imroz Adası see Gökçeada
Inagua Islands see Great Inagua
Inagua Islands see Little Inagua
Inarijärvi 62 D2 Lapp. Aanaarjävri, Swe. Enareträsk. Lake N Finland
Inawashiro-ko 109 D5 var. Inawasiro Ko. Lake Honshū, C Japan
Inawasiro Ko see Inawashiro-ko
İncesu 94 D3 Kayseri, C Turkey
Inch'ŏn 107 E4 off. Inch'ŏn-gwangyŏksi, Jap. Jinsen; prev. Chemulpo. NW South Korea
Incudine, Monte 69 E7 mountain Corse, France, C Mediterranean Sea
Indefatigable Island see Santa Cruz, Isla
Independence 23 F4 Missouri, C USA
Independence Fjord 61 E1 fjord N Greenland
Independence Mountains 24 C4 mountain range Nevada, W USA
India 102 B3 var. Indian Union, Union of India, Hind. Bhārat. Country S Asia
Indiana 18 B4 off. State of Indiana; also known as The Hoosier State. State N USA
Indianapolis 18 C4 state capital Indiana, N USA
Indian Church 30 C1 Orange Walk, N Belize
Indian Desert see Thar Desert
Indianola 23 F4 Iowa, C USA
Indigirka 93 F2 river NE Russian Federation
Indija 78 D3 Hung. India; prev. Indjija. Serbia, N Serbia and Montenegro (Yugo.)
Indira Point 110 G3 headland Andaman and Nicobar Islands, India, NE Indian Ocean
Indomed Fracture Zone 119 B6 tectonic feature SW Indian Ocean
Indonesia 116 B4 Ind. Republik Indonesia; prev. Dutch East Indies, Netherlands East Indies, United States of Indonesia. Country SE Asia
Indore 112 D4 Madhya Pradesh, C India
Indus 112 C2 Chin. Yindu He; prev. Yin-tu Ho. River S Asia
Indus Cone see Indus Fan
Indus Fan 90 C5 var. Indus Cone. Undersea feature N Arabian Sea
Indus, Mouths of the 112 B4 delta S Pakistan
İnebolu 94 C2 Kastamonu, N Turkey
Ineu 86 A4 Hung. Borosjenő; prev. Inău. Arad, W Romania
Infiernillo, Presa del 29 E4 reservoir S Mexico
Inglewood 24 D2 California, W USA
Ingolstadt 73 C6 Bayern, S Germany
Inhambane 57 E4 Inhambane, SE Mozambique
Inhulets' 87 F3 Rus. Ingulets. Dnipropetrovs'ka Oblast', E Ukraine
I-ning see Yining
Inis see Ennis
Inis Ceithleann see Enniskillen
Inn 73 C6 river C Europe
Innaanganeq 60 C1 var. Kap York. Headland NW Greenland
Inner Hebrides 66 B4 island group W Scotland, UK
Inner Islands 57 H1 var. Central Group. Island group NE Seychelles
Inner Mongolia 105 F3 var. Nei Mongol, Eng. Inner Mongolia, Inner Mongolian Autonomous Region; prev. Nei Monggol Zizhiqu. Admin. region autonomous region N China
Inner Mongolian Autonomous Region see Inner Mongolia
Innisfail 126 D3 Queensland, NE Australia
Inniskilling see Enniskillen
Innsbruch see Innsbruck
Innsbruck 73 C7 var. Innsbruch. Tirol, W Austria
Inoucdjouac see Inukjuak
Inowrocław 76 C3 Ger. Hohensalza; prev. Inowrazlaw. Kujawski-pomorskie, C Poland
I-n-Salah 48 D3 var. In Salah. C Algeria
In Salah see I-n-Salah
Insula see Lille
Inta 88 E3 Respublika Komi, NW Russian Federation
International Falls 23 F1 Minnesota, N USA
Inukjuak 16 D2 var. Inoucdjouac; prev. Port Harrison. Québec, NE Canada
Inuuvik see Inuvik
Inuvik 14 D3 var. Inuuvik. District capital Northwest Territories, NW Canada
Invercargill 129 A7 Southland, South Island, NZ
Inverness 66 C3 N Scotland, UK
Investigator Ridge 119 D5 undersea feature E Indian Ocean
Investigator Strait 127 B7 strait South Australia
Inyangani 56 D3 mountain NE Zimbabwe
Ioánnina 82 A4 var. Janina, Yannina. Ípeiros, W Greece
Iola 23 F5 Kansas, C USA
Ionia Basin see Ionian Basin
Ionian Basin 58 D5 var. Ionia Basin. Undersea feature Ionian Sea, C Mediterranean Sea
Ionian Islands see Iónioi Nísoi
Ionian Sea 81 E3 Gk. Iónio Pélagos, It. Mar Ionio. Sea C Mediterranean Sea
Iónioi Nísoi 83 A5 Eng. Ionian Islands. Island group W Greece
Íos 83 D6 var. Nio. Island Kykládes, Greece, Aegean Sea
Íos 83 D6 Íos, Kykládes, Greece, Aegean Sea
Iowa 23 F3 off. State of Iowa; also known as The Hawkeye State. State C USA
Iowa City 23 G3 Iowa, C USA
Iowa Falls 23 G3 Iowa, C USA
Ipel' 77 C6 var. Ipoly, Ger. Eipel. River Hungary/Slovakia
Ipiales 36 A4 Nariño, SW Colombia
Ipoh 116 B3 Perak, Peninsular Malaysia
Ipoly 77 C6 var. Ipel', Ger. Eipel. River Hungary/Slovakia
Ippy 54 C4 Ouaka, C Central African Republic
Ipswich 67 E6 hist. Gipeswic. E England, UK
Ipswich 127 E5 Queensland, E Australia
Iqaluit 15 H3 prev. Frobisher Bay. Baffin Island, Nunavut, NE Canada
Iquique 42 B1 Tarapacá, N Chile
Iquitos 38 C1 Loreto, N Peru
Irákleio 83 D7 var. Herakleion, Eng. Candia; prev. Iráklion. Kríti, Greece, E Mediterranean Sea
Iráklion see Irákleio
Iran 98 C3 prev. Persia. Country SW Asia
Iranian Plateau 98 D3 var. Plateau of Iran. plateau N Iran
Iran, Plateau of see Iranian Plateau
Irapuato 29 E4 Guanajuato, C Mexico
Iraq 98 B3 Ar. 'Irāq. Country SW Asia
Irbid 97 B5 Irbid, N Jordan
Irbīl see Arbīl
Ireland 58 C3 Lat. Hibernia. Island Ireland/UK
Ireland 67 A5 var. Republic of Ireland, Ir. Éire. Country NW Europe
Irian Barat see Papua
Irian Jaya see Papua
Irian, Teluk see Cenderawasih, Teluk
Iringa 51 C7 Iringa, C Tanzania
Iriomote-jima 108 A4 island Sakishima-shotō, SW Japan
Iriona 30 D2 Colón, NE Honduras
Irish Sea 67 C5 Ir. Muir Éireann. Sea C British Isles
Irkutsk 93 E4 Irkutskaya Oblast', S Russian Federation
Irminger Basin see Reykjanes Basin
Iroise 68 A3 sea NW France
Iron Mountain 18 B2 Michigan, N USA
Ironwood 18 B1 Michigan, N USA
Irrawaddy 114 B2 var. Ayeyarwady. River W Myanmar
Irrawaddy, Mouths of the 115 A5 delta SW Myanmar
Irtish see Irtysh
Irtysh 92 C4 var. Irtish, Kaz. Ertis. River C Asia
Irún 71 E1 País Vasco, N Spain
Iruña see Pamplona
Isabela, Isla 38 A5 var. Albemarle Island. Island Galapagos Islands, Ecuador, E Pacific Ocean
Isaccea 86 D4 Tulcea, E Romania
Isachsen 15 F1 Ellef Ringnes Island, Nunavut, N Canada
Ísafjördhur 61 E4 Vestfirdhir, NW Iceland
Isbarta see Ísparta
Ise 109 C6 Mie, Honshū, SW Japan
Isère 69 D5 river E France
Isernia 75 D5 var. Æsernia. Molise, C Italy
Ise-wan 109 C6 bay S Japan
Isha Baydhabo see Baydhabo
Ishigaki-jima 108 A4 var. Isigaki Zima. Island Sakishima-shotō, SW Japan
Ishikari-wan 108 C2 bay Hokkaidō, NE Japan
Ishim 92 C4 Kaz. Esil. River Kazakhstan/Russian Federation
Ishim 92 C4 Tyumenskaya Oblast', C Russian Federation
Ishinomaki 108 D4 var. Isinomaki. Miyagi, Honshū, C Japan
Ishkoshim 101 F3 Rus. Ishkashim. S Tajikistan
Isigaki Zima see Ishigaki-jima
Isinomaki see Ishinomaki
Isiro 55 E5 Orientale, NE Dem. Rep. Congo
Iskăr see Iskŭr
İskenderun 94 D4 Eng. Alexandretta. Hatay, S Turkey
İskenderun Körfezi 96 A2 Eng. Gulf of Alexandretta. Gulf S Turkey
Iskŭr 82 C2 var. Iskăr. River NW Bulgaria
Iskŭr, Yazovir 82 B2 prev. Yazovir Stalin. Reservoir W Bulgaria
Isla Cristina 70 C4 Andalucía, S Spain
Isla Gran Malvina see West Falkalnd
Islāmābād 112 C1 country capital (Pakistan) Federal Capital Territory Islāmābād, NE Pakistan
I-n-Sâkâne, 'Erg 53 E2 desert N Mali
Islas de los Galápagos see Galapagos Islands
Islas Malvinas see Falkland Islands
Islay 66 B4 island SW Scotland, UK
Isle 69 B5 river W France
Isle of Man 67 B5 UK crown dependency NW Europe
Ismailia see Ismâ'ilîya
Ismâ'ilîya 50 B1 var. Ismailia. N Egypt
Ismid see İzmit
Isna 50 B2 var. Esna. SE Egypt
Isoka 56 D1 Northern, NE Zambia
Isola Grossa see Dugi Otok
Isola Lunga see Dugi Otok
Isole Lipari see Eolie, Isole
Isparta 94 B4 var. Isbarta. Isparta, SW Turkey
İspir 95 E3 Erzurum, NE Turkey
Israel 97 A7 var. Medinat Israel, Heb. Yisrael, Yisra'el. Country SW Asia
Issiq Köl see Issyk-Kul', Ozero
Issoire 69 C5 Puy-de-Dôme, C France
Issyk-Kul', Ozero 101 G2 var. Issiq Köl, Kir. Ysyk-Köl. Lake E Kyrgyzstan
İstanbul 94 B2 Bul. Tsarigrad, Eng. Istanbul; prev. Constantinople, anc. Byzantium. İstanbul, NW Turkey
İstanbul Boğazı 94 B2 var. Bosporus Thracius, Eng. Bosphorus, Bosporus, Turk. Karadeniz Boğazı. Strait NW Turkey
Istra 78 A3 Eng. Istria, Ger. Istrien. Cultural region NW Croatia
Istra 74 D2 Eng. Istria. Peninsula NW Croatia
Itabuna 41 G3 Bahia, E Brazil
Itagüí 36 B3 Antioquia, W Colombia
Itaipú, Represa de 41 E4 reservoir Brazil/Paraguay
Itaituba 41 E2 Pará, NE Brazil**Italy** 74 C3 It. Italia, Republica Italiana. Country S Europe
Italy 74 C3 It. Italia, Republica Italiana. Country S Europe
Italy 58 D4 Texas, SW USA
Iténez, Río see Guaporé, Rio
Ithaca 19 E3 New York, NE USA
Itoigawa 109 C5 Niigata, Honshū, C Japan
Itseqqortoormiit see Ittoqqortoormiit
Ittoqqortoormiit 61 E3 var. Itseqqortoormiit, Dan. Scoresbysund, Eng. Scoresby Sound. C Greenland
Iturup, Ostrov 108 E1 island Kuril'skiye Ostrova, SE Russian Federation
Itzehoe 72 B2 Schleswig-Holstein, N Germany
Ivalo 62 D2 Lapp. Avveel, Avvil. Lappi, N Finland
Ivanava 85 B7 Pol. Janów, Janów Poleski, Rus. Ivanovo. Brestskaya Voblasts', SW Belarus
Ivanhoe 127 C6 New South Wales, SE Australia
Ivano-Frankivs'k 86 C2 Ger. Stanislau, Pol. Stanisławów, Rus. Ivano-Frankovsk; prev. Stanislav. Ivano-Frankivs'ka Oblast', W Ukraine
Ivanovo 89 B5 Ivanovskaya Oblast', W Russian Federation
Ivatsevichy 85 B6 Pol. Iwacewicze, Rus. Ivantsevichi, Ivatsevichi. Brestskaya Voblasts', SW Belarus
Ivigtut see Ivittuut
Ivittuut 60 B4 var. Ivigtut. S Greenland
Iviza see Eivissa
Ivory Coast see Côte d'Ivoire
Ivujivik 16 D1 Québec, NE Canada
Iwaki 109 D5 Fukushima, Honshū, N Japan
Iwakuni 109 B7 Yamaguchi, Honshū, SW Japan
Iwanai 108 C2 Hokkaidō, NE Japan
Iwate 108 D3 Iwate, Honshū, N Japan
Ixtapa 29 E5 Guerrero, S Mexico
Ixtepec 29 F5 Oaxaca, SE Mexico
Iyo-nada 109 B7 sea S Japan
Izabal, Lago de 30 B2 prev. Golfo Dulce. Lake E Guatemala
Īzad Khvāst 98 D3 Fārs, C Iran
Izegem 65 A6 prev. Iseghem. West-Vlaanderen, W Belgium
Izhevsk 89 D5 prev. Ustinov. Udmurtskaya Respublika, NW Russian Federation
Izmayil 86 D4 Rus. Izmail. Odes'ka Oblast', SW Ukraine
İzmir 94 A3 prev. Smyrna. İzmir, W Turkey
İzmit 94 B2 var. Ismid; anc. Astacus. Kocaeli, NW Turkey
İznik Gölü 94 B3 lake NW Turkey
Izu-hantō 109 D6 peninsula Honshū, S Japan
Izu Shichito see Izu-shotō
Izu-shotō 109 D6 var. Izu Shichito. Island group S Japan
Izvor 82 B2 Pernik, W Bulgaria
Izyaslav 86 C2 Khmel'nyts'ka Oblast', W Ukraine
Izyum 87 G2 Kharkivs'ka Oblast', E Ukraine

J

Jabal ash Shifā 98 A4 desert NW Saudi Arabia
Jabalpur 113 E4 prev. Jubbulpore. Madhya Pradesh, C India
Jabbūl, Sabkhat al 134 B2 salt flat NW Syria
Jablah 96 A3 var. Jeble, Fr. Djéblé. Al Lādhiqīyah, W Syria
Jaca 71 F1 Aragón, NE Spain
Jacaltenango 30 A2 Huehuetenango, W Guatemala
Jackson 20 B2 state capital Mississippi, S USA
Jackson 23 H5 Missouri, C USA
Jackson 20 C1 Tennessee, S USA
Jackson Head 129 A6 headland South Island, NZ
Jacksonville 21 E3 Florida, SE USA
Jacksonville 18 B4 Illinois, N USA
Jacksonville 21 F1 North Carolina, SE USA
Jacksonville 27 G3 Texas, SW USA
Jacmel 32 D3 var. Jaquemel. S Haiti
Jacobābād 112 B3 Sind, SE Pakistan
Jaén 70 D4 Andalucía, SW Spain
Jaén 38 B2 Cajamarca, N Peru
Jaffna 110 D3 Northern Province, N Sri Lanka
Jagannath see Puri
Jagdalpur 113 E5 Madhya Pradesh, C India
Jagdaqi 105 G1 Nei Mongol Zizhiqu, N China
Jagodina 78 D4 prev. Svetozarevo. Serbia, C Serbia and Montenegro (Yugo.)
Jahra see Al Jahrā'
Jaipur 112 D3 prev. Jeypore. Rājasthān, N India

Jaisalmer *112 C3* Rājasthān, NW India
Jajce *78 B3* Federacija Bosna I Hercegovina, W Bosnia and Herzegovina
Jakarta *116 C5 prev.* Djakarta, *Dut.* Batavia. *Country capital* (Indonesia) Jawa, C Indonesia
Jakobstad *62 D4 Fin.* Pietarsaari. Länsi-Suomi, W Finland
Jalālābād *101 F4 var.* Jalalabad, Jelalabad. Nangarhār, E Afghanistan
Jalandhar *112 D2 prev.* Jullundur. Punjab, N India
Jalapa *see* Xalapa
Jalapa *30 D3* Nueva Segovia, NW Nicaragua
Jalapa Enríquez *see* Xalapa
Jalpa *28 D4* Zacatecas, C Mexico
Jālū *49 G3 var.* Jūlā. NE Libya
Jaluit Atoll *122 D2 var.* Jālwōj. *Atoll* Ralik Chain, S Marshall Islands
Jālwōj *see* Jaluit Atoll
Jamaame *51 D6 It.* Giamame; *prev.* Margherita. Jubbada Hoose, S Somalia
Jamaica *32 A4 country* W West Indies
Jamaica *34 A1 island* W West Indies
Jamaica Channel *32 D3 channel* Haiti/Jamaica
Jamālpur *113 F3* Bihār, NE India
Jambi *116 B4 var.* Telanaipura; *prev.* Djambi. Sumatera, W Indonesia
James Bay *16 C3 bay* Ontario/Québec, E Canada
James River *23 E2 river* North Dakota/South Dakota, N USA
James River *19 E5 river* Virginia, NE USA
Jamestown *19 E3* New York, NE USA
Jamestown *23 E2* North Dakota, N USA
Jammu *112 D2 prev.* Jummoo. Jammu and Kashmir, NW India
Jammu and Kashmīr *112 D1 disputed region* India/Pakistan
Jāmnagar *112 C4 prev.* Navanagar. Gujarāt, W India
Jamshedpur *113 F4* Bihār, NE India
Jamuna *see* Brahmaputra
Janaúba *41 F3* Minas Gerais, SE Brazil
Janesville *18 B3* Wisconsin, N USA
Janīn *see* Jenīn
Janina *see* Ioánnina
Jan Mayen *61 F4 Norwegian dependency* N Atlantic Ocean
Jánoshalma *77 C7 SCr.* Jankovac. Bács-Kiskun, S Hungary
Japan *108 C4 var.* Nippon, *Jap.* Nihon. *Country* E Asia
Japan, Sea of *108 A4 var.* East Sea, *Rus.* Yapanskoye More. *Sea* NW Pacific Ocean *see also* East Sea
Japan Trench *103 F1 undersea feature* NW Pacific Ocean
Japiim *40 C2 var.* Máncio Lima. Acre, W Brazil
Japurá, Rio *40 C2 var.* Río Caquetá, Yapurá. *River* Brazil/Colombia *see also* Caquetá, Río
Jaqué *31 G5* Darién, SE Panama
Jaquemel *see* Jacmel
Jarablos *see* Jarābulus
Jarābulus *96 C2 var.* Jarablos, Jerablus, *Fr.* Djérablous. Ḩalab, N Syria
Jardines de la Reina, Archipiélago de los *32 B2 island group* C Cuba
Jarocin *76 C4* Wielkopolskie, C Poland
Jarosław *77 E5 Ger.* Jaroslau, *Rus.* Yaroslav. Podkarpackie, SE Poland
Jarqo'rg'on *101 E3 var.* Jarqŭrghon, *Rus.* Dzharkurgan. Surkhondaryo Wiloyati, S Uzbekistan
Jarqŭrghon *see* Jarqo'rg'on
Jarvis Island *123 G2 US unincorporated territory* C Pacific Ocean
Jasło *77 D5* Podkarpackie, SE Poland
Jastrzębie-Zdrój *77 C5* Śląskie, S Poland
Jataí *41 E3* Goiás, C Brazil
Játiva *see* Xátiva
Jauf *see* Al Jawf
Jaunpiebalga *84 D3* Gulbene, NE Latvia
Jaunpur *113 E3* Uttar Pradesh, N India
Java *130 A3 prev.* Djawa. *Island* C Indonesia
Javalambre *93 E3 mountain* E Spain
Javari, Rio *40 C2 var.* Yavarí. *River* Brazil/Peru
Java Sea *116 D4 Ind.* Laut Jawa. *Sea* W Indonesia
Java Trench *102 D5 var.* Sunda Trench. *Undersea feature* E Indian Ocean
Jawhar *51 D6 var.* Jowhar, *It.* Giohar. Shabeellaha Dhexe, S Somalia
Jaya, Puncak *139 G4 prev.* Puntjak Carstensz, Puntjak Sukarno. *Mountain* Papua, E Indonesia
Jayapura *117 H4 var.* Djajapura, *Dut.* Hollandia; *prev.* Kotabaru, Sukarnapura. Papua, E Indonesia
Jazā'ir Bin Ghalfān *see* Ḩalāniyāt, Juzur al
Jazīrat Jarbah *see* Jerba, Île de
Jazīreh-ye Qeshm *see* Qeshm
Jaz Mūriān, Hāmūn-e *98 E4 lake* SE Iran
Jebba *53 F4* Kwara, W Nigeria
Jebel esh Sharqi *see* Anti-Lebanon
Jebel Uweinat *see* 'Uwaynāt, Jabal al
Jeble *see* Jablah
Jedda *see* Jiddah
Jędrzejów *76 D4 Ger.* Endersdorf. Świętokrzyskie, C Poland
Jefferson City *23 G5 state capital* Missouri, C USA
Jega *53 F4* Kebbi, NW Nigeria
Jehol *see* Chengde
Jēkabpils *84 D4 Ger.* Jakobstadt. Jēkabpils, S Latvia
Jelalabad *see* Jalālābād
Jelenia Góra *76 B4 Ger.* Hirschberg, Hirschberg im Riesengebirge, Hirschberg in Riesengebirge, Hirschberg in Schlesien. Dolnośląskie, SW Poland
Jelgava *84 C3 Ger.* Mitau. Jelgava, C Latvia
Jemappes *87 B6* Hainaut, S Belgium
Jember *116 D5 prev.* Djember. Jawa, C Indonesia
Jena *72 C4* Thüringen, C Germany
Jenīn *97 A6 var.* Janīn, Jinīn; *anc.* Engannim. N West Bank
Jerablus *see* Jarābulus
Jerada *48 D2* NE Morocco
Jerba, Île de *49 F2 var.* Djerba, Jazīrat Jarbah. *Island* E Tunisia
Jérémie *32 D3* SW Haiti
Jerez *see* Jeréz de la Frontera
Jeréz de la Frontera *92 C5 var.* Jerez; *prev.* Xeres. Andalucía, SW Spain
Jeréz de los Caballeros *70 C4* Extremadura, W Spain
Jericho *97 B6 Ar.* Arīḩā, *Heb.* Yeriḥo. E West Bank
Jerid, Chott el 87 E2 var. Shaṭṭ al Jarīd. *Salt lake* SW Tunisia
Jersey *67 D8 UK dependent territory* NW Europe
Jerusalem *81 H4 Ar.* El Quds, *Heb.* Yerushalayim; *anc.* Hierosolyma. *Country capital* (Israel) Jerusalem, NE Israel
Jerusalem *90 A4* Admin. region *district* E Israel
Jesenice *73 D7 Ger.* Assling. NW Slovenia
Jessore *113 G4* Khulna, W Bangladesh
Jesús María *42 C3* Córdoba, C Argentina
Jhānsi *112 D3* Uttar Pradesh, N India
Jhārkand *113 F4* Admin. region *state* N India
Jhelum *112 C2* Punjab, NE Pakistan
Ji *see* Hebei
Ji *see* Jilin
Jiangmen *106 C6* Guangdong, S China
Jiangsu *106 D4 var.* Chiang-su, Jiangsu Sheng, Kiangsu, Su. Admin. region *province* E China
Jiangsu Sheng *see* Jiangsu
Jiangxi *106 C6 var.* Chiang-hsi, Gan, Jiangxi Sheng, Kiangsi. Admin. region *province* S China
Jiangxi Sheng *see* Jiangxi
Jiaxing *106 D5* Zhejiang, SE China
Jiayi *see* Chiai
Jibuti *see* Djibouti
Jiddah *99 A5 Eng.* Jedda. *Country capital* (Saudi Arabia) Makkah, W Saudi Arabia
Jih-k'a-tse *see* Xigazê
Jihlava *99 B5 Ger.* Iglau, *Pol.* Igława. Jihlavský Kraj, C Czech Republic
Jilib *51 D6 It.* Gelib. Jubbada Dhexe, S Somalia
Jilin *106 D3 var.* Chi-lin, Girin, Ji, Jilin Sheng, Kirin. Admin. region *province* NE China
Jilin *107 E3 var.* Chi-lin, Girin, Kirin; *prev.* Yungki, Yunki. Jilin, NE China
Jilin Sheng *see* Jilin
Jīma *51 C5 var.* Jimma, *It.* Gimma. C Ethiopia
Jimbolia *86 A4 Ger.* Hatzfeld, *Hung.* Zsombolya. Timiş, W Romania
Jiménez *28 D2* Chihuahua, N Mexico
Jimma *see* Jīma
Jimsar *104 C3* Xinjiang Uygur Zizhiqu, NW China
Jin *see* Shanxi
Jin *see* Tianjin Shi
Jinan *106 C4 var.* Chinan, Chi-nan, Tsinan. Shandong, E China
Jingdezhen *106 C5* Jiangxi, S China
Jinghong *106 A6 var.* Yunjinghong. Yunnan, SW China
Jinhua *106 D5* Zhejiang, SE China
Jinīn *see* Jenīn
Jining *105 F3* Shandong, E China
Jinja *51 C6* S Uganda
Jinotega *30 D3* Jinotega, NW Nicaragua
Jinotepe *30 D3* Carazo, SW Nicaragua
Jinsha Jiang *106 A5 river* SW China
Jinzhong *106 C4 var.* Yuci. Shanxi, C China
Jinzhou *106 D3 var.* Chin-chou, Chinchow; *prev.* Chinhsien. Liaoning, NE China
Jisr ash Shadadi *see* Ash Shadādah
Jiu *86 B5 Ger.* Schil, Schyl, *Hung.* Zsil, Zsily. *River* S Romania
Jiujiang *106 C5* Jiangxi, S China
Jixi *107 E2* Heilongjiang, NE China
Jīzān *99 B6 var.* Qīzān. Jīzān, SW Saudi Arabia
Jizzakh *101 E2 Rus.* Dzhizak. Jizzakh Wiloyati, C Uzbekistan
Jizzax *see* Jizzakh
João Pessoa *41 G2 prev.* Paraíba. *State capital* Paraíba, E Brazil
Jo'burg *see* Johannesburg
Jo-ch'iang *see* Ruoqiang
Jodhpur *112 C3* Rājasthān, NW India
Joensuu *85 E5* Itä-Suomi, E Finland
Jōetsu *109 C5 var.* Zyôetu. Niigata, Honshū, C Japan
Johanna Island *see* Anjouan
Johannesburg *56 D4 var.* Egoli, Erautini, Gauteng, *abbrev.* Jo'burg. Gauteng, NE South Africa
John Day River *24 C3 river* Oregon, NW USA
John o'Groats *66 C2* N Scotland, UK
Johnston Atoll *121 E1 US unincorporated territory* C Pacific Ocean
Johor Baharu *see* Johor Bahru
Johor Bahru *116 B3 var.* Johor Baharu, Johore Bahru. Johor, Peninsular Malaysia
Johore Bahru *see* Johor Bahru
Johore Strait *116 A1 Mal.* Selat Johor. *Strait* Malaysia/Singapore
Joinvile *see* Joinville
Joinville *41 E4 var.* Joinvile. Santa Catarina, S Brazil
Jokkmokk *62 C3* Norrbotten, N Sweden
Joliet *18 B3* Illinois, N USA
Jonava *84 B4 Ger.* Janow, *Pol.* Janów. Jonava, C Lithuania
Jonesboro *20 B1* Arkansas, C USA
Joniškis *84 C3 Ger.* Janischken. Joniškis, N Lithuania
Jönköping *63 B7* Jönköping, S Sweden
Jonquière *17 E4* Québec, SE Canada
Joplin *23 F5* Missouri, C USA
Jordan *97 B5 Ar.* Urdunn, *Heb.* HaYarden. *River* SW Asia
Jordan *97 B6 Ar.* Al Mamlakah al Urdunīyah al Hāshimīyah, Al Urdunn; *prev.* Transjordan. *Country* SW Asia
Jorhāt *113 H3* Assam, NE India
Jos *53 G4* Plateau, C Nigeria
Joseph Bonaparte Gulf *124 D2 gulf* N Australia
Jos Plateau *53 G4 plateau* C Nigeria
Jotunheimen *63 A5 mountain range* S Norway
Joûnié *96 A4 var.* Juniyah. W Lebanon
Joure *64 D2 Fris.* De Jouwer. Friesland, N Netherlands
Joutseno *63 E5* Etelä-Suomi, S Finland
Jowhar *see* Jawhar
JStorm Thurmond Reservoir *see* Clark Hill Lake
Juan Aldama *28 D3* Zacatecas, C Mexico
Juan de Fuca, Strait of *24 A1 strait* Canada/USA
Juan Fernández, Islas *35 A6 Eng.* Juan Fernandez Islands. *Island group* W Chile
Juazeiro *41 G2 prev.* Joazeiro. Bahia, E Brazil
Juazeiro do Norte *41 G2* Ceará, E Brazil
Juba *51 D6 Amh.* Genalē Wenz, *It.* Guiba, *Som.* Ganaane, Webi Jubba. *River* Ethiopia/Somalia
Juba *51 B5 var.* Jūbā. Bahr el Gabel, S Sudan
Júcar *71 E3 var.* Jucar. *River* C Spain
Juchitán *29 F5 var.* Juchitán de Zaragosa. Oaxaca, SE Mexico
Juchitán de Zaragosa *see* Juchitán
Judayyidat Hāmir *98 B3* S Iraq
Judenburg *73 D7* Steiermark, C Austria
Juigalpa *30 D3* Chontales, S Nicaragua
Juiz de Fora *41 F4* Minas Gerais, SE Brazil
Jujuy *see* San Salvador de Jujuy
Jūlā *see* Jālū
Juliaca *39 E4* Puno, SE Peru
Juliana Top *37 G3 mountain* C Suriname
Jumilla *71 E4* Murcia, SE Spain
Jumporn *see* Chumphon
Junction City *23 F4* Kansas, C USA
Juneau *14 D4 state capital* Alaska, USA
Junín *42 C4* Buenos Aires, E Argentina
Junīyah *see* Joûnié
Junkseylon *see* Phuket
Jur *51 B5 river* C Sudan
Jura *66 B4 island* SW Scotland, UK
Jura *73 A7 canton* NW Switzerland
Jura *68 D4 department* E France
Jurbarkas *84 B4 Ger.* Georgenburg, Jurburg. Jurbarkas, W Lithuania
Jūrmala *84 C3* Rīga, C Latvia
Juruá, Rio *40 C2 var.* Río Yuruá. *River* Brazil/Peru
Juruena, Rio *40 D3 river* W Brazil
Jutiapa *30 B2* Jutiapa, S Guatemala
Juticalpa *30 D2* Olancho, C Honduras
Juventud, Isla de la *32 A2 var.* Isla de Pinos, *Eng.* Isle of Youth; *prev.* The Isle of the Pines. *Island* W Cuba
Južna Morava *79 E5 Ger.* Südliche Morava. *River* SE Serbia and Montenegro (Yugo.)
Juzur Qarqannah *see* Kerkenah, Îles de
Jwaneng *56 C4* Southern, SE Botswana
Jylland *63 A7 Eng.* Jutland. *Peninsula* W Denmark
Jyväskylä *63 D5* Länsi-Suomi, W Finland

K

K2 *104 A4 Chin.* Qogir Feng, *Eng.* Mount Godwin Austen. *Mountain* China/Pakistan
Kaafu Atoll *see* Male' Atoll
Kaaimanston *37 G3* Sipaliwini, N Suriname
Kaakhka *see* Kaka
Kaala *see* Caála
Kaamanen *62 D2 Lapp.* Gámas. Lappi, N Finland
Kaapstad *see* Cape Town
Kaaresuvanto *62 C3 Lapp.* Gárassavon. Lappi, N Finland
Kabale *51 B6* SW Uganda
Kabinda *see* Cabinda
Kabinda *55 D7* Kasai Oriental, SE Dem. Rep. Congo
Kābol *see* Kābul
Kabompo *56 C2 river* W Zambia
Kābul *101 E4 var.* Kabul, *Per.* Kābol. *Country capital* (Afghanistan) Kābul, E Afghanistan
Kabul *see* Kābul
Kabwe *56 D2* Central, C Zambia
Kachchh, Gulf of *112 B4 var.* Gulf of Cutch, Gulf of Kutch. *Gulf* W India
Kachchh, Rann of *112 B4 var.* Rann of Kachh, Rann of Kutch. *Salt marsh* India/Pakistan
Kachh, Rann of *see* Kachchh, Rann of
Kadan Kyun *115 B5 prev.* King Island. *Island* Mergui Archipelago, S Myanmar
Kadavu *123 E4 prev.* Kandavu. *Island* S Fiji
Kadoma *56 D3 prev.* Gatooma. Mashonaland West, C Zimbabwe
Kadugli *50 B4* Southern Kordofan, S Sudan
Kaduna *53 G4* Kaduna, C Nigeria
Kadzhi-Say *101 G2 Kir.* Kajisay. Issyk-Kul'skaya Oblast', NE Kyrgyzstan
Kaédi *52 C3* Gorgol, S Mauritania
Kaffa *see* Feodosiya
Kafue *56 C2 river* C Zambia
Kafue *56 D2* Lusaka, SE Zambia
Kaga Bandoro *54 C4 prev.* Fort-Crampel. Nana-Grébizi, C Central African Republic
Kāghet *52 D1 var.* Karet. *Physical region* N Mauritania
Kagi *see* Chiai
Kagoshima *109 B8 var.* Kagosima. Kagoshima, Kyūshū, SW Japan
Kagoshima-wan *109 A8 bay* SW Japan
Kagosima *see* Kagoshima
Kahmard, Daryā-ye *101 E4 prev.* Darya-i-Surkhab. *River* NE Afghanistan
Kahraman Maraş *see* Kahramanmaraş
Kahramanmaraş *94 D4 var.* Kahraman Maraş, Maraş, Marash. Kahramanmaraş, S Turkey
Kaiapoi *129 C6* Canterbury, South Island, NZ
Kaifeng *106 C4* Henan, C China
Kai, Kepulauan *117 F4 prev.* Kei Islands. *Island group* Maluku, SE Indonesia
Kaikohe *128 C2* Northland, North Island, NZ
Kaikoura *129 C5* Canterbury, South Island, NZ
Kaikoura Peninsula *129 C5 peninsula* South Island, NZ
Kainji Lake *see* Kainji Reservoir
Kainji Reservoir *53 F4 var.* Kainji Lake. *Reservoir* W Nigeria
Kaipara Harbour *128 C2 harbour* North Island, NZ
Kairouan *49 E2 var.* Al Qayrawān. E Tunisia
Kaisaria *see* Kayseri
Kaiserslautern *73 A5* Rheinland-Pfalz, SW Germany
Kaišiadorys *85 B5* Kaišiadorys, S Lithuania
Kaitaia *128 C2* Northland, North Island, NZ
Kajaani *62 E4 Swe.* Kajana. Oulu, C Finland
Kaka *100 C2 var.* Kaakhka. Dashkhovuzskiy Velayat, N Turkmenistan
Kake *14 D4* Kupreanof Island, Alaska, USA
Kakhovka *87 F4* Khersons'ka Oblast', S Ukraine
Kakhovs'ka Vodoskhovyshche *87 F4 Rus.* Kakhovskoye Vodokhranilishche. *Reservoir* SE Ukraine
Kākināda *110 D1 prev.* Cocanada. Andhra Pradesh, E India
Kaktovik *14 D2* Alaska, USA
Kalahari Desert *56 B4 desert* Southern Africa
Kalamariá *82 B4* Kentrikí Makedonía, N Greece
Kalámata *83 B6 prev.* Kalámai. Pelopónnisos, S Greece
Kalamazoo *18 C3* Michigan, N USA
Kalambaka *see* Kalampáka
Kálamos *83 C5* Attikí, C Greece
Kalampáka *82 B4 var.* Kalambaka. Thessalía, C Greece
Kalanchak *87 F4* Khersons'ka Oblast', S Ukraine
Kalarash *see* Călăraşi
Kalasin *114 D4 var.* Muang Kalasin. Kalasin, E Thailand
Kalāt *101 E5 Per.* Qalāt. Zābul, S Afghanistan
Kālat *112 B2 var.* Kelat, Khelat. Baluchistān, SW Pakistan
Kalbarri *125 A5* Western Australia
Kalecik *94 C3* Ankara, N Turkey
Kalemie *55 E6 prev.* Albertville. Shaba, SE Dem. Rep. Congo
Kale Sultanie *see* Çanakkale
Kalgan *see* Zhangjiakou
Kalgoorlie *125 B6* Western Australia
Kalima *55 D6* Maniema, E Dem. Rep. Congo
Kalimantan *116 D4 Eng.* Indonesian Borneo. *Geopolitical region* Borneo, C Indonesia
Kálimnos *see* Kálymnos
Kaliningrad *see* Kaliningradskaya Oblast'
Kaliningrad *84 A4* Kaliningradskaya Oblast', W Russian Federation
Kaliningradskaya Oblast' *84 B4 var.* Kaliningrad. Admin. region *province and enclave* W Russian Federation
Kalinkavichy *85 C7 Rus.* Kalinkovichi. Homyel'skaya Voblasts', SE Belarus
Kalispell *44 B1* Montana, NW USA
Kalisz *76 C4 Ger.* Kalisch, *Rus.* Kalish; *anc.* Calisia. Wielkopolskie, C Poland
Kalix *62 D4* Norrbotten, N Sweden
Kalixälven *62 D3 river* N Sweden
Kallaste *84 E3 Ger.* Krasnogor. Tartumaa, SE Estonia
Kallavesi *63 E5 lake* SE Finland
Kalloní *83 D5* Lésvos, E Greece
Kalmar *63 C7 var.* Calmar. Kalmar, S Sweden
Kalmthout *65 C5* Antwerpen, N Belgium
Kalpáki *82 A4* Ípeiros, W Greece
Kalpeni Island *110 B3 island* Lakshadweep, India, N Indian Ocean
Kaluga *89 B5* Kaluzhskaya Oblast', W Russian Federation
Kalush *86 C2 Pol.* Kałusz. Ivano-Frankivs'ka Oblast', W Ukraine
Kalutara *110 D4* Western Province, SW Sri Lanka
Kalvarija *85 B5 Pol.* Kalwaria. Marijampolė, S Lithuania
Kalyān *112 C5* Mahārāshtra, W India
Kálymnos *83 D6 var.* Kálimnos. *Island* Dodekánisos, Greece, Aegean Sea
Kama *88 D4 river* NW Russian Federation
Kamarang *37 F3* W Guyana
Kamchatka *see* Kamchatka, Poluostrov
Kamchatka, Poluostrov *93 G3 Eng.* Kamchatka. *Peninsula* E Russian Federation
Kamensk-Shakhtinskiy *89 B6* Rostovskaya Oblast', SW Russian Federation
Kamina *55 D7* Shaba, S Dem. Rep. Congo
Kamishli *see* Al Qāmishlī
Kamloops *15 E5* British Columbia, SW Canada
Kammu Seamount *130 C2 undersea feature* N Pacific Ocean
Kampala *51 B6 country capital* (Uganda) S Uganda
Kâmpóng Cham *115 D6 prev.* Kompong Cham. Kâmpóng Cham, C Cambodia
Kâmpóng Chhnăng *115 D6 prev.* Kompong. Kâmpóng Chhnăng, C Cambodia
Kâmpóng Saôm *115 D6 prev.* Kompong Som, Sihanoukville. Kâmpóng Saôm, SW Cambodia
Kâmpóng Spoe *115 D6 prev.* Kompong Speu. Kâmpóng Spœ, S Cambodia
Kâmpôt *115 D6* Kâmpôt, SW Cambodia
Kam"yanets'-Podil's'kyy *86 C3 Rus.* Kamenets-Podol'skiy. Khmel'nyts'ka Oblast', W Ukraine
Kam"yanka-Dniprovs'ka *87 F3 Rus.* Kamenka Dneprovskaya. Zaporiz'ka Oblast', SE Ukraine
Kamyshin *89 B6* Volgogradskaya Oblast', SW Russian Federation
Kanaky *see* New Caledonia
Kananga *55 D6 prev.* Luluabourg. Kasai Occidental, S Dem. Rep. Congo
Kananur *see* Cannanore
Kanara *see* Karnātaka
Kanash *89 C5* Chuvashskaya Respublika, W Russian Federation
Kanazawa *109 C5* Ishikawa, Honshū, SW Japan
Kanbe *114 B4* Yangon, SW Myanmar
Kānchīpuram *110 C2 prev.* Conjeeveram. Tamil Nādu, SE India
Kandahār *101 E5 Per.* Qandahār. Kandahār, S Afghanistan
Kandalakša *see* Kandalaksha
Kandalaksha *88 B2 var.* Kandalakša, *Fin.* Kantalahti. Murmanskaya Oblast', NW Russian Federation
Kandangan *116 D4* Borneo, C Indonesia
Kandava *84 C3 Ger.* Kandau. Tukums, W Latvia
Kandi *53 F4* N Benin
Kandy *110 D3* Central Province, C Sri Lanka
Kane Fracture Zone *44 B4 tectonic feature* NW Atlantic Ocean
Kāne'ohe *25 A8 var.* Kaneohe. O'ahu, Hawai'i, USA, C Pacific Ocean
Kangān *98 D4* Būshehr, S Iran
Kangaroo Island *127 A7 island* South Australia
Kangertittivaq *61 E4 Dan.* Scoresby Sund. *Fjord* E Greenland
Kangikajik *61 E4 var.* Kap Brewster. *Headland* E Greenland
Kaniv *87 E2 Rus.* Kanëv. Cherkas'ka Oblast', C Ukraine
Kanivs'ke Vodoskhovyshche *87 E2 Rus.* Kanevskoye Vodokhranilishche. *Reservoir* C Ukraine
Kanjiža *78 D2 Ger.* Altkanischa, *Hung.* Magyarkanizsa, Ókanizsa; *prev.* Stara Kanjiža. Serbia, N Serbia and Montenegro (Yugo.)
Kankaanpää *63 D5* Länsi-Suomi, W Finland
Kankakee *18 B3* Illinois, N USA
Kankan *52 D4* Haute-Guinée, E Guinea
Kannur *see* Cannanore
Kano *53 G4* Kano, N Nigeria
Kānpur *113 E3 Eng.* Cawnpore. Uttar Pradesh, N India
Kansas *27 F1 off.* State of Kansas; also known as Jayhawker State, Sunflower State. *State* C USA
Kansas *23 F5* Kansas, C USA
Kansas City *23 F4* Kansas, C USA
Kansas City *23 F4* Missouri, C USA
Kansas River *23 F5 river* Kansas, C USA
Kansk *93 E4* Krasnoyarskiy Kray, S Russian Federation
Kansu *see* Gansu
Kantalahti *see* Kandalaksha
Kántanos *83 C7* Kríti, Greece, E Mediterranean Sea
Kantemirovka *89 B6* Voronezhskaya Oblast', W Russian Federation
Kanton *123 F3 var.* Abariringa, Canton Island; *prev.* Mary Island. *Atoll* Phoenix Islands, C Kiribati
Kanye *56 C4* Southern, SE Botswana
Kaohsiung *106 D6 var.* Gaoxiong, *Jap.* Takao, Takow. S Taiwan
Kaolack *52 B3 var.* Kaolak. W Senegal
Kaolak *see* Kaolack
Kaolan *see* Lanzhou
Kaoma *56 C2* Western, W Zambia
Kap Brewster *see* Kangikajik
Kapelle *65 B5* Zeeland, SW Netherlands
Kapellen *65 C5* Antwerpen, N Belgium
Kap Farvel *see* Uummannarsuaq
Kapka, Massif du *54 C2 mountain range* E Chad
Kaplangky, Plato *see* Gaplaňgyr Platosy
Kapoeta *51 C5* Eastern Equatoria, SE Sudan
Kaposvár *77 C7* Somogy, SW Hungary
Kappeln *72 B2* Schleswig-Holstein, N Germany
Kapstad *see* Cape Town
Kaptsevichy *85 C7 Rus.* Koptsevichi. Homyel'skaya Voblasts', SE Belarus
Kapuas, Sungai *116 C4 prev.* Kapoeas. *River* Borneo, C Indonesia
Kapuskasing *16 C4* Ontario, S Canada
Kapyl' *85 C6 Rus.* Kopyl'. Minskaya Voblasts', C Belarus
Kap York *see* Innaanganeq
Kara-Balta *101 F2* Chuyskaya Oblast', N Kyrgyzstan
Karabil', Vozvyshennost' *see* Garabil Belentligi
Kara-Bogaz-Gol, Zaliv *see* Garabogaz Aylagy
Karabük *94 C2* Karabük NW Turkey
Karāchi *112 B3* Sind, SE Pakistan
Karadeniz *see* Black Sea
Karadeniz Boğazı *see* İstanbul Boğazı
Karaferiye *see* Véroia
Karaganda *92 C4 Kaz.* Qaraghandy. Karaganda, C Kazakhstan
Karaginskiy, Ostrov *93 H2 island* E Russian Federation
Karak *see* Al Karak
Kara-Kala *see* Garrygala
Karakax *see* Moyu
Karakılısse *see* Ağrı
Karakol *101 G2 prev.* Przheval'sk. Issyk-Kul'skaya Oblast', NE Kyrgyzstan

Karakol *101 G2 var.* Karakolka. Issyk-Kul'skaya Oblast', NE Kyrgyzstan
Karakolka *see* Karakol
Karakoram Range *112 D1 mountain range* C Asia
Karaköse *see* Ağrı
Kara Kum *see* Garagum
Kara Kum Canal *see* Garagum Kanaly
Karakumskiy Kanal *see* Garagum Kanaly
Karakumy, Peski *see* Garagum
Karamai *see* Karamay
Karaman *94 C4* Karaman, S Turkey
Karamay *104 B2 var.* Karamai, Kelamayi, *prev. Chin.* K'o-la-ma-i. Xinjiang Uygur Zizhiqu, NW China
Karamea Bight *129 B5 gulf* South Island, NZ
Karapelit *82 E1 Rom.* Stejarul. Dobrich, NE Bulgaria
Kara-Say *101 G2* Issyk-Kul'skaya Oblast', NE Kyrgyzstan
Karasburg *56 B4* Karas, S Namibia
Kara Sea *see* Karskoye More
Karatau *92 C5 Kaz.* Qarataū. Zhambyl, S Kazakhstan
Karavás *83 B7* Kýthira, S Greece
Karbalā' *98 B3 var.* Kerbala, Kerbela. S Iraq
Kardhítsa *see* Kardítsa
Kardítsa *83 B5 var.* Kardhítsa. Thessalía, C Greece
Kärdla *84 C2 Ger.* Kertel. Hiiumaa, W Estonia
Karet *see* Kâgheț
Kargı *94 C2* Çorum, N Turkey
Kargilik *see* Yecheng
Kariba *56 D2* Mashonaland West, N Zimbabwe
Kariba, Lake *56 D3 reservoir* Zambia/Zimbabwe
Karibib *56 B3* Erongo, C Namibia
Karies *see* Karyés
Karigasniemi *62 D2 Lapp.* Garegegasnjárga. Lappi, N Finland
Karimata, Selat *116 C4 strait* W Indonesia
Karīmnagar *112 D5* Andhra Pradesh, C India
Karin *50 D4* Woqooyi Galbeed, N Somalia
Kariot *see* Ikaría
Káristos *see* Kárystos
Karkinits'ka Zatoka *87 E4 Rus.* Karkinitskiy Zaliv. *Gulf* S Ukraine
Karkūk *see* Kirkūk
Karlovac *78 B3 Ger.* Karlstadt, *Hung.* Károlyváros. Karlovac, C Croatia
Karlovy Vary *77 A5 Ger.* Karlsbad; prev. *Eng.* Carlsbad. Karlovarský Kraj, W Czech Republic
Karlskrona *63 C7* Blekinge, S Sweden
Karlsruhe *73 B6 var.* Carlsruhe. Baden-Württemberg, SW Germany
Karlstad *63 B6* Värmland, C Sweden
Karnāl *112 D2* Haryāna, N India
Karnātaka *110 C1 var.* Kanara; *prev.* Maisur, Mysore. Admin. region *state* W India
Karnobat *82 D2* Burgas, E Bulgaria
Karnul *see* Kurnool
Karpaten *see* Carpathian Mountains
Kárpathos *83 E7 It.* Scarpanto; *anc.* Carpathos, Carpathus. *Island* SE Greece
Kárpathos *83 E7* Kárpathos, SE Greece
Karpaty *see* Carpathian Mountains
Karpenísi *83 B5 prev.* Karpenísion. Stereá Ellás, C Greece
Kars *95 F2 var.* Qars. Kars, NE Turkey
Kārsava *84 D4 Ger.* Karsau; *prev.* Rus. Korsovka. Ludza, E Latvia
Karskiye Vorota, Proliv *88 E2 Eng.* Kara Strait. *Strait* N Russian Federation
Karskoye More *92 D2 Eng.* Kara Sea. *Sea* Arctic Ocean
Karyés *82 C4 var.* Karies. Ágion Óros, N Greece
Kárystos *83 C6 var.* Káristos. Évvoia, C Greece
Kasai *55 C6 var.* Cassai, Kassai. *River* Angola/Dem. Rep. Congo
Kasaji *55 D7* Shaba, S Dem. Rep. Congo
Kasama *56 D1* Northern, N Zambia
Kāsaragod *110 B2* Kerala, SW India
Kāshān *98 C3* Eşfahān, C Iran
Kashi *104 A3 Chin.* Kaxgar, K'o-shih, *Uigh.* Kashgar. Xinjiang Uygur Zizhiqu, NW China
Kasongo *55 D6* Maniema, E Dem. Rep. Congo
Kasongo-Lunda *55 C7* Bandundu, SW Dem. Rep. Congo
Kásos *83 D7 island* S Greece
Kaspiysk *89 B8* Respublika Dagestan, SW Russian Federation
Kassai *see* Kasai
Kassala *50 C4* Kassala, E Sudan
Kassel *72 B4 prev.* Cassel. Hessen, C Germany
Kasserine *49 E2 var.* Al Qaşrayn. W Tunisia
Kastamonu *94 C2 var.* Castamoni, Kastamuni. Kastamonu, N Turkey
Kastamuni *see* Kastamonu
Kastaneá *82 B4* Kentrikí Makedonía, N Greece
Kastélli *83 C7* Kríti, Greece, E Mediterranean Sea
Kastoría *82 B4* Dytikí Makedonía, N Greece
Kástro *83 C6* Sífnos, Kykládes, Greece, Aegean Sea
Kastsyukovichy *85 E7 Rus.* Kostyukovichi. Mahilyowskaya Voblasts', E Belarus
Kastsyukowka *85 D7 Rus.* Kostyukovka. Homyel'skaya Voblasts', SE Belarus
Kasulu *51 B7* Kigoma, W Tanzania
Kasumiga-ura *109 D5 lake* Honshū, S Japan
Katahdin, Mount *19 G1mountain* Maine, NE USA
Katalla *14 C3* Alaska, USA
Katana *see* Qaţanā
Katanning *125 B7* Western Australia
Katawaz *see* Zarghūn Shahr
Katchall Island *111 F3 island* Nicobar Islands, India, NE Indian Ocean
Kateríni *82 B4* Kentrikí Makedonía, N Greece
Katha *114 B2* Sagaing, N Myanmar
Katherine *126 A2* Northern Territory, N Australia
Kathmandu *102 C3 prev.* Kantipur. *Country capital* (Nepal) Central, C Nepal
Katikati *128 D3* Bay of Plenty, North Island, NZ
Katima Mulilo *56 C3* Caprivi, NE Namibia
Katiola *52 D4* C Côte d'Ivoire
Káto Achaïa *83 B5 var.* Kato Ahaia, Káto Akhaía. Dytikí Ellás, S Greece
Kato Ahaia *see* Káto Achaïa
Káto Akhaía *see* Káto Achaïa
Katoúna *83 A5* Dytikí Ellás, C Greece
Katowice *77 C5 Ger.* Kattowitz. Śląskie, S Poland
Katsina *53 G3* Katsina, N Nigeria
Kattaqo'rg'on *101 E2 var.* Kattaqŭrghon, *Rus.* Kattakurgan. Samarqand Wiloyati, C Uzbekistan
Kattaqŭrghon *see* Kattaqo'rg'on
Kattavía *83 E7* Ródos, Dodekánisos, Greece, Aegean Sea
Kattegat *63 B7 Dan.* Kattegatt. *Strait* N Europe
Kaua'i *25 A7 var.* Kauai. *Island* Hawaiian Islands, Hawai'i, USA, C Pacific Ocean
Kaufbeuren *73 C6* Bayern, S Germany
Kaunas *84 B4 Ger.* Kauen, *Pol.* Kowno; *prev.* Rus. Kovno. Kaunas, C Lithuania
Kavadarci *79 E6 Turk.* Kavadar. C FYR Macedonia
Kavajë *79 C6 It.* Cavaia, Kavaja. Tiranë, W Albania
Kavála *82 C3 prev.* Kavălla. Anatolikí Makedonía kai Thráki, NE Greece
Kāvali *110 D2* Andhra Pradesh, E India
Kavango *see* Cubango
Kavaratti Island *110 A3 island* Lakshadweep, India, N Indian Ocean
Kavarna *82 E2* Dobrich, NE Bulgaria
Kavengo *see* Cubango
Kavīr, Dasht-e *98 D3 var.* Great Salt Desert. *Salt pan* N Iran
Kavīr-e Lūt *see* Lūt, Dasht-e
Kawagoe *109 D5* Saitama, Honshū, S Japan
Kawasaki *108 A2* Kanagawa, Honshū, S Japan
Kawerau *128 E3* Bay of Plenty, North Island, NZ
Kaya *53 E3* C Burkina faso
Kayan *114 B4* Yangon, SW Myanmar
Kayan, Sungai *116 D3 prev.* Kajan. *River* Borneo, C Indonesia
Kayes *52 C3* Kayes, W Mali
Kayseri *94 D3 var.* Kaisaria; *anc.* Caesarea Mazaca, Mazaca. Kayseri, C Turkey
Kazach'ye *93 F2* Respublika Sakha (Yakutiya), NE Russian Federation
Kazakhskiy Melkosopochnik *92 C4 Eng.* Kazakh Uplands, Kirghiz Steppe, *Kaz.* Saryarqa. *Uplands* C Kazakhstan
Kazakhstan *92 B4 var.* Kazakstan, *Kaz.* Qazaqstan, Qazaqstan Respublikasy; *prev.* Kazakh Soviet Socialist Republic, *Rus.* Kazakhskaya SSR. *Country* C Asia
Kazakh Uplands *see* Kazakhskiy Melkosopochnik
Kazan' *89 C5* Respublika Tatarstan, W Russian Federation
Kazanlŭk *82 D2 prev.* Kazanlik. Stara Zagora, C Bulgaria
Kazbegi *see* Kazbek
Kazbek *95 F1 var.* Kazbegi, *Geor.* Mqinvartsveri. *Mountain* N Georgia
Kāzerūn *98 D4* Fārs, S Iran
Kazvin *see* Qazvīn
Kéa *83 C6 prev.* Kéos, *anc.* Ceos. *Island* Kykládes, Greece, Aegean Sea
Kéa *83 C6* Kéa, Kykládes, Greece, Aegean Sea
Kea, Mauna *25 B8 mountain* Hawai'i, USA, C Pacific Ocean
Kéamu *see* Aneityum
Kearney *23 E4* Nebraska, C USA
Keban Barajı *95 E3 reservoir* C Turkey
Kebkabiya *50 A4* Northern Darfur, W Sudan
Kebnekaise *62 C3 mountain* N Sweden
Kecskemét *77 D7* Bács-Kiskun, C Hungary
Kediri *116 D5* Jawa, C Indonesia
Kędzierzyn-Kole *77 C5 Ger.* Heydebrech. Opolskie, S Poland
Keelung *see* Chilung
Keetmanshoop *56 B4* Karas, S Namibia
Kefallinía *83 A5 var.* Kefallonía. *Island* Iónioi Nísoi, Greece, C Mediterranean Sea
Kefallonía *see* Kefallinía
Kefe *see* Feodosiya
Kehl *73 A6* Baden-Württemberg, SW Germany
Keila *84 D2 Ger.* Kegel. Harjumaa, NW Estonia
Keïta *53 F3* Tahoua, C Niger
Keitele *62 D4 lake* C Finland
Keith *127 B7* South Australia
Këk-Art *101 G2 prev.* Alaykel', Alay-Kuu. Oshskaya Oblast', SW Kyrgyzstan
Kékes *77 C6 mountain* N Hungary
Kelamayi *see* Karamay
Kelang *see* Klang
Kelat *see* Kālat
Kelifskiy Uzboy *see* Kelif Uzboÿy
Kelif Uzboÿy *100 D3 var.* Kelifskiy Uzboy. *Salt marsh* E Turkmenistan
Kelkit Çayı *95 E3 river* N Turkey
Kelmė *84 B4* Kelmė, C Lithuania
Kélo *54 B4* Tandjilé, SW Chad
Kelowna *15 E5* British Columbia, SW Canada
Kelso *24 B2* Washington, NW USA
Keluang *116 B3 var.* Kluang. Johor, Peninsular Malaysia
Kem' *88 B3* Respublika Kareliya, NW Russian Federation
Kemah *95 E3* Erzincan, E Turkey
Kemaman *see* Cukai
Kemerovo *92 D4 prev.* Shcheglovsk. Kemerovskaya Oblast', C Russian Federation
Kemi *62 D4* Lappi, NW Finland
Kemijärvi *62 D3 Swe.* Kemiträsk. Lappi, N Finland
Kemijoki *62 D3 river* NW Finland
Kemin *101 G2 prev.* Bystrovka. Chuyskaya Oblast', N Kyrgyzstan
Kempele *62 D4* Oulu, C Finland
Kempten *73 B7* Bayern, S Germany
Kendal *67 D5* NW England, UK
Kendari *117 E4* Sulawesi, C Indonesia
Kenedy *27 G4* Texas, SW USA
Kenema *52 C4* SE Sierra Leone
Këneurgench *see* Köneürgenç
Kenge *55 C6* Bandundu, SW Dem. Rep. Congo
Keng Tung *114 C3 var.* Kentung. Shan State, E Myanmar
Kénitra *48 C2 prev.* Port-Lyautey. NW Morocco
Kennett *23 H5* Missouri, C USA
Kennewick *24 C2* Washington, NW USA
Kenora *16 A3* Ontario, S Canada
Kenosha *18 B3* Wisconsin, N USA
Kentau *92 B5* Yuzhnyy Kazakhstan, S Kazakhstan
Kentucky *18 C5 off.* Commonwealth of Kentucky; also known as The Bluegrass State. *State* C USA
Kentucky Lake *18 B5 reservoir* Kentucky/Tennessee, S USA
Kentung *see* Keng Tung
Kenya *51 C6 Country* E Africa
Keokuk *23 G4* Iowa, C USA
Kępno *76 C4* Wielkopolskie, C Poland
Keppel Island *see* Niuatoputapu
Kepulauan Sangihe *see* Sangir, Kepulauan
Kerak *see* Al Karak
Kerala *110 C2 state* S India
Kerasunt *see* Giresun
Keratea *see* Keratéa
Keratéa *83 C6 var.* Keratea. Attikí, C Greece
Kerbala *see* Karbalā'
Kerbela *see* Karbalā'
Kerch *87 G5 Rus.* Kerch'. Respublika Krym, SE Ukraine
Kerchens'ka Protska *see* Kerch Strait
Kerchenskiy Proliv *see* Kerch Strait
Kerch Strait *87 G4 var.* Bosporus Cimmerius, Enikale Strait, *Rus.* Kerchenskiy Proliv, *Ukr.* Kerchens'ka Protska. *Strait* Black Sea/Sea of Azov
Kerguelen *119 C7 island* C French Southern and Antarctic Territories
Kerguelen Plateau *119 C7 undersea feature* S Indian Ocean
Kerí *83 A6* Zákynthos, Iónioi Nísoi, Greece, C Mediterranean Sea
Kerikeri *128 D2* Northland, North Island, NZ
Kerkenah, Îles de *80 D4 var.* Kerkenna Islands, *Ar.* Juzur Qarqannah. *Island group* E Tunisia
Kerkenna Islands *see* Kerkenah, Îles de
Kérkira *see* Kérkyra
Kerkrade *65 D6* Limburg, SE Netherlands
Kerkuk *see* Kirkūk
Kérkyra *82 A4 var.* Kérkira, *Eng.* Corfu. *Island* Iónioi Nísoi, Greece, C Mediterranean Sea
Kermadec Islands *130 C4 island group* NZ, SW Pacific Ocean
Kermadec Trench *121 E4 undersea feature* SW Pacific Ocean
Kermān *98 D3 var.* Kirman; *anc.* Carmana. Kermān, C Iran
Kermānshāh *98 C3 var.* Qahremānshahr; *prev.* Bākhtarān. Kermānshāh, W Iran
Kerrville *27 F4* Texas, SW USA
Kerulen *105 E2 Chin.* Herlen He, *Mong.* Herlen Gol. *River* China/Mongolia
Keryneia *80 C5 var.* Girne, Kyrenia. N Cyprus
Kesennuma *108 D4* Miyagi, Honshū, C Japan
Keszthely *77 C7* Zala, SW Hungary
Ketchikan *14 D4* Revillagigedo Island, Alaska, USA
Kętrzyn *76 D2 Ger.* Rastenburg. Warmiusko-Mazurskie, NE Poland
Kettering *67 D6* C England, UK
Kettering *18 C4* Ohio, N USA
Keuruu *63 D5* Länsi-Suomi, W Finland
Keweenaw Peninsula *18 B1 peninsula* Michigan, N USA
Key Largo *21 F5* Key Largo, Florida, SE USA
Key West *21 E5* Florida Keys, Florida, SE USA
Khabarovsk *93 G4* Khabarovskiy Kray, SE Russian Federation
Khadera *see* Hadera
Khairpur *112 B3* Sind, SE Pakistan
Khalīj al 'Aqabah *see* Aqaba, Gulf of
Khalīj al 'Arabī *see* Gulf, The
Khalīj-e Fars *see* Gulf, The
Khalkidhikí *see* Chalkidikí
Khalkís *see* Chalkída
Khambhāt, Gulf of *112 C4 Eng.* Gulf of Cambay. *Gulf* W India
Khamīs Mushayt *99 B6 var.* Hamīs Musait. 'Asīr, SW Saudi Arabia
Khānābād *101 E3* Kunduz, NE Afghanistan
Khān al Baghdādī *see* Al Baghdādī
Khandwa *112 D4* Madhya Pradesh, C India
Khanh *see* Soc Trăng
Khaniá *see* Chaniá
Khanka, Lake *107 E2 var.* Hsing-k'ai Hu, Lake Hanka, *Chin.* Xingkai Hu, *Rus.* Ozero Khanka. *Lake* China/Russian Federation
Khanthabouli *114 D4 prev.* Savannakhét. Savannakhét, S Laos
Khanty-Mansiysk *92 C3 prev.* Ostyako-Voguls'k. Khanty-Mansiyskiy Avtonomnyy Okrug, C Russian Federation
Khān Yūnis *97 A7 var.* Khān Yūnus. S Gaza Strip
Khān Yūnus *see* Khān Yūnis
Khanzi *see* Ghanzi
Kharagpur *113 F4* West Bengal, NE India
Kharbin *see* Harbin
Kharkiv *87 G2 Rus.* Khar'kov. Kharkivs'ka Oblast', NE Ukraine
Kharmanli *82 D3* Khaskovo, S Bulgaria
Khartoum *50 B4 var.* El Khartûm, Khartum. *Country capital* (Sudan) Khartoum, C Sudan
Khartum *see* Khartoum
Khasavyurt *89 B8* Respublika Dagestan, SW Russian Federation
Khāsh, Dasht-e *100 D5 Eng.* Khash Desert. *Desert* SW Afghanistan
Khashim Al Qirba *see* Khashm el Girba
Khashm al Qirbah *see* Khashm el Girba
Khashm el Girba *50 C4 var.* Khashim Al Qirba, Khashm al Qirbah. Kassala, E Sudan
Khaskovo *82 D3* Khaskovo, S Bulgaria
Khaydarkan *101 F2 var.* Khaydarken. Oshskaya Oblast', SW Kyrgyzstan
Khaydarken *see* Khaydarkan
Khelat *see* Kālat
Kherson *87 E4* Khersons'ka Oblast', S Ukraine
Kheta *93 E2 river* N Russian Federation
Khíos *see* Chíos
Khirbet el 'Aujā et Tahtā *119 E7 var.* 'Aujā et Tahtā. E West Bank
Khiva *see* Xiva
Khiwa *see* Xiva
Khmel'nyts'kyy *86 C2 Rus.* Khmel'nitskiy; *prev.* Proskurov. Khmel'nyts'ka Oblast', W Ukraine
Khodasy *85 E6 Rus.* Khodosy. Mahilyowskaya Voblasts', E Belarus
Khodoriv *86 C2 Pol.* Chodorów, *Rus.* Khodorov. L'vivs'ka Oblast', NW Ukraine
Khodzhent *see* Khŭjand
Khoi *see* Khvoy
Khojend *see* Khŭjand
Khokand *see* Qo'qon
Kholm *101 E3 var.* Tashqurghan, *Pash.* Khulm. Balkh, N Afghanistan
Kholon *see* Holon
Khoms *see* Al Khums
Khong Sedone *see* Muang Khôngxédôn
Khon Kaen *114 D4 var.* Muang Khon Kaen. Khon Kaen, E Thailand
Khor *93 G4* Khabarovskiy Kray, SE Russian Federation
Khorat *see* Nakhon Ratchasima
Khorugh *101 F3 Rus.* Khorog. S Tajikistan
Khotan *see* Hotan
Khouribga *48 B2* C Morocco
Khovd *see* Hovd
Khowst *101 F4* Paktīā, E Afghanistan
Khoy *see* Khvoy
Khoyniki *85 D8 Rus.* Khoyniki. Homyel'skaya Voblasts', SE Belarus
Khrebet Kolymskiy *see* Kolyma Range
Khrebet Kopetdag *see* Koppeh Dāgh
Khrebet Lomonsova *see* Lomonosov Ridge
Khudzhand *see* Khŭjand
Khŭjand *101 E2 var.* Khodzhent, Khojend, *Rus.* Khudzhand; *prev.* Leninabad, *Taj.* Leninobod. N Tajikistan
Khulm *see* Kholm
Khulna *113 G4* Khulna, SW Bangladesh
Khums *see* Al Khums
Khust *86 B3 Cz.* Chust, Husté, *Hung.* Huszt. Zakarpats'ka Oblast', W Ukraine
Khvoy *98 C2 var.* Khoi, Khoy. Āžarbāyjān-e Bākhtarī, NW Iran
Khyber Pass *112 C1 var.* Kowtal-e Khaybar. *Pass* Afghanistan/Pakistan
Kiangmai *see* Chiang Mai
Kiang-ning *see* Nanjing
Kiangsi *see* Jiangxi
Kiangsu *see* Jiangsu
Kiáto *83 B6 prev.* Kiáton. Pelopónnisos, S Greece
Kiayi *see* Chiai
Kibangou *55 B6* Le Niari, SW Congo
Kibombo *55 D6* Maniema, E Dem. Rep. Congo
Kičevo *79 D6* SW FYR Macedonia
Kidderminster *67 D6* C England, UK
Kiel *72 B2* Schleswig-Holstein, N Germany
Kielce *76 D4 Rus.* Keltsy. Świętokrzyskie, C Poland
Kieler Bucht *72 B2 bay* N Germany
Kiev *see* Kyyiv
Kiffa *52 C3* Assaba, S Mauritania
Kigali *51 B6 country capital* (Rwanda) C Rwanda
Kigoma *51 B7* Kigoma, W Tanzania
Kihnu *84 C2 var.* Kihnu Saar, *Ger.* Kühnö. *Island* SW Estonia
Kihnu Saar *see* Kihnu
Kii-suidō *109 C7 strait* S Japan
Kikinda *78 D3 Ger.* Grosskikinda, *Hung.* Nagykikinda; *prev.* Velika Kikinda. Serbia, N Serbia and Montenegro (Yugo.)
Kikládhes *see* Kykládes
Kikwit *55 C6* Bandundu, W Dem. Rep. Congo
Kilien Mountains *see* Qilian Shan
Kilimane *see* Quelimane
Kilimanjaro *51 C7 var.* Uhuru Peak. *Mountain* NE Tanzania
Kilimanjaro *47 E5 region* E Tanzania
Kilingi-Nõmme *84 D3 Ger.* Kurkund. Pärnumaa, SW Estonia
Kilis *94 D4* Kilis S Turkey
Kiliya *86 D4 Rom.* Chilia-Nouă. Odes'ka Oblast', SW Ukraine
Kilkenny *67 B6 Ir.* Cill Chainnigh. S Ireland
Kilkís *82 B3* Kentrikí Makedonía, N Greece
Killarney *67 A6 Ir.* Cill Airne. SW Ireland
Killeen *27 G3* Texas, SW USA
Kilmain *see* Quelimane
Kilmarnock *66 C4* W Scotland, UK
Kilwa *see* Kilwa Kivinje
Kilwa Kivinje *51 C7 var.* Kilwa. Lindi, SE Tanzania
Kimberley *56 C4* Northern Cape, C South Africa
Kimberley Plateau *124 C3 plateau* Western Australia
Kimch'aek *107 E3 prev.* Sŏngjin. E North Korea
Kinabalu, Gunung *116 D3 mountain* East Malaysia
Kindersley *15 F5* Saskatchewan, S Canada
Kindia *52 C4* Guinée-Maritime, SW Guinea
Kindley Field *20 A4 air base* E Bermuda
Kindu *55 D6 prev.* Kindu-Port-Empain. Maniema, C Dem. Rep. Congo
Kineshma *89 C5* Ivanovskaya Oblast', W Russian Federation
King Island *127 B8 island* Tasmania, SE Australia
Kingman *26 A1* Arizona, SW USA
Kingman Reef *123 E2 US territory* C Pacific Ocean
Kingsford Smith *126 E2 international airport* (Sydney) New South Wales, SE Australia
King's Lynn *67 E6 var.* Bishop's Lynn, Kings Lynn, Lynn, Lynn Regis. E England, UK
King Sound *124 B3 sound* Western Australia
Kingsport *21 E1* Tennessee, S USA
Kingston *32 B5 country capital* (Jamaica) E Jamaica
Kingston *19 F3* New York, NE USA
Kingston *16 D5* Ontario, SE Canada
Kingston upon Hull *67 D5 var.* Hull. E England, UK
Kingston upon Thames *67 A8* SE England, UK
Kingstown *33 H4 country capital* (Saint Vincent and the Grenadines) Saint Vincent, Saint Vincent and the Grenadines
Kingsville *27 G5* Texas, SW USA
King William Island *15 F3 island* Nunavut, N Canada Arctic Ocean
Kinrooi *65 D5* Limburg, NE Belgium
Kinshasa *55 B6 prev.* Léopoldville. *Country capital* (Congo (Zaire)) Kinshasa, W Dem. Rep. Congo
Kintyre *66 B4 peninsula* W Scotland, UK
Kinyeti *51 B5 mountain* S Sudan
Kiparissía *see* Kyparissía
Kipili *51 B7* Rukwa, W Tanzania
Kipushi *55 D8* Shaba, SE Dem. Rep. Congo
Kirdzhali *see* Kŭrdzhali
Kirghiz Range *101 F2 Rus.* Kirgizskiy Khrebet; *prev.* Alexander Range. *Mountain range* Kazakhstan/Kyrgyzstan
Kirghiz Steppe *see* Kazakhskiy Melkosopochnik
Kiriath-Arba *see* Hebron
Kiribati *123 F2 Country* C Pacific Ocean
Kırıkhan *94 D4* Hatay, S Turkey
Kırıkkale *94 C3* Kırıkkale, C Turkey
Kirin *see* Jilin
Kirinyaga *51 C6 prev.* Mount Kenya. *Volcano* C Kenya
Kirishi *88 B4 var.* Kirisi. Leningradskaya Oblast', NW Russian Federation
Kirisi *see* Kirishi
Kiritimati *123 G2 prev.* Christmas Island. *Atoll* Line Islands, E Kiribati
Kirkenes *62 E2 var.* Kirkkoniemi. Finnmark, N Norway
Kirkkoniemi *see* Kirkenes
Kirkland Lake *16 D4* Ontario, S Canada
Kırklareli *94 A2 prev.* Kirk-Kilissa. Kırklareli, NW Turkey
Kirkpatrick, Mount *132 B3 mountain* Antarctica
Kirksville *23 G4* Missouri, C USA
Kirkūk *98 B3 var.* Karkūk, Kerkuk. N Iraq
Kirkwall *66 C2* NE Scotland, UK
Kirkwood *23 G4* Missouri, C USA
Kirman *see* Kermān
Kir Moab *see* Al Karak
Kirov *89 C5 prev.* Vyatka. Kirovskaya Oblast', NW Russian Federation
Kirovo-Chepetsk *89 D5* Kirovskaya Oblast', NW Russian Federation
Kirovohrad *87 E3 Rus.* Kirovograd; *prev.* Kirovo, Yelizavetgrad, Zinov'yevsk. Kirovohrads'ka Oblast', C Ukraine
Kīrthar Range *112 B3 mountain range* S Pakistan
Kirun' *see* Chilung
Kiruna *62 C3* Norrbotten, N Sweden
Kisangani *55 D5 prev.* Stanleyville. Orientale, NE Dem. Rep. Congo
Kislovodsk *89 B7* Stavropol'skiy Kray, SW Russian Federation
Kismaayo *51 D6 var.* Chisimayu, Kismayu, *It.* Chisimaio. Jubbada Hoose, S Somalia
Kismayu *see* Kismaayo
Kissidougou *52 C4* Guinée-Forestière, S Guinea
Kissimmee, Lake *21 E4 lake* Florida, SE USA
Kisumu *51 C6 prev.* Port Florence. Nyanza, W Kenya
Kisvárda *77 E6 Ger.* Kleinwardein. Szabolcs-Szatmár-Bereg, E Hungary
Kita *52 D3* Kayes, W Mali
Kitakyūshū *109 A7 var.* Kitakyûsyû. Fukuoka, Kyūshū, SW Japan
Kitakyûsyû *see* Kitakyūshū
Kitami *108 D2* Hokkaidō, NE Japan
Kitchener *16 C5* Ontario, S Canada
Kíthira *see* Kýthira
Kíthnos *see* Kýthnos
Kitimat *14 D4* British Columbia, SW Canada
Kitinen *62 D3 river* N Finland
Kitob *101 E3 Rus.* Kitab. Qashqadaryo Wiloyati, S Uzbekistan
Kitwe *56 D2 var.* Kitwe-Nkana. Copperbelt, C Zambia

Kitwe-Nkana *see* Kitwe
Kitzbühler Alpen 73 C7 *mountain range* W Austria
Kivalina 14 C2 Alaska, USA
Kivalo 62 D3 *ridge* C Finland
Kivertsi 86 C1 *Pol.* Kiwerce, *Rus.* Kivertsy. Volyns'ka Oblast', NW Ukraine
Kivu, Lake 55 E6 *Fr.* Lac Kivu. *Lake* Rwanda/Dem. Rep. Congo
Kızıl Irmak 94 C3 *river* C Turkey
Kizil Kum *see* Kyzyl Kum
Kladno 77 A5 Středočesky Kraj, NW Czech Republic
Klagenfurt 73 D7 *Slvn.* Celovec. Kärnten, S Austria
Klaipėda 84 B3 *Ger.* Memel. Klaipėda, NW Lithuania
Klamath Falls 24 B4 Oregon, NW USA
Klamath Mountains 24 A4 *mountain range* California/Oregon, W USA
Klang 116 B3 *var.* Kelang; *prev.* Port Swettenham. Selangor, Peninsular Malaysia
Klarälven 63 B6 *river* Norway/Sweden
Klatovy 77 A5 *Ger.* Klattau. Plzeňský Kraj, W Czech Republic
Klazienaveen 64 E2 Drenthe, NE Netherlands
Klein Karas 56 B4 Karas, S Namibia
Kleisoúra 83 A5 Ípeiros, W Greece
Klerksdorp 56 D4 North-West, N South Africa
Klimavichy 85 E7 *Rus.* Klimovichi. Mahilyowskaya Voblasts', E Belarus
Klintsy 89 A5 Bryanskaya Oblast', W Russian Federation
Klisura 82 C2 Plovdiv, C Bulgaria
Ključ 78 B3 Federacija Bosna I Hercegovina, NW Bosnia and Herzegovina
Kłobuck 76 C4 Śląskie, S Poland
Klosters 73 B7 Graubünden, SE Switzerland
Kluang *see* Keluang
Kluczbork 76 C4 *Ger.* Kreuzburg, Kreuzburg in Oberschlesien. Opolskie, S Poland
Klyuchevskaya Sopka, Vulkan 93 H3 *volcano* E Russian Federation
Knin 78 B4 Šibenik-Knin, S Croatia
Knjaževac 78 E4 Serbia, E Serbia and Montenegro (Yugo.)
Knokke-Heist 65 A5 West-Vlaanderen, NW Belgium
Knoxville 20 D1 Tennessee, S USA
Knud Rasmussen Land 60 D1 *physical region* N Greenland
Kōbe 109 C6 Hyōgo, Honshū, SW Japan
København 63 B7 *Eng.* Copenhagen; *anc.* Hafnia. *Country capital* (Denmark) Sjælland, København, E Denmark
Kobenni 52 D3 Hodh el Gharbi, S Mauritania
Koblenz 73 A5 *prev.* Coblenz, *Fr.* Coblence, *anc.* Confluentes. Rheinland-Pfalz, W Germany
Kobryn 85 A6 *Pol.* Kobryn, *Rus.* Kobrin. Brestskaya Voblasts', SW Belarus
K'obulet'i 95 F2 W Georgia
Kočani 79 E6 NE FYR Macedonia
Kočevje 73 D8 *Ger.* Gottschee. S Slovenia
Koch Bihār 113 G3 West Bengal, NE India
Kōchi 109 B7 *var.* Kôti. Kōchi, Shikoku, SW Japan
Kochi *see* Cochin
Kochiu *see* Gejiu
Kodiak 14 C3 Kodiak Island, Alaska, USA
Kodiak Island 14 C3 *island* Alaska, USA
Koeln *see* Köln
Ko-erh-mu *see* Golmud
Koetai *see* Mahakam, Sungai
Koetaradja *see* Bandaaceh
Kōfu 109 D5 *var.* Kôhu. Yamanashi, Honshū, S Japan
Kogarah 126 E2 New South Wales, SE Australia
Kogon 100 D2 *Rus.* Kagan. Bukhoro Wiloyati, C Uzbekistan
Kohīma 113 H3 Nāgāland, E India
Koh I Noh *see* Büyükağrı Dağı
Kohtla-Järve 84 E2 Ida-Virumaa, NE Estonia
Kôhu *see* Kōfu
Kokand *see* Qo'qon
Kokkola 62 D4 *Swe.* Karleby; *prev. Swe.* Gamlakarleby. Länsi-Suomi, W Finland
Koko *see* Qinghai Hu
Koko 53 F4 Kebbi, W Nigeria
Kokomo 18 C4 Indiana, N USA
Koko Nor *see* Qinghai
Kokrines 14 C2 Alaska, USA
Kokshaal-Tau 101 G2 *Rus.* Khrebet Kakshaal-Too. *Mountain range* China/Kyrgyzstan
Kokshetau 92 C4 *Kaz.* Kökshetaū; *prev.* Kokchetav. Severnyy Kazakhstan, N Kazakhstan
Koksijde 65 A5 West-Vlaanderen, W Belgium
Koksoak 16 D2 *river* Québec, E Canada
Kokstad 56 D5 KwaZulu/Natal, E South Africa
Kola *see* Kol'skiy Poluostrov
Kolaka 117 E4 Sulawesi, C Indonesia
Kolam *see* Quilon
K'o-la-ma-i *see* Karamay
Kola Peninsula *see* Kol'skiy Poluostrov
Kolari 62 D3 Lappi, NW Finland
Kolárovo 77 C6 *Ger.* Gutta; *prev.* Guta, *Hung.* Gúta. Nitriansky Kraj, SW Slovakia
Kolda 52 C3 S Senegal
Kolding 63 A7 Vejle, C Denmark
Kölen 59 E1 *Nor.* Kjølen. *Mountain range* Norway/Sweden
Kolguyev, Ostrov 88 C2 *island* NW Russian Federation
Kolhāpur 110 B1 Mahārāshtra, SW India
Kolhumadulu Atoll 110 A5 *var.* Kolumadulu Atoll, Thaa Atoll. *Atoll* S Maldives
Kolín 77 B5 *Ger.* Kolin. Středočesky Kraj, C Czech Republic
Kolka 84 C2 Talsi, NW Latvia
Kolkasrags 84 C2 *prev. Eng.* Cape Domesnes. *Headland* NW Latvia
Kolkata *see* Calcutta
Kollam *see* Quilon
Köln 72 A4 *var.* Koeln, *Eng./Fr.* Cologne; *prev.* Cöln, *anc.* Colonia Agrippina, Oppidum Ubiorum. Nordrhein-Westfalen, W Germany
Koło 76 C3 Wielkopolskie, C Poland
Kołobrzeg 98 B2 *Ger.* Kolberg. Zachodniopomorskie, NW Poland
Kolokani 74 D3 Koulikoro, W Mali
Kolomna 89 B5 Moskovskaya Oblast', W Russian Federation
Kolomyya 86 C3 *Ger.* Kolomea. Ivano-Frankivs'ka Oblast', W Ukraine
Kolpa 78 A2 *Ger.* Kulpa, *SCr.* Kupa. *River* Croatia/Slovenia
Kolpino 88 B4 Leningradskaya Oblast', NW Russian Federation
Kólpos Ammóchostos 80 C5 *var.* Famagusta Bay, *bay* E Cyprus
Kol'skiy Poluostrov 88 C2 *Eng.* Kola Peninsula. *Peninsula* NW Russian Federation
Kolumadulu Atoll *see* Kolhumadulu Atoll
Kolwezi 55 D7 Shaba, S Dem. Rep. Congo
Kolyma 93 G2 *river* NE Russian Federation
Kolyma Range 91 G2 *var.* Khrebet Kolymskiy, *Eng.* Kolyma Range. *Mountain range* E Russian Federation
Komatsu 109 C5 *var.* Komatu. Ishikawa, Honshū, SW Japan
Komatu *see* Komatsu
Kommunizma Pik *see* Kommunizm, Qullai
Kommunizm, Qullai 101 F3 *var.* Qullai Garmo, *Eng.* Communism Peak, *Rus.* Kommunizma Pik; *prev.* Stalin Peak. *Mountain* E Tajikistan
Komoé 53 E4 *var.* Komoé Fleuve. *River* E Côte d'Ivoire
Komoé Fleuve *see* Komoé
Komotiní 82 D3 *var.* Gümüljina, *Turk.* Gümülcine. Anatolikí Makedonía kai Thráki, NE Greece
Komsomolets, Ostrov 93 E1 *island* Severnaya Zemlya, N Russian Federation
Komsomol'sk-na-Amure 93 G4 Khabarovskiy Kray, SE Russian Federation
Kondolovo 82 E3 Burgas, E Bulgaria
Kondopoga 88 B3 Respublika Kareliya, NW Russian Federation
Kondoz *see* Kunduz
Kondūz *see* Kunduz
Köneürgenç 100 C2 *Rus.* Këneurgench; *prev.* Kunya-Urgench. Dashkhovuzskiy Velayat, N Turkmenistan
Kong Christian IX Land 60 D4 *Eng.* King Christian IX Land. *Physical region* SE Greenland
Kong Frederik IX Land 60 C3 *Eng.* King Frederik IX Land. *Physical region* SW Greenland
Kong Frederik VIII Land 61 E2 *Eng.* King Frederik VIII Land. *Physical region* NE Greenland
Kong Frederik VI Kyst 60 C4 *Eng.* King Frederik VI Coast. *Physical region* SE Greenland
Kong Karls Land 61 G2 *Eng.* King Charles Islands. *Island group* SE Svalbard
Kongo *see* Congo
Kongolo 55 D6 Shaba, E Dem. Rep. Congo
Kongor 51 B5 Jonglei, SE Sudan
Kong Oscar Fjord 61 E3 *fjord* E Greenland
Kongsberg 63 B6 Buskerud, S Norway
Kông, Tônle 115 E5 *Lao.* Xê Kong. *River* Cambodia/Laos
Konia *see* Konya
Konieh *see* Konya
Konin 76 C3 *Ger.* Kuhnau. Wielkopolskie, C Poland
Konispol 79 C7 *var.* Konispoli. Vlorë, S Albania
Konispoli *see* Konispol
Kónitsa 82 A4 Ípeiros, W Greece
Konitz *see* Chojnice
Konjic 78 C4 Federacija Bosna I Hercegovina, S Bosnia and Herzegovina
Konosha 88 C4 Arkhangel'skaya Oblast', NW Russian Federation
Konotop 87 F1 Sums'ka Oblast', NE Ukraine
Konstanz 73 B7 *var.* Constanz, *Eng.* Constance; *hist.* Kostnitz, *anc.* Constantia. Baden-Württemberg, S Germany
Konstanza *see* Constanța
Konya 94 C4 *var.* Konieh; *prev.* Konia, *anc.* Iconium. Konya, C Turkey
Kopaonik 79 D5 *mountain range* S Serbia and Montenegro (Yugo.)
Koper 73 D8 *It.* Capodistria; *prev.* Kopar. SW Slovenia
Köpetdag Gershi 100 C3 *mountain range* Iran/Turkmenistan
Koppeh Dāgh 98 D2 *var.* Khrebet Kopetdag. *Mountain range* Iran/Turkmenistan
Koprivnica 78 B2 *Ger.* Kopreinitz, *Hung.* Kaproncza. Koprivnica-Križevci, N Croatia
Korat *see* Nakhon Ratchasima
Korat Plateau 114 D4 *plateau* E Thailand
Korba 113 E4 Madhya Pradesh, C India
Korça *see* Korçë
Korçë 79 D6 *var.* Korça, *Gk.* Korytsa, *It.* Corriza; *prev.* Koritsa. Korçë, SE Albania
Korčula 78 B4 *It.* Curzola; *anc.* Corcyra Nigra. *Island* S Croatia
Korea Bay 105 G3 *bay* China/North Korea
Korea Strait 109 A7 *Jap.* Chōsen-kaikyō, *Kor.* Taehan-haehyŏp. *Channel* Japan/South Korea
Korhogo 52 D4 N Côte d'Ivoire
Korinthiakós Kólpos 83 B5 *Eng.* Gulf of Corinth; *anc.* Corinthiacus Sinus. *Gulf* C Greece
Kórinthos 83 B6 *Eng.* Corinth; *anc.* Corinthus. Pelopónnisos, S Greece
Koritsa *see* Korçë
Kōriyama 109 D5 Fukushima, Honshū, C Japan
Korla 104 C3 *Chin.* K'u-erh-lo. Xinjiang Uygur Zizhiqu, NW China
Körmend 77 B7 Vas, W Hungary
Koróni 83 B6 Pelopónnisos, S Greece
Koror 122 A2 *var.* Oreor. *Country capital* (Palau) Oreor, N Palau
Korosten' 86 D1 Zhytomyrs'ka Oblast', NW Ukraine
Koro Toro 54 C2 Borkou-Ennedi-Tibesti, N Chad
Kortrijk 65 A6 *Fr.* Courtrai. West-Vlaanderen, W Belgium
Koryak Range *see* Koryakskoye Nagor'ye
Koryakskiy Khrebet *see* Koryakskoye Nagor'ye
Koryakskoye Nagor'ye 93 H2 *var.* Koryakskiy Khrebet, *Eng.* Koryak Range. *Mountain range* NE Russian Federation
Koryazhma 88 C4 Arkhangel'skaya Oblast', NW Russian Federation
Korytsa *see* Korçë
Kos 83 E6 *It.* Coo; *anc.* Cos. *Island* Dodekánisos, Greece, Aegean Sea
Kos 83 E6 Kos, Dodekánisos, Greece, Aegean Sea
Kō-saki 109 A7 *headland* Nagasaki, Tsushima, SW Japan
Kościan 76 B4 *Ger.* Kosten. Wielkopolskie, C Poland
Koscian *see* Lubań
Kościerzyna 76 C2 Pomorskie, NW Poland
Kosciusko, Mount *see* Kosciuszko, Mount
Kosciuszko, Mount 127 C7 *prev.* Mount Kosciusko. *Mountain* New South Wales, SE Australia
Koshikijima-rettō 109 A8 *var.* Kosikizima Rettô. *Island group* SW Japan
Košice 77 D6 *Ger.* Kaschau, *Hung.* Kassa. Košický Kraj, E Slovakia
Kosikizima Rettô *see* Koshikijima-rettō
Koson 101 E3 *Rus.* Kasan. Qashqadaryo Wiloyati, S Uzbekistan
Kosovo 79 D5 *prev.* Autonomous Province of Kosovo and Metohija. *Region* S Serbia and Montenegro (Yugo.)
Kosovo Polje 79 D5 Serbia, S Serbia and Montenegro (Yugo.)
Kosovska Mitrovica 79 D5 *Alb.* Mitrovicë; *prev.* Mitrovica, Titova Mitrovica. Serbia, S Serbia and Montenegro (Yugo.)
Kosrae 122 C2 *prev.* Kusaie. *Island* Caroline Islands, E Micronesia
Kossou, Lac de 52 D5 *lake* C Côte d'Ivoire
Kostanay 130 C4 *var.* Kustanay, *Kaz.* Qostanay. Kostanay, N Kazakhstan
Kosten *see* Lubań
Kostenets 82 C2 *prev.* Georgi Dimitrov. Sofiya, W Bulgaria
Kostnitz *see* Konstanz
Kostroma 88 B4 Kostromskaya Oblast', NW Russian Federation
Kostyantynivka 87 G3 *Rus.* Konstantinovka. Donets'ka Oblast', SE Ukraine
Koszalin 76 B2 *Ger.* Köslin. Zachodniopomorskie, NW Poland
Kota 112 D3 *prev.* Kotah. Rājasthān, N India
Kota Baharu *see* Kota Bharu
Kota Bahru *see* Kota Bharu
Kotabaru *see* Jayapura
Kota Bharu 116 B3 *var.* Kota Baharu, Kota Bahru. Kelantan, Peninsular Malaysia
Kotabumi 116 B4 *prev.* Kotaboemi. Sumatera, W Indonesia
Kota Kinabalu 116 D3 *prev.* Jesselton. Sabah, East Malaysia
Kotel'nyy, Ostrov 93 E2 *island* Novosibirskiye Ostrova, N Russian Federation
Kôti *see* Kōchi
Kotka 63 E5 Kymi, S Finland
Kotlas 88 C4 Arkhangel'skaya Oblast', NW Russian Federation
Kotonu *see* Cotonou
Kotor 79 C5 *It.* Cattaro. Montenegro, SW Serbia and Montenegro (Yugo.)
Kotovs'k 86 D3 *Rus.* Kotovsk. Odes'ka Oblast', SW Ukraine
Kotovsk *see* Hînceşti
Kotte *see* Sri Jayawardanapura
Kotto 54 D4 *river* Central African Republic/Dem. Rep. Congo
Kotuy 93 E2 *river* N Russian Federation
Koudougou 53 E4 C Burkina faso
Koulamoutou 55 B6 Ogooué-Lolo, C Gabon
Koulikoro 52 D3 Koulikoro, SW Mali
Koumra 54 C4 Moyen-Chari, S Chad
Kourou 37 H3 N French Guiana
Kousseir *see* Al Quşayr
Kousséri 54 B3 *prev.* Fort-Foureau. Extrême-Nord, NE Cameroon
Koutiala 52 D4 Sikasso, S Mali
Kouvola 63 E5 Kymi, S Finland
Kovel' 86 C1 *Pol.* Kowel. Volyns'ka Oblast', NW Ukraine
Kowloon 106 A2 *Chin.* Jiulong. Hong Kong, S China
Kowtal-e Barowghīl *see* Baroghil Pass
Kowtal-e Khaybar *see* Khyber Pass
Kozáni 82 B4 Dytikí Makedonía, N Greece
Kozara 78 B3 *mountain range* NW Bosnia and Herzegovina
Kozarska Dubica *see* Bosanska Dubica
Kozhikode *see* Calicut
Kōzu-shima 109 D6 *island* E Japan
Kozyatyn 86 D2 *Rus.* Kazatin. Vinnyts'ka Oblast', C Ukraine
Kpalimé 53 E5 *var.* Palimé. SW Togo
Krâchéh 115 D6 *prev.* Kratie. Krâchéh, E Cambodia
Kragujevac 78 D4 Serbia, C Serbia and Montenegro (Yugo.)
Kra, Isthmus of 115 B6 *isthmus* Malaysia/Thailand
Kraków 77 D5 *Eng.* Cracow, *Ger.* Krakau; *anc.* Cracovia. Małopolskie, S Poland
Krâlănh 115 D5 Siĕmréab, NW Cambodia
Kraljevo 78 D4 *prev.* Rankovićevo. Serbia, C Serbia and Montenegro (Yugo.)
Kramators'k 87 G3 *Rus.* Kramatorsk. Donets'ka Oblast', SE Ukraine
Kramfors 63 C5 Västernorrland, C Sweden
Kranéa 82 B4 Dytikí Makedonía, N Greece
Kranj 73 D7 *Ger.* Krainburg. NW Slovenia
Krāslava 84 D4 Krāslava, SE Latvia
Krasnaye 85 C5 *Rus.* Krasnoye. Minskaya Voblasts', C Belarus
Krasnoarmeysk 89 C6 Saratovskaya Oblast', W Russian Federation
Krasnodar 89 A7 *prev.* Ekaterinodar, Yekaterinodar. Krasnodarskiy Kray, SW Russian Federation
Krasnodon 87 H3 Luhans'ka Oblast', E Ukraine
Krasnohvardiys'ke 87 F4 *Rus.* Krasnogvardeyskoye. Respublika Krym, S Ukraine
Krasnokamensk 93 F4 Chitinskaya Oblast', S Russian Federation
Krasnokamsk 89 D5 Permskaya Oblast', W Russian Federation
Krasnoperekops'k 87 F4 *Rus.* Krasnoperekopsk. Respublika Krym, S Ukraine
Krasnoyarsk 92 D4 Krasnoyarskiy Kray, S Russian Federation
Krasnystaw 76 E4 *Rus.* Krasnostav. Lubelskie, E Poland
Krasnyy Kut 89 C6 Saratovskaya Oblast', W Russian Federation
Krasnyy Luch 87 H3 *prev.* Krindachevka. Luhans'ka Oblast', E Ukraine
Krâvanh, Chuŏr Phnum 115 C6 *Eng.* Cardamom Mountains, *Fr.* Chaîne des Cardamomes. *Mountain range* W Cambodia
Krefeld 72 A4 Nordrhein-Westfalen, W Germany
Kremenchuk 87 F2 *Rus.* Kremenchug. Poltavs'ka Oblast', NE Ukraine
Kremenchuts'ke Vodoskhovyshche 87 F2 *Eng.* Kremenchuk Reservoir, *Rus.* Kremenchugskoye Vodokhranilishche. *Reservoir* C Ukraine
Kremenets' 86 C2 *Pol.* Krzemieniec, *Rus.* Kremenets. Ternopil's'ka Oblast', W Ukraine
Kreminna 87 G2 *Rus.* Kremennaya. Luhans'ka Oblast', E Ukraine
Kresena *see* Kresna
Kresna 82 C3 *var.* Kresena. Blagoevgrad, SW Bulgaria
Kretikon Delagos *see* Kritikó Pélagos
Kretinga 84 B3 *Ger.* Krottingen. Kretinga, NW Lithuania
Krishna 110 C1 *prev.* Kistna. *River* C India
Krishnagiri 110 C2 Tamil Nādu, SE India
Kristiansand 63 A6 *var.* Christiansand. Vest-Agder, S Norway
Kristianstad 63 B7 Skåne, S Sweden
Kristiansund 62 A4 *var.* Christiansund. Møre og Romsdal, S Norway
Kríti 83 C7 *Eng.* Crete. *Island* Greece, Aegean Sea
Kritikó Pélagos 83 D7 *var.* Kretikon Delagos, *Eng.* Sea of Crete; *anc.* Mare Creticum. *Sea* Greece, Aegean Sea
Križevci 78 B2 *Ger.* Kreuz, *Hung.* Kőrös. Varaždin, NE Croatia
Krk 78 A3 *It.* Veglia; *anc.* Curieta. *Island* NW Croatia
Krolevets' 87 F1 *Rus.* Krolevets. Sums'ka Oblast', NE Ukraine
Kronach 73 C5 Bayern, E Germany
Kroonstad 56 D4 Free State, C South Africa
Kropotkin 89 A7 Krasnodarskiy Kray, SW Russian Federation
Krosno 77 D5 *Ger.* Krossen. Podkarpackie, SE Poland
Krosno Odrzańskie 76 B3 *Ger.* Crossen, Kreisstadt. Lubuskie, W Poland
Krško 73 E8 *Ger.* Gurkfeld; *prev.* Videm-Krško. E Slovenia
Kruhlaye 85 D6 *Rus.* Krugloye. Mahilyowskaya Voblasts', E Belarus
Kruja *see* Krujë
Krujë 79 C6 *var.* Kruja, *It.* Croia. Durrës, C Albania
Krummau *see* Český Krumlov
Krung Thep 115 C5 *var.* Krung Thep Mahanakhon, *Eng.* Bangkok. *Country capital* (Thailand) Bangkok, C Thailand
Krung Thep, Ao 115 C5 *var.* Bight of Bangkok. *Bay* S Thailand
Krung Thep Mahanakhon *see* Krung Thep
Krupki 85 D6 *Rus.* Krupki. Minskaya Voblasts', C Belarus
Krychaw 85 E7 *Rus.* Krichëv. Mahilyowskaya Voblasts', E Belarus
Krym *see* Crimea
Krymskaya Oblast' *see* Crimea
Kryms'ki Hory 87 F5 *mountain range* S Ukraine
Kryms'kyy Pivostriv 87 F5 *peninsula* S Ukraine
Krynica 77 D5 *Ger.* Tannenhof. Małopolskie, S Poland
Kryve Ozero 87 E3 Odes'ka Oblast', SW Ukraine
Kryvyy Rih 87 F3 *Rus.* Krivoy Rog. Dnipropetrovs'ka Oblast', SE Ukraine
Ksar al Kabir *see* Ksar-el-Kebir
Ksar al Soule *see* Er-Rachidia
Ksar-el-Kebir 48 C2 *var.* Alcázar, Ksar al Kabir, Ksar-el-Kébir, *Ar.* Al-Kasr al-Kebir, Al-Qsar al-Kbir, *Sp.* Alcazarquivir. NW Morocco
Ksar-el-Kébir *see* Ksar-el-Kebir
Kuala Dungun *see* Dungun
Kuala Lumpur 116 B3 *country capital* (Malaysia) Kuala Lumpur, Peninsular Malaysia
Kuala Terengganu 116 B3 *var.* Kuala Trengganu. Terengganu, Peninsular Malaysia
Kuala Trengganu *see* Kuala Terengganu
Kualatungkal 116 B4 Sumatera, W Indonesia
Kuang-chou *see* Guangzhou
Kuang-hsi *see* Guangxi Zhuangzu Zizhiqu
Kuang-tung *see* Guangdong
Kuang-yuan *see* Guangyuan
Kuantan 116 B3 Pahang, Peninsular Malaysia
Kuban' 87 G5 *var.* Hypanis. *River* SW Russian Federation
Kubango *see* Cubango
Kuching 116 C3 *prev.* Sarawak. Sarawak, East Malaysia
Kūchnay Darweyshān 100 D5 Helmand, S Afghanistan
Kuçova *see* Kuçovë
Kuçovë 79 C6 *var.* Kuçova; *prev.* Qyteti Stalin. Berat, C Albania
Kudara *see* Ghŭdara
Kudus 116 C5 *prev.* Koedoes. Jawa, C Indonesia
Kuei-chou *see* Guizhou
Kuei-lin *see* Guilin
Kuei-Yang *see* Guiyang
Kueyang *see* Guiyang
Kugluktuk 53 E3 *var.* Qurlurtuuq *prev.* Coppermine. Nunavut, NW Canada
Kuhmo 62 E4 Oulu, E Finland
Kühnö *see* Kihnu
Kuibyshev *see* Kuybyshevskoye Vodokhranilishche
Kuito 56 B2 *Port.* Silva Porto. Bié, C Angola
Kuji 108 D3 *var.* Kuzi. Iwate, Honshū, C Japan
Kukës 79 D5 *var.* Kukësi. Kukës, NE Albania
Kukësi *see* Kukës
Kukong *see* Shaoguan
Kukukhoto *see* Hohhot
Kula Kangri 113 G3 *var.* Kulhakangri. *Mountain* Bhutan/China
Kuldīga 84 B3 *Ger.* Goldingen. Kuldīga, W Latvia
Kuldja *see* Yining
Kulhakangri *see* Kula Kangri
Kullorsuaq 60 D2 *var.* Kuvdlorssuak. C Greenland
Kulmsee *see* Chełmża
Kŭlob 101 F3 *Rus.* Kulyab. SW Tajikistan
Kulu 94 C3 Konya, W Turkey
Kulunda Steppe 92 C4 *Kaz.* Qulyndy Zhazyghy, *Rus.* Kulundinskaya Ravnina. *Grassland* Kazakhstan/Russian Federation
Kum *see* Qom
Kuma 89 B7 *river* SW Russian Federation
Kumamoto 109 A7 Kumamoto, Kyūshū, SW Japan
Kumanovo 79 E5 *Turk.* Kumanova. N FYR Macedonia
Kumasi 53 E5 *prev.* Coomassie. C Ghana
Kumayri *see* Gyumri
Kumba 55 A5 Sud-Ouest, W Cameroon
Kumertau 89 D6 Respublika Bashkortostan, W Russian Federation
Kumo 53 G4 Gombe, E Nigeria
Kumon Range 114 B2 *mountain range* N Myanmar
Kumul *see* Hami
Kunashiri *see* Kunashir, Ostrov
Kunashir, Ostrov 108 E1 *var.* Kunashiri. *Island* Kuril'skiye Ostrova, SE Russian Federation
Kunda 84 E2 Lääne-Virumaa, NE Estonia
Kunduz 101 E3 *var.* Kondoz, Kundūz, Qondūz, *Per.* Kondūz. Kunduz, NE Afghanistan
Kuneitra *see* Al Qunayṭirah
Kunene *see* Cunene
Kungsbacka 63 B7 Halland, S Sweden
Kungur 89 D5 Permskaya Oblast', NW Russian Federation
Kunlun Mountains *see* Kunlun Shan
Kunlun Shan 104 B4 *Eng.* Kunlun Mountains. *Mountain range* NW China
Kunming 106 B6 *var.* K'un-ming; *prev.* Yunnan. Yunnan, SW China
K'un-ming *see* Kunming
Kununurra 124 D3 Western Australia
Kuopio 63 E5 Itä-Suomi, C Finland
Kupang 117 E5 *prev.* Koepang. Timor, C Indonesia
Kup"yans'k 87 G2 *Rus.* Kupyansk. Kharkivs'ka Oblast', E Ukraine
Kura 95 H3 *Az.* Kür, *Geor.* Mtkvari, *Turk.* Kura Nehri. *River* SW Asia
Kurashiki 109 B6 *var.* Kurasiki. Okayama, Honshū, SW Japan
Kurasiki *see* Kurashiki
Kurdistan 95 F4 *cultural region* SW Asia
Kŭrdzhali 82 D3 *var.* Kirdzhali. Kŭrdzhali, S Bulgaria
Kure 109 B7 Hiroshima, Honshū, SW Japan
Küre Dağları 94 C2 *mountain range* N Turkey
Kuressaare 84 C2 *Ger.* Arensburg; *prev.* Kingissepp. Saaremaa, W Estonia
Kureyka 90 D2 *river* N Russian Federation
Kuria Muria Islands *see* Ḩalāniyāt, Juzur al
Kurile Islands *see* Kuril'skiye Ostrova
Kurile-Kamchatka Depression *see* Kurile Trench
Kurile Trench 91 F3 *var.* Kurile-Kamchatka Depression. *Undersea feature* NW Pacific Ocean
Kuril'sk 108 E1 Kuril'skiye Ostrova, Sakhalinskaya Oblats', SE Russian Federation
Kuril'skiye Ostrova 93 H4 *Eng.* Kurile Islands. *Island group* SE Russian Federation

Ku-ring-gai *126 E1* New South Wales, SE Australia
Kurnool *110 C1 var.* Karnul. Andhra Pradesh, S India
Kursk *89 A6* Kurskaya Oblast', W Russian Federation
Kuršumlija *79 D5* Serbia, S Serbia and Montenegro (Yugo.)
Kuruktag *104 C3 mountain range* NW China
Kurume *109 A7* Fukuoka, Kyūshū, SW Japan
Kurupukari *37 F3* C Guyana
Kurzeme *84 B3 Eng.* Courland, *Ger.* Kurland. *Former province* W Latvia
Kushiro *108 D2 var.* Kusiro. Hokkaidō, NE Japan
Kusiro *see* Kushiro
Kuskokwim Mountains *14 C3 mountain range* Alaska, USA
Kuźnica *76 E2* Podlaskie, NE Poland
Kustanay *see* Kostanay
Küstence *see* Constanța
Küstendje *see* Constanța
Kütahya *94 B3 prev.* Kutaia. Kütahya, W Turkey
Kutai *see* Mahakam, Sungai
K'ut'aisi *95 F2* W Georgia
Kūt al 'Amārah *see* Al Kūt
Kut al Imara *see* Al Kūt
Kutaradja *see* Bandaaceh
Kutaraja *see* Bandaaceh
Kutch, Gulf of *see* Kachchh, Gulf of
Kutch, Rann of *see* Kachchh, Rann of
Kutina *78 B3* Sisak-Moslavina, NE Croatia
Kutno *76 C3* Łódzkie, C Poland
Kuujjuaq *17 E2 prev.* Fort-Chimo. Québec, E Canada
Kuusamo *62 E3* Oulu, Finland
Kuvango *see* Cubango
Kuvdlorssuak *see* Kullorsuaq
Kuwait *98 C4 var.* Dawlat al Kuwait, Koweit, Kuweit. *Country* SW Asia
Kuwait *see* Al Kuwayt
Kuwait City *see* Al Kuwayt
Kuwajleen *see* Kwajalein Atoll
Kuwayt *98 C3* E Iraq
Kuybyshev Reservoir *see* Kuybyshevskoye Vodokhranilishche
Kuybyshevskoye Vodokhranilishche *89 C5 var.* Kuibyshev, *Eng.* Kuybyshev Reservoir. *Reservoir* W Russian Federation
Kuytun *104 B2* Xinjiang Uygur Zizhiqu, NW China
Kuzi *see* Kuji
Kuznetsk *89 B6* Penzenskaya Oblast', W Russian Federation
Kvaløya *62 C2 island* N Norway
Kvarnbergsvattnet *62 B4 var.* Frostviken. *Lake* N Sweden
Kvarner *78 A3 var.* Carnaro, *It.* Quarnero. *Gulf* W Croatia
Kvitøya *61 G1 island* NE Svalbard
Kwajalein Atoll *122 C1 var.* Kuwajleen. *Atoll* Ralik Chain, C Marshall Islands
Kwando *see* Cuando
Kwangchow *see* Guangzhou
Kwangju *107 E4 off.* Kwangju-gwangyŏksi, *var.* Guangju, Kwangchu, *Jap.* Kōshū. SW South Korea
Kwango *55 C7 Port.* Cuango. *River* Angola/Dem. Rep. Congo *see also* Cuango
Kwango *see* Cuango
Kwangsi *see* Guangxi Zhuangzu Zizhiqu
Kwangsi Chuang Autonomous Region *see* Guangxi Zhuangzu Zizhiqu
Kwangtung *see* Guangdong
Kwangyuan *see* Guangyuan
Kwanza *see* Cuanza
Kweichow *see* Guizhou
Kweichu *see* Guiyang
Kweilin *see* Guilin
Kweisui *see* Hohhot
Kweiyang *see* Guiyang
Kwekwe *56 D3 prev.* Que Que. Midlands, C Zimbabwe
Kwesui *see* Hohhot
Kwidzyń *76 C2 Ger.* Marienwerder. Pomorskie, N Poland
Kwigillingok *14 C3* Alaska, USA
Kwilu *55 C6 river* W Dem. Rep. Congo
Kwito *see* Cuito
Kyabé *54 C4* Moyen-Chari, S Chad
Kyaikkami *115 B5 prev.* Amherst. Mon State, S Myanmar
Kyaiklat *114 B4* Irrawaddy, SW Myanmar
Kyaikto *114 B4* Mon State, S Myanmar
Kyakhta *93 E5* Respublika Buryatiya, S Russian Federation
Kyaukse *114 B3* Mandalay, C Myanmar
Kyjov *77 C5 Ger.* Gaya. Brněnský Kraj, SE Czech Republic
Kykládes *83 D6 var.* Kikládhes, *Eng.* Cyclades. *Island group* SE Greece
Kými *83 C5 prev.* Kími. Évvoia, C Greece
Kyōto *109 C6* Kyōto, Honshū, SW Japan
Kyparissía *83 B6 var.* Kiparissía. Pelopónnisos, S Greece
Kyrá Panagía *83 C5 island* Vóreioi Sporádes, Greece, Aegean Sea
Kyrenia *see* Kerýneia
Kyrgyzstan *101 F2 var.* Kirghizia; *prev.* Kirgizskaya SSR, Kirghiz SSR, Republic of Kyrgyzstan. *Country* C Asia
Kýthira *83 C7 var.* Kíthira, *It.* Cerigo; *Lat.* Cythera. *Island* S Greece
Kýthnos *83 C6 var.* Kíthnos, Thermiá, *It.* Termia; *anc.* Cythnos. *Island* Kykládes, Greece, Aegean Sea
Kýthnos *83 C6* Kýthnos, Kykládes, Greece, Aegean Sea
Kythréa *80 C5* N Cyprus
Kyūshū *109 B7 var.* Kyûsyû. *Island* SW Japan
Kyushu-Palau Ridge *103 F3 var.* Kyusyu-Palau Ridge. *Undersea feature* W Pacific Ocean
Kyustendil *82 B2 anc.* Pautalia. Kyustendil, W Bulgaria
Kyûsyû *see* Kyūshū
Kyusyu-Palau Ridge *see* Kyushu-Palau Ridge
Kyyiv *87 E2 Eng.* Kiev, *Rus.* Kiyev. *Country capital* (Ukraine) Kyyivs'ka Oblast', N Ukraine
Kyyivs'ke Vodoskhovyshche *87 E1 Eng.* Kiev Reservoir, *Rus.* Kiyevskoye Vodokhranilishche. *Reservoir* N Ukraine
Kyzyl *92 D4* Respublika Tyva, C Russian Federation
Kyzyl Kum *100 D2 var.* Kizil Kum, Qizil Qum, Qizilqum. *Desert* Kazakhstan/Uzbekistan
Kyzylorda *92 B5 var.* Kzyl-orda, Qizil Orda, *Kaz.* Qyzylorda; *prev.* Perovsk. Kyzylorda, S Kazakhstan
Kyzyl-Suu *101 G2 prev.* Pokrovka. Issyk-Kul'skaya Oblast', NE Kyrgyzstan
Kzyl-orda *see* Kyzylorda

L

La Algaba *70 C4* Andalucía, S Spain
Laamu Atoll *see* Hadhdhunmathi Atoll
Laarne *65 B5* Oost-Vlaanderen, NW Belgium
La Asunción *37 E1* Nueva Esparta, NE Venezuela
Laâyoune *48 B3 var.* Aaiún. *Dependent territory capital* (Western Sahara) NW Western Sahara
la Baule-Escoublac *68 A4* Loire-Atlantique, NW France
Labé *52 C4* Moyenne-Guinée, NW Guinea
La Blanquilla *see* Blanquilla, Isla
Laborec *77 E5 Hung.* Laborca. *River* E Slovakia
Labrador *17 F2 cultural region* Newfoundland and Labrador, SW Canada
Labrador Basin *12 E3 var.* Labrador Sea Basin. *Undersea feature* Labrador Sea
Labrador Sea *60 A4 sea* NW Atlantic Ocean
Labrador Sea Basin *see* Labrador Basin
Labutta *115 A5* Irrawaddy, SW Myanmar
Laç *79 C6 var.* Laci. Lezhë, C Albania
La Calera *42 B4* Valparaíso, C Chile
La Carolina *70 D4* Andalucía, S Spain
Laccadive Islands *see* Lakshadweep
La Ceiba *30 D2* Atlántida, N Honduras
Lachanás *82 B3* Kentrikí Makedonía, N Greece
La Chaux-de-Fonds *73 A7* Neuchâtel, W Switzerland
Lachlan River *127 C6 river* New South Wales, SE Australia
Laci *see* Laç
la Ciotat *69 D6 anc.* Citharista. Bouches-du-Rhône, SE France
La Concepción *36 C1* Zulia, NW Venezuela
La Concepción *31 E5 var.* Concepción. Chiriquí, W Panama
La Condamine *69 C8* NW Andorra
Laconia *19 G2* New Hampshire, NE USA
La Crosse *40 A2* Wisconsin, N USA
La Cruz *30 D4* Guanacaste, NW Costa Rica
Lacus Asphaltites *see* Dead Sea
Ladoga, Lake *see* Ladozhskoye Ozero
Ladozhskoye Ozero *88 B3 Eng.* Lake Ladoga, *Fin.* Laatokka. *Lake* NW Russian Federation
Ladysmith *18 B2* Wisconsin, N USA
Lae *122 B3* Morobe, W PNG
La Esperanza *30 C2* Intibucá, SW Honduras
Lafayette *18 C4* Indiana, N USA
Lafayette *20 B3* Louisiana, S USA
La Fé *32 A2* Pinar del Río, W Cuba
Lafia *53 G4* Nassarawa, C Nigeria
la Flèche *68 B4* Sarthe, NW France
Lagdo, Lac de *54 B4 lake* N Cameroon
Laghouat *48 D2* N Algeria
Lago dos Gansos *see* Goose Lake
Lago General Carrera *see* Buenos Aires, Lago
Lago Nyassa *see* Nyasa, Lake
Lago Pampa Aullagas *see* Poopó, Lago
Lagos *70 B5 anc.* Lacobriga. Faro, S Portugal
Lagos *53 F5* Lagos, SW Nigeria
Lagos de Moreno *29 E4* Jalisco, SW Mexico
Lagouira *48 A4* SW Western Sahara
La Grande *24 C3* Oregon, NW USA
La Guaira *44 B4* Distrito Federal, N Venezuela
Laguna Merín *see* Mirim Lagoon
Lagunas *42 B1* Tarapacá, N Chile
Lagunillas *39 G4* Santa Cruz, SE Bolivia
La Habana *32 B2 var.* Havana. *Country capital* (Cuba) Ciudad de La Habana, W Cuba
Lahat *116 B4* Sumatera, W Indonesia
La Haye *see* 's-Gravenhage
Laholm *63 B7* Halland, S Sweden
Lahore *112 D2* Punjab, NE Pakistan
Lahr *73 A6* Baden-Württemberg, S Germany
Lahti *63 D5 Swe.* Lahtis. Etelä-Suomi, S Finland
Laï *54 B4 prev.* Behagle, De Behagle. Tandjilé, S Chad
Lai Châu *114 D3* Lai Châu, N Vietnam
Laila *see* Laylá
La Junta *22 D5* Colorado, C USA
Lake Charles *20 A3* Louisiana, S USA
Lake City *21 E3* Florida, SE USA
Lake District *67 C5 physical region* NW England, UK
Lake Havasu City *26 A2* Arizona, SW USA
Lake Jackson *27 H4* Texas, SW USA
Lakeland *21 E4* Florida, SE USA
Lakeside *25 C8* California, W USA
Lakewood *22 D4* Colorado, C USA
Lakhnau *see* Lucknow
Lakonikós Kólpos *83 B7 gulf* S Greece
Lakselv *62 D2* Finnmark, N Norway
Lakshadweep *110 A3 Eng.* Laccadive Islands. *Island group* India, N Indian Ocean
la Laon *see* Laon
Lalibela *50 C4* N Ethiopia
La Libertad *30 B1* Petén, N Guatemala
La Ligua *42 B4* Valparaíso, C Chile
Lalín *70 C1* Galicia, NW Spain
Lalitpur *113 F3* Central, C Nepal
La Louvière *65 B6* Hainaut, S Belgium
La Maçana *see* La Massana
La Maddalena *74 A4* Sardegna, Italy, C Mediterranean Sea
la Manche *see* English Channel
Lamar *22 D5* Colorado, C USA
La Marmora, Punta *75 A5 mountain* Sardegna, Italy, C Mediterranean Sea
La Massana *69 A8 var.* La Maçana. W Andorra
Lambaréné *55 A6* Moyen-Ogooué, W Gabon
Lamego *70 C2* Viseu, N Portugal
Lamesa *27 E3* Texas, SW USA
Lamezia Terme *75 D6* Calabria, SE Italy
Lamía *83 B5* Stereá Ellás, C Greece
Lamoni *23 F4* Iowa, C USA
Lampang *114 C4 var.* Muang Lampang. Lampang, NW Thailand
Lámpeia *83 B6* Dytikí Ellás, S Greece
Lanbi Kyun *115 B6 prev.* Sullivan Island. *Island* Mergui Archipelago, S Myanmar
Lancang Jiang *see* Mekong
Lancaster *25 C7* California, W USA
Lancaster *67 D5* NW England, UK
Lancaster *19 F4* Pennsylvania, NE USA
Lancaster Sound *15 F2 sound* Nunavut, N Canada
Lan-chou *see* Lanzhou
Lan-chow *see* Lanzhou
Landen *65 C6* Vlaams Brabant, C Belgium
Lander *22 C3* Wyoming, C USA
Landerneau *68 A3* Finistère, NW France
Landes *69 B5 department* SW France
Land's End *67 B8 headland* SW England, UK
Landshut *73 C6* Bayern, SE Germany
Langar *101 E2 Rus.* Lyangar. Nawoiy Wiloyati, C Uzbekistan
Langfang *106 D4* Hebei, E China
Langkawi, Pulau *115 B7 island* Peninsular Malaysia
Langres *68 D4* Haute-Marne, N France
Langsa *116 A3* Sumatera, W Indonesia
Lang Shan *105 E3 mountain range* N China
Lang Sơn *114 D3 var.* Langson. Lang Sơn, N Vietnam
Langson *see* Lang Sơn
Lang Suan *115 B6* Chumphon, SW Thailand
Languedoc *69 C6 cultural region* S France
Länkäran *95 H3 Rus.* Lenkoran'. S Azerbaijan
Lansing *18 C3 state capital* Michigan, N USA
Lanta, Ko *115 B7 island* S Thailand
Lantau Island *106 A2 Cant.* Tai Yue Shan, *Chin.* Landao. *Island* Hong Kong, S China
Lan-ts'ang Chiang *see* Mekong
Lanzarote *48 B3 island* Islas Canarias, Spain, NE Atlantic Ocean
Lanzhou *106 B4 var.* Lan-chou, Lanchow, Lan-chow; *prev.* Kaolan. Gansu, C China
Lao Cai *114 D3* Lao Cai, N Vietnam
Laojunmiao *see* Yumen
Laon *68 D3 var.* la Laon; *anc.* Laudunum. Aisne, N France
La Orchila, Isla *36 D1 island* N Venezuela
La Oroya *38 C3* Junín, C Peru
Laos *114 D4 Country* SE Asia
La Palma *48 A3 island* Islas Canarias, Spain, NE Atlantic Ocean
La Palma *31 G5* Darién, SE Panama
La Paz *39 F4 var.* La Paz de Ayacucho. *Country capital* (Bolivia-legislative and administrative capital) La Paz, W Bolivia
La Paz *28 B3* Baja California Sur, NW Mexico
La Paz, Bahía de *28 B3 bay* W Mexico
La Paz de Ayacucho *see* La Paz
La Perouse Strait *108 D1 Jap.* Sōya-kaikyō, *Rus.* Proliv Laperuza. *Strait* Japan/Russian Federation
Lápithos *80 C5* NW Cyprus
Lapland *62 D3 Fin.* Lappi, *Swe.* Lappland. *Cultural region* N Europe
La Plata *42 D4* Buenos Aires, E Argentina
Lappeenranta *63 E5 Swe.* Villmanstrand. Etelä-Suomi, S Finland
Lappi *see* Lapland
Lappland *see* Lapland
Lapta *see* Lápithos
Laptev Sea *see* Laptevykh, More
Laptevykh, More *93 E2 Eng.* Laptev Sea. *Sea* Arctic Ocean
Lapua *63 D5 Swe.* Lappo. Länsi-Suomi, W Finland
La Puebla *see* Sa Pobla
Łapy *76 E3* Podlaskie
La Quiaca *42 C2* Jujuy, N Argentina
L'Aquila *74 C4 var.* Aquila, Aquila degli Abruzzo. Abruzzo, C Italy
Laracha *70 B1* Galicia, NW Spain
Laramie *22 C4* Wyoming, C USA
Laramie Mountains *22 C3 mountain range* Wyoming, C USA
Laredo *71 E1* Cantabria, N Spain
Laredo *27 F5* Texas, SW USA
Largo *21 E4* Florida, SE USA
Largo, Cayo *32 B2 island* W Cuba
Lario *see* Como, Lago di
La Rioja *71 E2* La Rioja, NW Argentina
Lárisa *82 B4 var.* Larissa. Thessalía, C Greece
Larissa *see* Lárisa
Lārkāna *112 B3 var.* Larkhana. Sind, SE Pakistan
Larkhana *see* Lārkāna
Larnaca *see* Lárnaka
Lárnaka *80 C5 var.* Larnaca, Larnax. SE Cyprus
Larnax *see* Lárnaka
la Rochelle *68 B4 anc.* Rupella. Charente-Maritime, W France
la Roche-sur-Yon *68 B4 prev.* Bourbon Vendée, Napoléon-Vendée. Vendée, NW France
La Roda *71 E3* Castilla-La Mancha, C Spain
La Romana *33 E3* E Dominican Republic
Larvotto *69 C8* N Monaco
La-sa *see* Lhasa
Las Cabezas de San Juan *70 C5* Andalucía, S Spain
Las Cruces *26 D3* New Mexico, SW USA
La See d'Urgel *71 G1 var.* La Seu d'Urgell, Seo de Urgel. Cataluña, NE Spain
La Serena *42 B3* Coquimbo, C Chile
La Seu d'Urgell *see* La See d'Urgel
la Seyne-sur-Mer *69 D6* Var, SE France
Lashio *114 B3* Shan State, E Myanmar
Lashkar Gāh *100 D5 var.* Lash-Kar-Gar'. Helmand, S Afghanistan
Lash-Kar-Gar' *see* Lashkar Gāh
La Sila *75 D6 mountain range* SW Italy
La Sirena *30 D3* Región Autónoma Atlántico Sur, E Nicaragua
Łask *76 C4* Łódzkie, C Poland
Las Lomitas *42 D2* Formosa, N Argentina
La Solana *71 E4* Castilla-La Mancha, C Spain
Las Palmas de Gran Canaria *48 A3* Gran Canaria, Islas Canarias, Spain, NE Atlantic Ocean
La Spezia *74 B3* Liguria, NW Italy
Lassa *see* Lhasa
Las Tablas *31 F5* Los Santos, S Panama
Las Tunas *32 C2 var.* Victoria de las Tunas. Las Tunas, E Cuba
Las Vegas *25 D7* Nevada, W USA
Latacunga *38 B1* Cotopaxi, C Ecuador
la Teste *69 B5* Gironde, SW France
Latina *75 C5 prev.* Littoria. Lazio, C Italy
La Tortuga, Isla *37 E1 var.* Isla Tortuga. *Island* N Venezuela
La Tuque *17 E4* Québec, SE Canada
Latvia *84 C3 Ger.* Lettland, *Latv.* Latvija,Latvijas Republika; *prev.* Latvian SSR, *Rus.* Latviyskaya SSR. *Country* NE Europe
Laudunum *see* Laon
Lauenburg *see* Lębork
Lauenburg in Pommern *see* Lębork
Lau Group *123 E4 island group* E Fiji
Launceston *127 C8* Tasmania, SE Australia
La Unión *71 F4* Murcia, SE Spain
La Unión *30 C2* Olancho, C Honduras
Laurel *20 C3* Mississippi, S USA
Laurel *22 C2* Montana, NW USA
Laurentian Highlands *see* Laurentian Mountains
Laurentian Mountains *17 E3 var.* Laurentian Highlands, *Fr.* Les Laurentides. *Plateau* Newfoundland and Labrador/Québec, Canada
Lauria *75 D6* Basilicata, S Italy
Laurinburg *21 F1* North Carolina, SE USA
Lauru *see* Choiseul
Lausanne *73 A7 It.* Losanna. Vaud, SW Switzerland
Laut Banda *see* Banda Sea
Laut, Pulau *116 D4 prev.* Laoet. *Island* Borneo, C Indonesia
Laval *68 B3* Mayenne, NW France
Laval *16 D4* Québec, SE Canada
La Vega *33 E3 var.* Concepción de la Vega. C Dominican Republic
La Vila Jojosa *see* Villajoyosa
Lávrio *83 C6 prev.* Lávrion. Attikí, C Greece
Lawrence *19 G3* Massachusetts, NE USA
Lawrenceburg *20 C1* Tennessee, S USA
Lawton *27 F2* Oklahoma, C USA
La Yarada *39 E4* Tacna, SW Peru
Laylá *99 C5 var.* Laila. Ar Riyāḍ, C Saudi Arabia
Lazarev Sea *132 B1 sea* Antarctica
Lázaro Cárdenas *29 E5* Michoacán de Ocampo, SW Mexico
Læsø *63 B7 island* N Denmark
Leamhcán *see* Lucan
Leamington *16 C5* Ontario, S Canada
Lebak *117 E3* Mindanao, S Philippines
Lebanon *96 A4 Ar.* Al Lubnān, *Fr.* Liban. *Country* SW Asia
Lebanon *23 G5* Missouri, C USA
Lebanon *19 G2* New Hampshire, NE USA
Lebanon *24 B3* Oregon, NW USA
Lebap *100 D2* Lebapskiy Velayat, NE Turkmenistan
Lebedyn *87 F2 Rus.* Lebedin. Sums'ka Oblast', NE Ukraine
Lębork *76 C2 var.* Lębórk, *Ger.* Lauenburg, Lauenburg in Pommern. Pomorskie, N Poland
Lebrija *70 C5* Andalucía, S Spain
Lebu *43 A5* Bío Bío, C Chile
le Cannet *69 D6* Alpes-Maritimes, SE France
Le Cap *see* Cap-Haïtien
Lecce *75 E6* Puglia, SE Italy
Lechainá *83 B6 var.* Lehena, Lekhainá. Dytikí Ellás, S Greece
Leduc *15 E5* Alberta, SW Canada
Leech Lake *23 F2 lake* Minnesota, N USA
Leeds *67 D5* N England, UK
Leek *64 E2* Groningen, NE Netherlands
Leer *72 A3* Niedersachsen, NW Germany
Leeuwarden *64 D1 Fris.* Ljouwert. Friesland, N Netherlands
Leeuwin, Cape *120 A5 headland* Western Australia
Leeward Islands *33 G3 island group* E West Indies
Leeward Islands *see* Sotavento, Ilhas de
Lefkáda *83 A5 It.* Santa Maura; *prev.* Levkás, *anc.* Leucas. *Island* Iónioi Nísoi, Greece, C Mediterranean Sea
Lefkáda *83 A5 prev.* Levkás. Lefkáda, Iónioi Nísoi, Greece, C Mediterranean Sea
Lefká Óri *83 C7 mountain range* Kríti, Greece, E Mediterranean Sea
Lefkímmi *83 A5 var.* Levkímmi. Kérkyra, Iónioi Nísoi, Greece, C Mediterranean Sea
Legaspi *117 E2 off.* Legaspi City. Luzon, N Philippines
Legnica *76 B4 Ger.* Liegnitz. Dolnośląskie
le Havre *68 B3 Eng.* Havre; *prev.* le Havre-de-Grâce. Seine-Maritime, N France
Lehena *see* Lechainá
Leicester *67 D6 Lat.* Batae Coritanorum. C England, UK
Leiden *64 B3 prev.* Leyden, *anc.* Lugdunum Batavorum. Zuid-Holland, W Netherlands
Leie *68 D2 Fr.* Lys. *River* Belgium/France
Leinster *67 B6 Ir.* Cúige Laighean. *Cultural region* E Ireland
Leipsoí *83 E6 island* Dodekánisos, Greece, Aegean Sea
Leipzig *72 C4 Pol.* Lipsk; *hist.* Leipsic, *anc.* Lipsia. Sachsen, E Germany
Leiria *70 B3 anc.* Collipo. Leiria, C Portugal
Leirvik *63 A6* Hordaland, S Norway
Lek *64 C4 river* SW Netherlands
Lekhainá *see* Lechainá
Lekhchevo *82 C2* Montana, NW Bulgaria
Leksand *63 C5* Kopparberg, C Sweden
Lelystad *64 D3* Flevoland, C Netherlands
le Mans *68 B3* Sarthe, NW France
Lemesós *80 C5 var.* Limassol. SW Cyprus
Lena *93 F3 river* NE Russian Federation
Lena Tablemount *119 B7 undersea feature* S Indian Ocean
Len Dao *106 C8 island* S Spratly Islands
Lengshuitan *106 C6* Hunan, S China
Leninabad *see* Khŭjand
Leninakan *see* Gyumri
Lenine *87 G5 Rus.* Lenino. Respublika Krym, S Ukraine
Leningorsk *92 D4 Kaz.* Leningor. Vostochnyy Kazakhstan, E Kazakhstan
Leningrad *see* Sankt-Peterburg
Leningradskaya *132 B4 Russian research station* Antarctica
Leninobod *see* Khŭjand
Leninpol' *101 F2* Talasskaya Oblast', NW Kyrgyzstan
Lenti *77 B7* Zala, SW Hungary
Leoben *73 E7* Steiermark, C Austria
León *29 E4 var.* León de los Aldamas. Guanajuato, C Mexico
León *70 D1* Castilla-León, NW Spain
León *30 C3* León, NW Nicaragua
León de los Aldamas *see* León
Leonídi *83 B6* Pelopónnisos, S Greece
Lepe *70 C4* Andalucía, S Spain
le Portel *68 C2* Pas-de-Calais, N France
le Puy *69 C5 prev.* le Puy-en-Velay, *hist.* Anicium, Podium Anicensis. Haute-Loire, C France
Léré *54 B4* Mayo-Kébbi, SW Chad
Lerma *92 D2* Castilla-León, N Spain
Léros *83 D6 island* Dodekánisos, Greece, Aegean Sea
Lerrnayin Gharabakh *see* Nagorno-Karabakh
Lerwick *66 D1* NE Scotland, UK
Lesbos *see* Lésvos
Les Cayes *see* Cayes
Les Gonaïves *see* Gonaïves
Lesh *see* Lezhë
Leshan *106 B5* Sichuan, C China
les Herbiers *68 B4* Vendée, NW France
Leshi *see* Lezhë
Leskovac *79 E5* Serbia, SE Serbia and Montenegro (Yugo.)
Les Laurentides *see* Laurentian Highlands
Lesnoy *92 C3* Sverdlovskaya Oblast', C Russian Federation
Lesotho *56 D4 prev.* Basutoland. *Country* S Africa
les Sables-d'Olonne *68 B4* Vendée, NW France
Lesser Antarctica *132 A3 var.* West Antarctica. *Physical region* Antarctica
Lesser Antilles *33 G4 island group* E West Indies
Lesser Caucasus *95 F2 Rus.* Malyy Kavkaz. *Mountain range* SW Asia
Lesser Sunda Islands *see* Nusa Tenggara
Lésvos *94 A3 anc.* Lesbos. *Island* E Greece
Leszno *76 B4 Ger.* Lissa. Wielkopolskie, C Poland
Lethbridge *15 E5* Alberta, SW Canada
Lethem *37 F3* S Guyana
Leti, Kepulauan *117 F5 island group* E Indonesia
Letpadan *114 B4* Pegu, SW Myanmar
Letsôk-aw Kyun *115 B6 var.* Letsutan Island; *prev.* Domel Island. *Island* Mergui Archipelago, S Myanmar
Letsutan Island *see* Letsôk-aw Kyun
Leuven *65 C6 Fr.* Louvain, *Ger.* Löwen. Vlaams Brabant, C Belgium
Leuze *see* Leuze-en-Hainaut
Leuze-en-Hainaut *65 B6 var.* Leuze. Hainaut, SW Belgium
Levanger *62 B4* Nord-Trøndelag, C Norway
Levelland *27 E2* Texas, SW USA
Leverkusen *72 A4* Nordrhein-Westfalen, W Germany
Levice *77 C6 Ger.* Lewentz, Lewenz, *Hung.* Léva. Nitriansky Kraj, SW Slovakia
Levin *128 D4* Manawatu-Wanganui, North Island, NZ
Levkímmi *see* Lefkímmi
Lewis, Isle of *66 B2 island* NW Scotland, UK
Lewis Range *22 B1 mountain range* Montana, NW USA
Lewiston *24 C2* Idaho, NW USA
Lewiston *19 G2* Maine, NE USA
Lewistown *22 C1* Montana, NW USA
Lexington *18 C5* Kentucky, S USA
Lexington *23 E4* Nebraska, C USA
Leyte *117 F2 island* C Philippines
Leżajsk *77 E5* Podkarpackie, SE Poland
Lezha *see* Lezhë
Lezhë *79 C6 var.* Lezha; *prev.* Lesh, Leshi. Lezhë, NW Albania
Lhasa *104 C5 var.* La-sa, Lassa. Xizang Zizhiqu, W China
Lhaviyani Atoll *see* Faadhippolhu Atoll
Lhazê *104 C5* Xizang Zizhiqu, W China

L'Hospitalet de Llobregat 71 G2 *var.* Hospitalet. Cataluña, NE Spain
Liancourt Rocks 109 A5 *Jap.* Take-shima, *Kor.* Tok-Do. *Island group* Japan/ South Korea
Lianyungang 106 D4 *var.* Xinpu. Jiangsu, E China
Liao *see* Liaoning
Liaodong Wan 105 G3 *Eng.* Gulf of Lantung, Gulf of Liaotung. *Gulf* NE China
Liao He 103 E1 *river* NE China
Liaoning 106 D3 *var.* Liao, Liaoning Sheng, Shengking; *hist.* Fengtien, Shenking. Admin. region *province* NE China
Liaoyuan 107 E3 *var.* Dongliao, Shuang-liao, *Jap.* Chengchiatun. Jilin, NE China
Liard *see* Fort Liard
Liban, Jebel 96 B4 *Ar.* Jabal al Gharbt, Jabal Lubnān, *Eng.* Mount Lebanon. *Mountain range* C Lebanon
Libby 22 A1 Montana, NW USA
Liberal 23 E5 Kansas, C USA
Liberec 76 B4 *Ger.* Reichenberg. Liberecký Kraj, N Czech Republic
Liberia 52 C5 *Country* W Africa
Liberia 30 D4 Guanacaste, NW Costa Rica
Libian Desert *see* Libyan Desert
Libourne 91 B5 Gironde, SW France
Libreville 55 A5 *country capital* (Gabon) Estuaire, NW Gabon
Libya 49 F3 *Ar.* Al Jamāhīrīyah al 'Arabīyah al Lībīyah ash Sha'bīyah al Ishtirākīyah; *prev.* Libyan Arab Republic. *Country* N Africa
Libyan Desert 49 H4 *var.* Libian Desert, *Ar.* Aş Şahrā' al Lībīyah. *Desert* N Africa
Libyan Plateau 81 F4 *var.* Aḍ Ḍiffah. *Plateau* Egypt/Libya
Lichtenfels 73 C5 Bayern, SE Germany
Lichtenvoorde 64 E4 Gelderland, E Netherlands
Lichuan 106 C5 Hubei, C China
Lida 85 B5 *Rus.* Lida. Hrodzyenskaya Voblasts', W Belarus
Lidköping 63 B6 Västra Götaland, S Sweden
Lidoríki 83 B5 *prev.* Lidhorikíon, Lidokhorikion. Stereá Ellás, C Greece
Lidzbark Warmiński 76 D2 *Ger.* Heilsberg. Warmińsko-Mazurskie, NE Poland
Liechtenstein 72 D1 *Country* C Europe
Liège 65 D6 *Dut.* Luik, *Ger.* Lüttich. Liège, E Belgium
Lienz 73 D7 Tirol, W Austria
Liepāja 84 B3 *Ger.* Libau. Liepāja, W Latvia
Liezen 95 D7 Steiermark, C Austria
Liffey 67 B6 *river* E Ireland
Lifou 122 D5 *island* Îles Loyauté, E New Caledonia
Liger *see* Loire
Ligure, Appennino 74 A2 *Eng.* Ligurian Mountains. *Mountain range* NW Italy
Ligurian Sea 74 A3 *Fr.* Mer Ligurienne, *It.* Mar Ligure. *Sea* N Mediterranean Sea
Līhu'e 25 A7 *var.* Lihue. Kaua'i, Hawai'i, USA, C Pacific Ocean
Lihula 84 D2 *Ger.* Leal. Läänemaa, W Estonia
Likasi 55 D7 *prev.* Jadotville. Shaba, SE Dem. Rep. Congo
Liknes 85 A6 Vest-Agder, S Norway
Lille 68 C2 *var.* l'Isle, *Dut.* Rijssel, *Flem.* Ryssel; *prev.* Lisle, *anc.* Insula. Nord, N France
Lillehammer 63 B5 Oppland, S Norway
Lillestrom 63 B6 Akershus, S Norway
Lilongwe 57 E2 *country capital* (Malawi) Central, W Malawi
Lima 38 C4 *country capital* (Peru) Lima, W Peru
Limanowa 77 D5 Małopolskie, S Poland
Limassol *see* Lemesós
Limerick 67 A6 *Ir.* Luimneach. SW Ireland
Límnos 81 F3 *anc.* Lemnos. *Island* E Greece
Limoges 69 C5 *anc.* Augustoritum Lemovicensium, Lemovices. Haute-Vienne, C France
Limón 31 E4 *var.* Puerto Limón. Limón, E Costa Rica
Limón 30 D2 Colón, NE Honduras
Limousin 69 C5 *cultural region* C France
Limoux 69 C6 Aude, S France
Limpopo 56 D3 *var.* Crocodile. *River* S Africa
Linares 70 D4 Andalucía, S Spain
Linares 42 B4 Maule, C Chile
Linares 29 E3 Nuevo León, NE Mexico
Lincoln 67 D5 *anc.* Lindum, Lindum Colonia. E England, UK
Lincoln 23 F4 *state capital* Nebraska, C USA
Lincoln 19 H2 Maine, NE USA
Lincoln Sea 12 D2 *sea* Arctic Ocean
Linden 37 F3 E Guyana
Líndhos *see* Líndos
Lindi 51 D8 Lindi, SE Tanzania
Líndos 83 E7 *var.* Líndhos. Ródos, Dodekánisos, Greece, Aegean Sea
Line Islands 123 G3 *island group* E Kiribati
Lingeh *see* Bandar-e Langeh
Lingen 72 A3 *var.* Lingen an der Ems. Niedersachsen, NW Germany
Lingen an der Ems *see* Lingen
Lingga, Kepulauan 116 B4 *island group* W Indonesia
Linköping 63 C6 Östergötland, S Sweden
Linz 73 D6 *anc.* Lentia. Oberösterreich, N Austria
Lion, Golfe du 69 C7 *Eng.* Gulf of Lion, Gulf of Lions; *anc.* Sinus Gallicus. *Gulf* S France
Lipari Islands *see* Eolie, Isole
Lipari, Isola 75 D6 *island* Isole Eolie, S Italy
Lipetsk 89 B5 Lipetskaya Oblast', W Russian Federation
Lipno 76 C3 Kujawsko-pomorskie, C Poland
Lipova 86 A4 *Hung.* Lippa. Arad, W Romania
Liqeni i Ohrit *see* Ohrid, Lake
Lira 51 B6 N Uganda
Lisala 55 C5 Equateur, N Dem. Rep. Congo
Lisboa 70 B4 *Eng.* Lisbon; *anc.* Felicitas Julia, Olisipo. *Country capital* (Portugal) Lisboa, W Portugal
Lisbon *see* Lisboa
Lisieux 68 B3 *anc.* Noviomagus. Calvados, N France
Liski 89 B6 *prev.* Georgiu-Dezh. Voronezhskaya Oblast', W Russian Federation
Lisle *see* Lille
l'Isle *see* Lille
Lismore 127 E5 Victoria, SE Australia
Lisse 64 C3 Zuid-Holland, W Netherlands
Litang 106 A5 Sichuan, C China
Lītani, Nahr el 135 B5 *var.* Nahr al Litant. *River* C Lebanon
Lithgow 127 D6 New South Wales, SE Australia
Lithuania 84 B4 *Ger.* Litauen, *Lith.* Lietuva, *Pol.* Litwa, *Rus.* Litva; *prev.* Lithuanian SSR, *Rus.* Litovskaya SSR. *Country* NE Europe
Litóchoro 82 B4 *var.* Litohoro, Litókhoron. Kentrikí Makedonía, N Greece
Litohoro *see* Litóchoro
Litókhoron *see* Litóchoro
Little Alföld 77 C6 *Ger.* Kleines Ungarisches Tiefland, *Hung.* Kisalföld, *Slvk.* Podunajská Rovina. *Plain* Hungary/Slovakia
Little Andaman 111 F2 *island* Andaman Islands, India, NE Indian Ocean
Little Barrier Island 128 D2 *island* N NZ
Little Bay 71 H5 *bay* S Gibraltar
Little Cayman 32 B3 *island* E Cayman Islands
Little Falls 23 F2 Minnesota, N USA
Littlefield 27 E2 Texas, SW USA
Little Inagua 32 D2 *var.* Inagua Islands. *Island* S Bahamas
Little Minch, The 66 B3 *strait* NW Scotland, UK
Little Missouri River 22 D2 *river* NW USA
Little Nicobar 111 G3 *island* Nicobar Islands, India, NE Indian Ocean
Little Rock 20 B1 *state capital* Arkansas, C USA
Little Saint Bernard Pass 69 D5 *Fr.* Col du Petit St-Bernard, *It.* Colle di Piccolo San Bernardo. *Pass* France/Italy
Little Sound 20 A5 *bay* Bermuda, NW Atlantic Ocean
Littleton 22 D4 Colorado, C USA
Liu-chou *see* Liuzhou
Liuchow *see* Liuzhou
Liuzhou 106 C6 *var.* Liu-chou, Liuchow. Guangxi Zhuangzu Zizhiqu, S China
Livanátes 83 B5 *prev.* Livanátai. Stereá Ellás, C Greece
Līvāni 84 D4 *Ger.* Lievenhof. Preiļi, SE Latvia
Liverpool 126 D2 New South Wales, SE Australia
Liverpool 17 F5 Nova Scotia, SE Canada
Liverpool 67 C5 NW England, UK
Livingston 22 B2 Montana, NW USA
Livingstone 56 C3 *var.* Maramba. Southern, S Zambia
Livingstone 27 H3 Texas, SW USA
Livingstone Mountains 129 A7 *mountain range* South Island, NZ
Livno 78 B4 Federacija Bosna I Hercegovina, SW Bosnia and Herzegovina
Livojoki 62 D4 *river* C Finland
Livonia 18 D3 Michigan, N USA
Livorno 74 B3 *Eng.* Leghorn. Toscana, C Italy
Lixoúri 83 A5 *prev.* Lixoúrion. Kefallinía, Iónioi Nísoi, Greece, C Mediterranean Sea
Lizarra *see* Estella
Ljubljana 73 D7 *Ger.* Laibach, *It.* Lubiana; *anc.* Aemona, Emona. *Country capital* (Slovenia) C Slovenia
Ljungby 63 B7 Kronoberg, S Sweden
Ljusdal 63 C5 Gävleborg, C Sweden
Ljusnan 63 C5 *river* C Sweden
Llanelli 67 C6 *prev.* Llanelly. SW Wales, UK
Llanes 70 D1 Asturias, N Spain
Llanos 36 D2 *physical region* Colombia/Venezuela
Lleida 71 F2 *Cast.* Lérida; *anc.* Ilerda. Cataluña, NE Spain
Lluchmayor *see* Llucmajor
Llucmajor 71 G3 *var.* Lluchmayor. Mallorca, Spain, W Mediterranean Sea
Loaita Island 106 C8 *island* W Spratly Islands
Loanda *see* Luanda
Lobatse 56 C4 *var.* Lobatsi. Kgatleng, SE Botswana
Lobatsi *see* Lobatse
Löbau 72 D4 Sachsen, E Germany
Lobito 56 B2 Benguela, W Angola
Lob Nor *see* Lop Nur
Loburi *see* Lop Buri
Locarno 73 B8 *Ger.* Luggarus. Ticino, S Switzerland
Lochem 64 E3 Gelderland, E Netherlands
Lockport 19 E3 New York, NE USA
Lodja 55 D6 Kasai Oriental, C Dem. Rep. Congo
Lodwar 51 C6 Rift Valley, NW Kenya
Łódź 76 D4 *Rus.* Lodz. Łódzkie, C Poland
Loei 114 C4 *var.* Loey, Muang Loei. Loei, C Thailand
Loey *see* Loei
Lofoten 62 B3 *var.* Lofoten Islands. *Island group* C Norway
Lofoten Islands *see* Lofoten
Logan 22 B3 Utah, W USA
Logan, Mount 14 D3 *mountain* Yukon Territory, W Canada
Logroño 71 E1 *anc.* Vareia, *Lat.* Juliobriga. La Rioja, N Spain
Loibl Pass 73 D7 *Ger.* Loiblpass, *Slvn.* Ljubelj. *Pass* Austria/Slovenia
Loi-Kaw 114 B4 Kayah State, C Myanmar
Loire 68 B4 *var.* Liger. *River* C France
Loja 38 B2 Loja, S Ecuador
Lokitaung 51 C5 Rift Valley, NW Kenya
Lokoja 53 G4 Kogi, C Nigeria
Loksa 84 E2 *Ger.* Loxa. Harjumaa, NW Estonia
Lolland 63 B8 *prev.* Laaland. *Island* S Denmark
Lom 82 C1 *prev.* Lom-Palanka. Montana, NW Bulgaria
Lomami 55 D6 *river* C Dem. Rep. Congo
Lomas 38 D4 Arequipa, SW Peru
Lomas de Zamora 42 D4 Buenos Aires, E Argentina
Lombardia 74 B2 *cultural region* N Italy
Lombok, Pulau 116 D5 *island* Nusa Tenggara, C Indonesia
Lomé 53 F5 *country capital* (Togo) S Togo
Lomela 55 D6 Kasai Oriental, C Dem. Rep. Congo
Lommel 87 C5 Limburg, N Belgium
Lomond, Loch 66 B4 *lake* C Scotland, UK
Lomonosov Ridge 133 B3 *var.* Harris Ridge, *Rus.* Khrebet Lomonsova. *Undersea feature* Arctic Ocean
Lompoc 25 B7 California, W USA
Lom Sak 114 C4 *var.* Muang Lom Sak. Phetchabun, C Thailand
Łomża 76 D3 *off.* Województwo Łomżyńskie, *Rus.* Lomzha. Podlaskie, NE Poland
Loncoche 43 B5 Araucanía, C Chile
London 67 A7 *anc.* Augusta, *Lat.* Londinium. *Country capital* (UK) SE England, UK
London 18 C5 Kentucky, S USA
London 16 C5 Ontario, S Canada
Londonderry 66 B4 *var.* Derry, *Ir.* Doire. NW Northern Ireland, UK
Londonderry, Cape 124 C2 *headland* Western Australia
Londrina 41 E4 Paraná, S Brazil
Longa, Proliv 93 G1 *Eng.* Long Strait. *Strait* NE Russian Federation
Long Bay 21 F2 *bay* North Carolina/South Carolina, E USA
Long Beach 25 C7 California, W USA
Longford 67 B5 *Ir.* An Longfort. C Ireland
Long Island 32 D2 *island* C Bahamas
Long Island 19 G4 *island* New York, NE USA
Long Island *see* Bermuda
Longlac 16 C3 Ontario, S Canada
Longmont 22 D4 Colorado, C USA
Longreach 126 C4 Queensland, E Australia
Long Strait *see* Longa, Proliv
Longview 27 H3 Texas, SW USA
Longview 24 B2 Washington, NW USA
Long Xuyên 115 D6 *var.* Longxuyen. An Giang, S Vietnam
Longxuyen *see* Long Xuyên
Longyan 106 D6 Fujian, SE China
Longyearbyen 61 G2 *dependent territory capital* (Svalbard) Spitsbergen, W Svalbard
Lons-le-Saunier 68 D4 *anc.* Ledo Salinarius. Jura, E France
Lop Buri 115 C5 *var.* Loburi. Lop Buri, C Thailand
Lop Nor *see* Lop Nur
Lop Nur 104 C3 *var.* Lob Nor, Lop Nor, Lo-pu Po. *Seasonal lake* NW China
Loppersum 64 E1 Groningen, NE Netherlands
Lo-pu Po *see* Lop Nur
Lorca 71 E4 *Ar.* Lurka; *anc.* Eliocroca, *Lat.* Illur co. Murcia, S Spain
Lord Howe Island 120 C4 *island* E Australia
Lord Howe Rise 120 C4 *undersea feature* SW Pacific Ocean
Loreto 28 B3 Baja California Sur, W Mexico
Lorient 68 A3 *prev.* l'Orient. Morbihan, NW France
Lorn, Firth of 66 B4 *inlet* W Scotland, UK
Loro Sae *see* East Timor
Lörrach 73 A7 Baden-Württemberg, S Germany
Lorraine 68 D3 *cultural region* NE France
Los Alamos 26 C1 New Mexico, SW USA
Los Amates 30 B2 Izabal, E Guatemala
Los Angeles 25 C7 California, W USA
Los Ángeles 43 B5 Bío Bío, C Chile
Lošinj 78 A3 *Ger.* Lussin, *It.* Lussino. *Island* W Croatia
Los Mochis 28 C3 Sinaloa, C Mexico
Los Roques, Islas 36 D1 *island group* N Venezuela
Los Testigos, Isla 33 G5 *island* NE Venezuela
Lost River Range 24 D3 *mountain range* Idaho, C USA
Lot 69 B5 *cultural region* C France
Lot 69 B5 *river* S France
Lotagipi Swamp 51 C5 *wetland* Kenya/Sudan
Louangnamtha 114 C3 *var.* Luong Nam Tha. Louang Namtha, N Laos
Louangphabang 102 D3 *var.* Louangphrabang, Luang Prabang. Louangphabang, N Laos
Louangphrabang *see* Louangphabang
Loudéac 68 A3 Côtes d'Armor, NW France
Loudi 106 C5 Hunan, S China
Louga 52 B3 NW Senegal
Louisiade Archipelago 122 B4 *island group* SE PNG
Louisiana 20 A2 *off.* State of Louisiana; also known as Creole State, Pelican State. *State* S USA
Louisville 18 C5 Kentucky, S USA
Louisville Ridge 121 E4 *undersea feature* S Pacific Ocean
Loup River 23 E4 *river* Nebraska, C USA
Lourdes 69 B6 Hautes-Pyrénées, S France
Louth 67 E5 E England, UK
Loutrá 82 C4 Kentrikí Makedonía, N Greece
Lóuva 56 C1 Lunda Norte, NE Angola
Louvain-la Neuve 65 C6 Wallon Brabant, C Belgium
Louviers 68 C3 Eure, N France
Lovech 82 C2 Lovech, N Bulgaria
Loveland 22 D4 Colorado, C USA
Lovosice 76 A4 *Ger.* Lobositz. Ústecký Kraj, NW Czech Republic
Lowell 19 G3 Massachusetts, NE USA
Lower California *see* Baja California
Lower Hutt 129 D5 Wellington, North Island, NZ
Lower Lough Erne 67 A5 *lake* SW Northern Ireland, UK
Lower Red Lake 23 F1 *lake* Minnesota, N USA
Lower Tunguska *see* Nizhnyaya Tunguska
Lowestoft 67 E6 E England, UK
Lo-yang *see* Luoyang
Loyauté, Îles 122 D5 *island group* S New Caledonia
Loyew 85 D8 *Rus.* Loyev. Homyel'skaya Voblasts', SE Belarus
Loznica 78 C3 Serbia, W Serbia and Montenegro (Yugo.)
Lu *see* Shandong
Lualaba 55 D6 *Fr.* Loualaba. *River* SE Dem. Rep. Congo
Luanda 56 A1 *var.* Loanda, *Port.* São Paulo de Loanda. *Country capital* (Angola) Luanda, NW Angola
Luang Prabang *see* Louangphabang
Luang, Thale 115 C7 *lagoon* S Thailand
Luangua, Rio *see* Luangwa
Luangwa 51 B8 *var.* Aruângua, Rio Luangua. *River* Mozambique/Zambia
Luanshya 56 D2 Copperbelt, C Zambia
Luarca 70 C1 Asturias, N Spain
Lubaczów 77 E5 *var.* Lúbaczów. Podkarpackie, SE Poland
Lubań 76 B4 *var.* Koscian, *Ger.* Kosten. Dolnośląskie, SW Poland
Lubānas Ezers *see* Lubāns
Lubango 56 B2 *Port.* Sá da Bandeira. Huíla, SW Angola
Lubāns 84 D4 *var.* Lubānas Ezers. *Lake* E Latvia
Lubao 55 D6 Kasai Oriental, C Dem. Rep. Congo
Lübben 72 D4 Brandenburg, E Germany
Lübbenau 72 D4 Brandenburg, E Germany
Lubbock 27 E2 Texas, SW USA
Lübeck 72 C2 Schleswig-Holstein, N Germany
Lubelska, Wyżyna 76 E4 *plateau* SE Poland
Lubin 76 B4 *Ger.* Lüben. Dolnośląskie, W Poland
Lublin 76 E4 *Rus.* Lyublin. Lubelskie, E Poland
Lubliniec 76 C4 Śląskie, S Poland
Lubny 87 F2 Poltavs'ka Oblast', NE Ukraine
Lubsko 76 B4 *Ger.* Sommerfeld. Lubuskie, W Poland
Lubumbashi 55 E8 *prev.* Élisabethville. Shaba, SE Dem. Rep. Congo
Lubutu 55 D6 Maniema, E Dem. Rep. Congo
Lucan 89 B5 *Ir.* Leamhcán. E Ireland
Lucano, Appennino 75 D5 *Eng.* Lucanian Mountains. *Mountain range* S Italy
Lucapa 56 C1 *var.* Lukapa. Lunda Norte, NE Angola
Lucca 74 B3 *anc.* Luca. Toscana, C Italy
Lucea 32 A4 W Jamaica
Lucena 117 E1 *off.* Lucena City. Luzon, N Philippines
Lucena 70 D4 Andalucía, S Spain
Lučenec 77 D6 *Ger.* Losontz, *Hung.* Losonc. Banskobystrický Kraj, C Slovakia
Luchow *see* Hefei
Lucknow 113 E3 *var.* Lakhnau. Uttar Pradesh, N India
Lüda *see* Dalian
Luda Kamchiya 82 D2 *river* E Bulgaria
Lüderitz 56 B4 *prev.* Angra Pequena. Karas, SW Namibia
Ludhiāna 112 D2 Punjab, N India
Ludington 18 C2 Michigan, N USA
Luduş 86 B4 *Ger.* Ludasch, *Hung.* Marosludas. Mureş, C Romania
Ludvika 63 C6 Kopparberg, C Sweden
Ludwiglust 72 C3 Mecklenburg-Vorpommern, N Germany
Ludwigsburg 73 B6 Baden-Württemberg, SW Germany
Ludwigsfelde 72 D3 Brandenburg, NE Germany
Ludwigshafen 73 B5 *var.* Ludwigshafen am Rhein. Rheinland-Pfalz, W Germany
Ludwigshafen am Rhein *see* Ludwigshafen
Ludza 84 D4 *Ger.* Ludsan. Ludza, E Latvia
Luebo 55 C6 Kasai Occidental, SW Dem. Rep. Congo
Luena 56 C2 *var.* Lwena, *Port.* Luso. Moxico, E Angola
Lufira 55 E7 *river* SE Dem. Rep. Congo
Lufkin 27 H3 Texas, SW USA
Luga 88 A4 Leningradskaya Oblast', NW Russian Federation
Lugano 73 B8 *Ger.* Lauis. Ticino, S Switzerland
Lugenda, Rio 57 E2 *river* N Mozambique
Lugo 70 C1 *anc.* Lugus Augusti. Galicia, NW Spain
Lugoj 86 A4 *Ger.* Lugosch, *Hung.* Lugos. Timiş, W Romania
Luhans'k 87 H3 *Rus.* Lugansk; *prev.* Voroshilovgrad. Luhans'ka Oblast', E Ukraine
Luimneach *see* Limerick
Lukapa *see* Lucapa
Lukenie 55 C6 *river* C Dem. Rep. Congo
Lukovit 82 C2 Lovech, NW Bulgaria
Łuków 76 E4 *Ger.* Bogendorf. Lubelskie, E Poland
Lukuga 55 D7 *river* SE Dem. Rep. Congo
Luleå 84 D4 Norrbotten, N Sweden
Luleälven 62 C3 *river* N Sweden
Lulonga 55 C5 *river* NW Dem. Rep. Congo
Lulua 55 D7 *river* S Dem. Rep. Congo
Lumbo 57 F2 Nampula, NE Mozambique
Lumsden 129 A7 Southland, South Island, NZ
Lund 63 B7 Skåne, S Sweden
Lüneburg 72 C3 Niedersachsen, N Germany
Lungkiang *see* Qiqihar
Lungué-Bungo 56 C2 *var.* Lungwebungu. *River* Angola/Zambia *see also* Lungwebungu
Lungwebungu *see* Lungué-Bungo
Luninyets 85 B7 *Pol.* Łuniniec, *Rus.* Luninets. Brestskaya Voblasts', SW Belarus
Lunteren 64 D4 Gelderland, C Netherlands
Luong Nam Tha *see* Louangnamtha
Luoyang 106 C4 *var.* Honan, Lo-yang. Henan, C China
Lúrio 57 F2 Nampula, NE Mozambique
Lúrio, Rio 57 E2 *river* NE Mozambique
Lusaka 56 D2 *country capital* (Zambia) Lusaka, SE Zambia
Lushnja *see* Lushnjë
Lushnjë 79 C6 *var.* Lushnja. Fier, C Albania
Luso *see* Luena
Lūt, Dasht-e 98 D3 *var.* Kavīr-e Lūt. *Desert* E Iran
Luton 67 D6 SE England, UK
Łutselk'e 15 F4 *prev.* Snowdrift. Northwest Territories, W Canada
Luts'k 86 C1 *Pol.* Łuck, *Rus.* Lutsk. Volyns'ka Oblast', NW Ukraine
Lutzow-Holm Bay *see* Lützow Holmbukta
Lützow Holmbukta 132 C2 *var.* Lutzow-Holm Bay. *Bay* Antarctica
Luuq 51 D6 *It.* Lugh Ganana. Gedo, SW Somalia
Luvua 55 D7 *river* SE Dem. Rep. Congo
Luwego 51 C8 *river* S Tanzania
Luxembourg 87 D8 *var.* Lëtzebuerg, Luxemburg. *Country* NW Europe
Luxembourg 65 D8 *country capital* (Luxembourg) Luxembourg, S Luxembourg
Luxor 50 B2 *Ar.* Al Uqşur. E Egypt
Luza 88 C4 Kirovskaya Oblast', NW Russian Federation
Luz, Costa de la 70 C5 *coastal region* SW Spain
Luzern 73 B7 *Fr.* Lucerne, *It.* Lucerna. Luzern, C Switzerland
Luzon 117 E1 *island* N Philippines
Luzon Strait 103 E3 *strait* Philippines/Taiwan
L'viv 86 B2 *Ger.* Lemberg, *Pol.* Lwów, *Rus.* L'vov. L'vivs'ka Oblast', W Ukraine
Lwena *see* Luena
Lyakhavichy 85 B6 *Rus.* Lyakhovichi. Brestskaya Voblasts', SW Belarus
Lycksele 62 C4 Västerbotten, N Sweden
Lycopolis *see* Asyût
Lyel'chytsy 85 C7 *Rus.* Lel'chitsy. Homyel'skaya Voblasts', SE Belarus
Lyepyel' 85 D5 *Rus.* Lepel'. Vitsyebskaya Voblasts', N Belarus
Lyme Bay 67 C7 *bay* S England, UK
Lynchburg 19 E5 Virginia, NE USA
Lynn Regis *see* King's Lynn
Lyon 69 D5 *Eng.* Lyons; *anc.* Lugdunum. Rhône, E France
Lyozna 85 E6 *Rus.* Liozno. Vitsyebskaya Voblasts', NE Belarus
Lypovets' 86 D2 *Rus.* Lipovets. Vinnyts'ka Oblast', C Ukraine
Lysychans'k 87 H3 *Rus.* Lisichansk. Luhans'ka Oblast', E Ukraine
Lyttelton 129 C6 Canterbury, South Island, NZ
Lyubotyn 87 G2 *Rus.* Lyubotin. Kharkivs'ka Oblast', E Ukraine
Lyulyakovo 82 E2 *prev.* Keremitlik. Burgas, E Bulgaria
Lyusina 85 B6 *Rus.* Lyusino. Brestskaya Voblasts', SW Belarus

M

Ma'ān 97 B7 Ma'ān, SW Jordan
Maardu 84 D2 *Ger.* Maart. Harjumaa, NW Estonia
Ma'aret-en-Nu'man *see* Ma'arrat an Nu'mān
Ma'arrat an Nu'mān 96 B3 *var.* Ma'aret-en-Nu'man, *Fr.* Maarret enn Naamâne. Idlib, NW Syria
Maarret enn Naamâne *see* Ma'arrat an Nu'mān
Maaseik 65 D5 *prev.* Maeseyck. Limburg, NE Belgium
Maastricht 65 D6 *var.* Maestricht; *anc.* Traietum ad Mosam, Traiectum Tungorum. Limburg, SE Netherlands
Macao 107 C6 *Chin.* Aomen, *Port.* Macao. S China
Macapá 41 E1 *state capital* Amapá, N Brazil
Macassar *see* Ujungpandang
MacCluer Gulf *see* Berau, Teluk
Macdonnell Ranges 124 D4 *mountain range* Northern Territory, C Australia
Macedonia, FYR 79 D6 *var.* Macedonia, *Mac.* Makedonija, *abbrev.* FYR Macedonia, FYROM. *Country* SE Europe
Maceió 41 G3 *state capital* Alagoas, E Brazil
Machachi 38 B1 Pichincha, C Ecuador
Machala 38 B2 El Oro, SW Ecuador
Machanga 57 E3 Sofala, E Mozambique

Machilīpatnam 110 D1 *var.* Bandar Masulipatnam. Andhra Pradesh, E India
Machiques 36 C2 Zulia, NW Venezuela
Macías Nguema Biyogo *see* Bioco, Isla de
Măcin 86 D5 Tulcea, SE Romania
Macizo de las Guayanas *see* Guiana Highlands
Mackay 126 D4 Queensland, NE Australia
Mackay, Lake 124 C4 *salt lake* Northern Territory/Western Australia
Mackenzie 15 E3 *river* Northwest Territories, NW Canada
Mackenzie Bay 132 D3 *bay* Antarctica
Mackenzie Mountains 14 D3 *mountain range* Northwest Territories, NW Canada
Macleod, Lake 124 A4 *lake* Western Australia
Macomb 18 A4 Illinois, N USA
Macomer 75 A5 Sardegna, Italy, C Mediterranean Sea
Macon 20 D2 Georgia, SE USA
Macon 23 G4 Missouri, C USA
Mâcon 69 D5 *anc.* Matisco, Matisco Ædourum. Saône-et-Loire, C France
Macquarie Ridge 132 C5 *undersea feature* SW Pacific Ocean
Macuspana 29 G4 Tabasco, SE Mexico
Ma'dabā 97 B6 *var.* Mādabā, Madeba; *anc.* Medeba. 'Ammān, NW Jordan
Madagascar 57 F3 *Malg.* Madagasikara; *prev.* Malagasy Republic. *Country* W Indian Ocean
Madagascar 57 F3 *island* W Indian Ocean
Madagascar Basin 47 E7 *undersea feature* W Indian Ocean
Madagascar Plateau 47 E7 *var.* Madagascar Ridge, Madagascar Rise, *Rus.* Madagaskarskiy Khrebet. *Undersea feature* W Indian Ocean
Madagascar Ridge *see* Madagascar Plateau
Madagascar Rise *see* Madagascar Plateau
Madagaskarskiy Khrebet *see* Madagascar Plateau
Madang 122 B3 Madang, N PNG
Madanīyīn *see* Médenine
Made 64 C4 Noord-Brabant, S Netherlands
Madeba *see* Ma'dabā
Madeira 48 A2 *var.* Ilha de Madeira. *Island* Portugal, NE Atlantic Ocean
Madeira 48 A2 *var.* Madeira, *Port.* Arquipélago da Madeira. *Island group* Portugal, NE Atlantic Ocean
Madeira Plain 44 C3 *undersea feature* E Atlantic Ocean
Madeira, Rio 40 D2 *Sp.* Río Madera. *River* Bolivia/Brazil *see also* Madera, Río
Madeleine, Îles de la 17 F4 *Eng.* Magdalen Islands. *Island group* Québec, E Canada
Madera 25 B6 California, W USA
Madhya Pradesh 113 E4 *prev.* Central Provinces and Berar. *Admin. region state* C India
Madīnat ath Thawrah 96 C2 *var.* Ath Thawrah. Ar Raqqah, N Syria Asia
Madison 18 B3 *state capital* Wisconsin, N USA
Madison 23 F3 South Dakota, N USA
Madiun 116 D5 *prev.* Madioen. Jawa, C Indonesia
Madona 84 D4 *Ger.* Modohn. Madona, E Latvia
Madras *see* Tamil Nādu
Madras *see* Chennai
Madre de Dios 34 B4 *off.* Departamento de Madre de Dios. *Department* E Peru
Madre de Dios, Río 39 E3 *river* Bolivia/Peru
Madre del Sur, Sierra 29 E5 *mountain range* S Mexico
Madre, Laguna 29 F3 *lagoon* NE Mexico
Madre, Laguna 27 G5 *lake* Texas, SW USA
Madre Occidental, Sierra 28 C3 *var.* Western Sierra Madre. *Mountain range* C Mexico
Madre Oriental, Sierra 29 E3 *var.* Eastern Sierra Madre. *Mountain range* C Mexico
Madrid 70 D3 *country capital* (Spain) Madrid, C Spain
Madurai 110 C3 *prev.* Madura, Mathurai. Tamil Nādu, S India
Madura, Pulau 116 D5 *prev.* Madoera. *Island* C Indonesia
Maebashi 109 D5 *var.* Maebasi, Mayebashi. Gunma, Honshū, S Japan
Maebasi *see* Maebashi
Mae Nam Khong *see* Mekong
Mae Nam Nan 114 C4 *river* NW Thailand
Mae Nam Yom 114 C4 *river* W Thailand
Maestricht *see* Maastricht
Maéwo 122 D4 *prev.* Aurora. *Island* C Vanuatu
Mafia 51 D7 *island* E Tanzania
Mafraq *see* Al Mafraq
Magadan 93 G3 Magadanskaya Oblast', E Russian Federation
Magangué 36 B2 Bolívar, N Colombia
Magdalena 34 A2 *off.* Departamento del Magdalena. *Province* N Colombia
Magdalena 39 F3 Beni, N Bolivia
Magdalena 28 B1 Sonora, NW Mexico
Magdalena, Isla 28 B3 *island* W Mexico
Magdalena, Río 36 B2 *river* C Colombia
Magdeburg 72 C4 Sachsen-Anhalt, C Germany
Magelang 116 C5 Jawa, C Indonesia
Magellan, Strait of 43 B8 *Sp.* Estrecho de Magallanes. *Strait* Argentina/Chile
Mageroy *see* Magerøya
Magerøya 62 D1 *var.* Magerøy. *Island* N Norway
Maggiore, Lake 74 B1 *It.* Lago Maggiore. *Lake* Italy/Switzerland
Maglaj 78 C3 Federacija Bosna I Hercegovina, N Bosnia and Herzegovina
Maglie 75 E6 Puglia, SE Italy
Magna 22 B4 Utah, W USA
Magnesia *see* Manisa
Magnitogorsk 92 B4 Chelyabinskaya Oblast', C Russian Federation
Magta' Lahjar 52 C3 *var.* Magta Lahjar, Magta' Lahjar, Magtá Lahjar. Brakna, SW Mauritania
Magway *see* Magwe
Magwe 114 A3 *var.* Magway. Magwe, W Myanmar
Mahajanga 57 F2 *var.* Majunga. Mahajanga, NW Madagascar
Mahakam, Sungai 116 D4 *var.* Koetai, Kutai. *River* Borneo, C Indonesia
Mahalapye 56 D3 *var.* Mahalatswe. Central, SE Botswana
Mahalatswe *see* Mahalapye
Mahān 98 D3 Kermān, E Iran
Mahānadi 113 F4 *river* E India
Mahārāshtra 112 D5 *state* W India
Mahbés *see* El Mahbas
Mahbūbnagar 112 D5 Andhra Pradesh, C India
Mahdia 49 F2 *var.* Al Mahdīyah, Mehdia. NE Tunisia
Mahé 57 H1 *island* Inner Islands, NE Seychelles
Mahia Peninsula 128 E4 *peninsula* North Island, NZ
Mahilyow 85 D6 *Rus.* Mogilëv. Mahilyowskaya Voblasts', E Belarus
Mahmūd-e 'Erāqī *see* Maḩmūd-e Rāqī
Maḩmūd-e Rāqī 101 E4 *var.* Mahmūd-e 'Erāqī. Kāpīsā, NE Afghanistan
Mahón 71 H3 *Cat.* Maó, *Eng.* Port Mahon; *anc.* Portus Magonis. Menorca, Spain, W Mediterranean Sea
Maicao 36 C1 La Guajira, N Colombia
Mai Ceu *see* Maych'ew
Mai Chio *see* Maych'ew
Maidstone 67 E7 SE England, UK
Maiduguri 53 H4 Borno, NE Nigeria
Maimāna *see* Meymaneh
Main 73 B5 *river* C Germany
Mai-Ndombe, Lac 55 C6 *prev.* Lac Léopold II. *Lake* W Dem. Rep. Congo
Maine 19 G2 *off.* State of Maine; also known as Lumber State, Pine Tree State. *State* NE USA
Maine 68 B3 *cultural region* NW France
Maine, Gulf of 19 H2 *gulf* NE USA
Main Island *see* Bermuda
Mainland 66 C2 *island* Orkney, N Scotland, UK
Mainland 66 D1 *island* Shetland, NE Scotland, UK
Mainz 73 B5 *Fr.* Mayence. Rheinland-Pfalz, SW Germany
Maio 52 A3 *var.* Mayo. *Island* Ilhas de Sotavento, SE Cape Verde
Maisur *see* Karnātaka
Maisur *see* Mysore
Maizhokunggar 104 C5 Xizang Zizhiqu, W China
Maíz, Islas del 31 E3 *var.* Corn Islands. *Island group* SE Nicaragua
Mājro *see* Majuro Atoll
Majunga *see* Mahajanga
Majuro Atoll 122 D2 *var.* Mājro. *Atoll* Ratak Chain, SE Marshall Islands
Makale *see* Mek'elē
Makarov Basin 133 B3 *undersea feature* Arctic Ocean
Makarska 78 B4 *It.* Macarsca. Split-Dalmacija, SE Croatia
Makasar *see* Ujungpandang
Makassar *see* Ujungpandang
Makassar Strait 116 D4 *Ind.* Selat Makasar. *Strait* C Indonesia
Makay 57 F3 *var.* Massif du Makay. *Mountain range* SW Madagascar
Makeni 52 C4 C Sierra Leone
Makhachkala 92 A4 *prev.* Petrovsk-Port. Respublika Dagestan, SW Russian Federation
Makin 122 D2 *prev.* Pitt Island. *Atoll* Tungaru, W Kiribati
Makira *see* San Cristobal
Makiyivka 87 G3 *Rus.* Makeyevka; *prev.* Dmitriyevsk. Donets'ka Oblast', E Ukraine
Makkah 99 A5 *Eng.* Mecca. Makkah, W Saudi Arabia
Makkovik 17 F2 Newfoundland and Labrador, NE Canada
Makó 77 D7 *Rom.* Macău. Csongrád, SE Hungary
Makoua 55 B5 Cuvette, C Congo
Makran Coast 98 E4 *coastal region* SE Iran
Makrany 85 A6 *Rus.* Mokrany. Brestskaya Voblasts', SW Belarus
Mākū 98 B2 Āžarbāyjān-e Bākhtarī, NW Iran
Makurdi 53 G4 Benue, C Nigeria
Mala *see* Malaita
Malabār Coast 110 B3 *coast* SW India
Malabo 55 A5 *prev.* Santa Isabel. *Country capital* (Equatorial Guinea) Isla de Bioco, NW Equatorial Guinea
Malacca *see* Melaka
Malacca, Strait of 116 B3 *Ind.* Selat Malaka. *Strait* Indonesia/Malaysia
Malacky 77 C6 *Hung.* Malacka. Bratislavský Kraj, W Slovakia
Maladzyechna 85 C5 *Pol.* Molodeczno, *Rus.* Molodechno. Minskaya Voblasts', C Belarus
Málaga 70 D5 *anc.* Malaca. Andalucía, S Spain
Malagarasi River 51 B7 *river* W Tanzania
Malaita 122 C3 *var.* Mala. *Island* N Solomon Islands
Malakal 51 B5 Upper Nile, S Sudan
Malakula *see* Malekula
Malang 116 D5 Jawa, C Indonesia
Malange *see* Malanje
Malanje 56 B1 *var.* Malange. Malanje, NW Angola
Mälaren 63 C6 *lake* C Sweden
Malatya 95 E4 *anc.* Melitene. Malatya, SE Turkey
Mala Vyska 87 E3 *Rus.* Malaya Viska. Kirovohrads'ka Oblast', S Ukraine
Malawi 57 E1 *prev.* Nyasaland, Nyasaland Protectorate. *Country* S Africa
Malawi, Lake *see* Nyasa, Lake
Malay Peninsula 102 D4 *peninsula* Malaysia/Thailand
Malaysia 116 B3 *var.* Federation of Malaysia; *prev.* the separate territories of Federation of Malaya, Sarawak and Sabah (North Borneo) and Singapore. *Country* SE Asia
Malaysia, Federation of *see* Malaysia
Malbork 76 C2 *Ger.* Marienburg, Marienburg in Westpreussen. Pomorskie, N Poland
Malchin 72 C3 Mecklenburg-Vorpommern, N Germany
Malden 23 H5 Missouri, C USA
Malden Island 123 G3 *prev.* Independence Island. *Atoll* E Kiribati
Maldives 110 A4 *Country* N Indian Ocean
Male' 110 B4 Male' Atoll, C Maldives
Male' Atoll 110 B4 *var.* Kaafu Atoll. *Atoll* C Maldives
Malekula 122 D4 *var.* Malakula; *prev.* Mallicolo. *Island* W Vanuatu
Malesína 83 C5 Stereá Ellás, E Greece
Malheur Lake 24 C3 *lake* Oregon, NW USA
Mali 53 E3 *Fr.* République du Mali; *prev.* French Sudan, Sudanese Republic. *Country* W Africa
Malik, Wadi al *see* Milk, Wadi el
Mali Kyun 115 B5 *var.* Tavoy Island. *Island* Mergui Archipelago, S Myanmar
Malindi 51 D7 Coast, SE Kenya
Malko Tŭrnovo 82 E3 Burgas, E Bulgaria
Mallaig 66 B3 N Scotland, UK
Mallawi 50 B2 C Egypt
Mallicolo *see* Malekula
Mallorca 71 G3 *Eng.* Majorca; *anc.* Baleares Major. *Island* Islas Baleares, Spain, W Mediterranean Sea
Malmberget 62 C3 Norrbotten, N Sweden
Malmédy 65 D6 Liège, E Belgium
Malmö 63 B7 Skåne, S Sweden
Maloelap *see* Maloelap Atoll
Maloelap Atoll 122 D1 *var.* Maloeļap. *Atoll* E Marshall Islands
Małopolska 76 D4 *plateau* S Poland
Malozemel'skaya Tundra 88 D3 *physical region* NW Russian Federation
Malta 75 C8 *Country* C Mediterranean Sea
Malta 75 C8 *island* Malta, C Mediterranean Sea
Malta 22 C1 Montana, NW USA
Malta 84 D4 Rēzekne, SE Latvia
Malta Channel 75 C8 *It.* Canale di Malta. *Strait* Italy/Malta
Maluku 117 F4 *Dut.* Molukken, *Eng.* Moluccas; *prev.* Spice Islands. *Island group* E Indonesia
Malung 63 B6 Kopparberg, C Sweden
Malyn 86 D2 *Rus.* Malin. Zhytomyrs'ka Oblast', N Ukraine
Mamberamo, Sungai 117 H4 *river* Papua, E Indonesia
Mambij *see* Manbij
Mamonovo 84 A4 *Ger.* Heiligenbeil. Kaliningradskaya Oblast', W Russian Federation
Mamoré, Rio 39 F3 *river* Bolivia/Brazil
Mamou 52 C4 Moyenne-Guinée, W Guinea
Mamoudzou 57 F2 *dependent territory capital* (Mayotte) C Mayotte
Mamuno 56 C3 Ghanzi, W Botswana
Manacor 71 G3 Mallorca, Spain, W Mediterranean Sea
Manado 117 F3 *prev.* Menado. Sulawesi, C Indonesia
Managua 30 D3 *country capital* (Nicaragua) Managua, W Nicaragua
Managua, Lago de 30 C3 *var.* Xolotlán. *Lake* W Nicaragua
Manakara 57 G4 Fianarantsoa, SE Madagascar
Manama *see* Al Manāmah
Mananjary 57 G3 Fianarantsoa, SE Madagascar
Manapouri, Lake 129 A7 *lake* South Island, NZ
Manar *see* Mannar
Manas, Gora 101 E2 *mountain* Kyrgyzstan/Uzbekistan
Manaus 40 D2 *prev.* Manáos. *State capital* Amazonas, NW Brazil
Manavgat 94 B4 Antalya, SW Turkey
Manbij 96 C2 *var.* Mambij, *Fr.* Membidj. Ḩalab, N Syria
Manchester 67 D5 *Lat.* Mancunium. NW England, UK
Manchester 19 G3 New Hampshire, NE USA
Man-chou-li *see* Manzhouli
Manchuria 103 E1 *cultural region* NE China
Máncio Lima *see* Japiim
Mand *see* Mand, Rūd-e
Mandalay 114 B3 Mandalay, C Myanmar
Mandan 23 E2 North Dakota, N USA
Mandeville 32 B5 C Jamaica
Mándra 83 C6 Attikí, C Greece
Mand, Rūd-e 98 D4 *var.* Mand. *River* S Iran
Mandurah 125 A6 Western Australia
Manduria 75 E5 Puglia, SE Italy
Mandya 110 C2 Karnātaka, C India
Manfredonia 75 D5 Puglia, SE Italy
Mangai 55 C6 Bandundu, W Dem. Rep. Congo
Mangaia 123 G5 *island group* S Cook Islands
Mangalia 86 D5 *anc.* Callatis. Constanţa, SE Romania
Mangalmé 54 C3 Guéra, SE Chad
Mangalore 110 B2 Karnātaka, W India
Mangaung *see* Bloemfontein
Mango *see* Sansanné-Mango
Mangoky 79 F3 *river* W Madagascar
Manhattan 23 F4 Kansas, C USA
Manicouagan, Réservoir 16 D3 *lake* Québec, E Canada
Manihiki 123 G4 *atoll* N Cook Islands
Manihiki Plateau 121 E3 *undersea feature* C Pacific Ocean
Maniitsoq 60 C3 *var.* Manîtsoq, *Dan.* Sukkertoppen. S Greenland
Manila 117 E1 *off.* City of Manila. *Country capital* (Philippines) Luzon, N Philippines
Manisa 94 A3 *var.* Manissa; *prev.* Saruhan, *anc.* Magnesia. Manisa, W Turkey
Manissa *see* Manisa
Manitoba 15 F5 *province* S Canada
Manitoba, Lake 15 F5 *lake* Manitoba, S Canada
Manitoulin Island 16 C4 *island* Ontario, S Canada
Manîtsoq *see* Maniitsoq
Manizales 36 B3 Caldas, W Colombia
Manjimup 125 A7 Western Australia
Mankato 23 F3 Minnesota, N USA
Manlleu 71 G2 Cataluña, NE Spain
Manly 126 E1 New South Wales, SE Australia
Manmād 112 C5 Mahārāshtra, W India
Mannar 110 C3 *var.* Manar. Northern Province, NW Sri Lanka
Mannar, Gulf of 110 C3 *gulf* India/Sri Lanka
Mannheim 73 B5 Baden-Württemberg, SW Germany
Manono 55 E7 Shabo, SE Dem. Rep. Congo
Manosque 69 D6 Alpes-de-Haute-Provence, SE France
Manra 123 F3 *prev.* Sydney Island. *Atoll* Phoenix Islands, C Kiribati
Mansa 56 D2 *prev.* Fort Rosebery. Luapula, N Zambia
Mansel Island 15 G3 *island* Nunavut, NE Canada
Mansfield 18 D4 Ohio, N USA
Manta 38 A2 Manabí, W Ecuador
Manteca 25 B6 California, W USA
Mantova 74 B2 *Eng.* Mantua, *Fr.* Mantoue. Lombardia, NW Italy
Manuae 123 G4 *island* S Cook Islands
Manurewa 128 D3 *var.* Manukau. Auckland, North Island, NZ
Manzanares 71 E3 Castilla-La Mancha, C Spain
Manzanillo 28 D4 Colima, SW Mexico
Manzanillo 32 C3 Granma, E Cuba
Manzhouli 105 F1 *var.* Man-chou-li. Nei Mongol Zizhiqu, N China
Mao 54 B3 Kanem, W Chad
Maoke, Pegunungan 117 H4 *Dut.* Sneeuw-gebergte, *Eng.* Snow Mountains. *Mountain range* Papua, E Indonesia
Maoming 106 C6 Guangdong, S China
Mapmaker Seamounts 103 H2 *undersea feature* N Pacific Ocean
Maputo 56 D4 *prev.* Lourenço Marques. *Country capital* (Mozambique) Maputo, S Mozambique
Marabá 41 F2 Pará, NE Brazil
Maracaibo 36 C1 Zulia, NW Venezuela
Maracaibo, Lago de 36 C2 *var.* Lake Maracaibo. *Inlet* NW Venezuela
Maracaibo, Lake *see* Maracaibo, Lago de
Maracay 36 D2 Aragua, N Venezuela
Marada *see* Marādah
Marādah 49 G3 *var.* Marada. N Libya
Maradi 53 G3 Maradi, S Niger
Maragha *see* Marāgheh
Marāgheh 98 C2 *var.* Maragha. Āžarbāyjān-e Khāvarī, NW Iran
Marajó, Baía de 41 F1 *bay* N Brazil
Marajó, Ilha de 41 E1 *island* N Brazil
Marakesh *see* Marrakech
Maramba *see* Livingstone
Maranhão 41 F2 *off.* Estado do Maranhão. *State* E Brazil
Marañón, Río 38 B2 *river* N Peru
Maraş *see* Kahramanmaraş
Marash *see* Kahramanmaraş
Marathon 16 C4 Ontario, S Canada
Marathónas 83 C5 *prev.* Marathón. Attikí, C Greece
Märäzä 95 H2 *Rus.* Maraza. E Azerbaijan
Marbella 70 D5 Andalucía, S Spain
Marble Bar 124 B4 Western Australia
Marburg an der Lahn 72 B4 *hist.* Marburg. Hessen, W Germany
March *see* Morava
Marche 69 C5 *cultural region* C France
Marche 96 C3 *cultural region* E Italy
Marche-en-Famenne 65 C7 Luxembourg, SE Belgium
Marchena, Isla 38 B5 *var.* Bindloe Island. *Island* Galapagos Islands, Ecuador, E Pacific Ocean
Mar Chiquita, Laguna 42 C3 *lake* C Argentina
Marcounda *see* Markounda
Mardān 112 C1 North-West Frontier Province, N Pakistan
Mar del Plata 43 D5 Buenos Aires, E Argentina
Mardin 95 E4 Mardin, SE Turkey
Maré 122 D5 *island* Îles Loyauté, E New Caledonia
Marea Neagră *see* Black Sea
Mare Creticum *see* Kritikó Pélagos
Mareeba 126 D3 Queensland, NE Australia
Margarita, Isla de 37 E1 *island* N Venezuela
Margate 67 E7 *prev.* Mergate. SE England, UK
Marghita 86 B3 *Hung.* Margitta. Bihor, NW Romania
Marhanets' 87 F3 *Rus.* Marganets. Dnipropetrovs'ka Oblast', E Ukraine
María Cleofas, Isla 28 C4 *island* C Mexico
Maria Island 127 C8 *island* Tasmania, SE Australia
María Madre, Isla 28 C4 *island* C Mexico
María Magdalena, Isla 28 C4 *island* C Mexico
Mariana Trench 103 G4 *undersea feature* W Pacific Ocean
Mariánské Lázně 77 A5 *Ger.* Marienbad. Karlovarský Kraj, W Czech Republic
Marías, Islas 28 C4 *island group* C Mexico
Maribor 73 E7 *Ger.* Marburg. NE Slovenia
Marica *see* Maritsa
Maridi 51 B5 Western Equatoria, SW Sudan
Marie Byrd Land 132 A3 *physical region* Antarctica
Marie-Galante 33 G4 *var.* Ceyre to the Caribs. *Island* SE Guadeloupe
Mariental 56 B4 Hardap, SW Namibia
Mariestad 63 B6 Västra Götaland, S Sweden
Marietta 20 D2 Georgia, SE USA
Marijampolė 84 B4 *prev.* Kapsukas. Marijampolė, S Lithuania
Marília 41 E4 São Paulo, S Brazil
Marín 70 B1 Galicia, NW Spain
Mar"ina Horka 85 C6 *Rus.* Mar'ina Gorka. Minskaya Voblasts', C Belarus
Maringá 41 E4 Paraná, S Brazil
Marion 23 G3 Iowa, C USA
Marion 18 D4 Ohio, N USA
Marion, Lake 21 E2 *reservoir* South Carolina, SE USA
Mariscal Estigarribia 42 D2 Boquerón, NW Paraguay
Maritsa 82 D3 *var.* Marica, *Gk.* Évros, *Turk.* Meriç; *anc.* Hebrus. *River* SW Europe *see also* Évros/Meriç
Maritzburg *see* Pietermaritzburg
Mariupol' 87 G4 *prev.* Zhdanov. Donets'ka Oblast', SE Ukraine
Marka 51 D6 *var.* Merca. Shabeellaha Hoose, S Somalia
Markham, Mount 132 B4 *mountain* Antarctica
Markounda 54 C4 *var.* Marcounda. Ouham, NW Central African Republic
Marktredwitz 73 C5 Bayern, E Germany
Marlborough 126 D4 Queensland, E Australia
Marmande 69 B5 *anc.* Marmanda. Lot-et-Garonne, SW France
Marmara Denizi 94 A2 *Eng.* Sea of Marmara. *Sea* NW Turkey
Marmara, Sea of *see* Marmara Denizi
Marmaris 94 A4 Muğla, SW Turkey
Marne 68 C3 *cultural region* N France
Marne 68 D3 *river* N France
Maro 54 C4 Moyen-Chari, S Chad
Maroantsetra 57 G2 Toamasina, NE Madagascar
Maromokotro 57 G2 *mountain* N Madagascar
Maroni River 37 G3 *Dut.* Marowijne. *River* French Guiana/Suriname
Maros *see* Mureş
Marosch *see* Mureş
Marotiri 121 F4 *var.* Îlots de Bass, Morotiri. *Island group* Îles Australes, SW French Polynesia
Maroua 54 B3 Extrême-Nord, N Cameroon
Marquesas Fracture Zone 131 E3 *tectonic feature* E Pacific Ocean
Marquesas Islands 131 E3 *island group* N French Polynesia
Marquette 18 B1 Michigan, N USA
Marrakech 48 C2 *var.* Marakesh, *Eng.* Marrakesh; *prev.* Morocco. W Morocco
Marrakesh *see* Marrakech
Marrawah 127 C8 Tasmania, SE Australia
Marree 127 B5 South Australia
Marsá al Burayqah 49 G3 *var.* Al Burayqah. N Libya
Marsabit 51 C6 Eastern, N Kenya
Marsala 75 B7 *anc.* Lilybaeum. Sicilia, Italy, C Mediterranean Sea
Marsberg 72 B4 Nordrhein-Westfalen, W Germany
Marseille 69 D6 *Eng.* Marseilles; *anc.* Massilia. Bouches-du-Rhône, SE France
Marshall 23 F2 Minnesota, N USA
Marshall 27 H2 Texas, SW USA
Marshall Islands 122 C1 *Country* W Pacific Ocean
Marshall Seamounts 103 H3 *undersea feature* SW Pacific Ocean
Marsh Harbour 32 C1 Great Abaco, W Bahamas
Martaban 114 B4 *var.* Moktama. Mon State, S Myanmar
Martha's Vineyard 19 G3 *island* Massachusetts, NE USA
Martigues 69 D6 Bouches-du-Rhône, SE France
Martin 77 C5 *Ger.* Sankt Martin, *Hung.* Turócszentmárton; *prev.* Turčianský Svätý Martin. Žilinský Kraj, N Slovakia
Martinique 33 G4 *French overseas department* E West Indies
Martinique Channel *see* Martinique Passage
Martinique Passage 33 G4 *var.* Dominica Channel, Martinique Channel. *Channel* Dominica/Martinique
Marton 128 D4 Manawatu-Wanganui, North Island, NZ
Martos 70 D4 Andalucía, S Spain
Marungu 55 E7 *mountain range* SE Dem. Rep. Congo
Mary 100 D3 *prev.* Merv. Maryyskiy Velayat, S Turkmenistan
Maryborough *see* Portlaoise
Maryborough 127 D4 Queensland, E Australia
Mary Island *see* Kanton

Maryland 19 E5 off. State of Maryland; also known as America in Miniature, Cockade State, Free State, Old Line State. State NE USA
Maryland 20 D1 Tennessee, S USA
Maryville 23 F4 Missouri, C USA
Masai Steppe 51 C7 grassland NW Tanzania
Masaka 51 B6 SW Uganda
Masallı 95 H3 Rus. Masally. S Azerbaijan
Masasi 51 C8 Mtwara, SE Tanzania
Masawa see Massawa
Masaya 30 D3 Masaya, W Nicaragua
Mascarene Basin 119 B5 undersea feature W Indian Ocean
Mascarene Islands 57 H4 island group W Indian Ocean
Mascarene Plain 119 B5 undersea feature W Indian Ocean
Mascarene Plateau 119 B5 undersea feature W Indian Ocean
Maseru 56 D4 country capital (Lesotho) W Lesotho
Mashhad 98 E2 var. Meshed. Khorāsān, NE Iran
Mas-ha 97 D7 W Bank
Masindi 51 B6 W Uganda
Masīra see Maşīrah, Jazīrat
Masira, Gulf of see Maşīrah, Khalīj
Maşīrah, Jazīrat 99 E5 var. Masīra. Island E Oman
Maşīrah, Khalīj 99 E5 var. Gulf of Masira. Bay E Oman
Masis see Büyükağrı Dağı
Maskat see Masqaţ
Mason City 23 F3 Iowa, C USA
Masqaţ 99 E5 var. Maskat, Eng. Muscat. Country capital (Oman) NE Oman
Massa 74 B3 Toscana, C Italy
Massachusetts 19 G3 off. Commonwealth of Massachusetts; also known as Bay State, Old Bay State, Old Colony State. State NE USA
Massawa 50 C4 var. Masawa, Amh. Mits'iwa. E Eritrea
Massenya 54 B3 Chari-Baguirmi, SW Chad
Massif Central 69 C5 plateau C France
Massif du Makay see Makay
Massoukou see Franceville
Masterton 129 D5 Wellington, North Island, NZ
Masty 85 B5 Rus. Mosty. Hrodzyenskaya Voblasts', W Belarus
Masuda 109 B6 Shimane, Honshū, SW Japan
Masuku see Franceville
Masvingo 56 D3 prev. Fort Victoria, Nyanda, Victoria. Masvingo, SE Zimbabwe
Maşyāf 96 B3 Fr. Misiaf. Ḩamāh, C Syria
Matadi 55 B6 Bas-Zaïre, W Dem. Rep. Congo
Matagalpa 30 D3 Matagalpa, C Nicaragua
Matale 110 D3 Central Province, C Sri Lanka
Matam 52 C3 NE Senegal
Matamata 128 D3 Waikato, North Island, NZ
Matamoros 28 D3 Coahuila de Zaragoza, NE Mexico
Matamoros 29 E2 Tamaulipas, C Mexico
Matane 17 E4 Québec, SE Canada
Matanzas 32 B2 Matanzas, NW Cuba
Matara 110 D4 Southern Province, S Sri Lanka
Mataram 116 D5 Pulau Lombok, C Indonesia
Mataró 71 G2 anc. Illuro. Cataluña, E Spain
Mataura 129 B7 river South Island, NZ
Mataura 129 B7 Southland, South Island, NZ
Mata Uta see Matā'utu
Matā'utu 123 E4 var. Mata Uta. Dependent territory capital (Wallis and Futuna) Île Uvea, Wallis and Futuna
Matera 75 E5 Basilicata, S Italy
Matías Romero 29 F5 Oaxaca, SE Mexico
Mato Grosso 41 E4 prev. Vila Bela da Santissima Trindade. Mato Grosso, W Brazil
Mato Grosso do Sul 41 E4 off. Estado de Mato Grosso do Sul. State S Brazil
Mato Grosso, Planalto de 34 C4 plateau C Brazil
Matosinhos 70 B2 prev. Matozinhos. Porto, NW Portugal
Matsue 109 B6 var. Matsuye, Matue. Shimane, Honshū, SW Japan
Matsumoto 109 C5 var. Matumoto. Nagano, Honshū, S Japan
Matsuyama 109 B7 var. Matuyama. Ehime, Shikoku, SW Japan
Matsuye see Matsue
Matterhorn 73 A8 It. Monte Cervino. Mountain Italy/Switzerland see also Cervino, Monte
Matthews Ridge 37 F2 N Guyana
Matthew Town 32 D2 Great Inagua, S Bahamas
Matucana 38 C4 Lima, W Peru
Matue see Matsue
Matumoto see Matsumoto
Maturín 37 E2 Monagas, NE Venezuela
Matuyama see Matsuyama
Mau 113 E3 var. Maunāth Bhanjan. Uttar Pradesh, N India
Maui 25 B8 island Hawai'i, USA, C Pacific Ocean
Maulmain see Moulmein
Maun 56 C3 Ngamiland, C Botswana
Maunāth Bhanjan see Mau
Mauren 72 E1 NE Liechtenstein
Mauritania 52 C2 Ar. Mūrītānīyah. Country W Africa
Mauritius 57 H3 Fr. Maurice. Country W Indian Ocean
Mauritius 119 B5 island W Indian Ocean
Mawlamyine see Moulmein
Mawson 132 D2 Australian research station Antarctica
Maya 30 B1 river E Russian Federation
Mayadin see Al Mayādīn
Mayaguana 32 D2 island SE Bahamas
Mayaguana Passage 32 D2 passage SE Bahamas
Mayagüez 33 F3 W Puerto Rico
Mayamey 98 D2 Semnān, N Iran
Maya Mountains 30 B2 Sp. Montañas Mayas. Mountain range Belize/Guatemala
Maych'ew 50 C4 var. Mai Chio, It. Mai Ceu. N Ethiopia
Maydān Shahr 101 E4 Wardag, E Afghanistan
Mayebashi see Maebashi
Mayfield 129 B6 Canterbury, South Island, NZ
Maykop 89 A7 Respublika Adygeya, SW Russian Federation
Maymana see Meymaneh
Maymyo 114 B3 Mandalay, C Myanmar
Mayo see Maio
Mayor Island 128 D3 island NE NZ
Mayor Pablo Lagerenza see Capitán Pablo Lagerenza
Mayotte 57 F2 French territorial collectivity E Africa
May Pen 32 B5 C Jamaica
Mazabuka 56 D2 Southern, S Zambia
Mazaca see Kayseri
Mazār-e Sharīf 101 E3 var. Mazār-i Sharif. Balkh, N Afghanistan
Mazār-i Sharif see Mazār-e Sharīf
Mazatlán 28 C3 Sinaloa, C Mexico
Mažeikiai 84 B3 Mažeikiai, NW Lithuania
Mazirbe 84 C2 Talsi, NW Latvia
Mazra'a see Al Mazra'ah
Mazury 76 D3 physical region NE Poland
Mazyr 85 C7 Rus. Mozyr'. Homyel'skaya Voblasts', SE Belarus
Mbabane 56 D4 country capital (Swaziland) NW Swaziland
Mbacké see Mbaké
M'Baiki see Mbaïki
Mbaïki 55 C5 var. M'Baiki. Lobaye, SW Central African Republic
Mbaké 52 B3 var. Mbacké. W Senegal
Mbala 56 D1 prev. Abercorn. Northern, NE Zambia
Mbale 51 C6 E Uganda
Mbandaka 55 C5 prev. Coquilhatville. Equateur, NW Dem. Rep. Congo
M'Banza Congo 56 B1 var. Mbanza Congo; prev. São Salvador, São Salvador do Congo. Zaire, NW Angola
Mbanza-Ngungu 55 B6 Bas-Zaïre, W Dem. Rep. Congo
Mbarara 51 B6 SW Uganda
Mbé 54 B4 Nord, N Cameroon
Mbeya 51 C7 Mbeya, SW Tanzania
Mbomou see Bomu
M'Bomu see Bomu
Mbour 52 B3 W Senegal
Mbuji-Mayi 55 D7 prev. Bakwanga. Kasai Oriental, S Dem. Rep. Congo
McAlester 27 G2 Oklahoma, C USA
McAllen 27 G5 Texas, SW USA
McCamey 27 E3 Texas, SW USA
McClintock Channel 15 F2 channel Nunavut, N Canada
McComb 20 B3 Mississippi, S USA
McCook 23 E4 Nebraska, C USA
McKean Island 123 E3 island Phoenix Islands, C Kiribati
McKinley, Mount 14 C3 var. Denali. Mountain Alaska, USA
McKinley Park 14 C3 Alaska, USA
McMinnville 24 B3 Oregon, NW USA
McMurdo Base 132 B4 US research station Antarctica
McPherson see Fort McPherson
McPherson 23 E5 Kansas, C USA
Mdantsane 56 D5 Eastern Cape, SE South Africa
Mead, Lake 25 D6 reservoir Arizona/Nevada, W USA
Meghālaya 91 G3 state, NE India
Mecca see Makkah
Mechelen 65 C5 Eng. Mechlin, Fr. Malines. Antwerpen, C Belgium
Mecklenburger Bucht 72 C2 bay N Germany
Mecsek 77 C7 mountain range SW Hungary
Medan 116 B3 Sumatera, E Indonesia
Medeba see Ma'dabā
Medellín 36 B3 Antioquia, NW Colombia
Médenine 49 F2 var. Madanīyīn. SE Tunisia
Medford 24 B4 Oregon, NW USA
Medgidia 86 D5 Constanţa, SE Romania
Mediaş 86 B4 Ger. Mediasch, Hung. Medgyes. Sibiu, C Romania
Medicine Hat 15 F5 Alberta, SW Canada
Medinaceli 71 E2 Castilla-León, N Spain
Medina del Campo 70 D2 Castilla-León, N Spain
Mediterranean Sea 80 D3 Fr. Mer Méditerranée. Sea Africa/Asia/Europe
Médoc 69 B5 cultural region SW France
Medvezh'yegorsk 88 B3 Respublika Kareliya, NW Russian Federation
Meekatharra 125 B5 Western Australia
Meemu Atoll see Mulaku Atoll
Meerssen 65 D6 var. Mersen. Limburg, SE Netherlands
Meerut 112 D2 Uttar Pradesh, N India
Mehdia see Mahdia
Meheso see Mī'ēso
Me Hka see Nmai Hka
Mehrīz 98 D3 Yazd, C Iran
Mehtar Lām see Mehtarlām
Mehtarlām 101 F4 var. Mehtar Lām, Meterlam, Methariam, Metharlam. Laghmān, E Afghanistan
Meiktila 114 B3 Mandalay, C Myanmar
Mejillones 42 B2 Antofagasta, N Chile
Mek'elē 50 C4 var. Makale. N Ethiopia
Mékhé 52 B3 NW Senegal
Mekong 102 D3 var. Lan-ts'ang Chiang, Cam. Mékôngk, Chin. Lancang Jiang, Lao. Mènam Khong, Th. Mae Nam Khong, Tib. Dza Chu, Vtn. Sông Tiên Giang. River SE Asia
Mékôngk see Mekong
Mekong, Mouths of the 115 E6 delta S Vietnam
Melaka 116 B3 var. Malacca. Melaka, Peninsular Malaysia
Melanesia 122 D3 island group W Pacific Ocean
Melanesian Basin 120 C2 undersea feature W Pacific Ocean
Melbourne 127 C7 state capital Victoria, SE Australia
Melbourne 21 E4 Florida, SE USA
Melghir, Chott 49 E2 var. Chott Melrhir. Salt lake E Algeria
Melilla 58 B5 anc. Rusaddir, Russadir. Melilla, Spain, N Africa
Melilla 48 D2 enclave Spain, N Africa
Melita 15 F5 Manitoba, S Canada
Melitopol' 87 F4 Zaporiz'ka Oblast', SE Ukraine
Melle 65 B5 Oost-Vlaanderen, NW Belgium
Mellerud 63 B6 Västra Götaland, S Sweden
Mellieha 80 B5 E Malta
Mellizo Sur, Cerro 43 A7 mountain S Chile
Melo 42 E4 Cerro Largo, NE Uruguay
Melsungen 72 B4 Hessen, C Germany
Melun 68 C3 anc. Melodunum. Seine-et-Marne, N France
Melville Island 124 D2 island Northern Territory, N Australia
Melville Island 15 E2 island Parry Islands, Northwest Territories/Nunavut, NW Canada
Melville, Lake 17 F2 lake Newfoundland and Labrador, E Canada
Melville Peninsula 15 G3 peninsula Northwest Territories, NE Canada
Membidj see Manbij
Memmingen 73 B6 Bayern, S Germany
Memphis 20 C1 Tennessee, S USA
Ménaka 53 F3 Goa, E Mali
Menaldum 64 D1 Fris. Menaam. Friesland, N Netherlands
Mènam Khong see Mekong
Mendaña Fracture Zone 131 F4 tectonic feature E Pacific Ocean
Mende 69 C5 anc. Mimatum. Lozère, S France
Mendeleyev Ridge 133 B2 undersea feature Arctic Ocean
Mendocino Fracture Zone 130 D2 tectonic feature NE Pacific Ocean
Mendoza 42 B4 Mendoza, W Argentina
Menemen 94 A3 İzmir, W Turkey
Menengiyn Tal 105 F2 plain E Mongolia
Menongue 56 B2 var. Vila Serpa Pinto, Port. Serpa Pinto. Cuando Cubango, C Angola
Menorca 71 H3 Eng. Minorca; anc. Balearis Minor. Island Islas Baleares, Spain, W Mediterranean Sea
Mentawai, Kepulauan 116 A4 island group W Indonesia
Meppel 64 D2 Drenthe, NE Netherlands
Merano 74 C1 Ger. Meran. Trentino-Alto Adige, N Italy
Merca see Marka
Mercedes see Villa Mercedes
Mercedes 42 D3 Corrientes, NE Argentina
Mercedes 42 D4 Soriano, SW Uruguay
Meredith, Lake 27 E1 reservoir Texas, SW USA
Merefa 87 G2 Kharkivs'ka Oblast', E Ukraine
Mergui 115 B6 Tenasserim, S Myanmar
Mergui Archipelago 115 B6 island group S Myanmar
Meriç see Maritsa
Mérida 70 C4 anc. Augusta Emerita. Extremadura, W Spain
Mérida 36 C2 Mérida, W Venezuela
Mérida 29 H3 Yucatán, SW Mexico
Meridian 20 C2 Mississippi, S USA
Mérignac 69 B5 Gironde, SW France
Merkinė 85 B5 Varėna, S Lithuania
Merowe 50 B3 desert W Sudan
Merredin 125 B6 Western Australia
Mersen see Meerssen
Mersey 67 D5 river NW England, UK
Mersin 94 C4 İçel, S Turkey
Mērsrags 84 C3 Talsi, NW Latvia
Meru 51 C6 Eastern, C Kenya
Merzifon 94 D2 Amasya, N Turkey
Merzig 73 A5 Saarland, SW Germany
Mesa 26 B2 Arizona, SW USA
Meshed see Mashhad
Mesopotamia 35 C5 var. Mesopotamia Argentina. Physical region NE Argentina
Mesopotamia Argentina see Mesopotamia
Messalo, Rio 57 E2 var. Mualo. River NE Mozambique
Messana see Messina
Messene see Messina
Messina 75 D7 var. Messana, Messene; anc. Zancle. Sicilia, Italy, C Mediterranean Sea
Messina see Musina
Messina, Stretto di 75 D7 Eng. Strait of Messina. Strait SW Italy
Messíni 83 B6 Pelopónnisos, S Greece
Mestghanem see Mostaganem
Mestia 95 F1 var. Mestiya. N Georgia
Mestiya see Mestia
Mestre 74 C2 Veneto, NE Italy
Meta 34 B2 off. Departamento del Meta. Province C Colombia
Metairie 20 B3 Louisiana, S USA
Metán 42 C2 Salta, N Argentina
Metapán 30 B2 Santa Ana, NW El Salvador
Meta, Río 36 D3 river Colombia/Venezuela
Meterlam see Mehtarlām
Methariam see Mehtarlām
Metharlam see Mehtarlām
Metković 78 B4 Dubrovnik-Neretva, SE Croatia
Métsovo 82 B4 prev. Métsovon. Ípeiros, C Greece
Metz 68 D3 anc. Divodurum Mediomatricum, Mediomatrica, Metis. Moselle, NE France
Meulaboh 116 A3 Sumatera, W Indonesia
Meuse 65 C6 Dut. Maas. River W Europe see also Maas
Meuse 90 D3 department NE France
Mexcala, Río see Balsas, Río
Mexicali 28 A1 Baja California, NW Mexico
Mexico 28 C3 var. Méjico, México, Sp. Estados Unidos Mexicanos. Country N Central America
Mexico 23 G4 Missouri, C USA
México 29 E4 var. Ciudad de México, Eng. Mexico City. Country capital (Mexico) México, C Mexico
Mexico City see México
Mexico, Gulf of 29 F2 Sp. Golfo de México. Gulf W Atlantic Ocean
Meyadine see Al Mayādīn
Meymaneh 100 D3 var. Maimāna, Maymana. Fāryāb, NW Afghanistan
Mezen' 88 D3 river NW Russian Federation
Mezőtúr 77 D7 Jász-Nagykun-Szolnok, E Hungary
Mġarr 80 A5 Gozo, N Malta
Miahuatlán 29 F5 var. Miahuatlán de Porfirio Díaz. Oaxaca, SE Mexico
Miahuatlán de Porfirio Díaz see Miahuatlán
Miami 21 F5 Florida, SE USA
Miami 27 G1 Oklahoma, C USA
Miami Beach 21 F5 Florida, SE USA
Mīāneh 98 C2 var. Miyāneh. Āžarbāyjān-e Khāvarī, NW Iran
Mianyang 106 B5 Sichuan, C China
Miastko 76 C2 Ger. Rummelsburg in Pommern. Pomorskie, N Poland
Mi Chai see Nong Khai
Michalovce 77 E5 Ger. Grossmichel, Hung. Nagymihály. Košický Kraj, E Slovakia
Michigan 18 C1 off. State of Michigan; also known as Great Lakes State, Lake State, Wolverine State. State N USA
Michigan, Lake 18 C2 lake N USA
Michurinsk 89 B5 Tambovskaya Oblast', W Russian Federation
Micoud 33 F2 SE Saint Lucia
Micronesia 122 B1 Country W Pacific Ocean
Micronesia 122 C1 island group W Pacific Ocean
Mid-Atlantic Cordillera see Mid-Atlantic Ridge
Mid-Atlantic Ridge 44 C3 var. Mid-Atlantic Cordillera, Mid-Atlantic Rise, Mid-Atlantic Swell. Undersea feature Atlantic Ocean
Mid-Atlantic Rise see Mid-Atlantic Ridge
Mid-Atlantic Swell see Mid-Atlantic Ridge
Middelburg 65 B5 Zeeland, SW Netherlands
Middelharnis 64 B4 Zuid-Holland, SW Netherlands
Middelkerke 65 A5 West-Vlaanderen, W Belgium
Middle America Trench 13 B7 undersea feature E Pacific Ocean
Middle Andaman 111 F2 island Andaman Islands, India, NE Indian Ocean
Middlesboro 18 C5 Kentucky, S USA
Middlesbrough 67 D5 N England, UK
Middletown 19 F4 New Jersey, NE USA
Middletown 19 F3 New York, NE USA
Mid-Indian Basin 119 C5 undersea feature N Indian Ocean
Mid-Indian Ridge 119 C5 var. Central Indian Ridge. Undersea feature C Indian Ocean
Midland 18 C3 Michigan, N USA
Midland 16 D5 Ontario, S Canada
Midland 27 E3 Texas, SW USA
Mid-Pacific Mountains 130 C2 var. Mid-Pacific Seamounts. Undersea feature NW Pacific Ocean
Mid-Pacific Seamounts see Mid-Pacific Mountains
Midway Islands 130 D2 US territory C Pacific Ocean
Miechów 77 D5 Małopolskie, S Poland
Międzyrzec Podlaski 76 E3 Lubelskie, E Poland
Międzyrzecz 76 B3 Ger. Meseritz. Lubuskie, W Poland
Mielec 77 D5 Podkarpackie, SE Poland
Miercurea-Ciuc 86 C4 Ger. Szeklerburg, Hung. Csíkszereda. Harghita, C Romania
Mieres del Camín see Mieres del Camino
Mieres del Camino 108 D1 var. Mieres del Camín. Asturias, NW Spain
Mieresch see Mureş
Mī'ēso 51 D5 var. Meheso, Miesso. C Ethiopia
Miesso see Mī'ēso
Miguel Asua 28 D3 var. Miguel Auza. Zacatecas, C Mexico
Miguel Auza see Miguel Asua
Mijdrecht 64 C3 Utrecht, C Netherlands
Mikashevichy 85 C7 Pol. Mikaszewicze, Rus. Mikashevichi. Brestskaya Voblasts', SW Belarus
Mikhaylovka 89 B6 Volgogradskaya Oblast', SW Russian Federation
Míkonos see Mýkonos
Mikre 82 C2 Lovech, N Bulgaria
Mikun' 88 D4 Respublika Komi, NW Russian Federation
Mikuni-sanmyaku 109 D5 mountain range Honshū, N Japan
Mikura-jima 109 D6 island E Japan
Milagro 38 B2 Guayas, SW Ecuador
Milan see Milano
Milange 57 E2 Zambézia, NE Mozambique
Milano 74 B2 Eng. Milan, Ger. Mailand; anc. Mediolanum. Lombardia, N Italy
Milas 94 A4 Muğla, SW Turkey
Milashavichy 85 C7 Rus. Milashevichi. Homyel'skaya Voblasts', SE Belarus
Mildura 127 C6 Victoria, SE Australia
Mile see Mili Atoll
Miles 127 D5 Queensland, E Australia
Miles City 22 C2 Montana, NW USA
Milford Haven 67 C6 prev. Milford. SW Wales, UK
Milford Sound 129 A6 inlet South Island, NZ
Milford Sound 129 A6 Southland, South Island, NZ
Mili Atoll 122 D2 var. Mile. Atoll Ratak Chain, SE Marshall Islands
Mil'kovo 93 H3 Kamchatskaya Oblast', E Russian Federation
Milk River 22 C1 river Montana, NW USA
Milk River 15 E5 Alberta, SW Canada
Milk, Wadi el 88 B4 var. Wadi al Malik. River C Sudan
Milledgeville 21 E2 Georgia, SE USA
Mille Lacs Lake 23 F2 lake Minnesota, N USA
Millennium Island 160 C8 prev. Caroline Island, Thornton Island. Atoll Line Islands, E Kiribati
Millerovo 89 B6 Rostovskaya Oblast', SW Russian Federation
Mílos 83 C7 island Kykládes, Greece, Aegean Sea
Mílos 83 C6 Mílos, Kykládes, Greece, Aegean Sea
Milton 129 B7 Otago, South Island, NZ
Milton Keynes 67 D6 SE England, UK
Milwaukee 18 B3 Wisconsin, N USA
Min see Fujian
Mīnā' Qābūs 118 B3 NE Oman
Minas Gerais 41 F3 off. Estado de Minas Gerais. State E Brazil
Minatitlán 29 F4 Veracruz-Llave, E Mexico
Minbu 114 A3 Magwe, W Myanmar
Minch, The 66 B3 var. North Minch. Strait NW Scotland, UK
Mindanao 117 F2 island S Philippines
Mindanao Sea see Bohol Sea
Mindelheim 73 C6 Bayern, S Germany
Mindello see Mindelo
Mindelo 52 A2 var. Mindello; prev. Porto Grande. São Vicente, N Cape Verde
Minden 72 B4 anc. Minthun. Nordrhein-Westfalen, NW Germany
Mindoro 117 E2 island N Philippines
Mindoro Strait 117 E2 strait W Philippines
Mineral Wells 27 F2 Texas, SW USA
Mingäçevir 95 G2 Rus. Mingechaur, Mingechevir. C Azerbaijan
Mingāora 112 C1 var. Mingora, Mongora. North-West Frontier Province, N Pakistan
Mingora see Mingāora
Minho 70 B2 former province N Portugal
Minho, Rio 70 B2 Sp. Miño. river Portugal/Spain see also Miño
Minicoy Island 110 B3 island SW India
Minius see Miño
Minna 53 G4 Niger, C Nigeria
Minneapolis 23 F2 Minnesota, N USA
Minnesota 23 F2 off. State of Minnesota; also known as Gopher State, New England of the West, North Star State. State N USA
Miño 70 B2 var. Mino, Minius, Port. Rio Minho. River Portugal/Spain see also Minho, Rio
Mino see Miño
Minot 23 E1 North Dakota, N USA
Minsk 85 C6 country capital (Belarus) Minskaya Voblasts', C Belarus
Minskaya Wzvyshsha 85 C6 mountain range C Belarus
Mińsk Mazowiecki 76 D3 var. Nowo-Minsk. Mazowieckie, C Poland
Minto, Lac 16 D2 lake Québec, C Canada
Minya see El Minya
Miraflores 28 C3 Baja California Sur, W Mexico
Miranda de Ebro 71 E1 La Rioja, N Spain
Miri 116 D3 Sarawak, East Malaysia
Mirim Lagoon 41 E5 var. Lake Mirim, Sp. Laguna Merín. Lagoon Brazil/Uruguay
Mirim, Lake see Mirim Lagoon
Mírina see Mýrina
Mīrjāveh 98 E4 Sīstān va Balūchestān, SE Iran
Mirny 132 C3 Russian research station Antarctica
Mirnyy 93 F3 Respublika Sakha (Yakutiya), NE Russian Federation
Mīrpur Khās 112 B3 Sind, SE Pakistan
Mirtóo Pélagos 83 C6 Eng. Mirtoan Sea; anc. Myrtoum Mare. Sea S Greece
Miskito Coast see Mosquito Coast
Miskitos, Cayos 31 E2 island group NE Nicaragua
Miskolc 77 D6 Borsod-Abaúj-Zemplén, NE Hungary
Misool, Pulau 117 F4 island Maluku, E Indonesia
Mişrātah 49 F2 var. Misurata. NW Libya
Mission 27 G5 Texas, SW USA
Mississippi 20 B2 off. State of Mississippi; also known as Bayou State, Magnolia State. State SE USA
Mississippi Delta 20 B4 delta Louisiana, S USA
Mississippi River 13 C6 river C USA
Missoula 22 B1 Montana, NW USA

Missouri 23 F5 off. State of Missouri; also known as Bullion State, Show Me State. State C USA
Missouri River 23 E3 river C USA
Mistassini, Lac 16 D3 lake Québec, SE Canada
Mistelbach an der Zaya 73 E6 Niederösterreich, NE Austria
Misti, Volcán 39 E4 mountain S Peru
Misurata see Mişrātah
Mitchell 127 D5 Queensland, E Australia
Mitchell 23 E3 South Dakota, N USA
Mitchell, Mount 21 E1 mountain North Carolina, SE USA
Mitchell River 126 C2 river Queensland, NE Australia
Mi Tho see My Tho
Mitilíni see Mytilíni
Mito 109 D5 Ibaraki, Honshū, S Japan
Mits'iwa see Massawa
Mitspe Ramon see Mizpé Ramon
Mitú 36 C4 Vaupés, SE Colombia
Mitumba, Monts 55 E7 var. Chaîne des Mitumba, Mitumba Range. Mountain range E Dem. Rep. Congo
Mitumba Range see Mitumba, Monts
Miyako 108 D4 Iwate, Honshū, C Japan
Miyako-jima 109 D6 island Sakishima-shotō, SW Japan
Miyakonojō 109 B8 var. Miyakonzyô. Miyazaki, Kyūshū, SW Japan
Miyakonzyô see Miyakonojō
Miyāneh see Mīāneh
Miyazaki 109 B8 Miyazaki, Kyūshū, SW Japan
Mizil 86 C5 Prahova, SE Romania
Miziya 82 C1 Vratsa, NW Bulgaria
Mizpé Ramon 97 A7 var. Mitspe Ramon. Southern, S Israel
Mjøsa 63 B6 var. Mjøsen. Lake S Norway
Mjøsen see Mjøsa
Mladenovac 78 D4 Serbia, C Serbia and Montenegro (Yugo.)
Mława 76 D3 Mazowieckie, C Poland
Mljet 79 B5 It. Meleda; anc. Melita. Island S Croatia
Mmabatho 56 C4 North-West, N South Africa
Moab 22 B5 Utah, W USA
Moab, Kir of see Al Karak
Moa Island 126 C1 island Queensland, NE Australia
Moanda 55 B6 var. Mouanda. Haut-Ogooué, SE Gabon
Moba 55 E7 Shaba, E Dem. Rep. Congo
Mobay see Montego Bay
Mobaye 55 C5 Basse-Kotto, S Central African Republic
Moberly 23 G4 Missouri, C USA
Mobile 20 C3 Alabama, S USA
Mobutu Sese Seko, Lac see Albert, Lake
Mochudi 56 C4 Kgatleng, SE Botswana
Mocímboa da Praia 57 F2 var. Vila de Mocímboa da Praia. Cabo Delgado, N Mozambique
Môco 56 B2 var. Morro de Môco. Mountain W Angola
Mocoa 36 A4 Putumayo, SW Colombia
Mocuba 57 E3 Zambézia, NE Mozambique
Modena 74 B3 anc. Mutina. Emilia-Romagna, N Italy
Modesto 25 B6 California, W USA
Modica 75 C7 anc. Motyca. Sicilia, Italy, C Mediterranean Sea
Modimolle 56 D4 var. Nylstroom, NE South Africa
Modriča 78 C3 Republika Srpska, N Bosnia and Herzegovina
Moe 127 C7 Victoria, SE Australia
Moero, Lac see Mweru, Lake
Mogadishu see Muqdisho
Mogilno 76 C3 Kujawski-pomorskie, C Poland
Mohammedia 48 C2 prev. Fédala. NW Morocco
Mohave, Lake 25 D7 reservoir Arizona/Nevada, W USA
Mohawk River 19 F3 river New York, NE USA
Mohéli 57 F2 var. Mwali, Mohilla, Mohila, Fr. Moili. Island S Comoros
Mohila see Mohéli
Mohilla see Mohéli
Mohns Ridge 61 F3 undersea feature Greenland Sea/Norwegian Sea
Moho 39 E4 Puno, SW Peru
Mohoro 51 C7 Pwani, E Tanzania
Mohyliv-Podil's'kyy 86 D3 Rus. Mogilev-Podol'skiy. Vinnyts'ka Oblast', C Ukraine
Moi 63 A6 Rogaland, S Norway
Moili see Mohéli
Mo i Rana 62 C3 Nordland, C Norway
Mõisaküla 84 D3 Ger. Moiseküll. Viljandimaa, S Estonia
Moissac 69 B6 Tarn-et-Garonne, S France
Mojácar 71 E5 Andalucía, S Spain
Mojave Desert 25 D7 plain California, W USA
Moktama see Martaban
Mol 65 C5 prev. Moll. Antwerpen, N Belgium
Moldavia see Moldova
Moldavian SSR/Moldavskaya SSR see Moldova
Molde 63 A5 Møre og Romsdal, S Norway
Moldo-Too, Khrebet 101 G2 prev. Khrebet Moldotau. Mountain range C Kyrgyzstan
Moldova 86 D3 var. Moldavia; prev. Moldavian SSR, Rus. Moldavskaya SSR. Country SE Europe
Moldova Nouă 86 A4 Ger. Neumoldowa, Hung. Újmoldova. Caraş-Severin, SW Romania
Moldoveanul see Vârful Moldoveanu
Molfetta 75 E5 Puglia, SE Italy
Mollendo 39 E4 Arequipa, SW Peru
Mölndal 63 B7 Västra Götaland, S Sweden
Molochans'k 87 G4 Rus. Molochansk. Zaporiz'ka Oblast', SE Ukraine
Molodezhnaya 132 C2 Russian research station Antarctica
Moloka'i 25 B8 var. Molokai. Island Hawai'i, USA, C Pacific Ocean
Molokai Fracture Zone 131 E2 tectonic feature NE Pacific Ocean
Molopo 56 C4 seasonal river Botswana/South Africa
Mólos 83 B5 Stereá Ellás, C Greece
Moluccas see Maluku
Molucca Sea 117 F4 Ind. Laut Maluku. Sea E Indonesia
Mombasa 51 D7 international airport Coast, SE Kenya
Mombasa 51 D7 Coast, SE Kenya
Mombetsu see Monbetsu
Momchilgrad 82 D3 prev. Mastanli. Kŭrdzhali, S Bulgaria
Møn 63 B8 prev. Möen. Island SE Denmark
Monaco 69 E6 Country W Europe
Monaco 69 C7 var. Monaco-Ville; anc. Monoecus. Country capital (Monaco) S Monaco
Monaco, Port de 69 C8 bay S Monaco
Monaco-Ville see Monaco
Monahans 27 E3 Texas, SW USA
Mona, Isla 33 E3 island W Puerto Rico
Mona Passage 33 E3 Sp. Canal de la Mona. Channel Dominican Republic/Puerto Rico
Monbetsu 108 D2 var. Mombetsu, Monbetu. Hokkaidō, NE Japan
Monbetu see Monbetsu
Moncalieri 74 A2 Piemonte, NW Italy
Monchegorsk 88 C2 Murmanskaya Oblast', NW Russian Federation
Monclova 28 D2 Coahuila de Zaragoza, NE Mexico
Moncton 17 F4 New Brunswick, SE Canada
Mondovì 74 A2 Piemonte, NW Italy
Monfalcone 74 D2 Friuli-Venezia Giulia, NE Italy
Monforte see Monforte de Lemos
Monforte de Lemos 92 C1 var. Monforte. Galicia, NW Spain
Mongo 54 C3 Guéra, C Chad
Mongolia 104 C2 Mong. Mongol Uls. Country E Asia
Mongolia, Plateau of 102 D1 plateau E Mongolia
Mongora see Mingāora
Mongu 56 C2 Western, W Zambia
Monkchester see Newcastle upon Tyne
Monkey Bay 57 E2 Southern, SE Malawi
Monkey River see Monkey River Town
Monkey River Town 30 C2 var. Monkey River. Toledo, SE Belize
Monoecus see Monaco
Mono Lake 25 C6 lake California, W USA
Monovar 71 F4 Cat. Monover. País Valenciano, E Spain
Monover see Monovar
Monroe 20 B2 Louisiana, S USA
Monrovia 52 C5 country capital (Liberia) W Liberia
Mons 65 B6 Dut. Bergen. Hainaut, S Belgium
Monselice 74 C2 Veneto, NE Italy
Montagnes Rocheuses see Rocky Mountains
Montana 22 B1 off. State of Montana; also known as Mountain State, Treasure State. State NW USA
Montana 82 C2 prev. Ferdinand, Mikhaylovgrad. Montana, NW Bulgaria
Montargis 68 C4 Loiret, C France
Montauban 69 B6 Tarn-et-Garonne, S France
Montbéliard 90 D4 Doubs, E France
Mont Cenis, Col du 69 D5 pass E France
Mont-de-Marsan 69 B6 Landes, SW France
Monteagudo 39 G4 Chuquisaca, S Bolivia
Monte-Carlo 69 C8 NE Monaco
Monte Caseros 42 D3 Corrientes, NE Argentina
Monte Cristi 32 D3 var. San Fernando de Monte Cristi. NW Dominican Republic
Montegiardino 74 E2 SE San Marino
Montego Bay 32 A4 var. Mobay. W Jamaica
Montélimar 69 D5 anc. Acunum Acusio, Montilium Adhemari. Drôme, E France
Montemorelos 29 E3 Nuevo León, NE Mexico
Montenegro 79 C5 Serb. Crna Gora. Admin. region republic SW Serbia and Montenegro (Yugo.)
Monte Patria 42 B3 Coquimbo, N Chile
Monterey see Monterrey
Monterey 25 B6 California, W USA
Monterey Bay 25 A6 bay California, W USA
Montería 36 B2 Córdoba, NW Colombia
Montero 39 G4 Santa Cruz, C Bolivia
Monterrey 29 E3 var. Monterey. Nuevo León, NE Mexico
Montes Claros 41 F3 Minas Gerais, SE Brazil
Montevideo 42 D4 country capital (Uruguay) Montevideo, S Uruguay
Montevideo 23 F2 Minnesota, N USA
Montgenèvre, Col de 69 D5 pass France/Italy
Montgomery 20 D2 state capital Alabama, S USA
Monthey 73 A7 Valais, SW Switzerland
Montluçon 68 C5 Allier, C France
Montoro 92 D4 Andalucía, S Spain
Montpelier 19 G2 state capital Vermont, NE USA
Montpellier 69 C6 Hérault, S France
Montréal 17 E4 Eng. Montreal. Québec, SE Canada
Montrose 22 C5 Colorado, C USA
Montrose 66 D3 E Scotland, UK
Montserrat 33 G3 var. Emerald Isle. UK dependent territory E West Indies
Monywa 114 B3 Sagaing, C Myanmar
Monza 74 B2 Lombardia, N Italy
Monze 56 D2 Southern, S Zambia
Monzón 71 F2 Aragón, NE Spain
Moonie 127 D5 Queensland, E Australia
Moora 125 A6 Western Australia
Moore 27 G1 Oklahoma, C USA
Moore, Lake 125 B6 lake Western Australia
Moorhead 45 F2 Minnesota, N USA
Moose 16 C3 river Ontario, S Canada
Moosehead Lake 19 G1 lake Maine, NE USA
Moosonee 16 C3 Ontario, SE Canada
Mopti 53 E3 Mopti, C Mali
Moquegua 39 E4 Moquegua, SE Peru
Mora 63 C5 Kopparberg, C Sweden
Morales 30 C2 Izabal, E Guatemala
Morant Bay 32 B5 E Jamaica
Moratalla 71 E4 Murcia, SE Spain
Morava 77 C5 var. March. River C Europe see also March
Morava see Velika Morava
Moravia 77 B5 Iowa, C USA
Moray Firth 66 C3 inlet N Scotland, UK
Morea see Pelopónnisos
Moreau River 22 D2 river South Dakota, N USA
Moree 127 D5 New South Wales, SE Australia
Morelia 29 E4 Michoacán de Ocampo, S Mexico
Morena, Sierra 70 C4 mountain range S Spain
Moreni 86 C5 Dâmboviţa, S Romania
Mórfou 80 C5 W Cyprus
Morgan City 20 B3 Louisiana, S USA
Morghāb, Daryā-ye 100 D3 var. Murgab, Murghab, Turkm. Murgap, Murgap Deryasy. River Afghanistan/Turkmenistan see also Murgap
Morioka 108 D4 Iwate, Honshū, C Japan
Morlaix 68 A3 Finistère, NW France
Mornington Abyssal Plain 45 A7 undersea feature SE Pacific Ocean
Mornington Island 126 B2 island Wellesley Islands, Queensland, N Australia
Morocco 48 B3 Ar. Al Mamlakah. Country N Africa
Morocco see Marrakech
Morogoro 51 C7 Morogoro, E Tanzania
Moro Gulf 117 E3 gulf S Philippines
Morón 32 C2 Ciego de Ávila, C Cuba
Mörön 104 D2 Hövsgöl, N Mongolia
Morondava 57 F3 Toliara, W Madagascar
Moroni 57 F2 country capital (Comoros) Grande Comore, NW Comoros
Morotai, Pulau 117 F3 island Maluku, E Indonesia
Morotiri see Marotiri
Morrinsville 128 D3 Waikato, North Island, NZ
Morris 23 F2 Minnesota, N USA
Morris Jesup, Kap 61 E1 headland N Greenland
Morro de Môco see Môco
Morvan 68 D4 physical region C France
Moscow see Moskva
Moscow 24 C2 Idaho, NW USA
Mosel 73 A5 Fr. Moselle. River W Europe see also Moselle
Moselle 65 E8 Ger. Mosel. River W Europe see also Mosel
Moselle 68 D3 department NE France
Mosgiel 129 B7 Otago, South Island, NZ
Moshi 51 C7 Kilimanjaro, NE Tanzania
Mosjøen 62 B4 Nordland, C Norway
Moskva 89 B5 Eng. Moscow. Country capital (Russian Federation) Gorod Moskva, W Russian Federation
Moskva 101 E3 Rus. Moskovskiy; prev. Chubek. SW Tajikistan
Mosonmagyaróvár 77 C6 Ger. Wieselburg-Ungarisch-Altenburg; prev. Moson and Magyaróvár, Ger. Wieselburg and Ungarisch-Altenburg. Győr-Moson-Sopron, NW Hungary
Mosquito Coast 31 E3 var. Miskito Coast. Coastal region E Nicaragua
Mosquitos, Golfo de los 31 F4 Eng. Mosquito Gulf. Gulf N Panama
Moss 63 B6 Østfold, S Norway
Mosselbaai 56 C5 var. Mosselbai, Eng. Mossel Bay. Western Cape, SW South Africa
Mossendjo 55 B6 Le Niari, SW Congo
Mossoró 41 G2 Rio Grande do Norte, NE Brazil
Most 76 A4 Ger. Brüx. Ústecký Kraj, NW Czech Republic
Mosta 80 B5 var. Musta. C Malta
Mostaganem 48 D2 var. Mestghanem. NW Algeria
Mostar 78 C4 Federacija Bosna I Hercegovina, S Bosnia and Herzegovina
Mosul see Al Mawşil
Mota del Cuervo 71 E3 Castilla-La Mancha, C Spain
Motagua, Río 30 B2 river Guatemala/Honduras
Motril 70 D5 Andalucía, S Spain
Motru 86 B4 Gorj, SW Romania
Motueka 129 C5 Tasman, South Island, NZ
Motul 29 H3 var. Motul de Felipe Carrillo Puerto. Yucatán, SE Mexico
Motul de Felipe Carrillo Puerto see Motul
Mouanda see Moanda
Mouhoun see Black Volta
Mouila 55 A6 Ngounié, C Gabon
Mould Bay 15 E2 Prince Patrick Island, Northwest Territories/Nunavut, N Canada
Moulins 68 C4 Allier, C France
Moulmein 114 B4 var. Maulmain, Mawlamyine. Mon State, S Myanmar
Moundou 54 B4 Logone-Occidental, SW Chad
Moŭng Roessei 115 D5 Bătdâmbâng, W Cambodia
Moun Hou see Black Volta
Mountain Home 20 B1 Arkansas, C USA
Mount Ara see Büyükağrı Dağı
Mount Cook 129 B6 Canterbury, South Island, NZ
Mount Desert Island 19 H2 island Maine, NE USA
Mount Fuji see Fuji-san
Mount Gambier 127 B7 South Australia
Mount Isa 126 B3 Queensland, C Australia
Mount Magnet 125 B5 Western Australia
Mount Pleasant 23 G4 Iowa, C USA
Mount Pleasant 18 C3 Michigan, N USA
Mount Vernon 18 B5 Illinois, N USA
Mount Vernon 24 B1 Washington, NW USA
Mourdi, Dépression du 54 C2 desert lowland Chad/Sudan
Mouscron 65 A6 Dut. Moeskroen. Hainaut, W Belgium
Mouse River see Souris River
Moussoro 54 B3 Kanem, W Chad
Moyen Atlas 48 C2 Eng. Middle Atlas. Mountain range N Morocco
Mo'ynoq 100 C1 var. Mŭynoq, Rus. Muynak. Qoraqalpoghiston Respublikasi, NW Uzbekistan
Moyobamba 38 B2 San Martín, NW Peru
Moyu 104 B3 var. Karakax. Xinjiang Uygur Zizhiqu, NW China
Moyynkum, Peski 101 F1 Kaz. Moyynqum. Desert S Kazakhstan
Mozambique 57 E3 prev. People's Republic of Mozambique, Portuguese East Africa. Country S Africa
Mozambique Basin see Natal Basin
Mozambique Channel 57 E3 Fr. Canal de Mozambique, Mal. Lakandranon' i Mozambika. Strait W Indian Ocean
Mozambique Plateau 47 D7 var. Mozambique Rise. Undersea feature SW Indian Ocean
Mozambique Rise see Mozambique Plateau
Mpama 55 B6 river C Congo
Mpika 56 D2 Northern, NE Zambia
Mqinvartsveri see Kazbek
Mrągowo 76 D2 Ger. Sensburg. Olsztyn, NE Poland
Mtwara 51 D8 Mtwara, SE Tanzania
Mualo see Messalo, Rio
Muang Chiang Rai see Chiang Rai
Muang Kalasin see Kalasin
Muang Không 115 D5 Champasak, S Laos
Muang Khôngxédôn 115 D5 var. Khong Sedone. Salavan, S Laos
Muang Khon Kaen see Khon Kaen
Muang Lampang see Lampang
Muang Loei see Loei
Muang Lom Sak see Lom Sak
Muang Nakhon Sawan see Nakhon Sawan
Muang Namo 114 C3 Oudômxai, N Laos
Muang Nan see Nan
Muang Phalan 114 D4 var. Muang Phalane. Savannakhét, S Laos
Muang Phalane see Muang Phalan
Muang Phayao see Phayao
Muang Phitsanulok see Phitsanulok
Muang Phrae see Phrae
Muang Roi Et see Roi Et
Muang Sakon Nakhon see Sakon Nakhon
Muang Samut Prakan see Samut Prakan
Muang Sing 114 C3 Louang Namtha, N Laos
Muang Ubon see Ubon Ratchathani
Muar 116 B3 var. Bandar Maharani. Johor, Peninsular Malaysia
Mucojo 57 F2 Cabo Delgado, N Mozambique
Mudanjiang 107 E3 var. Mu-tan-chiang. Heilongjiang, NE China
Mudon 115 B5 Mon State, S Myanmar
Muenchen see Munich
Muenster see Münster
Mufulira 56 D2 Copperbelt, C Zambia
Mughla see Muğla
Muğla 94 A4 var. Mughla. Muğla, SW Turkey
Mūḩ, Sabkhat al 134 C3 lake C Syria
Muir Éireann see Irish Sea
Muisne 38 A1 Esmeraldas, NW Ecuador
Mukacheve 86 B3 Hung. Munkács, Rus. Mukachevo. Zakarpats'ka Oblast', W Ukraine
Mukalla see Al Mukallā
Mula 71 E4 Murcia, SE Spain
Mulaku Atoll 110 B4 var. Meemu Atoll. Atoll C Maldives
Muleshoe 27 E2 Texas, SW USA
Mulhacén 71 E5 var. Cerro de Mulhacén. Mountain S Spain
Mulhouse 68 E4 Ger. Mülhausen. Haut-Rhin, NE France
Muller, Pegunungan 116 D4 Dut. Müller-gerbergte. Mountain range Borneo, C Indonesia
Müllheim 73 A6 Baden-Württemberg, SW Germany
Mull, Isle of 66 B4 island W Scotland, UK
Mulongo 55 D7 Shaba, SE Dem. Rep. Congo
Multān 112 C2 Punjab, E Pakistan
Mumbai 112 C5 prev. Bombay. Mahārāshtra, W India
Munamägi see Suur Munamägi
Münchberg 73 C5 Bayern, E Germany
Muncie 18 C4 Indiana, N USA
Mungbere 55 E5 Orientale, NE Dem. Rep. Congo
Mu Nggava see Rennell
Munich 58 D4 var. Muenchen, Bayern, SE Germany
Munkhafaḑ al Qaţţārah see Qaţţâra, Monkhafad el
Munster 67 A6 Ir. Cúige Mumhan. Cultural region S Ireland
Münster 72 A4 var. Muenster, Münster in Westfalen. Nordrhein-Westfalen, W Germany
Münster in Westfalen see Münster
Muong Xiang Ngeun 114 C4 var. Xieng Ngeun. Louangphabang, N Laos
Muonio 62 D3 Lappi, N Finland
Muonioälv 62 D3 river Finland/Sweden
Muqāţ 97 C5 Al Mafraq, E Jordan
Muqdisho 51 D6 Eng. Mogadishu, It. Mogadiscio. Country capital (Somalia) Banaadir, S Somalia
Mur 73 E7 SCr. Mura. River C Europe
Muradiye 95 F3 Van, E Turkey
Murapara see Murupara
Murata 74 E2 S San Marino
Murchison River 125 A5 river Western Australia
Murcia 71 E4 cultural region SE Spain
Murcia 71 F4 Murcia, SE Spain
Mureş 86 A4 var. Maros, Mureşul, Ger. Marosch, Mieresch. River Hungary/Romania see also Maros
Mureşul see Mureş
Murfreesboro 20 D1 Tennessee, S USA
Murgab see Murgap
Murgab see Morghāb, Daryā-ye/Murgap
Murgap 100 D3 var. Murgab. Maryyskiy Velayat, S Turkmenistan
Murgap 100 D3 var. Murgab, Murghab, Pash. Daryā-ye Morghāb, Turkm. Murgap Deryasy. River Afghanistan/Turkmenistan see also Morghāb, Daryā-ye
Murgap Deryasy see Morghāb, Daryā-ye/Murgap
Murghab see Morghāb, Daryā-ye/Murgap
Murghob 101 F3 Rus. Murgab. SE Tajikistan
Murgon 127 E5 Queensland, E Australia
Müritz 72 C3 var. Müritzee. Lake NE Germany
Müritzee see Müritz
Murmansk 88 C2 Murmanskaya Oblast', NW Russian Federation
Murmashi 88 C2 Murmanskaya Oblast', NW Russian Federation
Murom 89 B5 Vladimirskaya Oblast', W Russian Federation
Muroran 108 D3 Hokkaidō, NE Japan
Muros 70 B1 Galicia, NW Spain
Murray Fracture Zone 131 E2 tectonic feature NE Pacific Ocean
Murray Range see Murray Ridge
Murray Ridge 90 C5 var. Murray Range. Undersea feature N Arabian Sea
Murray River 127 B6 river SE Australia
Murrumbidgee River 127 C6 river New South Wales, SE Australia
Murska Sobota 73 E7 Ger. Olsnitz. NE Slovenia
Murupara 128 E3 var. Murapara. Bay of Plenty, North Island, NZ
Murviedro see Sagunto
Murwāra 113 E4 Madhya Pradesh, N India
Murwillumbah 127 E5 New South Wales, SE Australia
Murzuq, Idhān 49 F4 var. Edeyin Murzuq. Desert SW Libya
Mürzzuschlag 73 E7 Steiermark, E Austria
Muş 95 F3 var. Mush. Muş, E Turkey
Mûsa, Gebel 50 C2 mountain NE Egypt
Musala 82 B3 mountain W Bulgaria
Muscat see Masqaţ
Muscatine 23 G3 Iowa, C USA
Musgrave Ranges 125 D5 mountain range South Australia
Mush see Muş
Musina 56 D3 var. Messina. Northern, NE South Africa
Muskegon 18 C3 Michigan, N USA
Muskogee 27 G1 Oklahoma, C USA
Musoma 51 C6 Mara, N Tanzania
Musta see Mosta
Musters, Lago 43 B6 lake S Argentina
Muswellbrook 127 D6 New South Wales, SE Australia
Mut 94 C4 İçel, S Turkey
Mu-tan-chiang see Mudanjiang
Mutare 56 D3 var. Mutari; prev. Umtali. Manicaland, E Zimbabwe
Mutari see Mutare
Mutsu-wan 108 D3 bay N Japan
Muttonbird Islands 129 A8 island group SW NZ
Mu Us Shamo 105 E3 var. Ordos Desert. Desert N China
Muy Muy 30 D3 Matagalpa, C Nicaragua
Mŭynoq see Mo'ynoq
Mužlja 78 D3 Hung. Felsőmuzslya; prev. Gornja Mužlja. Serbia, N Serbia and Montenegro (Yugo.)
Mwali see Mohéli
Mwanza 51 B6 Mwanza, NW Tanzania
Mweka 55 C6 Kasai Occidental, C Dem. Rep. Congo
Mwene-Ditu 55 D7 Kasai Oriental, S Dem. Rep. Congo
Mweru, Lake 55 D7 var. Lac Moero. Lake Congo (Zaire)/Zambia
Mweru Wantipa, Lake 55 E7 lake N Zambia
Myadzyel 85 C5 Pol. Miadzioł Nowy, Rus. Myadel'. Minskaya Voblasts', N Belarus
Myanmar 114 A3 var. Burma. Country SE Asia
Myanaung 114 B4 Irrawaddy, SW Myanmar
Myaungmya 114 A4 Irrawaddy, SW Myanmar
Myerkulavichy 85 D7 Rus. Merkulovichi. Homyel'skaya Voblasts', SE Belarus

Myingyan 114 B3 Mandalay, C Myanmar
Myitkyina 114 B2 Kachin State, N Myanmar
Mykolayiv 87 E4 Rus. Nikolayev. Mykolayivs'ka Oblast', S Ukraine
Mýkonos 83 D6 var. Míkonos. Island Kykládes, Greece, Aegean Sea
Myrhorod 87 F2 Rus. Mirgorod. Poltavs'ka Oblast', NE Ukraine
Mýrina 82 D4 var. Mírina. Límnos, SE Greece
Myrtle Beach 21 F2 South Carolina, SE USA
Mýrtos 83 D8 Kríti, Greece, E Mediterranean Sea
Myślibórz 76 B3 Zachodniopomorskie, NW Poland
Mysore 110 C2 var. Maisur. Karnātaka, W India
Mysore see Karnātaka
My Tho 115 E6 var. Mi Tho. Tiên Giang, S Vietnam
Mytilene see Mytilíni
Mytilíni 83 D5 var. Mitilíni; anc. Mytilene. Lésvos, E Greece
Mzuzu 57 E2 Northern, N Malawi

N

Naberezhnyye Chelny 89 D5 prev. Brezhnev. Respublika Tatarstan, W Russian Federation
Nablus 97 A6 var. Nābulus, Heb. Shekhem; anc. Neapolis, Bibl. Shechem. N West Bank
Nābulus see Nablus
Nacala 57 F2 Nampula, NE Mozambique
Nada see Danzhou
Nadi 123 E4 prev. Nandi. Viti Levu, W Fiji
Nadur 80 A5 Gozo, N Malta
Nadvirna 86 C3 Pol. Nadwórna, Rus. Nadvornaya. Ivano-Frankivs'ka Oblast', W Ukraine
Nadvoitsy 88 B3 Respublika Kareliya, NW Russian Federation
Nadym 92 C3 Yamalo-Nenetskiy Avtonomnyy Okrug, N Russian Federation
Náfpaktos 83 B5 var. Návpaktos. Dytikí Ellás, C Greece
Náfplio 83 B6 prev. Návplion. Pelopónnisos, S Greece
Naga 117 E2 off. Naga City; prev. Nueva Caceres. Luzon, N Philippines
Nagano 109 C5 Nagano, Honshū, S Japan
Nagaoka 109 D5 Niigata, Honshū, C Japan
Nagara Pathom see Nakhon Pathom
Nagara Sridharmaraj see Nakhon Si Thammarat
Nagara Svarga see Nakhon Sawan
Nagasaki 109 A7 Nagasaki, Kyūshū, SW Japan
Nagato 109 A7 Yamaguchi, Honshū, SW Japan
Nāgercoil 110 C3 Tamil Nādu, SE India
Nagorno-Karabakh 95 G3 var. Nagorno-Karabakhskaya Avtonomnaya Oblast, Arm. Lerrnayin Gharabakh, Az. Dağliq Qarabağ, Rus. Nagornyy Karabakh. Former autonomous region SW Azerbaijan
Nagorno-Karabakhskaya Avtonomnaya Oblast see Nagorno-Karabakh
Nagornyy Karabakh see Nagorno-Karabakh
Nagoya 109 C6 Aichi, Honshū, SW Japan
Nāgpur 112 D4 Mahārāshtra, C India
Nagqu 104 C5 Chin. Na-ch'ii; prev. Hei-ho. Xizang Zizhiqu, W China
Nagykálló 77 E6 Szabolcs-Szatmár-Bereg, E Hungary
Nagykanizsa 77 C7 Ger. Grosskanizsa. Zala, SW Hungary
Nagykőrös 77 D7 Pest, C Hungary
Nagyszentmiklós see Sânnicolau Mare
Naha 108 A3 Okinawa, Okinawa, SW Japan
Nahariya see Nahariyya
Nahariyya 97 A5 var. Nahariya. Northern, N Israel
Nahr al 'Āṣī see Orantes
Nahr al Litant see Līṭani, Nahr el
Nahr an Nīl see Nile
Nahr el Aassi see Orantes
Nahuel Huapi, Lago 43 B5 lake W Argentina
Nā'īn 98 D3 Eşfahān, C Iran
Nain 17 F2 Newfoundland and Labrador, NE Canada
Nairobi 47 E5 country capital (Kenya) Nairobi Area, S Kenya
Nairobi 51 C6 international airport Nairobi Area, S Kenya
Najaf see An Najaf
Najima see Fukuoka
Najin 107 E3 NE North Korea
Najrān 99 B6 var. Abā as Su'ūd. Najrān, S Saudi Arabia
Nakambé see White Volta
Nakamura 109 B7 Kōchi, Shikoku, SW Japan
Nakatsugawa 109 C6 var. Nakatugawa. Gifu, Honshū, SW Japan
Nakatugawa see Nakatsugawa
Nakhodka 93 G5 Primorskiy Kray, SE Russian Federation
Nakhon Pathom 115 C5 var. Nagara Pathom, Nakorn Pathom. Nakhon Pathom, W Thailand
Nakhon Ratchasima 115 C5 var. Khorat, Korat. Nakhon Ratchasima, E Thailand
Nakhon Sawan 115 C5 var. Muang Nakhon Sawan, Nagara Svarga. Nakhon Sawan, W Thailand
Nakhon Si Thammarat 115 C7 var. Nagara Sridharmaraj, Nakhon Sithamnaraj. Nakhon Si Thammarat, SW Thailand
Nakhon Sithamnaraj see Nakhon Si Thammarat
Nakorn Pathom see Nakhon Pathom
Nakuru 51 C6 Rift Valley, SW Kenya
Nal'chik 89 B8 Kabardino-Balkarskaya Respublika, SW Russian Federation
Nālūt 49 F2 NW Libya
Namakan Lake 18 A1 lake Canada/USA
Namangan 101 F2 Namangan Wiloyati, E Uzbekistan
Nambala 56 D2 Central, C Zambia
Nam Co 104 C5 lake W China
Nam Định 114 D3 Nam Ha, N Vietnam
Namib Desert 56 B3 desert W Namibia
Namibe 56 A2 Port. Moçâmedes, Mossâmedes. Namibe, SW Angola
Namibia 56 B3 var. South West Africa, Afr. Suidwes-Afrika, Ger. Deutsch-Südwestafrika; prev. German Southwest Africa, South-West Africa. Country S Africa
Namo see Namu Atoll
Nam Ou 114 C3 river N Laos
Nampa 24 D3 Idaho, NW USA
Nampula 57 E2 Nampula, NE Mozambique
Namsos 62 B4 Nord-Trøndelag, C Norway
Nam Tha 114 C4 river N Laos
Namu Atoll 122 D2 var. Namo. Atoll Ralik Chain, C Marshall Islands
Namur 65 C6 Dut. Namen. Namur, SE Belgium
Namyit Island 106 C8 island S Spratly Islands
Nan 114 C4 var. Muang Nan. Nan, NW Thailand
Nanaimo 14 D5 Vancouver Island, British Columbia, SW Canada
Nanchang 106 C5 var. Nan-ch'ang, Nanch'ang-hsien. Jiangxi, S China
Nanch'ang-hsien see Nanchang
Nan-ching see Nanjing
Nancy 68 D3 Meurthe-et-Moselle, NE France
Nandaime 30 D3 Granada, SW Nicaragua
Nānded 112 D5 Mahārāshtra, C India
Nandyāl 110 C1 Andhra Pradesh, E India
Nanjing 106 D5 var. Nan-ching, Nanking; prev. Chianning, Chian-ning, Kiang-ning. Jiangsu, E China
Nanking see Nanjing
Nanning 106 B6 var. Nan-ning; prev. Yung-ning. Guangxi Zhuangzu Zizhiqu, S China
Nan-ning see Nanning
Nanortalik 60 C5 S Greenland
Nanpan Jiang 114 D2 river S China
Nanping 106 D6 var. Nan-p'ing; prev. Yenping. Fujian, SE China
Nanseí-Shotō 108 A2 var. Ryukyu Islands. Island group SW Japan
Nansei Syotō Trench see Ryukyu Trench
Nansen Basin 133 C4 undersea feature Arctic Ocean
Nansen Cordillera 133 B3 var. Arctic-Mid Oceanic Ridge, Nansen Ridge. Undersea feature Arctic Ocean
Nansen Ridge see Nansen Cordillera
Nanterre 68 D1 Hauts-de-Seine, N France
Nantes 68 B4 Bret. Naoned; anc. Condivincum, Namnetes. Loire-Atlantique, NW France
Nantucket Island 19 G3 island Massachusetts, NE USA
Nanumaga 123 E3 var. Nanumanga. Atoll NW Tuvalu
Nanumanga see Nanumaga
Nanumea Atoll 123 E3 atoll NW Tuvalu
Nanyang 106 C5 var. Nan-yang. Henan, C China
Napa 25 B6 California, W USA
Napier 128 E4 Hawke's Bay, North Island, NZ
Naples 58 D5 anc. Neapolis. Campania, S Italy
Naples 21 E5 Florida, SE USA
Napo 34 A3 province NE Ecuador
Napo, Río 38 C1 river Ecuador/Peru
Naracoorte 127 B7 South Australia
Naradhivas see Narathiwat
Narathiwat 115 C7 var. Naradhivas. Narathiwat, SW Thailand
Narbada see Narmada
Narbonne 69 C6 anc. Narbo Martius. Aude, S France
Narborough Island see Fernandina, Isla
Nares Abyssal Plain see Nares Plain
Nares Plain 13 E6 var. Nares Abyssal Plain. Undersea feature NW Atlantic Ocean
Nares Strait 60 D1 Dan. Nares Stræde. Strait Canada/Greenland
Narew 76 E3 river E Poland
Narmada 102 B3 var. Narbada. River C India
Narowlya 85 C8 Rus. Narovlya. Homyel'skaya Voblasts', SE Belarus
Närpes 63 D5 Fin. Närpiö. Länsi-Suomi, W Finland
Narrabri 127 D6 New South Wales, SE Australia
Narrogin 125 B6 Western Australia
Narva 84 E2 prev. Narova. River Estonia/Russian Federation
Narva 84 E2 Ida-Virumaa, NE Estonia
Narva Bay 84 E2 Est. Narva Laht, Ger. Narwa-Bucht, Rus. Narvskiy Zaliv. Bay Estonia/Russian Federation
Narva Reservoir 84 E2 Est. Narva Veehoidla, Rus. Narvskoye Vodokhranilishche. Reservoir Estonia/Russian Federation
Narvik 62 C3 Nordland, C Norway
Nar'yan-Mar 88 D3 prev. Beloshchel'ye, Dzerzhinskiy. Nenetskiy Avtonomnyy Okrug, NW Russian Federation
Naryn 101 G2 Narynskaya Oblast', C Kyrgyzstan
Năsăud 86 B3 Ger. Nussdorf, Hung. Naszód. Bistriţa-Năsăud, N Romania
Nase see Naze
Nāshik 112 C5 prev. Nāsik. Mahārāshtra, W India
Nashua 19 G3 New Hampshire, NE USA
Nashville 20 C1 state capital Tennessee, S USA
Näsijärvi 63 D5 lake SW Finland
Nāsiri see Ahvāz
Nasiriya see An Nāşirīyah
Nassau 32 C1 country capital (Bahamas) New Providence, N Bahamas
Nasser, Lake 50 B3 var. Buhayrat Nasir, Buḥayrat Nāşir, Buḥeiret Nâşir. Lake Egypt/Sudan
Nata 56 C3 Central, NE Botswana
Natal 41 G2 Rio Grande do Norte, E Brazil
Natal Basin 119 A6 var. Mozambique Basin. Undersea feature W Indian Ocean
Natanya see Netanya
Natchez 20 B3 Mississippi, S USA
Natchitoches 20 A2 Louisiana, S USA
Nathanya see Netanya
Natitingou 53 F4 NW Benin
Natsrat see Nazerat
Natuna Islands 102 D4 island group W Indonesia
Naturaliste Plateau 119 E6 undersea feature E Indian Ocean
Naugard see Nowogard
Naujamiestis 84 C4 Panevėžys, C Lithuania
Nauru 122 D2 prev. Pleasant Island. Country W Pacific Ocean
Nauta 38 C2 Loreto, N Peru
Navahrudak 85 C6 Pol. Nowogródek, Rus. Novogrudok. Hrodzyenskaya Voblasts', W Belarus
Navapolatsk 85 D5 Rus. Novopolotsk. Vitsyebskaya Voblasts', N Belarus
Navarra 71 E2 cultural region N Spain
Navassa Island 32 C3 US unincorporated territory C West Indies
Navoiy 101 E2 var. Nawoiy, Rus. Navoi. Nawoiy Wiloyati, C Uzbekistan
Navojoa 28 C2 Sonora, NW Mexico
Navolat see Navolato
Navolato 66 C3 var. Navolat. Sinaloa, C Mexico
Návpaktos see Náfpaktos
Nawabashah see Nawābshāh
Nawābshāh 112 B3 var. Nawabashah. Sind, S Pakistan
Nawoiy see Navoiy
Naxçıvan 95 G3 Rus. Nakhichevan'. SW Azerbaijan
Náxos 83 D6 var. Naxos. Náxos, Kykládes, Greece, Aegean Sea
Náxos 83 D6 island Kykládes, Greece, Aegean Sea
Nayoro 108 D2 Hokkaidō, NE Japan
Nazca 38 D4 Ica, S Peru
Nazca Ridge 35 A5 undersea feature E Pacific Ocean
Naze 108 B3 var. Nase. Kagoshima, Amami-ōshima, SW Japan
Nazerat 97 A5 var. Natsrat, Ar. En Nazira, Eng. Nazareth. Northern, N Israel
Nazilli 94 A4 Aydın, SW Turkey
Nazrēt 51 C5 var. Adama, Hadama. C Ethiopia
N'Dalatando 56 B1 Port. Salazar, Vila Salazar. Cuanza Norte, NW Angola
Ndélé 54 C4 Bamingui-Bangoran, N Central African Republic
Ndendé 55 B6 Ngounié, S Gabon
Ndindi 55 A6 Nyanga, S Gabon
Ndjamena 54 B3 var. N'Djamena; prev. Fort-Lamy. Country capital (Chad) Chari-Baguirmi, W Chad
Ndjolé 55 A5 Moyen-Ogooué, W Gabon
Ndola 56 D2 Copperbelt, C Zambia
Neagh, Lough 67 B5 lake E Northern Ireland, UK
Néa Moudanía 82 C4 var. Néa Moudhaniá. Kentrikí Makedonía, N Greece
Néa Moudhaniá see Néa Moudanía
Neápoli 82 B4 prev. Neápolis. Dytikí Makedonía, N Greece
Neápoli 83 D8 Kríti, Greece, E Mediterranean Sea
Neápoli 83 C7 Pelopónnisos, S Greece
Neapolis see Nablus
Near Islands 14 A2 island group Aleutian Islands, Alaska, USA
Néa Zíchni 82 C3 var. Néa Zíkhni; prev. Néa Zíkhna. Kentrikí Makedonía, NE Greece
Néa Zíkhna see Néa Zíchni
Néa Zíkhni see Néa Zíchni
Nebaj 30 B2 Quiché, W Guatemala
Neblina, Pico da 40 C1 mountain NW Brazil
Nebraska 22 D4 off. State of Nebraska; also known as Blackwater State, Cornhusker State, Tree Planters State. State C USA
Nebraska City 23 F4 Nebraska, C USA
Neches River 27 H3 river Texas, SW USA
Neckar 73 B6 river SW Germany
Necochea 43 D5 Buenos Aires, E Argentina
Neder Rijn 64 D4 Eng. Lower Rhine. River C Netherlands
Nederweert 65 D5 Limburg, SE Netherlands
Neede 64 E3 Gelderland, E Netherlands
Neerpelt 65 D5 Limburg, NE Belgium
Neftekamsk 89 D5 Respublika Bashkortostan, W Russian Federation
Negēlē 51 D5 var. Negelli, It. Neghelli. C Ethiopia
Negelli see Negēlē
Neghelli see Negēlē
Negomane 57 E2 var. Negomano. Cabo Delgado, N Mozambique
Negomano see Negomane
Negombo 110 C3 Western Province, SW Sri Lanka
Negotin 78 E4 Serbia, E Serbia and Montenegro (Yugo.)
Negra, Punta 38 A3 headland NW Peru
Negreşti-Oaş 86 B3 Hung. Avasfelsőfalu; prev. Negreşti. Satu Mare, NE Romania
Negro, Río 43 C5 river E Argentina
Negro, Rio 40 D1 river N South America
Negro, Río 42 D4 river Brazil/Uruguay
Negros 117 E2 island C Philippines
Nehbandān 98 E3 Khorāsān, E Iran
Neijiang 106 B5 Sichuan, C China
Nei Monggol Zizhiqu see Inner Mongolia
Nei Mongol see Inner Mongolia
Neiva 36 B3 Huila, S Colombia
Nellore 110 D2 Andhra Pradesh, E India
Nelson 15 G4 river Manitoba, C Canada
Nelson 129 C5 Nelson, South Island, NZ
Néma 52 D3 Hodh ech Chargui, SE Mauritania
Neman 84 A4 Bel. Nyoman, Ger. Memel, Lith. Nemunas, Pol. Niemen, Rus. Neman. River NE Europe
Neman 84 B4 Ger. Ragnit. Kaliningradskaya Oblast', W Russian Federation
Neméa 83 B6 Pelopónnisos, S Greece
Nemours 68 C3 Seine-et-Marne, N France
Nemuro 108 E2 Hokkaidō, NE Japan
Neochóri 83 B5 Dytikí Ellás, C Greece
Nepal 113 E3 Country S Asia
Nereta 84 C4 Aizkraukle, S Latvia
Neretva 78 C4 river Bosnia and Herzegovina/Croatia
Neringa 84 A3 var. Nida, Ger. Nidden. Neringa, SW Lithuania
Neris 85 C5 Bel. Viliya, Pol. Wilia; prev. Pol. Wilja. River Belarus/Lithuania
Nerva 70 C4 Andalucía, S Spain
Neryungri 93 F4 Respublika Sakha (Yakutiya), NE Russian Federation
Neskaupstadhur 61 E5 Austurland, E Iceland
Ness, Loch 66 C3 lake N Scotland, UK
Néstos 82 C3 Bul. Mesta, Turk. Kara Su. River Bulgaria/Greece see also Mesta
Netanya 97 A6 var. Natanya, Nathanya. Central, C Israel
Netherlands 64 C3 var. Holland, Dut. Koninkrijk der Nederlanden, Nederland. Country NW Europe
Netherlands Antilles 33 E5 prev. Dutch West Indies. Dutch autonomous region S Caribbean Sea
Netherlands New Guinea see Papua
Nettilling Lake 15 G3 lake Baffin Island, Nunavut, N Canada
Neubrandenburg 72 D3 Mecklenburg-Vorpommern, NE Germany
Neuchâtel 73 A7 Ger. Neuenburg. Neuchâtel, W Switzerland
Neuchâtel, Lac de A7 Ger. Neuenburger See. Lake W Switzerland
Neufchâteau 65 D8 Luxembourg, SE Belgium
Neumünster 72 B2 Schleswig-Holstein, N Germany
Neunkirchen 73 A5 Saarland, SW Germany
Neuquén 43 B5 Neuquén, SE Argentina
Neuruppin 72 C3 Brandenburg, NE Germany
Neusalz an der Oder see Nowa Sól
Neusiedler See 73 E6 Hung. Fertő. Lake Austria/Hungary
Neustadt an der Weinstrasse 73 B5 prev. Neustadt an der Haardt, hist. Niewenstat, anc. Nova Civitas. Rheinland-Pfalz, SW Germany
Neustrelitz 72 D3 Mecklenburg-Vorpommern, NE Germany
Neu-Ulm 73 B6 Bayern, S Germany
Neuwied 73 A5 Rheinland-Pfalz, W Germany
Neuzen see Terneuzen
Nevada 25 C5 off. State of Nevada; also known as Battle Born State, Sagebrush State, Silver State. State W USA
Nevada, Sierra 70 D5 mountain range S Spain
Nevers 68 C4 anc. Noviodunum. Nièvre, C France
Neves 54 E2 São Tomé, S Sao Tome and Principe
Nevinnomyssk 89 B7 Stavropol'skiy Kray, SW Russian Federation
Nevşehir 94 C3 var. Nevshehr. Nevşehir, C Turkey
Nevshehr see Nevşehir
Newala 73 C8 Mtwara, SE Tanzania
New Albany 18 C5 Indiana, N USA
New Amsterdam 37 G3 E Guyana
Newark 19 F4 New Jersey, NE USA
New Bedford 19 G3 Massachusetts, NE USA
Newberg 24 B3 Oregon, NW USA
New Bern 21 F1 North Carolina, SE USA
New Braunfels 27 G4 Texas, SW USA
Newbridge 67 B6 Ir. An Droichead Nua. C Ireland
New Britain 122 B3 island E PNG
New Brunswick 17 E4 Fr. Nouveau-Brunswick. Province SE Canada
New Caledonia 122 D4 var. Kanaky, Fr. Nouvelle-Calédonie. French overseas territory SW Pacific Ocean
New Caledonia 122 C5 island SW Pacific Ocean
New Caledonia Basin 120 C4 undersea feature W Pacific Ocean
Newcastle see Newcastle upon Tyne
Newcastle 127 D6 New South Wales, SE Australia
Newcastle upon Tyne 66 D4 var. Newcastle; hist. Monkchester, Lat. Pons Aelii. NE England, UK
New Delhi 112 D3 country capital (India) Delhi, N India
Newfoundland 17 G3 Fr. Terre-Neuve. Island Newfoundland, SE Canada
Newfoundland 17 F2 Fr. Terre Neuve. Province SE Canada
Newfoundland Basin 44 B3 undersea feature NW Atlantic Ocean
New Georgia Islands 122 C3 island group NW Solomon Islands
New Glasgow 17 F4 Nova Scotia, SE Canada
New Goa see Pānji
New Guinea 122 A3 Dut. Nieuw Guinea, Ind. Irian. Island Indonesia/PNG
New Hampshire 19 F2 off. State of New Hampshire; also known as The Granite State. State NE USA
New Haven 19 G3 Connecticut, NE USA
New Iberia 20 B3 Louisiana, S USA
New Ireland 122 C3 island NE PNG
New Jersey 19 F4 off. State of New Jersey; also known as The Garden State. State NE USA
Newman 124 B4 Western Australia
Newmarket 67 E6 E England, UK
New Mexico 26 C2 off. State of New Mexico; also known as Land of Enchantment, Sunshine State. State SW USA
New Orleans 20 B3 Louisiana, S USA
New Plymouth 128 C4 Taranaki, North Island, NZ
Newport 18 C4 Kentucky, S USA
Newport 67 D7 S England, UK
Newport 67 C7 SE Wales, UK
Newport 19 G2 Vermont, NE USA
Newport News 19 F5 Virginia, NE USA
New Providence 32 C1 island N Bahamas
Newquay 67 C7 SW England, UK
Newry 67 B5 Ir. An tIúr. SE Northern Ireland, UK
New Sarum see Salisbury
New Siberian Islands see Novosibirskiye Ostrova
New South Wales 127 C6 state SE Australia
Newton 23 G3 Iowa, C USA
Newtownabbey 67 B5 Ir. Baile na Mainistreach. E Northern Ireland, UK
New Ulm 23 F2 Minnesota, N USA
New York 19 F4 New York, NE USA
New York 19 F3 state NE USA
New Zealand 128 A4 abbrev. NZ. Country SW Pacific Ocean
Neyveli 110 C2 Tamil Nādu, SE India
Ngangzê Co 104 B5 lake W China
Ngaoundéré 54 B4 var. N'Gaoundéré. Adamaoua, N Cameroon
N'Giva 56 B3 var. Ondjiva, Port. Vila Pereira de Eça. Cunene, S Angola
Ngo 55 B6 Plateaux, SE Congo
Ngoko 55 B5 river Cameroon/Congo
Ngourti 53 H3 Diffa, E Niger
Nguigmi 53 H3 var. N'Guigmi. Diffa, SE Niger
Nguru 53 G3 Yobe, NE Nigeria
Nha Trang 115 E6 Khanh Hoa, S Vietnam
Niagara Falls 18 D3 waterfall Canada/USA
Niagara Falls 19 E3 New York, NE USA
Niagara Falls 16 D5 Ontario, S Canada
Niamey 53 F3 country capital (Niger) Niamey, SW Niger
Niangay, Lac 53 E3 lake E Mali
Nia-Nia 55 E5 Orientale, NE Dem. Rep. Congo
Nias, Pulau 116 A3 island W Indonesia
Nicaragua 30 D3 Country Central America
Nicaragua, Lago de 30 D4 var. Cocibolca, Gran Lago, Eng. Lake Nicaragua. Lake S Nicaragua
Nicaragua, Lake see Nicaragua, Lago de
Nicaria see Ikaría
Nice 69 D6 It. Nizza; anc. Nicaea. Alpes-Maritimes, SE France
Nicephorium see Ar Raqqah
Nicholas II Land see Severnaya Zemlya
Nicholls Town 32 C1 Andros Island, NW Bahamas
Nicobar Islands 102 B4 island group India, E Indian Ocean
Nicosia 80 C5 Gk. Lefkosia, Turk. Lefkoşa. Country capital (Cyprus) C Cyprus
Nicoya 30 D4 Guanacaste, W Costa Rica
Nicoya, Golfo de 30 D5 gulf W Costa Rica
Nicoya, Península de 30 D4 peninsula NW Costa Rica
Nida see Neringa
Nidden see Neringa
Nidzica 76 D3 Ger. Niedenburg. Warmińsko-Mazurskie, NE Poland
Niedere Tauern 77 A6 mountain range C Austria
Nieuw Amsterdam 37 G3 Commewijne, NE Suriname
Nieuw-Bergen 64 D4 Limburg, SE Netherlands
Nieuwegein 64 C4 Utrecht, C Netherlands
Nieuw Nickerie 37 G3 Nickerie, NW Suriname
Niğde 94 C4 Niğde, C Turkey
Niger 53 F3 Country W Africa
Niger 53 F4 river W Africa
Nigeria 53 F4 Country W Africa
Niger, Mouths of the 53 F5 delta S Nigeria
Nihon see Japan
Niigata 109 D5 Niigata, Honshū, C Japan
Niihama 109 B7 Ehime, Shikoku, SW Japan
Ni'ihau 25 A7 var. Niihau. Island Hawai'i, USA, C Pacific Ocean
Nii-jima 109 D6 island E Japan
Nijkerk 64 D3 Gelderland, C Netherlands
Nijlen 65 C5 Antwerpen, N Belgium
Nijmegen 64 D4 Ger. Nimwegen; anc. Noviomagus. Gelderland, SE Netherlands
Nikaria see Ikaría
Nikel' 88 C2 Murmanskaya Oblast', NW Russian Federation
Nikiniki 117 E5 Timor, S Indonesia
Nikopol' 87 F3 Pleven, N Bulgaria

INDEX

Nikšić 79 C5 Montenegro, SW Serbia and Montenegro (Yugo.)
Nikumaroro 123 E3 *prev.* Gardner Island, Kemins Island. *Atoll* Phoenix Islands, C Kiribati
Nikunau 123 E3 *var.* Nukunau; *prev.* Byron Island. *Atoll* Tungaru, W Kiribati
Nile 46 D3 *Ar.* Nahr an Nīl. *River* N Africa
Nile 50 B2 *former province* NW Uganda
Nile Delta 50 B1 *delta* N Egypt
Nîmes 69 C6 *anc.* Nemausus, Nismes. Gard, S France
Nine Degree Channel 110 B3 *channel* India/Maldives
Ninetyeast Ridge 119 D5 *undersea feature* E Indian Ocean
Ninety Mile Beach 128 C1 *beach* North Island, NZ
Ningbo 106 D5 *var.* Ning-po, Yin-hsien; *prev.* Ninghsien. Zhejiang, SE China
Ninghsien *see* Ningbo
Ning-po *see* Ningbo
Ningxia 106 B4 *off.* Ningxia Huizu Zizhiqu, *var.* Ning-hsia, Ningsia, *Eng.* Ningsia Hui, Ningsia Hui Autonomous Region. Admin. region *autonomous region* N China
Ningxia Huizu Zizhiqu *see* Ningxia
Nio *see* Íos
Niobrara River 23 E3 *river* Nebraska/Wyoming, C USA
Nioro 52 D3 *var.* Nioro du Sahel. Kayes, W Mali
Nioro du Sahel *see* Nioro
Niort 90 B4 Deux-Sèvres, W France
Nipigon 16 B4 Ontario, S Canada
Nipigon, Lake 16 B3 *lake* Ontario, S Canada
Nippon *see* Japan
Niš 79 E5 *Eng.* Nish, *Ger.* Nisch; *anc.* Naissus. Serbia, SE Serbia and Montenegro (Yugo.)
Nişab 98 B4 Al Ḩudūd ash Shamālīyah, N Saudi Arabia
Nisibin *see* Nusaybin
Nisiros *see* Nísyros
Nisko 76 E4 Podkarpackie, SE Poland
Nísyros 83 E7 *var.* Nisiros. *Island* Dodekánisos, Greece, Aegean Sea
Nitra 77 C6 *Ger.* Neutra, *Hung.* Nyitra. *River* W Slovakia
Nitra 77 C6 *Ger.* Neutra, *Hung.* Nyitra. Nitriansky Kraj, SW Slovakia
Niuatobutabu *see* Niuatoputapu
Niuatoputapu 123 E4 *var.* Niuatobutabu; *prev.* Keppel Island. *Island* N Tonga
Niue 123 F4 *self-governing territory in free association with NZ* S Pacific Ocean
Niulakita 123 E3 *var.* Nurakita. *Atoll* S Tuvalu
Niutao 123 E3 *atoll* NW Tuvalu
Nivernais 68 C4 *cultural region* C France
Nizāmābād 112 D5 Andhra Pradesh, C India
Nizhnekamsk 89 C5 Respublika Tatarstan, W Russian Federation
Nizhnevartovsk 92 D3 Khanty-Mansiyskiy Avtonomnyy Okrug, C Russian Federation
Nizhniy Novgorod 89 C5 *prev.* Gor'kiy. Nizhegorodskaya Oblast', W Russian Federation
Nizhniy Odes 88 D4 Respublika Komi, NW Russian Federation
Nizhnyaya Tunguska 93 E3 *Eng.* Lower Tunguska. *River* N Russian Federation
Nizhyn 87 E1 *Rus.* Nezhin. Chernihivs'ka Oblast', NE Ukraine
Njazidja *see* Grande Comore
Njombe 51 C8 Iringa, S Tanzania
Nkayi 55 B6 *prev.* Jacob. La Bouenza, S Congo
Nkongsamba 54 A4 *var.* N'Kongsamba. Littoral, W Cameroon
Nmai Hka 114 B2 *var.* Me Hka. *River* N Myanmar
Nobeoka 109 B7 Miyazaki, Kyūshū, SW Japan
Noboribetsu 108 D3 *var.* Noboribetu. Hokkaidō, NE Japan
Noboribetu *see* Noboribetsu
Nogales 26 B3 Arizona, SW USA
Nogales 28 B1 Sonora, NW Mexico
Nogal Valley *see* Dooxo Nugaaleed
Nokia 63 D5 Länsi-Suomi, W Finland
Nokou 54 B3 Kanem, W Chad
Nola 55 B5 Sangha-Mbaéré, SW Central African Republic
Nolinsk 89 C5 Kirovskaya Oblast', NW Russian Federation
Nongkaya *see* Nong Khai
Nong Khai 114 C4 *var.* Mi Chai, Nongkaya. Nong Khai, E Thailand
Nonouti 122 D2 *prev.* Sydenham Island. *Atoll* Tungaru, W Kiribati
Noord-Beveland 64 B4 *var.* North Beveland. *Island* SW Netherlands
Noordwijk aan Zee 64 C3 Zuid-Holland, W Netherlands
Nora 63 C6 Örebro, C Sweden
Norak 101 E3 *Rus.* Nurek. W Tajikistan
Nord 61 F1 N Greenland
Nordaustlandet 61 G1 *island* NE Svalbard
Norden 72 A3 Niedersachsen, NW Germany
Norderstedt 72 B3 Schleswig-Holstein, N Germany
Nordfriesische Inseln *see* North Frisian Islands
Nordhausen 72 C4 Thüringen, C Germany
Nordhorn 72 A3 Niedersachsen, NW Germany
Nordkapp 62 D1 *Eng.* North Cape. *Headland* N Norway
Norfolk 23 E3 Nebraska, C USA
Norfolk 19 F5 Virginia, NE USA
Norfolk Island 120 D4 *Australian external territory* SW Pacific Ocean
Norfolk Ridge 120 D4 *undersea feature* W Pacific Ocean
Norias 27 G5 Texas, SW USA
Noril'sk 92 D3 Taymyrskiy (Dolgano-Nenetskiy) Avtonomnyy Okrug, N Russian Federation
Norman 27 G1 Oklahoma, USA
Normandie 68 B3 *Eng.* Normandy. *Cultural region* N France
Normandy *see* Normandie
Normanton 126 C3 Queensland, NE Australia
Norrköping 63 C6 Östergötland, S Sweden
Norrtälje 63 C6 Stockholm, C Sweden
Norseman 125 B6 Western Australia
North Albanian Alps 79 C5 *Alb.* Bjeshkët e Namuna, *SCr.* Prokletije. *Mountain range* Albania/Serbia and Montenegro (Yugo.)
Northallerton 67 D5 N England, UK
Northam 125 A6 Western Australia
North America 12 *continent*
Northampton 67 D6 C England, UK
North Andaman 111 F2 *island* Andaman Islands, India, NE Indian Ocean
North Australian Basin 119 E5 *Fr.* Bassin Nord de l' Australie. *Undersea feature* E Indian Ocean
North Bay 16 D4 Ontario, S Canada
North Beveland *see* Noord-Beveland
North Cape 44 D1 *headland* New Ireland, NE PNG
North Cape 128 C1 *headland* North Island, NZ
North Cape *see* Nordkapp
North Carolina 21 E1 *off.* State of North Carolina; also known as Old North State, Tar Heel State, Turpentine State. *State* SE USA
North Channel 18 D2 *lake channel* Canada/USA
North Charleston 21 F2 South Carolina, SE USA
North Dakota 22 D2 *off.* State of North Dakota; also known as Flickertail State, Peace Garden State, Sioux State. *State* N USA
Northeast Providence Channel 32 C1 *channel* N Bahamas
Northeim 72 B4 Niedersachsen, C Germany
Northern Cook Islands 123 F4 *island group* N Cook Islands
Northern Cyprus, Turkish Republic of 80 D5 *disputed region* N Cyprus
Northern Dvina *see* Severnaya Dvina
Northern Ireland 66 B4 *var.* The Six Counties. *Political division* UK
Northern Mariana Islands 120 B1 *US commonwealth territory* W Pacific Ocean
Northern Sporades *see* Vóreioi Sporádes
Northern Territory 122 A5 *territory* N Australia
North European Plain 59 E3 *plain* N Europe
Northfield 23 F2 Minnesota, N USA
North Fiji Basin 120 D3 *undersea feature* N Coral Sea
North Frisian Islands 72 B2 *var.* Nordfriesische Inseln. *Island group* N Germany
North Huvadhu Atoll 110 B5 *var.* Gaafu Alifu Atoll. *Atoll* S Maldives
North Island 128 B2 *island* N NZ
North Korea 107 E3 *Kor.* Chosŏn-minjujuŭi-inmin-kanghwaguk. *Country* E Asia
North Little Rock 20 B1 Arkansas, C USA
North Minch *see* Minch, The
North Mole 71 G4 *harbour wall* NW Gibraltar
North Platte 23 E4 Nebraska, C USA
North Platte River 22 D4 *river* C USA
North Pole 133 B3 *pole* Arctic Ocean
North Saskatchewan 15 F5 *river* Alberta/Saskatchewan, S Canada
North Sea C3 *Dan.* Nordsøen, *Dut.* Noordzee, *Fr.* Mer du Nord, *Ger.* Nordsee, *Nor.* Nordsjøen; *prev.* German Ocean, *Lat.* Mare Germanicum. *Sea* NW Europe
North Siberian Lowland *see* Severo-Sibirskaya Nizmennost'
North Siberian Plain *see* Severo-Sibirskaya Nizmennost'
North Taranaki Bight 128 C3 *gulf* North Island, NZ
North Uist 66 B3 *island* NW Scotland, UK
Northwest Atlantic Mid-Ocean Canyon 12 E4 *undersea feature* N Atlantic Ocean
North West Highlands 66 C3 *mountain range* N Scotland, UK
Northwest Pacific Basin 91 G4 *undersea feature* NW Pacific Ocean
Northeast Providence Channel 32 C1 *channel* N Bahamas
Northwest Territories 15 E3 *Fr.* Territoires du Nord-Ouest. *Territory* NW Canada (the eastern part is now the territory of Nunavut)
Northwind Plain 133 B2 *undersea feature* Arctic Ocean
Norton Sound 14 C2 *inlet* Alaska, USA
Norway 63 A5 *Nor.* Norge. *Country* N Europe
Norwegian Basin 61 F4 *undersea feature* NW Norwegian Sea
Norwegian Sea 61 F4 *Nor.* Norske Havet. *Sea* NE Atlantic Ocean
Norwich 67 E6 E England, UK
Noshiro 108 D4 *var.* Nosiro; *prev.* Noshirominato. Akita, Honshū, C Japan
Noshirominato *see* Noshiro
Nosiro *see* Noshiro
Nosivka 87 E1 *Rus.* Nosovka. Chernihivs'ka Oblast', NE Ukraine
Noşratābād 98 E3 Sīstān va Balūchestān, E Iran
Nossob 56 C4 *river* E Namibia
Noteć 76 C3 *Ger.* Netze. *River* NW Poland
Nóties Sporádes *see* Dodekánisos
Nottingham 67 D6 C England, UK
Nouâdhibou 52 B2 *prev.* Port-Étienne. Dakhlet Nouâdhibou, W Mauritania
Nouakchott 52 B2 *country capital* (Mauritania) Nouakchott District, SW Mauritania
Nouméa 122 C5 *dependent territory capital* (New Caledonia) Province Sud, S New Caledonia
Nouvelle-Calédonie *see* New Caledonia
Nova Gorica 73 D8 W Slovenia
Nova Gradiška 78 C3 *Ger.* Neugradisk, *Hung.* Újgradiska. Brod-Posavina, NE Croatia
Nova Iguaçu 41 F4 Rio de Janeiro, SE Brazil
Novara 74 B2 *anc.* Novaria. Piemonte, NW Italy
Nova Scotia 17 F4 *Fr.* Nouvelle Écosse. *Province* SE Canada
Nova Scotia 13 E5 *physical region* SE Canada
Novaya Sibir', Ostrov 93 F1 *island* Novosibirskiye Ostrova, NE Russian Federation
Novaya Zemlya 88 D1 *island group* N Russian Federation
Novaya Zemlya Trench *see* East Novaya Zemlya Trench
Novgorod *see* Velikiy Novgorod
Novi Grad *see* Bosanski Novi
Novi Iskŭr 82 C2 Sofiya-Grad, W Bulgaria
Novi Pazar 79 D5 *Turk.* Yenipazar. Shumen, NE Bulgaria
Novi Sad 78 D3 *Ger.* Neusatz, *Hung.* Újvidék. Serbia, N Serbia and Montenegro (Yugo.)
Novoazovs'k 87 G4 *Rus.* Novoazovsk. Donets'ka Oblast', E Ukraine
Novocheboksarsk 89 C5 Chuvashskaya Respublika, W Russian Federation
Novocherkassk 89 B7 Rostovskaya Oblast', SW Russian Federation
Novodvinsk 88 C3 Arkhangel'skaya Oblast', NW Russian Federation
Novohrad-Volyns'kyy 86 D2 *Rus.* Novograd-Volynskiy. Zhytomyrs'ka Oblast', N Ukraine
Novokazalinsk *see* Ayteke Bi
Novokuznetsk 92 D4 *prev.* Stalinsk. Kemerovskaya Oblast', S Russian Federation
Novolazarevskaya 132 C2 *Russian research station* Antarctica
Novo mesto 73 E8 *Ger.* Rudolfswert; prev. *Ger.* Neustadtl. SE Slovenia
Novomoskovs'k 87 F3 *Rus.* Novomoskovsk. Dnipropetrovs'ka Oblast', E Ukraine
Novomoskovsk 89 B5 Tul'skaya Oblast', W Russian Federation
Novorossiysk 89 A7 Krasnodarskiy Kray, SW Russian Federation
Novoshakhtinsk 89 B6 Rostovskaya Oblast', SW Russian Federation
Novosibirsk 92 D4 Novosibirskaya Oblast', C Russian Federation
Novosibirskiye Ostrova 93 F1 *Eng.* New Siberian Islands. *Island group* N Russian Federation
Novotroitsk 89 D6 Orenburgskaya Oblast', W Russian Federation
Novotroyits'ke 87 F4 *Rus.* Novotroitskoye. Khersons'ka Oblast', S Ukraine
Novovolyns'k 86 C1 *Rus.* Novovolynsk. Volyns'ka Oblast', NW Ukraine
Novy Dvor 85 B6 *Rus.* Novyy Dvor. Hrodzyenskaya Voblasts', W Belarus
Novyy Buh 87 E3 *Rus.* Novyy Bug. Mykolayivs'ka Oblast', S Ukraine
Novyy Uzen' *see* Zhanaözen
Nowa Sól 76 B4 *var.* Nowasól, *Ger.* Neusalz an der Oder. Lubuskie, W Poland
Nowogard 76 B2 *var.* Nowógard, *Ger.* Naugard. Zachodniopomorskie, NW Poland
Nowógard *see* Nowogard
Nowo-Minsk *see* Mińsk Mazowiecki
Nowy Dwór Mazowiecki 76 D3 Mazowieckie, C Poland
Nowy Sącz 77 D5 *Ger.* Neu Sandec. Małopolskie, S Poland
Nowy Tomyśl 76 B3 *var.* Nowy Tomysl. Wielkopolskie, C Poland
Noyon 68 C3 Oise, N France
Nsanje 57 E3 Southern, S Malawi
Nsawam 53 E5 SE Ghana
Ntomba, Lac 55 C6 *var.* Lac Tumba. *Lake* NW Dem. Rep. Congo
Nubian Desert 50 B3 *desert* NE Sudan
Nu'eima 97 E7 E West Bank
Nueva Gerona 32 B2 Isla de la Juventud, S Cuba
Nueva Rosita 28 D2 Coahuila de Zaragoza, NE Mexico
Nuevitas 32 C2 Camagüey, E Cuba
Nuevo, Bajo 31 G1 *island* NW Colombia
Nuevo Casas Grandes 28 C1 Chihuahua, N Mexico
Nuevo, Golfo 43 C6 *gulf* S Argentina
Nuevo Laredo 29 E2 Tamaulipas, NE Mexico
Nui Atoll 123 E3 *atoll* W Tuvalu
Nûk *see* Nuuk
Nuku'alofa 123 E5 *country capital* (Tonga) Tongatapu, S Tonga
Nukufetau Atoll 123 E3 *atoll* C Tuvalu
Nukulaelae Atoll 123 E3 *var.* Nukulailai. *Atoll* E Tuvalu
Nukulailai *see* Nukulaelae Atoll
Nukunau *see* Nikunau
Nukunonu Atoll 123 E3 *island* C Tokelau
Nukus 100 C2 Qoraqalpoghiston Respublikasi, W Uzbekistan
Nullarbor Plain 125 C6 *plateau* South Australia/Western Australia
Nunap Isua 98 B5 *var* Uummannarsuaq, *Dan.* Kap Farvel, *Eng.* Cape Farewell. *Headland* S Greenland
Nunavut 37 F3 *territory* N Canada
Nuneaton 67 D6 C England, UK
Nunivak Island 14 B2 *island* Alaska, USA
Nunspeet 64 D3 Gelderland, E Netherlands
Nuoro 75 A5 Sardegna, Italy, C Mediterranean Sea
Nuquí 36 A3 Chocó, W Colombia
Nurakita *see* Niulakita
Nuremberg *see* Nürnberg
Nurmes 62 E4 Itä-Suomi, E Finland
Nürnberg 73 C5 *Eng.* Nuremberg. Bayern, S Germany
Nurota 101 E2 *Rus.* Nurata. Nawoiy Wiloyati, C Uzbekistan
Nusa Tenggara 117 E5 *Eng.* Lesser Sunda Islands. East Timor / C Indonesia
Nusaybin 95 F4 *var.* Nisibin. Manisa, SE Turkey
Nuuk 60 C4 *var.* Nûk, *Dan.* Godthaab, Godthåb. *Dependent territory capital* (Greenland) SW Greenland
Nyagan' 92 C3 Khanty-Mansiyskiy Avtonomnyy Okrug, N Russian Federation
Nyainqêntanglha Shan 104 C5 *mountain range* W China
Nyala 50 A4 Southern Darfur, W Sudan
Nyamapanda 56 D3 Mashonaland East, NE Zimbabwe
Nyamtumbo 51 C8 Ruvuma, S Tanzania
Nyandoma 88 C4 Arkhangel'skaya Oblast', NW Russian Federation
Nyantakara 51 B7 Kagera, NW Tanzania
Nyasa, Lake 57 E2 *var.* Lake Malawi; *prev.* Lago Nyassa. *Lake* E Africa
Nyasvizh 85 C6 *Pol.* Nieśwież, *Rus.* Nesvizh. Minskaya Voblasts', C Belarus
Nyaunglebin 114 B4 Pegu, SW Myanmar
Nyeri 51 C6 Central, C Kenya
Nyima 104 C5 Xizang Zizhiqu, W China
Nyíregyháza 77 D6 Szabolcs-Szatmár-Bereg, NE Hungary
Nykøbing 63 B8 Storstrøm, SE Denmark
Nyköping 63 C6 Södermanland, S Sweden
Nylstroom *see* Modimolle
Nyngan 127 D6 New South Wales, SE Australia
Nyurba 93 F3 Respublika Sakha (Yakutiya), NE Russian Federation
Nyzhn'ohirs'kyy 87 F4 *Rus.* Nizhnegorskiy. Respublika Krym, S Ukraine
Nzega 51 C7 Tabora, C Tanzania
Nzérékoré 52 D4 Guinée-Forestière, SE Guinea
Nzwani *see* Anjouan

O

O'ahu 25 A7 *var.* Oahu. *Island* Hawai'i, USA, C Pacific Ocean
Oak Harbor 24 B1 Washington, NW USA
Oakland 25 B6 California, W USA
Oamaru 129 B7 Otago, South Island, NZ
Oaxaca 29 F5 *var.* Oaxaca de Juárez; *prev.* Antequera. Oaxaca, SE Mexico
Oaxaca de Juárez *see* Oaxaca
Ob' 90 C2 *river* C Russian Federation
Obal' 85 D5 *Rus.* Obol'. Vitsyebskaya Voblasts', N Belarus
Oban *see* Halfmoon Bay
Oban 66 C4 W Scotland, UK
Obando *see* Puerto Inírida
Obeliai 84 C4 Rokiškis, NE Lithuania
Oberhollabrunn *see* Tulln
Ob, Gulf of *see* Obskaya Guba
Obihiro 108 D2 Hokkaidō, NE Japan
Obo 54 D4 Haut-Mbomou, E Central African Republic
Obock 50 D4 E Djibouti
Oborniki 76 C3 Wielkopolskie, C Poland
Obskaya Guba 92 D3 *Eng.* Gulf of Ob'. *Gulf* N Russian Federation
Ob' Tablemount 119 B7 *undersea feature* S Indian Ocean
Ocala 21 E4 Florida, SE USA
Ocaña 70 D3 Castilla-La Mancha, C Spain
Ocaña 36 B2 Norte de Santander, N Colombia
O Carballiño 108 C1 *var* Carballiño. Gallicia, NW Spain
Occidental, Cordillera 39 E4 *mountain range* W South America
Occidental, Cordillera 36 B2 *mountain range* W Colombia
Occidental, Cordillera 38 D4 *mountain range* W Peru
Ocean Falls 14 D5 British Columbia, SW Canada
Ocean Island *see* Banaba
Oceanside 25 C8 California, W USA
Ochakiv 87 E4 *Rus.* Ochakov. Mykolayivs'ka Oblast', S Ukraine
Och'amch'ire 95 E2 *Rus.* Ochamchira. W Georgia
Ocho Rios 32 B4 C Jamaica
Ochrida, Lake *see* Ohrid, Lake
Ocotal 30 D3 Nueva Segovia, NW Nicaragua
Ocozocuautla 29 G5 Chiapas, SE Mexico
Ocú 31 F5 Herrera, S Panama
Ōdate 108 D3 Akita, Honshū, C Japan
Oddur *see* Xuddur
Ödemiş 94 A4 İzmir, SW Turkey
Odense 63 B7 Fyn, C Denmark
Oder 76 B3 *Cz./Pol.* Odra. *River* C Europe
Oderhaff *see* Szczeciński, Zalew
Odesa 87 E4 *Rus.* Odessa. Odes'ka Oblast', SW Ukraine
Odessa 27 E3 Texas, SW USA
Odienné 52 D4 NW Côte d'Ivoire
Ôdôngk 115 D6 Kâmpóng Spoe, S Cambodia
Odoorn 64 E2 Drenthe, NE Netherlands
Of 95 E2 Trabzon, NE Turkey
Ofanto 75 D5 *river* S Italy
Offenbach 73 B5 *var.* Offenbach am Main. Hessen, W Germany
Offenbach am Main *see* Offenbach
Offenburg 73 B6 Baden-Württemberg, SW Germany
Ogaden 51 D5 *Som.* Ogaadeen. *Plateau* Ethiopia/Somalia
Ōgaki 109 C6 Gifu, Honshū, SW Japan
Ogallala 22 D4 Nebraska, C USA
Ogbomosho 53 F4 Oyo, W Nigeria
Ogden 22 B4 Utah, W USA
Ogdensburg 19 F2 New York, NE USA
Ogulin 78 A3 Karlovac, NW Croatia
Ohio 18 C4 *off.* State of Ohio; also known as The Buckeye State. *State* N USA
Ohio River 18 C4 *river* N USA
Ohrid 79 D6 *Turk.* Ochrida, Ohri. SW FYR Macedonia
Ohrid, Lake 79 D6 *var.* Lake Ochrida, *Alb.* Liqeni i Ohrit, *Mac.* Ohridsko Ezero. *Lake* Albania/FYR Macedonia
Ohridsko Ezero *see* Ohrid, Lake
Ohura 128 D3 Manawatu-Wanganui, North Island, NZ
Oirschot 65 C5 Noord-Brabant, S Netherlands
Oise 68 C3 *river* N France
Oistins 33 G2 S Barbados
Ōita 109 B7 Ōita, Kyūshū, SW Japan
Ojinaga 28 D2 Chihuahua, N Mexico
Ojos del Salado, Cerro 42 B3 *mountain* W Argentina
Okaihau 128 C2 Northland, North Island, NZ
Okāra 112 C2 Punjab, E Pakistan
Okavanggo *see* Cubango
Okavango *see* Cubango
Okavango 56 C3 *district* NW Namibia
Okavango Delta 56 C3 *wetland* N Botswana
Okayama 109 B6 Okayama, Honshū, SW Japan
Okazaki 109 C6 Aichi, Honshū, C Japan
Okeechobee, Lake 21 E4 *lake* Florida, SE USA
Okefenokee Swamp 21 E3 *wetland* Georgia, SE USA
Okhotsk 93 G3 Khabarovskiy Kray, E Russian Federation
Okhotskoye More 93 G3 *sea* NW Pacific Ocean
Okhotsk, Sea of 91 F3 *sea* NW Pacific Ocean
Okhtyrka 87 F2 *Rus.* Akhtyrka. Sums'ka Oblast', NE Ukraine
Oki-guntō *see* Oki-shotō
Okinawa 108 A3 *island* SW Japan
Okinawa-shotō 108 A3 *island group* SW Japan
Oki-shotō 109 B6 *var.* Oki-guntō. *Island group* SW Japan
Oklahoma 27 F2 *off.* State of Oklahoma; also known as The Sooner State. *State* C USA
Oklahoma City 27 G1 *state capital* Oklahoma, C USA
Okmulgee 27 G1 Oklahoma, C USA
Oko, Wadi 50 C3 *river* NE Sudan
Oktyabr'skiy 89 D6 Volgogradskaya Oblast', SW Russian Federation
Oktyabr'skoy Revolyutsii, Ostrov 93 E2 *Eng.* October Revolution Island. *Island* Severnaya Zemlya, N Russian Federation
Okulovka *see* Uglovka
Okushiri-tō 108 C3 *var.* Okusiri Tô. *Island* NE Japan
Okusiri Tô *see* Okushiri-tō
Öland 63 C7 *island* S Sweden
Olavarría 43 D5 Buenos Aires, E Argentina
Oława 76 C4 *Ger.* Ohlau. Dolnośląskie, SW Poland
Olbia 75 A5 *prev.* Terranova Pausania. Sardegna, Italy, C Mediterranean Sea
Oldebroek 64 D3 Gelderland, E Netherlands
Oldenburg 72 B3 Niedersachsen, NW Germany
Oldenburg 72 C2 Schleswig-Holstein, N Germany
Oldenzaal 64 E3 Overijssel, E Netherlands
Old Harbour 32 B5 C Jamaica
Olëkma 93 F4 *river* C Russian Federation
Olëkminsk 93 F3 Respublika Sakha (Yakutiya), NE Russian Federation
Oleksandrivka 87 E3 *Rus.* Aleksandrovka. Kirovohrads'ka Oblast', C Ukraine
Oleksandriya 87 F3 *Rus.* Aleksandriya. Kirovohrads'ka Oblast', C Ukraine
Olenegorsk 88 C2 Murmanskaya Oblast', NW Russian Federation
Olenëk 93 E3 Respublika Sakha (Yakutiya), NE Russian Federation
Olenëk 93 E3 *river* NE Russian Federation
Oléron, Île d' 69 A5 *island* W France
Olevs'k 86 D1 *Rus.* Olevsk. Zhytomyrs'ka Oblast', N Ukraine
Ölgiy 104 C2 Bayan-Ölgiy, W Mongolia
Olhão 70 B5 Faro, S Portugal
Olifa 56 B3 Kunene, NW Namibia
Ólimbos *see* Ólympos
Olimpo *see* Fuerte Olimpo
Oliva 71 F4 País Valenciano, E Spain
Olivet 68 C4 Loiret, C France
Olmaliq 101 E2 *Rus.* Almalyk. Toshkent Wiloyati, E Uzbekistan
Olomouc 77 C5 *Ger.* Olmütz, *Pol.* Ołomuniec. Olomoucký Kraj, E Czech Republic
Olonets 88 B3 Respublika Kareliya, NW Russian Federation
Olovyannaya 93 F4 Chitinskaya Oblast', S Russian Federation

Olpe 72 B4 Nordrhein-Westfalen, W Germany
Olsztyn 76 D2 *Ger.* Allenstein. Warmińsko-Mazurskie, NE Poland
Olt 86 B5 *var.* Oltul, *Ger.* Alt. *River* S Romania
Oltenița 86 C5 *prev. Eng.* Oltenitsa, *anc.* Constantiola. Călărași, SE Romania
Oltul *see* Olt
Olvera 70 D5 Andalucía, S Spain
Olympia 24 B2 *state capital* Washington, NW USA
Olympic Mountains 24 A2 *mountain range* Washington, NW USA
Ólympos 82 B4 *var.* Ólimbos, *Eng.* Mount Olympus. *Mountain* N Greece
Olympus, Mount *see* Ólympos
Omagh 67 B5 *Ir.* An Ómaigh. W Northern Ireland, UK
Omaha 23 F4 Nebraska, C USA
Oman 99 D6 *Ar.* Saltanat 'Umān; *prev.* Muscat and Oman. *Country* SW Asia
Oman, Gulf of 98 E4 *Ar.* Khalīj 'Umān. *Gulf* N Arabian Sea
Omboué 55 A6 Ogooué-Maritime, W Gabon
Omdurman 50 B4 *var.* Umm Durmān. Khartoum, C Sudan
Ometepe, Isla de 30 D4 *island* S Nicaragua
Ommen 64 E3 Overijssel, E Netherlands
Omsk 92 C4 Omskaya Oblast', C Russian Federation
Ōmuta 109 A7 Fukuoka, Kyūshū, SW Japan
Onda 71 F3 País Valenciano, E Spain
Ondjiva *see* N'Giva
Öndörhaan 105 E2 Hentiy, E Mongolia
Onega 88 B4 *river* NW Russian Federation
Onega 88 C3 Arkhangel'skaya Oblast', NW Russian Federation
Onega, Lake *see* Onezhskoye Ozero
Onex 73 A7 Genève, SW Switzerland
Onezhskoye Ozero 88 B4 *Eng.* Lake Onega. *Lake* NW Russian Federation
Ongole 110 D1 Andhra Pradesh, E India
Onitsha 53 G5 Anambra, S Nigeria
Onon Gol 105 E2 *river* N Mongolia
Onponte *see* Orantes
Onslow 124 A4 Western Australia
Onslow Bay 21 F1 *bay* North Carolina, E USA
Ontario 16 B3 *province* S Canada
Ontario, Lake 19 E3 *lake* Canada/USA
Onteniente *see* Ontinyent
Ontinyent 71 F4 *var.* Onteniente. País Valenciano, E Spain
Ontong Java Rise 103 H4 *undersea feature* W Pacific Ocean
Oostakker 65 B5 Oost-Vlaanderen, NW Belgium
Oostburg 65 B5 Zeeland, SW Netherlands
Oostende 65 A5 *Eng.* Ostend, *Fr.* Ostende. West-Vlaanderen, NW Belgium
Oosterbeek 64 D4 Gelderland, SE Netherlands
Oosterhout 64 C4 Noord-Brabant, S Netherlands
Opatija 78 A2 *It.* Abbazia. Primorje-Gorski Kotar, NW Croatia
Opava 77 C5 *Ger.* Troppau. Ostravský Kraj, E Czech Republic
Opelika 20 D2 Alabama, S USA
Opelousas 20 B3 Louisiana, S USA
Opmeer 64 C2 Noord-Holland, NW Netherlands
Opochka 88 A4 Pskovskaya Oblast', W Russian Federation
Opole 76 C4 *Ger.* Oppeln. Opolskie, S Poland
Opotiki 128 E3 Bay of Plenty, North Island, NZ
Oppidum Ubiorum *see* Köln
Oqtosh 101 E2 *Rus.* Aktash. Samarqand Wiloyati, C Uzbekistan
Oradea 86 B3 *prev.* Oradea Mare, *Ger.* Grosswardein, *Hung.* Nagyvárad. Bihor, NW Romania
Orahovac 79 D5 *Alb.* Rahovec. Serbia, S Serbia and Montenegro (Yugo.)
Oran 48 D2 *var.* Ouahran, Wahran. NW Algeria
Orange 69 D6 *anc.* Arausio. Vaucluse, SE France
Orange 127 D6 New South Wales, SE Australia
Orangeburg 21 E2 South Carolina, SE USA
Orange Cone *see* Orange Fan
Orange Fan 47 C7 *var.* Orange Cone. *Undersea feature* SW Indian Ocean
Orange Mouth *see* Oranjemund
Orangemund *see* Oranjemund
Orange River 56 B4 *Afr.* Oranjerivier. *River* S Africa
Orange Walk 30 C1 Orange Walk, N Belize
Oranienburg 72 D3 Brandenburg, NE Germany
Oranjemund 56 B4 *var.* Orangemund; *prev.* Orange Mouth. Karas, SW Namibia
Oranjestad 33 E5 *dependent territory capital* (Aruba) W Aruba
Orantes 96 B3 *var.* Ononte, *Ar.* Nahr el Aassi, Nahr al 'Aṣī. *River* SW Asia
Oravița 86 A4 *Ger.* Orawitza, *Hung.* Oravicabánya. Caraș-Severin, SW Romania
Orbetello 74 B4 Toscana, C Italy
Orcadas 132 A1 *Argentinian research station* South Orkney Islands, Antarctica
Orchard Homes 22 B1 Montana, NW USA
Ordino 69 A8 NW Andorra
Ordos Desert *see* Mu Us Shamo
Ordu 94 D2 *anc.* Cotyora. Ordu, N Turkey
Ordzhonikidze 87 F3 Dnipropetrovs'ka Oblast', E Ukraine
Orealla 37 G3 E Guyana
Örebro 63 C6 Örebro, C Sweden
Oregon 24 B3 *off.* State of Oregon; also known as Beaver State, Sunset State, Valentine State, Webfoot State. *State* NW USA
Oregon City 24 B3 Oregon, NW USA
Orël 89 B5 Orlovskaya Oblast', W Russian Federation
Orem 22 B4 Utah, W USA
Orenburg 89 D6 *prev.* Chkalov. Orenburgskaya Oblast', W Russian Federation
Orense *see* Ourense
Oreor *see* Koror
Orestiáda 82 D3 *prev.* Orestiás. Anatolikí Makedonía kai Thráki, NE Greece
Organ Peak 26 D3 *mountain* New Mexico, SW USA
Orgeyev *see* Orhei
Orhei 86 D3 *var.* Orheiu, *Rus.* Orgeyev. N Moldova
Orheiu *see* Orhei
Oriental, Cordillera 38 D3 *mountain range* Bolivia/Peru
Oriental, Cordillera 39 F4 *mountain range* C Bolivia
Oriental, Cordillera 36 B3 *mountain range* C Colombia
Orihuela 71 F4 País Valenciano, E Spain
Orikhiv 87 G3 *Rus.* Orekhov. Zaporiz'ka Oblast', SE Ukraine
Orinoco, Río 37 E2 *river* Colombia/Venezuela
Orissa 113 F4 *state* NE India
Orissaare 84 C2 *Ger.* Orissaar. Saaremaa, W Estonia
Oristano 75 A5 Sardegna, Italy, C Mediterranean Sea
Orito 36 A4 Putumayo, SW Colombia
Orizaba, Volcán Pico de 13 C7 *var.* Citlaltépetl. *Mountain* S Mexico
Orkney *see* Orkney Islands
Orkney Islands 66 C2 *var.* Orkney, Orkneys. *Island group* N Scotland, UK
Orkneys *see* Orkney Islands
Orlando 21 E4 Florida, SE USA
Orléanais 68 C4 *cultural region* C France
Orléans 68 C4 *anc.* Aurelianum. Loiret, C France
Orléansville *see* Chlef
Orly 68 E2 *international airport* (Paris) Essonne, N France
Orlya 85 B6 *Rus.* Orlya. Hrodzyenskaya Voblasts', W Belarus
Ormuz, Strait of *see* Hormuz, Strait of
Örnsköldsvik 63 C5 Västernorrland, C Sweden
Oromocto 17 F4 New Brunswick, SE Canada
Orona 123 F3 *prev.* Hull Island. *Atoll* Phoenix Islands, C Kiribati
Orosirá Rodhópis *see* Rhodope Mountains
Orpington 67 B8 SE England, UK
Orsha 85 E6 *Rus.* Orsha. Vitsyebskaya Voblasts', NE Belarus
Orsk 92 B4 Orenburgskaya Oblast', W Russian Federation
Orșova 86 A4 *Ger.* Orschowa, *Hung.* Orsova. Mehedinți, SW Romania
Orthez 69 B6 Pyrénées-Atlantiques, SW France
Ortona 74 D4 Abruzzo, C Italy
Oruba *see* Aruba
Oruro 39 F4 Oruro, W Bolivia
Ōsaka 109 C6 *hist.* Naniwa. Ōsaka, Honshū, SW Japan
Osa, Península de 31 E5 *peninsula* S Costa Rica
Osborn Plateau 119 D5 *undersea feature* E Indian Ocean
Osh 101 F2 Oshskaya Oblast', SW Kyrgyzstan
Oshawa 16 D5 Ontario, SE Canada
Oshikango 56 B3 Ohangwena, N Namibia
Ō-shima 109 D6 *island* S Japan
Oshkosh 18 B2 Wisconsin, N USA
Osijek 78 C3 *prev.* Osiek, Osjek, *Ger.* Esseg, *Hung.* Eszék. Osijek-Baranja, E Croatia
Oskaloosa 23 G4 Iowa, C USA
Oskarshamn 63 C7 Kalmar, S Sweden
Oskil 87 G2 *Rus.* Oskol. *River* Russian Federation/Ukraine
Oslo 63 B6 *prev.* Christiania, Kristiania. *Country capital* (Norway) Oslo, S Norway
Osmaniye 94 D4 Osmaniye, admin. region *province* S Turkey
Osnabrück 72 A3 Niedersachsen, NW Germany
Osogov Mountains 120 B3 *var.* Osogovske Planine, Osogovski Planina, *Mac.* Osogovski Planini. *mountain range* Bulgaria/FYR, Macedonia
Osogovske Planine/Osogovski Planina/Osogovski Planini *see* Osogov Mountains
Osorno 43 B5 Los Lagos, C Chile
Oss 64 D4 Noord-Brabant, S Netherlands
Ossa, Serra d' 70 C4 *mountain range* SE Portugal
Ossora 93 H2 Koryakskiy Avtonomnyy Okrug, E Russian Federation
Ostend *see* Oostende
Ostende *see* Oostende
Oster 87 E1 Chernihivs'ka Oblast', N Ukraine
Östersund 63 C5 Jämtland, C Sweden
Ostfriesische Inseln 72 A3 *Eng.* East Frisian Islands. *Island group* NW Germany
Ostiglia 74 C2 Lombardia, N Italy
Ostrava 77 C5 Ostravský Kraj, E Czech Republic
Ostróda 76 D3 *Ger.* Osterode, Osterode in Ostpreussen. Warmińsko-Mazurskie, NE Poland
Ostrołęka 76 D3 *Ger.* Wiesenhof, *Rus.* Ostrolenka. Mazowieckie, C Poland
Ostrov 88 A4 *Latv.* Austrava. Karlovarský Kraj, W Czech Republic
Ostrovets *see* Ostrowiec Świętokrzyski
Ostrovnoy 88 C2 Murmanskaya Oblast', NW Russian Federation
Ostrów *see* Ostrów Wielkopolski
Ostrowiec *see* Ostrowiec Świętokrzyski
Ostrowiec Świętokrzyski 76 D4 *var.* Ostrowiec, *Rus.* Ostrovets. Świętokrzyskie, C Poland
Ostrów Mazowiecka 76 D3 *var.* Ostrów Mazowiecki. Mazowieckie, C Poland
Ostrów Mazowiecki *see* Ostrów Mazowiecka
Ostrowo *see* Ostrów Wielkopolski
Ostrów Wielkopolski 76 C4 *var.* Ostrów, *Ger.* Ostrowo. Wielkopolskie, C Poland
Osum *see* Osumit, Lumi i
Ōsumi-shotō 109 A8 *island group* SW Japan
Osumit, Lumi i 79 D7 *var.* Osum. *River* SE Albania
Osuna 70 D4 Andalucía, S Spain
Oswego 19 F2 New York, NE USA
Otago Peninsula 129 B7 *peninsula* South Island, NZ
Otaki 128 D4 Wellington, North Island, NZ
Otaru 108 C2 Hokkaidō, NE Japan
Otavalo 38 B1 Imbabura, N Ecuador
Otavi 56 B3 Otjozondjupa, N Namibia
Oțelu Roșu 86 B4 *Ger.* Ferdinandsberg, *Hung.* Nándorhgy. Caras-Severin, SW Romania
Otepää 84 D3 *Ger.* Odenpäh. Valgamaa, SE Estonia
Oti 53 E4 *river* W Africa
Otira 129 C6 West Coast, South Island, NZ
Otjiwarongo 56 B3 Otjozondjupa, N Namibia
Otorohanga 128 D3 Waikato, North Island, NZ
Otranto, Strait of 79 C6 *It.* Canale d'Otranto. *Strait* Albania/Italy
Otrokovice 77 C5 *Ger.* Otrokowitz. Zlínský Kraj, E Czech Republic
Ōtsu 109 C6 *var.* Ōtu. Shiga, Honshū, SW Japan
Ottawa 19 E2 *Fr.* Outaouais. Admin. region *river* Ontario/Quebec, SE Canada
Ottawa 16 D5 *country capital* (Canada) Ontario, SE Canada
Ottawa 18 B3 Illinois, N USA
Ottawa 23 F5 Kansas, C USA
Ottawa Islands 16 C1 *island group* Northwest Territories, C Canada
Ottignies 65 C6 Wallon Brabant, C Belgium
Ottumwa 23 G4 Iowa, C USA
Ōtu *see* Ōtsu
Ouachita Mountains 20 A1 *mountain range* Arkansas/Oklahoma, C USA
Ouachita River 20 B2 *river* Arkansas/Louisiana, C USA
Ouadi Howa *see* Howar, Wādi
Ouagadougou 53 E4 *var.* Wagadugu. *Country capital* (Burkina Faso) C Burkina Faso
Ouahigouya 53 E3 NW Burkina faso
Ouahran *see* Oran
Oualata *see* Oualâta
Oualâta 52 D3 *var.* Oualata. Hodh ech Chargui, SE Mauritania
Ouanary 37 H3 E French Guiana
Ouanda Djallé 54 D4 Vakaga, NE Central African Republic
Ouarâne 52 D2 *desert* C Mauritania
Ouargla 49 E2 *var.* Wargla. NE Algeria
Ouarzazate 48 C3 S Morocco
Oubangui *see* Ubangi
Oubangui-Chari *see* Central African Republic
Ouessant, Île d' 68 A3 *Eng.* Ushant. *Island* NW France
Ouésso 55 B5 La Sangha, NW Congo
Oujda 48 D2 *Ar.* Oudjda, Ujda. NE Morocco
Oujeft 52 C2 Adrar, C Mauritania
Oulu 62 D4 *Swe.* Uleåborg. Oulu, C Finland
Oulujärvi 62 D4 *Swe.* Uleträsk. *Lake* C Finland
Oulujoki 62 D4 *Swe.* Uleälv. *River* C Finland
Ounasjoki 62 D3 *river* N Finland
Ounianga Kébir 54 C2 Borkou-Ennedi-Tibesti, N Chad
Oup *see* Auob
Oupeye 65 D6 Liège, E Belgium
Our 65 D6 *river* NW Europe
Ourense 70 C1 *var. Cast.* Orense; *Lat.* Aurium. Galicia, NW Spain
Ourique 70 B4 Beja, S Portugal
Ourthe 65 D7 *river* E Belgium
Ouse 67 D5 *river* N England, UK
Outer Hebrides 66 B3 *var.* Western Isles. *Island group* NW Scotland, UK
Outer Islands 57 G1 *island group* SW Seychelles
Outes 70 B1 Galicia, NW Spain
Ouvéa 122 D5 *island* Îles Loyauté, NE New Caledonia
Ouyen 127 C6 Victoria, SE Australia
Ovalle 42 B3 Coquimbo, N Chile
Ovar 70 B2 Aveiro, N Portugal
Overflakkee 64 B4 *island* SW Netherlands
Overijse 65 C6 Vlaams Brabant, C Belgium
Oviedo 70 C1 *anc.* Asturias. Asturias, NW Spain
Ovruch 86 D1 Zhytomyrs'ka Oblast', N Ukraine
Owando 55 B5 *prev.* Fort-Rousset. Cuvette, C Congo
Owase 109 C6 Mie, Honshū, SW Japan
Owatonna 23 F3 Minnesota, N USA
Owen Fracture Zone 118 B4 *tectonic feature* W Arabian Sea
Owen, Mount 129 C5 *mountain* South Island, NZ
Owensboro 18 B5 Kentucky, S USA
Owen Stanley Range 122 B3 *mountain range* S PNG
Owerri 53 G5 Imo, S Nigeria
Owo 53 F5 Ondo, SW Nigeria
Owyhee River 24 C4 *river* Idaho/Oregon, NW USA
Oxford 67 D6 *Lat.* Oxonia. S England, UK
Oxford 129 C6 Canterbury, South Island, NZ
Oxkutzcab 29 H4 Yucatán, SE Mexico
Oxnard 25 B7 California, W USA
Oyama 109 D5 Tochigi, Honshū, S Japan
Oyem 55 B5 Woleu-Ntem, N Gabon
Oyo 55 B6 Cuvette, C Congo
Oyo 53 F4 Oyo, W Nigeria
Ozark 20 D3 Alabama, S USA
Ozark Plateau 23 G5 *plain* Arkansas/Missouri, C USA
Ozarks, Lake of the 23 F5 *reservoir* Missouri, C USA
Ozbourn Seamount 130 D4 *undersea feature* W Pacific Ocean
Ózd 77 D6 Borsod-Abaúj-Zemplén, NE Hungary
Ozero Khanka *see* Khanka, Lake
Ozero Ubsu-Nur *see* Uvs Nuur
Ozieri 75 A5 Sardegna, Italy, C Mediterranean Sea

P

Paamiut 60 B4 *var.* Pâmiut, *Dan.* Frederikshåb. S Greenland
Pa-an 114 B4 Karen State, S Myanmar
Pabianice 76 C4 Łodz, C Poland
Pabna 113 G4 Rajshahi, W Bangladesh
Pachuca 29 E4 *var.* Pachuca de Soto. Hidalgo, C Mexico
Pachuca de Soto *see* Pachuca
Pacific-Antarctic Ridge 132 B5 *undersea feature* S Pacific Ocean
Pacific Ocean 130 D3 *ocean*
Padalung *see* Phatthalung
Padang 116 B4 Sumatera, W Indonesia
Paderborn 72 B4 Nordrhein-Westfalen, NW Germany
Padma *see* Brahmaputra
Padova 74 C2 *Eng.* Padua; *anc.* Patavium. Veneto, NE Italy
Padre Island 27 G5 *island* Texas, SW USA
Padua *see* Padova
Paducah 18 B5 Kentucky, S USA
Paeroa 128 D3 Waikato, North Island, NZ
Páfos 80 C5 *var.* Paphos. W Cyprus
Pag 78 A3 *It.* Pago. *Island* Zadar SW Croatia
Page 26 B1 Arizona, SW USA
Pago Pago 123 F4 *dependent territory capital* (American Samoa) Tutuila, W American Samoa
Pahiatua 128 D4 Manawatu-Wanganui, North Island, NZ
Pahsien *see* Chongqing
Paide 84 D2 *Ger.* Weissenstein. Järvamaa, N Estonia
Paihia 128 D2 Northland, North Island, NZ
Päijänne 63 D5 *lake* S Finland
Paine, Cerro 43 A7 *mountain* S Chile
Painted Desert 26 B1 *desert* Arizona, SW USA
Paisley 66 C4 W Scotland, UK
País Valenciano 71 F3 *cultural region* NE Spain
País Vasco 71 E1 *cultural region* N Spain
Paita 38 B3 Piura, NW Peru
Pakanbaru *see* Pekanbaru
Pakaraima Mountains 37 E3 *var.* Serra Pacaraim, Sierra Pacaraima. *Mountain range* N South America
Pakistan 112 A2 *var.* Islami Jamhuriya e Pakistan. *Country* S Asia
Paknam *see* Samut Prakan
Pakokku 114 A3 Magwe, C Myanmar
Pak Phanang 115 C7 *var.* Ban Pak Phanang. Nakhon Si Thammarat, SW Thailand
Pakruojis 84 C4 Pakruojis, N Lithuania
Paks 77 C7 Tolna, S Hungary
Pakxé *see* Pakxé
Pakxé 115 D5 *var.* Paksé. Champasak, S Laos
Palafrugell 71 G2 Cataluña, NE Spain
Palagruža 79 B5 *It.* Pelagosa. *Island* SW Croatia
Palaiá Epídavros 83 C6 Pelopónnisos, S Greece
Palaiseau 68 D2 Essonne, N France
Palamós 71 G2 Cataluña, NE Spain
Palamuse 84 E2 *Ger.* Sankt-Bartholomäi. Jõgevamaa, E Estonia
Pālanpur 112 C4 Gujarāt, W India
Palapye 56 D3 Central, SE Botswana
Palau 122 A2 *var.* Belau. *Country* W Pacific Ocean
Palawan 117 E2 *island* W Philippines
Palawan Passage 116 D2 *passage* W Philippines
Paldiski 84 D2 *prev.* Baltiski, *Eng.* Baltic Port, *Ger.* Baltischport. Harjumaa, NW Estonia
Palembang 116 B4 Sumatera, W Indonesia
Palencia 70 D2 *anc.* Palantia, Pallantia. Castilla-León, NW Spain
Palermo 75 C7 *Fr.* Palerme; *anc.* Panhormus, Panormus. Sicilia, Italy, C Mediterranean Sea
Pāli 112 C3 Rājasthān, N India
Palikir 122 C2 *country capital* (Micronesia) Pohnpei, E Micronesia
Palimé *see* Kpalimé
Palioúri, Akrotírio 82 C4 *var.* Akra Kanestron. *Headland* N Greece
Palk Strait 110 C3 *strait* India/Sri Lanka
Palliser, Cape 129 D5 *headland* North Island, NZ
Palma 71 G3 *var.* Palma de Mallorca. Mallorca, Spain, W Mediterranean Sea
Palma del Río 70 D4 Andalucía, S Spain
Palma de Mallorca *see* Palma
Palmar Sur 31 E5 Puntarenas, SE Costa Rica
Palma Soriano 32 C3 Santiago de Cuba, E Cuba
Palm Beach 126 E1 New South Wales, SE Australia
Palmer 132 A2 *US research station* Antarctica
Palmer Land 132 A3 *physical region* Antarctica
Palmerston 123 F4 *island* S Cook Islands
Palmerston North 128 D4 Manawatu-Wanganui, North Island, NZ
Palmi 75 D7 Calabria, SW Italy
Palmira 36 B3 Valle del Cauca, W Colombia
Palm Springs 25 D7 California, W USA
Palmyra *see* Tudmur
Palmyra Atoll 123 G2 *US privately owned unincorporated territory* C Pacific Ocean
Palo Alto 25 B6 California, W USA
Palu 117 E4 *prev.* Paloe. Sulawesi, C Indonesia
Pamiers 69 B6 Ariège, S France
Pamir *var.* Daryā-ye Pāmīr, *Taj.* Dar"yoi Pomir. *River* Afghanistan/Tajikistan *see also* Pāmīr, Daryā-ye
Pamirs 101 F3 *Pash.* Daryā-ye Pāmīr, *Rus.* Pamir. *Mountain range* C Asia
Pâmiut *see* Paamiut
Pamlico Sound 21 G1 *sound* North Carolina, SE USA
Pampa 27 E1 Texas, SW USA
Pampas 42 C4 *plain* C Argentina
Pamplona 71 E1 *Basq.* Iruña; *prev.* Pampeluna, *anc.* Pompaelo. Navarra, N Spain
Pamplona 36 C2 Norte de Santander, N Colombia
Panaji *see* Pānji
Panama 31 G5 *Country* Central America
Panamá 31 G4 *var.* Ciudad de Panamá, *Eng.* Panama City. *Country capital* (Panama) Panamá, C Panama
Panama Basin 13 C8 *undersea feature* E Pacific Ocean
Panama Canal 31 F4 *canal* E Panama
Panama City *see* Panamá
Panama City 20 D3 Florida, SE USA
Panamá, Golfo de 31 G5 *var.* Gulf of Panama. *Gulf* S Panama
Panama, Gulf of *see* Panamá, Golfo de
Panamá, Isthmus of *see* Panamá, Istmo de
Panamá, Istmo de 31 G4 *Eng.* Isthmus of Panama; *prev.* Isthmus of Darien. *Isthmus* E Panama
Panay Island 117 E2 *island* C Philippines
Pančevo 78 D3 *Ger.* Pantschowa, *Hung.* Pancsova. Serbia, N Serbia and Montenegro (Yugo.)
Paneas *see* Bāniyās
Panevėžys 84 C4 Panevėžys, C Lithuania
Pangim *see* Pānji
Pangkalpinang 116 C4 Pulau Bangka, W Indonesia
Pang-Nga *see* Phang-Nga
Panjim *see* Pānji
Pānji 110 B1 *var.* Pangim, Panaji, Panjim, New Goa. Goa, W India
Pánormos 83 C7 Kríti, Greece, E Mediterranean Sea
Pantanal 41 E3 *var.* Pantanalmato-Grossense. *Swamp* SW Brazil
Pantanalmato-Grossense *see* Pantanal
Pantelleria, Isola di 75 B7 *island* SW Italy
Pánuco 29 E3 Veracruz-Llave, E Mexico
Pao-chi *see* Baoji
Paoki *see* Baoji
Paola 80 B5 E Malta
Pao-shan *see* Baoshan
Pao-t'ou *see* Baotou
Paotow *see* Baotou
Papagayo, Golfo de 30 C4 *gulf* NW Costa Rica
Papakura 128 D3 Auckland, North Island, NZ
Papantla 29 F4 *var.* Papantla de Olarte. Veracruz-Llave, E Mexico
Papantla de Olarte *see* Papantla
Papeete 123 H4 *dependent territory capital* (French Polynesia) Tahiti, W French Polynesia
Paphos *see* Páfos
Papilė 84 B3 Akmenė, NW Lithuania
Papillion 23 F4 Nebraska, C USA
Papua 117 H4 *var.* Irian Barat, Irian Jaya, West Irian, West New Guinea, West Papua; *prev.* Dutch New Guinea, Netherlands New Guinea. Admin. region *province* E Indonesia
Papua, Gulf of 122 B3 *gulf* S PNG
Papua New Guinea 122 B3 *prev.* Territory of Papua and New Guinea, *abbrev.* PNG. *Country* NW Melanesia
Papuk 78 C3 *mountain range* NE Croatia
Pará 41 E2 *off.* Estado do Pará. *State* NE Brazil
Pará *see* Belém
Paracel Islands 103 E3 *disputed territory* SE Asia
Paraćin 78 D4 Serbia, C Serbia and Montenegro (Yugo.)
Paragua, Río 37 E3 *river* SE Venezuela
Paraguay 42 D2 *var.* Río Paraguay. *River* C South America
Paraguay 42 C2 *country* C South America
Paraguay, Río *see* Paraguay
Paraíba 41 G2 *off.* Estado da Paraíba; *prev.* Parahiba, Parahyba. *State* E Brazil
Parakou 53 F4 C Benin
Paramaribo 37 G3 *country capital* (Suriname) Paramaribo, N Suriname
Paramushir, Ostrov 93 H3 *island* SE Russian Federation
Paraná 41 E5 *off.* Estado do Paraná. *State* S Brazil
Paraná 35 C5 *var.* Alto Paraná. *River* C South America
Paraná 41 E4 Entre Ríos, E Argentina
Paranéstio 82 C3 Anatolikí Makedonía kai Thráki, NE Greece
Paraparaumu 129 D5 Wellington, North Island, NZ

INDEX

Parchim *72 C3* Mecklenburg-Vorpommern, N Germany
Parczew *76 E4* Lubelskie, E Poland
Pardubice *77 B5 Ger.* Pardubitz. Pardubický Kraj, C Czech Republic
Parechcha *85 B5 Rus.* Porech'ye. Hrodzyenskaya Voblasts', NE Belarus
Parecis, Chapada dos *40 D3 var.* Serra dos Parecis. *Mountain range* W Brazil
Parepare *117 E4* Sulawesi, C Indonesia
Párga *83 A5* Ípeiros, W Greece
Paria, Golfo de *see* Paria, Gulf of
Paria, Gulf of *37 E1 var.* Golfo de Paria. *Gulf* Trinidad and Tobago/Venezuela
Parika *37 F2* NE Guyana
Paris *68 D1 anc.* Lutetia, Lutetia Parisiorum, Parisii. *Country capital* (France) Paris, N France
Paris *27 G2* Texas, SW USA
Parkersburg *18 D4* West Virginia, NE USA
Parkes *127 D6* New South Wales, SE Australia
Parma *74 B2* Emilia-Romagna, N Italy
Parnahyba *see* Parnaíba
Parnaíba *41 F2 var.* Parnahyba. Piauí, E Brazil
Pärnu *84 D2 Ger.* Pernau, *Latv.* Pērnava; *prev.* Rus. Pernov. Pärnumaa, SW Estonia
Pärnu *84 D2 var.* Parnu Jõgi, *Ger.* Pernau. *River* SW Estonia
Pärnu-Jaagupi *84 D2 Ger.* Sankt-Jakobi. Pärnumaa, SW Estonia
Parnu Jõgi *see* Pärnu
Pärnu Laht *84 D2 Ger.* Pernauer Bucht. *Bay* SW Estonia
Páros *83 C6 island* Kykládes, Greece, Aegean Sea
Páros *83 D6* Páros, Kykládes, Greece, Aegean Sea
Parral *see* Hidalgo del Parral
Parral *42 B4* Maule, C Chile
Parramatta *126 D1* New South Wales, SE Australia
Parras *28 D3 var.* Parras de la Fuente. Coahuila de Zaragoza, NE Mexico
Parras de la Fuente *see* Parras
Parsons *23 F5* Kansas, C USA
Pasadena *25 C7* California, W USA
Pasadena *27 H4* Texas, SW USA
Paşcani *86 C3 Hung.* Páskán. Iaşi, NE Romania
Pasco *24 C2* Washington, NW USA
Pas de Calais *see* Dover, Strait of
Pasewalk *72 D3* Mecklenburg-Vorpommern, NE Germany
Pasinler *95 F3* Erzurum, NE Turkey
Pasłęk *76 D2 Ger.* Preußisch Holland. Warmińsko-Mazurskie, NE Poland
Pasni *112 A3* Baluchistān, SW Pakistan
Paso de Indios *43 B6* Chubut, S Argentina
Passau *73 D6* Bayern, SE Germany
Passo del Brennero *see* Brenner Pass
Passo Fundo *41 E5* Rio Grande do Sul, S Brazil
Pastavy *85 C5 Pol.* Postawy, *Rus.* Postavy. Vitsyebskaya Voblasts', NW Belarus
Pastaza, Río *38 B2 river* Ecuador/Peru
Pasto *36 A4* Nariño, SW Colombia
Pasvalys *84 C4* Pasvalys, N Lithuania
Patagonia *35 B7 physical region* Argentina/Chile
Patalung *see* Phatthalung
Patani *see* Pattani
Patavium *see* Padova
Patea *128 D4* Taranaki, North Island, NZ
Paterson *19 F3* New Jersey, NE USA
Pathein *see* Bassein
Pátmos *83 D6 island* Dodekánisos, Greece, Aegean Sea
Patna *113 F3 var.* Azimabad. Bihār, N India
Patnos *95 F3* Ağrı, E Turkey
Patos, Lagoa dos *41 E5 lagoon* S Brazil
Pátra *83 B5 Eng.* Patras; *prev.* Pátrai. Dytikí Ellás, S Greece
Pattani *115 C7 var.* Patani. Pattani, SW Thailand
Pattaya *115 C5* Chon Buri, S Thailand
Patuca, Río *30 D2 river* E Honduras
Pau *69 B6* Pyrénées-Atlantiques, SW France
Paulatuk *15 E3* Northwest Territories, NW Canada
Paungde *114 B4* Pegu, C Myanmar
Pavia *74 B2 anc.* Ticinum. Lombardia, N Italy
Pāvilosta *84 B3* Liepāja, W Latvia
Pavlikeni *82 D2* Veliko Tŭrnovo, N Bulgaria
Pavlodar *92 C4* Pavlodar, NE Kazakhstan
Pavlohrad *87 G3 Rus.* Pavlograd. Dnipropetrovs'ka Oblast', E Ukraine
Pawn *114 B3 river* C Myanmar
Paxoí *83 A5 island* Iónioi Nísoi, Greece, C Mediterranean Sea
Payo Obispo *see* Chetumal
Paysandú *42 D4* Paysandú, W Uruguay
Pazar *95 E2* Rize, NE Turkey
Pazardzhik *82 C3 prev.* Tatar Pazardzhik. Pazardzhik, C Bulgaria
Pearl River *20 B3 river* Louisiana/Mississippi, S USA
Pearsall *27 F4* Texas, SW USA
Peć *79 D5 Alb.* Pejë, *Turk.* Ipek. Serbia, S Serbia and Montenegro (Yugo.)
Pechora *88 D3 river* NW Russian Federation
Pechora *88 D3* Respublika Komi, NW Russian Federation
Pechorskoye More *88 D2 Eng.* Pechora Sea. *Sea* NW Russian Federation
Pecos *27 E3* Texas, SW USA
Pecos River *27 E3 river* New Mexico/Texas, SW USA
Pécs *77 C7 Ger.* Fünfkirchen; *Lat.* Sopianae. Baranya, SW Hungary
Pedra Lume *52 A3* Sal, NE Cape Verde
Pedro Cays *32 C3 island group* S Jamaica
Pedro Juan Caballero *42 D2* Amambay, E Paraguay
Peer *65 D5* Limburg, NE Belgium
Pegasus Bay *129 C6 bay* South Island, NZ
Pegu *114 B4 var.* Bago. Pegu, SW Myanmar
Pehuajó *42 C4* Buenos Aires, E Argentina
Pei-ching *see* Beijing
Peine *72 B3* Niedersachsen, C Germany
Pei-p'ing *see* Beijing
Peipus, Lake *E3 Est.* Peipsi Järv, *Ger.* Peipus-See, *Rus.* Chudskoye Ozero. *Lake* Estonia/Russian Federation
Peiraías *83 C6 prev.* Piraiévs, *Eng.* Piraeus. Attikí, C Greece
Pèk *114 D4 var.* Xieng Khouang; *prev.* Xiangkhoang. Xiangkhoang, N Laos
Pekalongan *116 C4* Jawa, C Indonesia
Pekanbaru *116 B3 var.* Pakanbaru. Sumatera, W Indonesia
Pekin *18 B4* Illinois, N USA
Peking *see* Beijing
Pelagie, Isole *75 B8 island group* SW Italy
Pelly Bay *15 G3* Nunavut, N Canada
Peloponnese *see* Pelopónnisos
Peloponnesus *see* Pelopónnisos
Pelopónnisos *83 B6 var.* Morea, *Eng.* Peloponnese; *anc.* Peloponnesus. *Peninsula* S Greece
Pematangsiantar *116 B3* Sumatera, W Indonesia
Pemba *57 F2 prev.* Port Amelia, Porto Amélia. Cabo Delgado, NE Mozambique
Pemba *51 D7 island* E Tanzania
Pembroke *16 D4* Ontario, SE Canada
Penang *see* George Town
Penang *see* Pinang, Pulau
Penas, Golfo de *43 A7 gulf* S Chile
Penderma *see* Bandırma
Pendleton *24 C3* Oregon, NW USA
Pend Oreille, Lake *24 D2 lake* Idaho, NW USA
Peneius *see* Pineiós
Peng-pu *see* Bengbu
Peniche *70 B3* Leiria, W Portugal
Péninsule de la Gaspésie *see* Gaspé, Péninsule de
Pennine Alps *73 A8 Fr.* Alpes Pennines, *It.* Alpi Pennine; *Lat.* Alpes Penninae. *Mountain range* Italy/Switzerland
Pennine Chain *see* Pennines
Pennines *67 D5 var.* Pennine Chain. *Mountain range* N England, UK
Pennsylvania *18 D3 off.* Commonwealth of Pennsylvania; also known as The Keystone State. *State* NE USA
Penobscot River *19 G2 river* Maine, NE USA
Penong *127 A6* South Australia
Penonomé *31 F5* Coclé, C Panama
Penrhyn *123 G3 atoll* N Cook Islands
Penrhyn Basin *121 F3 undersea feature* C Pacific Ocean
Penrith *126 D1* New South Wales, SE Australia
Penrith *67 D5* NW England, UK
Pensacola *20 C3* Florida, SE USA
Pentecost *122 D4 Fr.* Pentecôte. *Island* C Vanuatu
Penza *89 C6* Penzenskaya Oblast', W Russian Federation
Penzance *67 C7* SW England, UK
Peoria *18 B4* Illinois, N USA
Perchtoldsdorf *73 E6* Niederösterreich, NE Austria
Percival Lakes *124 C4 lakes* Western Australia
Perdido, Monte *71 F1 mountain* NE Spain
Perece Vela Basin *see* West Mariana Basin
Pereira *36 B3* Risaralda, W Colombia
Pergamino *42 C4* Buenos Aires, E Argentina
Périgueux *69 C5 anc.* Vesuna. Dordogne, SW France
Perito Moreno *43 B6* Santa Cruz, S Argentina
Perlas, Archipiélago de las *31 G5 Eng.* Pearl Islands. *Island group* SE Panama
Perlas, Laguna de *31 E3 Eng.* Pearl Lagoon. *Lagoon* E Nicaragua
Perleberg *72 C3* Brandenburg, N Germany
Perm' *92 C3 prev.* Molotov. Permskaya Oblast', NW Russian Federation
Pernambuco *41 G2 off.* Estado de Pernambuco. *State* E Brazil
Pernambuco Abyssal Plain *see* Pernambuco Plain
Pernambuco Plain *45 C5 var.* Pernambuco Abyssal Plain. *Undersea feature* E Atlantic Ocean
Pernau *see* Pärnu
Pernik *82 B2 prev.* Dimitrovo. Pernik, W Bulgaria
Perote *29 F4* Veracruz-Llave, E Mexico
Perovsk *see* Kyzylorda
Perpignan *69 C6* Pyrénées-Orientales, S France
Perryton *27 F1* Texas, SW USA
Perryville *23 H5* Missouri, C USA
Persian Gulf *see* Gulf, The
Perth *125 A6 state capital* Western Australia
Perth *66 C4* C Scotland, UK
Perth Basin *119 E6 undersea feature* SE Indian Ocean
Peru *38 C3 Country* W South America
Peru *see* Beru
Peru Basin *45 A5 undersea feature* E Pacific Ocean
Peru-Chile Trench *34 A4 undersea feature* E Pacific Ocean
Perugia *74 C4 Fr.* Pérouse; *anc.* Perusia. Umbria, C Italy
Péruwelz *65 B6* Hainaut, SW Belgium
Pervomays'k *87 E3 prev.* Ol'viopol'. Mykolayivs'ka Oblast', S Ukraine
Pervyy Kuril'skiy Proliv *93 H3 strait* E Russian Federation
Pesaro *74 C3 anc.* Pisaurum. Marche, C Italy
Pescara *74 D4 anc.* Aternum, Ostia Aterni. Abruzzo, C Italy
Peshāwar *112 C1* North-West Frontier Province, N Pakistan
Peshkopi *79 C6 var.* Peshkopia, Peshkopija. Dibër, NE Albania
Peshkopia *see* Peshkopi
Peshkopija *see* Peshkopi
Pessac *69 B5* Gironde, SW France
Petach-Tikva *see* Petaḥ Tiqwa
Petah Tiqva *see* Petaḥ Tiqwa
Petaḥ Tiqwa *97 A6 var.* Petach-Tikva, Petah Tiqva, Petakh Tikva. Tel Aviv, C Israel
Petakh Tikva *see* Petaḥ Tiqwa
Pétange *65 D8* Luxembourg, SW Luxembourg
Petchaburi *see* Phetchaburi
Peterborough *67 E6 prev.* Medeshamstede. E England, UK
Peterborough *16 D5* Ontario, SE Canada
Peterborough *127 B6* South Australia
Peterhead *66 D3* NE Scotland, UK
Peter I Island *132 A3 Norwegian dependency* Antarctica
Petermann Bjerg *61 E3 mountain* C Greenland
Petersburg *19 E5* Virginia, NE USA
Peters Mine *37 F3 var.* Peter's Mine. N Guyana
Peto *29 H4* Yucatán, SE Mexico
Petoskey *18 C2* Michigan, N USA
Petra *see* Wādī Mūsā
Petrich *82 C3* Blagoevgrad, SW Bulgaria
Petrinja *78 B3* Sisak-Moslavina, C Croatia
Petrodvorets *88 A4 Fin.* Pietarhovi. Leningradskaya Oblast', NW Russian Federation
Petrograd *see* Sankt-Peterburg
Petropavlovsk *92 C4 Kaz.* Petropavl. Severnyy Kazakhstan, N Kazakhstan
Petropavlovsk-Kamchatskiy *93 H3* Kamchatskaya Oblast', E Russian Federation
Petroşani *86 B4 var.* Petroşeni, *Ger.* Petroschen, *Hung.* Petrozsény. Hunedoara, W Romania
Petroschen *see* Petroşani
Petroşeni *see* Petroşani
Petrozavodsk *92 B2 Fin.* Petroskoi. Respublika Kareliya, NW Russian Federation
Petrozsény *see* Petroşani
Pevek *93 G1* Chukotskiy Avtonomnyy Okrug, NE Russian Federation
Pezinok *77 C6 Ger.* Bösing, *Hung.* Bazin. Bratislavský Kraj, W Slovakia
Pforzheim *73 B6* Baden-Württemberg, SW Germany
Pfungstadt *73 B5* Hessen, W Germany
Phangan, Ko *115 C6 island* SW Thailand
Phang-Nga *115 B7 var.* Pang-Nga, Phangnga. Phangnga, SW Thailand
Phangnga *see* Phang-Nga
Phanom Dang Raek *see* Dângrêk, Chuŏr Phnum
Phanom Dong Rak *see* Dângrêk, Chuŏr Phnum
Phan Rang *see* Phan Rang-Thap Cham
Phan Rang-Thap Cham *115 E6 var.* Phanrang, Phan Rang, Phan Rang Thap Cham. Ninh Thuận, S Vietnam
Phan Thiêt *115 E6* Binh Thuận, S Vietnam
Pharnacia *see* Giresun
Phatthalung *115 C7 var.* Padalung, Patalung. Phatthalung, SW Thailand
Phayao *114 C4 var.* Muang Phayao. Phayao, NW Thailand
Phenix City *20 D2* Alabama, S USA
Phet Buri *see* Phetchaburi
Phetchaburi *115 C5 var.* Bejraburi, Petchaburi, Phet Buri. Phetchaburi, SW Thailand
Philadelphia *see* 'Ammān
Philadelphia *19 F4* Pennsylvania, NE USA
Philippine Basin *103 F3 undersea feature* W Pacific Ocean
Philippines *117 E1 Country* SE Asia
Philippines *117 E1 island group* W Pacific Ocean
Philippine Sea *103 F3 sea* W Pacific Ocean
Philippine Trench *120 A1 undersea feature* W Philippine Sea
Phitsanulok *114 C4 var.* Bisnulok, Muang Phitsanulok, Pitsanulok. Phitsanulok, C Thailand
Phlórina *see* Flórina
Phnom Penh *see* Phnum Penh
Phnum Penh *115 D6 var.* Phnom Penh. *Country capital* (Cambodia) Phnum Penh, S Cambodia
Phoenix *26 B2 state capital* Arizona, SW USA
Phoenix Islands *123 E3 island group* C Kiribati
Phôngsali *114 C3 var.* Phong Saly. Phôngsali, N Laos
Phong Saly *see* Phôngsali
Phrae *114 C4 var.* Muang Phrae, Prae. Phrae, NW Thailand
Phra Nakhon Si Ayutthaya *see* Ayutthaya
Phra Thong, Ko *115 B6 island* SW Thailand
Phuket *115 B7 var.* Bhuket, Puket, *Mal.* Ujung Salang; *prev.* Junkseylon, Salang. Phuket, SW Thailand
Phuket, Ko *115 B7 island* SW Thailand
Phumĭ Kâmpóng Trâbêk *115 D5* Kâmpóng Chhnăng, N Cambodia
Phumĭ Sâmraông *115 D5* Poŭthĭsăt, NW Cambodia
Phu Vinh *see* Tra Vinh
Piacenza *74 B2 Fr.* Paisance; *anc.* Placentia. Emilia-Romagna, N Italy
Piatra-Neamţ *86 C4 Hung.* Karácsonkő. Neamţ, NE Romania
Piauí *41 F2 off.* Estado do Piauí; *prev.* Piauhy. *State* E Brazil
Picardie *68 C3 Eng.* Picardy. *Cultural region* N France
Pichilemu *42 B4* Libertador, C Chile
Pico *70 A5 var.* Ilha do Pico. *Island* Azores, Portugal, NE Atlantic Ocean
Picos *41 F2* Piauí, E Brazil
Picton *129 C5* Marlborough, South Island, NZ
Piedras Negras *29 E2 var.* Ciudad Porfirio Díaz. Coahuila de Zaragoza, NE Mexico
Pielinen *62 E4 var.* Pielisjärvi. *Lake* E Finland
Pielisjärvi *see* Pielinen
Piemonte *74 A2 Eng.* Piedmont. *Cultural region* NW Italy
Pierre *23 E3 state capital* South Dakota, N USA
Piešt'any *77 C6 Ger.* Pistyan, *Hung.* Pöstyén. Trnavský Kraj, W Slovakia
Pietermaritzburg *56 C5 var.* Maritzburg. KwaZulu/Natal, E South Africa
Pietersburg *see* Polokwane
Pigs, Bay of *see* Cochinos, Bahía de
Pijijiapán *29 G5* Chiapas, SE Mexico
Pikes Peak *22 C5 mountain* Colorado, C USA
Pikeville *18 D5* Kentucky, S USA
Pikinni *see* Bikini Atoll
Piła *76 B3 Ger.* Schneidemühl. Wielkopolskie, C Poland
Pilar *42 D3 var.* Villa del Pilar. Ñeembucú, S Paraguay
Pilcomayo *35 C5 river* C South America
Pílos *see* Pýlos
Pinang *see* George Town
Pinang, Pulau *116 B3 var.* Penang, Pinang; *prev.* Prince of Wales Island. *Island* Peninsular Malaysia
Pinar del Río *32 A2* Pinar del Río, W Cuba
Píndhos *see* Píndos
Píndhos Óros *see* Píndos
Píndos *82 A4 var.* Píndhos Óros, *Eng.* Pindus Mountains; *prev.* Píndhos. *Mountain range* C Greece
Pindus Mountains *see* Píndos
Pine Bluff *20 B2* Arkansas, C USA
Pine Creek *124 D2* Northern Territory, N Australia
Pinega *88 C3 river* NW Russian Federation
Pineiós *82 B4 var.* Piniós; *anc.* Peneius. *River* C Greece
Pineland *27 H3* Texas, SW USA
Pines, The Isle of the *see* Juventud, Isla de la
Pingdingshan *106 C4* Henan, C China
Pingkiang *see* Harbin
Ping, Mae Nam *114 B4 river* W Thailand
Piniós *see* Pineiós
Pinkiang *see* Harbin
Pínnes, Akrotírio *82 C4 headland* N Greece
Pinos, Isla de *see* Juventud, Isla de la
Pinotepa Nacional *29 F5 var.* Santiago Pinotepa Nacional. Oaxaca, SE Mexico
Pinsk *85 B7 Pol.* Pińsk. SW Belarus
Pinta, Isla *38 A5 var.* Abingdon. *Island* Galapagos Islands, Ecuador, E Pacific Ocean
Piombino *74 B3* Toscana, C Italy
Pioneer Mountains *24 D3 mountain range* Montana, N USA
Pionerskiy *84 A4 Ger.* Neukuhren. Kaliningradskaya Oblast', W Russian Federation
Piotrków Trybunalski *76 D4 Ger.* Petrikau, *Rus.* Petrokov. Łódzkie, C Poland
Piraeus *see* Peiraías
Pírgos *see* Pýrgos
Piripiri *41 F2* Piauí, E Brazil
Pirna *72 D4* Sachsen, E Germany
Pirot *79 E5* Serbia, SE Serbia and Montenegro (Yugo.)
Pisa *74 B3 var.* Pisae. Toscana, C Italy
Pisae *see* Pisa
Pisco *38 D4* Ica, SW Peru
Písek *77 A5* Budějovický Kraj, S Czech Republic
Pishan *104 A3 var.* Guma. Xinjiang Uygur Zizhiqu, NW China
Pishpek *see* Bishkek
Pistoia *74 B3 anc.* Pistoria, Pistoriæ. Toscana, C Italy
Pisz *76 D3 Ger.* Johannisburg. Warminsko-Mazurskie, NE Poland
Pita *52 C4* Moyenne-Guinée, NW Guinea
Pitalito *36 B4* Huila, S Colombia
Pitcairn Island *121 G4 island* S Pitcairn Islands
Pitcairn Islands *121 G4 UK dependent territory* C Pacific Ocean
Piteå *62 D4* Norrbotten, N Sweden
Piteşti *86 B5* Argeş, S Romania
Pitsanulok *see* Phitsanulok
Pittsburg *23 F5* Kansas, C USA
Pittsburgh *19 E4* Pennsylvania, NE USA
Pittsfield *19 F3* Massachusetts, NE USA
Piura *38 B2* Piura, NW Peru
Pivdennyy Buh *87 E3 Rus.* Yuzhnyy Bug. *River* S Ukraine
Placetas *32 B2* Villa Clara, C Cuba
Plainview *27 E2* Texas, SW USA
Planeta Rica *36 B2* Córdoba, NW Colombia
Planken *72 E1* C Liechtenstein
Plano *27 G2* Texas, SW USA
Plasencia *70 C3* Extremadura, W Spain
Plata, Río de la *42 D4 var.* River Plate. *Estuary* Argentina/Uruguay
Plateau du Bemaraha *see* Bemaraha
Platinum *14 C3* Alaska, USA
Plattensee *see* Balaton
Platte River *23 E4 river* Nebraska, C USA
Plattsburgh *19 F2* New York, NE USA
Plauen *73 C5 var.* Plauen im Vogtland. Sachsen, E Germany
Plauen im Vogtland *see* Plauen
Pļaviņas *84 D4 Ger.* Stockmannshof. Aizkraukle, S Latvia
Plây Cu *115 E5 var.* Pleiku. Gia Lai, C Vietnam
Pleiku *see* Plây Cu
Plenty, Bay of *128 E3 bay* North Island, NZ
Plérin *68 A3* Côtes d'Armor, NW France
Plesetsk *88 C3* Arkhangel'skaya Oblast', NW Russian Federation
Pleszew *76 C4* Wielkopolskie, C Poland
Pleven *82 C2 prev.* Plevna. Pleven, N Bulgaria
Pljevlja *78 C4 prev.* Plevlja, Plevlje. Montenegro, N Serbia and Montenegro (Yugo.)
Ploče *78 B4 It.* Plocce; *prev.* Kardeljevo. Dubrovnik-Neretva, SE Croatia
Płock *76 D3 Ger.* Plozk. Mazowieckie, C Poland
Plöcken Pass *73 C7 Ger.* Plöckenpass, *It.* Passo di Monte Croce Carnico. *Pass* SW Austria
Ploieşti *86 C5 prev.* Ploeşti. Prahova, SE Romania
Plomári *83 D5 prev.* Plomárion. Lésvos, E Greece
Płońsk *76 D3* Mazowieckie, C Poland
Plovdiv *82 C3 prev.* Eumolpias, *anc.* Evmolpia, Philippopolis, *Lat.* Trimontium. Plovdiv, C Bulgaria
Plungė *106 B3* Plungė, W Lithuania
Plyeshchanitsy *85 D5 Rus.* Pleshchenitsy. Minskaya Voblasts', N Belarus
Plymouth *33 G3 dependent territory capital* (Montserrat) SW Montserrat
Plymouth *67 C7* SW England, UK
Plzeň *77 A5 Ger.* Pilsen, *Pol.* Pilzno. Plzeňský Kraj, W Czech Republic
Po *58 D4 river* N Italy
Pobeda Peak *see* Pobedy, Pik
Pobedy, Pik *104 B3 var.* Pobeda Peak, *Chin.* Tomur Feng. *Mountain* China/Kyrgyzstan *see also* Tomur Feng
Pocahontas *20 B1* Arkansas, C USA
Pocatello *24 E4* Idaho, NW USA
Pochinok *89 A5* Smolenskaya Oblast', W Russian Federation
Pocking *73 D6* Bayern, SE Germany
Poděbrady *77 B5 Ger.* Podiebrad. Středočesky Kraj, C Czech Republic
Podgorica *79 C5 prev.* Titograd. Montenegro, SW Serbia and Montenegro (Yugo.)
Podil's'ka Vysochina *86 D3 Rus.* Podol'skaya Vozvyshennost'. *Mountain range* SW Ukraine
Podkarpackie admin. region *province* SE Poland
Podol'sk *89 B5* Moskovskaya Oblast', W Russian Federation
Podravska Slatina *see* Slatina.
Podujevo *79 D5* Serbia, S Serbia and Montenegro (Yugo.)
Po, Foci del *74 C2 var.* Bocche del Po. *River* NE Italy
Pogradec *79 D6 var.* Pogradeci. Korçë, SE Albania
Pogradeci *see* Pogradec
Pohnpei *122 C2 prev.* Ponape Ascension Island. *Island* E Micronesia
Poinsett, Cape *132 D4 headland* Antarctica
Pointe-à-Pitre *33 G3* Grande Terre, C Guadeloupe
Pointe-Noire *55 B6* Le Kouilou, S Congo
Point Lay *14 C2* Alaska, USA
Poitiers *68 B4 prev.* Poictiers, *anc.* Limonum. Vienne, W France
Poitou *68 B4 cultural region* W France
Pokhara *113 E3* Western, C Nepal
Pokrovs'ke *87 G3 Rus.* Pokrovskoye. Dnipropetrovs'ka Oblast', E Ukraine
Pola de Lena *70 D1* Asturias, N Spain
Poland *76 B4 var.* Polish Republic, *Pol.* Polska, Rzeczpospolita Polska; *prev. Pol.* Polska Rzeczpospolita Ludowa, Polish People's Republic. *Country* C Europe
Poland *59 E3* Kiritimati, E Kiribati
Polatlı *94 C3* Ankara, C Turkey
Polatsk *85 D5 Rus.* Polotsk. Vitsyebskaya Voblasts', N Belarus
Pol-e Khomrī *101 E4 var.* Pul-i-Khumri. Baghlān, NE Afghanistan
Poli *see* Pólis
Polikastro *see* Polýkastro
Políkastron *see* Polýkastro
Polikrayshte *82 D2* Veliko Tŭrnovo, N Bulgaria
Pólis *80 C5 var.* Poli. W Cyprus
Polkowice *76 B4 Ger.* Heerwegen. Dolnośląskie, SW Poland
Pollença *71 G3 var.* Pollensa. Mallorca, Spain, W Mediterranean Sea
Pollensa *see* Pollença
Polohy *87 G3 Rus.* Pologi. Zaporiz'ka Oblast', SE Ukraine
Polokwane *56 D4 Var.* Pietersburg, NE South Africa
Polonne *86 D2 Rus.* Polonnoye. Khmel'nyts'ka Oblast', NW Ukraine
Polsko Kosovo *82 D2* Ruse, N Bulgaria
Poltava *87 F2* Poltavs'ka Oblast', NE Ukraine
Põlva *84 E3 Ger.* Pölwe. Põlvamaa, SE Estonia
Polyarnyy *88 C2* Murmanskaya Oblast', NW Russian Federation
Polýkastro *82 B3 var.* Polikastro; *prev.* Políkastron. Kentrikí Makedonía, N Greece
Polynesia *121 F4 island group* C Pacific Ocean
Pomeranian Bay *72 D2 Ger.* Pommersche Bucht, *Pol.* Zatoka Pomorska. *Bay* Germany/Poland

Pomorskiy Proliv *88 D2 strait* NW Russian Federation
Pompano Beach *21 F5* Florida, SE USA
Ponca City *27 G1* Oklahoma, C USA
Ponce *33 F3* C Puerto Rico
Pondicherry *110 C2 var.* Puduchcheri, *Fr.* Pondichéry. Pondicherry, SE India
Pondichéry *see* Pondicherry
Ponferrada *70 C1* Castilla-León, NW Spain
Poniatowa *76 E4* Lublin, E Poland
Pons Aelii *see* Newcastle upon Tyne
Ponta Delgada *70 B5* São Miguel, Azores, Portugal, NE Atlantic Ocean
Ponta Grossa *41 E4* Paraná, S Brazil
Pontarlier *68 D4* Doubs, E France
Ponteareas *92 B2* Galicia, NW Spain
Ponte da Barca *70 B2* Viana do Castelo, N Portugal
Pontevedra *70 B1 anc.* Pons Vetus. Galicia, NW Spain
Pontiac *18 D3* Michigan, N USA
Pontianak *116 C4* Borneo, C Indonesia
Pontivy *68 A3* Morbihan, NW France
Pontoise *68 C3 anc.* Briva Isarae, Cergy-Pontoise, Pontisarae. Val-d'Oise, N France
Ponziane, Isole *75 C5 island* C Italy
Poole *67 D7* S England, UK
Poopó, Lago *39 F4 var.* Lago Pampa Aullagas. *Lake* W Bolivia
Popayán *36 B4* Cauca, SW Colombia
Poperinge *65 A6* West-Vlaanderen, W Belgium
Poplar Bluff *23 G5* Missouri, C USA
Popocatépetl *29 E4 volcano* S Mexico
Poprad *77 D5 Ger.* Deutschendorf, *Hung.* Poprád. Prešovský Kraj, E Slovakia
Poprad *77 D5 Ger.* Popper, *Hung.* Poprád. *River* Poland/Slovakia
Porbandar *112 B4* Gujarāt, W India
Porcupine Plain *58 B3 undersea feature* E Atlantic Ocean
Pordenone *74 C2 anc.* Portenau. Friuli-Venezia Giulia, NE Italy
Poreč *78 A2 It.* Parenzo. Istra, NW Croatia
Pori *63 D5 Swe.* Björneborg. Länsi-Suomi, W Finland
Porirua *129 D5* Wellington, North Island, NZ
Porkhov *88 A4* Pskovskaya Oblast', W Russian Federation
Porlamar *37 E1* Nueva Esparta, NE Venezuela
Póros *83 A5* Kefallinía, Iónioi Nísoi, Greece, C Mediterranean Sea
Póros *83 C6* Póros, S Greece
Porsangerfjorden *62 D2 fjord* N Norway
Porsgrunn *63 B6* Telemark, S Norway
Portachuelo *39 G4* Santa Cruz, C Bolivia
Portadown *67 B5 Ir.* Port An Dúnáin. S Northern Ireland, UK
Portalegre *70 C3 anc.* Ammaia, Amoea. Portalegre, E Portugal
Port Alexander *14 D4* Baranof Island, Alaska, USA
Port Alfred *56 D5* Eastern Cape, S South Africa
Port An Dúnáin *see* Portadown
Port Angeles *24 B1* Washington, NW USA
Port Antonio *32 B5* NE Jamaica
Port Arthur *27 H4* Texas, SW USA
Port Augusta *127 B6* South Australia
Port-au-Prince *32 D3 country capital* (Haiti) C Haiti
Port-au-Prince *13 D7 international airport* E Haiti
Port Blair *111 F2* Andaman and Nicobar Islands, SE India
Port Charlotte *21 E4* Florida, SE USA
Port d'Envalira *69 B8* E Andorra
Port Douglas *126 D3* Queensland, NE Australia
Port Elizabeth *56 C5* Eastern Cape, S South Africa
Porterville *25 C7* California, W USA
Port-Gentil *55 A6* Ogooué-Maritime, W Gabon
Port Harcourt *53 G5* Rivers, S Nigeria
Port Hardy *14 D5* Vancouver Island, British Columbia, SW Canada
Port Harrison *see* Inukjuak
Port Hedland *124 B4* Western Australia
Port Huron *18 D3* Michigan, N USA
Portimão *70 B4 var.* Vila Nova de Portimão. Faro, S Portugal
Port Jackson *126 E1 harbour* New South Wales, SE Australia
Port Láirge *see* Waterford
Portland *19 G2* Maine, NE USA
Portland *24 B3* Oregon, NW USA
Portland *27 G4* Texas, SW USA
Portland *127 B7* Victoria, SE Australia
Portland Bight *32 B5 bay* S Jamaica
Portlaoighise *see* Portlaoise
Portlaoise *67 B6 Ir.* Portlaoighise; *prev.* Maryborough. C Ireland
Port Lavaca *27 G4* Texas, SW USA
Port Lincoln *127 A6* South Australia
Port Louis *57 H3 country capital* (Mauritius) NW Mauritius
Port Macquarie *127 E6* New South Wales, SE Australia
Portmore *32 B5* C Jamaica
Port Moresby *122 B3 country capital* (PNG) Central/National Capital District, SW PNG
Port Musgrave *127 B9 bay* Queensland, N Australia
Port Natal *see* Durban
Porto *70 B2 Eng.* Oporto; *anc.* Portus Cale. Porto, NW Portugal
Porto Alegre *41 E5 var.* Pôrto Alegre. *State capital* Rio Grande do Sul, S Brazil
Porto Alegre *54 E2* São Tomé, S Sao Tome and Principe
Porto Bello *see* Portobelo
Portobelo *31 G4 var.* Porto Bello, Puerto Bello. Colón, N Panama
Port O'Connor *27 G4* Texas, SW USA
Porto Edda *see* Sarandë
Portoferraio *74 B4* Toscana, C Italy
Port-of-Spain *33 H5 country capital* (Trinidad and Tobago) Trinidad, Trinidad and Tobago
Porto Grande *see* Mindelo
Portogruaro *74 C2* Veneto, NE Italy
Porto-Novo *53 F5 country capital* (Benin) S Benin
Porto Santo *48 A2 var.* Ilha do Porto Santo. *Island* Madeira, Portugal, NE Atlantic Ocean
Porto Torres *75 A5* Sardegna, Italy, C Mediterranean Sea
Porto Velho *40 D2 var.* Velho. *State capital* Rondônia, W Brazil
Portoviejo *38 A2 var.* Puertoviejo. Manabí, W Ecuador
Port Pirie *127 B6* South Australia
Port Said *50 B1 Ar.* Būr Sa'īd. N Egypt
Portsmouth *19 G3* New Hampshire, NE USA
Portsmouth *18 D4* Ohio, N USA
Portsmouth *67 D7* S England, UK
Portsmouth *19 F5* Virginia, NE USA
Port Stanley *see* Stanley
Port Sudan *50 C3* Red Sea, NE Sudan
Port Swettenham *see* Klang
Port Talbot *67 C7* S Wales, UK
Portugal *70 B3 Country* SW Europe
Portuguese Timor *see* East Timor
Port-Vila *122 D4 var.* Vila. *Country capital* (Vanuatu) Éfaté, C Vanuatu
Porvenir *43 B8* Magallanes, S Chile
Porvenir *39 E3* Pando, NW Bolivia
Porvoo *63 E6 Swe.* Borgå. Etelä-Suomi, S Finland
Posadas *42 D3* Misiones, NE Argentina
Poschega *see* Požega
Posterholt *65 D5* Limburg, SE Netherlands
Postojna *73 D8 Ger.* Adelsberg, *It.* Postumia. SW Slovenia
Potamós *83 C7* Antikýthira, S Greece
Potenza *75 D5 anc.* Potentia. Basilicata, S Italy
P'ot'i *95 F2* W Georgia
Potiskum *53 G4* Yobe, NE Nigeria
Potomac River *19 E5 river* NE USA
Potosí *39 F4* Potosí, S Bolivia
Potsdam *72 D3* Brandenburg, NE Germany
Potwar Plateau *112 C2 plateau* NE Pakistan
Poŭthĭsăt *115 D6 prev.* Pursat. Poŭthĭsăt, W Cambodia
Po Valley *74 C2 It.* Valle del Po. *Valley* N Italy
Považská Bystrica *77 C5 Ger.* Waagbistritz, *Hung.* Vágbeszterce. Trenčiansky Kraj, W Slovakia
Poverty Bay *128 E4 inlet* North Island, NZ
Póvoa de Varzim *70 B2* Porto, NW Portugal
Powder River *22 D2 river* Montana/Wyoming, NW USA
Powell *22 C2* Wyoming, C USA
Powell, Lake *22 B5 lake* Utah, W USA
Požarevac *78 D4 Ger.* Passarowitz. Serbia, NE Serbia and Montenegro (Yugo.)
Poza Rica *29 F4 var.* Poza Rica de Hidalgo. Veracruz-Llave, E Mexico
Poza Rica de Hidalgo *see* Poza Rica
Požega *78 D4 prev.* Slavonska Požega. *Ger.* Poschega, *Hung.* Pozsega. Požega-Slavonija, NE Croatia
Pozsega *see* Požega
Poznań *76 C3 Ger.* Posen, Posnania. Wielkopolskie, C Poland
Pozoblanco *70 D4* Andalucía, S Spain
Pozzallo *75 C8* Sicilia, Italy, C Mediterranean Sea
Prachatice *77 A5 Ger.* Prachatitz. Budějovický Kraj, S Czech Republic
Prado del Ganso *see* Goose Green
Prae *see* Phrae
Prague *58 D3* Oklahoma, C USA
Praha *77 A5 Eng.* Prague, *Ger.* Prag, *Pol.* Praga. *Country capital* (Czech Republic) Středočesky Kraj, NW Czech Republic
Praia *52 A3 country capital* (Cape Verde) Santiago, S Cape Verde
Prato *74 B3* Toscana, C Italy
Pratt *23 E5* Kansas, C USA
Prattville *20 D2* Alabama, S USA
Pravda *82 D1 prev.* Dogrular. Silistra, NE Bulgaria
Pravia *70 C1* Asturias, N Spain
Prenzlau *72 D3* Brandenburg, NE Germany
Přerov *77 C5 Ger.* Prerau. Olomoucký Kraj, E Czech Republic
Presa de la Amistad *see* Amistad Reservoir
Preschau *see* Prešov
Prescott *26 B2* Arizona, SW USA
Preševo *79 D5* Serbia, SE Serbia and Montenegro (Yugo.)
Presidente Epitácio *41 E4* São Paulo, S Brazil
Prešov *77 D5 var.* Preschau, *Ger.* Eperies, *Hung.* Eperjes. Prešoský Kraj, E Slovakia
Prespa, Lake *79 D6 Alb.* Liqen i Prespës, *Gk.* Límni Megáli Préspa, Limni Prespa, *Mac.* Prespansko Ezero, *Serb.* Prespansko Jezero. *Lake* SE Europe
Presque Isle *19 H1* Maine, NE USA
Preston *67 D5* NW England, UK
Prestwick *66 C4* W Scotland, UK
Pretoria *56 D4 var.* Epitoli, Tshwane. *Country capital*(South Africa-administrative capital) Gauteng, NE South Africa
Préveza *83 A5* Ípeiros, W Greece
Pribilof Islands *14 A3 island group* Alaska, USA
Priboj *78 C4* Serbia, W Serbia and Montenegro (Yugo.)
Price *22 B4* Utah, W USA
Prichard *20 C3* Alabama, S USA
Priekulė *84 B3 Ger.* Prökuls. Gargždai, W Lithuania
Prienai *85 B5 Pol.* Preny. Prienai, S Lithuania
Prieska *56 C4* Northern Cape, C South Africa
Prijedor *78 B3* Republika Srpska, NW Bosnia and Herzegovina
Prijepolje *78 D4* Serbia, W Serbia and Montenegro (Yugo.)
Prilep *79 D6 Turk.* Perlepe. S FYR Macedonia
Primorsk *84 A4 Ger.* Fischhausen. Kaliningradskaya Oblast', W Russian Federation
Primorsko *82 E2 prev.* Keupriya. Burgas, E Bulgaria
Prince Albert *15 F5* Saskatchewan, S Canada
Prince Edward Island *17 F4 Fr.* Île-du Prince-Édouard. *Province* SE Canada
Prince Edward Islands *47 E8 island group* S South Africa
Prince George *15 E5* British Columbia, SW Canada
Prince of Wales Island *15 F2 island* Queen Elizabeth Islands, Nunavut, NW Canada
Prince of Wales Island *126 B1 island* Queensland, E Australia
Prince Patrick Island *15 E2 island* Parry Islands, Northwest Territories, NW Canada
Prince Rupert *14 D4* British Columbia, SW Canada
Prince's Island *see* Príncipe
Princess Charlotte Bay *126 C2 bay* Queensland, NE Australia
Princess Elizabeth Land *132 C3 physical region* Antarctica
Príncipe *55 A5 var.* Príncipe Island, *Eng.* Prince's Island. *Island* N Sao Tome and Principe
Príncipe Island *see* Príncipe
Prinzapolka *31 E3* Región Autónoma Atlántico Norte, NE Nicaragua
Pripet *85 C7 Bel.* Prypyats', *Ukr.* Pryp"yat'. *River* Belarus/Ukraine
Pripet Marshes *85 B7 wetland* Belarus/Ukraine
Priština *79 D5 Alb.* Prishtinë. Serbia, S Serbia and Montenegro (Yugo.)
Privas *69 D5* Ardèche, E France
Prizren *79 D5 Alb.* Prizreni. Serbia, S Serbia and Montenegro (Yugo.)
Probolinggo *116 D5* Jawa, C Indonesia
Progreso *29 H3* Yucatán, SE Mexico
Prokhladnyy *89 B8* Kabardino-Balkarskaya Respublika, SW Russian Federation
Prokuplje *79 D5* Serbia, SE Serbia and Montenegro (Yugo.)
Prome *114 B4 var.* Pyè. Pegu, C Myanmar
Promyshlennyy *88 E3* Respublika Komi, NW Russian Federation
Prostějov *77 C5 Ger.* Prossnitz, *Pol.* Prościejów. Olomoucký Kraj, E Czech Republic
Provence *69 D6 cultural region* SE France
Providence *see* Fort Providence
Providence *19 G3 state capital* Rhode Island, NE USA
Providencia, Isla de *31 F3 island* NW Colombia
Provideniya *172 B1* Chukotskiy Avtonomnyy Okrug, NE Russian Federation
Provo *22 B4* Utah, W USA
Prudhoe Bay *14 D2* Alaska, USA
Prusa *see* Bursa
Pruszków *76 D3 Ger.* Kaltdorf. Mazowieckie, C Poland
Prut *86 D4 Ger.* Pruth. *River* E Europe
Pruzhany *85 B6 Pol.* Prużana. Brestskaya Voblasts', SW Belarus
Prydz Bay *132 D3 bay* Antarctica
Pryluky *87 E2 Rus.* Priluki. Chernihivs'ka Oblast', NE Ukraine
Prymors'k *87 G4 Rus.* Primorsk; *prev.* Primorskoye. Zaporiz'ka Oblast', SE Ukraine
Przemysl *77 E5 Rus.* Peremyshl. Podkarpackie, SE Poland
Psará *83 D5 island* E Greece
Psël *87 F2 river* Russian Federation/Ukraine
Pskov *92 B2 Ger.* Pleskau, *Latv.* Pleskava. Pskovskaya Oblast', W Russian Federation
Pskov, Lake *E3 Est.* Pihkva Järv, *Ger.* Pleskauer See, *Rus.* Pskovskoye Ozero. *Lake* Estonia/Russian Federation
Ptsich *85 C7 Rus.* Ptich'. *River* SE Belarus
Ptsich *85 C7 Rus.* Ptich'. Homyel'skaya Voblasts', SE Belarus
Ptuj *73 E7 Ger.* Pettau; *anc.* Poetovio. NE Slovenia
Pucallpa *38 C3* Ucayali, C Peru
Puck *76 C2* Pomorskie, N Poland
Pudasjärvi *62 D4* Oulu, C Finland
Puduchcheri *see* Pondicherry
Puebla *29 F4 var.* Puebla de Zaragoza. Puebla, S Mexico
Puebla de Zaragoza *see* Puebla
Pueblo *22 D5* Colorado, C USA
Puerto Acosta *39 E4* La Paz, W Bolivia
Puerto Aisén *43 B6* Aisén, S Chile
Puerto Ángel *29 F5* Oaxaca, SE Mexico
Puerto Argentino *see* Stanley
Puerto Ayacucho *36 D3* Amazonas, SW Venezuela
Puerto Baquerizo Moreno *38 B5 var.* Baquerizo Moreno. Galapagos Islands, Ecuador, E Pacific Ocean
Puerto Barrios *30 C2* Izabal, E Guatemala
Puerto Bello *see* Portobelo
Puerto Berrío *36 B2* Antioquia, C Colombia
Puerto Cabello *36 D1* Carabobo, N Venezuela
Puerto Cabezas *31 E2 var.* Bilwi. Región Autónoma Atlántico Norte, NE Nicaragua
Puerto Carreño *36 D3* Vichada, E Colombia
Puerto Cortés *30 C2* Cortés, NW Honduras
Puerto Cumarebo *36 C1* Falcón, N Venezuela
Puerto Deseado *43 C7* Santa Cruz, SE Argentina
Puerto Escondido *29 F5* Oaxaca, SE Mexico
Puerto Francisco de Orellana *38 B1 var.* Coca. Napo, N Ecuador
Puerto Gallegos *see* Río Gallegos
Puerto Inírida *36 D3 var.* Obando. Guainía, E Colombia
Puerto La Cruz *37 E1* Anzoátegui, NE Venezuela
Puerto Lempira *31 E2* Gracias a Dios, E Honduras
Puerto Limón *see* Limón
Puertollano *70 D4* Castilla-La Mancha, C Spain
Puerto López *36 C1* La Guajira, N Colombia
Puerto Maldonado *39 E3* Madre de Dios, E Peru
Puerto México *see* Coatzacoalcos
Puerto Montt *43 B5* Los Lagos, C Chile
Puerto Natales *43 B7* Magallanes, S Chile
Puerto Obaldía *31 H5* San Blas, NE Panama
Puerto Plata *33 E3 var.* San Felipe de Puerto Plata. N Dominican Republic
Puerto Princesa *117 E2 off.* Puerto Princesa City. Palawan, W Philippines
Puerto Rico *33 F3 off.* Commonwealth of Puerto Rico; *prev.* Porto Rico. *US commonwealth territory* C West Indies
Puerto Rico *34 B1 island* C West Indies
Puerto Rico Trench *34 B1 undersea feature* NE Caribbean Sea
Puerto San José *see* San José
Puerto San Julián *43 B7 var.* San Julián. Santa Cruz, SE Argentina
Puerto Suárez *39 H4* Santa Cruz, E Bolivia
Puerto Vallarta *28 D4* Jalisco, SW Mexico
Puerto Varas *43 B5* Los Lagos, C Chile
Puerto Viejo *31 E4* Heredia, NE Costa Rica
Puertoviejo *see* Portoviejo
Puget Sound *24 B1 sound* Washington, NW USA
Puglia *75 E5 Eng.* Apulia. *Cultural region* SE Italy
Pukaki, Lake *129 B6 lake* South Island, NZ
Pukekohe *128 D3* Auckland, North Island, NZ
Puket *see* Phuket
Pukhavichy *85 C6 Rus.* Pukhovichi. Minskaya Voblasts', C Belarus
Pula *78 A3 It.* Pola; *prev.* Pulj. Istra, NW Croatia
Pulaski *18 D5* Virginia, NE USA
Pulau Butung *see* Buton, Pulau
Puławy *76 D4 Ger.* Neu Amerika. Lublin, E Poland
Pul-i-Khumri *see* Pol-e Khomrī
Pullman *24 C2* Washington, NW USA
Pułtusk *76 D3* Mazowieckie, C Poland
Puná, Isla *38 A2 island* SW Ecuador
Pune *112 C5 prev.* Poona. Mahārāshtra, W India
Punjab *112 C2 prev.* West Punjab, Western Punjab. *Province* E Pakistan
Puno *39 E4* Puno, SE Peru
Punta Alta *43 C5* Buenos Aires, E Argentina
Punta Arenas *43 B8 prev.* Magallanes. Magallanes, S Chile
Punta Gorda *31 E4* Región Autónoma Atlántico Sur, SE Nicaragua
Punta Gorda *30 C2* Toledo, SE Belize
Puntarenas *30 D4* Puntarenas, W Costa Rica
Punto Fijo *36 C1* Falcón, N Venezuela
Pupuya, Nevado *39 E4 mountain* W Bolivia
Puri *113 F5 var.* Jagannath. Orissa, E India
Puriramya *see* Buriram
Purmerend *64 C3* Noord-Holland, C Netherlands
Purus, Rio *40 C2 Sp.* Río Purús. *River* Brazil/Peru
Pusan *107 E4 off.* Pusan-gwangyŏksi, *var.* Busan, *Jap.* Fusan. SE South Korea
Püspökladány *77 D6* Hajdú-Bihar, E Hungary
Putorana Mountains *see* Putorana, Plato
Putorana, Plato *92 D3 var.* Gory Putorana, *Eng.* Putorana Mountains. *Mountain range* N Russian Federation
Putrajaya *116 B3 country capital* (Malaysia) Kuala Lumpur, Peninsular Malaysia
Puttalam *110 C3* North Western Province, W Sri Lanka
Puttgarden *72 C2* Schleswig-Holstein, N Germany
Putumayo, Río *36 B5 var.* Rio Içá. *River* NW South America *see also* Içá, Rio
Putumayo, Río *see* Içá, Rio
Puurmani *84 D2 Ger.* Talkhof. Jõgevamaa, E Estonia
Pyatigorsk *89 B7* Stavropol'skiy Kray, SW Russian Federation
P"yatykhatky *87 F3 Rus.* Pyatikhatki. Dnipropetrovs'ka Oblast', E Ukraine
Pyè *see* Prome
Pyetrykaw *85 C7 Rus.* Petrikov. Homyel'skaya Voblasts', SE Belarus
Pyinmana *114 B4* Mandalay, C Myanmar
Pýlos *83 B6 var.* Pilos. Pelopónnisos, S Greece
P'yŏngyang *107 E3 var.* P'yŏngyang-si, *Eng.* Pyongyang. *Country capital* (North Korea) SW North Korea
P'yŏngyang-si *see* P'yŏngyang
Pyramid Lake *25 C5 lake* Nevada, W USA
Pyrenees *80 B2 Fr.* Pyrénées, *Sp.* Pirineos; *anc.* Pyrenaei Montes. *Mountain range* SW Europe
Pýrgos *83 B6 var.* Pírgos. Dytikí Ellás, S Greece
Pyryatyn *87 E2 Rus.* Piryatin. Poltavs'ka Oblast', NE Ukraine
Pyrzyce *76 B3 Ger.* Pyritz. Zachodniopomorskie, NW Poland
Pyu *114 B4* Pegu, C Myanmar
Pyuntaza *114 B4* Pegu, SW Myanmar

Q

Qā' al Jafr *97 C7 lake* S Jordan
Qaanaaq *60 D1 var.* Qânâq, *Dan.* Thule. N Greenland
Qabātiya *97 E6* N West Bank
Qābis *see* Gabès
Qacentina *see* Constantine
Qafṣah *see* Gafsa
Qagan Us *see* Dulan
Qahremānshahr *see* Kermānshāh
Qaidam Pendi *104 C4 basin* C China
Qal'aikhum *101 F3 Rus.* Kalaikhum. S Tajikistan
Qal'at Bīshah *99 B5* 'Asīr, SW Saudi Arabia
Qalqīlya *97 D6* N West Bank
Qamdo *104 D5* Xizang Zizhiqu, W China
Qamishly *see* Al Qāmishlī
Qânâq *see* Qaanaaq
Qaqortoq *60 C4 Dan.* Julianehåb. S Greenland
Qara Qum *see* Garagum
Qarkilik *see* Ruoqiang
Qarokŭl *101 F3 Rus.* Karakul'. E Tajikistan
Qars *see* Kars
Qarshi *101 E3 Rus.* Karshi; *prev.* Bek-Budi. Qashqadaryo Wiloyati, S Uzbekistan
Qasigianguit *see* Qasigiannguit
Qasigiannguit *60 C3 var.* Qasigianguit, *Dan.* Christianshåb. C Greenland
Qasr Farâfra *50 B2* W Egypt
Qaṭanā *97 B5 var.* Katana. Dimashq, S Syria
Qatar *98 C4 Ar.* Dawlat Qaṭar. *Country* SW Asia
Qattara Depression *see* Qaṭṭâra, Monkhafad el
Qaṭṭâra, Monkhafad el 88 A1 var. Munkhafaḍ al Qaṭṭārah, *Eng.* Qattara Depression. *Desert* NW Egypt
Qazimämmäd *95 H3 Rus.* Kazi Magomed. SE Azerbaijan
Qazvīn *98 C2 var.* Kazvin. Qazvin, N Iran
Qena *50 B2 var.* Qinā; *anc.* Caene, Caenepolis. E Egypt
Qeqertarssuaq *see* Qeqertarsuaq
Qeqertarsuaq *60 C3 var.* Qeqertarssuaq, *Dan.* Godhavn. S Greenland
Qeqertarsuaq *60 C3 island* W Greenland
Qeqertarsuup Tunua *60 C3 Dan.* Disko Bugt. *Inlet* W Greenland
Qerveh *see* Qorveh
Qeshm *98 D4 var.* Jazīreh-ye Qeshm, Qeshm Island. *Island* S Iran
Qeshm Island *see* Qeshm
Qian *see* Guizhou
Qilian Shan *104 D3 var.* Kilien Mountains. *Mountain range* N China
Qimusseriarsuaq *60 C2 Dan.* Melville Bugt, *Eng.* Melville Bay. *Bay* NW Greenland
Qinā *see* Qena
Qing *see* Qinghai
Qingdao *106 D4 var.* Ching-Tao, Ch'ing-tao, Tsingtao, Tsintao, *Ger.* Tsingtau. Shandong, E China
Qinghai *104 C4 var.* Chinghai, Koko Nor, Qing, Qinghai Sheng, Tsinghai. Admin. region *province* C China
Qinghai Hu *104 D4 var.* Ch'ing Hai, Tsing Hai, *Mong.* Koko Nor. *lake* C China
Qinghai Sheng *see* Qinghai
Qingzang Gaoyuan *104 B4 var.* Xizang Gaoyuan, *Eng.* Plateau of Tibet. *Plateau* W China
Qinhuangdao *106 D3* Hebei, E China
Qinzhou *106 B6* Guangxi Zhuangzu Zizhiqu, S China
Qiong *see* Hainan
Qiqihar *106 D2 var.* Ch'i-ch'i-ha-erh, Tsitsihar; *prev.* Lungkiang. Heilongjiang, NE China
Qira *104 B4* Xinjiang Uygur Zizhiqu, NW China
Qitai *104 C3* Xinjiang Uygur Zizhiqu, NW China
Qīzān *see* Jīzān
Qizil Orda *see* Kyzylorda
Qizil Qum *see* Kyzyl Kum
Qizilrabot *101 G3 Rus.* Kyzylrabot. SE Tajikistan
Qom *98 C3 var.* Kum, Qum. Qom, N Iran
Qomul *see* Hami
Qondūz *see* Kunduz
Qo'qon *101 F2 var.* Khokand, Qŭqon, *Rus.* Kokand. Farghona Wiloyati, E Uzbekistan
Qorveh *98 C3 var.* Qerveh, Qurveh. Kordestān, W Iran
Qostanay *see* Kostanay
Qoubaïyât *96 B4 var.* Al Qubayyāt. N Lebanon
Qoussantîna *see* Constantine
Quang Ngai *115 E5 var.* Quangngai, Quang Nghia. Quang Ngai, C Vietnam
Quangngai *see* Quang Ngai
Quang Nghia *see* Quang Ngai
Quanzhou *106 D6 var.* Ch'uan-chou, Tsinkiang; *prev.* Chin-chiang. Fujian, SE China
Quanzhou *106 C6* Guangxi Zhuangzu Zizhiqu, S China
Qu'Appelle *15 F5 river* Saskatchewan, S Canada
Quarles, Pegunungan *117 E4 mountain range* Sulawesi, C Indonesia
Quarnero *see* Kvarner
Quartu Sant' Elena *75 A6* Sardegna, Italy, C Mediterranean Sea
Quba *95 H2 Rus.* Kuba. N Azerbaijan
Qubba *see* Ba'qūbah
Québec *17 E4 var.* Quebec. Québec, SE Canada
Quebec *16 D3 var.* Quebec. Admin. region *province* SE Canada
Queen Charlotte Islands *14 C5 Fr.* Îles de la Reine-Charlotte. *Island group* British Columbia, SW Canada

Queen Charlotte Sound 14 C5 sea area British Columbia, W Canada
Queen Elizabeth Islands 15 E1 Fr. Îles de la Reine-Élisabeth. Island group Northwest Territories/Nunavut, N Canada
Queensland 126 B4 state N Australia
Queenstown 56 D5 Eastern Cape, S South Africa
Queenstown 129 B7 Otago, South Island, NZ
Quelimane 57 E3 var. Kilimane, Kilmain, Quilimane. Zambézia, NE Mozambique
Quepos 31 E4 Puntarenas, S Costa Rica
Querétaro 29 E4 Querétaro de Arteaga, C Mexico
Quesada 31 E4 var. Ciudad Quesada, San Carlos. Alajuela, N Costa Rica
Quetta 112 B2 Baluchistān, SW Pakistan
Quetzalcoalco see Coatzacoalcos
Quetzaltenango see Quezaltenango
Quezaltenango 30 A2 var. Quetzaltenango. Quezaltenango, W Guatemala
Quibdó 36 A3 Chocó, W Colombia
Quilimane see Quelimane
Quillabamba 38 D3 Cusco, C Peru
Quilon 110 C3 var. Kolam, Kollam. Kerala, SW India
Quimper 68 A3 anc. Quimper Corentin. Finistère, NW France
Quimperlé 68 A3 Finistère, NW France
Quincy 18 A4 Illinois, N USA
Qui Nhon see Quy Nhơn
Quissico 57 E4 Inhambane, S Mozambique
Quito 38 B1 country capital (Ecuador) Pichincha, N Ecuador
Qullai Garmo see Kommunizm, Qullai
Qum see Qom
Qunaytra see Al Qunayţirah
Qŭqon see Qo'qon
Qurein see Al Kuwayt
Qŭrghonteppa 101 E3 Rus. Kurgan-Tyube. SW Tajikistan
Qurlurtuuq see Kugluktuk
Qurveh see Qorveh
Quşayr see Al Quşayr
Quy Nhơn 115 E5 var. Quinhon, Qui Nhon. Bình Đinh, C Vietnam
Qyteti Stalin see Kuçovë
Qyzylorda see Kyzylorda

R

Raab 78 B1 Hung. Rába. River Austria/Hungary see also Rába
Raahe 62 D4 Swe. Brahestad. Oulu, W Finland
Raalte 64 D3 Overijssel, E Netherlands
Raamsdonksveer 64 C4 Noord-Brabant, S Netherlands
Raasiku 84 D2 Ger. Rasik. Harjumaa, NW Estonia
Rába 77 B7 Ger. Raab. River Austria/Hungary see also Raab
Rabat 48 C2 var. al Dar al Baida. Country capital (Morocco) NW Morocco
Rabat see Victoria
Rabat 80 B5 W Malta
Rabbah Ammon see 'Ammān
Rabbath Ammon see 'Ammān
Rabinal 30 B2 Baja Verapaz, C Guatemala
Rabka 99 D5 Małopolskie, S Poland
Râbniţa see Rîbniţa
Rabyanāh, Ramlat 49 G4 var. Rebiana Sand Sea, şaḩrā' Rabyanāh. Desert SE Libya
Race, Cape 17 H3 headland Newfoundland, Newfoundland and Labrador, E Canada
Rach Gia 115 D6 Kiên Giang, S Vietnam
Rach Gia, Vinh 115 D6 bay S Vietnam
Racine 18 B3 Wisconsin, N USA
Rădăuţi 86 C3 Ger. Radautz, Hung. Rádóc. Suceava, N Romania
Radom 76 D4 Mazowieckie, C Poland
Radomsko 76 D4 Rus. Novoradomsk. Łódzkie, C Poland
Radomyshl' 86 D2 Zhytomyrs'ka Oblast', N Ukraine
Radoviš 79 E6 prev. Radovište. E FYR Macedonia
Radviliškis 84 B4 Radviliškis, N Lithuania
Radzyń Podlaski 76 E4 Lubelskie, E Poland
Rae-Edzo see Edzo
Raetihi 128 D4 Manawatu-Wanganui, North Island, NZ
Rafa see Rafah
Rafaela 42 C3 Santa Fe, E Argentina
Rafah 97 A7 var. Rafa, Rafaḩ, Heb. Rafiaḩ, Raphiah. SW Gaza Strip
Rafaḩ see Rafah
Rafḩah 98 B4 Al Ḩudūd ash Shamālīyah, N Saudi Arabia
Rafiaḩ see Rafah
Raga 51 A5 Western Bahr el Ghazal, SW Sudan
Ragged Island Range 32 C2 island group S Bahamas
Ragusa 75 C7 Sicilia, Italy, C Mediterranean Sea
Rahachow 85 D7 Rus. Rogachëv. Homyel'skaya Voblasts', SE Belarus
Rahaeng see Tak
Rahaţ, Ḩarrat 99 B5 lavaflow W Saudi Arabia
Rahīmyār Khān 112 C3 Punjab, SE Pakistan
Raiatea 123 G4 island Îles Sous le Vent, W French Polynesia
Rāichūr 110 C1 Karnātaka, C India
Rainier, Mount 12 A4 volcano Washington, NW USA
Rainy Lake 16 A4 lake Canada/USA
Raipur 113 E4 Madhya Pradesh, C India
Rājahmundry 113 E5 Andhra Pradesh, E India
Rajang see Rajang, Batang
Rajang, Batang 116 D3 var. Rajang. River East Malaysia
Rājapālaiyam 110 C3 Tamil Nādu, SE India
Rājasthān 112 C3 state NW India
Rājkot 112 C4 Gujarāt, W India
Rāj Nāndgaon 113 E4 Madhya Pradesh, C India
Rajshahi 113 G3 prev. Rampur Boalia. Rajshahi, W Bangladesh
Rakahanga 123 F3 atoll N Cook Islands
Rakaia 129 B6 river South Island, NZ
Rakka see Ar Raqqah
Rakke 84 E2 Lääne-Virumaa, NE Estonia
Rakvere 84 E2 Ger. Wesenberg. Lääne-Virumaa, N Estonia
Ralik Chain 122 D1 island group Ralik Chain, W Marshall Islands
Ramadi see Ar Ramādī
Ramlat Ahl Wahībah see Wahībah, Ramlat Āl
Ramlat Al Wahaybah see Wahībah, Ramlat Āl
Râmnicu Sărat 86 C4 prev. Râmnicul-Sărat, Rîmnicu-Sărat. Buzău, E Romania
Râmnicu Vâlcea 86 B4 prev. Rîmnicu Vîlcea. Vâlcea, C Romania
Ramree Island 114 A4 island W Myanmar
Ramtha see Ar Ramthā
Rancagua 42 B4 Libertador, C Chile
Rānchi 113 F4 Bihār, N India
Randers 63 B7 Århus, C Denmark
Rangiora 129 C6 Canterbury, South Island, NZ
Rangitikei 128 D4 river North Island, NZ
Rangoon see Yangon
Rangpur 113 G3 Rajshahi, N Bangladesh
Rankin Inlet 15 G3 Nunavut, C Canada
Ranong 115 B6 Ranong, SW Thailand
Rapa Nui see Easter Island
Raphiah see Rafah
Rapid City 22 D3 South Dakota, N USA
Rāpina 84 E3 Ger. Rappin. Põlvamaa, SE Estonia
Rapla 84 D2 Ger. Rappel. Raplamaa, NW Estonia
Rarotonga 123 G5 island S Cook Islands, C Pacific Ocean
Ras al 'Ain see Ra's al 'Ayn
Ra's al 'Ayn 96 D1 var. Ras al 'Ain. Al Ḩasakah, N Syria
Ra's an Naqb 97 B7 Ma'ān, S Jordan
Raseiniai 84 B4 Raseiniai, C Lithuania
Ras Hafun see Xaafuun, Raas
Rasht 98 C2 var. Resht. Gīlān, NW Iran
Râşnov 86 C4 prev. Rîşno, Rozsnyó, Hung. Barcarozsnyó. Braşov, C Romania
Ratak Chain 122 D1 island group Ratak Chain, E Marshall Islands
Rätan 63 C5 var. Ratan. Jämtland, C Sweden
Rat Buri see Ratchaburi
Ratchaburi 115 C5 var. Rat Buri. Ratchaburi, W Thailand
Rastenburg see Kętrzyn
Rat Islands 14 A2 island group Aleutian Islands, Alaska, USA
Ratlām 112 D4 prev. Rutlam. Madhya Pradesh, C India
Ratnapura 110 D4 Sabaragamuwa Province, S Sri Lanka
Raton 26 D1 New Mexico, SW USA
Rättvik 63 C5 Kopparberg, C Sweden
Raudhatain see Ar Rawḑatayn
Raufarhöfn 61 E4 Nordhurland Eystra, NE Iceland
Raukawa see Cook Strait
Raukumara Range 128 E3 mountain range North Island, NZ
Rāulakela 151 F4 var. Rāurkela, prev. Rourkela. Orissa, E India
Rauma 63 D5 Swe. Raumo. Länsi-Suomi, W Finland
Raurkela see Raulakela
Ravenna 74 C3 Emilia-Romagna, N Italy
Rāvi 112 C2 river India/Pakistan
Rāwalpindi 112 C1 Punjab, NE Pakistan
Rawa Mazowiecka 76 D4 Łódzkie, C Poland
Rawicz 76 C4 Ger. Rawitsch. Wielkopolskie, C Poland
Rawlins 22 C3 Wyoming, C USA
Rawson 43 C6 Chubut, SE Argentina
Rayak 96 B4 var. Rayaq, Riyāq. E Lebanon
Rayaq see Rayak
Rayleigh 21 F1 state capital North Carolina, SE USA
Rayong 115 C5 Rayong, S Thailand
Razāzah, Buḩayrat ar 98 B3 var. Baḩr al Milḩ. Lake C Iraq
Razgrad 82 D2 Razgrad, N Bulgaria
Razim, Lacul 86 D5 prev. Lacul Razelm. Lagoon NW Black Sea
Reading 19 F4 Pennsylvania, NE USA
Reading 67 D7 S England, UK
Realicó 42 C4 La Pampa, C Argentina
Reăng Kesei 115 D5 Bătdâmbâng, W Cambodia
Rebecca, Lake 125 C6 lake Western Australia
Rebiana Sand Sea see Rabyanāh, Ramlat
Rebun-tō 108 C2 island NE Japan
Rechytsa 85 D7 Rus. Rechitsa. Brestskaya Voblasts', SW Belarus
Recife 41 G2 prev. Pernambuco. State capital Pernambuco, E Brazil
Recklinghausen 72 A4 Nordrhein-Westfalen, W Germany
Recogne 65 C7 Luxembourg, SE Belgium
Reconquista 42 D3 Santa Fe, C Argentina
Red Deer 15 E5 Alberta, SW Canada
Redding 25 B5 California, W USA
Redon 68 B4 Ille-et-Vilaine, NW France
Red River 114 C2 var. Yuan, Chin. Yuan Jiang, Vtn. Sông Hông Hà. River China/Vietnam
Red River 23 E1 river Canada/USA
Red River 20 B3 river Louisiana, S USA
Red River 13 C6 river S USA
Red Sea 50 C3 anc. Sinus Arabicus. Sea Africa/Asia
Red Wing 23 G2 Minnesota, N USA
Reefton 129 C5 West Coast, South Island, NZ
Reese River 25 C5 river Nevada, W USA
Refahiye 95 E3 Erzincan, C Turkey
Regensburg 73 C6 Eng. Ratisbon, Fr. Ratisbonne; hist. Ratisbona, anc. Castra Regina, Reginum. Bayern, SE Germany
Regenstauf 73 C6 Bayern, SE Germany
Reggane 48 D3 C Algeria
Reggio see Reggio nell' Emilia
Reggio Calabria see Reggio di Calabria
Reggio di Calabria 75 D7 var. Reggio Calabria, Gk. Rhegion; anc. Regium, Rhegium. Calabria, SW Italy
Reggio Emilia see Reggio nell' Emilia
Reggio nell' Emilia 74 B2 var. Reggio Emilia, abbrev. Reggio; anc. Regium Lepidum. Emilia-Romagna, N Italy
Reghin 86 C4 Ger. Sächsisch-Reen, Hung. Szászrégen; prev. Reghinul Săsesc, Ger. Sächsisch-Regen. Mureş, C Romania
Regina 15 F5 Saskatchewan, S Canada
Registan see Rīgestān
Regium see Reggio di Calabria
Regium Lepidum see Reggio nell' Emilia
Rehoboth see Reḥovot
Rehoboth 56 B3 Hardap, C Namibia
Reḥovot 97 A6 var. Rehoboth, Rehovoth, Rekhovot. Central, C Israel
Rehovoth see Reḥovot
Reid 125 D6 Western Australia
Reikjavik see Reykjavík
Ré, Île de 68 A4 island W France
Reims 68 D3 Eng. Rheims; anc. Durocortorum, Remi. Marne, N France
Reindeer Lake 15 F4 lake Manitoba/Saskatchewan, C Canada
Reinga, Cape 128 C1 headland North Island, NZ
Reinosa 70 D1 Cantabria, N Spain
Rekhovot see Reḥovot
Reliance 15 F4 Northwest Territories, C Canada
Rendina see Rentína
Rendsburg 72 B2 Schleswig-Holstein, N Germany
Rengat 116 B4 Sumatera, W Indonesia
Reni 86 D4 Odes'ka Oblast', SW Ukraine
Rennell 122 C4 var. Mu Nggava. Island S Solomon Islands
Rennes 68 B3 Bret. Roazon; anc. Condate. Ille-et-Vilaine, NW France
Reno 25 C5 Nevada, W USA
Renqiu 106 C4 Hebei, E China
Rentína 83 B5 var. Rendina. Thessalía, C Greece
Republika Srpska Admin. region republic Bosnia and Herzegovina
République Centrafricaine see Central African Republic
Repulse Bay 15 G3 Nunavut, N Canada
Resht see Rasht
Resistencia 42 D3 Chaco, NE Argentina
Reşiţa 86 A4 Ger. Reschitza, Hung. Resicabánya. Caraş-Severin, W Romania
Resolute 15 F2 Cornwallis Island, Nunavut, N Canada
Resolution Island 17 E1 island Northwest Territories, NE Canada
Resolution Island 129 A7 island SW NZ
Réunion 57 H4 off. La Réunion. French overseas department W Indian Ocean
Réunion 119 B5 island W Indian Ocean
Reus 71 F2 Cataluña, E Spain
Reutlingen 73 B6 Baden-Württemberg, S Germany
Reuver 65 D5 Limburg, SE Netherlands
Revillagigedo Islands see Revillagigedo, Islas
Revillagigedo, Islas 28 B5 Eng. Revillagigedo Islands. Island group W Mexico
Rexburg 24 E3 Idaho, NW USA
Reyes 39 F3 Beni, NW Bolivia
Rey, Isla del 31 G5 island Archipiélago de las Perlas, SE Panama
Reykjanes Basin 60 C5 var. Irminger Basin. Undersea feature N Atlantic Ocean
Reykjanes Ridge 58 A1 undersea feature N Atlantic Ocean
Reykjavík 61 E5 var. Reikjavik. Country capital (Iceland) Höfudhborgarsvaedhi, W Iceland
Reynosa 29 E2 Tamaulipas, C Mexico
Rezé 68 A4 Loire-Atlantique, NW France
Rēzekne 84 D4 Ger. Rositten; prev. Rus. Rezhitsa. Rēzekne, SE Latvia
Rezovo 82 E3 Turk. Rezve. Burgas, E Bulgaria
Rhegion see Reggio di Calabria
Rhegium see Reggio di Calabria
Rhein see Rhine
Rheine 72 A3 var. Rheine in Westfalen. Nordrhein-Westfalen, NW Germany
Rheine in Westfalen see Rheine
Rheinisches Schiefergebirge 73 A5 var. Rhine State Uplands, Eng. Rhenish Slate Mountains. Mountain range W Germany
Rhenish Slate Mountains see Rheinisches Schiefergebirge
Rhine 58 D4 Dut. Rijn, Fr. Rhin, Ger. Rhein. River W Europe
Rhinelander 18 B2 Wisconsin, N USA
Rhine State Uplands see Rheinisches Schiefergebirge
Rho 74 B2 Lombardia, N Italy
Rhode Island 19 G3 off. State of Rhode Island and Providence Plantations; also known as Little Rhody, Ocean State. State NE USA
Rhodes see Ródos
Rhodope Mountains 82 C3 var. Rodhópi Óri, Bul. Rhodope Planina, Rodopi, Gk. Orosirá Rodhópis, Turk. Dospad Dagh. Mountain range Bulgaria/Greece
Rhodope Planina see Rhodope Mountains
Rhodos see Ródos
Rhône 58 C4 river France/Switzerland
Rhône 69 D6 department E France
Rhum 66 B3 var. Rum. Island W Scotland, UK
Ribble 67 D5 river NW England, UK
Ribeira 70 B1 Galicia, NW Spain
Ribeirão Preto 41 F4 São Paulo, S Brazil
Riberalta 39 F2 Beni, N Bolivia
Rîbniţa 86 D3 var. Râbniţa, Rus. Rybnitsa. NE Moldova
Rice Lake 18 A2 Wisconsin, N USA
Richard Toll 52 B3 N Senegal
Richfield 22 B4 Utah, W USA
Richland 24 C2 Washington, NW USA
Richmond 19 E5 state capital Virginia, NE USA
Richmond 18 C5 Kentucky, S USA
Richmond 129 C5 Tasman, South Island, NZ
Richmond Range 129 C5 mountain range South Island, NZ
Ricobayo, Embalse de 70 C2 reservoir NW Spain
Ridgecrest 25 C7 California, W USA
Ried see Ried im Innkreis
Ried im Innkreis 73 D6 var. Ried. Oberösterreich, NW Austria
Riemst 65 D6 Limburg, NE Belgium
Riesa 72 D4 Sachsen, E Germany
Rift Valley see Great Rift Valley
Rīga 84 C3 Eng. Riga. Country capital (Latvia) Rīga, C Latvia
Riga, Gulf of 84 C3 Est. Liivi Laht, Ger. Rigaer Bucht, Latv. Rīgas Jūras Līcis, Rus. Rizhskiy Zaliv; prev. Est. Riia Laht. Gulf Estonia/Latvia
Rīgān 98 E4 Kermān, SE Iran
Rīgestān 100 D5 var. Registan. Desert region S Afghanistan
Riihimäki 63 D5 Etelä-Suomi, S Finland
Rijeka 78 A2 Ger. Sankt Veit am Flaum, It. Fiume, Slvn. Reka; anc. Tarsatica. Primorje-Gorski Kotar, NW Croatia
Rijssel see Lille
Rijssen 64 E3 Overijssel, E Netherlands
Rimah, Wādī ar 98 B4 var. Wādī ar Rummah. Dry watercourse C Saudi Arabia
Rimini 74 C3 anc. Ariminum. Emilia-Romagna, N Italy
Rimouski 39 E4 Québec, SE Canada
Ringebu 63 B5 Oppland, S Norway
Ringkøbing Fjord 63 A7 fjord W Denmark
Ringvassøya 62 C2 island N Norway
Rio see Rio de Janeiro
Riobamba 38 B1 Chimborazo, C Ecuador
Rio Branco 34 B3 state capital Acre, W Brazil
Río Bravo 29 E2 Tamaulipas, C Mexico
Río Cuarto 42 C4 Córdoba, C Argentina
Rio de Janeiro 41 F4 var. Rio. State capital Rio de Janeiro, SE Brazil
Río Gallegos 43 B7 var. Gallegos, Puerto Gallegos. Santa Cruz, S Argentina
Rio Grande 41 E5 var. São Pedro do Rio Grande do Sul. Rio Grande do Sul, S Brazil
Río Grande 28 D3 Zacatecas, C Mexico
Rio Grande do Norte 41 G2 off. Estado do Rio Grande do Norte. State E Brazil
Rio Grande do Sul 41 E5 off. Estado do Rio Grande do Sul. State S Brazil
Rio Grande Plateau see Rio Grande Rise
Rio Grande Rise 35 E6 var. Rio Grande Plateau. Undersea feature SW Atlantic Ocean
Ríohacha 36 B1 La Guajira, N Colombia
Río Lagartos 29 H3 Yucatán, SE Mexico
Riom 69 C5 anc. Ricomagus. Puy-de-Dôme, C France
Río San Juan 31 E4 department S Nicaragua
Rioverde see Río Verde
Río Verde 29 E4 var. Rioverde. San Luis Potosí, C Mexico
Ripoll 71 G2 Cataluña, NE Spain
Rishiri-tō 108 C2 var. Risiri Tô. Island NE Japan
Risiri Tô see Rishiri-tō
Risti 84 D2 Ger. Kreuz. Läänemaa, W Estonia
Rivas 30 D4 Rivas, SW Nicaragua
Rivera 42 D3 Rivera, NE Uruguay
River Falls 18 A2 Wisconsin, N USA
River Plate see Plata, Río de la
Riverside 25 C7 California, W USA
Riverton 129 A7 Southland, South Island, NZ
Riverton 22 C3 Wyoming, C USA
Rivière-du-Loup 17 E4 Québec, SE Canada
Rivne 86 C2 Pol. Równe, Rus. Rovno. Rivnens'ka Oblast', NW Ukraine
Rivoli 74 A2 Piemonte, NW Italy
Riyadh see Ar Riyāḑ
Riyāq see Rayak
Rize 95 E2 Rize, NE Turkey
Rizhao 106 D4 Shandong, E China
Rkîz 52 C3 Trarza, W Mauritania
Road Town 33 F3 dependent territory capital (British Virgin Islands) Tortola, C British Virgin Islands
Roanne 69 C5 anc. Rodunma. Loire, E France
Roanoke 19 E5 Virginia, NE USA
Roanoke River 21 F1 river North Carolina/Virginia, SE USA
Roatán 30 C2 var. Coxen Hole, Coxin Hole. Islas de la Bahía, N Honduras
Robbie Ridge 121 E3 undersea feature W Pacific Ocean
Robert Williams see Caála
Robinson Range 125 B5 mountain range Western Australia
Robson, Mount 15 E5 mountain British Columbia, SW Canada
Robstown 27 G4 Texas, SW USA
Roca Partida, Isla 28 B5 island W Mexico
Rocas, Atol das 41 G2 island E Brazil
Rochefort 68 B4 var. Rochefort sur Mer. Charente-Maritime, W France
Rochefort 65 C7 Namur, SE Belgium
Rochefort sur Mer see Rochefort
Rochester 23 G3 Minnesota, N USA
Rochester 19 G2 New Hampshire, NE USA
Rochester 19 E3 New York, NE USA
Rockall Bank 58 B2 undersea feature N Atlantic Ocean
Rockall Trough 58 B2 undersea feature N Atlantic Ocean
Rockdale 126 E2 New South Wales, SE Australia
Rockford 18 B3 Illinois, N USA
Rockhampton 126 D4 Queensland, E Australia
Rock Hill 21 E1 South Carolina, SE USA
Rockies see Rocky Mountains
Rockingham 125 A6 Western Australia
Rock Island 18 B3 Illinois, N USA
Rock Sound 32 C1 Eleuthera Island, C Bahamas
Rock Springs 22 C3 Wyoming, C USA
Rockstone 37 F3 C Guyana
Rocky Mount 21 F1 North Carolina, SE USA
Rocky Mountains 12 B4 var. Rockies, Fr. Montagnes Rocheuses. Mountain range Canada/USA
Roden 64 E2 Drenthe, NE Netherlands
Rodez 69 C5 anc. Segodunum. Aveyron, S France
Rodhópi Óri see Rhodope Mountains
Ródhos see Ródos
Rodi see Ródos
Rodopi see Rhodope Mountains
Ródos 83 E7 var. Ródhos, Eng. Rhodes, It. Rodi; anc. Rhodos. Island Dodekánisos, Greece, Aegean Sea
Roermond 65 D5 Limburg, SE Netherlands
Roeselare 65 A6 Fr. Roulers; prev. Rousselaere. West-Vlaanderen, W Belgium
Rogatica 78 C4 Republika Srpska, SE Bosnia and Herzegovina
Rogers 20 A1 Arkansas, C USA
Roger Simpson Island see Abemama
Roi Ed see Roi Et
Roi Et 115 D5 var. Muang Roi Et, Roi Ed. Roi Et, E Thailand
Roja 84 C2 Talsi, NW Latvia
Rokiškis 84 C4 Rokiškis, NE Lithuania
Rokycany 77 A5 Ger. Rokytzan. Plzeňský Kraj, W Czech Republic
Rokytzan see Rokycany
Rôlas, Ilha das 54 E2 island S Sao Tome and Principe
Rolla 23 G5 Missouri, C USA
Roma 74 C4 Eng. Rome. Country capital (Italy) Lazio, C Italy
Roma 127 D5 Queensland, E Australia
Roman 86 C4 Hung. Románvásár. Neamţ, NE Romania
Roman 82 C2 Vratsa, NW Bulgaria
Romania 86 B4 Bul. Rumŭniya, Ger. Rumänien, Hung. Románia, Rom. România, SCr. Rumunjska, Ukr. Rumuniya; prev. Republica Socialistă România, Roumania, Rumania, Socialist Republic of Romania, Rom. Romînia. Country SE Europe
Rome see Roma
Rome 20 D2 Georgia, SE USA
Romny 87 F2 Sums'ka Oblast', NE Ukraine
Rømø 63 A7 Ger. Röm. Island SW Denmark
Roncador, Serra do 34 D4 mountain range C Brazil
Ronda 70 D5 Andalucía, S Spain
Rondônia 40 D3 off. Estado de Rondônia; prev. Território de Rondônia. State W Brazil
Rondonópolis 41 E3 Mato Grosso, W Brazil
Rongelap Atoll 122 D1 var. Rōnļap. Atoll Ralik Chain, NW Marshall Islands
Rõngu 84 D3 Ger. Ringen. Tartumaa, SE Estonia
Rōnļap see Rongelap Atoll
Rønne 63 B8 Bornholm, E Denmark
Ronne Ice Shelf 132 A3 ice shelf Antarctica
Roosendaal 65 C5 Noord-Brabant, S Netherlands
Roosevelt Island 132 B4 island Antarctica
Roraima 40 D1 off. Estado de Roraima; prev. Território de Rio Branco, Território de Roraima. State N Brazil
Roraima, Mount 37 E3 mountain N South America
Røros 63 B5 Sør-Trøndelag, S Norway
Rosa, Lake 32 D2 lake Great Inagua, S Bahamas
Rosario 42 D2 San Pedro, C Paraguay
Rosario 42 D4 Santa Fe, C Argentina
Rosarito 28 A1 Baja California, NW Mexico
Roscommon 18 C2 Michigan, N USA
Roseau 33 G4 prev. Charlotte Town. Country capital (Dominica) SW Dominica
Roseburg 24 B4 Oregon, NW USA
Rosenberg 27 G4 Texas, SW USA
Rosengarten 72 B3 Niedersachsen, N Germany
Rosenheim 73 C6 Bayern, S Germany
Rosia 71 H5 W Gibraltar
Rosia Bay 71 H5 bay SW Gibraltar
Roşiori de Vede 86 B5 Teleorman, S Romania
Roslavl' 89 A5 Smolenskaya Oblast', W Russian Federation
Rosmalen 64 C4 Noord-Brabant, S Netherlands
Ross 129 B6 West Coast, South Island, NZ
Rossano 75 E6 anc. Roscianum. Calabria, SW Italy
Ross Ice Shelf 132 B4 ice shelf Antarctica
Rosso 52 B3 Trarza, SW Mauritania
Rossosh' 89 B6 Voronezhskaya Oblast', W Russian Federation
Ross Sea 132 B4 sea Antarctica
Rostak see Ar Rustāq
Rostock 72 C2 Mecklenburg-Vorpommern, NE Germany
Rostov see Rostov-na-Donu
Rostov-na-Donu 89 B7 var. Rostov, Eng. Rostov-on-Don. Rostovskaya Oblast', SW Russian Federation
Rostov-on-Don see Rostov-na-Donu
Roswell 26 D2 New Mexico, SW USA
Rota 122 B1 island S Northern Mariana Islands

Rothera 132 A2 UK research station Antarctica
Rotorua 128 D3 Bay of Plenty, North Island, NZ
Rotorua, Lake 128 D3 lake North Island, NZ
Rotterdam 64 C4 Zuid-Holland, SW Netherlands
Rottweil 73 B6 Baden-Württemberg, S Germany
Rotuma 123 E4 island NW Fiji
Roubaix 68 C2 Nord, N France
Rouen 68 C3 anc. Rotomagus. Seine-Maritime, N France
Round Rock 27 G3 Texas, SW USA
Rourkela see Răulakela
Roussillon 69 C6 cultural region S France
Rouyn-Noranda 16 D4 Québec, SE Canada
Rovaniemi 84 D3 Lappi, N Finland
Rovigo 74 C2 Veneto, NE Italy
Rovinj 78 A3 It. Rovigno. Istra, NW Croatia
Rovuma, Rio 57 F2 var. Ruvuma. River Mozambique/Tanzania see also Ruvuma
Rovuma, Rio see Ruvuma
Roxas City 117 E2 Panay Island, C Philippines
Royale, Isle 18 B1 island Michigan, N USA
Royan 69 B5 Charente-Maritime, W France
Rozdol'ne 87 F4 Rus. Razdolnoye. Respublika Krym, S Ukraine
Rožňava 99 D6 Ger. Rosenau, Hung. Rozsnyó. Košický Kraj, E Slovakia
Ruapehu, Mount 128 D4 mountain North Island, NZ
Ruapuke Island 129 B8 island SW NZ
Ruatoria 128 E3 Gisborne, North Island, NZ
Ruawai 128 D2 Northland, North Island, NZ
Rubizhne 87 H3 Rus. Rubezhnoye. Luhans'ka Oblast', E Ukraine
Ruby Mountains 25 D5 mountain range Nevada, W USA
Rucava 84 B3 Liepāja, SW Latvia
Rūd-e Hīrmand see Helmand, Daryā-ye
Rūdiškės 85 B5 Trakai, S Lithuania
Rudnik 82 E2 Varna, E Bulgaria
Rudny see Rudnyy
Rudnyy 92 C4 var. Rudny. Kostanay, N Kazakhstan
Rudolf, Lake see Turkana, Lake
Rudolfswert see Novo Mesto
Rudzyensk 85 C6 Rus. Rudensk. Minskaya Voblasts', C Belarus
Rufiji 51 C7 river E Tanzania
Rufino 42 C4 Santa Fe, C Argentina
Rugāji 84 D4 Balvi, E Latvia
Rügen 94 D2 headland NE Germany
Ruggell 72 E1 N Liechtenstein
Ruhnu 84 C2 var. Ruhnu Saar, Swe. Runö. Island SW Estonia
Ruhnu Saar see Ruhnu
Rūjiena 84 D3 Est. Ruhja, Ger. Rujen. Valmiera, N Latvia
Rukwa, Lake 51 B7 lake SE Tanzania
Rum see Rhum
Ruma 78 D3 Serbia, N Serbia and Montenegro (Yugo.)
Rumadiya see Ar Ramādī
Rumbek 51 B5 El Buhayrat, S Sudan
Rum Cay 32 D2 island C Bahamas
Rumia 76 C2 Pomorskie, N Poland
Rummah, Wādī ar see Rimah, Wādī ar
Runanga 129 B5 West Coast, South Island, NZ
Runaway Bay 32 B4 C Jamaica
Rundu 56 C3 var. Runtu. Okavango, NE Namibia
Runö see Ruhnu
Runtu see Rundu
Ruoqiang 104 C3 var. Jo-ch'iang, Uigh. Charkhlik, Charkhliq, Qarkilik. Xinjiang Uygur Zizhiqu, NW China
Rupea 86 C4 Ger. Reps, Hung. Kőhalom; prev. Cohalm. Braşov, C Romania
Rupel 65 B5 river N Belgium
Rupert, Rivière de 16 D3 river Québec, C Canada
Ruschuk see Ruse
Rusçuk see Ruse
Ruse 82 D1 var. Ruschuk, Rustchuk, Turk. Rusçuk. Ruse, N Bulgaria
Rus Krymskaya ASSR see Crimea
Russellville 20 A1 Arkansas, C USA
Russian Federation 90 D2 var. Russia, Latv. Krievija, Rus. Rossiyskaya Federatsiya. Country Asia/Europe
Rustaq see Ar Rustāq
Rust'avi 95 G2 SE Georgia
Rustchuk see Ruse
Ruston 20 B2 Louisiana, S USA
Rutanzige |M, Lake see Edward, Lake
Rutba see Ar Ruţbah
Rutland 19 F2 Vermont, NE USA
Rutög 104 A4 var. Rutog, Rutok. Xizang Zizhiqu, W China
Rutok see Rutog
Ruvuma 47 E5 var. Rio Rovuma. River Mozambique/Tanzania see also Rovuma, Rio
Ruvuma see Rovuma, Rio
Ruwenzori 55 E5 mountain range Uganda/Dem. Rep. Congo
Ruzhany 85 B6 Rus. Ruzhany. Brestskaya Voblasts', SW Belarus
Ružomberok 77 C5 Ger. Rosenberg, Hung. Rózsahegy. Žilinsky Kraj, N Slovakia
Rwanda 51 B6 prev. Ruanda. Country C Africa
Ryazan' 89 B5 Ryazanskaya Oblast', W Russian Federation
Rybinsk 88 B4 prev. Andropov. Yaroslavskaya Oblast', W Russian Federation
Rybnik 77 C5 Śląskie, S Poland
Rybniţa see Rîbniţa
Ryde 126 E1 New South Wales, SE Australia
Ryki 76 D4 Lublin, E Poland
Rypin 76 C3 Kujawsko-pomorskie, C Poland
Ryssel see Lille
Rysy 77 C5 mountain S Poland
Ryukyu Islands 103 E3 island group SW Japan
Ryukyu Trench 103 F3 var. Nansei Syotō Trench. Undersea feature S East China Sea
Rzeszów 77 E5 Podkarpackie, SE Poland
Rzhev 88 B4 Tverskaya Oblast', W Russian Federation

S

Saale 72 C4 river C Germany
Saalfeld 73 C5 var. Saalfeld an der Saale. Thüringen, C Germany
Saalfeld an der Saale see Saalfeld
Saarbrücken 73 A6 Fr. Sarrebruck. Saarland, SW Germany
Säare 84 C2 var. Sjar. Saaremaa, W Estonia
Saaremaa 84 C2 Ger. Oesel, Ösel; prev. Saare. Island W Estonia
Saariselkä 62 D2 Lapp. Suoločielgi. Lappi, N Finland
Sab' Ābār 96 C4 var. Sab'a Biyar, Sa'b Bi'ār. Ḩimş, C Syria
Sab'a Biyar see Sab' Ābār
Šabac 78 D3 Serbia, W Serbia and Montenegro (Yugo.)
Sabadell 71 G2 Cataluña, E Spain
Sabah 116 D3 cultural region Borneo, SE Asia
Sabanalarga 36 B1 Atlántico, N Colombia
Sabaneta 36 C1 Falcón, N Venezuela
Sab'atayn, Ramlat as 99 C6 desert C Yemen
Sabaya 39 F4 Oruro, S Bolivia
Sa'b Bi'ār see Sab' Ābār
Şāberī, Hāmūn-e var. Daryācheh-ye Hāmūn, Daryācheh-ye Sīstān. Lake Afghanistan/Iran see also Sīstān, Daryācheh-ye
Sabhā 49 F3 C Libya
Sabi, Rio see Save, Rio
Sabinas 29 E2 Coahuila de Zaragoza, NE Mexico
Sabinas Hidalgo 29 E2 Nuevo León, NE Mexico
Sabine River 27 H3 river Louisiana/Texas, SW USA
Sabkha see As Sabkhah
Sable, Cape 21 E5 headland Florida, SE USA
Sable Island 17 G4 island Nova Scotia, SE Canada
Şabyā 99 B6 Jīzān, SW Saudi Arabia
Sabzawar see Sabzevār
Sabzevār 98 D2 var. Sabzawar. Khorāsān, NE Iran
Sachsen 72 D4 Eng. Saxony, Fr. Saxe. State E Germany
Sachs Harbour 15 E2 Banks Island, Northwest Territories, N Canada
Sacramento 25 B5 state capital California, W USA
Sacramento Mountains 26 D2 mountain range New Mexico, SW USA
Sacramento River 25 B5 river California, W USA
Sacramento Valley 25 B5 valley California, W USA
Şa'dah 99 B6 NW Yemen
Sado 109 C5 var. Sadoga-shima. Island C Japan
Sadoga-shima see Sado
Safad see Ẕefat
Safed see Ẕefat
Säffle 63 B6 Värmland, C Sweden
Safford 26 C3 Arizona, SW USA
Safi 48 B2 W Morocco
Safīd Kūh, Selseleh-ye 100 D4 Eng. Paropamisus Range. Mountain range W Afghanistan
Sagaing 114 B3 Sagaing, C Myanmar
Sagami-nada 109 D6 inlet SW Japan
Sagan see Żagań
Sāgar 112 D4 prev. Saugor. Madhya Pradesh, C India
Saghez see Saqqez
Saginaw 18 C3 Michigan, N USA
Saginaw Bay 18 D2 lake bay Michigan, N USA
Sagua la Grande 32 B2 Villa Clara, C Cuba
Sagunt see Sagunto
Sagunto 71 F3 var. Sagunt, Ar. Murviedro; anc. Saguntum. País Valenciano, E Spain
Saguntum see Sagunto
Sahara 46 B3 desert Libya/Algeria
Sahara el Gharbîya 50 B2 var. Aş Şaḩrā' al Gharbīyah, Eng. Western Desert. Desert C Egypt
Saharan Atlas see Atlas Saharien
Sahel 52 D3 physical region C Africa
Sāḩilīyah, Jibāl as 96 B3 mountain range NW Syria
Sāhīwāl 112 C2 prev. Montgomery. Punjab, E Pakistan
şaḩrā' Rabyanāh see Rabyanāh, Ramlat
Saïda 97 A5 var. Şaydā, Sayida; anc. Sidon. W Lebanon
Saidpur 113 G3 var. Syedpur. Rajshahi, NW Bangladesh
Saigon see Hô Chi Minh
Sai Hun see Syr Darya
Saimaa 63 E5 lake SE Finland
St Albans 67 E6 anc. Verulamium. E England, UK
Saint Albans 18 D5 West Virginia, NE USA
St Andrews 66 C4 E Scotland, UK
Saint Anna Trough see Svyataya Anna Trough
St.Ann's Bay 32 B4 C Jamaica
St.Anthony 17 G3 Newfoundland, Newfoundland and Labrador, SE Canada
Saint Augustine 21 E3 Florida, SE USA
St Austell 67 C7 SW England, UK
St-Brieuc 68 A3 Côtes d'Armor, NW France
St. Catharines 16 D5 Ontario, S Canada
St-Chamond 69 D5 Loire, E France
St.Clair, Lake 18 D3 Fr. Lac à L'Eau Claire. Lake Canada/USA
St-Claude 69 D5 anc. Condate. Jura, E France
Saint Cloud 23 F2 Minnesota, N USA
St Croix 33 F3 island S Virgin Islands (US)
Saint Croix River 18 A2 river Minnesota/Wisconsin, N USA
St David's Island 20 B5 island E Bermuda
St-Denis 57 G4 dependent territory capital (Réunion) NW Réunion
St-Dié 68 E4 Vosges, NE France
St-Egrève 69 D5 Isère, E France
Saintes 69 B5 anc. Mediolanum. Charente-Maritime, W France
St-Étienne 69 D5 Loire, E France
St-Flour 69 C5 Cantal, C France
Saint Gall see Sankt Gallen
St-Gall see Sankt Gallen
StGallen see Sankt Gallen
St-Gaudens 69 B6 Haute-Garonne, S France
St George 20 B4 N Bermuda
Saint George 127 D5 Queensland, E Australia
Saint George 22 A5 Utah, W USA
St.George's 33 G5 country capital (Grenada) SW Grenada
St-Georges 37 H3 E French Guiana
St-Georges 17 E4 Québec, SE Canada
St George's Channel 67 B6 channel Ireland/Wales, UK
St George's Island 20 B4 island E Bermuda
Saint Helena 47 B6 UK dependent territory C Atlantic Ocean
St.Helena Bay 56 B5 bay SW South Africa
St Helier 67 D8 dependent territory capital (Jersey) S Jersey, Channel Islands
Saint Ignace 18 C2 Michigan, N USA
St-Jean, Lac 17 E4 lake Québec, SE Canada
Saint Joe River 24 D2 river Idaho, NW USA
Saint John 19 H1 river Canada/USA
Saint John 17 F4 New Brunswick, SE Canada
St John's 33 G3 country capital (Antigua and Barbuda) Antigua, Antigua and Barbuda
St.John's 17 H3 Newfoundland, Newfoundland and Labrador, E Canada
Saint Joseph 23 F4 Missouri, C USA
St Julian's 80 B5 N Malta
St Kilda 66 A3 island NW Scotland, UK
Saint Kitts and Nevis 33 F3 var. Saint Christopher-Nevis. Country E West Indies
St-Laurent see St-Laurent-du-Maroni
St-Laurent-du-Maroni 37 H3 var. St-Laurent. NW French Guiana
St. Lawrence 17 E4 Fr. Fleuve St-Laurent. River Canada/USA
St. Lawrence, Gulf of 17 F3 gulf NW Atlantic Ocean
Saint Lawrence Island 14 B2 island Alaska, USA
St-Lô 68 B3 anc. Briovera, Laudus. Manche, N France
St-Louis 68 E4 Haut-Rhin, NE France
Saint Louis 23 G4 Missouri, C USA
Saint Louis 52 B3 NW Senegal
Saint Lucia 33 E1 country SE West Indies
Saint Lucia Channel 33 H4 channel Martinique/Saint Lucia
St-Malo 68 B3 Ille-et-Vilaine, NW France
St-Malo, Golfe de 68 A3 gulf NW France
St Matthew's Island see Zadetkyi Kyun
St.Matthias Group 122 B3 island group NE PNG
St-Maur-des-Fossés 68 E2 Val-de-Marne, N France
St.Moritz 73 B7 Ger. Sankt Moritz, Rmsch. San Murezzan. Graubünden, SE Switzerland
St-Nazaire 68 A4 Loire-Atlantique, NW France
St-Omer 68 C2 Pas-de-Calais, N France
Saint Paul 23 F2 state capital Minnesota, N USA
St-Paul, Île 119 C6 var. St.Paul Island. Island NE French Southern and Antarctic Territories
St.Paul Island see St-Paul, Île
St Peter Port 67 D8 dependent territory capital (Guernsey) C Guernsey, Channel Islands
Saint Petersburg see Sankt-Peterburg
Saint Petersburg 21 E4 Florida, SE USA
St-Pierre and Miquelon 17 G4 Fr. Îles St-Pierre et Miquelon. French territorial collectivity NE North America
St-Quentin 68 C3 Aisne, N France
Saint Vincent 33 G4 island N Saint Vincent and the Grenadines
Saint Vincent and the Grenadines 33 H4 country SE West Indies
Saint Vincent Passage 33 H4 passage Saint Lucia/Saint Vincent and the Grenadines
Saipan 120 B1 island country capital (Northern Mariana Islands) S Northern Mariana Islands
Sajama, Nevado 39 F4 mountain W Bolivia
Sajószentpéter 77 D6 Borsod-Abaúj-Zemplén, NE Hungary
Sakākah 98 B4 Al Jawf, NW Saudi Arabia
Sakakawea, Lake 22 D1 reservoir North Dakota, N USA
Sakata 108 D4 Yamagata, Honshū, C Japan
Sakhalin see Sakhalin, Ostrov
Sakhalin, Ostrov 93 G4 var. Sakhalin. Island SE Russian Federation
Sakhon Nakhon see Sakon Nakhon
Şäki 95 G2 Rus. Sheki; prev. Nukha. NW Azerbaijan
Sakishima-shotō 108 A3 var. Sakisima Syotô. Island group SW Japan
Sakisima Syotô see Sakishima-shotō
Sakiz see Saqqez
Sakiz-Adasi see Chíos
Sakon Nakhon 114 D4 var. Muang Sakon Nakhon, Sakhon Nakhon. Sakon Nakhon, E Thailand
Saky 87 F5 Rus. Saki. Respublika Krym, S Ukraine
Sal 52 A3 island Ilhas de Barlavento, NE Cape Verde
Sala 63 C6 Västmanland, C Sweden
Salacgrīva 84 C3 Est. Salatsi. Limbaži, N Latvia
Sala Consilina 75 D5 Campania, S Italy
Salado, Río 42 C3 river C Argentina
Salado, Río 40 D5 river E Argentina
Şalālah 99 D6 SW Oman
Salamá 30 B2 Baja Verapaz, C Guatemala
Salamanca 70 D2 anc. Helmantica, Salmantica. Castilla-León, NW Spain
Salamanca 42 B4 Coquimbo, C Chile
Salamīyah 96 B3 var. As Salamīyah. Ḩamāh, W Syria
Salang see Phuket
Salantai 84 B3 Kretinga, NW Lithuania
Salavan 115 D5 var. Saravan, Saravane. Salavan, S Laos
Salavat 89 D6 Respublika Bashkortostan, W Russian Federation
Sala y Gomez 131 F4 island Chile, E Pacific Ocean
Sala y Gomez Fracture Zone see Sala y Gomez Ridge
Sala y Gomez Ridge 131 G4 var. Sala y Gomez Fracture Zone. Tectonic feature SE Pacific Ocean
Šalčininkai 85 C5 Šalčininkai, SE Lithuania
Saldus 84 B3 Ger. Frauenburg. Saldus, W Latvia
Sale 127 C7 Victoria, SE Australia
Salé 48 C2 NW Morocco
Salekhard 92 D3 prev. Obdorsk. Yamalo-Nenetskiy Avtonomnyy Okrug, N Russian Federation
Salem 24 B3 state capital Oregon, NW USA
Salem 110 C2 Tamil Nādu, SE India
Salerno 75 D5 anc. Salernum. Campania, S Italy
Salerno, Golfo di 75 C5 Eng. Gulf of Salerno. Gulf S Italy
Salihorsk 85 C7 Rus. Soligorsk. Minskaya Voblasts', S Belarus
Salima 57 E2 Central, C Malawi
Salina 23 E5 Kansas, C USA
Salina Cruz 29 F5 Oaxaca, SE Mexico
Salinas 25 B6 California, W USA
Salinas 38 A2 Guayas, W Ecuador
Salisbury 67 D7 var. New Sarum. S England, UK
Sallyana see Salyan
Salmon River 24 D3 river Idaho, NW USA
Salmon River Mountains 24 D3 mountain range Idaho, NW USA
Salo 85 D6 Länsi-Suomi, W Finland
Salon-de-Provence 69 D6 Bouches-du-Rhône, SE France
Salonta 86 A3 Hung. Nagyszalonta. Bihor, W Romania
Sal'sk 89 B7 Rostovskaya Oblast', SW Russian Federation
Salt see As Salţ
Salta 42 C2 Salta, NW Argentina
Saltash 67 C7 SW England, UK
Saltillo 29 E3 Coahuila de Zaragoza, NE Mexico
Salt Lake City 22 B4 state capital Utah, W USA
Salto 42 D4 Salto, N Uruguay
Salton Sea 25 D8 lake California, W USA
Salvador 41 G3 prev. São Salvador. Bahia, E Brazil
Salween 102 C2 Bur. Thanlwin, Chin. Nu Chiang, Nu Jiang. River SE Asia
Salyan 113 E3 var. Sallyana. Mid Western, W Nepal
Salzburg 73 D6 anc. Juvavum. Salzburg, N Austria
Salzgitter 72 C4 prev. Watenstedt-Salzgitter. Niedersachsen, C Germany
Salzwedel 72 C3 Sachsen-Anhalt, N Germany
Šamac see Bosanski Šamac
Samakhixai 115 E5 var. Attapu, Attopeu. Attapu, S Laos
Samalayuca 28 C1 Chihuahua, N Mexico
Samar 117 F2 island C Philippines
Samara 92 B3 prev. Kuybyshev. Samarskaya Oblast', W Russian Federation
Samarang see Semarang
Samarinda 116 D4 Borneo, C Indonesia
Samarqand 101 E2 Rus. Samarkand. Samarqand Wiloyati, C Uzbekistan
Samawa see As Samāwah
Sambalpur 113 F4 Orissa, E India
Sambava 57 G2 Antsiraňana, NE Madagascar
Sambir 86 B2 Rus. Sambor. L'vivs'ka Oblast', NW Ukraine
Sambre 68 D2 river Belgium/France
Samfya 56 D2 Luapula, N Zambia
Saminatal 72 E2 valley Austria/Liechtenstein
Samnān see Semnān
Sam Neua see Xam Nua
Samoa 123 E4 var. Sāmoa; prev. Western Samoa. Country W Polynesia
Samoa Basin 121 E3 undersea feature W Pacific Ocean
Samobor 78 A2 Zagreb, N Croatia
Sámos 83 E6 prev. Limín Vathéos. Sámos, Dodekánisos, Greece, Aegean Sea
Sámos 83 D6 island Dodekánisos, Greece, Aegean Sea
Samosch see Someş
Samothráki 82 C4 anc. Samothrace. Island NE Greece
Samothráki 82 D4 Samothráki, NE Greece
Sampit 116 C4 Borneo, C Indonesia
Samsun 94 D2 anc. Amisus. Samsun, N Turkey
Samtredia 95 F2 W Georgia
Samui, Ko 115 C6 island SW Thailand
Samut Prakan 115 C5 var. Muang Samut Prakan, Paknam. Samut Prakan, C Thailand
San 77 E5 river SE Poland
San 52 D3 Ségou, C Mali
Şan'ā' 99 B6 Eng. Sana. Country capital (Yemen) W Yemen
Sana 78 B3 river NW Bosnia and Herzegovina
Sana see Şan'ā'
Sanae 132 B2 South African research station Antarctica
Sanaga 55 B5 river C Cameroon
San Ambrosio, Isla 35 A5 Eng. San Ambrosio Island. Island W Chile
Sanandaj 98 C3 prev. Sinneh. Kordestān, W Iran
San Andrés, Isla de 31 F3 island NW Colombia
San Andrés Tuxtla 29 F4 var. Tuxtla. Veracruz-Llave, E Mexico
San Angelo 27 F3 Texas, SW USA
San Antonio 27 F4 Texas, SW USA
San Antonio 30 B2 Toledo, S Belize
San Antonio 42 B4 Valparaíso, C Chile
San Antonio Oeste 43 C5 Río Negro, E Argentina
San Antonio River 27 G4 river Texas, SW USA
Sanāw 99 C6 var. Sanaw. NE Yemen
San Benedicto, Isla 28 B4 island W Mexico
San Benito 30 B1 Petén, N Guatemala
San Benito 27 G5 Texas, SW USA
San Bernardino 25 C7 California, W USA
San Blas 28 C3 Sinaloa, C Mexico
San Blas, Cape 20 D3 headland Florida, SE USA
San Blas, Cordillera de 31 G4 mountain range NE Panama
San Carlos see Quesada
San Carlos 26 B2 Arizona, SW USA
San Carlos 30 D4 Río San Juan, S Nicaragua
San Carlos de Bariloche 43 B5 Río Negro, SW Argentina
San Carlos del Zulia 36 C2 Zulia, W Venezuela
San Clemente Island 25 B8 island Channel Islands, California, W USA
San Cristobal 122 C4 var. Makira. Island SE Solomon Islands
San Cristóbal see San Cristóbal de Las Casas
San Cristóbal 36 C2 Táchira, W Venezuela
San Cristóbal de Las Casas 29 G5 var. San Cristóbal. Chiapas, SE Mexico
San Cristóbal, Isla 38 B5 var. Chatham Island. Island Galapagos Islands, Ecuador, E Pacific Ocean
Sancti Spíritus 32 B2 Sancti Spíritus, C Cuba
Sandakan 116 D3 Sabah, East Malaysia
Sandanski 82 C3 prev. Sveti Vrach. Blagoevgrad, SW Bulgaria
Sanday 66 D2 island NE Scotland, UK
Sanders 26 C2 Arizona, SW USA
Sand Hills 22 D3 mountain range Nebraska, C USA
San Diego 25 C8 California, W USA
Sandnes 63 A6 Rogaland, S Norway
Sandomierz 76 D4 Rus. Sandomir. Świętokrzyskie, C Poland
Sandoway 114 A4 Arakan State, W Myanmar
Sandpoint 24 C1 Idaho, NW USA
Sand Springs 27 G1 Oklahoma, C USA
Sandusky 18 D3 Ohio, N USA
Sandvika 63 A6 Akershus, S Norway
Sandviken 63 C6 Gävleborg, C Sweden
Sandy Bay 71 H5 bay E Gibraltar
Sandy City 22 B4 Utah, W USA
Sandy Lake 16 B3 lake Ontario, C Canada
San Esteban 30 D2 Olancho, C Honduras
San Felipe 36 D1 Yaracuy, NW Venezuela
San Felipe de Puerto Plata see Puerto Plata
San Félix, Isla 35 A5 Eng. San Felix Island. Island W Chile
San Fernando 70 C5 prev. Isla de León. Andalucía, S Spain
San Fernando 36 D2 var. San Fernando de Apure. Apure, C Venezuela
San Fernando 24 D1 California, W USA
San Fernando 33 H5 Trinidad, Trinidad and Tobago
San Fernando de Apure see San Fernando
San Fernando del Valle de Catamarca 42 C3 var. Catamarca. Catamarca, NW Argentina
San Fernando de Monte Cristi see Monte Cristi
San Francisco 25 B6 California, W USA
San Francisco del Oro 28 C2 Chihuahua, N Mexico
San Francisco de Macorís 33 E3 C Dominican Republic
San Gabriel 38 B1 Carchi, N Ecuador
San Gabriel Mountains 24 E1 mountain range California, W USA
Sangir, Kepulauan 117 F3 var. Kepulauan Sangihe. Island group N Indonesia
Sāngli 132 B1 Mahārāshtra, W India
Sangmélima 77 B5 Sud, S Cameroon
Sangre de Cristo Mountains 26 D1 mountain range Colorado/New Mexico, C USA
San Ignacio 30 B1 prev. Cayo, El Cayo. Cayo, W Belize
San Ignacio 28 B2 Baja California Sur, W Mexico
San Ignacio 39 F3 Beni, N Bolivia
San Joaquin Valley 25 B7 valley California, W USA
San Jorge, Golfo 43 C6 var. Gulf of San Jorge. Gulf S Argentina

INDEX

San Jorge, Gulf of *see* San Jorge, Golfo
San José *see* San José del Guaviare
San Jose 25 *B6* California, W USA
San José 30 *B3 var.* Puerto San José. Escuintla, S Guatemala
San José 39 *G3 var.* San José de Chiquitos. Santa Cruz, E Bolivia
San José 31 *E4 country capital* (Costa Rica) San José, C Costa Rica
San José de Chiquitos *see* San José
San José de Cúcuta *see* Cúcuta
San José del Guaviare 36 *C4 var.* San José. Guaviare, S Colombia
San Juan 33 *F3 dependent territory capital* (Puerto Rico) NE Puerto Rico
San Juan *see* San Juan de los Morros
San Juan 42 *B4* San Juan, W Argentina
San Juan Bautista 42 *D3* Misiones, S Paraguay
San Juan Bautista Tuxtepec *see* Tuxtepec
San Juan de Alicante 71 *F4* País Valenciano, E Spain
San Juan del Norte 31 *E4 var.* Greytown. Río San Juan, SE Nicaragua
San Juan de los Morros 36 *D2 var.* San Juan. Guárico, N Venezuela
San Juanito, Isla 28 *C4 island* C Mexico
San Juan Mountains 26 *D1 mountain range* Colorado, C USA
San Juan River 26 *C1 river* Colorado/Utah, W USA
San Julián *see* Puerto San Julián
Sankt Gallen 73 *B7 var.* St.Gallen, *Eng.* Saint Gall, *Fr.* St-Gall. Sankt Gallen, NE Switzerland
Sankt-Peterburg 88 *B4 prev.* Leningrad, Petrograd, *Eng.* Saint Petersburg, *Fin.* Pietari. Leningradskaya Oblast', NW Russian Federation
Sankt Pölten 73 *E6* Niederösterreich, N Austria
Sankuru 55 *D6 river* C Dem. Rep. Congo
Şanlıurfa 95 *E4 prev.* Sanli Urfa, Urfa, *anc.* Edessa. Şanlıurfa, S Turkey
San Lorenzo 38 *A1* Esmeraldas, N Ecuador
San Lorenzo 39 *G5* Tarija, S Bolivia
San Lorenzo, Isla 38 *C4 island* W Peru
Sanlúcar de Barrameda 70 *C5* Andalucía, S Spain
San Luis 28 *A1 var.* San Luis Río Colorado. Sonora, NW Mexico
San Luis 30 *B2* Petén, NE Guatemala
San Luis 42 *C4* San Luis, C Argentina
San Luis Obispo 25 *B7* California, W USA
San Luis Potosí 29 *E3* San Luis Potosí, C Mexico
San Luis Río Colorado *see* San Luis
San Marcos 30 *A2* San Marcos, W Guatemala
San Marcos 27 *G4* Texas, SW USA
San Marino 74 *E1 country capital* (San Marino) C San Marino
San Marino 74 *D1 Country* S Europe
San Martín 132 *A2 Argentinian research station* Antarctica
San Mateo 37 *E2* Anzoátegui, NE Venezuela
San Matías 39 *H3* Santa Cruz, E Bolivia
San Matías, Golfo 43 *C5 var.* Gulf of San Matías. *Gulf* E Argentina
San Matías, Gulf of *see* San Matías, Golfo
Sanmenxia 106 *C4 var.* Shan Xian. Henan, C China
Sânmiclăuş Mare *see* Sânnicolau Mare
San Miguel 28 *D2* Coahuila de Zaragoza, N Mexico
San Miguel 30 *C3* San Miguel, SE El Salvador
San Miguel de Ibarra *see* Ibarra
San Miguel de Tucumán 42 *C3 var.* Tucumán. Tucumán, N Argentina
San Miguelito 31 *G4* Panamá, C Panama
San Miguel, Río 39 *G3 river* E Bolivia
Sannār *see* Sennar
Sânnicolaul-Mare *see* Sânnicolau Mare
Sânnicolau Mare 86 *A4 var.* Sânnicolaul-Mare, *Hung.* Nagyszentmiklós; *prev.* Sânmiclăuş Mare, Sînnicolau Mare. Timiş, W Romania
Sanok 77 *E5* Podkarpackie, SE Poland
San Pablo 39 *F5* Potosí, S Bolivia
San Pedro 28 *D3 var.* San Pedro de las Colonias. Coahuila de Zaragoza, NE Mexico
San Pedro 30 *C1* Corozal, NE Belize
San-Pédro 52 *D5* S Côte d'Ivoire
San Pedro de la Cueva 28 *C2* Sonora, NW Mexico
San Pedro de las Colonias *see* San Pedro
San Pedro de Lloc 38 *B3* La Libertad, NW Peru
San Pedro Mártir, Sierra 28 *A1 mountain range* NW Mexico
San Pedro Sula 30 *C2* Cortés, NW Honduras
San Rafael 42 *B4* Mendoza, W Argentina
San Rafael Mountains 25 *C7 mountain range* California, W USA
San Ramón de la Nueva Orán 42 *C2* Salta, N Argentina
San Remo 74 *A3* Liguria, NW Italy
San Salvador 30 *B3 country capital* (El Salvador) San Salvador, SW El Salvador
San Salvador de Jujuy 42 *C2 var.* Jujuy. Jujuy, N Argentina
San Salvador, Isla 38 *A4 prev.* Watlings Island. *Island* E Bahamas
Sansanné-Mango 53 *E4 var.* Mango. N Togo
Sansepolcro 74 *C3* Toscana, C Italy
San Severo 75 *D5* Puglia, SE Italy
Santa Ana 39 *F3* Beni, N Bolivia
Santa Ana 24 *D2* California, W USA
Santa Ana 30 *B3* Santa Ana, NW El Salvador
Santa Ana Mountains 24 *E2 mountain range* California, W USA
Santa Barbara 25 *C7* California, W USA
Santa Barbara 28 *C2* Chihuahua, N Mexico
Santa Catalina Island 25 *B8 island* Channel Islands, California, W USA
Santa Catarina 41 *E5 off.* Estado de Santa Catarina. *State* S Brazil
Santa Clara 32 *B2* Villa Clara, C Cuba
Santa Clarita 24 *D1* California, W USA
Santa Comba 70 *B1* Galicia, NW Spain
Santa Cruz 39 *G4 var.* Santa Cruz de la Sierra. Santa Cruz, C Bolivia
Santa Cruz 25 *B6* California, W USA
Santa Cruz 54 *E2* São Tomé, C Sao Tome and Principe
Santa Cruz Barillas *see* Barillas
Santa Cruz de la Sierra *see* Santa Cruz
Santa Cruz del Quiché 30 *B2* Quiché, W Guatemala
Santa Cruz de Tenerife 48 *A3* Tenerife, Islas Canarias, Spain, NE Atlantic Ocean
Santa Cruz, Isla 38 *B5 var.* Indefatigable Island, Isla Chávez. *Island* Galapagos Islands, Ecuador, E Pacific Ocean
Santa Cruz Islands 122 *D3 island group* E Solomon Islands
Santa Cruz, Río 43 *B7 river* S Argentina
Santa Elena 30 *B1* Cayo, W Belize
Santa Fe 26 *D1 state capital* New Mexico, SW USA
Santa Fe 42 *C4* Santa Fe, C Argentina
Santa Genoveva 28 *B3 mountain* W Mexico
Santa Isabel 122 *C3 var.* Bughotu. *Island* N Solomon Islands
Santa Lucia Range 25 *B7 mountain range* California, W USA
Santa Margarita, Isla 28 *B3 island* W Mexico
Santa Maria 70 *A5 island* Azores, Portugal, NE Atlantic Ocean
Santa Maria 25 *B7* California, W USA
Santa Maria 41 *E5* Rio Grande do Sul, S Brazil
Santa María, Isla 38 *A5 var.* Isla Floreana, Charles Island. *Island* Galapagos Islands, Ecuador, E Pacific Ocean
Santa Marta 36 *B1* Magdalena, N Colombia
Santa Monica 24 *D1* California, W USA
Santana 54 *E2* São Tomé, S Sao Tome and Principe
Santander 70 *D1* Cantabria, N Spain
Santanilla, Islas 31 *E1 Eng.* Swan Islands. *Island* NE Honduras
Santarém 70 *B3 anc.* Scalabis. Santarém, W Portugal
Santarém 41 *E2* Pará, N Brazil
Santa Rosa *see* Santa Rosa de Copán s
Santa Rosa 42 *C4* La Pampa, C Argentina
Santa Rosa de Copán 30 *C2 var.* Santa Rosa. Copán, W Honduras
Santa Rosa Island 25 *B8 island* California, W USA
Sant Carles de la Rápida *see* Sant Carles de la Ràpita
Sant Carles de la Ràpita 71 *F3 var.* Sant Carles de la Rápida. Cataluña, NE Spain
Santiago 42 *B4 var.* Gran Santiago. *Country capital* (Chile) Santiago, C Chile
Santiago 70 *B1 var.* Santiago de Compostela, *Eng.* Compostella; *anc.* Campus Stellae. Galicia, NW Spain
Santiago 33 *E3 var.* Santiago de los Caballeros. N Dominican Republic
Santiago 52 *A3 var.* São Tiago. *Island* Ilhas de Sotavento, S Cape Verde
Santiago *see* Santiago de Cuba
Santiago 31 *F5* Veraguas, S Panama
Santiago de Compostela *see* Santiago
Santiago de Cuba 32 *C3 var.* Santiago. Santiago de Cuba, E Cuba
Santiago de Guayaquil *see* Guayaquil
Santiago del Estero 42 *C3* Santiago del Estero, C Argentina
Santiago de los Caballeros *see* Santiago
Santiago Pinotepa Nacional *see* Pinotepa Nacional
Santiago, Río 38 *B2 river* N Peru
Santi Quaranta *see* Sarandë
Santissima Trinidad *see* Chilung
Sant Julià de Lòria 69 *A8* SW Andorra
Santo *see* Espiritu Santo
Santo Antão 52 *A2 island* Ilhas de Barlavento, N Cape Verde
Santo António 54 *E1* Príncipe, N Sao Tome and Principe
Santo Domingo 32 *D3 prev.* Ciudad Trujillo. *Country capital* (Dominican Republic) SE Dominican Republic
Santo Domingo de los Colorados 38 *B1* Pichincha, NW Ecuador
Santo Domingo Tehuantepec *see* Tehuantepec
Santos 41 *F4* São Paulo, S Brazil
Santos Plateau 35 *D5 undersea feature* SW Atlantic Ocean
Santo Tomé 42 *D3* Corrientes, NE Argentina
San Valentín, Cerro 43 *A6 mountain* S Chile
San Vicente 30 *C3* San Vicente, C El Salvador
São Francisco, Rio 41 *F3 river* E Brazil
Sao Hill 51 *C7* Iringa, S Tanzania
São João da Madeira 70 *B2* Aveiro, N Portugal
São Jorge 70 *A5 island* Azores, Portugal, NE Atlantic Ocean
São Luís 41 *F2 state capital* Maranhão, NE Brazil
São Mandol *see* São Manuel, Rio
São Manuel, Rio 41 *E3 var.* São Mandol, Teles Pirés. *River* C Brazil
São Marcos, Baía de 41 *F1 bay* N Brazil
São Miguel 70 *A5 island* Azores, Portugal, NE Atlantic Ocean
Saona, Isla 33 *E3 island* SE Dominican Republic
Saône 69 *D5 river* E France
São Nicolau 52 *A3 Eng.* Saint Nicholas. *Island* Ilhas de Barlavento, N Cape Verde
São Paulo 41 *E4 off.* Estado de São Paulo. *State* S Brazil
São Paulo 41 *E4 state capital* São Paulo, S Brazil
São Paulo de Loanda *see* Luanda
São Pedro do Rio Grande do Sul *see* Rio Grande
São Roque, Cabo de 41 *G2 headland* E Brazil
São Salvador *see* M'Banza Congo
São Salvador do Congo *see* M'Banza Congo
São Tiago *see* Santiago
São Tomé 54 *E2 Eng.* Saint Thomas. *Island* S Sao Tome and Principe
São Tomé 55 *A5 country capital* (Sao Tome and Principe) São Tomé, S Sao Tome and Principe
Sao Tome and Principe 54 *D1 Country* E Atlantic Ocean
São Tomé, Pico de 54 *D2 mountain* São Tomé, S Sao Tome and Principe
São Vicente, Cabo de 70 *B5 Eng.* Cape Saint Vincent, *Port.* Cabo de São Vicente. *Headland* S Portugal
São Vicente 52 *A3 Eng.* Saint Vincent. *Island* Ilhas de Barlavento, N Cape Verde
Sápai *see* Sápes
Sapele 53 *F5* Delta, S Nigeria
Sápes 82 *D3 var.* Sápai. Anatolikí Makedonía kai Thráki, NE Greece
Sapir *see* Sappir
Sa Pobla 71 *G3 var.* La Puebla. Mallorca, Spain, W Mediterranean Sea
Sappir 97 *B7 var.* Sapir. Southern, S Israel
Sapporo 108 *D2* Hokkaidō, NE Japan
Sapri 75 *D6* Campania, S Italy
Sapulpa 27 *G1* Oklahoma, C USA
Saqqez 98 *C2 var.* Saghez, Sakiz, Saqqiz. Kordestān, NW Iran
Saqqiz *see* Saqqez
Sara Buri 115 *C5 var.* Saraburi. Saraburi, C Thailand
Saragt *see* Sarahs
Saraguro 38 *B2* Loja, S Ecuador
Sarahs 100 *D3 var.* Saragt, Serakhs. Akhalskiy Velayat, S Turkmenistan
Sarajevo 78 *C4 country capital* (Bosnia and Herzegovina) Federacija Bosna I Hercegovina, SE Bosnia and Herzegovina
Sarakhs 98 *E2* Khorāsān, NE Iran
Saraktash 89 *D6* Orenburgskaya Oblast', W Russian Federation
Saran' 92 *C4 Kaz.* Saran. Karaganda, C Kazakhstan
Saranda *see* Sarandë
Sarandë 79 *C7 var.* Saranda, *It.* Porto Edda; *prev.* Santi Quaranta. Vlorë, S Albania
Saransk 89 *C5* Respublika Mordoviya, W Russian Federation
Sarasota 21 *E4* Florida, SE USA
Saratov 92 *B3* Saratovskaya Oblast', W Russian Federation
Saravan *see* Salavan
Saravane *see* Salavan
Sarawak 116 *D3 cultural region* Borneo, SE Asia
Sarawak and Sabah (North Borneo) and Singapore *see* Malaysia
Sarcelles 68 *D1* Val-d'Oise, N France
Sardegna 75 *A5 Eng.* Sardinia. *Island* Italy, C Mediterranean Sea
Sardinia *see* Sardegna
Sarera, Teluk *see* Cenderawasih, Teluk
Sargasso Sea 44 *B4 sea* W Atlantic Ocean
Sargodha 112 *C2* Punjab, NE Pakistan
Sarh 54 *C4 prev.* Fort-Archambault. Moyen-Chari, S Chad
Sārī 98 *D2 var.* Sari, Sāri. Māzandarān, N Iran
Saría 83 *E7 island* SE Greece
Sarıkamış 95 *F3* Kars, NE Turkey
Sarikol Range 101 *G3 Rus.* Sarykol'skiy Khrebet. *Mountain range* China/Tajikistan
Sark 67 *D8 Fr.* Sercq. *Island* Channel Islands
Şarkışla 94 *D3* Sivas, C Turkey
Sarmiento 43 *B6* Chubut, S Argentina
Sarnia 16 *C5* Ontario, S Canada
Sarny 86 *C1* Rivnens'ka Oblast', NW Ukraine
Sarochyna 85 *D5 Rus.* Sorochino. Vitsyebskaya Voblasts', N Belarus
Sarov 89 *C5 prev.* Sarova. Respublika Mordoviya, SW Russian Federation
Sarova *see* Sarov
Sarpsborg 85 *B6* Østfold, S Norway
Sartène 69 *E7* Corse, France, C Mediterranean Sea
Sarthe 68 *B4 cultural region* N France
Sárti 82 *C4* Kentrikí Makedonía, N Greece
Saruhan *see* Manisa
Saryesik-Atyrau, Peski 101 *G1 desert* E Kazakhstan
Sary-Tash 101 *F2* Oshskaya Oblast', SW Kyrgyzstan
Sasebo 109 *A7* Nagasaki, Kyūshū, SW Japan
Saskatchewan 15 *F5 river* Manitoba/Saskatchewan, C Canada
Saskatchewan 15 *F5 province* SW Canada
Saskatoon 15 *F5* Saskatchewan, S Canada
Sasovo 89 *B5* Ryazanskaya Oblast', W Russian Federation
Sassandra 52 *D5 var.* Ibo, Sassandra Fleuve. *River* S Côte d'Ivoire
Sassandra 52 *D5* S Côte d'Ivoire
Sassandra Fleuve *see* Sassandra
Sassari 75 *A5* Sardegna, Italy, C Mediterranean Sea
Sassenheim 64 *C3* Zuid-Holland, W Netherlands
Sassnitz 72 *D2* Mecklenburg-Vorpommern, NE Germany
Sátoraljaújhely 77 *D6* Borsod-Abaúj-Zemplén, NE Hungary
Sātpura Range 112 *D4 mountain range* C India
Satsunan-shotō 108 *A3 var.* Satunan Syotō. *Island group* SW Japan
Sattanen 62 *D3* Lappi, NE Finland
Satu Mare 86 *B3 Ger.* Sathmar, *Hung.* Szatmárnémeti. Satu Mare, NW Romania
Satunan Syotô *see* Satsunan-shotō
Saudi Arabia 99 *B5 Ar.* Al 'Arabīyah as Su'ūdīyah, Al Mamlakah al 'Arabīyah as Su'ūdīyah. *Country* SW Asia
Sauer *see* Sûre
Saulkrasti 84 *C3* Rīga, C Latvia
Sault Sainte Marie 18 *C1* Michigan, N USA
Sault Ste.Marie 16 *C4* Ontario, S Canada
Saumur 68 *B4* Maine-et-Loire, NW France
Saurimo 56 *C1 Port.* Henrique de Carvalho, Vila Henrique de Carvalho. Lunda Sul, NE Angola
Sava 78 *B3 Eng.* Save, *Ger.* Sau, *Hung.* Száva. *River* SE Europe
Sava 85 *E6 Rus.* Sava. Mahilyowskaya Voblasts', E Belarus
Savá 30 *D2* Colón, N Honduras
Savai'i 123 *E4 island* NW Samoa
Savannah 21 *E2* Georgia, SE USA
Savannah River 21 *E2 river* Georgia/South Carolina, SE USA
Savanna-La-Mar 32 *A5* W Jamaica
Save, Rio 57 *E3 var.* Rio Sabi. *River* Mozambique/Zimbabwe
Saverne 68 *E3 var.* Zabern; *anc.* Tres Tabernae. Bas-Rhin, NE France
Savigliano 74 *A2* Piemonte, NW Italy
Savigsivik *see* Savissivik
Savinski *see* Savinskiy
Savinskiy 88 *C3 var.* Savinski. Arkhangel'skaya Oblast', NW Russian Federation
Savissivik 60 *D1 var.* Savigsivik. N Greenland
Savoie 69 *D5 cultural region* E France
Savona 74 *A2* Liguria, NW Italy
Savu Sea 117 *E5 Ind.* Laut Sawu. *Sea* S Indonesia
Sawakin *see* Suakin
Sawdirī *see* Sodiri
Sawhāj *see* Sohâg
Şawqirah 99 *D6 var.* Suqrah. S Oman
Sayanskiy Khrebet 90 *D3 mountain range* S Russian Federation
Saýat 100 *D3 var.* Sayat. Lebapskiy Velayat, E Turkmenistan
Sayaxché 52 *B2* Petén, N Guatemala
Şaydā *see* Saïda
Sayhūt 99 *D6* E Yemen
Sayida *see* Saïda
Saynshand 105 *E2* Dornogovĭ, SE Mongolia
Sayre 19 *E3* Pennsylvania, NE USA
Say'ūn 99 *C6 var.* Saywūn. C Yemen
Saywūn *see* Say'ūn
Scandinavia 44 *D2 geophysical region* NW Europe
Scarborough 89 *D5* N England, UK
Schaan 72 *E1* W Liechtenstein
Schaerbeek 65 *C6* Brussels, C Belgium
Schaffhausen 73 *B7 Fr.* Schaffhouse. Schaffhausen, N Switzerland
Schagen 64 *C2* Noord-Holland, NW Netherlands
Schebschi Mountains *see* Shebshi Mountains
Scheessel 72 *B3* Niedersachsen, NW Germany
Schefferville 17 *E2* Québec, E Canada
Scheldt 65 *B5 Dut.* Schelde, *Fr.* Escaut. *River* W Europe
Schell Creek Range 25 *D5 mountain range* Nevada, W USA
Schenectady 19 *F3* New York, NE USA
Schertz 27 *G4* Texas, SW USA
Schiermonnikoog 64 *D1 Fris.* Skiermûntseach. *Island* Waddeneilanden, N Netherlands
Schijndel 64 *D4* Noord-Brabant, S Netherlands
Schiltigheim 68 *E3* Bas-Rhin, NE France
Schleswig 72 *B2* Schleswig-Holstein, N Germany
Schleswig-Holstein 72 *B2 cultural region* N Germany
Schönebeck 72 *C4* Sachsen-Anhalt, C Germany
Schooten *see* Schoten
Schoten 65 *C5 var.* Schooten. Antwerpen, N Belgium
Schouwen 64 *B4 island* SW Netherlands
Schwabenalb *see* Schwäbische Alb
Schwäbische Alb 73 *B6 var.* Schwabenalb, *Eng.* Swabian Jura. *Mountain range* S Germany
Schwandorf 73 *C5* Bayern, SE Germany
Schwarzwald 73 *B6 Eng.* Black Forest. *Mountain range* SW Germany
Schwaz 73 *C7* Tirol, W Austria
Schweinfurt 73 *B5* Bayern, SE Germany
Schwerin 72 *C3* Mecklenburg-Vorpommern, N Germany
Schwiz *see* Schwyz
Schwyz 73 *B7 var.* Schwiz. Schwyz, C Switzerland
Scilly, Isles of 67 *B8 island group* SW England, UK
Scio *see* Chíos
Scoresby Sound *see* Ittoqqortoormiit
Scoresbysund *see* Ittoqqortoormiit
Scotia Sea 35 *C8 sea* SW Atlantic Ocean
Scotland 66 *C3 national region* UK
Scott Base 132 *B4 NZ research station* Antarctica
Scott Island 132 *B5 island* Antarctica
Scottsbluff 22 *D3* Nebraska, C USA
Scottsboro 20 *D1* Alabama, S USA
Scottsdale 26 *B2* Arizona, SW USA
Scranton 19 *F3* Pennsylvania, NE USA
Scupi *see* Skopje
Scutari *see* Shkodër
Scutari, Lake 79 *C5 Alb.* Liqeni i Shkodrës, *SCr.* Skadarsko Jezero. *Lake* Albania/Serbia and Montenegro (Yugo.)
Scyros *see* Skýros
Searcy 20 *B1* Arkansas, C USA
Seattle 24 *B2* Washington, NW USA
Sébaco 30 *D3* Matagalpa, W Nicaragua
Sebastían Vizcaíno, Bahía 28 *A2 bay* NW Mexico
Sechura, Bahía de 38 *A3 bay* NW Peru
Secunderābād 112 *D5 var.* Sikandarabad. Andhra Pradesh, C India
Sedan 68 *D3* Ardennes, N France
Seddon 129 *D5* Marlborough, South Island, NZ
Seddonville 129 *C5* West Coast, South Island, NZ
Sédhiou 52 *B3* SW Senegal
Sedona 26 *B2* Arizona, SW USA
Seesen 72 *B4* Niedersachsen, C Germany
Segestica *see* Sisak
Segezha 88 *B3* Respublika Kareliya, NW Russian Federation
Ségou 52 *D3 var.* Segu. Ségou, C Mali
Segovia 70 *D2* Castilla-León, C Spain
Segoviao Wangkí *see* Coco, Río
Segu *see* Ségou
Séguédine 53 *H2* Agadez, NE Niger
Seguin 27 *G4* Texas, SW USA
Segura 71 *E4 river* S Spain
Seinäjoki 63 *D5 Swe.* Östermyra. Länsi-Suomi, W Finland
Seine 68 *D1 river* N France
Seine, Baie de la 68 *B3 bay* N France
Sekondi *see* Sekondi-Takoradi
Sekondi-Takoradi 53 *E5 var.* Sekondi. S Ghana
Selat Balabac *see* Balabac Strait
Selenga 105 *E1 Mong.* Selenge Mörön. *River* Mongolia/Russian Federation
Sélestat 68 *E4 Ger.* Schlettstadt. Bas-Rhin, NE France
Selfoss 61 *E5* Sudhurland, SW Iceland
Sélibabi 52 *C3 var.* Sélibaby. Guidimaka, S Mauritania
Sélibaby *see* Sélibabi
Selma 25 *C6* California, W USA
Selway River 24 *D2 river* Idaho, NW USA
Selwyn Range 126 *B3 mountain range* Queensland, C Australia
Selzaete *see* Zelzate
Semarang 116 *C5 var.* Samarang. Jawa, C Indonesia
Sembé 55 *B5* La Sangha, NW Congo
Semey *see* Semipalatinsk
Seminole 27 *E3* Texas, SW USA
Seminole, Lake 20 *D3 reservoir* Florida/Georgia, SE USA
Semipalatinsk 92 *D4 Kaz.* Semey. Vostochnyy kazakhstan, E Kazakhstan
Semnān 98 *D3 var.* Samnān. Semnān, N Iran
Semois 65 *C8 river* SE Belgium
Sendai 109 *A8* Kagoshima, Kyūshū, SW Japan
Sendai 108 *D4* Miyagi, Honshū, C Japan
Sendai-wan 108 *D4 bay* E Japan
Senec 77 *C6 Ger.* Wartberg, *Hung.* Szenc; *prev.* Szempcz. Bratislavský Kraj, W Slovakia
Senegal 52 *C3 Fr.* Sénégal. *River* W Africa
Senegal 52 *B3 Fr.* Sénégal. *Country* W Africa
Senftenberg 72 *D4* Brandenburg, E Germany
Senica 77 *C6 Ger.* Senitz, *Hung.* Szenice. Trnavský Kraj, W Slovakia
Senj 78 *A3 Ger.* Zengg, *It.* Segna; *anc.* Senia. Lika-Senj, NW Croatia
Senja 62 *C2 prev.* Senjen. *Island* N Norway
Senkaku-shotō 108 *A3 island group* SW Japan
Senlis 68 *C3* Oise, N France
Sennar 50 *C4 var.* Sannār. Sinnar, C Sudan
Sens 68 *C3 anc.* Agendicum, Senones. Yonne, C France
Sên, Stœng 115 *D5 river* C Cambodia
Senta 78 *D3 Hung.* Zenta. Serbia, N Serbia and Montenegro (Yugo.)
Seo de Urgel *see* La See d'Urgel
Seoul *see* Sŏul
Sept-Îles 17 *E3* Québec, SE Canada
Seraing 65 *D6* Liège, E Belgium
Serakhs *see* Sarahs
Seram, Pulau 117 *F4 var.* Serang, *Eng.* Ceram. *Island* Maluku, E Indonesia
Serang *see* Seram, Pulau
Serang 116 *C5* Jawa, C Indonesia
Serasan, Selat 116 *C3 strait* Indonesia/Malaysia
Serbia 78 *D4 Ger.* Serbien, *Serb.* Srbija. Admin. region *republic* Serbia and Montenegro (Yugo.)
Serbia and Montenegro (Yugo.) 78 *D4 SCr.* Jugoslavija, Savezna Republika Jugoslavija. *Country* SE Europe
Serdar 100 *C2 prev.* Gyzylarbat, Kizyl-Arvat. Balkanskiy Velayat, W Turkmenistan
Serdica *see* Sofiya
Serenje 56 *D2* Central, E Zambia
Seres *see* Sérres
Seret *see* Siret
Sereth *see* Siret
Serhetabat 100 *D4 prev.* Gushgy, Kushka. Maryyskiy Velayat, S Turkmenistan
Sérifos 83 *C6 anc.* Seriphos. *Island* Kykládes, Greece, Aegean Sea
Serov 92 *C3* Sverdlovskaya Oblast', C Russian Federation
Serowe 56 *D3* Central, SE Botswana
Serpa Pinto *see* Menongue
Serpent's Mouth, The 37 *F2 Sp.* Boca de la Serpiente. *Strait* Trinidad and Tobago/Venezuela
Serpukhov 89 *B5* Moskovskaya Oblast', W Russian Federation
Serra dos Parecis *see* Parecis, Chapada dos
Sérrai *see* Sérres
Serrana, Cayo de 31 *F2 island group* NW Colombia
Serranilla, Cayo de 31 *F2 island group* NW Colombia
Serra Pacaraim *see* Pakaraima Mountains
Serra Tumucumaque *see* Tumuc Humac Mountains

Serravalle *74 E1* N San Marino
Sérres *82 C3 var.* Seres; *prev.* Sérrai. Kentrikí Makedonía, NE Greece
Sert *see* Siirt
Sesto San Giovanni *74 B2* Lombardia, N Italy
Sesvete *78 B2* Zagreb, N Croatia
Setabis *see* Xàtiva
Sète *69 C6 prev.* Cette. Hérault, S France
Setesdal *63 A6 valley* S Norway
Sétif *49 E2 var.* Stif. N Algeria
Setté Cama *55 A6* Ogooué-Maritime, SW Gabon
Setúbal *70 B4 Eng.* Saint Ubes, Saint Yves. Setúbal, W Portugal
Setúbal, Baía de *70 B4 bay* W Portugal
Seul, Lac *16 B3 lake* Ontario, S Canada
Sevan *95 G2* C Armenia
Sevana Lich *95 G3 Eng.* Lake Sevan, *Rus.* Ozero Sevan. *Lake* E Armenia
Sevastopol' *87 F5 Eng.* Sebastopol. Respublika Krym, S Ukraine
Severn *67 D6 Wel.* Hafren. *River* England/Wales, UK
Severn *16 B2 river* Ontario, S Canada
Severnaya Dvina *88 C4 var.* Northern Dvina. *River* NW Russian Federation
Severnaya Zemlya *93 E2 var.* Nicholas II Land. *Island group* N Russian Federation
Severnyy *88 E3* Respublika Komi, NW Russian Federation
Severodvinsk *88 C3 prev.* Molotov, Sudostroy. Arkhangel'skaya Oblast', NW Russian Federation
Severomorsk *88 C2* Murmanskaya Oblast', NW Russian Federation
Severo-Sibirskaya Nizmennost' *93 E2 var.* North Siberian Plain, *Eng.* North Siberian Lowland. *Lowlands* N Russian Federation
Seversk *92 D4* Tomskaya Oblast', C Russian Federation
Severskiy Donets *see* Donets
Sevier Lake *22 A4 lake* Utah, W USA
Sevilla *70 C4 Eng.* Seville; *anc.* Hispalis. Andalucía, SW Spain
Seville *see* Sevilla
Sevlievo *82 D2* Gabrovo, N Bulgaria
Seychelles *57 G1 Country* W Indian Ocean
Seydhisfjördhur *61 E5* Austurland, E Iceland
Seýdi *100 D2 var.* Seydi; *prev.* Neftezavodsk. Lebapskiy Velayat, E Turkmenistan
Seyhan *see* Adana
Sfákia *83 C8* Kriti, Greece, E Mediterranean Sea
Sfântu Gheorghe *86 C4 Ger.* Sankt-Georgen, *Hung.* Sepsiszentgyőrgy; *prev.* Şepşi-Sângeorz, Sfîntu Gheorghe. Covasna, C Romania
Sfax *49 F2 Ar.* Şafāqis. E Tunisia
's-Gravenhage *64 B4 var.* Den Haag, *Eng.* The Hague, *Fr.* La Haye. *Country capital* (Netherlands-seat of government) Zuid-Holland, W Netherlands
's-Gravenzande *64 B4* Zuid-Holland, W Netherlands
Shaan *see* Shaanxi
Shaanxi *106 B5 var.* Shaan, Shaanxi Sheng, Shan-hsi, Shenshi, Shensi. Admin. region *province* C China
Shaanxi Sheng *see* Shaanxi
Shache *104 A3 var.* Yarkant. Xinjiang Uygur Zizhiqu, NW China
Shackleton Ice Shelf *132 D3 ice shelf* Antarctica
Shaddādī *see* Ash Shadādah
Shāhābād *see* Eslāmābād
Shahjahanabad *see* Delhi
Shahr-e Kord *98 C3 var.* Shahr Kord. Chahār Maḩall va Bakhtīārī, C Iran
Shahr Kord *see* Shahr-e Kord
Shāhrūd *98 D2 prev.* Emāmrūd, Emāmshahr. Semnān, N Iran
Shalkar *92 B4 var.* Chelkar. Aktyubinsk, W Kazakhstan
Shandī *see* Shendi
Shandong *106 D4 var.* Lu, Shandong Sheng, Shantung. Admin. region *province* E China
Shandong Sheng *see* Shandong
Shanghai *106 D5 var.* Shang-hai. Shanghai Shi, E China
Shang-hai *see* Shanghai
Shangrao *106 D5* Jiangxi, S China
Shan-hsi *see* Shaanxi
Shan-hsi *see* Shanxi
Shannon *67 A6 Ir.* An tSionainn. *River* W Ireland
Shan Plateau *114 B3 plateau* E Myanmar
Shansi *see* Shanxi
Shantarskiye Ostrova *93 G3 Eng.* Shantar Islands. *Island group* E Russian Federation
Shantou *106 D6 var.* Shan-t'ou, Swatow. Guangdong, S China
Shantung *see* Shandong
Shanxi *106 C4 var.* Jin, Shan-hsi, Shansi, Shanxi Sheng. Admin. region *province* C China
Shan Xian *see* Sanmenxia
Shanxi Sheng *see* Shanxi
Shaoguan *106 C6 var.* Shao-kuan, *Cant.* Kukong; *prev.* Ch'u-chiang. Guangdong, S China
Shao-kuan *see* Shaoguan
Shaqrā *see* Shuqrah
Shaqrā' *98 B4* Ar Riyāḑ, C Saudi Arabia
Shar *130 D5 var.* Charsk. Vostochnyy Kazakhstan, E Kazakhstan
Shari *see* Chari
Shari *108 D2* Hokkaidō, NE Japan
Shark Bay *125 A5 bay* Western Australia
Shashe *56 D3 var.* Shashi. *River* Botswana/Zimbabwe
Shashi *see* Shashe
Shatsky Rise *103 G1 undersea feature* N Pacific Ocean
Shatt al-Hodna *see* Hodna, Chott El
Shaţţ al Jarīd *see* Jerid, Chott el
Shawnee *27 G1* Oklahoma, C USA
Shchadryn *85 D7 Rus.* Shchedrin. Homyel'skaya Voblasts', SE Belarus
Shchëkino *89 B5* Tul'skaya Oblast', W Russian Federation
Shchors *87 E1* Chernihivs'ka Oblast', N Ukraine
Shchuchinsk *92 C4 prev.* Shchuchye. Severnyy kazakhstan, N Kazakhstan
Shchuchyn *85 B5 Pol.* Szczuczyn Nowogródzki, *Rus.* Shchuchin. Hrodzyenskaya Voblasts', W Belarus
Shebekino *89 A6* Belgorodskaya Oblast', W Russian Federation
Shebeli *51 D5 Amh.* Wabē Shebelē Wenz, *It.* Scebeli, *Som.* Webi Shabeelle. *River* Ethiopia/Somalia
Sheberghān *101 E3 var.* Shibarghān, Shiberghan, Shiberghān. Jowzjān, N Afghanistan
Sheboygan *18 B2* Wisconsin, N USA
Shebshi Mountains *54 A4 var.* Schebschi Mountains. *Mountain range* E Nigeria
Shechem *see* Nablus
Shedadi *see* Ash Shadādah
Sheffield *67 D5* N England, UK
Shekhem *see* Nablus
Shelby *22 B1* Montana, NW USA
Sheldon *23 F3* Iowa, C USA
Shelekhov Gulf *see* Shelikhova, Zaliv
Shelikhova, Zaliv *93 G2 Eng.* Shelekhov Gulf. *Gulf* E Russian Federation
Shendi *50 C4 var.* Shandī. River Nile, NE Sudan
Shengking *see* Liaoning
Shenking *see* Liaoning
Shenshi *see* Shaanxi
Shensi *see* Shaanxi
Shenyang *106 D3 Chin.* Shen-yang, *Eng.* Moukden, Mukden; *prev.* Fengtien. Liaoning, NE China
Shepetivka *86 D2 Rus.* Shepetovka. Khmel'nyts'ka Oblast', NW Ukraine
Shepparton *127 C7* Victoria, SE Australia
Sherbrooke *17 E4* Québec, SE Canada
Shereik *50 C3* River Nile, N Sudan
Sheridan *22 C2* Wyoming, C USA
Sherman *27 G2* Texas, SW USA
's-Hertogenbosch *64 C4 Fr.* Bois-le-Duc, *Ger.* Herzogenbusch. Noord-Brabant, S Netherlands
Shetland Islands *66 D1 island group* NE Scotland, UK
Shibarghān *see* Sheberghān
Shiberghān *see* Sheberghān
Shibetsu *108 D2 var.* Sibetu. Hokkaidō, NE Japan
Shibh Jazīrat Sīnā' *see* Sinai
Shibushi-wan *109 B8 bay* SW Japan
Shigatse *see* Xigazê
Shih-chia-chuang *see* Shijiazhuang
Shihezi *104 C2* Xinjiang Uygur Zizhiqu, NW China
Shihmen *see* Shijiazhuang
Shijiazhuang *106 C4 var.* Shih-chia-chuang; *prev.* Shihmen. Hebei, E China
Shikārpur *112 B3* Sind, S Pakistan
Shikoku *109 C7 var.* Sikoku. *Island* SW Japan
Shikoku Basin *103 F2 var.* Sikoku Basin. *Undersea feature* N Philippine Sea
Shikotan, Ostrov *108 E2 Jap.* Shikotan-tō. *Island* NE Russian Federation
Shilabo *51 D5* E Ethiopia
Shiliguri *113 F3 prev.* Siliguri. West Bengal, NE India
Shilka *93 F4 river* S Russian Federation
Shillong *113 G3* E India
Shimbir Berris *see* Shimbiris
Shimbiris *50 E4 var.* Shimbir Berris. *Mountain* N Somalia
Shimoga *110 C2* Karnātaka, W India
Shimonoseki *109 A7 var.* Simonoseki; *hist.* Akamagaseki, Bakan. Yamaguchi, Honshū, SW Japan
Shinano-gawa *109 C5 var.* Sinano Gawa. *River* Honshū, C Japan
Shīndand *100 D4* Farāh, W Afghanistan
Shingū *109 C6 var.* Singû. Wakayama, Honshū, SW Japan
Shinjō *108 D4 var.* Sinzyô. Yamagata, Honshū, C Japan
Shinyanga *51 C7* Shinyanga, NW Tanzania
Shiprock *26 C1* New Mexico, SW USA
Shīrāz *98 D4 var.* Shīrāz. Fārs, S Iran
Shivpuri *112 D3* Madhya Pradesh, C India
Shizugawa *108 D4* Miyagi, Honshū, NE Japan
Shizuoka *109 D6 var.* Sizuoka. Shizuoka, Honshū, S Japan
Shklow *85 D6 Rus.* Shklov. Mahilyowskaya Voblasts', E Belarus
Shkodër *79 C5 var.* Shkodra, *It.* Scutari, *SCr.* Skadar. Shkodër, NW Albania
Shkodra *see* Shkodër
Shkubinit, Lumi i *79 C6 var.* Shkumbî, Shkumbin. *River* C Albania
Shkumbî *see* Shkubinit, Lumi i
Shkumbin *see* Shkubinit, Lumi i
Sholāpur *see* Solāpur
Shostka *87 F1* Sums'ka Oblast', NE Ukraine
Show Low *26 B2* Arizona, SW USA
Shpola *87 E3* Cherkas'ka Oblast', N Ukraine
Shreveport *20 A2* Louisiana, S USA
Shrewsbury *67 D6 hist.* Scrobesbyrig'. W England, UK
Shu *92 C5 Kaz.* Shū. Zhambyl, SE Kazakhstan
Shuang-liao *see* Liaoyuan
Shumagin Islands *14 B3 island group* Alaska, USA
Shumen *82 D2* Shumen, NE Bulgaria
Shumilina *85 E5 Rus.* Shumilino. Vitsyebskaya Voblasts', NE Belarus
Shuqrah *99 B7 var.* Shaqrā. SW Yemen
Shwebo *114 B3* Sagaing, C Myanmar
Shyichy *85 C7 Rus.* Shiichi. Homyel'skaya Voblasts', SE Belarus
Shymkent *92 B5 prev.* Chimkent. Yuzhnyy Kazakhstan, S Kazakhstan
Shyshchytsy *85 C6 Rus.* Shishchitsy. Minskaya Voblasts', C Belarus
Si *see* Syr Darya
Siam, Gulf of *see* Thailand, Gulf of
Sian *see* Xi'an
Siang *see* Brahmaputra
Siangtan *see* Xiangtan
Šiauliai *84 B4 Ger.* Schaulen. Šiauliai, N Lithuania
Sibay *89 D6* Respublika Bashkortostan, W Russian Federation
Šibenik *116 B4 It.* Sebenico. Šibenik-Knin, S Croatia
Siberia *see* Sibir'
Siberut, Pulau *116 A4 prev.* Siberoet. *Island* Kepulauan Mentawai, W Indonesia
Sibetu *see* Shibetsu
Sibi *112 B2* Baluchistān, SW Pakistan
Sibir' *93 E3 var.* Siberia. *Physical region* NE Russian Federation
Sibiti *55 B6* La Lékoumou, S Congo
Sibiu *86 B4 Ger.* Hermannstadt, *Hung.* Nagyszeben. Sibiu, C Romania
Sibolga *116 B3* Sumatera, W Indonesia
Sibu *116 D3* Sarawak, East Malaysia
Sibut *54 C4 prev.* Fort-Sibut. Kémo, S Central African Republic
Sibuyan Sea *117 E2 sea* C Philippines
Sichon *115 C6 var.* Ban Sichon, Si Chon. Nakhon Si Thammarat, SW Thailand
Sichuan *106 B5 var.* Chuan, Sichuan Sheng, Ssu-ch'uan, Szechuan, Szechwan. Admin. region *province* C China
Sichuan Pendi *106 B5 depression* C China
Sichuan Sheng *see* Sichuan
Sicilia *75 C7 Eng.* Sicily; *anc.* Trinacria. *Island* Italy, C Mediterranean Sea
Sicilian Channel *see* Sicily, Strait of
Sicily *see* Sicilia
Sicily, Strait of *75 B7 var.* Sicilian Channel. *Strait* C Mediterranean Sea
Sicuani *39 E4* Cusco, S Peru
Sidári *82 A4* Kérkyra, Iónioi Nísoi, Greece, C Mediterranean Sea
Sidas *116 C4* Borneo, C Indonesia
Siderno *75 D7* Calabria, SW Italy
Sîdi Barrâni *50 A1* NW Egypt
Sidi Bel Abbès *48 D2 var.* Sidi bel Abbès, Sidi-Bel-Abbès. NW Algeria
Sidirókastro *82 C3 prev.* Sidhirókastron. Kentrikí Makedonía, NE Greece
Sidley, Mount *132 B4 mountain* Antarctica
Sidney *22 D1* Montana, NW USA
Sidney *22 D4* Nebraska, C USA
Sidney *18 C4* Ohio, N USA
Sidon *see* Saïda
Sidra *see* Surt
Siedlce *76 E3 Ger.* Sedlez, *Rus.* Sesdlets. Mazowieckie, C Poland
Siegen *72 B4* Nordrhein-Westfalen, W Germany
Siemiatycze *76 E3* Podlaskie
Siena *74 B3 Fr.* Sienne; *anc.* Saena Julia. Toscana, C Italy
Sieradz *76 C4* Łódzkie, C Poland
Sierpc *76 D3* Mazowieckie, C Poland
Sierra de Soconusco *see* Sierra Madre
Sierra Leone *52 C4 Country* W Africa
Sierra Leone Basin *44 C4 undersea feature* E Atlantic Ocean
Sierra Leone Ridge *see* Sierra Leone Rise
Sierra Leone Rise *44 C4 var.* Sierra Leone Ridge, Sierra Leone Schwelle. *Undersea feature* E Atlantic Ocean
Sierra Leone Schwelle *see* Sierra Leone Rise
Sierra Madre *30 B2 var.* Sierra de Soconusco. *Mountain range* Guatemala/Mexico
Sierra Madre *see* Madre Occidental, Sierra
Sierra Nevada *25 C6 mountain range* W USA
Sierra Pacaraima *see* Pakaraima Mountains
Sierra Vieja *26 D3 mountain range* Texas, SW USA
Sierra Vista *26 B3* Arizona, SW USA
Sífnos *83 C6 anc.* Siphnos. *Island* Kykládes, Greece, Aegean Sea
Sigli *116 A3* Sumatera, W Indonesia
Siglufjördhur *61 E4* Nordhurland Vestra, N Iceland
Signal Peak *26 A2 mountain* Arizona, SW USA
Signan *see* Xi'an
Signy *132 A2 UK research station* South Orkney Islands, Antarctica
Siguatepeque *30 C2* Comayagua, W Honduras
Siguiri *52 D4* Haute-Guinée, NE Guinea
Siilinjärvi *62 E4* Itä-Suomi, C Finland
Siirt *95 F4 var.* Sert; *anc.* Tigranocerta. Siirt, SE Turkey
Sikandarabad *see* Secunderābād
Sikasso *52 D4* Sikasso, S Mali
Sikeston *23 H5* Missouri, C USA
Sikhote-Alin', Khrebet *93 G4 mountain range* SE Russian Federation
Siking *see* Xi'an
Siklós *77 C7* Baranya, SW Hungary
Sikoku *see* Shikoku
Sikoku Basin *see* Shikoku Basin
Šilalė *84 B4* Šilalė, W Lithuania
Silchar *113 G3* Assam, NE India
Silesia *76 B4 physical region* SW Poland
Silifke *94 C4 anc.* Seleucia. İçel, S Turkey
Siling Co *104 C5 lake* W China
Silinhot *see* Xilinhot
Silistra *82 E1 var.* Silistria; *anc.* Durostorum. Silistra, NE Bulgaria
Silistria *see* Silistra
Sillamäe *84 E2 Ger.* Sillamäggi. Ida-Virumaa, NE Estonia
Šilutė *84 B4 Ger.* Heydekrug. Šilutė, W Lithuania
Silvan *95 E4* Dıyarbakır, SE Turkey
Silverek *95 E4* Şanlıurfa, SE Turkey
Simanggang *see* Sri Aman
Simanichy *85 C7 Rus.* Simonichi. Homyel'skaya Voblasts', SE Belarus
Simav *94 B3* Kütahya, W Turkey
Simav Çayı *94 A3 river* NW Turkey
Simeto *75 C7 river* Sicilia, Italy, C Mediterranean Sea
Simeulue, Pulau *116 A3 island* NW Indonesia
Simferopol' *87 F5* Respublika Krym, S Ukraine
Simitli *82 C3* Blagoevgrad, SW Bulgaria
Şimleu Silvaniei *86 B3 Hung.* Szilágsomlyó; *prev.* Şimlăul Silvaniei, Şimleul Silvaniei. Sălaj, NW Romania
Simonoseki *see* Shimonoseki
Simpelveld *65 D6* Limburg, SE Netherlands
Simplon Pass *73 B8 pass* S Switzerland
Simpson *see* Fort Simpson
Simpson Desert *126 B4 desert* Northern Territory/South Australia
Sīnā' *see* Sinai
Sinai *50 C2 var.* Sinai Peninsula, *Ar.* Shibh Jazīrat Sīnā', Sīnā'. *Physical region* NE Egypt
Sinaia *86 C4* Prahova, SE Romania
Sinai Peninsula *see* Sinai
Sinano Gawa *see* Shinano-gawa
Sincelejo *36 B2* Sucre, NW Colombia
Sind *112 B3 var.* Sindh. Admin. region *province* SE Pakistan
Sindelfingen *73 B6* Baden-Württemberg, SW Germany
Sindh *see* Sind
Sindi *84 D2 Ger.* Zintenhof. Pärnumaa, SW Estonia
Sines *70 B4* Setúbal, S Portugal
Singan *see* Xi'an
Singapore *116 A1 Country* SE Asia
Singapore *116 B3 country capital* (Singapore) S Singapore
Singen *73 B6* Baden-Württemberg, S Germany
Singida *51 C7* Singida, C Tanzania
Singkang *117 E4* Sulawesi, C Indonesia
Singkawang *116 C3* Borneo, C Indonesia
Singora *see* Songkhla
Singû *see* Shingū
Sining *see* Xining
Siniscola *75 A5* Sardegna, Italy, C Mediterranean Sea
Sinj *78 B4* Split-Dalmacija, SE Croatia
Sinkiang *see* Xinjiang Uygur Zizhiqu
Sinkiang Uighur Autonomous Region *see* Xinjiang Uygur Zizhiqu
Sinnamarie *see* Sinnamary
Sinnamary *37 H3 var.* Sinnamarie. N French Guiana
Sînnicolau Mare *see* Sânnicolau Mare
Sinoie, Lacul *86 D5 prev.* Lacul Sinoe. *Lagoon* SE Romania
Sinop *94 D2 anc.* Sinope. Sinop, N Turkey
Sinsheim *73 B6* Baden-Württemberg, SW Germany
Sint Maarten *33 G3 Eng.* Saint Martin. *Island* N Netherlands Antilles
Sint-Michielsgestel *64 C4* Noord-Brabant, S Netherlands
Sint-Niklaas *65 B5 Fr.* Saint-Nicolas. Oost-Vlaanderen, N Belgium
Sint-Pieters-Leeuw *65 B6* Vlaams Brabant, C Belgium
Sintra *70 B3 prev.* Cintra. Lisboa, W Portugal
Sinujiif *51 E5* Nugaal, NE Somalia
Sinus Aelaniticus *see* Aqaba, Gulf of
Sinyang *see* Xinyang
Sinzyô *see* Shinjō
Sion *73 A7 Ger.* Sitten; *anc.* Sedunum. Valais, SW Switzerland
Sioux City *23 F3* Iowa, C USA
Sioux Falls *23 F3* South Dakota, N USA
Siping *106 D3 var.* Ssu-p'ing, Szeping; *prev.* Ssu-p'ing-chieh. Jilin, NE China
Siple, Mount *132 A4 mountain* Siple Island, Antarctica
Siquirres *31 E4* Limón, E Costa Rica
Siracusa *75 D7 Eng.* Syracuse. Sicilia, Italy, C Mediterranean Sea
Sir Darya *see* Syr Darya
Sir Edward Pellew Group *126 B2 island group* Northern Territory, NE Australia
Siret *86 C3 var.* Siretul, *Ger.* Sereth, *Rus.* Seret, *Ukr.* Siret. *River* Romania/Ukraine
Siret *see* Siret
Siretul *see* Siret
Sirikit Reservoir *114 C4 lake* N Thailand
Sīrjān *98 D4 prev.* Sa'īdābād. Kermān, S Iran
Sirna *see* Sýrna
Şırnak *95 F4* Şırnak, SE Turkey
Síros *see* Sýros
Sirte *see* Surt
Sirte, Gulf of *see* Surt, Khalīj
Sisak *78 B3 var.* Siscia, *Ger.* Sissek, *Hung.* Sziszek; *anc.* Segestica. Sisak-Moslavina, C Croatia
Siscia *see* Sisak
Sisimiut *60 C3 var.* Holsteinborg, Holsteinsborg, Holstenborg, Holstensborg. S Greenland
Sissek *see* Sisak
Sistema Penibético *see* Béticos, Sistemas
Siteía *83 D8 var.* Sitía. Kríti, Greece, E Mediterranean Sea
Sitges *71 G2* Cataluña, NE Spain
Sitía *see* Siteía
Sittang *114 B4 var.* Sittoung. *River* S Myanmar
Sittard *65 D5* Limburg, SE Netherlands
Sittoung *see* Sittang
Sittwe *114 A3 var.* Akyab. Arakan State, W Myanmar
Siuna *30 D3* Región Autónoma Atlántico Norte, NE Nicaragua
Siut *see* Asyût
Sivas *94 D3 anc.* Sebastia, Sebaste. Sivas, C Turkey
Sivers'kyy Donets' *see* Donets
Siwa *50 A2 var.* Sīwah. NW Egypt
Sīwah *see* Siwa
Six-Fours-les-Plages *69 D6* Var, SE France
Siyäzän *95 H2 Rus.* Siazan'. NE Azerbaijan
Sizuoka *see* Shizuoka
Sjar *see* Säärе
Sjælland *B8 Eng.* Zealand, *Ger.* Seeland. *Island* E Denmark
Sjenica *79 D5 Turk.* Seniça. Serbia, SW Serbia and Montenegro (Yugo.)
Skadar *see* Shkodër
Skagerak *see* Skagerrak
Skagerrak *63 A6 var.* Skagerak. *Channel* N Europe
Skagit River *24 B1 river* Washington, NW USA
Skalka *62 C3 lake* N Sweden
Skarżysko-Kamienna *76 D4* Świętokrzyskie, C Poland
Skaudvilė *84 B4* Tauragė, SW Lithuania
Skegness *67 E6* E England, UK
Skellefteå *62 D4* Västerbotten, N Sweden
Skellefteälven *62 C4 river* N Sweden
Ski *63 B6* Akershus, S Norway
Skíathos *83 C5* Skíathos, Vóreioi Sporádes, Greece, Aegean Sea
Skidal' *85 B5 Rus.* Skidel'. Hrodzyenskaya Voblasts', W Belarus
Skierniewice *76 D3* Lodzkie, C Poland
Skiftet *84 C1 Fin.* Kihti. *Strait* Gulf of Bothnia/Gulf of Finland
Skíros *see* Skýros
Skópelos *83 C5* Skópelos, Vóreioi Sporádes, Greece, Aegean Sea
Skopje *79 D6 var.* Üsküb, *Turk.* Üsküp; *prev.* Skoplje, *anc.* Scupi. *Country capital* (FYR Macedonia) N FYR Macedonia
Skoplje *see* Skopje
Skovorodino *93 F4* Amurskaya Oblast', SE Russian Federation
Skuodas *84 B3 Ger.* Schoden, *Pol.* Szkudy. Skuodas, NW Lithuania
Skye, Isle of *66 B3 island* NW Scotland, UK
Skýros *83 C5 var.* Skíros. Skýros, Vóreioi Sporádes, Greece, Aegean Sea
Skýros *83 C5 var.* Skíros; *anc.* Scyros. *Island* Vóreioi Sporádes, Greece, Aegean Sea
Slagelse *63 B7* Vestsjælland, E Denmark
Slatina *86 B5* Olt, S Romania
Slatina *78 C3 Hung.* Szlatina, *prev.* Podravska Slatina. Virovtica-Podravina, NE Croatia
Slavonska Požega *see* Požega
Slavonski Brod *78 C3 Ger.* Brod, *Hung.* Bród; *prev.* Brod, Brod na Savi. Brod-Posavina, NE Croatia
Slavuta *86 C2* Khmel'nyts'ka Oblast', NW Ukraine
Slawharad *85 E7 Rus.* Slavgorod. Mahilyowskaya Voblasts', E Belarus
Sławno *76 C2* Zachodniopomorskie, NW Poland
Sléibhte Chill Mhantáin *see* Wicklow Mountains
Slēmānī *see* As Sulaymānīyah
Sliema *80 B5* N Malta
Sligeach *see* Sligo
Sligo *67 A5 Ir.* Sligeach. NW Ireland
Sliven *82 D2 var.* Slivno. Sliven, C Bulgaria
Slivnitsa *82 B2* Sofiya, W Bulgaria
Slivno *see* Sliven
Slobozia *86 C5* Ialomiţa, SE Romania
Slonim *85 B6 Pol.* Słonim, *Rus.* Slonim. Hrodzyenskaya Voblasts', W Belarus
Slovakia *77 C6 Ger.* Slowakei, *Hung.* Szlovákia, *Slvk.* Slovensko. *Country* C Europe
Slovak Ore Mountains *see* Slovenské rudohorie
Slovenia *73 D8 Ger.* Slowenien, *Slvn.* Slovenija. *Country* SE Europe
Slovenské rudohorie *77 D6 Eng.* Slovak Ore Mountains, *Ger.* Slowakisches Erzgebirge, Ungarisches Erzgebirge. *Mountain range* C Slovakia
Slov"yans'k *87 G3 Rus.* Slavyansk. Donets'ka Oblast', E Ukraine
Slowakisches Erzgebirge *see* Slovenské rudohorie
Słubice *76 B3 Ger.* Frankfurt. Lubuskie, W Poland
Sluch *86 D1 river* NW Ukraine
Słupsk *76 C2 Ger.* Stolp. Pomorskie, N Poland
Slutsk *85 C6 Rus.* Slutsk. Minskaya Voblasts', S Belarus
Smallwood Reservoir *17 F2 lake* Newfoundland and Labrador, S Canada
Smara *48 B3 var.* Es Semara. N Western Sahara
Smarhon' *85 C5 Pol.* Smorgonie, *Rus.* Smorgon'. Hrodzyenskaya Voblasts', W Belarus
Smederevo *78 D4 Ger.* Semendria. Serbia, N Serbia and Montenegro (Yugo.)
Smederevska Palanka *78 D4* Serbia, C Serbia and Montenegro (Yugo.)
Smila *87 E2 Rus.* Smela. Cherkas'ka Oblast', C Ukraine
Smiltene *84 D3 Ger.* Smilten. Valka, N Latvia
Smøla *62 A4 island* W Norway
Smolensk *89 A5* Smolenskaya Oblast', W Russian Federation
Snake *12 B4 river* Yukon Territory, NW Canada
Snake River *24 C3 river* NW USA
Snake River Plain *24 D4 plain* Idaho, NW USA
Sneek *64 D2* Friesland, N Netherlands
Sněžka *76 B4 Ger.* Schneekoppe. *Mountain* N Czech Republic

INDEX

Śniardwy, Jezioro *114 D2 Ger.* Spirdingsee. *Lake* NE Poland
Snina *77 E5 Hung.* Szinna. Prešovský Kraj, E Slovakia
Snowdonia *67 C6 mountain range* NW Wales, UK
Snyder *27 F3* Texas, SW USA
Sobradinho, Represa de *41 F2 var.* Barragem de Sobradinho. *Reservoir* E Brazil
Sochi *89 A7* Krasnodarskiy Kray, SW Russian Federation
Société, Archipel de la *123 G4 var.* Archipel de Tahiti, Îles de la Société, *Eng.* Society Islands. *Island group* W French Polynesia
Society Islands *see* Société, Archipel de la
Socorro *26 D2* New Mexico, SW USA
Socorro, Isla *28 B5 island* W Mexico
Socotra *see* Suquṭrā
Soc Trăng *115 D6 var.* Khanh. Soc Trăng, S Vietnam
Socuéllamos *71 E3* Castilla-La Mancha, C Spain
Sodankylä *62 D3* Lappi, N Finland
Sodari *see* Sodiri
Söderhamn *63 C5* Gävleborg, C Sweden
Södertälje *63 C6* Stockholm, C Sweden
Sodiri *50 B4 var.* Sawdirī, Sodari. Northern Kordofan, C Sudan
Sofia *see* Sofiya
Sofiya *82 C2 var.* Sophia, *Eng.* Sofia; *Lat.* Serdica. *Country capital* (Bulgaria) Sofiya-Grad, W Bulgaria
Sogamoso *36 B3* Boyacá, C Colombia
Sognefjorden *63 A5 fjord* NE North Sea
Sohâg *50 B2 var.* Sawhāj, Suliag. C Egypt
Sohar *see* Şuḩār
Sohm Plain *44 B3 undersea feature* NW Atlantic Ocean
Sohrau *see* Żory
Sokal' *86 C2 Rus.* Sokal. L'vivs'ka Oblast', NW Ukraine
Söke *94 A4* Aydın, SW Turkey
Sokhumi *95 E1 Rus.* Sukhumi. NW Georgia
Sokodé *53 F4* C Togo
Sokol *88 C4* Vologodskaya Oblast', NW Russian Federation
Sokółka *76 E3* Białystok, NE Poland
Sokolov *77 A5 Ger.* Falkenau an der Eger; *prev.* Falknov nad Ohří. Karlovarský Kraj, W Czech Republic
Sokone *52 B3* W Senegal
Sokoto *53 F4 river* NW Nigeria
Sokoto *53 F3* Sokoto, NW Nigeria
Sokotra *see* Suquṭrā
Solāpur *102 B3 var.* Sholāpur. Mahārāshtra, W India
Solca *86 C3 Ger.* Solka. Suceava, N Romania
Sol, Costa del *70 D5 coastal region* S Spain
Soldeu *69 B7* NE Andorra
Solec Kujawski *76 C3* Kujawski-pomorskie, C Poland
Soledad, Isla *see* East Falkland
Soledad *36 B1* Anzoátegui, NE Venezuela
Solikamsk *92 C3* Permskaya Oblast', NW Russian Federation
Sol'-Iletsk *89 D6* Orenburgskaya Oblast', W Russian Federation
Solingen *72 A4* Nordrhein-Westfalen, W Germany
Sollentuna *63 C6* Stockholm, C Sweden
Solok *116 B4* Sumatera, W Indonesia
Solomon Islands *122 C3 prev.* British Solomon Islands Protectorate. *Country* W Pacific Ocean
Solomon Islands *122 C3 island group* PNG/Solomon Islands
Solomon Sea *122 B3 sea* W Pacific Ocean
Soltau *72 B3* Niedersachsen, NW Germany
Sol'tsy *88 A4* Novgorodskaya Oblast', W Russian Federation
Solwezi *56 D2* North Western, NW Zambia
Sōma *108 D4* Fukushima, Honshū, C Japan
Somalia *51 D5 Som.* Jamuuriyada Demuqraadiga Soomaaliyeed, Soomaaliya; *prev.* Italian Somaliland, Somaliland Protectorate. *Country* E Africa
Somali Basin *47 E5 undersea feature* W Indian Ocean
Sombor *78 C3 Hung.* Zombor. Serbia, NW Serbia and Montenegro (Yugo.)
Someren *65 D5* Noord-Brabant, SE Netherlands
Somerset *20 A5 var.* Somerset Village. W Bermuda
Somerset *18 C5* Kentucky, S USA
Somerset Island *15 F2 island* Queen Elizabeth Islands, Nunavut, NW Canada
Somerset Island *20 A5 island* W Bermuda
Somerset Village *see* Somerset
Somers Islands *see* Bermuda
Somerton *26 A2* Arizona, SW USA
Someş *86 B3 var.* Somesch, Someşul, Szamos, *Ger.* Samosch. *River* Hungary/Romania
Somesch *see* Someş
Someşul *see* Someş
Somme *68 C2 river* N France
Somotillo *30 C3* Chinandega, NW Nicaragua
Somoto *30 D3* Madriz, NW Nicaragua
Songea *51 C8* Ruvuma, S Tanzania
Sông Hông Hà *see* Red River
Songkhla *115 C7 var.* Songkla, *Mal.* Singora. Songkhla, SW Thailand
Songkla *see* Songkhla
Sông Srepok *see* Srêpôk, Tônle
Sông Tiên Giang *see* Mekong
Sonoran Desert *26 A3 var.* Desierto de Altar. *Desert* Mexico/USA *see also* Altar, Desierto de
Sonsonate *30 B3* Sonsonate, W El Salvador
Soochow *see* Suzhou
Sop Hao *114 D3* Houaphan, N Laos
Sophia *see* Sofiya
Sopot *76 C2 Ger.* Zoppot. Plovdiv, C Bulgaria
Sopron *77 B6 Ger.* Ödenburg. Győr-Moson-Sopron, NW Hungary
Sorgues *69 D6* Vaucluse, SE France
Sorgun *94 D3* Yozgat, C Turkey
Soria *71 E2* Castilla-León, N Spain
Soroca *86 D3 Rus.* Soroki. N Moldova
Sorong *117 F4* Papua, E Indonesia
Sørøy *see* Sørøya
Sørøya *62 C2 var.* Sørøy. *Island* N Norway
Sortavala *88 B3* Respublika Kareliya, NW Russian Federation
Sotavento, Ilhas de *52 A3 var.* Leeward Islands. *Island group* S Cape Verde
Sotkamo *62 E4* Oulu, C Finland
Souanké *55 B5* La Sangha, NW Congo
Soueida *see* As Suwaydā'
Souflí *82 D3 prev.* Souflíon. Anatolikí Makedonía kai Thráki, NE Greece
Soufrière *33 F2 volcano* S Dominica
Soukhné *see* As Sukhnah
Sŏul *107 E4 off.* Sŏul-t'ŭkpyŏlsi, *Eng.* Seoul, *Jap.* Keijō; *prev.* Kyŏngsŏng. *Country capital* (South Korea) NW South Korea
Soûr *97 A5 var.* Şūr; *anc.* Tyre. SW Lebanon
Souris River *23 E1 var.* Mouse River. *River* Canada/USA
Sourpi *83 B5* Thessalía, C Greece
Sousse *49 F2 var.* Sūsah. NE Tunisia
South Africa *56 C4 Afr.* Suid-Afrika. *Country* S Africa
South America *34 continent*
Southampton *67 D7 hist.* Hamwih, *Lat.* Clausentum. S England, UK
Southampton Island *15 G3 island* Nunavut, NE Canada
South Andaman *111 F2 island* Andaman Islands, India, NE Indian Ocean
South Australia *127 A5 state* S Australia
South Australian Basin *120 B5 undersea feature* SW Indian Ocean
South Bend *18 C3* Indiana, N USA
South Beveland *see* Zuid-Beveland
South Bruny Island *127 C8 island* Tasmania, SE Australia
South Carolina *21 E2 off.* State of South Carolina; also known as The Palmetto State. *State* SE USA
South Carpathians *see* Carpaţii Meridionali
South China Basin *103 E4 undersea feature* SE South China Sea
South China Sea *102 D4 Chin.* Nan Hai, *Ind.* Laut Cina Selatan, *Vtn.* Biên Đông. *Sea* SE Asia
South Dakota *22 D2 off.* State of South Dakota; also known as The Coyote State, Sunshine State. *State* N USA
Southeast Indian Ridge *119 D7 undersea feature* Indian Ocean/Pacific Ocean
Southeast Pacific Basin *131 E5 var.* Belling Hausen Mulde. *Undersea feature* SE Pacific Ocean
South East Point *127 C7 headland* Victoria, S Australia
Southend-on-Sea *67 E6* E England, UK
Southern Alps *129 B6 mountain range* South Island, NZ
Southern Cook Islands *123 F4 island group* S Cook Islands
Southern Cross *125 B6* Western Australia
Southern Indian Lake *15 F4 lake* Manitoba, C Canada
Southern Ocean *45 B7 ocean*
Southern Uplands *66 C4 mountain range* S Scotland, UK
South Fiji Basin *120 D4 undersea feature* S Pacific Ocean
South Geomagnetic Pole *132 B3 pole* Antarctica
South Georgia *35 D8 island* South Georgia and the South Sandwich Islands, SW Atlantic Ocean
South Goulburn Island *124 E2 island* Northern Territory, N Australia
South Huvadhu Atoll *110 A5 var.* Gaafu Dhaalu Atoll. *Atoll* S Maldives
South Indian Basin *119 D7 undersea feature* Indian Ocean/Pacific Ocean
South Island *129 C6 island* S NZ
South Korea *107 E4 Kor.* Taehan Min'guk. *Country* E Asia
South Lake Tahoe *25 C5* California, W USA
South Orkney Islands *132 A2 island group* Antarctica
South Ossetia *95 F2 former autonomous region* SW Georgia
South Pacific Basin *see* Southwest Pacific Basin
South Platte River *22 D4 river* Colorado/Nebraska, C USA
South Pole *132 B3 pole* Antarctica
South Sandwich Islands *35 D8 island group* SE South Georgia and South Sandwich Islands
South Sandwich Trench *35 E8 undersea feature* SW Atlantic Ocean
South Shetland Islands *132 A2 island group* Antarctica
South Shields *66 D4* NE England, UK
South Sioux City *23 F3* Nebraska, C USA
South Taranaki Bight *128 C4 bight* SE Tasman Sea
South Tasmania Plateau *see* Tasman Plateau
South Uist *66 B3 island* NW Scotland, UK
South West Cape *129 A8 headland* Stewart Island, NZ
Southwest Indian Ocean Ridge *see* Southwest Indian Ridge
Southwest Indian Ridge *119 B6 var.* Southwest Indian Ocean Ridge. *Undersea feature* SW Indian Ocean
Southwest Pacific Basin *121 E4 var.* South Pacific Basin. *Undersea feature* SE Pacific Ocean
Sovereign Base Area *80 C5 UK military installation* E Cyprus
Sovereign Base Area *80 C5 UK military installation* S Cyprus
Soweto *56 D4* Gauteng, NE South Africa
Spain *70 D3 Sp.* España; *anc.* Hispania, Iberia, *Lat.* Hispana. *Country* SW Europe
Spanish Town *32 B5 hist.* St.Iago de la Vega. C Jamaica
Sparks *25 C5* Nevada, W USA
Spartanburg *21 E1* South Carolina, SE USA
Spárti *83 B6 Eng.* Sparta. Pelopónnisos, S Greece
Spearfish *22 D2* South Dakota, N USA
Speightstown *33 G1* NW Barbados
Spencer *23 F3* Iowa, C USA
Spencer Gulf *127 B6 gulf* South Australia
Spey *66 C3 river* NE Scotland, UK
Spiess Seamount *45 C7 undersea feature* S Atlantic Ocean
Spijkenisse *64 B4* Zuid-Holland, SW Netherlands
Spíli *83 C8* Kríti, Greece, E Mediterranean Sea
Spīn Būldak *101 E5* Kandahār, S Afghanistan
Spirdingsee *see* Śniardwg, Jezioro
Spitsbergen *61 F2 island* NW Svalbard
Split *78 B4 It.* Spalato. Split-Dalmacija, S Croatia
Špoģi *84 D4* Daugvapils, SE Latvia
Spokane *24 C2* Washington, NW USA
Spratly Islands *116 B2 Chin.* Nansha Qundao. *Disputed territory* SE Asia
Spree *72 D4 river* E Germany
Springfield *18 B4 state capital* Illinois, N USA
Springfield *19 G3* Massachusetts, NE USA
Springfield *23 G5* Missouri, C USA
Springfield *18 C4* Ohio, N USA
Springfield *24 B3* Oregon, NW USA
Spring Garden *37 F2* NE Guyana
Spring Hill *21 E4* Florida, SE USA
Springs Junction *129 C5* West Coast, South Island, NZ
Springsure *126 D4* Queensland, E Australia
Spruce Knob *19 E4 mountain* West Virginia, NE USA
Srbinje *see* Foča
Srbobran *see* Donji Vakuf
Srebrenica *78 C4* Republika Srpska, E Bosnia and Herzegovina
Sredets *82 E2 prev.* Grudovo. Burgas, E Bulgaria
Sredets *82 D2 prev.* Syulemeshlii. Stara Zagora, C Bulgaria
Srednerusskaya Vozvyshennost' *87 G1 Eng.* Central Russian Upland. *Mountain range* W Russian Federation
Srednesibirskoye Ploskogor'ye *92 D3 var.* Central Siberian Uplands, *Eng.* Central Siberian Plateau. *Mountain range* N Russian Federation
Sremska Mitrovica *78 C3 prev.* Mitrovica, *Ger.* Mitrowitz. Serbia, NW Serbia and Montenegro(Yugo.)
Srêpôk, Tônle *115 E5 var.* Sông Srepok. *River* Cambodia/Vietnam
Sri Aman *116 C3 var.* Bandar Sri Aman, Simanggang. Borneo, East Malaysia
Sri Jayawardanapura *110 D3 var.* Sri Jayawardenepura; *prev.* Kotte. Western Province, W Sri Lanka
Sri Jayawardenepura *see* Sri Jayawardanapura
Srīkākulam *113 F5* Andhra Pradesh, E India
Sri Lanka *110 D3 prev.* Ceylon. *Country* S Asia
Srpska, Republika *78 B3* Admin. region *republic* NE Bosnia and Herzegovina
Srinagarind Reservoir *115 C5 lake* W Thailand
Ssu-ch'uan *see* Sichuan
Ssu-p'ing *see* Siping
Ssu-p'ing-chieh *see* Siping
Stabroek *65 B5* Antwerpen, N Belgium
Stade *72 B3* Niedersachsen, NW Germany
Stadskanaal *64 E2* Groningen, NE Netherlands
Stafford *67 D6* C England, UK
Staicele *84 D3* Limbaži, N Latvia
Stakhanov *87 H3* Luhans'ka Oblast', E Ukraine
Stalinabad *see* Dushanbe
Stalingrad *see* Volgograd
Stalinobod *see* Dushanbe
Stalin Peak *see* Kommunizm, Qullai
Stalowa Wola *76 E4* Podkarpackie, SE Poland
Stamford *19 F3* Connecticut, NE USA
Stampalia *see* Astypálaia
Stanley *43 D7 var.* Port Stanley, Puerto Argentino. *Dependent territory capital* (Falkland Islands) East Falkland, Falkland Islands
Stanovoy Khrebet *91 E3 mountain range* SE Russian Federation
Stanthorpe *127 D5* Queensland, E Australia
Staphorst *64 D2* Overijssel, E Netherlands
Starachowice *76 D4* Świętokrzyskie, C Poland
Stara Pazova *78 D3 Ger.* Altpasua, *Hung.* Ópazova. Serbia, N Serbia and Montenegro (Yugo.)
Stara Zagora *82 D2 Lat.* Augusta Trajana. Stara Zagora, C Bulgaria
Starbuck Island *123 G3 prev.* Volunteer Island. *Island* E Kiribati
Stargard Szczeciński *76 B3 Ger.* Stargard in Pommern. Zachodniopomorskie, NW Poland
Starobil's'k *87 H2 Rus.* Starobel'sk. Luhans'ka Oblast', E Ukraine
Starobyn *85 C7 Rus.* Starobin. Minskaya Voblasts', S Belarus
Starogard Pomorskiei *76 C2 Ger.* Preussisch-Stargard. Pomorskie, N Poland
Starokostyantyniv *86 D2 Rus.* Starokonstantinov. Khmel'nyts'ka Oblast', NW Ukraine
Starominskaya *89 A7* Krasnodarskiy Kray, SW Russian Federation
Staryya Darohi *85 C6 Rus.* Staryye Dorogi. Minskaya Voblasts', S Belarus
Staryy Oskol *89 B6* Belgorodskaya Oblast', W Russian Federation
State College *19 E4* Pennsylvania, NE USA
Statesboro *21 E2* Georgia, SE USA
Staunton *19 E5* Virginia, NE USA
Stavanger *63 A6* Rogaland, S Norway
Stavers Island *see* Vostok Island
Stavropol' *89 B7 prev.* Voroshilovsk. Stavropol'skiy Kray, SW Russian Federation
Steamboat Springs *22 C4* Colorado, C USA
Steenwijk *64 D2* Overijssel, N Netherlands
Steier *see* Steyr
Steinkjer *62 B4* Nord-Trøndelag, C Norway
Stendal *72 C3* Sachsen-Anhalt, C Germany
Stephenville *27 F3* Texas, SW USA
Sterling *22 D4* Colorado, C USA
Sterling *18 B3* Illinois, N USA
Sterlitamak *92 B3* Respublika Bashkortostan, W Russian Federation
Stettiner Haff *see* Szczeciński, Zalew
Stevenage *67 E6* E England, UK
Stevens Point *18 B2* Wisconsin, N USA
Stewart Island *129 A8 island* S NZ
Steyr *73 D6 var.* Steier. Oberösterreich, N Austria
Stif *see* Sétif
Stillwater *27 G1* Oklahoma, C USA
Stirling *66 C4* C Scotland, UK
Stjørdalshalsen *62 B4* Nord-Trøndelag, C Norway
Stockach *73 B6* Baden-Württemberg, S Germany
Stockholm *63 C6 country capital* (Sweden) Stockholm, C Sweden
Stockton *25 B6* California, W USA
Stockton Plateau *27 E4 plain* Texas, SW USA
Stœng Trêng *115 D5 prev.* Stung Treng. Stœng Trêng, NE Cambodia
Stoke *see* Stoke-on-Trent
Stoke-on-Trent *67 D6 var.* Stoke. C England, UK
Stómio *82 B4* Thessalía, C Greece
Stony Tunguska *90 D2 river* C Russian Federation
Store Bælt *see* Storebælt
Storebælt *63 B8 var.* Store Bælt, *Eng.* Great Belt, Storebelt. *Channel* Baltic Sea/Kattegat
Storebelt *see* Storebælt
Støren *63 B5* Sør-Trøndelag, S Norway
Storfjorden *61 G2 fjord* S Norway
Stornoway *88 B2* NW Scotland, UK
Storsjön *63 B5 lake* C Sweden
Storuman *62 C4 lake* N Sweden
Storuman *62 C4* Västerbotten, N Sweden
Stowbtsy *85 C6 Pol.* Stolbce, *Rus.* Stolbtsy. Minskaya Voblasts', C Belarus
Strabane *67 B5 Ir.* An Srath Bán. W Northern Ireland, UK
Strakonice *77 A5 Ger.* Strakonitz. Budějovický Kraj, S Czech Republic
Stralsund *72 D2* Mecklenburg-Vorpommern, NE Germany
Stranraer *67 C5* S Scotland, UK
Strasbourg *68 E3 Ger.* Strassburg; *anc.* Argentoratum. Bas-Rhin, NE France
Străşeni *86 D3 var.* Strasheny. C Moldova
Strasheny *see* Străşeni
Stratford *128 D4* Taranaki, North Island, NZ
Strathfield *126 E2* New South Wales, SE Australia
Straubing *73 C6* Bayern, SE Germany
Strehaia *86 B5* Mehedinţi, SW Romania
Strelka *92 D4* Krasnoyarskiy Kray, C Russian Federation
Strofilia *see* Strofyliá
Strofyliá *83 C5 var.* Strofilia. Évvoia, C Greece
Stromboli, Isola *75 D6 island* Isole Eolie, S Italy
Stromeferry *66 C3* N Scotland, UK
Strömstad *63 B6* Västra Götaland, S Sweden
Strömsund *62 C4* Jämtland, C Sweden
Struga *79 D6* SW FYR Macedonia
Strumica *79 E6* E FYR Macedonia
Strumyani *82 C3* Blagoevgrad, SW Bulgaria
Strymónas *82 C3 Bul.* Struma. *River* Bulgaria/Greece *see also* Struma
Stryy *86 B2* L'vivs'ka Oblast', NW Ukraine
Studholme *129 B6* Canterbury, South Island, NZ
Sturgis *22 D3* South Dakota, N USA
Stuttgart *73 B6* Baden-Württemberg, SW Germany
Stykkishólmur *61 E4* Vesturland, W Iceland
Styr *86 C1 Rus.* Styr'. *River* Belarus/Ukraine
Su *see* Jiangsu
Suakin *50 C3 var.* Sawakin. Red Sea, NE Sudan
Subačius *84 C4* Kupiškis, NE Lithuania
Subaykhān *96 E3* Dayr az Zawr, E Syria
Subotica *78 D2 Ger.* Maria-Theresiopel, *Hung.* Szabadka. Serbia, N Serbia and Montenegro (Yugo.)
Suceava *86 C3 Ger.* Suczawa, *Hung.* Szucsava. Suceava, NE Romania
Su-chou *see* Suzhou
Suchow *see* Xuzhou
Sucre *39 F4 hist.* Chuquisaca, La Plata. *Country capital* (Bolivia-legal capital) Chuquisaca, S Bolivia
Sudan *50 A4 Ar.* Jumhuriyat as-Sudan; *prev.* Anglo-Egyptian *Sudan. country* N Africa
Sudbury *16 C4* Ontario, S Canada
Sudd *51 B5 swamp region* S Sudan
Sudeten *76 B4 var.* Sudetes, Sudetic Mountains, *Cz./Pol.* Sudety. *Mountain range* Czech Republic/Poland
Sudetes *see* Sudeten
Sudetic Mountains *see* Sudeten
Sudety *see* Sudeten
Südkarpaten *see* Carpaţii Meridionali
Sue *51 B5 river* S Sudan
Sueca *71 F3* País Valenciano, E Spain
Sue Wood Bay *20 B5 bay* W Bermuda
Suez *50 B1 Ar.* As Suways, El Suweis. NE Egypt
Suez Canal *50 B1 Ar.* Qanāt as Suways. *Canal* NE Egypt
Suez, Gulf of *50 B2 Ar.* Khalīj as Suways. *Gulf* NE Egypt
Suğla Gölü *94 C4 lake* SW Turkey
Şuḩār *99 D5 var.* Sohar. N Oman
Sühbaatar *105 E1* Selenge, N Mongolia
Suhl *73 C5* Thüringen, C Germany
Suixi *106 C6* Guangdong, S China
Sujāwal *112 B3* Sind, SE Pakistan
Sukabumi *116 C5 prev.* Soekaboemi. Jawa, C Indonesia
Sukagawa *109 D5* Fukushima, Honshū, C Japan
Sukarnapura *see* Jayapura
Sukhne *see* As Sukhnah
Sukhona *88 C4 var.* Tot'ma. *River* NW Russian Federation
Sukkertoppen *see* Maniitsoq
Sukkur *112 B3* Sind, SE Pakistan
Sukumo *109 B7* Kōchi, Shikoku, SW Japan
Sulaimaniya *see* As Sulaymānīyah
Sulaimān Range *112 C2 mountain range* C Pakistan
Sula, Kepulauan *117 E4 island group* C Indonesia
Sulawesi *117 E4 Eng.* Celebes. *Island* C Indonesia
Sulechów *76 B3 Ger.* Züllichau. Lubuskie, W Poland
Suliag *see* Sohâg
Sullana *38 B2* Piura, NW Peru
Sulphur Springs *27 G2* Texas, SW USA
Sulu Archipelago *117 E3 island group* SW Philippines
Sulu Sea *117 E2 Ind.* Laut Sulu. *Sea* SW Philippines
Sulyukta *101 E2 Kir.* Sülüktü. Oshskaya Oblast', SW Kyrgyzstan
Sumatera *115 B8 Eng.* Sumatra. *Island* W Indonesia
Sumatra *see* Sumatera
Sumba, Pulau *117 E5 Eng.* Sandalwood Island; *prev.* Soemba. *Island* Nusa Tenggara, C Indonesia
Sumba, Selat *117 E5 strait* Nusa Tenggara, S Indonesia
Sumbawanga *51 B7* Rukwa, W Tanzania
Sumbe *56 B2 prev.* N'Gunza, *Port.* Novo Redondo. Cuanza Sul, W Angola
Sumeih *51 B5* Southern Darfur, S Sudan
Summer Lake *24 B4 lake* Oregon, NW USA
Summit *93 H5 mountain* C Gibraltar
Sumqayıt *95 H2 Rus.* Sumgait. E Azerbaijan
Sumy *87 F2* Sums'ka Oblast', NE Ukraine
Sunbury *127 C7* Victoria, SE Australia
Sunda Islands *see* Greater Sunda Islands
Sunda, Selat *116 B5 strait* Jawa/Sumatera, SW Indonesia
Sunda Trench *see* Java Trench
Sunderland *66 D4 var.* Wearmouth. NE England, UK
Sundsvall *63 C5* Västernorrland, C Sweden
Sungaipenuh *116 B4 prev.* Soengaipenoeh. Sumatera, W Indonesia
Sunnyvale *25 A6* California, W USA
Suntar *93 F3* Respublika Sakha (Yakutiya), NE Russian Federation
Sunyani *53 E5* W Ghana
Suomussalmi *62 E4* Oulu, E Finland
Suŏng *115 D6* Kâmpóng Cham, C Cambodia
Suoyarvi *88 B3* Respublika Kareliya, NW Russian Federation
Supe *38 C3* Lima, W Peru
Superior *18 A1* Wisconsin, N USA
Superior, Lake *18 B1 Fr.* Lac Supérieur. *Lake* Canada/USA
Suqrah *see* Şawqirah
Suquṭrā *99 C7 var.* Sokotra, *Eng.* Socotra. *Island* SE Yemen
Şūr *see* Soûr
Şūr *99 E5* NE Oman
Surabaya *116 D5 prev.* Soerabaja, Surabaja. Jawa, C Indonesia
Surakarta *116 C5 Eng.* Solo; *prev.* Soerakarta. Jawa, S Indonesia
Šurany *77 C6 Hung.* Nagysurány. Nitriansky Kraj, SW Slovakia
Sūrat *112 C4* Gujarāt, W India
Suratdhani *see* Surat Thani
Surat Thani *115 C6 var.* Suratdhani. Surat Thani, SW Thailand
Surazh *85 E5 Rus.* Surazh. Vitsyebskaya Voblasts', NE Belarus
Surdulica *79 E5* Serbia, SE Serbia and Montenegro (Yugo.)
Sûre *65 D7 var.* Sauer. *River* W Europe *see also* Sauer
Surendranagar *112 C4* Gujarāt, W India
Surfers Paradise *127 E5* Queensland, E Australia
Surgut *92 D3* Khanty-Mansiyskiy Avtonomnyy Okrug, C Russian Federation
Surin *115 D5* Surin, E Thailand
Surinam *see* Suriname
Suriname *37 G3 var.* Surinam; *prev.* Dutch Guiana, Netherlands Guiana. *Country* N S America
Surkhob *101 F3 river* C Tajikistan
Surt *49 G2 var.* Sidra, Sirte. N Libya
Surt, Khalīj *49 F2 Eng.* Gulf of Sidra, Gulf of Sirti, Sidra. *Gulf* N Libya
Surtsey *61 E5 island* S Iceland
Suruga-wan *109 D6 bay* SE Japan
Susa *74 A2* Piemonte, NE Italy
Sūsah *see* Sousse
Susanville *25 B5* California, W USA
Susitna *14 C3* Alaska, USA

Susteren 65 D5 Limburg, SE Netherlands
Susuman 93 G3 Magadanskaya Oblast', E Russian Federation
Sutherland 126 E2 New South Wales, SE Australia
Sutlej 112 C2 river India/Pakistan
Suur Munamägi 84 D3 var. Munamägi, Ger. Eier-Berg. Mountain SE Estonia
Suur Väin 84 C2 Ger. Grosser Sund. Strait W Estonia
Suva 123 E4 country capital (Fiji) Viti Levu, W Fiji
Suwałki 76 E2 Lith. Suvalkai, Rus. Suvalki. Podlaskie, NE Poland
Şuwār see Aş Şuwār
Suweida see As Suwaydā'
Suzhou 106 D5 var. Soochow, Su-chou, Suchow; prev. Wuhsien. Jiangsu, E China
Svalbard 61 E1 Norwegian dependency Arctic Ocean
Svartisen 62 C3 glacier C Norway
Svay Riĕng 115 D6 Svay Riĕng, S Cambodia
Sveg 63 B5 Jämtland, C Sweden
Svenstavik 63 C5 Jämtland, C Sweden
Svetlograd 89 B7 Stavropol'skiy Kray, SW Russian Federation
Svilengrad 82 D3 prev. Mustafa-Pasha. Khaskovo, S Bulgaria
Svitlovods'k 87 F3 Rus. Svetlovodsk. Kirovohrads'ka Oblast', C Ukraine
Svobodnyy 93 G4 Amurskaya Oblast', SE Russian Federation
Svyataya Anna Trough 172 C4 var. Saint Anna Trough. Undersea feature N Kara Sea
Svyetlahorsk 85 D7 Rus. Svetlogorsk. Homyel'skaya Voblasts', SE Belarus
Swabian Jura see Schwäbische Alb
Swakopmund 56 B3 Erongo, W Namibia
Swansea 67 C7 Wel. Abertawe. S Wales, UK
Swarzędz 76 C3 Wielkopolskie, C Poland
Swatow see Shantou
Swaziland 56 D4 Country S Africa
Sweden 62 B4 Swe. Sverige. Country N Europe
Swed Ormsö see Vormsi
Sweetwater 27 F3 Texas, SW USA
Świdnica 76 B4 Ger. Schweidnitz. Wałbrzych, SW Poland
Świdwin 76 B2 Ger. Schivelbein. Zachodniopomorskie, NW Poland
Świebodzice 76 B4 Ger. Freiburg in Schlesien, Swiebodzice. Wałbrzych, SW Poland
Świebodzin 76 B3 Ger. Schwiebus. Lubuskie, W Poland
Świecie 76 C3 Ger. Schwertberg. Kujawski-pomorskie, C Poland
Swindon 67 D7 S England, UK
Świnoujście 76 B2 Ger. Swinemünde. Zachodniopomorskie, NW Poland
Switzerland 73 A7 Fr. La Suisse, Ger. Schweiz, It. Svizzera; anc. Helvetia. Country C Europe
Sycaminum see Hefa
Sydney 126 D1 state capital New South Wales, SE Australia
Sydney 17 G4 Cape Breton Island, Nova Scotia, SE Canada
Syedpur see Saidpur
Syemyezhava 85 C6 Rus. Semezhevo. Minskaya Voblasts', C Belarus
Syene see Aswân
Syeverodonets'k 87 H3 Rus. Severodonetsk. Luhans'ka Oblast', E Ukraine
Syktyvkar 88 D4 prev. Ust'-Sysol'sk. Respublika Komi, NW Russian Federation
Sylhet 113 G3 Chittagong, NE Bangladesh
Synel'nykove 87 G3 Dnipropetrovs'ka Oblast', E Ukraine
Syowa 132 C2 Japanese research station Antarctica
Syracuse 19 E3 New York, NE USA
Syrdariya see Syr Darya
Syr Darya 92 B4 var. Sai Hun, Sir Darya, Syrdarya, Kaz. Syrdariya, Rus. Syrdar'ya, Uzb. Sirdaryo; anc. Jaxartes. River C Asia
Syria 96 B3 var. Siria, Syrie, Ar. Al-Jumhūrīyah al-'Arabīyah as-Sūrīyah, Sūrīya. Country SW Asia
Syrian Desert 97 D5 Ar. Al Hamad, Bādiyat ash Shām. Desert SW Asia
Sýrna 83 E7 var. Sirna. Island Kykládes, Greece, Aegean Sea
Sýros 83 C6 var. Síros. Island Kykládes, Greece, Aegean Sea
Syvash, Zatoka 87 F4 Rus. Zaliv Syvash. Inlet S Ukraine
Syzran' 89 C6 Samarskaya Oblast', W Russian Federation
Szamos see Someş
Szamotuły 76 B3 Wielkopolskie, C Poland
Szczecin 76 B3 Eng./Ger. Stettin. Zachodniopomorskie, NW Poland
Szczecinek 76 B2 Ger. Neustettin. Zachodniopomorskie, NW Poland
Szczeciński, Zalew 76 A2 var. Stettiner Haff, Ger. Oderhaff. Bay Germany/Poland
Szczytno 76 D3 Ger. Ortelsburg. Olsztyn, NE Poland
Szechuan see Sichuan
Szechwan see Sichuan
Szeged 77 D7 Ger. Szegedin, Rom. Seghedin. Csongrád, SE Hungary
Székesfehérvár 77 C6 Ger. Stuhlweissenberg; anc. Alba Regia. Fejér, W Hungary
Szekszárd 77 C7 Tolna, S Hungary
Szenttamás see Srbobran
Szeping see Siping
Sziszek see Sisak
Szlatina see Slatina
Szolnok 77 D6 Jász-Nagykun-Szolnok, C Hungary
Szombathely 77 B6 Ger. Steinamanger; anc. Sabaria, Savaria. Vas, W Hungary
Szprotawa 76 B4 Ger. Sprottau. Lubuskie, W Poland

T

Table Rock Lake 27 G1 reservoir Arkansas/Missouri, C USA
Tábor 77 B5 Budějovický Kraj, S Czech Republic
Tabora 51 B7 Tabora, W Tanzania
Tabrīz 98 C2 var. Tebriz; anc. Tauris. Āžarbāyjān-e Khāvarī, NW Iran
Tabuaeran 123 G2 prev. Fanning Island. Atoll Line Islands, E Kiribati
Tabūk 98 A4 Tabūk, NW Saudi Arabia
Täby 63 C6 Stockholm, C Sweden
Tachov 77 A5 Ger. Tachau. Plzeňský Kraj, W Czech Republic
Tacloban 117 F2 off. Tacloban City. Leyte, C Philippines
Tacna 39 E4 Tacna, SE Peru
Tacoma 24 B2 Washington, NW USA
Tacuarembó 42 D4 prev. San Fructuoso. Tacuarembó, C Uruguay
Tademaït, Plateau du 48 D3 plateau C Algeria
Tadmor see Tudmur
Tadmur see Tudmur
Tādpatri 110 C2 Andhra Pradesh, E India
Taegu 107 E4 off. Taegu-gwangyŏksi, var. Daegu, Jap. Taikyū. SE South Korea
Taejŏn 107 E4 off. Taejŏn-gwangyŏksi, Jap. Taiden. C South Korea
Tafassâset, Ténéré du 53 G2 desert N Niger
Tafila see Aṭ Ṭafilah
Taganrog 89 A7 Rostovskaya Oblast', SW Russian Federation
Taganrog, Gulf of 87 G4 Rus. Taganrogskiy Zaliv, Ukr. Tahanroz'ka Zatoka. Gulf Russian Federation/Ukraine
Taguatinga 41 F3 Tocantins, C Brazil
Tagus 70 C3 Port. Rio Tejo, Sp. Río Tajo. River Portugal/Spain
Tagus Plain 58 A4 undersea feature E Atlantic Ocean
Tahat 49 E4 mountain SE Algeria
Tahiti 123 H4 island Îles du Vent, W French Polynesia
Tahlequah 27 G1 Oklahoma, C USA
Tahoe, Lake 25 B5 lake California/Nevada, W USA
Tahoua 53 F3 Tahoua, W Niger
T'aichung 106 D6 Jap. Taichū; prev. Taiwan. C Taiwan
Taieri 129 B7 river South Island, NZ
Taihape 128 D4 Manawatu-Wanganui, North Island, NZ
Tailem Bend 127 B7 South Australia
T'ainan 106 D6 Jap. Tainan; prev. Dainan. S Taiwan
T'aipei 106 D6 Jap. Taihoku; prev. Daihoku. Country capital (Taiwan) N Taiwan
Taiping 116 B3 Perak, Peninsular Malaysia
Taiwan 106 D6 var. Formosa, Formo'sa. Country E Asia
T'aiwan Haihsia see Taiwan Strait
Taiwan Haixia see Taiwan Strait
Taiwan Strait 106 D6 var. Formosa Strait, Chin. T'aiwan Haihsia, Taiwan Haixia. Strait China/Taiwan
Taiyuan 106 C4 prev. T'ai-yuan, T'ai-yüan, Yangku. Shanxi, C China
Ta'izz 99 B7 SW Yemen
Tajikistan 101 E3 Rus. Tadzhikistan, Taj. Jumhurii Tojikiston; prev. Tajik S.S.R. Country C Asia
Tak 114 C4 var. Rahaeng. Tak, W Thailand
Takao see Kaohsiung
Takaoka 109 C5 Toyama, Honshū, SW Japan
Takapuna 128 D2 Auckland, North Island, NZ
Takhiatosh see Taxiatosh
Takhtakŭpir see Taxtako'pir
Takikawa 108 D2 Hokkaidō, NE Japan
Takla Makan Desert see Taklimakan Shamo
Taklimakan Shamo 104 B3 Eng. Takla Makan Desert. Desert NW China
Takow see Kaohsiung
Takutea 123 G4 island S Cook Islands
Talachyn 85 D6 Rus. Tolochin. Vitsyebskaya Voblasts', NE Belarus
Talamanca, Cordillera de 31 E5 mountain range S Costa Rica
Talara 38 B2 Piura, NW Peru
Talas 101 F2 Talasskaya Oblast', NW Kyrgyzstan
Talaud, Kepulauan 117 F3 island group E Indonesia
Talavera de la Reina 70 D3 anc. Caesarobriga, Talabriga. Castilla-La Mancha, C Spain
Talca 42 B4 Maule, C Chile
Talcahuano 43 B5 Bío Bío, C Chile
Taldykorgan 92 C5 Kaz. Taldyqorghan; prev. Taldy-Kurgan. Almaty, SE Kazakhstan
Taldy-Kurgan/Taldyqorghan see Taldykorgan
Ta-lien see Dalian
Taliq-an see Tāloqān
Tal'ka 85 C6 Rus. Tal'ka. Minskaya Voblasts', C Belarus
Tallahassee 20 D3 prev. Muskogean. State capital Florida, SE USA
Tall al Abyaḍ see At Tall al Abyaḍ
Tallinn 84 D2 Ger. Reval, Rus. Tallin; prev. Revel. Country capital (Estonia) Harjumaa, NW Estonia
Tall Kalakh 96 B4 var. Tell Kalakh. Ḥimṣ, C Syria
Tallulah 20 B2 Louisiana, S USA
Talnakh 92 D3 Taymyrskiy (Dolgano-Nenetskiy) Avtonomnyy Okrug, N Russian Federation
Tal'ne 87 E3 Rus. Tal'noye. Cherkas'ka Oblast', C Ukraine
Taloga 27 F1 Oklahoma, C USA
Tāloqān 101 E3 var. Taliq-an. Takhār, NE Afghanistan
Talsi 84 C3 Ger. Talsen. Talsi, NW Latvia
Taltal 42 B2 Antofagasta, N Chile
Talvik 62 D2 Finnmark, N Norway
Tamabo, Banjaran 116 D3 mountain range East Malaysia
Tamale 53 E4 C Ghana
Tamana 123 E3 prev. Rotcher Island. Atoll Tungaru, W Kiribati
Tamanrasset 49 E4 var. Tamenghest. S Algeria
Tamar 67 C7 river SW England, UK
Tamar see Tudmur
Tamatave see Toamasina
Tamazunchale 29 E4 San Luis Potosí, C Mexico
Tambacounda 52 C3 SE Senegal
Tambov 89 B6 Tambovskaya Oblast', W Russian Federation
Tambura 51 B5 Western Equatoria, SW Sudan
Tamchaket see Tâmchekkeṭ
Tâmchekkeṭ 52 C3 var. Tamchaket. Hodh el Gharbi, S Mauritania
Tamenghest see Tamanrasset
Tamiahua, Laguna de 29 F4 lagoon E Mexico
Tamil Nādu 110 C3 prev. Madras. State SE India
Tam Ky 115 E5 Quang Nam-Đa Nẵng, C Vietnam
Tampa 21 E4 Florida, SE USA
Tampa Bay 21 E4 bay Florida, SE USA
Tampere 63 D5 Swe. Tammerfors. Länsi-Suomi, W Finland
Tampico 29 E3 Tamaulipas, C Mexico
Tamworth 127 D6 New South Wales, SE Australia
Tana see Deatnu/Tenojoki
Tanabe 109 C7 Wakayama, Honshū, SW Japan
Tana Bru 62 D2 Finnmark, N Norway
T'ana Hāyk' 50 C4 Eng. Lake Tana. Lake NW Ethiopia
Tanais see Don
Tanami Desert 124 D3 desert Northern Territory, N Australia
Țăndărei 86 D5 Ialomița, SE Romania
Tandil 43 D5 Buenos Aires, E Argentina
Tanega-shima 109 B8 island Nansei-shotō, SW Japan
Tane Range 114 B4 Bur. Tanen Taunggyi. Mountain range W Thailand
Tanezrouft 48 D4 desert Algeria/Mali
Ṭanf, Jabal aṭ 96 D4 mountain SE Syria
Tanga 47 E5 Tanga, E Tanzania
Tanga 51 C7 region E Tanzania
Tanganyika, Lake 51 B7 lake E Africa
Tangeh-ye Hormoz see Hormuz, Strait of
Tanger 48 C2 var. Tangiers, Tangier, Fr./Ger. Tangerk, Sp. Tánger; anc. Tingis. NW Morocco
Tangerk see Tanger
Tanggula Shan 104 C4 var. Dangla, Tangla Range. Mountain range W China
Tangier see Tanger
Tangiers see Tanger
Tangla Range see Tanggula Shan
Tangra Yumco 104 B5 var. Tangro Tso. Lake W China
Tangro Tso see Tangra Yumco
Tangshan 106 D3 var. T'ang-shan. Hebei, E China
T'ang-shan see Tangshan
Tanimbar, Kepulauan 117 F5 island group Maluku, E Indonesia
Tanna 122 D4 island S Vanuatu
Tannenhof see Krynica
Tan-Tan 48 B3 SW Morocco
Tan-tung see Dandong
Tanzania 51 C7 Swa. Jamhuri ya Muungano wa Tanzania; prev. German East Africa, Tanganyika and Zanzibar. Country E Africa
Taoudenit see Taoudenni
Taoudenni 53 E2 var. Taoudenit. Tombouctou, N Mali
Tapa 84 E2 Ger. Taps. Lääne-Virumaa, NE Estonia
Tapachula 29 G5 Chiapas, SE Mexico
Tapajós, Rio 41 E2 var. Tapajóz. River NW Brazil
Tapajóz see Tapajós, Rio
Țarābulus 49 F2 var. Țarābulus al Gharb, Eng. Tripoli. Country capital (Libya) NW Libya
Tarābulus see Tripoli
Țarābulus al Gharb see Țarābulus
Țarābulus ash Shām see Tripoli
Taraclia 86 D4 Rus. Tarakilya. S Moldova
Taranaki, Mount 128 C4 var. Egmont, Mount. Mountain North Island, NZ
Tarancón 71 E3 Castilla-La Mancha, C Spain
Taranto 75 E5 var. Tarentum. Puglia, SE Italy
Taranto, Golfo di 75 E6 Eng. Gulf of Taranto. Gulf S Italy
Tarapoto 38 C2 San Martín, N Peru
Tarare 69 D5 Rhône, E France
Tarascon 69 D6 Bouches-du-Rhône, SE France
Tarawa 122 D2 atoll Tungaru, W Kiribati
Taraz 92 C5 prev. Aulie Ata, Auliye-Ata, Dzhambul, Zhambyl. Zhambyl, S Kazakhstan
Tarazona 71 E2 Aragón, NE Spain
Tarbes 69 B6 anc. Bigorra. Hautes-Pyrénées, S France
Tarcoola 127 A6 South Australia
Taree 127 D6 New South Wales, SE Australia
Tarentum see Taranto
Târgovişte 86 C5 prev. Tîrgovişte. Dâmbovița, S Romania
Târgu Jiu 86 B4 prev. Tîrgu Jiu. Gorj, W Romania
Târgul-Neamț see Târgu-Neamț
Târgu Mureş 86 B4 prev. Oşorhei, Tîrgu Mures, Ger. Neumarkt, Hung. Marosvásárhely. Mureş, C Romania
Târgu-Neamț 86 C3 var. Târgul-Neamț; prev. Tîrgu-Neamț. Neamț, NE Romania
Târgu Ocna 86 C4 Hung. Aknavásár; prev. Tîrgu Ocna. Bacău, E Romania
Târgu Secuiesc 86 C4 Ger. Neumarkt, Szekler Neumarkt, Hung. Kezdivásárhely; prev. Chezdi-Oşorheiu, Târgul-Săcuiesc, Tîrgu Secuiesc. Covasna, E Romania
Tarija 39 G5 Tarija, S Bolivia
Tarīm 99 C6 C Yemen
Tarim Basin 102 C2 basin NW China
Tarim He 104 B3 river NW China
Tarma 38 C3 Junín, C Peru
Tarn 69 C6 cultural region S France
Tarn 69 C6 river S France
Tarnobrzeg 76 D4 Podkarpackie, SE Poland
Tarnów 77 D5 Małopolskie, S Poland
Tarragona 71 G2 anc. Tarraco. Cataluña, E Spain
Tàrrega 71 F2 var. Tarrega. Cataluña, NE Spain
Tarsus 94 C4 İçel, S Turkey
Tartu 84 D3 Ger. Dorpat; prev. Rus. Yurev, Yur'yev. Tartumaa, SE Estonia
Țarțūs 96 A3 Fr. Tartouss; anc. Tortosa. Țarțūs, W Syria
Ta Ru Tao, Ko 115 B7 island S Thailand
Tarvisio 74 D2 Friuli-Venezia Giulia, NE Italy
Tashi Chho Dzong see Thimphu
Tashkent see Toshkent
Tash-Kumyr 101 F2 Kir. Tash-Kömür. Dzhalal-Abadskaya Oblast', W Kyrgyzstan
Tashqurghan see Kholm
Tasikmalaya 116 C5 prev. Tasikmalaja. Jawa, C Indonesia
Tasman Basin 120 C5 var. East Australian Basin. Undersea feature S Tasman Sea
Tasman Bay 129 C5 inlet South Island, NZ
Tasmania 127 B8 prev. Van Diemen's Land. State SE Australia
Tasmania 130 B4 island SE Australia
Tasman Plateau 120 C5 var. South Tasmania Plateau. Undersea feature SW Tasman Sea
Tasman Sea 120 C5 sea SW Pacific Ocean
Tassili-n-Ajjer 49 E4 plateau E Algeria
Tatabánya 77 C6 Komárom-Esztergom, NW Hungary
Tathlīth 99 B5 'Asīr, S Saudi Arabia
Tatra Mountains 77 D5 Ger. Tatra, Hung. Tátra, Pol./Slvk. Tatry. Mountain range Poland/Slovakia
Ta-t'ung see Datong
Tatvan 95 F3 Bitlis, SE Turkey
Ta'ū 123 F4 var. Tau. Island Manua Islands, E American Samoa
Tau see Ta'ū
Taukum, Peski 101 G1 desert SE Kazakhstan
Taumarunui 128 D4 Manawatu-Wanganui, North Island, NZ
Taungdwingyi 114 B3 Magwe, C Myanmar
Taunggyi 114 B3 Shan State, C Myanmar
Taunton 67 C7 SW England, UK
Taupo 128 D3 Waikato, North Island, NZ
Taupo, Lake 128 D3 lake North Island, NZ
Tauragė 84 B4 Ger. Tauroggen. Tauragė, SW Lithuania
Tauranga 128 D3 Bay of Plenty, North Island, NZ
Tauris see Tabrīz
Tavas 94 B4 Denizli, SW Turkey
Tavira 70 C5 Faro, S Portugal
Tavoy 115 B5 var. Dawei. Tenasserim, S Myanmar
Tavoy Island see Mali Kyun
Tawakoni, Lake 27 G2 reservoir Texas, SW USA
Tawau 116 D3 Sabah, East Malaysia
Țawkar see Tokar
Tawzar see Tozeur
Taxco 29 E4 var. Taxco de Alarcón. Guerrero, S Mexico
Taxco de Alarcón see Taxco
Taxiatosh 100 C2 var. Takhiatosh, Rus. Takhiatash. Qoraqalpoghiston Respublikasi, W Uzbekistan
Taxtako'pir 100 D1 var. Takhtakŭpir, Rus. Takhtakupyr. Qoraqalpoghiston Respublikasi, NW Uzbekistan
Tay 66 C3 river C Scotland, UK
Taylor 27 G3 Texas, SW USA
Taymā' 98 A4 Tabūk, NW Saudi Arabia
Taymyr, Ozero 93 E2 lake N Russian Federation
Taymyr, Poluostrov 93 E2 peninsula N Russian Federation
Taz 92 D3 river N Russian Federation
T'bilisi 95 G2 Eng. Tiflis. Country capital (Georgia) SE Georgia
T'bilisi 90 B4 international airport S Georgia
Tchien see Zwedru
Tchongking see Chongqing
Tczew 76 C2 Ger. Dirschau. Pomorskie, N Poland
Te Anau 129 A7 Southland, South Island, NZ
Te Anau, Lake 129 A7 lake South Island, NZ
Teapa 29 G4 Tabasco, SE Mexico
Teate see Chieti
Tebingtinggi 116 B3 Sumatera, N Indonesia
Tebriz see Tabrīz
Techirghiol 86 D5 Constanța, SE Romania
Tecomán 28 D4 Colima, SW Mexico
Tecpan 29 E5 var. Tecpan de Galeana. Guerrero, S Mexico
Tecpan de Galeana see Tecpan
Tecuci 86 C4 Galați, E Romania
Tedzhen see Tejen
Tedzhen see Harīrūd
Tees 67 D5 river N England, UK
Tefé 40 D2 Amazonas, N Brazil
Tegal 116 C4 Jawa, C Indonesia
Tegelen 65 D5 Limburg, SE Netherlands
Tegucigalpa 30 C3 country capital (Honduras) Francisco Morazán, SW Honduras
Teheran see Tehrān
Tehrān 98 C3 var. Teheran. Country capital (Iran) Tehrān, N Iran
Tehuacán 29 F4 Puebla, S Mexico
Tehuantepec 29 F5 var. Santo Domingo Tehuantepec. Oaxaca, SE Mexico
Tehuantepec, Golfo de 29 F5 var. Gulf of Tehuantepec. Gulf S Mexico
Tehuantepec, Gulf of see Tehuantepec, Golfo de
Tehuantepec, Isthmus of see Tehuantepec, Istmo de
Tehuantepec, Istmo de 29 F5 var. Isthmus of Tehuantepec. Isthmus SE Mexico
Tejen 100 C3 Rus. Tedzhen. Akhalskiy Velayat, S Turkmenistan
Tejen see Harīrūd
Te Kao 128 C1 Northland, North Island, NZ
Tekax 29 H4 var. Tekax de Álvaro Obregón. Yucatán, SE Mexico
Tekax de Álvaro Obregón see Tekax
Tekeli 92 C5 Almaty, SE Kazakhstan
Tekirdağ 94 A2 It. Rodosto; anc. Bisanthe, Raidestos, Rhaedestus. Tekirdağ, NW Turkey
Te Kuiti 128 D3 Waikato, North Island, NZ
Tela 30 C2 Atlántida, NW Honduras
Telanaipura see Jambi
Tel Aviv-Jaffa see Tel Aviv-Yafo
Tel Aviv-Yafo 97 A6 var. Tel Aviv-Jaffa. Tel Aviv, C Israel
Teles Pirés see São Manuel, Rio
Telish 82 C2 prev. Azizie. Pleven, NW Bulgaria
Tell Abiad see At Tall al Abyaḍ
Tell Abyad see At Tall al Abyaḍ
Tell Kalakh see Tall Kalakh
Tell Shedadi see Ash Shadādah
Telšiai 84 B3 Ger. Telschen. Telšiai, NW Lithuania
Teluk Irian see Cenderawasih, Teluk
Teluk Serera see Cenderawasih, Teluk
Temerin 78 D3 Serbia, N Serbia and Montenegro (Yugo.)
Temirtau 92 C4 prev. Samarkandski, Samarkandskoye. Karaganda, C Kazakhstan
Tempio Pausania 75 A5 Sardegna, Italy, C Mediterranean Sea
Temple 27 G3 Texas, SW USA
Temuco 43 B5 Araucanía, C Chile
Temuka 129 B6 Canterbury, South Island, NZ
Tenasserim 115 B6 Tenasserim, S Myanmar
Ténenkou 52 D3 Mopti, C Mali
Ténéré 53 G3 physical region C Niger
Tenerife 48 A3 island Islas Canarias, Spain, NE Atlantic Ocean
Tengger Shamo 105 E3 desert N China
Tengréla 52 D4 var. Tingréla. N Côte d'Ivoire
Tenkodogo 53 E4 S Burkina faso
Tennant Creek 126 A3 Northern Territory, C Australia
Tennessee 20 C1 off. State of Tennessee; also known as The Volunteer State. State SE USA
Tennessee River 20 C1 river S USA
Tenojoki see Deatnu/Tana
Tepelena see Tepelenë
Tepelenë 79 C7 var. Tepelena, It. Tepeleni. Gjirokastër, S Albania
Tepeleni see Tepelenë
Tepic 28 D4 Nayarit, C Mexico
Teplice 76 A4 Ger. Teplitz; prev. Teplice-Sanov, Teplitz-Schönau. Ústecký Kraj, NW Czech Republic
Tequila 28 D4 Jalisco, SW Mexico
Teraina 123 G2 prev. Washington Island. Atoll Line Islands, E Kiribati
Teramo 74 C4 anc. Interamna. Abruzzo, C Italy
Tercan 95 E3 Erzincan, NE Turkey
Terceira 70 A5 var. Ilha Terceira. Island Azores, Portugal, NE Atlantic Ocean
Teresina 41 F2 var. Therezina. State capital Piauí, NE Brazil
Termia see Kýthnos
Términos, Laguna de 29 G4 lagoon SE Mexico
Termiz 101 E3 Rus. Termez. Surkhondaryo Wiloyati, S Uzbekistan
Termoli 74 D4 Molise, C Italy
Terneuzen 65 B5 var. Neuzen. Zeeland, SW Netherlands
Terni 74 C4 anc. Interamna Nahars. Umbria, C Italy
Ternopil' 86 C2 Pol. Tarnopol, Rus. Ternopol'. Ternopil's'ka Oblast', W Ukraine
Terracina 75 C5 Lazio, C Italy
Terrassa 71 G2 Cast. Tarrasa. Cataluña, E Spain
Terre Adélie 132 C4 disputed region SE Antarctica
Terre Haute 18 B4 Indiana, N USA
Territoire du Yukon see Yukon Territory
Terschelling 64 C1 Fris. Skylge. Island Waddeneilanden, N Netherlands
Teruel 71 F3 anc. Turba. Aragón, E Spain
Tervel 82 E1 prev. Kurtbunar, Rom. Curtbunar. Dobrich, NE Bulgaria
Tervueren see Tervuren
Tervuren 65 C6 var. Tervueren. Vlaams Brabant, C Belgium
Teseney 50 C4 var. Tessenei. W Eritrea
Tessalit 53 E2 Kidal, NE Mali
Tessaoua 53 G3 Maradi, S Niger
Tessenderlo 65 C5 Limburg, NE Belgium
Tessenei see Teseney
Testigos, Islas los 37 E1 island group N Venezuela
Tete 57 E2 Tete, NW Mozambique
Teterow 72 C3 Mecklenburg-Vorpommern, NE Germany
Tétouan 48 C2 var. Tetouan, Tetuán. N Morocco
Tetovo 79 D5 Alb. Tetova, Tetovë, Turk. Kalkandelen. Razgrad, N Bulgaria
Tetuán see Tétouan
Tevere 74 C4 Eng. Tiber. River C Italy
Teverya 97 B5 var. Tiberias, Tverya. Northern, N Israel
Te Waewae Bay 129 A7 bay South Island, NZ
Texarkana 20 A2 Arkansas, C USA

INDEX

Texarkana 27 H2 Texas, SW USA
Texas 27 F3 off. State of Texas; also known as The Lone Star State. State S USA
Texas City 27 H4 Texas, SW USA
Texel 64 C2 island Waddeneilanden, NW Netherlands
Texoma, Lake 27 G2 reservoir Oklahoma/Texas, C USA
Teziutlán 29 F4 Puebla, S Mexico
Thaa Atoll see Kolhumadulu Atoll
Thai Binh 114 D3 Thai Binh, N Vietnam
Thailand 115 C5 Th. Prathet Thai; prev. Siam. Country SE Asia
Thailand, Gulf of 115 C6 var. Gulf of Siam, Th. Ao Thai, Vtn. Vinh Thai Lan. Gulf SE Asia
Thai Nguyên 114 D3 Băc Thai, N Vietnam
Thakhèk 114 D4 prev. Muang Khammouan. Khammouan, C Laos
Thamarīd see Thamarīt
Thamarīt 99 D6 var. Thamarīd, Thumrayt. SW Oman
Thames 67 B8 river S England, UK
Thames 128 D3 Waikato, North Island, NZ
Thanh Hoa 114 D3 Vinh Phu, N Vietnam
Thanintari Taungdan see Bilauktaung Range
Thar Desert 112 C3 var. Great Indian Desert, Indian Desert. Desert India/Pakistan
Tharthār, Buḩayrat ath 98 B3 lake C Iraq
Thásos 82 C4 island E Greece
Thásos 82 C4 Thásos, E Greece
Thaton 114 B4 Mon State, S Myanmar
Thayetmyo 114 A4 Magwe, C Myanmar
The Crane 33 H2 var. Crane. S Barbados
The Dalles 24 B3 Oregon, NW USA
The Flatts Village see Flatts Village
The Hague see 's-Gravenhage
Theodosia see Feodosiya
The Pas 15 F5 Manitoba, C Canada
Therezina see Teresina
Thérma 83 D6 Ikaría, Dodekánisos, Greece, Aegean Sea
Thermaïkós Kólpos 82 B4 Eng. Thermaic Gulf; anc. Thermaicus Sinus. Gulf N Greece
Thermiá see Kýthnos
Thérmo 83 B5 Dytikí Ellás, C Greece
The Rock 71 H4 E Gibraltar
The Six Counties see Northern Ireland
Thessaloníki 82 C3 Eng. Salonica, Salonika, SCr. Solun, Turk. Selânik. Kentrikí Makedonía, N Greece
The Valley 33 G3 dependent territory capital (Anguilla) E Anguilla
The Village 27 G1 Oklahoma, C USA
Thiamis see Thýamis
Thibet see Xizang Zizhiqu
Thief River Falls 23 F1 Minnesota, N USA
Thienen see Tienen
Thiers 69 C5 Puy-de-Dôme, C France
Thiès 52 B3 W Senegal
Thimbu see Thimphu
Thimphu 113 G3 var. Thimbu; prev. Tashi Chho Dzong. Country capital (Bhutan) W Bhutan
Thionville 68 D3 Ger. Diedenhofen. Moselle, NE France
Thíra 83 D7 prev. Santorin, Santoríni, anc. Thera. Island Kykládes, Greece, Aegean Sea
Thíra 83 D7 Thíra, Kykládes, Greece, Aegean Sea
Thiruvanathapuram see Trivandrum
Thitu Island 106 C8 island NW Spratly Islands
Tholen 64 B4 island SW Netherlands
Thomasville 20 D3 Georgia, SE USA
Thompson 15 F4 Manitoba, C Canada
Thonon-les-Bains 69 D5 Haute-Savoie, E France
Thorlákshöfn 61 E5 Sudhurland, SW Iceland
Thornton Island see Millennium Island
Thouars 68 B4 Deux-Sèvres, W France
Thracian Sea 82 D4 Gk. Thrakikó Pélagos; anc. Thracium Mare. Sea Greece/Turkey
Three Kings Islands 128 C1 island group N NZ
Thrissur see Trichūr
Thuin 65 B7 Hainaut, S Belgium
Thule see Qaanaaq
Thumrayt see Thamarīt
Thun 73 A7 Fr. Thoune. Bern, W Switzerland
Thunder Bay 16 B4 Ontario, S Canada
Thuner See 73 A7 lake C Switzerland
Thung Song 115 C7 var. Cha Mai. Nakhon Si Thammarat, SW Thailand
Thurso 66 C2 N Scotland, UK
Thýamis 82 A4 var. Thiamis. River W Greece
Tianjin 106 D4 var. Tientsin. Tianjin Shi, E China
Tianjin see Tianjin Shi
Tianjin Shi 106 D4 var. Jin, Tianjin, T'ien-ching, Tientsin. Admin. region municipality E China
Tianshui 106 B4 Gansu, C China
Tiba see Chiba
Tiberias see Teverya
Tiberias, Lake 97 B5 var. Chinnereth, Sea of Bahr Tabariya, Sea of Galilee, Ar. Bahrat Tabariya, Heb. Yam Kinneret. Lake N Israel
Tibesti 54 C2 var. Tibesti Massif, Ar. Tibistī. Mountain range N Africa
Tibesti Massif see Tibesti
Tibet see Xizang Zizhiqu
Tibetan Autonomous Region see Xizang Zizhiqu
Tibet, Plateau of see Qingzang Gaoyuan
Tibistī see Tibesti
Tibnī see At Tibnī
Tiburón, Isla 28 B2 var. Isla del Tiburón. Island NW Mexico
Tiburón, Isla del see Tiburón, Isla
Tîchît 52 D2 var. Tichitt. Tagant, C Mauritania
Tichitt see Tîchît
Ticul 29 H3 Yucatán, SE Mexico
Tidjikdja see Tidjikja
Tidjikja 52 C2 var. Tidjikdja; prev. Fort-Cappolani. Tagant, C Mauritania
T'ien-ching see Tianjin Shi
Tienen 65 C6 var. Thienen, Fr. Tirlemont. Vlaams Brabant, C Belgium
Tien Shan 104 B3 Chin. Thian Shan, Tian Shan, T'ien Shan, Rus. Tyan'-Shan'. Mountain range C Asia
Tientsin see Tianjin Shi
Tierp 63 C6 Uppsala, C Sweden
Tierra del Fuego 43 B8 off. Provincia de la Tierra del Fuego. Admin. region province S Argentina
Tierra del Fuego 35 B8 island Argentina/Chile
Tifton 20 D3 Georgia, SE USA
Tifu 117 F4 Pulau Buru, E Indonesia
Tighina 86 D4 Rus. Bendery; prev. Bender. E Moldova
Tigranocerta see Siirt
Tigris 98 B2 Ar. Dijlah, Turk. Dicle. River Iraq/Turkey
Tiguentourine 49 E3 E Algeria
Ti-hua see Ürümqi
Tihwa see Ürümqi
Tijuana 28 A1 Baja California, NW Mexico
Tikhoretsk 89 A7 Krasnodarskiy Kray, SW Russian Federation
Tikhvin 88 B4 Leningradskaya Oblast', NW Russian Federation
Tiki Basin 121 G3 undersea feature S Pacific Ocean
Tiksi 93 F2 Respublika Sakha (Yakutiya), NE Russian Federation
Tilburg 64 C4 Noord-Brabant, S Netherlands
Tilimsen see Tlemcen
Tillabéri 53 F3 var. Tillabéry. Tillabéri, W Niger
Tillabéry see Tillabéri
Tílos 83 E7 island Dodekánisos, Greece, Aegean Sea
Timanskiy Kryazh 88 D3 Eng. Timan Ridge. Ridge NW Russian Federation
Timaru 129 B6 Canterbury, South Island, NZ
Timbaki see Tympáki
Timbákion see Tympáki
Timbedgha 52 D3 var. Timbédra. Hodh ech Chargui, SE Mauritania
Timbédra see Timbedgha
Timbuktu see Tombouctou
Timiş 86 A4 river W Romania
Timişoara 86 A4 Ger. Temeschwar, Temeswar, Hung. Temesvár; prev. Temeschburg. Timiş, W Romania
Timmins 16 C4 Ontario, S Canada
Timor 103 F5 island Nusa Tenggara, East Timor/Indonesia
Timor Timur see East Timor
Timor Sea 103 F5 sea E Indian Ocean
Timor Trench see Timor Trough
Timor Trough 103 F5 var. Timor Trench. Undersea feature NE Timor Sea
Timrå 63 C5 Västernorrland, C Sweden
Tindouf 48 C3 W Algeria
Tineo 70 C1 Asturias, N Spain
Tingis | **MM** see Tanger
Tingo María 38 C3 Huánuco, C Peru
Tingréla see Tengréla
Tinhosa Grande 54 E2 island N Sao Tome and Principe
Tinhosa Pequena 54 E1 island N Sao Tome and Principe
Tinian 122 B1 island S Northern Mariana Islands
Tínos 83 D6 anc. Tenos. Island Kykládes, Greece, Aegean Sea
Tínos 83 D6 Tínos, Kykládes, Greece, Aegean Sea
Tip 79 E6 Papua, E Indonesia
Tipitapa 30 D3 Managua, W Nicaragua
Tip Top Mountain 16 C4 mountain Ontario, S Canada
Tirana see Tiranë
Tiranë 79 C6 var. Tirana. Country capital (Albania) Tiranë, C Albania
Tiraspol 86 D4 Rus. Tiraspol'. E Moldova
Tiree 66 B3 island W Scotland, UK
Tîrgu-Neamţ see Târgu-Neamţ
Tirlemont see Tienen
Tírnavos see Týrnavos
Tirol 73 C7 cultural region Austria/Italy
Tiruchchirāppalli 110 C3 prev. Trichinopoly. Tamil Nādu, SE India
Tiruppattūr 110 C2 Tamil Nādu, SE India
Tisza 81 F1 Ger. Theiss, Rom./Slvn./SCr. Tisa, Rus. Tissa, Ukr. Tysa. River SE Europe see also Tisa
Tiszakécske 77 D7 Bács-Kiskun, C Hungary
Titano, Monte 74 E1 mountain C San Marino
Titicaca, Lake 39 E4 lake Bolivia/Peru
Titose see Chitose
Titu 86 C5 Dâmboviţa, S Romania
Titule 55 D5 Orientale, N Dem. Rep. Congo
Tiverton 67 C7 SW England, UK
Tivoli 74 C4 anc. Tiber. Lazio, C Italy
Tizimín 29 H3 Yucatán, SE Mexico
Tizi Ouzou 49 E1 var. Tizi-Ouzou. N Algeria
Tiznit 48 B3 SW Morocco
Tlaquepaque 28 D4 Jalisco, C Mexico
Tlascala see Tlaxcala
Tlaxcala 29 F4 var. Tlascala, Tlaxcala de Xicohténcatl. Tlaxcala, C Mexico
Tlaxcala de Xicohténcatl see Tlaxcala
Tlemcen 48 D2 var. Tilimsen, Tlemsen. NW Algeria
Tlemsen see Tlemcen
Toamasina 57 G3 var. Tamatave. Toamasina, E Madagascar
Toba, Danau 116 B3 lake Sumatera, W Indonesia
Tobago 33 H5 island NE Trinidad and Tobago
Tobol 92 C4 Kaz. Tobyl. River Kazakhstan/Russian Federation
Tobol'sk 92 C3 Tyumenskaya Oblast', C Russian Federation
Tocantins 41 E3 off. Estado do Tocantins. State C Brazil
Tocantins, Rio 41 F2 river N Brazil
Tocoa 30 D2 Colón, N Honduras
Tocopilla 42 B2 Antofagasta, N Chile
Todi 74 C4 Umbria, C Italy
Todos os Santos, Baía de 41 G3 bay E Brazil
Toetoes Bay 129 B8 bay South Island, NZ
Tofua 123 E4 island Ha'apai Group, C Tonga
Togo 53 E4 French Togoland. Country W Africa
Tokanui 129 B7 Southland, South Island, NZ
Tokar 50 C3 var. Ţawkar. Red Sea, NE Sudan
Tokat 94 D3 Tokat, N Turkey
Tokelau 123 E3 NZ overseas territory W Polynesia
Tokio see Tōkyō
Tokmak 101 G2 Kir. Tokmok. Chuyskaya Oblast', N Kyrgyzstan
Tokmak 87 G4 var. Velykyy Tokmak. Zaporiz'ka Oblast', SE Ukraine
Tokoroa 128 D3 Waikato, North Island, NZ
Tokounou 52 C4 Haute-Guinée, C Guinea
Tokushima 109 C6 var. Tokusima. Tokushima, Shikoku, SW Japan
Tokusima see Tokushima
Tōkyō 108 A1 var. Tokio. Country capital (Japan) Tōkyō, Honshū, S Japan
Tōkyō Bay 108 A2 bay SW Japan
Toledo 70 D3 anc. Toletum. Castilla-La Mancha, C Spain
Toledo 18 D3 Ohio, N USA
Toledo Bend Reservoir 27 G3 reservoir Louisiana/Texas, SW USA
Toliara 57 F4 var. Toliary; prev. Tuléar. Toliara, SW Madagascar
Toliary see Toliara
Tolmin 73 D7 Ger. Tolmein, It. Tolmino. W Slovenia
Tolna 77 C7 Ger. Tolnau. Tolna, S Hungary
Tolosa 71 E1 País Vasco, N Spain
Toluca 29 E4 var. Toluca de Lerdo. México, S Mexico
Toluca de Lerdo see Toluca
Tol'yatti 89 C6 prev. Stavropol'. Samarskaya Oblast', W Russian Federation
Tomah 18 B2 Wisconsin, N USA
Tomakomai 108 D2 Hokkaidō, NE Japan
Tomar 70 B3 Santarém, W Portugal
Tomaschow see Tomaszów Mazowiecki
Tomaszów see Tomaszów Mazowiecki
Tomaszów Lubelski 76 E4 Ger. Tomaschow. Lubelskie, E Poland
Tomaszów Mazowiecka see Tomaszów Mazowiecki
Tomaszów Mazowiecki 76 D4 var. Tomaszów Mazowiecka; prev. Tomaszów, Ger. Tomaschow. Łódzkie, C Poland
Tombigbee River 20 C3 river Alabama/Mississippi, S USA
Tombouctou 53 E3 Eng. Timbuktu. Tombouctou, N Mali
Tombua 56 A2 Port. Porto Alexandre. Namibe, SW Angola
Tomelloso 71 E3 Castilla-La Mancha, C Spain
Tomini, Gulf of 117 E4 var. Teluk Tomini; prev. Teluk Gorontalo. Bay Sulawesi, C Indonesia
Tomini, Teluk see Tomini, Gulf of
Tomsk 92 D4 Tomskaya Oblast', C Russian Federation
Tomur Feng see Pobedy, Pik
Tonga 123 E4 var. Friendly Islands. Country SW Pacific Ocean
Tongatapu 123 E5 island Tongatapu Group, S Tonga
Tonga Trench 121 E3 undersea feature S Pacific Ocean
Tongchuan 106 C4 Shaanxi, C China
Tongeren 65 D6 Fr. Tongres. Limburg, NE Belgium
Tongking, Gulf of 106 B7 Chin. Beibu Wan, Vtn. Vinh Băc Bô. Gulf China/Vietnam
Tongliao 105 G2 Nei Mongol Zizhiqu, N China
Tongshan see Xuzhou
Tongtian He 104 C4 river C China
Tonj 51 B5 Warab, SW Sudan
Tônlé Sap 115 D5 Eng. Great Lake. Lake W Cambodia
Tonopah 25 C6 Nevada, W USA
Tonyezh 85 C7 Rus. Tonezh. Homyel'skaya Voblasts', SE Belarus
Tooele 22 B4 Utah, W USA
Toowoomba 127 E5 Queensland, E Australia
Topeka 23 F4 state capital Kansas, C USA
Topliţa 86 C3 Ger. Töplitz, Hung. Maroshévíz; prev. Topliţa Română, Hung. Oláh-Toplicza, Toplicza. Harghita, C Romania
Topoľčany 77 C6 Hung. Nagytapolcsány. Nitriansky Kraj, SW Slovakia
Topolovgrad 82 D3 prev. Kavakli. Khaskovo, S Bulgaria
Top Springs Roadhouse 124 D3 Northern Territory, N Australia
Torez 87 H3 Donets'ka Oblast', SE Ukraine
Torgau 72 D4 Sachsen, E Germany
Torhout 65 A5 West-Vlaanderen, W Belgium
Torino 74 A2 Eng. Turin. Piemonte, NW Italy
Tornacum see Tournai
Torneälven see Tornionjoki
Torneträsk 62 C3 lake N Sweden
Tornio 62 D4 Swe. Torneå. Lappi, NW Finland
Tornionjoki see Tornionjoki
Tornionjoki 62 D3 var. Torniojoki, Swe. Torneälven. River Finland/Sweden
Toro 70 D2 Castilla-León, N Spain
Toronto 16 D5 Ontario, S Canada
Toros Dağları 94 C4 Eng. Taurus Mountains. Mountain range S Turkey
Torquay 67 C7 SW England, UK
Torrance 24 D2 California, W USA
Torre, Alto da 70 B3 mountain C Portugal
Torre del Greco 75 D5 Campania, S Italy
Torrejón de Ardoz 71 E3 Madrid, C Spain
Torrelavega 70 D1 Cantabria, N Spain
Torrens, Lake 127 A6 salt lake South Australia
Torrent 71 F3 var. Torrent de l'Horta, Cas. Torrente. País Valenciano, E Spain
Torrent de l'Horta see Torrent
Torrente see Torrent
Torreón 28 D3 Coahuila de Zaragoza, NE Mexico
Torres Strait 126 C1 strait Australia/PNG
Torres Vedras 70 B3 Lisboa, C Portugal
Torrington 22 D3 Wyoming, C USA
Tórshavn 61 F5 Dan. Thorshavn. Dependent territory capital (Faeroe Islands) N Faeroe Islands
To'rtko'l 100 D2 var. Türtkül, Rus. Turtkul'; prev. Petroaleksandrovsk. Qoraqalpoghiston Respublikasi, W Uzbekistan
Tortoise Islands see Galapagos Islands
Tortosa 71 F2 anc. Dertosa. Cataluña, E Spain
Tortue, Montagne 37 H3 mountain range C French Guiana
Tortuga, Isla see La Tortuga, Isla
Toruń 76 C3 Ger. Thorn. Kujawskie-pomorskie, C Poland
Tõrva 84 D3 Ger. Törwa. Valgamaa, S Estonia
Torzhok 88 B4 Tverskaya Oblast', W Russian Federation
Tosa-wan 109 B7 bay SW Japan
Toscana 74 B3 Eng. Tuscany. Cultural region C Italy
Toscano, Archipelago 74 B4 Eng. Tuscan Archipelago. Island group C Italy
Toshkent 101 E2 Eng./Rus. Tashkent. Country capital (Uzbekistan) Toshkent Wiloyati, E Uzbekistan
Totana 71 E4 Murcia, SE Spain
Tot'ma see Sukhona
Totness 37 G3 Coronie, N Suriname
Tottori 109 B6 Tottori, Honshū, SW Japan
Touâjîl 52 C2 Tiris Zemmour, N Mauritania
Touggourt 49 E2 NE Algeria
Toukoto 52 C3 Kayes, W Mali
Toul 68 D3 Meurthe-et-Moselle, NE France
Toulon 69 D6 anc. Telo Martius, Tilio Martius. Var, SE France
Toulouse 69 B6 anc. Tolosa. Haute-Garonne, S France
Toungoo 114 B4 Pegu, C Myanmar
Touraine 68 B4 cultural region C France
Tourcoing 68 C2 Nord, N France
Tournai 65 A6 var. Tournay, Dut. Doornik; anc. Tornacum. Hainaut, SW Belgium
Tournay see Tournai
Tours 68 B4 anc. Caesarodunum, Turoni. Indre-et-Loire, C France
Tovarkovskiy 89 B5 Tul'skaya Oblast', W Russian Federation
Tower Island see Genovesa, Isla
Townsville 126 D3 Queensland, NE Australia
Towraghoudī 100 D4 Herāt, NW Afghanistan
Towson 19 F4 Maryland, NE USA
Towuti, Danau 117 E4 Dut. Towoeti Meer. Lake Sulawesi, C Indonesia
Toyama 109 C5 Toyama, Honshū, SW Japan
Toyama-wan 109 B5 bay W Japan
Toyota 109 C6 Aichi, Honshū, SW Japan
Tozeur 49 E2 var. Tawzar. W Tunisia
Trâblous see Tripoli
Trabzon 95 E2 Eng. Trebizond; anc. Trapezus. Trabzon, NE Turkey
Traiectum Tungorum see Maastricht
Traietum ad Mosam see Maastricht
Traiskirchen 73 E6 Niederösterreich, NE Austria
Trakai 85 C5 Ger. Traken, Pol. Troki. Trakai, SE Lithuania
Tralee 67 A6 Ir. Trá Lí. SW Ireland
Trá Lí see Tralee
Tralles see Aydın
Trang 115 C7 Trang, S Thailand
Transantarctic Mountains 132 B3 mountain range Antarctica
Transsylvanische Alpen see Carpaţii Meridionali
Transylvania 86 B4 Eng. Ardeal, Transilvania, Ger. Siebenbürgen, Hung. Erdély. Cultural region NW Romania
Transylvanian Alps see Carpaţii Meridionali
Trapani 75 B7 anc. Drepanum. Sicilia, Italy, C Mediterranean Sea
Trâpeăng Vêng 115 D5 Kâmpóng Thum, C Cambodia
Traralgon 127 C7 Victoria, SE Australia
Trasimeno, Lago C4 Eng. Lake of Perugia, Ger. Trasimenischersee. Lake C Italy
Traverse City 18 C2 Michigan, N USA
Tra Vinh 115 D6 var. Phu Vinh. Tra Vinh, S Vietnam
Travis, Lake 27 F3 reservoir Texas, SW USA
Travnik 78 C4 Federacija Bosna I Hercegovina, C Bosnia and Herzegovina
Trbovlje 73 E7 Ger. Trifail. C Slovenia
Třebíč 77 B5 Ger. Trebitsch. Jihlavský Kraj, C Czech Republic
Trebinje 79 C5 Republika Srpska, S Bosnia and Herzegovina
Trebišov 77 D6 Hung. Tőketerebes. Košický Kraj, E Slovakia
Trélazé 68 B4 Maine-et-Loire, NW France
Trelew 43 C6 Chubut, SE Argentina
Tremelo 65 C5 Vlaams Brabant, C Belgium
Trenčín 77 C5 Ger. Trentschin, Hung. Trencsén. Trenčiansky Kraj, W Slovakia
Trenque Lauquen 42 C4 Buenos Aires, E Argentina
Trento 74 C2 Eng. Trent, Ger. Trient; anc. Tridentum. Trentino-Alto Adige, N Italy
Trenton 19 F4 state capital New Jersey, NE USA
Tres Arroyos 43 D5 Buenos Aires, E Argentina
Treskavica 78 C4 mountain range SE Bosnia and Herzegovina
Tres Tabernae see Saverne
Treviso 74 C2 anc. Tarvisium. Veneto, NE Italy
Trichūr 110 C3 var. Thrissur. Kerala, SW India
Trier 73 A5 Eng. Treves, Fr. Trèves; anc. Augusta Treverorum. Rheinland-Pfalz, SW Germany
Triesen 72 E2 SW Liechtenstein
Triesenberg 94 E2 SW Liechtenstein
Trieste 74 D2 Slvn. Trst. Friuli-Venezia Giulia, NE Italy
Tríkala 82 B4 prev. Trikkala. Thessalía, C Greece
Trincomalee 110 D3 var. Trinkomali. Eastern Province, NE Sri Lanka
Trindade, Ilha da 45 C5 island Brazil, W Atlantic Ocean
Trinidad 33 H5 island C Trinidad and Tobago
Trinidad 39 F3 Beni, N Bolivia
Trinidad 22 D5 Colorado, C USA
Trinidad 42 D4 Flores, S Uruguay
Trinidad and Tobago 33 H5 Country SE West Indies
Trinité, Montagnes de la 37 H3 mountain range C French Guiana
Trinity River 27 G3 river Texas, SW USA
Trinkomali see Trincomalee
Tripoli 96 B4 var. Tarābulus, Ţarābulus ash Shām, Trâblous; anc. Tripolis. N Lebanon
Tripoli see Ţarābulus
Trípoli 83 B6 prev. Trípolis. Pelopónnisos, S Greece
Tripolis see Tripoli
Tristan da Cunha 47 B7 dependency of Saint Helena SE Atlantic Ocean
Triton Island 106 B7 island S Paracel Islands
Trivandrum 110 C3 var. Thiruvanathapuram. Kerala, SW India
Trnava 77 C6 Ger. Tyrnau, Hung. Nagyszombat. Trnavský Kraj, W Slovakia
Trogir 78 B4 It. Traù. Split-Dalmacija, S Croatia
Troglav 78 B4 mountain Bosnia and Herzegovina/Croatia
Trois-Rivières 17 E4 Québec, SE Canada
Trollhättan 63 B6 Västra Götaland, S Sweden
Tromsø 62 C2 Fin. Tromssa. Troms, N Norway
Trondheim 62 B4 Ger. Drontheim; prev. Nidaros, Trondhjem. Sør-Trøndelag, S Norway
Trondheimsfjorden 62 B4 fjord S Norway
Troódos 80 C5 var. Troodos Mountains. Mountain range C Cyprus
Troodos Mountains see Troódos
Troy 20 D3 Alabama, S USA
Troy 19 F3 New York, NE USA
Troyan 82 C2 Lovech, N Bulgaria
Troyes 68 D3 anc. Augustobona Tricassium. Aube, N France
Trstenik 78 E4 Serbia, C Serbia and Montenegro (Yugo.)
Trujillo 30 D2 Colón, NE Honduras
Trujillo 70 C3 Extremadura, W Spain
Trujillo 38 B3 La Libertad, NW Peru
Truk Islands see Chuuk Islands
Trŭn 82 B2 Pernik, W Bulgaria
Truro 17 F4 Nova Scotia, SE Canada
Truro 67 C7 SW England, UK
Trzcianka 76 B3 Ger. Schönlanke. Wielkopolskie, C Poland
Trzebnica 76 C4 Ger. Trebnitz. Dolnośląskie, SW Poland
Tsalka 95 F2 S Georgia
Tsamkong see Zhanjiang
Tsangpo see Brahmaputra
Tsarevo 82 E2 prev. Michurin. Burgas, E Bulgaria
Tsaritsyn see Volgograd
Tsefat see Zefat
Tsetserleg 104 D2 Arhangay, C Mongolia
Tsevat see Zefat
Tshela 55 B6 Bas-Zaïre, W Dem. Rep. Congo
Tshikapa 55 C7 Kasai Occidental, SW Dem. Rep. Congo
Tshuapa 55 D6 river C Dem. Rep. Congo
Tshwane see Pretoria
Tsinan see Jinan
Tsing Hai see Qinghai Hu
Tsingtao see Qingdao
Tsingtau see Qingdao
Tsinkiang see Quanzhou
Tsintao see Qingdao
Tsitsihar see Qiqihar
Tsu 109 C6 var. Tu. Mie, Honshū, SW Japan
Tsugaru-kaikyō 108 C3 strait N Japan
Tsumeb 56 B3 Otjikoto, N Namibia
Tsuruga 109 C6 var. Turuga. Fukui, Honshū, SW Japan
Tsuruoka 108 D4 var. Turuoka. Yamagata, Honshū, C Japan
Tsushima 109 A7 var. Tsushima-tō, Tusima. Island group SW Japan
Tsushima-tō see Tsushima
Tsyerakhowka 85 D8 Rus. Terekhovka. Homyel'skaya Voblasts', SE Belarus
Tsyurupyns'k 87 E4 Rus. Tsyurupinsk. Khersons'ka Oblast', S Ukraine
Tu see Tsu
Tuamotu Fracture Zone 121 H3 tectonic feature E Pacific Ocean
Tuamotu, Îles 123 H4 var. Archipel des Tuamotu, Dangerous Archipelago, Tuamotu Islands. Island group N French Polynesia

Tuamotu Islands *see* Tuamotu, Îles
Tuapi *31 E2* Región Autónoma Atlántico Norte, NE Nicaragua
Tuapse *89 A7* Krasnodarskiy Kray, SW Russian Federation
Tuba City *26 B1* Arizona, SW USA
Tubbergen *64 E3* Overijssel, E Netherlands
Tubize *65 B6 Dut.* Tubeke. Wallon Brabant, C Belgium
Tubmanburg *52 C5* NW Liberia
Ţubruq *49 H2 Eng.* Tobruk, *It.* Tobruch. NE Libya
Tubuai Islands *see* Australes, Îles
Tucker's Town *20 B5* E Bermuda
Tucson *26 B3* Arizona, SW USA
Tucumán *see* San Miguel de Tucumán
Tucumcari *27 E2* New Mexico, SW USA
Tucupita *37 E2* Delta Amacuro, NE Venezuela
Tucuruí, Represa de *41 F2 reservoir* NE Brazil
Tudela *71 E2 Basq.* Tutera; *anc.* Tutela. Navarra, N Spain
Tudmur *96 C3 var.* Tadmur, Tamar, *Gk.* Palmyra; *Bibl.* Tadmor. Ḩimş, C Syria
Tuguegarao *117 E1* Luzon, N Philippines
Tuktoyaktuk *15 E3* Northwest Territories, NW Canada
Tukums *84 C3 Ger.* Tuckum. Tukums, W Latvia
Tula *89 B5* Tul'skaya Oblast', W Russian Federation
Tulancingo *29 E4* Hidalgo, C Mexico
Tulare Lake Bed *25 C7 salt flat* California, W USA
Tulcán *38 B1* Carchi, N Ecuador
Tulcea *86 D5* Tulcea, E Romania
Tul'chyn *86 D3 Rus.* Tul'chin. Vinnyts'ka Oblast', C Ukraine
Tuléar *see* Toliara
Tulia *27 E2* Texas, SW USA
Tulle *69 C5 anc.* Tutela. Corrèze, C France
Tulln *73 E6 var.* Oberhollabrunn. Niederösterreich, NE Austria
Tully *126 D3* Queensland, NE Australia
Tulsa *27 G1* Oklahoma, C USA
Tuluá *36 B3* Valle del Cauca, W Colombia
Tulun *93 E4* Irkutskaya Oblast', S Russian Federation
Tumaco *36 A4* Nariño, SW Colombia
Tumba, Lac *see* Ntomba, Lac
Tumbes *38 A2* Tumbes, NW Peru
Tumkūr *132 C2* Karnātaka, W India
Tumuc Humac Mountains *41 E1 var.* Serra Tumucumaque. *Mountain range* N South America
Tunduru *51 C8* Ruvuma, S Tanzania
Tundzha *82 D3 Turk.* Tunca Nehri. *River* Bulgaria/Turkey *see also* Tunca Nehri
Tungabhadra Reservoir *110 C2 lake* S India
Tungaru *123 E2 prev.* Gilbert Islands. *Island group* W Kiribati
T'ung-shan *see* Xuzhou
Tungsten *14 D4* Northwest Territories, W Canada
Tung-t'ing Hu *see* Dongting Hu
Tunis *49 E1 var.* Tūnis. *Country capital* (Tunisia) NE Tunisia
Tūnis *see* Tunis
Tunis, Golfe de *80 D3 Ar.* Khalīj Tūnis. *Gulf* NE Tunisia
Tunisia *49 F2 Ar.* Al Jumhūrīyah at Tūnisīyah, *Fr.* République Tunisienne. *Country* N Africa
Tunja *36 B3* Boyacá, C Colombia
Tuong Buong *see* T,ong Đ,ong
Tupelo *20 C2* Mississippi, S USA
Tupiza *39 G5* Potosí, S Bolivia
Turabah *99 B5* Makkah, W Saudi Arabia
Turangi *128 D4* Waikato, North Island, NZ
Turan Lowland *100 C2 var.* Turan Plain, *Kaz.* Turan Oypaty, *Rus.* Turanskaya Nizmennost', *Turk.* Turan Pesligi, *Uzb.* Turon Pasttekisligi. *Plain* C Asia
Turan Oypaty *see* Turan Lowland
Turan Pesligi *see* Turan Lowland
Turan Plain *see* Turan Lowland
Turanskaya Nizmennost' *see* Turan Lowland
Ţurayf *98 A3* Al Ḩudūd ash Shamālīyah, NW Saudi Arabia
Turbat *112 A3* Baluchistān, SW Pakistan
Turda *86 B4 Ger.* Thorenburg, *Hung.* Torda. Cluj, NW Romania
Turek *76 C3* Wielkopolskie, C Poland
Turfan *see* Turpan
Turin *see* Torino
Turkana, Lake *89 C6 var.* Lake Rudolf. *Lake* N Kenya
Turkish Republic of Northern Cyprus *80 D5 Ger.* Dependent territory, *disputed territory.* Cyprus
Turkestan *92 B5 Kaz.* Türkistan. Yuzhnyy Kazakhstan, S Kazakhstan
Turkey *94 B3 Turk.* Türkiye Cumhuriyeti. *Country* SW Asia
Türkmenabat *100 D3 prev.* Chardzhev, Chardzhou, Chardzhui, Leninsk-Turkmenski, *Turkm.* Chärjew. Lebapskiy Velayat, E Turkmenistan
Turkmen Aylagy *100 B2 Rus.* Turkmenskiy Zaliv. *Lake gulf* W Turkmenistan
Turkmenbashi *see* Türkmenbaşy
Türkmenbaşy *100 B2 var.* Turkmenbashi; *prev.* Krasnovodsk. Balkanskiy Velayat, W Turkmenistan
Türkmenbaşy Aylagy *100 A2 prev.* Krasnovodskiy Zaliv, Krasnowodsk Aylagy. *Lake gulf* W Turkmenistan
Turkmenistan *100 B2 prev.* Turkmenskaya Soviet Socialist Republic. *Country* C Asia
Turkmenskiy Zaliv *see* Türkmen Aylagy
Turks and Caicos Islands *33 E2 UK dependent territory* N West Indies
Turlock *25 B6* California, W USA
Turnagain, Cape *128 D4 headland* North Island, NZ
Turnhout *65 C5* Antwerpen, N Belgium
Turnov *76 B4 Ger.* Turnau. Liberecký Kraj, N Czech Republic
Turnu Măgurele *86 B5 var.* Turnu-Măgurele. Teleorman, S Romania
Turon Pasttekisligi *see* Turan Lowland
Turpan *104 C3 var.* Turfan. Xinjiang Uygur Zizhiqu, NW China
Turpan Pendi *104 C3 Eng.* Turpan Depression. *Depression* NW China
Türtkül *see* To'rtko'l
Turuga *see* Tsuruga
Turuoka *see* Tsuruoka
Tuscaloosa *20 C2* Alabama, S USA
Tusima *see* Tsushima
Tuticorin *110 C3* Tamil Nādu, SE India
Tutrakan *82 D1* Silistra, NE Bulgaria
Tutuila *123 F4 island* W American Samoa
Tuvalu *123 E3 prev.* Ellice Islands. *Country* SW Pacific Ocean
Ţuwayq, Jabal *99 C5 mountain range* C Saudi Arabia
Tuxpán *29 F4 var.* Tuxpán de Rodríguez Cano. Veracruz-Llave, E Mexico
Tuxpan *28 D4* Jalisco, C Mexico
Tuxpan *28 D4* Nayarit, C Mexico
Tuxpán de Rodríguez Cano *see* Tuxpán
Tuxtepec *29 F4 var.* San Juan Bautista Tuxtepec. Oaxaca, S Mexico
Tuxtla *29 G5 var.* Tuxtla Gutiérrez. Chiapas, SE Mexico
Tuxtla *see* San Andrés Tuxtla
Tuxtla Gutiérrez *see* Tuxtla
Tuy Hoa *115 E5* Phu Yên, S Vietnam
Tuz Gölü *94 C3 lake* C Turkey
Tuzla *78 C3* Federacija Bosna I Hercegovina, NE Bosnia and Herzegovina
Tver' *88 B4 prev.* Kalinin. Tverskaya Oblast', W Russian Federation
Tverya *see* Teverya
Twin Falls *24 D4* Idaho, NW USA
Tychy *77 D5 Ger.* Tichau. Śląskie, S Poland
Tyler *27 G3* Texas, SW USA
Tympáki *83 C8 var.* Timbaki; *prev.* Timbákion. Kríti, Greece, E Mediterranean Sea
Tynda *93 F4* Amurskaya Oblast', SE Russian Federation
Tyne *66 D4 river* N England, UK
Tyôsi *see* Chōshi
Tyre *see* Soûr
Týrnavos *82 B4 var.* Tírnavos. Thessalía, C Greece
Tyrrhenian Sea *75 B6 It.* Mare Tirreno. *Sea* N Mediterranean Sea
Tyumen' *92 C3* Tyumenskaya Oblast', C Russian Federation
Tyup *101 G2 Kir.* Tüp. Issyk-Kul'skaya Oblast', NE Kyrgyzstan
Tywyn *67 C6* W Wales, UK
Tzekung *see* Zigong
T,ong Đ,ong *114 D4 var.* Tuong Buong. Nghê An, N Vietnam

U

Uanle Uen *see* Wanlaweyn
Uaupés, Rio *see* Vaupés, Río
Ubangi *55 C5 Fr.* Oubangui. *River* C Africa
Ubangi-Shari *see* Central African Republic
Ube *109 B7* Yamaguchi, Honshū, SW Japan
Ubeda *71 E4* Andalucía, S Spain
Uberaba *41 F4* Minas Gerais, SE Brazil
Uberlândia *41 F4* Minas Gerais, SE Brazil
Ubol Rajadhani *see* Ubon Ratchathani
Ubol Ratchathani *see* Ubon Ratchathani
Ubon Ratchathani *115 D5 var.* Muang Ubon, Ubol Rajadhani, Ubol Ratchathani, Udon Ratchathani. Ubon Ratchathani, E Thailand
Ubrique *70 D5* Andalucía, S Spain
Ucayali, Río *38 D3 river* C Peru
Uchiura-wan *108 D3 bay* NW Pacific Ocean
Uchquduq *100 D2 Rus.* Uchkuduk. Nawoiy Wiloyati, N Uzbekistan
Uchtagan, Peski *see* Uçtagan Gumy
Uçtagan Gumy *100 C2 Rus.* Peski Uchtagan. *Desert* NW Turkmenistan
Udaipur *112 C3 prev.* Oodeypore. Rājasthān, N India
Uddevalla *63 B6* Västra Götaland, S Sweden
Udine *74 D2 anc.* Utina. Friuli-Venezia Giulia, NE Italy
Udintsev Fracture Zone *132 A5 tectonic feature* S Pacific Ocean
Udipi *see* Udupi
Udon Ratchathani *see* Ubon Ratchathani
Udon Thani *114 C4 var.* Ban Mak Khaeng, Udorndhani. Udon Thani, N Thailand
Udorndhani *see* Udon Thani
Udupi *110 B2 var.* Udipi. Karnātaka, SW India
Uele *55 D5 var.* Welle. *River* NE Dem. Rep. Congo
Uelzen *72 C3* Niedersachsen, N Germany
Ufa *89 D6* Respublika Bashkortostan, W Russian Federation
Ugāle *84 C2* Ventspils, NW Latvia
Uganda *51 B6 Country* E Africa
Uglovka *88 B4 var.* Okulovka. Novgorodskaya Oblast', W Russian Federation
Uhuru Peak *see* Kilimanjaro
Uíge *56 B1 Port.* Carmona, Vila Marechal Carmona. Uíge, NW Angola
Uinta Mountains *22 B4 mountain range* Utah, W USA
Uitenhage *56 C5* Eastern Cape, S South Africa
Uithoorn *64 C3* Noord-Holland, C Netherlands
Ujelang Atoll *122 C1 var.* Wujlān. *Atoll* Ralik Chain, W Marshall Islands
Ujungpandang *117 E4 var.* Macassar, Makassar; *prev.* Makasar. Sulawesi, C Indonesia
Ujung Salang *see* Phuket
Ukhta *92 C3* Respublika Komi, NW Russian Federation
Ukiah *25 B5* California, W USA
Ukmergė *84 C4 Pol.* Wiłkomierz. Ukmergė, C Lithuania
Ukraine *86 C2 Ukr.* Ukrayina; *prev.* Ukrainian Soviet Socialist Republic, Ukrainskaya S.S.R. *Country* SE Europe
Ulaanbaatar *105 E2 Eng.* Ulan Bator. *Country capital* (Mongolia) Töv, C Mongolia
Ulaangom *104 C2* Uvs, NW Mongolia
Ulan Bator *see* Ulaanbaatar
Ulanhad *see* Chifeng
Ulan-Ude *93 E4 prev.* Verkhneudinsk. Respublika Buryatiya, S Russian Federation
Ulft *64 E4* Gelderland, E Netherlands
Ullapool *66 C3* N Scotland, UK
Ulm *73 B6* Baden-Württemberg, S Germany
Ulsan *107 E4 Jap.* Urusan. SE South Korea
Ulster *67 B5 cultural region* N Ireland
Ulungur Hu *104 B2 lake* NW China
Uluru *125 D5 var.* Ayers Rock. *Rocky outcrop* Northern Territory, C Australia
Ulyanivka *87 E3 Rus.* Ul'yanovka. Kirovohrads'ka Oblast', C Ukraine
Ul'yanovsk *89 C5 prev.* Simbirsk. Ul'yanovskaya Oblast', W Russian Federation
Uman' *87 E3 Rus.* Uman. Cherkas'ka Oblast', C Ukraine
Umán *29 H3* Yucatán, SE Mexico
Umanak *see* Uummannaq
Umanaq *see* Uummannaq
Umbro-Marchigiano, Appennino *74 C3 Eng.* Umbrian-Machigian Mountains. *Mountain range* C Italy
Umeå *62 C4* Västerbotten, N Sweden
Umeälven *62 C4 river* N Sweden
Umiat *14 D2* Alaska, USA
Umm Buru *50 A4* Western Darfur, W Sudan
Umm Durmān *see* Omdurman
Umm Ruwaba *50 C4 var.* Umm Ruwābah, Um Ruwāba. Northern Kordofan, C Sudan
Umm Ruwābah *see* Umm Ruwaba
Umnak Island *14 A3 island* Aleutian Islands, Alaska, USA
Um Ruwāba *see* Umm Ruwaba
Umtali *see* Mutare
Umtata *56 D5* Eastern Cape, SE South Africa
Una *78 B3 river* Bosnia and Herzegovina/Croatia
Unac *78 B3 river* W Bosnia and Herzegovina
Unalaska Island *14 A3 island* Aleutian Islands, Alaska, USA
'Unayzah *98 B4 var.* Anaiza. Al Qaşīm, C Saudi Arabia
Uncía *39 F4* Potosí, C Bolivia
Uncompahgre Peak *22 B5 mountain* Colorado, C USA
Ungarisches Erzgebirge *see* Slovenské rudohorie
Ungava Bay *17 E1 bay* Québec, E Canada
Ungava, Péninsule d' *16 D1 peninsula* Québec, SE Canada
Ungheni *86 D3 Rus.* Ungeny. W Moldova
Üngüz Angyrsyndaky Garagum *122 C2 Rus.* Zaunguzskiye Garagumy. *Desert* N Turkmenistan
Unimak Island *14 B3 island* Aleutian Islands, Alaska, USA
Union *21 E1* South Carolina, SE USA
Union City Tennessee, S USA
United Arab Emirates *99 C5 Ar.* Al Imārāt al 'Arabīyah al Muttaḩidah, *abbrev.* UAE; *prev.* Trucial States. *Country* SW Asia
United Kingdom *67 B5 abbrev.* UK. *Country* NW Europe
United States of America *13 B5 var.* America, The States, *abbrev.* U.S., USA. *Country*
Unst *66 D1 island* NE Scotland, UK
Ünye *94 D2* Ordu, W Turkey
Upala *30 D4* Alajuela, NW Costa Rica
Upata *37 E2* Bolívar, E Venezuela
Upemba, Lac *55 D7 lake* SE Dem. Rep. Congo
Upernavik *60 C2 var.* Upernivik. C Greenland
Upernivik *see* Upernavik
Upington *56 C4* Northern Cape, W South Africa
Upolu *123 F4 island* SE Samoa
Upper Klamath Lake *24 A4 lake* Oregon, NW USA
Upper Lough Erne *67 A5 lake* SW Northern Ireland, UK
Upper Red Lake *23 F1 lake* Minnesota, N USA
Uppsala *63 C6* Uppsala, C Sweden
Ural *90 B3 Kaz.* Zayyq. *River* Kazakhstan/Russian Federation
Ural Mountains *see* Ural'skiye Gory
Ural'sk *92 B3 Kaz.* Oral. Zapadnyy Kazakhstan, NW Kazakhstan
Ural'skiye Gory *92 C3 var.* Ural'skiy Khrebet, *Eng.* Ural Mountains. *Mountain range* Kazakhstan/Russian Federation
Ural'skiy Khrebet *see* Ural'skiye Gory
Uraricoera *40 D1* Roraima, N Brazil
Urbandale *23 F3* Iowa, C USA
Uren' *89 C5* Nizhegorodskaya Oblast', W Russian Federation
Urganch *100 D2 Rus.* Urgench; *prev.* Novo-Urgench. Khorazm Wiloyati, W Uzbekistan
Urgut *101 E3* Samarqand Wiloyati, C Uzbekistan
Uroševac *79 D5 Alb.* Ferizaj. Serbia, S Serbia and Montenegro (Yugo.)
Üroteppa *101 E2 Rus.* Ura-Tyube. NW Tajikistan
Uruapan *29 E4 var.* Uruapan del Progreso. Michoacán de Ocampo, SW Mexico
Uruapan del Progreso *see* Uruapan
Uruguai, Rio *see* Uruguay
Uruguay *42 D4 prev.* La Banda Oriental. *Country* E South America
Uruguay *42 D3 var.* Rio Uruguai, Río Uruguay. *River* E South America
Uruguay, Río *see* Uruguay
Urumchi *see* Ürümqi
Urumqi *see* Ürümqi
Ürümqi *104 C3 var.* Tihwa, Urumchi, Urumqi, Urumtsi, Wu-lu-k'o-mu-shi, Wu-lu-mu-ch'i; *prev.* Ti-hua. *Autonomous region capital* Xinjiang Uygur Zizhiqu, NW China
Urumtsi *see* Ürümqi
Urup, Ostrov *93 H4 island* Kuril'skiye Ostrova, SE Russian Federation
Urziceni *86 C5* Ialomiţa, SE Romania
Usa *88 E3 river* NW Russian Federation
Uşak *94 B3 prev.* Ushak. Uşak, W Turkey
Ushuaia *43 B8* Tierra del Fuego, S Argentina
Usinsk *88 E3* Respublika Komi, NW Russian Federation
Üsküb *see* Skopje
Üsküp *see* Skopje
Usmas Ezers *84 B3 lake* NW Latvia
Usol'ye-Sibirskoye *93 E4* Irkutskaya Oblast', C Russian Federation
Ussel *69 C5* Corrèze, C France
Ussuriysk *93 G5 prev.* Nikol'sk, Nikol'sk-Ussuriyskiy, Voroshilov. Primorskiy Kray, SE Russian Federation
Ustica, Isola d' *75 B6 island* S Italy
Ust'-Ilimsk *93 E4* Irkutskaya Oblast', C Russian Federation
Ústí nad Labem *76 A4 Ger.* Aussig. Ústecký Kraj, NW Czech Republic
Ustka *76 C2 Ger.* Stolpmünde. Pomorskie, N Poland
Ust'-Kamchatsk *93 H2* Kamchatskaya Oblast', E Russian Federation
Ust'-Kamenogorsk *92 D5 Kaz.* Öskemen. Vostochnyy Kazakhstan, E Kazakhstan
Ust'-Kut *93 E4* Irkutskaya Oblast', C Russian Federation
Ust'-Olenëk *93 E3* Respublika Sakha (Yakutiya), NE Russian Federation
Ustrzyki Dolne *77 E5* Podkarpackie, SE Poland
Ust Urt *see* Ustyurt Plateau
Ustyurt Plateau *100 B1 var.* Ust Urt, *Uzb.* Ustyurt Platosi. *Plateau* Kazakhstan/Uzbekistan
Ustyurt Platosi *see* Ustyurt Plateau
Usulután *30 C3* Usulután, SE El Salvador
Usumacinta, Río *30 B1 river* Guatemala/Mexico
Utah *26 A1 off.* State of Utah; also known as Beehive State, Mormon State. *State* W USA
Utah Lake *22 B4 lake* Utah, W USA
Utena *84 C4* Utena, E Lithuania
Utica *19 F3* New York, NE USA
Utrecht *64 C4 Lat.* Trajectum ad Rhenum. Utrecht C Netherlands
Utsunomiya *109 D5 var.* Utunomiya. Tochigi, Honshū, S Japan
Uttaranchal *113 E2* Admin. region *state* N India
Uttar Pradesh *113 E3 prev.* United Provinces, United Provinces of Agra and Oudh. *State* N India
Utunomiya *see* Utsunomiya
Uulu *84 D2* Pärnumaa, SW Estonia
Uummannaq *60 C3 var.* Umanak, Umanaq. C Greenland
Uummannarsuaq *see* Nunap Isua
Uvalde *27 F4* Texas, SW USA
Uvaravichy *85 D7 Rus.* Uvarovichi. Homyel'skaya Voblasts', SE Belarus
Uvea, Île *123 E4 island* N Wallis and Futuna
Uvs Nuur *104 C1 var.* Ozero Ubsu-Nur. *Lake* Mongolia/Russian Federation
'Uwaynāt, Jabal al *88 A3 var.* Jebel Uweinat. *Mountain* Libya/Sudan
Uyo *53 G5* Akwa Ibom, S Nigeria
Uyuni *39 F5* Potosí, W Bolivia
Uzbekistan *100 D2 Country* C Asia
Uzhhorod *86 B2 Rus.* Uzhgorod; *prev.* Ungvár. Zakarpats'ka Oblast', W Ukraine
Užice *78 D4 prev.* Titovo Užice. Serbia, W Serbia and Montenegro (Yugo.)

V

Vaal *56 D4 river* C South Africa
Vaals *65 D6* Limburg, SE Netherlands
Vaasa *63 D5 Swe.* Vasa; *prev.* Nikolainkaupunki. Länsi-Suomi, W Finland
Vaassen *64 D3* Gelderland, E Netherlands
Vác *77 C6 Ger.* Waitzen. Pest, N Hungary
Vadodara *112 C4 prev.* Baroda. Gujarāt, W India
Vaduz *72 E2 country capital* (Liechtenstein) W Liechtenstein
Váh *77 C5 Ger.* Waag, *Hung.* Vág. *River* W Slovakia
Väinameri *84 C2 prev.* Muhu Väin, *Ger.* Moon-Sund. *Sea* E Baltic Sea
Valachia *see* Wallachia
Valday *88 B4* Novgorodskaya Oblast', W Russian Federation
Valdecañas, Embalse de *70 D3 reservoir* W Spain
Valdepeñas *71 E4* Castilla-La Mancha, C Spain
Valdés, Península *43 C6 peninsula* SE Argentina
Valdez *14 C3* Alaska, USA
Valdia *see* Weldiya
Valdivia *43 B5* Los Lagos, C Chile
Val-d'Or *16 D4* Québec, SE Canada
Valdosta *21 E3* Georgia, SE USA
Valence *69 D5 anc.* Valentia, Valentia Julia, Ventia. Drôme, E France
Valencia *24 D1* California, W USA
Valencia *36 D1* Carabobo, N Venezuela
Valencia *71 F3* País Valenciano, E Spain
Valencia, Golfo de *71 F3 var.* Gulf of Valencia. *Gulf* E Spain
Valencia, Gulf of *see* Valencia, Golfo de
Valenciennes *90 D2* Nord, N France
Valera *36 C2* Trujillo, NW Venezuela
Valga *84 D3 Ger.* Walk, *Latv.* Valka. Valgamaa, S Estonia
Valira *69 A8 river* Andorra/Spain
Valjevo *78 C4* Serbia, W Serbia and Montenegro (Yugo.)
Valjok *see* Válljohka
Valka *84 D3 Ger.* Walk. Valka, N Latvia
Valkenswaard *65 D5* Noord-Brabant, S Netherlands
Valladolid *70 D2* Castilla-León, NW Spain
Valladolid *29 H3* Yucatán, SE Mexico
Vall d'Uxó *71 F3* País Valenciano, E Spain
Valle de La Pascua *36 D2* Guárico, N Venezuela
Valledupar *36 B1* Cesar, N Colombia
Vallejo *25 B6* California, W USA
Vallenar *42 B3* Atacama, N Chile
Valletta *75 C8 prev.* Valetta. *Country capital* (Malta) E Malta
Valley City *23 E2* North Dakota, N USA
Válljohka *62 D2 var.* Valjok. Finnmark, N Norway
Valls *71 G2* Cataluña, NE Spain
Valmiera *84 D3 Est.* Volmari, *Ger.* Wolmar. Valmiera, N Latvia
Valozhyn *85 C5 Pol.* Wołożyn, *Rus.* Volozhin. Minskaya Voblasts', C Belarus
Valparaiso *18 C3* Indiana, N USA
Valparaíso *42 B4* Valparaíso, C Chile
Valverde del Camino *70 C4* Andalucía, S Spain
Van *95 F3* Van, E Turkey
Vanadzor *95 F2 prev.* Kirovakan. N Armenia
Vancouver *14 D5* British Columbia, SW Canada
Vancouver *24 B3* Washington, NW USA
Vancouver Island *14 D5 island* British Columbia, SW Canada
Van Diemen Gulf *124 D2 gulf* Northern Territory, N Australia
Vänern *63 B6 Eng.* Lake Vaner; *prev.* Lake Vener. *Lake* S Sweden
Vangaindrano *57 G4* Fianarantsoa, SE Madagascar
Van Gölü *95 F3 Eng.* Lake Van; *anc.* Thospitis. *Salt lake* E Turkey
Van Horn *26 D3* Texas, SW USA
Van, Lake *see* Van Gölü
Vannes *68 A3 anc.* Dariorigum. Morbihan, NW France
Vantaa *63 D6 Swe.* Vanda. Etelä-Suomi, S Finland
Vanua Levu *123 E4 island* N Fiji
Vanuatu *122 C4 prev.* New Hebrides. *Country* SW Pacific Ocean
Van Wert *18 C4* Ohio, N USA
Varakļani *84 D4* Madona, C Latvia
Vārānasi *113 E3 prev.* Banaras, Benares, *hist.* Kasi. Uttar Pradesh, N India
Varangerfjorden *62 E2 fjord* N Norway
Varangerhalvøya *62 D2 peninsula* N Norway
Varannó *see* Vranov nad Topl'ou
Varaždin *78 B2 Ger.* Warasdin, *Hung.* Varasd. Varaždin, N Croatia
Varberg *63 B7* Halland, S Sweden
Vardar *79 E6 Gk.* Axiós. *River* FYR Macedonia/Greece *see also* Axiós
Varde *63 A7* Ribe, W Denmark
Varėna *85 B5 Pol.* Orany. Varėna, S Lithuania
Varese *74 B2* Lombardia, N Italy
Vârful Moldoveanu *86 B4 var.* Moldoveanul; *prev.* Vîrful Moldoveanu. *Mountain* C Romania
Varkaus *85 E5* Itä-Suomi, C Finland
Varna *82 E2 prev.* Stalin, *anc.* Odessus. Varna, E Bulgaria
Varnenski Zaliv *82 E2 prev.* Stalinski Zaliv. *Bay* E Bulgaria
Vasilikí *83 A5* Lefkáda, Iónioi Nísoi, Greece, C Mediterranean Sea
Vasilishki *85 B5 Pol.* Wasiliszki, *Rus.* Vasilishki. Hrodzyenskaya Voblasts', W Belarus
Vaslui *86 D4* Vaslui, C Romania
Västerås *63 C6* Västmanland, C Sweden
Vasyl'kiv *87 E2 Rus.* Vasil'kov. Kyyivs'ka Oblast', N Ukraine
Vaté *see* Efate
Vatican City *75 A7 Country* S Europe
Vatnajökull *61 E5 glacier* SE Iceland
Vättern *63 B6 Eng.* Lake Vatter; *prev.* Lake Vetter. *Lake* S Sweden
Vaughn *26 D2* New Mexico, SW USA
Vaupés, Río *36 C4 var.* Rio Uaupés. *River* Brazil/Colombia *see also* Uaupés, Rio
Vava'u Group *123 E4 island group* N Tonga
Vavuniya *110 D3* Northern Province, N Sri Lanka
Vawkavysk *85 B6 Pol.* Wołkowysk, *Rus.* Volkovysk. Hrodzyenskaya Voblasts', W Belarus
Växjö *63 C7 var.* Vexiö. Kronoberg, S Sweden
Vaygach, Ostrov *88 E2 island* NW Russian Federation
Veendam *64 E2* Groningen, NE Netherlands
Veenendaal *64 D4* Utrecht, C Netherlands
Vega *62 B4 island* C Norway
Veisiejai *85 B5* Lazdijai, S Lithuania
Vejer de la Frontera *70 C5* Andalucía, S Spain
Veldhoven *65 D5* Noord-Brabant, S Netherlands
Velebit *78 A3 mountain range* C Croatia
Velenje *73 E7 Ger.* Wöllan. N Slovenia
Veles *79 E6 Turk.* Köprülü. C FYR Macedonia
Velho *see* Porto Velho
Velika Morava *78 D4 var.* Glavn'a Morava, Morava, *Ger.* Grosse Morava. *River* C Serbia and Montenegro (Yugo.)
Velikaya *91 G2 river* NE Russian Federation

Velikiye Luki 88 A4 Pskovskaya Oblast', W Russian Federation
Velikiy Novgorod 88 B4 prev. Novgorod. Novgorodskaya Oblast', W Russian Federation
Veliko Tŭrnovo 82 D2 prev. Tirnovo, Trnovo, Tŭrnovo. Veliko Tŭrnovo, N Bulgaria
Velingrad 82 C3 Pazardzhik, C Bulgaria
Vel'ký Krtíš 77 D6 Banskobystrický Kraj, C Slovakia
Vellore 110 C2 Tamil Nādu, SE India
Velobriga see Viana do Castelo
Velsen see Velsen-Noord
Velsen-Noord 64 C3 var. Velsen. Noord-Holland, W Netherlands
Vel'sk 88 C4 var. Velsk. Arkhangel'skaya Oblast', NW Russian Federation
Velsk see Vel'sk
Velvendós see Velvendós
Velvendós 82 B4 var. Velvendos. Dytikí Makedonía, N Greece
Velykyy Tokmak see Tokmak
Vendôme 68 C4 Loir-et-Cher, C France
Venezia 74 C2 Eng. Venice, Fr. Venise, Ger. Venedig; anc.Venetia. Veneto, NE Italy
Venezuela 36 D2 prev. Estados Unidos de Venezuela, United States of Venezuela. Country N South America
Venezuela, Golfo de 36 C1 Eng. Gulf of Maracaibo, Gulf of Venezuela. Gulf NW Venezuela
Venezuelan Basin 34 B1 undersea feature E Caribbean Sea
Venice see Venezia
Venice 20 C4 Louisiana, S USA
Venice, Gulf of 74 C2 It. Golfo di Venezia, Slvn. Beneški Zaliv. Gulf N Adriatic Sea
Venlo 65 D5 prev. Venloo. Limburg, SE Netherlands
Venta 84 B3 Ger. Windau. River Latvia/Lithuania
Ventimiglia 74 A3 Liguria, NW Italy
Ventspils 84 B2 Ger. Windau. Ventspils, NW Latvia
Vera 42 D3 Santa Fe, C Argentina
Veracruz 29 F4 var. Veracruz Llave. Veracruz-Llave, E Mexico
Veracruz Llave see Veracruz
Vercelli 74 A2 anc. Vercellae. Piemonte, NW Italy
Verdal see Verdalsøra
Verdalsøra 62 B4 var. Verdal. Nord-Trøndelag, C Norway
Verde, Costa 70 D1 coastal region N Spain
Verden 72 B3 Niedersachsen, NW Germany
Veria see Véroia
Verkhoyanskiy Khrebet 93 F3 mountain range NE Russian Federation
Vermillion 23 F3 South Dakota, N USA
Vermont 19 F2 off. State of Vermont; also known as The Green Mountain State. State NE USA
Vernal 22 B4 Utah, W USA
Vernon 27 F2 Texas, SW USA
Véroia 82 B4 var. Veria, Veroia, Turk. Karaferiye. Kentrikí Makedonía, N Greece
Verona 74 C2 Veneto, NE Italy
Vérroia see Véroia
Versailles 90 D1 Yvelines, N France
Verviers 65 D6 Liège, E Belgium
Vesdre 65 D6 river E Belgium
Veselinovo 82 D2 Shumen, NE Bulgaria
Vesoul 68 D4 anc. Vesulium, Vesulum. Haute-Saône, E France
Vesterålen 62 B2 island group N Norway
Vestfjorden 62 C3 fjord C Norway
Vestmannaeyjar 61 E5 Suðurland, S Iceland
Vesuvio 75 D5 Eng. Vesuvius. Volcano S Italy
Veszprém 77 C7 Ger. Veszprim. Veszprém, W Hungary
Vetrino 82 E2 Varna, E Bulgaria
Veurne 65 A5 var. Furnes. West-Vlaanderen, W Belgium
Vexiö see Växjö
Viacha 37 F4 La Paz, W Bolivia
Viana de Castelo see Viana do Castelo
Viana do Castelo 70 B2 var. Viana de Castelo; anc. Velobriga. Viana do Castelo, NW Portugal
Vianen 64 C4 Zuid-Holland, C Netherlands
Viangchan 114 C4 Eng./Fr. Vientiane. Country capital (Laos) C Laos
Viangphoukha 114 C3 var. Vieng Pou Kha. Louang Namtha, N Laos
Viareggio 74 B3 Toscana, C Italy
Viborg 85 A7 Viborg, NW Denmark
Vic 71 G2 var. Vich; anc. Ausa, Vicus Ausonensis. Cataluña, NE Spain
Vich see Vic
Vicenza 74 C2 anc. Vicentia. Veneto, NE Italy
Vichy 69 C5 Allier, C France
Vicksburg 20 B2 Mississippi, S USA
Victoria 80 A5 var. Rabat. Gozo, NW Malta
Victoria 57 H1 country capital (Seychelles) Mahé, SW Seychelles
Victoria 27 G4 Texas, SW USA
Victoria 14 D5 Vancouver Island, British Columbia, SW Canada
Victoria 127 C7 state SE Australia
Victoria Bank see Vitória Seamount
Victoria de Durango see Durango
Victoria de las Tunas see Las Tunas
Victoria Falls 56 C2 waterfall Zambia/Zimbabwe
Victoria Falls 56 C3 Matabeleland North, W Zimbabwe
Victoria Island 15 F3 island Northwest Territories/Nunavut, NW Canada
Victoria, Lake 51 B6 var. Victoria Nyanza. Lake E Africa
Victoria Land 132 C4 physical region Antarctica
Victoria Nyanza see Victoria, Lake

Victoria River 124 D3 river Northern Territory, N Australia
Victorville 25 C7 California, W USA
Vicus Ausonensis see Vic
Vidalia 21 E2 Georgia, SE USA
Vidin 82 B1 anc. Bononia. Vidin, NW Bulgaria
Vidzy 85 C5 Rus. Vidzy. Vitsyebskaya Voblasts', NW Belarus
Viedma 43 C5 Río Negro, E Argentina
Vieng Pou Kha see Viangphoukha
Vienna see Wien
Vienne 69 D5 anc. Vienna. Isère, E France
Vienne 68 B4 river W France
Vientiane see Viangchan
Vierzon 68 C4 Cher, C France
Viesïte 84 D4 Ger. Eckengraf. Jēkabpils, S Latvia
Vietnam 114 D4 Vtn. Cộng Hoa Xa Hôi Chu Nghia Viêt Nam. Country SE Asia
Vietri see Viêt Tri
Viêt Tri 114 D3 var. Vietri. Vinh Phu, N Vietnam
Vieux Fort 33 F2 S Saint Lucia
Vigo 70 B2 Galicia, NW Spain
Vijayawāda 111 D1 prev. Bezwada. Andhra Pradesh, SE India
Vijosa see Vjosës, Lumi i
Vijosë see Vjosës, Lumi i
Vila see Port-Vila
Vila Artur de Paiva see Cubango
Vila da Ponte see Cubango
Vila de Mocímboa da Praia see Mocímboa da Praia
Vila do Conde 70 B2 Porto, NW Portugal
Vila do Zumbo 56 D2 prev. Vila do Zumbu, Zumbo. Tete, NE Mozambique
Vilafranca del Penedès 71 G2 var. Villafranca del Panadés. Cataluña, NE Spain
Vila General Machado see Camacupa
Vijaka 84 D4 Ger. Marienhausen. Balvi, NE Latvia
Vilalba 70 C1 Galicia, NW Spain
Vila Nova de Gaia 70 B2 Porto, NW Portugal
Vila Nova de Portimão see Portimão
Vila Pereira de Eça see N'Giva
Vila Real 70 C2 var. Vila Rial. Vila Real, N Portugal
Vila Rial see Vila Real
Vila Robert Williams see Caála
Vila Serpa Pinto see Menongue
Vilhelmina 62 C4 Västerbotten, N Sweden
Vilhena 40 D3 Rondônia, W Brazil
Vília 83 C5 Attikí, C Greece
Viliya 85 C5 Lith. Neris, Rus. Viliya. River W Belarus
Viljandi 84 D2 Ger. Fellin. Viljandimaa, S Estonia
Vilkaviškis 84 B4 Pol. Wyłkowyszki. Vilkaviškis, SW Lithuania
Villa Acuña 28 D2 var. Cuidad Acuña. Coahuila de Zaragoza, NE Mexico
Villa Bella 39 F2 Beni, N Bolivia
Villacarrillo 71 E4 Andalucía, S Spain
Villa Cecilia see Ciudad Madero
Villach 73 D7 Slvn. Beljak. Kärnten, S Austria
Villacidro 75 A5 Sardegna, Italy, C Mediterranean Sea
Villa Concepción see Concepción
Villa del Pilar see Pilar
Villafranca de los Barros 70 C4 Extremadura, W Spain
Villafranca del Panadés see Vilafranca del Penedès
Villahermosa 29 G4 prev. San Juan Bautista. Tabasco, SE Mexico
Villajoyosa 71 F4 var. La Vila Jojosa. País Valenciano, E Spain
Villarrica 42 D2 Guairá, SE Paraguay
Villavicencio 36 B3 Meta, C Colombia
Villaviciosa 70 D1 Asturias, N Spain
Villazón 39 G5 Potosí, S Bolivia
Villena 71 F4 País Valenciano, E Spain
Villeurbanne 69 D5 Rhône, E France
Villingen-Schwenningen 73 B6 Baden-Württemberg, S Germany
Vilnius 85 C5 Pol. Wilno, Ger. Wilna; prev. Rus. Vilna. Country capital (Lithuania) Vilnius, SE Lithuania
Vil'shanka 87 E3 Rus. Olshanka. Kirovohrads'ka Oblast', C Ukraine
Vilvoorde 65 C6 Fr. Vilvorde. Vlaams Brabant, C Belgium
Vilyeyka 85 C5 Pol. Wilejka, Rus. Vileyka. Minskaya Voblasts', NW Belarus
Vilyuy 93 F3 river NE Russian Federation
Viña del Mar 42 B4 Valparaíso, C Chile
Vinarös 71 F3 País Valenciano, E Spain
Vincennes 18 B4 Indiana, N USA
Vindhya Mountains see Vindhya Range
Vindhya Range 112 D4 var. Vindhya Mountains. Mountain range N India
Vineland 19 F4 New Jersey, NE USA
Vinh 114 D4 Nghê An, N Vietnam
Vinh Loi see Bac Liêu
Vinh Than Lan see Thailand, Gulf of
Vinishte 82 C2 Montana, NW Bulgaria
Vinita 27 G1 Oklahoma, C USA
Vinkovci 78 C3 Ger. Winkowitz, Hung. Vinkovce. Vukovar-Srijem, E Croatia
Vinnytsya 86 D2 Rus. Vinnitsa. Vinnyts'ka Oblast', C Ukraine
Vinson Massif 132 A3 mountain Antarctica
Virandşehir 95 E4 Şanlıurfa, SE Turkey
Vîrful Moldoveanu see Vârful Moldoveanu

Virginia 19 E5 off. Commonwealth of Virginia; also known as Mother of Presidents, Mother of States, Old Dominion. State NE USA
Virginia 23 G1 Minnesota, N USA
Virginia Beach 19 F5 Virginia, NE USA
Virgin Islands see British Virgin Islands
Virgin Islands (US) 33 F3 var. Virgin Islands of the United States; prev. Danish West Indies. US unincorporated territory E West Indies
Virgin Islands of the United States see Virgin Islands (US)
Virôchey 115 E5 Rôtânôkiri, NE Cambodia
Virovitica 78 C2 Ger. Virovititz, Hung. Verőcze; prev. Ger. Werowitz. Virovitica-Podravina, NE Croatia
Virton 65 D8 Luxembourg, SE Belgium
Virtsu 84 D2 Ger. Werder. Läänemaa, W Estonia
Vis 78 B4 It. Lissa; anc. Issa. Island S Croatia
Vis see Fish
Visaginas 84 C4 prev. Sniečkus. Ignalina, E Lithuania
Visākhapatnam 113 E5 Andhra Pradesh, SE India
Visalia 25 C6 California, W USA
Visby 63 C7 Ger. Wisby. Gotland, SE Sweden
Viscount Melville Sound 15 F2 prev. Melville Sound. Sound Northwest Territories/Nunavut, N Canada
Visé 65 D6 Liège, E Belgium
Viseu 70 C2 prev. Vizeu. Viseu, N Portugal
Visoko 78 C4 Federacija Bosna I Hercegovina, C Bosnia and Herzegovina
Vistasjohka 62 D3 Swe. Kalixälven. River N Sweden
Vistula see Wisła
Vistula Lagoon 76 C2 Ger. Frisches Haff, Pol. Zalew Wiślany, Rus. Vislinskiy Zaliv. Lagoon Poland/Russian Federation
Viterbo 74 C4 anc. Vicus Elbii. Lazio, C Italy
Viti Levu 123 E4 island W Fiji
Vitim 93 F4 river C Russian Federation
Vitoria see Vitoria-Gasteiz
Vitória 41 F4 Espírito Santo, SE Brazil
Vitória Bank see Vitória Seamount
Vitória da Conquista 41 F3 Bahia, E Brazil
Vitoria-Gasteiz 71 E1 var. Vitoria, Eng. Vittoria. País Vasco, N Spain
Vitória Seamount 45 B5 var. Victoria Bank, Vitoria Bank. Undersea feature C Atlantic Ocean
Vitré 68 B3 Ille-et-Vilaine, NW France
Vitsyebsk 85 E5 Rus. Vitebsk. Vitsyebskaya Voblasts', NE Belarus
Vittoria see Vitoria-Gasteiz
Vittoria 75 C7 Sicilia, Italy, C Mediterranean Sea
Vizianagaram 113 E5 var. Vizianagram. Andhra Pradesh, E India
Vizianagram see Vizianagaram
Vjosës, Lumi i 79 C7 var. Vijosa, Vijosë, Gk. Aóos. River Albania/Greece see also Aóos
Vlaardingen 64 B4 Zuid-Holland, SW Netherlands
Vladikavkaz 89 B8 prev. Dzaudzhikau, Ordzhonikidze. Severnaya Osetiya-Alaniya, SW Russian Federation
Vladimir 89 B5 Vladimirskaya Oblast', W Russian Federation
Vladivostok 93 G5 Primorskiy Kray, SE Russian Federation
Vlagtwedde 64 E2 Groningen, NE Netherlands
Vlasotince 79 E5 Serbia, SE Serbia and Montenegro (Yugo.)
Vlieland 64 C1 Fris. Flylân. Island Waddeneilanden, N Netherlands
Vlijmen 64 C4 Noord-Brabant, S Netherlands
Vlissingen 65 B5 Eng. Flushing, Fr. Flessingue. Zeeland, SW Netherlands
Vlorë 79 C7 prev. Vlonë, It. Valona, Vlora. Vlorë, SW Albania
Vöcklabruck 73 D6 Oberösterreich, NW Austria
Vohimena, Tanjona 57 F4 Fr. Cap Sainte Marie. Headland S Madagascar
Voiron 69 D5 Isère, E France
Vojvodina 78 D3 Ger. Wojwodina. Region N Serbia and Montenegro (Yugo.)
Volcán de Chiriquí see Barú, Volcán
Volga 89 B7 river NW Russian Federation
Volga Delta 59 G4 delta Astrakhanskaya Oblast', SW Russian Federation
Volga Uplands 59 G3 Russ. Privolzhskaya Vozvyshennost' mountain range W Russian Federation
Volgodonsk 89 B7 Rostovskaya Oblast', SW Russian Federation
Volgograd 89 B7 prev. Stalingrad, Tsaritsyn. Volgogradskaya Oblast', SW Russian Federation
Volkhov 88 B4 Leningradskaya Oblast', NW Russian Federation
Volnovakha 87 G3 Donets'ka Oblast', SE Ukraine
Volodymyr-Volyns'kyy 86 C1 Pol. Włodzimierz, Rus. Vladimir-Volynskiy. Volyns'ka Oblast', NW Ukraine
Vologda 88 B4 Vologodskaya Oblast', W Russian Federation
Vólos 83 B5 Thessalía, C Greece
Vol'sk 89 C6 Saratovskaya Oblast', W Russian Federation
Volta 53 E5 river SE Ghana
Volta Blanche see White Volta
Volta, Lake 53 E5 reservoir SE Ghana
Volta Noire see Black Volta
Volturno 75 D5 river S Italy
Volzhskiy 89 B6 Volgogradskaya Oblast', SW Russian Federation
Võnnu 84 E3 Ger. Wendau. Tartumaa, SE Estonia
Voorst 64 D3 Gelderland, E Netherlands

Voranava 85 C5 Pol. Werenów, Rus. Voronovo. Hrodzyenskaya Voblasts', W Belarus
Vorderrhein 73 B7 river SE Switzerland
Vóreioi Sporádhes 83 C5 var. Vórioi Sporádhes, Eng. Northern Sporades. Island group E Greece
Vórioi Sporádhes see Vóreioi Sporádhes
Vorkuta 92 C2 Respublika Komi, NW Russian Federation
Vormsi 84 C2 var. Vormsi Saar, Ger. Worms, Swed. Ormsö. Island W Estonia
Vormsi Saar see Vormsi
Voronezh 89 B6 Voronezhskaya Oblast', W Russian Federation
Võru 84 D3 Ger. Werro. Võrumaa, SE Estonia
Vosges 68 E4 mountain range NE France
Vostochno-Sibirskoye More 93 F1 Eng. East Siberian Sea. Sea Arctic Ocean
Vostok Island see Vostok Island
Vostok 132 C3 Russian research station Antarctica
Vostok Island 123 G3 var. Vostock Island; prev. Stavers Island. Island Line Islands, SE Kiribati
Voznesens'k 87 E3 Rus. Voznesensk. Mykolayivs'ka Oblast', S Ukraine
Vrangelya, Ostrov 93 F1 Eng. Wrangel Island. Island NE Russian Federation
Vranje 79 E5 Serbia, SE Serbia and Montenegro (Yugo.)
Vranov see Vranov nad Topl'ou
Vranov nad Topl'ou 77 D5 var. Vranov, Hung. Varannó. Prešovský Kraj, E Slovakia
Vratsa 82 C2 Vratsa, NW Bulgaria
Vrbas 78 C3 river N Bosnia and Herzegovina
Vrbas 78 C3 Serbia, NW Serbia and Montenegro (Yugo.)
Vsetín 77 C5 Ger. Wsetin. Zlínský Kraj, E Czech Republic
Vučitrn 79 D5 Serbia, S Serbia and Montenegro (Yugo.)
Vukovar 78 C3 Hung. Vukovár. Vukovar-Srijem, E Croatia
Vulcano, Isola 75 C7 island Isole Eolie, S Italy
Vung Tau 115 E6 prev. Fr. Cape Saint Jacques, Cap Saint-Jacques. Ba Ria-Vung Tau, S Vietnam
Vyatka 89 C5 river NW Russian Federation
Vyborg 88 B3 Fin. Viipuri. Leningradskaya Oblast', NW Russian Federation
Vyerkhnyadzvinsk 85 D5 Rus. Verkhnedvinsk. Vitsyebskaya Voblasts', N Belarus
Vyetryna 85 D5 Rus. Vetrino. Vitsyebskaya Voblasts', N Belarus
Vynohradiv 86 B3 Cz. Sevluš, Hung. Nagyszőllős, Rus. Vinogradov; prev. Sevlyush. Zakarpats'ka Oblast', W Ukraine

W

Wa 53 E4 NW Ghana
Waal 64 C4 river S Netherlands
Wabash 18 C4 Indiana, N USA
Wabash River 18 B5 river N USA
Waco 27 G3 Texas, SW USA
Waddān 49 F3 NW Libya
Waddeneilanden 64 C1 var. West Frisian Islands. Island group N Netherlands
Waddenzee 64 C1 var. Wadden Zee. Sea SE North Sea
Waddington, Mount 14 D5 mountain British Columbia, SW Canada
Wādī as Sīr 97 B6 var. Wadi es Sir. 'Ammān, NW Jordan
Wadi es Sir see Wādī as Sīr
Wadi Halfa 50 B3 var. Wādī Ḥalfā'. Northern, N Sudan
Wādī Mūsā 97 B7 var. Petra. Ma'ān, S Jordan
Wad Madanī see Wad Medani
Wad Medani 50 C4 var. Wad Madanī. Gezira, C Sudan
Waflia 117 F4 Pulau Buru, E Indonesia
Wagadugu see Ouagadougou
Wagga Wagga 127 C7 New South Wales, SE Australia
Wagin 125 B7 Western Australia
Wāh 112 C1 Punjab, NE Pakistan
Wahai 117 F4 Pulau Seram, E Indonesia
Wahiawā 25 A8 var. Wahiawa. O'ahu, Hawai'i, USA, C Pacific Ocean
Wahibah, Ramlat Āl 99 E5 var. Ramlat Ahl Wahībah, Ramlat Al Wahaybah, Eng. Wahibah Sands. Desert N Oman
Wahibah Sands see Wahībah, Ramlat Āl
Wahpeton 23 F2 North Dakota, N USA
Wahran see Oran
Waiau 129 A7 river South Island, NZ
Waigeo, Pulau 117 G4 island Maluku, E Indonesia
Waikaremoana, Lake 128 E4 lake North Island, NZ
Wailuku 25 B8 Maui, Hawai'i, USA, C Pacific Ocean
Waimate 129 B6 Canterbury, South Island, NZ
Waiouru 128 D4 Manawatu-Wanganui, North Island, NZ
Waipara 129 C6 Canterbury, South Island, NZ
Waipawa 128 E4 Hawke's Bay, North Island, NZ
Waipukurau 128 D4 Hawke's Bay, North Island, NZ
Wairau 129 C5 river South Island, NZ
Wairoa 128 D2 river North Island, NZ
Wairoa 128 E4 Hawke's Bay, North Island, NZ
Waitaki 129 B6 river South Island, NZ
Waitara 128 D3 Taranaki, North Island, NZ
Waiuku 128 D3 Auckland, North Island, NZ
Wakasa-wan 109 C6 bay C Japan
Wakatipu, Lake 129 A7 lake South Island, NZ

Wakayama 109 C6 Wakayama, Honshū, SW Japan
Wake Island 120 D1 atoll NW Pacific Ocean
Wake Island 130 C2 US unincorporated territory NW Pacific Ocean
Wakkanai 108 C1 Hokkaidō, NE Japan
Walachei see Wallachia
Walachia see Wallachia
Wałbrzych 76 B4 Ger. Waldenburg, Waldenburg in Schlesien. Dolnośląskie, SW Poland
Walcourt 65 C7 Namur, S Belgium
Wałcz 76 B3 Ger. Deutsch Krone. Zachodniopomorskie, NW Poland
Waldia see Weldiya
Wales 67 C6 Wel. Cymru. National region UK
Wales 14 C2 Alaska, USA
Wales Island, Prince of see Pinang, Pulau
Walgett 127 D5 New South Wales, SE Australia
Walker Lake 25 C5 lake Nevada, W USA
Wallachia 86 B5 var. Walachia, Ger. Walachei, Rom. Valachia. Cultural region S Romania
Walla Walla 24 C2 Washington, NW USA
Wallis and Futuna 123 E4 Fr. Territoire de Wallis et Futuna. French overseas territory C Pacific Ocean
Walnut Ridge 20 B1 Arkansas, C USA
Walthamstow 67 B7 SE England, UK
Walvis Bay 56 A4 Afr. Walvisbaai. Erongo, NW Namibia
Walvish Ridge see Walvis Ridge
Walvis Ridge 47 B7 var. Walvish Ridge. Undersea feature E Atlantic Ocean
Wan see Wanxian
Wanaka 129 B6 Otago, South Island, NZ
Wanaka, Lake 129 A6 lake South Island, NZ
Wanchuan see Zhangjiakou
Wandel Sea 61 E4 sea Arctic Ocean
Wandsworth 89 A8 SE England, UK
Wanganui 128 D4 Manawatu-Wanganui, North Island, NZ
Wangaratta 127 C7 Victoria, SE Australia
Wanki, Río see Coco, Río
Wanlaweyn 51 D6 var. Wanle Weyn, It. Uanle Uen. Shabeellaha Hoose, SW Somalia
Wanle Weyn see Wanlaweyn
Wanxian 106 B5 Chongqing, C China
Warangal 113 E5 Andhra Pradesh, C India
Warburg 72 B4 Nordrhein-Westfalen, W Germany
Ware 15 E4 British Columbia, W Canada
Waremme 65 C6 Liège, E Belgium
Waren 72 C3 Mecklenburg-Vorpommern, NE Germany
Wargla see Ouargla
Warkworth 128 D2 Auckland, North Island, NZ
Warnemünde 72 C2 Mecklenburg-Vorpommern, NE Germany
Warner 27 G1 Oklahoma, C USA
Warnes 39 G4 Santa Cruz, C Bolivia
Warrego River 127 C5 seasonal river New South Wales/Queensland, E Australia
Warren 18 D3 Michigan, N USA
Warren 18 D3 Ohio, N USA
Warren 19 E3 Pennsylvania, NE USA
Warri 53 F5 Delta, S Nigeria
Warrnambool 127 B7 Victoria, SE Australia
Warsaw see Mazowieckie
Warszawa 76 D3 Eng. Warsaw, Ger. Warschau, Rus. Varshava. Country capital (Poland) Mazowieckie, C Poland
Warta 76 B4 Ger. Warthe. River W Poland
Warwick 127 E5 Queensland, E Australia
Washington 22 A2 off. State of Washington; also known as Chinook State, Evergreen State. State NW USA
Washington D. C. 19 E4 country capital (USA) District of Columbia, NE USA
Washington, Mount 19 G2 mountain New Hampshire, NE USA
Wash, The 67 E6 inlet E England, UK
Waspam 31 E2 var. Waspán. Región Autónoma Atlántico Norte, NE Nicaragua
Waspán see Waspam
Watampone 117 E4 var. Bone. Sulawesi, C Indonesia
Waterbury 19 F3 Connecticut, NE USA
Waterford 67 B6 Ir. Port Láirge. S Ireland
Waterloo 18 D3 Iowa, C USA
Watertown 19 F2 New York, NE USA
Watertown 23 F2 South Dakota, N USA
Waterville 19 G2 Maine, NE USA
Watford 67 A7 SE England, UK
Watsa 55 E5 Orientale, NE Dem. Rep. Congo
Watts Bar Lake reservoir Tennessee, S USA
Wau 51 B5 var. Wāw. Western Bahr el Ghazal, S Sudan
Waukegan 18 B3 Illinois, N USA
Waukesha 18 B3 Wisconsin, N USA
Wausau 18 B2 Wisconsin, N USA
Waverly 23 G3 Iowa, C USA
Wavre 65 C6 Wallon Brabant, C Belgium
Wāw see Wau
Wawa 16 C4 Ontario, S Canada
Waycross 21 E3 Georgia, SE USA
Wearmouth see Sunderland
Webster City 23 F3 Iowa, C USA
Weddell Plain 132 A2 undersea feature SW Atlantic Ocean
Weddell Sea 132 A2 sea SW Atlantic Ocean
Weener 72 A3 Niedersachsen, NW Germany
Weert 65 D5 Limburg, SE Netherlands
Weesp 64 C3 Noord-Holland, C Netherlands
Węgorzewo 76 D2 Ger. Angerburg. Warmińsko-Mazurskie, NE Poland
Weimar 72 C4 Thüringen, C Germany
Weissenburg see Wissembourg in Bayern
Weissenburg in Bayern 73 C6 var. Weißenburg. Bayern, SE Germany
Weiswampach 65 D7 Diekirch, N Luxembourg
Wejherowo 76 C2 Pomorskie, NW Poland